KEY TO WORLD MAP PAGES

- **Large scale maps**
  (> 1:2 500 000)
- **Medium scale maps**
  (1:2 800 000–1:9 000 000)
- **Small scale maps**
  (< 1:10 000 000)

ASIA
44-69

NORTH AMERICA
94-117

SOUTH AMERICA
118-128

COUNTRIES

Afghanistan	60	Laos	58
Albania	38–39	Latvia	40
Algeria	74–75	Lebanon	69
Angola	80–81	Lesotho	85
Argentina	126, 128	Liberia	78
Armenia	67	Libya	73
Australia	88–91	Lithuania	40
Austria	19, 20–21	Luxembourg	17
Azerbaijan	67		
		Macedonia	38–39
Bahamas	116–117	Madagascar	85
Bangladesh	61	Malawi	83
Barbados	117	Malaysia	55–56
Belgium	17	Mali	78–79
Belize	116	Malta	37
Belorussia	40	Mauritania	78
Benin	79	Mauritius	71
Bhutan	61	Mexico	114–115
Bolivia	124–125	Moldavia	42
Bosnia-		Mongolia	54
Herzegovina	21	Morocco	74
Botswana	84–85	Mozambique	83
Brazil	120–127		
Brunei	55	Namibia	84
Bulgaria	38–39	Nepal	63
Burkina Faso	78–79	Netherlands	16–17
Burma	61	New Zealand	87
Burundi	82	Nicaragua	116
		Niger	79
Cambodia	58–59	Nigeria	79
Cameroon	82	Northern Ireland	15
Canada	96–101	Norway	8–9
Central African			
Republic	82	Oman	68
Chad	73		
Chile	126, 128	Pakistan	62
China	50–54	Panama	116
Colombia	120	Papua New Guinea	86
Congo	82	Paraguay	126–127
Costa Rica	116	Peru	124
Croatia	21	Philippines	55
Cuba	116–117	Poland	20
Cyprus	37	Portugal	30–31
Czech Republic	20–21	Puerto Rico	117
Denmark	11	Qatar	65
Djibouti	68		
Dominican Republic	117	Romania	38
		Russia	40–45
Ecuador	120	Rwanda	82
Egypt	76		
El Salvador	116	Saudi Arabia	68
England	12–13	Scotland	14
Equatorial Guinea	82	Senegal	78
Estonia	40	Sierra Leone	78
Ethiopia	68, 77	Singapore	59
		Slovak Republic	20–21
Fiji	87	Slovenia	33
Finland	8–9	Somali Republic	68
France	24–27	South Africa	84–85
French Guiana	121	Spain	28–31
		Sri Lanka	60
Gabon	80	Sudan	77
Gambia	78	Surinam	121
Georgia	43	Swaziland	85
Germany	18–19	Sweden	8–9
Ghana	78–79	Switzerland	22–23
Greece	39	Syria	67
Greenland	4		
Guatemala	116	Taiwan	53
Guinea	78	Tajikistan	44
Guinea-Bissau	78	Tanzania	82–83
Guyana	121	Thailand	58–59
		Togo	79
Haiti	117	Trinidad and	
Honduras	116	Tobago	117
Hong Kong	53	Tunisia	75
Hungary	21	Turkey	66–67
		Turkmenistan	44
Iceland	8		
India	60–63	Uganda	82
Indonesia	56–57	Ukraine	42
Iran	64–65	United Arab Emirates	65
Iraq	64–65	United Kingdom	12–15
Irish Republic	15	USA	102–113
Israel	69	Uruguay	126–127
Italy	32–35	Uzbekistan	44
Ivory Coast	78		
		Venezuela	120–121
Jamaica	116	Vietnam	58–59
Japan	48–49		
Jordan	69	Wales	12–13
Kazakhstan	44	Yemen	68
Kenya	82	Yugoslavia	38–39
Kirghizia	44		
Korea, North	51	Zaïre	80–81
Korea, South	51	Zambia	83
Kuwait	64–65	Zimbabwe	83

PHILIP'S

CONCISE WORLD ATLAS

First published in Great Britain in 1993
by George Philip Limited,
an imprint of Reed Consumer Books Limited,
Michelin House, 81 Fulham Road, London SW3 6RB,
and Auckland, Melbourne, Singapore and Toronto

Cartography by Philip's

Copyright © 1993 Reed International Books Limited

ISBN 0-540-05744-4

A CIP catalogue record for this book is available from
the British Library

Printed in Great Britain

PHILIP'S

CONCISE WORLD ATLAS

CONTENTS

WORLD STATISTICS

Countries vi
Physical
Dimensions vii
Philip's World Maps viii

WORLD MAPS

1-128

Map Symbols
1

The World: Political
1:71 100 000
2-3

Arctic Ocean 1:31 100 000
4

Antarctica 1:31 100 000
5

EUROPE

Europe: Physical
1:17 800 000
6

Europe: Political
1:17 800 000
7

Scandinavia and the Baltic Lands 1:4 400 000

8-9

Denmark and Southern Sweden 1:2 200 000
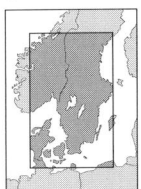
10-11

England and Wales
1:1 800 000

12-13

Scotland 1:1 800 000
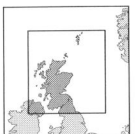
14

Ireland 1:1 800 000

15

Netherlands, Belgium and Luxembourg 1:1 100 000

16-17

Germany 1:2 200 000
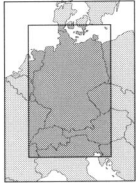
18-19

Middle Europe 1:3 100 000
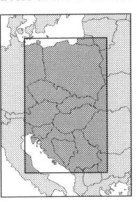
20-21

Switzerland 1:900 000
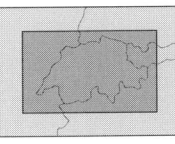
22-23

Northern France 1:2 200 000
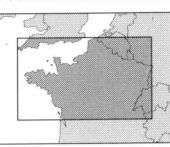
24-25

Southern France 1:2 200 000
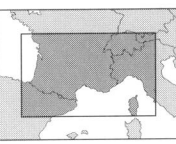
26-27

Eastern Spain 1:2 200 000

28-29

Western Spain and Portugal 1:2 200 000

30-31

Northern Italy, Slovenia and Croatia
1:2 200 000
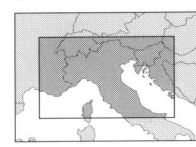
32-33

Southern Italy 1:2 200 000
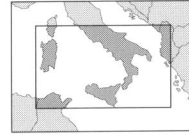
34-35

Balearics, Canaries and Madeira 1:900 000 / 1:1 800 000

36

Malta, Crete, Corfu, Rhodes and Cyprus
1:900 000 / 1:1 200 000

37

The Balkans 1:3 100 000

38-39

Western Russia, Belorussia and the Baltic States 1:4 400 000
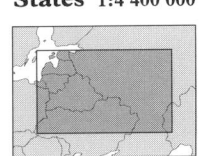
40-41

Ukraine, Moldavia and the Caucasus
1:4 400 000
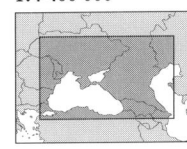
42-43

ASIA

Russia and Central Asia
1:17 800 000
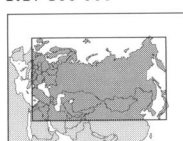
44-45

Asia: Physical
1:44 400 000
46

Asia: Political
1:44 400 000
47

Japan 1:4 400 000

48-49

Northern China and Korea
1:5 300 000
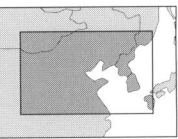
50-51

Southern China 1:5 300 000
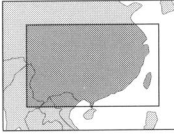
52-53

China 1:17 800 000
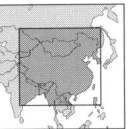
54

Philippines 1:6 700 000

55

Indonesia 1:11 100 000
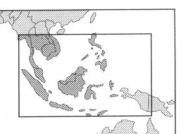
56-57

Mainland South-East Asia
1:5 300 000

58-59

South Asia 1:8 900 000
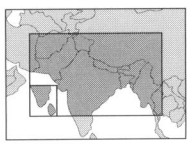
60-61

The Indo-Gangetic Plain
1:5 300 000
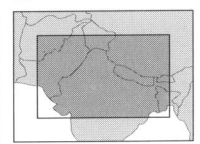
62-63

The Middle East 1:6 200 000

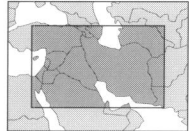

64-65

Turkey 1:4 400 000

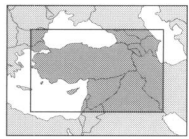

66-67

Arabia and the Horn of Africa 1:13 300 000

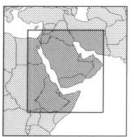

68

The Near East 1:2 200 000

69

AFRICA

Africa: Physical
1:36 000 000
70

Africa: Political
1:36 000 000
71

Northern Africa 1:13 300 000

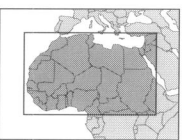

72-73

North-West Africa
1:7 100 000

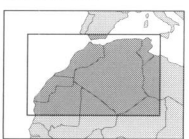

74-75

The Nile Valley 1:7 100 000
The Nile Delta 1:3 600 000

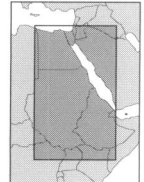

76-77

West Africa 1:7 100 000

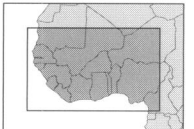

78-79

Central and Southern Africa 1:13 300 000

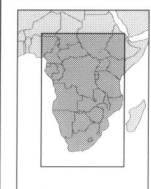

80-81

East Africa 1:7 100 000

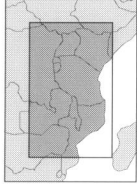

82-83

Southern Africa 1:7 100 000
Madagascar 1:7 100 000

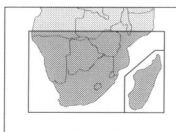

84-85

AUSTRALIA AND OCEANIA

Australia and Oceania: Physical and Political
1:36 000 000
86

New Zealand 1:5 300 000

87

Western Australia
1:7 100 000

88-89

Eastern Australia 1:7 100 000

90-91

Pacific Ocean 1:48 000 000
92-93

NORTH AMERICA

North America: Physical
1:31 100 000
94

North America: Political
1:31 100 000
95

Canada 1:13 300 000
Alaska 1:26 700 000

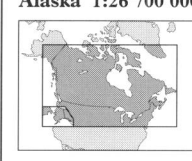

96-97

Eastern Canada 1:6 200 000

98-99

Western Canada 1:6 200 000

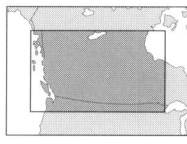

100-101

United States 1:10 700 000
Hawaii 1:8 900 000

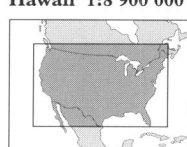

102-103

Eastern United States
1:5 300 000

104-105

North-Eastern United States 1:2 200 000

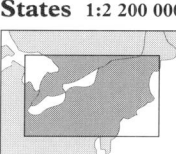

106-107

Middle United States
1:5 300 000

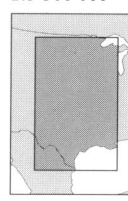

108-109

Western United States
1:5 300 000

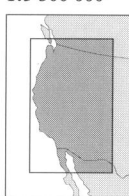

110-111

Central and Southern California and Washington 1:2 200 000

112-113

Mexico 1:7 100 000

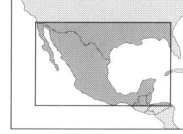

114-115

Central America and the West Indies 1:7 100 000

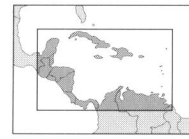

116-117

SOUTH AMERICA

South America: Physical
1:26 700 000
118

South America: Political
1:26 700 000
119

South America – North-West 1:7 100 000

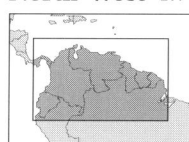

120-121

Eastern Brazil 1:7 100 000

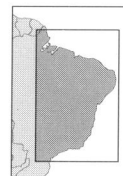

122-123

South America – West
1:7 100 000

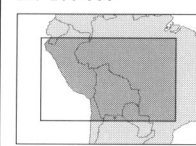

124-125

Central South America
1:7 100 000

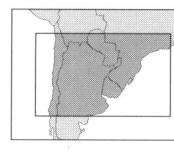

126-127

Southern Chile and Argentina 1:7 100 000

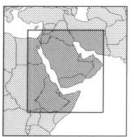

128

INDEX TO WORLD MAPS
129-224

V

WORLD STATISTICS: COUNTRIES

This alphabetical list includes all the countries and territories of the world. If a territory is not completely independent, then the country it is associated with is named. The area figures give the total area of land, inland water and ice. Units for areas and populations are thousands. The annual income is the Gross National Product per capita in US dollars. The figures are the latest available, usually 1991.

Country/Territory	Area km² Thousands	Area miles² Thousands	Population Thousands	Capital	Annual Income US $
Adélie Land (Fr.)	432	167	0.03	-	-
Afghanistan	652	252	16,433	Kabul	450
Albania	28.8	11.1	3,250	Tirana	1,000
Algeria	2,382	920	24,960	Algiers	2,020
American Samoa (US)	0.20	0.08	39	Pago Pago	6,000
Amsterdam Is. (Fr.)	0.05	0.02	0.03	-	-
Andorra	0.45	0.17	52	Andorre-la-Vella	-
Angola	1,247	481	10,020	Luanda	620
Anguilla (UK)	0.09	0.04	8	The Valley	-
Antigua & Barbuda	0.44	0.17	77	St John's	4,770
Argentina	2,767	1,068	32,322	Buenos Aires	2,780
Armenia	29.8	11.5	3,416	Yerevan	2,150
Aruba (Neths.)	0.19	0.07	60	Oranjestad	6,000
Ascension Is. (UK)	0.09	0.03	1.5	Georgetown	-
Australia	7,687	2,968	17,086	Canberra	16,590
Australian Antarctic Territory	6,120	2,363	0	-	-
Austria	83.9	32.4	7,712	Vienna	20,380
Azerbaijan	86.6	33.4	7,451	Baku	1,670
Azores (Port.)	2.2	0.87	260	Ponta Delgada	-
Bahamas	13.9	5.4	253	Nassau	11,720
Bahrain	0.68	0.26	503	Manama	6,910
Bangladesh	144	56	115,594	Dacca	220
Barbados	0.43	0.17	255	Bridgetown	6,630
Belau (US)	0.46	0.18	15	Koror	-
Belgium	30.5	11.8	9,845	Brussels	19,300
Belize	23	8.9	188	Belmopan	2,050
Belorussia	207.6	80.1	10,374	Minsk	3,110
Benin	113	43	4,736	Porto-Novo	380
Bermuda (UK)	0.05	0.02	61	Hamilton	25,000
Bhutan	47	18.1	1,517	Thimphu	180
Bolivia	1,099	424	7,400	La Paz/Sucre	650
Bosnia-Herzegovina	51.2	19.8	4,364	Sarajevo	-
Botswana	582	225	1,291	Gaborone	2,590
Bouvet Is. (Nor.)	0.05	0.02	0.02	-	-
Brazil	8,512	3,286	153,322	Brasilia	2,920
British Antarctic Terr. (UK)	1,709	660	0.3	Stanley	-
British Indian Ocean Terr. (UK)	0.08	0.03	3	-	-
Brunei	5.8	2.2	266	Bandar Seri Begawan	6,000
Bulgaria	111	43	9,011	Sofia	1,840
Burkina Faso	274	106	9,001	Ouagadougou	350
Burma (Myanmar)	677	261	41,675	Rangoon	500
Burundi	27.8	10.7	5,438	Bujumbura	210
Cambodia	181	70	8,246	Phnom Penh	200
Cameroon	475	184	11,834	Yaoundé	940
Canada	9,976	3,852	26,522	Ottawa	21,260
Canary Is. (Spain)	7.3	2.8	1,700	Las Palmas/Santa Cruz	-
Cape Verde Is.	4	1.6	370	Praia	750
Cayman Is. (UK)	0.26	0.10	27	Georgetown	-
Central African Republic	623	241	3,039	Bangui	390
Chad	1,284	496	5,679	Ndjamena	220
Chatham Is. (NZ)	0.96	0.37	0.05	Waitangi	-
Chile	757	292	13,386	Santiago	2,160
China	9,597	3,705	1,139,060	Beijing (Peking)	370
Christmas Is. (Aus.)	0.14	0.05	2.3	The Settlement	-
Cocos (Keeling) Is. (Aus.)	0.01	0.005	0.70	-	-
Colombia	1,139	440	32,987	Bogotá	1,280
Comoros	2.2	0.86	551	Moroni	500
Congo	342	132	2,271	Brazzaville	1,120
Cook Is. (NZ)	0.24	0.09	18	Avarua	900
Costa Rica	51.1	19.7	2,994	San José	1,930
Croatia	56.5	21.8	4,784	Zagreb	-
Crozet Is. (Fr.)	0.51	0.19	35	-	-
Cuba	111	43	10,609	Havana	3,000
Cyprus	9.3	3.6	702	Nicosia	8,640
Czech Republic	78.9	30.4	10,299	Prague	2,370
Denmark	43.1	16.6	5,140	Copenhagen	23,660
Djibouti	23.2	9	409	Djibouti	1,000
Dominica	0.75	0.29	83	Roseau	2,440
Dominican Republic	48.7	18.8	7,170	Santo Domingo	950
Ecuador	284	109	10,782	Quito	1,020
Egypt	1,001	387	53,153	Cairo	620
El Salvador	21	8.1	5,252	San Salvador	1,070
Equatorial Guinea	28.1	10.8	348	Malabo	330
Estonia	44.7	17.3	1,600	Tallinn	3,830
*Ethiopia	1,222	472	50,974	Addis Ababa	120
Falkland Is. (UK)	12.2	4.7	2	Stanley	-
Faroe Is. (Den.)	1.4	0.54	47	Tórshavn	23,660
Fiji	18.3	7.1	765	Suva	1,830
Finland	338	131	4,986	Helsinki	24,400
France	552	213	56,440	Paris	20,600
French Guiana (Fr.)	90	34.7	99	Cayenne	2,500
French Polynesia (Fr.)	4	1.5	206	Papeete	6,000
Gabon	268	103	1,172	Libreville	3,780
Gambia, The	11.3	4.4	861	Banjul	360
Georgia	69.7	26.9	5,571	Tbilisi	1,640
Germany	357	138	79,479	Berlin	17,000
Ghana	239	92	15,028	Accra	400
Gibraltar (UK)	0.007	0.003	31	-	4,000
Greece	132	51	10,269	Athens	6,230
Greenland (Den.)	2,176	840	57	Godthåb	6,000
Grenada	0.34	0.13	85	St George's	2,180
Guadeloupe (Fr.)	1.7	0.66	344	Basse-Terre	7,000
Guam (US)	0.55	0.21	119	Agana	6,000
Guatemala	109	42	9,197	Guatemala City	930
Guinea	246	95	5,756	Conakry	450
Guinea-Bissau	36.1	13.9	965	Bissau	190
Guyana	215	83	796	Georgetown	290
Haiti	27.8	10.7	6,486	Port-au-Prince	370
Honduras	112	43	5,105	Tegucigalpa	570
Hong Kong (UK)	1.1	0.40	5,801	-	13,200
Hungary	93	35.9	10,344	Budapest	2,690
Iceland	103	40	255	Reykjavik	22,580
India	3,288	1,269	843,931	Delhi	330
Indonesia	1,905	735	179,300	Jakarta	610
Iran	1,648	636	58,031	Tehran	2,320
Iraq	438	169	18,920	Baghdad	2,000
Ireland	70.3	27.1	3,523	Dublin	10,780
Israel	27	10.3	4,659	Jerusalem	11,330
Italy	301	116	57,663	Rome	18,580
Ivory Coast	322	125	11,998	Abidjan	690
Jamaica	11	4.2	2,420	Kingston	1,380
Jan Mayen Is. (Nor.)	0.38	0.15	0.06	-	-
Japan	378	146	123,537	Tokyo	26,920
Johnston Is. (US)	0.002	0.0009	0.30	-	-
Jordan	89.2	34.4	4,009	Amman	1,120
Kazakhstan	2,717	1,049	17,104	Alma Ata	2,470
Kenya	580	224	24,032	Nairobi	340
Kerguelen Is. (Fr.)	7.2	2.8	0	-	-
Kermadec Is. (NZ)	0.03	0.01	0	-	-
Kirghizia	198.5	76.6	4,568	Bishkek	1,550
Kiribati	0.72	0.28	66	Tarawa	750
Korea, North	121	47	21,773	Pyongyang	900
Korea, South	99	38.2	43,302	Seoul	6,340
Kuwait	17.8	6.9	2,143	Kuwait City	16,380
Laos	237	91	4,139	Vientiane	230
Latvia	63.1	24.4	2,700	Riga	3,410
Lebanon	10.4	4	2,701	Beirut	2,000
Lesotho	30.4	11.7	1,774	Maseru	580
Liberia	111	43	2,607	Monrovia	500
Libya	1,760	679	4,545	Tripoli	5,800
Liechtenstein	0.16	0.06	29	Vaduz	33,000
Lithuania	65.2	25.2	3,751	Vilnius	2,710
Luxembourg	2.6	1	384	Luxembourg	31,080
Macau (Port.)	0.02	0.006	479	-	2,000
Macedonia	25.3	9.8	2,174	Skopje	-
Madagascar	587	227	11,197	Antananarivo	210
Madeira (Port.)	0.81	0.31	280	Funchal	-
Malawi	118	46	8,556	Lilongwe	230
Malaysia	330	127	17,861	Kuala Lumpur	2,490
Maldives	0.30	0.12	215	Malé	460
Mali	1,240	479	8,156	Bamako	280
Malta	0.32	0.12	354	Valletta	6,850
Mariana Is. (US)	0.48	0.18	22	Saipan	-
Marshall Is.	0.18	0.07	42	Dalap-Uliga-Darrit	-
Martinique (Fr.)	1.1	0.42	341	Fort-de-France	4,000
Mauritania	1,025	396	2,050	Nouakchott	510
Mauritius	1.9	0.72	1,075	Port Louis	2,420
Mayotte (Fr.)	0.37	0.14	84	Mamoundzou	-
Mexico	1,958	756	86,154	Mexico City	2,870
Micronesia, Fed. States	0.70	0.27	103	Palikir	-
Midway Is. (US)	0.005	0.002	0.45	-	-
Moldavia	33.7	13	4,458	Kishinev	2,170
Monaco	0.002	0.0001	29	-	20,000
Mongolia	1,567	605	2,190	Ulan Bator	400
Montserrat (UK)	0.10	0.04	13	Plymouth	-
Morocco	447	172	25,061	Rabat	1,030
Mozambique	802	309	15,656	Maputo	70
Namibia	824	318	1,781	Windhoek	1,120
Nauru	0.02	0.008	10	Domaneab	-
Nepal	141	54	18,916	Katmandu	180
Netherlands	41.9	16.2	15,019	Amsterdam	18,560
Neths. Antilles (Neths.)	0.99	0.38	189	Willemstad	6,000
New Caledonia (Fr.)	19	7.3	168	Nouméa	4,000
New Zealand	269	104	3,429	Wellington	12,140
Nicaragua	130	50	3,871	Managua	340
Niger	1,267	489	7,732	Niamey	300
Nigeria	924	357	108,542	Lagos/Abuja	290
Niue (NZ)	0.26	0.10	3	Alofi	-
Norfolk Is. (Aus.)	0.03	0.01	2	Kingston	-
Norway	324	125	4,242	Oslo	24,160
Oman	212	82	1,502	Muscat	5,220
Pakistan	796	307	112,050	Islamabad	400
Panama	77.1	29.8	2,418	Panama City	2,180
Papua New Guinea	463	179	3,699	Port Moresby	820
Paraguay	407	157	4,277	Asunción	1,210
Peru	1,285	496	22,332	Lima	1,020
Peter 1st Is. (Nor.)	0.18	0.07	0	-	-
Philippines	300	116	61,480	Manila	740
Pitcairn Is. (UK)	0.03	0.01	0.06	Adamstown	-
Poland	313	121	38,180	Warsaw	1,830
Portugal	92.4	35.7	10,525	Lisbon	5,620
Puerto Rico (US)	8.9	3.4	3,599	San Juan	6,330
Qatar	11	4.2	368	Doha	15,860
Queen Maud Land (Nor.)	2,800	1,081	0	-	-
Réunion (Fr.)	2.5	0.97	599	St-Denis	4,000
Romania	238	92	23,200	Bucharest	1,340
Ross Dependency (NZ)	435	168	0	-	-
Russia	17,075	6,592	149,527	Moscow	3,220
Rwanda	26.3	10.2	7,181	Kigali	260
St Christopher/Nevis	0.36	0.14	44	Basseterre	3,960
St Helena (UK)	0.12	0.05	7	Jamestown	-
St Lucia	0.62	0.24	151	Castries	2,500
St Paul Is. (Fr.)	0.007	0.003	0	-	-
St Pierre & Miquelon (Fr.)	0.24	0.09	7	St-Pierre	-
St Vincent/Grenadines	0.39	0.15	116	Kingstown	1,730
San Marino	0.06	0.02	24	San Marino	-
São Tomé & Príncipe	0.96	0.37	121	São Tomé	350
Saudi Arabia	2,150	830	14,870	Riyadh	7,070
Senegal	197	76	7,327	Dakar	720
Seychelles	0.46	0.18	67	Victoria	5,110
Sierra Leone	71.7	27.7	4,151	Freetown	210
Singapore	0.62	0.24	3,003	Singapore	12,890
Slovak Republic	49	18.9	5,269	Bratislava	1,650
Slovenia	20.3	7.8	1,963	Ljubljana	-
Solomon Is.	28.9	11.2	321	Honiara	560
Somalia	638	246	7,497	Mogadishu	150
South Africa	1,221	471	35,282	Pretoria	2,530
South Georgia (UK)	3.8	1.4	0.05	-	-
South Sandwich Is. (UK)	0.38	0.15	0	-	-
Spain	505	195	38,959	Madrid	12,460
Sri Lanka	65.6	25.3	16,993	Colombo	500
Sudan	2,506	967	25,204	Khartoum	400
Surinam	163	63	422	Paramaribo	3,610
Svalbard (Nor.)	62.9	24.3	4	Longyearbyen	-
Swaziland	17.4	6.7	768	Mbabane	1,060
Sweden	450	174	8,618	Stockholm	25,490
Switzerland	41.3	15.9	6,712	Bern	33,510
Syria	185	71	12,116	Damascus	1,110
Taiwan	36	13.9	20,300	Taipei	6,600
Tajikistan	143.1	55.2	5,680	Dushanbe	1,050
Tanzania	945	365	25,635	Dar es Salaam	100
Thailand	513	198	57,196	Bangkok	1,580
Togo	56.8	21.9	3,531	Lomé	410
Tokelau (NZ)	0.01	0.005	2	Nukunonu	-
Tonga	0.75	0.29	95	Nuku'alofa	1,100
Trinidad & Tobago	5.1	2	1,227	Port of Spain	3,620
Tristan da Cunha (UK)	0.11	0.04	0.33	Edinburgh	-
Tunisia	164	63	8,180	Tunis	1,510
Turkey	779	301	57,326	Ankara	1,820
Turkmenistan	488.1	188.5	3,838	Ashkhabad	1,700
Turks & Caicos Is. (UK)	0.43	0.17	10	Grand Turk	-
Tuvalu	0.03	0.01	10	Funafuti	600
Uganda	236	91	18,795	Kampala	160
Ukraine	603.7	233.1	51,940	Kiev	2,340
United Arab Emirates	83.6	32.3	1,589	Abu Dhabi	19,860
United Kingdom	243.3	94	54,889	London	16,750
United States	9,373	3,619	249,975	Washington	22,560
Uruguay	177	68	3,094	Montevideo	2,860
Uzbekistan	447.4	172.7	21,627	Tashkent	1,350
Vanuatu	12.2	4.7	147	Port Vila	1,120
Vatican City	0.0004	0.0002	1	-	-
Venezuela	912	352	19,735	Caracas	2,610
Vietnam	332	127	66,200	Hanoi	300
Virgin Is. (UK)	0.15	0.06	13	Road Town	-
Virgin Is. (US)	0.34	0.13	117	Charlotte Amalie	12,000
Wake Is.	0.008	0.003	0.30	-	-
Wallis & Futuna Is. (Fr.)	0.20	0.08	18	Mata-Utu	-
Western Sahara	266	103	179	El Aaiún	-
Western Samoa	2.8	1.1	164	Apia	930
Yemen	528	204	11,282	Sana	540
Yugoslavia	102.3	39.5	10,642	Belgrade	2,940
Zaïre	2,345	906	35,562	Kinshasa	230
Zambia	753	291	8,073	Lusaka	420
Zimbabwe	391	151	9,369	Harare	620

** Eritrea formally declared full independence from Ethiopia on 24th May 1993*

World Statistics: Physical Dimensions

Each topic list is divided into continents and within a continent the items are listed in size order. The order of the continents is as in the atlas, Europe through to South America. Certain lists down to this mark > are complete; below they are selective. The world top ten are shown in square brackets; in the case of mountains this has not been done because the world top 30 are all in Asia. The figures are rounded as appropriate.

World, Continents, Oceans

	km²	miles²	%
The World	509,450,000	196,672,000	-
Land	149,450,000	57,688,000	29.3
Water	360,000,000	138,984,000	70.7
Asia	44,500,000	17,177,000	29.8
Africa	30,302,000	11,697,000	20.3
North America	24,241,000	9,357,000	16.2
South America	17,793,000	6,868,000	11.9
Antarctica	14,100,000	5,443,000	9.4
Europe	9,957,000	3,843,000	6.7
Australia & Oceania	8,557,000	3,303,000	5.7
Pacific Ocean	179,679,000	69,356,000	49.9
Atlantic Ocean	92,373,000	35,657,000	25.7
Indian Ocean	73,917,000	28,532,000	20.5
Arctic Ocean	14,090,000	5,439,000	3.9

Mountains

Europe

		m	ft
Mont Blanc	*France/Italy*	4,807	15,771
Monte Rosa	*Italy/Switz.*	4,634	15,203
Dom	*Switzerland*	4,545	14,911
Weisshorn	*Switzerland*	4,505	14,780
Matterhorn/Cervino	*Italy/Switz.*	4,478	14,691
Mt Maudit	*France/Italy*	4,465	14,649
Finsteraarhorn	*Switzerland*	4,275	14,025
Aletschhorn	*Switzerland*	4,182	13,720
Jungfrau	*Switzerland*	4,158	13,642
Barre des Ecrins	*France*	4,103	13,461
Gran Paradiso	*Italy*	4,061	13,323
Piz Bernina	*Italy/Switz.*	4,052	13,294
Ortles	*Italy*	3,899	12,792
Monte Viso	*Italy*	3,841	12,602
Grossglockner	*Austria*	3,797	12,457
Wildspitze	*Austria*	3,774	12,382
Weisskügel	*Austria/Italy*	3,736	12,257
Dammastock	*Switzerland*	3,640	11,942
Tödi	*Switzerland*	3,623	11,886
Presanella	*Italy*	3,556	11,667
Monte Adamello	*Italy*	3,554	11,660
Mulhacén	*Spain*	3,478	11,411
Pico de Aneto	*Spain*	3,404	11,168
Marmolada	*Italy*	3,342	10,964
Etna	*Italy*	3,340	10,958
>Olympus	*Greece*	2,917	9,570
Galdhöpiggen	*Norway*	2,469	8,100
Pietrosul	*Romania*	2,305	7,562
Hvannadalshnúkur	*Iceland*	2,119	6,952
Narodnaya	*Russia*	1,894	6,214
Ben Nevis	*UK*	1,343	4,406

Asia

		m	ft
Everest	*China/Nepal*	8,848	29,029
Godwin Austen (K2)	*China/Kashmir*	8,611	28,251
Kanchenjunga	*India/Nepal*	8,598	28,208
Lhotse	*China/Nepal*	8,516	27,939
Makalu	*China/Nepal*	8,481	27,824
Cho Oyu	*China/Nepal*	8,201	26,906
Dhaulagiri	*Nepal*	8,172	26,811
Manaslu	*Nepal*	8,156	26,758
Nanga Parbat	*Kashmir*	8,126	26,660
Annapurna	*Nepal*	8,078	26,502
Gasherbrum	*China/Kashmir*	8,068	26,469
Broad Peak	*India*	8,051	26,414
Gosainthan	*China*	8,012	26,286
Disteghil Sar	*Kashmir*	7,885	25,869
Nuptse	*Nepal*	7,879	25,849
Masherbrum	*Kashmir*	7,826	25,676
Nanda Devi	*India*	7,817	25,646
Rakaposhi	*Kashmir*	7,788	25,551
Kamet	*India*	7,756	25,446
Namcha Barwa	*China*	7,756	25,446
Gurla Mandhata	*China*	7,728	25,354
Muztag	*China*	7,723	25,338
Kongur Shan	*China*	7,719	25,324
Tirich Mir	*Pakistan*	7,690	25,229
Saser	*Kashmir*	7,672	25,170
>Pik Kommunizma	*Tajikistan*	7,495	24,590
Aling Gangri	*China*	7,315	23,999
Elbrus	*Russia*	5,633	18,481
Demavand	*Iran*	5,604	18,386
Ararat	*Turkey*	5,165	16,945
Gunong Kinabalu	*Borneo*	4,101	13,455
Yu Shan	*Taiwan*	3,997	13,113
Fuji-san	*Japan*	3,776	12,388
Rinjani	*Indonesia*	3,726	12,224
Mt Rajang	*Philippines*	3,364	11,037
Pidurutalagala	*Sri Lanka*	2,524	8,281

Africa

		m	ft
Kilimanjaro	*Tanzania*	5,895	19,340
Mt Kenya	*Kenya*	5,199	17,057
Ruwenzori	*Uganda/Zaïre*	5,109	16,762
Ras Dashan	*Ethiopia*	4,620	15,157
Meru	*Tanzania*	4,565	14,977
Karisimbi	*Rwanda/Zaïre*	4,507	14,787
Mt Elgon	*Kenya/Uganda*	4,321	14,176
Batu	*Ethiopia*	4,307	14,130
Gughe	*Ethiopia*	4,200	13,779
Toubkal	*Morocco*	4,165	13,665
Irhil Mgoun	*Morocco*	4,071	13,356
Mt Cameroon	*Cameroon*	4,070	13,353
Teide	*Spain (Tenerife)*	3,718	12,198
Thabana Ntlenyana	*Lesotho*	3,482	11,424
Emi Kussi	*Chad*	3,415	11,204

Oceania

		m	ft
Puncak Jaya	*Indonesia*	5,029	16,499
Puncak Mandala	*Indonesia*	4,760	15,617
Puncak Trikora	*Indonesia*	4,750	15,584
Mt Wilhelm	*Papua N. Guinea*	4,508	14,790
>Mauna Kea	*USA (Hawaii)*	4,208	13,806
Mauna Loa	*USA (Hawaii)*	4,169	13,678
Mt Cook	*New Zealand*	3,753	12,313
Mt Balbi	*Solomon Is.*	2,743	8,999
Mt Kosciusko	*Australia*	2,230	7,316

North America

		m	ft
Mt McKinley	*USA (Alaska)*	6,194	20,321
Mt Logan	*Canada*	6,050	19,849
Citlaltepetl	*Mexico*	5,700	18,701
Mt St Elias	*USA/Canada*	5,489	18,008
Popocatepetl	*Mexico*	5,452	17,887
Mt Foraker	*USA (Alaska)*	5,304	17,401
Ixtaccihuatl	*Mexico*	5,286	17,342
Lucania	*USA (Alaska)*	5,226	17,145
Mt Steele	*Canada*	5,011	16,440
Mt Bona	*USA (Alaska)*	5,005	16,420
Mt Blackburn	*USA (Alaska)*	4,996	16,391
Mt Sanford	*USA (Alaska)*	4,949	16,237
Mt Wood	*Canada*	4,848	15,905
Nevado de Toluca	*Mexico*	4,670	15,321
Mt Fairweather	*USA (Alaska)*	4,663	15,298
Mt Whitney	*USA*	4,418	14,495
Mt Elbert	*USA*	4,399	14,432
Mt Harvard	*USA*	4,395	14,419
Mt Rainier	*USA*	4,392	14,409
Blanca Peak	*USA*	4,364	14,317
Long's Peak	*USA*	4,345	14,255
Nevado de Colima	*Mexico*	4,339	14,235
Mt Shasta	*USA*	4,317	14,163
Tajumulco	*Guatemala*	4,217	13,835
>Gannett Peak	*USA*	4,202	13,786
Mt Waddington	*Canada*	3,994	13,104
Mt Robson	*Canada*	3,954	12,972
Chirripó Grande	*Costa Rica*	3,837	12,589
Loma Tinta	*Haiti*	3,175	10,417

South America

		m	ft
Aconcagua	*Argentina*	6,960	22,834
Illimani	*Bolivia*	6,882	22,578
Bonete	*Argentina*	6,872	22,546
Ojos del Salado	*Argentina/Chile*	6,863	22,516
Tupungato	*Argentina/Chile*	6,800	22,309
Pissis	*Argentina*	6,779	22,241
Mercedario	*Argentina/Chile*	6,770	22,211
Huascaran	*Peru*	6,768	22,204
Llullaillaco	*Argentina/Chile*	6,723	22,057
Nudo de Cachi	*Argentina*	6,720	22,047
Yerupaja	*Peru*	6,632	21,758
N. de Tres Cruces	*Argentina/Chile*	6,620	21,719
Incahuasi	*Argentina/Chile*	6,601	21,657
Ancohuma	*Bolivia*	6,550	21,489
Sajama	*Bolivia*	6,520	21,391
Coropuna	*Peru*	6,425	21,079
Ausangate	*Peru*	6,384	20,945
Cerro del Toro	*Argentina*	6,380	20,932
Ampato	*Peru*	6,310	20,702
>Chimborasso	*Ecuador*	6,267	20,561
Cotopaxi	*Ecuador*	5,897	19,347
Cayambe	*Ecuador*	5,796	19,016
S. Nev. de S. Marta	*Colombia*	5,775	18,947
Pico Bolivar	*Venezuela*	5,007	16,427

Antarctica

	m	ft
Vinson Massif	4,897	16,066
Mt Kirkpatrick	4,528	14,855

Ocean Depths

Atlantic Ocean

	m	ft
Puerto Rico (Milwaukee) Deep [7]	9,200	30,183
Cayman Trench [10]	7,680	25,197
Gulf of Mexico	5,203	17,070
Mediterranean Sea	5,121	16,801
Black Sea	2,211	7,254
North Sea	310	1,017
Baltic Sea	294	965
Hudson Bay	111	364

Indian Ocean

	m	ft
Java Trench	7,450	24,442
Red Sea	2,266	7,434
Persian Gulf	73	239

Pacific Ocean

	m	ft
Mariana Trench [1]	11,022	36,161
Tonga Trench [2]	10,822	35,505
Japan Trench [3]	10,554	34,626
Kuril Trench [4]	10,542	34,586
Mindanao Trench [5]	10,497	34,439
Kermadec Trench [6]	10,047	32,962
Peru-Chile Trench [8]	8,050	26,410
Aleutian Trench [9]	7,822	25,662
Middle American Trench	6,662	21,857

Arctic Ocean

	m	ft
Molloy Deep	5,608	18,399

Land Lows

		m	ft
Caspian Sea	*Europe*	-28	-92
Dead Sea	*Asia*	-400	-1,312
Lake Assal	*Africa*	-156	-512
Lake Eyre North	*Oceania*	-16	-52
Death Valley	*N. America*	-86	-282
Valdés Peninsula	*S. America*	-40	-131

Rivers

Europe

		km	miles
Volga	*Caspian Sea*	3,700	2,300
Danube	*Black Sea*	2,850	1,770
Ural	*Caspian Sea*	2,535	1,574
Dnieper	*Volga*	2,285	1,420
Kama	*Volga*	2,030	1,260
Don	*Volga*	1,990	1,240
Petchora	*Arctic Ocean*	1,790	1,110
Oka	*Volga*	1,480	920
Belaya	*Kama*	1,420	880
Dniester	*Black Sea*	1,400	870
Vyatka	*Kama*	1,370	850
Rhine	*North Sea*	1,320	820
N. Dvina	*Arctic Ocean*	1,290	800
Desna	*Dnieper*	1,190	740
Elbe	*North Sea*	1,145	710
>Vistula	*Baltic Sea*	1,090	675
Loire	*Atlantic Ocean*	1,020	635
W. Dvina	*Baltic Sea*	1,019	633

Asia

		km	miles
Yangtze [3]	*Pacific Ocean*	6,380	3,960
Yenisey-Angara [5]	*Arctic Ocean*	5,550	3,445
Ob-Irtysh [6]	*Arctic Ocean*	5,410	3,360
Hwang Ho [7]	*Pacific Ocean*	4,840	3,005
Amur [9]	*Pacific Ocean*	4,510	2,800
Mekong [10]	*Pacific Ocean*	4,500	2,795
Lena	*Arctic Ocean*	4,400	2,730
Irtysh	*Ob*	4,250	2,640
Yenisey	*Arctic Ocean*	4,090	2,540
Ob	*Arctic Ocean*	3,680	2,285
Indus	*Indian Ocean*	3,100	1,925
Brahmaputra	*Indian Ocean*	2,900	1,800
Syr Darya	*Aral Sea*	2,860	1,775
Salween	*Indian Ocean*	2,800	1,740
Euphrates	*Indian Ocean*	2,700	1,675
Vilyuy	*Lena*	2,650	1,645
Kolyma	*Arctic Ocean*	2,600	1,615
Amu Darya	*Aral Sea*	2,540	1,575
Ural	*Caspian Sea*	2,535	1,575
Ganges	*Indian Ocean*	2,510	1,560
>Si Kiang	*Pacific Ocean*	2,100	1,305
Irrawaddy	*Indian Ocean*	2,010	1,250
Tigris	*Indian Ocean*	1,900	1,180
Angara	*Yenisey*	1,830	1,135
Yamuna	*Indian Ocean*	1,400	870

Africa

		km	miles
Nile [1]	*Mediterranean*	6,670	4,140
Zaïre/Congo [8]	*Atlantic Ocean*	4,670	2,900
Niger	*Atlantic Ocean*	4,180	2,595
Zambezi	*Indian Ocean*	2,740	1,700
Oubangi/Uele	*Zaïre*	2,250	1,400
Kasai	*Zaïre*	1,950	1,210
Shaballe	*Indian Ocean*	1,930	1,200
Orange	*Atlantic Ocean*	1,860	1,155
Cubango	*Okavango*	1,800	1,120
Limpopo	*Indian Ocean*	1,600	995
>Senegal	*Atlantic Ocean*	1,600	995
Volta	*Atlantic Ocean*	1,500	930
Benue	*Niger*	1,350	840

Australia

		km	miles
Murray-Darling	*Indian Ocean*	3,720	2,310
Darling	*Murray*	3,070	1,905
Murray	*Indian Ocean*	2,575	1,600
Murrumbidgee	*Murray*	1,690	1,050

North America

		km	miles
Mississ.-Missouri [4]	*Gulf of Mexico*	6,020	3,740
Mackenzie	*Arctic Ocean*	4,240	2,630
Mississippi	*Gulf of Mexico*	3,780	2,350
Missouri	*Mississippi*	3,725	2,310
Yukon	*Pacific Ocean*	3,185	1,980
Rio Grande	*Gulf of Mexico*	3,030	1,880
Arkansas	*Mississippi*	2,340	1,450
Colorado	*Pacific Ocean*	2,330	1,445
Red	*Mississippi*	2,040	1,270
Columbia	*Pacific Ocean*	1,950	1,210
Saskatchewan	*Lake Winnipeg*	1,940	1,205
Snake	*Columbia*	1,670	1,040
Churchill	*Hudson Bay*	1,600	990
Ohio	*Mississippi*	1,580	980
Brazos	*Gulf of Mexico*	1,400	870
>St Lawrence	*Atlantic Ocean*	1,170	730

South America

		km	miles
Amazon [2]	*Atlantic Ocean*	6,430	3,990
Paraná-Plate	*Atlantic Ocean*	4,000	2,480
Purus	*Amazon*	3,350	2,080
Madeira	*Amazon*	3,200	1,990
São Francisco	*Atlantic Ocean*	2,900	1,800
Paraná	*Plate*	2,800	1,740
Tocantins	*Atlantic Ocean*	2,640	1,640
Paraguay	*Paraná*	2,550	1,580
Orinoco	*Atlantic Ocean*	2,500	1,550
Pilcomayo	*Paraná*	2,500	1,550
Araguaia	*Tocantins*	2,250	1,400
Juruá	*Amazon*	2,000	1,240
Xingu	*Amazon*	1,980	1,230
Ucayali	*Amazon*	1,900	1,180
Maranón	*Amazon*	1,600	990
>Uruguay	*Plate*	1,600	990
Magdalena	*Caribbean Sea*	1,540	960

Lakes

Europe

		km²	miles²
Lake Ladoga	*Russia*	18,400	7,100
Lake Onega	*Russia*	9,700	3,700
Saimaa system	*Finland*	8,000	3,100
Vänern	*Sweden*	5,500	2,100
Rybinsk Res.	*Russia*	4,700	1,800

Asia

		km²	miles²
Caspian Sea [1]	*Asia*	371,000	143,000
Aral Sea [6]	*Kazakh./Uzbek.*	36,000	13,900
Lake Baykal [9]	*Russia*	31,500	12,200
Tonlé Sap	*Cambodia*	20,000	7,700
Lake Balkhash	*Kazakhstan*	18,500	7,100
>Dongting Hu	*China*	12,000	4,600
Issyk Kul	*Kirghizia*	6,200	2,400
Lake Urmia	*Iran*	5,900	2,300
Koko Nur	*China*	5,700	2,200
Poyang Hu	*China*	5,000	1,900
Lake Khanka	*China/Russia*	4,400	1,700
Lake Van	*Turkey*	3,500	1,400
Ubsa Nur	*China*	3,400	1,300

Africa

		km²	miles²
Lake Victoria [3]	*E. Africa*	68,000	26,000
Lake Tanganyika [7]	*C. Africa*	33,000	13,000
Lake Malawi [10]	*E. Africa*	29,000	11,000
Lake Chad	*C. Africa*	25,000	9,700
Lake Turkana	*Ethiop./Kenya*	8,500	3,300
Lake Volta	*Ghana*	8,500	3,300
Lake Bangweulu	*Zambia*	8,000	3,100
Lake Rukwa	*Tanzania*	7,000	2,700
Lake Mai-Ndombe	*Zaïre*	6,500	2,500
>Lake Kariba	*Zamb./Zimbab.*	5,300	2,000
Lake Mobutu	*Uganda/Zaïre*	5,300	2,000
Lake Nasser	*Egypt/Sudan*	5,200	2,000
Lake Mweru	*Zambia/Zaïre*	4,900	1,900
Lake Kyoga	*Uganda*	4,400	1,700
Lake Tana	*Ethiopia*	3,630	1,400

Australia

		km²	miles²
Lake Eyre	*Australia*	9,000	3,500
Lake Torrens	*Australia*	5,800	2,200

North America

		km²	miles²
Lake Superior [2]	*Canada/USA*	82,200	31,700
Lake Huron [4]	*Canada/USA*	59,600	23,000
Lake Michigan [5]	*USA*	58,000	22,400
Great Bear Lake [8]	*Canada*	31,500	12,200
Great Slave Lake	*Canada*	28,700	11,100
Lake Erie	*Canada/USA*	25,700	9,900
Lake Winnipeg	*Canada*	24,400	9,400
Lake Ontario	*Canada/USA*	19,500	7,500
Lake Nicaragua	*Nicaragua*	8,200	3,200
>Lake Athabasca	*Canada*	8,000	3,100
Smallwood Res.	*Canada*	6,530	2,520
Reindeer Lake	*Canada*	6,400	2,500
Lake Winnipegosis	*Canada*	5,400	2,100
Nettilling Lake	*Canada*	5,500	2,100

South America

		km²	miles²
Lake Titicaca	*Bolivia/Peru*	8,200	3,200
Lake Poopo	*Peru*	2,800	1,100

Islands

Europe

		km²	miles²
Great Britain [8]	*UK*	229,880	88,700
Iceland	*Atlantic*	103,000	39,800
Ireland	*Ireland/UK*	84,400	32,600
Novaya Zemlya (N.)	*Russia*	48,200	18,600
W. Spitzbergen	*Norway*	39,000	15,100
Novaya Zemlya (S.)	*Russia*	33,200	12,800
Sicily	*Italy*	25,500	9,800
Sardinia	*Italy*	24,000	9,300
N. E. Spitzbergen	*Norway*	15,000	5,600
Corsica	*France*	8,700	3,400
Crete	*Greece*	8,350	3,200
Zealand	*Denmark*	6,850	2,600

Asia

		km²	miles²
Borneo [3]	*S. E. Asia*	737,000	284,000
Sumatra [6]	*Indonesia*	425,000	164,000
Honshu [7]	*Japan*	230,000	88,800
Celebes	*Indonesia*	189,000	73,000
Java	*Indonesia*	126,700	48,900
Luzon	*Philippines*	104,700	40,400
Mindanao	*Philippines*	95,000	36,700
Hokkaido	*Japan*	78,400	30,300
Sakhalin	*Russia*	76,400	29,500
Sri Lanka	*Indian Ocean*	65,600	25,300
Taiwan	*Pacific Ocean*	36,000	13,900
Kyushu	*Japan*	35,700	13,800
Hainan	*China*	34,000	13,100
Timor	*Indonesia*	33,600	13,000
Shikoku	*Japan*	18,800	7,300
Halmahera	*Indonesia*	18,000	6,900
Ceram	*Indonesia*	17,150	6,600
Sumbawa	*Indonesia*	15,450	6,000
Flores	*Indonesia*	15,200	5,900
Samar	*Philippines*	13,100	5,100
>Negros	*Philippines*	12,700	4,900
Bangka	*Indonesia*	12,000	4,600
Panay	*Philippines*	11,500	4,400
Sumba	*Indonesia*	11,100	4,300
Mindoro	*Philippines*	9,750	3,800
Bali	*Indonesia*	5,600	2,200
Cyprus	*Mediterranean*	3,570	1,400
Wrangel Is.	*Russia*	2,800	1,000

Africa

		km²	miles²
Madagascar [4]	*Indian Ocean*	587,000	226,600
Socotra	*Indian Ocean*	3,600	1,400
Réunion	*Indian Ocean*	2,500	965
Tenerife	*Atlantic Ocean*	2,350	900
Mauritius	*Indian Ocean*	1,865	720

Oceania

		km²	miles²
New Guinea [2]	*Ind./Pap. NG*	780,000	301,080
New Zealand (S.)	*New Zealand*	150,500	58,100
New Zealand (N.)	*New Zealand*	114,400	44,200
Tasmania	*Australia*	67,800	26,200
New Britain	*Papua NG*	37,800	14,600
New Caledonia	*Pacific Ocean*	16,100	6,200
Viti Levu	*Fiji*	10,500	4,100
Hawaii	*Pacific Ocean*	10,450	4,000
Bougainville	*Papua NG*	9,600	3,700
Guadalcanal	*Solomon Is.*	6,500	2,500
>Vanua Levu	*Fiji*	5,550	2,100
New Ireland	*Papua NG*	3,200	1,200

North America

		km²	miles²
Greenland [1]	*Greenland*	2,175,600	839,800
Baffin Is. [5]	*Canada*	508,000	196,100
Victoria Is. [9]	*Canada*	212,200	81,900
Ellesmere Is. [10]	*Canada*	212,000	81,800
Cuba	*Cuba*	114,500	44,200
Newfoundland	*Canada*	96,000	37,100
Hispaniola	*Atlantic Ocean*	76,200	29,400
Banks Is.	*Canada*	67,000	25,900
Devon Is.	*Canada*	54,500	21,000
Melville Is.	*Canada*	42,400	16,400
>Vancouver Is.	*Canada*	32,150	12,400
Somerset Is.	*Canada*	24,300	9,400
Jamaica	*Caribbean Sea*	11,400	4,400
Puerto Rico	*Atlantic Ocean*	8,900	3,400
Cape Breton Is.	*Canada*	4,000	1,500

South America

		km²	miles²
Tierra del Fuego	*Argent./Chile*	47,000	18,100
Falkland Is. (E.)	*Atlantic Ocean*	6,800	2,600
South Georgia	*Atlantic Ocean*	4,200	1,600
Galapagos (Isabela)	*Pacific Ocean*	2,250	870

PHILIP'S WORLD MAPS

The reference maps which form the main body of this atlas have been prepared in accordance with the highest standards of international cartography to provide an accurate and detailed representation of the earth. The scales and projections used have been carefully chosen to give balanced coverage of the world, while emphasizing the most densely populated and economically significant regions. A hallmark of Philip's mapping is the use of hill shading and relief colouring to create a graphic impression of landforms: this makes the maps exceptionally easy to read. However, knowledge of the key features employed in the construction and presentation of the maps will enable the reader to derive the fullest benefit from the atlas.

Map sequence

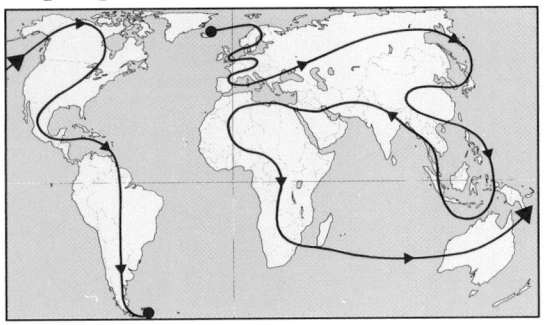

The atlas covers the earth continent by continent: first Europe; then its land neighbour Asia (mapped north before south, in a clockwise sequence), then Africa, Australia and Oceania, North America and South America. This is the classic arrangement adopted by most cartographers since the 16th century. For each continent, there are maps at a variety of scales. First, physical relief and political maps of the whole continent. Then a series of larger-scale maps of the regions within the continent, each followed, where required, by still larger-scale maps of the most important or densely populated areas. The governing principle is that by turning the pages of the atlas, the reader moves steadily from north to south through each continent, with each map overlapping its neighbours. A key map showing this sequence, and the area covered by each map, can be found on the endpapers of the atlas.

Map presentation

With very few exceptions (eg for the Arctic and Antarctic), the maps are drawn with north at the top, regardless of whether they are presented upright or sideways on the page. In the borders will be found the map title; a locator diagram showing the area covered and the page numbers for maps of adjacent areas; the scale; the projection used; the degrees of latitude and longitude; and the letters and figures used in the index for locating place names and geographical features. Physical relief maps also have a height reference panel identifying the colours used for each layer of contouring.

Map symbols

Each map contains a vast amount of detail which can only be conveyed clearly and accurately by the use of symbols. Points and circles of varying sizes locate and identify the relative importance of towns and cities; different styles of type are employed for administrative, geographical and regional place names. A variety of pictorial symbols denote landscape features such as glaciers, marshes and reefs, and man-made structures including roads, railways, airports, canals and dams. International borders are shown by red lines. Where neighbouring countries are in dispute, for example in the Middle East, the maps show the *de facto* boundary between nations, regardless of the legal or historical situation. The symbols are explained on the first page of the World Maps section of the atlas.

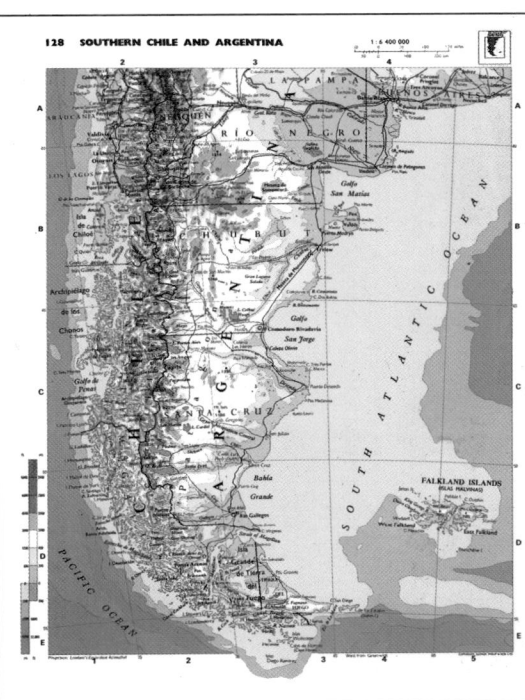

128 SOUTHERN CHILE AND ARGENTINA

Map scales

1: 16 000 000
1 inch = 252 statute miles

The scale of each map is given in the numerical form known as the 'representative fraction'. The first figure is always one, signifying one unit of distance on the map; the second figure, usually in millions, is the number by which the map unit must be multiplied to give the equivalent distance on the earth's surface. Calculations can easily be made in centimetres and kilometres, by dividing the earth units figure by 100 000 (ie deleting the last five 0s). Thus 1:1 000 000 means 1 cm = 10 km. The calculation for inches and miles is more laborious, but 1 000 000 divided by 63 360 (the number of inches in a mile) shows that 1:1 000 000 means approximately 1 inch = 16 miles. The table below provides distance equivalents for scales down to 1:50 000 000.

LARGE SCALE		
1: 1 000 000	1 cm = 10 km	1 inch = 16 miles
1: 2 500 000	1 cm = 25 km	1 inch = 39.5 miles
1: 5 000 000	1 cm = 50 km	1 inch = 79 miles
1: 6 000 000	1 cm = 60 km	1 inch = 95 miles
1: 8 000 000	1 cm = 80 km	1 inch = 126 miles
1: 10 000 000	1 cm = 100 km	1 inch = 158 miles
1: 15 000 000	1 cm = 150 km	1 inch = 237 miles
1: 20 000 000	1 cm = 200 km	1 inch = 316 miles
1: 50 000 000	1 cm = 500 km	1 inch = 790 miles
SMALL SCALE		

Measuring distances

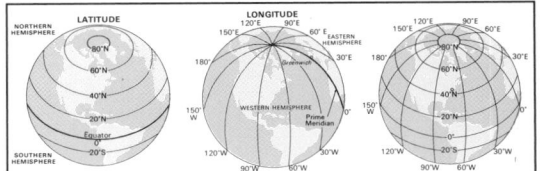

Although each map is accompanied by a scale bar, distances cannot always be measured with confidence because of the distortions involved in portraying the curved surface of the earth on a flat page. As a general rule, the larger the map scale (ie the lower the number of earth units in the representative fraction), the more accurate and reliable will be the distance measured. On small-scale maps such as those of the world and of entire continents, measurement may only be accurate along the 'standard parallels', or central axes, and should not be attempted without considering the map projection.

Map projections

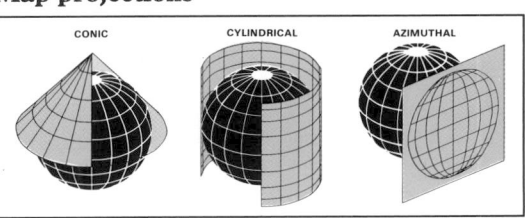

Unlike a globe, no flat map can give a true scale representation of the world in terms of area, shape and position of every region. Each of the numerous systems that have been devised for projecting the curved surface of the earth on to a flat page involves the sacrifice of accuracy in one or more of these elements. The variations in shape and position of landmasses such as Alaska, Greenland and Australia, for example, can be quite dramatic when different projections are compared.

For this atlas, the guiding principle has been to select projections that involve the least distortion of size and distance. The projection used for each map is noted in the border. Most fall into one of three categories - conic, cylindrical or azimuthal - whose basic concepts are shown above. Each involves plotting the forms of the earth's surface on a grid of latitude and longitude lines, which may be shown as parallels, curves or radiating spokes.

Latitude and longitude

Accurate positioning of individual points on the earth's surface is made possible by reference to the geometrical system of latitude and longitude. Latitude *parallels* are drawn west-east around the earth and numbered by degrees north and south of the Equator, which is designated 0° of latitude. Longitude *meridians* are drawn north-south and numbered by degrees east and west of the *prime meridian*, 0° of longitude, which passes through Greenwich in England. By referring to these co-ordinates and their sub-divisions of minutes (1/60th of a degree) and seconds (1/60th of a minute), any place on earth can be located to within a few hundred yards. Latitude and longitude are indicated by blue lines on the maps; they are straight or curved according to the projection employed. Reference to these lines is the easiest way of determining the relative positions of places on different maps, and for plotting compass directions.

Name forms

For ease of reference, both English and local name forms appear in the atlas. Oceans, seas and countries are shown in English throughout the atlas; country names may be abbreviated to their commonly accepted form (eg Germany, not Federal Republic of Germany). Conventional English forms are also used for place names on the smaller-scale maps of the continents. However, local name forms are used on all large-scale and regional maps, with the English form given in brackets only for important cities - the large-scale map of European Russia thus shows Moskva (Moscow). For countries which do not use a Roman script, place names have been transcribed according to the systems adopted by the British and US Geographic Names Authorities. For China, the Pin Yin system has been used, with some more widely known forms appearing in brackets, as with Beijing (Peking). Both English and local names appear in the index, the English form being cross-referenced to the local form.

WORLD MAPS

MAP SYMBOLS

SETTLEMENTS

⬗ PARIS   ◼ Berne   ◉ Livorno   ◉ Brugge   ◉ Algeciras   ○ Fréjus   ○ Oberammergau   ○ Thira

Settlement symbols and type styles vary according to the scale of each map and indicate the importance
of towns on the map rather than specific population figures

∴   Ruins or Archæological Sites   ˅   Wells in Desert

--- ADMINISTRATION ---

————— International Boundaries

− − − International Boundaries
(Undefined or Disputed)

·—··—···· Internal Boundaries

⬭ National Parks

Country Names

NICARAGUA

Administrative
Area Names

KENT

CALABRIA

International boundaries show the *de facto* situation where there are rival claims to territory

--- COMMUNICATIONS ---

————— Principal Roads

∿ Other Roads

-·-·-· Trails and Seasonal Roads

⋊ Passes

⌑ Airfields

— Principal Railways

-·-·- Railways
Under Construction

∿ Other Railways

∃---E Railway Tunnels

····· Principal Canals

--- PHYSICAL FEATURES ---

∿ Perennial Streams

-·-·- Intermittent Streams

⬭ Perennial Lakes

⬭ Intermittent Lakes

Swamps and Marshes

Permanent Ice
and Glaciers

▲ 8848 Elevations in metres

▼ 8050 Sea Depths in metres

1134 Height of Lake Surface
Above Sea Level
in metres

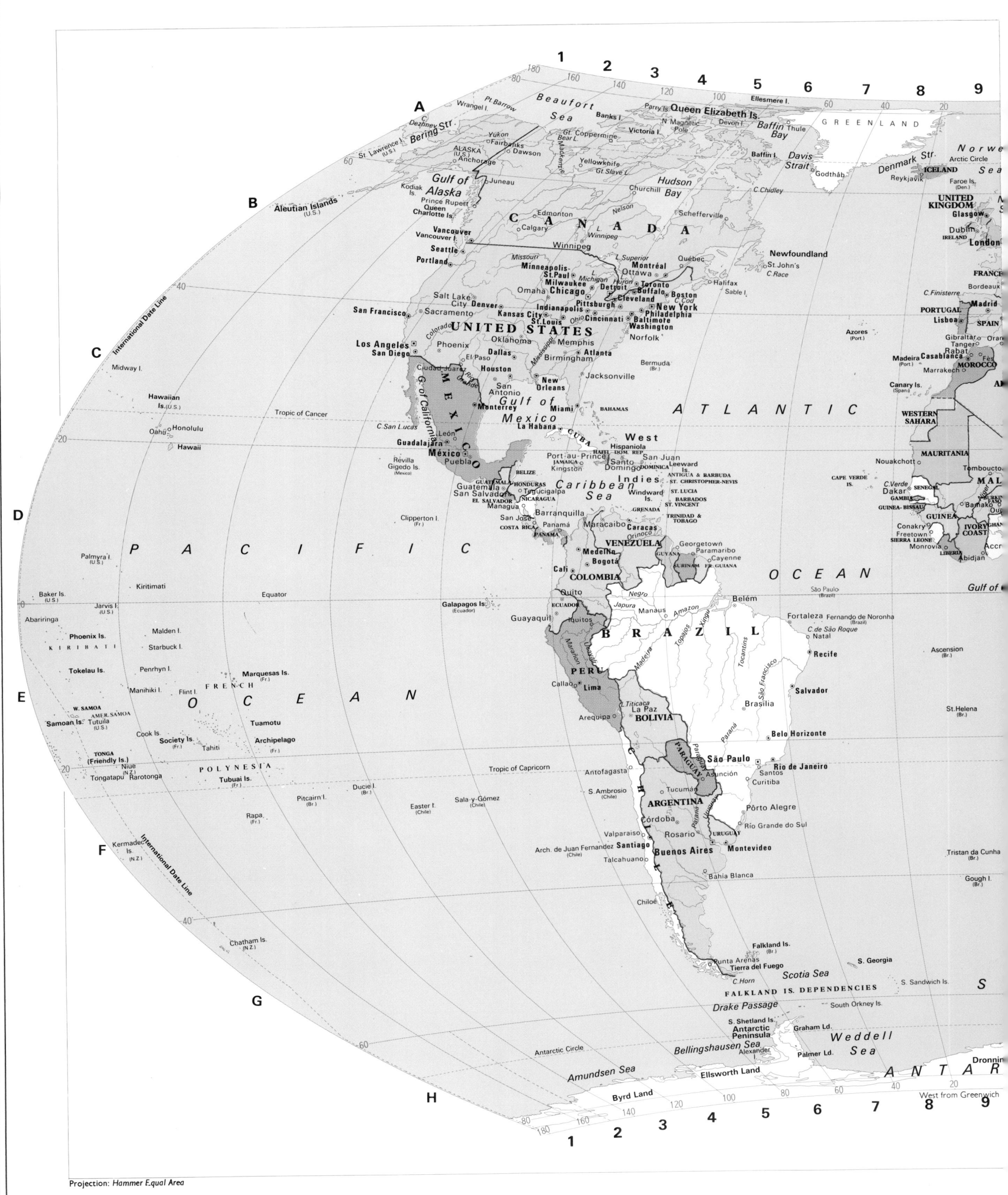

Projection: *Hammer Equal Area*

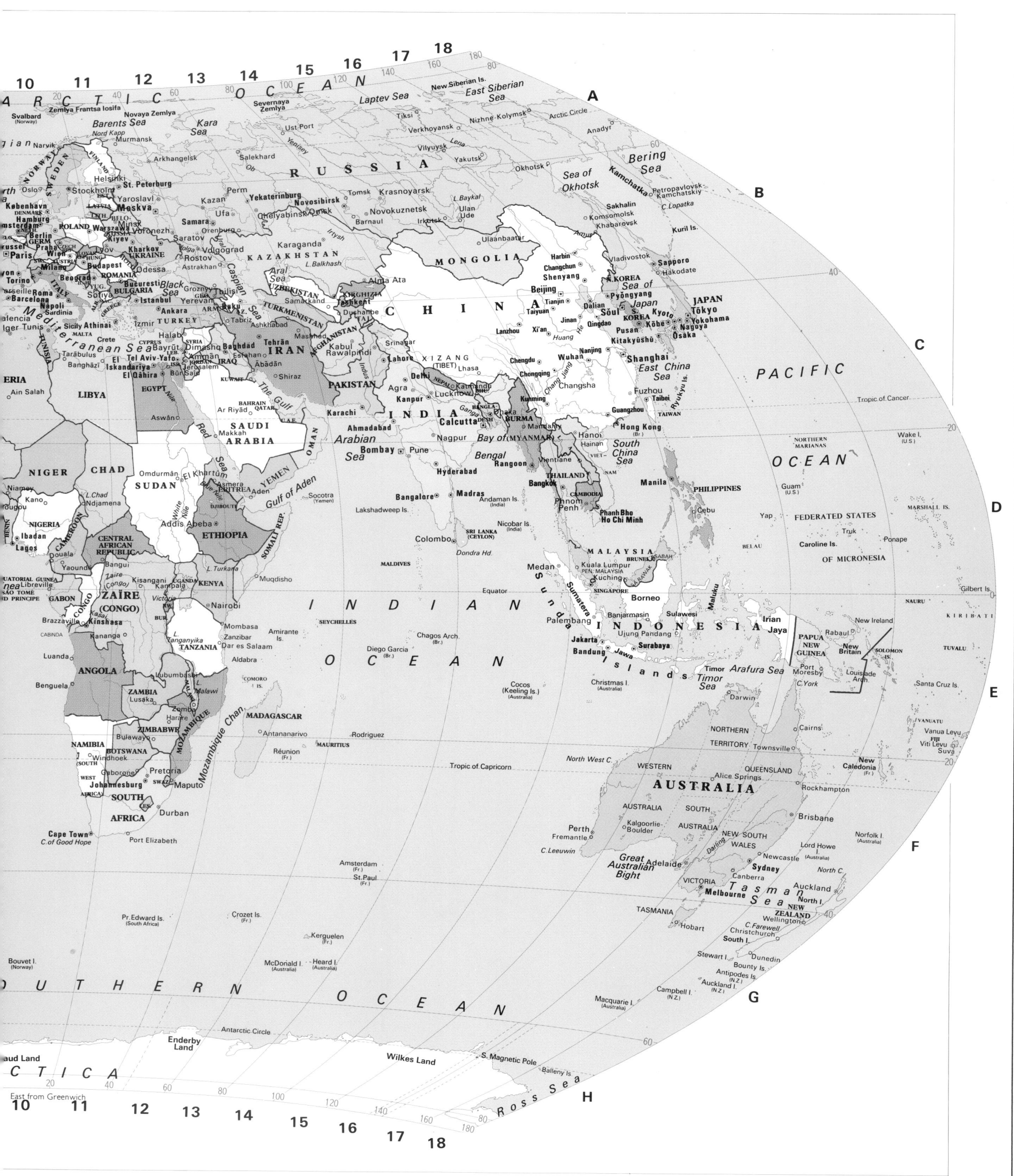

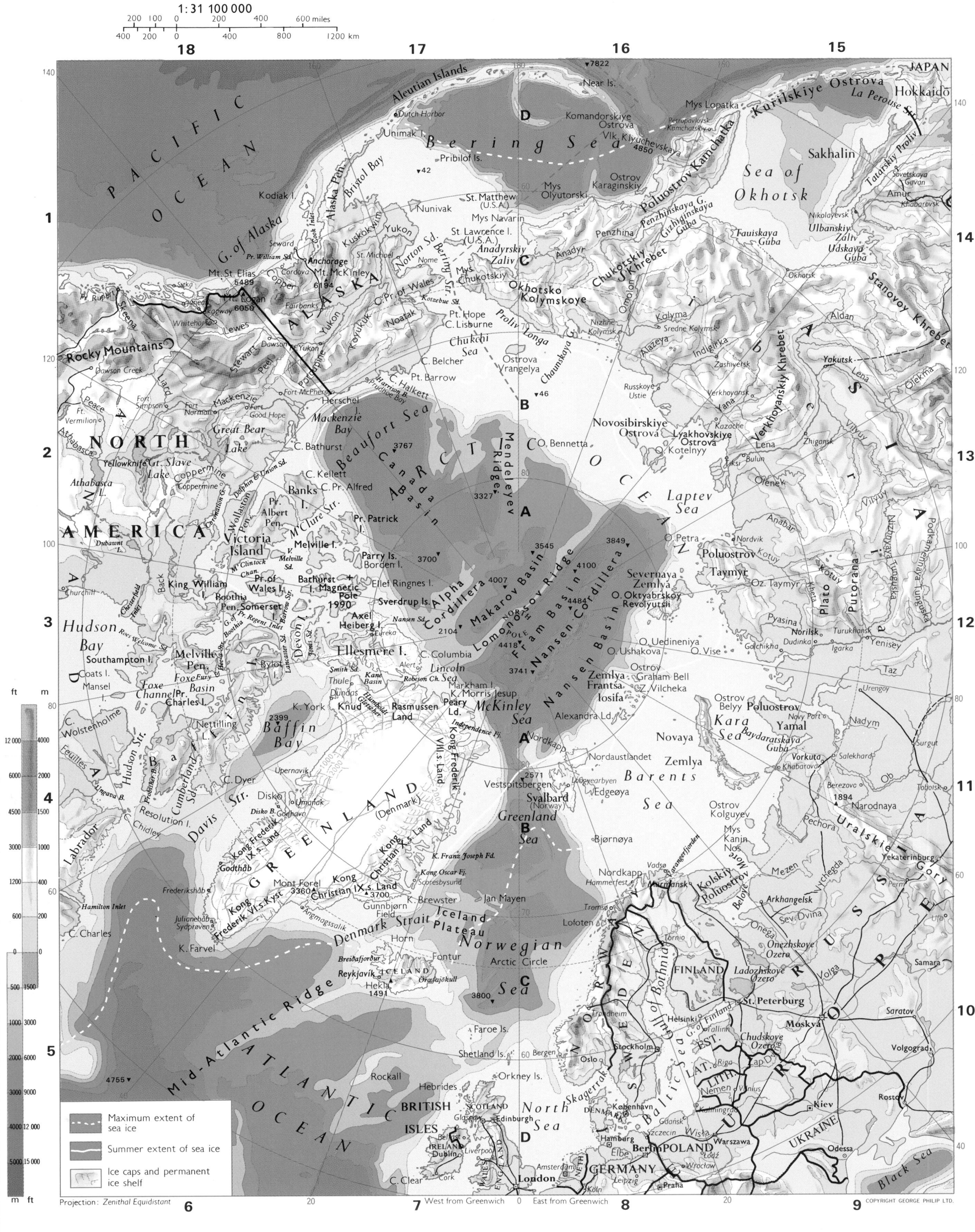

1:31 100 000

Projection: Zenithal Equidistant

COPYRIGHT GEORGE PHILIP LTD.

Maximum extent of sea ice

Summer extent of sea ice

Ice caps and permanent ice shelf

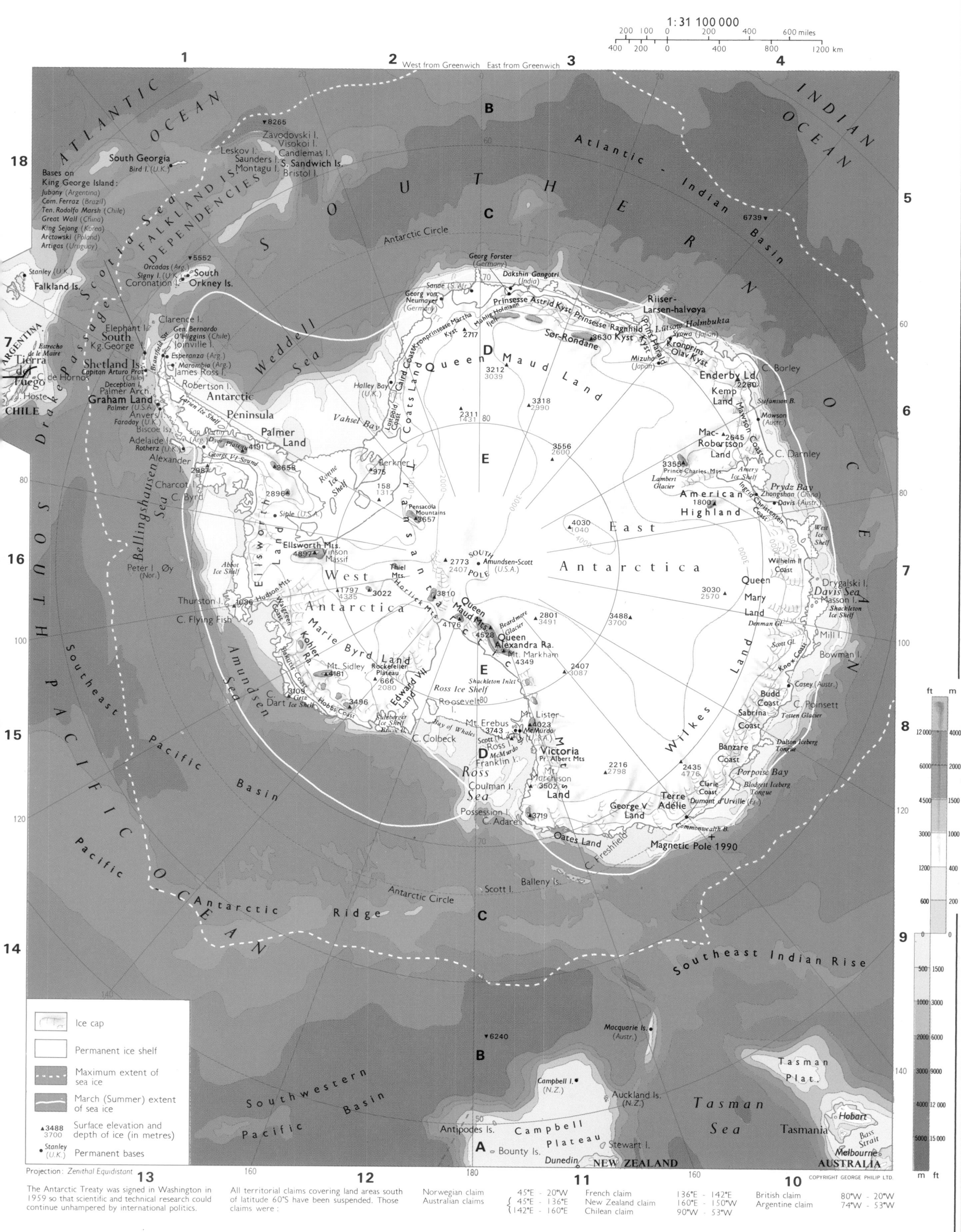

1:17 800 000

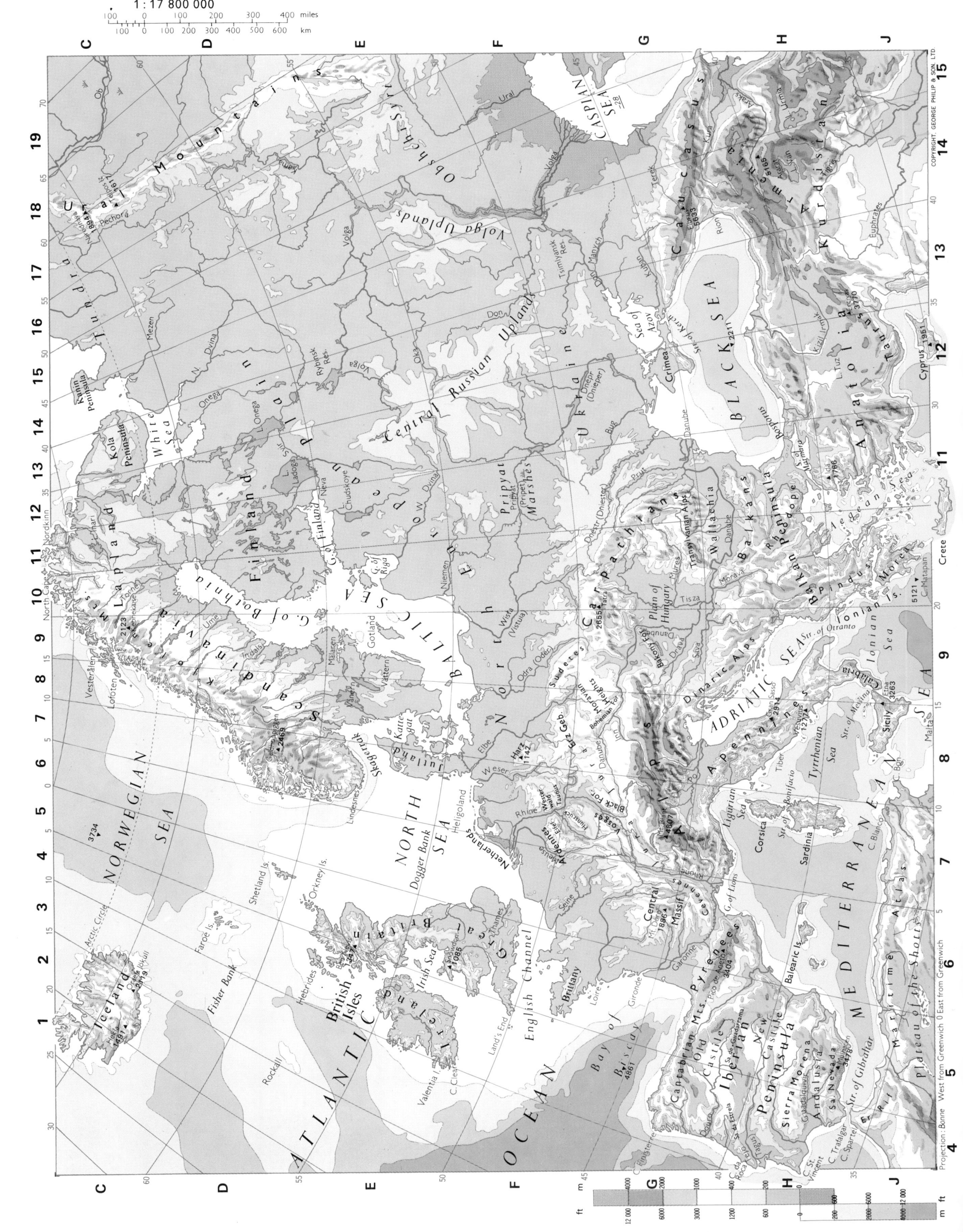

Projection: Bonne   West from Greenwich 0 East from Greenwich

1 : 17 800 000

Scale bar: 100 0 100 200 300 400 miles
100 0 100 200 300 400 500 600 km

COPYRIGHT GEORGE PHILIP & SON LTD

ATLANTIC OCEAN

ICELAND
Reykjavik

NORWAY
Oslo
Bergen
Stavanger
Trondheim
Narvik
Hammerfest
Tromsø

SWEDEN
Stockholm
Göteborg
Malmö
Kiruna

FINLAND
Helsinki
Tampere
Turku

DENMARK
COPENHAGEN
Århus
Ålborg

UNITED KINGDOM
SCOTLAND
Edinburgh
Glasgow
Aberdeen
Dundee
Newcastle
ENGLAND
LONDON
Birmingham
Manchester
Liverpool
Leeds
Sheffield
Bristol
Cardiff
WALES
Southampton
Plymouth
Hull
IRELAND
Dublin
Belfast
Cork

NORTH SEA
BALTIC SEA

ESTONIA
Tallinn
LATVIA
Riga
LITHUANIA
Kaunas
Kaliningrad

BELORUSSIA
Minsk

POLAND
WARSAW
Łódź
Kraków
Wrocław
Gdańsk
Poznań
Szczecin
Katowice

GERMANY
BERLIN
Hamburg
Munich
Cologne
Frankfurt
Stuttgart
Hanover
Bremen
Leipzig
Dresden
Dortmund
Essen
Bonn
Nuremberg

NETHERLANDS
Amsterdam
The Hague
Rotterdam

BELGIUM
BRUSSELS
Antwerp

LUX.

FRANCE
PARIS
Marseille
Lyons
Bordeaux
Nantes
Toulouse
Strasbourg
Nice
Rouen
Le Havre
St. Étienne

SWITZERLAND
Zürich
Basel
Geneva

AUSTRIA
VIENNA
Graz

CZECH REP.
PRAGUE

SLOVAK REP.
Bratislava

HUNGARY
BUDAPEST

SPAIN
MADRID
Barcelona
Valencia
Sevilla
Zaragoza
Málaga
Bilbao
Granada
Córdoba
Valladolid
Murcia

PORTUGAL
Lisbon
Oporto

ITALY
Rome
Milan
Naples
Turin
Genoa
Florence
Venice
Palermo
Catania
Bologna
Bari
Sicily
Sardinia

ROMANIA
BUCHAREST
Cluj-Napoca
Timișoara
Brașov
Constanța

BULGARIA
Sofia
Plovdiv
Varna

YUGOSLAVIA
Belgrade

CROATIA
Zagreb

BOSNIA HERZ.
Sarajevo

MACEDONIA
Skopje

ALBANIA
Tiranë

GREECE
ATHENS
Thessaloníki

MOLDAVIA

UKRAINE
Kiev
Kharkov
Odessa
Dnepropetrovsk
Donetsk
Lvov

RUSSIA
MOSCOW
St. Petersburg
Nizhniy Novgorod
Kazan
Samara
Saratov
Volgograd
Rostov
Perm
Ufa
Voronezh
Murmansk
Arkhangelsk
Yekaterinburg
Chelyabinsk
Omsk

KAZAKHSTAN

GEORGIA
Tbilisi

ARMENIA
Yerevan

AZERBAIJAN
Baku

TURKEY
Ankara
Istanbul
Izmir
Bursa
Adana
Konya

CYPRUS
Nicosia
Limassol

SYRIA
Aleppo

IRAQ
Baghdad
Mosul

IRAN
Tabriz

MOROCCO
Rabat

ALGERIA
Algiers
Oran

TUNISIA
Tunis

MALTA
Valletta

MEDITERRANEAN SEA
ADRIATIC SEA
TYRRHENIAN SEA
IONIAN SEA
AEGEAN SEA
BLACK SEA
CASPIAN SEA
WHITE SEA
NORTH SEA
BAY OF BISCAY
English Channel
Kattegat
Gulf of Bothnia
Skagerrak

Crete
Corsica

LONDON Capital Cities

Projection: Bonne
West from Greenwich 0 East from Greenwich

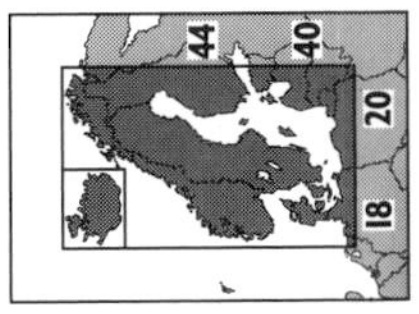

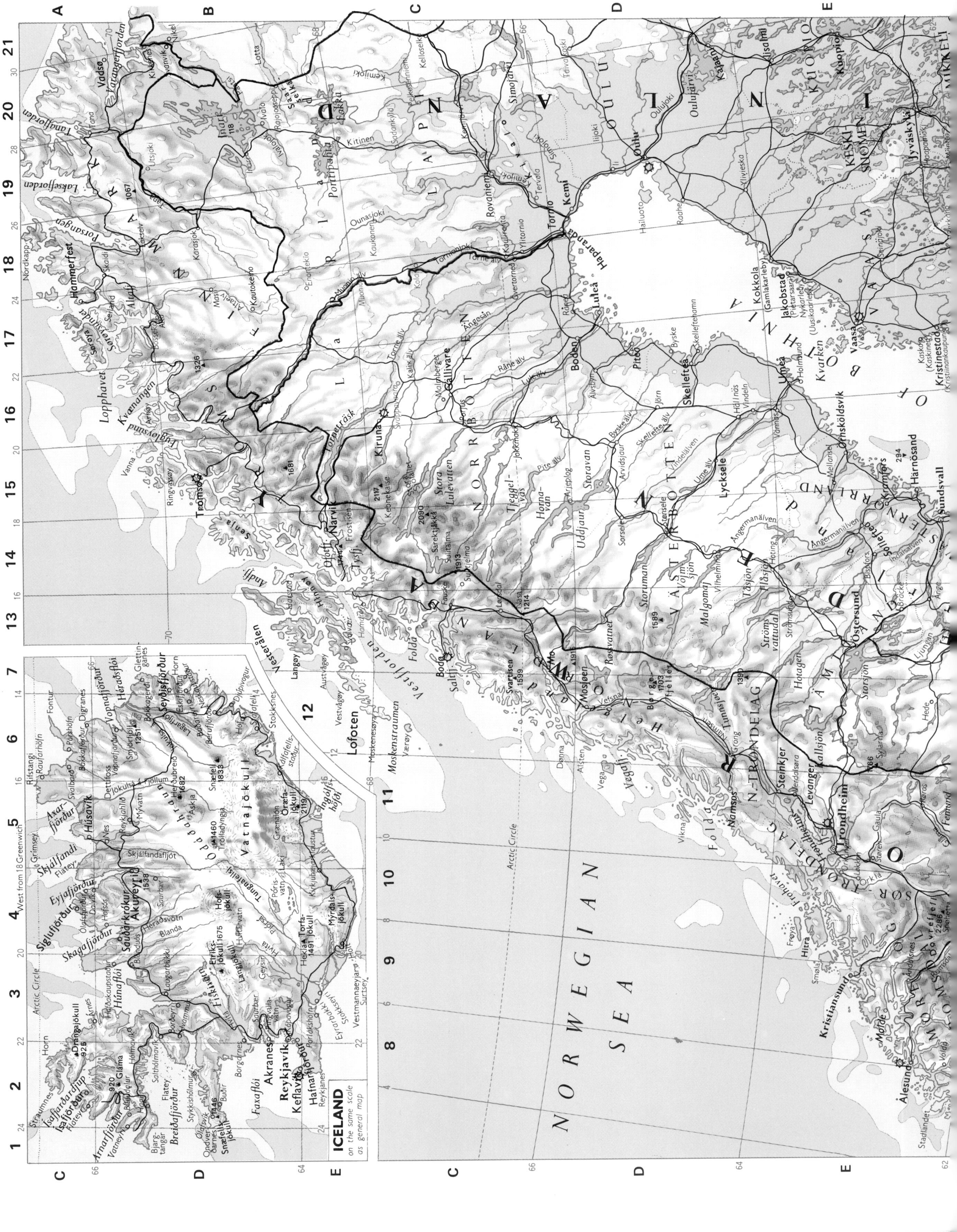

ICELAND
on the same scale
as general map

West from 18 Greenwich

NORWEGIAN SEA

Arctic Circle

Lofoten

Vesterålen

Moskenstraumen

FINLAND

LAPPLAND

NORRBOTTEN

VÄSTERBOTTEN

ÅNGERMANLAND

JÄMTLAND

N.-TRÖNDELAG

SØR-TRÖNDELAG

POHJOIS-SUOMI

KESKI-SUOMI

Hammerfest
Vadsö
Tromsö
Narvik
Bodö
Mosjøen
Trondheim
Steinkjer
Namsos
Ålesund
Kristiansund
Molde
Levanger

Kiruna
Gällivare
Boden
Luleå
Piteå
Skellefteå
Umeå
Lycksele
Östersund
Härnösand
Sundsvall

Rovaniemi
Kemi
Tornio
Haparanda
Oulu
Kokkola
Jakobstad
Vaasa
Kristinestad
Kuopio
Mikkeli
Jyväskylä

Reykjavik
Keflavik
Akranes
Akureyri
Húsavík
Siglufjördur
Saudárkrókur
Seydisfjördur
Vopnafjördur

Vatnajökull
Hofsjökull
Langjökull
Myrdalsjökull
Drangajökull
Snæfellsjökull
Eiriksjökull
Torfajökull

Storuman
Storavan
Uddjaur

BOTHNIA

GULF OF BOTHNIA

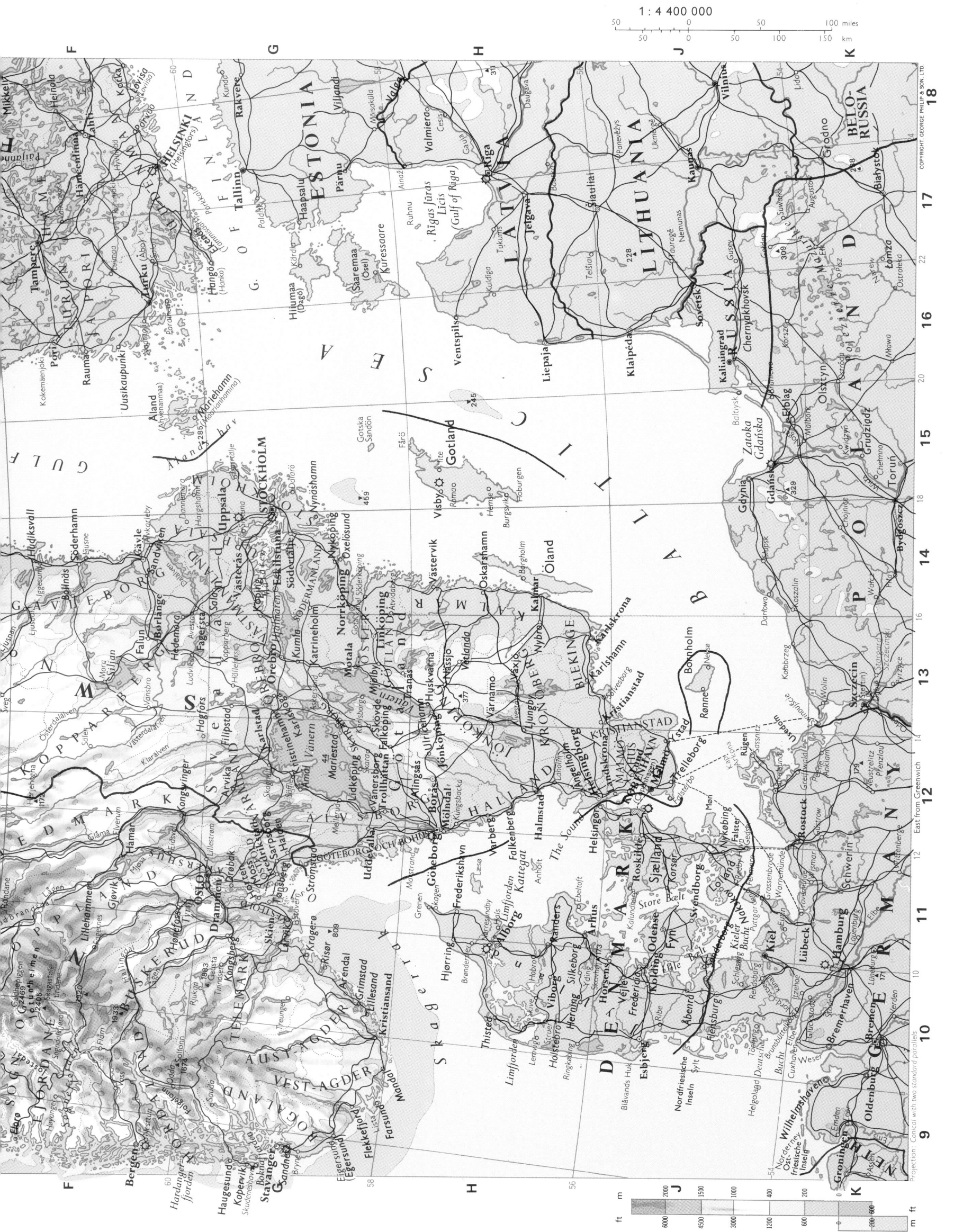

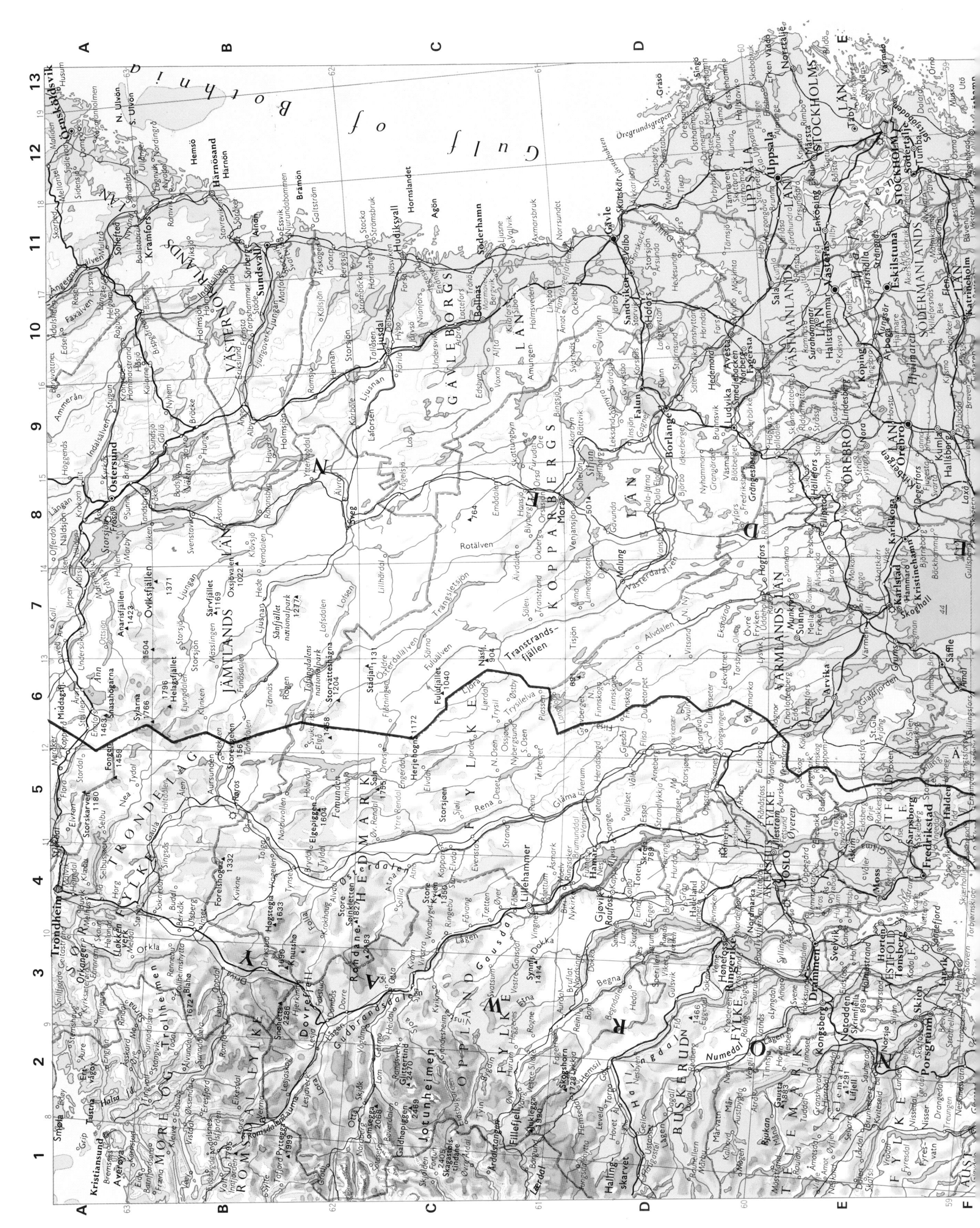

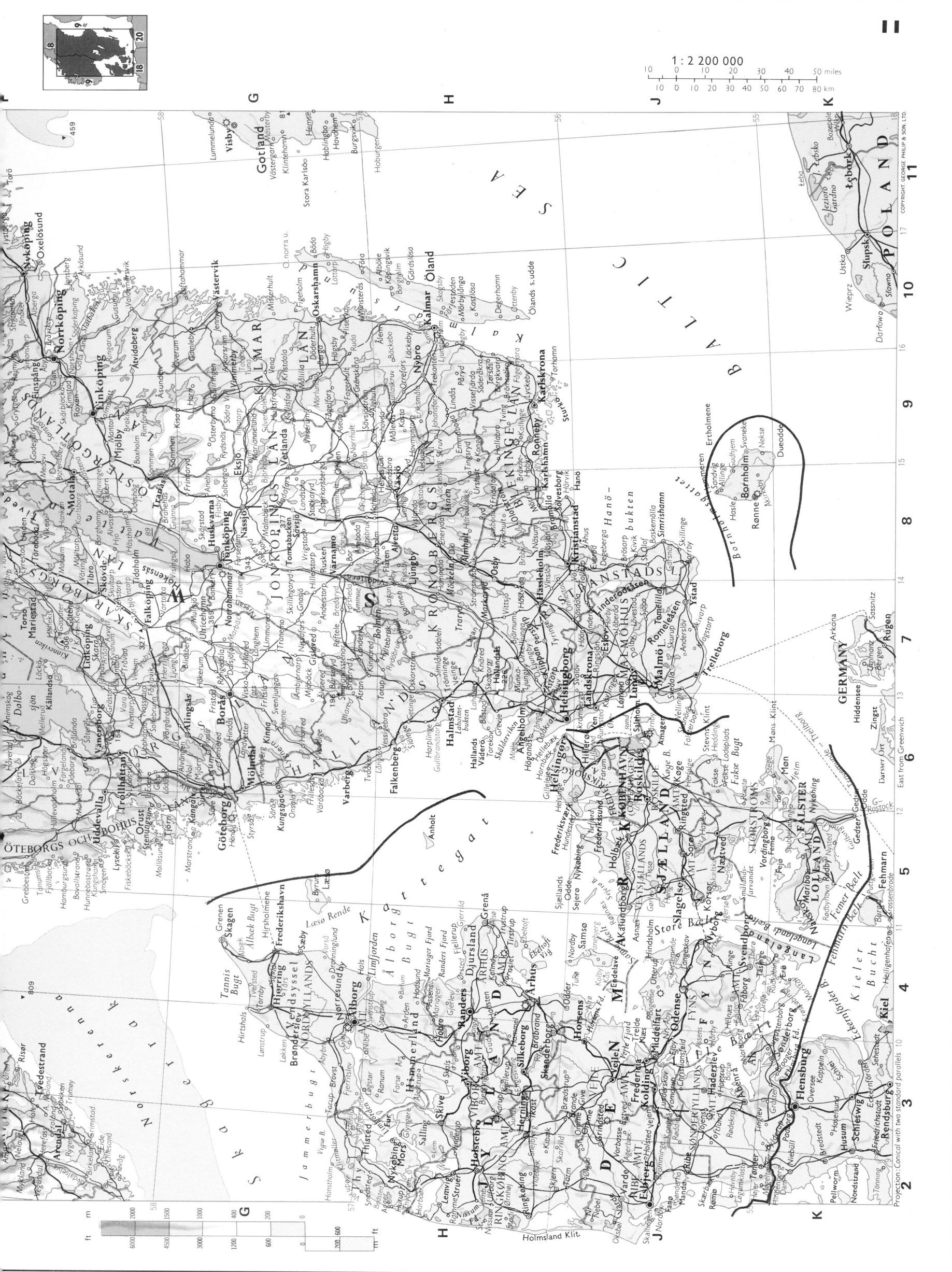

N O R T H   S E A

I R I S H   S E A

S C O T L A N D

NORTHUMBERLAND

P e n n i n e s

S o u t h e r n   U p l a n d s

North Channel

Galloway

CUMBRIA

Cumbrian Mts.

DURHAM

CLEVELAND

TYNE & WEAR

N. YORK MOORS

NORTH YORKSHIRE

LANCASHIRE

MERSEYSIDE

CHESHIRE

GT. MANCHESTER

SOUTH YORKSHIRE

WEST YORKSHIRE

HUMBERSIDE

DERBY

NOTTS

LINCOLN

STAFFORD

CLWYD

GWYNEDD

NORFOLK

Lincoln Wolds

Cheviot Hills

The Cheviot 816

Skiddaw 931

Sca Fell 978

Helvellyn 950

Cross Fell 893

Pen-y-Ghent 693

The Wash

ISLE OF MAN

Snaefell 620

Anglesey

Merrick 843

Goat Fell 874

Broad Law 840

Ochil Hills

Edinburgh

Glasgow

Paisley

Greenock

Dumbarton

Clydebank

Rutherglen

Hamilton

Motherwell

Wishaw

Airdrie

Coatbridge

Falkirk

Stirling

Dunfermline

Kirkcaldy

Leith

Musselburgh

Haddington

Dunbar

Peebles

Galashiels

Selkirk

Hawick

Jedburgh

Kelso

Coldstream

Berwick-upon-Tweed

Eyemouth

Duns

Holy I.

Farne Is.

Alnwick

Morpeth

Ashington

Blyth

Newcastle

Gateshead

Tynemouth

South Shields

Sunderland

Consett

Durham

Bishop Auckland

Hartlepool

Stockton

Billingham

Middlesbrough

Redcar

Darlington

Northallerton

Thirsk

Richmond

Scarborough

Filey

Bridlington

Whitby

Pickering

Malton

York

Selby

Goole

Leeds

Bradford

Harrogate

Knaresborough

Keighley

Halifax

Huddersfield

Wakefield

Barnsley

Rotherham

Sheffield

Doncaster

Scunthorpe

Grimsby

Cleethorpes

Louth

Skegness

Mablethorpe

Hornsea

Withernsea

Spurn Hd.

Hull

Beverley

Driffield

Lincoln

Gainsborough

Worksop

Mansfield

Chesterfield

Matlock

Buxton

Glossop

Stockport

Manchester

Salford

Bolton

Bury

Rochdale

Oldham

Wigan

St. Helens

Warrington

Liverpool

Bootle

Birkenhead

Wallasey

Southport

Blackpool

Fleetwood

Preston

Blackburn

Burnley

Nelson

Colne

Lancaster

Morecambe

Heysham

Barrow

Millom

Whitehaven

Workington

Maryport

Carlisle

Penrith

Kendal

Windermere

Ambleside

Keswick

Cockermouth

Dumfries

Annan

Langholm

Lockerbie

Moffat

Sanquhar

Ayr

Kilmarnock

Saltcoats

Irvine

Newton Stewart

Stranraer

Castle Douglas

Kirkcudbright

Douglas

Ramsey

Peel

Castletown

Holyhead

Caernarfon

Bangor

Conwy

Llandudno

Rhyl

Colwyn Bay

Denbigh

Mold

Wrexham

Flint

Llangollen

Stoke-on-Trent

Newcastle-under-Lyme

Crewe

Nantwich

Macclesfield

Congleton

Derby

Nottingham

Stafford

Burton-on-Trent

Uttoxeter

Cromer

Great Yarmouth

Kings Lynn

Hunstanton

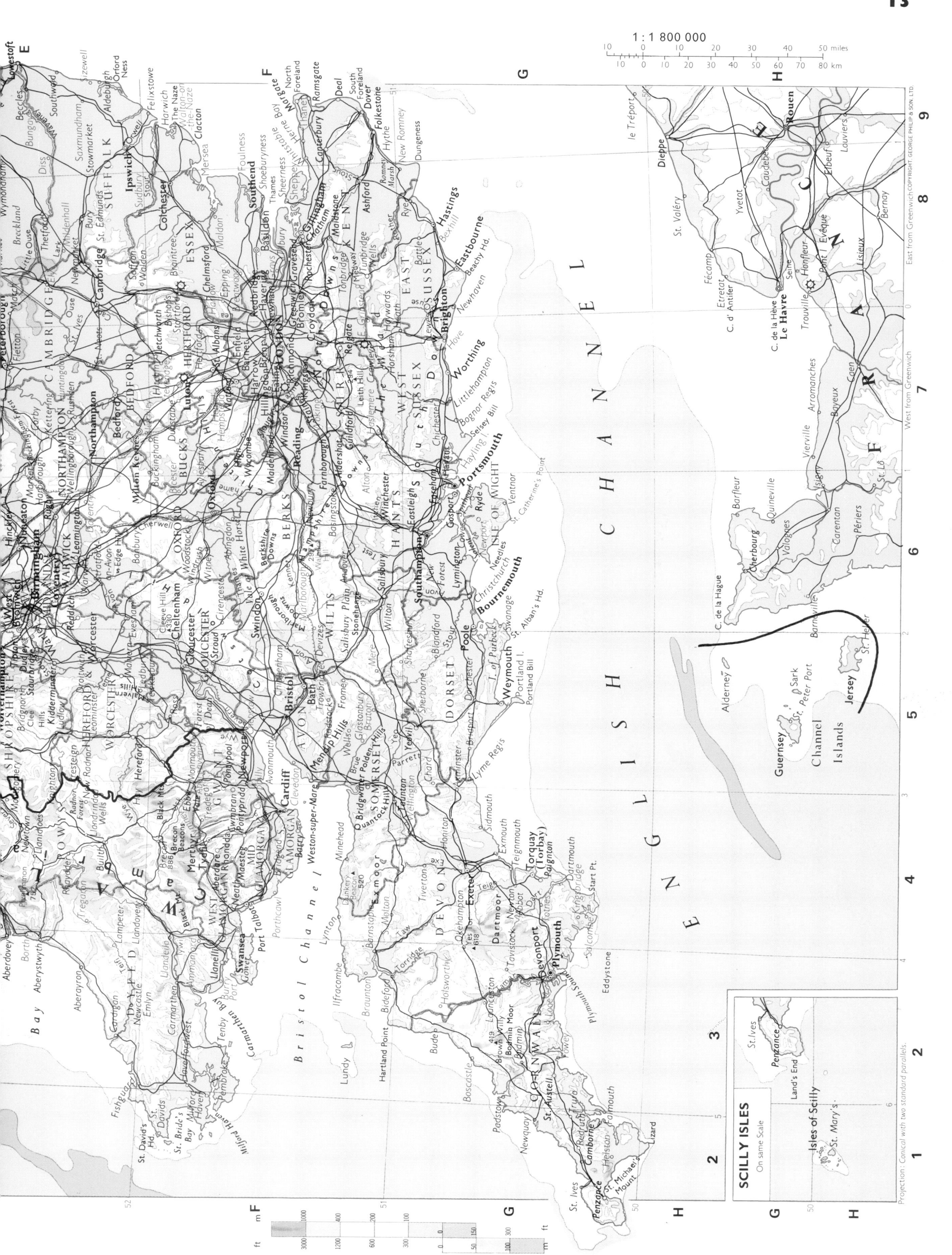

1 : 1 800 000

SCILLY ISLES
On same Scale

Projection: Conical with two standard parallels.

East from Greenwich COPYRIGHT GEORGE PHILIP & SON LTD.

14 SCOTLAND

1 : 1 800 000

1 : 1 800 000

10 20 30 40 50 miles
10 0 10 20 30 40 50 60 70 80 km

ATLANTIC OCEAN

NORTH CHANNEL

IRISH SEA

St. George's Channel

Provinces and Counties

DONEGAL
NORTHERN IRELAND
ULSTER
Sperrin Mts.
Londonderry
Coleraine
Ballymoney
Ballycastle
Giant's Causeway
Rathlin I.
Ballymena
Larne
Antrim
Carrickfergus
Belfast
Lisburn
Bangor
Newtownards
Ards Pen.
Armagh
Banbridge
Downpatrick
Dundrum
Newcastle
Mourne Mts.
Slieve Donard 852
Warrenpoint
Newry
Castleblayney
Carlingford L.
Greenore
Dundalk
Dundalk Bay

Malin Hd.
Inishowen Pen.
Carndonagh
Moville
Buncrana
Bloody Foreland
Tory I.
Horn Hd.
Sheep Haven
Lough Swilly
Gweedore Mts.
Errigal 752
Aran I.
Derryveagh Mts.
Letterkenny
Glenties
Gweebarra B.
Loughros More B.
Rossan Pt.
Rathlin O Birne I.
Killybegs
Donegal
Bundoran
Ballyshannon
Lifford
Strabane
Mourne
Omagh
Irvinestown
Lower L. Erne
Enniskillen
Upper L. Erne
Clones
Monaghan
Cootehill
Cavan
Carrickmacross
Kingscourt
Sawel 683
Magherafelt
Cookstown
Dungannon
Blackwater
Portadown
Lurgan (Craigavon)
Lough Neagh
Bann
Main

DONEGAL BAY
Downpatrick Hd.
Killala B.
Erris Hd.
Broad Haven
Belmullet
Mullet Peninsula
Blacksod Bay
Achill Hd.
Achill I.
Achill
Clare I.
Clew Bay
Croagh Patrick 765
Mweelrea 819
Inishbofin
Slyne Hd.
Twelve Pins
Connemara
Cliffs
Killala
Ballina
Nephin 806
L. Conn
L. Cullin
Castlebar
Westport
Newport
L. Mask
Clifden
Ballinrobe
Robe
Cong
L. Corrib
Galway
Galway Bay
Inishmore
Aran Is.
Kilkieran B.

SLIGO
Sligo B.
Sligo
Colloney
L. Allen
Leitrim
Arrow
Boyle
Carrick-on-Shannon
ROSCOMMON
Castlereagh
Roscommon
LONGFORD
Longford
Granard
Gowna
L. Sheelin
Oldcastle
Ceanannus Mor (Kells)
An Uaimh (Navan)
Trim
MEATH
Drogheda
Balbriggan
Swords
Lambay I.
Howth Head
DUBLIN
Ireland's Eye
Dublin (Baile Atha Cliath)
Dublin Bay
Dun Laoghaire
Bray

CONNACHT
MAYO
GALWAY
Tuam
Claremorris
Athenry
Loughrea
Ballinasloe
Portumna
Slieve Aughty
Gort
Ennistymon
Lahinch

IRELAND

WESTMEATH
Mullingar
Athlone
Maynooth
Clara
Tullamore
OFFALY
Edenderry
Daingean
Philipstown
Portarlington
Mountmellick
Port Laoise
LAOIS
LEINSTER
KILDARE
Naas
Kildare
Newbridge
Droichead Nua
Poulaphouca Res.
Kilcullen 754
Athy
WICKLOW
Lugnaquillia 923
Wicklow
Wicklow Hd.
Rathdrum
Avoca
Arklow
Mizen Hd.

CLARE
Mal Bay
Miltown Malbay
Ennis
Kilkee
Loop Hd.
Kilrush
R. Shannon
Foynes
Rineanna
Ardnacrusha
Killaloe
Keeper 694
Nenagh
Templemore
Thurles
TIPPERARY
Cashel
Tipperary
Golden Vale
Gallymore 920
Galty Mts.
Caher
Clonmel
Carrick-on-Suir
Comeragh Mts.
Slievenamon 722
Knockmealdown Mts.

LIMERICK
Limerick
Rathkeale
Newcastle
Rath Luirc (Charleville)
Listowel
MUNSTER
Abbeyfeale
Newmarket
Mitchelstown
Fermoy
Mallow
Kanturk
Blackwater
Lismore
Dungarvan
WATERFORD
Waterford
Dungarvan Bay
Tramore
Youghal
Youghal Harbour
Midleton
Cobh
Cork
Blarney
Passage West
Crosshaven
Cork Harbour
Kinsale
Bandon
Clonakilty
Clonakilty Bay
Skibbereen
Old Head of Kinsale

KERRY
Tralee
Dingle
Dingle Bay
Brandon Mt. 953
Brandon Hd.
Tralee Bay
Sl. Mish
Maine
Laune
Killarney
Lakes of Killarney
Macgillycuddy's Reeks
Carrauntoohill 1040
Kenmare
Kenmare River
Cahirciveen
Valentia I.
Valentia Harbour
Skellig Rocks
Ballinskelligs B.
Bolus Hd.
Crow Hd.
Dursey I.
Bear I.
Bantry Bay
Caha Mts.
Glengarriff
Bantry
Dunmanus Bay
Mizen Hd.
Skull
Baltimore
Clear I.
C. Clear
Fastnet Rock
Crookhaven

Macroom
Boggeragh Mts.
Lee
CORK
Gt. Blasket I.

WEXFORD
Enniscorthy
New Ross
Wexford
Wexford Harbour
Rosslare
Greenore Pt.
Tuscar Rock
Carnsore Pt.
Saltee Is.
Hook Hd.
Waterford Harbour
St. David's Hd.
Cahore Pt.
Gorey
Shillelagh
Mt. Leinster 796
Muine Bheag
CARLOW
Carlow
KILKENNY
Kilkenny
Callan

Kintyre
Campbeltown
Mull of Kintyre
Arran
Ailsa Craig
Fair Hd.
Stranraer
Portpatrick
I. Magee
Portrush

LOUTH
Louth
Ardee
Boyne

MAP KEY — Northern Ireland Districts

Towns underlined in Northern Ireland give their names to the Districts in which they stand

The remaining Districts are:—

1 Fermanagh
2 Moyle
3 Newtownabbey
4 North Down
5 Castlereagh
6 Ards
7 Down
8 Newry & Mourne

ft | m
3000 | 1000
1200 | 400
600 | 200
300 | 100
0 | 0
100 | 300
200 | 600
m | ft

Projection: Conical with two standard parallels.

West from Greenwich

COPYRIGHT. GEORGE PHILIP & SON. LTD.

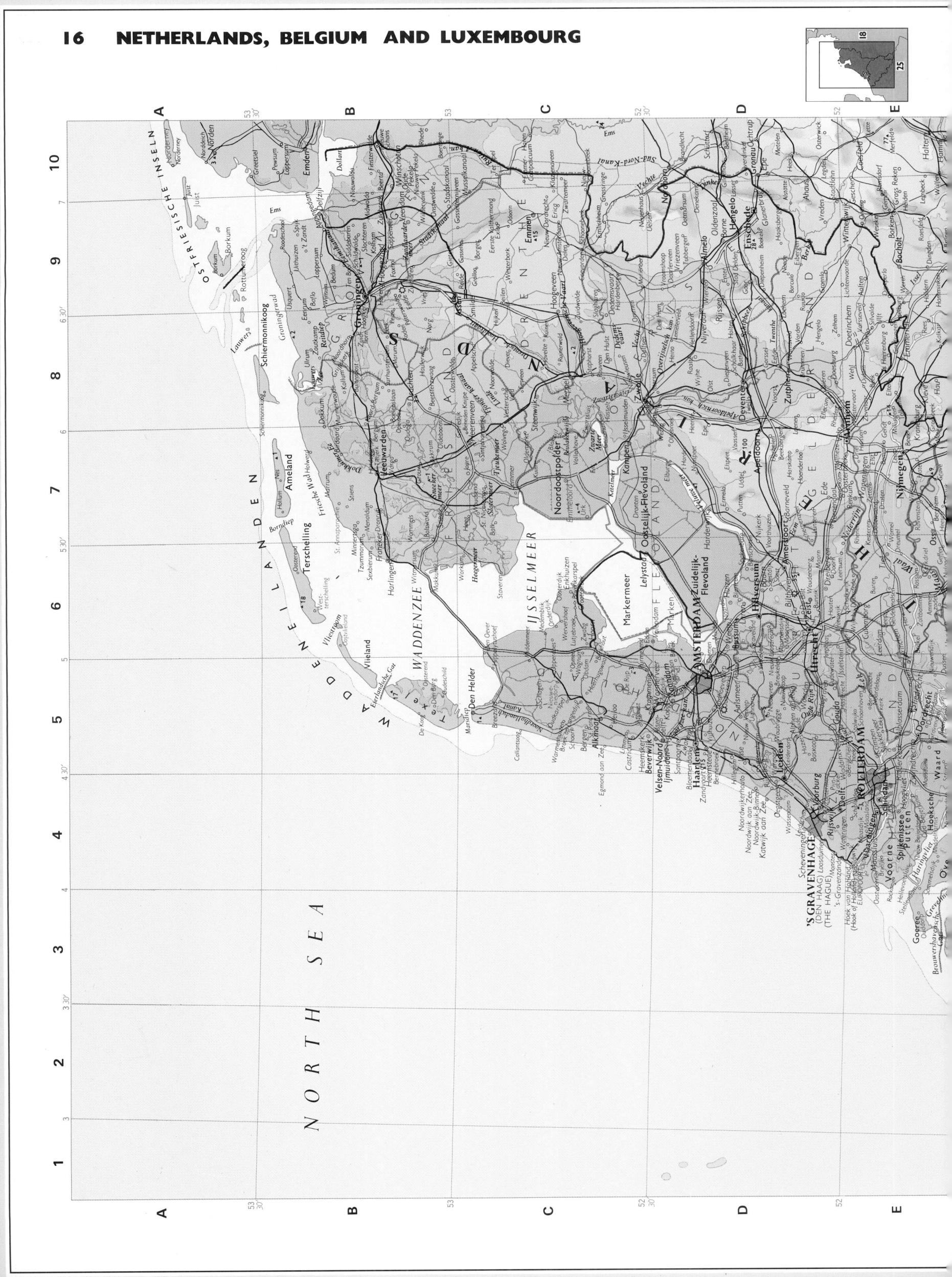

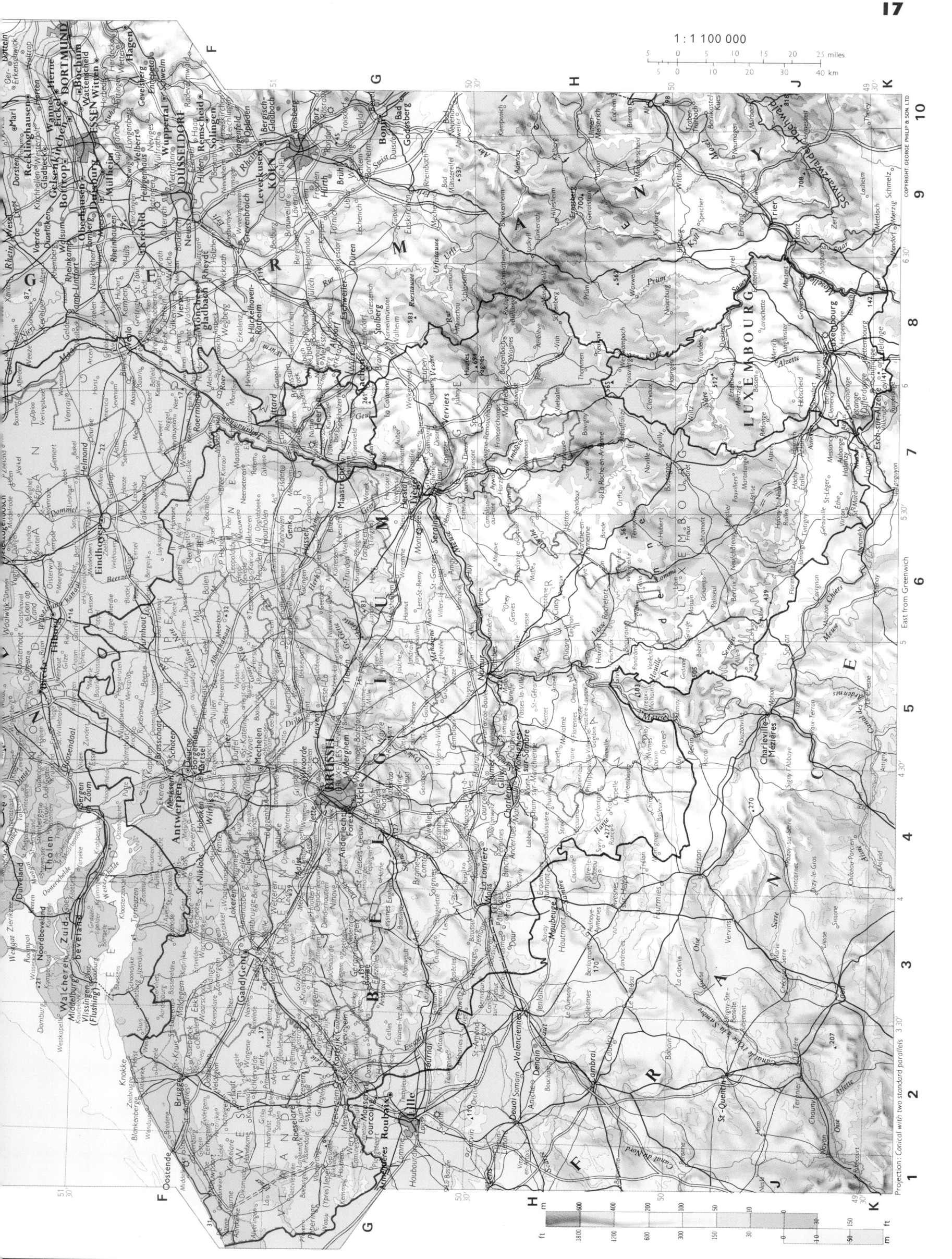

1 : 1 100 000

Projection: Conical with two standard parallels

East from Greenwich

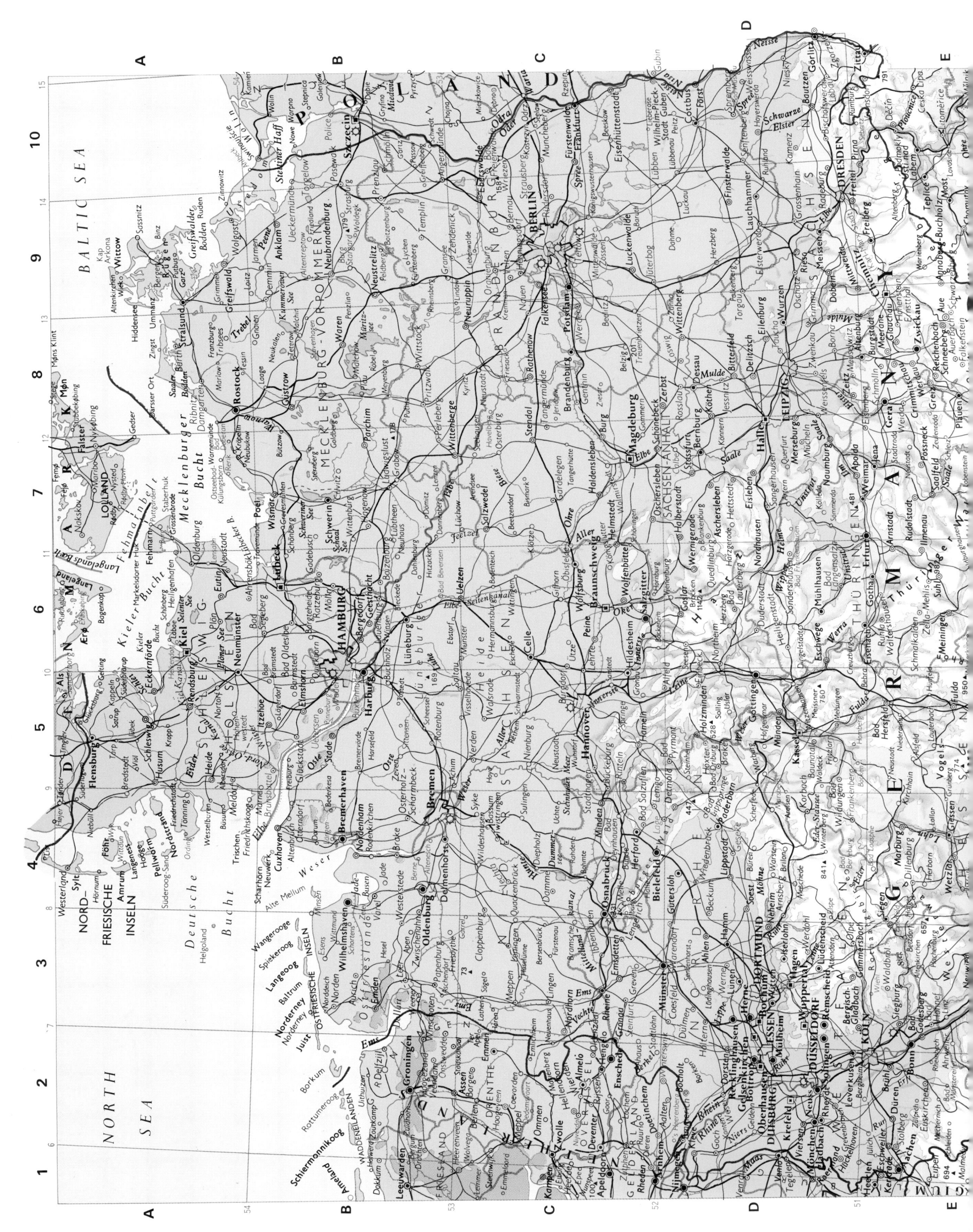

1 : 2 200 000

East from Greenwich

Projection: Conical with two standard parallels.

40
38
39
11
18
19
32
33

BALTIC SEA
BELORUSSIA
LITHUANIA
(RUSSIA)
UKRAINE
DENMARK
POLAND
GERMANY
Kaliningrad (Königsberg)
Grodno
Brest
Białystok
Gdańsk
Gdynia
Szczecin
Bydgoszcz
Toruń
Poznań
WARSZAWA
Łódź
Lublin
Radom
Kielce
Częstochowa
Kraków
Katowice
WROCŁAW
BERLIN
Potsdam
Frankfurt
Cottbus
DRESDEN
LEIPZIG
Halle
Chemnitz
PRAHA
Plzeň
Brno
Ostrava
Olomouc
Košice
Uzhgorod
Lvov
Rzeszów
Przemyśl
Rostock
Stralsund

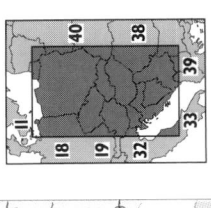

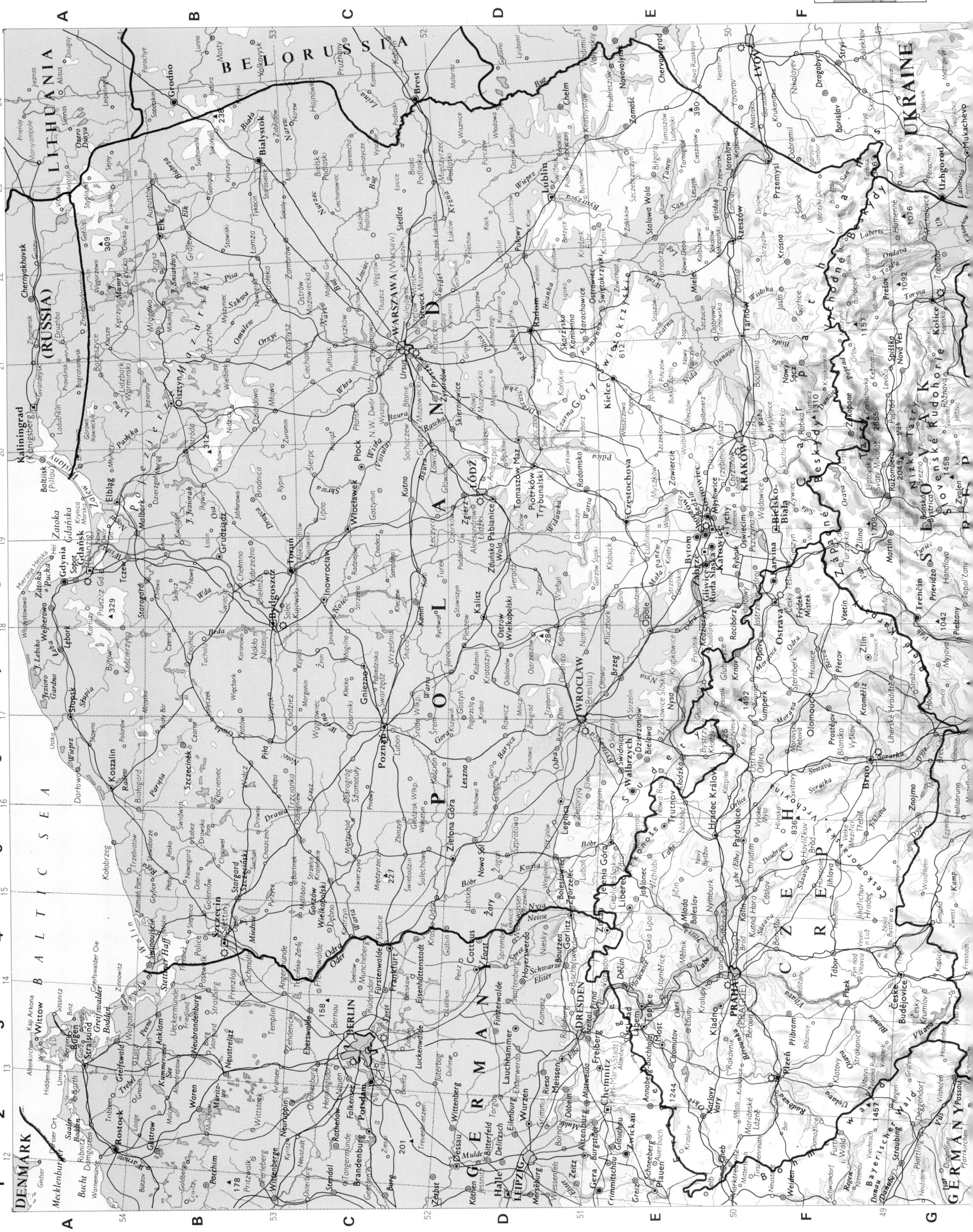

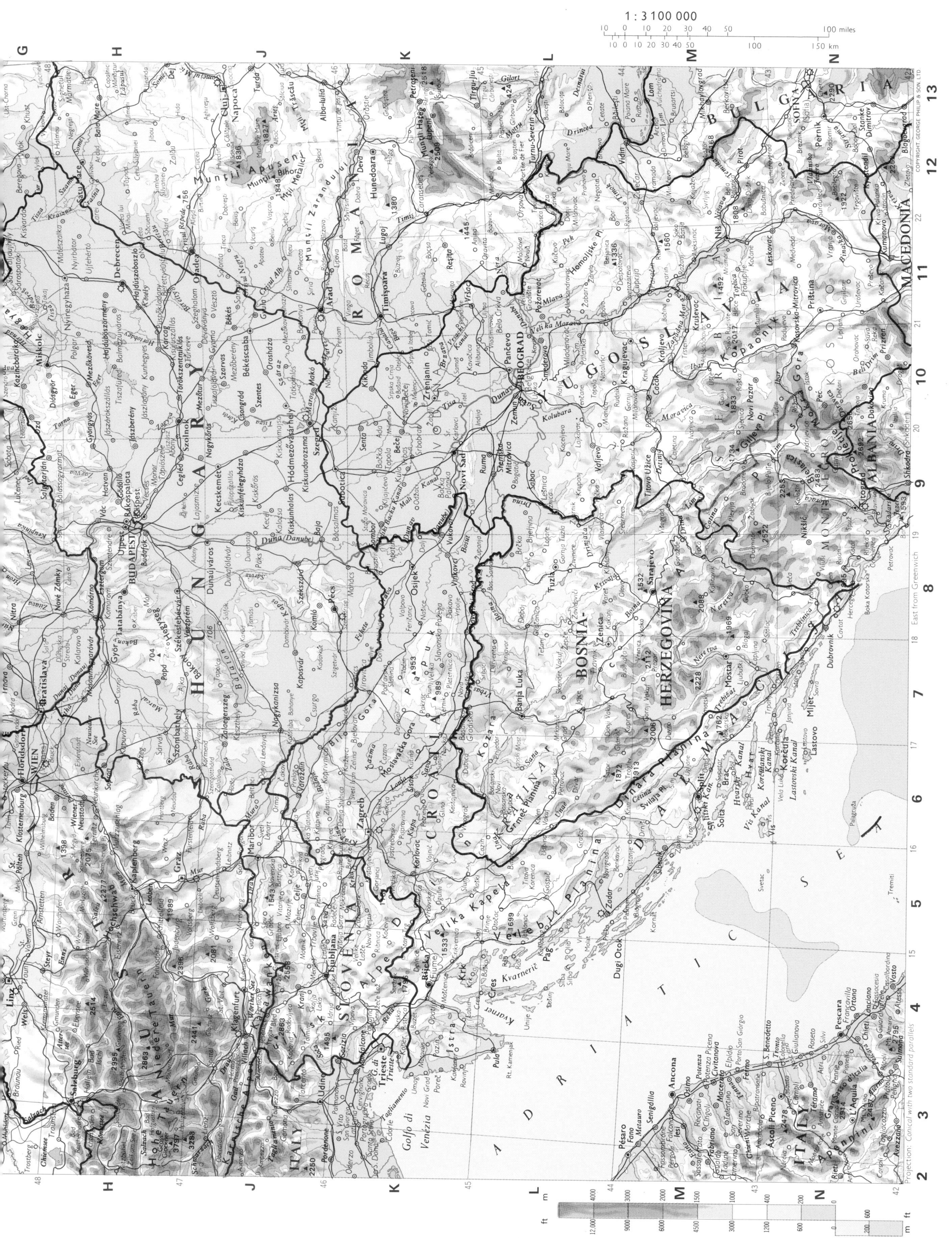

Projection: Conical with two standard parallels

FRANCE

HAUTE-SAÔNE

JURA

DOUBS

MULHOUSE

BELFORT

BESANÇON

BASEL (BASLE)

LANDSCHAFT

AARGAU

Olten

Solothurn

Grenchen

Biel (Bienne)

La Chaux-de-Fonds

Le Locle

NEUCHÂTEL

Neuchâtel

Pontarlier

Ste-Croix

Yverdon

FRIBOURG

Fribourg (Freibourg)

BERN (BERNE)

Bulle

Gruyère

Thun

Thunersee

Brienzersee

LAUSANNE

Morges

Vevey

Montreux

Lac Léman (L. Geneva)

OBERLAND

BERNER ALPEN

Morez

St-Claude

Nyon

Thonon-les-Bains

Evian-les-Bains

GENÈVE (GENEVA)

Annemasse

HAUTE-SAVOIE

Martigny

Sion

Sierre

VALAIS

Brig

Zermatt

Matterhorn (Mte Cervino)

Monte Rosa

Oyonnax

Bellegarde-s.-V.

Annecy

Lac d'Annecy

Rumilly

Aix-les-Bains

Lac du Bourget

SAVOIE

Albertville

Chamonix-Mont-Blanc

Col du Gd St-Bernard

VALLE D'AOSTA

Aosta

Dora Baltea

LUZERN

Burgdorf

PENNINE ALPES

1 : 900 000

East from Greenwich

COPYRIGHT. GEORGE PHILIP & SON, LTD.

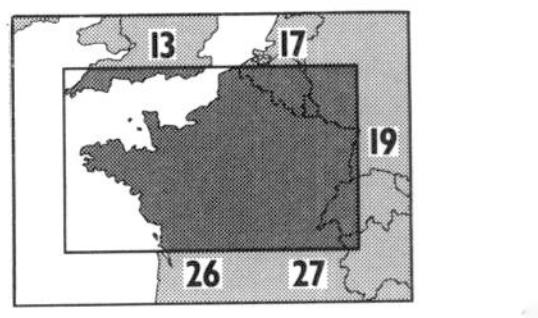

ENGLAND

English Channel

CHANNEL ISLANDS
Guernsey
St. Peter Port
Jersey
St. Helier
Alderney

Baie de la Seine
Cherbourg
Le Havre
Rouen
Dieppe
Caen
Bayeux
St-Lô
Coutances
Granville
Avranches
Le Mont-St-Michel

NORMANDIE
Collines de Normandie
Alençon
Évreux
Dreux

Golfe de St-Malo
St-Malo
Dinard
Dinan
St-Brieuc
Guingamp
Morlaix
Lannion
Paimpol

Brest
Ile d'Ouessant
Mer d'Iroise
Quimper
Douarnenez
Châteaulin
Landerneau

Monts d'Arrée 391
Montagne Noire 326

BRETAGNE
CÔTES-DU-NORD
Lamballe
Pontivy
Rennes
Vitré
Laval
Le Mans
Mayenne

Lorient
Vannes
MORBIHAN
Auray
Quiberon
Belle-Ile
Presqu'île de Quiberon
Ile de Groix

St-Nazaire
Nantes
Angers
LOIRE-ATLANTIQUE
Baie de Bourgneuf
Ile de Noirmoutier
Ile d'Yeu
La Roche-sur-Yon
Les Sables-d'Olonne

Cholet
Saumur
Tours
Châtellerault
Poitiers
DEUX-SÈVRES
Niort
VENDÉE
Fontenay-le-Comte
Luçon

La Rochelle
Ile de Ré
Rochefort
Ile d'Oléron
Saintes
Cognac
Angoulême
AUNIS
CHARENTE-MARITIME
ANGOUMOIS
LIMOUSIN
HAUTE-VIENNE
Limoges

Pointe de Grave
Pointe de la Coubre
Royan

Scale
ft   m
12 000 4000
9000   3000
6000   2000
4500   1500
3000   1000
1200   400
600   200
0   0
200   600
2000   6000
m   ft

DÉPARTEMENTS IN THE PARIS AREA
1 Ville de Paris   3 Val-de-Marne
2 Seine-St-Denis   4 Hauts-de-Seine

Projection: Conical with two standard parallels

West from Greenwich   East from Greenwich

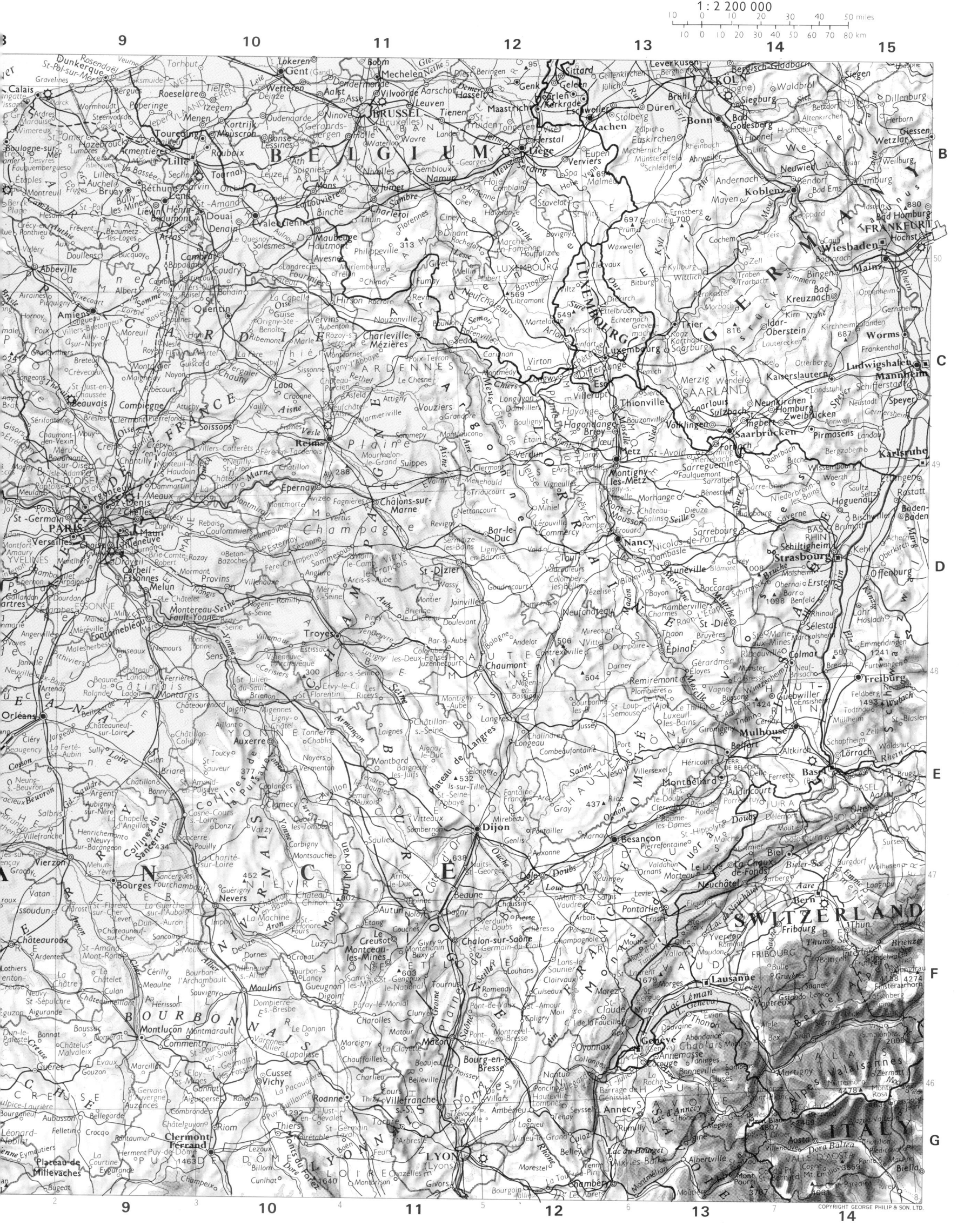

1 : 2 200 000

1 : 2 200 000

26
75
30
31

BAY OF BISCAY
Golfe de Gascogne
ANDORRA
BARCELONA
Zaragoza (Saragossa)
MADRID
Pamplona
San Sebastián
Bilbao
Vitoria
Logroño
Burgos
Huesca
Lérida
Tarragona
Gerona
Perpignan
Toulouse
Carcassonne
Narbonne
Béziers
Tarbes
Pau
Bayonne
Biarritz
Castellón de la Plana
Teruel
Cuenca
Guadalajara
Soria
Menorca (Minorca)
Mallorca (Majorca)
Palma
Mahón
Ciudadela
ROUSSILLON
NAVARRA
Sierra de la Peña
Montes Universales
Sierra de Guara
Golfo de San Jorge

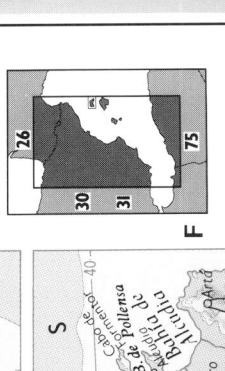

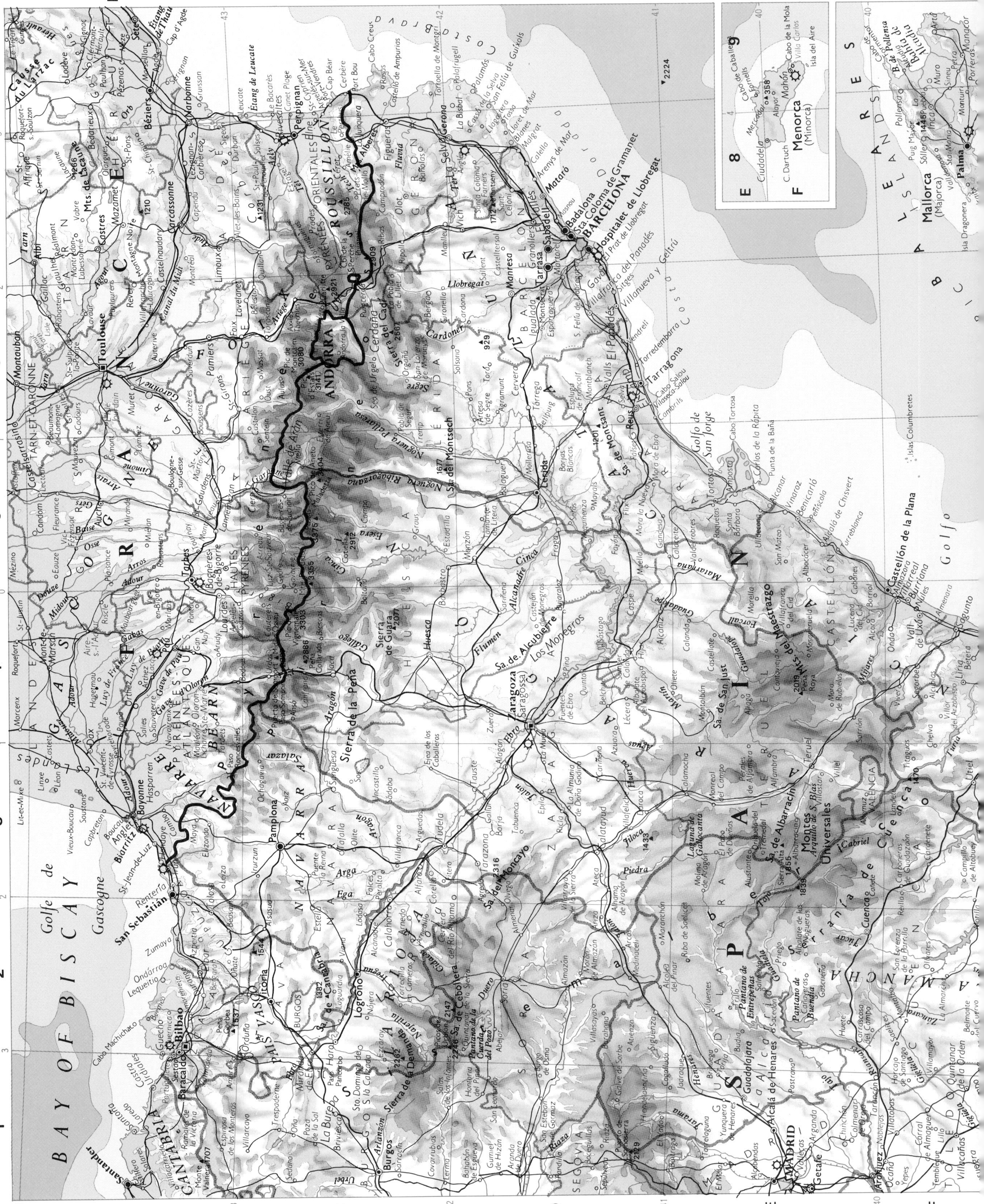

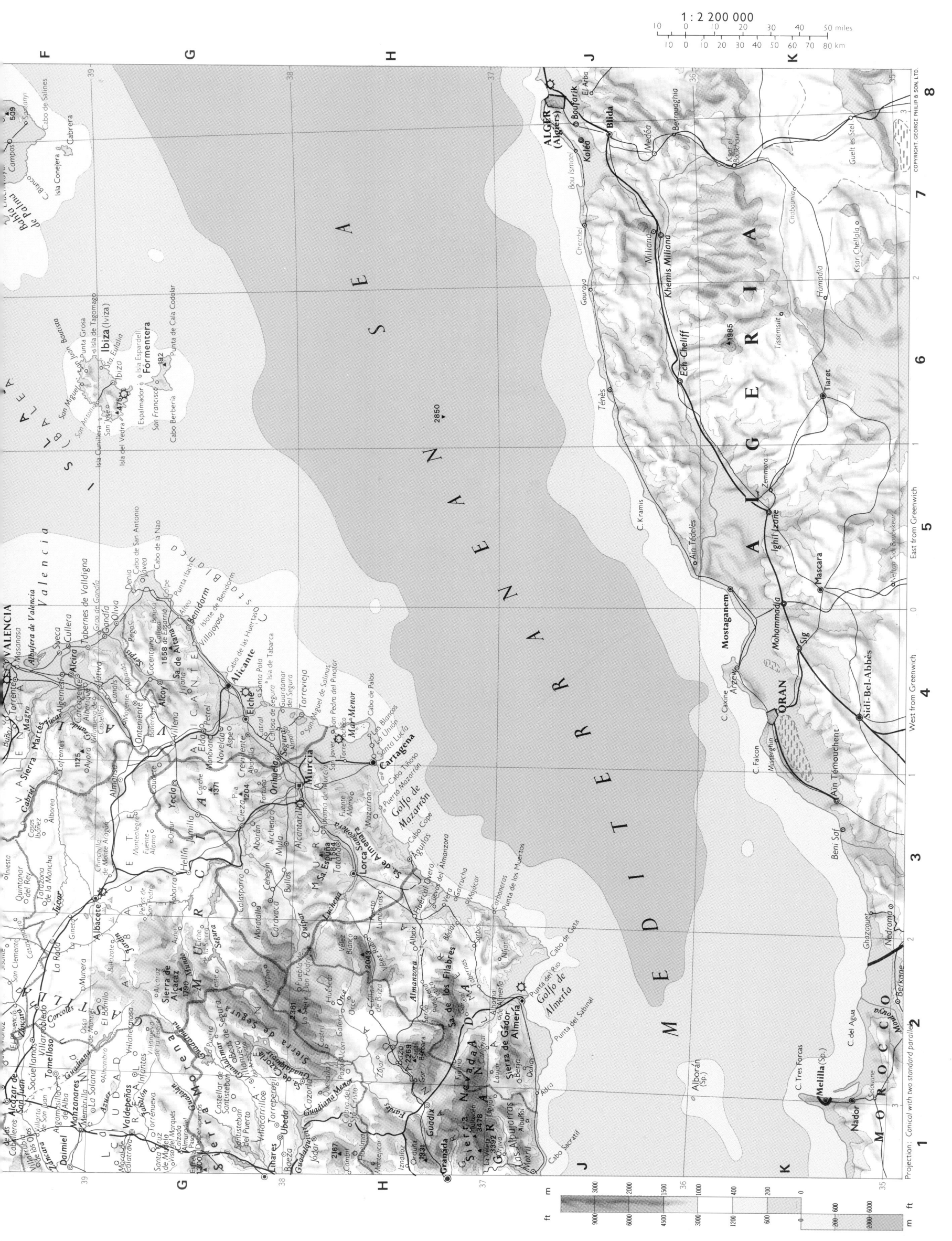

29

1 : 2 200 000

10   20   30   40   50 miles

10   0   10   20   30   40   50   60   70   80 km

MEDITERRANEAN SEA

BALEARIC ISLANDS

Ibiza
Formentera

VALENCIA
Valencia
Alicante
Elche
Murcia
Cartagena
Lorca
Almería

ALGERIA

ALGER (Algiers)
Blida
Médéa
Khemis Miliana
Ech Cheliff
Tiaret
Mostaganem
ORAN
Sidi-Bel-Abbès
Mascara

MOROCCO

Melilla (Sp.)
Nador

Projection: Conical with two standard parallels

m   ft
3000   9000
2000   6000
1500   4500
1000   3000
400   1200
200   600
0   0

ft   m
0   0
600   200
6000   2000

BAY OF BISCAY
ATLANTIC OCEAN
San Sebastián
Bilbao
Santander
Oviedo
Gijón
León
Burgos
Logroño
Vitoria
Valladolid
Palencia
Zamora
Salamanca
Ávila
Segovia
MADRID
Toledo
Guadalajara
Lugo
Orense
La Coruña (Corunna)
El Ferrol
Santiago de Compostela
Vigo
Pontevedra
Porto (Oporto)
Coimbra
Aveiro
Braga
Bragança
Viseu
Guarda
Cordillera Cantábrica
Picos de Europa
Sierra de Gredos
Sierra de Guadarrama
Sierra de Gata
Duero
Douro
Tajo
Miño

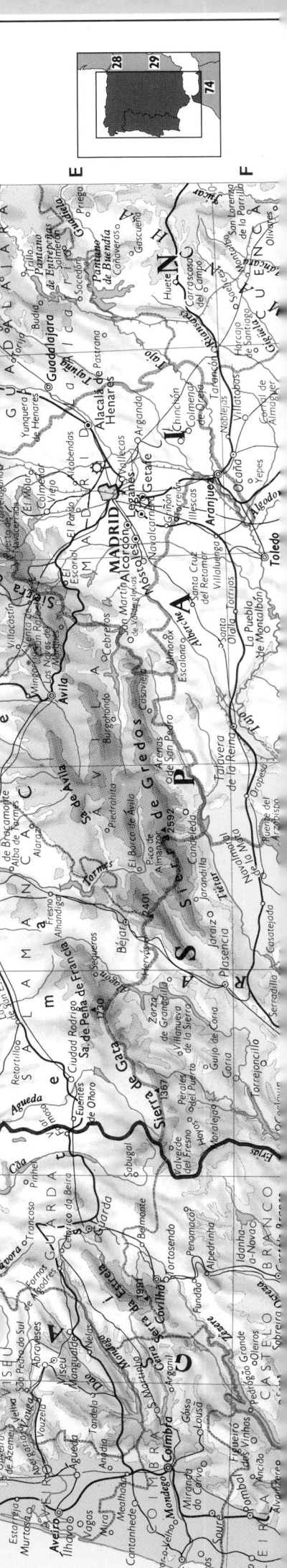

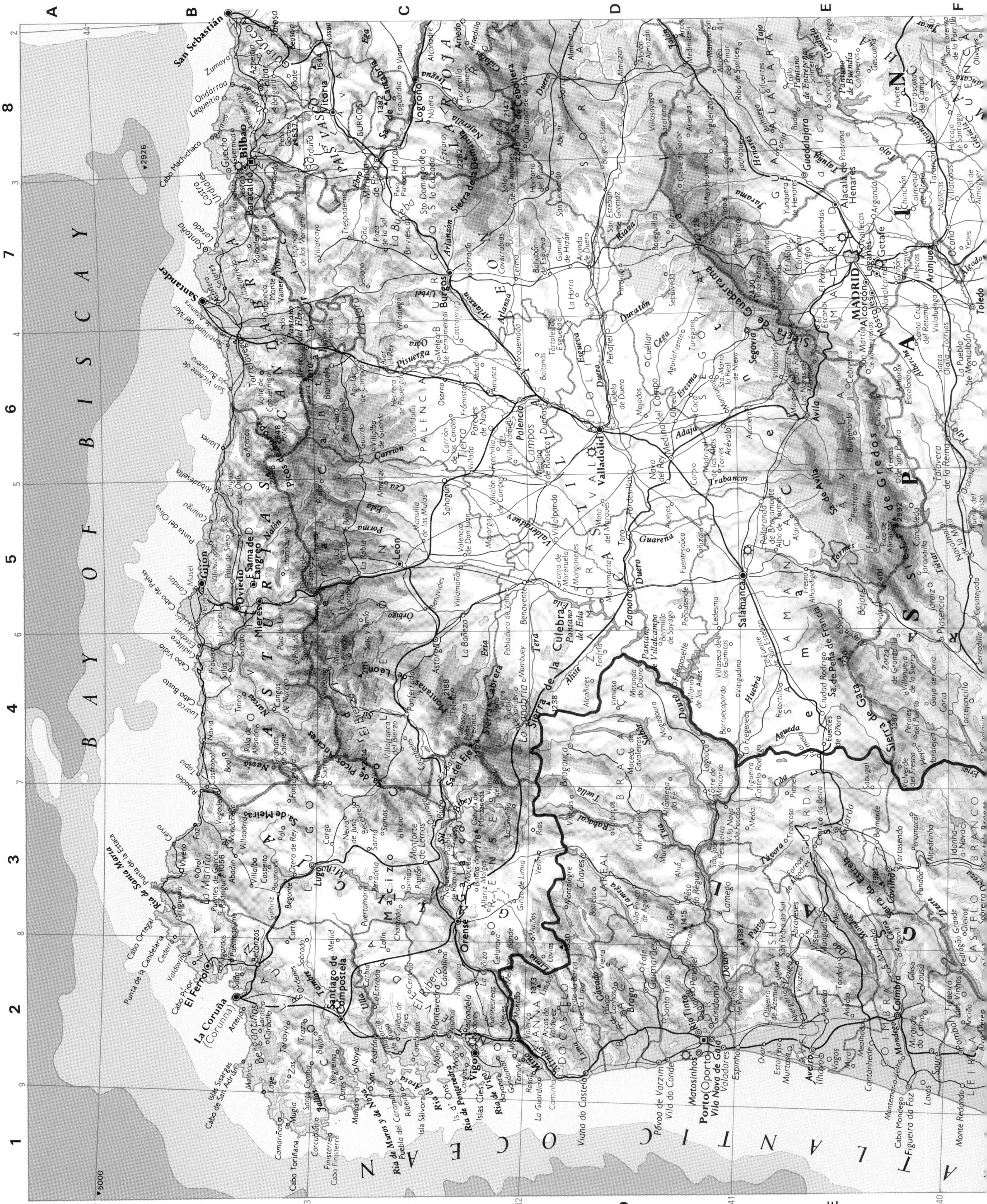

1 : 2 200 000

Projection: Conical with two standard parallels

COPYRIGHT. GEORGE PHILIP & SON. LTD.

Projection: Conical with two standard parallels

East from Greenwich

32 33
38
75 39

1 **2** **3** **4** **5** **6**

A

Iles Sanguinaires
G. d'Ajaccio
Tarabo
C. di Muro
Petreto
2136
Zonza
Solenzara
Propriano
Levie
Favone
CORSE
Sartène
Porto-Vecchio
CORSICA
CORSE-DU-SUD
Iles Cerbicales
Bonifacio
I. de Cavallo
Bouches de Bonifacio
Maddalena
Santa Teresa Gallura
Caprera

ROMA
(Rome)
Vatican City
Tivoli
Subiaco
Conca del Fucino
Fregene
Palestrina
Lido di Óstia
(Lido di Roma)
Anagni
Alatri
Sora
Prática di Mare
Albano
Lazio
Velletri
Cori
Ferentino
Monte S. Giova
Aprilia
Latina
Cisterna di Latina
Ceccano
Ceprano
Cassino
Nettuno
Anzio
Priverno
Sonnino
Pontecel
Sabáudia
Monte Circeo
541
Fondi
1633
Terracina
Gaeta
Fórmia
Mintúrno
Liri

41

Punta dello Scorno
Asinara
Golfo dell'
Asinara
Costa
Smeralda
La Maddalena
Arzachena
Pto. Cervo
Golfo Aranci
Porto Tórres
C. dell'Argentiera
Sássari
Coghinas
Ággius
Calangiánus
Tempio Pausania
1362
Olbia
G. di Ólbia
Tavolara
Sorso
Sennori
Ósilo
Oschiri
al Coghinas
Tanaurella
Golfo di
Gaeta
Zannone
Palmarola
Ponza
Ísole
Ponziane
283
Ventotene
Volturno
Casal
Giúglia
788
 Íschia
(Nap)

B

Ittiri
Alghero
Villanova
Monteleone
Bosa
Temo
Macomer
Bonorva
1259
Ozieri
Púttoda
Buddusò
1058
Bitti
Orune
Núoro
Bargali
Siniscola
C. Comino
Oliena
Golfo di
Orosei

40

C. Mannu
L. del Tirso
Ghilarza
Sórgono
SARDEGNA
Monti del
1834
Gennargentu
Baunei
C. di Monte Santu
3719
T Y R R H E N I A N

Cábras
Oristano
SARDEGNA
M. Arci
812
Golfo di
Oristano
Arbórea
Terralba
Lácon
Nurri
Láconi
Arbatax
SARDINIA
Ánela
Ierzu

C

S. Gávino
Monreale
Gúspini
Arbus
Gonnosfanadiga
1236
M. Línas
Villacidro
Sanluri
Sénorbi
V. Sáto
Villaputzu
Muravera
C. Ferrato
S E A
C. Pécora
Fluminimaggiore
Iglésias
Guerri
Assémini
Siliqua
Dolianova
Pta. Serpeddi
1068
Settimo
Sérramanna

Portoscuso
Gonnesa
Carbónia
1116
Sestu
Sinnai
Selargius
3589
San Pietro
Carloforte
Quartu Sant'Elena
Santadi
Cágliari
39

Sant'Antíoco
Sant'
Antíoco
Porto Botte
Pula
Teulada
Golfo di
Cágliari
C. Carbonara
Serpentara
G. di Palmas
C. Spartivento

D

Ústica

38

C. San Vito
Castellammare del Golfo
G. di Castellammare
Favarotta
Favorita
C. Gallo
PALERMO
Monreale
Bagheria
Ter
Levanzo
Trápani
1110
Érice
Aléamo
Giuseppe
Maríneo
E

Iles de la
Galite
Marettimo
Isole Égadi
Favignana
Stagnone
Salemi
Paceco
Calatafimi
lato
Gibellina
Camporeale
Corleone
1613
Belsto
Marsala
Partanna
Bisacquino
Prizzi
Lercara
Fríddi
Alia
Castelvetrano
Sambuca
di Sicilia
SICI
Mazara
del Vallo
Menfi
Belíce
Mussomeli
Cas
Campobello di Mazara
Sciacca
Cattólica
Eraclea
Caltabellotta
Ribera
Búrgio
Platani
Racalmuto
San Cataro
Calta
3000
Siculiana
Raffadali
Sicília
Agrigento
Favard
Ngro

37

Bizerte
(Binzert)
C. Blanc
Cani
C. Serrat
Menzel-Bourguiba
Plane
Porto Empédocle
Cattólica Eraclea
Licata
Palma di Montechiaro
Campobello di
Lic

Mateur
Zembra
C. Bon
Sicilian Channel
El Kala
Tabarka
Téboursouk
Téburba
TUNIS
Halq el Oued
Golfe de Tunis
Kelibia
Menzel-
Temime
F

Bou Salem
Béja
Medjerda
Soliman
Pantelleria
836
Pantelleria
(It.)
M E D I T E R
Téboursouk
Zaghouan
Hammamet
Nabeul
1319

ft m
9000 3000
6000 2000
4500 1500
3000 1000
1200 400
600 200
0 37
m ft
200 600
2000 6000
4000 12.000

Projection: Conical with two standard parallels
East from Greenwich

1 **2** **3** **4** **5** **6**

1 : 2 200 000

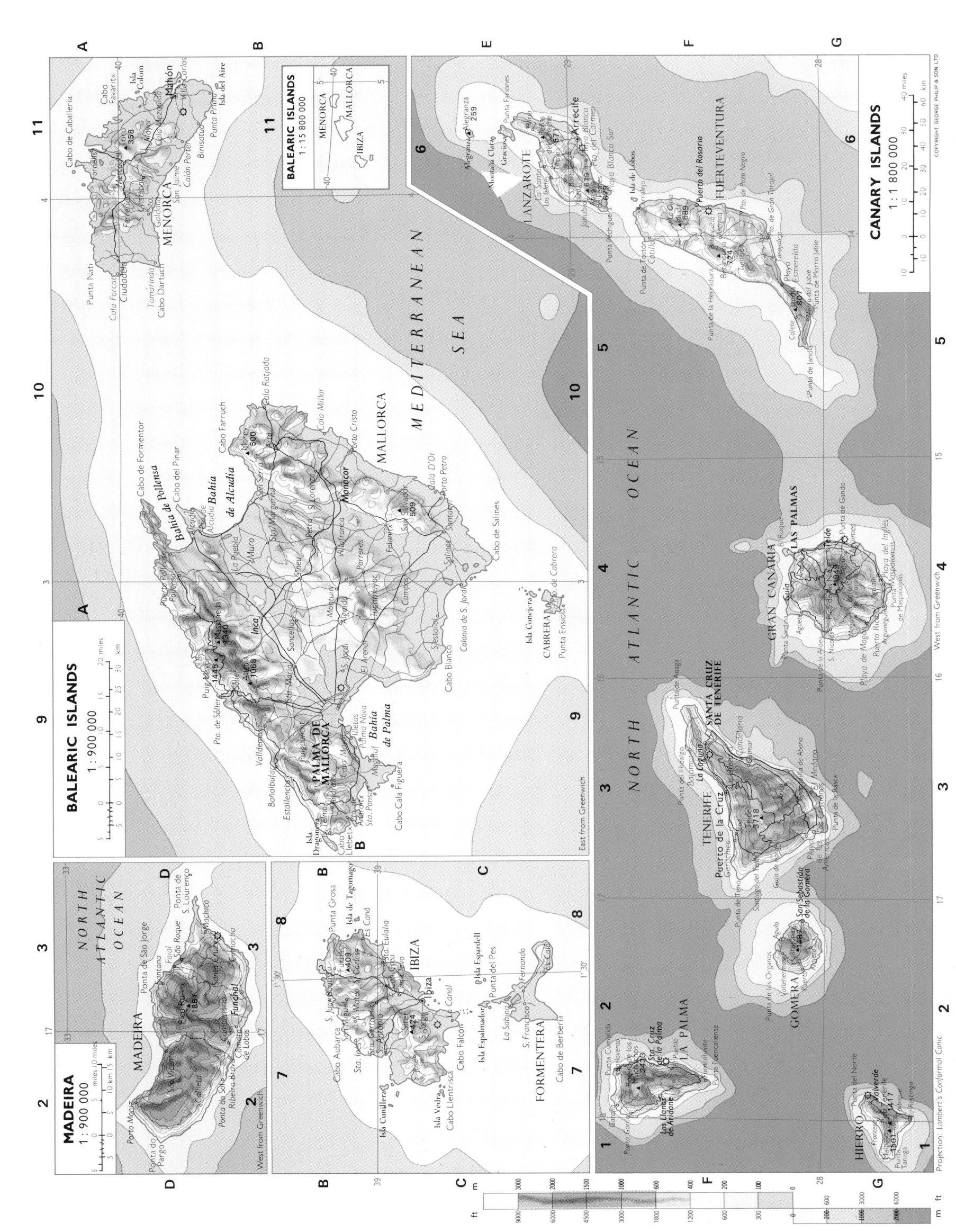

BALEARIC ISLANDS
1 : 15 800 000

MENORCA
MALLORCA
IBIZA

MENORCA
Cabo de Caballeria
Isla Colom
Mahón
Villa Carlos
Cabo Favaritx
Ciudadela
San Jaime
Punta Prima
Isla del Aire
Punta Nati
Cala Forcat
Tamarinda
Cabo Dartuch
358

MEDITERRANEAN SEA

MALLORCA
Cabo de Formentor
Bahia de Alcudia
Cabo del Pinar
Alcudia
Cala Ratjada
Cabo Farruch
Cala Millor
Porto Cristo
Manacor
500
509
Felanitx
Cabo de Salines
Cabo Blanco
PALMA DE MALLORCA
Bahia de Palma
Inca
Isla Dragonera
Cabo Cala Figuera

CABRERA
Punta Ensiola
Isla Conejera

BALEARIC ISLANDS
1 : 900 000

MADEIRA
1 : 900 000

NORTH ATLANTIC OCEAN

MADEIRA
Funchal
Santa Cruz
Porto Moniz
Ponta de São Jorge
Ponta de São Lourenço
1861

West from Greenwich

IBIZA
IBIZA
Punta Grosa
Sta. Eulalia
San Antonio
424
FORMENTERA
Cabo de Berberia
Isla Vedra

CANARY ISLANDS
1 : 1 800 000

LANZAROTE
Alegranza
259
Graciosa
Arrecife
671
FUERTEVENTURA
Puerto del Rosario
724
807

NORTH ATLANTIC OCEAN

GRAN CANARIA
LAS PALMAS
1949

TENERIFE
SANTA CRUZ DE TENERIFE
La Laguna
Puerto de la Cruz
3718

GOMERA
San Sebastián de la Gomera
1467

LA PALMA
Sta. Cruz de la Palma

HIERRO
Valverde
1501
1417

Projection: Lambert's Conformal Conic
Copyright: GEORGE PHILIP & SON LTD.

ft m
9000 3000
6000 2000
4500 1500
3000 600
1800 400
1200 200
600 100
300 0
0
200 600
1200 3000
2000 6000

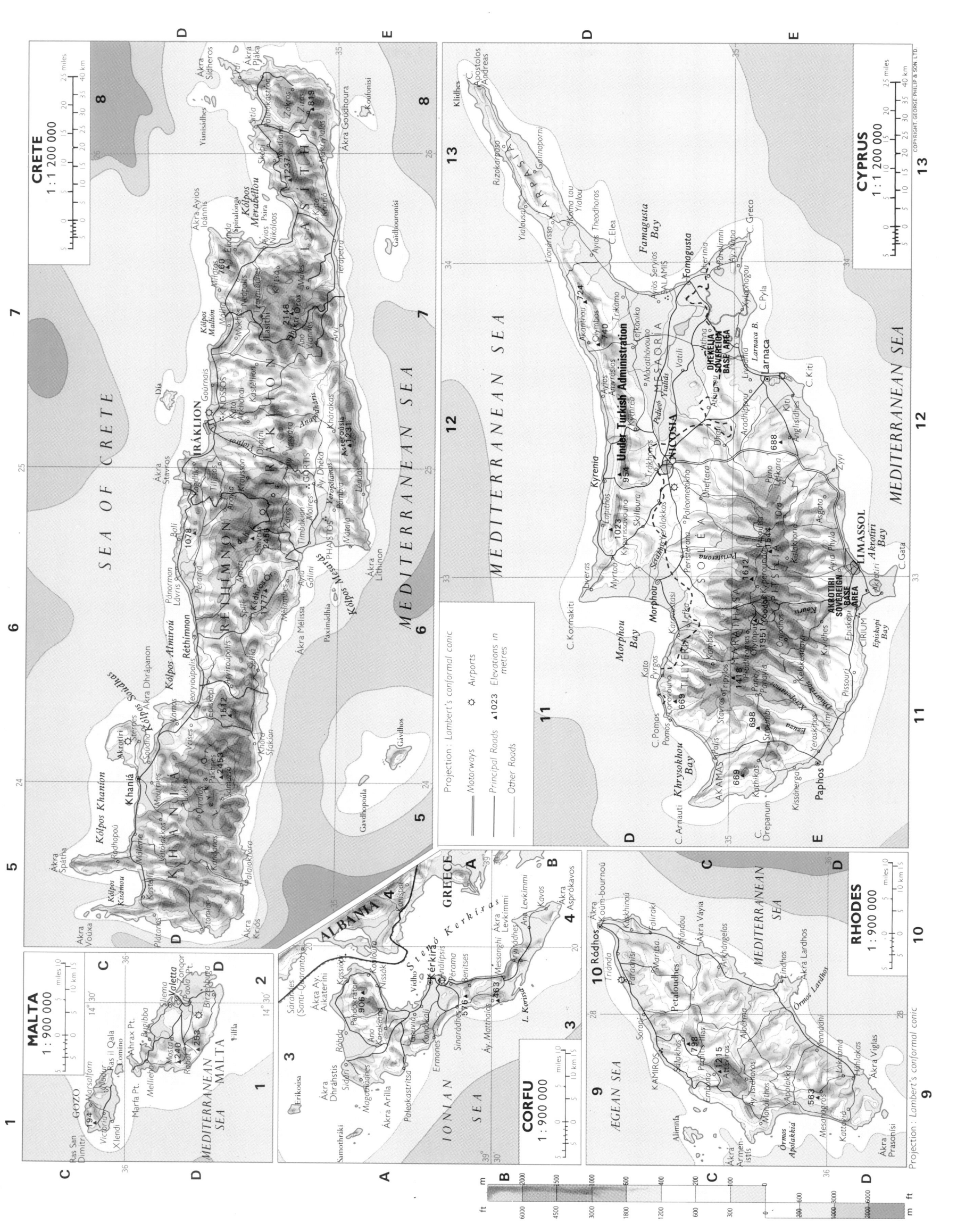

1:3 100 000

Projection: Conical with two standard parallels

COPYRIGHT GEORGE PHILIP & SON LTD.

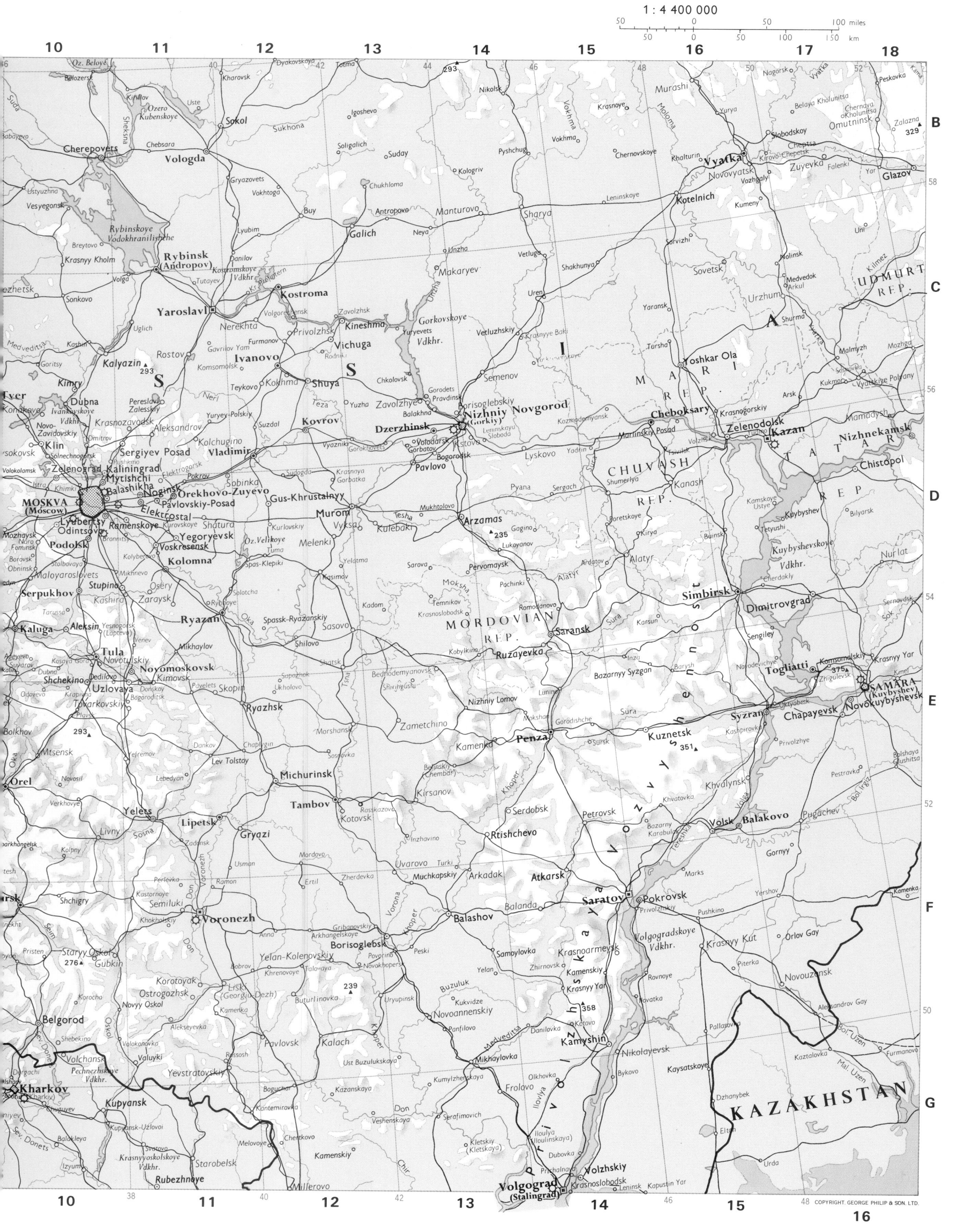

1 : 4 400 000

COPYRIGHT. GEORGE PHILIP & SON. LTD.

Projection: Conical with two standard parallels

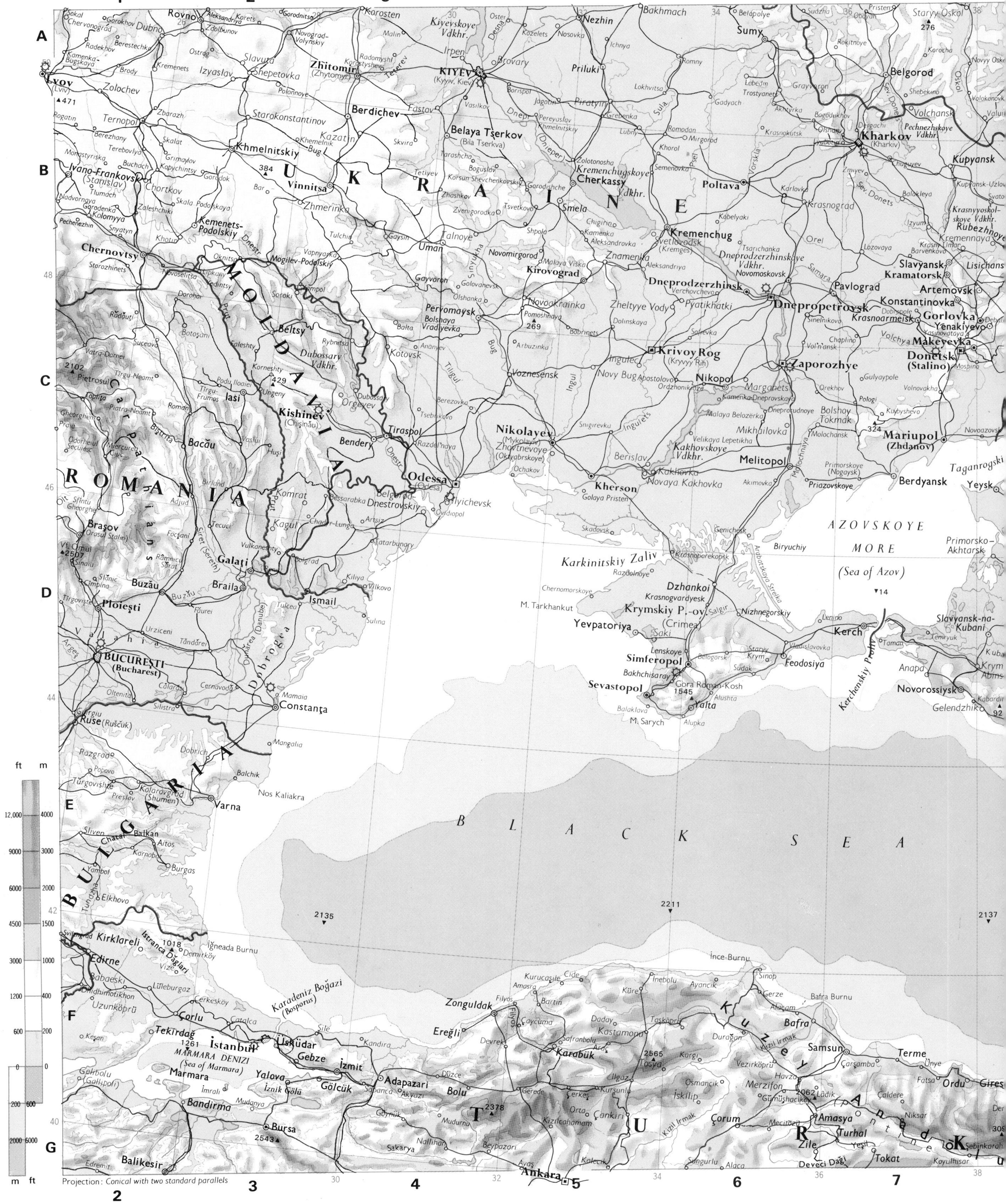

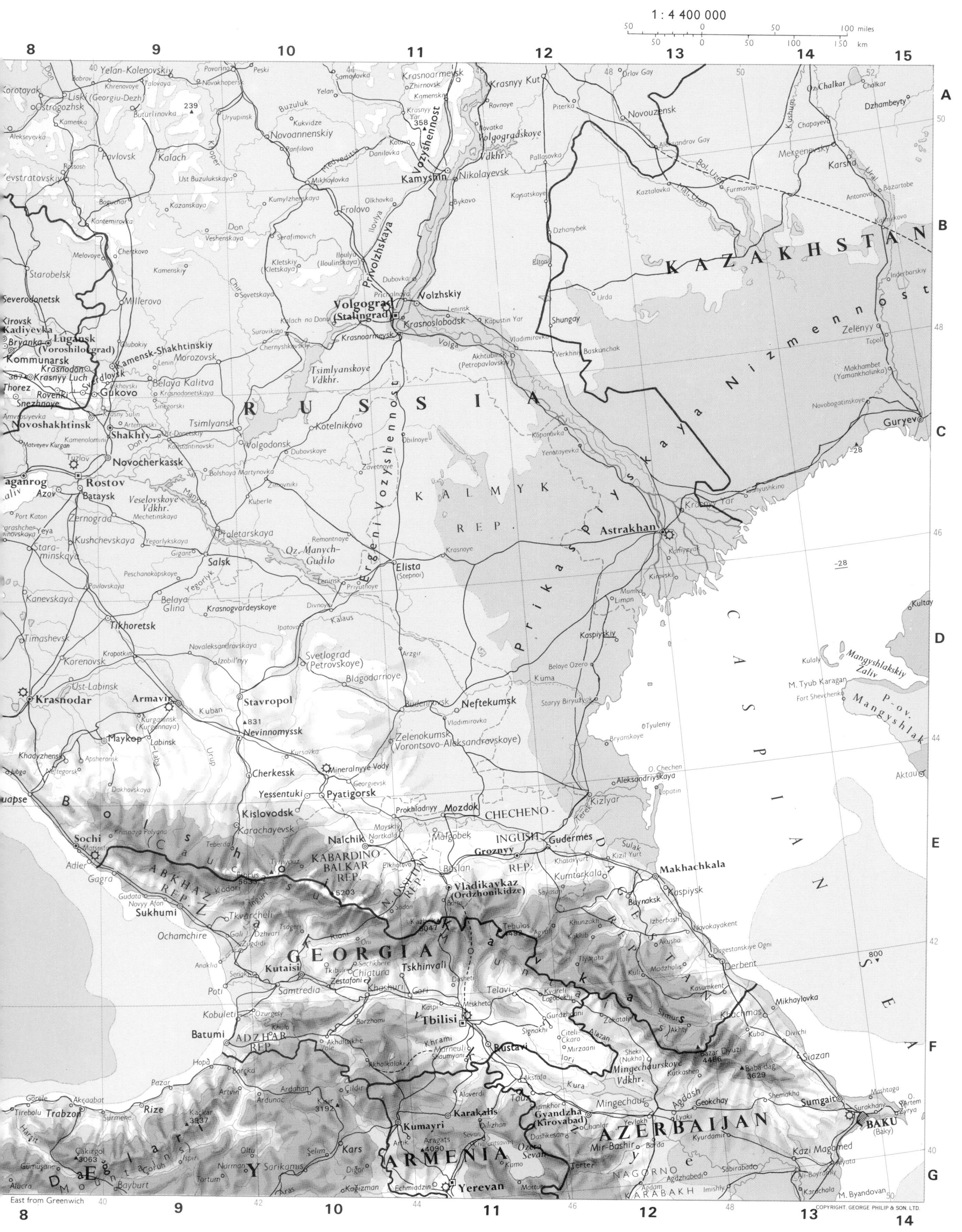

1 : 4 400 000

50   0   50   100 miles

50   0   50   100   150 km

COPYRIGHT. GEORGE PHILIP & SON. LTD.

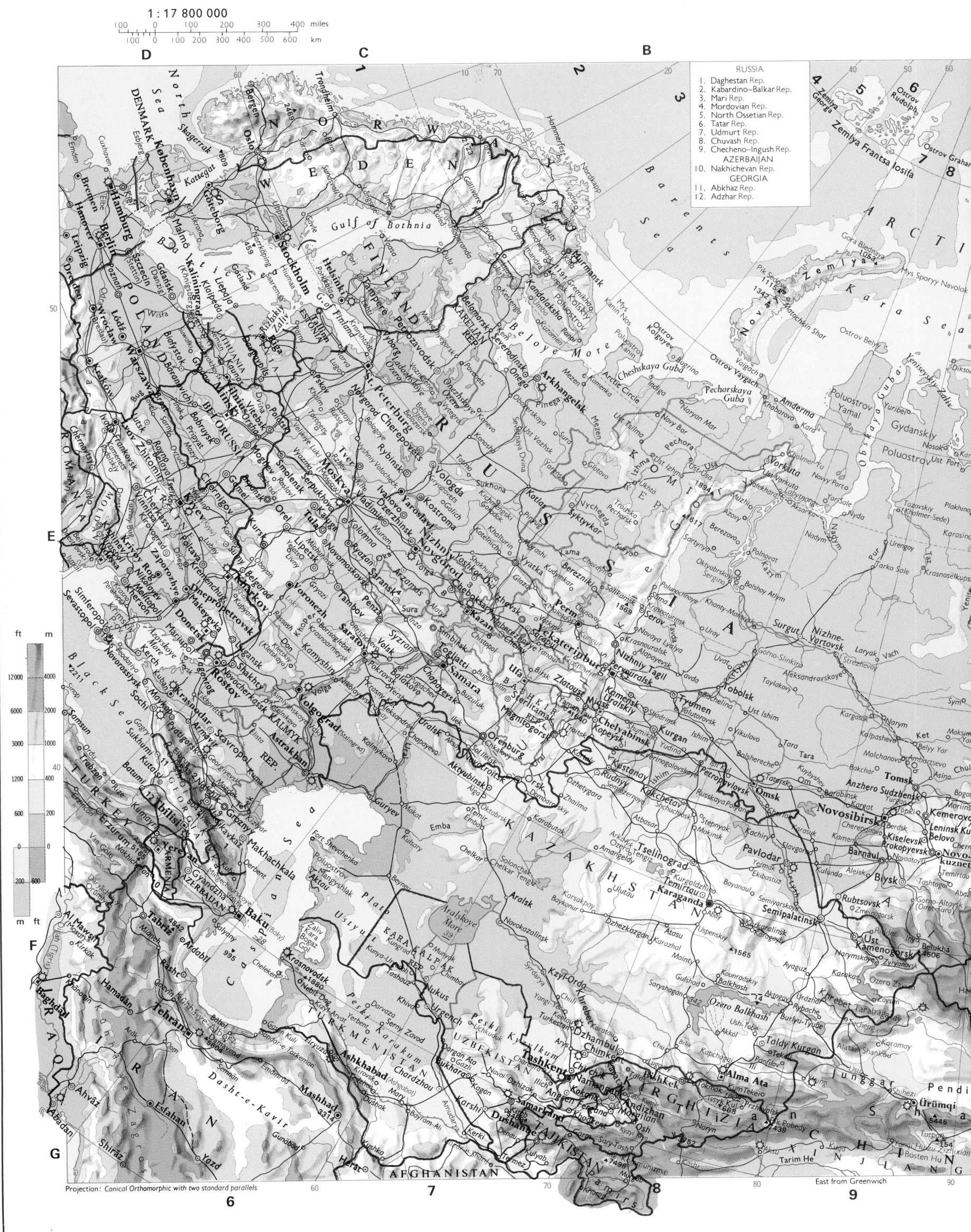

Projection: Conical Orthomorphic with two standard parallels

East from Greenwich

A B C

70 80 90 100 110 120 130 140 150 16 17 170 18 19

10 11

9 12 13 14 3800 15

Mys Arkticheskiy

Ostrov
Shmidta

Ostrov
Komsomolets

Ostrov
Pioner Ostrov Oktyabrskoy
965 Revolyutsii

Severnaya
Zemlya Ostrov Bolshevik

Proliv Vilkitskogo

Mys Dezhneva
(East C.)

Chukotskoye
More St. Lawrence I.
(U.S.A.)

Anadyrskiy
Zaliv

Chukotskiy Khrebet

60

OCEAN

Laptev
Sea Ostrova
Ostrov De Long
Henrietta

v Novosibirskiye Ostrova

Ostrov Faddeyevskiy

Ostrov
Bennett

Ostrova Zhokhova

Ostrov
Novaya Sibir

East Siberian Sea

Ostrov Vrangelya

Poluostrov
Gory 1146
Byrranga

Taymyr Oz. Taymyr

Nordvik

Ostrov Bolshoy
Begichev

Ostrov Belkovskiy

Ostrov Kotelny

Ostrov Stolbovoy

Ostrov Malyy
Lyakhovskiy Ostrov Bolshoy
Lyakhovskiy

Lyakhovskiye Ostrova

Proliv Dmitriya Lapteva

Mys Buorkhaya

Bolshoy Anyuy

Omolon

D

Bering
Sea

Koryakskiy Khrebet 2562

Srednnny Khrebet

Poluostrov
Kamchatka

Norilsk

Gory
Putorana
1701

Ust Olenek
Dryung-Khaya Tit-Ary Tiksi

Saskylakh

Novorybnoye

Popigay

Khatanga

Kheta

Volochanka

Agapa

Pyasina

Nordvik

Olenek

Bulun

Kyusyur

Tit-Ary

Kel

(Bysyttakh)

Zhigansk

Verkhoyansk 2389

Khrebet Cherskogo 3147

Srednekolymsk

Kolyma

Indigirka

Erchda

Chokurdakh

Nizhne Kolymsk

Ostrova
Medvezhi

Okhotsko Kolymskoye

Gizhiga

Penzhinskaya Guba

Gizhiginskaya
Guba

Magadan

Zaliv
Shelikhova

Poluostrov
Kamchatka

Petropavlovsk-
Kamchatskiy

Achinsk Kansk

Krasnoyarsk

ARCTIC CIRCLE

962

Shologontsy

Vilyuy

Vilyuysk Vilyuy

Verkhnevilyuysk

Nyurba

Suntar

Yakutsk

Pokrovskoye

Amga

Ust Maya

Maya

Okhotsk

Sea of
Okhotsk 1780

R U S S I A N REP.

Lensk
(Mukhtuya)

Olekminsk

Aldan 2246

Khrebet Dzhugdzhur

Ayan

Nikolayevsk-
na-Am.

Sakhalin

Khrebet Sikhote Alin

50

Bratsk

Krasnoyarsk

Kirensk

Ust-Ilimsk

Ust-Kut

Nizhneangarsk

2840

2999

Yepukdan

Nagornyy

3482

Chulman

Tynda

Stanovoy Khrebet

Komsomolsk 2078

Khabarovsk

Yuzhno-Sakhalinsk

Sovetskaya Gavan

Hokkaido Sapporo

E

Irkutsk 1620

Ulan Ude

Chita

Shilka

Nerchinsk

Da Hinggan Ling

Blagoveshchensk

Amur

1054

Birobidzhan

Jiamusi 3669

Ussuriysk

Vladivostok Nakhodka

Hakodate

40

MONGOLIA

Ulaanbaatar
(Ulan Bator)

2800

Hentiyn Nuruu

Qiqihar

Harbin

Dongbei

Jilin

Changchun

Siping

Chongjin

Sea of JAPAN

Honshu

Niigata

F

G O B I

3957

Edrengiyn Nuruu

4266

Saynshand

Linxi

Chifeng

Fushun 2744

Shenyang Anshan

Dandong

Yingkou

NORTH
KOREA

Wonsan

Pyongyang

Chongjin

Kanazawa To-yama

1949

Baotou Hohhot Zhangjiakou Beijing

Chengde

Dalian

Chinnampo

Inch'on Soul

SOUTH KOREA Taejon

Taegu

Pusan

Boundaries of
Autonomous
Republics

10 100 11 110 12 120 13 130 14

1 : 44 400 000

250   0   250   500   750   1000 miles
250   0   500   1000   1500   km

Projection: Bonne

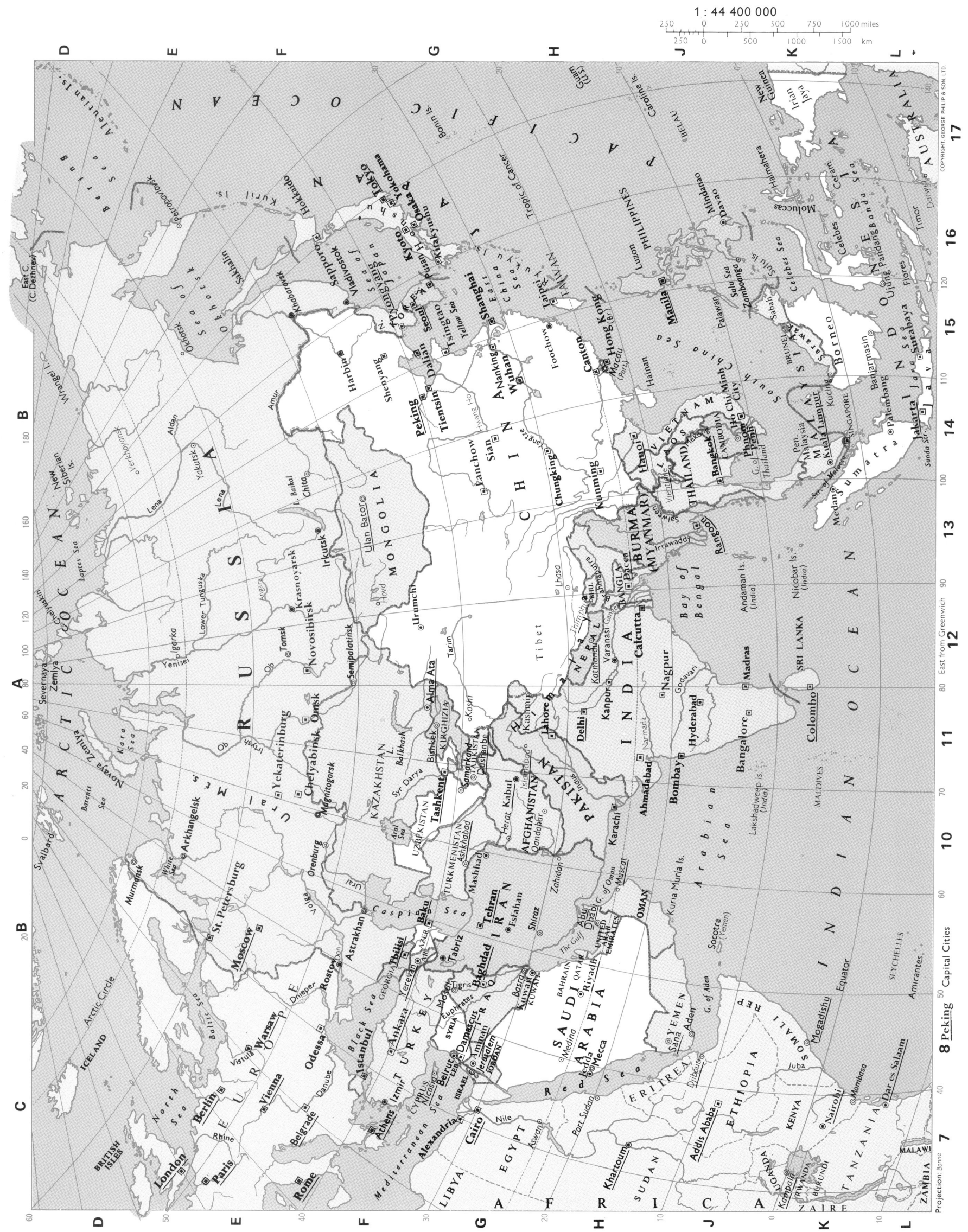

SEA OF OKHOTSK

Sakhalin

La Pérouse Strait
Sōya-Kaikyō

HOKKAIDO

SAPPORO

Wakkanai
Rebun-Tō
Rishiri-Tō
Teshio
Embetsu
Haboro
Rumoi
Otaru
Ishikari-Wan
(Otaru-Wan)
Iwonai
Suttsu
Setana
Kan'ui-Misaki
Esashi
Ōmu
Mombetsu
Yūbetsu
Noyoro
Kitami
Asahigawa
Ashibetsu
Bibai
Furano
Yūbari
Tomakomai
Shikoh-Ko
Uchiura-Wan
Muroran
Atsuta
Ebetsu
Shiraoi
Shirioi
Horobetsu
Esashi
Okushiri-Tō
Hakodate
Matsumai-Misaki
Shiragami-Misaki

Abashiri-Wan
Abashiri
Shiretoko-Misaki
Rausu-Dake 1661
Nemuro-Kaikyō
Kunashir
Ostrov Kunashir
Nemuro
Nemuro
Kushiro
Kushiro
Obihiro
Tokachi
Hiroo
Urakawa
Erimo-Misaki

Sammyaku
Daisetsu-Zan 2290
Tokachi-Dake 2077
Hidaka-Sammyaku

HOKKAIDO

Shirya-Zaki
Esan-Misaki
Ōma
Shimokita
Mutsu-Wan
Hachinohe
Misawa
Noshiro
Oga-Hantō
AKITA
Akita
Honjo
Sakata
Tsuruoka
Murakami
Niitsu
Niigata
Sado
Ryōtsu
Aikawa

TŌHOKU
Miyako
Morioka
Kamaishi
Kesennuma
Ishinomaki
Sendai
Sendai-Wan
Shiogama
Furukawa
Ōfunato
YAMAGATA
Yonezawa
Fukushima
Aizu-Wakamatsu

SEA OF JAPAN

RUSSIA

Bikin
Lesopilnoye
Dalnerechensk
Lesozovodsk
Novokachalinsk
Ozero Khanka
Kamen-Rybolov
Pogranichny
Spassk-Dalniy
Liporcy
Morzovka
Ussuriysk
Artem
Vladivostok
Nakhodka
Zaliv Petra Velikogo
Slavyanka
Kraskino
Khasan

Svetlaya
Amgu
Velikaya Kema
Terney
Plastun
Tetyukhe Pristan
Dalnegorsk
Kavalerovo
Krasnorechenskiy
Lifudzin
Olga
Margaritovo
Valentin
Preobrazheniye

Sikhote-Alin

CHINA

NORTH KOREA
Najin
Chongjin
Unggi

OCEAN

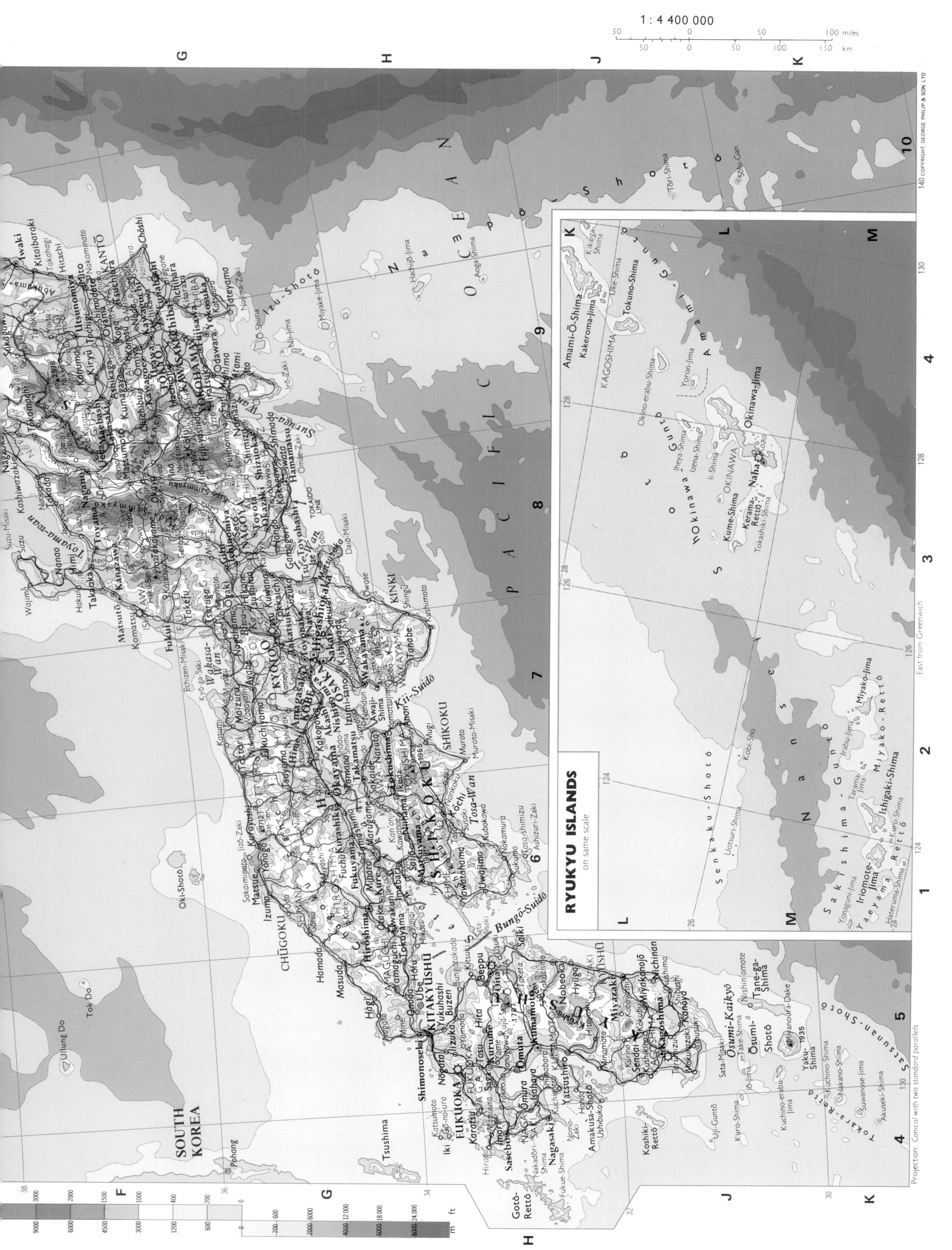

1 : 4 400 000

50   0   50   100 miles

50   0   50   100   150 km

SOUTH
KOREA

PACIFIC OCEAN

RYUKYU ISLANDS
on same scale

Amami-Ō-Shima
KAGOSHIMA
OKINAWA
Naha

Nansei-Guntō

Sakishima-Guntō
Miyako-Rettō
Ishigaki-Shima
Yaeyama-Rettō

Senkaku-Shotō

East from Greenwich

Projection: Conical with two standard parallels

140 COPYRIGHT GEORGE PHILIP & SON LTD.

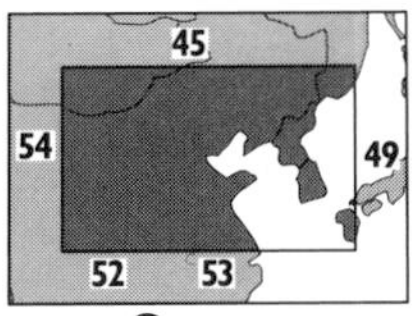

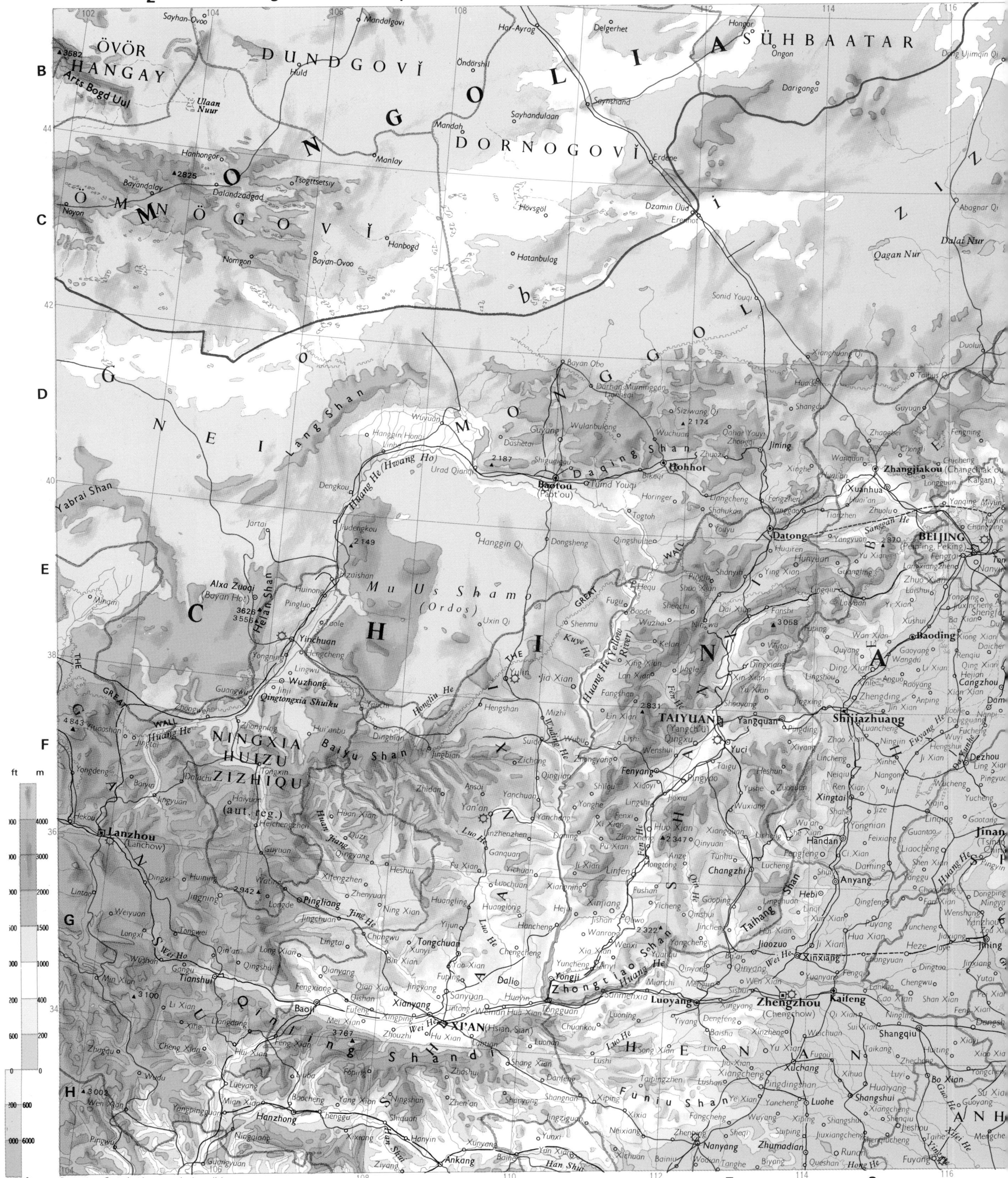

ÖVÖR HANGAY
Arts Bogd Uul
ÖMNÖGOVĬ
DUNDGOVĬ
DORNOGOVĬ
MONGOLIA
SÜHBAATAR
ZIZ

NEI MONGGOL
CHINA
NINGXIA HUIZU ZIZHIQU (aut. reg.)
SHANXI
SHAANXI
HEBEI
HENAN
ANHUI
SHANDONG

Mu Us Shamo (Ordos)
Helan Shan
Yabrai Shan
Lang Shan
Daqing Shan
Qin Ling
Zhongtiao Shan
Taihang Shan
Funiu Shan
Bai Yu Shan

THE GREAT WALL

Huang He (Hwang Ho)
Huang He / Yellow River
Wei He
Han Shui

BEIJING (Peiping, Peking)
Hohhot
Baotou (Paot'ou)
Datong
Zhangjiakou (Changchiak'ou, Kalgan)
Baoding
Shijiazhuang
TAIYUAN (Yangch'u)
Lanzhou (Lanchow)
Yinchuan
Xi'an (Hsian, Sian)
Zhengzhou (Chengchow)
Kaifeng
Luoyang
Jinan (Tsinan)
Xingtai
Handan
Anyang
Changzhi
Tianshui
Pingliang
Baoji
Hanzhong
Nanyang
Zhumadian
Dezhou
Cangzhou

Dalandzadgad
Mandalgovi
Sayhan-Ovoo
Dzamin Uud
Erenhot
Bayan Obo
Qagan Nur
Dalai Nur
Ulaan Nuur

Projection: Conical with two standard parallels

ft	m
	4000
	3000
	2000
	1500
	1000
	400
	200
	0
	600
	6000
m	ft

1 : 5 300 000

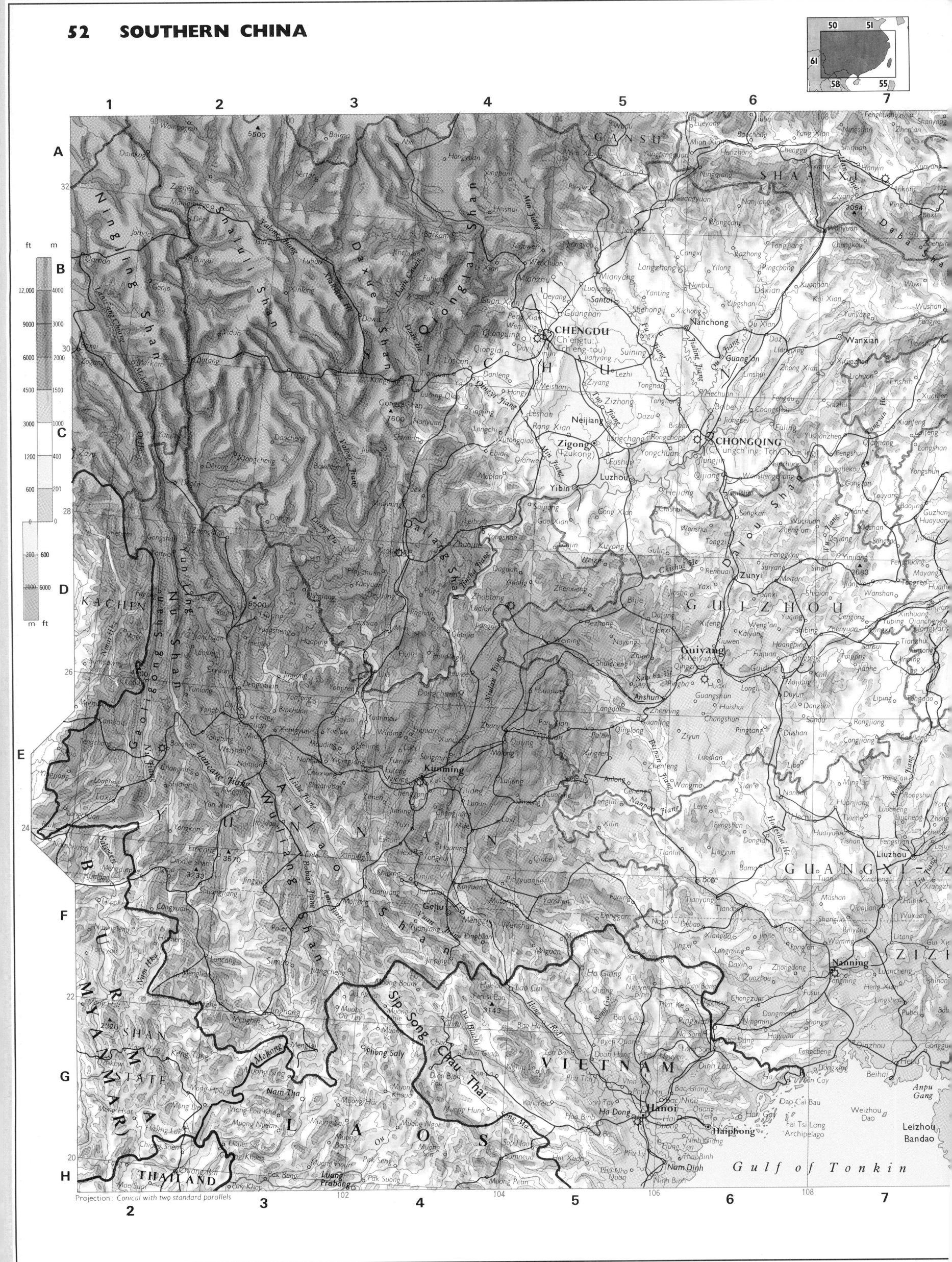

1 : 5 300 000

50   0   50   100   150 miles

50   0   50   100   150   200
km

8   9   10   11   12   13   14

112   120   122

A

HENAN   Bengbu
Huainan   **JIANGSU**   Gaoyou

Nanyang   Yangzhou   Taizhou   Nantong   32

Zhenjiang
(Chenchiang)   Haimen

Xiangfan   Huai He   NANJING   Changzhou   Wuxi   SHANGHAI
HUBEI   Hefei   Nanching   Suzhou   (Changhai)   **B**
                Chao Hu   (Suchou)
Yichang   Songjiang

ANHUI   Wuhu   Hangzhou
Hankou   **WUHAN**   (Hangchou; Hanchow)   Hangzhou   Zhoushan   30
Wou-han   Anqing   Shaoxing   Ningbo   Dao
Huangshi   (Ningpo)

Jiujiang   Putuo

ZHEJIANG   **C**

Dongting   Jingdezhen
Hu   Poyang
Changde   Hu   Wenzhou
Changsha   Nanchang   Wenchow   28

Xiangtan   **JIANGXI**   Wenzhou
Zhuzhou
HUNAN   Linchuan

Hengyang   Nanping   **D**
                                                                        26

Shaoyang   **FUJIAN**

Fuzhou
(Foochow; Fuchou)   **E**

Ganzhou   Changting   Sanming

Guilin   Quanzhou   TAIBEI
(Ch'uanchou)   (Taipei)

Shaoguan   Quannan   Zhangzhou   Xinzhu   **TAIWAN**
Xiamen   Zhanghua   Taizhong   **F**
(Hsiamen; Amoy)   Jinmen Dao   (Taichung)   24
GUANGDONG   Mei Xian   Jinmen Dao
Tropic of Cancer   Tainan
GUANGZHOU   Shantou   **(FORMOSA)**
Guangzhou   (Swatow)
Foshan   Gaoxiong   Pingdong
(Canton)   Honghai Wan   Tainan   (Kaohsiung)   Fangliao

HONG KONG (U.K.)   22
Macau   Kowloon   Dangan Liedao
(Macao)
(Port.)   Lan Yu

Gaolan
Dao   Shangchuan   **Luzon**   **G**
Dao   Strait

Zhanjiang

Donghai Dao

S O U T H   C H I N A   S E A   20

H

8   9   10   11   12   13
112   114   116   118
120 COPYRIGHT. GEORGE PHILIP & SON. LTD.

1 : 17 800 000

1 : 6 700 000

50 0 50 100 150 200 miles
50 0 50 100 150 200 250 300 km

A

Itbayat Batanes Is.
Batan

Balintang Channel

Calayan Babuyan

B

Dalupiri Babuyan Camiguin
Islands
Fuga
Mayraira Pt. *Babuyan Channel*
Bangui Claveria
Bacarra Ballesteros Aparri Port San Vicente
San Nicolas Laoag Gonzaga
Batac Kabugao Gattaran
Santa 2360 Tuao Tuguegarao
Vigan Banna Cabagao Chico Cresta
Santa Lubuagan 1672
Maria Bontoc Ilagan
Candon Roxas San Mateo Palanan Pt.
Taguding Luna Santiago Palanan

C

PACIFIC

San Fernando Cordon
Lingayen Gulf Pulog Solano Casiguran
Bolinao Baguio 2929 Bayombong
Alaminos Rosario Dagupan Anacuao C. San Ildefonso
Lingayen 1850
San Carlos Bayambang San Manuel Baler Bay
Santa Cruz Moncada Cuyapo San Jose

OCEAN

D

Palauig Camiling Victoria Baler **LUZON**
2038 Tarlac La Dingalan
Iba Capas Paz Gapan
Sapangbato Angeles Polillo Str. **Polillo Is.**
San Narciso San Fernando Patnanongan
San Antonio Malaban Jomalig
Olongapo Orani Caloocan
Bataan Manila Quezon City
Cavite **MANILA** Lamon Bay
Trece Martires Pasay Santa Cruz Larap Paracale Pandan
Tagaytay Lucban Atimonan Labo Payo
Nasugbu San Pablo Daet Calabanga Catanduanes
Balayan Lipa Lucena Lopez Naga Iriga Virac
Lemery Batangas Tayabas Bay Catanauan Nabua Rapu Rapu
Lubang Bauan Boac Calauag Ligao Tabaco
Verde I. Pass. Marinduque Mayon Legazpi Sorsogon
Mamburao Calapan Pola Bui Irosin Gubat
MINDORO Pinamalayan Romblon Ticao Lavezares Laoang
Baco Tablas Str. **SIBUYAN** Masbate San Bernardino Str.
2488 Sablayan Sibuyan Mandaon Catarman Gamay
Bongabong Tablas Aroroy **MASBATE** Calbayog
Busuanga Roxas Odiongan Masbate **SAMAR**
Ilin San Jose *SEA* Wright Borongan

E

SOUTH

CHINA

SEA

F

Culion Semirara Is. Placer Taft
Calamian Pandan Kalibo Catbalogan Sta. Rita Maydolong
Group Roxas **VISAYAN** Biliran Calbiga General MacArthur
Linapacan Str. Sigma *SEA* Gutusan San Antonio Guiuan
Libro Pt. Tibiao 2117 Ajuy Bantayan Cangara Homonhon
Cuyo West Pass **PANAY** Estancia Palompon **LEYTE** Tacloban
Taytay Bugasong Pototan Silay Cadiz Bogo Ormoc Dulag
Cuyo Is. San Jose **Iloilo** Victorias Camotes Is. Abuyog
Cuyo de Buenavista San Carlos **Cebu** *Camotes* Baybay
Guimaras 2465 **Bacolod** Mandaue *Sea* Sogod
Dumaran Jordan La Carcar Matalom
PALAWAN Hinigaran Carlota Calamba Maasin

G

ft m

Mantalingajan Caliling Binalbagan Kabankalan Dinagat
1593 Himamaylan Baso Bohol Surigao
Irahuan Honda B. Cagayan Sipalay Dumaguete 10 497
Puerto Princesa **NEGROS** Tanjay Oslob Tagbilaran Siargao
Bayawan Bais **BOHOL** Bucas Grande
Bonawan Siquijor L. Carrascal
Mantalingajan Zamboanguita Camiguin Mainit Lanuza
2085 Talisayan 1837 Tandag
C. Bulilayan Bugsuk Dapitan Hilonghilong Tago
Balabac Strait Dipolog **Butuan** Marihatag
Balabac Manucan Iligan Nasipit Esperanza Lianga

H

SULU

SEA

Mindanao Trench

Kudat Oroquieta Bay Opol Talacogon San Juan
Sindangan Iligan **Cagayan de Oro** Malaybalay Mangagoy
SABAH Ozamiz Malabang **MINDANAO**
Kota Belud Tubod L. Lanao Bunawan Cateel
Tuaran Kinabalu Pagadian 2896 Baganga
Kinabalu 4101 Sibuguey Marawi 2815 Panabo Tagum
Kota Penampang Malabang Parang Tagum
Papar Cotabato Datu Piang Pikit **Davao** Manay
Beaufort **Zamboanga** Moro Gulf Apo 2954 Davao Gulf
Isabela Salaman Digos Koronadal Malita Batobato
Basilan Lebok C. San Agustin

J

CELEBES

SEA

Projection: Lambert's Conformal Conic   East from Greenwich   COPYRIGHT. GEORGE PHILIP & SON. LTD.

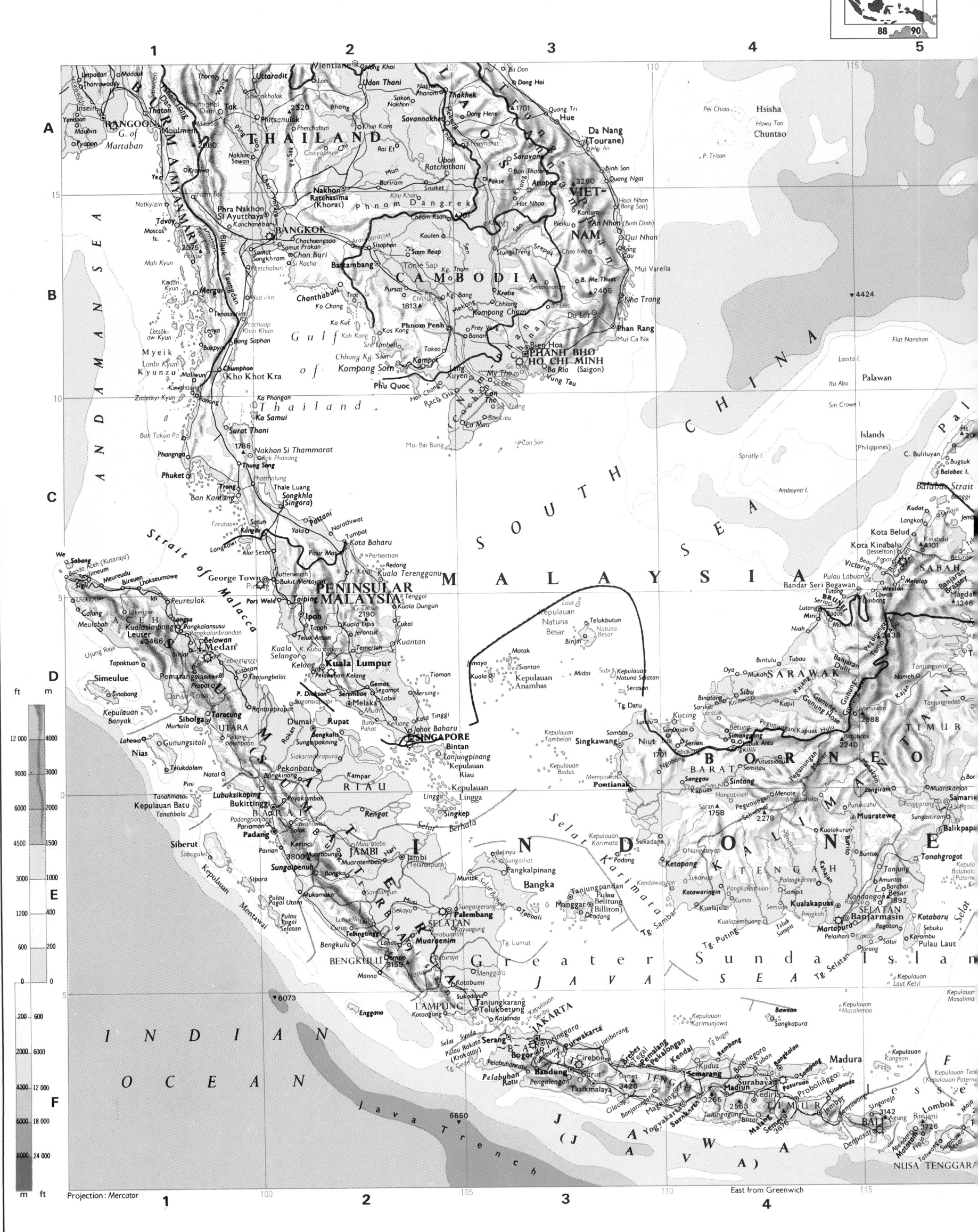

Projection: Mercator

East from Greenwich

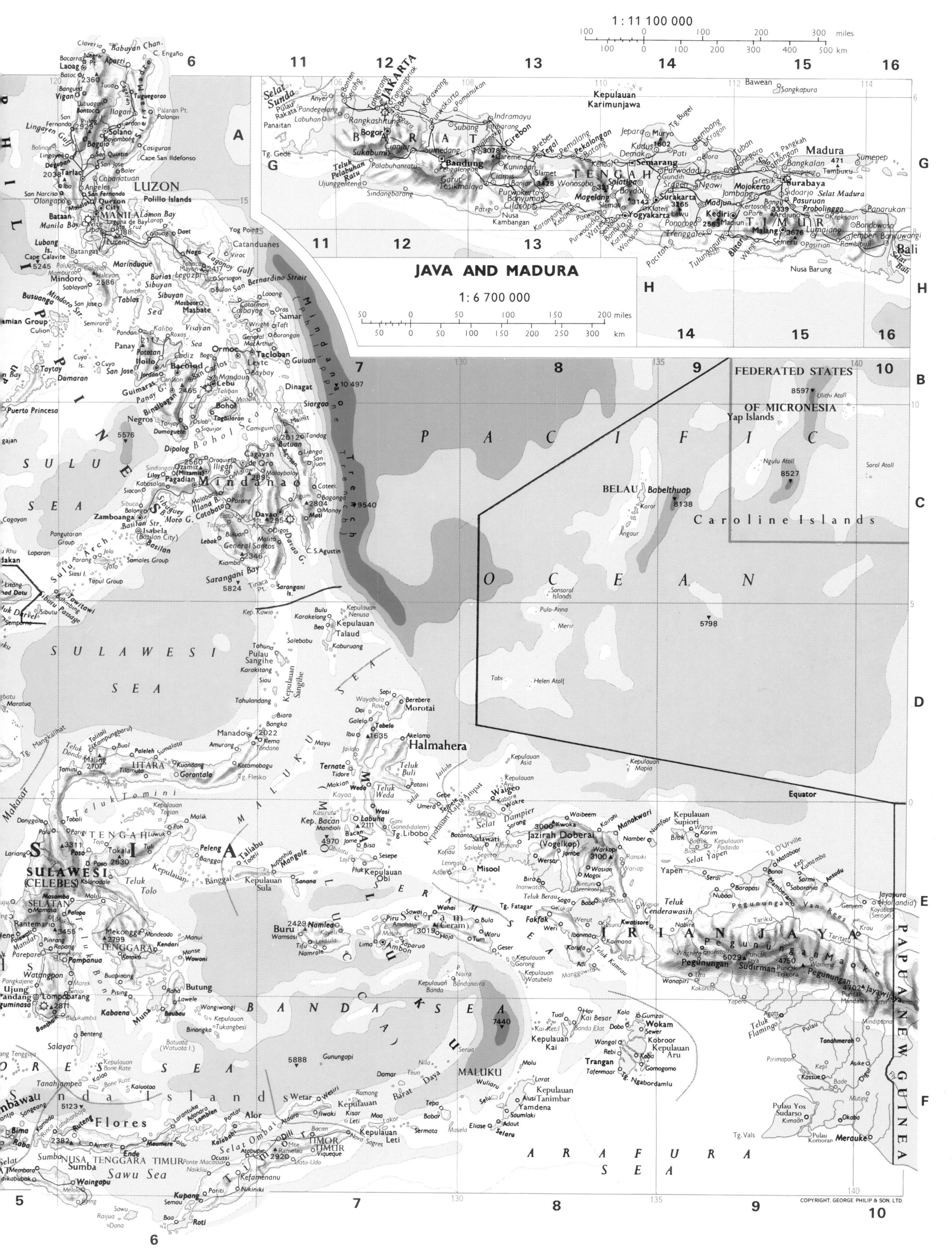

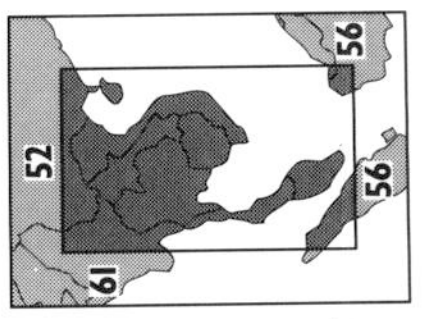

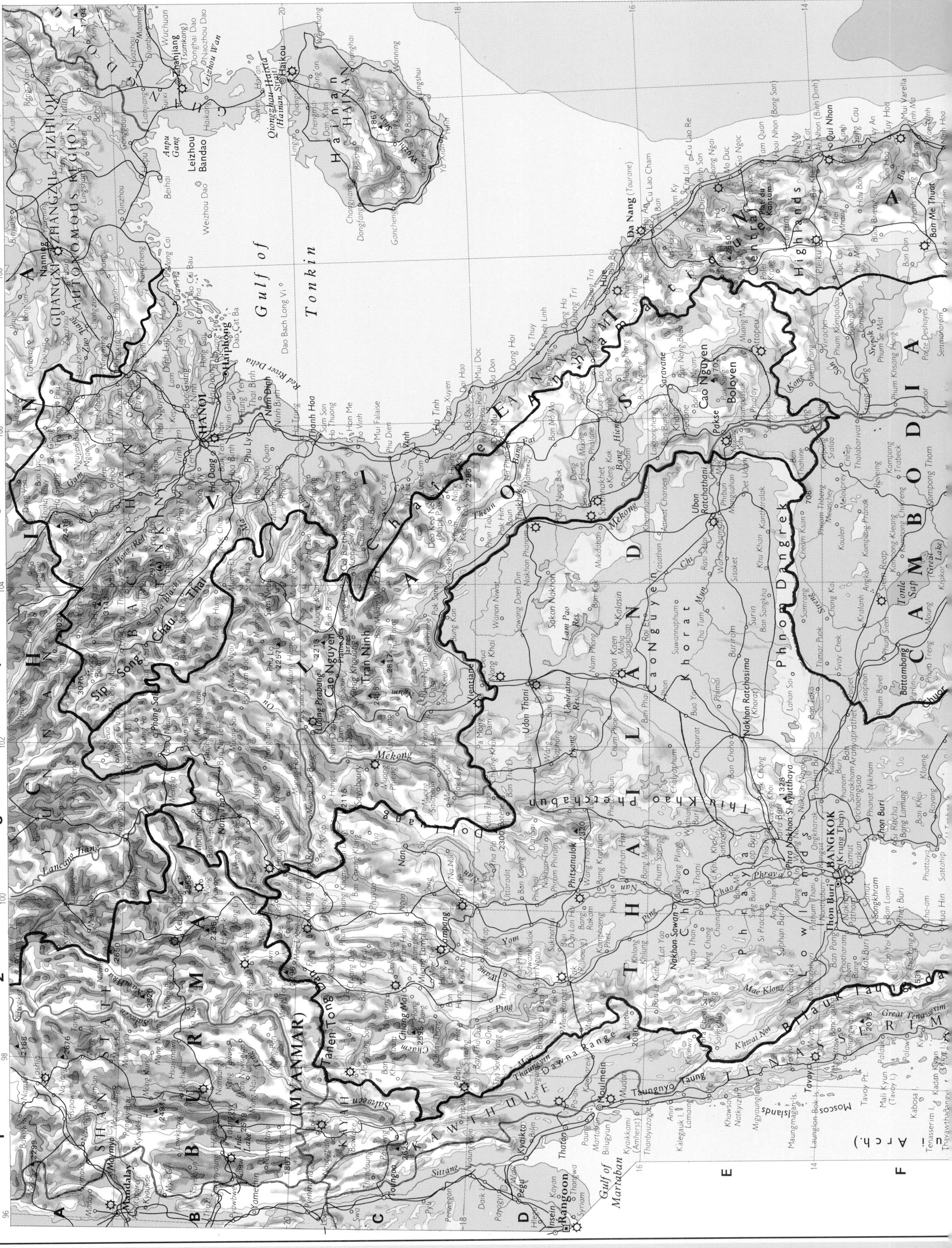

Gulf of Tonkin

HAINAN

GUANGXI ZHUANGZU ZIZHIQU AUTONOMOUS REGION

YUNNAN

VIETNAM

LAOS

THAILAND

CAMBODIA

BURMA (MYANMAR)

SHAN STATE

KAYAH

KAWTHULE

TENASSERIM

Annam

Chaîne Annamitique

Central Highlands

Cao Nguyen Boloven

Plateau Khorat

Phnom Dangrek

Thiu Khao Phetchabun

Dawna Range

Taungnyo Range

HANOI
Haiphong
Red River Delta
Nam Dinh
Thanh Hoa
Vinh
Ha Tinh
Dong Hoi
Hue
Da Nang (Tourane)
Qui Nhon
Nha Trang
Luang Prabang
Vientiane
Savanakhet
Pakse
Udon Thani
Nong Khai
Ubon Ratchathani
Surin
Buriram
Nakhon Ratchasima (Khorat)
Khon Kaen
Phitsanulok
Sukhothai
Chiang Mai
Chiang Rai
Lampang
Nakhon Sawan
BANGKOK (Krung Thep)
Thon Buri
Ayutthaya
Hua Hin
Battambang
Tonle Sap
Siem Reap
Mandalay
Rangoon
Pegu
Moulmein
Thaton
Tavoy (Dawei)
Mergui

Zhanjiang (Tsamkong)
Haikou
Leizhou Bandao
Beihai
Nanning

Mekong
Salween
Chao Phraya
Ping
Nan
Yom

Gulf of Martaban

Hainan Strait (Qiongzhou Haixia)

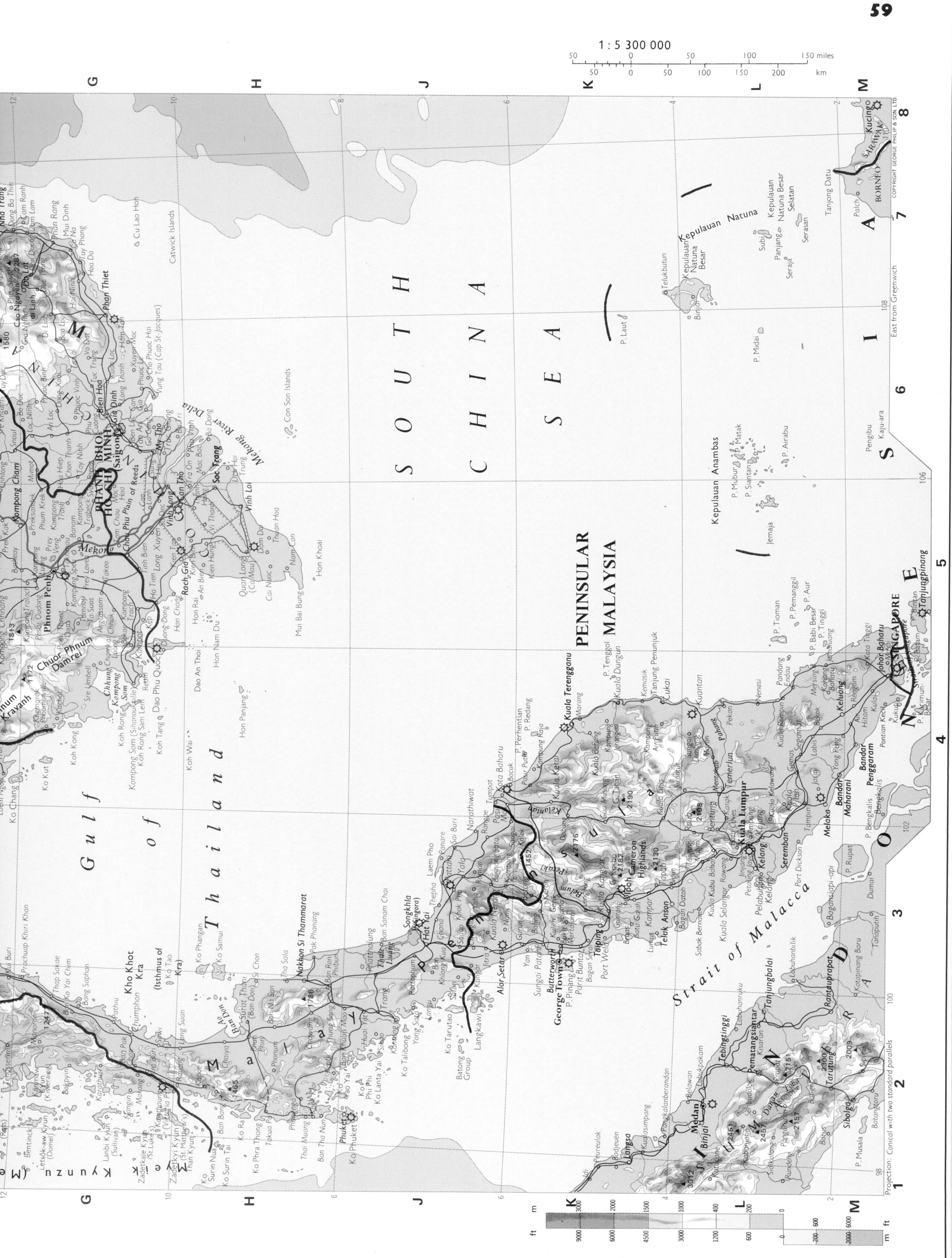

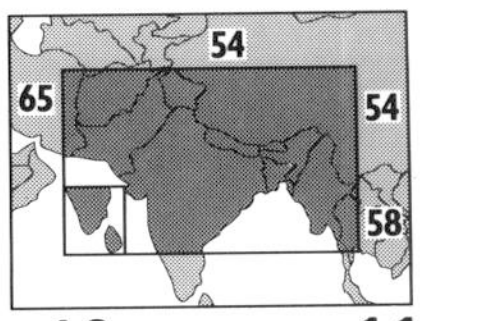

Grid references (top): 1 2 3 4 5 6 7 8 9 10 11

Row labels (left): B C D E F G H M N P Q R

AFGHANISTAN — Herāt, Kābul, Kandahār, Ghaznī, Jalālābād, Gardēz

IRAN — Zāhedān (Duzdab), Zābol, Bampūr

PAKISTAN — Peshāwar, Rāwalpindi, Islāmābād, Quetta, Sukkur, Hyderabad, KARACHI, Lahōre, Faisalābād, Multān, Nawabshah

JAMMU AND KASHMIR — Srinagar, Leh

HIMACHAL PRADESH — Simla, Mandi

PUNJAB — Amritsar, Ludhiana, Chandigarh, Patiala

HARYANA — Rohtak, Hisar

DELHI — DELHI

RAJASTHAN — Jaipur, Jodhpur, Ajmer, Bikaner, Udaipur, Kota, Bharatpur

GUJARAT — Ahmadabad, Rajkot, Jamnagar, Vadodara (Baroda), Surat, Bhavnagar, Junagadh, Bhuj

MADHYA PRADESH — Bhopal, Indore, Ujjain, Gwalior, Jabalpur, Ratlam, Sagar, Nagpur

MAHARASHTRA — BOMBAY, Pune (Poona), Nagpur, Nasik, Aurangabad, Solapur, Kolhapur, Amravati, Akola, Nanded

KARNATAKA — Bangalore, Mysore, Mangalore, Hubli, Bellary, Gulbarga, Bijapur, Belgaum

ANDHRA PRADESH — Hyderabad, Secunderabad, Kurnool, Raichur

TAMIL NADU — Madras, Madurai, Coimbatore, Salem, Tiruchchirappalli, Tirunelveli, Vellore, Thanjavur

KERALA — Cochin, Ernakulam, Calicut (Kozhikode), Trivandrum, Quilon, Alleppey, Trichur

GOA — Panaji (Panjim), Marmagao

SRI LANKA (CEYLON) — Colombo, Kandy, Mt. Lavinia, Moratuwa, Galle, Trincomalee, Anuradhapura, Negombo

Water bodies: ARABIAN SEA, Gulf of Kachchh, Gulf of Khambhat, Palk Strait, Palk Bay, Gulf of Mannar (Manaar), Tropic of Cancer, Mouths of the Indus

Physical features: Hindu Kush, Karakoram Range, Himalaya, Thar Desert (Great Indian Desert), Rann of Kachchh, Little Rann, Kathiawar, Makran Coast Range, Central Makran Range, Kirthar Range, Siahan Range, Satpura, Ajanta Range, Balaghat Range, Western Ghats, Malabar Coast, Coromandel Coast, Cape Comorin, Dondra Head, Adam's Bridge, Adam's Peak

Rivers: Indus, Narmada, Tapi, Krishna, Cauvery, Godavari, Bhima, Tungabhadra

Elevation points: Mt. Everest area peaks — 7690, 7788, 8575, 7135, 5143, 4148, 2886, 4042, 2093, 2146, 1580

Continuation Southwards on same scale

Projection: Conical with two standard parallels

Elevation scale (ft / m): 18 000 / 6000, 12 000 / 4000, 9000 / 3000, 4500 / 1500, 1200 / 400, 600 / 200, 0, 200 / 600

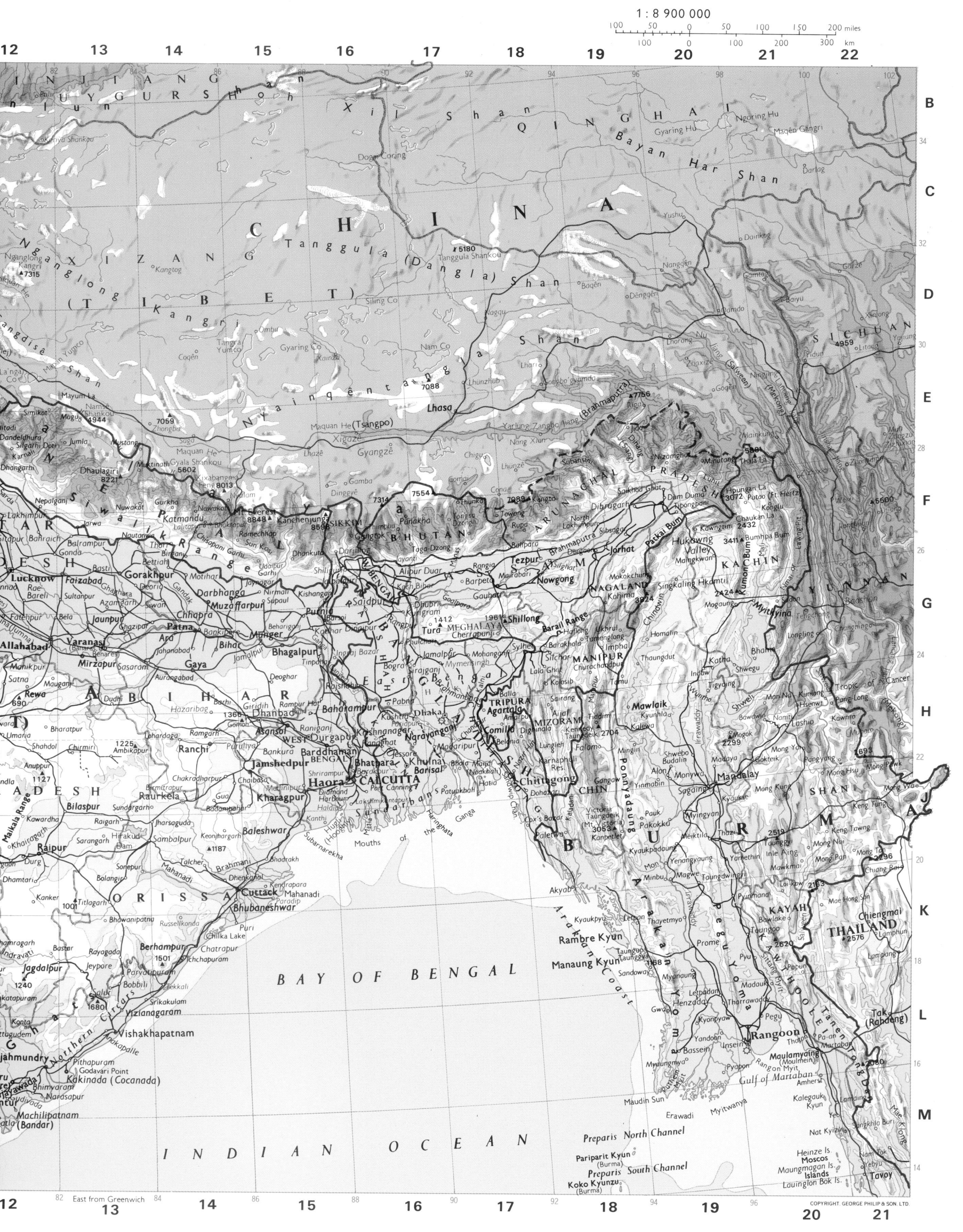

1 : 8 900 000

East from Greenwich

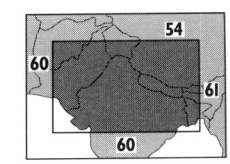

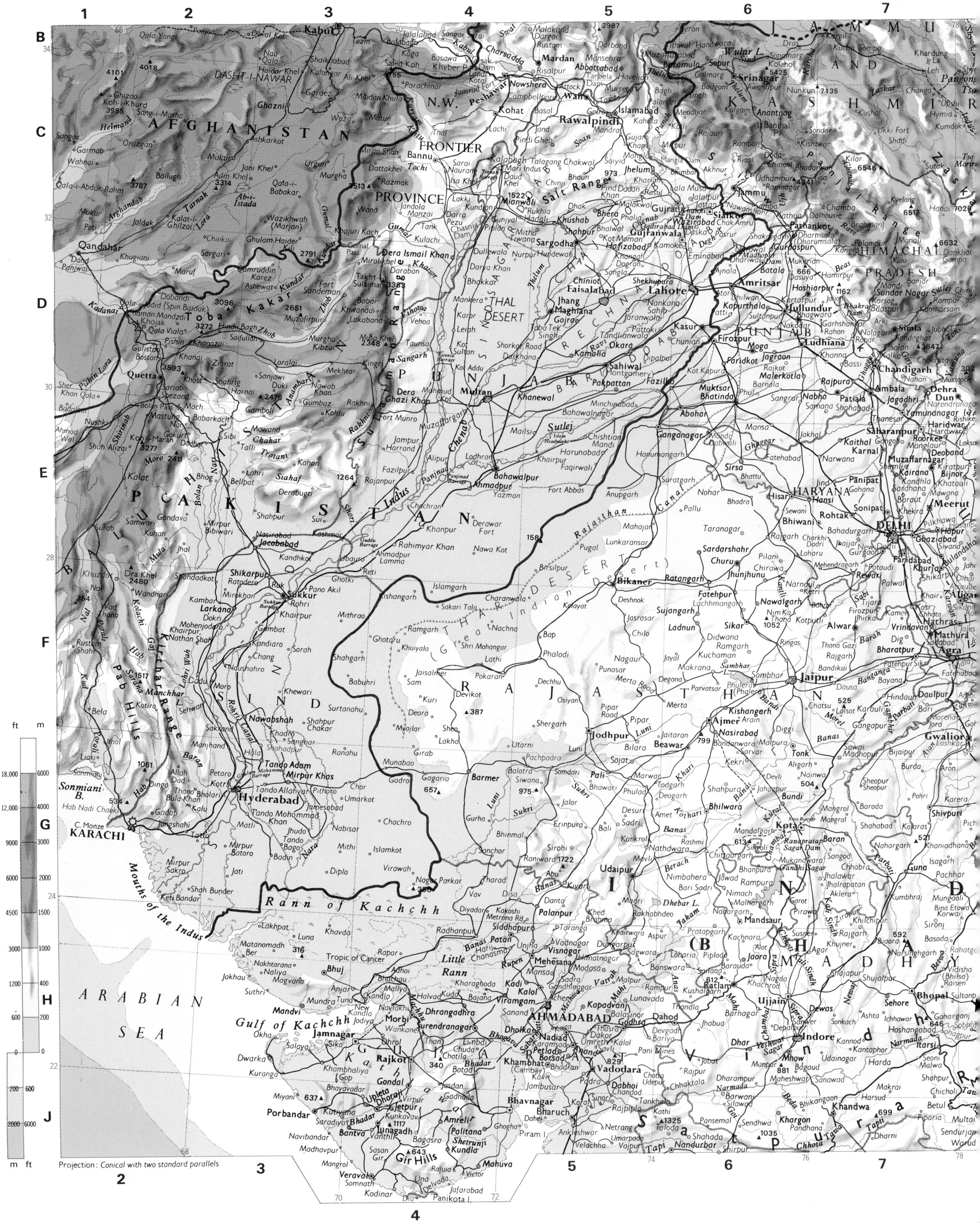

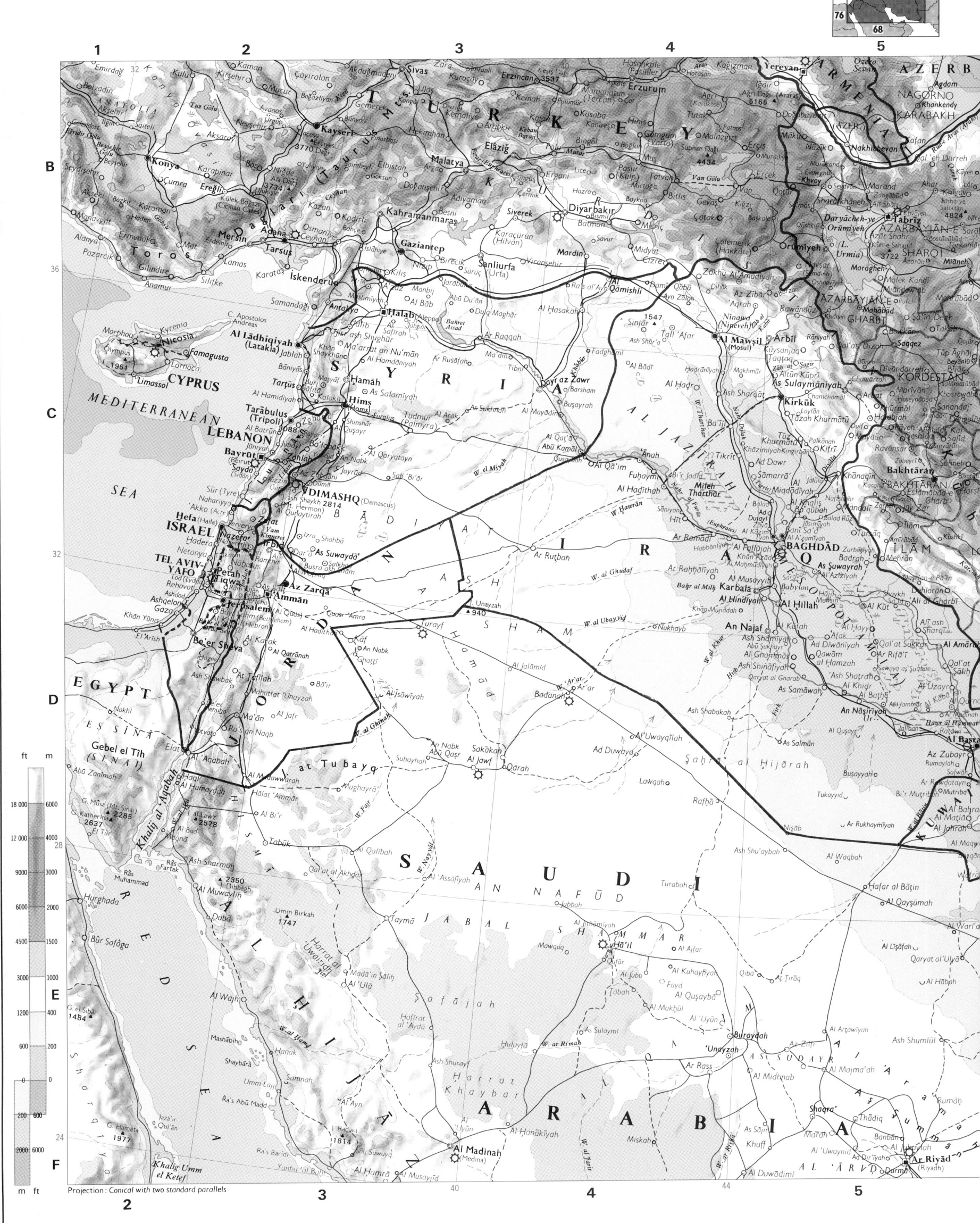

Projection: Conical with two standard parallels

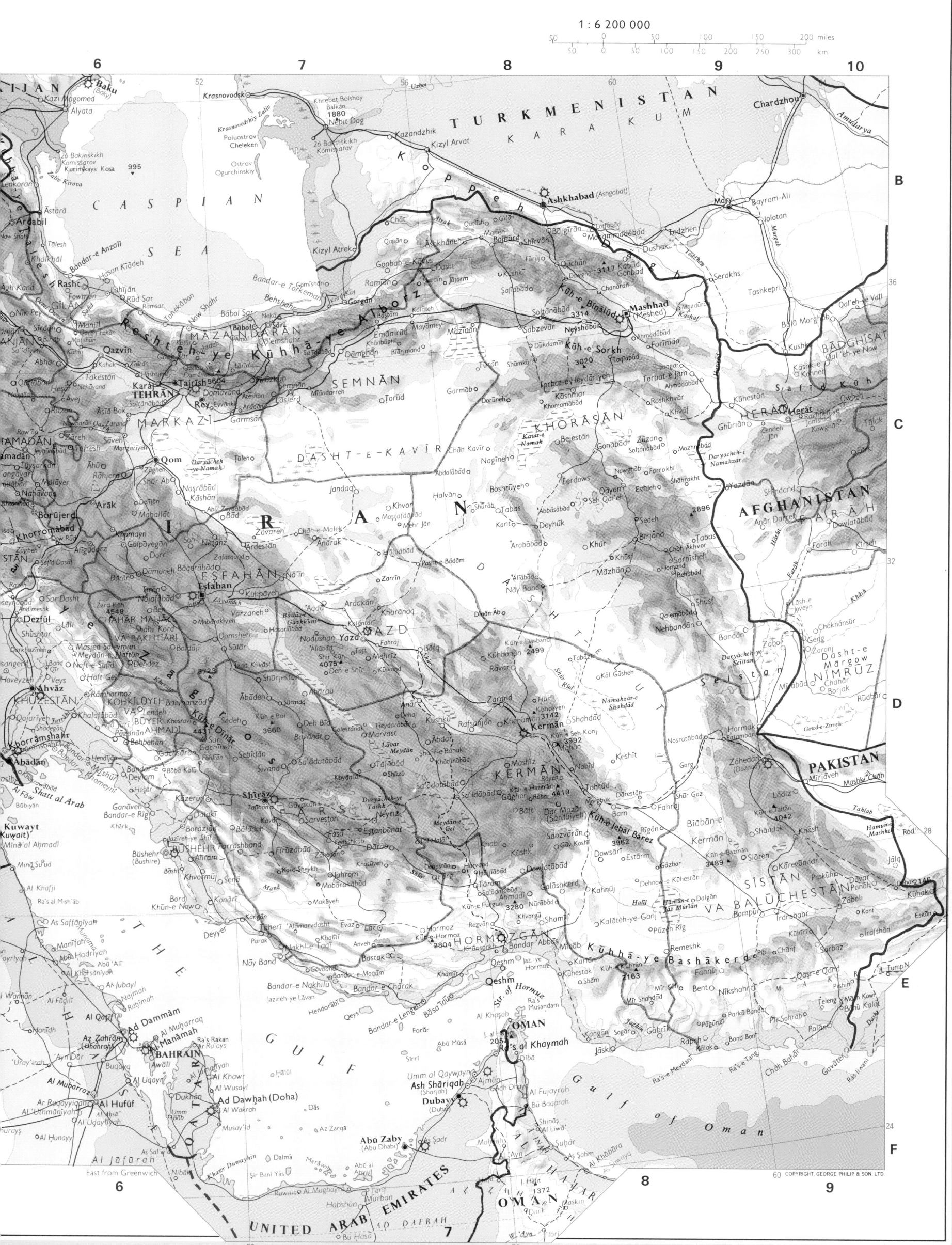

1 : 6 200 000

B L A C K   S E A

BULGARIA

GREECE   THRACE

MEDITERRANEAN   SEA

CYPRUS

LEBANON

1 : 4 400 000

East from Greenwich

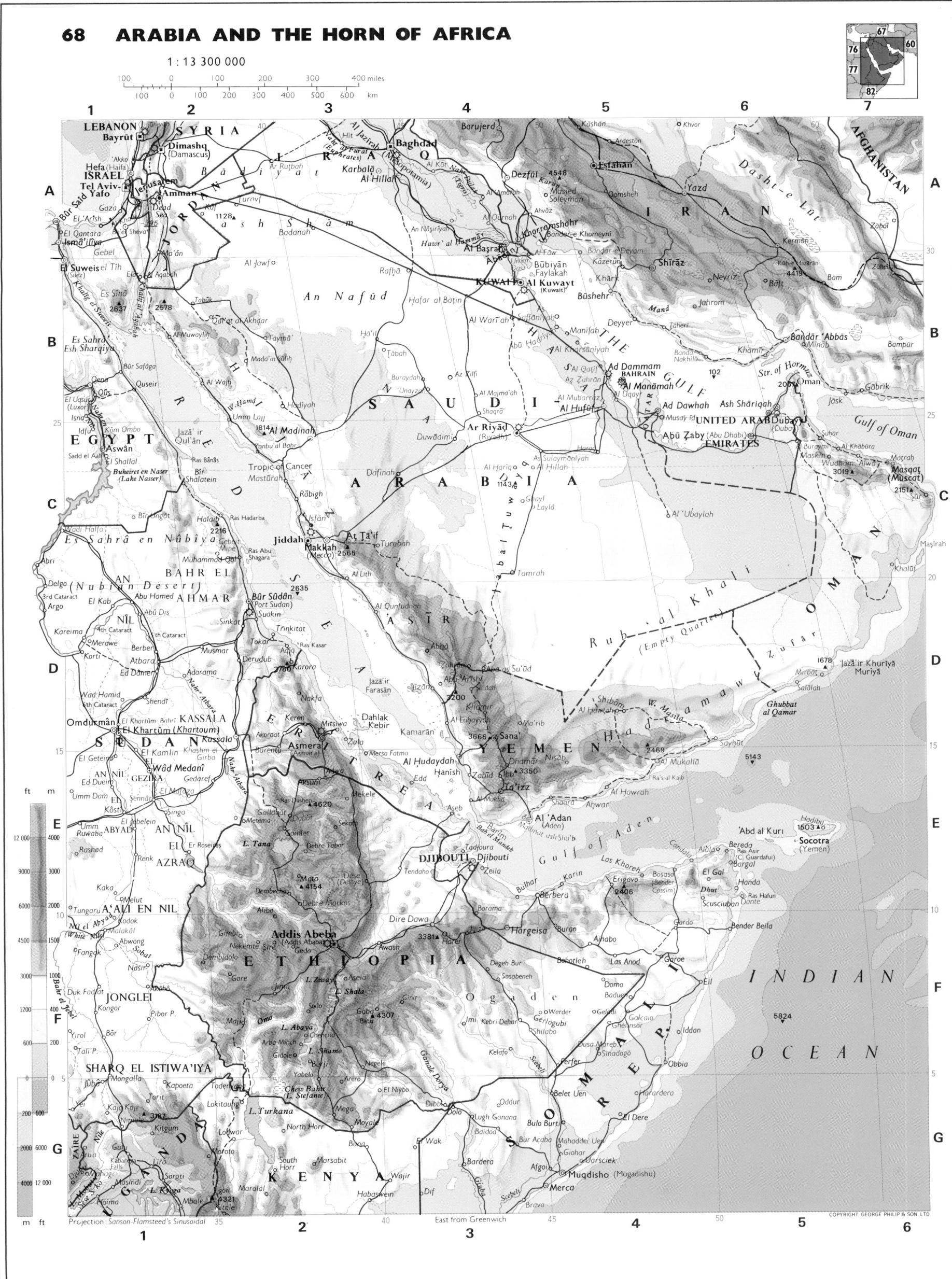

1 : 13 300 000

Projection: Sanson-Flamsteed's Sinusoidal

East from Greenwich

COPYRIGHT GEORGE PHILIP & SON LTD

1 : 2 200 000

10   0   10   20   30   40   50 miles
10 0 10 20 30 40 50 60 70 80 km

A

CYPRUS

Paphos
Episkopi
Limassol
Akrotiri
Episkopi Bay
Akrotiri Bay
C. Gata

M E D I T E R R A N E A N

S E A

Al Hamidîya
Al Mînâ'
Tarâbulus (Tripoli)
Hims (Homs)
Tell Kalakh
Shinshâr
Furklus
1075
Halba
Al Quşayr
HIMŞ
Al Qaryatayn
Al Hirmil
Al Burayj
Bîr Ghadîr
Al Batrûn
Dûma
3088
Qurnat as Sawdâ'
Qartaba
Ba'labakk
An Nabk
Jubayl
2616
Khân Abû Shâmât
2628
Yabrûde
BAYRÛT (Beirut)
Bikfayyā
Shaqrā
SYRIA
J. az Zubaydîyah
1406
Ash Shuwayfāt
Zaḥlah
LEBANON
2420
Az Zabadânî
Al Qutayfah
Saydâ (Sidon)
Khirbat Qanâfâr
Al Barûk 1942
Dûma
DIMASHQ (Damascus)
An Nabatîyah at Tahta
2814
DIMASHQ
Jazzin
Ash Shaykh
Qaţanâ
A'zaj
Al Kiswah
Al Hijânah
AL JANÛB
Şûr (Tyre)
Buraq
As Sanamayn
Qiryat Shemona
DARʻĀ
Shahbâ
Nahariyya
1197
Al Qunayţirah
W. al Harîr
AS SUWAYDĀ
'Akko (Acre)
HAZOR
Zefat
Golan Hts.
Izra'
As Suwaydâ'
Mifraz Hefa
Sakhnîn
Mughār
1800
Şalah
Hefa (Haifa)
Qiryat Yam
Qiryat Ata Teverya
Yam
Şahm al Jawlân
Tirat Karmel
Nazerat (Nazareth)
Kinneret
Dar'â
Salkhad
Umm al Faḥm
Dâliyat el Karmel
HEFA
HAZAFON
Ţafas
Yarmûk
Jabal ad Durûz
TEL MEGIDDO
'Afula
Ar Ramthā
Buşrá ash Shâm
Umm al Qittayn
CAESAREA
Shē'an
IRBID
Hadera
Pardes Hanna
Jenin
Irbid
Al Mafraq
ISRAEL
SHÔMRÔN
'Ajlûn
Umm ad Daraj
Netanya
Țûbâs
Herzliyya
SAMARIA
Jarash
HAMERKAZ
NÂBULUS
Bene Beraq
Nâbulus
Under Israeli
Az Zarqâ'
Petah Tiqwa
SHILO
Administration
AL BALQĀ
Tel Aviv-Yafo
Ramat Gan
Az Zarqâ'
Bat Yam
West Bank
As Salt
Rishon le Ziyyon
1016
AMMĀN
N. Soreq
Lod
Ramla
Ram Allâh
(Jericho)
Na'ûr
Rehovot
AL QUDS
289
Ashdod
Yavne
Jerusalem (Yerushalayim) (Al Quds)
Ma'dabā
Qiryat Mal'akhi
Bêt Shemesh
Bayt Laḥm (Bethlehem)
AL ʻĀŞIMAH
Ashqelon
Qiryat Gat
TEL LAKHISH
Al Khalîl (Hebron)
W. al Haydān
Gaza
N. Shiqma
AL KHALIL
Dhîbân
Gaza Strip
Sederot
Az Zâhirîya
1065
W. al Mawjib
Khân Yûnus
HAR YEHUDA
Rafah
Bûr Sa'îd (Port Said)
Bûr Fu'ad
Al Karak
Bîr el Garârât
Al Qaţrânah
981
Khalîg el Tîna
Sabkhet el Bardawil
Bir Laḥfân
Bor Mashash
'Arad
W. al Mazâr
Romani
Bîr el Duweidar
Bîr el 'Abd
Bîr Kaseiba
'Arad
1305
W. al Ḥasâ
AL KARAK
El Qanţara
Bîr el Jafar
El 'Arîsh
Dimona
33
Aţ Ţafîlah
W. Bâ'ir
El Daḥeir
Wâḥid
Bîr Madkûr
W. el 'Arîsh
Bā'ir
Ismâ'ilîya
-121
HADAROM
Az Zubayrâ
JORDAN
Birein
Muweilih
El Quşeima
Mizpe Ramon
At Tunayaj
J. ash Shawmari
1072
Khamsa
El Buheirat el Murrat el Kubra (Gt. Bitter L.)
Bîr Hasana
Bîr Beida
Niţil
892
1094 G. Yi 'Allâq
Bîr el Thamâda
W. el Brûk
Hanegev (Negev Desert)
Bi'r ad Dabbâghāt
Maḥattat 'Unayzah
W. Abu Şafâr
EL SUWEIS
E G Y P T
W. Qiratya
El 'Agrûd
N. Paran
Rijm Tal'at al Jamâl'â
1736
Qā' el Jafr
W. Mahashm
N. Ḥiyyon
PETRA
Al Jafr
875
Ginaifa
Bîr Gebel Hisn
W. Maḥashm
Bi'r al Mârî
El Suweis (Suez)
Bîr Taufîq
W. el 'Agaba
Nakhl
El Qunţilla
Ma'ân
MAʻĀN
Uyûn Mûsa
W. el Ruqq
W. el Tamâdnî
Ra's an Naqb
Maḥattat ash Shîdîyah
Bîr Bad
G. el Kabrît 948
W. Varga
Gebel el Tîh
El Thamad
Bîr Abu Mujammad
'En Avrona
Bi'r al Buţayyinah
Ra's an Naqb 1435
Râs Bad
S I N A I P e n i n s u l a
1592
Jazîrat Tubayq
Bîr Abu Şandûq
1272
Bîr el Biarât
Bîr Ţaba
Ilat
952
SAUDI
Matarma
W. Abu Ga'da
Bîr el Heisi
W. an Nuwaybi'
ARABIA
1165

Projection: Polyconic

East from Greenwich

COPYRIGHT. GEORGE PHILIP & SON. LTD.

- - - - 1949 Armistice Line, 1967 and 1974 Cease Fire Lines

ft   m
9000   3000
6000   2000
4500   1500
3000   1000
1200   400
600   200
0   0
200   600
2000   6000
m   ft

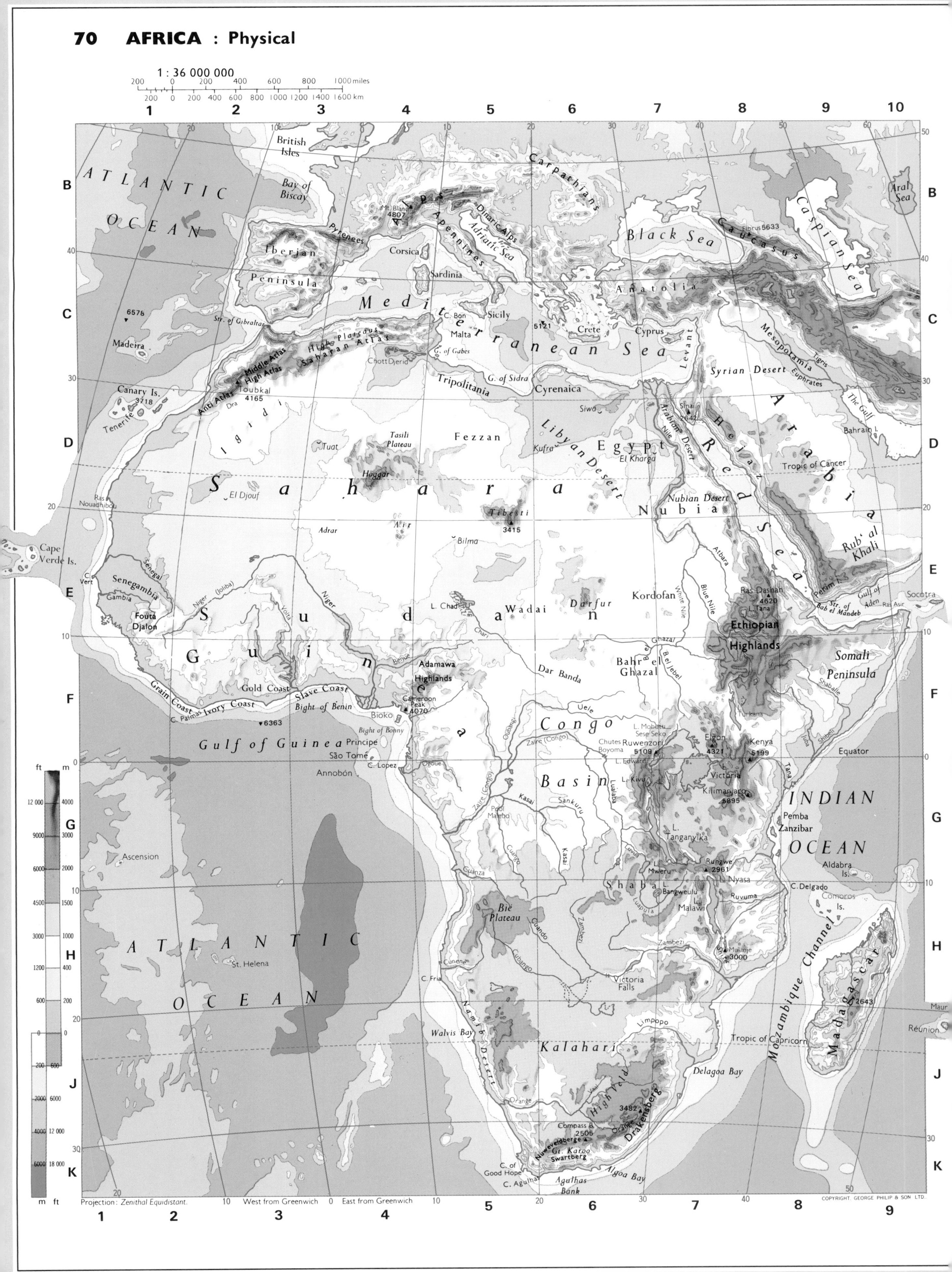

1 : 36 000 000

Projection: Zenithal Equidistant.

COPYRIGHT. GEORGE PHILIP & SON LTD.

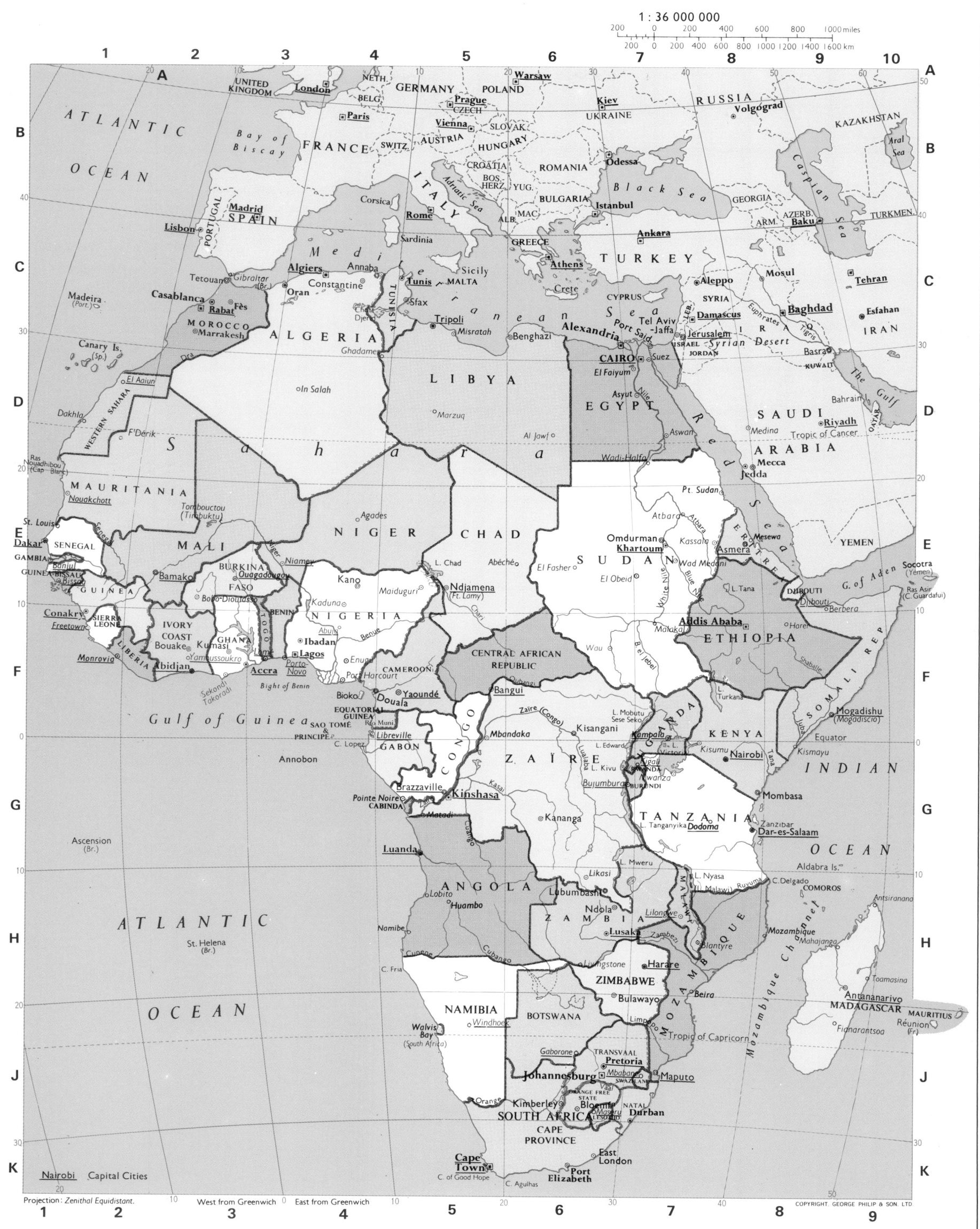

1 : 36 000 000

200   0   200   400   600   800   1000 miles
200   0   200 400 600 800 1000 1200 1400 1600 km

Projection : Zenithal Equidistant.   West from Greenwich   East from Greenwich   COPYRIGHT. GEORGE PHILIP & SON. LTD.

<u>Nairobi</u>   Capital Cities

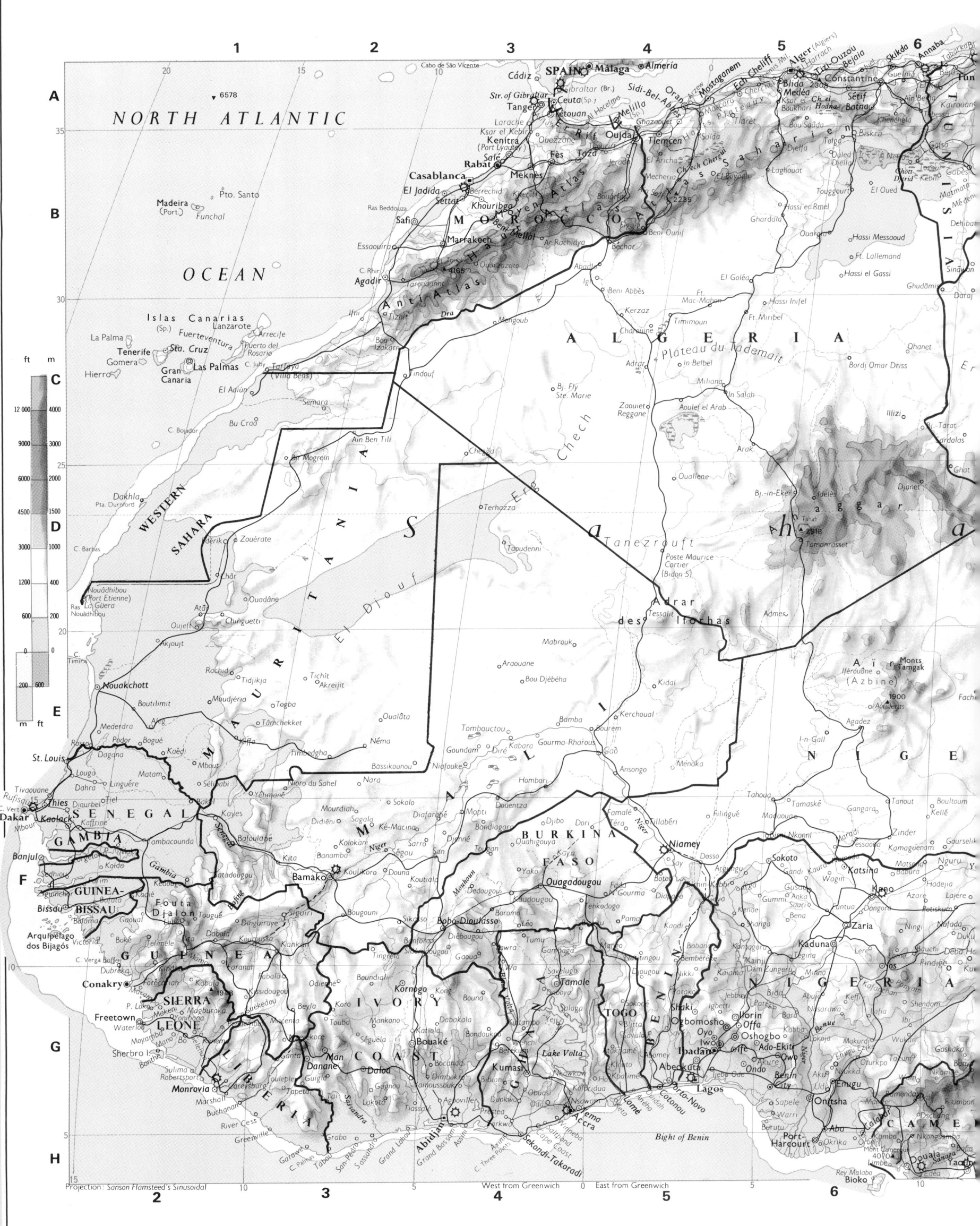

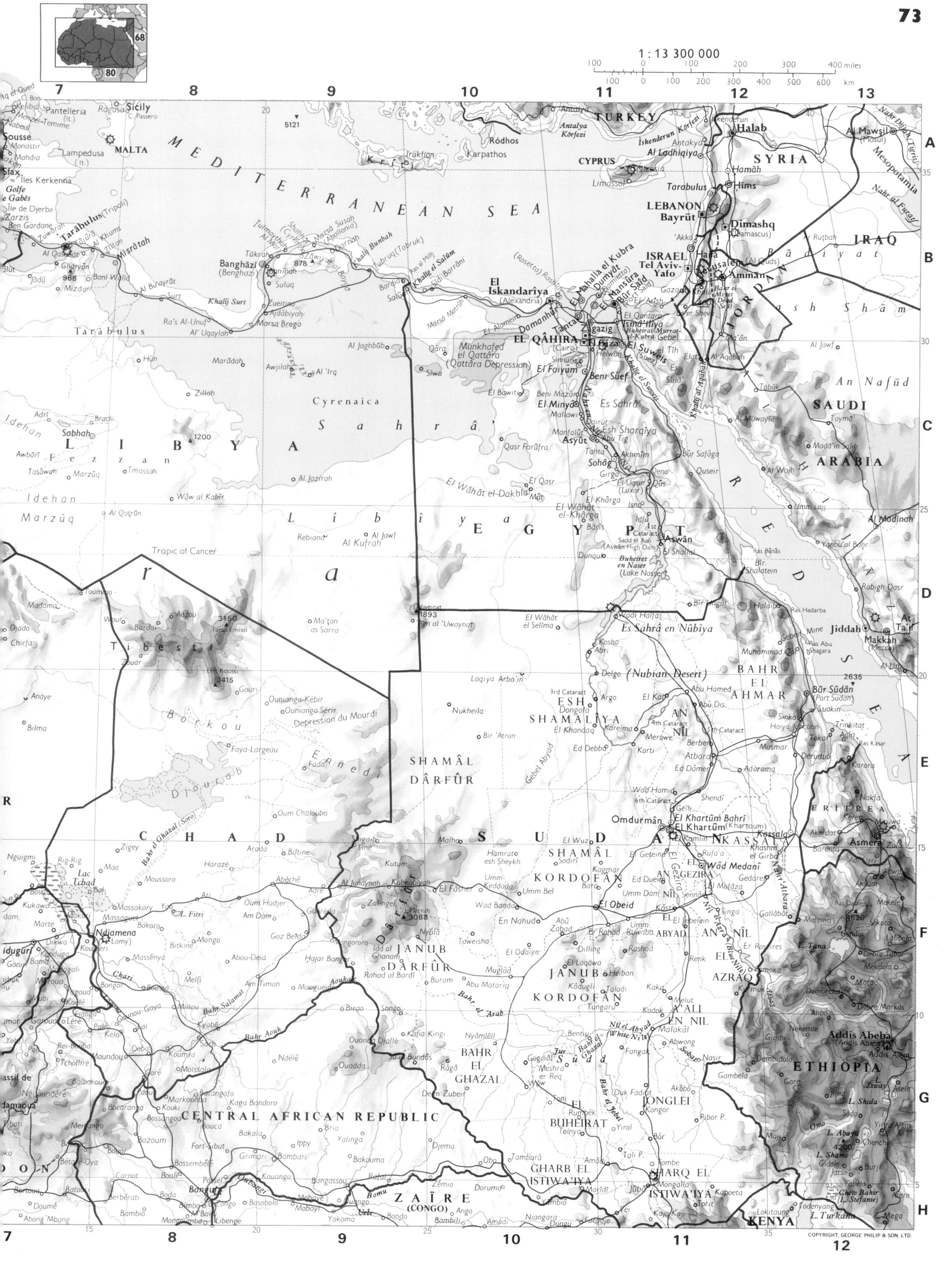

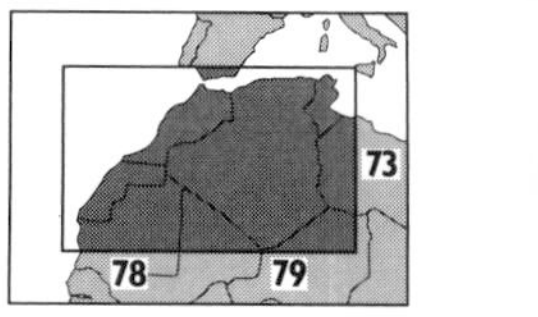

73

78 79

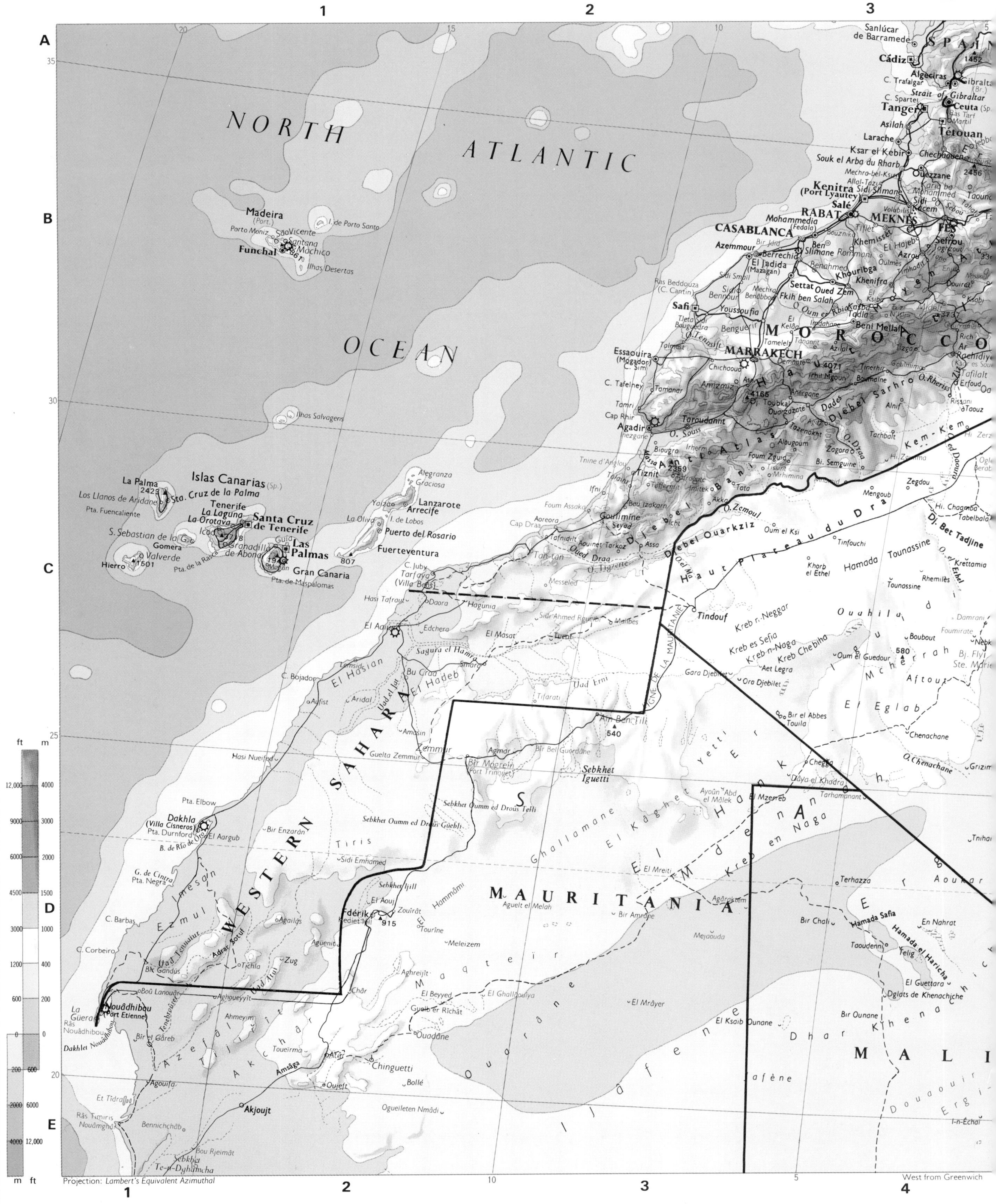

NORTH ATLANTIC OCEAN

Madeira (Port.)
I. de Porto Santo
Porto Moniz
SãoVicente
Santana
Mochico
Funchal
Ilhas Desertas

Ilhas Salvagens

Islas Canarias (Sp.)
La Palma 2423
Los Llanos de Aridane
Sta. Cruz de la Palma
Pta. Fuencaliente
Tenerife
La Laguna
La Orotava
Santa Cruz de Tenerife
S. Sebastian de los G.
Icod
3718
Gomera
Granadilla
de Abona
Las Palmas
Valverde
1501
Hierro
Pta. de la Rasca
Gran Canaria
Pta. de Maspalomas

Alegranza
Graciosa
Yaizao
Lanzarote
Arrecife
La Oliva
I. de Lobos
Puerto del Rosario
807
Fuerteventura

SPAIN
Sanlúcar de Barramede
Cádiz
C. Trafalgar
Algeciras
Gibraltar
1452
C. Spartel
Strait of Gibraltar
Ceuta (Sp.)
Tanger
Ras Tarf
Asilah
Tétouan
Larache
Chechaouen
Ksar el Kebir
Souk el Arba du Rharb
Mechra-bel-Ksiri
Ouezzane
2486
Allal-Tazi
Kenitra (Port Lyautey)
Sidi Slimane
Salé
RABAT
MEKNÈS
FÈS
Sefrou
Mohammedia (Fedala)
CASABLANCA
Azemmour
Berrechid
Ben Slimane
Rommani
El Hajeb
Azrou
El Jadida (Mazagan)
Khemisset
Sidi Smail
Settat
Oued Zem
Khouribga
Khenifra
Safi
Youssoufia
Fkih ben Salah
Beni Mellal
Tleta
MARRAKECH
MOROCCO
Chichaoua
Demnate
4071
Essaouira (Mogador)
C. Tafelney
Tamanar
Amizmiz
4165
Toubkal
Ouarzazate
Djebel Sarhro
Rachidiya
Tafilalt
Erfoud
Rissani
Taouz
Cap Rhir
Agadir
Taroudannt
Tata
Zagora
Kem-Kem

MOROCCO

Tiznit
Goulimine
Tan-tan
C. Juby
Tarfaya (Villa Bens)

WESTERN SAHARA
El Aaiún
Daora
Edchera
El Masat
Smara
Bu Craa
El Hadeb
Tindouf

MAURITANIA
Dakhla (Villa Cisneros)
Pta. Durnford
El Aargub
Bir Enzarán
Tiris
Sidi Emhamed
C. Barbas
C. Corbeiro
Fdérik
915
Zouîrât
Tourîne
Bir Amrane
MAURITANIA
Chingueti
Atar
Akjoujt
Nouâdhibou (Port Etienne)
La Güera
Ras Nouâdhibou
Dakhlet Nouâdhibou
Ras Timiris

MALI
Taoudenni
Hamada el Haricha
MALI

Projection: Lambert's Equivalent Azimuthal

West from Greenwich

1 : 7 100 000

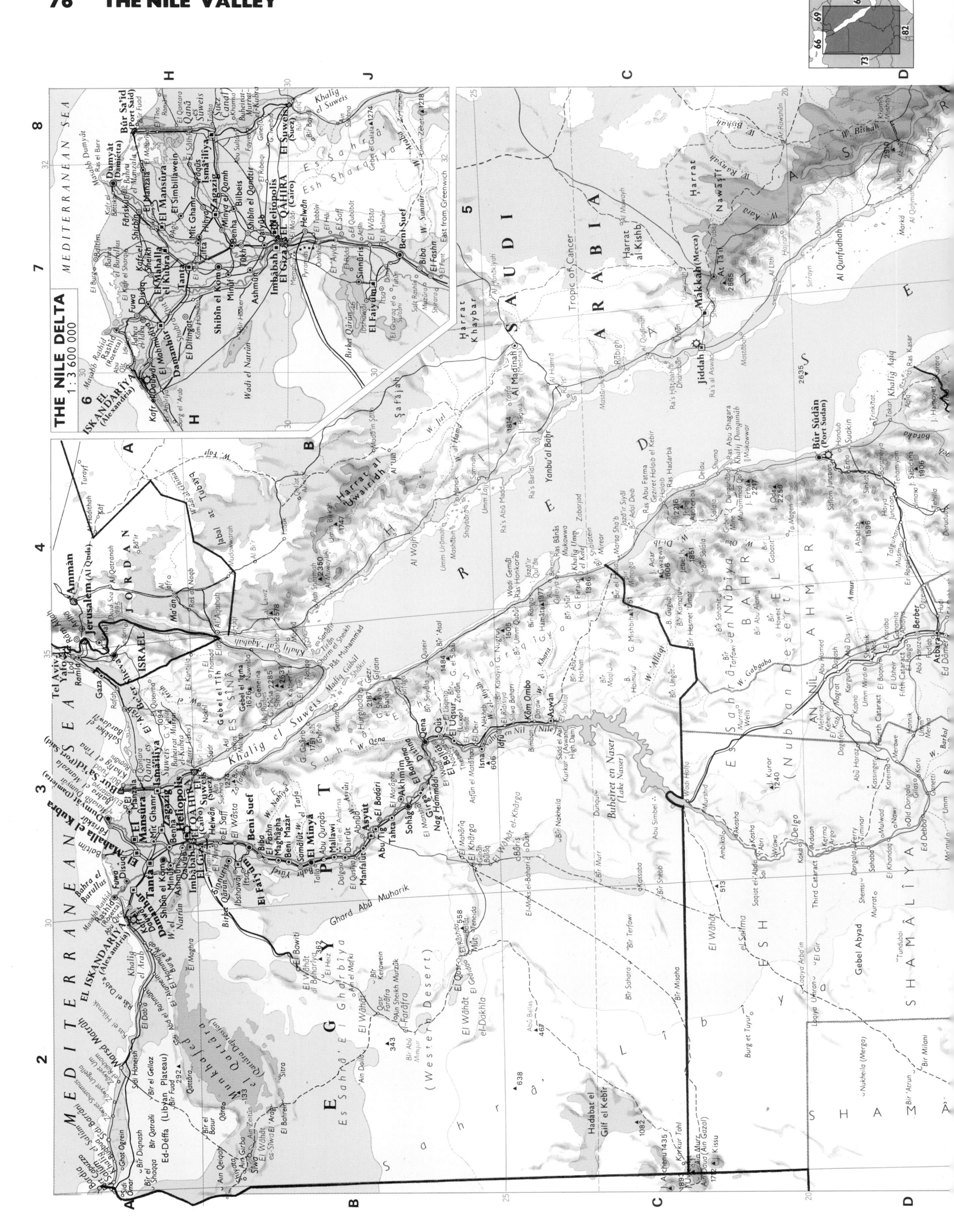

THE NILE DELTA
1 : 3 600 000

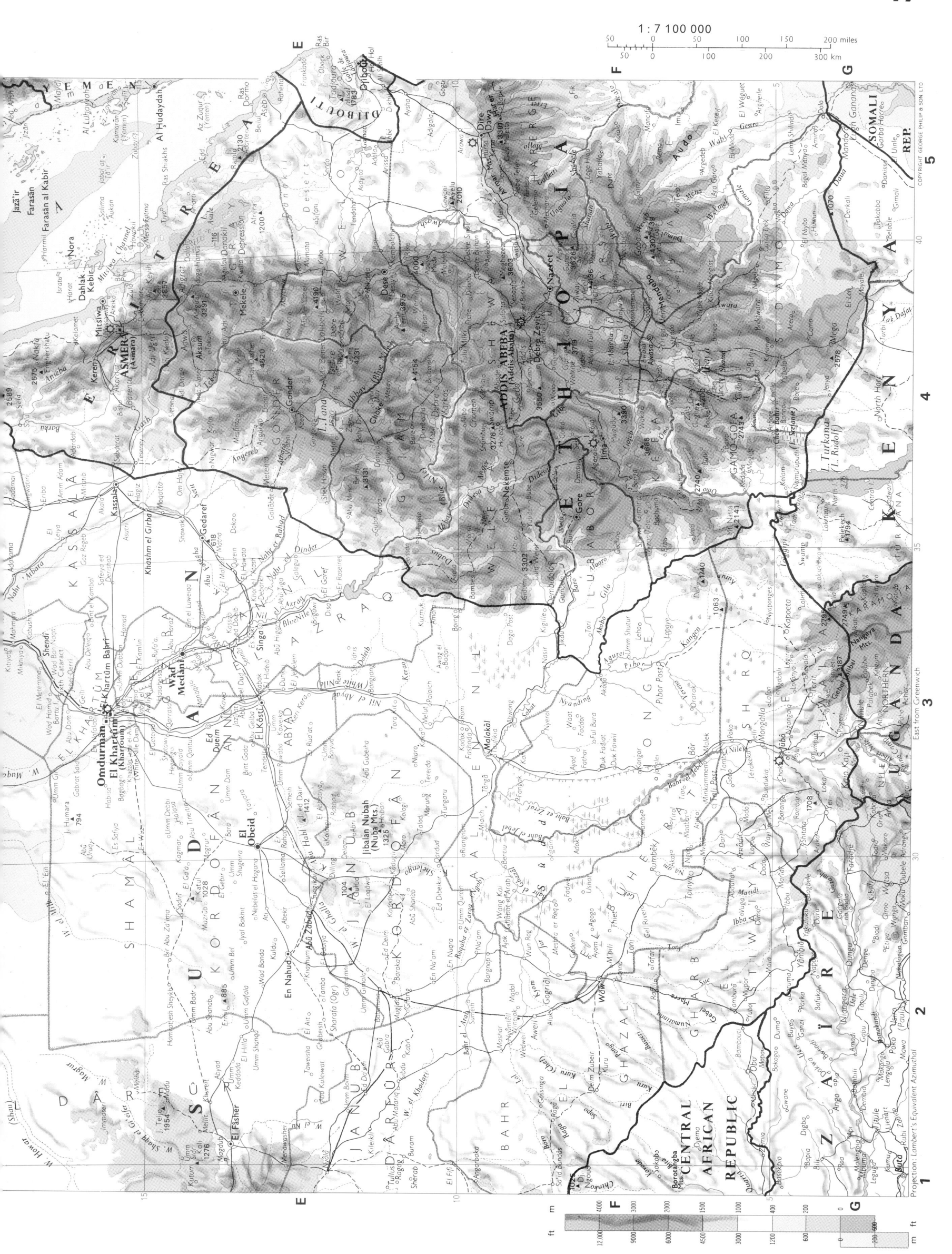

1 : 7 100 000

Projection: Lambert's Equivalent Azimuthal

East from Greenwich

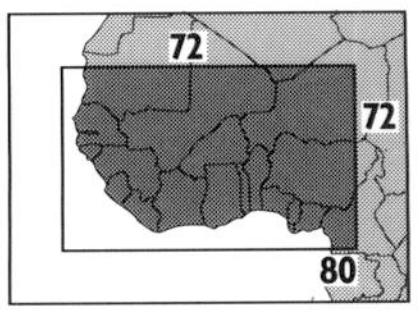

MAURITANIA

SENEGAL

GAMBIA

GUINEA-BISSAU
Arquipélago dos Bijagós

GUINEA

SIERRA LEONE
NORTHERN
EASTERN
WESTERN
SOUTHERN

LIBERIA

IVORY COAST

BURKINA FASO

MALI

Nouakchott
St. Louis
DAKAR
Thies
Rufisque
Diourbel
Mbour
Fatick
Kaolack
Banjul
Bissau
Conakry
Freetown
Monrovia
Bamako
Bobo-Dioulasso
Ouagadougou
Mopti
Ségou
Korhogo
Bouaké
Abidjan
Tombouctou (Timbuktu)
Goundam

Grain Coast

Ivory Coast

GUL

Projection: Lambert's Equivalent Azimuthal
West from Greenw

ft m
12 000 4000
9000 3000
6000 2000
4500 1500
3000 1000
1200 400
600 200
0 0
200 600
2000 6000
4000 12 000
6000 18 000
m ft

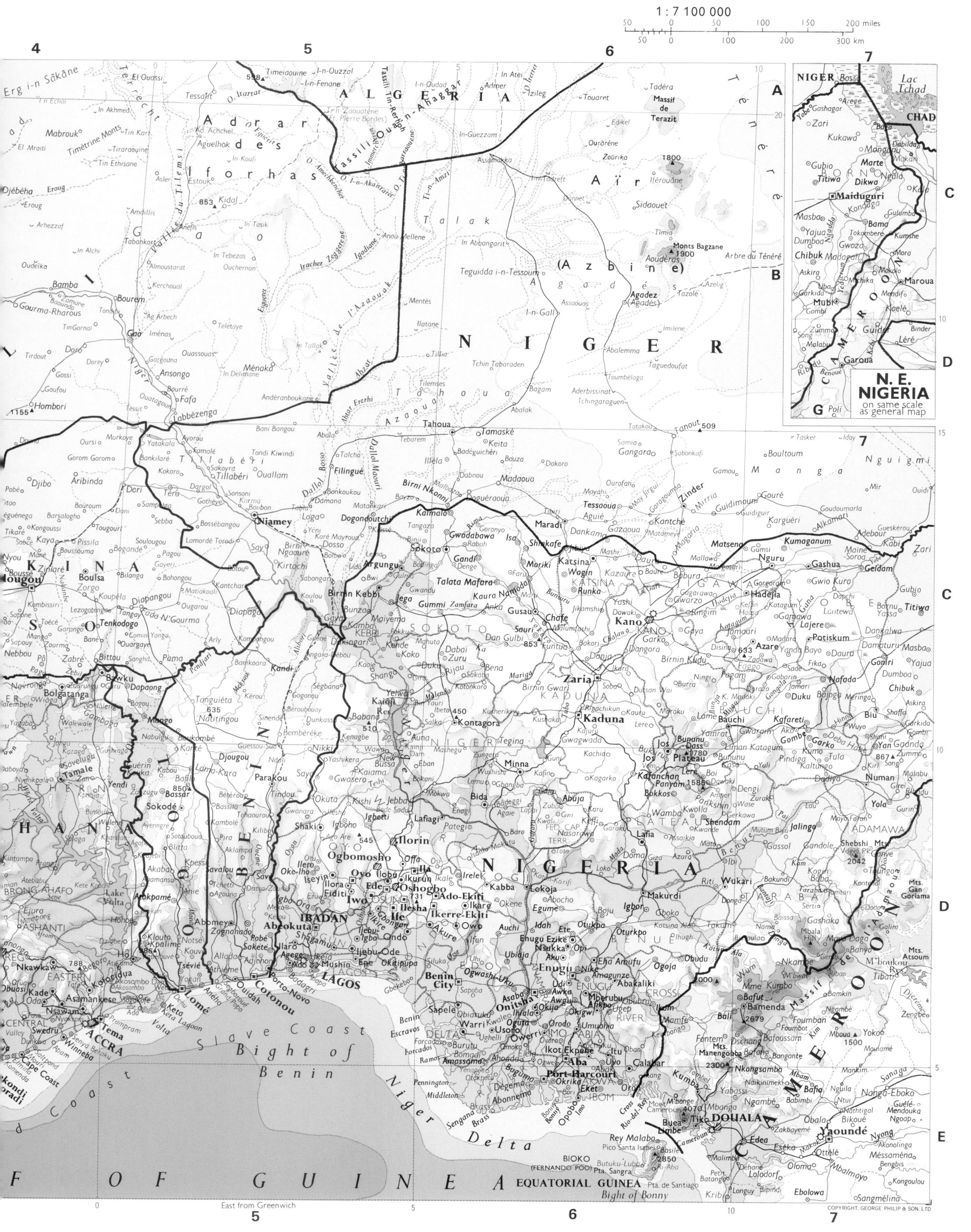

1 : 7 100 000

50   0   50   100   150   200 miles
50   0   100   200   300 km

N. E.
NIGERIA
on same scale
as general map

East from Greenwich

COPYRIGHT. GEORGE PHILIP & SON. LTD.

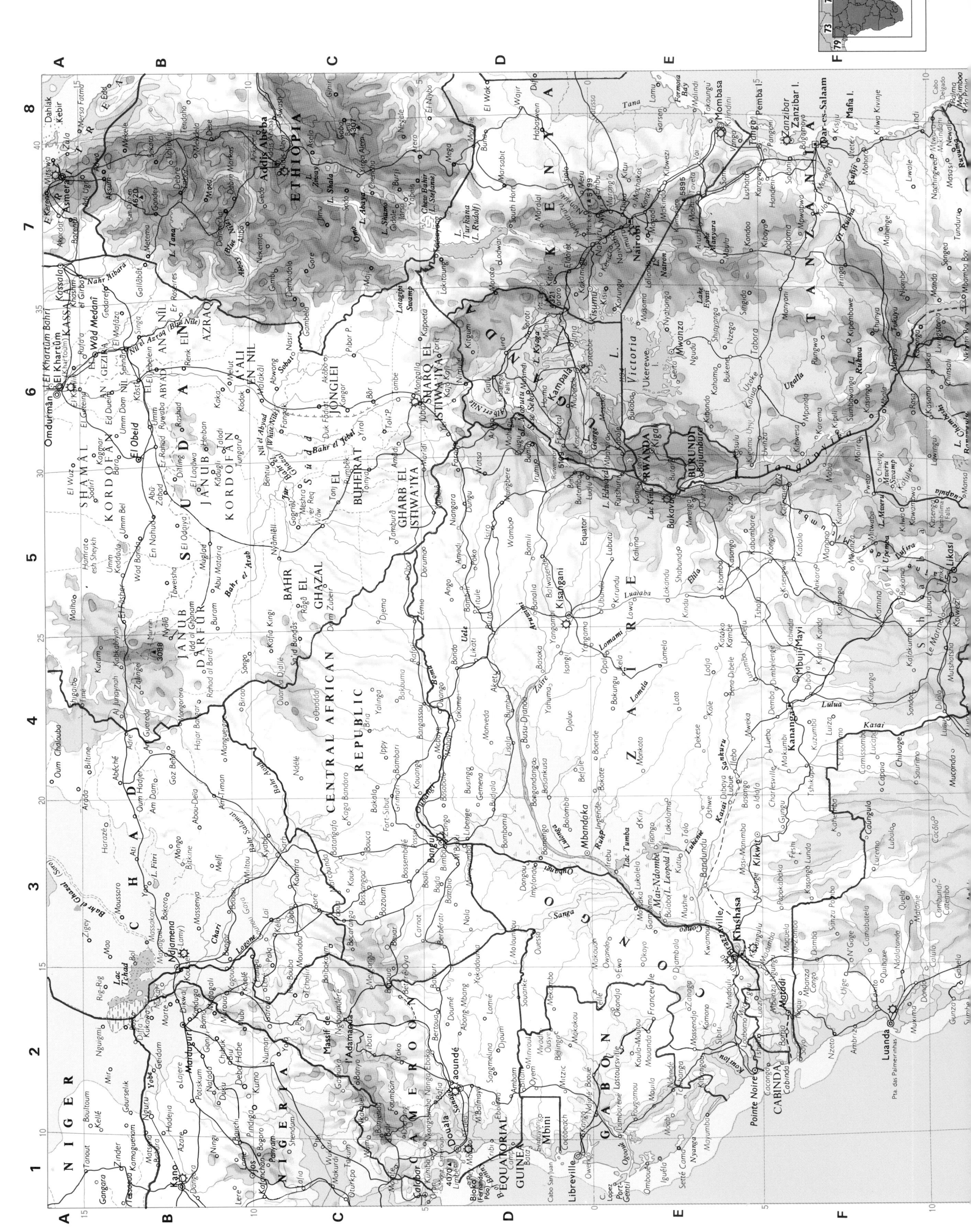

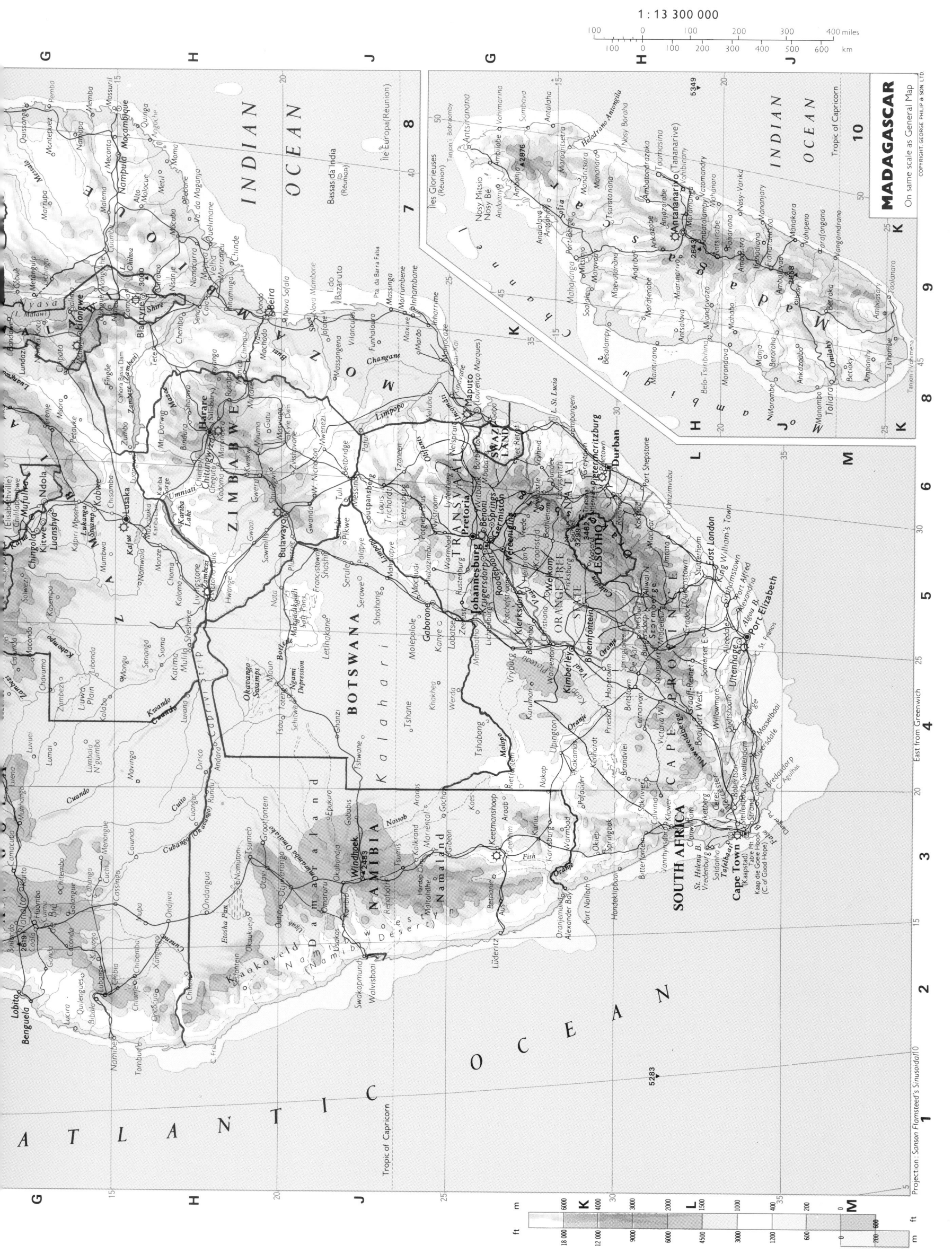

1 : 13 300 000

100   0   100   200   300   400 miles
100   0   100   200   300   400   500   600 km

MADAGASCAR
On same scale as General Map

COPYRIGHT GEORGE PHILIP & SON LTD

INDIAN OCEAN

INDIAN OCEAN

Tropic of Capricorn

ATLANTIC OCEAN

Tropic of Capricorn

ZIMBABWE

BOTSWANA

NAMIBIA

SOUTH AFRICA

Kalahari

CAPE PROVINCE

ORANGE FREE STATE

TRANSVAAL

NATAL

LESOTHO

SWAZILAND

Johannesburg
Pretoria
Bulawayo
Harare
Windhoek
Cape Town
Port Elizabeth
Durban
Pietermaritzburg
Maputo
Bloemfontein
Kimberley
Gaborone

Antananarivo
(Tananarive)

East from Greenwich

Projection: Sanson Flamsteed's Sinusoidal

m   ft
6000 18 000
4000 12 000
3000   9000
2000   6000
1500   4500
1000   3000
400   1200
200   600
0   0

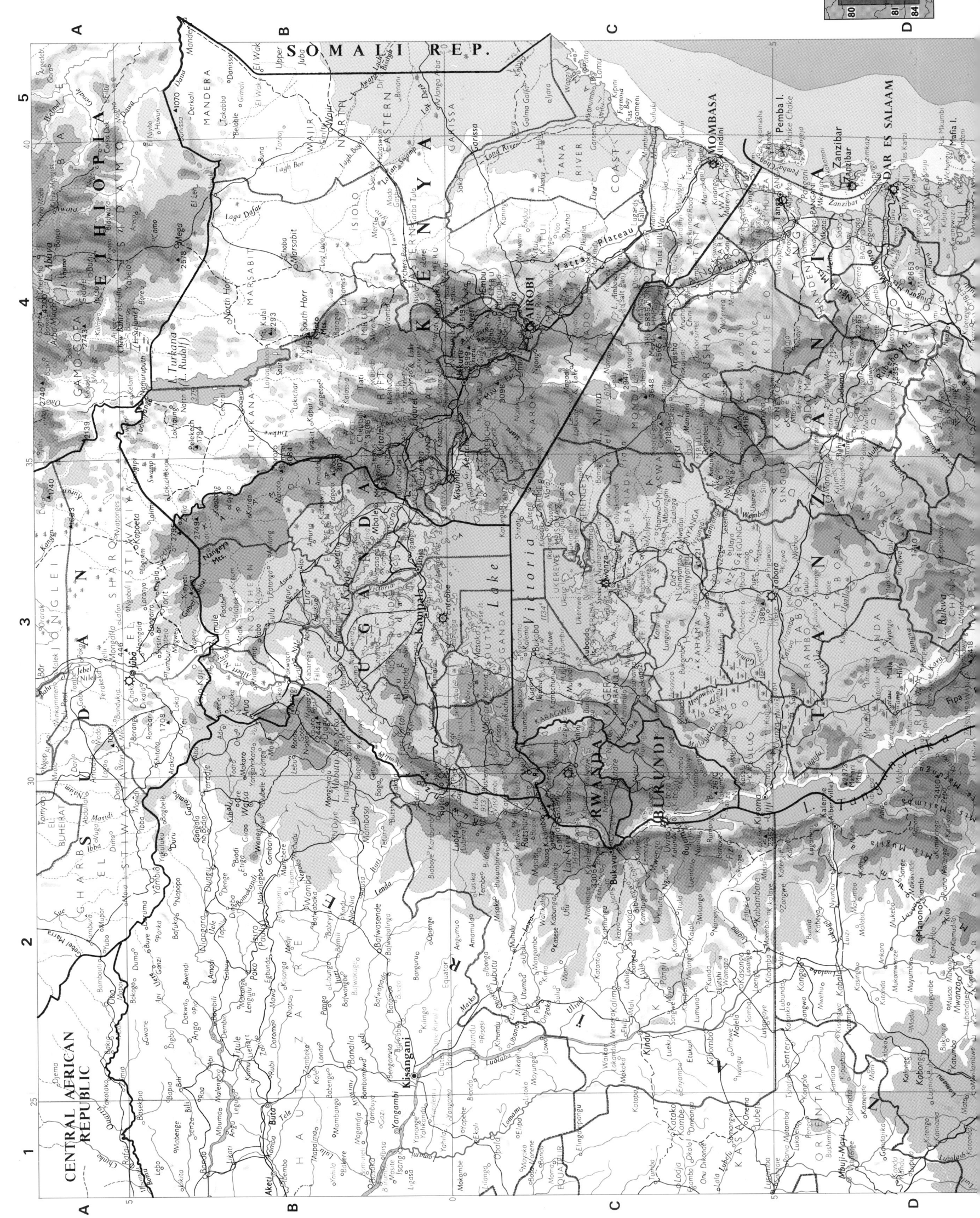

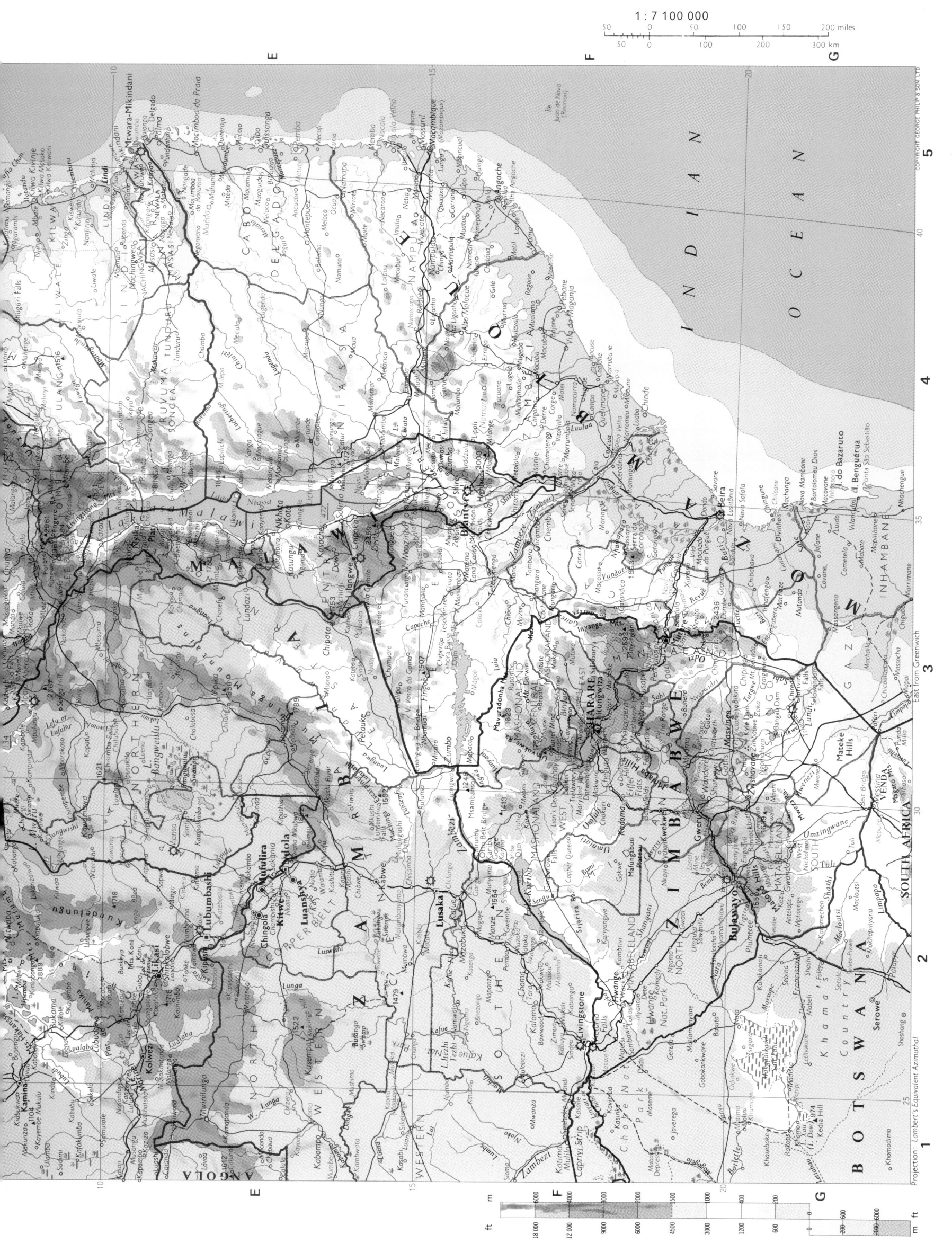

1 : 7 100 000

Projection: Lambert's Equivalent Azimuthal

East from Greenwich

81 83

1 2 3 4

ANGOLA

CUANDO CUBANGO

ZAMBIA

SOUTH

WESTERN Zambezi

Caprivi Strip

NAMIBIA

Etosha Pan

Tsumeb
Grootfontein
Otavi

Tsodilo Hill ▲1300

Okavango Swamps

Ngami Depression

Ghanzi

BOTSWANA

Kaukauveld

Sandveld

Rooiboklaagte

Windhoek
Khomas Hochland

Gobabis

Kalahari

Tropic of Capricorn

Sandwich B.

Conception B.

Namaland

Schwarzrand

Namib Desert

Kalahari Gemsbok National Park

Mariental

Keetmanshoop

Lüderitz
Lüderitzbaai

Groot Karasberge

Fish

Oranjemund
Alexander Bay

Orange

SOUTH AFRICA

ATLANTIC

OCEAN

Port Nolloth

Springbok
Namaqualand

ORANGE FREE STATE

Kimberley

Bloemfontein

CAPE PROVINCE

Great Karoo

De Aar

Beaufort West

CISKEI

Cradock

Vredenburg
Saldanha

Worcester

Paarl

CAPE TOWN (Kaapstad)
Table Mt. 1086

Stellenbosch
Strand

Kaap die Goeie Hoop
(Cape of Good Hope)

C. Agulhas

PORT ELIZABETH

Algoa Bay

ft m

9000
6000
4500
3000
1200
600
0

D m
3000
2000
1500
1000
400
200
0

Projection: Lambert's Equivalent Azimuthal

1 : 7 100 000

50   0   50   100   150   200 miles
50   0   100   200   300 km

MALAWI

MOZAMBIQUE CHANNEL

ZIMBABWE

ZAMBÉZIA

HARARE
Chitungwiza

Bulawayo

MASHONALAND

MOZAMBIQUE

Beira

VENDA

PRETORIA
JOHANNESBURG

SWAZILAND

Maputo
(Lourenço Marques)

MAPUTO

NATAL

LESOTHO

PIETERMARITZBURG
DURBAN
Umlazi

INDIAN

OCEAN

East London

MADAGASCAR

Antsiranana

Mahajanga

ANTANANARIVO

Antsirabe

FIANARANTSOA

Toliara

Tropic of Capricorn

Taolanaro

East from Greenwich

MADAGASCAR

On same scale as General Map

COPYRIGHT. GEORGE PHILIP & SON. LTD.

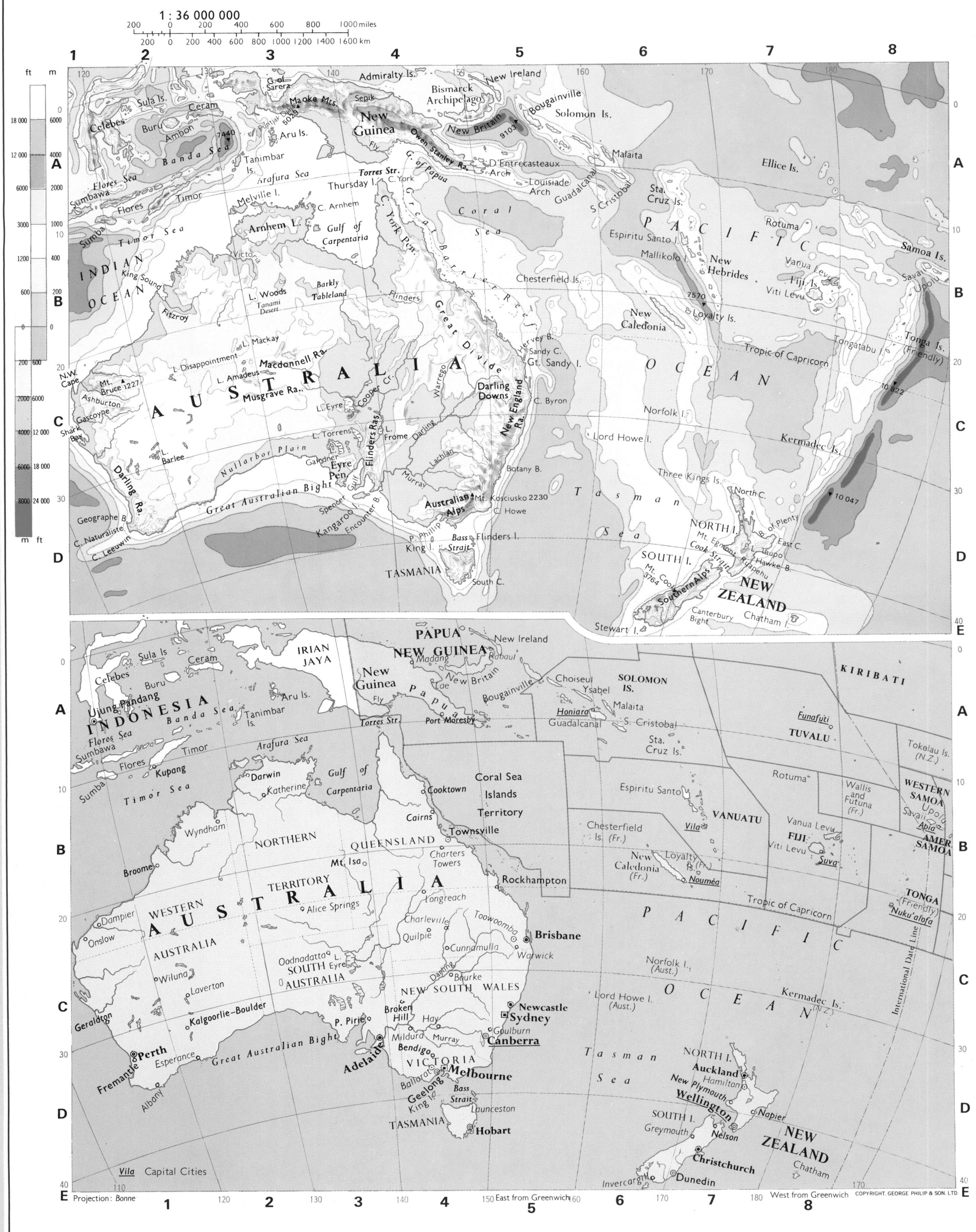

1 : 36 000 000

Projection: *Bonne*

Vila Capital Cities

East from Greenwich

West from Greenwich COPYRIGHT. GEORGE PHILIP & SON, LTD

1 : 5 300 000

20   0   20   40   60   80   100 miles
20   0   40   80   120   160 km

NEW ZEALAND & S.W. PACIFIC
1 : 53 000 000

200   0   200   400   600   800 miles
200   0   400   800   1200 km

SAMOA ISLANDS
1 : 10 700 000

FIJI AND TONGA ISLANDS
1 : 10 700 000

50   0   50   100   150 miles
50   0   50   100   150   200   250 km

Projection: Conical with two standard parallels

COPYRIGHT. GEORGE PHILIP & SON LTD.

NORTHERN TERRITORY

Tanami Desert

TIMOR SEA

Timor

INDONESIA

Sumba
Sumbawa
Lombok
Roti
Sawa
Semau
Danu
Raidjea

INDIAN OCEAN

Melville I.
Bathurst I.
Darwin
Van Diemen Gulf
Cobourg Pen.
C. Croker
C. Don
Dundas Str.
Port Darwin
C. Gambier
Clarence Str.
C. Hotham
P. Essington
C. Van Diemen
Gordan B.
Pt. Fawcett
C. Ford
Field I.
Rum Jungle
Adelaide River
Batchelor
Peron Is.
Anson B.
C. Scott
C. Hay
Pt. Blaze
Mt. Greenwood
Daly
Daly River
Greenwood
Katherine
Mataranka
Larrimah
Birdum
Birdum Creek
Tindal
Maranboy
Millaroo
Venn
Katherine R.
Oenpelly
Jabiru
Nourlangie
Mt. Gilruth
480
486
Birdum

Joseph Bonaparte Gulf
Cambridge Gulf
Queen's Channel
C. Hay
C. Dussejour
Buckle Hd.
Ord R.
Wyndham
Carr Boyd Ra.
Cockburn Ra.
Black Ra.
Chamberlain Ra.
Durack Ra.
Durack
Gibb River
Bedford Downs
Alice Downs
Springvale
Turkey Creek
Elvire
Albert Edward Ra.
McClintock Ra.
Mueller Ra.
Margaret
Bohemia Downs
Christmas Creek
Halls Creek
Nicholson
Gordon Downs
Sturt Creek
Lewis Ra.
Tanami
Balgo
Gregory Lake
Stansmore Ra.
L. White
L. Hazlett
Lake Mackay
Mt. Leisler 901
Mt. Liebig 1524
Mt. Zeil 1540
MACDONNELL RANGES
Stuart Bluff Ra.
Reynolds Ra.
Yuendumu
Mt. Singleton 808
Hooker Creek
Winnecke Cr.
Horden Hills
Landor
Willowra
Anningie
Hermannsburg
Missionbug
James Ranges
Palmer Temp
George Gill Ra.
L. Neale
L. Amadeus
Tropic of Capricorn

KING LEOPOLD RANGES
Napier Downs
Mt. Ord 1057
Fitzroy
Fitzroy Crossing
Leopold Downs
Noonkanbah
Christmas Creek
Gibson Desert
Percival Lakes
L. Auld
L. George
L. Blanche
L. Dora
L. Tobin
Waukarlycarly
McKay Ra.
Paterson Ra.
Throssell Ra.
Broadhurst Ra.
Poisonbush Ra.
Lake Disappointment
Robertson Ra.
Rudall
Baron Ra.
Angas Hills
Hopkins
Bonython Ra.
Macdonald

Bonaparte Archipelago
Admiralty Gulf
Montague Snd.
C. Bougainville
C. Voltaire
Long Reef
York Snd.
Prince Regent R.
Brunswick B.
St. George B.
Camden Snd.
Collier B.
King Sound
Yampi Sd.
Buccaneer Archipelago
Cape Leveque
Pender B.
Beagle Bay
Lombadina
Cygnet B.
Sunday Is.
Adele I.
C. Boileau
Carnot B.
Broome
Roebuck B.
Roebuck Plains
Lagrange B.
Lagrange
C. Latouche Treville
Lacepede Is.
Frazier Downs
Anna Plains
Eighty Mile Beach
Wallal Downs
Spay Gap
Isabella Ra.
Gregory Ra.
Nullagine
Bonney Downs
Roy Hill
Ethel Creek
Ophthalmia Ra.
Newman 1053
Mt. Meharry 1251
Hamersley Range
Mt. Bruce 1235
Wittenoom
Marble Bar
Hillside
Woodstock
Shaw
De Grey
Warrawagine
Eel
Goldsworthy
Port Hedland
C. Keraudren
C. Thouin
Pippingarra
Mallina
De Grey
Strelley
Yule
Yarrie
Bamboo Creek
Duck Cr.
Tom Price
Paraburdoo
Mt. Windell
Mt. Florence
Fortescue
Rocklea
Yandeearra
Pippingarra
Wyloo
Ashburton
Glenflorrie
Ningaloo
Murrilla
Bulldra
Exmouth Gulf
North West C.
Exmouth
Learmonth
Coates B.
Ningaloo
Rough Range
Barrow I.
Monte Bello Is.
Dampier Archipelago
Dampier
Karratha
Roebourne
Cossack
Legendre I.
Delambre I.
Dixon I.
Depuch I.
Preston I.
C. Preston
Pasco I.
Yarraloola
Red Hill
Pannawonica
Onslow
Rowley Shoals
Mermaid Reef
Clerke Reef
Imperieuse Reef
Scott Reef
Seringapatan Reef
Ashmore Reef
Cartier I.
Hibernia Reef
Browse I.
Lynher Reef
Lesuer I.
Ruthieres
C. Rulhieres
Eclipse Is.
Hamilton B.
Sir Graham Moore Is.
Napier Broome B.
Talbot
Londonderry
Kuri Bay
Kalumburu
Oombulgurri
C. Whiskey
Drysdale
Mount Elizabeth
King Edward R.
Sir John Hann
Mt. Hann 776
Charnley R.
Hooley
Barnett R.
Tableland
Hann
Mount House
Mornington
Glenroy
Myalls Bore
Kimberley Downs
Meda
Derby
Liveringa
Myroodah
Geegully Cr.
Jubilee Downs
Go Go
Cherrabun
Bulka
Margaret R.
Mt. Amhurst
Lansdowne
Bow River
Lissadell
Argyle Downs
Ivanhoe
Newry
Auvergne
Rosewood
Inverway
Waterloo
Nicholson
Bulloo River
Negri
Duncan Hwy.
Limbunya
Humbert River
West Baines R.
Victoria River Downs
Timber Creek
Victoria River
Coolibah
Wave Hill
Montejinni
Victoria Hwy.
Monte

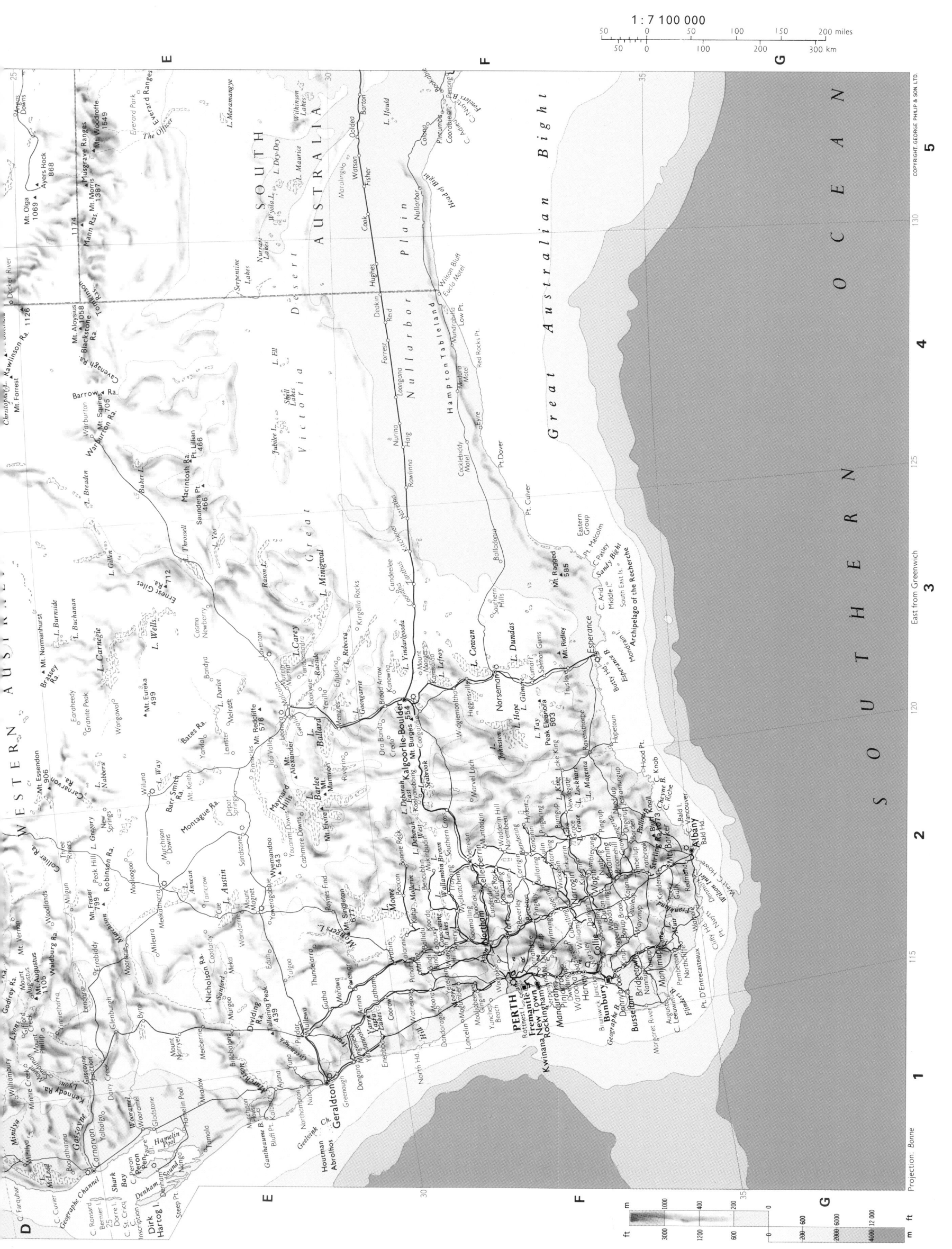

1 : 7 100 000

50   0   50   100   150   200 miles

50   0   100   200   300 km

D

E

WESTERN AUSTRALIA

SOUTH

AUSTRALIA

Great

Victoria

Desert

Nullarbor Plain

Hampton Tableland

Great   Australian   Bight

S O U T H E R N

O C E A N

Christopher R.
Rawlinson Ra. 1126
Mt. Forrest

Mt. Aloysius
1058   Mt. Squires
Blackstone   705
Ra.   Warburton Ra.

Barrow
Ra.

Cavenagh Ra.

Warburton
Ra.

Macintosh Ra.   Pt. Lillah
Saunders Pt.   466
466

Throssell

Ernest Giles
Ra.   712

L. Yeo

Jubilee L.

Shell
Lakes

Rason L.

L. Minigwal

L. Carey

L. Rebecca

L. Raeside

L. Cowan

L. Dundas

Esperance

Archipelago of the Recherche

Everard Park
The Officer
Everard Ranges
Deter River

Musgrave Ranges
Mt Woodroffe
1549

Ayers Rock
868

Mt. Olga
1069

Mann Ras.   Mt Morris 1387
1174

L. Meramangye

L. Day-Dey

L. Maurice

Wilkinson
Lakes

Coldea   Barton

L. Ifould

Cobog

C. North
Pintumba   Forrest B.
Coordee   Penong B.
Adelong B.

Serpentine

Nurrari
Lakes

Marslingva   Watson   Fisher

Cook   Hughes   Deakin   Reid

Maralbinna

Loongana   Nurina   Hing
Naretha

Haig

Zanthus

Wooaldabi
Naretha

Rowinna

Cocklebiddy
Motel

Eucla Motel

Mundrabilla   Low Pt.
Eyre

Madura
Motel

Wilson Bluff

Red Rocks Pt.

Pt. Dover

Pt. Culver

Eastern
Group

Pt. Malcolm

Sandy Bight   Hd.

C. Arid   C. Pasley

Middle I.

South East Is.

Balladonia

Cundeelee

Kingella Rocks

Kambalda

Widgiemooltha

Higginsville

Norseman

Cosmo
Newberry

Laverton

Bandya

Darlot

Melrose

Mt. Redcliffe
576

Yandil

Lemitter

L. Way

Yundamindera

Ida Valley
Pinnacles

Lawlers

Leonora   Gwalia   Murrin
Murrin

Malcolm

Mt. Alexander

L. Carey

Menzies

Ora Banda
Credo

Broad Arrow

Kanowna   Gindalbie

Kalgoorlie-Boulder   254
Mt Burges

East
Kookynie   Kurnalpi   Mt Monger

Coolgardie

Seabrook

Bonnie Rock

Widgiemooltha

L. Lefroy

Marvel Loch

Johnston

L. Hope

L. Cowan

L. Tay

Peak Eleanora   503

Buldania

Esperance B.
Batty Hd. B

Mt Ridley

Mondrain I.

C. Arid

Mt Ragged
585

Hopetoun

Ravensthorpe

Starvation Boat
Harbour

Hood Pt.

C. Knob

Bald Hd.

Albany

West Home

Stirling Ra. 1073
Chester B.

Cheyne B.

Bald I.

C. Vancouver

Projection. Bonne

E

F

G

1   2   115   3   120   4   125   5   130

COPYRIGHT GEORGE PHILIP & SON LTD.

East from Greenwich

25

30

35

m   ft
3000   12 000
             6000
1200   4000
             2000
400   600
200
0   0
                200
             600

EASTERN AUSTRALIA

TASMANIA

Bass Strait
Kent Group
Deal I.
Flinders Island
Furneaux Group
Cape Barren I.
Curtis Group
C. Wickham
King Island
Three Hummock I.
Robbins I.
Stanley
Smithton
Wynyard
Burnie
Ulverstone
Devonport
Georgetown
Launceston
Scottsdale
Bridport
St. Helens
Eddystone Pt.
St. Marys
Swansea
Campbell Town
Waratah
Rosebery
Zeehan
Queenstown
Strahan
Mt. Ossa 1617
Great Lake
New Norfolk
Glenorchy
Hobart
Richmond
Sorell
Bruny I.
S.E. Cape
Port Davey
Bathurst Harb.
S.W. Cape
Storm Bay
Tasman Pen.
Port Arthur
Maria I.
Schouten I.
Freycinet Pen.
Forester Pen.

CORAL SEA
Great Barrier Reef
Willis Group
Magdelaine Cays
Coringa Is.
Diamond Is.
Lihou Reefs & Cays
Tregrosse Is.
Abington Reef
Herald Cays
Holmes Reefs
Moore Reefs
Flinders Reefs
Bougainville Reef
Osprey Reef
Lizard I.
C. Flattery
Cooktown

Gulf of Carpentaria
Arnhem Land
NORTHERN TERRITORY
Groote Eylandt
Wessel Is.
Sir Edward Pellew Group
Mornington I.
Wellesley Is.
Bentinck I.

Cape York Peninsula
Gt. Dividing Range
McIlwraith Ra.
Thursday I.
Prince of Wales
Horn I.
C. York
Bamaga
Weipa
Aurukun Mission
Pera Hd.
Coen
Port Stewart
Princess Charlotte Bay

Normanton
Croydon
Georgetown
Burketown
Karumba
Cloncurry
Mount Isa
Cairns
Mareeba
Atherton
Innisfail
Tully
Cardwell
Ingham
Halifax
Townsville
Ayr
Home Hill
Bowen
Proserpine
Mackay
Sarina

GREAT DIVIDING RANGE
Charters Towers
Hughenden
Richmond
Winton
Longreach
Barcaldine
Blackall
Emerald
Clermont
Blackwater
Rockhampton
Yeppoon
Gladstone
P. Curtis
Capricorn Group
Hervey Bay
Lady Elliott I.

Tropic of Capricorn
Alice Springs
Macdonnell Ranges
Todd
Finke
Simpson Desert
Toko Range
Barkly Tableland
Davenport Range

1 : 7 100 000

50   0   50   100   150   200 miles
50   0   100   200   300 km

Projection: Bonne

East from Greenwich

COPYRIGHT. GEORGE PHILIP & SON. LTD.

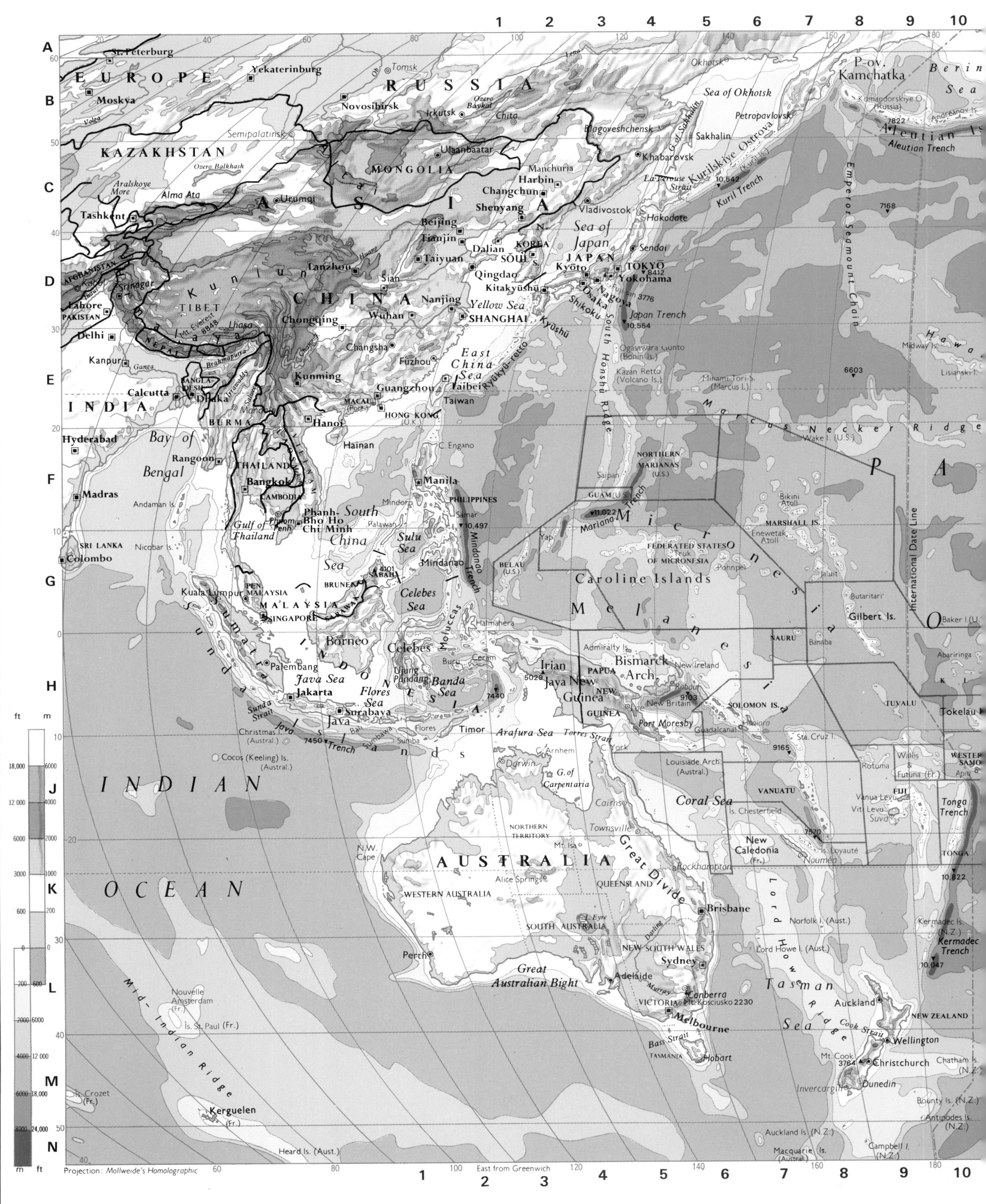

Projection: Mollweide's Homolographic

1 : 48 000 000

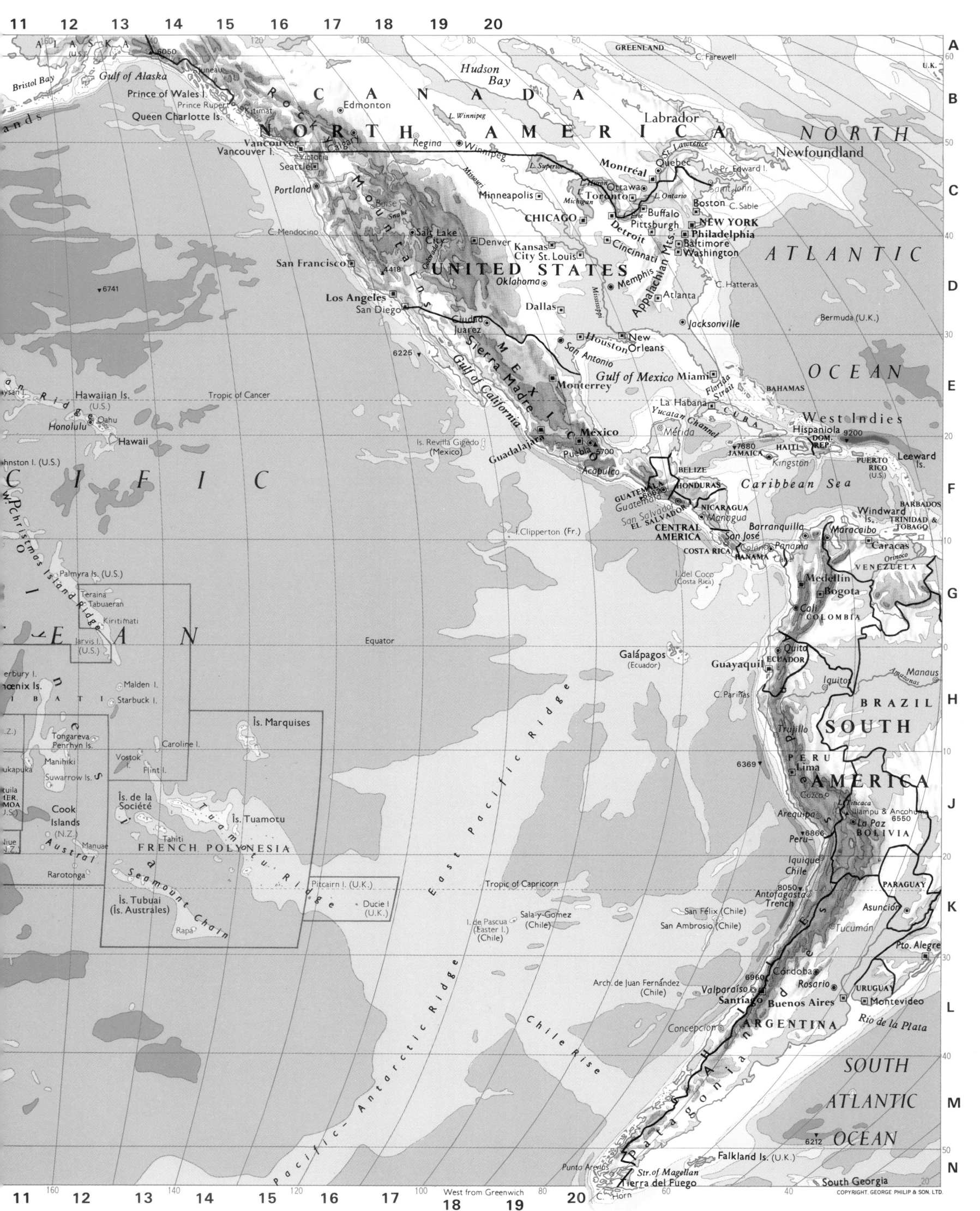

1 : 31 100 000

200   0   200   400   600   800 miles
400   0   400   800   1200 km

ARCTIC OCEAN

Asia
Bering Strait
Bering Sea
Beaufort Sea
Brook's Range
Alaska Range
Mt McKinley 6194
Alaska Pen.
Gulf of Alaska
Mt St Elias 5489
Mt Logan 6050
Alexander Archipelago
Queen Charlotte Islands
Queen Charlotte Sound
Vancouver I.
Juan de Fuca Strait
C. Flattery
Mackenzie Mts.
Great Bear L.
Great Slave L.
Athabasca L.
Reindeer L.
Lake Winnipeg
Arctic Circle

Queen Elizabeth Islands
Axel Heiberg
Sverdrup Land
Parry Is.
Melville I.
Banks I.
Victoria I.
Prince of Wales
Devon I.
Ellesmere I.
Kane Basin
Thule

Greenland
Iceland
Denmark Strait

Baffin Island
Baffin Bay
Davis Strait
Cumberland Sound
Frobisher Bay
Hudson Strait
Southampton
Foxe Basin
Foxe Channel
Boothia Pen.
Melville Pen.
Chesterfield Inlet

Hudson Bay
James Bay
Ungava Peninsula
Labrador
Hamilton Inlet
Laurentian Plateau
Newfoundland

Rocky Mountains
Mt Robson 3954
Yellowhead Pass
Kicking Horse Pass
Selkirk Mts.
Calgary
Edmonton
Crowsnest Pass
N. Saskatchewan
S. Saskatchewan
Regina
Winnipeg
Minneapolis

Seattle
Mt Rainier 4399
Portland
Columbia
C. Blanco
C. Mendocino
Mt Shasta 4317
San Francisco
Sacramento
Great Salt Lake
Coast Range
Cascade Range
Sierra Nevada
Mt Whitney 4418
Los Angeles
Grand Canyon
Colorado Plateau
Great Basin
Wasatch Mountains
Mt Elbert 4399
Denver
Blanca Pk 4378
Snake
N. Platte
S. Platte

L. Superior
L. Michigan
L. Huron
L. Erie
L. Ontario
Toronto
Detroit
Chicago
Hamilton
Niagara Falls
Ottawa
Montréal
Québec
Mt Washington 1917
Lake Champlain
New York
Philadelphia
Washington
Chesapeake Bay
Appalachian Mts.
Allegheny Mts.
Tennessee
Blue Ridge 2037
Cumberland Plateau
Ozark Plateau
St. Louis
Kansas City
Memphis
Atlanta
Dallas
Red
Arkansas
Missouri
Mississippi

ATLANTIC OCEAN
Bermuda
C. Hatteras

PACIFIC OCEAN

Murray Seascarp
Mendocino Seascarp
Clarion Fracture Zone

Tropic of Cancer

Great Plains
Llano Estacado
Lower California
Gulf of California
Western Sierra Madre
Eastern Sierra Madre
Mexican Plateau
Revilla Gigedo Is.
Monterrey
Guadalajara
Santiago
México
Popocatepetl 5452
Citlaltepec 5700
Puebla
Isthmus of Tehuantepec
G. of Tehuantepec
Guatemala Trench
Guatemala 6662

New Orleans
Houston
Mississippi Delta
Gulf of Mexico
Gulf of Campeche
Yucatán Peninsula
Bahama Islands
Florida
Florida Strait
Cuba
Havana
Jamaica
Hispaniola
Puerto Rico
Milwaukee Deep 9700
Greater Antilles
Cayman Trough 7680
Caribbean Sea
Colombian Basin
Venezuelan Basin
Lesser Antilles
Panama Canal
G. of Darien
G. of Panama
Andes
Sierra de Merida

ft / m elevation scale:
12 000 / 4000
6000 / 2000
3000 / 1000
1200 / 400
600 / 200
0 / 0
m / ft depth scale:
200 / 600
2000 / 6000
4000 / 12 000
6000 / 18 000
8000 / 24 000

1 : 31 100 000

200   0   200   400   600   800 miles
400   0   400   800   1200 km

West from Greenwich

COPYRIGHT. GEORGE PHILIP & SON. LTD.

102 103

4 5 6 7 8 9 10

B Fairbanks

Anchorage

Mt. McKinley

ALASKA

YUKON TERRITORY

Dawson

Whitehorse

Fairbanks

Old Crow

Ft. McPherson

Arctic Red R.

INUVIK

Inuvik

Tuktoyaktuk

C. Bathurst

Banks Island

Amundsen Gulf

Prince Albert Pen.

Victoria Island

C. Baring

Coronation Gulf

Coppermine

Wollaston Pen.

KITIKMEOT

Boothia Pen.

Somerset Island

Prince of Wales Island

McClintock Channel

Melville Sound

Viscount

Mackenzie

NORTH WEST

Norman Wells

Ft. Good Hope

Ft. Norman

Gt. Bear Lake

Ft. Franklin

Echo Bay

Port Radium

Bathurst Inlet

Chantrey Inlet

Queen Maud Gulf

King William

Spence Bay

Pelly

Macdougall

Gt. Bear

Fort Providence

Yellowknife

Great Slave L.

Ft. Resolution

Ft. Smith

Fort Reliance

Snowdrift

Dubawnt L.

Baker Lake

Chesterfield In.

Rankin Inlet

KEEW

Whale Cove

Eskimo Pt.

C

PACIFIC OCEAN

Mt. Fairweather

Juneau

Skagway

Chichagof I.

Baranof I.

Sitka

Prince of Wales I.

Dixon Entrance

Queen Charlotte Is.

Pr. Rupert

Hecate Str.

BRITISH COLUMBIA

Rocky Mountains

Stikine

Fort Nelson

Ft. Liard

Trout L.

Liard

Peace

Ft. Vermilion

Fort McMurray

Fort Mackay

Lake Athabasca

Uranium City

Fond-du-Lac

Wholdaia L.

Nueltin

C. Church

50

Queen Charlotte Sd.

Vancouver I.

Vancouver

Victoria

Seattle

Tacoma

Olympia

WASHINGTON

Spokane

Prince George

Kamloops

Kelowna

ALBERTA

Edmonton

Leduc

Red Deer

Calgary

High River

Lethbridge

Medicine Hat

SASKATCHEWAN

Prince Albert

Saskatoon

Moose Jaw

Regina

Weyburn

Lake Athabasca

Reindeer Lake

Lynn Lake

MANITOBA

Flin Flon

The Pas

Churchill

Port Nelson

Nelson

Cedar Lake

Lake Winnipegosis

Lake Manitoba

Lake Winnipeg

Dauphin

Winnipeg

D

C. Flattery

Bellingham

Everett

MONTANA

WYOMING

NORTH DAKOTA

Bismarck

Fargo

SOUTH DAKOTA

Rapid City

Pierre

NEBRASKA

North Platte

Omaha

UNITED STATES

MINNESOTA

Minneapolis

St. Paul

Duluth

IOWA

Des Moines

Sioux City

WISCONSIN

Superior

Lake of the Woods

Rainy

Kenora

Fort Frances

7

Projection: Bonne

ALASKA

1 : 26 700 000

100 0 100 200 300 miles

100 0 200 400 km

1 2 3 4 5 6

BERING SEA

RUSSIA

Koryakskij Khr.

Anadyr

Providenija

St. Lawrence I.

Nome

Seward Pen.

Barrow

Prudhoe Bay

Brooks Range

Arctic Circle

Baird Mts.

Kotzebue

Fairbanks

College

Yukon

ALASKA

Anchorage

Valdez

Cordova

Seward

Homer

Kodiak

Kodiak I.

Afognak I.

Bristol Bay

Alaska Peninsula

Aleutian Is.

Unimak I.

Dutch Harbor

Shumagin Is.

GULF OF ALASKA

Mt. Fairweather

Juneau

Sitka

Chichagof I.

Baranof I.

Prince of Wales Is.

Alexander Archipelago

Ketchikan

Dixon Entrance

Graham I.

Queen Charlotte Is.

Moresby

PACIFIC OCEAN

West from Greenwich

1 2 3 4 5 6

ft m

9000 3000

6000 2000

4500 1500

3000 1000

1200 400

600 200

0

600 200

6000 2000

m ft

1 : 13 300 000

100   200   300   400 miles
100   0   100   200   300   400   500   600   km

Devon Island
Lancaster Sound
Baffin Bay
GREENLAND
Angmagssalik
Brodeur
Peninsula
Arctic Bay
Bylot I.
Pond Inlet
Svartenhuk
Halvø
Disko
Kong Frederik VI Kyst
ATLANTIC
Milne
Inlet
C. Hewett
Christianshåb
2850
Søndre Strømfjord
Julianehåb
Clyde
Godthåb
Frederikshåb
Ivigtut
Cumberland
Peninsula
2591
C. Dyer
Cape
Dyer
Holsteinsborg
Sukkertoppen
Nanortalik
Kap Farvel
Igloolik
Committee B.
Hall
Lake
Melville
Peninsula
Prince
Charles
I.
Cumberland Sd.
C. Merchison
Southampton
Foxe
Basin
Nettilling
L.
BAFFIN
Coral Harbour
Rae Isthmus
Circle
C. Dorchester
Frobisher Bay
Resolution I.
Coats
I.
Amadjuak
L.
3809
Foxe
Channel
Cape Dorset
Hudson   Strait
Digges Is.
Invujuk (Sugluk)
Koartac
(Notre Dame
de Koartoc)
C. Chidley
Mansel
I.
Maricourt
(Wakeham)
D'Akpatok
Bell
Pen.
Ungava
Arnaud (Bellin)
(Payne Bay)
2678
Port Nouveau Quebec
Hudson
Payne
Ottawa Is.
Ungava Bay
Hebron
Nutak
257
Portland
Promontory
Inoucdjouac
(Port Harrison)
Feuilles
NEW
Nain
Bay
Peninsula
Whale
Kaniapiskau
C. Harrison
Indian Harbour
Sleeper Is.
Minto
L.
Mélèzes
Hopedale
Rigolet
King
George Is.
Koksoak
Kuujjuaq
Makkovik
King George Is.
Baker's
Dozen
Is.
Lac Bienville
Schefferville
George
North West
River
Cartwright
Bottle Hbr.
Belle Isle
Ft. Severn
C. Henrietta
Maria
Belcher
Is.
Grand Baleine
Poste-de-la-Baleine
(Great Whale River)
Petitsikapau
L.
COAST OF LABRADOR
Churchill
Falls
Churchill
Natashquan
Twillingate
Lewisporte
Gander
Severn
Winisk
Kanaaupscow
Ft. George
Ashuanipi
L.
St. Augustin
Saguenay
NEWFOUNDLAND
Grand
Falls
Bonavista
Big
Trout L.
Kaniapiskau
James Bay
Nouveau Comptoir
(Paint Hills)
1128
Gagnon
Moisie
Natashquan
Mingan
I. d'Anticosti
St. John's
Attawapiskat
Akimiski I.
Eastmain
QUEBEC
Cagnon
1140
Manicouagan
Sept-Îles
Port-Cartier
Harbour Grace
Carbonear
Trepassey
C. Race
Ft. Albany
Charlton
Fort Rupert
(Rupert House)
Rupert L.
L. Albanel
Péribonca
Baie-Comeau
Gaspé
Is. de la Madeleine
Cape Breton I.
ST.-PIERRE
et MIQUELON
(Fr.)
Albany
Albany
Moosonee
Mistassini L.
Chibougamau
Matane
Pen. de Gaspé
Gulf of
Port aux
Basques
Missinaibi
Nottaway
Harricana
Rés. de Gouin
Dolbeau
St-Jean
Rimouski
Campbellton
Bathurst
Chatham
St. Lawrence
Cabot Str.
Cape North
Ray
Nakina
Hearst
Mattagami
Senneterre
Roberval
Jonquière
Chicoutimi
Rivière-
du-Loup
Newcastle
PR. EDWARD I.
Charlottetown
Summerside
Glace Bay
Sydney
Nipigon
Longlac
Cochrane
L. Abitibi
Taschereau
La Tuque
Saguenay
Edmundston
St. Leonard
Moncton
Amherst
NOVA
Port Hawkesbury
Mulgrave
Thunder Bay
Heron Bay
Oba
Timmins
Kirkland Lake
d'Or
Shawinigan
QUEBEC
Lévis
Thetford Mines
Woodstock
NEW
BRUNSWICK
Kentville
Truro
New Glasgow
Michipicoten
Franz
Haileybury
Cobalt
Témiscamingue L.
Trois-Rivières
Rés. de
Cabonga
Joliette
St. Hyacinthe
Sherbrooke
Fredericton
Saint
John
Windsor
Dartmouth
Sault Ste. Marie
Sudbury
North
Bay
MONTRÉAL
Lachine
MAINE
Bangor
B. of Fundy
NOVA SCOTIA
Halifax
Lake Superior
Calumet
Keweenaw
Marquette
Copper Cliff
Sault Ste. Marie
North Chan.
Pembroke
Hull
Ottawa
Cornwall
Augusta
Lewiston
Liverpool
Shelburne
Sable I.
(Nova Scotia)
6309
Georgian
Bay
Arnprior
L. Champlain
VERMONT
NEW
HAMPSHIRE
Concord
Manchester
Portland
C. Sable
Yarmouth
Menominee
Escanaba
Cheboygan
Parry
Sound
Bellevie
Kingston
Burlington
Watertown
Antigo
Iron Mt.
Green
Bay
Traverse
Owen Sound
Orillia
Cobourg
Oshawa
Peterboro
Syracuse
Utica
Worcester
MASS.
Boston
Wausau
Appleton
Cadillac
Georgian Bay
TORONTO
Ontario
Rochester
CONN.
Providence
Manitowoc
Saginaw
Guelph
Kitchener
Hamilton
NEW YORK
Albany
Springfield
R.I.
Sheboygan
Muskegon
Stratford
Brantford
Niagara Falls
Buffalo
Scranton
Waterbury
New Haven
Milwaukee
Grand
Rapids
London
Binghamton
Elmira
Bridgeport
Racine
Kalamazoo
Windsor
Erie
Williamsport
NEW YORK
Evanston
DETROIT
Jamestown
PENNSYLVANIA
Newark
Jersey City
CHICAGO
Gary
South Bend
Toledo
Cleveland
Youngstown
Reading
Trenton
ILLINOIS
INDIANA
OHIO
Akron
NEW JERSEY
Allentown
L. Michigan
Thunder Bay

West from Greenwich

COPYRIGHT. GEORGE PHILIP & SON. LTD.

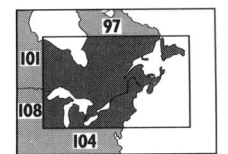

MANITOBA

N.W. TERRITORIES

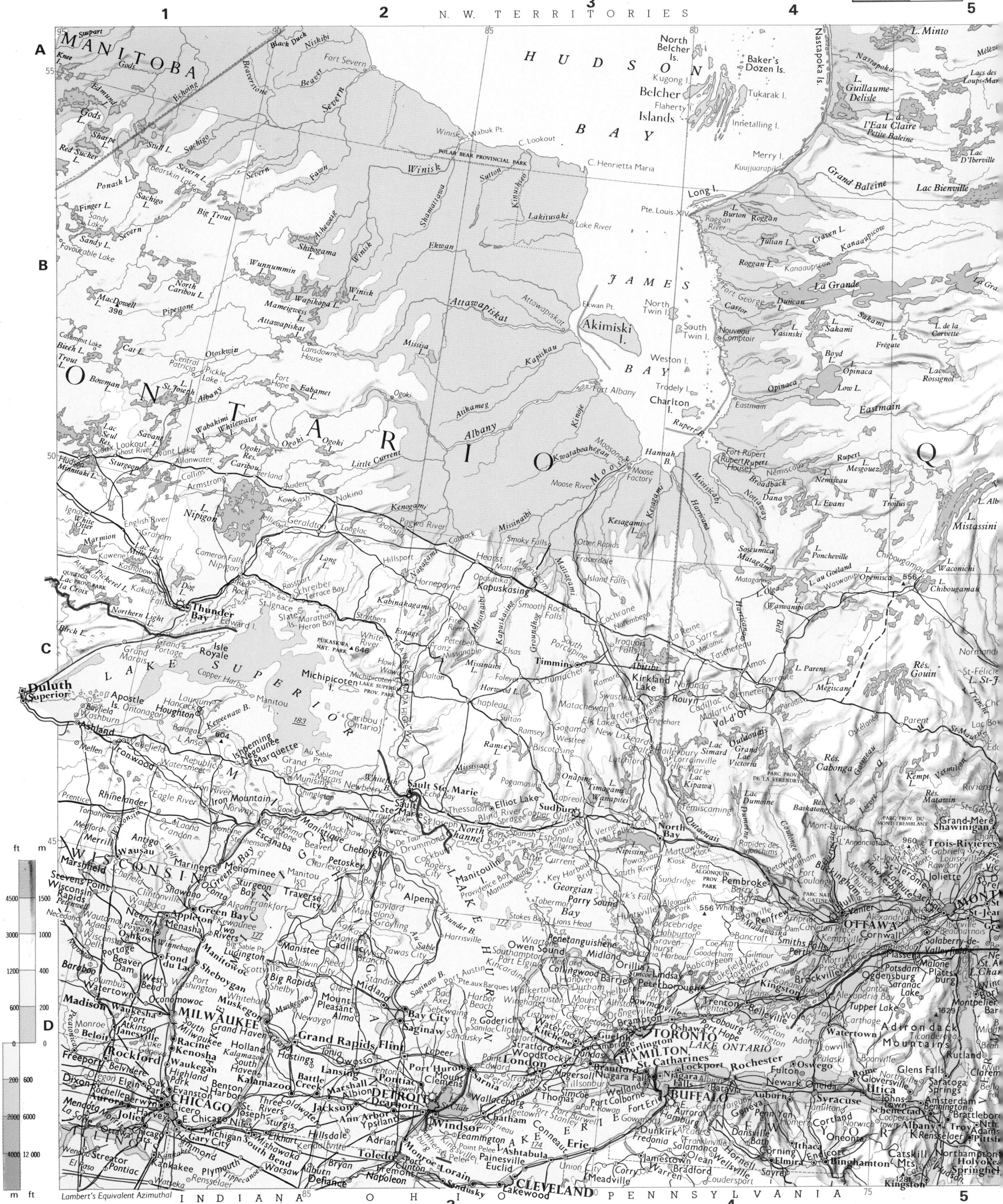

HUDSON BAY

JAMES BAY

ONTARIO

Q (QUÉBEC)

LAKE SUPERIOR

LAKE HURON

LAKE MICHIGAN

LAKE ONTARIO

LAKE ERIE

Georgian Bay

WISCONSIN

INDIANA

OHIO

PENNSYLVANIA

Adirondack Mountains

Belcher Islands

Akimiski I.

Duluth · Superior

Thunder Bay

Isle Royale

Timmins

Kirkland Lake

Sudbury

North Bay

Ottawa

Toronto

Hamilton

Buffalo

Rochester

Syracuse

Utica

Chicago

Milwaukee

Green Bay

Detroit

Windsor

Cleveland

Toledo

Sault Ste. Marie

Marquette

Grand Rapids

Flint

Saginaw

Bay City

Lansing

Kalamazoo

Rockford

Madison

London

Kitchener

St. Catharines

Niagara Falls

Kingston

Peterborough

Trois-Rivières

Grand-Mère

Pembroke

Parry Sound

Algonquin Prov. Park

ALGONQUIN PROV. PARK

Lambert's Equivalent Azimuthal

ft m
4500 1500
3000 1000
1200 400
600 200
0 0
200 600
2000 6000
4000 12 000
m ft

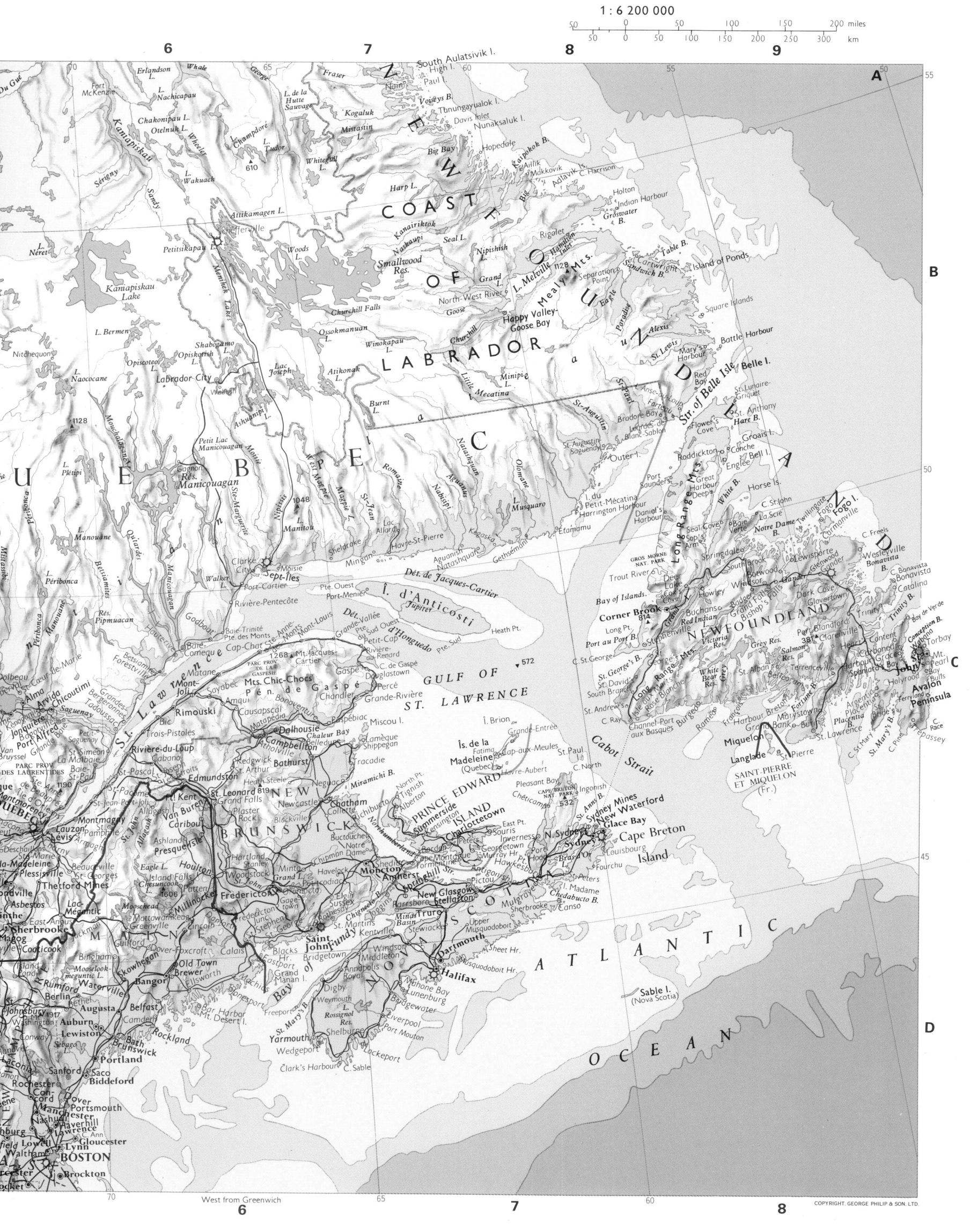

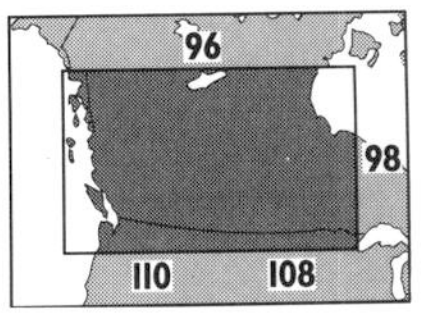

YUKON TERRITORY

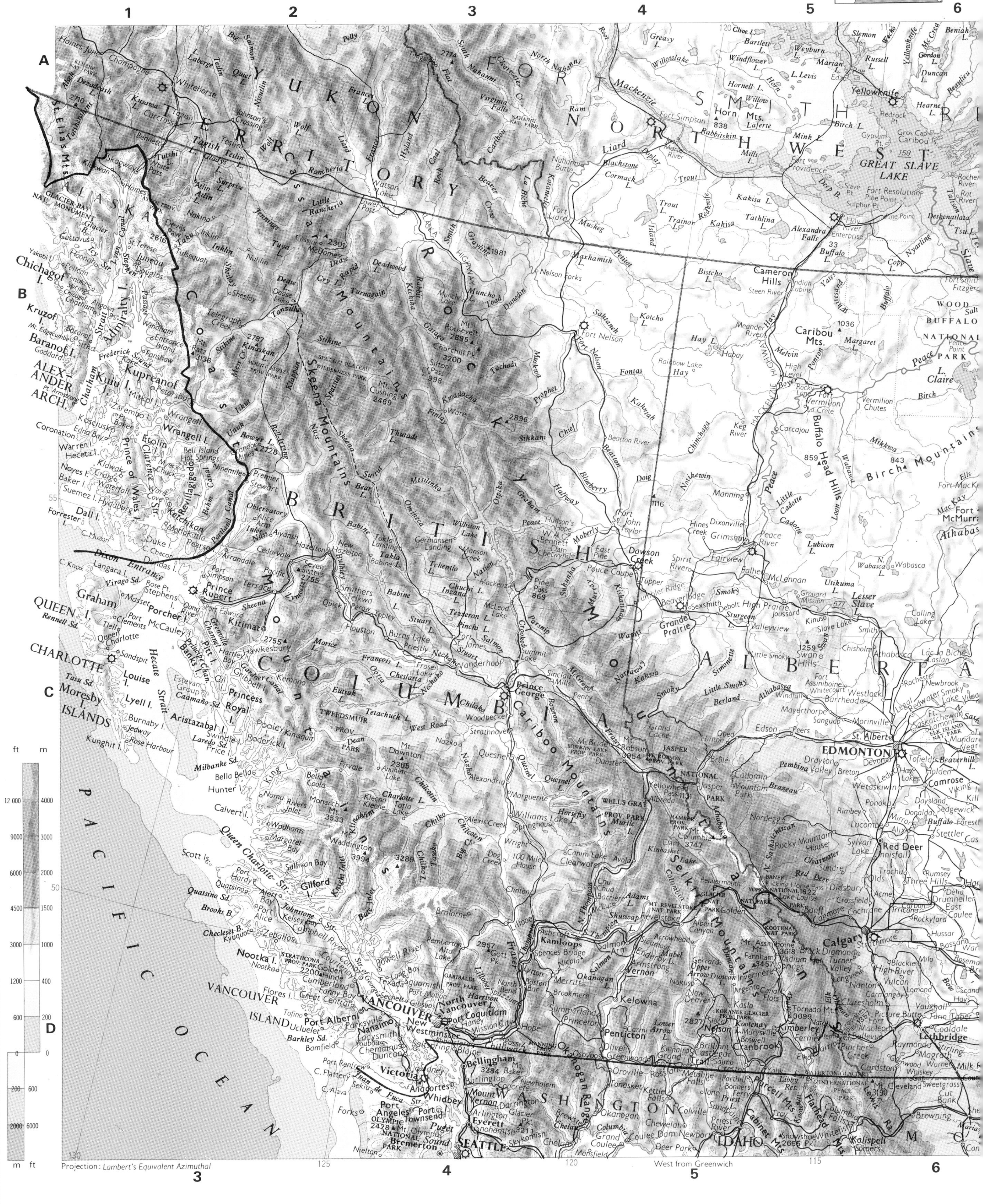

NORTH WEST TERRITORIES

FORT SMITH

GREAT SLAVE LAKE

ALASKA

BRITISH COLUMBIA

ALBERTA

WOOD BUFFALO NATIONAL PARK

QUEEN CHARLOTTE ISLANDS

VANCOUVER ISLAND

PACIFIC OCEAN

WASHINGTON

IDAHO

MONTANA

ALEXANDER ARCH.

Rocky Mountains

Skeena Mountains

Selkirk Mountains

Coast Mountains

Cities and places (selection):
Whitehorse, Carcross, Atlin, Juneau, Sitka, Ketchikan, Prince Rupert, Kitimat, Terrace, Smithers, Prince George, Quesnel, Williams Lake, Kamloops, Kelowna, Penticton, Vancouver, New Westminster, North Vancouver, Victoria, Nanaimo, Port Alberni, Powell River, Hope, Chilliwack, Merritt, Vernon, Revelstoke, Golden, Banff, Lake Louise, Calgary, Red Deer, EDMONTON, Camrose, Wetaskiwin, Ponoka, Lethbridge, Medicine, Dawson Creek, Fort St. John, Grande Prairie, Peace River, Fort Nelson, Fort McMurray, Athabasca, Yellowknife, Fort Simpson, Fort Providence, Fort Resolution, Hay River, High Level, Seattle, Everett, Bremerton, Bellingham

Mt. Robson 3954, Mt. Waddington 3994, Mt. Assiniboine 3618, Mt. Revelstoke, Churchill Pk. 3200, Mt. Cushing 2469

Caribou Mts., Birch Mountains, Buffalo Head Hills, Cameron Hills, Caribou Mts.

Lesser Slave Lake, Williston Lake, Great Slave Lake

Projection: Lambert's Equivalent Azimuthal

West from Greenwich

Scale bar:
ft / m
12 000 / 4000
9000 / 3000
6000 / 2000
4500 / 1500
3000 / 1000
1200 / 400
600 / 200
0 / 0
600 / 200
2000 / 6000
m ft

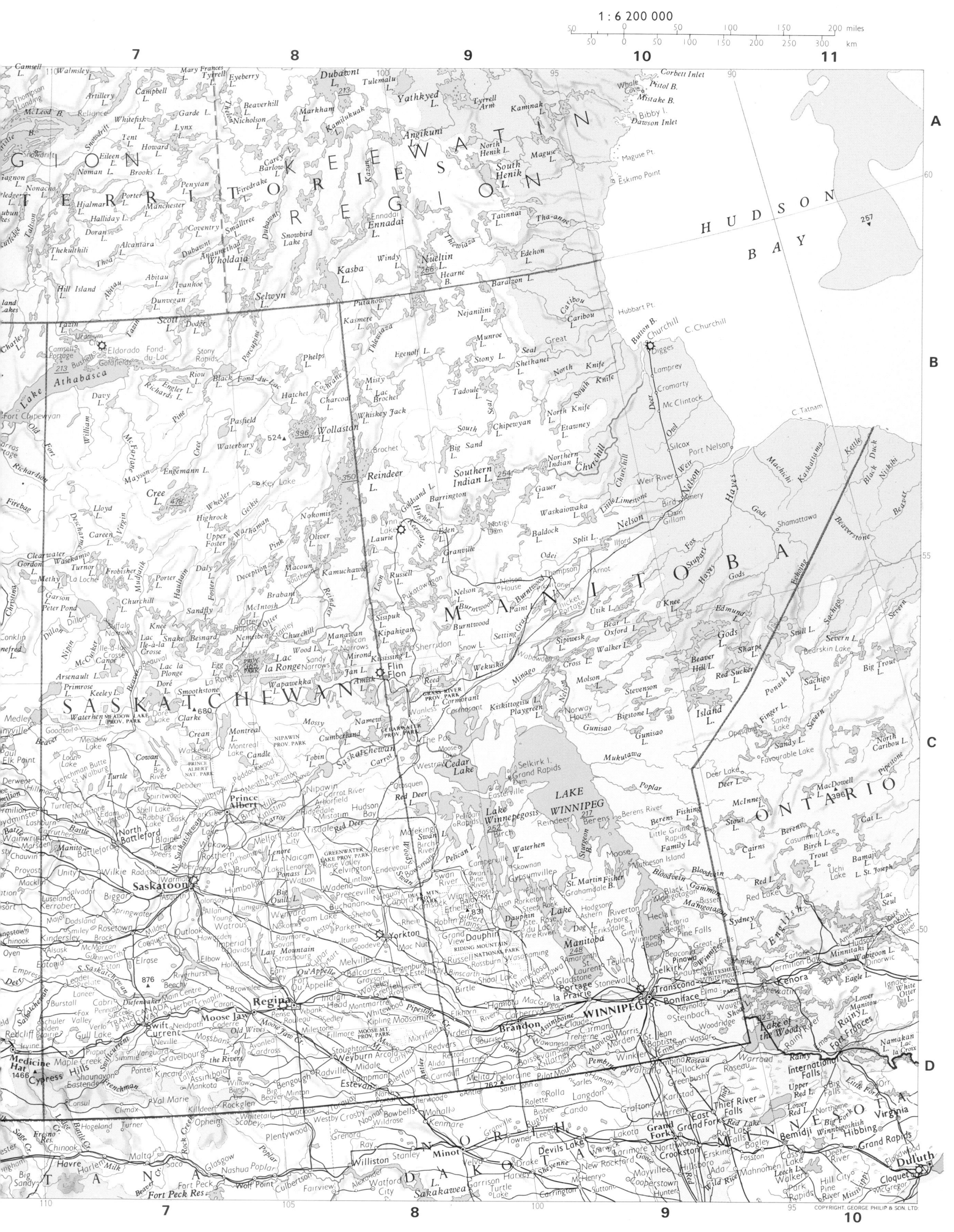

1 : 6 200 000

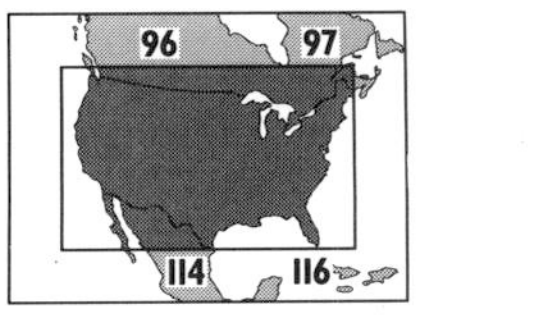

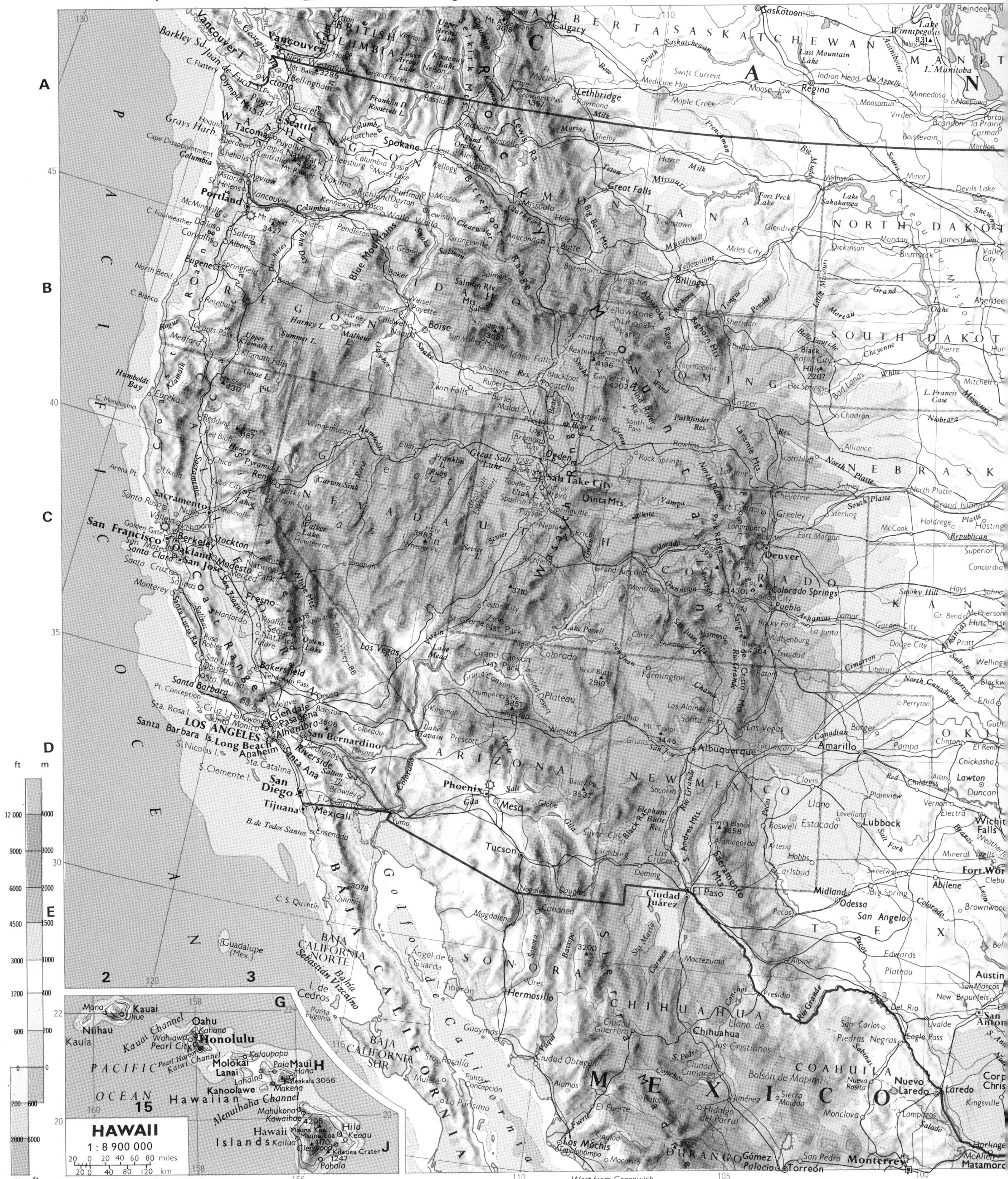

1
2
3
4
5
6
A
B
C
D
E
BRITISH COLUMBIA
ALBERTA
SASKATCHEWAN
C A N A D A
Vancouver
Victoria
Calgary
Lethbridge
Regina
Saskatoon
Moose Jaw
Medicine Hat
L. Manitoba
Lake Winnipegosis
P A C I F I C   O C E A N
W A S H I N G T O N
O R E G O N
C A L I F O R N I A
N E V A D A
I D A H O
M O N T A N A
W Y O M I N G
U T A H
C O L O R A D O
A R I Z O N A
N E W   M E X I C O
T E X A S
N O R T H   D A K O T A
S O U T H   D A K O T A
N E B R A S K A
K A N S A S
O K L A H O M A
M E X I C O
S O N O R A
C H I H U A H U A
C O A H U I L A
D U R A N G O
BAJA CALIFORNIA NORTE
BAJA CALIFORNIA SUR
Golfo de California
Seattle
Tacoma
Spokane
Portland
Salem
Eugene
Boise
Great Falls
Helena
Butte
Billings
Missoula
Bismarck
Pierre
Casper
Cheyenne
Denver
Colorado Springs
Pueblo
Salt Lake City
Ogden
Provo
Reno
Carson City
Sacramento
San Francisco
Oakland
Berkeley
San Jose
Stockton
Modesto
Fresno
Bakersfield
Santa Barbara
LOS ANGELES
Long Beach
Pasadena
Glendale
San Bernardino
Riverside
Anaheim
Santa Ana
San Diego
Tijuana
Mexicali
Las Vegas
Phoenix
Mesa
Tucson
Albuquerque
Santa Fe
El Paso
Ciudad Juárez
Amarillo
Lubbock
Midland
Odessa
San Angelo
Abilene
Hermosillo
Chihuahua
Monterrey
Torreón
Nuevo Laredo
Laredo
Great Salt Lake
Lake Powell
Lake Mead
Yellowstone National Park
Grand Canyon Nat. Park
Death Valley
Rocky Mts.
Sierra Nevada
Cascade Ra.
Coast Ranges
Uinta Mts.
Wasatch Ra.
Bighorn Mts.
Black Hills
Colorado Plateau
Great Basin
Llano Estacado
Columbia
Snake
Missouri
Yellowstone
Colorado
Rio Grande
Pecos
Arkansas
Platte
Mt. Rainier 4392
Mt. Hood 3427
Mt. Shasta 4317
Lassen Pk. 3187
Mt. Whitney 4418
Pikes Pk. 4301
Blanca Pk. 4364
Gannett Pk. 4202
Grand Teton 4196
Humphreys Pk. 3851
Wheeler Pk. 3982
Bald Pk. 3532
Sierra Blanca 3658
Guadalupe (Mex.)
HAWAII
1 : 8 900 000
miles
km
Kauai
Niihau
Oahu
Honolulu
Molokai
Lanai
Maui
Kahoolawe
Hawaii
Haleakala 3056
Mauna Kea 4205
Mauna Loa 4170
Kilauea Crater 1247
Hilo
Kaula
Kauai Channel
Kaiwi Channel
Alenuihaha Channel
PACIFIC OCEAN
Hawaiian Islands
ft
m
12 000
9000
6000
4500
3000
1200
600
0
200
2000
4000
3000
2000
1500
1000
400
200
0
600
6000
Projection: Albers Equal Area
West from Greenwich
16
17

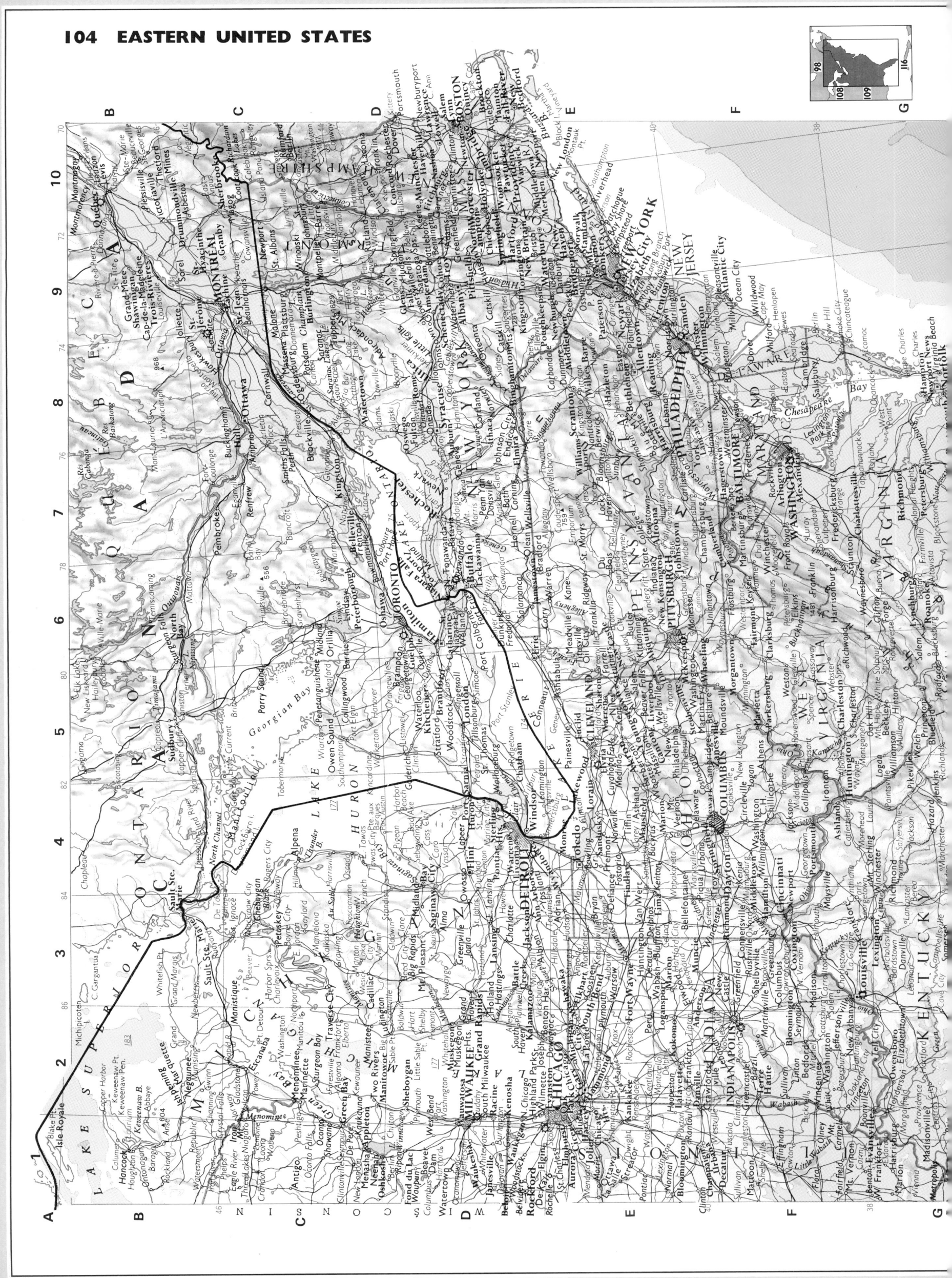

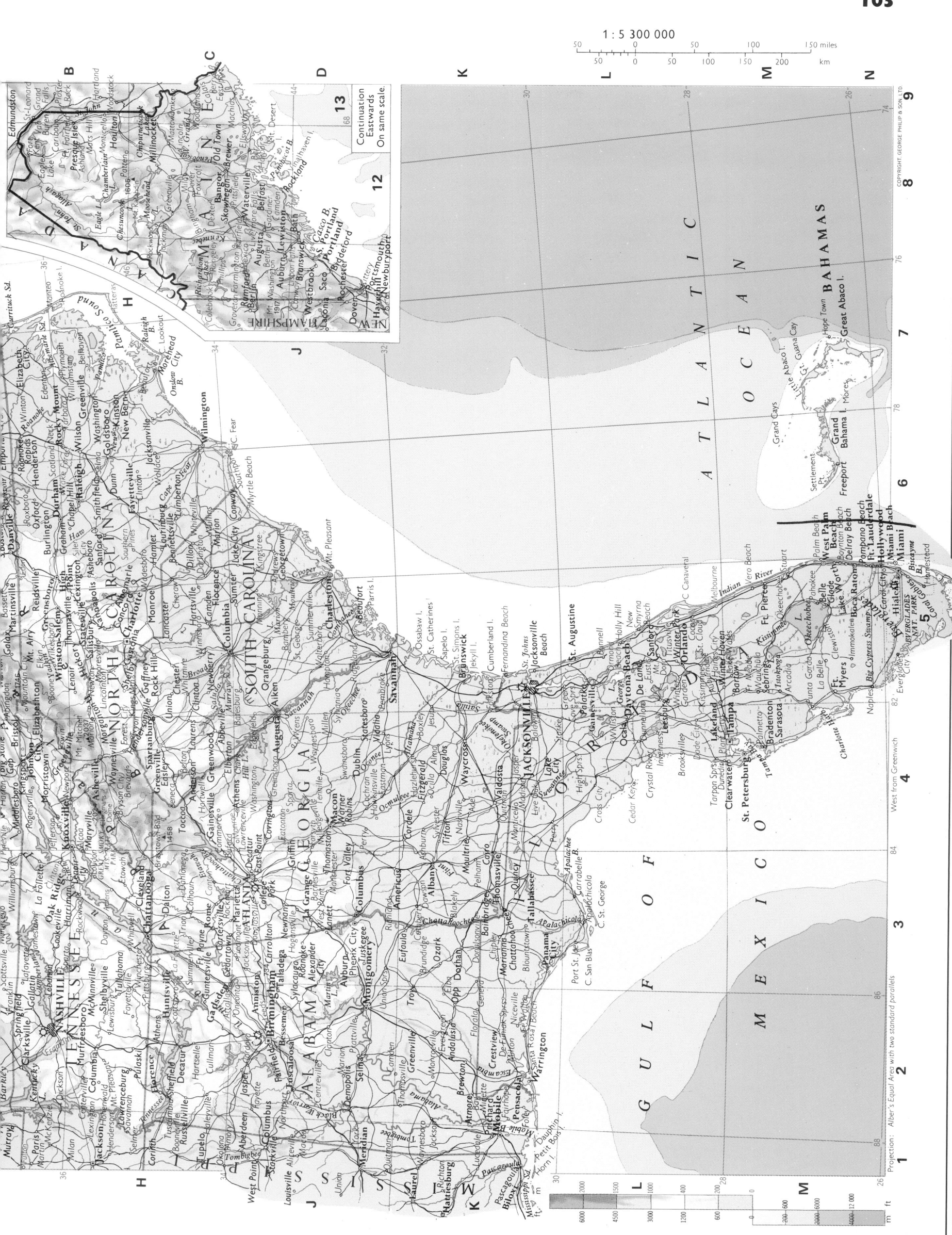

1 : 5 300 000

50   0   50   100   150 miles
50   0   50   100   150   200 km

Continuation Eastwards
On same scale.

13

12

M A I N E

B

C

D

K

Edmundston
St-Léonard
Grand
Falls
Eagle L.
Fort Kent
Burnt I.
Plaster
Rock
Van Buren
Woodstock
Presque Isle
Ken
Caribou
Houlton
Chesuncook
Millinocket
Chiputneticook
Lakes
1606
Patten
Old Town
Brewer
Bangor
Skowhegan
Waterville
Belfast
Augusta
Lewiston
Brunswick
Bath
Casco B.
Portland
Biddeford
Dover
Portsmouth
Haverhill
Newburyport

N E W
H A M P S H I R E

A T L A N T I C

O C E A N

B A H A M A S

Little Abaco I.
Great Abaco I.
Hope Town
Gt. Guana Cay
Grand Cays
Settlement Pt.
Grand
Bahama I.
Freeport

Pamlico Sound
Albemarle Sd.
Currituck Sd.
C. Hatteras
Raleigh
Wilmington
C. Fear
C. Lookout
Morehead City
New Bern
Kinston
Goldsboro
Greenville
Washington
Rocky Mount
Roanoke
Henderson
Durham
Chapel Hill
Raleigh
Fayetteville
Lumberton
Southport
Myrtle Beach
Conway
Georgetown
Florence
Lake City
Sumter
Camden
Charlotte
Columbia
Orangeburg
Charleston
Beaufort
Parris I.
Savannah
Brunswick
Jekyll I.
St. Simons I.
Sapelo I.
St. Catherines I.
Ossabaw I.
Cumberland I.
Fernandina Beach
Jacksonville
Jacksonville Beach
St. Augustine
Daytona Beach
New Smyrna
Cape Canaveral
Melbourne
Vero Beach
Ft. Pierce
Stuart
West Palm Beach
Palm Beach
Boynton Beach
Delray Beach
Pompano Beach
Ft. Lauderdale
Hollywood
Miami Beach
Miami
Hialeah
Homestead

N O R T H   C A R O L I N A

S O U T H   C A R O L I N A

G E O R G I A

F L O R I D A

T E N N E S S E E

A L A B A M A

M I S S I S S I P P I

Atlanta
Macon
Columbus
Albany
Valdosta
Tallahassee
Jacksonville
Gainesville
Ocala
Orlando
Tampa
St. Petersburg
Lakeland
Winter Haven
Sarasota
Bradenton
Ft. Myers
Naples
Everglades City
Everglades Nat. Park
Big Cypress Swamp
L. Okeechobee
L. George
Indian River
St. Johns R.

G U L F

O F

M E X I C O

G U L F   O F   M E X I C O

Mobile
Pensacola
Panama City
Apalachicola
C. San Blas
C. St. George
Port St. Joe
Mississippi Sd.
Biloxi
Pascagoula
Mobile B.
Dauphin I.
Horn I.
Petit Bois I.

Nashville
Knoxville
Chattanooga
Memphis
Birmingham
Montgomery
Mobile
Hattiesburg
Laurel
Meridian
Tupelo

West from Greenwich
74
76
78
82
84
86
88
30
28
26

9
8
7
6
5
4
3
2
1

L
M
N
K
H
J

Projection: Alber's Equal Area with two standard parallels
COPYRIGHT GEORGE PHILIP & SON LTD

ft.   m
12 000   4000
6000   2000
4500   1500
3000   1000
1200   400
600   200
0   0
200   600
2000   6000

98
104   104

1   2   3   4   5   6   7

A

Georgian Bay

C A N

Thunder Bay
North Pt.
South Pt.
Blackriver

Bruce Peninsula

Lucas Channel
Cove I.
Tobermory
C. Hurd
Dyer Bay

Fitzwilliam I.
Yeo I.
Flowerpot I.

B

L A K E   H U R O N

Harrisville
Greenbush
Oscoda
Au Sable
Au Sable Pt.

Owen Sound
Nottawasaga
Meaford Bay
Thornbury
Collingwood
Wasaga Beach
Stayner

O N T A R I

Parry Sound
Huntsville
Bracebridge
Gravenhurst
L. Muskoka

Haliburton
Wilberforce
Bancroft

Westmeikoon L.

Combermere
Madawaska
Griffith

44

Port Austin
Kinde
Bad Axe
Harbor Beach

Barrie
L. Simcoe
Orillia
Beaverton

Lindsay
Peterborough
Keene
Rice L.

Belleville
Trenton

C

MICHIGAN

Sandusky
Carsonville
Port Sanilac

Waterloo
Kitchener
Stratford
Guelph

TORONTO
Mississauga

L A K E   O N T A R I O

Oshawa
Whitby
Port Hope
Cobourg

43

Port Huron
Sarnia

London

Hamilton
Burlington
St. Catharines
Niagara Falls
N. Tonawanda

Lockport
Rochester
Greece
Brighton

N E W

D

DETROIT
Windsor
Lake St. Clair

Chatham

BUFFALO
Lackawanna
West Seneca

Dunkirk
Fredonia

Hornell
Corning
Elmira

42

L A K E   E R I E

Erie

Jamestown
Olean
Bradford

Wellsville

RONDEAU PROV. PK.
Pte aux Pins

PT. PELEE NAT. PK.

Pelee I.

E

CLEVELAND
Lakewood
Euclid
Shaker Hts.

Ashtabula
Conneaut

Meadville
Titusville
Oil City

Warren
Ridgway
Emporium

F

O H I O

Akron
Canton
Youngstown
New Castle

P E N N S Y L V A

Oil City
Franklin
Butler
Kittanning

Altoona
State College

41

Mansfield

Massillon
Alliance

New Castle
Beaver Falls

Indiana
Ebensburg
Johnstown

G

Newark
Zanesville
Cambridge

PITTSBURGH
Steubenville
Weirton
McKeesport
Washington

Wheeling
W. VA.

Connellsville
Somerset

40

Projection: Bonne

82   3   81   4   80   5   79   6   78   7   77

ft m

6000 2000
4500 1500
3000 1000
1200 400
600 200
0   0
200 600

m ft

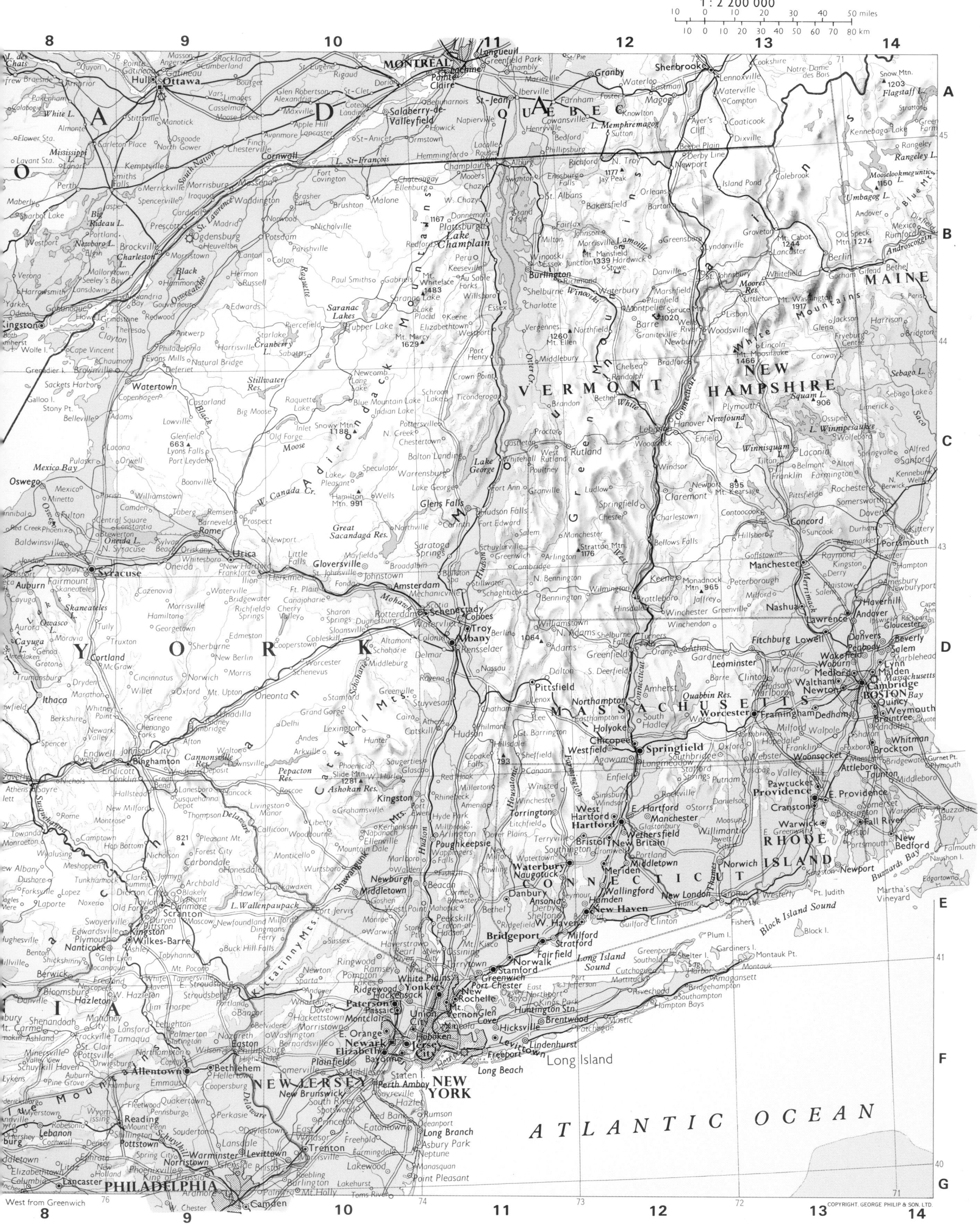

1 : 2 200 000

ATLANTIC OCEAN

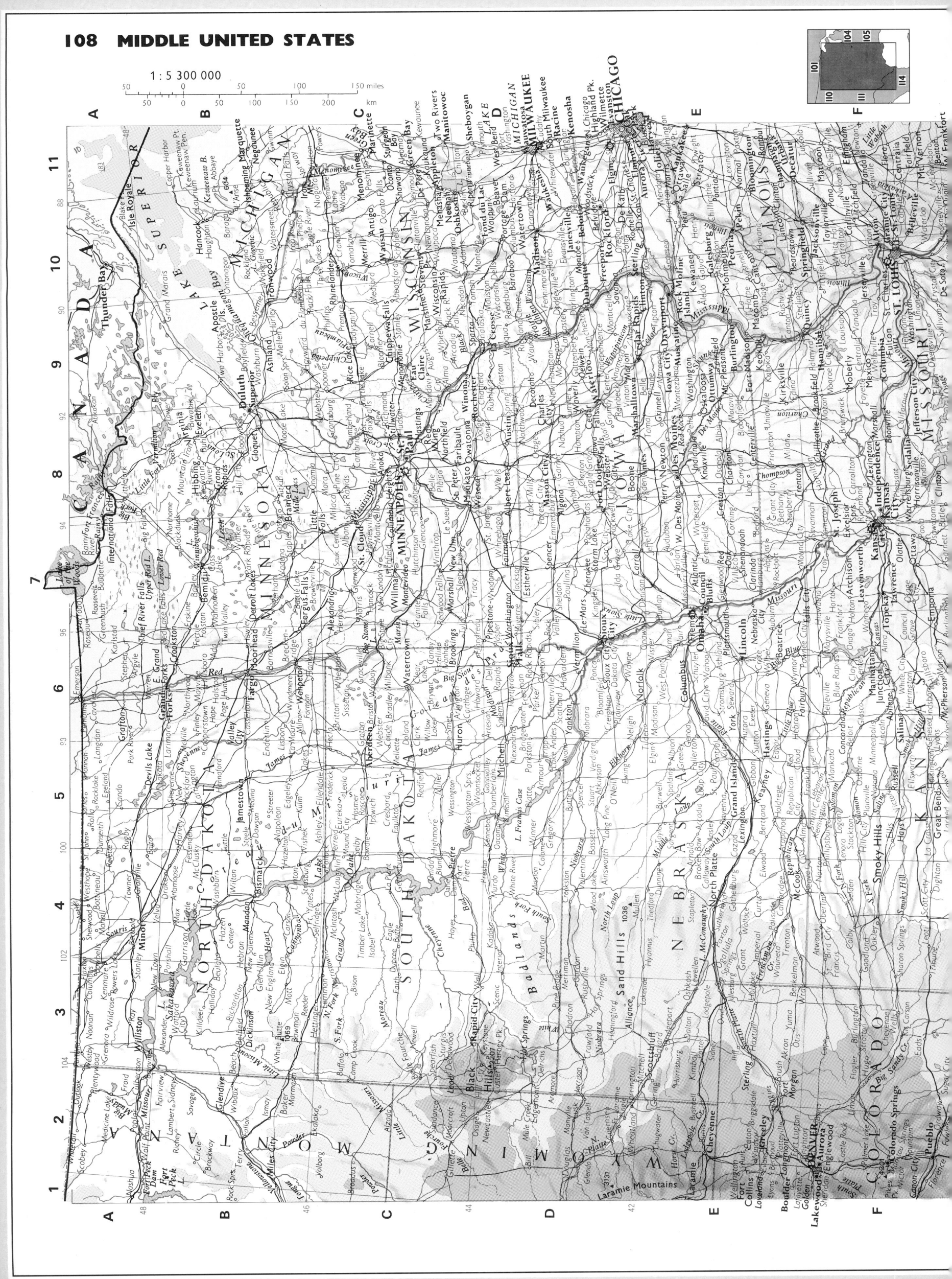

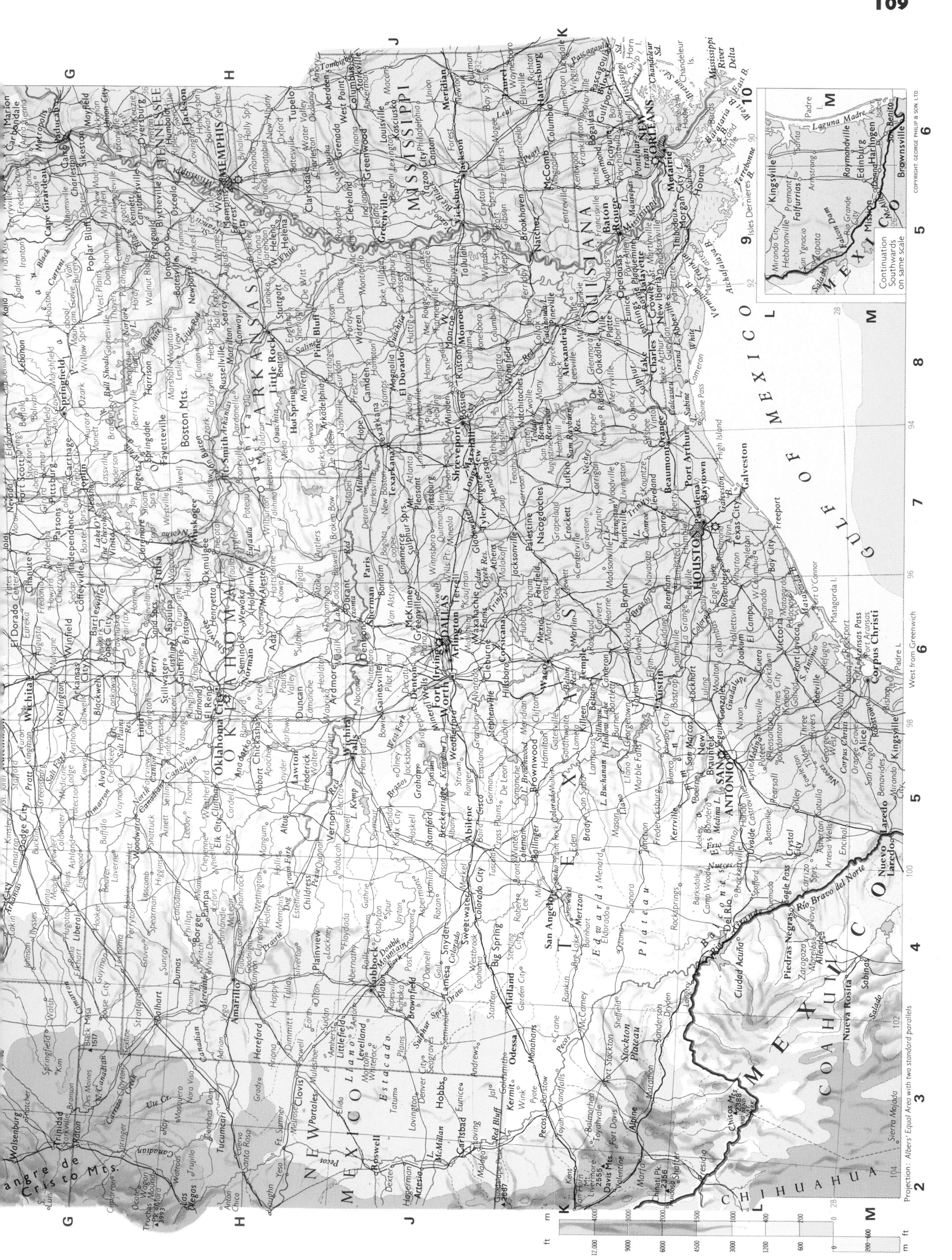

1 : 5 300 000

50   0   50   100 miles
50   0   50   100   150 km

COPYRIGHT. GEORGE PHILIP & SON, LTD.

COLORADO

NEW MEXICO

TEXAS

ARIZONA

CALIFORNIA

NEW ... (UTAH)

MEXICO

SONORA

CHIHUAHUA

BAJA CALIFORNIA

Sangre de Cristo Mts.
San Juan Mts.
Uncompahgre Plat.
Colorado Plateau
Painted Desert
Mogollon Rim
Gila
Sonora Desert
Desierto de Altar
Gran Desierto
Death Valley
Mojave Desert

LOS ANGELES
San Diego
PHOENIX
Tucson
El Paso
Ciudad Juárez
Albuquerque
Santa Fe
Las Vegas
Flagstaff
Hermosillo

Golfo de California

PACIFIC OCEAN

I. de Guadalupe (Mexico)

Projection: Albers' Equal Area with two standard parallels

West from Greenwich

ft
m
12,000
9000
6000
4500
3000
1500
600
0
m ft
200 600
2000 6000
4000 12,000

SEATTLE-PORTLAND REGION
On same scale
PACIFIC OCEAN
CANADA
WASHINGTON
OREGON
VANCOUVER
SEATTLE
PORTLAND
SAN FRANCISCO
SAN JOSE
Sacramento
Stockton
Fresno
Reno

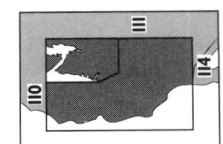

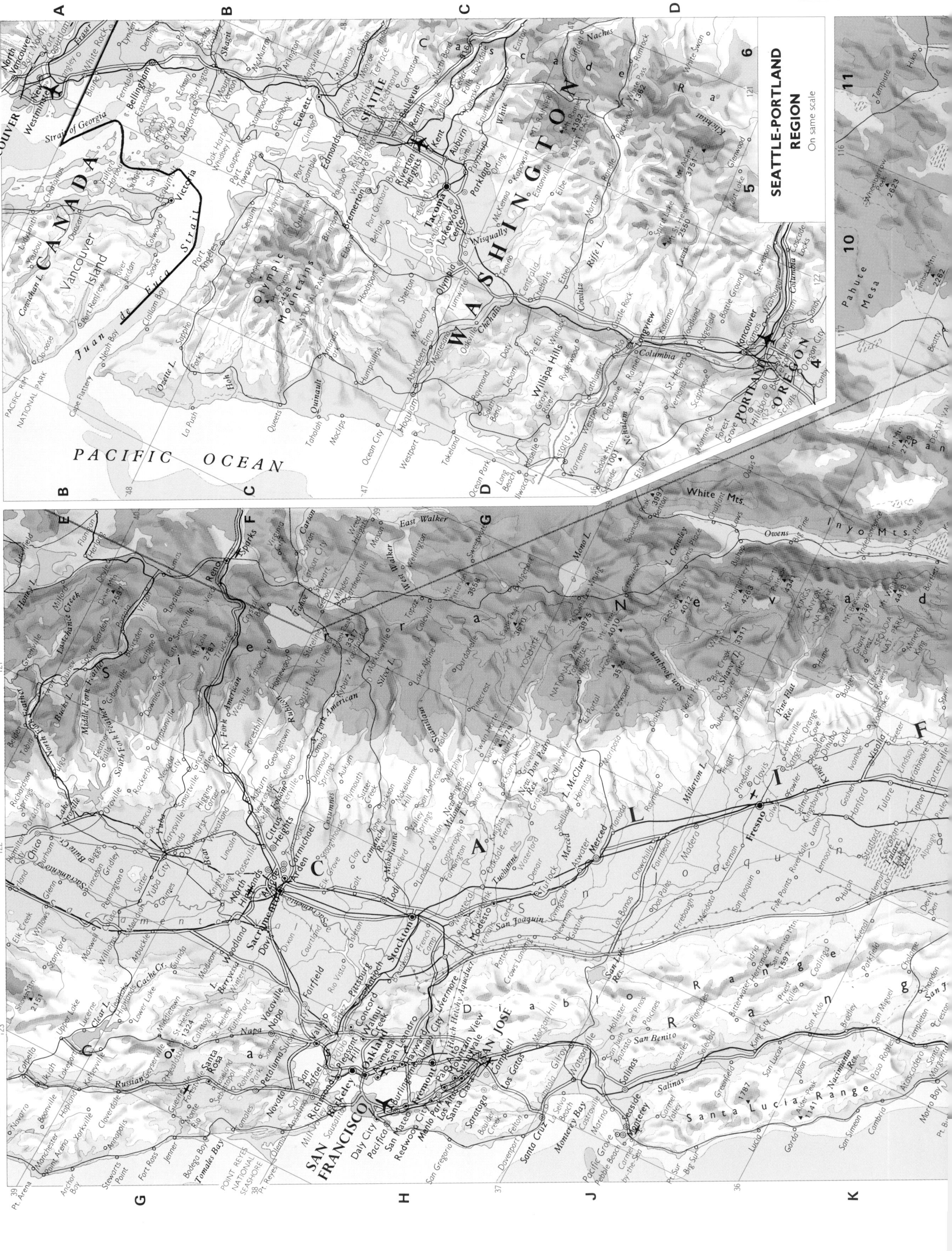

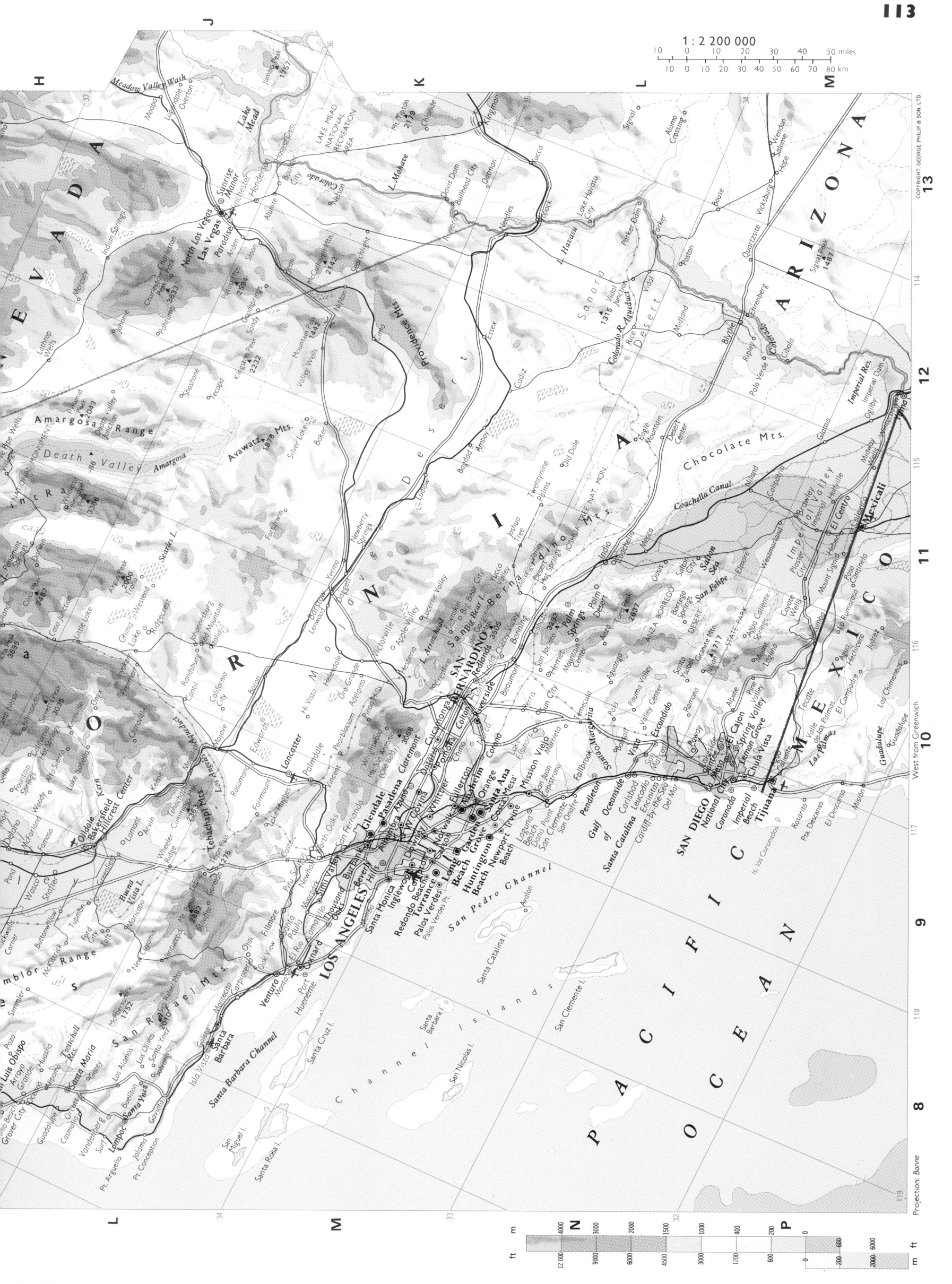

1 : 2 200 000

10 0 10 20 30 40 50 miles

10 0 10 20 30 40 50 60 70 80 km

Projection: Bonne

West from Greenwich

N E V A D A

A R I Z O N A

C A L I F O R N I A

M E X I C O

P A C I F I C   O C E A N

LOS ANGELES

SAN DIEGO

San Bernardino

Mexicali

Tijuana

Las Vegas

Death Valley

Colorado Desert

Mojave Desert

Chocolate Mts.

Santa Barbara Channel

San Pedro Channel

Channel Islands

Lake Mead

m
ft
4000   12 000
3000   9000
2000   6000
1500   4500
1000   3000
400   1200
200   600
0   0

ft   m
12 000
9000
6000
4500
3000   600
1200   200
600   0
0
2000
6000

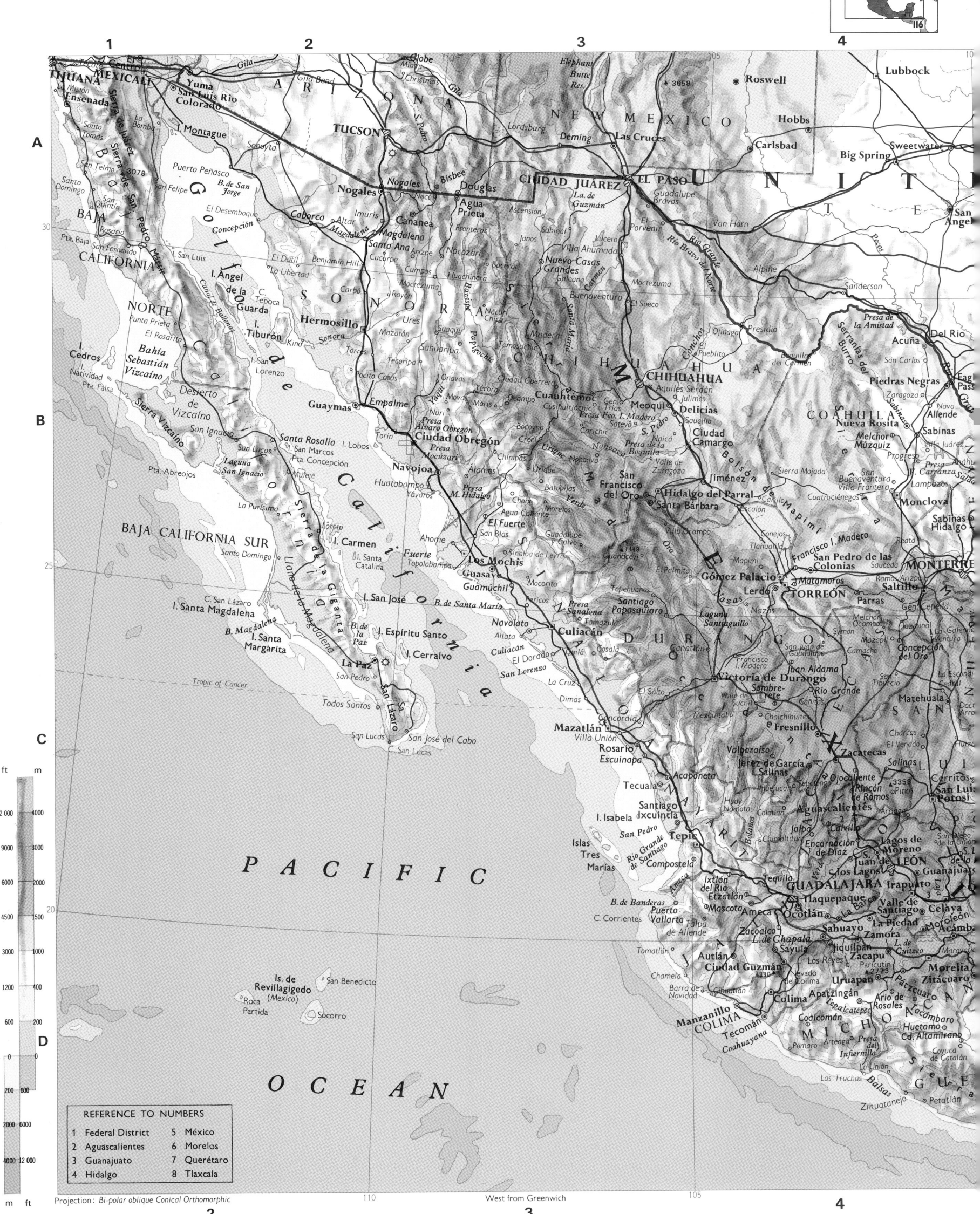

REFERENCE TO NUMBERS

1 Federal District	5 México
2 Aguascalientes	6 Morelos
3 Guanajuato	7 Querétaro
4 Hidalgo	8 Tlaxcala

Projection: Bi-polar oblique Conical Orthomorphic

West from Greenwich

1 : 7 100 000

50   0   50   100   150   200 miles
50   0   100   200   300 km

5

Wichita
Falls
Denison
Sherman   Paris   Red   Hope
Texarkana   90
Denton Greenville Texarkana El Dorado Camden Greenville
FORT WORTH   DALLAS   Marshall   ARKANSAS   Camden
Abilene
Ranger   Cleburne   Longview   Shreveport   Monroe   Tallulah   Vicksburg   MISSISSIPPI   Tuscaloosa   Opelika
Hillsboro   Corsicana   Tyler   S   Natchez   Jackson   Meridian   Selma   Montgomery   Phenix City   Columbus
Brownwood   Waco   Palestine   Toledo   Nacogdoches   O   Laurel   Troy   A   B   A   M   A   Americus   Cordele
Temple   Huntsville   Lufkin   Sam   Alexandria   Baton   Bogalusa   Hattiesburg   Flomaton   Dothan   Chattahoochee   Valdosta
Austin   Bryan   Rosenberg   Beaumont   Lake Charles   Lafayette   NEW   Gulfport   MOBILE   Pensacola   Panama City   Apalachee   Lake City
HOUSTON   Port   ORLEANS   Mobile Bay   C. San Blas   Bay   Suwannee
SAN   Victoria   Arthur   Atchafalaya   Breton Sound   FLORIDA
ANTONIO   Galveston   Bay   Terrebonne B.   Mississippi Delta   Clearwater

GULF   OF

Alice
Corpus Christi

Laredo   Laguna Madre
Kingsville
Nuevo Laredo   Harlingen   MEXICO
Reynosa   Brownsville
Matamoros   CUBA
Valle Hermoso
Montemorelos   Laguna Madre   Tropic of Cancer
Linares   La Esperanza
Guane
La Fé
Ciudad   Soto la Marina
Victoria   Canal de Yucatán   C. San Antonio   Corrientes

Ciudad Mante   Isla   C. Catoche
Desterrada   Río Lagartos   Cancún
Ciudad Madero   Isla Pérez   Pta.   El Cuyo   Pto. Juárez
Tampico   Yalkubul   Temax   Tizimín
Ciudad de   Progreso   Dzilam   Izamal   Espita   Puerto Morelos
Valles   de Bravo   Motul   YUCATÁN   Valladolid   Isla
Laguna de Tamiahua   MÉRIDA   Sotuta   Cozumel
Maxcanú   Ficul   Peto   B. de la Ascensión
Tuxpan   Tekax   QUINTANA
Poza Rica   C. Rojo   Tenabo   ROO   B. del Espíritu Santo
Papantla   Campeche   Hopelchén
Huauchinango   Champotón   Felipe Carrillo   Banco
Tulancingo   Chenkán   Puerto   Chinchorro
Pachuca   Jalapa   Vigía Chico   Bacalar
Enríquez   Ciudad del   Laguna de Términos   Chetumal   B. de
MÉXICO   Veracruz   Carmen   Frontera   CAMPECHE   Corozal   Chetumal
Coatepec   Llave   Coatzacoalcos   Orange Walk   Ambergris Cay
PUEBLA   Alvarado   Paraíso   Palizada   Hondo   Turneffe Is.
Córdoba   San Andrés   Concepción   Uaxactún   Belize   BELIZE
Cuernavaca   Cosamaloapan   Tuxtla   Villahermosa   City   Belmopan
TABASCO   Tikal   Benque   Dangriga   Islas de
Tehuacán   Acayucan   Cárdenas   Viejo   la Bahía
Iguala   Minatitlán   L. Petén Itzá   Roatán   Puerto
Cosamaloapan   La Libertad   Puerto Cortés   Cortés
Oaxaca   Istmo   Flores   Monkey River   La Ceiba
Chilpancingo   de   Tuxtla   San Cristóbal de   GUATEMALA
Tehuantepec   Gutiérrez   las Casas   La Independencia   San Pedro Sula   HONDURAS
Acapulco   Ixtepec   CHIAPAS   Comitán   Puerto Barrios   El Progreso
Salina Cruz   Mar Muerto   Livingston   Santa Rosa de Copán
Golfo de   GUATEMALA   Cobán   Zacapa   Tegucigalpa
Tehuantepec   Huehuetenango   Sa. de las Minas   Chiquimula de   Jutiapa
Tapachula   GUATEMALA   La Paz

6   **7**   **8**

COPYRIGHT. GEORGE PHILIP & SON, LTD

GULF OF MEXICO

U.S.A.
Fort Myers
Boca Raton
Fort Lauderdale
West Palm Beach
West End
Grand Bahama I.
Freeport
Hope Town
Great Abaco I.
Naples
C. Romano
Everglades
Hialeah
MIAMI
Bimini Is.
Berry Is.
Andros Island
New Providence
Nassau
Eleuthera I.
BAH
Great Exuma I.

Everglades
C. Sable
Florida Bay
Key West
Dry Tortugas
Florida Keys
Straits of Florida

Isla Desterrada
Isla Pérez

Canal de Yucatán
C. Catoche
Pta. Yalkubul
Río Lagartos
El Cuyo
C. San Antonio
Guane
La Fé
Pinar del Río
San Luis
Los Palacios
San Antonio de los Baños
Guanabacoa
(Havana) **LA HABANA**
MARIANAO
Matanzas
Cárdenas
Jovellanos
Colón
Güines
Bahía Honda
La Esperanza
Batabanó
Jagüey Grande
Playa Larga
Cienfuegos
Santa Clara
Sagua la Grande
Caibarién
Placetas
Morón
Cay Sal Bank
Canal Nicolás
Canal Viejo de Bahama
Jumentos Cays
Duncan Town
GREAT BAHAMA BANK

Great Guana Cay
Northeast Providence Channel
Northwest Providence Channel

Progreso
Dzilam de Bravo
Temax
Tizimín
Izamal
Motul
Mérida
Valladolid
Pto. Juárez
Cancún
Puerto Morelos
Isla Cozumel
YUCATAN
Ticul
Tekax
Chichén Itzá
Mayapán
Peto
Maxcanú
Sotuta
Campeche
Champotón
Chenkán
Hopelchén
Vigía Chico
B. de la Ascensión
B. del Espíritu Santo
QUINTANA ROO
Pedro Antonio Santos
Banco Chinchorro
Juárez

Archipiélago de los Canarreos
Nueva Gerona
Isla de la Juventud
Corrientes
Trinidad
Sancti-Spíritus
Ciego de Ávila
Florida
Camagüey
Júcaro
Tunas de Zaza
Arch. de los Jardines de la Reina
Santa Cruz del Sur
Nuevitas
Puerto Manati
Puerto Padr
Gibara
Victoria de las Tunas
Holguí
Bayamo
Palma Soriano
SANTIAGO DE CUBA
Manzanillo
Golfo de Guacanayabo
Sierra Maestra
C. Cruz
GREATER
CUBA

Ciudad del Carmen
Laguna de Términos
Palizada
Champotón
Concepción
San José Carpizo
CAMPECHE
Matamoros
Tenabo
Candelaria
Palenque
Chetumal
B. de Chetumal
Corozal
Orange Walk
Hondo
Ambergris Cay
BELIZE
Belize City
Belmopan
Turneffe Is.
Middlesex
Dangriga

Cayman Islands (Br.)
Cayman Brac
Little Cayman
Georgetown
Grand Cayman
7680

Montego Bay
Lucea
Falmouth
St. Ann's Bay
Annotto Bay
Port Antonio
South Negril Pt.
Savanna la Mar
Black River
Mandeville
May Pen
Spanish Town
KINGSTON
Morant
Mora Cay (Jamaica)
JAMAICA

Ocosingo
Comitán
L. Petén Itzá
La Libertad
Flores
Benque Viejo
Uaxactún
Tikal
San Luis
Punta Gorda
Maya Mts.
San Antonio
Monkey River
Golfo de Honduras
Islas de la Bahía
Roatán
Utila
Puerto Cortés
Puerto Barrios
Livingston
Morales
Tela
La Ceiba
Trujillo
Iriona
Pta. Patuca
C. Camarón
Bonacca
Bruss Laguna
GUATEMALA
Cuchumatanes
Cobán
Huehuetenango
San Marcos
Totonicapán
Sololá
Antigua
Jalapa
Zacapa
Chiquimula
GUATEMALA
Amatitlán
Escuintla
Santa Ana
Suchitoto
Cojutepeque
Zacatecoluca
Ahuachapán
Acajutla
Nueva San Salvador
Santa Tecla
SAN SALVADOR
Usulután
EL SALVADOR
San Miguel
Golfo de Fonseca
Chinandega
Corinto
León
La Paz Centro
HONDURAS
San Pedro Sula
El Progreso
Santa Bárbara
Arenal
Yoro
Olanchito
Comayagua
Tegucigalpa
Danlí
Juticalpa
Catacamas
Patuca
Coco
Segovia
Puerto Cabo Gracias á Dios
Kisalaya
Cayos Miskitos (Nicaragua)
Pta. Gorda
Puerto Cabezas
Laguna Caratasca
Mosquitia
C. Falso
C. Gracias á Dios
Ocotal
Somoto
Estelí
Condega
Jinotega
Matagalpa
El Sauce
Boaco
NICARAGUA
MANAGUA
Masaya
Granada
Diriamba
Jinotepe
Rivas
San Juan del Sur
B. de Salinas
C. Sta. Elena
Golfo de Papagayo
C. Velas
Santa Cruz
Nicoya
Pen. de Nicoya
C. Blanco
Golfo de Nicoya
Puntarenas
Esparta
COSTA RICA
Alajuela
San José
Cartago
Heredia
Limón
Golfito
Golfo Dulce
Puerto Armuelles
Pta. Burica
Pta. Mariato

Siuna
Bonanza
Prinzapolca
Río Grande
Tungla
San Pedro del Norte
Muy Muy
Siquia
Santo Domingo
Rama
Pta. de Perlas
Bluefields
El Bluff
Cord. de Yolaina
Islas del Maiz (Nicaragua, U.S.A.)
Pta. Mico
Lago de Nicaragua
Isla de Ometepe
San Carlos
San Juan
San Juan del Norte
Bahía de San Juan del Norte

Swan Islands (U.S.A. & Honduras)
Bajo Nuevo (Colombia)
CARIB
I. de Providencia (Colombia)
Cayos Roncador (U.S.A. & Colombia)
I. de San Andrés (Colombia)
Cayos de Albuquerque (Colombia)

Cord. Central
Guápiles
Siquirres
Cord. de Talamanca
Buenos Aires
Volcán Barú
Boquete
Bocas del Toro
Almirante
David
Remedios
Santiago
Chitré
Las Tablas
Pocri
Pen. de Azuero
I. de Coiba
I. de Cebaco
I. Jicarón
Golfo de Chiriqui
Laguna de Chiriquí
Golfo de los Mosquitos
La Chorrera
Gatun L.
Balboa
PANAMÁ
Colón
Nombre de Dios
Portobelo
Penonomé
Aguadulce
Río Hato
Chiman
San Miguel
Arch. de las Perlas
I. del Rey
Garachine
La Palma
El Real
Serranía de Tabasará
Sierra de Darién
Archipiélago de las Mulatas
Golfo del Darién
Golfo de Panamá
Serranía del Darién
CARTAG
G. de Morrosqu
Is. de San Bernardo
Pta. Manzanillo
Lori
Cére
Monterí
Turbo
G. de Uraba

1 : 7 100 000

50   0   50   100   150   200 miles
50   0   50   100   200   300 km

A T L A N T I C

O C E A N

Tropic of Cancer

ft   m

12,000   4000

9000   3000

6000   2000

4500   1500

3000   1000

1200   400

600   200

0

200   600

2000   6000

4000   12,000

6000   18,000

8000   24,000

m   ft

BAMAS

Arthur's Town

The Bight
Cat I.

San Salvador
(Watling I., Guanahani)

Conception I.

Rum Cay

Long I.

Clarence
Town

 andy

ay

Cay Verde

Crooked I. Passage

Crooked I.

Richmond

Albert
Town

Snug
Corner

Acklins I.

Mira por vos Cay

Hogsty Reefs

Plana Cays

Mayaguana I.

Caicos Passage

Cay Santa
Domingo

anes

antilla

Mayari

Moa

Lake Rose

Little Inagua I.

Matthew
Town

Great
Inagua I.

Turks I. Passage

Caicos
Islands
(Br.)

Turks Islands
(Br.)

Baracoa

Pta. de
Anis.

I. de la
Tortue

Port-de-Paix

Cap-Haïtien

Guantánamo

Pta. de
Maisi

Jean-Rabel

Fort-Liberté

Monte Cristi

La Isabela

Puerto Plata

C. Frances Viejo

San Francisco de Macorís

Nagua

Milwaukee
Deep
9200

Puerto Rico Trench

Paso de los Vientos
(Windward Passage)

Cap-à-Foux

Gonaïves

Hinche

Santiago de
los Cabelleros

La Vega

Sánchez

Sabana de la Mar

Bayamón

San Juan

Anegada

Virgin Gorda

Virgin Is.
(Br.)

Sombrero (Anguilla)

Golfe de la
Gonâve

St.-Marc

Cord.
Central

3175

Hato Mayor

Carolina

Arecibo

Tortola

Road Town

Anegada Passage

Anguilla (Br.)

Jérémie

I. de la Gonâve

Port-
AU-PRINCE

San Juan

San Pedro
de Macorís

C. Engano

Aguadilla

1338

Ponce

Fajardo

St. Thomas

Virgin Is.
(U.S.A.)

St.-Martin (Guad.)

St-Barthélemy
(Fr.)

Navassa I.
(U.S.A.)

Damé

HAITI

DOMINICAN
REP.

Higuey

B. de
Yuma

Mayagüez

Caguas

Guayama

Charlotte Amalie

St. Maarten
(Neth.)

Saba (Neth.)

St.
Barbuda

casse

Les Cayes

Massif de la Hotte

2280

Jacmel

Enriquillo

L.

Baní

San Cristóbal

La Romana

Isla
Mona
(U.S.A.)

PUERTO
RICO
(U.S.A.)

Frederiksted

St. Croix

St. Eustatius
(Neth.)

Basse-Terre

Nevis

CHRISTOPHER-
NEVIS

ANTIGUA
& BARBUDA

St.
Johns

Antigua

Aquin

Pointe-à-Gravois

I. à-Vache

Pedernales

Barahona

Cuenca de
Composteila

San José de
Ocoa

SANTO DOMINGO

Canal de la Mona

Christiansted

Redonda

Montserrat

LEEWARD ISLANDS

Guadeloupe Passage

Ste-Rose

Moule

Désirade

H I S P A N I O L A

I. Beata

C. Beata

A N T I L L E S

(Fr.) GUADELOUPE

Pointe-a-Pitre

Basse-Terre

Marie-Galante (Fr.)
Grand-Bourge

I. des Saintes
(Guad.)

Dominica Passage

I. de Aves
(Bird I.)
(Venezuela)

Portsmouth

Roseau

DOMINICA

Martinique Passage

B E A N   **S E A**

Mt. Pelée
1397

Ste-Marie
François

Fort-de-France

MARTINIQUE

Rivière-Pil

WINDWARD ISLANDS

St. Lucia Channel
(Fr.)

Castries

ST. LUCIA

Soufrière

Soufrière 1234

St. Vincent Passage

ST. VINCENT

Speightstown

Kingstown

Bridgetown

THE
BARBADOS

L E S S E R   A N T I L L E S

Hillsborough

The Grenadines

GRENADINES

St. George's

GRENADA

Aruba
(Neth.)

Curaçao

Bonaire

NETH.
ANTILLES

Willemstad

I. Blanquilla (Ven.)

I. Los Hermanos
(Ven.)

I. Los Testigos
(Ven.)

Tobago

Pta. Gallinas

C. San Román

Pen. de
Paraguaná

Is. de Aves
(Ven.)

Is. Los Roques
(Ven.)

I. Orchila
(Ven.)

Scarborough

Pen. de la
Guajira

Pta.
Espada

Punto Fijo

I. Margarita

La Asunción

Galera
Pt.

Ríohacha

Uribia

GUAJIRA

San
Rafael

Golfo de
Venezuela

Punta
Cardón

Coro

La Vela de Coro

I. La Tortuga
(Ven.)

NUEVA
ESPARTA

Porlamar

Pen. de Paria

Pta. Mejillon s

Port of
Spain

C. San Juan
de Guia

Altagracia

Mene de Mauroa

FALCÓN

Tucacas

Puerto
Cabello

Maracay

La Guaira

Maiquetia

CARACAS

DISTRITO
FEDERAL

Carúpano

Río
Caribe

Güira

Golfo de Paria

Trinidad

Arima

ARRAN-
QUILLA

Santa
Marta

Cienaga

Sa. Nevada de
Santa Marta
5800

Punto Fijo

San Felipe

Baragua

YARACUY

Guatire

MIRANDA

Los Teques

Higuerote

Puerto
La Cruz

Cumaná

SUCRE

Caripito

Río Claro

TRINIDAD
& TOBAGO

San Fernando

Baranoa

Soledad

Sabanalarga

Fundación

Calamar

La
Concepción

Cabimas

Santa Rita

Carora

LARA

Mariara
Valencia

S. Juan de
los Morros

Villa
de Cura

Ocumare del Tuy

Río Chico

Serpent's Mouth

ANT-
LANTIC

Valledupar

Villa del
Rosario

Ciudad
Ojeda

Lago de
Maracaibo

Grande

BARQUISIMETO

El Tocuyo

Maritagua de
los Morros

San Carlos

Aragua de
Barcelona

Barcelona

Caicara

ANACO

Maturín

MONAGAS

Magdalen
Plato

Agustin
Codazzi

CÉSAR

Machiques

TRUJILLO

Trujillo

COJEDES

GUÁRICO

El Sombrero

Cantaura

El Tigre

DELTA

Tucupita

AMACUR

Carmen
Bolívar

ijo

Zambrano

El Banco

ZULIA

Betijoque

Valera

Acarigua

PORTUGUESA

Guanare

El Baúl

Valle de la
Pascua

Unare

ANZOATEGUI

Soledad

El Pao

Ciudad Guayana

Sierra Imataca

Sahagún

San
Marcos

laneta
ica

CA

BOLÍVAR

Mompós

Simití

MÉRIDA

Mérida

Cord. de
Mérida

Barinas

BARINAS

Libertad

Ciudad
Bolivia

Santa María
de Ipire

Pariaguán

GUASIPATI

Upata

P. Coroz

Sincé

El Barco

NORTE
DE

SANTANDER

Cúcuta

TÁCHIRA

San Carlos
del Zulia

Catatumbo

Encontrados

Santa
Bárbara

VENEZUELA

San
Fernando de
Apure

APURE

Ciudad
Bolívar

Guasipati

Embarcadero

Tumeremo

El Callao

Sao

Caucasia

Ayapel

San
Fernando
de

Magangué

Guásipati

West from Greenwich

5   6   65   7

COPYRIGHT. GEORGE PHILIP & SON, LTD.

1 : 26 700 000

100   0   100   200   300   400   500 miles
100   0   200   400   600   800 km

ft   m

18 000   6000
12 000   4000
9000   3000
6000   2000
3000   1000
1200   400
600   200
0   0

200   600
2000   6000
4000   12 000
6000   18 000
8000   24 000

m   ft

Projection: Lambert's Equivalent Azimuthal

COPYRIGHT. GEORGE PHILIP & SON. LTD.

1 : 26 700 000

100   0   100 200 300   400   500 miles
100   0   200   400   600   800 km

Projection: Lambert's Equivalent Azimuthal

West from Greenwich

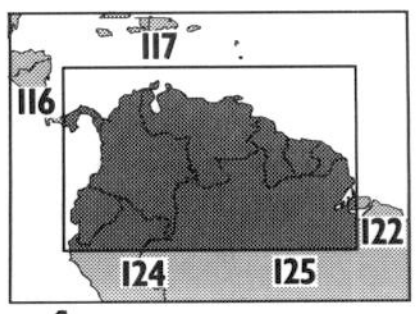

CARIBBEAN SEA

PACIFIC OCEAN

PANAMA

COLOMBIA

VENEZUELA

ECUADOR

PERU

Projection: Lambert's Equivalent Azimuthal

1 : 7 100 000

50   50   0   50   100   150   200 miles
50   0   100   200   300 km

5   6   7

La Blanquilla (Ven.)
Los Hermanos (Ven.)
St. George's GRENADA
Tobago

A

ATLANTIC

NUEVA ESPARTA
Margarita
La Asunción
Porlamar
I. La
Tortuga (Ven.)
Coche
Pta.
Araya
Carúpano
Río Caribe
Pen. de
Paria
Boca del Dragón
Port of
Spain
Arima
Scarborough

TRINIDAD AND TOBAGO

Cumaná
SUCRE
Güiria
Golfo de San
Fernando
Trinidad

OCEAN

Puerto
La Cruz
Barcelona
2596
Cariaco
Caripito
Maturín
MONAGAS
Pariaguán
DELTA
Tucupita
Boca Grande
I. Corocoro

10

ANZOATEGUI
El Tigre
Orinoco
Ciudad
Guayana
AMACURO
Morawhanna
Mabaruma

Ciudad
Bolívar
Guri Dam
Upata
El Palmar
La Horqueta
Barima
Charity

B

BOLIVAR
Serranía
Turagua
El Callao
Tumeremo
Matthew's
Ridge
Kokerite
Anna Regina
Suddie

Angel Falls
2580
El Dorado
Cuyuni
GUYANA
Parika
Georgetown
Buxton
Mahaicony

La Gran
Sabana
Pakaraima
Mt.
Roraima
2772
Kaieteur
Falls
Peter's
Mine
Bartica
Hyde
Park
Rosignol
New Amsterdam
Port Mourant

Orinduik
Mazaruni
Issano
Wismar
Linden
(Mackenzie)
Mara
Skeldon
Nieuw Nickerie
Totness
Paramaribo
Nieuw Amsterdam

5

SURINAM
FRENCH
GUIANA

Cayenne

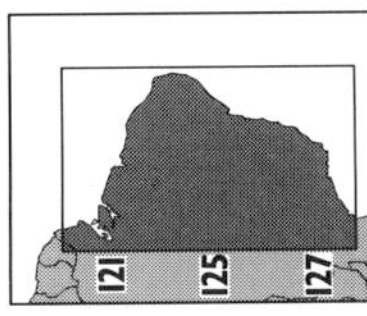

ATLANTIC OCEAN

AMAPÁ
I. de Maracá
Macapá
Ilha de Marajó
Cabo Maguarinho
Baía de Marajó
I. Mexiana
I. Caviana
BELÉM
Tocantins

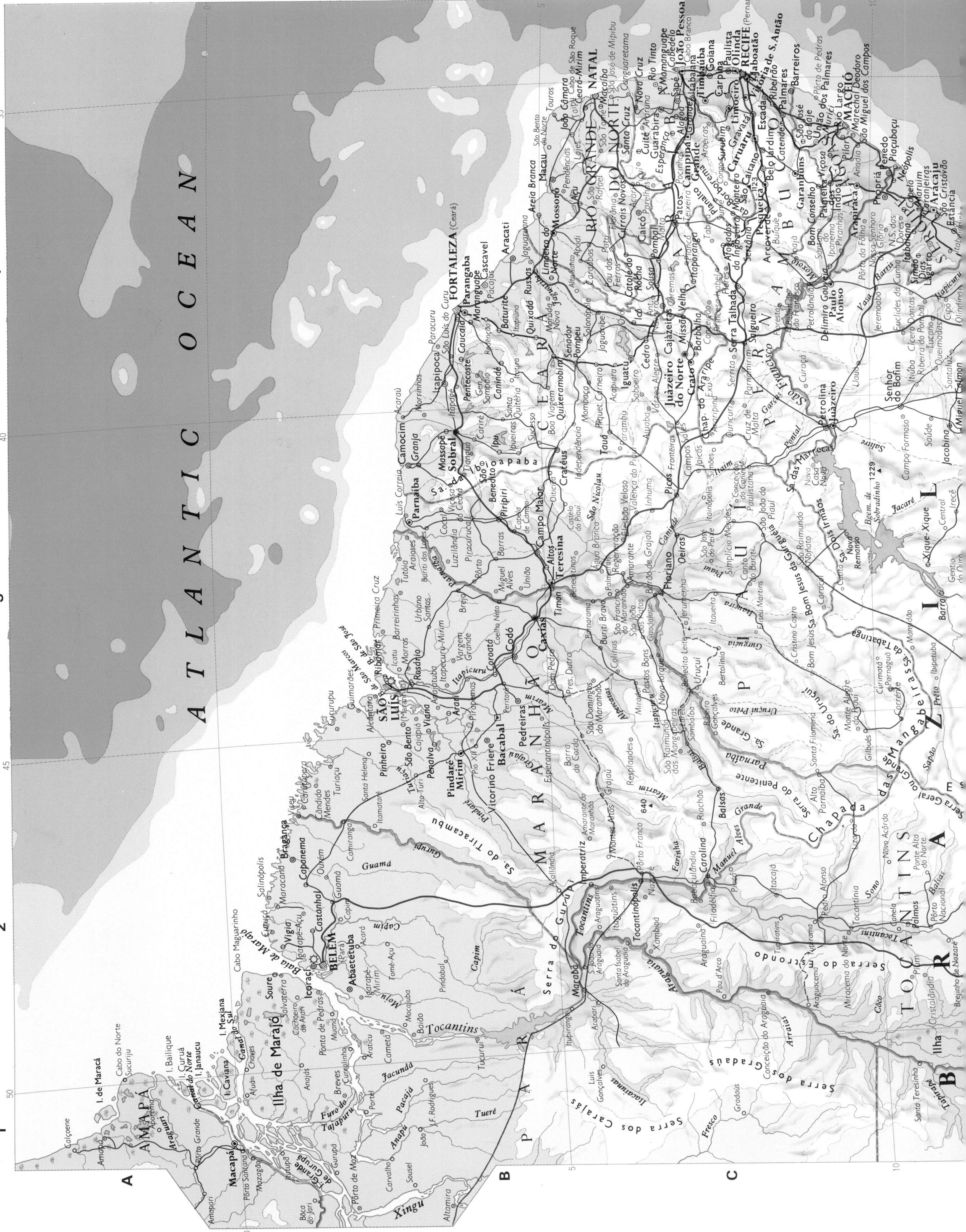

PARÁ

FORTALEZA (Ceará)
Parangaba
Maranguape
Cascavel
Aracati

CEARÁ

Camocim
Granja
Sobral
Massapê
Parnaíba
Crateús
Quixeramobim
Senador
Pompeu

SÃO LUÍS
Bacabal
Caxias
Teresina
Timon
Codó
Pedreiras

MARANHÃO

PIAUÍ

Floriano
Oeiras
Picos
Juazeiro
do Norte
Crato

RIO GRANDE DO NORTE
NATAL
Macau
Mossoró

PARAÍBA
JOÃO PESSOA (Paraíba)
Campina Grande

PERNAMBUCO
RECIFE (Pernambuco)
Olinda
Caruaru

ALAGOAS
MACEIÓ
Penedo

SERGIPE
Aracaju
Estância

BAHIA

São Francisco
Petrolina
Juazeiro
Senhor do Bonfim

TOCANTINS

Chapada das Mangabeiras
Serra dos Carajás
Serra do Tiracambu
Serra do Gurupi

Xingu

1 : 7 100 000

50   0   50   100   150   200 miles
50   0   100   200   300 km

ATLANTIC OCEAN

SALVADOR (Bahia)

ESPIRITO SANTO

Tropic of Capricorn

RIO DE JANEIRO

NITERÓI

SÃO PAULO

CURITIBA

BRASÍLIA

GOIÁS

GOIÂNIA

PARANÁ

MINAS GERAIS

BELO HORIZONTE

CAMPINAS

SANTO ANDRÉ

SANTOS

CAMPOS

West from Greenwich

Projection : Lambert's Equivalent Azimuthal 50

COPYRIGHT. GEORGE PHILIP & SON LTD

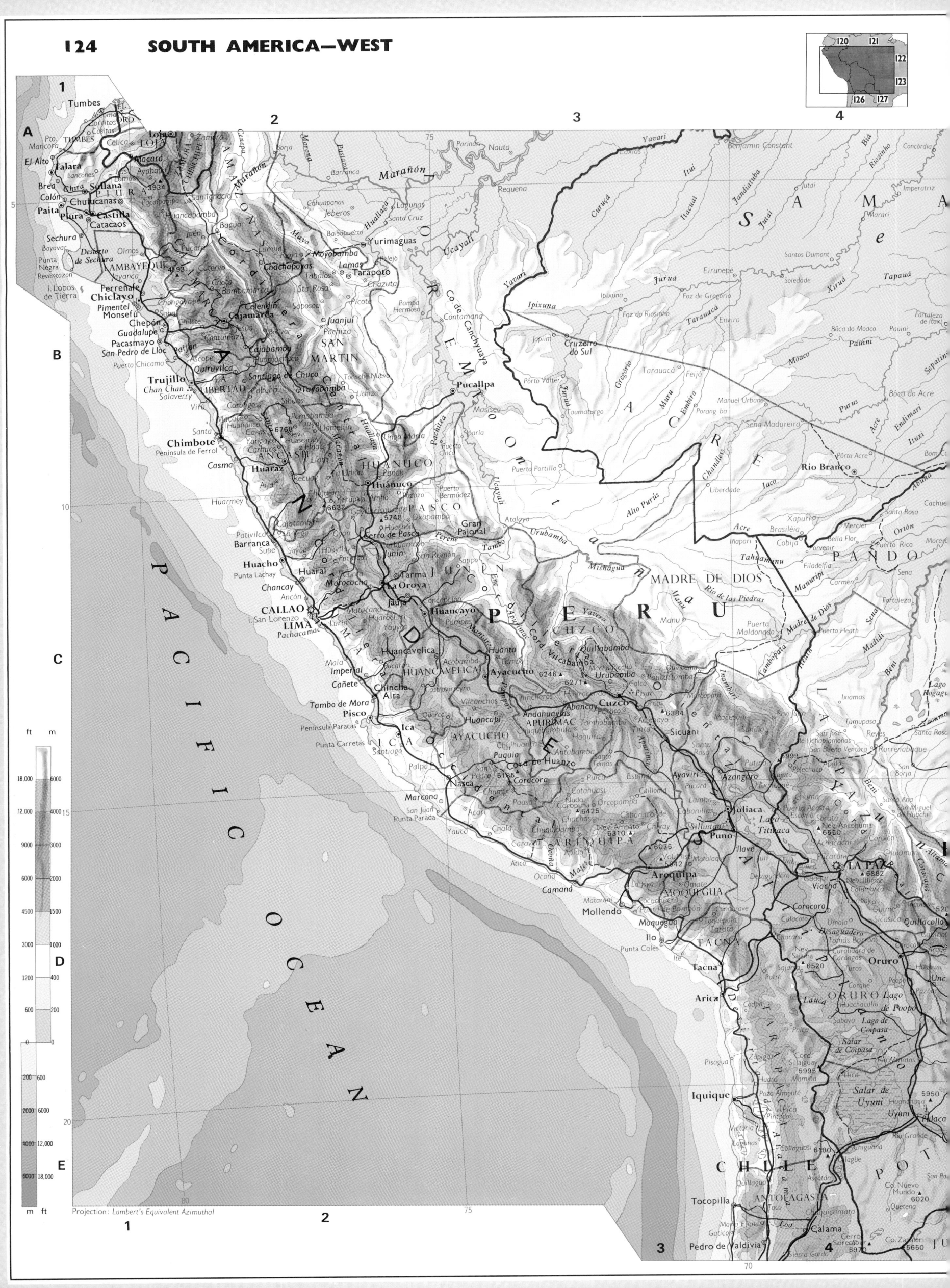

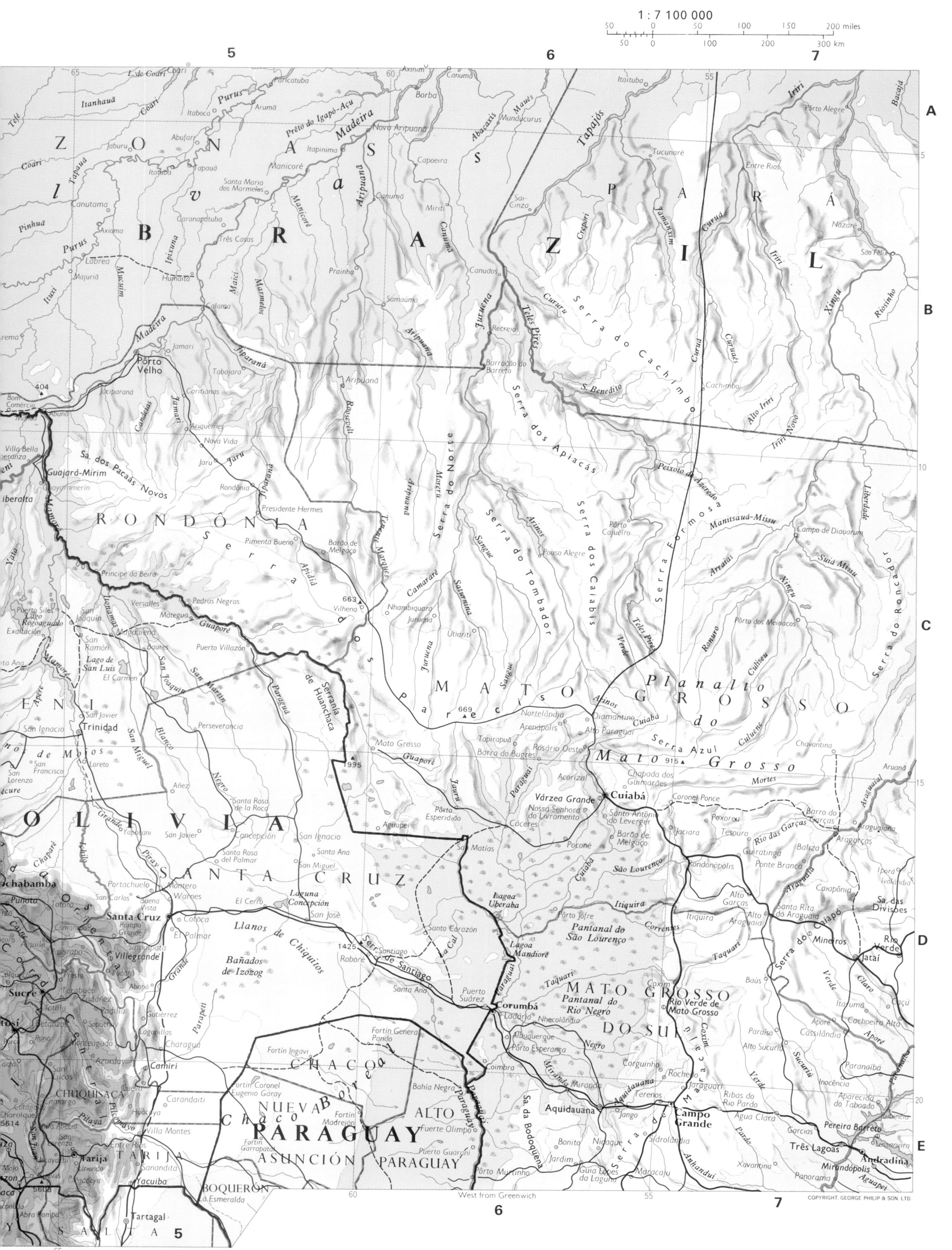

1 : 7 100 000

50   0   50   100   150   200 miles

50   0   50   100   200   300 km

5   6   7

A

5

B

10

C

15

D

E

West from Greenwich

6   7

COPYRIGHT. GEORGE PHILIP & SON. LTD.

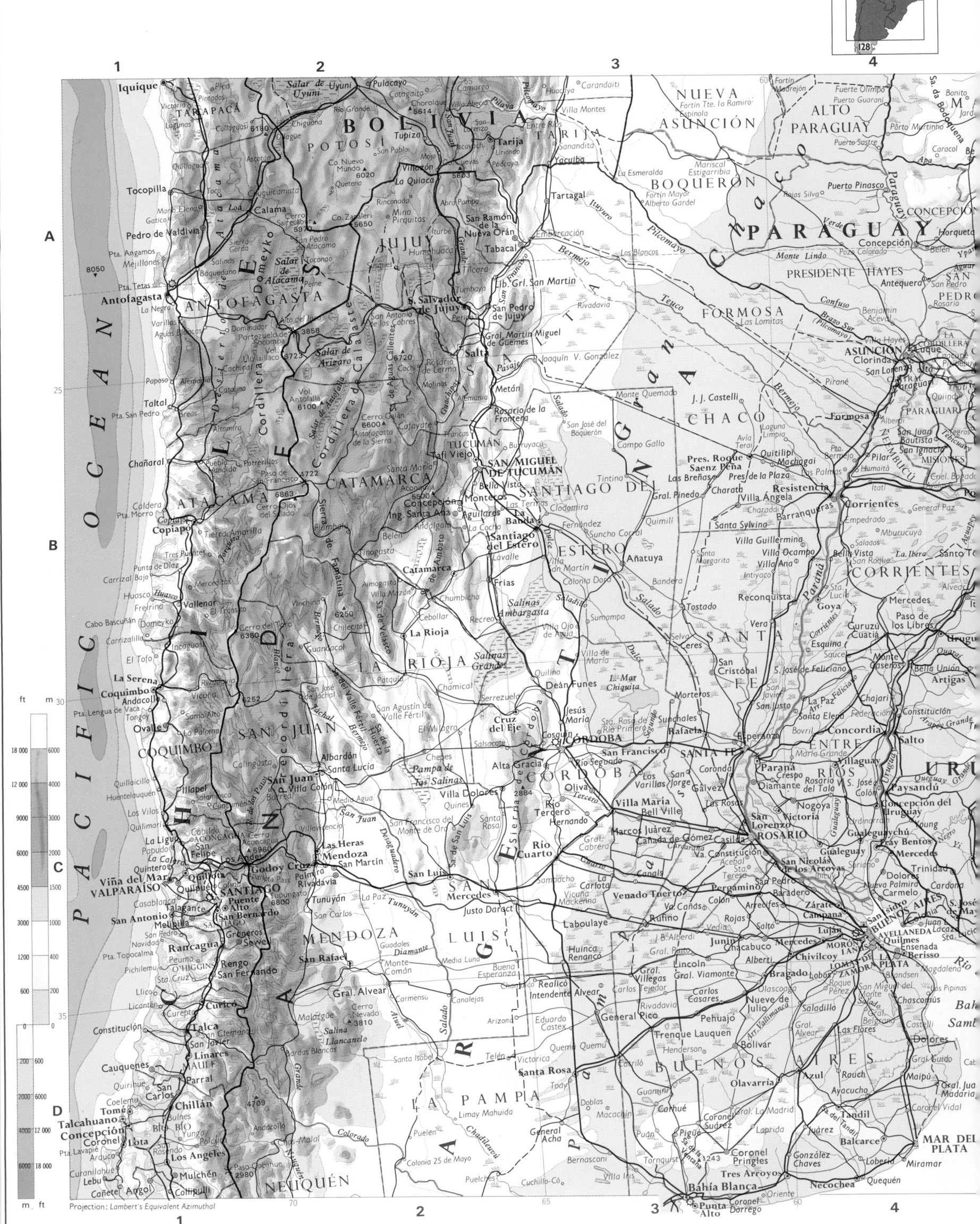

Projection: Lambert's Equivalent Azimuthal

1 : 7 100 000

50   0   50   100   150   200 miles
50   0   100   200   300 km

ATLANTIC

OCEAN

BRAZIL

RIO GRANDE
DO SUL

SANTA
CATARINA

PARANÁ

SÃO PAULO

RIO DE JANEIRO

BELO HORIZONTE

Tropic of Capricorn

West from Greenwich

COPYRIGHT. GEORGE PHILIP & SON LTD

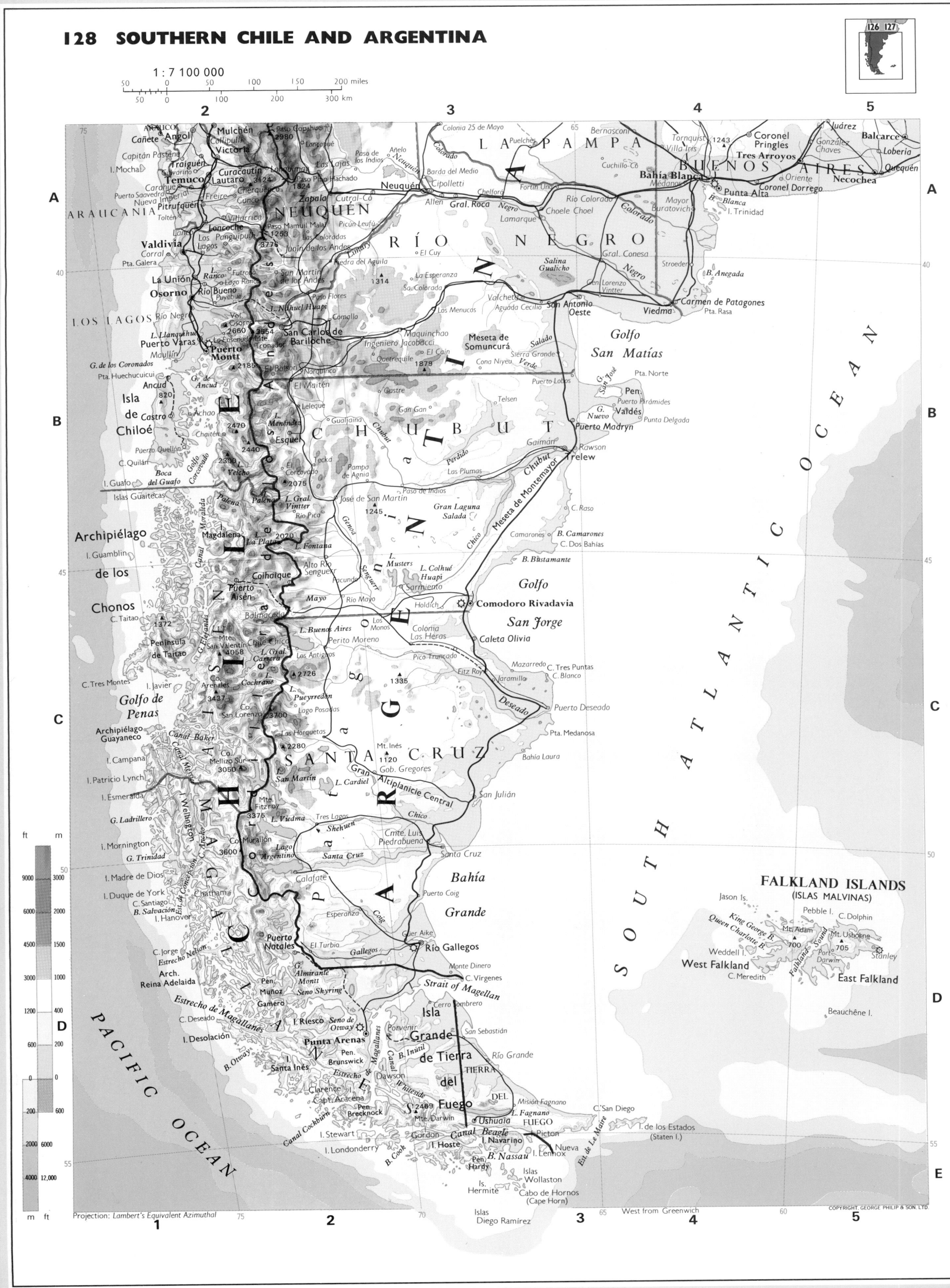

1 : 7 100 000

PACIFIC OCEAN

SOUTH ATLANTIC OCEAN

LA PAMPA

RÍO NEGRO

NEUQUÉN

ARAUCANIA

LOS LAGOS

CHUBUT

SANTA CRUZ

PATAGONIA

MAGALLANES

TIERRA DEL FUEGO

FALKLAND ISLANDS
(ISLAS MALVINAS)

West Falkland

East Falkland

BUENOS AIRES

Golfo
San Matías

Golfo
San Jorge

Bahía
Grande

Strait of Magellan

Cabo de Hornos
(Cape Horn)

Projection: Lambert's Equivalent Azimuthal

COPYRIGHT. GEORGE PHILIP & SON. LTD.

West from Greenwich

INDEX

The index contains the names of all the principal places and features shown on the World Maps. Each name is followed by an additional entry in italics giving the country or region within which it is located. The alphabetical order of names composed of two or more words is governed primarily by the first word and then by the second. This is an example of the rule:

Mīr Kūh, *Iran* **65** **E8**
Mīr Shahdād, *Iran* **65** **E8**
Miraj, *India* **60** **L9**
Miram Shah, *Pakistan* **62** **C4**
Miramar, *Mozam.* **85** **C6**

Physical features composed of a proper name (Erie) and a description (Lake) are positioned alphabetically by the proper name. The description is positioned after the proper name and is usually abbreviated:

Erie, L., *N. Amer.* **106** **D3**

Where a description forms part of a settlement or administrative name however, it is always written in full and put in its true alphabetic position:

Mount Morris, *U.S.A.* **106** **D7**

Names beginning with M' and Mc are indexed as if they were spelt Mac. Names beginning St. are alphabetised under Saint, but Sankt, Sint, Sant', Santa and San are all spelt in full and are alphabetised accordingly. If the same place name occurs two or more times in the index and all are in the same country, each is followed by the name of the administrative subdivision in which it is located. The names are placed in the alphabetical order of the subdivisions. For example:

Jackson, *Ky., U.S.A.* **104** **G4**
Jackson, *Mich., U.S.A.* **104** **D3**
Jackson, *Minn., U.S.A.* **108** **D7**

The number in bold type which follows each name in the index refers to the number of the map page where that feature or place will be found. This is usually the largest scale at which the place or feature appears. The letter and figure which are in bold type immediately after the page number give the grid square on the map page, within which the feature is situated. The letter represents the latitude and the figure the longitude.

In some cases the feature itself may fall within the specified square, while the name is outside. This is usually the case only with features which are larger than a grid square. Rivers are indexed to their mouths or confluences, and carry the symbol ➝ after their names. A solid square ■ follows the name of a country while, an open square □ refers to a first order administrative area.

ABBREVIATIONS USED IN THE INDEX

A.C.T. — Australian Capital Territory
Afghan. — Afghanistan
Ala. — Alabama
Alta. — Alberta
Amer. — America(n)
Arch. — Archipelago
Ariz. — Arizona
Ark. — Arkansas
Atl. Oc. — Atlantic Ocean
B. — Baie, Bahía, Bay, Bucht, Bugt
B.C. — British Columbia
Bangla. — Bangladesh
Barr. — Barrage
Bos.-H. — Bosnia-Herzegovina
C. — Cabo, Cap, Cape, Coast
C.A.R. — Central African Republic
C. Prov. — Cape Province
Calif. — California
Cent. — Central
Chan. — Channel
Colo. — Colorado
Conn. — Connecticut
Cord. — Cordillera
Cr. — Creek
Czech. — Czech Republic
D.C. — District of Columbia
Del. — Delaware
Dep. — Dependency
Des. — Desert
Dist. — District
Dj. — Djebel
Domin. — Dominica
Dom. Rep. — Dominican Republic
E. — East
El Salv. — El Salvador

Eq. Guin. — Equatorial Guinea
Fla. — Florida
Falk. Is. — Falkland Is.
G. — Golfe, Golfo, Gulf, Guba, Gebel
Ga. — Georgia
Gt. — Great, Greater
Guinea-Biss. — Guinea-Bissau
H.K. — Hong Kong
H.P. — Himachal Pradesh
Hants. — Hampshire
Harb. — Harbor, Harbour
Hd. — Head
Hts. — Heights
I.(s). — Île, Ilha, Insel, Isla, Island, Isle
Ill. — Illinois
Ind. — Indiana
Ind. Oc. — Indian Ocean
Ivory C. — Ivory Coast
J. — Jabal, Jebel, Jazira
Junc. — Junction
K. — Kap, Kapp
Kans. — Kansas
Kep. — Kepulauan
Ky. — Kentucky
L. — Lac, Lacul, Lago, Lagoa, Lake, Limni, Loch, Lough
La. — Louisiana
Liech. — Liechtenstein
Lux. — Luxembourg
Mad. P. — Madhya Pradesh
Madag. — Madagascar
Man. — Manitoba
Mass. — Massachusetts
Md. — Maryland

Me. — Maine
Medit. S. — Mediterranean Sea
Mich. — Michigan
Minn. — Minnesota
Miss. — Mississippi
Mo. — Missouri
Mont. — Montana
Moza. — Mozambique
Mt.(e). — Mont, Monte, Monti, Montaña, Mountain
N. — Nord, Norte, North, Northern, Nouveau
N.B. — New Brunswick
N.C. — North Carolina
N. Cal. — New Caledonia
N. Dak. — North Dakota
N.H. — New Hampshire
N.I. — North Island
N.J. — New Jersey
N. Mex. — New Mexico
N.S. — Nova Scotia
N.S.W. — New South Wales
N.W.T. — North West Territory
N.Y. — New York
N.Z. — New Zealand
Nebr. — Nebraska
Neths. — Netherlands
Nev. — Nevada
Nfld. — Newfoundland
Nic. — Nicaragua
O. — Oued, Ouadi
Occ. — Occidentale
O.F.S. — Orange Free State
Okla. — Oklahoma
Ont. — Ontario
Or. — Orientale

Oreg. — Oregon
Os. — Ostrov
Oz. — Ozero
P. — Pass, Passo, Pasul, Pulau
P.E.I. — Prince Edward Island
Pa. — Pennsylvania
Pac. Oc. — Pacific Ocean
Papua N.G. — Papua New Guinea
Pass. — Passage
Pen. — Peninsula, Péninsule
Phil. — Philippines
Pk. — Park, Peak
Plat. — Plateau
P-ov. — Poluostrov
Prov. — Province, Provincial
Pt. — Point
Pta. — Ponta, Punta
Pte. — Pointe
Qué. — Québec
Queens. — Queensland
R. — Rio, River
R.I. — Rhode Island
Ra.(s). — Range(s)
Raj. — Rajasthan
Reg. — Region
Rep. — Republic
Res. — Reserve, Reservoir
S. — San, South, Sea
Si. Arabia — Saudi Arabia
S.C. — South Carolina
S. Dak. — South Dakota
S.I. — South Island
S. Leone — Sierra Leone
Sa. — Serra, Sierra
Sask. — Saskatchewan
Scot. — Scotland

Sd. — Sound
Sev. — Severnaya
Sib. — Siberia
Sprs. — Springs
St. — Saint, Sankt, Sint
Sta. — Santa, Station
Ste. — Sainte
Sto. — Santo
Str. — Strait, Stretto
Switz. — Switzerland
Tas. — Tasmania
Tenn. — Tennessee
Tex. — Texas
Tg. — Tanjung
Trin. & Tob. — Trinidad & Tobago
U.A.E. — United Arab Emirates
U.K. — United Kingdom
U.S.A. — United States of America
Ut. P. — Uttar Pradesh
Va. — Virginia
Vdkhr. — Vodokhranilishche
Vf. — Vîrful
Vic. — Victoria
Vol. — Volcano
Vt. — Vermont
W. — Wadi, West
W. Va. — West Virginia
Wash. — Washington
Wis. — Wisconsin
Wlkp. — Wielkopolski
Wyo. — Wyoming
Yorks. — Yorkshire
Yug. — Yugoslavia

A Coruña

A

A Coruña = La Coruña, Spain 30 B2
Aachen, Germany 18 E2
Aadorf, Switz. 23 B7
Aalborg = Ålborg, Denmark 11 G3
Aalen, Germany 19 G6
A'âli en Nîl □, Sudan 77 F3
Aalsmeer, Neths. 16 D5
Aalst, Belgium 17 G4
Aalst, Neths. 17 F6
Aalten, Neths. 16 E9
Aalter, Belgium 17 F2
Aarau, Switz. 22 B6
Aarberg, Switz. 22 B4
Aardenburg, Belgium 17 F2
Aare →, Switz. 22 A6
Aargau □, Switz. 22 B6
Aarhus = Århus, Denmark 11 H4
Aarle, Neths. 17 E7
Aarschot, Belgium 17 G5
Aarsele, Belgium 17 G2
Aartrijke, Belgium 17 F2
Aarwangen, Switz. 22 B5
Aba, China 52 A3
Aba, Nigeria 79 D6
Aba, Zaïre 82 B3
Âbâ, Jazîrat, Sudan 77 E3
Abacaxis →, Brazil 121 D6
Ābādān, Iran 65 D6
Abade, Ethiopia 77 F4
Ābādeh, Iran 65 D7
Abadin, Spain 30 B3
Abadla, Algeria 75 B4
Abaeté, Brazil 123 E2
Abaeté →, Brazil 123 E2
Abaetetuba, Brazil 122 B2
Abagnar Qi, China 50 C9
Abai, Paraguay 127 B4
Abak, Nigeria 79 E6
Abakaliki, Nigeria 79 D6
Abakan, Russia 45 D10
Abalemma, Niger 79 B6
Abana, Turkey 66 C6
Abancay, Peru 124 C3
Abanilla, Spain 29 G3
Abano Terme, Italy 33 C8
Abapó, Bolivia 125 D5
Abarán, Spain 29 G3
Abariringa, Kiribati 92 H10
Abarqū, Iran 65 D7
Abashiri, Japan 48 B12
Abashiri-Wan, Japan 48 B12
Abaújszántó, Hungary 21 G11
Abay, Kazakhstan 44 E8
Abaya, L., Ethiopia 77 F4
Abaza, Russia 44 D10
Abbadia San Salvatore, Italy 33 F8
'Abbāsābād, Iran 65 C8
Abbay = Nîl el Azraq →, Sudan 77 D3
Abbaye, Pt., U.S.A. 104 B1
Abbé, L., Ethiopia 77 E5
Abbeville, France 25 B8
Abbeville, La., U.S.A. 109 K8
Abbeville, S.C., U.S.A. 105 H4
Abbiategrasso, Italy 32 C5
Abbieglassie, Australia 91 D4
Abbot Ice Shelf, Antarctica 5 D16
Abbotsford, Canada 100 D4
Abbotsford, U.S.A. 108 C9
Abbottabad, Pakistan 62 B5
Abcoude, Neths. 16 D5
Abd al Kūrī, Ind. Oc. 68 E5
Ābdar, Iran 65 D7
'Abdolābād, Iran 65 C8
Abéché, Chad 73 F9
Abejar, Spain 28 D2
Abekr, Sudan 77 E2
Abêlessa, Algeria 75 D5
Abengourou, Ivory C. 78 D4
Åbenrå, Denmark 11 J3
Abensberg, Germany 19 G7
Abeokuta, Nigeria 79 D5
Aber, Uganda 82 B3
Aberaeron, U.K. 13 E3
Aberayron = Aberaeron, U.K. 13 E3
Abercorn = Mbala, Zambia 83 D3
Abercorn, Australia 91 D5
Aberdare, U.K. 13 F4
Aberdare Ra., Kenya 82 C4
Aberdeen, Australia 91 E5
Aberdeen, Canada 101 C7
Aberdeen, S. Africa 84 E3
Aberdeen, U.K. 14 D6
Aberdeen, Ala., U.S.A. 105 J1
Aberdeen, Idaho, U.S.A. 110 E7
Aberdeen, S. Dak., U.S.A. 108 C5
Aberdeen, Wash., U.S.A. 112 D3
Aberdovey = Aberdyfi, U.K. 13 E3
Aberdyfi, U.K. 13 E3
Aberfeldy, U.K. 14 E5
Abergaria-a-Velha, Portugal 30 E2
Abergavenny, U.K. 13 F4
Abernathy, U.S.A. 109 J4
Abert, L., U.S.A. 110 E3
Aberystwyth, U.K. 13 E3
Abha, Si. Arabia 76 D5
Abhar, Iran 65 B6
Abhayapuri, India 63 F14
Abia □, Nigeria 79 D6
Abidiya, Sudan 76 D3
Abidjan, Ivory C. 78 D4
Abilene, Kans., U.S.A. 108 F6
Abilene, Tex., U.S.A. 109 J5
Abingdon, U.K. 13 F6
Abingdon, Ill., U.S.A. 108 E9
Abingdon, Va., U.S.A. 105 G5
Abington Reef, Australia 90 B4
Abitau →, Canada 101 B7
Abitau L., Canada 101 A7
Abitibi L., Canada 98 C4
Abiy Adi, Ethiopia 77 E4
Abkhaz Republic □, Georgia 43 E9
Abkit, Russia 45 C16
Abminga, Australia 91 D1
Abnûb, Egypt 76 B3
Abocho, Nigeria 79 D6
Abohar, India 62 D6
Aboisso, Ivory C. 78 D4
Abomey, Benin 79 D5
Abondance, France 27 B10
Abong-Mbang, Cameroon 80 D2
Abonnema, Nigeria 79 E6
Abony, Hungary 21 H10
Aboso, Ghana 78 D4
Abou-Deïa, Chad 73 F8
Aboyne, U.K. 14 D6
Abra Pampa, Argentina 126 A2
Abrantes, Portugal 31 F2
Abraveses, Portugal 30 E3
Abreojos, Pta., Mexico 114 B2
Abreschviller, France 25 D14
Abri, Esh Shamâliya, Sudan 76 C3
Abri, Janub Kordofân, Sudan 77 E3
Abrolhos, Banka, Brazil 123 E4
Abruzzi □, Italy 33 F10
Absaroka Range, U.S.A. 110 D9
Abū al Khaşīb, Iraq 65 D6
Abū 'Alī, Si. Arabia 65 E6
Abū 'Alī →, Lebanon 69 A4
Abu 'Arīsh, Si. Arabia 68 D3
Abû Ballas, Egypt 76 C2
Abu Deleiq, Sudan 77 D3
Abu Dhabi = Abū Ẓāby, U.A.E. 65 E7
Abû Dis, Sudan 76 D3
Abû Dom, Sudan 77 D3
Abū Du'ān, Syria 64 B3
Abu el Gairi, W. →, Egypt 69 F2
Abû Gabra, Sudan 77 E2
Abu Ga'da, W. →, Egypt 69 F1
Abû Gubeiha, Sudan 77 E3
Abu Habl, Khawr →, Sudan 77 E3
Abū Ḩadrīyah, Si. Arabia 65 E6
Abu Hamed, Sudan 76 D3
Abu Haraz, An Nîl el Azraq, Sudan 77 E3
Abû Haraz, Esh Shamâliya, Sudan 76 D3
Abû Higar, Sudan 77 E3
Abū Kamāl, Syria 64 C4
Abū Madd, Ra's, Si. Arabia 64 E3
Abu Matariq, Sudan 77 E2
Abu Qir, Egypt 76 H7
Abu Qireiya, Egypt 76 C4
Abu Qurqâs, Egypt 76 J7
Abu Şafāt, W. →, Jordan 69 E5
Abû Simbel, Egypt 76 C3
Abū Şukhayr, Iraq 64 D5
Abu Tig, Egypt 76 B3
Abû Tiga, Sudan 77 E3
Abû Zabad, Sudan 77 E2
Abū Ẓāby, U.A.E. 65 E7
Abū Zeydābād, Iran 65 C6
Abufari, Brazil 125 B5
Abuja, Nigeria 79 D6
Abukuma-Gawa →, Japan 48 E10
Abukuma-Sammyaku, Japan 48 F10
Abunã, Brazil 125 B4
Abunã →, Brazil 125 B4
Aburo, Zaïre 82 B3
Abut Hd., N.Z. 87 K3
Abwong, Sudan 77 F3
Åby, Sweden 11 F10
Aby, Lagune, Ivory C. 78 D4
Acacías, Colombia 120 C3
Acajutla, El Salv. 116 D2
Açailândia, Brazil 122 C2
Acámbaro, Mexico 114 C4
Acaponeta, Mexico 114 C3
Acapulco, Mexico 115 D5
Acarai, Serra, Brazil 121 C6
Acaraú, Brazil 122 B3
Acari, Brazil 122 C4
Acarí, Peru 124 D3
Acarigua, Venezuela 120 B4
Acatlán, Mexico 115 D5
Acayucan, Mexico 115 D6
Accéglio, Italy 32 D3
Accomac, U.S.A. 104 G8
Accous, France 26 E3
Accra, Ghana 79 D4
Accrington, U.K. 12 D5
Acebal, Argentina 126 C3
Aceh □, Indonesia 56 D1
Acerenza, Italy 35 B8
Acerra, Italy 35 B7
Aceuchal, Spain 31 G4
Achacachi, Bolivia 124 D4
Achaguas, Venezuela 120 B4
Achalpur, India 60 J10
Achao, Chile 128 B2
Achel, Belgium 17 F6
Acheng, China 51 B14
Achenkirch, Austria 19 H7
Achensee, Austria 19 H7
Acher, India 62 H5
Achern, Germany 19 G4
Achill, Ireland 15 C2
Achill Hd., Ireland 15 C1
Achill I., Ireland 15 C1
Achill Sd., Ireland 15 C2
Achim, Germany 18 B5
Achinsk, Russia 45 D10
Achol, Sudan 77 F3
Acıgöl, Turkey 66 E3
Acireale, Italy 35 E8
Ackerman, U.S.A. 109 J10
Acklins I., Bahamas 117 B5
Acme, Canada 100 C6
Acobamba, Peru 124 C3
Acomayo, Peru 124 C3
Aconcagua □, Chile 126 C1
Aconcagua, Cerro, Argentina 126 C2
Aconquija, Mt., Argentina 126 B2
Acopiara, Brazil 122 C4
Açores, Is. dos = Azores, Atl. Oc. 2 C8
Acorizal, Brazil 125 D6
Acquapendente, Italy 33 F8
Acquasanta, Italy 33 F10
Acquaviva delle Fonti, Italy 35 B9
Acqui, Italy 32 D5
Acraman, L., Australia 91 E2
Acre = 'Akko, Israel 69 C4
Acre □, Brazil 124 B3
Acre →, Brazil 124 B4
Acri, Italy 35 C9
Acs, Hungary 21 H8
Acton, Canada 106 C4
Açu, Brazil 122 C4
Ad Dammām, Si. Arabia 65 E6
Ad Dawhah, Qatar 65 E6
Ad Dawr, Iraq 64 C4
Ad Dir'īyah, Si. Arabia 64 E5
Ad Dīwānīyah, Iraq 64 D5
Ad Dujayl, Iraq 64 C5
Ad Durūz, J., Jordan 69 C5
Ada, Ghana 79 D5
Ada, Serbia 21 K10
Ada, Minn., U.S.A. 108 B6
Ada, Okla., U.S.A. 109 H6
Adaja →, Spain 30 D6
Ådalslinden, Sweden 10 A10
Adam, Mt., Falk. Is. 128 D4
Adamantina, Brazil 123 F1
Adamaoua, Massif de l', Cameroon 79 D7
Adamawa □, Nigeria 79 D7
Adamawa Highlands = Adamaoua, Massif de l', Cameroon 79 D7
Adamello, Mt., Italy 32 B7
Adami Tulu, Ethiopia 77 F4
Adaminaby, Australia 91 F4
Adams, Mass., U.S.A. 107 D11
Adams, N.Y., U.S.A. 107 C8
Adams, Wis., U.S.A. 108 D10
Adam's Bridge, Sri Lanka 60 Q11
Adams L., Canada 100 C5
Adams Mt., U.S.A. 112 D5
Adam's Peak, Sri Lanka 60 R12
Adamuz, Spain 31 G6
Adana, Turkey 66 E6
Adana □, Turkey 66 E6
Adanero, Spain 30 E6
Adapazarı, Turkey 66 C4
Adarama, Sudan 77 D3
Adare, C., Antarctica 5 D11
Adaut, Indonesia 57 F8
Adavale, Australia 91 D3
Adda →, Italy 32 C6
Addis Ababa = Addis Abeba, Ethiopia 77 F4
Addis Abeba, Ethiopia 77 F4
Addis Alem, Ethiopia 77 F4
Addison, U.S.A. 106 D7
Addo, S. Africa 84 E4
Adebour, Niger 79 C7
Ādeh, Iran 64 B5
Adel, U.S.A. 105 K4
Adelaide, Australia 91 E2
Adelaide, Bahamas 116 A4
Adelaide, S. Africa 84 E4
Adelaide I., Antarctica 5 C17
Adelaide Pen., Canada 96 B10
Adelaide River, Australia 88 B5
Adelanto, U.S.A. 113 L9
Adelboden, Switz. 22 D5
Adele I., Australia 88 C3
Adélie, Terre, Antarctica 5 C10
Adélie Land = Adélie, Terre, Antarctica 5 C10
Ademuz, Spain 28 E3
Aden = Al 'Adan, Yemen 68 E4
Aden, G. of, Asia 68 E4
Adendorp, S. Africa 84 E3
Adh Dhayd, U.A.E. 65 E7
Adhoi, India 62 H4
Adi, Indonesia 57 E8
Adi Daro, Ethiopia 77 E4
Adi Keyih, Eritrea 77 E4
Adi Kwala, Eritrea 77 E4
Adi Ugri, Eritrea 77 E4
Adieu, C., Australia 89 F5
Adieu Pt., Australia 88 C3
Adigala, Ethiopia 77 E5
Adige →, Italy 33 C9
Adigrat, Ethiopia 77 E4
Adilabad, India 60 K11
Adin, U.S.A. 110 F3
Adin Khel, Afghan. 60 C6
Adinkerke, Belgium 17 F1
Adirondack Mts., U.S.A. 107 C10
Adıyaman, Turkey 67 E8
Adiyaman □, Turkey 67 E8
Adjim, Tunisia 75 B7
Adjohon, Benin 79 D5
Adjud, Romania 38 C10
Adjumani, Uganda 82 B3
Adlavik Is., Canada 99 B8
Adler, Russia 43 E8
Adliswil, Switz. 23 B7
Admer, Algeria 75 D6
Admer, Erg d', Algeria 75 D6
Admiralty G., Australia 88 B4
Admiralty I., U.S.A. 96 C6
Admiralty Inlet, U.S.A. 110 C2
Admiralty Is., Papua N. G. 92 H6
Ado, Nigeria 79 D5
Ado Ekiti, Nigeria 79 D6
Adok, Sudan 77 F3
Adola, Ethiopia 77 E5
Adonara, Indonesia 57 F6
Adoni, India 60 M10
Adony, Hungary 21 H8
Adour →, France 26 E2
Adra, India 63 H12
Adra, Spain 29 J1
Adrano, Italy 35 E7
Adrar, Algeria 75 C4
Adré, Chad 73 F9
Adrī, Libya 73 C7
Ádria, Italy 33 C9
Adrian, Mich., U.S.A. 104 E3
Adrian, Tex., U.S.A. 109 H3
Adriatic Sea, Europe 6 G9
Adua, Indonesia 57 E7
Adula, Switz. 23 D8
Adwa, Ethiopia 77 E4
Adzhar Republic □, Georgia 43 F10
Adzopé, Ivory C. 78 D4
Ægean Sea, Europe 39 L8
Æolian Is. = Eólie, Is., Italy 35 D7
Aerhtai Shan, Mongolia 54 B4
Ærø, Denmark 11 K4
Ærøskøbing, Denmark 11 K4
Aesch, Switz. 22 B5
'Afak, Iraq 64 C5
Afándou, Greece 37 C10
Afarag, Erg, Algeria 75 D5
Afars & Issas, Terr. of = Djibouti ■, Africa 68 E3
Affreville = Khemis Miliana, Algeria 75 A5
Afghanistan ■, Asia 60 C4
Afgoi, Somali Rep. 68 G3
Afikpo, Nigeria 79 D6
Aflou, Algeria 75 B5
Afogados da Ingàzeira, Brazil 122 C4
Afognak I., U.S.A. 96 C4
Afragola, Italy 35 B7
Afrera, Ethiopia 77 E5
Africa 70 E6
'Afrīn, Syria 64 B3
Afşin, Turkey 66 D7
Afton, U.S.A. 107 D9
Aftout, Algeria 74 C4
Afuá, Brazil 121 D7
Afula, Israel 69 C4
Afyonkarahisar, Turkey 66 D4
Afyonkarahisar □, Turkey 66 D4
Aga, Egypt 76 H7
Agadès = Agadez, Niger 79 B6
Agadez, Niger 79 B6
Agadir, Morocco 74 B3
Agaete, Canary Is. 36 F4
Agailás, Mauritania 74 D2
Agapa, Russia 45 B9
Agar, India 62 H7
Agaro, Ethiopia 77 F4
Agartala, India 61 H17
Agassiz, Canada 100 D4
Agats, Indonesia 57 F9
Agbélouvé, Togo 79 D5
Agboville, Ivory C. 78 D4
Agdam, Azerbaijan 43 G12
Agdash, Azerbaijan 43 F12
Agde, France 26 E7
Agde, C. d', France 26 E7
Agdz, Morocco 74 B3
Agdzhabedi, Azerbaijan 43 F12
Agen, France 26 D4
Agersø, Denmark 11 J5
Ageyevo, Russia 41 D10
Agger, Denmark 11 H2
Ággius, Italy 34 B2
Āgh Kand, Iran 65 B6
Aghoueyyît, Mauritania 74 D1
Aginskoye, Russia 45 D12
Agira, Italy 35 E7
Ağlasun, Turkey 66 E4
Agly →, France 26 F7
Agnibilékrou, Ivory C. 78 D4
Agnita, Romania 38 D7
Agnone, Italy 35 A7
Agofie, Ghana 79 D5
Agogna →, Italy 32 C5
Agogo, Sudan 77 F2
Agon, France 24 C5
Agön, Sweden 10 C11
Agordo, Italy 33 B9
Agout →, France 26 E5
Agra, India 62 F7
Agramunt, Spain 28 D6
Agreda, Spain 28 D3
Ağri, Turkey 67 D10
Ağri □, Turkey 67 D10
Agri →, Italy 35 B9
Ağrı Dağı, Turkey 67 D11
Ağrı Karakose, Turkey 67 D10
Agrigento, Italy 34 E6
Agrinion, Greece 39 L4
Agrópoli, Italy 35 B7
Água Branca, Brazil 122 C3
Agua Caliente, Baja Calif. N., Mexico 113 N10
Agua Caliente, Sinaloa, Mexico 114 B3
Agua Caliente Springs, U.S.A. 113 N10
Água Clara, Brazil 125 E7
Agua Hechicero, Mexico 113 N10
Agua Preta →, Brazil 121 D5
Agua Prieta, Mexico 114 A3
Aguachica, Colombia 120 B3
Aguada Cecilio, Argentina 128 B3
Aguadas, Colombia 120 B2
Aguadilla, Puerto Rico 117 C6
Aguadulce, Panama 116 E3
Aguanga, U.S.A. 113 M10
Aguanish, Canada 99 B7
Aguanus →, Canada 99 B7
Aguapeí, Brazil 125 D6
Aguapeí →, Brazil 123 F1
Aguapey →, Argentina 126 B4
Aguaray Guazú →, Paraguay 126 A4
Aguarico →, Ecuador 120 D2
Aguas →, Spain 28 D4
Aguas Blancas, Chile 126 A2
Aguas Calientes, Sierra de, Argentina 126 B2
Águas Formosas, Brazil 123 E3
Aguascalientes, Mexico 114 C4
Aguascalientes □, Mexico 114 C4
Agudo, Spain 31 G6
Águeda, Portugal 30 E2
Agueda →, Spain 30 D4
Aguié, Niger 79 C6
Aguilafuente, Spain 30 D6
Aguilar, Spain 31 H6
Aguilar de Campóo, Spain 30 C6
Aguilares, Argentina 126 B2
Aguilas, Spain 29 H3
Agüimes, Canary Is. 36 G4
Aguja, C. de la, Colombia 120 A3
Agulaa, Ethiopia 77 E4
Agulhas, C., S. Africa 84 E3
Agulo, Canary Is. 36 F2
Agung, Indonesia 56 F5
Agur, Uganda 82 B3
Agusan →, Phil. 55 G6
Agustín Codazzi, Colombia 120 A3
Agvali, Russia 43 E12
Aha Mts., Botswana 84 B3
Ahaggar, Algeria 75 D6
Ahamansu, Ghana 79 D5
Ahar, Iran 64 B5
Ahaus, Germany 18 C3
Ahelledjem, Algeria 75 C6
Ahipara B., N.Z. 87 F4
Ahiri, India 60 K12
Ahlen, Germany 18 D3
Ahmad Wal, Pakistan 62 E1
Ahmadabad, India 62 H5
Aḩmadābād, Khorāsān, Iran 65 C9
Aḩmadābād, Khorāsān, Iran 65 C8
Aḩmadī, Iran 65 E8
Ahmadnagar, India 60 K9
Ahmadpur, Pakistan 62 E4
Ahmar, Ethiopia 77 F5
Ahmedabad = Ahmadabad, India 62 H5
Ahmednagar = Ahmadnagar, India 60 K9
Ahoada, Nigeria 79 D6
Ahome, Mexico 114 B3
Ahr →, Germany 18 E3
Ahram, Iran 65 D6
Ahrax Pt., Malta 37 D1
Ahrensbök, Germany 18 A6
Ahrweiler, Germany 18 E3
Āhū, Iran 65 C6
Ahuachapán, El Salv. 116 D2
Ahvāz, Iran 65 D6
Ahvenanmaa = Åland, Finland 9 F16
Aḩwar, Yemen 68 E4
Ahzar, Mali 79 B5
Aiari →, Brazil 120 C4
Aichach, Germany 19 G7
Aichi □, Japan 49 G8

Aidone, *Italy* 35 E7
Aiello Cálabro, *Italy* 35 C9
Aigle, *Switz.* 22 D3
Aignay-le-Duc, *France* .. 25 E11
Aigoual, Mt., *France* 26 D7
Aigre, *France* 26 C4
Aigua, *Uruguay* 127 C5
Aigueperse, *France* 26 B7
Aigues →, *France* 27 D8
Aigues-Mortes, *France* .. 27 E8
Aigues-Mortes, G. d',
  France 27 E8
Aiguilles, *France* 27 D10
Aiguillon, *France* 26 D4
Aigurande, *France* 26 B5
Aihui, *China* 54 A7
Aija, *Peru* 124 B2
Aikawa, *Japan* 48 E9
Aiken, *U.S.A.* 105 J5
Ailao Shan, *China* 52 F3
Aillant-sur-Tholon, *France* 25 E10
Aillik, *Canada* 99 A8
Ailly-sur-Noye, *France* .. 25 C9
Ailsa Craig, *U.K.* 14 F3
'Ailūn, *Jordan* 69 C4
Aim, *Russia* 45 D14
Aimere, *Indonesia* 57 F6
Aimogasta, *Argentina* ... 126 B2
Aimorés, *Brazil* 123 E3
Ain □, *France* 27 B9
Ain →, *France* 27 C9
Aïn Beïda, *Algeria* 75 A6
Aïn Ben Khellil, *Algeria* . 75 B4
Aïn Ben Tili, *Mauritania* . 74 C3
Aïn Beni Mathar, *Morocco* 75 B4
Aïn Benian, *Algeria* 75 A5
Ain Dalla, *Egypt* 76 B2
Ain el Mafki, *Egypt* 76 B2
Ain Girba, *Egypt* 76 B2
Aïn M'lila, *Algeria* 75 A6
Ain Qeiqab, *Egypt* 76 B1
Aïn-Sefra, *Algeria* 75 B4
Ain Sheikh Murzûk, *Egypt* 76 B2
'Ain Sudr, *Egypt* 76 J8
Aïn Tédelès, *Algeria* 75 A5
Aïn-Témouchent, *Algeria* . 75 A4
Aïn Touta, *Algeria* 75 A6
Aïn Zeitûn, *Egypt* 76 B2
Aïn Zorah, *Morocco* 75 B4
Ainabo, *Somali Rep.* 68 F4
Ainaži, *Latvia* 40 C4
Aínos Óros, *Greece* 39 L3
Ainsworth, *U.S.A.* 108 D5
Aipe, *Colombia* 120 C2
Aiquile, *Bolivia* 125 D4
Aïr, *Niger* 79 B6
Air Hitam, *Malaysia* 59 M4
Airaines, *France* 25 C8
Airão, *Brazil* 121 D5
Airdrie, *U.K.* 14 F5
Aire →, *France* 25 C11
Aire →, *U.K.* 12 D7
Aire, I. del, *Spain* 36 B11
Aire-sur-la-Lys, *France* .. 25 B9
Aire-sur-l'Adour, *France* . 26 E3
Airlie Beach, *Australia* .. 90 C4
Airolo, *Switz.* 23 C7
Airvault, *France* 24 F6
Aisch →, *Germany* 19 F7
Aisen □, *Chile* 128 C2
Aisne □, *France* 25 C10
Aisne →, *France* 25 C9
Aitana, Sierra de, *Spain* . 29 G4
Aitkin, *U.S.A.* 108 B8
Aitolikón, *Greece* 39 L4
Aiuaba, *Brazil* 122 C3
Aiud, *Romania* 38 C6
Aix-en-Provence, *France* . 27 E9
Aix-la-Chapelle = Aachen,
  Germany 18 E2
Aix-les-Bains, *France* ... 27 C9
Aixe-sur-Vienne, *France* . 26 C5
Aiyansh, *Canada* 100 B3
Áyina, *Greece* 39 M6
Aiyínion, *Greece* 39 J5
Aiyion, *Greece* 39 L5
Aizawl, *India* 61 H18
Aizenay, *France* 24 F5
Aizpute, *Latvia* 40 C2
Aizuwakamatsu, *Japan* .. 48 F9
Ajaccio, *France* 27 G12
Ajaccio, G. d', *France* .. 27 G12
Ajaju →, *Colombia* 120 C3
Ajalpan, *Mexico* 115 D5
Ajanta Ra., *India* 60 J9
Ajari Rep. = Adzhar
  Republic □, *Georgia* . 43 F10
Ajax, *Canada* 106 C5
Ajdâbiyah, *Libya* 73 B9
Ajdovščina, *Slovenia* ... 33 C10
Ajibar, *Ethiopia* 77 E4
Ajka, *Hungary* 21 H7
'Ajmān, *U.A.E.* 65 E7
Ajmer, *India* 62 F6
Ajo, *U.S.A.* 111 K7
Ajoie, *Switz.* 22 B4
Ajok, *Sudan* 77 F2
Ajuy, *Phil.* 55 F5
Ak Dağ, *Antalya, Turkey* . 66 E4
Ak Dağ, *Sivas, Turkey* .. 66 D7
Akaba, *Togo* 79 D5
Akabira, *Japan* 48 C11
Akabli, *Algeria* 75 C5
Akaki Beseka, *Ethiopia* .. 77 F4

Akala, *Sudan* 77 D4
Akamas □, *Cyprus* 37 D11
Akanthou, *Cyprus* 37 D12
Akaroa, *N.Z.* 87 K4
Akasha, *Sudan* 76 C3
Akashi, *Japan* 49 G7
Akbou, *Algeria* 75 A5
Akçaabat, *Turkey* 67 C8
Akçakoca, *Turkey* 66 C4
Akchâr, *Mauritania* 74 D2
Akdağmadeni, *Turkey* .. 66 D6
Akelamo, *Indonesia* 57 D7
Akershus fylke □, *Norway* 10 E5
Aketi, *Zaïre* 80 D4
Akhalkalaki, *Georgia* ... 43 F10
Akhaltsikhe, *Georgia* ... 43 F10
Akharnaí, *Greece* 39 L6
Akhelóös →, *Greece* 39 L4
Akhendria, *Greece* 39 Q8
Akhéron →, *Greece* 39 K3
Akhladhókambos, *Greece* . 39 M5
Akhmîm, *Egypt* 76 B3
Akhnur, *India* 63 C6
Akhtubinsk, *Russia* 43 B12
Akhty, *Russia* 43 F12
Akhtyrka, *Ukraine* 40 F9
Aki, *Japan* 49 H6
Akimiski I., *Canada* 98 B3
Akimovka, *Ukraine* 42 C6
Akita, *Japan* 48 E10
Akita □, *Japan* 48 E10
Akjoujt, *Mauritania* 78 B2
Akka, *Morocco* 74 C3
Akkeshi, *Japan* 48 C12
'Akko, *Israel* 69 C4
Akkol, *Kazakhstan* 44 E8
Akkrum, *Neths.* 16 B7
Aklampa, *Benin* 79 D5
Aklavik, *Canada* 96 B6
Akmolinsk = Tselinograd,
  Kazakhstan 44 D8
Akmonte, *Spain* 31 H4
Aknoul, *Morocco* 75 B4
Akō, *Japan* 49 G7
Ako, *Nigeria* 79 C7
Akobo →, *Ethiopia* 77 F3
Akola, *India* 60 J10
Akonolinga, *Cameroon* .. 79 E7
Akordat, *Eritrea* 77 D4
Akosombo Dam, *Ghana* . 79 D5
Akot, *Sudan* 77 F3
Akpatok I., *Canada* 97 B13
Akranes, *Iceland* 8 D3
Akreïjit, *Mauritania* 78 B3
Akrítas Venétiko, Ákra,
  Greece 39 N4
Akron, *Colo., U.S.A.* ... 108 E3
Akron, *Ohio, U.S.A.* ... 106 E3
Akrotíri, *Cyprus* 37 E11
Akrotíri, Ákra, *Greece* .. 39 J8
Akrotiri Bay, *Cyprus* ... 37 E12
Aksai Chih, *India* 63 B8
Aksaray, *Turkey* 66 D6
Aksarka, *Russia* 44 C7
Aksay, *Kazakhstan* 44 D6
Akşehir, *Turkey* 66 D4
Akşehir Gölü, *Turkey* ... 66 D4
Aksenovo Zilovskoye,
  Russia 45 D12
Akstafa, *Azerbaijan* 43 F11
Aksu, *China* 54 B3
Aksu →, *Turkey* 66 E4
Aksum, *Ethiopia* 77 E4
Aktogay, *Kazakhstan* ... 44 E8
Aktyubinsk, *Kazakhstan* . 44 D6
Aku, *Nigeria* 79 D6
Akure, *Nigeria* 79 D6
Akureyri, *Iceland* 8 D4
Akuseki-Shima, *Japan* .. 49 K4
Akusha, *Russia* 43 E12
Akwa-Ibom □, *Nigeria* . 79 E6
Akyab = Sittwe, *Burma* . 61 J18
Akyazı, *Turkey* 66 C4
Al 'Adan, *Yemen* 68 E4
Al Ahsā, *Si. Arabia* 65 E6
Al Ajfar, *Si. Arabia* 64 E4
Al Amādīyah, *Iraq* 64 B4
Al Amārah, *Iraq* 64 D5
Al 'Aqabah, *Jordan* 69 F4
Al Arak, *Syria* 64 C3
Al 'Aramah, *Si. Arabia* .. 64 E5
Al Arṭāwīyah, *Si. Arabia* . 64 E5
Al 'Āṣimah □, *Jordan* .. 69 D5
Al' Assāfiyah, *Si. Arabia* . 64 D3
Al 'Ayn, *Oman* 65 E7
Al 'Ayn, *Si. Arabia* 64 E3
Al A'zamīyah, *Iraq* 64 C5
Al 'Azīzīyah, *Iraq* 64 C5
Al 'Azīzīyah, *Libya* 75 B7
Al Bāb, *Syria* 64 B3
Al Bad', *Si. Arabia* 64 D2
Al Bādī, *Iraq* 64 C4
Al Balqā' □, *Jordan* 69 C4
Al Barkāt, *Libya* 75 D7
Al Bārūk, J., *Lebanon* .. 69 B4
Al Başrah, *Iraq* 64 D5
Al Baṭḥā, *Iraq* 64 D5
Al Batrūn, *Lebanon* 69 A4
Al Bi'r, *Si. Arabia* 64 D3
Al Bu'ayrāt, *Libya* 73 B8
Al Burayj, *Syria* 69 A5
Al Fallūjah, *Iraq* 64 C4
Al Fāw, *Iraq* 65 D6
Al Fujayrah, *U.A.E.* 65 E8

Al Ghadaf, W. →, *Jordan* 69 D5
Al Ghammās, *Iraq* 64 D5
Al Hābah, *Si. Arabia* ... 64 E5
Al Ḥadīthah, *Iraq* 64 C4
Al Ḥadīthah, *Si. Arabia* . 64 D3
Al Ḥājānah, *Syria* 69 B5
Al Ḥāmad, *Si. Arabia* .. 64 D3
Al Hamdānīyah, *Syria* .. 64 C3
Al Hamīdīyah, *Syria* ... 69 A4
Al Hammādah al Ḥamrā',
  Libya 75 C7
Al Ḥammār, *Iraq* 64 D5
Al Ḥarīr, W. →, *Syria* .. 69 C4
Al Ḥasā, W. →, *Jordan* . 69 D4
Al Ḥasakah, *Syria* 64 B4
Al Ḥawrah, *Yemen* 68 E4
Al Ḥaydān, W. →, *Jordan* 69 D4
Al Ḥayy, *Iraq* 64 C5
Al Ḥijāz, *Si. Arabia* 68 B2
Al Ḥillah, *Iraq* 64 C5
Al Ḥillah, *Si. Arabia* ... 68 C4
Al Hirmil, *Lebanon* 69 A5
Al Hoceïma, *Morocco* .. 74 A4
Al Ḥudaydah, *Yemen* .. 68 E3
Al Hufūf, *Si. Arabia* ... 65 E6
Al Ḥumaydah, *Si. Arabia* . 64 D2
Al Ḥunayy, *Si. Arabia* .. 65 E6
Al Irq, *Libya* 73 C9
Al Īsāwīyah, *Si. Arabia* .. 64 D3
Al Ittihad = Madīnat ash
  Sha'b, *Yemen* 68 E3
Al Jafr, *Jordan* 69 E5
Al Jaghbūb, *Libya* 73 C9
Al Jahrah, *Kuwait* 64 D5
Al Jalāmīd, *Si. Arabia* .. 64 D3
Al Jamalīyah, *Qatar* 65 E6
Al Janūb □, *Lebanon* .. 69 B4
Al Jawf, *Libya* 73 D9
Al Jawf, *Si. Arabia* 64 D3
Al Jazirah, *Iraq* 64 C5
Al Jazirah, *Libya* 73 C9
Al Jithāmīyah, *Si. Arabia* . 64 E4
Al Jubayl, *Si. Arabia* ... 65 E6
Al Jubaylah, *Si. Arabia* . 64 E5
Al Jubb, *Si. Arabia* 64 E4
Al Junaynah, *Sudan* 73 F9
Al Kabā'ish, *Iraq* 64 D5
Al Karak, *Jordan* 69 D4
Al Karak □, *Jordan* ... 69 D5
Al Kāzim Tyah, *Iraq* ... 64 C5
Al Khalīl, *Jordan* 69 D4
Al Khalīl □, *Jordan* 69 D4
Al Khawr, *Qatar* 65 E6
Al Khiḍr, *Iraq* 64 D5
Al Khiyām, *Lebanon* ... 69 B4
Al Kiswah, *Syria* 69 B5
Al Kufrah, *Libya* 73 D9
Al Kuhayfiyah, *Si. Arabia* . 64 E4
Al Kūt, *Iraq* 64 C5
Al Kuwayt, *Kuwait* 64 D5
Al Labwah, *Lebanon* ... 69 A5
Al Lādhiqīyah, *Syria* ... 64 C2
Al Līth, *Si. Arabia* 76 C5
Al Liwā', *Oman* 65 E8
Al Luḥayyah, *Yemen* ... 68 D3
Al Madīnah, *Iraq* 64 D5
Al Madīnah, *Si. Arabia* . 64 E3
Al-Mafraq, *Jordan* 69 C5
Al Maḥmūdīyah, *Iraq* .. 64 C5
Al Majma'ah, *Si. Arabia* . 64 E5
Al Makhruq, W. →,
  Jordan 69 D6
Al Makhūl, *Si. Arabia* .. 64 E4
Al Manāmah, *Bahrain* .. 65 E6
Al Maqwa', *Kuwait* 64 D5
Al Marj, *Libya* 73 B9
Al Maṭlā, *Kuwait* 64 D5
Al Mawjib, W. →, *Jordan* 69 D4
Al Mawṣil, *Iraq* 64 B4
Al Mayādin, *Syria* 64 C4
Al Mazār, *Jordan* 69 D4
Al Midhnab, *Si. Arabia* . 64 E5
Al Minā', *Lebanon* 69 A4
Al Miqdādīyah, *Iraq* ... 64 C5
Al Mubarraz, *Si. Arabia* . 65 E6
Al Mughayrā', *U.A.E.* .. 65 E7
Al Muḥarraq, *Bahrain* .. 65 E6
Al Mukallā, *Yemen* 68 E4
Al Mukhā, *Yemen* 68 E3
Al Musayjīd, *Si. Arabia* . 64 E3
Al Musayyib, *Iraq* 64 C5
Al Muwaylih, *Si. Arabia* . 64 E2
Al Owuho = Otukpa,
  Nigeria 79 D6
Al Qā'im, *Iraq* 64 C4
Al Qalībah, *Si. Arabia* .. 64 D3
Al Qaryatayn, *Syria* 69 A6
Al Qaṣabát, *Libya* 73 B7
Al Qaṭ'ā, *Syria* 64 C4
Al Qaṭīf, *Si. Arabia* 65 E6
Al Qaṭrānah, *Jordan* ... 69 D5
Al Qaṭrūn, *Libya* 73 D8
Al Qayṣūmah, *Si. Arabia* . 64 D5
Al Quds = Jerusalem,
  Israel 69 D4
Al Quds □, *Jordan* 69 D4
Al Qunayṭirah, *Syria* ... 69 C4
Al Qunfudhah, *Si. Arabia* 76 D5
Al Qurnah, *Iraq* 64 D5
Al Quṣayr, *Iraq* 64 D5
Al Quṣayr, *Syria* 69 A5
Al Quṭayfah, *Syria* 69 B5
Al' Uḏaylīyah, *Si. Arabia* . 65 E6
Al 'Ulā, *Si. Arabia* 64 E3
Al Uqaylah ash Sharqīgah,
  Libya 73 B8

Al Uqayr, *Si. Arabia* 65 E6
Al 'Uwaynid, *Si. Arabia* .. 64 E5
Al' 'Uwayqīlah, *Si. Arabia* 64 D4
Al 'Uyūn, *Si. Arabia* 64 E4
Al 'Uyūn, *Si. Arabia* 64 E3
Al Wajh, *Si. Arabia* 64 E3
Al Wakrah, *Qatar* 65 E6
Al Wannān, *Si. Arabia* .. 65 E6
Al Waqbah, *Si. Arabia* .. 64 D5
Al Wari'āh, *Si. Arabia* .. 64 E5
Al Wāṭiyah, *Libya* 75 B7
Al Wusayl, *Qatar* 65 E6
Ala, *Italy* 32 C8
Ala Dağları, *Turkey* 67 D10
Alabama □, *U.S.A.* 105 J2
Alabama →, *U.S.A.* ... 105 K2
Alaca, *Turkey* 66 C6
Alaçam, *Turkey* 66 C6
Alaçam Dağları, *Turkey* . 66 D3
Alaejos, *Spain* 30 D5
Alaérma, *Greece* 37 C9
Alagna Valsésia, *Italy* ... 32 C4
Alagoa Grande, *Brazil* .. 122 C4
Alagoas □, *Brazil* 122 C4
Alagoinhas, *Brazil* 123 D4
Alagón, *Spain* 28 D3
Alagón →, *Spain* 31 F4
Alajero, *Canary Is.* 36 F2
Alajuela, *Costa Rica* ... 116 D3
Alakamisy, *Madag.* 85 C8
Alalapura, *Surinam* 121 C6
Alalaú →, *Brazil* 121 D5
Alameda, *Spain* 31 H6
Alameda, *Calif., U.S.A.* . 112 H4
Alameda, *N. Mex., U.S.A.* 111 J10
Alaminos, *Phil.* 55 C3
Alamo, *U.S.A.* 113 J11
Alamo Crossing, *U.S.A.* . 113 L13
Alamogordo, *U.S.A.* ... 111 K11
Alamos, *Mexico* 114 B3
Alamosa, *U.S.A.* 111 H11
Åland, *Finland* 9 F16
Alandroal, *Portugal* 31 G3
Ålands hav, *Sweden* 9 G15
Alandur, *India* 60 N12
Alange, Presa de, *Spain* . 31 G4
Alanís, *Spain* 31 G5
Alanya, *Turkey* 66 E4
Alaotra, Farihin', *Madag.* 85 B8
Alapayevsk, *Russia* 44 D7
Alar del Rey, *Spain* 30 C6
Alaraz, *Spain* 30 E5
Alaşehir, *Turkey* 66 D3
Alaska □, *U.S.A.* 96 B5
Alaska, G. of, *Pac. Oc.* . 96 C5
Alaska Highway, *Canada* . 100 B3
Alaska Peninsula, *U.S.A.* . 96 C4
Alaska Range, *U.S.A.* .. 96 B4
Alássio, *Italy* 32 D5
Alataw Shankou, *China* . 54 B3
Alatri, *Italy* 34 A6
Alatyr, *Russia* 41 D15
Alatyr →, *Russia* 41 D15
Alausi, *Ecuador* 120 D2
Álava □, *Spain* 28 C2
Alava, C., *U.S.A.* 110 B1
Alaverdi, *Armenia* 43 F11
Alawoona, *Australia* 91 E3
'Alayh, *Lebanon* 69 B4
Alazan →, *Azerbaijan* .. 43 F12
Alba, *Italy* 32 D5
Alba de Tormes, *Spain* .. 30 E5
Alba Iulia, *Romania* 38 C6
Albac, *Romania* 38 C6
Albacete, *Spain* 29 G3
Albacete □, *Spain* 29 G3
Albacutya, L., *Australia* . 91 F3
Ålbæk, *Denmark* 11 G4
Ålbæk Bugt, *Denmark* .. 11 G4
Albaida, *Spain* 29 G4
Albalate de las Nogueras,
  Spain 28 E2
Albalate del Arzobispo,
  Spain 28 D4
Albania ■, *Europe* 39 J3
Albano Laziale, *Italy* ... 34 A5
Albany, *Australia* 89 G2
Albany, *Ga., U.S.A.* ... 105 K3
Albany, *Minn., U.S.A.* . 108 C7
Albany, *N.Y., U.S.A.* .. 107 D11
Albany, *Oreg., U.S.A.* . 110 D2
Albany, *Tex., U.S.A.* .. 109 J5
Albany →, *Canada* 98 B3
Albardón, *Argentina* ... 126 C2
Albarracín, *Spain* 28 E3
Albarracín, Sierra de, *Spain* 28 E3
Albatross B., *Australia* .. 90 A3
Albegna →, *Italy* 33 F8
Albemarle, *U.S.A.* 105 H5
Albemarle Sd., *U.S.A.* .. 105 H7
Albenga, *Italy* 32 D5
Alberche →, *Spain* 30 F6
Alberdi, *Paraguay* 126 B4
Alberes, Mts., *Spain* 28 C7
Alberique, *Spain* 29 F4
Albersdorf, *Germany* ... 18 A5
Albert, *France* 25 B9
Albert, L. = Mobutu Sese
  Seko, L., *Africa* 82 B3
Albert, L., *Australia* 91 F2
Albert Canyon, *Canada* . 100 C5
Albert Edward Ra.,
  Australia 88 C4
Albert Lea, *U.S.A.* 108 D8

Albert Nile →, *Uganda* .. 82 B3
Albert Town, *Bahamas* .. 117 B5
Alberta □, *Canada* 100 C6
Alberti, *Argentina* 126 D3
Albertinia, *S. Africa* 84 E3
Albertkanaal →, *Belgium* 17 F4
Alberton, *Canada* 99 C7
Albertville = Kalemie,
  Zaïre 82 D2
Albertville, *France* 27 C10
Albi, *France* 26 E6
Albia, *U.S.A.* 108 E8
Albina, *Surinam* 121 B7
Albina, Ponta, *Angola* .. 84 B1
Albino, *Italy* 32 C6
Albion, *Idaho, U.S.A.* .. 110 E7
Albion, *Mich., U.S.A.* .. 104 D3
Albion, *Nebr., U.S.A.* .. 108 E5
Albion, *Pa., U.S.A.* 106 E4
Alblasserdam, *Neths.* ... 16 E5
Albocácer, *Spain* 28 E5
Alborán, *Medit. S.* 31 K7
Ålborg, *Denmark* 11 G3
Ålborg Bugt, *Denmark* .. 11 H4
Alborz, Reshteh-ye Kūhhā-
  ye, *Iran* 65 C7
Albox, *Spain* 29 H2
Albreda, *Canada* 100 C5
Albufeira, *Portugal* 31 H2
Albula →, *Switz.* 23 C8
Albuñol, *Spain* 29 J1
Albuquerque, *Brazil* ... 125 D6
Albuquerque, *U.S.A.* .. 111 J10
Albuquerque, Cayos de,
  Caribbean 116 D3
Alburg, *U.S.A.* 107 B11
Alburno, Mte., *Italy* ... 35 B8
Alburquerque, *Spain* ... 31 F4
Albury, *Australia* 91 F4
Alby, *Sweden* 10 B9
Alcácer do Sal, *Portugal* . 31 G2
Alcáçovas, *Portugal* 31 G2
Alcalá de Chisvert, *Spain* . 28 E5
Alcalá de Guadaira, *Spain* 31 H5
Alcalá de Henares, *Spain* . 28 E1
Alcalá de los Gazules,
  Spain 31 J5
Alcalá la Real, *Spain* ... 31 H7
Álcamo, *Italy* 34 E5
Alcanadre →, *Spain* 28 D4
Alcanar, *Spain* 28 E5
Alcanede, *Portugal* 31 F2
Alcanena, *Portugal* 31 F2
Alcañices, *Spain* 30 D4
Alcañiz, *Spain* 28 D4
Alcântara, *Brazil* 122 B3
Alcântara, *Spain* 31 F4
Alcantara L., *Canada* ... 101 A7
Alcantarilla, *Spain* 29 H3
Alcaracejos, *Spain* 31 G6
Alcaraz, *Spain* 29 G2
Alcaraz, Sierra de, *Spain* . 29 G2
Alcaudete, *Spain* 31 H6
Alcázar de San Juan, *Spain* 29 F1
Alchevsk = Kommunarsk,
  Ukraine 43 B8
Alcira, *Spain* 29 F4
Alcoa, *U.S.A.* 105 H4
Alcobaça, *Portugal* 31 F2
Alcobendas, *Spain* 28 E1
Alcolea del Pinar, *Spain* . 28 D2
Alcora, *Spain* 28 E4
Alcorcón, *Spain* 30 E7
Alcoutim, *Portugal* 31 H3
Alcova, *U.S.A.* 110 E10
Alcoy, *Spain* 29 G4
Alcubierre, Sierra de, *Spain* 28 D4
Alcublas, *Spain* 28 F4
Alcudia, *Spain* 36 B10
Alcudia, B. de, *Spain* ... 36 B10
Alcudia, Sierra de la, *Spain* 31 G6
Aldabra Is., *Seychelles* .. 71 G8
Aldama, *Mexico* 115 C5
Aldan, *Russia* 45 D13
Aldan →, *Russia* 45 C13
Aldea, Pta. de la,
  Canary Is. 36 G4
Aldeburgh, *U.K.* 13 E9
Aldeia Nova, *Portugal* .. 31 H3
Alder, *U.S.A.* 110 D7
Alder Pk., *U.S.A.* 112 K5
Alderney, *Chan. Is.* 13 H5
Aldershot, *U.K.* 13 F7
Aledo, *U.S.A.* 108 E9
Alefa, *Ethiopia* 77 E4
Aleg, *Mauritania* 78 B2
Alegranza, *Canary Is.* ... 36 E6
Alegranza, I., *Canary Is.* . 36 E6
Alegre, *Brazil* 123 F3
Alegrete, *Brazil* 127 B4
Aleisk, *Russia* 44 D9
Aleksandriya, *Ukraine* .. 40 F5
Aleksandriya, *Ukraine* .. 42 B5
Aleksandriyskaya, *Russia* 43 E12
Aleksandrov, *Russia* ... 41 C11
Aleksandrov, *Serbia* ... 21 G11
Aleksandrovka, *Ukraine* . 42 B5
Aleksandrovo, *Bulgaria* . 38 F7
Aleksandrovsk-
  Sakhalinskiy, *Russia* ... 45 D15
Aleksandrovskiy Zavod,
  Russia 45 D12
Aleksandrovskoye, *Russia* 44 C8

Aleksandrów Kujawski,
  Poland 20 C8
Aleksandrów Łódzki,
  Poland 20 D9
Alekseyevka, Russia 41 F11
Aleksin, Russia 41 D10
Aleksinac, Serbia 21 M11
Além Paraíba, Brazil ... 123 F3
Alemania, Argentina 126 B2
Alemania, Chile 126 B2
Ålen, Norway 10 B5
Alençon, France 24 D7
Alenuihaha Channel,
  U.S.A. 102 H17
Aleppo = Ḥalab, Syria .. 64 B3
Aléria, France 27 F13
Alert Bay, Canada 100 C3
Alès, France 27 D8
Aleşd, Romania 38 B5
Alessándria, Italy 32 D5
Ålestrup, Denmark 11 H3
Ålesund, Norway 8 E9
Alet-les-Bains, France . 26 F6
Aletschhorn, Switz. 22 D6
Aleutian Is., Pac. Oc. . 96 C2
Aleutian Trench, Pac. Oc. 96 B10
Alexander, U.S.A. 108 B3
Alexander, Mt., Australia 89 E3
Alexander Arch., U.S.A. . 100 B2
Alexander B., S. Africa . 84 D2
Alexander Bay, S. Africa 84 D2
Alexander City, U.S.A. . 105 J3
Alexander I., Antarctica 5 C17
Alexandra, Australia ... 91 F4
Alexandra, N.Z. 87 L2
Alexandra Falls, Canada 100 A5
Alexandretta =
  İskenderun, Turkey ... 66 E7
Alexandria = El
  Iskandarîya, Egypt ... 76 H6
Alexandria, Australia .. 90 B2
Alexandria, B.C., Canada 100 C4
Alexandria, Ont., Canada 98 C5
Alexandria, Romania 38 F8
Alexandria, S. Africa .. 84 E4
Alexandria, Ind., U.S.A. 104 E3
Alexandria, La., U.S.A. 109 K8
Alexandria, Minn., U.S.A. 108 C7
Alexandria, S. Dak.,
  U.S.A. 108 D6
Alexandria, Va., U.S.A. 104 F7
Alexandria Bay, U.S.A. . 107 B9
Alexandrina, L., Australia 91 F2
Alexandroúpolis, Greece 39 J8
Alexis →, Canada 99 B8
Alexis Creek, Canada ... 100 C4
Alfabia, Spain 36 B9
Alfambra, Spain 28 E3
Alfândega da Fé, Portugal 30 D4
Alfaro, Spain 28 C3
Alfeld, Germany 18 D5
Alfenas, Brazil 127 A6
Alfiós →, Greece 39 M4
Alfonsine, Italy 33 D9
Alford, U.K. 14 D6
Alfred, Maine, U.S.A. .. 107 C14
Alfred, N.Y., U.S.A. ... 106 D7
Alfreton, U.K. 12 D6
Alga, Kazakhstan 44 E6
Algaida, Spain 36 B9
Algar, Spain 31 J5
Algarinejo, Spain 31 H6
Algarve, Portugal 31 J2
Algeciras, Spain 31 J5
Algemesí, Spain 29 F4
Alger, Algeria 75 A5
Algeria ■, Africa 75 C5
Alghero, Italy 34 B1
Algiers = Alger, Algeria 75 A5
Algoa B., S. Africa 84 E4
Algodonales, Spain 31 J5
Algodor →, Spain 30 F7
Algoma, U.S.A. 104 C2
Algona, U.S.A. 108 D7
Algonac, U.S.A. 106 D2
Alhama de Almería, Spain 29 J2
Alhama de Aragón, Spain 28 D3
Alhama de Granada, Spain 31 J7
Alhama de Murcia, Spain . 29 H3
Alhambra, Spain 29 G1
Alhambra, U.S.A. 113 L8
Alhaurín el Grande, Spain 31 J6
Alhucemas = Al Hoceïma,
  Morocco 74 A4
'Alī al Gharbī, Iraq ... 64 C5
'Alī ash Sharqī, Iraq .. 64 C5
Ali Bayramly, Azerbaijan 43 G13
'Alī Khēl, Afghan. 62 C3
Ali Sahîh, Djibouti 77 E5
Ali Shāh, Iran 64 B5
Ália, Italy 34 E6
'Alīābād, Khorāsān, Iran 65 C8
Alīābād, Kordestān, Iran 64 C5
'Alīābād, Yazd, Iran ... 65 D7
Aliaga, Spain 28 E4
Aliağa, Turkey 66 C2
Aliákmon →, Greece 39 J5
Alibo, Ethiopia 77 F4
Alibunar, Serbia 21 K10
Alicante, Spain 29 G4
Alicante □, Spain 29 G4
Alice, S. Africa 84 E4
Alice, U.S.A. 109 M5
Alice →, Queens.,
  Australia 90 C3

Alice →, Queens.,
  Australia 90 B3
Alice, Punta dell', Italy 35 C10
Alice Arm, Canada 100 B3
Alice Downs, Australia . 88 C4
Alice Springs, Australia 90 C1
Alicedale, S. Africa ... 84 E4
Aliceville, U.S.A. 105 J1
Alick Cr. →, Australia . 90 C3
Alida, Canada 101 D8
Aligarh, Raj., India ... 62 G7
Aligarh, Ut. P., India . 62 F8
Alīgūdarz, Iran 65 C6
Alijó, Portugal 30 D3
Alimena, Italy 35 E7
Alimnía, Greece 37 C9
Alingsås, Sweden 11 G6
Alipur, Pakistan 62 E4
Alipur Duar, India 61 F16
Aliquippa, U.S.A. 106 F4
Aliste →, Spain 30 D5
Alitus, Lithuania 40 D4
Alivérion, Greece 39 L7
Aliwal North, S. Africa 84 E4
Alix, Canada 100 C6
Aljezur, Portugal 31 H2
Aljustrel, Portugal 31 H2
Alkamari, Niger 79 C7
Alken, Belgium 17 G6
Alkmaar, Neths. 16 C5
All American Canal,
  U.S.A. 111 K6
Allada, Benin 79 D5
Allah Dad, Pakistan 62 G2
Allahabad, India 63 G9
Allakh-Yun, Russia 45 C14
Allal Tazi, Morocco 74 B3
Allan, Canada 101 C7
Allanche, France 26 C6
Allanmyo, Burma 61 K19
Allanridge, S. Africa .. 84 D4
Allanwater, Canada 98 B1
Allaqi, Wadi →, Egypt .. 76 C3
Allariz, Spain 30 C3
Allassac, France 26 C5
Alle, Belgium 17 J5
Allegan, U.S.A. 104 D3
Allegany, U.S.A. 106 D6
Alleghany →, U.S.A. 106 F5
Allegheny Plateau, U.S.A. 104 G6
Allegheny Reservoir,
  U.S.A. 106 E6
Allègre, France 26 C7
Allen, Argentina 128 A3
Allen, Bog of, Ireland . 15 C4
Allen, L., Ireland 15 B3
Allende, Mexico 114 B4
Allentown, U.S.A. 107 F9
Alleppey, India 60 Q10
Aller →, Germany 18 C5
Alleur, Belgium 17 G7
Allevard, France 27 C10
Alliance, Surinam 121 B7
Alliance, Nebr., U.S.A. 108 D3
Alliance, Ohio, U.S.A. . 106 F3
Allier □, France 26 B6
Allier →, France 25 F10
Allingåbro, Denmark 11 H4
Alliston, Canada 98 D4
Alloa, U.K. 14 E5
Allora, Australia 91 D5
Allos, France 27 D10
Alluitsup Paa = Sydprøven,
  Greenland 4 C5
Alma, Canada 99 C5
Alma, Ga., U.S.A. 105 K4
Alma, Kans., U.S.A. 108 F6
Alma, Mich., U.S.A. 104 D3
Alma, Nebr., U.S.A. 108 E5
Alma, Wis., U.S.A. 108 C9
Alma Ata, Kazakhstan ... 44 E8
Almada, Portugal 31 G1
Almadén, Australia 90 B3
Almadén, Spain 31 G6
Almagro, Spain 31 G7
Almanor, L., U.S.A. 110 F3
Almansa, Spain 29 G3
Almanza, Spain 30 C5
Almanzor, Pico de, Spain 30 E5
Almanzora →, Spain 29 H3
Almas, Brazil 123 D2
Almaty, Alma Ata,
  Kazakhstan 44 E8
Almazán, Spain 28 D2
Almazora, Spain 28 F4
Almeirim, Brazil 121 D7
Almeirim, Portugal 31 F2
Almelo, Neths. 16 D9
Almenar, Spain 28 D2
Almenara, Brazil 123 E3
Almenara, Spain 28 F4
Almenara, Sierra de, Spain 29 H3
Almendralejo, Spain 31 G4
Almería, Spain 29 J2
Almería □, Spain 29 H2
Almería, G. de, Spain .. 29 J2
Almirante, Panama 116 E3
Almirós, Greece 39 K5
Almiroú, Kólpos, Greece 37 D6
Almodôvar, Portugal 31 H2
Almodóvar del Campo,
  Spain 31 G6
Almogia, Spain 31 J6

Almonaster la Real, Spain 31 H4
Almont, U.S.A. 106 D1
Almonte, Canada 107 A8
Almonte →, Spain 31 F4
Almora, India 63 E8
Almoradí, Spain 29 G4
Almorox, Spain 30 E6
Almoustarat, Mali 79 B5
Almuñécar, Spain 31 J7
Alnif, Morocco 74 B3
Alnwick, U.K. 12 B6
Aloi, Uganda 82 B3
Alon, Burma 61 H19
Alor, Indonesia 57 F6
Alor Setar, Malaysia ... 59 J3
Alora, Spain 31 J6
Alosno, Spain 31 H3
Alougoum, Morocco 74 B3
Aloysius, Mt., Australia 89 E4
Alpaugh, U.S.A. 112 K7
Alpedrinha, Portugal ... 30 E3
Alpena, U.S.A. 104 C4
Alpercatas →, Brazil ... 122 C3
Alpes-de-Haute-
  Provence □, France ... 27 D10
Alpes-Maritimes □, France 27 E11
Alpha, Australia 90 C4
Alphen, Neths. 17 F5
Alphen aan den Rijn,
  Neths. 16 D5
Alpiarça, Portugal 31 F2
Alpine, Ariz., U.S.A. .. 111 K9
Alpine, Calif., U.S.A. . 113 N10
Alpine, Tex., U.S.A. ... 109 K3
Alpnach, Switz. 23 C6
Alps, Europe 6 F7
Alpu, Turkey 66 D4
Alrø, Denmark 11 J4
Alroy Downs, Australia . 90 B2
Alsace, France 25 D14
Alsask, Canada 101 C7
Alsásua, Spain 28 C2
Alsen, Sweden 10 A7
Alsfeld, Germany 18 E5
Alsten, Norway 8 D12
Alta, Norway 8 B17
Alta, Sierra, Spain 28 E3
Alta Gracia, Argentina . 126 C3
Alta Lake, Canada 100 C4
Alta Sierra, U.S.A. 113 K8
Altaelva →, Norway 8 B17
Altafjorden, Norway 8 A17
Altagracia, Venezuela .. 120 A3
Altagracia de Orituco,
  Venezuela 120 B4
Altai = Aerhtai Shan,
  Mongolia 54 B4
Altamachi →, Bolivia ... 124 D4
Altamaha →, U.S.A. 105 K5
Altamira, Brazil 121 D7
Altamira, Chile 126 B2
Altamira, Colombia 120 C2
Altamira, Mexico 115 C5
Altamira, Cuevas de, Spain 30 B6
Altamont, U.S.A. 107 D10
Altamura, Italy 35 B9
Altanbulag, Mongolia ... 54 A5
Altar, Mexico 114 A2
Altata, Mexico 114 C3
Altavista, U.S.A. 104 G6
Altay, China 54 B3
Altdorf, Switz. 23 C7
Alte Mellum, Germany ... 18 B4
Altea, Spain 29 G4
Altenberg, Germany 18 E9
Altenbruch, Germany 18 B4
Altenburg, Germany 18 E8
Altenkirchen,
  Mecklenburg-Vorpommern,
  Germany 18 A9
Altenkirchen, Rhld-Pfz.,
  Germany 18 E3
Altenteptow, Germany ... 18 B9
Alter do Chão, Portugal 31 F3
Altıntaş, Turkey 66 D4
Altiplano, Bolivia 124 D4
Altkirch, France 25 E14
Altmühl →, Germany 19 G7
Alto Adige = Trentino-
  Alto Adige □, Italy .. 32 B8
Alto Araguaia, Brazil .. 125 D7
Alto Cuchumatanes =
  Cuchumatanes, Sierra de
  los, Guatemala 116 C1
Alto del Inca, Chile ... 126 A2
Alto Garças, Brazil 125 D7
Alto Iriri →, Brazil ... 125 B7
Alto Ligonha, Mozam. ... 83 F4
Alto Molocue, Mozam. ... 83 F4
Alto Paraguai, Brazil .. 125 C6
Alto Paraguay □, Paraguay 126 A4
Alto Paraná □, Paraguay 127 B5
Alto Parnaíba, Brazil .. 122 C2
Alto Purús →, Peru 124 B3
Alto Río Senguerr,
  Argentina 128 C2
Alto Santo, Brazil 122 C4
Alto Sucuriú, Brazil ... 125 D7
Alto Turi, Brazil 122 B2
Alton, Canada 106 C4
Alton, U.S.A. 108 F9
Alton Downs, Australia . 91 D2
Altoona, U.S.A. 106 F6
Altopáscio, Italy 32 E7
Altos, Brazil 122 C3

Altötting, Germany 19 G8
Altstätten, Switz. 23 B9
Altun Kŭprī, Iraq 64 C5
Altun Shan, China 54 C3
Alturas, U.S.A. 110 F3
Altus, U.S.A. 109 H5
Alubijid, Phil. 55 G6
Alucra, Turkey 43 F8
Alŭksne, Latvia 40 C5
Alŭla, Somali Rep. 68 E5
Alunite, U.S.A. 113 K12
Alupka, Ukraine 42 D6
Alushta, Ukraine 42 D6
Alusi, Indonesia 57 F8
Alustante, Spain 28 E3
Al'Uzayr, Iraq 64 D5
Alva, U.S.A. 109 G5
Alvaiázere, Portugal ... 30 F2
Älvängen, Sweden 11 G6
Alvarado, Mexico 115 D5
Alvarado, U.S.A. 109 J6
Alvarães, Brazil 121 D5
Alvaro Obregón, Presa,
  Mexico 114 B3
Alvdal, Norway 10 B4
Alvear, Argentina 126 B4
Alverca, Portugal 31 G1
Alveringen, Belgium 17 F1
Alvesta, Sweden 9 H13
Alvie, Australia 91 F3
Alvin, U.S.A. 109 L7
Alvinston, Canada 106 D3
Alvito, Portugal 31 G3
Älvkarleby, Sweden 9 F14
Älvros, Sweden 10 B8
Älvsborgs län □, Sweden 11 F6
Älvsbyn, Sweden 8 D16
Alvsered, Sweden 11 G6
Alwar, India 62 F7
Alxa Zuoqi, China 50 E3
Alyaskitovyy, Russia ... 45 C15
Alyata, Azerbaijan 43 G13
Alyth, U.K. 14 E5
Alzada, U.S.A. 108 C2
Alzano Lombardo, Italy . 32 C6
Alzette →, Lux. 17 J8
Alzey, Germany 19 F4
Am Dam, Chad 73 F9
Am-Timan, Chad 73 F9
Amacuro □, Venezuela ... 121 B5
Amadeus, L., Australia . 89 D5
Amâdi, Sudan 77 F3
Amadi, Zaïre 82 B2
Amadjuak, Canada 97 B12
Amadjuak L., Canada 97 B12
Amadora, Portugal 31 G1
Amagasaki, Japan 49 G7
Amager, Denmark 11 J6
Amakusa-Shotō, Japan ... 49 H5
Amalfi, Colombia 120 B2
Amalfi, Italy 35 B7
Amaliás, Greece 39 M4
Amalner, India 60 J9
Amambaí, Brazil 127 A4
Amambaí →, Brazil 127 A5
Amambay □, Paraguay 127 A4
Amambay, Cordillera de,
  S. Amer. 127 A4
Amami-Guntō, Japan 49 L4
Amami-Ō-Shima, Japan ... 49 L4
Amana →, Venezuela 121 B5
Amaná, L., Brazil 121 D5
Amanda Park, U.S.A. 112 C3
Amándola, Italy 33 F10
Amangeldy, Kazakhstan .. 44 D7
Amantea, Italy 35 C9
Amapá, Brazil 121 C7
Amapá □, Brazil 121 C7
Amapari, Brazil 121 C7
Amara, Sudan 77 E3
Amarante, Brazil 122 C3
Amarante, Portugal 30 D2
Amarante do Maranhão,
  Brazil 122 C2
Amaranth, Canada 101 C9
Amareleja, Portugal 31 G3
Amargosa, Brazil 123 D4
Amargosa →, U.S.A. 113 J10
Amargosa Range, U.S.A. . 113 J10
Amári, Greece 37 D6
Amarillo, U.S.A. 109 H4
Amaro, Mt., Italy 33 F11
Amaro Leite, Brazil 123 D2
Amarpur, India 63 G12
Amasra, Turkey 66 C5
Amassama, Nigeria 79 D6
Amasya, Turkey 66 C6
Amasya □, Turkey 66 C6
Amataurá, Brazil 120 D4
Amatikulu, S. Africa ... 85 D5
Amatitlán, Guatemala ... 116 D1
Amatrice, Italy 33 F10
Amay, Belgium 17 G6
Amazon = Amazonas →,
  S. Amer. 121 D7
Amazonas □, Brazil 125 B5
Amazonas □, Peru 124 B2
Amazonas □, Venezuela .. 120 C4
Amazonas →, S. Amer. ... 121 D7
Ambahakily, Madag. 85 C7
Ambala, India 62 D7
Ambalavao, Madag. 85 C8
Ambalindum, Australia .. 90 C2
Ambam, Cameroon 80 D2
Ambanja, Madag. 85 A8

Ambarchik, Russia 45 C17
Ambarijeby, Madag. 85 A8
Ambaro, Helodranon',
  Madag. 85 A8
Ambartsevo, Russia 44 D9
Ambato, Ecuador 120 D2
Ambato, Sierra de,
  Argentina 126 B2
Ambato Boeny, Madag. ... 85 B8
Ambatofinandrahana,
  Madag. 85 C8
Ambatolampy, Madag. 85 B8
Ambatondrazaka, Madag. . 85 B8
Ambatosoratra, Madag. .. 85 B8
Ambenja, Madag. 85 B8
Amberg, Germany 19 F7
Ambergris Cay, Belize .. 115 D7
Ambérieu-en-Bugey,
  France 27 C9
Amberley, N.Z. 87 K4
Ambert, France 26 C7
Ambidédi, Mali 78 C2
Ambikapur, India 63 H10
Ambikol, Sudan 76 C3
Ambilobé, Madag. 85 A8
Ambinanindrano, Madag. . 85 C8
Ambjörnarp, Sweden 11 G7
Ambleside, U.K. 12 C5
Amblève, Belgium 17 H8
Amblève →, Belgium 17 H7
Ambo, Ethiopia 77 F4
Ambo, Peru 124 C2
Ambodifototra, Madag. .. 85 B8
Ambodilazana, Madag. ... 85 B8
Ambohimahasoa, Madag. .. 85 C8
Ambohimanga, Madag. 85 C8
Ambohitra, Madag. 85 A8
Ambon, Indonesia 57 E7
Amboseli L., Kenya 82 C4
Ambositra, Madag. 85 C8
Ambovombé, Madag. 85 D8
Amboy, U.S.A. 113 L11
Amboyna I., S. China Sea 56 C4
Ambridge, U.S.A. 106 F4
Ambriz, Angola 80 F2
Amby, Australia 91 D4
Amchitka I., U.S.A. 96 C1
Amderma, Russia 44 C7
Ameca, Mexico 114 C4
Ameca →, Mexico 114 C3
Amecameca, Mexico 115 D5
Ameland, Neths. 16 B7
Amélia, Italy 33 F9
Amélie-les-Bains-Palalda,
  France 26 F6
Amen, Russia 45 C18
Amendolaro, Italy 35 C9
America, Neths. 17 F7
American Falls, U.S.A. . 110 E7
American Falls Reservoir,
  U.S.A. 110 E7
American Highland,
  Antarctica 5 D6
American Samoa ■,
  Pac. Oc. 87 B13
Americana, Brazil 127 A6
Americus, U.S.A. 105 J3
Amersfoort, Neths. 16 D6
Amersfoort, S. Africa .. 85 D4
Amery, Australia 89 F2
Amery, Canada 101 B10
Amery Ice Shelf, Antarctica 5 C6
Ames, U.S.A. 108 E8
Amesbury, U.S.A. 107 D14
Amfíklia, Greece 39 L5
Amfilokhía, Greece 39 L4
Amga, Russia 45 C14
Amga →, Russia 45 C14
Amgu, Russia 45 E14
Amgun →, Russia 45 D14
Amherst, Burma 61 L20
Amherst, Canada 99 C7
Amherst, Mass., U.S.A. . 107 D12
Amherst, N.Y., U.S.A. .. 106 D6
Amherst, Ohio, U.S.A. .. 106 E2
Amherst, Tex., U.S.A. .. 109 H3
Amherst I., Canada 107 B8
Amherstburg, Canada 98 D3
Amiata, Mte., Italy 33 F8
Amiens, France 25 C9
Amindaion, Greece 39 J4
Amīrābād, Iran 64 C5
Amirante Is., Seychelles 3 E12
Amisk L., Canada 101 C8
Amistad, Presa de la,
  Mexico 114 B4
Amite, U.S.A. 109 K9
Amizmiz, Morocco 74 B3
Åmli, Norway 11 F2
Amlwch, U.K. 12 D3
Amm Adam, Sudan 77 D4
'Ammān, Jordan 69 D4
Ammanford, U.K. 13 F3
Ammassalik =
  Angmagssalik, Greenland 4 C6
Ammerån, Sweden 10 A10
Ammerån →, Sweden 10 A10
Ammersee, Germany 19 G7
Ammerzoden, Neths. 16 E6
Amnat Charoen, Thailand 58 E5
Amo Jiang →, China 52 F3
Åmol, Iran 65 B7
Amorebieta, Spain 28 B2
Amorgós, Greece 39 N8
Amory, U.S.A. 105 J1

Amos, *Canada* 98 C4
Åmot, *Buskerud, Norway* . 10 E3
Åmot, *Telemark, Norway* . 10 E2
Åmotsdal, *Norway* 10 E2
Amour, Djebel, *Algeria* .. 75 B5
Amoy = Xiamen, *China* .. 53 E12
Ampang, *Malaysia* 59 L3
Ampanihy, *Madag.* 85 C7
Ampasindava,
　Helodranon', *Madag.* . 85 A8
Ampasindava, Saikanosy,
　Madag. 85 A8
Ampato, Nevado, *Peru* .. 124 D3
Ampenan, *Indonesia* 56 F5
Amper, *Nigeria* 79 D6
Amper →, *Germany* 19 G7
Ampère, *Algeria* 75 A6
Ampezzo, *Italy* 33 B9
Amposta, *Spain* 28 E5
Ampotaka, *Madag.* 85 D7
Ampoza, *Madag.* 85 C7
Amqui, *Canada* 99 C6
Amravati, *India* 60 J10
Amreli, *India* 62 J4
Amrenene el Kasba,
　Algeria 75 D5
Amriswil, *Switz.* 23 A8
Amritsar, *India* 62 D6
Amroha, *India* 63 E8
Amrum, *Germany* 18 A4
Amsel, *Algeria* 75 D6
Amsterdam, *Neths.* 16 D5
Amsterdam, *U.S.A.* 107 D10
Amsterdam, I., *Ind. Oc.* .. 3 F13
Amstetten, *Austria* 21 G4
Amudarya →, *Uzbekistan* 44 E6
Amundsen Gulf, *Canada* . 96 A7
Amundsen Sea, *Antarctica* 5 D15
Amuntai, *Indonesia* 56 E5
Amur →, *Russia* 45 D15
Amurang, *Indonesia* 57 D6
Amuri Pass, *N.Z.* 87 K4
Amurrio, *Spain* 28 B1
Amursk, *Russia* 45 D14
Amurzet, *Russia* 45 E14
Amusco, *Spain* 30 C6
Amvrakikós Kólpos, *Greece* 39 L4
Amvrosiyevka, *Ukraine* ... 43 C8
Amyderya =
　Amudarya →,
　Uzbekistan 44 E6
Amzeglouf, *Algeria* 75 C5
An Bien, *Vietnam* 59 H5
An Hoa, *Vietnam* 58 E7
An Khe, *Vietnam* 58 F7
An Nabaţiyah at Taḩta,
　Lebanon 69 B4
An Nabk, *Si. Arabia* 64 D3
An Nabk, *Syria* 69 A5
An Nabk Abū Qaşr,
　Si. Arabia 64 D3
An Nafūd, *Si. Arabia* ... 64 D4
An Najaf, *Iraq* 64 C5
An Nāşirīyah, *Iraq* 64 D5
An Nhon, *Vietnam* 58 F7
An Nîl □, *Sudan* 76 D3
An Nîl el Abyaḑ □, *Sudan* 77 E3
An Nîl el Azraq □, *Sudan* 77 E3
An Nu'ayrīyah, *Si. Arabia* 65 E6
An Nuwayb'ī, W. →,
　Si. Arabia 69 F3
An Thoi, Dao, *Vietnam* .. 59 H4
An Uaimh, *Ireland* 15 C5
Anabar →, *Russia* 45 B12
'Anabtā, *Jordan* 69 C4
Anaco, *Venezuela* 121 B5
Anaconda, *U.S.A.* 110 C7
Anacortes, *U.S.A.* 112 B4
Anacuao, Mt., *Phil.* 55 C4
Anadarko, *U.S.A.* 109 H5
Anadia, *Brazil* 122 C4
Anadia, *Portugal* 30 E2
Anadolu, *Turkey* 66 D4
Anadyr, *Russia* 45 C18
Anadyr →, *Russia* 45 C18
Anadyrskiy Zaliv, *Russia* 45 C19
Anáfi, *Greece* 39 N8
Anafópoulo, *Greece* 39 N8
Anaga, Pta. de, *Canary Is.* 36 F3
Anagni, *Italy* 34 A6
'Ānah, *Iraq* 64 C4
Anaheim, *U.S.A.* 113 M9
Anahim Lake, *Canada* .. 100 C3
Anáhuac, *Mexico* 114 B4
Anajás, *Brazil* 122 B2
Anajatuba, *Brazil* 122 B3
Anakapalle, *India* 61 L13
Anakie, *Australia* 90 C4
Anaklia, *Georgia* 43 E9
Analalava, *Madag.* 85 A8
Análipsis, *Greece* 37 A3
Anamã, *Brazil* 121 D5
Anambar →, *Pakistan* .. 62 D3
Anambas, Kepulauan,
　Indonesia 56 D3
Anambas Is. = Anambas,
　Kepulauan, *Indonesia* . 56 D3
Anambra □, *Nigeria* 79 D6
Anamoose, *U.S.A.* 108 B4
Anamosa, *U.S.A.* 108 D9
Anamur, *Turkey* 66 E5
Anamur Burnu, *Turkey* . 66 E5
Anan, *Japan* 49 H7
Anand, *India* 62 H5
Anantnag, *India* 63 C6

Ananyev, *Ukraine* 42 C3
Anapa, *Russia* 42 D7
Anapodháris →, *Greece* . 37 E7
Anápolis, *Brazil* 123 E2
Anapu →, *Brazil* 121 D7
Anār, *Iran* 65 D7
Anārak, *Iran* 65 C7
Anatolia = Anadolu,
　Turkey 66 D4
Anatone, *U.S.A.* 110 C5
Anatsogno, *Madag.* 85 C7
Añatuya, *Argentina* 126 B3
Anauá →, *Brazil* 121 C5
Anaunethad L., *Canada* . 101 A8
Anavilhanas, Arquipélago
　das, *Brazil* 121 D5
Anaye, *Niger* 73 E7
Anbyŏn, *N. Korea* 51 E14
Ancash □, *Peru* 124 B2
Ancenis, *France* 24 E5
Ancho, Canal, *Chile* 128 D2
Anchor Bay, *U.S.A.* 112 G3
Anchorage, *U.S.A.* 96 B5
Anci, *China* 50 E9
Ancohuma, Nevada,
　Bolivia 124 D4
Ancón, *Peru* 124 C2
Ancona, *Italy* 33 E10
Ancud, *Chile* 128 B2
Ancud, G. de, *Chile* 128 B2
Andacollo, *Argentina* ... 126 D1
Andacollo, *Chile* 126 C1
Andado, *Australia* 90 D2
Andahuaylas, *Peru* 124 C3
Andalgalá, *Argentina* ... 126 B2
Åndalsnes, *Norway* 10 B1
Andalucía □, *Spain* 31 H6
Andalusia □ =
　Andalucía □, *Spain* ... 31 H6
Andalusia, *U.S.A.* 105 K2
Andaman Is., *Ind. Oc.* .. 46 H13
Andaman Sea, *Ind. Oc.* . 56 B1
Andara, *Namibia* 84 B3
Andaraí, *Brazil* 123 D3
Andeer, *Switz.* 23 C8
Andelfingen, *Switz.* 23 A7
Andelot, *France* 25 D12
Andenne, *Belgium* 17 H6
Andéranboukane, *Mali* .. 79 B5
Anderlecht, *Belgium* 17 G4
Anderlues, *Belgium* 17 H4
Andermatt, *Switz.* 23 C7
Andernach, *Germany* ... 18 E3
Andernos-les-Bains, *France* 26 D2
Anderslöv, *Sweden* 11 J7
Anderson, *Calif., U.S.A.* 110 F2
Anderson, *Ind., U.S.A.* . 104 E3
Anderson, *Mo., U.S.A.* . 109 G7
Anderson, *S.C., U.S.A.* . 105 H4
Anderson →, *Canada* ... 96 B7
Anderson, Mt., *S. Africa* 85 D5
Andes = Andes, Cord. de
　los, *S. Amer.* 124 C3
Andes, *S. Amer.* 124 C2
Andes, Cord. de los,
　S. Amer. 124 C3
Andfjorden, *Norway* 8 B14
Andhra Pradesh □, *India* 60 L11
Andijon = Andizhan,
　Uzbekistan 44 E8
Andikíthira, *Greece* 39 P6
Andīmeshk, *Iran* 65 C6
Andímilos, *Greece* 39 N7
Andípaxoi, *Greece* 39 K3
Andizhan, *Uzbekistan* .. 44 E8
Andoany, *Madag.* 85 A8
Andoas, *Peru* 120 D2
Andong, *S. Korea* 51 F15
Andongwei, *China* 51 G10
Andorra ■, *Europe* 28 C6
Andorra La Vella, *Andorra* 28 C6
Andover, *U.K.* 13 F6
Andover, *Mass., U.S.A.* . 107 D13
Andover, *N.Y., U.S.A.* .. 106 D7
Andover, *Ohio, U.S.A.* .. 106 E4
Andradina, *Brazil* 123 F1
Andrahary, Mt., *Madag.* 85 A8
Andraitx, *Spain* 36 B9
Andramasina, *Madag.* .. 85 B8
Andranopasy, *Madag.* .. 85 C7
Andreanof Is., *U.S.A.* .. 96 C2
Andreapol, *Russia* 40 C8
Andrewilla, *Australia* ... 91 D2
Andrews, *S.C., U.S.A.* . 105 J6
Andrews, *Tex., U.S.A.* . 109 J3
Ándria, *Italy* 35 A9
Andriba, *Madag.* 85 B8
Andrijevica, *Montenegro* 21 N9
Andrítsaina, *Greece* 39 M4
Androka, *Madag.* 85 C7
Andropov = Rybinsk,
　Russia 41 B11
Ándros, *Greece* 39 M7
Andros I., *Bahamas* 116 B4
Andros Town, *Bahamas* . 116 B4
Andújar, *Spain* 31 G6
Andulo, *Angola* 80 G3
Anegada, B., *Argentina* . 128 B4
Anegada I., *Virgin Is.* .. 117 C7
Anegada Passage,
　W. Indies 117 C7
Aného, *Togo* 79 D5
Añelo, *Argentina* 128 A3
Anergane, *Morocco* 74 B3

Aneto, Pico de, *Spain* ... 28 C5
Añez, *Bolivia* 125 D5
Anfu, *China* 53 D10
Ang Thong, *Thailand* ... 58 E3
Ang'angxi, *China* 54 B7
Angara →, *Russia* 45 D10
Angarab, *Ethiopia* 77 E4
Angarsk, *Russia* 45 D11
Angas Downs, *Australia* . 89 E5
Angas Hills, *Australia* .. 88 D4
Angaston, *Australia* 91 E2
Ånge, *Sweden* 10 B9
Ángel de la Guarda, I.,
　Mexico 114 B2
Angel Falls, *Venezuela* . 121 B5
Angeles, *Phil.* 55 D4
Ängelholm, *Sweden* 11 H6
Angellala, *Australia* 91 D4
Angels Camp, *U.S.A.* .. 111 G3
Anger →, *Ethiopia* 77 F4
Angereb →, *Ethiopia* .. 77 E4
Ångermanälven →,
　Sweden 10 B12
Angermünde, *Germany* .. 18 B10
Angers, *Canada* 107 A9
Angers, *France* 24 E6
Angerville, *France* 25 D8
Ängesån →, *Sweden* ... 8 C17
Anghiari, *Italy* 33 E9
Angical, *Brazil* 123 D3
Angikuni L., *Canada* ... 101 A9
Angkor, *Cambodia* 58 F4
Anglés, *Spain* 28 D7
Anglesey, *U.K.* 12 D3
Anglet, *France* 26 E2
Angleton, *U.S.A.* 109 L7
Angleur, *Belgium* 17 G7
Anglin →, *France* 26 B4
Anglisidhes, *Cyprus* 37 E12
Anglure, *France* 25 D10
Angmagssalik, *Greenland* 4 C6
Ango, *Zaïre* 82 B2
Angoche, *Mozam.* 83 F4
Angoche, I., *Mozam.* ... 83 F4
Angol, *Chile* 126 D1
Angola, *Ind., U.S.A.* ... 104 E3
Angola, *N.Y., U.S.A.* ... 106 D5
Angola ■, *Africa* 81 G3
Angoon, *U.S.A.* 100 B2
Angoulême, *France* 26 C4
Angoumois, *France* 26 C4
Angra dos Reis, *Brazil* . 127 A7
Angren, *Uzbekistan* 44 E8
Angtassom, *Cambodia* .. 59 G5
Angu, *Zaïre* 82 B1
Anguang, *China* 51 B12
Anguilla ■, *W. Indies* .. 117 C7
Anguo, *China* 50 E8
Angurugu, *Australia* ... 90 A2
Angus, Braes of, *U.K.* .. 14 E5
Anhée, *Belgium* 17 H5
Anholt, *Denmark* 11 H5
Anhua, *China* 53 C8
Anhui □, *China* 53 B11
Anhwei □ = Anhui □,
　China 53 B11
Anichab, *Namibia* 84 C1
Anicuns, *Brazil* 123 E2
Anídhros, *Greece* 39 N8
Anie, *Togo* 79 D5
Animas, *U.S.A.* 111 L9
Animskog, *Sweden* 11 F6
Anina, *Romania* 38 D4
Anivorano, *Madag.* 85 B8
Anjar, *India* 62 H4
Anjidiv I., *India* 60 M9
Anjou, *France* 24 E6
Anjozorobe, *Madag.* 85 B8
Anju, *N. Korea* 51 E13
Anka, *Nigeria* 79 C6
Ankaboa, Tanjona, *Madag.* 85 C7
Ankang, *China* 50 H5
Ankara, *Turkey* 66 D5
Ankara →, *Turkey* 66 D5
Ankaramena, *Madag.* .. 85 C8
Ankazoabo, *Madag.* 85 C7
Ankazobe, *Madag.* 85 B8
Ankisabe, *Madag.* 85 B8
Anklam, *Germany* 18 B9
Ankober, *Ethiopia* 77 F4
Ankoro, *Zaïre* 82 D2
Anlong, *China* 52 E5
Anlu, *China* 53 B9
Anmyŏn-do, *S. Korea* .. 51 F14
Ann, C., *U.S.A.* 107 D14
Ann Arbor, *U.S.A.* 104 D4
Anna, *Russia* 41 F12
Anna, *U.S.A.* 109 G10
Anna Plains, *Australia* .. 88 C3
Anna Regina, *Guyana* .. 121 B6
Annaba, *Algeria* 75 A6
Annaberg-Buchholz,
　Germany 18 E8
Annalee →, *Ireland* 15 B4
Annam = Trung-Phan,
　Vietnam 58 E7
Annamitique, Chaîne, *Asia* 58 D6
Annan, *U.K.* 14 G5
Annan →, *U.K.* 14 G5
Annapolis, *U.S.A.* 104 F7
Annapolis Royal, *Canada* 99 D6
Annapurna, *Nepal* 63 E10

Annean, L., *Australia* ... 89 E2
Anneberg, *Sweden* 11 G6
Annecy, *France* 27 C10
Annecy, L. d', *France* .. 27 C10
Annemasse, *France* 27 B10
Anning, *China* 52 E4
Anningie, *Australia* 88 D5
Anniston, *U.S.A.* 105 J3
Annobón, *Atl. Oc.* 71 G4
Annonay, *France* 27 C8
Annot, *France* 27 E10
Annotto Bay, *Jamaica* .. 116 C4
Annuello, *Australia* 91 E3
Annville, *U.S.A.* 107 F8
Annweiler, *Germany* 19 F3
Áno Viánnos, *Greece* ... 37 D7
Anoka, *U.S.A.* 108 C8
Anorotsangana, *Madag.* . 85 A8
Anóyia, *Greece* 37 D6
Anping, *Hebei, China* .. 50 E8
Anping, *Liaoning, China* 51 D12
Anpu Gang, *China* 52 G7
Anqing, *China* 53 B11
Anqiu, *China* 51 F10
Anren, *China* 53 D9
Ans, *Belgium* 17 G7
Ansai, *China* 50 F5
Ansbach, *Germany* 19 F6
Anseba →, *Eritrea* 77 D4
Anserma, *Colombia* 120 B2
Anseroeul, *Belgium* 17 G3
Anshan, *China* 54 B7
Anshan, *Liaoning, China* 51 D12
Anshun, *China* 52 D5
Ansião, *Portugal* 30 F2
Ansirabe, *Madag.* 85 B8
Ansley, *U.S.A.* 108 E5
Ansó, *Spain* 28 C4
Anson, *U.S.A.* 109 J5
Anson B., *Australia* 88 B5
Ansongo, *Mali* 79 B5
Ansonia, *U.S.A.* 107 E11
Anstruther, *U.K.* 14 E6
Ansudu, *Indonesia* 57 E9
Antabamba, *Peru* 124 C3
Antakya, *Turkey* 66 E7
Antalaha, *Madag.* 85 A9
Antalya, *Turkey* 66 E4
Antalya □, *Turkey* 66 E4
Antalya Körfezi, *Turkey* . 66 E4
Antananarivo, *Madag.* .. 85 B8
Antananarivo □, *Madag.* 85 B8
Antanimbaribe, *Madag.* . 85 C7
Antarctic Pen., *Antarctica* 5 C18
Antarctica ■ 5 E3
Antelope, *Zimbabwe* ... 83 G2
Antenor Navarro, *Brazil* 122 C4
Antequera, *Paraguay* ... 126 A4
Antequera, *Spain* 31 H6
Antero, Mt., *U.S.A.* 111 G10
Anthony, *Kans., U.S.A.* 109 G5
Anthony, *N. Mex., U.S.A.* 111 K10
Anthony Lagoon, *Australia* 90 B2
Anti Atlas, *Morocco* 74 C2
Anti-Lebanon = Ash
　Sharqi, Al Jabal,
　Lebanon 69 B5
Antibes, *France* 27 E11
Antibes, C. d', *France* .. 27 E11
Anticosti, I. d', *Canada* . 99 C7
Antifer, C. d', *France* ... 24 C7
Antigo, *U.S.A.* 108 C10
Antigonish, *Canada* 99 C7
Antigua, *Canary Is.* 36 F5
Antigua, *Guatemala* 116 D1
Antigua, *W. Indies* 117 C7
Antigua & Barbuda ■,
　W. Indies 117 C7
Antilla, *Cuba* 116 B4
Antimony, *U.S.A.* 111 G8
Antioch, *U.S.A.* 112 G5
Antioche, Pertuis d',
　France 26 B2
Antioquia, *Colombia* ... 120 B2
Antioquia □, *Colombia* . 120 B2
Antipodes Is., *Pac. Oc.* . 92 M9
Antler, *U.S.A.* 108 A4
Antler →, *Canada* 101 D8
Antlers, *U.S.A.* 109 H7
Antofagasta, *Chile* 126 A1
Antofagasta □, *Chile* ... 126 A2
Antofagasta de la Sierra,
　Argentina 126 B2
Antofalla, *Argentina* ... 126 B2
Antofalla, Salar de,
　Argentina 126 B2
Antoing, *Belgium* 17 G2
Anton, *U.S.A.* 109 J3
Anton Chico, *U.S.A.* ... 111 J11
Antongila, Helodrano,
　Madag. 85 B8
Antonibé, *Madag.* 85 B8
Antonibé, Presqu'île d',
　Madag. 85 A8
Antonina, *Brazil* 127 B6
Antonito, *U.S.A.* 111 H10
Antonovo, *Kazakhstan* .. 43 B14
Antrain, *France* 24 D5
Antrim, *U.K.* 15 B5
Antrim □, *U.K.* 15 B5
Antrim, Mts. of, *U.K.* .. 15 B5
Antrim Plateau, *Australia* 88 C4
Antrodoco, *Italy* 33 F10
Antropovo, *Russia* 41 B13
Antsalova, *Madag.* 85 B7

Antsiranana, *Madag.* ... 85 A8
Antsohihy, *Madag.* 85 A8
Antsohimbondrona
　Seranana, *Madag.* ... 85 A8
Antu, *China* 51 C15
Antwerp = Antwerpen,
　Belgium 17 F4
Antwerp, *U.S.A.* 107 B9
Antwerpen, *Belgium* ... 17 F4
Antwerpen □, *Belgium* . 17 F5
Anupgarh, *India* 62 E5
Anuradhapura, *Sri Lanka* 60 Q12
Anvers = Antwerpen,
　Belgium 17 F4
Anvers I., *Antarctica* ... 5 C17
Anveh, *Iran* 65 E7
Anxi, *Fujian, China* 53 E12
Anxi, *Gansu, China* 54 B4
Anxiang, *China* 53 C9
Anxious B., *Australia* ... 91 E1
Anyama, *Ivory C.* 78 D4
Anyang, *China* 50 F8
Anyi, *Jiangxi, China* ... 53 C10
Anyi, *Shanxi, China* ... 50 G6
Anyuan, *China* 53 E10
Anza, *U.S.A.* 113 M10
Anze, *China* 50 F7
Anzhero-Sudzhensk, *Russia* 44 D9
Ánzio, *Italy* 34 A5
Anzoátegui □, *Venezuela* 121 B5
Aoga-Shima, *Japan* 49 H9
Aoiz, *Spain* 28 C3
Aomori, *Japan* 48 D10
Aomori □, *Japan* 48 D10
Aonla, *India* 63 E8
Aosta, *Italy* 32 C4
Aoudéras, *Niger* 79 B6
Aouinet Torkoz, *Morocco* 74 C3
Aoukar, *Mali* 74 D4
Aouker, *Mauritania* 78 B3
Aoulef el Arab, *Algeria* . 75 C5
Apa →, *S. Amer.* 126 A4
Apache, *U.S.A.* 109 H5
Apalachee B., *U.S.A.* .. 105 L3
Apalachicola, *U.S.A.* ... 105 L3
Apalachicola →, *U.S.A.* 105 L3
Apapa, *Nigeria* 79 D5
Apaporis →, *Colombia* . 120 D4
Aparecida do Taboado,
　Brazil 123 F1
Aparri, *Phil.* 55 B4
Aparurén, *Venezuela* ... 121 B5
Apateu, *Romania* 38 C4
Apatin, *Serbia* 21 K8
Apatzingán, *Mexico* 114 D4
Apeldoorn, *Neths.* 16 D7
Apeldoornsch Kanal →,
　Neths. 16 D8
Apen, *Germany* 18 B3
Apennines = Appennini,
　Italy 32 D7
Apere →, *Bolivia* 125 C4
Apia, *W. Samoa* 87 A13
Apiacás, Serra dos, *Brazil* 125 B6
Apiaú →, *Brazil* 121 C5
Apiaú, Serra do, *Brazil* . 121 C5
Apidiá →, *Brazil* 125 C5
Apinajé, *Brazil* 123 D2
Apizaco, *Mexico* 115 D5
Aplao, *Peru* 124 D3
Apo, Mt., *Phil.* 57 C7
Apodi, *Brazil* 122 C4
Apolakkiá, *Greece* 37 C9
Apolakkiá, Órmos, *Greece* 37 C9
Apolda, *Germany* 18 D7
Apollonia = Marsá Susah,
　Libya 73 B9
Apollonia, *Greece* 39 N7
Apolo, *Bolivia* 124 C4
Apónguao →, *Venezuela* 121 C5
Aporé, *Brazil* 125 D7
Aporé →, *Brazil* 123 E1
Aporema, *Brazil* 122 A1
Apostle Is., *U.S.A.* 108 B9
Apostolos Andreas, C.,
　Cyprus 37 D13
Apostolovo, *Ukraine* ... 42 C5
Apoteri, *Guyana* 121 C6
Appalachian Mts., *U.S.A.* 104 G6
Appelscha, *Neths.* 16 C8
Appennini, *Italy* 32 D7
Appennino Ligure, *Italy* . 32 D6
Appenzell, *Switz.* 23 B8
Appenzell-Ausser
　Rhoden □, *Switz.* 23 B8
Appenzell-Inner
　Rhoden □, *Switz.* 23 B8
Appiano, *Italy* 33 B8
Appingedam, *Neths.* ... 16 B9
Apple Hill, *Canada* 107 A10
Apple Valley, *U.S.A.* ... 113 L9
Appleby, *U.K.* 12 C5
Appleton, *U.S.A.* 104 C1
Approuague, *Fr. Guiana* 121 C7
Approuague →,
　Fr. Guiana 121 C7
Apricena, *Italy* 35 A8
Aprigliano, *Italy* 35 C9
Aprília, *Italy* 34 A5
Apsheronsk, *Russia* 43 D8
Apt, *France* 27 E9
Apuane, Alpi, *Italy* 32 D7
Apuaú, *Brazil* 121 D5
Apucarana, *Brazil* 127 A5

Apulia

Apulia = Púglia □, *Italy* 35 B9
Apure □, *Venezuela* 120 B4
Apure →, *Venezuela* 120 B4
Apurímac □, *Peru* 124 C3
Apurimac →, *Peru* 124 C3
Apuseni, Munţii, *Romania* 38 C5
Aqabah = Al 'Aqabah, *Jordan* 69 F4
'Aqabah, Khalīj al, *Red Sea* 64 D2
'Aqdā, *Iran* 65 C7
Aqîq, *Sudan* 76 D4
Aqîq, Khalîg, *Sudan* 76 D4
Aqmola = Tselinograd, *Kazakhstan* 44 D8
Aqrah, *Iraq* 64 B4
Aqtöbe = Aktyubinsk, *Kazakhstan* 44 D6
Aquidauana, *Brazil* 125 E6
Aquidauana →, *Brazil* 125 D6
Aquiles Serdán, *Mexico* 114 B3
Aquin, *Haiti* 117 C5
Ar Rachidiya, *Morocco* 74 B4
Ar Rafīd, *Syria* 69 C4
Ar Raḥḥālīyah, *Iraq* 64 C4
Ar Ramādī, *Iraq* 64 C4
Ar Ramthā, *Jordan* 69 C5
Ar Raqqah, *Syria* 64 C3
Ar Rass, *Si. Arabia* 64 E4
Ar Rifā'ī, *Si. Arabia* 64 D5
Ar Riyāḍ, *Si. Arabia* 64 E5
Ar Ru'ays, *Qatar* 65 E6
Ar Rukhaymīyah, *Iraq* 64 D5
Ar Ruqayyidah, *Si. Arabia* 65 E6
Ar Ruşāfah, *Syria* 64 C3
Ar Ruţbah, *Iraq* 64 C4
Ara, *India* 63 G11
'Arab, Bahr el →, *Sudan* 77 F2
Arab, Khalîg el, *Egypt* 76 H6
'Arabābād, *Iran* 65 C8
Araban, *Turkey* 67 E7
Arabatskaya Strelka, *Ukraine* 42 D6
Arabba, *Italy* 33 B8
Arabelo, *Venezuela* 121 C5
Arabia, *Asia* 68 C4
Arabian Desert = Es Sahrâ' Esh Sharqîya, *Egypt* 76 B3
Arabian Gulf = Gulf, The, *Asia* 65 E6
Arabian Sea, *Ind. Oc.* 46 H10
Araç, *Turkey* 66 C5
Aracaju, *Brazil* 122 D4
Aracataca, *Colombia* 120 A3
Aracati, *Brazil* 122 B4
Araçatuba, *Brazil* 127 A5
Aracena, *Spain* 31 H4
Aracena, Sierra de, *Spain* 31 H4
Araçuaí, *Brazil* 123 E3
Araçuaí →, *Brazil* 123 E3
'Arad, *Israel* 69 D4
Arad, *Romania* 38 C4
Arada, *Chad* 73 F9
Aradhippou, *Cyprus* 37 E12
Arafura Sea, *E. Indies* 57 F8
Aragarças, *Brazil* 125 D7
Aragats, *Armenia* 43 F11
Aragón □, *Spain* 28 D4
Aragón →, *Spain* 28 C3
Aragona, *Italy* 34 E6
Aragua □, *Venezuela* 120 B4
Aragua de Barcelona, *Venezuela* 121 B5
Araguacema, *Brazil* 122 C2
Araguaçu, *Brazil* 123 D2
Araguaia →, *Brazil* 122 C2
Araguaiana, *Brazil* 125 D7
Araguaína, *Brazil* 122 C2
Araguari, *Brazil* 123 E2
Araguari →, *Brazil* 121 C8
Araguatins, *Brazil* 122 C2
Araioses, *Brazil* 122 B3
Arak, *Algeria* 75 C5
Arāk, *Iran* 65 C6
Arakan Coast, *Burma* 61 K19
Arakan Yoma, *Burma* 61 K19
Arakli, *Turkey* 67 C9
Araks = Aras, Rūd-e →, *Iran* 64 B5
Aral Sea = Aralskoye More, *Asia* 44 E7
Aralsk, *Kazakhstan* 44 E7
Aralskoye More, *Asia* 44 E7
Aramac, *Australia* 90 C4
Arambag, *India* 63 H12
Aran I., *Ireland* 15 B3
Aran Is., *Ireland* 15 C2
Aranda de Duero, *Spain* 28 D1
Arandān, *Iran* 64 C5
Aranjuez, *Spain* 30 E7
Aranos, *Namibia* 84 C2
Aransas Pass, *U.S.A.* 109 M6
Aranzazu, *Colombia* 120 B2
Araouane, *Mali* 78 B4
Arapahoe, *U.S.A.* 108 E5
Arapari, *Brazil* 122 C2
Arapey Grande →, *Uruguay* 126 C4
Arapiraca, *Brazil* 122 C4
Arapkir, *Turkey* 67 D8
Arapongas, *Brazil* 127 A5
Ar'ar, *Si. Arabia* 64 D4
Araracuara, *Colombia* 120 D3
Araranguá, *Brazil* 127 B6
Araraquara, *Brazil* 123 F2
Ararás, Serra das, *Brazil* 127 B5
Ararat, *Australia* 91 F3
Ararat, Mt. = Ağrı Dağı, *Turkey* 67 D11
Arari, *Brazil* 122 B3
Araria, *India* 63 F12
Araripe, Chapada do, *Brazil* 122 C3
Araripina, *Brazil* 122 C3
Araruama, L. de, *Brazil* 123 F3
Araruna, *Brazil* 122 C4
Aras, Rūd-e →, *Iran* 64 B5
Araticu, *Brazil* 122 B2
Arauca, *Colombia* 120 B3
Arauca □, *Colombia* 120 B3
Arauca →, *Venezuela* 120 B4
Arauco, *Chile* 126 D1
Arauco □, *Chile* 126 D1
Araújos, *Brazil* 123 E2
Arauquita, *Colombia* 120 B3
Araure, *Venezuela* 120 B4
Arawa, *Ethiopia* 77 F5
Araxá, *Brazil* 123 E2
Araya, Pen. de, *Venezuela* 121 A5
Arba Minch, *Ethiopia* 77 F4
Arbat, *Iraq* 64 C5
Arbatax, *Italy* 34 C2
Arbaza, *Russia* 45 D10
Arbedo, *Switz.* 23 D8
Arbīl, *Iraq* 64 B5
Arbois, *France* 25 F12
Arboletes, *Colombia* 120 B2
Arbon, *Switz.* 23 A8
Arbore, *Ethiopia* 77 F4
Arborea, *Italy* 34 C1
Arborfield, *Canada* 101 C8
Arborg, *Canada* 101 C9
Arbrå, *Sweden* 10 C10
Arbroath, *U.K.* 14 E6
Arbuckle, *U.S.A.* 112 F4
Arbus, *Italy* 34 C1
Arbuzinka, *Ukraine* 42 C4
Arc, *France* 25 E12
Arc →, *France* 27 C10
Arcachon, *France* 26 D2
Arcachon, Bassin d', *France* 26 D2
Arcade, *U.S.A.* 106 D6
Arcadia, *Fla., U.S.A.* 105 M5
Arcadia, *La., U.S.A.* 109 J8
Arcadia, *Nebr., U.S.A.* 108 E5
Arcadia, *Pa., U.S.A.* 106 F6
Arcadia, *Wis., U.S.A.* 108 C9
Arcata, *U.S.A.* 110 F1
Arcévia, *Italy* 33 E9
Archangel = Arkhangelsk, *Russia* 44 C5
Archar, *Bulgaria* 38 F5
Archbald, *U.S.A.* 107 E9
Archena, *Spain* 29 G3
Archer →, *Australia* 90 A3
Archer B., *Australia* 90 A3
Archers Post, *Kenya* 82 B4
Archidona, *Spain* 31 H6
Arci, Monte, *Italy* 34 C1
Arcidosso, *Italy* 33 F8
Arcila = Asilah, *Morocco* 74 A3
Arcis-sur-Aube, *France* 25 D11
Arckaringa, *Australia* 91 D1
Arckaringa Cr. →, *Australia* 91 D2
Arco, *Italy* 32 C7
Arco, *U.S.A.* 110 E7
Arcola, *Canada* 101 D8
Arcos, *Spain* 28 D2
Arcos de los Frontera, *Spain* 31 J5
Arcos de Valdevez, *Portugal* 30 D2
Arcot, *India* 60 N11
Arcoverde, *Brazil* 122 C4
Arctic Bay, *Canada* 97 A11
Arctic Ocean, *Arctic* 4 B18
Arctic Red River, *Canada* 96 B6
Arda →, *Bulgaria* 39 H9
Arda →, *Italy* 32 D6
Ardabīl, *Iran* 65 B6
Ardahan, *Turkey* 67 C10
Ardakān = Sepīdān, *Iran* 65 D7
Ardales, *Spain* 31 J6
Årdalstangen, *Norway* 10 C1
Ardatov, *Russia* 41 D15
Ardea, *Greece* 39 J5
Ardèche □, *France* 27 D8
Ardèche →, *France* 27 D8
Ardee, *Ireland* 15 C5
Arden, *Canada* 106 B8
Arden, *Denmark* 11 H3
Arden, *Calif., U.S.A.* 112 G5
Arden, *Nev., U.S.A.* 113 J11
Ardenne, *Belgium* 25 C12
Ardennes = Ardenne, *Belgium* 25 C12
Ardennes □, *France* 25 C11
Ardentes, *France* 25 F8
Ardeşen, *Turkey* 67 C9
Ardestān, *Iran* 65 C7
Ardgour, *U.K.* 14 E3
Árdhas →, *Greece* 39 H9
Ardila →, *Portugal* 31 G3
Ardlethan, *Australia* 91 E4
Ardmore, *Australia* 90 C2
Ardmore, *Okla., U.S.A.* 109 H6
Ardmore, *Pa., U.S.A.* 107 G9
Ardmore, *S. Dak., U.S.A.* 108 D3
Ardnacrusha, *Ireland* 15 D3
Ardnamurchan, Pt. of, *U.K.* 14 E2
Ardoie, *Belgium* 17 G2
Ardore Marina, *Italy* 35 D9
Ardres, *France* 25 B8
Ardrossan, *Australia* 91 E2
Ardrossan, *U.K.* 14 F4
Ards □, *U.K.* 15 B6
Ards Pen., *U.K.* 15 B6
Ardud, *Romania* 38 B5
Ardunac, *Turkey* 43 F10
Åre, *Sweden* 10 A7
Arecibo, *Puerto Rico* 117 C6
Areia Branca, *Brazil* 122 B4
Arena, Pt., *U.S.A.* 112 G3
Arenales, Cerro, *Chile* 128 C2
Arenápolis, *Brazil* 125 C6
Arenas, *Spain* 30 B6
Arenas de San Pedro, *Spain* 30 E5
Arendal, *Norway* 11 F2
Arendonk, *Belgium* 17 F6
Arendsee, *Germany* 18 C7
Arenillas, *Ecuador* 120 D1
Arenys de Mar, *Spain* 28 D7
Arenzano, *Italy* 32 D5
Areópolis, *Greece* 39 N5
Arequipa, *Peru* 124 D3
Arequipa □, *Peru* 124 D3
Arere, *Brazil* 121 D7
Arero, *Ethiopia* 77 G4
Arès, *France* 26 D2
Arévalo, *Spain* 30 D6
Arezzo, *Italy* 33 E8
Arga →, *Spain* 28 C3
Argalastí, *Greece* 39 K6
Argamakmur, *Indonesia* 56 E2
Argamasilla de Alba, *Spain* 29 F1
Arganda, *Spain* 28 E1
Arganil, *Portugal* 30 E2
Argelès-Gazost, *France* 26 F3
Argelès-sur-Mer, *France* 26 F7
Argens →, *France* 27 E10
Argent-sur-Sauldre, *France* 25 E9
Argenta, *Italy* 33 D8
Argentan, *France* 24 D6
Argentário, Mte., *Italy* 33 F8
Argentat, *France* 26 C5
Argentera, *Italy* 32 D3
Argentera, Monte del, *Italy* 32 D4
Argenteuil, *France* 25 D9
Argentia, *Canada* 99 C9
Argentiera, C. dell', *Italy* 34 B1
Argentière, Aiguilles d', *Switz.* 22 E4
Argentina ■, *S. Amer.* 128 B3
Argentina Is., *Antarctica* 5 C17
Argentino, L., *Argentina* 128 D2
Argenton-Château, *France* 24 F6
Argenton-sur-Creuse, *France* 26 B5
Argeş →, *Romania* 38 E9
Arghandab →, *Afghan.* 62 D1
Argo, *Sudan* 76 D3
Argolikós Kólpos, *Greece* 39 M5
Argonne, *France* 25 C12
Árgos, *Greece* 39 M5
Argostólion, *Greece* 39 L3
Arguedas, *Spain* 28 C3
Arguello, Pt., *U.S.A.* 113 L6
Arguineguín, *Canary Is.* 36 G4
Argun →, *Russia* 45 D13
Argungu, *Nigeria* 79 C5
Argus Pk., *U.S.A.* 113 K9
Argyle, *U.S.A.* 108 A6
Argyle, L., *Australia* 88 C4
Arhavi, *Turkey* 67 C9
Århus, *Denmark* 11 H4
Århus Amtskommune □, *Denmark* 11 H4
Ariadnoye, *Russia* 48 B7
Ariamsvlei, *Namibia* 84 D2
Ariana, *Tunisia* 75 A7
Ariano Irpino, *Italy* 35 A8
Ariano nel Polèsine, *Italy* 33 D9
Ariari →, *Colombia* 120 C3
Aribinda, *Burkina Faso* 79 C4
Arica, *Chile* 124 D3
Arica, *Colombia* 120 D3
Arico, *Canary Is.* 36 F3
Arid, C., *Australia* 89 F3
Arida, *Japan* 49 G7
Ariège □, *France* 26 F5
Ariège →, *France* 26 E5
Arieş →, *Romania* 38 C6
Arīḥā, *Syria* 64 C3
Arílla, Ákra, *Greece* 37 A3
Arima, *Trin. & Tob.* 117 D7
Arinos →, *Brazil* 125 C6
Ario de Rosales, *Mexico* 114 D4
Aripuanã, *Brazil* 125 B5
Aripuanã →, *Brazil* 125 B5
Ariquemes, *Brazil* 125 B5
Arisaig, *U.K.* 14 E3
Arîsh, W. el →, *Egypt* 76 H8
Arismendi, *Venezuela* 120 B4
Arissa, *Ethiopia* 77 E5
Aristazabal I., *Canada* 100 C3
Arivaca, *U.S.A.* 111 L8
Arivonimamo, *Madag.* 85 B8
Ariza, *Spain* 28 D2
Arizaro, Salar de, *Argentina* 126 A2
Arizona, *Argentina* 126 D2
Arizona □, *U.S.A.* 111 J8
Arizpe, *Mexico* 114 A2
Arjeplog, *Sweden* 8 C15
Arjona, *Colombia* 120 A2
Arjona, *Spain* 31 H6
Arjuno, *Indonesia* 57 G15
Arka, *Russia* 45 C15
Arkadak, *Russia* 41 F13
Arkadelphia, *U.S.A.* 109 H8
Arkaig, L., *U.K.* 14 E3
Arkalyk, *Kazakhstan* 44 D7
Arkansas □, *U.S.A.* 109 H8
Arkansas →, *U.S.A.* 109 J9
Arkansas City, *U.S.A.* 109 G6
Árkathos →, *Greece* 39 K4
Arkhángelos, *Greece* 37 C10
Arkhangelsk, *Russia* 44 C5
Arkhangelskoye, *Russia* 41 F12
Arkiko, *Eritrea* 77 D4
Arklow, *Ireland* 15 D5
Arkona, Kap, *Germany* 18 A9
Arkösund, *Sweden* 11 F10
Arkticheskiy, Mys, *Russia* 45 A10
Arkul, *Russia* 41 C17
Arlanc, *France* 26 C7
Arlanza →, *Spain* 30 C6
Arlanzón →, *Spain* 30 C6
Arlberg Pass, *Austria* 19 H6
Arlee, *U.S.A.* 110 C6
Arles, *France* 27 E8
Arlesheim, *Switz.* 22 B5
Arlington, *S. Africa* 85 D4
Arlington, *Oreg., U.S.A.* 110 D3
Arlington, *S. Dak., U.S.A.* 108 C6
Arlington, *Va., U.S.A.* 104 F7
Arlington, *Wash., U.S.A.* 112 B4
Arlon, *Belgium* 17 J7
Arlöv, *Sweden* 11 J7
Arly, *Burkina Faso* 79 C5
Armagh, *U.K.* 15 B5
Armagh □, *U.K.* 15 B5
Armagnac, *France* 26 E4
Armançon →, *France* 25 E10
Armavir, *Russia* 43 D9
Armenia, *Colombia* 120 C2
Armenia ■, *Asia* 43 F11
Armenistís, Ákra, *Greece* 37 C9
Armentières, *France* 25 B9
Armidale, *Australia* 91 E5
Armour, *U.S.A.* 108 D5
Armstrong, *B.C., Canada* 100 C5
Armstrong, *Ont., Canada* 98 B2
Armstrong, *U.S.A.* 109 M6
Armstrong →, *Australia* 88 C5
Arnarfjörður, *Iceland* 8 D2
Arnaud →, *Canada* 97 B12
Arnauti, C., *Cyprus* 37 D11
Arnay-le-Duc, *France* 25 E11
Arnedillo, *Spain* 28 C2
Arnedo, *Spain* 28 C2
Arnemuiden, *Neths.* 17 F3
Árnes, *Iceland* 8 C3
Årnes, *Norway* 10 D5
Arnett, *U.S.A.* 109 G5
Arnhem, *Neths.* 16 E7
Arnhem, C., *Australia* 90 A2
Arnhem B., *Australia* 90 A2
Arnhem Land, *Australia* 90 A1
Arno →, *Italy* 32 E7
Arno Bay, *Australia* 91 E2
Arnold, *Calif., U.S.A.* 112 G6
Arnold, *Nebr., U.S.A.* 108 E4
Arnoldstein, *Austria* 21 J3
Arnon →, *France* 25 E9
Arnot, *Canada* 101 B9
Arnøy, *Norway* 8 A16
Arnprior, *Canada* 98 C4
Arnsberg, *Germany* 18 D4
Arnstadt, *Germany* 18 E6
Aro →, *Venezuela* 121 B5
Aroab, *Namibia* 84 D2
Aroche, *Spain* 31 H4
Aroeiras, *Brazil* 122 C4
Arolla, *Switz.* 22 D4
Arolsen, *Germany* 18 D5
Aron →, *France* 26 B7
Arona, *Italy* 32 C5
Aroroy, *Phil.* 55 E5
Arosa, *Switz.* 23 C9
Arosa, Ria de, *Spain* 30 C2
Arpajon, *France* 25 D9
Arpajon-sur-Cère, *France* 26 D6
Arpino, *Italy* 34 A6
Arque, *Bolivia* 124 D4
Arrabury, *Australia* 91 D3
Arrah = Ara, *India* 63 G11
Arraias, *Brazil* 123 D2
Arraias →, *Mato Grosso, Brazil* 125 C7
Arraias →, *Pará, Brazil* 122 C2
Arraiolos, *Portugal* 31 G3
Arran, *U.K.* 14 F3
Arrandale, *Canada* 100 C3
Arras, *France* 25 B9
Arrats →, *France* 26 D4
Arreau, *France* 26 F4
Arrecife, *Canary Is.* 36 F6
Arrecifes, *Argentina* 126 C3
Arrée, Mts. d', *France* 24 D3
Arriaga, *Chiapas, Mexico* 115 D6
Arriaga, *San Luis Potosí, Mexico* 114 C4
Arrilalah P.O., *Australia* 90 C3
Arrino, *Australia* 89 E2
Arrojado →, *Brazil* 123 D3
Arromanches-les-Bains, *France* 24 C6
Arronches, *Portugal* 31 F3
Arros →, *France* 26 E3
Arrou, *France* 24 D8
Arrow, L., *Ireland* 15 B3
Arrow Rock Res., *U.S.A.* 110 E6
Arrowhead, *Canada* 100 C5
Arrowhead, L., *U.S.A.* 113 L9
Arrowtown, *N.Z.* 87 L2
Arroyo de la Luz, *Spain* 31 F4
Arroyo Grande, *U.S.A.* 113 K6
Års, *Denmark* 11 H3
Ars, *Iran* 64 B5
Ars-en-Ré, *France* 26 B2
Ars-sur-Moselle, *France* 25 C13
Arsenault L., *Canada* 101 B7
Arsenev, *Russia* 48 B6
Arsi □, *Ethiopia* 77 F4
Arsiero, *Italy* 33 C8
Arsin, *Turkey* 67 C8
Arsk, *Russia* 41 C16
Árta, *Greece* 39 K4
Artá, *Spain* 36 B10
Arteaga, *Mexico* 114 D4
Arteche, *Phil.* 55 E6
Arteijo, *Spain* 30 B2
Artem, *Russia* 48 C6
Artem, Ostrov, *Azerbaijan* 43 F14
Artemovsk, *Russia* 45 D10
Artemovsk, *Ukraine* 42 B8
Artemovski, *Russia* 43 C9
Artenay, *France* 25 D8
Artern, *Germany* 18 D7
Artesa de Segre, *Spain* 28 D6
Artesia = Mosomane, *Botswana* 84 C4
Artesia, *U.S.A.* 109 J2
Artesia Wells, *U.S.A.* 109 L5
Artesian, *U.S.A.* 108 C6
Arth, *Switz.* 23 B7
Arthez-de-Béarn, *France* 26 E3
Arthington, *Liberia* 78 D2
Arthur →, *Australia* 90 G3
Arthur Cr. →, *Australia* 90 C2
Arthur Pt., *Australia* 90 C5
Arthur's Pass, *N.Z.* 87 K3
Arthur's Town, *Bahamas* 117 B4
Artigas, *Uruguay* 126 C4
Artik, *Armenia* 43 F10
Artillery L., *Canada* 101 A7
Artois, *France* 25 B9
Artsiz, *Ukraine* 42 C3
Artvin, *Turkey* 43 F9
Artvin □, *Turkey* 67 C9
Aru, Kepulauan, *Indonesia* 57 F8
Aru Is. = Aru, Kepulauan, *Indonesia* 57 F8
Aru Meru □, *Tanzania* 82 C4
Arua, *Uganda* 82 B3
Aruanã, *Brazil* 123 D1
Aruba ■, *W. Indies* 117 D6
Arucas, *Canary Is.* 36 F4
Arudy, *France* 26 E3
Arumã, *Brazil* 121 D5
Arumpo, *Australia* 91 E3
Arun →, *Nepal* 63 F12
Arunachal Pradesh □, *India* 61 E19
Arusha, *Tanzania* 82 C4
Arusha □, *Tanzania* 82 C4
Arusha Chini, *Tanzania* 82 C4
Aruwimi →, *Zaïre* 82 B1
Arvada, *U.S.A.* 110 D10
Arvayheer, *Mongolia* 54 B5
Arve →, *France* 27 B10
Árvi, *Greece* 37 E7
Arvida, *Canada* 99 C5
Arvidsjaur, *Sweden* 8 D15
Arvika, *Sweden* 9 G12
Arvin, *U.S.A.* 113 K8
Arxan, *China* 54 B6
Aryirádhes, *Greece* 37 B3
Aryiroúpolis, *Greece* 37 D6
Arys, *Kazakhstan* 44 E7
Arzachena, *Italy* 34 A2
Arzamas, *Russia* 41 D13
Arzew, *Algeria* 75 A4
Arzgir, *Russia* 43 D11
Arzignano, *Italy* 33 C8
As, *Belgium* 17 F7
Aş Şadr, *U.A.E.* 65 E7
Aş Şafā, *Syria* 69 B6
'As Saffānīyah, *Si. Arabia* 65 D6
As Safīrah, *Syria* 64 B3
Aş Şahm, *Oman* 65 E8
As Sājir, *Si. Arabia* 64 E5
As Salamīyah, *Syria* 64 C3
As Salt, *Jordan* 69 C4
As Sal'w'a, *Qatar* 65 E6
As Samāwah, *Iraq* 64 D5
As Sanamayn, *Syria* 69 B5
As Sukhnah, *Syria* 64 C3
As Sulaymānīyah, *Iraq* 64 C5
As Sulaymī, *Si. Arabia* 64 E4
As Summān, *Si. Arabia* 64 E5
As Suwaydā', *Syria* 69 C5
As Suwaydā' □, *Syria* 69 C5
Aş Şuwayrah, *Iraq* 64 C5
Asab, *Namibia* 84 D2
Asaba, *Nigeria* 79 D6
Asafo, *Ghana* 78 D4
Asahi-Gawa →, *Japan* 49 G6
Asahigawa, *Japan* 48 C11
Asale, L., *Ethiopia* 77 E5

Asamankese, *Ghana* 79 D4
Asansol, *India* 63 H12
Åsarna, *Sweden* 10 B8
Asbe Teferi, *Ethiopia* ... 77 F5
Asbesberge, *S. Africa* 84 D3
Asbestos, *Canada* 99 C5
Asbury Park, *U.S.A.* 107 F10
Ascensión, *Mexico* 114 A3
Ascensión, B. de la, *Mexico* 115 D7
Ascension I., *Atl. Oc.* .. 2 E9
Aschaffenburg, *Germany* . 19 F5
Aschendorf, *Germany* .. 18 B3
Aschersleben, *Germany* .. 18 D7
Asciano, *Italy* 33 E8
Áscoli Piceno, *Italy* 33 F10
Áscoli Satriano, *Italy* ... 35 A8
Ascona, *Switz.* 23 D7
Ascope, *Peru* 124 B2
Ascotán, *Chile* 126 A2
Aseb, *Eritrea* 68 E3
Asedjrad, *Algeria* 75 D5
Asela, *Ethiopia* 77 F4
Asenovgrad, *Bulgaria* 39 G7
Asfeld, *France* 25 C11
Asfûn el Matâ'na, *Egypt* . 76 B3
Åsgårdstrand, *Norway* .. 10 E4
Asgata, *Cyprus* 37 E12
Ash Fork, *U.S.A.* 111 J7
Ash Grove, *U.S.A.* 109 G8
Ash Shamāl □, *Lebanon* . 69 A5
Ash Shāmiyah, *Iraq* 64 D5
Ash Shāriqah, *U.A.E.* 65 E7
Ash Sharmah, *Si. Arabia* . 64 D2
Ash Sharqāt, *Iraq* 64 C4
Ash Sharqi, Al Jabal, *Lebanon* 69 B5
Ash Shaṭrah, *Iraq* 64 D5
Ash Shawbak, *Jordan* ... 64 D2
Ash Shawmari, J., *Jordan* 69 E5
Ash Shaykh, J., *Lebanon* . 69 B4
Ash Shināfiyah, *Iraq* ... 64 D5
Ash Shu'aybah, *Si. Arabia* 64 E5
Ash Shumlūl, *Si. Arabia* . 64 E5
Ash Shūr'a, *Iraq* 64 C4
Ash Shurayf, *Si. Arabia* . 64 E3
Ash Shuwayfāt, *Lebanon* . 69 B4
Ashanti □, *Ghana* 79 D4
Ashau, *Vietnam* 58 D6
Ashburn, *U.S.A.* 105 K4
Ashburton, *N.Z.* 87 K3
Ashburton →, *Australia* .. 88 D1
Ashburton Downs, *Australia* 88 D2
Ashby de la Zouch, *U.K.* . 12 E6
Ashcroft, *Canada* 100 C4
Ashdod, *Israel* 69 D3
Asheboro, *U.S.A.* 105 H6
Asherton, *U.S.A.* 109 L5
Asheville, *U.S.A.* 105 H4
Asheweig →, *Canada* .. 98 B2
Ashford, *Australia* 91 D5
Ashford, *U.K.* 13 F8
Ashford, *U.S.A.* 110 C2
Ashgabat = Ashkhabad, *Turkmenistan* 44 F6
Ashibetsu, *Japan* 48 C11
Ashikaga, *Japan* 49 F9
Ashizuri-Zaki, *Japan* ... 49 H6
Ashkarkot, *Afghan.* 62 C2
Ashkhabad, *Turkmenistan* 44 F6
Ashland, *Kans., U.S.A.* . 109 G5
Ashland, *Ky., U.S.A.* ... 104 F4
Ashland, *Maine, U.S.A.* . 99 C6
Ashland, *Mont., U.S.A.* . 110 D10
Ashland, *Nebr., U.S.A.* . 108 E6
Ashland, *Ohio, U.S.A.* . 106 F2
Ashland, *Oreg., U.S.A.* . 110 E2
Ashland, *Pa., U.S.A.* ... 107 F8
Ashland, *Va., U.S.A.* ... 104 G7
Ashland, *Wis., U.S.A.* .. 108 B9
Ashley, *N. Dak., U.S.A.* . 108 B5
Ashley, *Pa., U.S.A.* 107 E9
Ashmont, *Canada* 100 C6
Ashmore Reef, *Australia* . 88 B3
Ashmûn, *Egypt* 76 H7
Ashq'elon, *Israel* 69 D3
Ashtabula, *U.S.A.* 106 E4
Ashton, *S. Africa* 84 E3
Ashton, *U.S.A.* 110 D8
Ashton under Lyne, *U.K.* 12 D5
Ashuanipi, L., *Canada* .. 99 B6
Asia 46 E11
Asia, Kepulauan, *Indonesia* 57 D8
Āsīā Bak, *Iran* 65 C6
Asiago, *Italy* 33 C8
Asidonhoppo, *Surinam* . 121 C6
Asifabad, *India* 60 K11
Asike, *Indonesia* 57 F10
Asilah, *Morocco* 74 A3
Asinara, *Italy* 34 A1
Asinara, G. dell', *Italy* .. 34 B1
Asino, *Russia* 44 D9
'Asīr □, *Si. Arabia* 68 D3
'Asīr, Ras, *Somali Rep.* .. 68 E5
Aşkale, *Turkey* 67 D9
Asker, *Norway* 10 E4
Askersund, *Sweden* 11 F8
Askham, *S. Africa* 84 D3
Askim, *Norway* 10 E5
Askja, *Iceland* 8 D5
Asl, *Egypt* 76 J8
Asmara = Asmera, *Eritrea* 77 D4
Asmera, *Eritrea* 77 D4

Asnæs, *Denmark* 11 J5
Asni, *Morocco* 74 B3
Ásola, *Italy* 32 C7
Asoteriba, Jebel, *Sudan* . 76 C4
Asotin, *U.S.A.* 110 C5
Aspe, *Spain* 29 G4
Aspen, *U.S.A.* 111 G10
Aspendos, *Turkey* 66 E4
Aspermont, *U.S.A.* 109 J4
Aspiring, Mt., *N.Z.* 87 L2
Aspres-sur-Buëch, *France* . 27 D9
Asprókavos, Ákra, *Greece* 37 B4
Aspromonte, *Italy* 35 D8
Aspur, *India* 62 H6
Asquith, *Canada* 101 C7
Assa, *Morocco* 74 C3
Assâba, *Mauritania* 78 B2
Assam □, *India* 61 F18
Assamakka, *Niger* 79 B6
Asse, *Belgium* 17 H4
Assebroek, *Belgium* 17 F2
Assekrem, *Algeria* 75 D6
Assémini, *Italy* 34 C2
Assen, *Neths.* 16 C9
Assendelft, *Neths.* 16 D5
Assenede, *Belgium* 17 F3
Assens, *Århus, Denmark* . 11 H4
Assens, *Fyn, Denmark* .. 11 J3
Assesse, *Belgium* 17 H6
Assini, *Ivory C.* 78 D4
Assiniboia, *Canada* 101 D7
Assiniboine →, *Canada* . 101 D9
Assis, *Brazil* 127 A5
Assisi, *Italy* 33 E9
Assynt, L., *U.K.* 14 C3
Astaffort, *France* 26 D4
Astara, *Azerbaijan* 67 D13
Asten, *Neths.* 17 F7
Asterousia, *Greece* 37 E7
Asti, *Italy* 32 D5
Astipálaia, *Greece* 39 N9
Astorga, *Spain* 30 C4
Astoria, *U.S.A.* 112 D3
Åstorp, *Sweden* 11 H6
Astrakhan, *Russia* 43 C13
Astudillo, *Spain* 30 C6
Asturias □, *Spain* 30 B5
Asunción, *Paraguay* ... 126 B4
Asunción Nochixtlán, *Mexico* 115 D5
Asutri, *Sudan* 77 D4
Aswa →, *Uganda* 82 B3
Aswad, Ras al, *Si. Arabia* 76 C4
Aswân, *Egypt* 76 C3
Aswân High Dam = Sadd el Aali, *Egypt* 76 C3
Asyût, *Egypt* 76 B3
Asyûti, Wadi →, *Egypt* . 76 B3
Aszód, *Hungary* 21 H9
At Ṭafīlah, *Jordan* 69 E4
At Ṭā'if, *Si. Arabia* ... 68 C3
Aṭ Ṭirāq, *Si. Arabia* ... 64 E5
Atacama, *Chile* 126 B2
Atacama, Desierto de, *Chile* 126 A2
Atacama, Salar de, *Chile* 126 A2
'Ataco, *Colombia* 120 C2
Atakor, *Algeria* 75 D6
Atakpamé, *Togo* 79 D5
Ataländi, *Greece* 39 L5
Atalaya, *Peru* 124 C3
Atalaya de Femes, *Canary Is.* 36 F6
Ataléia, *Brazil* 123 E3
Atami, *Japan* 49 G9
Atapupu, *Indonesia* ... 57 F6
Atâr, *Mauritania* 74 D2
Atara, *Russia* 45 C13
Ataram, Erg n-, *Algeria* . 75 D5
Atarfe, *Spain* 31 H7
Atascadero, *Calif., U.S.A.* 111 J3
Atascadero, *Calif., U.S.A.* 112 K6
Atasu, *Kazakhstan* 44 E8
Atauro, *Indonesia* 57 F7
Atbara, *Sudan* 77 D3
'Atbara →, *Sudan* 76 D3
Atbasar, *Kazakhstan* ... 44 D7
Atchafalaya B., *U.S.A.* . 109 L9
Atchison, *U.S.A.* 108 F7
Atebubu, *Ghana* 79 D4
Ateca, *Spain* 28 D3
Aterno →, *Italy* 33 F10
Atesine, Alpi, *Italy* ... 32 B8
Atessa, *Italy* 33 F11
Ath, *Belgium* 17 G3
Athabasca, *Canada* ... 100 C6
Athabasca →, *Canada* . 101 B6
Athabasca, L., *Canada* . 101 B7
Athboy, *Ireland* 15 C5
Athenry, *Ireland* 15 C3
Athens = Athínai, *Greece* 39 M6
Athens, *Ala., U.S.A.* .. 105 H2
Athens, *Ga., U.S.A.* .. 105 J4
Athens, *N.Y., U.S.A.* . 107 D11
Athens, *Ohio, U.S.A.* . 104 F4
Athens, *Pa., U.S.A.* ... 107 E8
Athens, *Tenn., U.S.A.* . 105 H3
Athens, *Tex., U.S.A.* .. 109 J7
Atherley, *Canada* 106 B5
Atherton, *Australia* ... 90 B4
Athiéme, *Benin* 79 D5
Athienou, *Cyprus* 37 D12
Athínai, *Greece* 39 M6
Athlone, *Ireland* 15 C4
Athna, *Cyprus* 37 D12

Atholl, Forest of, *U.K.* ... 14 E5
Atholville, *Canada* 99 C6
Áthos, *Greece* 39 J7
Athus, *Belgium* 17 J7
Athy, *Ireland* 15 D5
Ati, *Chad* 73 F8
Ati, *Sudan* 77 E2
Atiak, *Uganda* 82 B3
Atico, *Peru* 124 D3
Atienza, *Spain* 28 D2
Atikokan, *Canada* 98 C1
Atikonak L., *Canada* .. 99 B7
Atimonan, *Phil.* 55 E4
Atka, *Russia* 45 C16
Atkarsk, *Russia* 41 F14
Atkinson, *U.S.A.* 108 D5
Atlanta, *Ga., U.S.A.* .. 105 J3
Atlanta, *Tex., U.S.A.* .. 109 J7
Atlantic, *U.S.A.* 108 E7
Atlantic City, *U.S.A.* .. 104 F8
Atlantic Ocean 2 E9
Atlántico □, *Colombia* . 120 A2
Atlas Mts. = Haut Atlas, *Morocco* 74 B3
Atlin, *Canada* 100 B2
Atlin, L., *Canada* 100 B2
Atmore, *U.S.A.* 105 K2
Atoka, *U.S.A.* 109 H6
Atokos, *Greece* 39 L3
Atolia, *U.S.A.* 113 K9
Atouguia, *Portugal* ... 31 F1
Atoyac →, *Mexico* ... 115 D5
Atrak →, *Iran* 65 B8
Atran, *Sweden* 11 G6
Atrato →, *Colombia* .. 120 B2
Atrauli, *India* 62 E8
Atri, *Italy* 33 F10
Atsbi, *Ethiopia* 77 E4
Atsoum, Mts., *Cameroon* 79 D7
Atsuta, *Japan* 48 C10
Attalla, *U.S.A.* 105 H2
Attáviros, *Greece* 37 C9
Attawapiskat, *Canada* . 98 B3
Attawapiskat →, *Canada* 98 B3
Attawapiskat, L., *Canada* 98 B2
Attendorn, *Germany* .. 18 D3
Attert, *Belgium* 17 J7
Attica, *U.S.A.* 104 E2
Attichy, *France* 25 C10
Attigny, *France* 25 C11
Attikamagen L., *Canada* 99 A6
Attleboro, *U.S.A.* 107 E13
Attock, *Pakistan* 62 C5
Attopeu, *Laos* 58 E6
Attur, *India* 60 P11
Atuel →, *Argentina* .. 126 D2
Atvacik, *Turkey* 66 D2
Åtvidaberg, *Sweden* .. 11 F10
Atwater, *U.S.A.* 111 H3
Atwood, *Canada* 106 C3
Atwood, *U.S.A.* 108 F4
Atyrau, *Kazakhstan* ... 43 C14
Au Sable →, *U.S.A.* .. 104 C4
Au Sable Pt., *U.S.A.* .. 98 C2
Aubagne, *France* 27 E9
Aubange, *Belgium* ... 17 J7
Aubarca, C., *Spain* ... 36 B7
Aube □, *France* 25 D11
Aube →, *France* 25 D10
Aubel, *Belgium* 17 G7
Aubenas, *France* 27 D8
Aubenton, *France* 25 C11
Auberry, *U.S.A.* 112 H7
Aubigny-sur-Nère, *France* 25 E9
Aubin, *France* 26 D6
Aubrac, Mts. d', *France* . 26 D7
Auburn, *Ala., U.S.A.* .. 105 J3
Auburn, *Calif., U.S.A.* . 112 G5
Auburn, *Ind., U.S.A.* .. 104 E3
Auburn, *N.Y., U.S.A.* .. 107 D8
Auburn, *Nebr., U.S.A.* . 108 E7
Auburn, *Wash., U.S.A.* . 112 C4
Auburn Ra., *Australia* . 91 D5
Auburndale, *U.S.A.* ... 105 L5
Aubusson, *France* 26 C6
Auch, *France* 26 E4
Auchel, *France* 25 B9
Auchi, *Nigeria* 79 D6
Auckland, *N.Z.* 87 G5
Auckland Is., *Pac. Oc.* . 92 N8
Aude □, *France* 26 E6
Aude →, *France* 26 E7
Auden, *Canada* 98 B2
Auderghem, *Belgium* . 17 G4
Auderville, *France* ... 24 C5
Audierne, *France* 24 D2
Audincourt, *France* .. 25 E13
Audo, *Ethiopia* 77 F5
Audubon, *U.S.A.* 108 E7
Aue, *Germany* 18 E8
Auerbach, *Germany* .. 18 E8
Aueti Paraná →, *Brazil* . 120 D4
Aufist, *W. Sahara* 74 C2
Augathella, *Australia* . 91 D4
Augrabies Falls, *S. Africa* 84 D3
Augsburg, *Germany* .. 19 G6
Augusta, *Italy* 35 E8
Augusta, *Ark., U.S.A.* . 109 H9
Augusta, *Ga., U.S.A.* . 105 J5
Augusta, *Kans., U.S.A.* 109 G6
Augusta, *Maine, U.S.A.* 99 D6
Augusta, *Mont., U.S.A.* 110 C7
Augusta, *Wis., U.S.A.* . 108 C9
Augustenborg, *Denmark* 11 K3
Augustów, *Poland* 20 B12

Augustus, Mt., *Australia* .. 88 D2
Augustus Downs, *Australia* 90 B2
Augustus I., *Australia* .. 88 C3
Aukan, *Eritrea* 77 D5
Aukum, *U.S.A.* 112 G6
Auld, L., *Australia* 88 D3
Aulla, *Italy* 32 D6
Aulnay, *France* 26 B3
Aulne →, *France* 24 D2
Aulnoye-Aymeries, *France* 25 B10
Ault, *France* 24 B8
Ault, *U.S.A.* 108 E2
Aulus-les-Bains, *France* . 26 F5
Aumale, *France* 25 C8
Aumont-Aubrac, *France* . 26 D7
Auna, *Nigeria* 79 C5
Aunis, *France* 26 B3
Auponhia, *Indonesia* .. 57 E7
Aups, *France* 27 E10
Aur, P., *Malaysia* 59 L5
Auragh, *France* 24 E4
Auraiya, *India* 63 F8
Aurangabad, *Bihar, India* 63 G11
Aurangabad, *Maharashtra, India* 60 K9
Auray, *France* 24 E4
Aurès, *Algeria* 75 A6
Aurich, *Germany* 18 B3
Aurilândia, *Brazil* ... 123 E1
Aurillac, *France* 26 D6
Auronza, *Italy* 33 B9
Aurora, *S. Africa* 84 E2
Aurora, *Colo., U.S.A.* . 108 F2
Aurora, *Ill., U.S.A.* .. 104 E1
Aurora, *Mo., U.S.A.* . 109 G8
Aurora, *Nebr., U.S.A.* . 108 E6
Aurora, *Ohio, U.S.A.* . 106 E3
Aursmoen, *Norway* .. 10 E5
Aurukun Mission, *Australia* 90 A3
Aus, *Namibia* 84 D2
Auschwitz = Oświecim, *Poland* 20 E9
Aust-Agder fylke □, *Norway* 9 G9
Austin, *Minn., U.S.A.* . 108 D8
Austin, *Nev., U.S.A.* .. 110 G5
Austin, *Pa., U.S.A.* ... 106 E6
Austin, *Tex., U.S.A.* .. 109 K6
Austin, L., *Australia* .. 89 E2
Austral Downs, *Australia* 90 C2
Austral Is. = Tubuai Is., *Pac. Oc.* 93 K12
Austral Seamount Chain, *Pac. Oc.* 93 K13
Australia ■, *Oceania* 92 K5
Australian Alps, *Australia* 91 F4
Australian Capital Territory □, *Australia* .. 91 F4
Austria ■, *Europe* 21 H4
Austvågøy, *Norway* ... 8 B13
Autazes, *Brazil* 121 D6
Autelbas, *Belgium* ... 17 J7
Auterive, *France* 26 E5
Authie →, *France* ... 25 B8
Authon-du-Perche, *France* 24 D7
Autlán, *Mexico* 114 D4
Autun, *France* 25 F11
Auvelais, *Belgium* ... 17 H5
Auvergne, *Australia* .. 88 C5
Auvergne, *France* ... 26 C7
Auvergne, Mts. d', *France* 26 C6
Auvézère →, *France* . 26 C4
Auxerre, *France* 25 E10
Auxi-le-Château, *France* 25 B9
Auxonne, *France* 25 E12
Auzances, *France* ... 26 B6
Auzat-sur-Allier, *France* 26 C7
Avallon, *France* 25 E10
Avalon, *U.S.A.* 113 M8
Avalon Pen., *Canada* . 99 C9
Avaré, *Brazil* 127 A6
Ávas, *Greece* 39 J8
Avawatz Mts., *U.S.A.* . 113 K10
Aveiro, *Brazil* 121 D6
Aveiro, *Portugal* 30 E2
Aveiro □, *Portugal* .. 30 E2
Āvej, *Iran* 65 C6
Avelgem, *Belgium* ... 17 G2
Avellaneda, *Argentina* . 126 C4
Avellino, *Italy* 35 B7
Avenal, *U.S.A.* 112 K6
Avenches, *Switz.* 22 C4
Averøya, *Norway* ... 10 A1
Aversa, *Italy* 35 B7
Avery, *U.S.A.* 110 C6
Aves, I. de, *W. Indies* . 117 C7
Aves, Is. de, *Venezuela* 117 D6
Avesnes-sur-Helpe, *France* 25 B10
Avesta, *Sweden* 9 F14
Aveyron □, *France* .. 26 D6
Aveyron →, *France* .. 26 D5
Avezzano, *Italy* 33 F10
Aviá Terai, *Argentina* . 126 B3
Aviano, *Italy* 33 B9
Avigliana, *Italy* 32 C4
Avigliano, *Italy* 35 B8
Avignon, *France* 27 E8
Ávila, *Spain* 30 E6
Ávila □, *Spain* 30 E6
Ávila, Sierra de, *Spain* . 30 E5
Avila Beach, *U.S.A.* .. 113 K6
Avilés, *Spain* 30 B5
Avisio →, *Italy* 33 B8
Aviz, *Portugal* 31 F3
Avize, *France* 25 D11

Avoca, *Ireland* 15 D5
Avoca, *U.S.A.* 106 D7
Avoca →, *Australia* ... 91 F3
Avola, *Canada* 100 C5
Avola, *Italy* 35 F8
Avon, *N.Y., U.S.A.* ... 106 D7
Avon, *S. Dak., U.S.A.* . 108 D5
Avon □, *U.K.* 13 F5
Avon →, *Australia* ... 89 F2
Avon →, *Avon, U.K.* .. 13 F5
Avon →, *Hants., U.K.* . 13 G6
Avon →, *Warks., U.K.* . 13 F5
Avondale, *Zimbabwe* .. 83 F3
Avonlea, *Canada* 101 D7
Avonmore, *Canada* ... 107 A10
Avonmouth, *U.K.* 13 F5
Avranches, *France* ... 24 D5
Avre →, *France* 24 D8
Awag el Baqar, *Sudan* . 77 E3
A'waj →, *Syria* 69 B5
Awaji-Shima, *Japan* .. 49 G7
'Awālī, *Bahrain* 65 E6
Awantipur, *India* 63 C6
Awasa, L., *Ethiopia* .. 77 F4
Awash, *Ethiopia* 68 F3
Awash →, *Ethiopia* .. 77 E5
Awaso, *Ghana* 78 D4
Awatere →, *N.Z.* 87 J5
Awbārī, *Libya* 75 C7
Awbārī □, *Libya* 75 C7
Awe, L., *U.K.* 14 E3
Aweil, *Sudan* 77 F2
Awgu, *Nigeria* 79 D6
Awjilah, *Libya* 73 C9
Ax-les-Thermes, *France* 26 F5
Axarfjörður, *Iceland* .. 8 C5
Axel, *Neths.* 17 F3
Axel Heiberg I., *Canada* 4 B3
Axim, *Ghana* 78 E4
Axinim, *Brazil* 121 D6
Axintele, *Romania* ... 38 E9
Axioma, *Brazil* 125 B5
Axiós →, *Greece* 39 J5
Axminster, *U.K.* 13 G4
Axvall, *Sweden* 11 F7
Aÿ, *France* 25 C11
Ayabaca, *Peru* 124 A2
Ayabe, *Japan* 49 G7
Ayacucho, *Argentina* . 126 D4
Ayacucho, *Peru* 124 C3
Ayaguz, *Kazakhstan* .. 44 E9
Ayamonte, *Spain* ... 31 H3
Ayan, *Russia* 45 D14
Ayancık, *Turkey* 42 F6
Ayapel, *Colombia* ... 120 B2
Ayas, *Turkey* 42 F5
Ayaviri, *Peru* 124 C3
Aybastı, *Turkey* 66 C7
Aydın, *Turkey* 66 E2
Aydın □, *Turkey* 66 E2
Aye, *Belgium* 17 H6
Ayenngré, *Togo* 79 D5
Ayer's Cliff, *Canada* . 107 A12
Ayers Rock, *Australia* . 89 E5
Ayiá, *Greece* 39 K5
Ayía Aikateríni, Ákra, *Greece* 37 A3
Ayia Dhéka, *Greece* .. 37 D6
Ayia Gálini, *Greece* .. 37 D6
Ayía Marína, *Greece* .. 39 M9
Ayia Napa, *Cyprus* .. 37 E13
Ayía Paraskeví, *Greece* 39 K9
Ayia Phyla, *Cyprus* .. 37 E12
Ayía Rouméli, *Greece* . 39 P6
Ayía Varvára, *Greece* . 37 D7
Áyios Amvrósios, *Cyprus* 37 D12
Áyios Andréas, *Greece* . 39 M5
Áyios Evstrátios, *Greece* 39 K7
Áyios Ioánnis, Ákra, *Greece* 37 D7
Áyios Isidoros, *Greece* . 37 C9
Áyios Kiríkos, *Greece* . 39 M9
Áyios Matthaíos, *Greece* 37 B3
Áyios Mírono, *Greece* . 39 P8
Áyios Nikólaos, *Greece* . 37 D7
Áyios Seryios, *Cyprus* . 37 D12
Áyios Theodhoros, *Cyprus* 37 D13
Aykathonísi, *Greece* .. 39 M9
Aylesbury, *U.K.* 13 F7
Aylmer, *Canada* 106 D4
Aylmer, L., *Canada* .. 96 B8
Ayna, *Spain* 29 G2
Ayolas, *Paraguay* ... 126 B4
Ayom, *Sudan* 77 F2
Ayon, Ostrov, *Russia* . 45 C17
Ayora, *Spain* 29 F3
Ayr, *Australia* 90 B4
Ayr, *U.K.* 14 F4
Ayr →, *U.K.* 14 F4
Ayrancı, *Turkey* 66 E5
Ayre, Pt. of, *U.K.* ... 12 C3
Aysha, *Ethiopia* 77 E5
Aytos, *Bulgaria* 38 G10
Ayu, Kepulauan, *Indonesia* 57 D8
Ayutla, *Guatemala* .. 116 D1
Ayutla, *Mexico* 115 D5
Ayvacık, *Turkey* 66 C7
Ayvalık, *Turkey* 66 E2
Aywaille, *Belgium* ... 17 H7
Az Zabdānī, *Syria* ... 69 B5
Az Zāhirīyah, *Jordan* . 69 D3
Aẓ Ẓahrān, *Si. Arabia* . 65 E6
Az Zarqā, *Jordan* ... 69 C5
Az Zāwiyah, *Libya* ... 75 B7
Az Zībār, *Iraq* 64 B5

Az-Zilfī

Az-Zilfī, *Si. Arabia* 64 E5
Az Zubayr, *Iraq* 64 D5
Azambuja, *Portugal* 31 F2
Azamgarh, *India* 63 F10
Azangaro, *Peru* 124 C3
Azaouak, Vallée de l', *Mali* 79 B5
Āzār Shahr, *Iran* 64 B5
Azärbayjan = Azerbaijan ■, *Asia* 43 F12
Āzarbāyjān-e Gharbī □, *Iran* 64 B5
Āzarbāyjān-e Sharqī □, *Iran* 64 B5
Azare, *Nigeria* 79 C7
Azay-le-Rideau, *France* 24 E7
A'zāz, *Syria* 64 B3
Azazga, *Algeria* 75 A5
Azbine = Aïr, *Niger* 79 B6
Azefal, *Mauritania* 74 D2
Azeffoun, *Algeria* 75 A5
Azemmour, *Morocco* 74 B3
Azerbaijan ■, *Asia* 43 F12
Azerbaijchan = Azerbaijan ■, *Asia* 43 F12
Azezo, *Ethiopia* 77 E4
Azimganj, *India* 63 G13
Aznalcóllar, *Spain* 31 H4
Azogues, *Ecuador* 120 D2
Azores, *Atl. Oc.* 2 C8
Azov, *Russia* 43 C8
Azov, Sea of = Azovskoye More, *Europe* 42 C7
Azovskoye More, *Europe* 42 C7
Azovy, *Russia* 44 C7
Azpeitia, *Spain* 28 B2
Azrou, *Morocco* 74 B3
Aztec, *U.S.A.* 111 H10
Azúa, *Dom. Rep.* 117 C5
Azuaga, *Spain* 31 G5
Azuara, *Spain* 28 D4
Azuay □, *Ecuador* 120 D2
Azuer →, *Spain* 31 F7
Azuero, Pen. de, *Panama* 116 E3
Azul, *Argentina* 126 D4
Azul, Serra, *Brazil* 125 C7
Azurduy, *Bolivia* 125 D5
Azusa, *U.S.A.* 113 L9
Azzaba, *Algeria* 75 A6
Azzano Décimo, *Italy* 33 C9
'Azzūn, *Jordan* 69 C4

B

Ba Don, *Vietnam* 58 D6
Ba Dong, *Vietnam* 59 H6
Ba Ngoi = Cam Lam, *Vietnam* 59 G7
Ba Ria, *Vietnam* 59 G6
Ba Tri, *Vietnam* 59 G6
Ba Xian, *China* 50 E9
Baa, *Indonesia* 57 F6
Baamonde, *Spain* 30 B3
Baar, *Switz.* 23 B7
Baarle Nassau, *Belgium* 17 F5
Baarlo, *Neths.* 17 F8
Baarn, *Neths.* 16 D6
Bab el Mandeb, *Red Sea* 68 E3
Baba Burnu, *Turkey* 66 D2
Baba dag, *Azerbaijan* 43 F13
Bābā Kalū, *Iran* 65 D6
Babaçulândia, *Brazil* 122 C2
Babadag, *Romania* 38 E11
Babadayhan = Kirovsk, *Turkmenistan* 44 F7
Babaeski, *Turkey* 66 C2
Babahoyo, *Ecuador* 120 D2
Babakin, *Australia* 89 F2
Babana, *Nigeria* 79 C5
Babar, *Algeria* 75 A6
Babar, *Indonesia* 57 F7
Babar, *Pakistan* 62 D3
Babarkach, *Pakistan* 62 E2
Babayevo, *Russia* 41 B9
Babb, *U.S.A.* 110 B7
Babenhausen, *Germany* 19 F4
Babi Besar, P., *Malaysia* 59 L4
Babian Jiang →, *China* 52 F3
Babile, *Ethiopia* 77 F5
Babinda, *Australia* 90 B4
Babine, *Canada* 100 B3
Babine →, *Canada* 100 B3
Babine L., *Canada* 100 C3
Babo, *Indonesia* 57 E8
Bābol, *Iran* 65 B7
Bābol Sar, *Iran* 65 B7
Baboua, *C.A.R.* 80 C2
Babruysk = Bobruysk, *Belorussia* 40 E6
Babura, *Nigeria* 79 C6
Babusar Pass, *Pakistan* 63 B5
Babušnica, *Serbia* 21 M12
Babuyan Chan., *Phil.* 55 B4
Babuyan Is., *Phil.* 55 B4
Babylon, *Iraq* 64 C5
Bac Can, *Vietnam* 58 A5
Bac Giang, *Vietnam* 58 B6
Bac Ninh, *Vietnam* 58 B6
Bac Phan, *Vietnam* 58 B5
Bac Quang, *Vietnam* 58 A5
Bacabal, *Brazil* 122 B3
Bacajá →, *Brazil* 121 D7
Bacalar, *Mexico* 115 D7
Bacan, *Indonesia* 57 F7
Bacan, Kepulauan, *Indonesia* 57 E7
Bacan, Pulau, *Indonesia* 57 E7
Bacarra, *Phil.* 55 B4
Bacău, *Romania* 38 C9
Baccarat, *France* 25 D13
Bacerac, *Mexico* 114 A3
Băceşti, *Romania* 38 C10
Bach Long Vi, Dao, *Vietnam* 58 B6
Bachaquero, *Venezuela* 120 B3
Bacharach, *Germany* 19 E3
Bachelina, *Russia* 44 D7
Bachuma, *Ethiopia* 77 F4
Bačina, *Serbia* 21 M11
Back →, *Canada* 96 B9
Bačka Palanka, *Serbia* 21 K9
Bačka Topola, *Serbia* 21 K9
Bäckefors, *Sweden* 11 F6
Backnang, *Germany* 19 G5
Backstairs Passage, *Australia* 91 F2
Baco, Mt., *Phil.* 55 E4
Bacolod, *Phil.* 55 F5
Bacqueville-en-Caux, *France* 24 C8
Bácsalmás, *Hungary* 21 J9
Bacuag, *Phil.* 55 G6
Bacuk, *Malaysia* 59 J4
Bād, *Iran* 65 C7
Bad →, *U.S.A.* 108 C4
Bad Axe, *U.S.A.* 106 C2
Bad Bergzabern, *Germany* 19 F4
Bad Berleburg, *Germany* 18 D4
Bad Bevensen, *Germany* 18 B6
Bad Bramstedt, *Germany* 18 B5
Bad Brückenau, *Germany* 19 E5
Bad Doberan, *Germany* 18 A7
Bad Driburg, *Germany* 18 D5
Bad Ems, *Germany* 19 E3
Bad Frankenhausen, *Germany* 18 D7
Bad Freienwalde, *Germany* 18 C10
Bad Godesberg, *Germany* 18 E3
Bad Hersfeld, *Germany* 18 E5
Bad Hofgastein, *Austria* 21 H3
Bad Homburg, *Germany* 19 E4
Bad Honnef, *Germany* 18 E3
Bad Ischl, *Austria* 21 H3
Bad Kissingen, *Germany* 19 E6
Bad Königshofen, *Germany* 19 E6
Bad Kreuznach, *Germany* 19 F3
Bad Laasphe, *Germany* 18 E4
Bad Lands, *U.S.A.* 108 D3
Bad Langensalza, *Germany* 18 D6
Bad Lauterberg, *Germany* 18 D6
Bad Lippspringe, *Germany* 18 D4
Bad Mergentheim, *Germany* 19 F5
Bad Münstereifel, *Germany* 18 E2
Bad Muskau, *Germany* 18 D10
Bad Nauheim, *Germany* 19 E4
Bad Oeynhausen, *Germany* 18 C4
Bad Oldesloe, *Germany* 18 B6
Bad Orb, *Germany* 19 E5
Bad Pyrmont, *Germany* 18 D5
Bad Ragaz, *Switz.* 23 B9
Bad Reichenhall, *Germany* 19 H8
Bad Säckingen, *Germany* 19 H3
Bad Salzuflen, *Germany* 18 C4
Bad Segeberg, *Germany* 18 B6
Bad Tölz, *Germany* 19 H7
Bad Urach, *Germany* 19 G5
Bad Waldsee, *Germany* 19 H5
Bad Wildungen, *Germany* 18 D5
Bad Wimpfen, *Germany* 19 F5
Bad Windsheim, *Germany* 19 F6
Badagara, *India* 60 P9
Badagri, *Nigeria* 79 D5
Badajós, L., *Brazil* 121 D5
Badajoz, *Spain* 31 G4
Badajoz □, *Spain* 31 G4
Badalona, *Spain* 28 D7
Badalzai, *Afghan.* 62 E1
Badampahar, *India* 61 H15
Badanah, *Si. Arabia* 64 D4
Badarinath, *India* 63 D8
Badas, *Brunei* 56 D4
Badas, Kepulauan, *Indonesia* 56 D3
Baddo →, *Pakistan* 60 F4
Bade, *Indonesia* 57 F9
Baden, *Austria* 21 G6
Baden, *Switz.* 23 B6
Baden-Baden, *Germany* 19 G4
Baden-Württemberg □, *Germany* 19 G5
Badenoch, *U.K.* 14 E4
Badger, *Canada* 99 C8
Badger, *U.S.A.* 112 J7
Bādghīsāt □, *Afghan.* 60 B3
Badgom, *India* 63 B6
Badhoevedorp, *Neths.* 16 D5
Badia Polèsine, *Italy* 33 C8
Badin, *Pakistan* 62 G3
Badogo, *Mali* 78 C3
Badong, *China* 53 B8
Baduen, *Somali Rep.* 68 F4
Badulla, *Sri Lanka* 60 R12
Baena, *Spain* 31 H6
Baexem, *Neths.* 17 F7
Baeza, *Ecuador* 120 D2
Baeza, *Spain* 29 H1
Bafa Gölü, *Turkey* 66 E2
Bafang, *Cameroon* 79 D7
Bafatá, *Guinea-Biss.* 78 C2
Baffin B., *Canada* 4 B4
Baffin I., *Canada* 97 B12
Bafia, *Cameroon* 79 E7
Bafilo, *Togo* 79 D5
Bafing →, *Mali* 78 C2
Bafliyūn, *Syria* 64 B3
Baflo, *Neths.* 16 B9
Bafoulabé, *Mali* 78 C2
Bafoussam, *Cameroon* 79 D7
Bāfq, *Iran* 65 D7
Bafra, *Turkey* 42 F6
Bafra Burnu, *Turkey* 42 F6
Bāft, *Iran* 65 D8
Bafut, *Cameroon* 79 D7
Bafwasende, *Zaïre* 82 B2
Bagamoyo, *Tanzania* 82 D4
Bagamoyo □, *Tanzania* 82 D4
Bagan Datoh, *Malaysia* 59 L3
Bagan Serai, *Malaysia* 59 K3
Baganga, *Phil.* 55 H7
Bagani, *Namibia* 84 B3
Bagansiapiapi, *Indonesia* 56 D2
Bagasra, *India* 62 J4
Bagawi, *Sudan* 77 E3
Bagdad, *U.S.A.* 113 L11
Bagdarin, *Russia* 45 D12
Bagé, *Brazil* 127 C5
Bagenalstown = Muine Bheag, *Ireland* 15 D5
Baggs, *U.S.A.* 110 F10
Bagh, *Pakistan* 63 C5
Baghdād, *Iraq* 64 C5
Bagheria, *Italy* 34 D6
Baghlān, *Afghan.* 60 A6
Bagley, *U.S.A.* 108 B7
Bagnacavallo, *Italy* 33 D8
Bagnara Cálabra, *Italy* 35 D8
Bagnères-de-Bigorre, *France* 26 E4
Bagnères-de-Luchon, *France* 26 F4
Bagni di Lucca, *Italy* 32 D7
Bagno di Romagna, *Italy* 33 E8
Bagnoles-de-l'Orne, *France* 24 D6
Bagnoli di Sopra, *Italy* 33 C8
Bagnolo Mella, *Italy* 32 C7
Bagnols-sur-Cèze, *France* 27 D8
Bagnorégio, *Italy* 33 F9
Bagolino, *Italy* 32 C7
Bagotville, *Canada* 99 C5
Bagua, *Peru* 124 B2
Baguio, *Phil.* 55 C4
Bahabón de Esgueva, *Spain* 28 D1
Bahadurgarh, *India* 62 E7
Bahama, Canal Viejo de, *W. Indies* 116 B4
Bahamas ■, *N. Amer.* 117 B5
Baharampur, *India* 63 G13
Baharîya, El Wâhât al, *Egypt* 76 J6
Bahau, *Malaysia* 59 L4
Bahawalnagar, *Pakistan* 62 D5
Bahawalpur, *Pakistan* 62 E4
Bahçe, *Turkey* 66 E7
Baheri, *India* 63 E8
Bahi, *Tanzania* 82 D4
Bahi Swamp, *Tanzania* 82 D4
Bahía = Salvador, *Brazil* 123 D4
Bahía □, *Brazil* 123 D3
Bahía, Is. de la, *Honduras* 116 C2
Bahía Blanca, *Argentina* 126 D3
Bahía de Caráquez, *Ecuador* 120 D1
Bahía Honda, *Cuba* 116 B3
Bahía Laura, *Argentina* 128 C3
Bahía Negra, *Paraguay* 125 E6
Bahir Dar, *Ethiopia* 77 E4
Bahmanzād, *Iran* 65 D6
Bahmer, *Algeria* 75 C4
Bahönye, *Hungary* 21 J7
Bahr Aouk →, *C.A.R.* 80 C3
Bahr el Ahmar □, *Sudan* 76 C3
Bahr el Ghazâl □, *Sudan* 77 F2
Bahr Salamat →, *Chad* 73 G8
Bahr Yûsef →, *Egypt* 76 J7
Bahra el Burullus, *Egypt* 76 H7
Bahraich, *India* 63 F9
Bahrain ■, *Asia* 65 E6
Bahret Assad, *Syria* 64 C3
Bahror, *India* 62 F7
Bāhū Kalāt, *Iran* 65 E9
Bai, *Mali* 78 C4
Bai Bung, Mui, *Vietnam* 59 H5
Bai Duc, *Vietnam* 58 C5
Bai Thuong, *Vietnam* 58 C5
Baia Mare, *Romania* 38 B6
Baia-Sprie, *Romania* 38 B6
Baião, *Brazil* 122 B2
Baïbokoum, *Chad* 73 G8
Baicheng, *China* 51 B12
Baidoa, *Somali Rep.* 68 G3
Baie Comeau, *Canada* 99 C6
Baie-St-Paul, *Canada* 99 C5
Baie Trinité, *Canada* 99 C6
Baie Verte, *Canada* 99 C8
Baignes-Ste.-Radegonde, *France* 26 C3
Baigneux-les-Juifs, *France* 25 E11
Baihe, *China* 50 H6
Baihe, *Taiwan* 53 F13
Ba'ījī, *Iraq* 64 C4
Baikal, L. = Baykal, Oz., *Russia* 45 D11
Baile Atha Cliath = Dublin, *Ireland* 15 C5
Bailei, *Ethiopia* 77 F5
Bailén, *Spain* 31 G7
Băileşti, *Romania* 38 E6
Baileux, *Belgium* 17 H4
Bailique, Ilha, *Brazil* 122 A2
Bailleul, *France* 25 B9
Bailundo, *Angola* 81 G3
Baima, *China* 52 A3
Bain-de-Bretagne, *France* 24 E5
Bainbridge, *Ga., U.S.A.* 105 K3
Bainbridge, *N.Y., U.S.A.* 107 D9
Baing, *Indonesia* 57 F6
Bainiu, *China* 50 H7
Bainville, *U.S.A.* 108 A2
Bā'ir, *Jordan* 69 E5
Baird, *U.S.A.* 109 J5
Baird Mts., *U.S.A.* 96 B3
Bairin Youqi, *China* 51 C10
Bairin Zuoqi, *China* 51 C10
Bairnsdale, *Australia* 91 F4
Bais, *Phil.* 55 G5
Baisha, *China* 50 G7
Baïsole →, *France* 26 E4
Baissa, *Nigeria* 79 D7
Baitadi, *Nepal* 63 E9
Baixa Grande, *Brazil* 123 D3
Baiyin, *China* 50 F3
Baiyü, *China* 52 B2
Baiyu Shan, *China* 50 F4
Baiyuda, *Sudan* 76 D3
Baj Baj, *India* 63 H13
Baja, *Hungary* 21 J8
Baja, Pta., *Mexico* 114 B1
Baja California, *Mexico* 114 A1
Bajamar, *Canary Is.* 36 F3
Bajana, *India* 62 H4
Bājgīrān, *Iran* 65 B8
Bajimba, Mt., *Australia* 91 D5
Bajo Nuevo, *Caribbean* 116 C4
Bajoga, *Nigeria* 79 C7
Bajool, *Australia* 90 C5
Bakala, *C.A.R.* 73 G9
Bakar, *Croatia* 33 C11
Bakchar, *Russia* 44 D9
Bakel, *Neths.* 17 E7
Bakel, *Senegal* 78 C2
Baker, *Calif., U.S.A.* 113 K10
Baker, *Mont., U.S.A.* 108 B2
Baker, *Oreg., U.S.A.* 110 D5
Baker, Canal, *Chile* 128 C2
Baker, L., *Canada* 96 B10
Baker I., *Pac. Oc.* 92 G10
Baker L., *Australia* 89 E4
Baker Lake, *Canada* 96 B10
Baker Mt., *U.S.A.* 110 B3
Bakers Creek, *Australia* 90 C4
Baker's Dozen Is., *Canada* 98 A4
Bakersfield, *Calif., U.S.A.* 113 K7
Bakersfield, *Vt., U.S.A.* 107 B12
Bakhchisaray, *Ukraine* 42 D5
Bakhmach, *Ukraine* 40 F8
Bākhtarān, *Iran* 64 C5
Bākhtarān □, *Iran* 64 C5
Bakırdaği, *Turkey* 66 D6
Bakırköy, *Turkey* 39 H11
Bakkafjörður, *Iceland* 8 C6
Bakkagerði, *Iceland* 8 D7
Bakony →, *Hungary* 21 H7
Bakony Forest = Bakony Hegyseg, *Hungary* 21 H7
Bakony Hegyseg, *Hungary* 21 H7
Bakori, *Nigeria* 79 C6
Bakouma, *C.A.R.* 73 G9
Baku, *Azerbaijan* 43 F13
Bakutis Coast, *Antarctica* 5 D15
Baky = Baku, *Azerbaijan* 43 F13
Bala, *Canada* 106 A5
Bâlâ, *Turkey* 66 D5
Bala, L., *U.K.* 12 E4
Balabac I., *Phil.* 55 H2
Balabac Str., *E. Indies* 56 C5
Balabagh, *Afghan.* 62 B4
Balabakk, *Lebanon* 69 A5
Balabalangan, Kepulauan, *Indonesia* 56 E5
Bălăciţa, *Romania* 38 E6
Balad, *Iraq* 64 C5
Balad Rūz, *Iraq* 64 C5
Bālādeh, *Fārs, Iran* 65 D6
Baladeh, *Māzandaran, Iran* 65 B6
Balaghat, *India* 60 J12
Balaghat Ra., *India* 60 K10
Balaguer, *Spain* 28 D5
Balakhna, *Russia* 41 C13
Balaklava, *Australia* 91 E2
Balaklava, *Ukraine* 42 D5
Balakleya, *Ukraine* 42 B7
Balakovo, *Russia* 41 E15
Balancán, *Mexico* 115 D6
Balanda, *Russia* 41 F14
Balashikha, *Russia* 41 D10
Balashov, *Russia* 41 F13
Balasinor, *India* 62 H5
Balasore = Baleshwar, *India* 61 J15
Balassagyarmat, *Hungary* 21 G9
Balât, *Egypt* 76 B2
Balaton, *Hungary* 21 J7
Balayan, *Phil.* 55 E4
Balazote, *Spain* 29 G2
Balboa, *Panama* 116 E4
Balbriggan, *Ireland* 15 C5
Balcarce, *Argentina* 126 D4
Balcarres, *Canada* 101 C8
Balchik, *Bulgaria* 38 F11
Balclutha, *N.Z.* 87 M2
Bald Hd., *Australia* 89 G2
Bald I., *Australia* 89 F2
Bald Knob, *U.S.A.* 109 H9
Baldock L., *Canada* 101 B9
Baldwin, *Fla., U.S.A.* 105 K4
Baldwin, *Mich., U.S.A.* 104 D3
Baldwinsville, *U.S.A.* 107 C8
Baldy Peak, *U.S.A.* 111 K9
Bale, *Croatia* 33 C10
Bale □, *Ethiopia* 77 F5
Baleares □, *Spain* 28 F7
Baleares, Is., *Spain* 36 B10
Balearic Is. = Baleares, Is., *Spain* 36 B10
Baleia, Pta. da, *Brazil* 123 E4
Balen, *Belgium* 17 F6
Baler, *Phil.* 55 D4
Baler Bay, *Phil.* 55 D4
Balerna, *Switz.* 23 E8
Baleshwar, *India* 61 J15
Balfate, *Honduras* 116 C2
Balfe's Creek, *Australia* 90 C4
Balfour, *S. Africa* 85 D4
Bali, *Cameroon* 79 D6
Balí, *Greece* 37 D6
Bali, *Indonesia* 56 F5
Bali □, *Indonesia* 56 F5
Bali, Selat, *Indonesia* 57 H16
Baligród, *Poland* 20 F12
Balık Gölü, *Turkey* 67 D10
Balikeşir, *Turkey* 66 D2
Balikeşir □, *Turkey* 66 D2
Balikpapan, *Indonesia* 56 E5
Balimbing, *Phil.* 57 C5
Baling, *Malaysia* 59 K3
Balintang Channel, *Phil.* 55 B4
Balipara, *India* 61 F18
Baliza, *Brazil* 125 D7
Balk, *Neths.* 16 C7
Balkan Mts. = Stara Planina, *Bulgaria* 38 F6
Balkan Peninsula, *Europe* 6 G10
Balkhash, *Kazakhstan* 44 E8
Balkhash, Ozero, *Kazakhstan* 44 E8
Balla, *Bangla.* 61 G17
Ballachulish, *U.K.* 14 E3
Balladonia, *Australia* 89 F3
Ballarat, *Australia* 91 F3
Ballard, L., *Australia* 89 E3
Ballater, *U.K.* 14 D5
Ballenas, Canal de, *Mexico* 114 B2
Balleny Is., *Antarctica* 5 C11
Ballesteros, *Phil.* 55 B4
Ballia, *India* 63 G11
Ballidu, *Australia* 89 F2
Ballina, *Australia* 91 D5
Ballina, *Mayo, Ireland* 15 B2
Ballina, *Tipp., Ireland* 15 D3
Ballinasloe, *Ireland* 15 C3
Ballinger, *U.S.A.* 109 K5
Ballinrobe, *Ireland* 15 C2
Ballinskelligs B., *Ireland* 15 E1
Ballon, *France* 24 D7
Ballycastle, *U.K.* 15 A5
Ballymena, *U.K.* 15 B5
Ballymena □, *U.K.* 15 B5
Ballymoney, *U.K.* 15 A5
Ballymoney □, *U.K.* 15 A5
Ballyshannon, *Ireland* 15 B3
Balmaceda, *Chile* 128 C2
Balmazújváros, *Hungary* 21 H11
Balmhorn, *Switz.* 22 D5
Balmoral, *Australia* 91 F3
Balmoral, *U.K.* 14 D5
Balmorhea, *U.S.A.* 109 K3
Balonne →, *Australia* 91 D4
Balqash Kol = Balkhash, Ozero, *Kazakhstan* 44 E8
Balrampur, *India* 63 F10
Balranald, *Australia* 91 E3
Balş, *Romania* 38 E7
Balsapuerto, *Peru* 124 B2
Balsas, *Mexico* 115 D5
Balsas →, *Goiás, Brazil* 122 C2
Balsas →, *Maranhão, Brazil* 122 C3
Balsas →, *Mexico* 114 D4
Bålsta, *Sweden* 10 E11
Balsthal, *Switz.* 22 B5
Balston Spa, *U.S.A.* 107 D11
Balta, *Romania* 38 E5
Balta, *Russia* 43 E11
Balta, *Ukraine* 42 B3
Balta, *U.S.A.* 108 A4
Baltanás, *Spain* 30 D6
Bălţi = Beltsy, *Moldavia* 42 C3
Baltic Sea, *Europe* 9 H15
Baltîm, *Egypt* 76 H7
Baltimore, *Ireland* 15 E2
Baltimore, *U.S.A.* 104 F7
Baltit, *Pakistan* 63 A6
Baltrum, *Germany* 18 B3
Baluchistan □, *Pakistan* 60 F4
Balurghat, *India* 63 G13
Balya, *Turkey* 66 D2
Balygychan, *Russia* 45 C16
Balzar, *Ecuador* 120 D2
Bam, *Iran* 65 D8
Bama, *China* 52 E6
Bama, *Nigeria* 79 C7
Bamako, *Mali* 78 C3

Bamba, *Mali* 79 B4
Bambamarca, *Peru* 124 B2
Bambari, *C.A.R.* 73 G9
Bambaroo, *Australia* 90 B4
Bamberg, *Germany* 19 F6
Bamberg, *U.S.A.* 105 J5
Bambesi, *Ethiopia* 77 F3
Bambey, *Senegal* 78 C1
Bambili, *Zaïre* 82 B2
Bambuí, *Brazil* 123 F2
Bamenda, *Cameroon* 79 D7
Bamfield, *Canada* 100 D3
Bāmīān □, *Afghan.* 60 B5
Bamiancheng, *China* ... 51 C13
Bamkin, *Cameroon* 79 D7
Bampūr, *Iran* 65 E9
Ban Aranyaprathet,
  Thailand 58 F4
Ban Ban, *Laos* 58 C4
Ban Bang Hin, *Thailand* .. 59 H2
Ban Chiang Klang,
  Thailand 58 C3
Ban Chik, *Laos* 58 D4
Ban Choho, *Thailand* .. 58 E4
Ban Dan Lan Hoi,
  Thailand 58 D2
Ban Don = Surat Thani,
  Thailand 59 H2
Ban Don, *Vietnam* ... 58 F6
Ban Don, Ao, *Thailand* .. 59 H2
Ban Dong, *Thailand* .. 58 C3
Ban Hong, *Thailand* .. 58 C2
Ban Kaeng, *Thailand* .. 58 D3
Ban Keun, *Laos* 58 C4
Ban Khai, *Thailand* .. 58 F3
Ban Kheun, *Laos* 58 B3
Ban Khlong Kua, *Thailand* 59 J3
Ban Khuan Mao, *Thailand* 59 J2
Ban Khun Yuam, *Thailand* 58 C1
Ban Ko Yai Chim,
  Thailand 59 G2
Ban Kok, *Thailand* .. 58 D4
Ban Laem, *Thailand* .. 58 F2
Ban Lao Ngam, *Laos* .. 58 E6
Ban Le Kathe, *Thailand* .. 58 E2
Ban Mae Chedi, *Thailand* 58 C2
Ban Mae Laeng, *Thailand* 58 B2
Ban Mae Sariang, *Thailand* 58 C1
Ban Mê Thuôt = Buon Me
  Thuot, *Vietnam* 58 F7
Ban Mi, *Thailand* 58 E3
Ban Muong Mo, *Laos* .. 58 C4
Ban Na Mo, *Laos* 58 D5
Ban Na San, *Thailand* .. 59 H2
Ban Na Tong, *Laos* ... 58 B3
Ban Nam Bac, *Laos* .. 58 B4
Ban Nam Ma, *Laos* ... 58 A3
Ban Ngang, *Laos* 58 E6
Ban Nong Bok, *Laos* .. 58 D5
Ban Nong Boua, *Laos* .. 58 E6
Ban Nong Pling, *Thailand* 58 E3
Ban Pak Chan, *Thailand* . 59 G2
Ban Phai, *Thailand* .. 58 D4
Ban Pong, *Thailand* .. 58 F2
Ban Ron Phibun, *Thailand* 59 H2
Ban Sanam Chai, *Thailand* 59 J3
Ban Sangkha, *Thailand* .. 58 E4
Ban Tak, *Thailand* ... 58 D2
Ban Tako, *Thailand* .. 58 E4
Ban Tha Dua, *Thailand* .. 58 D2
Ban Tha Li, *Thailand* .. 58 D3
Ban Tha Nun, *Thailand* .. 59 H2
Ban Thahine, *Laos* ... 58 E5
Ban Xien Kok, *Laos* .. 58 B3
Ban Yen Nhan, *Vietnam* . 58 B6
Baña, Punta de la, *Spain* .. 28 E5
Banaba, *Kiribati* 92 H8
Bañalbufar, *Spain* 36 B9
Banalia, *Zaïre* 82 B2
Banam, *Cambodia* 59 G5
Banamba, *Mali* 78 C3
Banana, *Australia* 90 C5
Bananal, I. do, *Brazil* .. 123 D1
Banaras = Varanasi, *India* 63 G10
Banas →, *Gujarat, India* .. 62 H4
Banas →, *Mad. P., India* .. 63 G9
Bânâs, Ras, *Egypt* 76 C4
Banaz, *Turkey* 66 D3
Banbān, *Si. Arabia* ... 64 E5
Banbridge, *U.K.* 15 B5
Banbridge □, *U.K.* ... 15 B5
Banbury, *U.K.* 13 E6
Banchory, *U.K.* 14 D6
Bancroft, *Canada* 98 C4
Band Boni, *Iran* 65 E8
Band Qīr, *Iran* 65 D6
Banda, *India* 63 G9
Banda, Kepulauan,
  Indonesia 57 E7
Banda Aceh, *Indonesia* .. 56 C1
Banda Banda, Mt.,
  Australia 91 E5
Banda Elat, *Indonesia* .. 57 F8
Banda Is. = Banda,
  Kepulauan, *Indonesia* .. 57 E7
Banda Sea, *Indonesia* .. 57 F7
Bandai-San, *Japan* ... 48 F10
Bandama →, *Ivory C.* .. 78 D3
Bandān, *Iran* 65 D9
Bandanaira, *Indonesia* .. 57 E7
Bandanwara, *India* ... 62 F6
Bandar = Machilipatnam,
  India 61 L12
Bandar 'Abbās, *Iran* ... 65 E8
Bandar-e Anzalī, *Iran* .. 65 B6

Bandar-e Chārak, *Iran* ... 65 E7
Bandar-e Deylam, *Iran* .. 65 D6
Bandar-e Khomeyni, *Iran* . 65 D6
Bandar-e Lengeh, *Iran* .. 65 E7
Bandar-e Maqām, *Iran* .. 65 E7
Bandar-e Ma'shur, *Iran* .. 65 D6
Bandar-e Nakhīlū, *Iran* .. 65 E7
Bandar-e Rīg, *Iran* ... 65 D6
Bandar-e Torkeman, *Iran* . 65 B7
Bandar Maharani = Muar,
  Malaysia 59 L4
Bandar Penggaram = Batu
  Pahat, *Malaysia* 59 M4
Bandar Seri Begawan,
  Brunei 56 C4
Bandawe, *Malawi* 83 E3
Bande, *Belgium* 17 H6
Bande, *Spain* 30 C3
Bandeira, Pico da, *Brazil* . 123 F3
Bandeirante, *Brazil* ... 123 D1
Bandera, *Argentina* ... 126 B3
Bandera, *U.S.A.* 109 L5
Banderas, B. de, *Mexico* . 114 C3
Bandiagara, *Mali* 78 C4
Bandırma, *Turkey* ... 66 C3
Bandon, *Ireland* 15 E3
Bandon →, *Ireland* .. 15 E3
Bandula, *Mozam.* 83 F3
Bandundu, *Zaïre* 80 E3
Bandung, *Indonesia* .. 57 G12
Bandya, *Australia* ... 89 E3
Bāneh, *Iran* 64 C5
Bañeres, *Spain* 29 G4
Banes, *Cuba* 117 B4
Banff, *Canada* 100 C5
Banff, *U.K.* 14 D6
Banff Nat. Park, *Canada* . 100 C5
Banfora, *Burkina Faso* .. 78 C4
Bang Fai →, *Laos* ... 58 D5
Bang Hieng →, *Laos* .. 58 D5
Bang Krathum, *Thailand* .. 58 D3
Bang Lamung, *Thailand* . 58 F3
Bang Mun Nak, *Thailand* . 58 D3
Bang Pa In, *Thailand* .. 58 E3
Bang Rakam, *Thailand* .. 58 D3
Bang Saphan, *Thailand* . 59 G2
Bangala Dam, *Zimbabwe* . 83 G3
Bangalore, *India* 60 N10
Bangante, *Cameroon* .. 79 D7
Bangaon, *India* 63 H13
Bangassou, *C.A.R.* ... 80 D4
Banggai, Kepulauan,
  Indonesia 57 E6
Banggi, P., *Malaysia* .. 56 C5
Banghāzī, *Libya* 73 B9
Bangil, *Indonesia* ... 57 G15
Bangjang, *Sudan* 77 E3
Bangka, P., *Sulawesi,
  Indonesia* 57 D7
Bangka, P., *Sumatera,
  Indonesia* 56 E3
Bangka, Selat, *Indonesia* . 56 E3
Bangkalan, *Indonesia* .. 57 G15
Bangkinang, *Indonesia* .. 56 D2
Bangko, *Indonesia* ... 56 E2
Bangkok, *Thailand* ... 58 F3
Bangladesh ■, *Asia* ... 61 H17
Bangolo, *Ivory C.* ... 78 D3
Bangong Co, *India* ... 63 B8
Bangor, *Down, U.K.* .. 15 B6
Bangor, *Gwynedd, U.K.* .. 12 D3
Bangor, *Maine, U.S.A.* . 99 D6
Bangor, *Pa., U.S.A.* .. 107 F9
Bangued, *Phil.* 55 C4
Bangui, *C.A.R.* 80 D3
Bangui, *Phil.* 55 B4
Banguru, *Zaïre* 82 B2
Bangweulu, L., *Zambia* .. 83 E3
Bangweulu Swamp, *Zambia* 83 E3
Bani, *Dom. Rep.* 117 C5
Bani →, *Mali* 78 C4
Bani, Djebel, *Morocco* .. 74 C3
Bani Bangou, *Niger* .. 79 B5
Bani Sa'd, *Iraq* 64 C5
Banī Walīd, *Libya* ... 73 B7
Bania, *Ivory C.* 78 D4
Banihal Pass, *India* .. 63 C6
Banīnah, *Libya* 73 B9
Bāniyās, *Syria* 64 C3
Banja Luka, *Bos.-H.* .. 21 L7
Banjar, *Indonesia* ... 57 G13
Banjarmasin, *Indonesia* . 56 E4
Banjarnegara, *Indonesia* . 57 G13
Banjul, *Gambia* 78 C1
Banka Banka, *Australia* . 90 B1
Banket, *Zimbabwe* ... 83 F3
Bankilaré, *Niger* 79 C5
Bankipore, *India* 63 G11
Banks I., *B.C., Canada* . 100 C3
Banks I., *N.W.T., Canada* . 96 A7
Banks Pen., *N.Z.* 87 K4
Banks Str., *Australia* .. 90 G4
Bankura, *India* 63 H12
Bann →, *Down, U.K.* . 15 B5
Bann →, *L'derry., U.K.* . 15 A5
Banna, *Phil.* 55 C4
Bannalec, *France* 24 E3
Bannang Sata, *Thailand* . 59 J3
Banning, *U.S.A.* 113 M10
Banningville = Bandundu,
  Zaïre 80 E3
Bannockburn, *Canada* .. 106 B7
Bannockburn, *U.K.* .. 14 E5
Bannockburn, *Zimbabwe* . 83 G2
Bannu, *Pakistan* 60 C7

Bañolas, *Spain* 28 C7
Banon, *France* 27 D9
Baños de la Encina, *Spain* . 31 G7
Baños de Molgas, *Spain* . 30 C3
Banská Bystrica,
  Slovak Rep. 20 G9
Banská Štiavnica,
  Slovak Rep. 21 G8
Banswara, *India* 62 H6
Bantayan, *Phil.* 55 F5
Banten, *Indonesia* ... 57 G12
Bantry, *Ireland* 15 E2
Bantry B., *Ireland* ... 15 E2
Bantul, *Indonesia* ... 57 G14
Banu, *India* 60 B6
Banyak, Kepulauan,
  Indonesia 56 D1
Banyo, *Cameroon* 79 D7
Banyuls-sur-Mer, *France* . 26 F7
Banyumas, *Indonesia* .. 57 G13
Banyuwangi, *Indonesia* . 57 H16
Banzare Coast, *Antarctica* 5 C9
Banzyville = Mobayi, *Zaïre* 80 D4
Bao Ha, *Vietnam* 58 A5
Bao Lac, *Vietnam* ... 58 A5
Bao Loc, *Vietnam* ... 59 G6
Bao'an, *China* 53 F10
Baocheng, *China* 50 H4
Baode, *China* 50 E6
Baodi, *China* 51 E9
Baoding, *China* 50 E8
Baoji, *China* 50 G4
Baojing, *China* 52 C7
Baokang, *China* 53 B8
Baoshan, *Shanghai, China* 53 B13
Baoshan, *Yunnan, China* . 52 E2
Baotou, *China* 50 D6
Baoying, *China* 51 H10
Bap, *India* 62 F5
Bapatla, *India* 61 M12
Bapaume, *France* 25 B9
Bāqerābād, *Iran* 65 C6
Ba'qūbah, *Iraq* 64 C5
Baquedano, *Chile* ... 126 A2
Bar, *Montenegro* 21 N9
Bar, *Ukraine* 42 B2
Bar Bigha, *India* 63 G11
Bar Harbor, *U.S.A.* .. 99 D6
Bar-le-Duc, *France* ... 25 D12
Bar-sur-Aube, *France* .. 25 D11
Bar-sur-Seine, *France* .. 25 D11
Barabai, *Indonesia* ... 56 E5
Barabinsk, *Russia* ... 44 D8
Baraboo, *U.S.A.* 108 D10
Baracaldo, *Spain* 28 B2
Baracoa, *Cuba* 117 B5
Baradero, *Argentina* .. 126 C4
Baraga, *U.S.A.* 108 B10
Barahona, *Dom. Rep.* .. 117 C5
Barahona, *Spain* 28 D2
Barail Range, *India* .. 61 G18
Baraka →, *Sudan* 76 D4
Barakhola, *India* 61 G18
Barakot, *India* 63 J11
Barakpur, *India* 63 H13
Barakula, *Australia* .. 91 D5
Baralaba, *Australia* .. 90 C4
Baralzon L., *Canada* .. 101 B9
Barameiya, *Sudan* ... 76 D4
Baramula, *India* 63 B6
Baran, *India* 62 G7
Baranavichy =
  Baranovichi, *Belorussia* . 40 E5
Baranoa, *Colombia* ... 120 A3
Baranof I., *U.S.A.* ... 100 B1
Baranovichi, *Belorussia* . 40 E5
Barão de Cocais, *Brazil* . 123 E3
Barão de Grajaú, *Brazil* . 122 C3
Barão de Melgaço,
  Mato Grosso, Brazil .. 125 D6
Barão de Melgaço,
  Rondônia, Brazil 125 C5
Baraolt, *Romania* 38 C8
Barapasi, *Indonesia* .. 57 E9
Barasat, *India* 63 H13
Barat Daya, Kepulauan,
  Indonesia 57 F7
Barataria B., *U.S.A.* .. 109 L10
Baraut, *India* 62 E7
Baraya, *Colombia* ... 120 C2
Barbacena, *Brazil* ... 123 F3
Barbacoas, *Colombia* .. 120 C2
Barbacoas, *Venezuela* . 120 B4
Barbados ■, *W. Indies* . 117 D8
Barbalha, *Brazil* 122 C4
Barban, *Croatia* 33 C11
Barbastro, *Spain* 28 C5
Barbate, *Spain* 31 J5
Barberino di Mugello, *Italy* 33 D8
Barberton, *S. Africa* .. 85 D5
Barberton, *U.S.A.* ... 106 E3
Barbezieux, *France* ... 26 C3
Barbosa, *Colombia* ... 120 B3
Barbourville, *U.S.A.* .. 105 G4
Barbuda, *W. Indies* .. 117 C7
Barcaldine, *Australia* .. 90 C4
Barcarrota, *Spain* ... 31 G4
Barcellona Pozzo di Gotto,
  Italy 35 D8
Barcelona □, *Spain* .. 28 D7
Barcelona, *Venezuela* . 121 A5
Barcelona □, *Spain* .. 28 D7
Barcelonette, *France* .. 27 D10
Barcelos, *Brazil* 121 D5

Barcoo →, *Australia* .. 90 D3
Barcs, *Hungary* 21 K7
Barda, *Azerbaijan* ... 43 F12
Barda del Medio, *Argentina* 128 A3
Bardas Blancas, *Argentina* 126 D2
Bardai, *Chad* 73 D8
Barddhaman, *India* ... 63 H12
Bardejov, *Slovak Rep.* .. 20 F11
Bardera, *Somali Rep.* .. 68 G3
Bardi, *Italy* 32 D6
Bardīya, *Libya* 73 B9
Bardolino, *Italy* 32 C7
Bardsey I., *U.K.* 12 E3
Bareilly, *India* 63 E8
Barentin, *France* 24 C7
Barenton, *France* 24 D6
Barents Sea, *Arctic* .. 4 B9
Barentu, *Eritrea* 77 D4
Barfleur, *France* 24 C5
Barfleur, Pte. de, *France* . 24 C5
Barga, *China* 54 C3
Barga, *Italy* 32 D7
Bargal, *Somali Rep.* .. 68 E5
Bargara, *Australia* ... 90 C5
Barge, *Italy* 32 D4
Bargnop, *Sudan* 77 F2
Bargteheide, *Germany* .. 18 B6
Barguzin, *Russia* 45 D11
Barh, *India* 63 G11
Barhaj, *India* 63 F10
Barhi, *India* 63 G11
Bari, *India* 62 F7
Bari, *Italy* 35 A9
Bari Doab, *Pakistan* .. 62 D5
Bariadi □, *Tanzania* .. 82 C3
Barīm, *Yemen* 68 E3
Barinas, *Venezuela* .. 120 B3
Barinas □, *Venezuela* . 120 B4
Baring, C., *Canada* ... 96 B8
Baringo, *Kenya* 82 B4
Baringo □, *Kenya* ... 82 B4
Baringo, L., *Kenya* .. 82 B4
Barinitas, *Venezuela* . 120 B3
Bariri, *Brazil* 123 F2
Bârîs, *Egypt* 76 C3
Barisal, *Bangla.* 61 H17
Barisan, Bukit, *Indonesia* . 56 E2
Barito →, *Indonesia* .. 56 E4
Barjac, *France* 27 D8
Barjols, *France* 27 E10
Barjūj, Wadi →, *Libya* .. 75 C7
Bark L., *Canada* 106 A7
Barka = Baraka →, *Sudan* 76 D4
Barkam, *China* 52 B4
Barker, *U.S.A.* 106 C6
Barkley Sound, *Canada* . 100 D3
Barkly Downs, *Australia* . 90 C2
Barkly East, *S. Africa* .. 84 E4
Barkly Tableland, *Australia* 90 B2
Barkly West, *S. Africa* .. 84 D3
Barkol, Wadi →, *Sudan* . 76 D3
Barksdale, *U.S.A.* ... 109 L4
Barlee, L., *Australia* .. 89 E2
Barlee, Mt., *Australia* .. 89 D4
Barletta, *Italy* 35 A9
Barlinek, *Poland* 20 C5
Barlovento, *Canary Is.* . 36 F2
Barlow L., *Canada* ... 101 A8
Barmedman, *Australia* . 91 E4
Barmer, *India* 62 G4
Barmera, *Australia* ... 91 E3
Barmouth, *U.K.* 12 E3
Barnagar, *India* 62 H6
Barnard Castle, *U.K.* .. 12 C6
Barnato, *Australia* ... 91 E3
Barnaul, *Russia* 44 D9
Barnesville, *U.S.A.* .. 105 J3
Barnet, *U.K.* 13 F7
Barneveld, *Neths.* ... 16 D7
Barneveld, *U.S.A.* ... 107 C9
Barneville-Cartevert,
  France 24 C5
Barngo, *Australia* ... 90 D4
Barnhart, *U.S.A.* 109 K4
Barnsley, *U.K.* 12 D6
Barnstaple, *U.K.* 13 F3
Barnsville, *U.S.A.* ... 108 B6
Baro, *Nigeria* 79 D6
Baro →, *Ethiopia* ... 77 F3
Baroda = Vadodara, *India* 62 H5
Baroda = India 62 G7
Baroe, *S. Africa* 84 E3
Baron Ra., *Australia* .. 88 D4
Barpeta, *India* 61 F17
Barques, Pt. Aux, *U.S.A.* . 104 C4
Barquinha, *Portugal* .. 31 F2
Barquísimeto, *Venezuela* 120 A4
Barr, *France* 25 D14
Barra, *Brazil* 122 D3
Barra, *U.K.* 14 E1
Barra, Sd. of, *U.K.* .. 14 D1
Barra da Estiva, *Brazil* . 123 D3
Barra de Navidad, *Mexico* 114 D4
Barra de Corda, *Brazil* . 122 C2
Barra do Mendes, *Brazil* . 123 D3
Barra do Piraí, *Brazil* . 123 F3
Barra Falsa, Pta. da,
  Mozam. 85 C6
Barra Hd., *U.K.* 14 E1
Barra Mansa, *Brazil* .. 123 F3
Barraba, *Australia* ... 91 E5
Barracão do Barreto, *Brazil* 125 B6

Barrackpur = Barakpur,
  India 63 H13
Barrafranca, *Italy* ... 35 E7
Barranca, *Lima, Peru* . 124 C2
Barranca, *Loreto, Peru* . 120 D2
Barrancabermeja, *Colombia* 120 B3
Barrancas, *Colombia* .. 120 A3
Barrancas, *Venezuela* . 121 B5
Barrancos, *Portugal* .. 31 G4
Barranqueras, *Argentina* . 126 B4
Barranquilla, *Colombia* . 120 A3
Barras, *Brazil* 122 B3
Barras, *Colombia* ... 120 D3
Barraute, *Canada* ... 98 C4
Barre, *Mass., U.S.A.* . 107 D12
Barre, *Vt., U.S.A.* .. 107 B12
Barre do Bugres, *Brazil* . 125 C6
Barreal, *Argentina* ... 126 C2
Barreiras, *Brazil* 123 D3
Barreirinha, *Brazil* .. 121 D6
Barreirinhas, *Brazil* .. 122 B3
Barreiro, *Portugal* ... 31 G1
Barreiros, *Brazil* 122 C4
Barrême, *France* 27 E10
Barren, Nosy, *Madag.* .. 85 B7
Barretos, *Brazil* 123 F2
Barrhead, *Canada* ... 100 C6
Barrie, *Canada* 98 D4
Barrier Ra., *Australia* . 91 E3
Barrière, *Canada* 100 C4
Barrington, *U.S.A.* .. 107 E13
Barrington L., *Canada* . 101 B8
Barrington Tops, *Australia* 91 E5
Barringun, *Australia* .. 91 D4
Barro do Garças, *Brazil* . 125 D7
Barrow, *U.S.A.* 96 A4
Barrow →, *Ireland* .. 15 D4
Barrow, C., *U.S.A.* .. 94 B4
Barrow Creek, *Australia* . 90 C1
Barrow-in-Furness, *U.K.* . 12 C4
Barrow I., *Australia* .. 88 D2
Barrow Pt., *Australia* . 90 A3
Barrow Ra., *Australia* . 89 E4
Barrow Str., *Canada* .. 4 B3
Barruecopardo, *Spain* . 30 D4
Barruelo, *Spain* 30 C6
Barry, *U.K.* 13 F4
Barry's Bay, *Canada* .. 98 C4
Barsalogho, *Burkina Faso* 79 C4
Barsat, *Pakistan* 63 A5
Barsham, *Syria* 64 C4
Barsi, *India* 60 K9
Barsø, *Denmark* 11 J3
Barsoi, *India* 61 G15
Barstow, *Calif., U.S.A.* . 113 L9
Barstow, *Tex., U.S.A.* . 109 K3
Barth, *Germany* 18 A8
Barthélemy, Col, *Vietnam* 58 C5
Bartica, *Guyana* 121 B6
Bartin, *Turkey* 66 C5
Bartlesville, *U.S.A.* .. 109 G7
Bartlett, *Calif., U.S.A.* . 112 J8
Bartlett, *Tex., U.S.A.* . 109 K6
Bartlett, L., *Canada* .. 100 A5
Bartolomeu Dias, *Mozam.* 83 G4
Barton, *Australia* ... 89 F5
Barton upon Humber, *U.K.* 12 D7
Bartoszyce, *Poland* ... 20 A10
Bartow, *U.S.A.* 105 M5
Barú, I. de, *Colombia* .. 120 A2
Barú, Volcan, *Panama* . 116 E3
Barumba, *Zaïre* 82 B1
Baruth, *Germany* 18 C9
Barvaux, *Belgium* ... 17 H6
Barvenkovo, *Ukraine* .. 42 B7
Barwani, *India* 62 H6
Barysaw = Borisov,
  Belorussia 40 D6
Barysh, *Russia* 41 E15
Barzān, *Iraq* 64 B5
Bas-Rhin □, *France* .. 25 D14
Bašaid, *Serbia* 21 K10
Bāsa'idū, *Iran* 65 E7
Basal, *Pakistan* 62 C5
Basankusa, *Zaïre* 80 D3
Basawa, *Afghan.* 62 B4
Bascharage, *Lux.* 17 J7
Bascuñán, C., *Chile* .. 126 B1
Basècles, *Belgium* ... 17 G3
Basel, *Switz.* 22 A5
Basel-Stadt □, *Switz.* . 22 A5
Baselland □, *Switz.* .. 22 B5
Basento →, *Italy* 35 B9
Bāshī, *Iran* 65 D6
Bashi Channel, *Phil.* .. 54 D7
Bashkir Republic □, *Russia* 44 D6
Bashkortostan □, *Russia*
  Republic □, *Russia* .. 44 D6
Basilan, *Phil.* 55 H5
Basilan Str., *Phil.* ... 55 H5
Basildon, *U.K.* 13 F8
Basilicata □, *Italy* ... 35 B9
Basim = Washim, *India* . 60 J10
Basin, *U.S.A.* 110 D9
Basingstoke, *U.K.* ... 13 F6
Baška, *Croatia* 33 D11
Başkale, *Turkey* 67 D10
Baskatong, Rés., *Canada* . 98 C4
Basle = Basel, *Switz.* . 22 A5
Basoda, *India* 62 H7
Basoka, *Zaïre* 82 B1
Basongo, *Zaïre* 80 E4
Basque, Pays, *France* .. 26 E2
Basque Provinces = País
  Vasco □, *Spain* 28 C2

Basra

Basra = Al Başrah, *Iraq* .. 64 D5
Bass Rock, *U.K.* 14 E6
Bass Str., *Australia* 90 F4
Bassano, *Canada* 100 C6
Bassano del Grappa, *Italy* 33 C8
Bassar, *Togo* 79 D5
Bassas da India, *Ind. Oc.* . 81 J7
Basse Santa-Su, *Gambia* .. 78 C2
Basse-Terre, *Guadeloupe* . 117 C7
Bassecourt, *Switz.* 22 B4
Bassein, *Burma* 61 L19
Basseterre,
St. Christopher-Nevis ... 117 C7
Bassett, *Nebr., U.S.A.* ... 108 D5
Bassett, *Va., U.S.A.* 105 G6
Bassevelde, *Belgium* 17 F3
Bassi, *India* 62 D7
Bassigny, *France* 25 E12
Bassikounou, *Mauritania* . 78 B3
Bassilly, *Belgium* 17 G3
Bassum, *Germany* 18 C4
Båstad, *Sweden* 11 H6
Bastak, *Iran* 65 E7
Baştām, *Iran* 65 B7
Bastar, *India* 61 K12
Bastelica, *France* 27 F13
Basti, *India* 63 F10
Bastia, *France* 27 F13
Bastia Umbra, *Italy* 33 E9
Bastogne, *Belgium* 17 H7
Bastrop, *U.S.A.* 109 K6
Bat Yam, *Israel* 69 C3
Bata, *Eq. Guin.* 80 D1
Bata, *Romania* 38 C5
Bataan, *Phil.* 55 D4
Batabanó, *Cuba* 116 B3
Batabanó, G. de, *Cuba* ... 116 B3
Batac, *Phil.* 55 B4
Batagoy, *Russia* 45 C14
Batak, *Bulgaria* 39 H7
Batalha, *Portugal* 31 F2
Batama, *Zaïre* 82 B2
Batamay, *Russia* 45 C13
Batan I., *Phil.* 55 A4
Batanes Is., *Phil.* 55 A4
Batang, *China* 52 B2
Batang, *Indonesia* 57 G13
Batangafo, *C.A.R.* 73 G8
Batangas, *Phil.* 55 E4
Batanta, *Indonesia* 57 E8
Batatais, *Brazil* 127 A6
Batavia, *U.S.A.* 106 D6
Bataysk, *Russia* 43 C8
Batchelor, *Australia* 88 B5
Bateman's B., *Australia* .. 91 F5
Batemans Bay, *Australia* .. 91 F5
Bates Ra., *Australia* 89 E3
Batesburg, *U.S.A.* 105 J5
Batesville, *Ark., U.S.A.* .. 109 H9
Batesville, *Miss., U.S.A.* . 109 H10
Batesville, *Tex., U.S.A.* .. 109 L5
Bath, *U.K.* 13 F5
Bath, *Maine, U.S.A.* 99 D6
Bath, *N.Y., U.S.A.* 106 D7
Batheay, *Cambodia* 59 G5
Bathgate, *U.K.* 14 F5
Bathmen, *Neths.* 16 D8
Bathurst = Banjul, *Gambia* 78 C1
Bathurst, *Australia* 91 E4
Bathurst, *Canada* 99 C6
Bathurst, *S. Africa* 84 E4
Bathurst, C., *Canada* 96 A7
Bathurst B., *Australia* 90 A3
Bathurst Harb., *Australia* . 90 G4
Bathurst I., *Australia* 88 B5
Bathurst I., *Canada* 4 B2
Bathurst Inlet, *Canada* ... 96 B9
Batie, *Burkina Faso* 78 D4
Batlow, *Australia* 91 F4
Batman, *Turkey* 67 E9
Batna, *Algeria* 75 A6
Batobato, *Phil.* 55 H7
Batoka, *Zambia* 83 F2
Baton Rouge, *U.S.A.* 109 K9
Batong, Ko, *Thailand* 59 J2
Batopilas, *Mexico* 114 B3
Batouri, *Cameroon* 80 D2
Battambang, *Cambodia* ... 58 F4
Batticaloa, *Sri Lanka* 60 R12
Battice, *Belgium* 17 G7
Battipáglia, *Italy* 35 B7
Battle, *U.K.* 13 G8
Battle →, *Canada* 101 C7
Battle Camp, *Australia* ... 90 B3
Battle Creek, *U.S.A.* 104 D3
Battle Ground, *U.S.A.* ... 112 E4
Battle Harbour, *Canada* .. 99 B8
Battle Lake, *U.S.A.* 108 B7
Battle Mountain, *U.S.A.* . 110 F5
Battlefields, *Zimbabwe* ... 83 F2
Battleford, *Canada* 101 C7
Battonya, *Hungary* 21 J11
Batu, *Ethiopia* 68 F2
Batu, Kepulauan, *Indonesia* 56 E1
Batu Caves, *Malaysia* 59 L3
Batu Gajah, *Malaysia* 59 K3
Batu Is. = Batu,
Kepulauan, *Indonesia* .. 56 E1
Batu Pahat, *Malaysia* 59 M4
Batuata, *Indonesia* 57 F6
Batumi, *Georgia* 43 F9
Baturaja, *Indonesia* 56 E2
Baturité, *Brazil* 122 B4
Bau, *Malaysia* 56 D4
Baubau, *Indonesia* 57 F6
Bauchi, *Nigeria* 79 C6
Bauchi □, *Nigeria* 79 C6
Baud, *France* 24 E3
Baudette, *U.S.A.* 108 A7
Baudour, *Belgium* 17 H3
Bauer, C., *Australia* 91 E1
Baugé, *France* 24 E6
Bauhinia Downs, *Australia* 90 C4
Bauma, *Switz.* 23 B7
Baume-les-Dames, *France* 25 E13
Baunatal, *Germany* 18 D5
Baunei, *Italy* 34 B2
Baures, *Bolivia* 125 C5
Bauru, *Brazil* 127 A6
Baús, *Brazil* 125 D7
Bauska, *Latvia* 40 C4
Bautzen, *Germany* 18 D10
Bavānāt, *Iran* 65 D7
Bavaria = Bayern □,
Germany 19 F7
Båven, *Sweden* 10 F10
Bavi Sadri, *India* 62 G6
Bavispe →, *Mexico* 114 B3
Bawdwin, *Burma* 61 H20
Bawean, *Indonesia* 56 F4
Bawku, *Ghana* 79 C4
Bawlake, *Burma* 61 K20
Bawolung, *China* 52 C3
Baxley, *U.S.A.* 105 K4
Baxoi, *China* 52 B1
Baxter Springs, *U.S.A.* ... 109 G7
Bay, L. de, *Phil.* 57 B6
Bay Bulls, *Canada* 99 C9
Bay City, *Mich., U.S.A.* .. 104 D4
Bay City, *Oreg., U.S.A.* .. 110 D2
Bay City, *Tex., U.S.A.* ... 109 L7
Bay de Verde, *Canada* ... 99 C9
Bay Minette, *U.S.A.* 105 K2
Bay St. Louis, *U.S.A.* 109 K10
Bay Springs, *U.S.A.* 109 K10
Bay View, *N.Z.* 87 H6
Baya, *Zaïre* 83 E2
Bayamo, *Cuba* 116 B4
Bayamón, *Puerto Rico* ... 117 C6
Bayan Har Shan, *China* .. 54 C4
Bayan Hot = Alxa Zuoqi,
China 50 E3
Bayan Obo, *China* 50 D5
Bayan-Ovoo, *Mongolia* ... 50 C4
Bayana, *India* 62 F7
Bayanaul, *Kazakhstan* 44 D8
Bayandalay, *Mongolia* 50 C2
Bayanhongor, *Mongolia* .. 54 B5
Bayard, *U.S.A.* 108 E3
Bayawan, *Phil.* 55 G5
Baybay, *Phil.* 55 F6
Bayburt, *Turkey* 67 C9
Bayerischer Wald,
Germany 19 F8
Bayern □, *Germany* 19 F7
Bayeux, *France* 24 C6
Bayfield, *Canada* 106 C3
Bayfield, *U.S.A.* 108 B9
Bayındır, *Turkey* 66 D2
Baykal, Oz., *Russia* 45 D11
Baykit, *Russia* 45 C10
Baykonur, *Kazakhstan* 44 E7
Baynes Mts., *Namibia* 84 B1
Bayombong, *Phil.* 55 C4
Bayon, *France* 25 D13
Bayona, *Spain* 30 C2
Bayonne, *France* 26 E2
Bayonne, *U.S.A.* 107 F10
Bayovar, *Peru* 124 B1
Bayram-Ali, *Turkmenistan* 44 F7
Bayramiç, *Turkey* 66 D2
Bayreuth, *Germany* 19 F7
Bayrischzell, *Germany* ... 19 H8
Bayrūt, *Lebanon* 69 B4
Bayt Lahm, *Jordan* 69 D4
Baytown, *U.S.A.* 109 L7
Bayzo, *Niger* 79 C5
Baza, *Spain* 29 H2
Bazar Dyuzi, *Russia* 43 F12
Bazarny Karabulak, *Russia* 41 E15
Bazarnyy Syzgan, *Russia* .. 41 E15
Bazartobe, *Kazakhstan* ... 43 B14
Bazaruto, I. do, *Mozam.* . 85 C6
Bazas, *France* 26 D3
Bazhong, *China* 52 B6
Bazmān, Kūh-e, *Iran* 65 D9
Beach, *U.S.A.* 108 B3
Beach City, *U.S.A.* 106 F3
Beachport, *Australia* 91 F2
Beachy Hd., *U.K.* 13 G8
Beacon, *Australia* 89 F2
Beacon, *U.S.A.* 107 E11
Beaconia, *Canada* 101 C9
Beagle, Canal, *S. Amer.* . 128 E3
Beagle Bay, *Australia* 88 C3
Bealanana, *Madag.* 85 A8
Beamsville, *Canada* 106 C5
Bear →, *U.S.A.* 112 G5
Béar, C., *France* 26 F7
Bear I., *Ireland* 15 E2
Bear L., *B.C., Canada* ... 100 B3
Bear L., *Man., Canada* ... 101 B9
Bear L., *U.S.A.* 110 E8
Bearcreek, *U.S.A.* 110 D9
Beardmore, *Canada* 98 C2
Beardmore Glacier,
Antarctica 5 E11
Beardstown, *U.S.A.* 108 F9
Béarn, *France* 26 E3
Bearpaw Mts., *U.S.A.* 110 B9
Bearskin Lake, *Canada* ... 98 B1
Beas de Segura, *Spain* 29 G2
Beasain, *Spain* 28 B2
Beata, C., *Dom. Rep.* 117 C5
Beata, I., *Dom. Rep.* 117 C5
Beatrice, *U.S.A.* 108 E6
Beatrice, *Zimbabwe* 83 F3
Beatrice, C., *Australia* 90 A2
Beatton →, *Canada* 100 B4
Beatton River, *Canada* ... 100 B4
Beatty, *U.S.A.* 111 H5
Beaucaire, *France* 27 E8
Beauce, Plaine de la,
France 25 D8
Beauceville, *Canada* 99 C5
Beauchêne, I., *Falk. Is.* .. 128 D5
Beaudesert, *Australia* 91 D5
Beaufort, *Malaysia* 56 C5
Beaufort, *N.C., U.S.A.* ... 105 H7
Beaufort, *S.C., U.S.A.* ... 105 J5
Beaufort Sea, *Arctic* 4 B1
Beaufort West, *S. Africa* . 84 E3
Beaugency, *France* 25 E8
Beauharnois, *Canada* 98 C5
Beaujeu, *France* 27 B8
Beaulieu →, *Canada* 100 A6
Beaulieu-sur-Dordogne,
France 26 D5
Beaulieu-sur-Mer, *France* . 27 E11
Beauly, *U.K.* 14 D4
Beauly →, *U.K.* 14 D4
Beaumaris, *U.K.* 12 D3
Beaumetz-lès-Loges, *France* 25 B9
Beaumont, *Belgium* 17 H4
Beaumont, *France* 26 D4
Beaumont, *Calif., U.S.A.* . 113 M10
Beaumont, *Tex., U.S.A.* . 109 K7
Beaumont-de-Lomagne,
France 26 E4
Beaumont-le-Roger, *France* 24 C7
Beaumont-sur-Oise, *France* 25 C9
Beaumont-sur-Sarthe,
France 24 D7
Beaune, *France* 25 E11
Beaune-la-Rolande, *France* 25 D9
Beaupréau, *France* 24 E6
Beauraing, *Belgium* 17 H5
Beauséjour, *Canada* 101 C9
Beauvais, *France* 25 C9
Beauval, *Canada* 101 B7
Beauvoir-sur-Mer, *France* . 24 F4
Beauvoir-sur-Niort, *France* 26 B3
Beaver, *Alaska, U.S.A.* .. 96 B5
Beaver, *Okla., U.S.A.* ... 109 G4
Beaver, *Pa., U.S.A.* 106 F4
Beaver, *Utah, U.S.A.* 111 G7
Beaver →, *B.C., Canada* 100 B4
Beaver →, *Ont., Canada* . 98 A2
Beaver →, *Sask., Canada* 101 B7
Beaver City, *U.S.A.* 108 E5
Beaver Dam, *U.S.A.* 108 D10
Beaver Falls, *U.S.A.* 106 F4
Beaver Hill L., *Canada* ... 101 C10
Beaver I., *U.S.A.* 104 C3
Beaverhill L., *Alta.,*
Canada 100 C6
Beaverhill L., *N.W.T.,*
Canada 101 A8
Beaverlodge, *Canada* 100 B5
Beavermouth, *Canada* ... 100 C5
Beaverstone →, *Canada* . 98 B2
Beaverton, *Canada* 106 B5
Beaverton, *U.S.A.* 112 E4
Beawar, *India* 62 F6
Bebedouro, *Brazil* 127 A6
Beboa, *Madag.* 85 B7
Bebra, *Germany* 18 E5
Beccles, *U.K.* 13 E9
Bečej, *Serbia* 21 K10
Becerreá, *Spain* 30 C3
Béchar, *Algeria* 75 B4
Beckley, *U.S.A.* 104 G5
Beckum, *Germany* 18 D4
Bečva →, *Czech.* 20 F7
Bédar, *Spain* 29 H3
Bédarieux, *France* 26 E7
Bédarrides, *France* 27 D8
Beddouza, Ras, *Morocco* . 74 B3
Bedele, *Ethiopia* 77 F4
Bederkesa, *Germany* 18 B4
Bedeso, *Ethiopia* 77 F5
Bedford, *Canada* 98 C5
Bedford, *S. Africa* 84 E4
Bedford, *U.K.* 13 E7
Bedford, *Ind., U.S.A.* ... 104 F2
Bedford, *Iowa, U.S.A.* .. 108 E7
Bedford, *Ohio, U.S.A.* ... 106 E3
Bedford, *Pa., U.S.A.* 106 F6
Bedford, *Va., U.S.A.* 104 G6
Bedford, C., *Australia* ... 90 B4
Bedford Downs, *Australia* 88 C4
Bedfordshire □, *U.K.* 13 E7
Będków, *Poland* 20 D9
Bednja →, *Croatia* 33 B13
Bednodemyanovsk, *Russia* 41 E13
Bedónia, *Italy* 32 D6
Bedourie, *Australia* 90 C2
Bedretto, *Switz.* 23 C7
Bedum, *Neths.* 16 B9
Będzin, *Poland* 20 E9
Beech Grove, *U.S.A.* 104 F2
Beechy, *Canada* 101 C7
Beek, *Gelderland, Neths.* . 16 E8
Beek, *Limburg, Neths.* ... 17 G7
Beek, *Noord-Brabant,*
Neths. 17 E7
Beekbergen, *Neths.* 16 D7
Beelitz, *Germany* 18 C8
Beenleigh, *Australia* 91 D5
Be'er Menuha, *Israel* 64 D2
Be'er Sheva', *Israel* 69 D3
Beersheba = Be'er Sheva',
Israel 69 D3
Beerta, *Neths.* 16 B10
Beerze →, *Neths.* 16 E6
Beesd, *Neths.* 16 E6
Beeskow, *Germany* 18 C10
Beeston, *U.K.* 12 E6
Beetaloo, *Australia* 90 B1
Beetsterzwaag, *Neths.* ... 16 B8
Beetzendorf, *Germany* ... 18 C7
Beeville, *U.S.A.* 109 L6
Befale, *Zaïre* 80 D4
Befandriana, *Madag.* 85 C7
Befotaka, *Madag.* 85 C8
Bega, *Australia* 91 F4
Bega, Canalul, *Romania* .. 38 D3
Bégard, *France* 24 D3
Bègles, *France* 26 D3
Begna →, *Norway* 10 D4
Begonte, *Spain* 30 B3
Begusarai, *India* 63 G12
Behābād, *Iran* 65 C8
Behara, *Madag.* 85 C8
Behbehān, *Iran* 65 D6
Behshahr, *Iran* 65 B7
Bei Jiang →, *China* 53 F9
Bei'an, *China* 54 B7
Beibei, *China* 54 D5
Beigang, *Taiwan* 53 F13
Beihai, *China* 52 G7
Beijing, *China* 50 E9
Beijing □, *China* 50 E9
Beilen, *Neths.* 16 C8
Beiliu, *China* 53 F8
Beilngries, *Germany* 19 F7
Beilpajah, *Australia* 91 E3
Beilul, *Eritrea* 77 E5
Beipiao, *China* 51 D11
Beira, *Mozam.* 83 F3
Beirut = Bayrūt, *Lebanon* 69 B4
Beitaolaizhao, *China* 51 B13
Beitbridge, *Zimbabwe* 83 G3
Beiuş, *Romania* 38 C5
Beizhen, *Liaoning, China* . 51 D11
Beizhen, *Shandong, China* 51 F10
Beizhengzhen, *China* 51 B12
Beja, *Portugal* 31 G3
Béja, *Tunisia* 75 A6
Beja □, *Portugal* 31 H3
Bejaia, *Algeria* 75 A6
Béjar, *Spain* 30 E5
Bejestān, *Iran* 65 C8
Bekasi, *Indonesia* 57 G12
Békés, *Hungary* 21 J11
Békéscsaba, *Hungary* 21 J11
Bekily, *Madag.* 85 C8
Bekkevoort, *Belgium* 17 G5
Bekoji, *Ethiopia* 77 F4
Bekok, *Malaysia* 59 L4
Bekwai, *Ghana* 79 D4
Bela, *India* 63 G9
Bela, *Pakistan* 62 F2
Bela Crkva, *Serbia* 21 L11
Bela Palanka, *Serbia* 21 M12
Bela Vista, *Brazil* 126 A4
Bela Vista, *Mozam.* 85 D5
Bélâbre, *France* 26 B5
Belalcázar, *Spain* 31 G5
Belarus = Belorussia ■,
Europe 40 E5
Belau ■, *Pac. Oc.* 92 G5
Belavenona, *Madag.* 85 C8
Belawan, *Indonesia* 56 D1
Belaya, *Ethiopia* 77 E4
Belaya Glina, *Russia* 43 C9
Belaya Kalitva, *Russia* ... 43 B9
Belaya Kholunitsa, *Russia* 41 B17
Belaya Tserkov, *Ukraine* . 40 G7
Belcher Is., *Canada* 97 C12
Belchite, *Spain* 28 D4
Belden, *U.S.A.* 112 E5
Belém, *Brazil* 122 B2
Belém de São Francisco,
Brazil 122 C4
Belén, *Argentina* 126 B2
Belén, *Colombia* 120 C2
Belén, *Paraguay* 126 A4
Belen, *U.S.A.* 111 J10
Bélesta, *France* 26 F5
Belet Uen, *Somali Rep.* .. 68 G4
Belev, *Russia* 41 E10
Belfair, *U.S.A.* 112 C4
Belfast, *S. Africa* 85 D5
Belfast, *U.K.* 15 B6
Belfast, *Maine, U.S.A.* .. 99 D6
Belfast, *N.Y., U.S.A.* 106 D6
Belfast □, *U.K.* 15 B6
Belfast L., *U.K.* 15 B6
Belfeld, *Neths.* 17 F8
Belfield, *U.S.A.* 108 B3
Belfort, *France* 25 E13
Belfort, Territoire de □,
France 25 E13
Belfry, *U.S.A.* 110 D9
Belgaum, *India* 60 M9
Belgioioso, *Italy* 32 C6
Belgium ■, *Europe* 17 G5
Belgorod, *Russia* 41 F10
Belgorod-Dnestrovskiy,
Ukraine 42 C4
Belgrade = Beograd,
Serbia 21 L10
Belgrade, *U.S.A.* 110 D8
Belhaven, *U.S.A.* 105 H7
Beli Drim →, *Europe* 21 N10
Beli Manastir, *Croatia* ... 21 K8
Belice →, *Italy* 34 E5
Belin-Béliet, *France* 26 D3
Belinga, *Gabon* 80 D2
Belinskiy, *Russia* 41 E13
Belinyu, *Indonesia* 56 E3
Beliton Is. = Belitung,
Indonesia 56 E3
Belitung, *Indonesia* 56 E3
Beliu, *Romania* 38 C5
Belize ■, *Cent. Amer.* 115 D7
Belize City, *Belize* 115 D7
Beljanica, *Serbia* 21 L11
Belkovskiy, Ostrov, *Russia* 45 B14
Bell →, *Canada* 98 C4
Bell Bay, *Australia* 90 G4
Bell I., *Canada* 99 B8
Bell-Irving →, *Canada* .. 100 B3
Bell Peninsula, *Canada* ... 97 B11
Bell Ville, *Argentina* 126 C3
Bella Bella, *Canada* 100 C3
Bella Coola, *Canada* 100 C3
Bella Flor, *Bolivia* 124 C4
Bella Unión, *Uruguay* 126 C4
Bella Vista, *Corrientes,*
Argentina 126 B4
Bella Vista, *Tucuman,*
Argentina 126 B2
Bellac, *France* 26 B5
Bellágio, *Italy* 32 C6
Bellaire, *U.S.A.* 106 F4
Bellary, *India* 60 M10
Bellata, *Australia* 91 D4
Belle Fourche, *U.S.A.* ... 108 C3
Belle Fourche →, *U.S.A.* 108 C3
Belle Glade, *U.S.A.* 105 M5
Belle-Ile, *France* 24 E3
Belle Isle, *Canada* 99 B8
Belle Isle, Str. of, *Canada* 99 B8
Belle-Isle-en-Terre, *France* 24 D3
Belle Plaine, *Iowa, U.S.A.* 108 E8
Belle Plaine, *Minn., U.S.A.* 108 C8
Belle Yella, *Liberia* 78 D3
Belledonne, Chaîne de,
France 27 C10
Belledune, *Canada* 99 C6
Bellefontaine, *U.S.A.* 104 E4
Bellefonte, *U.S.A.* 106 F7
Bellegarde, *France* 25 E9
Bellegarde-en-Marche,
France 26 C6
Bellegarde-sur-Valserine,
France 27 B9
Bellême, *France* 24 D7
Belleoram, *Canada* 99 C8
Belleville, *Canada* 98 D4
Belleville, *France* 27 B8
Belleville, *Ill., U.S.A.* ... 108 F10
Belleville, *Kans., U.S.A.* . 108 F6
Belleville, *N.Y., U.S.A.* .. 107 C8
Belleville-sur-Vie, *France* . 24 F5
Bellevue, *Canada* 100 D6
Bellevue, *Idaho, U.S.A.* .. 110 E6
Bellevue, *Ohio, U.S.A.* ... 106 E2
Bellevue, *Wash., U.S.A.* . 112 C4
Belley, *France* 27 C9
Bellin, *Canada* 97 B13
Bellingen, *Australia* 91 E5
Bellingham, *U.S.A.* 112 B4
Bellingshausen Sea,
Antarctica 5 C17
Bellinzona, *Switz.* 23 D8
Bello, *Colombia* 120 B2
Bellows Falls, *U.S.A.* 107 C12
Bellpat, *Pakistan* 62 E3
Bellpuig, *Spain* 28 D6
Belluno, *Italy* 33 B9
Bellville, *U.S.A.* 109 L6
Bellwood, *U.S.A.* 106 F6
Bélmez, *Spain* 31 G5
Belmont, *Australia* 91 E5
Belmont, *Canada* 106 D3
Belmont, *S. Africa* 84 D3
Belmont, *U.S.A.* 106 D6
Belmonte, *Brazil* 123 E4
Belmonte, *Portugal* 30 E3
Belmonte, *Spain* 28 F2
Belmopan, *Belize* 115 D7
Belmullet, *Ireland* 15 B2
Belo Horizonte, *Brazil* ... 123 E3
Belo Jardim, *Brazil* 122 C4
Belo-sur-Mer, *Madag.* 85 C7
Belo-Tsiribihina, *Madag.* . 85 B7
Belogorsk, *Russia* 45 D13
Belogorsk, *Ukraine* 42 D6
Belogradchik, *Bulgaria* ... 38 F5
Beloha, *Madag.* 85 D8
Beloit, *Kans., U.S.A.* 108 F5
Beloit, *Wis., U.S.A.* 108 D10
Belokorovichi, *Ukraine* ... 40 F6
Belomorsk, *Russia* 44 C4
Belonia, *India* 61 H17
Belopolye, *Ukraine* 40 F9
Belorussia ■, *Europe* 40 E5
Belovo, *Russia* 44 D9
Beloye More, *Russia* 44 C4
Beloye Ozero, *Russia* 43 D12
Belozersk, *Russia* 41 A10
Belpasso, *Italy* 35 E7
Belsele, *Belgium* 17 F4

Bijnor

Belsito, *Italy* 34 E6
Beltana, *Australia* 91 E2
Belterra, *Brazil* 121 D7
Beltinci, *Slovenia* 33 B13
Belton, *S.C., U.S.A.* 105 H4
Belton, *Tex., U.S.A.* 109 K6
Belton Res., *U.S.A.* 109 K6
Beltsy, *Moldavia* 42 C3
Belturbet, *Ireland* 15 B4
Belukha, *Russia* 44 E9
Beluran, *Malaysia* 56 C5
Belvedere Marittimo, *Italy* 35 C8
Belvès, *France* 26 D5
Belvidere, *Ill., U.S.A.* 108 D10
Belvidere, *N.J., U.S.A.* 107 F9
Belvis de la Jara, *Spain* 31 F6
Belyando →, *Australia* 90 C4
Belyy, *Russia* 40 D8
Belyy, Ostrov, *Russia* 44 B8
Belyy Yar, *Russia* 44 D9
Belzig, *Germany* 18 C8
Belzoni, *U.S.A.* 109 J9
Bemaraha, Lembalemban' i, *Madag.* 85 B7
Bemarivo, *Madag.* 85 C7
Bemarivo →, *Madag.* 85 B8
Bemavo, *Madag.* 85 C8
Bembéréke, *Benin* 79 C5
Bembesi, *Zimbabwe* 83 F2
Bembesi →, *Zimbabwe* 83 F2
Bembézar →, *Spain* 31 H5
Bemidji, *U.S.A.* 108 B7
Bemmel, *Neths.* 16 E7
Ben, *Iran* 65 C6
Ben Cruachan, *U.K.* 14 E3
Ben Dearg, *U.K.* 14 D4
Ben Gardane, *Tunisia* 75 B7
Ben Hope, *U.K.* 14 C4
Ben Lawers, *U.K.* 14 E4
Ben Lomond, *N.S.W., Australia* 91 E5
Ben Lomond, *Tas., Australia* 90 G4
Ben Lomond, *U.K.* 14 E4
Ben Luc, *Vietnam* 59 G6
Ben Macdhui, *U.K.* 14 D5
Ben Mhor, *U.K.* 14 D1
Ben More, *Central, U.K.* 14 E4
Ben More, *Strath., U.K.* 14 E2
Ben More Assynt, *U.K.* 14 C4
Ben Nevis, *U.K.* 14 E4
Ben Quang, *Vietnam* 58 D6
Ben Slimane, *Morocco* 74 B3
Ben Tre, *Vietnam* 59 G6
Ben Vorlich, *U.K.* 14 E4
Ben Wyvis, *U.K.* 14 D4
Bena, *Nigeria* 79 C6
Bena Dibele, *Zaïre* 80 E4
Benagalbón, *Spain* 31 J6
Benagerie, *Australia* 91 E3
Benahmed, *Morocco* 74 B3
Benalla, *Australia* 91 F4
Benambra, Mt., *Australia* 91 F4
Benamejí, *Spain* 31 H6
Benares = Varanasi, *India* 63 G10
Bénat, C., *France* 27 E10
Benavente, *Portugal* 31 G2
Benavente, *Spain* 30 C5
Benavides, *Spain* 30 C5
Benavides, *U.S.A.* 109 M5
Benbecula, *U.K.* 14 D1
Benbonyathe, *Australia* 91 E2
Bencubbin, *Australia* 89 F2
Bend, *U.S.A.* 110 D3
Bender Beila, *Somali Rep.* 68 F5
Bendering, *Australia* 89 F2
Bendery, *Moldavia* 42 C3
Bendigo, *Australia* 91 F3
Bendorf, *Germany* 18 E3
Benē Beraq, *Israel* 69 C3
Beneden Knijpe, *Neths.* 16 C7
Beneditinos, *Brazil* 122 C3
Benedito Leite, *Brazil* 122 C3
Bénéna, *Mali* 78 C4
Benenitra, *Madag.* 85 C8
Benešöv, *Czech.* 20 F4
Bénestroff, *France* 25 D13
Benet, *France* 26 B3
Benevento, *Italy* 35 A7
Benfeld, *France* 25 D14
Benga, *Mozam.* 83 F3
Bengal, Bay of, *Ind. Oc.* 61 K16
Bengbu, *China* 51 H9
Benghazi = Banghāzī, *Libya* 73 B9
Bengkalis, *Indonesia* 56 D2
Bengkulu, *Indonesia* 56 E2
Bengkulu □, *Indonesia* 56 E2
Bengough, *Canada* 101 D7
Benguela, *Angola* 81 G2
Benguerir, *Morocco* 74 B3
Benguérua, I., *Mozam.* 85 C6
Benha, *Egypt* 76 H7
Beni, *Zaïre* 82 B2
Beni □, *Bolivia* 125 C4
Beni →, *Bolivia* 125 C4
Beni Abbès, *Algeria* 75 B4
Beni-Haoua, *Algeria* 75 A5
Beni Mazâr, *Egypt* 76 J7
Beni Mellal, *Morocco* 74 B3
Beni Ounif, *Algeria* 75 B4
Beni Saf, *Algeria* 75 A4
Beni Suef, *Egypt* 76 J7
Beniah L., *Canada* 100 A6
Benicarló, *Spain* 28 E5
Benicia, *U.S.A.* 112 G4
Benidorm, *Spain* 29 G4
Benidorm, Islote de, *Spain* 29 G4
Benin ■, *Africa* 79 D5
Benin, Bight of, *W. Afr.* 79 D5
Benin City, *Nigeria* 79 D6
Benisa, *Spain* 29 G5
Benitses, *Greece* 37 A3
Benjamin Aceval, *Paraguay* 126 A4
Benjamin Constant, *Brazil* 120 D3
Benjamin Hill, *Mexico* 114 A2
Benkelman, *U.S.A.* 108 E4
Benkovac, *Croatia* 33 D12
Benlidi, *Australia* 90 C3
Bennebroek, *Neths.* 16 D5
Bennekom, *Neths.* 16 D7
Bennett, *Canada* 100 B2
Bennett, L., *Australia* 88 D5
Bennett, Ostrov, *Russia* 45 B15
Bennettsville, *U.S.A.* 105 H6
Bennington, *U.S.A.* 107 D11
Bénodet, *France* 24 E2
Benoni, *S. Africa* 85 D4
Benoud, *Algeria* 75 B5
Benque Viejo, *Belize* 115 D7
Bensheim, *Germany* 19 F4
Benson, *U.S.A.* 111 L8
Bent, *Iran* 65 E8
Benteng, *Indonesia* 57 F6
Bentinck I., *Australia* 90 B2
Bentiu, *Sudan* 77 F2
Bento Gonçalves, *Brazil* 127 B5
Benton, *Ark., U.S.A.* 109 H8
Benton, *Calif., U.S.A.* 112 H8
Benton, *Ill., U.S.A.* 108 F10
Benton Harbor, *U.S.A.* 104 D2
Bentu Liben, *Ethiopia* 77 F4
Bentung, *Malaysia* 59 L3
Benue □, *Nigeria* 79 D6
Benue →, *Nigeria* 79 D6
Benxi, *China* 51 D12
Benzdorp, *Surinam* 121 C7
Beo, *Indonesia* 57 D7
Beograd, *Serbia* 21 L10
Beowawe, *U.S.A.* 110 F5
Bepan Jiang →, *China* 52 E6
Beppu, *Japan* 49 H5
Berati, *Albania* 39 J2
Berau, Teluk, *Indonesia* 57 E8
Berber, *Sudan* 76 D3
Berbera, *Somali Rep.* 68 E4
Berbérati, *C.A.R.* 80 D3
Berberia, C. del, *Spain* 36 C7
Berbice →, *Guyana* 121 B6
Berceto, *Italy* 32 D7
Berchtesgaden, *Germany* 19 H8
Berdichev, *Ukraine* 42 B3
Berdsk, *Russia* 44 D9
Berdyansk, *Ukraine* 42 C7
Berdychiv = Berdichev, *Ukraine* 42 B3
Berea, *U.S.A.* 104 G3
Berebere, *Indonesia* 57 D7
Bereda, *Somali Rep.* 68 E5
Berekum, *Ghana* 78 D4
Berenice, *Egypt* 76 C4
Berens →, *Canada* 101 C9
Berens I., *Canada* 101 C9
Berens River, *Canada* 101 C9
Berestechko, *Ukraine* 40 F4
Bereşti, *Romania* 38 C10
Beretău →, *Romania* 38 B4
Berettyo →, *Hungary* 21 J11
Berettyóújfalu, *Hungary* 21 H11
Berevo, *Mahajanga, Madag.* 85 B7
Berevo, *Toliara, Madag.* 85 B7
Bereza, *Belorussia* 40 E4
Berezhany, *Ukraine* 40 G4
Berezina →, *Belorussia* 40 E7
Berezna, *Ukraine* 40 F7
Berezniki, *Russia* 44 D6
Berezovka, *Ukraine* 42 C4
Berezovo, *Russia* 44 C7
Berga, *Spain* 28 C6
Bergama, *Turkey* 66 D2
Bergambacht, *Neths.* 16 E5
Bérgamo, *Italy* 32 C6
Bergantiños, *Spain* 30 B2
Bergara, *Spain* 28 B2
Bergedorf, *Germany* 18 B6
Bergeijk, *Neths.* 17 F6
Bergen, *Germany* 18 A9
Bergen, *Neths.* 16 C5
Bergen, *Norway* 9 F8
Bergen, *U.S.A.* 106 C7
Bergen-op-Zoom, *Neths.* 17 F4
Bergerac, *France* 26 D4
Bergheim, *Germany* 18 E2
Berghem, *Neths.* 16 E7
Bergisch-Gladbach, *Germany* 18 E3
Bergschenhoek, *Neths.* 16 E5
Bergsjö, *Sweden* 10 C11
Bergues, *France* 25 B9
Bergum, *Neths.* 16 B7
Bergville, *S. Africa* 85 D4
Berhala, Selat, *Indonesia* 56 E2
Berhampore = Baharampur, *India* 63 G13
Berhampur, *India* 61 K14
Berheci →, *Romania* 38 C10
Bering Sea, *Pac. Oc.* 96 C1
Bering Strait, *U.S.A.* 96 B3
Beringen, *Belgium* 17 F6
Beringen, *Switz.* 23 A7
Beringovskiy, *Russia* 45 C18
Berislav, *Ukraine* 42 C5
Berisso, *Argentina* 126 C4
Berja, *Spain* 29 J2
Berkane, *Morocco* 75 B4
Berkel →, *Neths.* 16 D8
Berkeley, *U.K.* 13 F5
Berkeley, *U.S.A.* 112 H4
Berkeley Springs, *U.S.A.* 104 F6
Berkhout, *Neths.* 16 C5
Berkner I., *Antarctica* 5 D18
Berkovitsa, *Bulgaria* 38 F6
Berkshire □, *U.K.* 13 F6
Berlaar, *Belgium* 17 F5
Berland →, *Canada* 100 C5
Berlanga, *Spain* 31 G5
Berlare, *Belgium* 17 F4
Berlenga, I., *Portugal* 31 F1
Berlin, *Germany* 18 C9
Berlin, *Md., U.S.A.* 104 F8
Berlin, *N.H., U.S.A.* 107 B13
Berlin, *Wis., U.S.A.* 104 D1
Bermeja, Sierra, *Spain* 31 J5
Bermejo →, *Formosa, Argentina* 126 B4
Bermejo →, *San Juan, Argentina* 126 C2
Bermeo, *Spain* 28 B2
Bermillo de Sayago, *Spain* 30 D4
Bermuda ■, *Atl. Oc.* 2 C6
Bern, *Switz.* 22 C4
Bern □, *Switz.* 22 C5
Bernado, *U.S.A.* 111 J10
Bernalda, *Italy* 35 B9
Bernalillo, *U.S.A.* 111 J10
Bernardo de Irigoyen, *Argentina* 127 B5
Bernardo O'Higgins □, *Chile* 126 C1
Bernasconi, *Argentina* 126 D3
Bernau, *Bayern, Germany* 19 H8
Bernau, *Brandenburg, Germany* 18 C9
Bernay, *France* 24 C7
Bernburg, *Germany* 18 D7
Berne = Bern, *Switz.* 22 C4
Berne = Bern □, *Switz.* 22 C5
Berner Alpen, *Switz.* 22 D5
Bernese Oberland = Oberland, *Switz.* 22 C5
Bernier I., *Australia* 89 D1
Bernina, Piz, *Switz.* 23 D9
Bernina, Pizzo, *Switz.* 23 D9
Bernissart, *Belgium* 17 H3
Bernkastel-Kues, *Germany* 19 F3
Beroroha, *Madag.* 85 C8
Béroubouay, *Benin* 79 C5
Beroun, *Czech.* 20 F4
Berounka →, *Czech.* 20 F4
Berovo, *Macedonia* 39 H5
Berrahal, *Algeria* 75 A6
Berre, Étang de, *France* 27 E9
Berrechid, *Morocco* 74 B3
Berri, *Australia* 91 E3
Berriane, *Algeria* 75 B5
Berrouaghia, *Algeria* 75 A5
Berry, *Australia* 91 E5
Berry, *France* 25 F8
Berry Is., *Bahamas* 116 A4
Berryessa L., *U.S.A.* 112 G4
Berryville, *U.S.A.* 109 G8
Bersenbrück, *Germany* 18 C3
Berthold, *U.S.A.* 108 A4
Berthoud, *U.S.A.* 108 E2
Bertincourt, *France* 25 B9
Bertoua, *Cameroon* 80 D2
Bertrand, *U.S.A.* 108 E5
Bertrange, *Lux.* 17 J8
Bertrix, *Belgium* 17 J6
Berufjörður, *Iceland* 8 D6
Beruri, *Brazil* 121 D5
Berwick, *U.S.A.* 107 E8
Berwick-upon-Tweed, *U.K.* 12 B5
Berwyn Mts., *U.K.* 12 E4
Berzasca, *Romania* 38 E4
Besal, *Pakistan* 63 B5
Besalampy, *Madag.* 85 B7
Besançon, *France* 25 E13
Besar, *Indonesia* 56 E5
Beshenkovichi, *Belorussia* 40 D6
Beslan, *Russia* 43 E11
Besnard L., *Canada* 101 B7
Besni, *Turkey* 67 E7
Besor, N. →, *Egypt* 69 D3
Bessarabiya, *Moldavia* 38 B11
Bessarabka, *Moldavia* 42 C3
Bessèges, *France* 27 D8
Bessemer, *Ala., U.S.A.* 105 J2
Bessemer, *Mich., U.S.A.* 108 B9
Bessin, *France* 24 C5
Bessines-sur-Gartempe, *France* 26 B5
Best, *Neths.* 17 E6
Bet She'an, *Israel* 69 C4
Bet Shemesh, *Israel* 69 D3
Bet Tadjine, Djebel, *Algeria* 74 C4
Betafo, *Madag.* 85 B8
Betancuria, *Canary Is.* 36 F5
Betanzos, *Bolivia* 125 D4
Betanzos, *Spain* 30 B2
Bétaré Oya, *Cameroon* 80 C2
Bétera, *Spain* 28 F4
Bethal, *S. Africa* 85 D4
Bethanien, *Namibia* 84 D2
Bethany, *S. Africa* 84 D4
Bethany, *U.S.A.* 108 E7
Bethel, *Alaska, U.S.A.* 96 B3
Bethel, *Vt., U.S.A.* 107 C12
Bethel Park, *U.S.A.* 106 F4
Bethlehem = Bayt Lahm, *Jordan* 69 D4
Bethlehem, *S. Africa* 85 D4
Bethlehem, *U.S.A.* 107 F9
Bethulie, *S. Africa* 84 E4
Béthune, *France* 25 B9
Béthune →, *France* 24 C8
Bethungra, *Australia* 91 E4
Betijoque, *Venezuela* 120 B3
Betim, *Brazil* 123 E3
Betioky, *Madag.* 85 C7
Beton-Bazoches, *France* 25 D10
Betong, *Thailand* 59 K3
Betoota, *Australia* 90 D3
Betroka, *Madag.* 85 C8
Betsiamites, *Canada* 99 C6
Betsiamites →, *Canada* 99 C6
Betsiboka →, *Madag.* 85 B8
Betsjoeanaland, *S. Africa* 84 D3
Bettembourg, *Lux.* 17 J8
Bettiah, *India* 63 F11
Bèttola, *Italy* 32 D6
Betul, *India* 60 J10
Betung, *Malaysia* 56 D4
Betzdorf, *Germany* 18 E3
Beuca, *Romania* 38 E7
Beuil, *France* 27 D10
Beulah, *U.S.A.* 108 B4
Beuvron →, *France* 24 E8
Beveren, *Belgium* 17 F4
Beverley, *Australia* 89 F2
Beverley, *U.K.* 12 D7
Beverlo, *Belgium* 17 F6
Beverly, *Mass., U.S.A.* 107 D14
Beverly, *Wash., U.S.A.* 110 C4
Beverly Hills, *U.S.A.* 113 L8
Beverwijk, *Neths.* 16 D5
Bex, *Switz.* 22 D4
Bey Dağları, *Turkey* 66 E4
Beyānlū, *Iran* 64 C5
Beyin, *Ghana* 78 D4
Beyla, *Guinea* 78 D3
Beynat, *France* 26 C5
Beyneu, *Kazakhstan* 44 E6
Beypazarı, *Turkey* 66 C4
Beyşehir Gölü, *Turkey* 66 E4
Beytüşşebap, *Turkey* 67 E10
Bezhetsk, *Russia* 41 C10
Bezhitsa, *Russia* 40 E9
Béziers, *France* 26 E7
Bezwada = Vijayawada, *India* 61 L12
Bhachau, *India* 60 H7
Bhadarwah, *India* 63 C6
Bhadrakh, *India* 61 J15
Bhadravati, *India* 60 N9
Bhagalpur, *India* 63 G12
Bhakkar, *Pakistan* 62 D4
Bhakra Dam, *India* 62 D7
Bhamo, *Burma* 61 G20
Bhandara, *India* 60 J11
Bhanrer Ra., *India* 62 H8
Bharat = India ■, *Asia* 60 K11
Bharatpur, *India* 62 F7
Bhatinda, *India* 62 D6
Bhatpara, *India* 63 H13
Bhaun, *Pakistan* 62 C5
Bhaunagar = Bhavnagar, *India* 62 J5
Bhavnagar, *India* 62 J5
Bhawanipatna, *India* 61 K12
Bhera, *Pakistan* 62 C5
Bhilsa = Vidisha, *India* 62 H7
Bhilwara, *India* 62 G6
Bhima →, *India* 60 L10
Bhimavaram, *India* 61 L12
Bhimbar, *Pakistan* 63 C6
Bhind, *India* 63 F8
Bhiwandi, *India* 60 K8
Bhiwani, *India* 62 E7
Bhola, *Bangla.* 61 H17
Bhopal, *India* 62 H7
Bhubaneshwar, *India* 61 J14
Bhuj, *India* 62 H3
Bhumiphol Dam = Phumiphon, Khuan, *Thailand* 58 D2
Bhusaval, *India* 60 J9
Bhutan ■, *Asia* 61 F17
Biá →, *Brazil* 120 D4
Biafra, B. of = Bonny, Bight of, *Africa* 79 E6
Biak, *Indonesia* 57 E9
Biała →, *Poland* 20 E10
Biała Podlaska, *Poland* 20 C13
Białogard, *Poland* 20 A5
Białystok, *Poland* 20 B13
Biancavilla, *Italy* 35 E7
Bīārjmand, *Iran* 65 B7
Biaro, *Indonesia* 57 D7
Biarritz, *France* 26 E2
Biasca, *Switz.* 23 D7
Biba, *Egypt* 76 J7
Bibai, *Japan* 48 C10
Bibala, *Angola* 81 G2
Bibane, Bahiret el, *Tunisia* 75 B7
Bibbiena, *Italy* 33 E8
Bibby I., *Canada* 101 A10
Biberach, *Germany* 19 G5
Biberist, *Switz.* 22 B5
Bibey →, *Spain* 30 C3
Bibiani, *Ghana* 78 D4
Biboohra, *Australia* 90 B4
Bibungwa, *Zaïre* 82 C2
Bic, *Canada* 99 C6
Bicaz, *Romania* 38 C9
Biccari, *Italy* 35 A8
Bichena, *Ethiopia* 77 E4
Bickerton I., *Australia* 90 A2
Bicknell, *Ind., U.S.A.* 104 F2
Bicknell, *Utah, U.S.A.* 111 G8
Bida, *Nigeria* 79 D6
Bidar, *India* 60 L10
Biddeford, *U.S.A.* 99 D5
Biddwara, *Ethiopia* 77 F4
Bideford, *U.K.* 13 F3
Bidon 5 = Poste Maurice Cortier, *Algeria* 75 D5
Bidor, *Malaysia* 59 K3
Bié, Planalto de, *Angola* 81 G3
Bieber, *U.S.A.* 110 F3
Biel, *Switz.* 22 B4
Bielawa, *Poland* 20 E6
Bielé Karpaty, *Europe* 20 F7
Bielefeld, *Germany* 18 C4
Bielersee, *Switz.* 22 B4
Biella, *Italy* 32 C5
Bielsk Podlaski, *Poland* 20 C13
Bielsko-Biała, *Poland* 20 F9
Bien Hoa, *Vietnam* 59 G6
Bienfait, *Canada* 101 D8
Bienne = Biel, *Switz.* 22 B4
Bienvenida, *Spain* 31 G4
Bienvenue, *Fr. Guiana* 121 C7
Bienville, L., *Canada* 98 A5
Biescas, *Spain* 28 C4
Biese →, *Germany* 18 C7
Biesiesfontein, *S. Africa* 84 E2
Bietigheim, *Germany* 19 G5
Bievre, *Belgium* 17 J6
Biferno →, *Italy* 35 A8
Big →, *Canada* 99 B8
Big B., *Canada* 99 A7
Big Bear City, *U.S.A.* 113 L10
Big Bear Lake, *U.S.A.* 113 L10
Big Beaver, *Canada* 101 D7
Big Belt Mts., *U.S.A.* 110 C8
Big Bend, *Swaziland* 85 D5
Big Bend National Park, *U.S.A.* 109 L3
Big Black →, *U.S.A.* 109 J9
Big Blue →, *U.S.A.* 108 F6
Big Cr. →, *Canada* 100 C4
Big Creek, *U.S.A.* 112 H7
Big Cypress Swamp, *U.S.A.* 105 M5
Big Falls, *U.S.A.* 108 A8
Big Fork →, *U.S.A.* 108 A8
Big Horn Mts. = Bighorn Mts., *U.S.A.* 110 D10
Big Lake, *U.S.A.* 109 K4
Big Moose, *U.S.A.* 107 C10
Big Muddy Cr. →, *U.S.A.* 108 A2
Big Pine, *U.S.A.* 111 H4
Big Piney, *U.S.A.* 110 E8
Big Quill L., *Canada* 101 C8
Big Rapids, *U.S.A.* 104 D3
Big River, *Canada* 101 C7
Big Run, *U.S.A.* 106 F6
Big Sable Pt., *U.S.A.* 104 C2
Big Sand L., *Canada* 101 B9
Big Sandy, *U.S.A.* 110 B8
Big Sandy Cr. →, *U.S.A.* 108 F3
Big Sioux →, *U.S.A.* 108 D6
Big Spring, *U.S.A.* 109 J4
Big Springs, *U.S.A.* 108 E3
Big Stone City, *U.S.A.* 108 C6
Big Stone Gap, *U.S.A.* 105 G4
Big Stone L., *U.S.A.* 108 C6
Big Sur, *U.S.A.* 112 J5
Big Timber, *U.S.A.* 110 D9
Big Trout L., *Canada* 98 B1
Biğa, *Turkey* 66 C2
Bigadiç, *Turkey* 66 D3
Biganos, *France* 26 D3
Bigfork, *U.S.A.* 110 B6
Biggar, *Canada* 101 C7
Biggar, *U.K.* 14 F5
Bigge I., *Australia* 88 B4
Biggenden, *Australia* 91 D5
Biggs, *U.S.A.* 112 F5
Bighorn, *U.S.A.* 110 C10
Bighorn →, *U.S.A.* 110 C10
Bighorn Mts., *U.S.A.* 110 D10
Bignona, *Senegal* 78 C1
Bigorre, *France* 26 E4
Bigstone L., *Canada* 101 C9
Bigwa, *Tanzania* 82 D4
Bihać, *Bos.-H.* 33 D12
Bihar, *India* 63 G11
Bihar □, *India* 63 G11
Biharamulo, *Tanzania* 82 C3
Biharamulo □, *Tanzania* 82 C3
Bihor, Munţii, *Romania* 38 C5
Bijagós, Arquipélago dos, *Guinea-Biss.* 78 C1
Bijaipur, *India* 62 F7
Bijapur, *Karnataka, India* 60 L9
Bijapur, *Mad. P., India* 61 K12
Bījār, *Iran* 64 C5
Bijeljina, *Bos.-H.* 21 L9
Bijelo Polje, *Montenegro* 21 M9
Bijie, *China* 52 D5
Bijnor, *India* 62 E8

Bikaner

Bikaner, *India* 62 E5
Bikapur, *India* 63 F10
Bikeqi, *China* 50 D6
Bikfayyā, *Lebanon* 69 B4
Bikin, *Russia* 45 E14
Bikin →, *Russia* 48 A7
Bikini Atoll, *Pac. Oc.* 92 F8
Bikoué, *Cameroon* 79 E7
Bila Tserkva = Belaya Tserkov, *Ukraine* 40 G7
Bilara, *India* 62 F5
Bilaspur, *Mad. P., India* 63 H10
Bilaspur, *Punjab, India* 62 D7
Bilauk Taungdan, *Thailand* 58 F2
Bilbao, *Spain* 28 B2
Bilbeis, *Egypt* 76 H7
Bilbo = Bilbao, *Spain* 28 B2
Bilbor, *Romania* 38 B8
Bîldudalur, *Iceland* 8 D2
Bileća, *Bos.-H.* 21 N8
Bilecik, *Turkey* 66 C4
Bilecik □, *Turkey* 66 C4
Biłgoraj, *Poland* 20 E12
Bilibino, *Russia* 45 C17
Bilibiza, *Mozam.* 83 E5
Bilir, *Russia* 45 C14
Biliran I., *Phil.* 55 F6
Bill, *U.S.A.* 108 D2
Billabalong, *Australia* 89 E2
Billiluna, *Australia* 88 C4
Billingham, *U.K.* 12 C6
Billings, *U.S.A.* 110 D9
Billiton Is. = Belitung, *Indonesia* 56 E3
Billom, *France* 26 C7
Bilma, *Niger* 73 E7
Bilo Gora, *Croatia* 21 K7
Biloela, *Australia* 90 C5
Biloku, *Guyana* 121 C6
Biloxi, *U.S.A.* 109 K10
Bilpa Morea Claypan, *Australia* 90 D2
Bilthoven, *Neths.* 16 D6
Biltine, *Chad* 73 F9
Bilyana, *Australia* 90 B4
Bilyarsk, *Russia* 41 D17
Bilzen, *Belgium* 17 G7
Bima, *Indonesia* 57 F5
Bimban, *Egypt* 76 C3
Bimbila, *Ghana* 79 D5
Bimbo, *C.A.R.* 80 D3
Bimini Is., *Bahamas* 116 A4
Bin Xian, *Heilongjiang, China* 51 B14
Bin Xian, *Shaanxi, China* 50 G5
Bina-Etawah, *India* 62 G8
Bināb, *Iran* 65 B6
Binalbagan, *Phil.* 55 F5
Binalong, *Australia* 91 E4
Bīnālūd, Kūh-e, *Iran* 65 B8
Binatang, *Malaysia* 56 D4
Binbee, *Australia* 90 C4
Binche, *Belgium* 17 H4
Binchuan, *China* 52 E3
Binda, *Australia* 91 D4
Bindle, *Australia* 91 D4
Bindura, *Zimbabwe* 83 F3
Bingara, *N.S.W., Australia* 91 D5
Bingara, *Queens., Australia* 91 D3
Bingen, *Germany* 19 F3
Bingerville, *Ivory C.* 78 D4
Bingham, *U.S.A.* 99 C6
Bingham Canyon, *U.S.A.* 110 F7
Binghamton, *U.S.A.* 107 D9
Bingöl, *Turkey* 67 D9
Bingöl □, *Turkey* 67 D9
Bingöl Dağları, *Turkey* 67 D9
Binh Dinh = An Nhon, *Vietnam* 58 F7
Binh Khe, *Vietnam* 58 F7
Binh Son, *Vietnam* 58 E7
Binhai, *China* 51 G10
Binisatua, *Spain* 36 B11
Binjai, *Indonesia* 56 D1
Binnaway, *Australia* 91 E4
Binongko, *Indonesia* 57 F6
Binscarth, *Canada* 101 C8
Bintan, *Indonesia* 56 D2
Bintulu, *Malaysia* 56 D4
Bintuni, *Indonesia* 57 E8
Binyang, *China* 52 F7
Binz, *Germany* 18 A9
Binzert = Bizerte, *Tunisia* 75 A6
Bío Bío □, *Chile* 126 D1
Biograd, *Croatia* 33 E12
Bioko, *Eq. Guin.* 79 E6
Biougra, *Morocco* 74 B3
Bir, *India* 60 K9
Bir, Ras, *Djibouti* 77 E5
Bîr Abu Hashim, *Egypt* 76 C3
Bîr Abu M'nqar, *Egypt* 76 B2
Bîr Abu Muḩammad, *Egypt* 69 F3
Bi'r ad Dabbāghāt, *Jordan* 69 E4
Bîr Adal Deib, *Sudan* 76 C4
Bi'r al Butayyihāt, *Jordan* 69 F4
Bi'r al Mārī, *Jordan* 69 E4
Bi'r al Qattār, *Jordan* 69 F4
Bir Aouine, *Tunisia* 75 B6
Bîr 'Asal, *Egypt* 76 B3
Bir Autrun, *Sudan* 76 D2
Bîr Beiḍa, *Egypt* 69 E3
Bîr Diqnash, *Egypt* 76 A2
Bir el Abbes, *Algeria* 74 C3
Bîr el 'Abd, *Egypt* 69 D2
Bir el Ater, *Algeria* 75 B6
Bîr el Basur, *Egypt* 76 B2
Bîr el Biarât, *Egypt* 69 F3
Bîr el Duweidar, *Egypt* 69 E1
Bîr el Garârât, *Egypt* 69 D2
Bîr el Gellaz, *Egypt* 76 A2
Bîr el Heisi, *Egypt* 69 F3
Bîr el Jafir, *Egypt* 69 E1
Bîr el Mâlḩi, *Egypt* 69 E2
Bîr el Shaqqa, *Egypt* 76 A2
Bîr el Thamâda, *Egypt* 69 E2
Bîr Fuad, *Egypt* 76 A2
Bîr Gebeil Ḩişn, *Egypt* 69 E2
Bi'r Ghadīr, *Syria* 69 A6
Bîr Haimur, *Egypt* 76 C3
Bîr Ḩasana, *Egypt* 69 E2
Bi'r Jadīd, *Iraq* 64 C4
Bir Jdid, *Morocco* 74 B3
Bîr Kanayis, *Egypt* 76 C3
Bîr Kaseiba, *Egypt* 69 E2
Bîr Kerawein, *Egypt* 76 B2
Bîr Lahfân, *Egypt* 69 D2
Bîr Lahrache, *Algeria* 75 B6
Bîr Madkûr, *Egypt* 69 E1
Bîr Maql, *Egypt* 76 C3
Bîr Misaha, *Egypt* 76 C2
Bir Mogrein, *Mauritania* 74 C2
Bîr Murr, *Egypt* 76 C3
Bi'r Muţribah, *Kuwait* 64 D5
Bîr Nakheila, *Egypt* 76 C3
Bîr Qaţia, *Egypt* 69 E1
Bîr Qatrani, *Egypt* 76 A2
Bîr Ranga, *Egypt* 76 C4
Bîr Sahara, *Egypt* 76 C2
Bîr Seiyâla, *Egypt* 76 B3
Bir Semguine, *Morocco* 74 B3
Bîr Shalatein, *Egypt* 76 C4
Bîr Shebb, *Egypt* 76 C2
Bîr Shût, *Egypt* 76 C4
Bîr Terfawi, *Egypt* 76 C2
Bîr Umm Qubûr, *Egypt* 76 C3
Bîr Ungât, *Egypt* 76 C3
Bîr Za'farâna, *Egypt* 76 J8
Bîr Zeidûn, *Egypt* 76 B3
Bira, *Indonesia* 57 E8
Bîra, *Romania* 38 B10
Biramféro, *Guinea* 78 C3
Birao, *C.A.R.* 73 F9
Birawa, *Zaïre* 82 C2
Bîrca, *Romania* 38 F6
Birch Hills, *Canada* 101 C7
Birch I., *Canada* 101 C9
Birch L., *N.W.T., Canada* 100 A5
Birch L., *Ont., Canada* 98 B1
Birch L., *U.S.A.* 98 C1
Birch Mts., *Canada* 100 B6
Birch River, *Canada* 101 C8
Birchip, *Australia* 91 F3
Bird, *Canada* 101 B10
Bird City, *U.S.A.* 108 F4
Bird I. = Aves, I. de, *W. Indies* 117 C7
Bird I., *S. Africa* 84 E2
Birdaard, *Neths.* 16 B7
Birdlip, *U.K.* 13 F5
Birdsville, *Australia* 90 D2
Birdum, *Australia* 88 C5
Birein, *Israel* 69 E3
Bireuen, *Indonesia* 56 C1
Birifo, *Gambia* 78 C2
Birigui, *Brazil* 127 A5
Birkenfeld, *Germany* 19 F3
Birkenhead, *U.K.* 12 D4
Birket Qârûn, *Egypt* 76 J7
Birkhadem, *Algeria* 75 A5
Bîrlad, *Romania* 38 C10
Birmingham, *U.K.* 13 E6
Birmingham, *U.S.A.* 105 J2
Birmitrapur, *India* 61 H14
Birni Ngaouré, *Niger* 79 C5
Birni Nkonni, *Niger* 79 C6
Birnin Gwari, *Nigeria* 79 C6
Birnin Kebbi, *Nigeria* 79 C5
Birnin Kudu, *Nigeria* 79 C6
Birobidzhan, *Russia* 45 E14
Birr, *Ireland* 15 C4
Birrie →, *Australia* 91 D4
Birs →, *Switz.* 22 B5
Birsilpur, *India* 62 E5
Birsk, *Russia* 44 D6
Birtin, *Romania* 38 C5
Birtle, *Canada* 101 C8
Birur, *India* 60 N9
Biryuchiy, *Ukraine* 42 C6
Biržai, *Lithuania* 40 C4
Bîrzava, *Romania* 38 C4
Birzebugga, *Malta* 37 D2
Bisa, *Indonesia* 57 E7
Bisáccia, *Italy* 35 A8
Bisacquino, *Italy* 34 E6
Bisalpur, *India* 63 E8
Bisbee, *U.S.A.* 111 L9
Biscarrosse et de Parentis, Étang de, *France* 26 D2
Biscay, B. of, *Atl. Oc.* 6 F5
Biscayne B., *U.S.A.* 105 N5
Biscéglie, *Italy* 35 A9
Bischofshofen, *Austria* 21 H3
Bischofswerda, *Germany* 18 D10
Bischofszell, *Switz.* 23 B8
Bischwiller, *France* 25 D14
Biscoe Bay, *Antarctica* 5 D13
Biscoe Is., *Antarctica* 5 C17
Biscostasing, *Canada* 98 C3
Biscucuy, *Venezuela* 120 B4
Biševo, *Croatia* 33 F13
Bisha, *Eritrea* 77 D4
Bishah, W. →, *Si. Arabia* 76 C5
Bishan, *China* 52 C6
Bishkek, *Kirghizia* 44 E8
Bishnupur, *India* 63 H12
Bisho, *S. Africa* 85 E4
Bishop, *Calif., U.S.A.* 111 H4
Bishop, *Tex., U.S.A.* 109 M6
Bishop Auckland, *U.K.* 12 C6
Bishop's Falls, *Canada* 99 C8
Bishop's Stortford, *U.K.* 13 F8
Bisignano, *Italy* 35 C9
Bisina, L., *Uganda* 82 B3
Biskra, *Algeria* 75 B6
Bislig, *Phil.* 57 C7
Bismarck, *U.S.A.* 108 B4
Bismarck Arch., *Papua N. G.* 92 H6
Bismark, *Germany* 18 C7
Biso, *Uganda* 82 B3
Bison, *U.S.A.* 108 C3
Bīsotūn, *Iran* 64 C5
Bispfors, *Sweden* 8 E14
Bispgården, *Sweden* 10 A10
Bissagos = Bijagós, Arquipélago dos, *Guinea-Biss.* 78 C1
Bissau, *Guinea-Biss.* 78 C1
Bissett, *Canada* 101 C9
Bissikrima, *Guinea* 78 C2
Bistcho L., *Canada* 100 B5
Bistreţu, *Romania* 38 F6
Bistrica = Ilirska-Bistrica, *Slovenia* 33 C11
Bistriţa, *Romania* 38 B7
Bistriţa →, *Romania* 38 C9
Bistriţei, Munţii, *Romania* 38 B8
Biswan, *India* 63 F9
Bitam, *Gabon* 80 D2
Bitburg, *Germany* 19 F2
Bitche, *France* 25 C14
Bithynia, *Turkey* 66 C4
Bitkine, *Chad* 73 F8
Bitlis, *Turkey* 67 D10
Bitlis □, *Turkey* 67 D10
Bitola, *Macedonia* 39 H4
Bitolj = Bitola, *Macedonia* 39 H4
Bitonto, *Italy* 35 A9
Bitter Creek, *U.S.A.* 110 F9
Bitter L. = Buheirat-Murrat-el-Kubra, *Egypt* 76 H8
Bitterfeld, *Germany* 18 D8
Bitterfontein, *S. Africa* 84 E2
Bitterroot →, *U.S.A.* 110 C6
Bitterroot Range, *U.S.A.* 110 D6
Bitterwater, *U.S.A.* 112 J6
Bitti, *Italy* 34 B2
Bittou, *Burkina Faso* 79 C4
Biu, *Nigeria* 79 C7
Bivolari, *Romania* 38 B10
Biwa-Ko, *Japan* 49 G8
Biwabik, *U.S.A.* 108 B8
Bixad, *Romania* 38 B6
Biyang, *China* 50 H7
Biysk, *Russia* 44 D9
Bizana, *S. Africa* 85 E4
Bizen, *Japan* 49 G7
Bizerte, *Tunisia* 75 A6
Bjargtangar, *Iceland* 8 D1
Bjelasica, *Montenegro* 21 N9
Bjelovar, *Croatia* 21 K6
Bjerringbro, *Denmark* 11 H3
Bjørnøya, *Arctic* 4 B8
Bjuv, *Sweden* 11 H6
Blace, *Serbia* 21 M11
Black = Da →, *Vietnam* 58 B5
Black →, *Canada* 106 B5
Black →, *Ark., U.S.A.* 109 H9
Black →, *N.Y., U.S.A.* 107 C8
Black →, *Wis., U.S.A.* 108 D9
Black Diamond, *Canada* 100 C6
Black Forest = Schwarzwald, *Germany* 19 H4
Black Hills, *U.S.A.* 108 C3
Black I., *Canada* 101 C9
Black L., *Canada* 101 B7
Black L., *U.S.A.* 104 C3
Black Mesa, *U.S.A.* 109 G3
Black Mt. = Mynydd Du, *U.K.* 13 F4
Black Mts., *U.K.* 13 F4
Black Range, *U.S.A.* 111 K10
Black River, *Jamaica* 116 C4
Black River Falls, *U.S.A.* 108 C9
Black Sea, *Europe* 42 E6
Black Volta →, *Africa* 78 D4
Black Warrior →, *U.S.A.* 105 J2
Blackall, *Australia* 90 C4
Blackball, *N.Z.* 87 K3
Blackbull, *Australia* 90 B3
Blackburn, *U.K.* 12 D5
Blackduck, *U.S.A.* 108 B7
Blackfoot, *U.S.A.* 110 E7
Blackfoot →, *U.S.A.* 110 C7
Blackfoot River Reservoir, *U.S.A.* 110 E8
Blackie, *Canada* 100 C6
Blackpool, *U.K.* 12 D4
Blackriver, *U.S.A.* 106 B1
Blacks Harbour, *Canada* 99 C6
Blacksburg, *U.S.A.* 104 G5
Blacksod B., *Ireland* 15 B2
Blackstone, *U.S.A.* 104 G6
Blackstone →, *Canada* 100 A4
Blackstone Ra., *Australia* 89 E4
Blackville, *Canada* 99 C6
Blackwater, *Australia* 90 C4
Blackwater →, *Ireland* 15 E4
Blackwater →, *U.K.* 15 B5
Blackwater Cr. →, *Australia* 91 D3
Blackwell, *U.S.A.* 109 G6
Blackwells Corner, *U.S.A.* 113 K7
Bladel, *Neths.* 17 F6
Blaenau Ffestiniog, *U.K.* 12 E4
Blagodarnoye, *Russia* 43 D10
Blagoevgrad, *Bulgaria* 39 G6
Blagoveshchensk, *Russia* 45 D13
Blain, *France* 24 E5
Blaine, *U.S.A.* 112 B4
Blaine Lake, *Canada* 101 C7
Blainville-sur-l'Eau, *France* 25 D13
Blair, *U.S.A.* 108 E6
Blair Athol, *Australia* 90 C4
Blair Atholl, *U.K.* 14 E5
Blairgowrie, *U.K.* 14 E5
Blairmore, *Canada* 100 D6
Blairsden, *U.S.A.* 112 F6
Blairsville, *U.S.A.* 106 F5
Blaj, *Romania* 38 C6
Blake Pt., *U.S.A.* 108 A10
Blakely, *U.S.A.* 105 K3
Blâmont, *France* 25 D13
Blanc, C., *Tunisia* 75 A6
Blanc, Mont, *Alps* 27 C10
Blanca, B., *Argentina* 128 A4
Blanca Peak, *U.S.A.* 111 H11
Blanchard, *U.S.A.* 109 H6
Blanche, C., *Australia* 91 E1
Blanche, L., *S. Austral., Australia* 91 D2
Blanche, L., *W. Austral., Australia* 88 D3
Blanco, *S. Africa* 84 E3
Blanco, *U.S.A.* 109 K5
Blanco →, *Argentina* 126 C2
Blanco, C., *U.S.A.* 110 E1
Blanco, C., *Costa Rica* 116 E2
Blanco, C., *Spain* 36 B9
Blanda →, *Iceland* 8 D4
Blandford Forum, *U.K.* 13 G5
Blanding, *U.S.A.* 111 H9
Blanes, *Spain* 28 D7
Blangy-sur-Bresle, *France* 25 C8
Blanice →, *Czech.* 20 F4
Blankenberge, *Belgium* 17 F2
Blankenburg, *Germany* 18 D6
Blanquefort, *France* 26 D3
Blanquillo, *Uruguay* 127 C4
Blansko, *Czech.* 20 F6
Blantyre, *Malawi* 83 F4
Blaricum, *Neths.* 16 D6
Blarney, *Ireland* 15 E3
Blato, *Croatia* 33 F13
Blatten, *Switz.* 22 D5
Blaubeuren, *Germany* 19 G5
Blåvands Huk, *Denmark* 9 J10
Blaydon, *U.K.* 12 C6
Blaye, *France* 26 C3
Blaye-les-Mines, *France* 26 D6
Blayney, *Australia* 91 E4
Blaze, Pt., *Australia* 88 B5
Bleckede, *Germany* 18 B6
Bled, *Slovenia* 33 B11
Blednaya, Gora, *Russia* 44 B7
Bléharis, *Belgium* 17 G2
Blejeşti, *Romania* 38 E8
Blekinge län □, *Sweden* 9 H13
Blenheim, *Canada* 106 D2
Blenheim, *N.Z.* 87 J4
Bléone →, *France* 27 D10
Blerick, *Neths.* 17 F8
Bletchley, *U.K.* 13 F7
Blida, *Algeria* 75 A5
Blidet Amor, *Algeria* 75 B6
Blidö, *Sweden* 10 E12
Bligh Sound, *N.Z.* 87 L1
Blind River, *Canada* 98 C3
Blinnenhorn, *Switz.* 23 D6
Blitar, *Indonesia* 57 H15
Blitta, *Togo* 79 D5
Block I., *U.S.A.* 107 E13
Block Island Sd., *U.S.A.* 107 E13
Blodgett Iceberg Tongue, *Antarctica* 5 C9
Bloemendaal, *Neths.* 16 D5
Bloemfontein, *S. Africa* 84 D4
Bloemhof, *S. Africa* 84 D4
Blois, *France* 24 E8
Blokziji, *Neths.* 16 C7
Blönduós, *Iceland* 8 D3
Bloodvein →, *Canada* 101 C9
Bloody Foreland, *Ireland* 15 A3
Bloomer, *U.S.A.* 108 C9
Bloomfield, *Australia* 90 B4
Bloomfield, *Canada* 106 C7
Bloomfield, *Iowa, U.S.A.* 108 E8
Bloomfield, *N. Mex., U.S.A.* 111 H10
Bloomfield, *Nebr., U.S.A.* 108 D6
Bloomington, *Ill., U.S.A.* 108 E10
Bloomington, *Ind., U.S.A.* 104 F2
Bloomsburg, *U.S.A.* 107 F8
Blora, *Indonesia* 57 G14
Blossburg, *U.S.A.* 106 E7
Blouberg, *S. Africa* 85 C4
Blountstown, *U.S.A.* 105 K3
Bludenz, *Austria* 19 H5
Blue Island, *U.S.A.* 104 E2
Blue Lake, *U.S.A.* 110 F2
Blue Mesa Reservoir, *U.S.A.* 111 G10
Blue Mts., *Oreg., U.S.A.* 110 D4
Blue Mts., *Pa., U.S.A.* 107 F8
Blue Mud B., *Australia* 90 A2
Blue Nile = An Nîl el Azraq □, *Sudan* 77 E3
Blue Nile = Nîl el Azraq →, *Sudan* 77 D3
Blue Rapids, *U.S.A.* 108 F6
Blue Ridge Mts., *U.S.A.* 105 G5
Blue Stack Mts., *Ireland* 15 B3
Blueberry →, *Canada* 100 B4
Bluefield, *U.S.A.* 104 G5
Bluefields, *Nic.* 116 D3
Bluff, *Australia* 90 C4
Bluff, *N.Z.* 87 M2
Bluff, *U.S.A.* 111 H9
Bluff Knoll, *Australia* 89 F2
Bluff Pt., *Australia* 89 E1
Bluffton, *U.S.A.* 104 E3
Blumenau, *Brazil* 127 B6
Blümisalphorn, *Switz.* 22 D5
Blunt, *U.S.A.* 108 C4
Bly, *U.S.A.* 110 E3
Blyth, *Canada* 106 C3
Blyth, *U.K.* 12 B6
Blyth Bridge, *U.K.* 12 E5
Blythe, *U.S.A.* 113 M12
Bø, *Norway* 10 E3
Bo, *S. Leone* 78 D2
Bo Duc, *Vietnam* 59 G6
Bo Hai, *China* 51 E10
Bo Xian, *China* 50 H8
Boa Esperança, *Brazil* 121 C5
Boa Nova, *Brazil* 123 D3
Boa Viagem, *Brazil* 122 C4
Boa Vista, *Brazil* 121 C5
Boac, *Phil.* 55 E4
Boaco, *Nic.* 116 D2
Bo'ai, *China* 50 G7
Boal, *Spain* 30 B4
Boardman, *U.S.A.* 106 E4
Boatman, *Australia* 91 D4
Bobadah, *Australia* 91 E4
Bobai, *China* 52 F7
Bobbili, *India* 61 K13
Bóbbio, *Italy* 32 D6
Bobcaygeon, *Canada* 98 D4
Böblingen, *Germany* 19 G5
Bobo-Dioulasso, *Burkina Faso* 78 C4
Boboc, *Romania* 38 D9
Bobonaza →, *Ecuador* 120 D2
Bobov Dol, *Bulgaria* 38 G5
Bóbr →, *Poland* 20 C5
Bobraomby, Tanjon' i, *Madag.* 85 A8
Bobrinets, *Ukraine* 42 B5
Bobrov, *Russia* 41 F12
Bobruysk, *Belorussia* 40 E6
Bobures, *Venezuela* 120 B3
Boca de Drago, *Venezuela* 121 A5
Bôca do Acre, *Brazil* 124 B4
Bôca do Jari, *Brazil* 121 D7
Bôca do Moaco, *Brazil* 124 B4
Boca Grande, *Venezuela* 121 B5
Boca Raton, *U.S.A.* 105 M5
Bocaiúva, *Brazil* 123 E3
Bocanda, *Ivory C.* 78 D4
Bocaranga, *C.A.R.* 73 G8
Bocas del Toro, *Panama* 116 E3
Boceguillas, *Spain* 28 D1
Bochnia, *Poland* 20 F10
Bocholt, *Belgium* 17 F7
Bocholt, *Germany* 18 D2
Bochum, *Germany* 18 D3
Bockenem, *Germany* 18 C6
Bocognano, *France* 27 F13
Boconó, *Venezuela* 120 B3
Boconó →, *Venezuela* 120 B4
Bocoyna, *Mexico* 114 B3
Bocq →, *Belgium* 17 H5
Boda, *C.A.R.* 80 D3
Bodaybo, *Russia* 45 D12
Boddington, *Australia* 89 F2
Bodega Bay, *U.S.A.* 112 G3
Bodegraven, *Neths.* 16 D5
Boden, *Sweden* 8 D16
Bodensee, *Europe* 23 A8
Bodenteich, *Germany* 18 C6
Bodhan, *India* 60 K10
Bodinga, *Nigeria* 79 C6
Bodio, *Switz.* 23 D7
Bodmin, *U.K.* 13 G3
Bodmin Moor, *U.K.* 13 G3
Bodoquena, Serra da, *Brazil* 125 E6
Bodrog →, *Hungary* 21 G11
Bodrum, *Turkey* 66 E2
Boechout, *Belgium* 17 F5
Boegoebergdam, *S. Africa* 84 D3
Boekelo, *Neths.* 16 D9
Boelenslaan, *Neths.* 16 B8
Boën, *France* 27 C8
Boende, *Zaïre* 80 E4
Boerne, *U.S.A.* 109 L5
Boertange, *Neths.* 16 B10
Boezinge, *Belgium* 17 G1
Boffa, *Guinea* 78 C2
Bogalusa, *U.S.A.* 109 K10
Bogan Gate, *Australia* 91 E4
Bogantungan, *Australia* 90 C4
Bogata, *U.S.A.* 109 J7
Bogatić, *Serbia* 21 L9

Name	Page	Grid
Boğazlıyan, *Turkey*	66	D6
Bogense, *Denmark*	11	J4
Boggabilla, *Australia*	91	D5
Boggabri, *Australia*	91	E5
Boggeragh Mts., *Ireland*	15	D3
Bognor Regis, *U.K.*	13	G7
Bogø, *Denmark*	11	K6
Bogo, *Phil.*	55	F6
Bogodukhov, *Ukraine*	42	A6
Bogong, Mt., *Australia*	91	F4
Bogor, *Indonesia*	57	G12
Bogoroditsk, *Russia*	41	E11
Bogorodsk, *Russia*	41	C13
Bogorodskoye, *Russia*	45	D15
Bogoso, *Ghana*	78	D4
Bogotá, *Colombia*	120	C3
Bogotol, *Russia*	44	D9
Bogra, *Bangla.*	61	G16
Boguchany, *Russia*	45	D10
Boguchar, *Russia*	43	B9
Bogué, *Mauritania*	78	B2
Boguslav, *Ukraine*	42	B4
Bohain-en-Vermandois, *France*	25	C10
Bohemia Downs, *Australia*	88	C4
Bohemian Forest = Böhmerwald, *Germany*	19	F8
Bohena Cr. →, *Australia*	91	E4
Bohinjska Bistrica, *Slovenia*	33	B11
Böhmerwald, *Germany*	19	F8
Bohmte, *Germany*	18	C4
Bohol, *Phil.*	55	G6
Bohol Sea, *Phil.*	57	C6
Bohotleh, *Somali Rep.*	68	F4
Boi, *Nigeria*	79	D6
Boi, Pta. de, *Brazil*	127	A6
Boiaçu, *Brazil*	121	D5
Boiano, *Italy*	35	A7
Boileau, C., *Australia*	88	C3
Boipeba, I. de, *Brazil*	123	D4
Bois →, *Brazil*	123	E1
Boischot, *Belgium*	17	F5
Boise, *U.S.A.*	110	E5
Boise City, *U.S.A.*	109	G3
Boissevain, *Canada*	101	D8
Boite →, *Italy*	33	B9
Boitzenburg, *Germany*	18	B9
Boizenburg, *Germany*	18	B6
Bojador C., *W. Sahara*	74	C2
Bojnūrd, *Iran*	65	B8
Bojonegoro, *Indonesia*	57	G14
Boju, *Nigeria*	79	D6
Boka Kotorska, *Montenegro*	21	N8
Bokala, *Ivory C.*	78	D4
Boké, *Guinea*	78	C2
Bokhara →, *Australia*	91	D4
Bokkos, *Nigeria*	79	D6
Boknafjorden, *Norway*	9	G8
Bokoro, *Chad*	73	F8
Bokote, *Zaïre*	80	E4
Boksitogorsk, *Russia*	40	B8
Bokungu, *Zaïre*	80	E4
Bol, *Chad*	73	F7
Bol, *Croatia*	33	E13
Bolama, *Guinea-Biss.*	78	C1
Bolan Pass, *Pakistan*	60	E5
Bolaños →, *Mexico*	114	C4
Bolbec, *France*	24	C7
Boldājī, *Iran*	65	D6
Boldeşti, *Romania*	38	D9
Bole, *China*	54	B3
Bole, *Ethiopia*	77	F4
Bolekhov, *Ukraine*	40	G3
Bolesławiec, *Poland*	20	D5
Bolgatanga, *Ghana*	79	C4
Bolgrad, *Ukraine*	42	D3
Boli, *Sudan*	77	F2
Bolinao, *Phil.*	55	C3
Bolinao C., *Phil.*	57	A5
Bolívar, *Argentina*	126	D3
Bolívar, *Antioquía, Colombia*	120	B3
Bolívar, *Cauca, Colombia*	120	C2
Bolívar, *Peru*	124	B2
Bolivar, *Mo., U.S.A.*	109	G8
Bolivar, *Tenn., U.S.A.*	109	H10
Bolívar □, *Colombia*	120	B3
Bolívar □, *Ecuador*	120	D2
Bolívar □, *Venezuela*	121	B5
Bolivia ■, *S. Amer.*	125	D5
Bolivian Plateau, *S. Amer.*	118	D3
Bolkhov, *Russia*	41	E10
Bollène, *France*	27	D8
Bollnäs, *Sweden*	10	C10
Bollon, *Australia*	91	D4
Bollstabruk, *Sweden*	10	A11
Bollullos, *Spain*	31	H4
Bolobo, *Zaïre*	80	E3
Bologna, *Italy*	33	D8
Bologne, *France*	25	D12
Bologoye, *Russia*	40	C9
Bolomba, *Zaïre*	80	D3
Bolonchenticul, *Mexico*	115	D7
Bolong, *Phil.*	57	C6
Boloven, Cao Nguyen, *Laos*	58	E6
Bolpur, *India*	63	H12
Bolsena, *Italy*	33	F8
Bolsena, L. di, *Italy*	33	F8
Bolshaya Glushitsa, *Russia*	41	E17
Bolshaya Martynovka, *Russia*	43	C9
Bolshaya Vradiyevka, *Ukraine*	42	C4
Bolsshereche, *Russia*	44	D8
Bolshevik, Ostrov, *Russia*	45	B11
Bolshoi Kavkas, *Asia*	43	E11
Bolshoy Anyuy →, *Russia*	45	C17
Bolshoy Atlym, *Russia*	44	C7
Bolshoy Begichev, Ostrov, *Russia*	45	B12
Bolshoy Lyakhovskiy, Ostrov, *Russia*	45	B15
Bolshoy Tokmak, *Ukraine*	42	C6
Bol'shoy Tyuters, *Estonia*	40	B5
Bolsward, *Neths.*	16	B7
Boltaña, *Spain*	28	C5
Boltigen, *Switz.*	22	C4
Bolton, *Canada*	106	C5
Bolton, *U.K.*	12	D5
Bolu, *Turkey*	66	C4
Bolu □, *Turkey*	66	C4
Boluo, *China*	53	F10
Bolvadin, *Turkey*	66	D4
Bolzano, *Italy*	33	B8
Bom Comércio, *Brazil*	125	B4
Bom Conselho, *Brazil*	122	C4
Bom Despacho, *Brazil*	123	E2
Bom Jesus, *Brazil*	122	C3
Bom Jesus da Gurguéia, Serra, *Brazil*	122	C3
Bom Jesus da Lapa, *Brazil*	123	D3
Boma, *Zaïre*	80	F2
Bomaderry, *Australia*	91	E5
Bombala, *Australia*	91	F4
Bombarral, *Portugal*	31	F1
Bombay, *India*	60	K8
Bomboma, *Zaïre*	80	D3
Bombombwa, *Zaïre*	82	B2
Bomi Hills, *Liberia*	78	D2
Bomili, *Zaïre*	82	B2
Bomokandi →, *Zaïre*	82	B2
Bomongo, *Zaïre*	80	D3
Bomu →, *C.A.R.*	80	D4
Bon, C., *Tunisia*	75	A7
Bon Sar Pa, *Vietnam*	58	F6
Bonaduz, *Switz.*	23	C8
Bonaire, *Neth. Ant.*	117	D6
Bonang, *Australia*	91	F4
Bonanza, *Nic.*	116	D3
Bonaparte Arch., *Australia*	88	B3
Boñar, *Spain*	30	C5
Bonaventure, *Canada*	99	C6
Bonavista, *Canada*	99	C9
Bonavista, C., *Canada*	99	C9
Bonawan, *Phil.*	55	G5
Bondeno, *Italy*	33	D8
Bondo, *Zaïre*	82	B1
Bondoukou, *Ivory C.*	78	D4
Bondowoso, *Indonesia*	57	G15
Bone, Teluk, *Indonesia*	57	E6
Bone Rate, *Indonesia*	57	F6
Bone Rate, Kepulauan, *Indonesia*	57	F6
Bonefro, *Italy*	35	A7
Bo'ness, *U.K.*	14	E5
Bong Son = Hoai Nhon, *Vietnam*	58	E7
Bongabong, *Phil.*	55	E4
Bongandanga, *Zaïre*	80	D4
Bongor, *Chad*	73	F8
Bongouanou, *Ivory C.*	78	D4
Bonham, *U.S.A.*	109	J6
Bonheiden, *Belgium*	17	F5
Bonifacio, *France*	27	G13
Bonifacio, Bouches de, *Medit. S.*	34	A2
Bonin Is. = Ogasawara Gunto, *Pac. Oc.*	92	E6
Bonke, *Ethiopia*	77	F4
Bonn, *Germany*	18	E3
Bonnat, *France*	26	B5
Bonne Terre, *U.S.A.*	109	G9
Bonners Ferry, *U.S.A.*	110	B5
Bonnétable, *France*	24	D7
Bonneuil-Matours, *France*	24	F7
Bonneval, *France*	24	D8
Bonneville, *France*	27	B10
Bonney, L., *Australia*	91	F3
Bonnie Downs, *Australia*	90	C3
Bonnie Rock, *Australia*	89	F2
Bonny, *Nigeria*	79	E6
Bonny →, *Nigeria*	79	E6
Bonny, Bight of, *Africa*	79	E6
Bonny-sur-Loire, *France*	25	E9
Bonnyville, *Canada*	101	C6
Bonoi, *Indonesia*	57	E9
Bonorva, *Italy*	34	B1
Bonsall, *U.S.A.*	113	M9
Bontang, *Indonesia*	56	D5
Bonthain, *Indonesia*	57	F5
Bonthe, *S. Leone*	78	D2
Bontoc, *Phil.*	55	C4
Bonyeri, *Ghana*	78	D4
Bonython Ra., *Australia*	88	D4
Bookabie, *Australia*	89	F5
Booker, *U.S.A.*	109	G4
Boolaboolka L., *Australia*	91	E3
Booligal, *Australia*	91	E3
Boom, *Belgium*	17	F4
Boonah, *Australia*	91	D5
Boone, *Iowa, U.S.A.*	108	D8
Boone, *N.C., U.S.A.*	105	G5
Booneville, *Ark., U.S.A.*	109	H8
Booneville, *Miss., U.S.A.*	105	H1
Boonville, *Calif., U.S.A.*	112	F3
Boonville, *Ind., U.S.A.*	104	F2
Boonville, *Mo., U.S.A.*	108	F8
Boonville, *N.Y., U.S.A.*	107	C9
Boorindal, *Australia*	91	E4
Boorowa, *Australia*	91	E4
Boothia, Gulf of, *Canada*	97	A11
Boothia Pen., *Canada*	96	A10
Bootle, *Cumb., U.K.*	12	C4
Bootle, *Mersey., U.K.*	12	D4
Booué, *Gabon*	80	E2
Bophuthatswana □, *S. Africa*	84	D4
Boppard, *Germany*	19	E3
Boquerón □, *Paraguay*	125	E5
Boquete, *Panama*	116	E3
Boquilla, Presa de la, *Mexico*	114	B3
Boquillas del Carmen, *Mexico*	114	B4
Bor, *Czech.*	20	F2
Bor, *Serbia*	21	L12
Bôr, *Sudan*	77	F3
Bor, *Turkey*	66	E6
Bor Mashash, *Israel*	69	D3
Boradā →, *Syria*	69	B5
Borah Peak, *U.S.A.*	110	D7
Borama, *Somali Rep.*	68	F3
Borang, *Sudan*	77	G3
Borås, *Sweden*	11	G6
Borāzjān, *Iran*	65	D6
Borba, *Brazil*	121	D6
Borba, *Portugal*	31	G3
Borborema, Planalto da, *Brazil*	122	C4
Borçka, *Turkey*	43	F9
Borculo, *Neths.*	16	D9
Bord Khūn-e Now, *Iran*	65	D6
Borda, C., *Australia*	91	F2
Bordeaux, *France*	26	D3
Borden, *Australia*	89	F2
Borden, *Canada*	99	C7
Borden I., *Canada*	4	B2
Borders □, *U.K.*	14	F6
Bordertown, *Australia*	91	F3
Borðeyri, *Iceland*	8	D3
Bordighera, *Italy*	32	E4
Bordj bou Arreridj, *Algeria*	75	A5
Bordj Bourguiba, *Tunisia*	75	B7
Bordj el Hobra, *Algeria*	75	B5
Bordj Fly Ste. Marie, *Algeria*	74	C4
Bordj-in-Eker, *Algeria*	75	D6
Bordj Menaiel, *Algeria*	75	A5
Bordj Messouda, *Algeria*	75	B6
Bordj Nili, *Algeria*	75	B5
Bordj Omar Driss, *Algeria*	75	C6
Bordj-Tarat, *Algeria*	75	C6
Bordj Zelfana, *Algeria*	75	B5
Borensberg, *Sweden*	11	F9
Borga, *Finland*	9	F18
Borgarnes, *Iceland*	8	D3
Børgefjellet, *Norway*	8	D12
Borger, *Neths.*	16	C9
Borger, *U.S.A.*	109	H4
Borgerhout, *Belgium*	17	F4
Borgharen, *Neths.*	17	G7
Borgholm, *Sweden*	9	H14
Bórgia, *Italy*	35	D9
Borgloon, *Belgium*	17	G6
Borgo San Dalmazzo, *Italy*	32	D4
Borgo San Lorenzo, *Italy*	33	E8
Borgo Valsugana, *Italy*	33	B8
Borgomanero, *Italy*	32	C5
Borgonovo Val Tidone, *Italy*	32	C6
Borgorose, *Italy*	33	F10
Borgosésia, *Italy*	32	C5
Borgvattnet, *Sweden*	10	A9
Borikhane, *Laos*	58	C4
Borislav, *Ukraine*	40	G3
Borisoglebsk, *Russia*	41	F13
Borisoglebskiy, *Russia*	41	C13
Borisov, *Belorussia*	40	D6
Borispol, *Ukraine*	40	F7
Borja, *Peru*	120	D2
Borja, *Spain*	28	D3
Borjas Blancas, *Spain*	28	D5
Borken, *Germany*	18	D2
Borkou, *Chad*	73	E8
Borkum, *Germany*	18	B2
Borlänge, *Sweden*	9	F13
Borley, C., *Antarctica*	5	C5
Bórmio, *Italy*	32	B7
Born, *Neths.*	17	F7
Borna, *Germany*	18	D8
Borndiep, *Neths.*	16	B7
Borne, *Neths.*	16	D9
Bornem, *Belgium*	17	F4
Borneo, *E. Indies*	56	D5
Bornholm, *Denmark*	9	J13
Borno □, *Nigeria*	79	C7
Bornos, *Spain*	31	J5
Bornu Yassa, *Nigeria*	79	C7
Borobudur, *Indonesia*	57	G14
Borodino, *Russia*	40	D9
Borogontsy, *Russia*	45	C14
Boromo, *Burkina Faso*	78	C4
Boron, *U.S.A.*	113	L9
Borongan, *Phil.*	55	F6
Bororen, *Australia*	90	C5
Borotangba Mts., *C.A.R.*	77	F1
Borovan, *Bulgaria*	38	F6
Borovichi, *Russia*	40	B8
Borovsk, *Russia*	41	D10
Borrego Springs, *U.S.A.*	113	M10
Borriol, *Spain*	28	E4
Borroloola, *Australia*	90	B2
Borşa, *Romania*	38	B7
Borssele, *Neths.*	17	F3
Bort-les-Orgues, *France*	26	C6
Borth, *U.K.*	13	E3
Borujerd, *Iran*	65	C6
Borzhomi, *Georgia*	43	F10
Borzna, *Ukraine*	40	F8
Borzya, *Russia*	45	D12
Bosa, *Italy*	34	B1
Bosanska Dubica, *Bos.-H.*	33	C13
Bosanska Gradiška, *Bos.-H.*	21	K7
Bosanska Kostajnica, *Bos.-H.*	33	C13
Bosanska Krupa, *Bos.-H.*	33	D13
Bosanski Novi, *Bos.-H.*	33	C13
Bosanski Šamac, *Bos.-H.*	21	K8
Bosansko Grahovo, *Bos.-H.*	33	D13
Bosansko Petrovac, *Bos.-H.*	33	D13
Bosaso, *Somali Rep.*	68	E4
Boscastle, *U.K.*	13	G3
Boscotrecase, *Italy*	35	B7
Bose, *China*	52	F6
Boshan, *China*	51	F9
Boshoek, *S. Africa*	84	D4
Boshof, *S. Africa*	84	D4
Boshrūyeh, *Iran*	65	C8
Bosilegrad, *Serbia*	21	N12
Boskoop, *Neths.*	16	D5
Bosna →, *Bos.-H.*	21	K8
Bosna i Hercegovina = Bosnia-Herzegovina ■, *Europe*	21	L7
Bosnia-Herzegovina ■, *Europe*	21	L7
Bosnik, *Indonesia*	57	E9
Bosobolo, *Zaïre*	80	D3
Bosporus = Karadeniz Boğazı, *Turkey*	66	C3
Bossangoa, *C.A.R.*	73	G8
Bossekop, *Norway*	8	B17
Bossembélé, *C.A.R.*	73	G8
Bossier City, *U.S.A.*	109	J8
Bosso, *Niger*	79	C7
Bostānābād, *Iran*	64	B5
Bosten Hu, *China*	54	B3
Boston, *U.K.*	12	E7
Boston, *U.S.A.*	107	D13
Boston Bar, *Canada*	100	D4
Bosut →, *Croatia*	21	K8
Boswell, *Canada*	100	D5
Boswell, *Okla., U.S.A.*	109	H7
Boswell, *Pa., U.S.A.*	106	F5
Botad, *India*	62	H4
Botan →, *Turkey*	67	E9
Botany B., *Australia*	91	E5
Botene, *Laos*	58	D3
Botevgrad, *Bulgaria*	38	G6
Bothaville, *S. Africa*	84	D4
Bothnia, G. of, *Europe*	8	E16
Bothwell, *Australia*	90	G4
Bothwell, *Canada*	106	D3
Boticas, *Portugal*	30	D3
Botletle →, *Botswana*	84	C3
Botoşani, *Romania*	38	B9
Botro, *Ivory C.*	78	D3
Botswana ■, *Africa*	84	C3
Botucatu, *Brazil*	127	A6
Botwood, *Canada*	99	C8
Bou Alam, *Algeria*	75	B5
Bou Ali, *Algeria*	75	C4
Bou Djébéha, *Mali*	78	B4
Bou Guema, *Algeria*	75	C5
Bou Ismael, *Algeria*	75	A5
Bou Izakarn, *Morocco*	74	C3
Boû Lanouâr, *Mauritania*	74	D1
Bou Saâda, *Algeria*	75	A5
Bou Salem, *Tunisia*	75	A6
Bouaké, *Ivory C.*	78	D3
Bouar, *C.A.R.*	80	C3
Bouârfa, *Morocco*	75	B4
Bouca, *C.A.R.*	73	G8
Boucau, *France*	26	E2
Boucaut B., *Australia*	90	A1
Bouches-du-Rhône □, *France*	27	E9
Bouda, *Algeria*	75	C4
Boudenib, *Morocco*	74	B4
Boudry, *Switz.*	22	C3
Boufarik, *Algeria*	75	A5
Bougainville, C., *Australia*	88	B4
Bougainville Reef, *Australia*	90	B4
Bougaroun, C., *Algeria*	75	A6
Bougie = Bejaia, *Algeria*	75	A6
Bougouni, *Mali*	78	C3
Bouillon, *Belgium*	17	J6
Bouïra, *Algeria*	75	A5
Boulder, *Colo., U.S.A.*	108	E2
Boulder, *Mont., U.S.A.*	110	C7
Boulder City, *U.S.A.*	113	K12
Boulder Creek, *U.S.A.*	112	H4
Boulder Dam = Hoover Dam, *U.S.A.*	113	K12
Bouli, *Mauritania*	78	B2
Boulia, *Australia*	90	C2
Bouligny, *France*	25	C12
Boulogne →, *France*	24	E5
Boulogne-sur-Gesse, *France*	26	E4
Boulogne-sur-Mer, *France*	25	B8
Bouloire, *France*	24	E7
Boulsa, *Burkina Faso*	79	C4
Boultoum, *Niger*	79	C7
Boumalne, *Morocco*	74	B3
Boun Neua, *Laos*	58	B3
Boun Tai, *Laos*	58	B3
Bouna, *Ivory C.*	78	D4
Boundary Peak, *U.S.A.*	112	H8
Boundiali, *Ivory C.*	78	D3
Bountiful, *U.S.A.*	110	F8
Bounty Is., *Pac. Oc.*	92	M9
Bourbon-Lancy, *France*	26	B7
Bourbon-l'Archambault, *France*	26	B7
Bourbonnais, *France*	26	B7
Bourbonne-les-Bains, *France*	25	E12
Bourem, *Mali*	79	B4
Bourg, *France*	26	C3
Bourg-Argental, *France*	27	C8
Bourg-de-Péage, *France*	27	C9
Bourg-en-Bresse, *France*	27	B9
Bourg-St.-Andéol, *France*	27	D8
Bourg-St.-Maurice, *France*	27	C10
Bourg-St.-Pierre, *Switz.*	22	E4
Bourganeuf, *France*	26	C5
Bourges, *France*	25	E9
Bourget, *Canada*	107	A9
Bourget, L. du, *France*	27	C9
Bourgneuf, B. de, *France*	24	E4
Bourgneuf-en-Retz, *France*	24	E5
Bourgogne, *France*	25	F11
Bourgoin-Jallieu, *France*	27	C9
Bourgueil, *France*	24	E7
Bourke, *Australia*	91	E4
Bournemouth, *U.K.*	13	G6
Bourriot-Bergonce, *France*	26	D3
Bouse, *U.S.A.*	113	M13
Boussac, *France*	26	B6
Boussens, *France*	26	E4
Bousso, *Chad*	73	F8
Boussu, *Belgium*	17	H3
Boutilimit, *Mauritania*	78	B2
Bouvet I. = Bouvetøya, *Antarctica*	3	G10
Bouvetøya, *Antarctica*	3	G10
Bouznika, *Morocco*	74	B3
Bouzonville, *France*	25	C13
Bova Marina, *Italy*	35	E8
Bovalino Marina, *Italy*	35	D9
Bovec, *Slovenia*	33	B10
Bovenkarspel, *Neths.*	16	C6
Bovigny, *Belgium*	17	H7
Bovill, *U.S.A.*	110	C5
Bovino, *Italy*	35	A8
Bow Island, *Canada*	100	D6
Bowbells, *U.S.A.*	108	A3
Bowdle, *U.S.A.*	108	C5
Bowelling, *Australia*	89	F2
Bowen, *Australia*	90	C4
Bowen Mts., *Australia*	91	F4
Bowie, *Ariz., U.S.A.*	111	K9
Bowie, *Tex., U.S.A.*	109	J6
Bowkān, *Iran*	64	B5
Bowland, Forest of, *U.K.*	12	D5
Bowling Green, *Ky., U.S.A.*	104	G2
Bowling Green, *Ohio, U.S.A.*	104	E4
Bowling Green, C., *Australia*	90	B4
Bowman, *U.S.A.*	108	B3
Bowman I., *Antarctica*	5	C8
Bowmans, *Australia*	91	E2
Bowmanville, *Canada*	98	D4
Bowmore, *U.K.*	14	F2
Bowral, *Australia*	91	E5
Bowraville, *Australia*	91	E5
Bowron →, *Canada*	100	C4
Bowser L., *Canada*	100	B3
Bowsman, *Canada*	101	C8
Bowwood, *Zambia*	83	F2
Boxholm, *Sweden*	11	F9
Boxmeer, *Neths.*	17	E7
Boxtel, *Neths.*	17	E6
Boyabat, *Turkey*	42	F6
Boyaca = Casanare □, *Colombia*	120	B3
Boyce, *U.S.A.*	109	K8
Boyer →, *Canada*	100	B5
Boyle, *Ireland*	15	C3
Boyne →, *Ireland*	15	C5
Boyne City, *U.S.A.*	104	C3
Boynton Beach, *U.S.A.*	105	M5
Boyoma, Chutes, *Zaïre*	82	B2
Boyup Brook, *Australia*	89	F2
Boz Dağ, *Turkey*	66	E3
Boz Dağları, *Turkey*	66	D3
Bozburun, *Turkey*	66	E3
Bozcaada, *Turkey*	66	D2
Bozdoğan, *Turkey*	66	E3
Bozeman, *U.S.A.*	110	D8
Bozen = Bolzano, *Italy*	33	B8
Bozkır, *Turkey*	66	E5
Bozouls, *France*	26	D6
Bozova, *Turkey*	67	E8
Bozovici, *Romania*	38	E5
Bozüyük, *Turkey*	66	D4
Bra, *Italy*	32	D4
Brabant □, *Belgium*	17	G5
Brabant L., *Canada*	101	B8
Brabrand, *Denmark*	11	H4
Brač, *Croatia*	33	E13
Bracadale, L., *U.K.*	14	D2
Bracciano, *Italy*	33	F9

Bracciano, L. di, *Italy*	33	F9
Bracebridge, *Canada*	98	C4
Brach, *Libya*	73	C7
Bracieux, *France*	25	E8
Bräcke, *Sweden*	10	B9
Brackettville, *U.S.A.*	109	L4
Brački Kanal, *Croatia*	33	E13
Brad, *Romania*	38	C5
Brádano →, *Italy*	35	B9
Bradenton, *U.S.A.*	105	M4
Bradford, *Canada*	106	B5
Bradford, *U.K.*	12	D6
Bradford, *Pa., U.S.A.*	106	E6
Bradford, *Vt., U.S.A.*	107	C12
Brădiceni, *Romania*	38	D6
Bradley, *Ark., U.S.A.*	109	J8
Bradley, *Calif., U.S.A.*	112	K6
Bradley, *S. Dak., U.S.A.*	108	C6
Bradley Institute, *Zimbabwe*	83	F3
Bradore Bay, *Canada*	99	B8
Bradshaw, *Australia*	88	C5
Brady, *U.S.A.*	109	K5
Brædstrup, *Denmark*	11	J3
Braemar, *Australia*	91	E2
Braeside, *Canada*	107	A8
Braga, *Portugal*	30	D2
Braga □, *Portugal*	30	D2
Bragado, *Argentina*	126	D3
Bragança, *Brazil*	122	B2
Bragança, *Portugal*	30	D4
Bragança □, *Portugal*	30	D4
Bragança Paulista, *Brazil*	127	A6
Brahmanbaria, *Bangla.*	61	H17
Brahmani →, *India*	61	J15
Brahmaputra →, *India*	63	G13
Braich-y-pwll, *U.K.*	12	E3
Braidwood, *Australia*	91	F4
Brăila, *Romania*	38	D10
Braine-l'Alleud, *Belgium*	17	G4
Braine-le-Comte, *Belgium*	17	G4
Brainerd, *U.S.A.*	108	B7
Braintree, *U.K.*	13	F8
Braintree, *U.S.A.*	107	D14
Brak →, *S. Africa*	84	D3
Brake, *Niedersachsen, Germany*	18	B4
Brake, *Nordrhein-Westfalen, Germany*	18	D5
Brakel, *Neths.*	16	E6
Brakwater, *Namibia*	84	C2
Brålanda, *Sweden*	11	F6
Bralorne, *Canada*	100	C4
Bramberg, *Germany*	19	E6
Bramminge, *Denmark*	11	J2
Brämön, *Sweden*	10	B11
Brampton, *Canada*	98	D4
Bramsche, *Germany*	18	C3
Bramwell, *Australia*	90	A3
Branco →, *Brazil*	121	D5
Branco, C., *Brazil*	122	C5
Brande, *Denmark*	11	J3
Brandenburg = Neubrandenburg, *Germany*	18	B9
Brandenburg, *Germany*	18	C8
Brandenburg □, *Germany*	18	C9
Brandfort, *S. Africa*	84	D4
Brandon, *Canada*	101	D9
Brandon, *U.S.A.*	107	C11
Brandon B., *Ireland*	15	D1
Brandon Mt., *Ireland*	15	D1
Brandsen, *Argentina*	126	D4
Brandval, *Norway*	10	D6
Brandvlei, *S. Africa*	84	E3
Brandýs, *Czech.*	20	E4
Branford, *U.S.A.*	107	E12
Braniewo, *Poland*	20	A9
Bransfield Str., *Antarctica*	5	C18
Branson, *Colo., U.S.A.*	109	G3
Branson, *Mo., U.S.A.*	109	G8
Brantford, *Canada*	98	D3
Brantôme, *France*	26	C4
Branxholme, *Australia*	91	F3
Branzi, *Italy*	32	B6
Bras d'Or, L., *Canada*	99	C7
Brasiléia, *Brazil*	124	C4
Brasília, *Brazil*	123	E2
Brasília Legal, *Brazil*	121	D6
Braslav, *Belorussia*	40	D5
Braslovce, *Slovenia*	33	B12
Brașov, *Romania*	38	D8
Brass, *Nigeria*	79	E6
Brass →, *Nigeria*	79	E6
Brassac-les-Mines, *France*	26	C7
Brasschaat, *Belgium*	17	F4
Brassey, Banjaran, *Malaysia*	56	D5
Brassey Ra., *Australia*	89	E3
Brasstown Bald, *U.S.A.*	105	H4
Bratislava, *Slovak Rep.*	21	G7
Bratsk, *Russia*	45	D11
Brattleboro, *U.S.A.*	107	D12
Braunau, *Austria*	21	G3
Braunschweig, *Germany*	18	C6
Braunton, *U.K.*	13	F3
Brava, *Somali Rep.*	68	G3
Bråviken, *Sweden*	10	F10
Bravo del Norte →, *Mexico*	114	B5
Brawley, *U.S.A.*	113	N11
Bray, *Ireland*	15	C5
Bray, Mt., *Australia*	90	A1
Bray, Pays de, *France*	25	C8
Bray-sur-Seine, *France*	25	D10
Brazeau →, *Canada*	100	C5
Brazil, *U.S.A.*	104	F2
Brazil ■, *S. Amer.*	123	D2
Brazo Sur →, *S. Amer.*	126	B4
Brazos →, *U.S.A.*	109	L7
Brazzaville, *Congo*	80	E3
Brčko, *Bos.-H.*	21	L8
Brea, *Peru*	124	A1
Breadalbane, *Australia*	90	C2
Breadalbane, *U.K.*	14	E4
Breaden, L., *Australia*	89	E4
Breaksea Sd., *N.Z.*	87	L1
Bream B., *N.Z.*	87	F5
Bream Hd., *N.Z.*	87	F5
Breas, *Chile*	126	B1
Brebes, *Indonesia*	57	G13
Brechin, *Canada*	106	B5
Brechin, *U.K.*	14	E6
Brecht, *Belgium*	17	F5
Breckenridge, *Colo., U.S.A.*	110	G10
Breckenridge, *Minn., U.S.A.*	108	B6
Breckenridge, *Tex., U.S.A.*	109	J5
Breckland, *U.K.*	13	E8
Brecknock, Pen., *Chile*	128	D2
Břeclav, *Czech.*	20	G6
Brecon, *U.K.*	13	F4
Brecon Beacons, *U.K.*	13	F4
Breda, *Neths.*	17	E5
Bredasdorp, *S. Africa*	84	E3
Bredbo, *Australia*	91	F4
Bredene, *Belgium*	17	F1
Bredstedt, *Germany*	18	A4
Bree, *Belgium*	17	F7
Breezand, *Neths.*	16	C5
Bregalnica →, *Macedonia*	39	H5
Bregenz, *Austria*	19	H5
Bréhal, *France*	24	D5
Bréhat, Î. de, *France*	24	D4
Breiðafjörður, *Iceland*	8	D2
Breil-sur-Roya, *France*	27	E11
Breisach, *Germany*	19	G3
Brejinho de Nazaré, *Brazil*	122	D2
Brejo, *Brazil*	122	B3
Bremen, *Germany*	18	B4
Bremen □, *Germany*	18	B4
Bremer I., *Australia*	90	A2
Bremerhaven, *Germany*	18	B4
Bremerton, *U.S.A.*	112	C4
Bremervörde, *Germany*	18	B5
Bremsnes, *Norway*	10	A1
Brenes, *Spain*	31	H5
Brenham, *U.S.A.*	109	K6
Brenner Pass, *Austria*	19	H7
Breno, *Italy*	32	C7
Brent, *Canada*	98	C4
Brent, *U.K.*	13	F7
Brenta →, *Italy*	33	C9
Brentwood, *U.K.*	13	F8
Brentwood, *U.S.A.*	107	F11
Bréscia, *Italy*	32	C7
Breskens, *Neths.*	17	F3
Breslau = Wrocław, *Poland*	20	D7
Bresle →, *France*	24	B8
Bresles, *France*	25	C9
Bressanone, *Italy*	33	B8
Bressay, *U.K.*	14	A7
Bresse, *France*	25	F12
Bressuire, *France*	24	F6
Brest, *Belorussia*	40	E3
Brest, *France*	24	D2
Brest-Litovsk = Brest, *Belorussia*	40	E3
Bretagne, *France*	24	D4
Bretçu, *Romania*	38	C9
Breteuil, *Eure, France*	24	D7
Breteuil, *Oise, France*	25	C9
Breton, *Canada*	100	C6
Breton, Pertuis, *France*	26	B2
Breton Sd., *U.S.A.*	109	L10
Brett, C., *N.Z.*	87	F5
Bretten, *Germany*	19	F4
Brevard, *U.S.A.*	105	H4
Breves, *Brazil*	122	B1
Brevik, *Norway*	10	E3
Brewarrina, *Australia*	91	D4
Brewer, *U.S.A.*	99	D6
Brewer, Mt., *U.S.A.*	112	J8
Brewster, *N.Y., U.S.A.*	107	E11
Brewster, *Wash., U.S.A.*	110	B4
Brewster, Kap, *Greenland*	4	B6
Brewton, *U.S.A.*	105	K2
Breyten, *S. Africa*	85	D4
Breytovo, *Russia*	41	B10
Brezhnev = Naberezhnyye Chelny, *Russia*	44	D6
Brežice, *Slovenia*	33	C12
Brézina, *Algeria*	75	B5
Březnice, *Czech.*	20	F3
Breznik, *Bulgaria*	38	G5
Brezno, *Slovak Rep.*	20	G9
Bria, *C.A.R.*	73	G9
Briançon, *France*	27	D10
Briare, *France*	25	E9
Bribie I., *Australia*	91	D5
Bricquebec, *France*	24	C5
Bridgehampton, *U.S.A.*	107	F12
Bridgend, *U.K.*	13	F4
Bridgeport, *Calif., U.S.A.*	111	G4
Bridgeport, *Conn., U.S.A.*	107	E11
Bridgeport, *Nebr., U.S.A.*	108	E3
Bridgeport, *Tex., U.S.A.*	109	J6
Bridger, *U.S.A.*	110	D9
Bridgeton, *U.S.A.*	104	F8
Bridgetown, *Australia*	89	F2
Bridgetown, *Barbados*	117	D8
Bridgetown, *Canada*	99	D6
Bridgewater, *Canada*	99	D7
Bridgewater, *Mass., U.S.A.*	107	E14
Bridgewater, *S. Dak., U.S.A.*	108	D6
Bridgewater, C., *Australia*	91	F3
Bridgnorth, *U.K.*	13	E5
Bridgton, *U.S.A.*	107	B14
Bridgwater, *U.K.*	13	F4
Bridlington, *U.K.*	12	C7
Bridport, *Australia*	90	G4
Bridport, *U.K.*	13	G5
Brie, Plaine de la, *France*	25	D10
Brie-Comte-Robert, *France*	25	D9
Briec, *France*	24	D2
Brielle, *Neths.*	16	E4
Brienne-le-Château, *France*	25	D11
Brienon-sur-Armançon, *France*	25	E10
Brienz, *Switz.*	22	C6
Brienzersee, *Switz.*	22	C5
Brig, *Switz.*	22	D5
Brigg, *U.K.*	12	D7
Briggsdale, *U.S.A.*	108	E2
Brigham City, *U.S.A.*	110	F7
Bright, *Australia*	91	F4
Brighton, *Australia*	91	F2
Brighton, *Canada*	98	D4
Brighton, *U.K.*	13	G7
Brighton, *U.S.A.*	108	F2
Brignogan-Plage, *France*	24	D2
Brignoles, *France*	27	E10
Brihuega, *Spain*	28	E2
Brikama, *Gambia*	78	C1
Brilliant, *Canada*	100	D5
Brilliant, *U.S.A.*	106	F4
Brilon, *Germany*	18	D4
Bríndisi, *Italy*	35	B10
Brinje, *Croatia*	33	D12
Brinkley, *U.S.A.*	109	H9
Brinkworth, *Australia*	91	E2
Brinnon, *U.S.A.*	112	C4
Brion, I., *Canada*	99	C7
Brionne, *France*	24	C7
Brionski, *Croatia*	33	D10
Brioude, *France*	26	C7
Briouze, *France*	24	D6
Brisbane, *Australia*	91	D5
Brisbane →, *Australia*	91	D5
Brisighella, *Italy*	33	D8
Bristol, *U.K.*	13	F5
Bristol, *Conn., U.S.A.*	107	E12
Bristol, *Pa., U.S.A.*	107	F10
Bristol, *R.I., U.S.A.*	107	E13
Bristol, *S. Dak., U.S.A.*	108	C6
Bristol, *Tenn., U.S.A.*	105	G4
Bristol B., *U.S.A.*	96	C4
Bristol Channel, *U.K.*	13	F3
Bristol I., *Antarctica*	5	B1
Bristol L., *U.S.A.*	111	J5
Bristow, *U.S.A.*	109	H6
British Columbia □, *Canada*	100	C3
British Guiana = Guyana ■, *S. Amer.*	121	B6
British Honduras = Belize ■, *Cent. Amer.*	115	D7
British Isles, *Europe*	6	E5
Brits, *S. Africa*	85	D4
Britstown, *S. Africa*	84	E3
Britt, *Canada*	98	C3
Brittany = Bretagne, *France*	24	D4
Britton, *U.S.A.*	108	C6
Brive-la-Gaillarde, *France*	26	C5
Briviesca, *Spain*	28	C1
Brixton, *Australia*	90	C3
Brlik, *Kazakhstan*	44	E8
Brno, *Czech.*	20	F6
Bro, *Sweden*	10	E11
Broad →, *U.S.A.*	105	J5
Broad Arrow, *Australia*	89	F3
Broad B., *U.K.*	14	C2
Broad Haven, *Ireland*	15	B2
Broad Law, *U.K.*	14	F5
Broad Sd., *Australia*	90	C4
Broadhurst Ra., *Australia*	88	D3
Broads, The, *U.K.*	12	E9
Broadus, *U.S.A.*	108	C2
Broadview, *Canada*	101	C8
Broager, *Denmark*	11	K3
Broaryd, *Sweden*	11	G7
Brochet, *Canada*	101	B8
Brochet, L., *Canada*	101	B8
Brock, *Canada*	101	C7
Brocken, *Germany*	18	D6
Brockport, *U.S.A.*	106	C7
Brockton, *U.S.A.*	107	D13
Brockville, *Canada*	98	D4
Brockway, *Mont., U.S.A.*	108	B2
Brockway, *Pa., U.S.A.*	106	E6
Brocton, *U.S.A.*	106	D5
Brod, *Macedonia*	39	H4
Brodarevo, *Serbia*	21	M9
Brodick, *U.K.*	14	F3
Brodnica, *Poland*	20	B9
Brody, *Ukraine*	40	F4
Brodeur Pen., *Canada*	97	A11
Broek, *Neths.*	16	D6
Broek op Langedijk, *Neths.*	16	C5
Brogan, *U.S.A.*	110	D5
Broglie, *France*	24	C7
Broken Bow, *Nebr., U.S.A.*	108	E5
Broken Bow, *Okla., U.S.A.*	109	H7
Broken Hill = Kabwe, *Zambia*	83	E2
Broken Hill, *Australia*	91	E3
Brokind, *Sweden*	11	F9
Brokopondo, *Surinam*	121	B7
Brokopondo □, *Surinam*	121	C6
Bromfield, *U.K.*	13	E5
Bromley, *U.K.*	13	F8
Brønderslev, *Denmark*	11	G3
Brong-Ahafo □, *Ghana*	78	D4
Bronkhorstspruit, *S. Africa*	85	D4
Bronnitsy, *Russia*	41	D11
Bronte, *Italy*	35	E7
Bronte, *U.S.A.*	109	K4
Bronte Park, *Australia*	90	G4
Brook Park, *U.S.A.*	106	E4
Brookfield, *U.S.A.*	108	F8
Brookhaven, *U.S.A.*	109	K9
Brookings, *Oreg., U.S.A.*	110	E1
Brookings, *S. Dak., U.S.A.*	108	C6
Brooklin, *Canada*	106	C6
Brookmere, *Canada*	100	D4
Brooks, *Canada*	100	C6
Brooks B., *Canada*	100	C3
Brooks L., *Canada*	101	A7
Brooks Ra., *U.S.A.*	96	B5
Brooksville, *U.S.A.*	105	L4
Brookville, *U.S.A.*	104	F3
Brooloo, *Australia*	91	D5
Broom, L., *U.K.*	14	D3
Broome, *Australia*	88	C3
Broomehill, *Australia*	89	F2
Broons, *France*	24	D4
Brora, *U.K.*	14	C5
Brora →, *U.K.*	14	C5
Brosna →, *Ireland*	15	C4
Broșteni, *Romania*	38	C8
Brotas de Macaúbas, *Brazil*	123	D3
Brothers, *U.S.A.*	110	E3
Brøttum, *Norway*	10	C4
Brou, *France*	24	D8
Brough, *U.K.*	12	C5
Broughton Island, *Canada*	97	B13
Broughty Ferry, *U.K.*	14	E6
Brouwershavensche Gat, *Neths.*	16	E3
Brouwershaven, *Neths.*	16	E3
Brovary, *Ukraine*	40	F7
Brovst, *Denmark*	11	G3
Browerville, *U.S.A.*	108	B7
Brown, Pt., *Australia*	91	E1
Brown Willy, *U.K.*	13	G3
Brownfield, *U.S.A.*	109	J3
Browning, *U.S.A.*	110	B7
Brownlee, *Canada*	101	C7
Brownsville, *Oreg., U.S.A.*	110	D2
Brownsville, *Tenn., U.S.A.*	109	H10
Brownsville, *Tex., U.S.A.*	109	N6
Brownsweg, *Surinam*	121	B6
Brownwood, *U.S.A.*	109	K5
Brownwood, L., *U.S.A.*	109	K5
Browse I., *Australia*	88	B3
Broye →, *Switz.*	22	C3
Brozas, *Spain*	31	F4
Bruas, *Malaysia*	59	K3
Bruay-en-Artois, *France*	25	B9
Bruce, Mt., *Australia*	88	D2
Bruce Pen., *Canada*	106	A3
Bruce Rock, *Australia*	89	F2
Bruche →, *France*	25	D14
Bruchsal, *Germany*	19	F4
Bruck an der Leitha, *Austria*	21	G6
Bruck an der Mur, *Austria*	21	H5
Brue →, *U.K.*	13	F5
Brugelette, *Belgium*	17	G3
Bruges = Brugge, *Belgium*	17	F2
Brugg, *Switz.*	22	B6
Brugge, *Belgium*	17	F2
Brühl, *Germany*	18	E2
Bruinisse, *Neths.*	17	E4
Brûlé, *Canada*	100	C5
Brûlon, *France*	24	E6
Brûly, *Belgium*	17	J5
Brumado, *Brazil*	123	D3
Brumado →, *Brazil*	123	D3
Brumath, *France*	25	D14
Brummen, *Neths.*	16	D8
Brumunddal, *Norway*	10	D4
Brunchilly, *Australia*	90	B1
Brundidge, *U.S.A.*	105	K3
Bruneau, *U.S.A.*	110	E6
Bruneau →, *U.S.A.*	110	E6
Brunei = Bandar Seri Begawan, *Brunei*	56	C4
Brunei ■, *Asia*	56	D4
Brunette Downs, *Australia*	90	B2
Brunflo, *Sweden*	10	A8
Brunico, *Italy*	33	B8
Brünig, P., *Switz.*	22	C6
Brunkeberg, *Norway*	10	E2
Brunna, *Sweden*	10	E11
Brunnen, *Switz.*	23	C7
Brunner, L., *N.Z.*	87	K3
Bruno, *Canada*	101	C7
Brunsbüttel, *Germany*	18	B5
Brunssum, *Neths.*	17	G7
Brunswick = Braunschweig, *Germany*	18	C6
Brunswick, *Ga., U.S.A.*	105	K5
Brunswick, *Maine, U.S.A.*	99	D6
Brunswick, *Md., U.S.A.*	104	F7
Brunswick, *Mo., U.S.A.*	108	F8
Brunswick, *Ohio, U.S.A.*	106	E3
Brunswick, Pen. de, *Chile*	128	D2
Brunswick B., *Australia*	88	C3
Brunswick Junction, *Australia*	89	F2
Bruntál, *Czech.*	20	F7
Bruny I., *Australia*	90	G4
Brus Laguna, *Honduras*	116	C3
Brusartsi, *Bulgaria*	38	F6
Brush, *U.S.A.*	108	E3
Brushton, *U.S.A.*	107	B10
Brusio, *Switz.*	23	D10
Brusque, *Brazil*	127	B6
Brussel, *Belgium*	17	G4
Brussels = Brussel, *Belgium*	17	G4
Brussels, *Canada*	106	C3
Brustem, *Belgium*	17	G6
Bruthen, *Australia*	91	F4
Bruxelles = Brussel, *Belgium*	17	G4
Bruyères, *France*	25	D13
Bryan, *Ohio, U.S.A.*	104	E3
Bryan, *Tex., U.S.A.*	109	K6
Bryan, Mt., *Australia*	91	E2
Bryanka, *Ukraine*	43	B8
Bryansk, *Russia*	40	E9
Bryanskoye, *Russia*	43	D12
Bryant, *U.S.A.*	108	C6
Bryne, *Norway*	9	G11
Bryson City, *U.S.A.*	105	H4
Brza Palanka, *Serbia*	21	L12
Brzava →, *Serbia*	21	K10
Brzeg, *Poland*	20	E7
Brzeg Din, *Poland*	20	D7
Bsharri, *Lebanon*	69	A5
Bū Baqarah, *U.A.E.*	65	E8
Bū Ḥasā, *U.A.E.*	65	F7
Bu Craa, *W. Sahara*	74	C2
Bū Yai, *Thailand*	58	E4
Buapinang, *Indonesia*	57	E6
Buayan, *Phil.*	57	C7
Buba, *Guinea-Biss.*	78	C2
Bubanza, *Burundi*	82	C2
Būbiyān, *Kuwait*	65	D6
Bucak, *Turkey*	66	E4
Bucaramanga, *Colombia*	120	B3
Bucas Grande I., *Phil.*	55	G6
Buccaneer Arch., *Australia*	88	C3
Bucchiánico, *Italy*	33	F11
Bucecea, *Romania*	38	B9
Buchach, *Ukraine*	40	G4
Buchan, *U.K.*	14	D6
Buchan Ness, *U.K.*	14	D7
Buchanan, *Canada*	101	C8
Buchanan, *Liberia*	78	D2
Buchanan, L., *Queens., Australia*	90	C4
Buchanan, L., *W. Austral., Australia*	89	E3
Buchanan, L., *U.S.A.*	109	K5
Buchanan Cr. →, *Australia*	90	B2
Buchans, *Canada*	99	C8
Bucharest = București, *Romania*	38	E9
Buchholz, *Germany*	18	B5
Buchloe, *Germany*	19	G6
Buchon, Pt., *U.S.A.*	112	K6
Buchs, *Switz.*	23	B8
Bückeburg, *Germany*	18	C5
Buckeye, *U.S.A.*	111	K7
Buckhannon, *U.S.A.*	104	F5
Buckhaven, *U.K.*	14	E5
Buckie, *U.K.*	14	D6
Buckingham, *Canada*	98	C4
Buckingham, *U.K.*	13	F7
Buckingham B., *Australia*	90	A2
Buckinghamshire □, *U.K.*	13	F7
Buckle Hd., *Australia*	88	B4
Buckleboo, *Australia*	91	E2
Buckley, *U.S.A.*	110	C2
Buckley →, *Australia*	90	C2
Bucklin, *U.S.A.*	109	G5
Bucks L., *U.S.A.*	112	F5
Bucquoy, *France*	25	B9
Buctouche, *Canada*	99	C7
București, *Romania*	38	E9
Bucyrus, *U.S.A.*	104	E4
Budafok, *Hungary*	21	H9
Budalin, *Burma*	61	H19
Budapest, *Hungary*	21	H9
Budaun, *India*	63	E8
Budd Coast, *Antarctica*	5	C8
Buddusò, *Italy*	34	B2
Bude, *U.K.*	13	G3
Budel, *Neths.*	17	F7
Budennovsk, *Russia*	43	D11
Budești, *Romania*	38	E9
Budge Budge = Baj Baj, *India*	63	H13
Budgewoi, *Australia*	91	E5
Búðareyri, *Iceland*	8	D6
Búðir, *Iceland*	8	D2
Budia, *Spain*	28	E2
Budjala, *Zaïre*	80	D3
Búdrio, *Italy*	33	D8
Buea, *Cameroon*	79	E6
Buellton, *U.S.A.*	113	L6
Buena Vista, *Bolivia*	125	D5
Buena Vista, *Colo., U.S.A.*	111	G10
Buena Vista, *Va., U.S.A.*	104	G6

Buena Vista L., *U.S.A.* .. 113 K7
Buenaventura, *Colombia* . 120 C2
Buenaventura, *Mexico* .. 114 B3
Buenaventura, B. de, *Colombia* 120 C2
Buendía, Pantano de, *Spain* 28 E2
Buenópolis, *Brazil* 123 E3
Buenos Aires, *Argentina* . 126 C4
Buenos Aires, *Colombia* . 120 C3
Buenos Aires, *Costa Rica* . 116 E3
Buenos Aires □, *Argentina* 126 B4
Buenos Aires, L., *Chile* .. 128 C2
Buesaco, *Colombia* 120 C2
Buffalo, *Mo., U.S.A.* 109 G8
Buffalo, *N.Y., U.S.A.* 106 D6
Buffalo, *Okla., U.S.A.* 109 G5
Buffalo, *S. Dak., U.S.A.* .. 108 C3
Buffalo, *Wyo., U.S.A.* 110 D10
Buffalo →, *Canada* 100 A5
Buffalo Head Hills, *Canada* 100 B5
Buffalo L., *Canada* 100 C6
Buffalo Narrows, *Canada* . 101 B7
Buffels →, *S. Africa* 84 D2
Buford, *U.S.A.* 105 H4
Bug →, *Poland* 20 C11
Bug →, *Ukraine* 42 C4
Buga, *Colombia* 120 C2
Buganda, *Uganda* 82 C3
Buganga, *Uganda* 82 C3
Bugasong, *Phil.* 55 F5
Bugeat, *France* 26 C5
Bugel, Tanjung, *Indonesia* 56 F4
Buggenhout, *Belgium* 17 F4
Bugibba, *Malta* 37 D1
Bugsuk, *Phil.* 55 G2
Buguma, *Nigeria* 79 E6
Bugun Shara, *Mongolia* .. 54 B5
Buguruslan, *Russia* 44 D6
Buhăeşti, *Romania* 38 C10
Buheirat-Murrat-el-Kubra, *Egypt* 76 H8
Buhl, *Idaho, U.S.A.* 110 E6
Buhl, *Minn., U.S.A.* 108 B8
Buick, *U.S.A.* 109 G9
Builth Wells, *U.K.* 13 E4
Buinsk, *Russia* 41 D16
Buíque, *Brazil* 122 C4
Buir Nur, *Mongolia* 54 B6
Buis-les-Baronnies, *France* 27 D9
Buitenpost, *Neths.* 16 B8
Buitrago, *Spain* 30 E7
Bujalance, *Spain* 31 H6
Buján, *Spain* 30 C2
Bujaraloz, *Spain* 28 D4
Buje, *Croatia* 33 C10
Bujumbura, *Burundi* 82 C2
Bukachacha, *Russia* 45 D12
Bukama, *Zaïre* 83 D2
Bukavu, *Zaïre* 82 C2
Bukene, *Tanzania* 82 C3
Bukhara, *Uzbekistan* 44 F7
Bukhoro = Bukhara, *Uzbekistan* 44 F7
Bukima, *Tanzania* 82 C3
Bukit Mertajam, *Malaysia* 59 K3
Bukittinggi, *Indonesia* 56 E2
Bukoba, *Tanzania* 82 C3
Bukoba □, *Tanzania* 82 C3
Bukuru, *Nigeria* 79 D6
Bukuya, *Uganda* 82 B3
Bula, *Guinea-Biss.* 78 C1
Bula, *Indonesia* 57 E8
Bülach, *Switz.* 23 A7
Bulahdelah, *Australia* 91 E5
Bulan, *Phil.* 55 E5
Bulancak, *Turkey* 67 C8
Bulandshahr, *India* 62 E7
Bulanık, *Turkey* 67 D10
Bûlâq, *Egypt* 76 B3
Bulawayo, *Zimbabwe* 83 G2
Buldan, *Turkey* 66 D3
Bulgan, *Mongolia* 54 B5
Bulgaria ■, *Europe* 38 G8
Bulgroo, *Australia* 91 D3
Bulgunnia, *Australia* 91 E1
Bulhar, *Somali Rep.* 68 E3
Buli, Teluk, *Indonesia* 57 D7
Buliluyan, C., *Phil.* 55 G2
Bulki, *Ethiopia* 77 F4
Bulkley →, *Canada* 100 B3
Bull Shoals L., *U.S.A.* .. 109 G8
Bullange, *Belgium* 17 H8
Bullaque →, *Spain* 31 G6
Bullara, *Australia* 88 D1
Bullaring, *Australia* 89 F2
Bullas, *Spain* 29 G3
Bulle, *Switz.* 22 C4
Bulli, *Australia* 91 E5
Bullock Creek, *Australia* . 90 B3
Bulloo →, *Australia* 91 D3
Bulloo Downs, *Queens., Australia* 91 D3
Bulloo Downs, *W. Austral., Australia* 88 D2
Bulloo L., *Australia* 91 D3
Bulls, *N.Z.* 87 J5
Bully-les-Mines, *France* .. 25 B9
Bulnes, *Chile* 126 D1
Bulo Burti, *Somali Rep.* . 68 G4
Bulsar = Valsad, *India* .. 60 J8
Bultfontein, *S. Africa* 84 D4
Bulu Karakelong, *Indonesia* 57 D7
Bulukumba, *Indonesia* 57 F6
Bulun, *Russia* 45 B13
Bumba, *Zaïre* 80 D4

Bumbiri I., *Tanzania* 82 C3
Bumhpa Bum, *Burma* 61 F20
Bumi →, *Zimbabwe* 83 F2
Buna, *Kenya* 82 B4
Bunawan, *Agusan del S., Phil.* 55 G6
Bunawan, *Davao del S., Phil.* 55 H6
Bunazi, *Tanzania* 82 C3
Bunbah, Khalīj, *Libya* 73 B9
Bunbury, *Australia* 89 F2
Bundaberg, *Australia* 91 C5
Bünde, *Germany* 18 C4
Bundey →, *Australia* 90 C2
Bundi, *India* 62 G6
Bundooma, *Australia* 90 C1
Bundoran, *Ireland* 15 B3
Bundukia, *Sudan* 77 F3
Bung Kan, *Thailand* 58 C4
Bungatakada, *Japan* 49 H5
Bungil Cr. →, *Australia* . 90 D4
Bungo-Suidō, *Japan* 49 H6
Bungoma, *Kenya* 82 B3
Bungu, *Tanzania* 82 D4
Bunia, *Zaïre* 82 B3
Bunji, *Pakistan* 63 B6
Bunkie, *U.S.A.* 109 K8
Bunnell, *U.S.A.* 105 L5
Bunnik, *Neths.* 16 D6
Buñol, *Spain* 29 F4
Bunsbeek, *Belgium* 17 G5
Bunschoten, *Neths.* 16 D6
Buntok, *Indonesia* 56 E4
Bununu, *Nigeria* 79 D6
Bununu Dass, *Nigeria* .. 79 C6
Bünyan, *Turkey* 66 D6
Bunyu, *Indonesia* 56 D5
Bunza, *Nigeria* 79 C5
Buol, *Indonesia* 57 D6
Buon Brieng, *Vietnam* .. 58 F7
Buon Me Thuot, *Vietnam* 58 F7
Buong Long, *Cambodia* .. 58 F6
Buorkhaya, Mys, *Russia* . 45 B14
Buqayq, *Si. Arabia* 65 E6
Buqbuq, *Egypt* 76 A2
Bur Acaba, *Somali Rep.* . 68 G3
Bûr Fuad, *Egypt* 76 H8
Bûr Safâga, *Egypt* 76 B3
Bûr Sa'îd, *Egypt* 76 H8
Bûr Sûdân, *Sudan* 76 D4
Bûr Taufiq, *Egypt* 76 J8
Bura, *Kenya* 82 C4
Burao, *Somali Rep.* 68 F4
Buras, *U.S.A.* 109 L10
Buraydah, *Si. Arabia* 64 E5
Burbank, *U.S.A.* 113 L8
Burcher, *Australia* 91 E4
Burdekin →, *Australia* .. 90 B4
Burdett, *Canada* 100 D6
Burdur, *Turkey* 66 E4
Burdur □, *Turkey* 66 E4
Burdur Gölü, *Turkey* .. 66 E4
Burdwan = Barddhaman, *India* 63 H12
Bure, *Ethiopia* 77 E4
Bure →, *U.K.* 12 E9
Büren, *Germany* 18 D4
Buren, *Neths.* 16 E6
Bureya →, *Russia* 45 E13
Burford, *Canada* 106 C4
Burg, *Sachsen-Anhalt, Germany* 18 C7
Burg, *Schleswig-Holstein, Germany* 18 A7
Burg el Arab, *Egypt* 76 H6
Burg et Tuyur, *Sudan* .. 76 C2
Burg Stargard, *Germany* . 18 B9
Burgas, *Bulgaria* 38 G10
Burgdorf, *Germany* 18 C5
Burgdorf, *Switz.* 22 B5
Burgeo, *Canada* 99 C8
Burgersdorp, *S. Africa* .. 84 E4
Burges, Mt., *Australia* .. 89 F3
Burghausen, *Germany* .. 19 G8
Búrgio, *Italy* 34 E6
Bürglen, *Switz.* 23 C7
Burglengenfeld, *Germany* . 19 F8
Burgo de Osma, *Spain* .. 28 D1
Burgohondo, *Spain* 30 E6
Burgos, *Spain* 28 C1
Burgos □, *Spain* 28 C1
Burgstädt, *Germany* 18 E8
Burgsvik, *Sweden* 9 H15
Burguillos del Cerro, *Spain* 31 G4
Burgundy = Bourgogne, *France* 25 E11
Burhanpur, *India* 60 J10
Burhou, *U.K.* 24 C4
Buri Pen., *Eritrea* 77 D4
Burias, *Phil.* 55 E5
Burica, Pta., *Costa Rica* . 116 E3
Burigi, L., *Tanzania* 82 C3
Burin, *Canada* 99 C8
Buriram, *Thailand* 58 E4
Buriti Alegre, *Brazil* 123 E2
Buriti Bravo, *Brazil* 122 C3
Buriti dos Lopes, *Brazil* . 122 B3
Burj Sāfitā, *Syria* 64 C3
Burji, *Ethiopia* 77 F4
Burkburnett, *U.S.A.* 109 H5
Burke, *U.S.A.* 110 C6
Burke →, *Australia* 90 C2
Burketown, *Australia* 90 B2

Burkina Faso ■, *Africa* ... 78 C4
Burk's Falls, *Canada* 98 C4
Burley, *U.S.A.* 110 E7
Burlingame, *U.S.A.* 112 H4
Burlington, *Canada* 106 C5
Burlington, *Colo., U.S.A.* 108 F3
Burlington, *Iowa, U.S.A.* 108 E9
Burlington, *Kans., U.S.A.* 108 F7
Burlington, *N.C., U.S.A.* 105 G6
Burlington, *N.J., U.S.A.* 107 F10
Burlington, *Vt., U.S.A.* 107 B11
Burlington, *Wash., U.S.A.* 112 B4
Burlington, *Wis., U.S.A.* 104 D1
Burlyu-Tyube, *Kazakhstan* 44 E8
Burma ■, *Asia* 61 J20
Burnaby I., *Canada* 100 C2
Burnet, *U.S.A.* 109 K5
Burney, *U.S.A.* 110 F3
Burngup, *Australia* 89 F2
Burnham, *U.S.A.* 106 F7
Burnie, *Australia* 90 G4
Burnley, *U.K.* 12 D5
Burns, *Oreg., U.S.A.* ..110 E4
Burns, *Wyo., U.S.A.* ..108 E2
Burns Lake, *Canada* 100 C3
Burnside →, *Canada* 96 B9
Burnside, L., *Australia* .. 89 E3
Burnt River, *Canada* 106 B6
Burntwood →, *Canada* .. 101 B9
Burntwood L., *Canada* .. 101 B8
Burqān, *Kuwait* 64 D5
Burqin, *China* 54 B3
Burra, *Australia* 91 E2
Burramurra, *Australia* .. 90 C2
Burren Junction, *Australia* 91 E4
Burreli, *Albania* 39 H3
Burriana, *Spain* 28 F4
Burrendong Dam, *Australia* 91 E4
Burrinjuck Res., *Australia* 91 F4
Burro, Serranías del, *Mexico* 114 B4
Burruyacú, *Argentina* .. 126 B3
Burry Port, *U.K.* 13 F3
Bursa, *Turkey* 66 C3
Bursa □, *Turkey* 66 C3
Burseryd, *Sweden* 11 G7
Burstall, *Canada* 101 C7
Burton L., *Canada* 98 B4
Burton upon Trent, *U.K.* 12 E6
Burtundy, *Australia* 91 E3
Buru, *Indonesia* 57 E7
Burullus, Bahra el, *Egypt* 76 H7
Burûn, Râs, *Egypt* 69 D2
Burundi ■, *Africa* 82 C3
Bururi, *Burundi* 82 C2
Burutu, *Nigeria* 79 D6
Burwell, *U.S.A.* 108 E5
Bury, *U.K.* 12 D5
Bury St. Edmunds, *U.K.* . 13 E8
Buryat Republic □, *Russia* 45 D11
Buryn, *Ukraine* 40 F8
Busalla, *Italy* 32 D5
Busango Swamp, *Zambia* . 83 E2
Buşayrah, *Syria* 64 C4
Buşayyah, *Iraq* 64 D5
Busca, *Italy* 32 D4
Büshehr, *Iran* 65 D6
Büshehr □, *Iran* 65 D6
Bushell, *Canada* 101 B7
Bushenyi, *Uganda* 82 C3
Bushire = Büshehr, *Iran* . 65 D6
Bushnell, *Ill., U.S.A.* ..108 E9
Bushnell, *Nebr., U.S.A.* . 108 E3
Busia □, *Kenya* 82 B3
Busie, *Ghana* 78 C4
Businga, *Zaïre* 80 D4
Buskerud fylke □, *Norway* 10 D3
Busko Zdrój, *Poland* 20 E10
Busoga □, *Uganda* 82 B3
Busovača, *Bos.-H.* 21 L7
Busra ash Shām, *Syria* .. 69 C5
Bussang, *France* 25 E13
Busselton, *Australia* 89 F2
Busseto, *Italy* 32 D7
Bussigny, *Switz.* 22 C3
Bussum, *Neths.* 16 D6
Bustamante, B., *Argentina* 128 C3
Busto, C., *Spain* 30 B4
Busto Arsizio, *Italy* 32 C5
Busu-Djanoa, *Zaïre* 80 D4
Busuanga, *Phil.* 55 E4
Büsum, *Germany* 18 A4
Buta, *Zaïre* 82 B1
Butare, *Rwanda* 82 C2
Butaritari, *Kiribati* 92 G9
Bute, *U.K.* 14 F3
Bute Inlet, *Canada* 100 C4
Butemba, *Uganda* 82 B3
Butembo, *Zaïre* 82 B2
Butera, *Italy* 35 E7
Bütgenbach, *Belgium* .. 17 H8
Butha Qi, *China* 54 B7
Butiaba, *Uganda* 82 B3
Butler, *Mo., U.S.A.* ..108 F7
Butler, *Pa., U.S.A.* 106 F5
Bütschwil, *Switz.* 23 B8
Butte, *Mont., U.S.A.* ..110 C7
Butte, *Nebr., U.S.A.* ..108 D5
Butte Creek →, *U.S.A.* . 112 F5
Butterworth = Gcuwa, *S. Africa* 85 E4
Butterworth, *Malaysia* .. 59 K3
Buttfield, Mt., *Australia* . 89 E4
Button B., *Canada* 101 B10
Buttonwillow, *U.S.A.* .. 113 K7

Butty Hd., *Australia* 89 F3
Butuan, *Phil.* 55 G6
Butuku-Luba, *Eq. Guin.* . 79 E6
Butung, *Indonesia* 57 E6
Buturlinovka, *Russia* 41 F12
Butzbach, *Germany* 18 E4
Bützow, *Germany* 18 B7
Buxar, *India* 63 G10
Buxton, *S. Africa* 84 D3
Buxton, *U.K.* 12 D6
Buxy, *France* 25 F11
Buy, *Russia* 41 B12
Buyaga, *Russia* 45 D13
Buynaksk, *Russia* 43 E12
Büyük Menderes →, *Turkey* 66 E2
Büyükçekmece, *Turkey* . 39 H11
Buzançais, *France* 24 F8
Buzău, *Romania* 38 D10
Buzău →, *Romania* 38 D10
Buzău, Pasul, *Romania* .. 38 D9
Buzen, *Japan* 49 H5
Buzet, *Croatia* 33 C10
Buzi →, *Mozam.* 83 F3
Buziaş, *Romania* 38 D4
Buzuluk, *Russia* 44 D6
Buzuluk →, *Russia* 41 F13
Buzzards Bay, *U.S.A.* .. 107 E14
Bwana Mkubwe, *Zaïre* .. 83 E2
Byala, *Bulgaria* 38 F8
Byala Slatina, *Bulgaria* .. 38 F6
Byandovan, Mys, *Azerbaijan* 43 G13
Bychawa, *Poland* 20 D12
Bydgoszcz, *Poland* 20 B8
Byelarus = Belorussia ■, *Europe* 40 E5
Byelorussia = Belorussia ■, *Europe* 40 E5
Byers, *U.S.A.* 108 F2
Byesville, *U.S.A.* 106 G3
Byhalia, *U.S.A.* 109 H10
Bykhov, *Belorussia* 40 E7
Bykovo, *Russia* 43 B11
Bylas, *U.S.A.* 111 K8
Bylderup, *Denmark* 11 K3
Bylot I., *Canada* 97 A12
Byrd, *U.S.A.* 5 C17
Byro, *Australia* 89 E2
Byrock, *Australia* 91 E4
Byron Bay, *Australia* .. 91 D5
Byrranga, Gory, *Russia* .. 45 B11
Byrranga Mts. = Byrranga, Gory, *Russia* 45 B11
Byrum, *Denmark* 11 G5
Byske, *Sweden* 8 D16
Byske älv →, *Sweden* .. 8 D16
Bystrzyca Kłodzka, *Poland* 20 E6
Byten, *Belorussia* 40 E4
Bytom, *Poland* 20 E8
Bytów, *Poland* 20 A7
Byumba, *Rwanda* 82 C3

C

C.I.S. = Commonwealth of Independent States ■, *Eurasia* 45 D11
Ca →, *Vietnam* 58 C5
Ca Mau = Quan Long, *Vietnam* 59 H5
Ca Mau, Mui = Bai Bung, Mui, *Vietnam* 59 H5
Ca Na, *Vietnam* 59 G7
Caacupé, *Paraguay* 126 B4
Caála, *Angola* 81 G3
Caamano Sd., *Canada* .. 100 C3
Caapiranga, *Brazil* 121 D5
Caazapá, *Paraguay* 126 B4
Caazapá □, *Paraguay* .. 127 B4
Cabadbaran, *Phil.* 55 G6
Cabalian, *Phil.* 55 F6
Caballeria, C. de, *Spain* . 36 A11
Cabana, *Peru* 124 B2
Cabanaconde, *Peru* 124 D3
Cabañaquinta, *Spain* 30 B5
Cabanatuan, *Phil.* 55 D4
Cabanes, *Spain* 28 E5
Cabanillas, *Peru* 124 D3
Cabano, *Canada* 99 C6
Čabar, *Croatia* 33 C11
Cabazon, *U.S.A.* 113 M10
Cabedelo, *Brazil* 122 C5
Cabeza del Buey, *Spain* . 31 G5
Cabildo, *Chile* 126 C1
Cabimas, *Venezuela* 120 A3
Cabinda, *Angola* 80 F2
Cabinda □, *Angola* 80 F2
Cabinet Mts., *U.S.A.* .. 110 C6
Cabo Blanco, *Argentina* . 128 C3
Cabo Frio, *Brazil* 123 F3
Cabo Pantoja, *Peru* 120 D2
Cabo Raso, *Argentina* .. 128 B3
Cabonga, Réservoir, *Canada* 98 C4
Cabool, *U.S.A.* 109 G8
Caboolture, *Australia* .. 91 D5
Cabora Bassa Dam = Cahora Bassa Dam, *Mozam.* 83 F3
Caborca, *Mexico* 114 A2

Cabot, Mt., *U.S.A.* 107 B13
Cabot Str., *Canada* 99 C8
Cabra, *Spain* 31 H6
Cabra del Santo Cristo, *Spain* 29 H1
Cábras, *Italy* 34 C1
Cabrera, I., *Spain* 36 B9
Cabrera, Sierra, *Spain* .. 30 C4
Cabri, *Canada* 101 C7
Cabriel →, *Spain* 29 F3
Cabruta, *Venezuela* 120 B4
Cabugao, *Phil.* 55 C4
Cabuyaro, *Colombia* .. 120 C3
Cacabelos, *Spain* 30 C4
Čačak, *Serbia* 21 M10
Cacao, *Fr. Guiana* 121 C7
Cáceres, *Brazil* 125 D6
Cáceres, *Colombia* 120 B2
Cáceres, *Spain* 31 F4
Cáceres □, *Spain* 31 F4
Cache Bay, *Canada* 98 C4
Cache Cr. →, *U.S.A.* .. 112 G5
Cachepo, *Portugal* 31 H3
Cachéu, *Guinea-Biss.* .. 78 C1
Cachi, *Argentina* 126 B2
Cachimbo, *Brazil* 125 B7
Cachimbo, Serra do, *Brazil* 125 B6
Cachoeira, *Brazil* 123 D4
Cachoeira Alta, *Brazil* .. 123 E1
Cachoeira de Itapemirim, *Brazil* 123 F3
Cachoeira do Sul, *Brazil* . 127 C5
Cachoeiro do Arari, *Brazil* 122 B2
Cachopo, *Portugal* 31 H3
Cachuela Esperanza, *Bolivia* 125 C4
Cacólo, *Angola* 80 G3
Caconda, *Angola* 81 G3
Cacongo, *Angola* 80 F2
Caçu, *Brazil* 123 E1
Caculé, *Brazil* 123 D3
Cadarache, *France* 27 E9
Čadca, *Slovak Rep.* 20 F8
Caddo, *U.S.A.* 109 H6
Cadell Cr. →, *Australia* . 90 C3
Cadenazzo, *Switz.* 23 D7
Cader Idris, *U.K.* 12 E4
Cadí, Sierra del, *Spain* .. 28 C6
Cadibarrawirracanna, L., *Australia* 91 D2
Cadillac, *Canada* 98 C4
Cadillac, *France* 26 D3
Cadillac, *U.S.A.* 104 C3
Cadiz, *Phil.* 55 F5
Cádiz, *Spain* 31 J4
Cadiz, *U.S.A.* 106 F4
Cádiz □, *Spain* 31 J5
Cádiz, G. de, *Spain* 31 J4
Cadney Park, *Australia* . 91 D1
Cadomin, *Canada* 100 C5
Cadotte →, *Canada* 100 B5
Cadours, *France* 26 E5
Cadoux, *Australia* 89 F2
Caen, *France* 24 C6
Caernarfon, *U.K.* 12 D3
Caernarfon B., *U.K.* .. 12 D3
Caernarvon = Caernarfon, *U.K.* 12 D3
Caerphilly, *U.K.* 13 F4
Caesarea, *Israel* 69 C3
Caeté, *Brazil* 123 E3
Caetité, *Brazil* 123 D3
Cafayate, *Argentina* 126 B2
Cafifi, *Colombia* 120 B3
Cafu, *Angola* 84 B2
Cagayan →, *Phil.* 55 B4
Cagayan de Oro, *Phil.* .. 55 G6
Cagayan Is., *Phil.* 55 G4
Cagayan Sulu I., *Phil.* .. 55 H3
Cagli, *Italy* 33 E9
Cágliari, *Italy* 34 C2
Cágliari, G. di, *Italy* 34 C2
Cagnano Varano, *Italy* .. 35 A8
Cagnes-sur-Mer, *France* . 27 E11
Caguán →, *Colombia* .. 120 D3
Caguas, *Puerto Rico* .. 117 C6
Caha Mts., *Ireland* 15 E2
Cahama, *Angola* 84 B1
Caher, *Ireland* 15 D4
Cahersiveen, *Ireland* .. 15 E1
Cahora Bassa Dam, *Mozam.* 83 F3
Cahore Pt., *Ireland* 15 D5
Cahors, *France* 26 D5
Cahuapanas, *Peru* 124 B2
Cahuinari →, *Colombia* . 120 D3
Cai Bau, Dao, *Vietnam* . 58 B6
Cai Nuoc, *Vietnam* 59 H5
Caia, *Mozam.* 83 F4
Caiabis, Serra dos, *Brazil* . 125 C6
Caianda, *Angola* 83 E1
Caiapó, Serra do, *Brazil* . 125 D7
Caiapônia, *Brazil* 125 D7
Caibarién, *Cuba* 116 B4
Caibiran, *Phil.* 55 F6
Caicara, *Bolívar, Venezuela* 120 B4
Caicara, *Monagas, Venezuela* 121 B5
Caicó, *Brazil* 122 C4
Caicos Is., *W. Indies* 117 B5
Caicos Passage, *W. Indies* 117 B5
Cailloma, *Peru* 124 D3
Caine →, *Bolivia* 125 D4
Caird Coast, *Antarctica* .. 5 D1
Cairn Gorm, *U.K.* 14 D5

Cairn Toul

Cairn Toul, *U.K.* 14 D5
Cairngorm Mts., *U.K.* 14 D5
Cairns, *Australia* 90 B4
Cairo = El Qâhira, *Egypt* 76 H7
Cairo, *Ga., U.S.A.* 105 K3
Cairo, *Ill., U.S.A.* 109 G10
Cairo Montenotte, *Italy* 32 D5
Caithness, Ord of, *U.K.* 14 C5
Caiundo, *Angola* 81 H3
Caiza, *Bolivia* 125 E4
Cajabamba, *Peru* 124 B2
Cajamarca, *Peru* 124 B2
Cajamarca □, *Peru* 124 B2
Cajapió, *Brazil* 122 B3
Cajarc, *France* 26 D5
Cajatambo, *Peru* 124 C2
Cajàzeiras, *Brazil* 122 C4
Čajetina, *Serbia* 21 M9
Çakirgol, *Turkey* 43 F8
Čakovec, *Croatia* 33 B13
Çal, *Turkey* 66 D3
Cala, *Spain* 31 H4
Cala →, *Spain* 31 H4
Cala Cadolar, Punta de, *Spain* 29 G6
Cala d'Or, *Spain* 36 B10
Cala Figuera, C., *Spain* 36 B9
Cala Forcat, *Spain* 36 A10
Cala Mayor, *Spain* 36 B9
Cala Mezquida, *Spain* 36 B11
Cala Millor, *Spain* 36 B10
Cala Ratjada, *Spain* 36 B10
Calabanga, *Phil.* 55 E5
Calabar, *Nigeria* 79 E6
Calabozo, *Venezuela* 120 B4
Calábria □, *Italy* 35 C9
Calaburras, Pta. de, *Spain* 31 J6
Calaceite, *Spain* 28 D5
Calacota, *Bolivia* 124 D4
Calafate, *Argentina* 128 D2
Calahorra, *Spain* 28 C3
Calais, *France* 25 B8
Calais, *U.S.A.* 99 C6
Calais, Pas de, *France* 25 B8
Calalaste, Cord. de, *Argentina* 126 B2
Calama, *Brazil* 125 B5
Calama, *Chile* 126 A2
Calamar, *Bolívar, Colombia* 120 A3
Calamar, *Vaupés, Colombia* 120 C3
Calamarca, *Bolivia* 124 D4
Calamba, *Phil.* 55 F5
Calamian Group, *Phil.* 55 F3
Calamocha, *Spain* 28 E3
Calán Porter, *Spain* 36 B11
Calañas, *Spain* 31 H4
Calanda, *Spain* 28 E4
Calang, *Indonesia* 56 D1
Calangiánus, *Italy* 34 B2
Calapan, *Phil.* 55 E4
Călăraşi, *Romania* 38 E10
Calasparra, *Spain* 29 G3
Calatafimi, *Italy* 34 E5
Calatayud, *Spain* 28 D3
Calato = Kálathos, *Greece* 39 N11
Calauag, *Phil.* 55 E5
Calavà, C., *Italy* 35 D7
Calavite, C., *Phil.* 55 E4
Calayan, *Phil.* 55 B4
Calbayog, *Phil.* 55 E6
Calbe, *Germany* 18 D7
Calca, *Peru* 124 C3
Calcasieu L., *U.S.A.* 109 L8
Calci, *Italy* 32 E7
Calcutta, *India* 63 H13
Caldaro, *Italy* 33 B8
Caldas □, *Colombia* 120 B2
Caldas da Rainha, *Portugal* 31 F1
Caldas de Reyes, *Spain* 30 C2
Caldas Novas, *Brazil* 123 E2
Calder →, *U.K.* 12 D6
Caldera, *Chile* 126 B1
Caldwell, *Idaho, U.S.A.* 110 E5
Caldwell, *Kans., U.S.A.* 109 G6
Caldwell, *Tex., U.S.A.* 109 K6
Caledon, *S. Africa* 84 E2
Caledon →, *S. Africa* 84 E4
Caledon B., *Australia* 90 A2
Caledonia, *Canada* 106 C5
Caledonia, *U.S.A.* 106 D7
Calella, *Spain* 28 D7
Calemba, *Angola* 84 B2
Calenzana, *France* 27 F12
Caleta Olivia, *Argentina* 128 C3
Calexico, *U.S.A.* 113 N11
Calf of Man, *U.K.* 12 C3
Calgary, *Canada* 100 C6
Calheta, *Madeira* 36 D2
Calhoun, *U.S.A.* 105 H3
Cali, *Colombia* 120 C2
Calicut, *India* 60 P9
Caliente, *U.S.A.* 111 H6
California, *Mo., U.S.A.* 108 F8
California, *Pa., U.S.A.* 106 F5
California □, *U.S.A.* 111 H4
California, Baja, *Mexico* 114 A1
California, Baja, T.N. □, *Mexico* 114 B2
California, Baja, T.S. □, *Mexico* 114 B2
California, G. de, *Mexico* 114 B2
California City, *U.S.A.* 113 K9
California Hot Springs, *U.S.A.* 113 K8
Călimăneşti, *Romania* 38 D7
Călimani, Munţii, *Romania* 38 B8
Călineşti, *Romania* 38 D7
Calingasta, *Argentina* 126 C2
Calipatria, *U.S.A.* 113 M11
Calistoga, *U.S.A.* 112 G4
Calitri, *Italy* 35 B8
Calitzdorp, *S. Africa* 84 E3
Callabonna, L., *Australia* 91 D3
Callac, *France* 24 D3
Callan, *Ireland* 15 D4
Callander, *U.K.* 14 E4
Callantsoog, *Neths.* 16 C5
Callao, *Peru* 124 C2
Callaway, *U.S.A.* 108 E5
Calles, *Mexico* 115 C5
Callide, *Australia* 90 C5
Calling Lake, *Canada* 100 B6
Calliope, *Australia* 90 C5
Callosa de Ensarriá, *Spain* 29 G4
Callosa de Segura, *Spain* 29 G4
Calola, *Angola* 84 B2
Calolbon, *Phil.* 55 E6
Caloocan, *Phil.* 55 D4
Calore →, *Italy* 35 A7
Caloundra, *Australia* 91 D5
Calpe, *Spain* 29 G5
Calpella, *U.S.A.* 112 F3
Calpine, *U.S.A.* 112 F6
Calstock, *Canada* 98 C3
Caltabellotta, *Italy* 34 E6
Caltagirone, *Italy* 35 E7
Caltanissetta, *Italy* 35 E7
Calulo, *Angola* 80 G2
Calumet, *U.S.A.* 104 B1
Calunda, *Angola* 81 G4
Caluso, *Italy* 32 C4
Calvados □, *France* 24 C6
Calvert, *U.S.A.* 109 K6
Calvert →, *Australia* 90 B2
Calvert Hills, *Australia* 90 B2
Calvert I., *Canada* 100 C3
Calvert Ra., *Australia* 88 D3
Calvi, *France* 27 F12
Calvillo, *Mexico* 114 C4
Calvinia, *S. Africa* 84 E2
Calw, *Germany* 19 G4
Calwa, *U.S.A.* 112 J7
Calzada Almuradiel, *Spain* 29 G1
Calzada de Calatrava, *Spain* 31 G7
Cam →, *U.K.* 13 E8
Cam Lam, *Vietnam* 59 G7
Cam Pha, *Vietnam* 58 B6
Cam Ranh, *Vietnam* 59 G7
Cam Xuyen, *Vietnam* 58 C6
Camabatela, *Angola* 80 F3
Camacã, *Brazil* 123 E4
Camaçari, *Brazil* 123 D4
Camacha, *Madeira* 36 D3
Camacho, *Mexico* 114 C4
Camacupa, *Angola* 81 G3
Camaguán, *Venezuela* 120 B4
Camagüey, *Cuba* 116 B4
Camaiore, *Italy* 32 E7
Camamu, *Brazil* 123 D4
Camaná, *Peru* 124 D3
Camanche Reservoir, *U.S.A.* 112 G6
Camaquã →, *Brazil* 127 C5
Câmara de Lobos, *Madeira* 36 D3
Camararé →, *Brazil* 125 C6
Camarat, C., *France* 27 E10
Camaret, *France* 24 D2
Camargo, *Bolivia* 125 E4
Camargue, *France* 27 E8
Camarillo, *U.S.A.* 113 L7
Camariñas, *Spain* 30 B1
Camarón, C., *Honduras* 116 C2
Camarones, *Argentina* 128 B3
Camarones, B., *Argentina* 128 B3
Camas, *U.S.A.* 112 E4
Camas Valley, *U.S.A.* 110 E2
Cambados, *Spain* 30 C2
Cambará, *Brazil* 127 A5
Cambay = Khambhat, *India* 62 H5
Cambay, G. of = Khambat, G. of, *India* 62 J5
Cambil, *Spain* 29 H1
Cambo-les-Bains, *France* 26 E2
Cambodia ■, *Asia* 58 F5
Camborne, *U.K.* 13 G2
Cambrai, *France* 25 B10
Cambria, *U.S.A.* 111 J3
Cambrian Mts., *U.K.* 13 E4
Cambridge, *Canada* 98 D3
Cambridge, *Jamaica* 116 C4
Cambridge, *N.Z.* 87 G5
Cambridge, *U.K.* 13 E8
Cambridge, *Idaho, U.S.A.* 110 D5
Cambridge, *Mass., U.S.A.* 107 D13
Cambridge, *Md., U.S.A.* 104 F7
Cambridge, *Minn., U.S.A.* 108 C8
Cambridge, *N.Y., U.S.A.* 107 C11
Cambridge, *Nebr., U.S.A.* 108 E4
Cambridge, *Ohio, U.S.A.* 106 F3
Cambridge Bay, *Canada* 96 B9
Cambridge G., *Australia* 88 B4
Cambridge Springs, *U.S.A.* 106 E4
Cambridgeshire □, *U.K.* 13 E8
Cambrils, *Spain* 28 D6
Cambuci, *Brazil* 123 F3
Cambundi-Catembo, *Angola* 80 G3
Camden, *Ala., U.S.A.* 105 K2
Camden, *Ark., U.S.A.* 109 J8
Camden, *Maine, U.S.A.* 99 D6
Camden, *N.J., U.S.A.* 107 G9
Camden, *S.C., U.S.A.* 105 H5
Camden Sd., *Australia* 88 C3
Camdenton, *U.S.A.* 109 F8
Çameli, *Turkey* 66 E3
Camembert, *France* 24 D7
Cámeri, *Italy* 32 C5
Camerino, *Italy* 33 E10
Cameron, *Ariz., U.S.A.* 111 J8
Cameron, *La., U.S.A.* 109 L8
Cameron, *Mo., U.S.A.* 108 F7
Cameron, *Tex., U.S.A.* 109 K6
Cameron Falls, *Canada* 98 C2
Cameron Highlands, *Malaysia* 59 K3
Cameron Hills, *Canada* 100 B5
Cameroon ■, *Africa* 73 G7
Camerota, *Italy* 35 B8
Cameroun →, *Cameroon* 79 E6
Cameroun, Mt., *Cameroon* 79 E6
Cametá, *Brazil* 122 B2
Camiguin □, *Phil.* 55 G6
Camiguin I., *Phil.* 55 B4
Camiling, *Phil.* 55 D4
Caminha, *Portugal* 30 D2
Camino, *U.S.A.* 112 G6
Camira Creek, *Australia* 91 D5
Camiranga, *Brazil* 122 B2
Camiri, *Bolivia* 125 E5
Camissombo, *Angola* 80 F4
Cammal, *U.S.A.* 106 E7
Camocim, *Brazil* 122 B3
Camogli, *Italy* 32 D6
Camooweal, *Australia* 90 B2
Camopi, *Fr. Guiana* 121 C7
Camopi →, *Fr. Guiana* 121 C7
Camotes Is., *Phil.* 55 F6
Camotes Sea, *Phil.* 55 F6
Camp Crook, *U.S.A.* 108 C3
Camp Nelson, *U.S.A.* 113 J8
Camp Wood, *U.S.A.* 109 L4
Campagna, *Italy* 35 B8
Campana, *Argentina* 126 C4
Campana, I., *Chile* 128 C1
Campanário, *Madeira* 36 D2
Campanario, *Spain* 31 G5
Campania □, *Italy* 35 B7
Campbell, *S. Africa* 84 D3
Campbell, *Calif., U.S.A.* 112 H5
Campbell, *Ohio, U.S.A.* 106 E4
Campbell I., *Pac. Oc.* 92 N8
Campbell L., *Canada* 101 A7
Campbell River, *Canada* 100 C3
Campbell Town, *Australia* 90 G4
Campbellford, *Canada* 106 B7
Campbellpur, *Pakistan* 62 C5
Campbellsville, *U.S.A.* 104 G3
Campbellton, *Canada* 99 C6
Campbelltown, *Australia* 91 E5
Campbeltown, *U.K.* 14 F3
Campeche, *Mexico* 115 D6
Campeche □, *Mexico* 115 D6
Campeche, B. de, *Mexico* 115 D6
Camperdown, *Australia* 91 F3
Camperville, *Canada* 101 C8
Campi Salentina, *Italy* 35 B11
Campidano, *Italy* 34 C1
Campíglia Maríttima, *Italy* 32 E7
Campillo de Altobuey, *Spain* 28 F3
Campillo de Llerena, *Spain* 31 G5
Campillos, *Spain* 31 H6
Campina Grande, *Brazil* 122 C4
Campina Verde, *Brazil* 123 E2
Campinas, *Brazil* 127 A6
Campine, *Belgium* 17 F6
Campli, *Italy* 33 F10
Campo, *Cameroon* 80 D1
Campo, *Spain* 28 C5
Campo Belo, *Brazil* 123 F2
Campo de Criptana, *Spain* 29 F1
Campo de Diauarum, *Brazil* 125 C7
Campo de Gibraltar, *Spain* 31 J5
Campo Flórido, *Brazil* 123 E2
Campo Formoso, *Brazil* 122 D3
Campo Grande, *Brazil* 125 E7
Campo Maíor, *Brazil* 122 B3
Campo Maior, *Portugal* 31 G3
Campo Mourão, *Brazil* 127 A5
Campo Tencia, *Switz.* 23 D7
Campo Túres, *Italy* 33 B8
Campoalegre, *Colombia* 120 C2
Campobasso, *Italy* 35 A7
Campobello di Licata, *Italy* 34 E6
Campobello di Mazara, *Italy* 34 E5
Campofelice, *Italy* 34 E6
Camporeale, *Italy* 34 E6
Campos, *Brazil* 123 F3
Campos Altos, *Brazil* 123 E2
Campos Belos, *Brazil* 123 D2
Campos del Puerto, *Spain* 36 B10
Campos Novos, *Brazil* 127 B5
Campos Sales, *Brazil* 122 C3
Camprodón, *Spain* 28 C7
Camptonville, *U.S.A.* 112 F5
Campuya →, *Peru* 120 D3
Camrose, *Canada* 100 C6
Camsell Portage, *Canada* 101 B7
Çan, *Turkey* 66 C2
Can Clavo, *Spain* 36 C7
Can Creu, *Spain* 36 C7
Can Gio, *Vietnam* 59 G6
Can Tho, *Vietnam* 59 G5
Canaan, *U.S.A.* 107 D11
Canada ■, *N. Amer.* 96 C10
Cañada de Gómez, *Argentina* 126 C3
Canadian, *U.S.A.* 109 H4
Canadian →, *U.S.A.* 109 H7
Canadian Shield, *Canada* 97 C10
Çanakkale, *Turkey* 39 J9
Çanakkale □, *Turkey* 66 C2
Çanakkale Boğazı, *Turkey* 66 C2
Canal Flats, *Canada* 100 C5
Canalejas, *Argentina* 126 D2
Canals, *Argentina* 126 C3
Canals, *Spain* 29 G4
Canandaigua, *U.S.A.* 106 D7
Cananea, *Mexico* 114 A2
Cañar, *Ecuador* 120 D2
Cañar □, *Ecuador* 120 D2
Canarias, Is., *Atl. Oc.* 36 F4
Canarreos, Arch. de los, *Cuba* 116 B3
Canary Is. = Canarias, Is., *Atl. Oc.* 36 F4
Canastra, Serra da, *Brazil* 123 F2
Canatlán, *Mexico* 114 C4
Canaveral, C., *U.S.A.* 105 L5
Cañaveras, *Spain* 28 E2
Canavieiras, *Brazil* 123 E4
Canbelego, *Australia* 91 E4
Canberra, *Australia* 91 F4
Canby, *Calif., U.S.A.* 110 F3
Canby, *Minn., U.S.A.* 108 C6
Canby, *Oreg., U.S.A.* 112 E4
Cancale, *France* 24 D5
Canche →, *France* 25 B8
Canchyuaya, Cordillera de, *Peru* 124 B3
Cancún, *Mexico* 115 C7
Candala, *Somali Rep.* 68 E4
Candarave, *Peru* 124 D3
Candas, *Spain* 30 B5
Candé, *France* 24 E5
Candeias →, *Brazil* 125 B5
Candela, *Italy* 35 A8
Candelaria, *Argentina* 127 B4
Candelaria, *Canary Is.* 36 F3
Candelaria, Pta. de la, *Spain* 30 B2
Candeleda, *Spain* 30 E5
Candelo, *Australia* 91 F4
Candia = Iráklion, *Greece* 37 D7
Candia, Sea of = Crete, Sea of, *Greece* 39 N8
Cândido de Abreu, *Brazil* 123 F1
Cândido Mendes, *Brazil* 122 B2
Candle L., *Canada* 101 C7
Candlemas I., *Antarctica* 5 B1
Cando, *U.S.A.* 108 A5
Candon, *Phil.* 55 C4
Canea = Khaniá, *Greece* 37 D6
Canela, *Brazil* 122 D2
Canelli, *Italy* 32 D5
Canelones, *Uruguay* 127 C4
Canet-Plage, *France* 26 F7
Cañete, *Chile* 126 D1
Cañete, *Peru* 124 C2
Cañete, *Spain* 28 E3
Cañete de las Torres, *Spain* 31 H6
Canfranc, *Spain* 28 C4
Cangas, *Spain* 30 C2
Cangas de Narcea, *Spain* 30 B4
Cangas de Onís, *Spain* 30 B5
Canguaretama, *Brazil* 122 C4
Canguçu, *Brazil* 127 C5
Cangxi, *China* 52 B5
Cangyuan, *China* 52 F2
Cangzhou, *China* 50 E9
Cani, I., *Tunisia* 75 A7
Canicattì, *Italy* 34 E6
Canicattini, *Italy* 35 E8
Canim Lake, *Canada* 100 C4
Canindé, *Brazil* 122 B4
Canindé →, *Brazil* 122 C3
Canindeyu □, *Paraguay* 127 A4
Canipaan, *Phil.* 56 C5
Canisteo, *U.S.A.* 106 D7
Canisteo →, *U.S.A.* 106 D7
Cañitas, *Mexico* 114 C4
Cañizal, *Spain* 30 D5
Canjáyar, *Spain* 29 H2
Çankırı, *Turkey* 66 C5
Çankırı □, *Turkey* 66 C5
Cankuzo, *Burundi* 82 C3
Canmore, *Canada* 100 C5
Cann River, *Australia* 91 F4
Canna, *U.K.* 14 D2
Cannanore, *India* 60 P9
Cannes, *France* 27 E11
Canning Town = Port Canning, *India* 63 H13
Cannington, *Canada* 106 B5
Cannock, *U.K.* 12 E5
Cannon Ball →, *U.S.A.* 108 B4
Cannondale Mt., *Australia* 90 D4
Caño Colorado, *Colombia* 120 C4
Canoas, *Brazil* 127 B5
Canoe L., *Canada* 101 B7
Canon City, *U.S.A.* 108 F2
Canora, *Canada* 101 C8
Canosa di Púglia, *Italy* 35 A9
Canowindra, *Australia* 91 E4
Canso, *Canada* 99 C7
Canta, *Peru* 124 C2
Cantabria □, *Spain* 30 B6
Cantabria, Sierra de, *Spain* 28 C2
Cantabrian Mts. = Cantábrica, Cordillera, *Spain* 30 C5
Cantábrica, Cordillera, *Spain* 30 C5
Cantal □, *France* 26 C6
Cantal, Plomb du, *France* 26 C6
Cantanhede, *Portugal* 30 E2
Cantaura, *Venezuela* 121 B5
Cantavieja, *Spain* 28 E4
Canterbury, *Australia* 90 D3
Canterbury, *U.K.* 13 F9
Canterbury □, *N.Z.* 87 K3
Canterbury Bight, *N.Z.* 87 L3
Canterbury Plains, *N.Z.* 87 K3
Cantil, *U.S.A.* 113 K9
Cantillana, *Spain* 31 H5
Canto do Buriti, *Brazil* 122 C3
Canton = Guangzhou, *China* 53 F9
Canton, *Ga., U.S.A.* 105 H3
Canton, *Ill., U.S.A.* 108 E9
Canton, *Miss., U.S.A.* 109 J9
Canton, *Mo., U.S.A.* 108 E9
Canton, *N.Y., U.S.A.* 107 B9
Canton, *Ohio, U.S.A.* 106 F3
Canton, *Okla., U.S.A.* 109 G5
Canton, *S. Dak., U.S.A.* 108 D6
Canton L., *U.S.A.* 109 G5
Cantù, *Italy* 32 C6
Canudos, *Brazil* 125 B6
Canumã, *Amazonas, Brazil* 121 D6
Canumã, *Amazonas, Brazil* 125 B5
Canumã →, *Brazil* 125 A6
Canutama, *Brazil* 125 B5
Canutillo, *U.S.A.* 111 L10
Canyon, *Tex., U.S.A.* 109 H4
Canyon, *Wyo., U.S.A.* 110 D8
Canyonlands National Park, *U.S.A.* 111 G9
Canyonville, *U.S.A.* 110 E2
Canzo, *Italy* 32 C6
Cao Bang, *Vietnam* 58 A6
Cao He →, *China* 51 D13
Cao Lanh, *Vietnam* 59 G5
Cao Xian, *China* 50 G8
Cáorle, *Italy* 33 C9
Cap-aux-Meules, *Canada* 99 C7
Cap-Chat, *Canada* 99 C6
Cap-de-la-Madeleine, *Canada* 98 C5
Cap-Haïtien, *Haiti* 117 C5
Cap St.-Jacques = Vung Tau, *Vietnam* 59 G6
Capa, *Vietnam* 58 A4
Capa Stilo, *Italy* 35 D9
Capáccio, *Italy* 35 B8
Capaia, *Angola* 80 F4
Capanaparo →, *Venezuela* 120 B4
Capanema, *Brazil* 122 B2
Caparo →, *Barinas, Venezuela* 120 B3
Caparo →, *Bolívar, Venezuela* 121 B5
Capatárida, *Venezuela* 120 A3
Capbreton, *France* 26 E2
Capdenac, *France* 26 D6
Cape →, *Australia* 90 C4
Cape Barren I., *Australia* 90 G4
Cape Breton Highlands Nat. Park, *Canada* 99 C7
Cape Breton I., *Canada* 99 C7
Cape Charles, *U.S.A.* 104 G8
Cape Coast, *Ghana* 79 D4
Cape Dorset, *Canada* 97 B12
Cape Dyer, *Canada* 97 B13
Cape Fear →, *U.S.A.* 105 H6
Cape Girardeau, *U.S.A.* 109 G10
Cape Jervis, *Australia* 91 F2
Cape May, *U.S.A.* 104 F8
Cape May Point, *U.S.A.* 103 C12
Cape Palmas, *Liberia* 78 E3
Cape Province □, *S. Africa* 84 E3
Cape Tormentine, *Canada* 99 C7
Cape Town, *S. Africa* 84 E2
Cape Verde Is. ■, *Atl. Oc.* 2 D8
Cape Vincent, *U.S.A.* 107 B8
Cape York Peninsula, *Australia* 90 A3
Capela, *Brazil* 122 D4
Capela de Campo, *Brazil* 122 B3
Capelinha, *Brazil* 123 E3
Capella, *Australia* 90 C4
Capendu, *France* 26 E6
Capestang, *France* 26 E7
Capim, *Brazil* 122 B2
Capim →, *Brazil* 122 B2
Capinópolis, *Brazil* 123 E2
Capinota, *Bolivia* 124 D4
Capitan, *U.S.A.* 111 K11
Capitán Aracena, I., *Chile* 128 D2
Capitán Pastene, *Chile* 128 A2
Capitola, *U.S.A.* 112 J5
Capivara, Serra da, *Brazil* 123 D3
Capizzi, *Italy* 35 E7
Čapljina, *Bos.-H.* 21 M7
Capoche →, *Mozam.* 83 F3
Capoeira, *Brazil* 125 B6
Cappadocia, *Turkey* 66 D6
Capraia, *Italy* 32 E6
Caprarola, *Italy* 33 F9
Capreol, *Canada* 98 C3

Caprera, *Italy* 34 A2
Capri, *Italy* 35 B7
Capricorn Group, *Australia* 90 C5
Capricorn Ra., *Australia* .. 88 D2
Caprino Veronese, *Italy* .. 32 C7
Caprivi Strip, *Namibia* .. 84 B3
Captainganj, *India* 63 F10
Captain's Flat, *Australia* .. 91 F4
Captieux, *France* 26 D3
Cápua, *Italy* 35 A7
Caquetá □, *Colombia* 120 C3
Caquetá →, *Colombia* 120 D4
Carabobo, *Venezuela* 120 A4
Carabobo □, *Venezuela* .. 120 A4
Caracal, *Romania* 38 E7
Caracaraí, *Brazil* 121 C5
Caracas, *Venezuela* 120 A4
Caracol, *Brazil* 122 C3
Caracollo, *Bolivia* 124 D4
Caradoc, *Australia* 91 E3
Caráglio, *Italy* 32 D4
Carahue, *Chile* 128 A2
Caraí, *Brazil* 123 E3
Carajás, Serra dos, *Brazil* . 122 C1
Caranapatuba, *Brazil* ... 125 B5
Carandaiti, *Bolivia* 125 E5
Carangola, *Brazil* 123 F3
Carani, *Australia* 89 F2
Caransebeş, *Romania* ... 38 D5
Carantec, *France* 24 D3
Caraparaná →, *Colombia* 120 D3
Carapelle →, *Italy* 35 A8
Caras, *Peru* 124 B2
Caratasca, L., *Honduras* 116 C3
Caratinga, *Brazil* 123 E3
Caraúbas, *Brazil* 122 C4
Caravaca, *Spain* 29 G3
Caravággio, *Italy* 32 C6
Caravelas, *Brazil* 123 E4
Caraveli, *Peru* 124 D3
Caràzinho, *Brazil* 127 B5
Carballino, *Spain* 30 C2
Carballo, *Spain* 30 B2
Carberry, *Canada* 101 D9
Carbia, *Spain* 30 C2
Carbó, *Mexico* 114 B2
Carbon, *Canada* 100 C6
Carbonara, C., *Italy* 34 C2
Carbondale, *Colo., U.S.A.* 110 G10
Carbondale, *Ill., U.S.A.* 109 G10
Carbondale, *Pa., U.S.A.* 107 E9
Carbonear, *Canada* 99 C9
Carboneras, *Spain* 29 J3
Carboneras de Guadazón,
  Spain 28 F3
Carbonia, *Italy* 34 C1
Carcabuey, *Spain* 31 H6
Carcagente, *Spain* 29 F4
Carcajou, *Canada* 100 B5
Carcar, *Phil.* 55 F5
Carcasse, C., *Haiti* 117 C5
Carche, *Spain* 29 G3
Carchi □, *Ecuador* 120 C2
Carcross, *Canada* 96 B6
Cardabia, *Australia* 88 D1
Çardak, *Turkey* 66 E3
Cardamon Hills, *India* .. 60 Q10
Cárdenas, *Cuba* 116 B3
Cárdenas, *San Luis Potosí,
  Mexico* 115 C5
Cárdenas, *Tabasco, Mexico* 115 D6
Cardenete, *Spain* 28 F3
Cardiel, L., *Argentina* .. 128 C2
Cardiff, *U.K.* 13 F4
Cardiff-by-the-Sea, *U.S.A.* 113 M9
Cardigan, *U.K.* 13 E3
Cardigan B., *U.K.* 13 E3
Cardinal, *Canada* 107 B9
Cardón, Punta, *Venezuela* 120 A3
Cardona, *Spain* 28 D6
Cardona, *Uruguay* 126 C4
Cardoner →, *Spain* 28 D6
Cardross, *Canada* 101 D7
Cardston, *Canada* 100 D6
Cardwell, *Australia* 90 B4
Careen L., *Canada* 101 B7
Carei, *Romania* 38 B5
Careiro, *Brazil* 121 D6
Careme, *Indonesia* 57 G13
Carentan, *France* 24 C5
Carey, *Idaho, U.S.A.* ... 110 E7
Carey, *Ohio, U.S.A.* 104 E4
Carey, L., *Australia* 89 E3
Carey L., *Canada* 101 A8
Careysburg, *Liberia* 78 D2
Cargèse, *France* 27 F12
Carhaix-Plouguer, *France* . 24 D3
Carhuamayo, *Peru* 124 C2
Carhuas, *Peru* 124 B2
Carhué, *Argentina* 126 D3
Caria, *Turkey* 66 E3
Cariacica, *Brazil* 123 F3
Caribbean Sea, *W. Indies* 117 C5
Cariboo Mts., *Canada* ... 100 C4
Caribou, *U.S.A.* 99 C6
Caribou →, *Man., Canada* 101 B10
Caribou →, *N.W.T.,
  Canada* 100 A3
Caribou I., *Canada* 98 C2
Caribou Is., *Canada* 100 A6
Caribou L., *Man., Canada* 101 B9
Caribou L., *Ont., Canada* 98 B2
Caribou Mts., *Canada* ... 100 B5
Carichic, *Mexico* 114 B3

Carigara, *Phil.* 55 F6
Carignan, *France* 25 C12
Carignano, *Italy* 32 D4
Carillo, *Mexico* 114 B4
Cariñena, *Spain* 28 D3
Carinhanha, *Brazil* 123 D3
Carinhanha →, *Brazil* ... 123 D3
Carini, *Italy* 34 D6
Carinola, *Italy* 34 A6
Caripito, *Venezuela* 121 A5
Caritianas, *Brazil* 125 B5
Carlbrod = Dimitrovgrad,
  Serbia 21 M12
Carlentini, *Italy* 35 E8
Carleton Place, *Canada* . 98 C4
Carletonville, *S. Africa* . 84 D4
Carlin, *U.S.A.* 110 F5
Carlingford, L., *Ireland* . 15 B5
Carlinville, *U.S.A.* 108 F10
Carlisle, *U.K.* 12 C5
Carlisle, *U.S.A.* 106 F7
Carlit, Pic, *France* 26 F5
Carloforte, *Italy* 34 C1
Carlos Casares, *Argentina* 126 D3
Carlos Chagas, *Brazil* .. 123 E3
Carlos Tejedor, *Argentina* 126 D3
Carlow, *Ireland* 15 D5
Carlow □, *Ireland* 15 D5
Carlsbad, *Calif., U.S.A.* 113 M9
Carlsbad, *N. Mex., U.S.A.* 109 J2
Carlyle, *Canada* 101 D8
Carlyle, *U.S.A.* 108 F10
Carmacks, *Canada* 96 B6
Carmagnola, *Italy* 32 D4
Carman, *Canada* 101 D9
Carmangay, *Canada* 100 C6
Carmanville, *Canada* 99 C9
Carmarthen, *U.K.* 13 F3
Carmarthen B., *U.K.* 13 F3
Carmaux, *France* 26 D6
Carmel, *U.S.A.* 107 E11
Carmel-by-the-Sea, *U.S.A.* 111 H3
Carmel Valley, *U.S.A.* .. 112 J5
Carmelo, *Uruguay* 126 C4
Carmen, *Bolivia* 124 C4
Carmen, *Colombia* 120 B2
Carmen, *Paraguay* 127 B4
Carmen →, *Mexico* 114 A3
Carmen, I., *Mexico* 114 B2
Carmen de Patagones,
  Argentina 128 B4
Cármenes, *Spain* 30 C5
Carmensa, *Argentina* 126 D2
Carmi, *U.S.A.* 104 F1
Carmichael, *U.S.A.* 112 G5
Carmila, *Australia* 90 C4
Carmona, *Spain* 31 H5
Carnarvon, *Queens.,
  Australia* 90 C4
Carnarvon, *W. Austral.,
  Australia* 89 D1
Carnarvon, *S. Africa* ... 84 E3
Carnarvon Ra., *Queens.,
  Australia* 90 D4
Carnarvon Ra.,
  W. Austral., Australia . 89 E3
Carnation, *U.S.A.* 112 C5
Carnaxide, *Portugal* 31 G1
Carndonagh, *Ireland* 15 A4
Carnduff, *Canada* 101 D8
Carnegie, *U.S.A.* 106 F4
Carnegie, L., *Australia* .. 89 E3
Carnic Alps = Karnische
  Alpen, *Europe* 21 J3
Carniche Alpi = Karnische
  Alpen, *Europe* 21 J3
Carnot, *C.A.R.* 80 D3
Carnot, C., *Australia* ... 91 E2
Carnot B., *Australia* 88 C3
Carnsore Pt., *Ireland* ... 15 D5
Caro, *U.S.A.* 104 D4
Carol City, *U.S.A.* 105 N5
Carolina, *Brazil* 122 C2
Carolina, *Puerto Rico* ... 117 C6
Carolina, *S. Africa* 85 D5
Caroline I., *Kiribati* 93 H12
Caroline Is., *Pac. Oc.* .. 92 G6
Caron, *Canada* 101 C7
Caroni →, *Venezuela* ... 121 B5
Caroona, *Australia* 91 E5
Carora, *Venezuela* 120 A3
Carovigno, *Italy* 35 B10
Carpathians, *Europe* 20 F11
Carpaţii Meridionali,
  Romania 38 D8
Carpenédolo, *Italy* 32 C7
Carpentaria, G. of,
  Australia 90 A2
Carpentaria Downs,
  Australia 90 B3
Carpentras, *France* 27 D9
Carpi, *Italy* 32 D7
Carpina, *Brazil* 122 C4
Carpino, *Italy* 35 A8
Carpinteria, *U.S.A.* 113 L7
Carpolac = Morea,
  Australia 91 F3
Carr Boyd Ra., *Australia* 88 C4
Carrabelle, *U.S.A.* 105 L3
Carranya, *Australia* 88 C4
Carrara, *Italy* 32 D7
Carrascal, *Phil.* 55 G6
Carrascosa del Campo,
  Spain 28 E2

Carrauntoohill, *Ireland* ... 15 E2
Carretas, Punta, *Peru* ... 124 C2
Carrick-on-Shannon,
  Ireland 15 C3
Carrick-on-Suir, *Ireland* .. 15 D4
Carrickfergus, *U.K.* 15 B6
Carrickfergus □, *U.K.* ... 15 B6
Carrickmacross, *Ireland* .. 15 C5
Carrieton, *Australia* 91 E2
Carrington, *U.S.A.* 108 B5
Carrión →, *Spain* 30 D6
Carrión de los Condes,
  Spain 30 C6
Carrizal Bajo, *Chile* 126 B1
Carrizalillo, *Chile* 126 B1
Carrizo Cr. →, *U.S.A.* .. 109 G3
Carrizo Springs, *U.S.A.* . 109 L5
Carrizozo, *U.S.A.* 111 K11
Carroll, *U.S.A.* 108 D7
Carrollton, *Ga., U.S.A.* . 105 J3
Carrollton, *Ill., U.S.A.* . 108 F9
Carrollton, *Ky., U.S.A.* . 104 F3
Carrollton, *Mo., U.S.A.* . 108 F8
Carrollton, *Ohio, U.S.A.* 106 F3
Carron →, *U.K.* 14 D3
Carron, L., *U.K.* 14 D3
Carrot →, *Canada* 101 C8
Carrot River, *Canada* 101 C8
Carrouges, *France* 24 D6
Carruthers, *Canada* 101 C7
Çarşamba, *Turkey* 66 C7
Carse of Gowrie, *U.K.* .. 14 E5
Carsoli, *Italy* 33 F10
Carson, *Calif., U.S.A.* .. 113 M8
Carson, *N. Dak., U.S.A.* 108 B4
Carson →, *U.S.A.* 112 F8
Carson City, *U.S.A.* 112 F7
Carson Sink, *U.S.A.* 110 G4
Carstairs, *U.K.* 14 F5
Cartagena, *Colombia* 120 A2
Cartagena, *Spain* 29 H4
Cartago, *Colombia* 120 C2
Cartago, *Costa Rica* 116 E3
Cartaxo, *Portugal* 31 F2
Cartaya, *Spain* 31 H3
Carteret, *France* 24 C5
Cartersville, *U.S.A.* 105 H3
Carterton, *N.Z.* 87 J5
Carthage, *Ark., U.S.A.* . 109 H8
Carthage, *Ill., U.S.A.* .. 108 E9
Carthage, *Mo., U.S.A.* . 109 G7
Carthage, *S. Dak., U.S.A.* 108 C6
Carthage, *Tex., U.S.A.* . 109 J7
Cartier I., *Australia* 88 B3
Cartwright, *Canada* 99 B8
Caruaru, *Brazil* 122 C4
Carúpano, *Venezuela* ... 121 A5
Carutapera, *Brazil* 122 B2
Caruthersville, *U.S.A.* ... 109 G10
Carvalho, *Brazil* 121 D7
Carvin, *France* 25 B5
Carvoeiro, *Brazil* 121 D5
Carvoeiro, C., *Portugal* .. 31 F1
Casa Branca, *Brazil* 123 F2
Casa Branca, *Portugal* .. 31 G2
Casa Grande, *U.S.A.* 111 K8
Casablanca, *Chile* 126 C1
Casablanca, *Morocco* 74 B3
Casalbordino, *Italy* 33 F11
Casal di Principe, *Italy* .. 35 B7
Casale Monferrato, *Italy* 32 C5
Casalmaggiore, *Italy* 32 D7
Casalpusterlengo, *Italy* . 32 C6
Casamance →, *Senegal* .. 78 C1
Casamássima, *Italy* 35 B9
Casanare □, *Colombia* ... 120 B3
Casanare □, *Colombia* ... 120 B3
Casanare →, *Colombia* ... 120 B4
Casarano, *Italy* 35 B11
Casares, *Spain* 31 J5
Casas Grandes, *Mexico* . 114 A3
Casas Ibáñez, *Spain* 29 F3
Casasimarro, *Spain* 29 F2
Casatejada, *Spain* 30 F5
Casavieja, *Spain* 30 E6
Cascade, *Idaho, U.S.A.* . 110 D5
Cascade, *Mont., U.S.A.* . 110 C8
Cascade Locks, *U.S.A.* .. 112 E5
Cascade Ra., *U.S.A.* 112 D5
Cascais, *Portugal* 31 G1
Cascavel, *Brazil* 127 A5
Cáscina, *Italy* 32 E7
Caselle Torinese, *Italy* .. 32 C4
Caserta, *Italy* 35 A7
Cashel, *Ireland* 15 D4
Cashmere, *U.S.A.* 110 C3
Cashmere Downs, *Australia* 89 E2
Casibare →, *Colombia* ... 120 C3
Casiguran, *Phil.* 55 C5
Casilda, *Argentina* 126 C3
Casino, *Australia* 91 D5
Casiquiare →, *Venezuela* 120 C4
Casitas, *Peru* 124 A1
Caslan, *Canada* 100 C6
Čáslav, *Czech.* 20 F5
Casma, *Peru* 124 B2
Casmalia, *U.S.A.* 113 L6
Casola Valsenio, *Italy* ... 33 D8
Cásoli, *Italy* 33 F11
Caspe, *Spain* 28 D4
Casper, *U.S.A.* 110 E10
Caspian Sea, *Asia* 44 E6
Casquets, *Chan. Is.* 24 C4
Cass City, *U.S.A.* 104 D4

Cass Lake, *U.S.A.* 108 B7
Cassá de la Selva, *Spain* . 28 D7
Cassano Iónio, *Italy* 35 C9
Cassel, *France* 25 B9
Casselman, *Canada* 107 A9
Casselton, *U.S.A.* 108 B6
Cassiar, *Canada* 100 B3
Cassiar Mts., *Canada* ... 100 B2
Cassilândia, *Brazil* 125 D7
Cassinga, *Angola* 81 H3
Cassino, *Italy* 34 A6
Cassville, *U.S.A.* 109 G8
Cástagneto Carducci, *Italy* 32 E7
Castaic, *U.S.A.* 113 L8
Castanhal, *Brazil* 122 B2
Casteau, *Belgium* 17 G4
Castejón de Monegros,
  Spain 28 D4
Castel di Sangro, *Italy* .. 33 G11
Castel San Giovanni, *Italy* 32 C6
Castel San Pietro, *Italy* .. 33 D8
Castelbuono, *Italy* 35 E7
Casteldelfino, *Italy* 32 D4
Castelfiorentino, *Italy* .. 32 E7
Castelfranco Emília, *Italy* 32 D8
Castelfranco Véneto, *Italy* 33 C8
Casteljaloux, *France* 26 D4
Castellabate, *Italy* 35 B7
Castellammare, G. di, *Italy* 34 D5
Castellammare del Golfo,
  Italy 34 D5
Castellammare di Stábia,
  Italy 35 B7
Castellamonte, *Italy* 32 C4
Castellana Grotte, *Italy* .. 35 B10
Castellane, *France* 27 E10
Castellaneta, *Italy* 35 B9
Castellar de Santisteban,
  Spain 29 G1
Castelleone, *Italy* 32 C6
Castelli, *Argentina* 126 D4
Castelló de Ampurias,
  Spain 28 C8
Castellón □, *Spain* 28 E4
Castellón de la Plana, *Spain* 28 E4
Castellote, *Spain* 28 E4
Castelltersol, *Spain* 28 D7
Castelmáuro, *Italy* 35 A7
Castelnau-de-Médoc,
  France 26 C3
Castelnaudary, *France* ... 26 E5
Castelnovo ne' Monti, *Italy* 32 D7
Castelnuovo di Val di
  Cécina, *Italy* 32 E7
Castelo, *Brazil* 123 F3
Castelo Branco, *Portugal* . 30 F3
Castelo Branco □, *Portugal* 30 F3
Castelo de Paiva, *Portugal* 30 D2
Castelo de Vide, *Portugal* . 31 F3
Castelo do Piauí, *Brazil* . 122 C3
Castelsarrasin, *France* ... 26 D5
Casteltérmini, *Italy* 34 E6
Castelvetrano, *Italy* 34 E5
Casterton, *Australia* 91 F3
Castets, *France* 26 E2
Castiglione del Lago, *Italy* 33 E9
Castiglione della Pescáia,
  Italy 32 F7
Castiglione della Stiviere,
  Italy 32 C7
Castiglione Fiorentino, *Italy* 33 E8
Castilblanco, *Spain* 31 F5
Castilla, *Peru* 124 B1
Castilla, Playa de, *Spain* . 31 H4
Castilla La Mancha □,
  Spain 31 F7
Castilla La Nueva =
  Castilla La Mancha □,
  Spain 31 F7
Castilla La Vieja = Castilla
  y León □, *Spain* 30 D6
Castilla y León □, *Spain* 30 D6
Castillon, Barr. de, *France* 27 E10
Castillon-en-Couserans,
  France 26 F5
Castillon-la-Bataille, *France* 26 D3
Castillonès, *France* 26 D4
Castillos, *Uruguay* 127 C5
Castle Dale, *U.S.A.* 110 G8
Castle Douglas, *U.K.* 14 G5
Castle Rock, *Colo., U.S.A.* 108 F2
Castle Rock, *Wash.,
  U.S.A.* 112 D4
Castlebar, *Ireland* 15 C2
Castleblaney, *Ireland* ... 15 B5
Castlegar, *Canada* 100 D5
Castlemaine, *Australia* .. 91 F3
Castlereagh, *Ireland* 15 C3
Castlereagh □, *U.K.* 15 B6
Castlereagh →, *Australia* 91 E4
Castlereagh B., *Australia* 90 A2
Castletown, *I. of Man* ... 12 C3
Castletown Bearhaven,
  Ireland 15 E2
Castlevale, *Australia* 90 C4
Castor, *Canada* 100 C6
Castres, *France* 26 E6
Castries, *St. Lucia* 117 D7
Castril, *Spain* 29 H2
Castro, *Brazil* 127 A5
Castro, *Chile* 128 B2
Castro Alves, *Brazil* 123 D4

Castro del Río, *Spain* 31 H6
Castro Marim, *Portugal* . 31 H3
Castro Urdiales, *Spain* ... 28 B1
Castro Verde, *Portugal* .. 31 H2
Castrojeriz, *Spain* 30 C6
Castropol, *Spain* 30 B3
Castroreale, *Italy* 35 D8
Castrovillari, *Italy* 35 C9
Castroville, *Calif., U.S.A.* 112 J5
Castroville, *Tex., U.S.A.* 109 L5
Castrovirreyna, *Peru* 124 C2
Castuera, *Spain* 31 G5
Çat, *Turkey* 67 D9
Cat Ba, Dao, *Vietnam* ... 58 B6
Cat I., *Bahamas* 117 B4
Cat I., *U.S.A.* 109 K10
Cat L., *Canada* 98 B1
Catacamas, *Honduras* ... 116 D2
Catacáos, *Peru* 124 B1
Cataguases, *Brazil* 123 F3
Catahoula L., *U.S.A.* 109 K8
Çatak, *Turkey* 67 D10
Catalão, *Brazil* 123 E2
Catalca, *Turkey* 66 C3
Catalina, *Canada* 99 C9
Catalonia = Cataluña □,
  Spain 28 D6
Cataluña □, *Spain* 28 D6
Çatalzeytin, *Turkey* 66 C6
Catamarca, *Argentina* ... 126 B2
Catamarca □, *Argentina* . 126 B2
Catanauan, *Phil.* 55 E5
Catanduanes, *Phil.* 55 E6
Catanduva, *Brazil* 127 A6
Catánia, *Italy* 35 E8
Catánia, G. di, *Italy* 35 E8
Catanzaro, *Italy* 35 D9
Cataonia, *Turkey* 66 E6
Catarman, *Phil.* 55 E6
Catbalogan, *Phil.* 55 F6
Cateel, *Phil.* 55 H7
Catende, *Brazil* 122 C4
Cathcart, *S. Africa* 84 E4
Cathlamet, *U.S.A.* 112 D3
Catio, *Guinea-Biss.* 78 C1
Catismiña, *Venezuela* ... 121 C5
Catita, *Brazil* 122 C3
Catlettsburg, *U.S.A.* 104 F4
Catoche, C., *Mexico* 115 C7
Catolé do Rocha, *Brazil* . 122 C4
Catral, *Spain* 29 G4
Catria, Mt., *Italy* 33 E9
Catrimani, *Brazil* 121 C5
Catrimani →, *Brazil* 121 C5
Catskill, *U.S.A.* 107 D11
Catskill Mts., *U.S.A.* ... 107 D10
Catt, Mt., *Australia* 90 A1
Cattaraugus, *U.S.A.* 106 D6
Cáttólica, *Italy* 33 E9
Cáttólica Eraclea, *Italy* .. 34 E6
Catu, *Brazil* 123 D4
Catuala, *Angola* 84 B2
Catur, *Mozam.* 83 E4
Catwick Is., *Vietnam* 59 G7
Cauca □, *Colombia* 120 C2
Cauca →, *Colombia* 120 B3
Caucaia, *Brazil* 122 B4
Caucasia, *Colombia* 120 B2
Caucasus = Bolshoi
  Kavkas, *Asia* 43 E11
Caudebec-en-Caux, *France* 24 C7
Caudete, *Spain* 29 G3
Caudry, *France* 25 B10
Caulnes, *France* 24 D4
Caulónia, *Italy* 35 D9
Caúngula, *Angola* 80 F3
Cauquenes, *Chile* 126 D1
Caura →, *Venezuela* 121 B5
Caurés →, *Brazil* 121 D5
Cauresi →, *Mozam.* 83 F3
Causapscal, *Canada* 99 C6
Caussade, *France* 26 D5
Causse-Méjean, *France* .. 26 D7
Cauterets, *France* 26 F3
Cautín □, *Chile* 128 A2
Cauvery →, *India* 60 P11
Caux, Pays de, *France* ... 24 C7
Cava dei Tirreni, *Italy* ... 35 B7
Cávado →, *Portugal* 30 D2
Cavaillon, *France* 27 E9
Cavalaire-sur-Mer, *France* 27 E10
Cavalcante, *Brazil* 123 D2
Cavalese, *Italy* 33 B8
Cavalier, *U.S.A.* 108 A6
Cavalla = Cavally →,
  Africa 78 E3
Cavallo, I. de, *France* ... 27 G13
Cavally →, *Africa* 78 E3
Cavan, *Ireland* 15 C4
Cavan □, *Ireland* 15 C4
Cavárzere, *Italy* 33 C9
Cave City, *U.S.A.* 104 G3
Cavendish, *Australia* 91 F3
Caviana, I., *Brazil* 121 C7
Cavite, *Phil.* 55 D4
Cavour, *Italy* 32 D4
Cavtat, *Croatia* 21 N8
Cavuşcu Gölü, *Turkey* ... 66 D4
Cawndilla L., *Australia* .. 91 E3
Cawnpore = Kanpur, *India* 63 F9
Caxias, *Brazil* 122 B3
Caxias do Sul, *Brazil* 127 B5
Caxine, C., *Algeria* 75 A4

Caxito, Angola 80 F2
Çay, Turkey 66 D4
Çay Sal Bank, Bahamas .. 116 B3
Cayambe, Ecuador 120 C2
Cayambe, Ecuador 120 C2
Çaycuma, Turkey 66 C5
Çayeli, Turkey 67 C9
Cayenne, Fr. Guiana 121 B7
Cayenne □, Fr. Guiana .. 121 C7
Cayeux-sur-Mer, France .. 25 B8
Çayıralan, Turkey 66 D6
Caylus, France 26 D5
Cayman Brac, Cayman Is. 116 C4
Cayman Is. ■, W. Indies . 116 C3
Cayo Romano, Cuba 117 B4
Cayuga, Canada 106 D5
Cayuga, U.S.A. 107 D8
Cayuga L., U.S.A. 107 D8
Cazalla de la Sierra, Spain 31 H5
Căzănești, Romania 38 E10
Cazaux et de Sanguinet,
  Étang de, France 26 D2
Cazères, France 26 E5
Cazin, Bos.-H. 33 D12
Čazma, Croatia 33 C13
Čazma →, Croatia 33 C13
Cazombo, Angola 81 G4
Cazorla, Spain 29 H1
Cazorla, Venezuela 120 B4
Cazorla, Sierra de, Spain . 29 G2
Cea →, Spain 30 C5
Ceanannus Mor, Ireland . 15 C5
Ceará = Fortaleza, Brazil 122 B4
Ceará □, Brazil 122 C4
Ceará Mirim, Brazil ... 122 C4
Cebaco, I. de, Panama .. 116 E3
Cebollar, Argentina ... 126 B2
Cebollera, Sierra de, Spain 28 D2
Cebreros, Spain 30 E6
Cebu, Phil. 55 F5
Ceccano, Italy 34 A6
Cechi, Ivory C. 78 D4
Čechy, Czech. 19 F9
Cecil Plains, Australia .. 91 D5
Cécina, Italy 32 E7
Cécina →, Italy 32 E7
Ceclavin, Spain 30 F4
Cedar →, U.S.A. 108 E9
Cedar City, U.S.A. 111 H7
Cedar Creek Reservoir,
  U.S.A. 109 J6
Cedar Falls, Iowa, U.S.A. 108 D8
Cedar Falls, Wash., U.S.A. 112 C5
Cedar Key, U.S.A. 105 L4
Cedar L., Canada 101 C8
Cedar Rapids, U.S.A. .. 108 E9
Cedartown, U.S.A. 105 H3
Cedarvale, Canada 100 B3
Cedarville, S. Africa ... 85 E4
Cedarville, U.S.A. 110 F3
Cedeira, Spain 30 B2
Cedral, Mexico 114 C4
Cedrino →, Italy 34 B2
Cedro, Brazil 122 C4
Cedros, I. de, Mexico ... 114 B1
Ceduna, Australia 91 E1
Cefalù, Italy 35 D7
Cega →, Spain 30 D6
Cegléd, Hungary 21 H9
Céglie Messápico, Italy . 35 B10
Cehegín, Spain 29 G3
Ceheng, China 52 E5
Cehu-Silvaniei, Romania . 38 B6
Ceira →, Portugal 30 E2
Cekhira, Tunisia 75 B7
Celano, Italy 33 F10
Celanova, Spain 30 C3
Celaya, Mexico 114 C4
Celbridge, Ireland 15 C5
Celebes = Sulawesi □,
  Indonesia 57 E6
Celebes Sea = Sulawesi
  Sea, Indonesia 57 D6
Celendín, Peru 124 B2
Čelić, Bos.-H. 21 L8
Celica, Ecuador 120 D2
Celina, U.S.A. 104 E3
Celje, Slovenia 33 B12
Celle, Germany 18 C6
Celles, Belgium 17 G2
Celorico da Beira, Portugal 30 E3
Cement, U.S.A. 109 H5
Çemişgezek, Turkey ... 67 D8
Cenepa →, Peru 120 D2
Cengong, China 52 D7
Ceno →, Italy 32 D7
Centallo, Italy 32 D4
Centenário do Sul, Brazil 123 F1
Center, N. Dak., U.S.A. . 108 B4
Center, Tex., U.S.A. ... 109 K7
Centerfield, U.S.A. 111 G8
Centerville, Calif., U.S.A. 112 J7
Centerville, Iowa, U.S.A. 108 E8
Centerville, Pa., U.S.A. . 106 F5
Centerville, S. Dak.,
  U.S.A. 108 D6
Centerville, Tenn., U.S.A. 105 H2
Centerville, Tex., U.S.A. 109 K7
Cento, Italy 33 D8
Central, Brazil 122 D3
Central, U.S.A. 111 K9
Central □, Kenya 82 C4
Central □, Malawi 83 E3
Central □, U.K. 14 E4
Central □, Zambia 83 E2

Central, Cordillera, Bolivia 125 D5
Central, Cordillera,
  Colombia 120 C2
Central, Cordillera,
  Costa Rica 116 D3
Central, Cordillera,
  Dom. Rep. 117 C5
Central, Cordillera, Peru . 124 B2
Central, Cordillera, Phil. . 55 C4
Central, Sistema, Spain . 30 E5
Central African Rep. ■,
  Africa 73 G9
Central City, Ky., U.S.A. . 104 G2
Central City, Nebr., U.S.A. 108 E5
Central I., Kenya 82 B4
Central Makran Range,
  Pakistan 60 F4
Central Patricia, Canada . 98 B1
Central Russian Uplands,
  Europe 6 E13
Central Siberian Plateau,
  Russia 46 C14
Centralia, Ill., U.S.A. ... 108 F10
Centralia, Mo., U.S.A. .. 108 F8
Centralia, Wash., U.S.A. . 112 D4
Centreville, Ala., U.S.A. . 105 J2
Centreville, Miss., U.S.A. 109 K9
Centúripe, Italy 35 E7
Cephalonia = Kefallinía,
  Greece 39 L3
Ceprano, Italy 34 A6
Cepu, Indonesia 57 G14
Ceram = Seram, Indonesia 57 E7
Ceram Sea = Seram Sea,
  Indonesia 57 E7
Cerbère, France 26 F7
Cerbicales, Is., France .. 27 G13
Cercal, Portugal 31 H2
Cercemaggiore, Italy ... 35 A7
Cerdaña, Spain 28 C6
Cerdedo, Spain 30 C2
Cère →, France 26 D5
Cerea, Italy 33 C8
Ceres, Argentina 126 B3
Ceres, Brazil 123 E2
Ceres, Italy 32 C4
Ceres, S. Africa 84 E2
Ceres, U.S.A. 112 H6
Céret, France 26 F6
Cereté, Colombia 120 B2
Cerfontaine, Belgium .. 17 H4
Cerignola, Italy 35 A8
Cerigo = Kíthira, Greece . 39 N7
Cérilly, France 25 B6
Cerisiers, France 25 D10
Cerizay, France 24 F6
Çerkeş, Turkey 66 C5
Çerkezköy, Turkey ... 66 C2
Čerknica, Slovenia 33 C11
Çermik, Turkey 67 D8
Cerna →, Romania ... 38 E7
Cernavodă, Romania .. 38 E11
Cernay, France 25 E14
Cernik, Croatia 21 K7
Cerralvo, I., Mexico ... 114 C3
Cerreto Sannita, Italy .. 35 A7
Cerritos, Mexico 114 C4
Cerro Sombrero, Chile . 128 D3
Certa, Colombia 120 B3
Ceraldo, Italy 32 E8
Cervaro →, Italy 35 A8
Cervera, Spain 28 D6
Cervera de Pisuerga, Spain 30 C6
Cervera del Río Alhama,
  Spain 28 C3
Cérvia, Italy 33 D9
Cervignano del Friuli, Italy 33 C10
Cervione, France 27 F13
Cervo, Spain 30 B3
César □, Colombia 120 B3
Cesaro, Italy 35 E7
Cesena, Italy 33 D9
Cesenático, Italy 33 D9
Cēsis, Latvia 40 C4
Česká Lípa, Czech. 20 E4
České Budějovice, Czech. 20 G4
Českomoravská Vrchovina,
  Czech. 20 F5
Český Brod, Czech. 20 E4
Český Krumlov, Czech. . 20 G4
Český Těšin, Czech. ... 20 F8
Çeşme, Turkey 66 D2
Cessnock, Australia ... 91 E5
Cestos →, Liberia 78 D3
Cétin Grad, Croatia ... 33 C12
Cetina →, Croatia 33 E13
Cetraro, Italy 35 C8
Ceuta, Morocco 74 A3
Ceva, Italy 32 D5
Cévennes, France 26 D7
Ceyhan, Turkey 66 E6
Ceyhan →, Turkey ... 66 E6
Ceylânpınar, Turkey .. 67 E9
Ceylon = Sri Lanka ■,
  Asia 60 R12
Cèze →, France 27 D8
Cha-am, Thailand 58 F2
Chaam, Neths. 17 E5
Chabeuil, France 27 D9
Chablais, France 27 B10
Chablis, France 25 E10
Chabounia, Algeria .. 75 A5
Chacabuco, Argentina . 126 C3
Chachapoyas, Peru ... 124 B2
Chachasp, Peru 124 D3

Chachoengsao, Thailand .. 58 F3
Chachran, Pakistan ... 60 E7
Chachro, Pakistan 62 G4
Chaco □, Argentina .. 126 B3
Chaco □, Paraguay ... 126 B3
Chad ■, Africa 73 E8
Chad, L. = Tchad, L.,
  Chad 73 F7
Chadan, Russia 45 D10
Chadileuvú →, Argentina 126 D2
Chadiza, Zambia 83 E3
Chadron, U.S.A. 108 D3
Chadyr-Lunga, Moldavia . 42 C3
Chae Hom, Thailand .. 58 C2
Chaem →, Thailand .. 58 C2
Chaeryŏng, N. Korea .. 51 E13
Chagai Hills, Afghan. .. 60 E3
Chagda, Russia 45 D14
Chagny, France 25 F11
Chagoda, Russia 40 B9
Chagos Arch., Ind. Oc. .. 46 K11
Chāh Ākhvor, Iran ... 65 C8
Chāh Bahār, Iran 65 E9
Chāh-e-Malek, Iran ... 65 D8
Chāh Kavīr, Iran 65 D7
Chahar Burjak, Afghan. . 60 D3
Chaibasa, India 61 H14
Chaillé-les-Marais, France 26 B2
Chainat, Thailand ... 58 E3
Chaitén, Chile 128 B2
Chaiya, Thailand 59 H2
Chaj Doab, Pakistan .. 62 C5
Chajari, Argentina ... 126 C4
Chake Chake, Tanzania . 82 D4
Chakhānsūr, Afghan. .. 60 D3
Chakonipau, L., Canada . 99 A6
Chakradharpur, India .. 63 H11
Chakwal, Pakistan ... 62 C5
Chala, Peru 124 D3
Chalais, France 26 C4
Chalchihuites, Mexico . 114 C4
Chalcis = Khalkís, Greece 39 L6
Chaleur B., Canada ... 99 C6
Chalfant, U.S.A. 112 H8
Chalhuanca, Peru 124 C3
Chalindrey, France ... 25 E12
Chaling, China 53 D9
Chalisgaon, India ... 60 J9
Chalkar, Kazakhstan .. 43 A14
Chalkar, Ozero,
  Kazakhstan 43 A14
Chalky Inlet, N.Z. 87 M1
Challans, France 24 F5
Challapata, Bolivia ... 124 D4
Challis, U.S.A. 110 D6
Chalna, India 63 H13
Chalon-sur-Saône, France . 25 F11
Chalonnes-sur-Loire,
  France 24 E6
Châlons-sur-Marne, France 25 D11
Châlus, France 26 C4
Chalyaphum, Thailand . 58 E4
Cham, Germany 19 F8
Cham, Switz. 23 B6
Cham, Cu Lao, Vietnam . 58 E7
Chama, U.S.A. 111 H10
Chaman, Pakistan ... 60 D5
Chamba, India 62 C7
Chamba, Tanzania ... 83 E4
Chambal →, India .. 63 F8
Chamberlain, U.S.A. . 108 D5
Chamberlain →, Australia 88 C4
Chambers, U.S.A. ... 111 J9
Chambersburg, U.S.A. . 104 F7
Chambéry, France ... 27 C9
Chambly, Canada ... 107 A11
Chambord, Canada .. 99 C5
Chamchamal, Iraq ... 64 C5
Chamela, Mexico ... 114 D3
Chamical, Argentina . 126 C2
Chamkar Luong, Cambodia 59 G4
Chamonix-Mont-Blanc,
  France 27 C10
Champa, India 63 H10
Champagne, Canada . 100 A1
Champagne, France .. 25 D11
Champagne, Plaine de,
  France 25 D11
Champagnole, France . 25 F12
Champaign, U.S.A. ... 104 E1
Champassak, Laos ... 58 E5
Champaubert, France . 25 D10
Champdeniers, France . 26 B3
Champeix, France ... 26 C7
Champlain, Canada .. 104 B9
Champlain, U.S.A. .. 107 B11
Champlain, L., U.S.A. . 107 B11
Champotón, Mexico .. 115 D6
Chamusca, Portugal .. 31 F2
Chan Chan, Peru ... 124 B2
Chana, Thailand 59 J3
Chañaral, Chile 126 B1
Chanārān, Iran 65 B8
Chanasma, India ... 62 H5
Chancay, Peru 124 C2
Chanco, Chile 126 D1
Chand, India 63 J8
Chandigarh, India .. 62 D7
Chandler, Australia .. 91 D1
Chandler, Canada ... 99 C7
Chandler, Ariz., U.S.A. . 111 K8
Chandler, Okla., U.S.A. . 109 H6

Chandless →, Brazil 124 B4
Chandmani, Mongolia .. 54 B4
Chandpur, Bangla. ... 61 H17
Chandpur, India 62 E8
Chandrapur, India ... 60 K11
Chānf, Iran 65 E9
Chang, Pakistan 62 F3
Chang, Ko, Thailand .. 59 F4
Ch'ang Chiang = Chang
  Jiang →, China 53 B13
Chang Jiang →, China . 53 B13
Changa, India 63 C7
Changanacheri, India . 60 Q10
Changane →, Mozam. . 85 C5
Changbai, China 51 D15
Changbai Shan, China . 51 C15
Changchiak'ou =
  Zhangjiakou, China .. 50 D8
Changchun, China ... 51 C13
Changchunling, China . 51 B13
Changde, China 53 C8
Changdo-ri, N. Korea .. 51 E14
Changfeng, China ... 53 A11
Changhai = Shanghai,
  China 53 B13
Changhua, China ... 53 B12
Changhǔng, S. Korea .. 51 G14
Changhǔngni, N. Korea . 51 D15
Changjiang, China ... 54 E5
Changjin, N. Korea ... 51 D14
Changjin-chōsuji, N. Korea 51 D14
Changle, China 53 E12
Changli, China 51 E10
Changling, China 51 B12
Changlun, Malaysia .. 59 J3
Changning, Hunan, China 53 D9
Changning, Yunnan, China 52 E2
Changping, China ... 50 D9
Changsha, China 53 C9
Changshan, China ... 53 C12
Changshou, China ... 52 C6
Changshu, China 53 B13
Changshun, China ... 52 D6
Changtai, China 53 E11
Changting, China ... 53 E11
Changwu, China 50 G4
Changxing, China ... 53 B12
Changyang, China ... 53 B8
Changyi, China 51 F10
Changyǒn, N. Korea .. 51 E13
Changyuan, China ... 50 G8
Changzhi, China 50 F7
Changzhou, China ... 53 B12
Chanhanga, Angola .. 84 B1
Chanlar, Azerbaijan .. 43 F12
Channapatna, India .. 60 N10
Channel Is., U.K. 13 H5
Channel Is., U.S.A. .. 113 M7
Channel-Port aux Basques,
  Canada 99 C8
Channing, Mich., U.S.A. . 104 B1
Channing, Tex., U.S.A. . 109 H3
Chantada, Spain 30 C3
Chanthaburi, Thailand . 58 F4
Chantilly, France 25 C9
Chantonnay, France .. 24 F5
Chantrey Inlet, Canada .. 96 B10
Chanute, U.S.A. 109 G7
Chanza →, Spain ... 31 H3
Chao Hu, China 53 B11
Chao Phraya →, Thailand 58 F3
Chao Phraya Lowlands,
  Thailand 58 E3
Chao Xian, China ... 53 B11
Chao'an, China 53 F11
Chaocheng, China ... 50 F8
Chaoyang, Guangdong,
  China 53 F11
Chaoyang, Liaoning, China 51 D11
Chapada dos Guimarães,
  Brazil 125 D6
Chapala, Mozam. 83 F4
Chapala, L. de, Mexico .. 114 C4
Chaparé →, Bolivia .. 125 D5
Chaparral, Colombia .. 120 C2
Chapayevo, Kazakhstan . 43 A14
Chapayevsk, Russia .. 41 E16
Chapecó, Brazil 127 B5
Chapel Hill, U.S.A. .. 105 H6
Chapleau, Canada ... 98 C3
Chaplin, Canada 101 C7
Chaplino, Ukraine ... 42 B7
Chaplygin, Russia ... 41 E12
Chapra = Chhapra, India . 63 G11
Châr, Mauritania ... 74 D2
Chara, Russia 45 D12
Charadai, Argentina .. 126 B4
Charagua, Bolivia ... 125 D5
Charalá, Colombia ... 120 B3
Charambirá, Punta,
  Colombia 120 C2
Charaña, Bolivia 124 D4
Charapita, Colombia .. 120 D3
Charata, Argentina ... 126 B3
Charcas, Mexico 114 C4
Charcoal L., Canada .. 101 B8
Chard, U.K. 13 G5
Chardara, Kazakhstan . 44 E7
Chardon, U.S.A. 106 E3
Chardzhou, Turkmenistan . 44 F7
Charente □, France .. 26 C4
Charente →, France .. 26 C2
Charente-Maritime □,
  France 26 C3

Charentsavan, Armenia ... 43 F11
Chari →, Chad 73 F7
Chārīkār, Afghan. ... 60 B6
Chariton →, U.S.A. .. 108 F8
Charity, Guyana 121 B6
Chärjew = Chardzhou,
  Turkmenistan 44 F7
Charkhari, India 63 G8
Charkhi Dadri, India .. 62 E7
Charleroi, Belgium ... 17 H4
Charleroi, U.S.A. ... 106 F5
Charles, C., U.S.A. .. 104 G8
Charles City, U.S.A. .. 108 D8
Charles L., Canada .. 101 B6
Charles Town, U.S.A. . 104 F7
Charleston, Ill., U.S.A. . 104 F1
Charleston, Miss., U.S.A. 109 H9
Charleston, Mo., U.S.A. . 109 G10
Charleston, S.C., U.S.A. . 105 J6
Charleston, W. Va., U.S.A. 104 F5
Charleston Peak, U.S.A. . 113 J11
Charlestown, S. Africa .. 85 D4
Charlestown, U.S.A. .. 104 F3
Charlesville, Zaïre ... 80 F4
Charleville = Rath Luirc,
  Ireland 15 D3
Charleville, Australia .. 91 D4
Charleville-Mézières,
  France 25 C11
Charlevoix, U.S.A. ... 104 C3
Charlieu, France 27 B8
Charlotte, Mich., U.S.A. . 104 D3
Charlotte, N.C., U.S.A. . 105 H5
Charlotte Amalie,
  Virgin Is. 117 C7
Charlotte Harbor, U.S.A. . 105 M4
Charlottesville, U.S.A. . 104 F6
Charlottetown, Canada . 99 C7
Charlton, Australia ... 91 F3
Charlton, U.S.A. 108 E8
Charlton I., Canada .. 98 B4
Charmes, France 25 D13
Charny, Canada 99 C5
Charolles, France ... 27 B8
Chârost, France 25 F9
Charouine, Algeria ... 75 C4
Charre, Mozam. 83 F4
Charroux, France ... 26 B4
Charsadda, Pakistan .. 62 B4
Charters Towers, Australia 90 C4
Chartres, France 24 D8
Chascomús, Argentina . 126 D4
Chasefu, Zambia 83 E3
Chasovnya-Uchurskaya,
  Russia 45 D14
Chasseneuil-sur-Bonnieure,
  France 26 C4
Chāt, Iran 65 B7
Chatal Balkan = Udvoy
  Balkan, Bulgaria 38 G9
Château-Arnoux, France . 27 D10
Château-Chinon, France . 25 E10
Château d'Oex, Switz. .. 22 D4
Château-du-Loir, France . 24 E7
Château-Gontier, France . 24 E6
Château-la-Vallière, France 24 E7
Château-Landon, France . 25 D9
Château-Porcien, France . 25 C11
Château-Renault, France . 24 E7
Château-Salins, France . 25 D13
Château-Thierry, France . 25 C10
Châteaubourg, France .. 24 D5
Châteaubriant, France .. 24 E5
Châteaudun, France .. 24 D8
Châteaugiron, France .. 24 D5
Châteaulin, France ... 24 D2
Châteaumeillant, France . 26 B6
Châteauneuf-du-Faou,
  France 24 D3
Châteauneuf-en-Thymerais,
  France 24 D8
Châteauneuf-sur-Charente,
  France 26 C3
Châteauneuf-sur-Cher,
  France 25 F9
Châteauneuf-sur-Loire,
  France 25 E9
Châteaurenard,
  Bouches-du-Rhône,
  France 27 E8
Châteaurenard, Loiret,
  France 25 E9
Châteauroux, France .. 25 F8
Châtel-St.-Denis, Switz. . 22 D3
Châtelaillon-Plage, France 26 B2
Châtelaudren, France .. 24 D3
Chatelet, Belgium ... 17 H5
Châtelguyon, France .. 26 C7
Châtellerault, France .. 24 F7
Châtelus-Malvaleix, France 26 B6
Chatham, U.S.A. 108 E9
Chatham, N.B., Canada . 99 C6
Chatham, Ont., Canada . 98 D3
Chatham, U.K. 13 F8
Chatham, La., U.S.A. .. 109 J8
Chatham, N.Y., U.S.A. . 107 D11
Chatham, I., Chile ... 128 D2
Chatham, Is., Pac. Oc. .. 92 M10
Chatham Str., U.S.A. .. 100 B2
Chatillon, Italy 32 C4
Châtillon-Coligny, France . 25 E9
Châtillon-en-Bazois, France 25 E10
Châtillon-en-Diois, France 27 D9
Châtillon-sur-Indre, France 24 F7
Châtillon-sur-Loire, France 25 E9

Châtillon-sur-Marne, France	25	C10	
Châtillon-sur-Seine, France	25	E11	
Chatmohar, Bangla.	63	G13	
Chatra, India	63	G11	
Chatrapur, India	61	K14	
Chats, L. des, Canada	107	A8	
Chatsworth, Canada	106	B4	
Chatsworth, Zimbabwe	83	F3	
Chattahoochee →, U.S.A.	105	K3	
Chattanooga, U.S.A.	105	H3	
Chaturat, Thailand	58	E3	
Chau Doc, Vietnam	59	G5	
Chaudanne, Barr. de, France	27	E10	
Chaudes-Aigues, France	26	D7	
Chauffailles, France	27	B8	
Chauk, Burma	61	J19	
Chaukan La, Burma	61	F20	
Chaulnes, France	25	C9	
Chaumont, France	25	D12	
Chaumont, U.S.A.	107	B8	
Chaumont-en-Vexin, France	25	C8	
Chaumont-sur-Loire, France	24	E8	
Chaunay, France	26	B4	
Chauny, France	25	C10	
Chausey, Is., France	24	D5	
Chaussin, France	25	F12	
Chautauqua L., U.S.A.	106	D5	
Chauvigny, France	24	F7	
Chauvin, Canada	101	C6	
Chavantina, Brazil	125	C7	
Chaves, Brazil	122	B2	
Chaves, Portugal	30	D3	
Chavuma, Zambia	81	G4	
Chawang, Thailand	59	H2	
Chazelles-sur-Lyon, France	27	C8	
Chazuta, Peru	124	B2	
Chazy, U.S.A.	107	B11	
Cheb, Czech.	20	E2	
Cheboksary, Russia	41	C15	
Cheboygan, U.S.A.	104	C3	
Chebsara, Russia	41	B11	
Chech, Erg, Africa	74	D4	
Chechaouen, Morocco	74	A3	
Chechen, Os., Russia	43	E12	
Checheno-Ingush Republic □, Russia	43	E11	
Chechon, S. Korea	51	F15	
Chęciny, Poland	20	E10	
Checleset B., Canada	100	C3	
Checotah, U.S.A.	109	H7	
Cheduba I., Burma	61	K18	
Cheepie, Australia	91	D4	
Chef-Boutonne, France	26	B3	
Chegdomyn, Russia	45	D14	
Chegga, Mauritania	74	C3	
Chegutu, Zimbabwe	83	F3	
Chehalis, U.S.A.	112	D4	
Cheiron, Mt., France	27	E10	
Cheju Do, S. Korea	51	H14	
Chekalin, Russia	41	D10	
Chekiang = Zhejiang □, China	53	C13	
Chel = Kuru, Bahr el →, Sudan	77	F2	
Chela, Sa. da, Angola	84	B1	
Chelan, U.S.A.	110	C4	
Chelan, L., U.S.A.	110	C3	
Cheleken, Turkmenistan	44	F6	
Chelforó, Argentina	128	A3	
Chéliff, O. →, Algeria	75	A5	
Chelkar, Kazakhstan	44	E6	
Chelkar Tengiz, Solonchak, Kazakhstan	44	E7	
Chellala Dahrania, Algeria	75	B5	
Chelles, France	25	D9	
Chełm, Poland	20	D13	
Chełmek, Poland	20	E9	
Chełmno, Poland	20	B8	
Chelmsford, U.K.	13	F8	
Chelmsford Dam, S. Africa	85	D4	
Chełmża, Poland	20	B8	
Chelsea, Okla., U.S.A.	109	G7	
Chelsea, Vt., U.S.A.	107	C12	
Cheltenham, U.K.	13	F5	
Chelva, Spain	28	F4	
Chelyabinsk, Russia	44	D7	
Chelyuskin, C., Russia	46	B14	
Chemainus, Canada	100	D4	
Chembar = Belinskiy, Russia	41	E13	
Chemillé, France	24	E6	
Chemnitz, Germany	18	E8	
Chemult, U.S.A.	110	E3	
Chen, Gora, Russia	45	C15	
Chen Xian, China	53	E9	
Chenab →, Pakistan	62	D4	
Chenachane, O. →, Algeria	74	C4	
Chenango Forks, U.S.A.	107	D9	
Chencha, Ethiopia	77	F4	
Chenchiang = Zhenjiang, China	53	A12	
Chênée, Belgium	17	G7	
Cheney, U.S.A.	110	C5	
Cheng Xian, China	50	H3	
Chengbu, China	53	D8	
Chengcheng, China	50	G5	
Chengchou = Zhengzhou, China	50	G7	
Chengde, China	51	D9	
Chengdong Hu, China	53	A11	
Chengdu, China	52	B5	
Chenggong, China	52	E4	
Chenggu, China	50	H4	
Chengjiang, China	52	E4	
Chengkou, China	52	B7	
Ch'engtu = Chengdu, China	52	B5	
Chengwu, China	50	G8	
Chengxi Hu, China	53	A11	
Chengyang, China	51	F11	
Chenjiagang, China	51	G10	
Chenkán, Mexico	115	D6	
Chenxi, China	53	C8	
Cheo Reo, Vietnam	58	F7	
Cheom Ksan, Cambodia	58	E5	
Chepelare, Bulgaria	39	H7	
Chepén, Peru	124	B2	
Chepes, Argentina	126	C2	
Chepo, Panama	116	E4	
Cheptsa →, Russia	41	B17	
Cheptulil, Mt., Kenya	82	B4	
Chequamegon B., U.S.A.	108	B9	
Cher □, France	25	E9	
Cher →, France	24	E7	
Cherasco, Italy	32	D4	
Cheratte, Belgium	17	G7	
Cheraw, U.S.A.	105	H6	
Cherbourg, France	24	C5	
Cherchell, Algeria	75	A5	
Cherdakly, Russia	41	D16	
Cherdyn, Russia	44	C6	
Cheremkhovo, Russia	45	D11	
Cherepanovo, Russia	44	D9	
Cherepovets, Russia	41	B10	
Chergui, Chott ech, Algeria	75	B5	
Cherikov, Belorussia	40	E7	
Cherkassy, Ukraine	42	B5	
Cherkasy = Cherkassy, Ukraine	42	B5	
Cherkessk, Russia	43	D10	
Cherlak, Russia	44	D8	
Chernaya Kholunitsa, Russia	41	B17	
Cherni, Bulgaria	38	G6	
Chernigov, Russia	40	F7	
Chernihiv = Chernigov, Ukraine	40	F7	
Chernivtsi = Chernovtsy, Ukraine	42	B1	
Chernobyl, Ukraine	40	F7	
Chernogorsk, Russia	45	D10	
Chernomorskoye, Ukraine	42	D5	
Chernovskoye, Russia	41	B15	
Chernovtsy, Ukraine	42	B1	
Chernoye, Russia	45	B9	
Chernyakhovsk, Russia	40	D2	
Chernyshkovskiy, Russia	43	B10	
Chernyshovskiy, Russia	45	C12	
Cherokee, Iowa, U.S.A.	108	D7	
Cherokee, Okla., U.S.A.	109	G5	
Cherokees, Lake O' The, U.S.A.	109	G7	
Cherquenco, Chile	128	A2	
Cherrapunji, India	61	G17	
Cherry Creek, U.S.A.	110	G6	
Cherry Valley, U.S.A.	113	M10	
Cherryvale, U.S.A.	109	G7	
Cherskiy, Russia	45	C17	
Cherskogo Khrebet, Russia	45	C15	
Chertkovo, Russia	43	B9	
Cherven, Belorussia	40	E6	
Cherven-Bryag, Bulgaria	38	F7	
Chervonograd, Ukraine	40	F4	
Cherwell →, U.K.	13	F6	
Chesapeake, U.S.A.	104	G7	
Chesapeake B., U.S.A.	104	F7	
Cheshire □, U.K.	12	D5	
Cheshskaya Guba, Russia	44	C5	
Cheslatta L., Canada	100	C3	
Chesley, Canada	106	B3	
Cheste, Spain	29	F4	
Chester, U.K.	12	D5	
Chester, Calif., U.S.A.	110	F3	
Chester, Ill., U.S.A.	109	G10	
Chester, Mont., U.S.A.	110	B8	
Chester, Pa., U.S.A.	104	F8	
Chester, S.C., U.S.A.	105	H5	
Chesterfield, U.K.	12	D6	
Chesterfield, Is., N. Cal.	92	J7	
Chesterfield Inlet, Canada	96	B10	
Chesterton Ra., Australia	91	D4	
Chesterville, Canada	107	A9	
Chestertown, Canada	99	C6	
Chetaibi, Algeria	75	A6	
Chéticamp, Canada	99	C7	
Chetumal, Mexico	115	D7	
Chetumal, B. de, Mexico	115	D7	
Chetwynd, Canada	100	B4	
Chevanceaux, France	26	C3	
Cheviot, The, U.K.	12	B5	
Cheviot Hills, U.K.	12	B5	
Cheviot Ra., Australia	90	D3	
Chew Bahir, Ethiopia	77	G4	
Chewelah, U.S.A.	110	B5	
Cheyenne, Okla., U.S.A.	109	H5	
Cheyenne, Wyo., U.S.A.	108	E2	
Cheyenne →, U.S.A.	108	C4	
Cheyenne Wells, U.S.A.	108	F3	
Cheyne B., Australia	89	F2	
Chhabra, India	62	G7	
Chhapra, India	63	G11	
Chhata, India	62	F7	
Chhatarpur, India	63	G8	
Chhep, Cambodia	58	F5	
Chhindwara, India	63	H8	
Chhlong, Cambodia	59	F5	
Chhuk, Cambodia	59	G5	
Chi →, Thailand	58	E5	
Chiamis, Indonesia	57	G13	
Chiamussu = Jiamusi, China	54	B8	
Chiang Dao, Thailand	58	C2	
Chiang Kham, Thailand	58	C3	
Chiang Khan, Thailand	58	D3	
Chiang Khong, Thailand	58	B3	
Chiang Mai, Thailand	58	C2	
Chiang Saen, Thailand	58	B3	
Chiange, Angola	81	H2	
Chiapa →, Mexico	115	D6	
Chiapa de Corzo, Mexico	115	D6	
Chiapas □, Mexico	115	D6	
Chiaramonte Gulfi, Italy	35	E7	
Chiaravalle, Italy	33	E10	
Chiaravalle Centrale, Italy	35	D9	
Chiari, Italy	32	C6	
Chiasso, Switz.	23	E8	
Chiatura, Georgia	43	E10	
Chiautla, Mexico	115	D5	
Chiávari, Italy	32	D6	
Chiavenna, Italy	32	B6	
Chiba, Japan	49	G10	
Chiba □, Japan	49	G10	
Chibabava, Mozam.	85	C5	
Chibemba, Cunene, Angola	81	H2	
Chibemba, Huila, Angola	84	B2	
Chibia, Angola	81	H2	
Chibougamau, Canada	98	C5	
Chibougamau L., Canada	98	C5	
Chibuk, Nigeria	79	C7	
Chic-Chocs, Mts., Canada	99	C6	
Chicacole = Srikakulam, India	61	K13	
Chicago, U.S.A.	104	E2	
Chicago Heights, U.S.A.	104	E2	
Chichagof I., U.S.A.	100	B1	
Chichaoua, Morocco	74	B3	
Chicheng, China	50	D8	
Chichester, U.K.	13	G7	
Chichibu, Japan	49	F9	
Chickasha, U.S.A.	109	H5	
Chiclana de la Frontera, Spain	31	J4	
Chiclayo, Peru	124	B2	
Chico, U.S.A.	112	F5	
Chico →, Chubut, Argentina	128	B3	
Chico →, Santa Cruz, Argentina	128	C3	
Chicomo, Mozam.	85	C5	
Chicontepec, Mexico	115	C5	
Chicopee, U.S.A.	107	D12	
Chicoutimi, Canada	99	C5	
Chicualacuala, Mozam.	85	C5	
Chidambaram, India	60	P11	
Chidenguele, Mozam.	85	C5	
Chidley, C., Canada	97	B13	
Chiede, Angola	84	B2	
Chiefs Pt., Canada	106	B3	
Chiem Hoa, Vietnam	58	A5	
Chiemsee, Germany	19	H8	
Chiengi, Zambia	83	D2	
Chiengmai = Chiang Mai, Thailand	58	C2	
Chienti →, Italy	33	E10	
Chieri, Italy	32	D4	
Chiers →, France	25	C11	
Chiese →, Italy	32	C7	
Chieti, Italy	33	F11	
Chièvres, Belgium	17	G3	
Chifeng, China	51	C10	
Chigirin, Ukraine	42	B5	
Chignecto B., Canada	99	C7	
Chigorodó, Colombia	120	B2	
Chiguana, Bolivia	126	A2	
Chiha-ri, N. Korea	51	E14	
Chihli, G. of = Bo Hai, China	51	E10	
Chihuahua, Mexico	114	B3	
Chihuahua □, Mexico	114	B3	
Chiili, Kazakhstan	44	E7	
Chik Bollapur, India	60	N10	
Chikmagalur, India	60	N9	
Chilako →, Canada	100	C4	
Chilam Chavki, Pakistan	63	B6	
Chilanga, Zambia	83	F2	
Chilapa, Mexico	115	D5	
Chilas, Pakistan	63	B6	
Chilaw, Sri Lanka	60	R11	
Chilcotin →, Canada	100	C4	
Childers, Australia	91	D5	
Childress, U.S.A.	109	H4	
Chile ■, S. Amer.	128	D2	
Chile Chico, Chile	128	C2	
Chile Rise, Pac. Oc.	93	L18	
Chilecito, Argentina	126	B2	
Chilete, Peru	124	B2	
Chilia, Braţul →, Romania	38	D12	
Chililabombwe, Zambia	83	E2	
Chilin = Jilin, China	51	C14	
Chilka L., India	61	K14	
Chillicothe, Ohio, U.S.A.	104	F4	
Chilliwack, Canada	100	D4	
Chilo, India	62	F5	
Chiloane, I., Mozam.	85	C5	
Chiloé □, Chile	128	B2	
Chiloé, I. de, Chile	128	B2	
Chilpancingo, Mexico	115	D5	
Chiltern Hills, U.K.	13	F7	
Chilton, U.S.A.	104	C1	
Chiluage, Angola	80	F4	
Chilubi, Zambia	83	E2	
Chilubula, Zambia	83	E3	
Chilumba, Malawi	83	E3	
Chilwa, L., Malawi	83	F4	
Chimaltitán, Mexico	114	C4	
Chimán, Panama	116	E4	
Chimay, Belgium	17	H4	
Chimbay, Uzbekistan	44	E6	
Chimborazo, Ecuador	120	D2	
Chimborazo □, Ecuador	120	D2	
Chimbote, Peru	124	B2	
Chimkent, Kazakhstan	44	E7	
Chimoio, Mozam.	83	F3	
Chimpembe, Zambia	83	D2	
Chin □, Burma	61	J18	
Chin Ling Shan = Qinling Shandi, China	50	H5	
China, Mexico	115	B5	
China ■, Asia	50	E3	
China Lake, U.S.A.	113	K9	
Chinacota, Colombia	120	B3	
Chinan = Jinan, China	50	F9	
Chinandega, Nic.	116	D2	
Chinati Peak, U.S.A.	109	K2	
Chincha Alta, Peru	124	C2	
Chinchilla, Australia	91	D5	
Chinchilla de Monte Aragón, Spain	29	G3	
Chinchón, Spain	28	E1	
Chinchorro, Banco, Mexico	115	D7	
Chinchou = Jinzhou, China	51	D11	
Chincoteague, U.S.A.	104	G8	
Chinde, Mozam.	83	F4	
Chindo, S. Korea	51	G14	
Chindwin →, Burma	61	J19	
Chineni, India	63	C6	
Chinga, Mozam.	83	F4	
Chingola, Zambia	83	E2	
Chingole, Malawi	83	E3	
Ch'ingtao = Qingdao, China	51	F11	
Chinguetti, Mauritania	74	D2	
Chingune, Mozam.	85	C5	
Chinhae, S. Korea	51	G15	
Chinhanguanine, Mozam.	85	D5	
Chinhoyi, Zimbabwe	83	F3	
Chiniot, Pakistan	62	D5	
Chínipas, Mexico	114	B3	
Chinju, S. Korea	51	G15	
Chinle, U.S.A.	111	H9	
Chinnampo, N. Korea	51	E13	
Chino, Japan	49	G9	
Chino, U.S.A.	113	L9	
Chino Valley, U.S.A.	111	J7	
Chinon, France	24	E7	
Chinook, Canada	101	C6	
Chinook, U.S.A.	110	B9	
Chinsali, Zambia	83	E3	
Chióggia, Italy	33	C9	
Chipata, Zambia	83	E3	
Chipewyan L., Canada	101	B9	
Chipinge, Zimbabwe	83	G3	
Chipiona, Spain	31	J4	
Chipley, U.S.A.	105	K3	
Chipman, Canada	99	C6	
Chipoka, Malawi	83	E3	
Chippenham, U.K.	13	F5	
Chippewa →, U.S.A.	108	C8	
Chippewa Falls, U.S.A.	108	C9	
Chiquián, Peru	124	C2	
Chiquimula, Guatemala	116	D2	
Chiquinquira, Colombia	120	B3	
Chiquitos, Llanos de, Bolivia	125	D5	
Chir →, Russia	43	B10	
Chirala, India	60	M12	
Chiramba, Mozam.	83	F3	
Chirawa, India	62	E6	
Chirchik, Uzbekistan	44	E7	
Chirgua →, Venezuela	120	B4	
Chiricahua Peak, U.S.A.	111	L9	
Chiriquí, G. de, Panama	116	E3	
Chiriquí, L. de, Panama	116	E3	
Chirivira Falls, Zimbabwe	83	G3	
Chirmiri, India	61	H13	
Chiromo, Malawi	81	H7	
Chirpan, Bulgaria	38	G8	
Chirripó Grande, Cerro, Costa Rica	116	E3	
Chisamba, Zambia	83	E2	
Chisapani Garhi, Nepal	61	F14	
Chisholm, Canada	100	C6	
Chishtian Mandi, Pakistan	62	E5	
Chishui, China	52	C5	
Chishui He →, China	52	C5	
Chisimba Falls, Zambia	83	E3	
Chişinău = Kishinev, Moldavia	42	C3	
Chisone →, Italy	32	D4	
Chisos Mts., U.S.A.	109	L3	
Chistopol, Russia	41	D17	
Chita, Colombia	120	B3	
Chita, Russia	45	D12	
Chitado, Angola	81	H2	
Chitembo, Angola	81	G3	
Chitipa, Malawi	83	D3	
Chitose, Japan	48	C10	
Chitral, Pakistan	60	B7	
Chitré, Panama	116	E3	
Chittagong, Bangla.	61	H17	
Chittagong □, Bangla.	61	G17	
Chittaurgarh, India	62	G6	
Chittoor, India	60	N11	
Chitungwiza, Zimbabwe	83	F3	
Chiusa, Italy	33	B8	
Chiusi, Italy	33	E8	
Chiva, Spain	29	F4	
Chivacoa, Venezuela	120	A4	
Chivasso, Italy	32	C4	
Chivay, Peru	124	D3	
Chivhu, Zimbabwe	83	F3	
Chivilcoy, Argentina	126	C4	
Chiwanda, Tanzania	83	E3	
Chixi, China	53	G9	
Chizera, Zambia	83	E1	
Chkalov = Orenburg, Russia	44	D6	
Chkolovsk, Russia	41	C13	
Chloride, U.S.A.	113	K12	
Cho Bo, Vietnam	58	B5	
Cho-do, N. Korea	51	E13	
Cho Phuoc Hai, Vietnam	59	G6	
Choba, Kenya	82	B4	
Chobe National Park, Botswana	84	B3	
Chochiwŏn, S. Korea	51	F14	
Chociwel, Poland	20	B5	
Chocó □, Colombia	120	B2	
Chocontá, Colombia	120	B3	
Choctawhatchee B., U.S.A.	103	D9	
Chodecz, Poland	20	C9	
Chodziez, Poland	20	C6	
Choele Choel, Argentina	128	A3	
Choisy-le-Roi, France	25	D9	
Choix, Mexico	114	B3	
Chojnice, Poland	20	B7	
Chojnów, Poland	20	D5	
Chōkai-San, Japan	48	E10	
Choke, Ethiopia	77	E4	
Chokurdakh, Russia	45	B15	
Cholame, U.S.A.	112	K6	
Cholet, France	24	E6	
Choluteca, Honduras	116	D2	
Choluteca →, Honduras	116	D2	
Chom Bung, Thailand	58	F2	
Chom Thong, Thailand	58	C2	
Choma, Zambia	83	F2	
Chomen Swamp, Ethiopia	77	F4	
Chomun, India	62	F6	
Chomutov, Czech.	20	E3	
Chon Buri, Thailand	58	F3	
Chon Thanh, Vietnam	59	G6	
Chonan, S. Korea	51	F14	
Chone, Ecuador	120	D2	
Chong Kai, Cambodia	58	F4	
Chong Mek, Thailand	58	E5	
Chong'an, China	53	D12	
Chongde, China	53	B13	
Chŏngdo, S. Korea	51	G15	
Chŏngha, S. Korea	51	F15	
Chongjin, N. Korea	51	D15	
Chŏngju, N. Korea	51	E13	
Chŏngju, S. Korea	51	F14	
Chongli, China	50	D8	
Chongming, China	53	B13	
Chongming Dao, China	53	B13	
Chongoyape, Peru	124	B2	
Chongqing, Sichuan, China	52	C5	
Chongqing, Sichuan, China	52	B4	
Chongren, China	53	D11	
Chŏngup, S. Korea	51	G14	
Chongzuo, China	52	F6	
Chŏnju, S. Korea	51	G14	
Chonos, Arch. de los, Chile	128	C2	
Chopim →, Brazil	127	B5	
Chorbat La, India	63	B7	
Chorley, U.K.	12	D5	
Chornobyl = Chernobyl, Ukraine	40	F7	
Cholorque, Cerro, Bolivia	126	A2	
Chorregon, Australia	90	C3	
Chortkov, Ukraine	40	G4	
Chŏrwŏn, S. Korea	51	E14	
Chorzów, Poland	20	E8	
Chos-Malal, Argentina	126	D1	
Chosan, N. Korea	51	D13	
Choszczno, Poland	20	B5	
Chota, Peru	124	B2	
Choteau, U.S.A.	110	C7	
Chotila, India	62	H4	
Chowchilla, U.S.A.	111	H3	
Choybalsan, Mongolia	54	B6	
Christchurch, N.Z.	87	K4	
Christchurch, U.K.	13	G6	
Christian I., Canada	106	B4	
Christiana, S. Africa	84	D4	
Christiansfeld, Denmark	11	J3	
Christiansted, Virgin Is.	117	C7	
Christie B., Canada	101	A6	
Christina →, Canada	101	B6	
Christmas Cr. →, Australia	88	C4	
Christmas Creek, Australia	88	C4	
Christmas I. = Kiritimati, Kiribati	93	G12	
Christmas I., Ind. Oc.	92	J2	
Christopher L., Australia	89	D4	
Chrudim, Czech.	20	F5	
Chrzanów, Poland	20	E9	
Chtimba, Malawi	83	E3	

Chu, *Kazakhstan* 44 E8
Chu →, *Vietnam* 58 C5
Chu Chua, *Canada* 100 C4
Chu Lai, *Vietnam* 58 E7
Chu Xian, *China* 53 A12
Ch'uanchou = Quanzhou,
  China 53 E12
Chuankou, *China* 50 G6
Chūbu □, *Japan* 49 F8
Chubut □, *Argentina* 128 B3
Chubut →, *Argentina* ... 128 B3
Chuchi L., *Canada* 100 B4
Chudovo, *Russia* 40 B7
Chudskoye, Oz., *Estonia* . 40 B5
Chūgoku □, *Japan* 49 G6
Chūgoku-Sanchi, *Japan* .. 49 G6
Chuguyev, *Ukraine* 42 B7
Chugwater, *U.S.A.* 108 E2
Chukhloma, *Russia* 41 B13
Chukotskiy Khrebet, *Russia* 45 C18
Chukotskoye More, *Russia* 45 C19
Chula Vista, *U.S.A.* 113 N9
Chulman, *Russia* 45 D13
Chulucanas, *Peru* 124 B1
Chulumani, *Bolivia* 124 D4
Chulym →, *Russia* 44 D9
Chum Phae, *Thailand* 58 D4
Chum Saeng, *Thailand* ... 58 E3
Chuma, *Bolivia* 124 D4
Chumar, *India* 63 C8
Chumbicha, *Argentina* ... 126 B2
Chumerna, *Bulgaria* 38 G8
Chumikan, *Russia* 45 D14
Chumphon, *Thailand* 59 G2
Chumpi, *Peru* 124 D3
Chumuare, *Mozam.* 83 E3
Chumunjin, *S. Korea* 51 F15
Chuna →, *Russia* 45 D10
Chun'an, *China* 53 C12
Chunchŏn, *S. Korea* 51 F14
Chunchura, *India* 63 H13
Chunga, *Zambia* 83 F2
Chunggang-ŭp, *N. Korea* . 51 D14
Chunghwa, *N. Korea* 51 E13
Chungju, *S. Korea* 51 F14
Chungking = Chongqing,
  China 52 C6
Chungmu, *S. Korea* 51 G15
Chungt'iaoshan =
  Zhongtiao Shan, *China* . 50 G6
Chunian, *Pakistan* 62 D6
Chunya, *Tanzania* 83 D3
Chunya □, *Tanzania* 82 D3
Chunyang, *China* 51 C15
Chuquibamba, *Peru* 124 D3
Chuquibambilla, *Peru* ... 124 C3
Chuquicamata, *Chile* 126 A2
Chuquisaca □, *Bolivia* .. 125 E5
Chur, *Switz.* 23 C9
Churachandpur, *India* ... 61 G18
Churchill, *Canada* 101 B10
Churchill →, *Man.,*
  Canada 101 B10
Churchill →, *Nfld.,*
  Canada 99 B7
Churchill, C., *Canada* ... 101 B10
Churchill Falls, *Canada* . 99 B7
Churchill L., *Canada* 101 B7
Churchill Pk., *Canada* ... 100 B3
Churfisten, *Switz.* 23 B8
Churu, *India* 62 E6
Churwalden, *Switz.* 23 C9
Chushal, *India* 63 C8
Chusovoy, *Russia* 44 D6
Chuuronjang, *N. Korea* .. 51 D15
Chuvash Republic □,
  Russia 41 D15
Chuwārtah, *Iraq* 64 C5
Chuxiong, *China* 52 E3
Ci Xian, *China* 50 F8
Ciacova, *Romania* 38 D4
Cianjur, *Indonesia* 57 G12
Cibadok, *Indonesia* 57 G12
Cibatu, *Indonesia* 57 G12
Cibola, *U.S.A.* 113 M12
Cicero, *U.S.A.* 104 E2
Cícero Dantas, *Brazil* ... 122 D4
Cidacos →, *Spain* 28 C3
Cide, *Turkey* 42 F5
Ciechanów, *Poland* 20 C10
Ciego de Avila, *Cuba* 116 B4
Ciénaga, *Colombia* 120 A3
Ciénaga de Oro, *Colombia* 120 B2
Cienfuegos, *Cuba* 116 B3
Cieplice Śląskie Zdrój,
  Poland 20 E5
Cierp, *France* 26 F4
Cíes, Is., *Spain* 30 C2
Cieszyn, *Poland* 20 F8
Cieza, *Spain* 29 G3
Çifteler, *Turkey* 66 D4
Cifuentes, *Spain* 28 E2
Cihanbeyli, *Turkey* 66 D5
Cihuatlán, *Mexico* 114 D4
Cijara, Pantano de, *Spain* . 31 F6
Cijulang, *Indonesia* 57 G13
Cikajang, *Indonesia* 57 G12
Cikampek, *Indonesia* 57 G12
Cilacap, *Indonesia* 57 G13
Çıldır, *Turkey* 43 F10
Çıldır Gölü, *Turkey* 67 C10
Cili, *China* 53 C8
Cilicia, *Turkey* 66 E6
Cilo Dağı, *Turkey* 67 E10
Cima, *U.S.A.* 113 K11

Cimahi, *Indonesia* 57 G12
Cimarron, *Kans., U.S.A.* . 109 G4
Cimarron, *N. Mex., U.S.A.* 109 G2
Cimarron →, *U.S.A.* 109 G6
Cimone, Mte., *Italy* 32 D7
Cîmpina, *Romania* 38 D8
Cîmpulung, *Argeş,*
  Romania 38 D8
Cîmpulung, *Suceava,*
  Romania 38 B8
Çınar, *Turkey* 67 E9
Cinca →, *Spain* 28 D5
Cincinnati, *U.S.A.* 104 F3
Cîndeşti, *Romania* 38 D9
Çine, *Turkey* 66 E3
Ciney, *Belgium* 17 H6
Cíngoli, *Italy* 33 E10
Cinigiano, *Italy* 33 F8
Cinto, Mte., *France* 27 F12
Ciorani, *Romania* 38 E9
Ćiovo, *Croatia* 33 E13
Cipó, *Brazil* 122 D4
Circeo, Monte, *Italy* ... 34 A6
Çirçir, *Turkey* 66 C7
Circle, *Alaska, U.S.A.* . 96 B5
Circle, *Mont., U.S.A.* .. 108 B2
Circleville, *Ohio, U.S.A.* 104 F4
Circleville, *Utah, U.S.A.* . 111 G7
Cirebon, *Indonesia* 57 G13
Cirencester, *U.K.* 13 F6
Cirey-sur-Vezouze, *France* 25 D13
Ciriè, *Italy* 32 C4
Cirium, *Cyprus* 37 E11
Cirò, *Italy* 35 C10
Ciron →, *France* 26 D3
Cisco, *U.S.A.* 109 J5
Ciskei □, *S. Africa* 85 E4
Cislău, *Romania* 38 D9
Cisneros, *Colombia* 120 B2
Cisterna di Latina, *Italy* . 34 A5
Cisternino, *Italy* 35 B10
Citaré →, *Brazil* 121 C7
Citeli-Ckaro, *Georgia* .. 43 F12
Citlaltépetl, *Mexico* ... 115 D5
Citrus Heights, *U.S.A.* . 112 G5
Citrusdal, *S. Africa* ... 84 E2
Città della Pieve, *Italy* . 33 F9
Città di Castello, *Italy* . 33 E9
Città Sant' Angelo, *Italy* . 33 F11
Cittadella, *Italy* 33 C8
Cittaducale, *Italy* 33 F9
Cittanova, *Italy* 35 D9
Ciucaş, *Romania* 38 D8
Ciudad Altamirano, *Mexico* 114 D4
Ciudad Bolívar, *Venezuela* 121 B5
Ciudad Camargo, *Mexico* . 114 B3
Ciudad Chetumal, *Mexico* . 115 D7
Ciudad de Valles, *Mexico* . 115 C5
Ciudad del Carmen, *Mexico* 115 D6
Ciudad Delicias = Delicias,
  Mexico 114 B3
Ciudad Guayana,
  Venezuela 121 B5
Ciudad Guerrero, *Mexico* . 114 B3
Ciudad Guzmán, *Mexico* .. 114 D4
Ciudad Juárez, *Mexico* .. 114 A3
Ciudad Madero, *Mexico* .. 115 C5
Ciudad Mante, *Mexico* ... 115 C5
Ciudad Obregón, *Mexico* . 114 B3
Ciudad Ojeda, *Venezuela* . 120 A3
Ciudad Real, *Spain* 31 G7
Ciudad Real □, *Spain* ... 31 G7
Ciudad Rodrigo, *Spain* .. 30 E4
Ciudad Trujillo = Santo
  Domingo, *Dom. Rep.* ... 117 C6
Ciudad Victoria, *Mexico* . 115 C5
Ciudadela, *Spain* 36 B10
Ciulniţa, *Romania* 38 E10
Civa Burnu, *Turkey* 66 C7
Cividale del Friuli, *Italy* 33 B10
Cívita Castellana, *Italy* . 33 F9
Civitanova Marche, *Italy* . 33 E10
Civitavécchia, *Italy* ... 33 F8
Civitella del Tronto, *Italy* 33 F10
Civray, *France* 26 B4
Çivril, *Turkey* 66 D3
Cixerri →, *Italy* 34 C1
Cizre, *Turkey* 67 E10
Clacton-on-Sea, *U.K.* ... 13 F9
Clain →, *France* 24 F7
Claire, L., *Canada* 100 B6
Clairemont, *U.S.A.* 109 J4
Clairton, *U.S.A.* 106 F5
Clairvaux-les-Lacs, *France* 27 B9
Clallam Bay, *U.S.A.* 112 B2
Clamecy, *France* 25 E10
Clanton, *U.S.A.* 105 J2
Clanwilliam, *S. Africa* . 84 E2
Clara, *Ireland* 15 C4
Clara →, *Australia* 90 B3
Claraville, *U.S.A.* 113 K8
Clare, *Australia* 91 E2
Clare □, *Ireland* 15 D3
Clare →, *Ireland* 15 C2
Clare I., *Ireland* 15 C1
Claremont, *Calif., U.S.A.* . 113 L9
Claremont, *N.H., U.S.A.* . 107 C12
Claremont Pt., *Australia* . 90 A3
Claremore, *U.S.A.* 109 G7
Claremorris, *Ireland* ... 15 C3
Clarence →, *Australia* .. 91 D5
Clarence →, *N.Z.* 87 K4
Clarence, I., *Chile* 128 D2
Clarence I., *Antarctica* . 5 C18

Clarence Str., *Australia* . 88 B5
Clarence Str., *U.S.A.* .. 100 B2
Clarence Town, *Bahamas* . 117 B5
Clarendon, *Ark., U.S.A.* . 109 H9
Clarendon, *Tex., U.S.A.* . 109 H4
Clarenville, *Canada* 99 C9
Claresholm, *Canada* 100 C6
Clarie Coast, *Antarctica* . 5 C9
Clarinda, *U.S.A.* 108 E7
Clarion, *Iowa, U.S.A.* .. 108 D8
Clarion, *Pa., U.S.A.* ... 106 E5
Clarion →, *U.S.A.* 106 E5
Clark, *U.S.A.* 108 C6
Clark, Pt., *Canada* 106 B3
Clark Fork, *U.S.A.* 110 B5
Clark Fork →, *U.S.A.* ... 110 B5
Clark Hill Res., *U.S.A.* . 105 J4
Clarkdale, *U.S.A.* 111 J7
Clarke City, *Canada* 99 B6
Clarke I., *Australia* ... 90 G4
Clarke L., *Canada* 101 C7
Clarke Ra., *Australia* .. 90 C4
Clark's Fork →, *U.S.A.* . 110 D9
Clark's Harbour, *Canada* . 99 D6
Clarks Summit, *U.S.A.* .. 107 E9
Clarksburg, *U.S.A.* 104 F5
Clarksdale, *U.S.A.* 109 H9
Clarkston, *U.S.A.* 110 C5
Clarksville, *Ark., U.S.A.* 109 H8
Clarksville, *Tenn., U.S.A.* 105 G2
Clarksville, *Tex., U.S.A.* 109 J7
Claro →, *Brazil* 123 E1
Clatskanie, *U.S.A.* 112 D3
Claude, *U.S.A.* 109 H4
Claveria, *Phil.* 55 B4
Clay, *U.S.A.* 112 G5
Clay Center, *U.S.A.* 108 F6
Claypool, *U.S.A.* 111 K8
Claysville, *U.S.A.* 106 F4
Clayton, *Idaho, U.S.A.* . 110 D6
Clayton, *N. Mex., U.S.A.* 109 G3
Cle Elum, *U.S.A.* 110 C3
Clear, C., *Ireland* 15 E2
Clear I., *Ireland* 15 E2
Clear L., *U.S.A.* 112 F4
Clear Lake, *S. Dak.,*
  U.S.A. 108 C6
Clear Lake, *Wash., U.S.A.* 110 B2
Clear Lake Reservoir,
  U.S.A. 110 F3
Clearfield, *Pa., U.S.A.* . 104 E6
Clearfield, *Utah, U.S.A.* . 110 F7
Clearlake Highlands,
  U.S.A. 112 G4
Clearmont, *U.S.A.* 110 D10
Clearwater, *Canada* 100 C4
Clearwater, *U.S.A.* 105 M4
Clearwater →, *Alta.,*
  Canada 100 C6
Clearwater →, *Alta.,*
  Canada 101 B6
Clearwater Cr. →, *Canada* 100 A3
Clearwater Mts., *U.S.A.* . 110 C6
Clearwater Prov. Park,
  Canada 101 C8
Cleburne, *U.S.A.* 109 J6
Cleethorpes, *U.K.* 12 D7
Cleeve Hill, *U.K.* 13 F6
Clelles, *France* 27 D9
Clemency, *Lux.* 17 J7
Clerke Reef, *Australia* . 88 C2
Clermont, *Australia* 90 C4
Clermont, *France* 25 C9
Clermont-en-Argonne,
  France 25 C12
Clermont-Ferrand, *France* 26 C7
Clermont-l'Hérault, *France* 26 E7
Clerval, *France* 25 E13
Clervaux, *Lux.* 17 H8
Cléry-St.-André, *France* . 25 E8
Cles, *Italy* 32 B8
Cleveland, *Australia* ... 91 D5
Cleveland, *Miss., U.S.A.* 109 J9
Cleveland, *Ohio, U.S.A.* . 106 E3
Cleveland, *Okla., U.S.A.* 109 G6
Cleveland, *Tenn., U.S.A.* 105 H3
Cleveland, *Tex., U.S.A.* . 109 K7
Cleveland □, *U.K.* 12 C9
Cleveland, C., *Australia* . 90 B4
Cleveland Heights, *U.S.A.* 106 E3
Clevelândia, *Brazil* 127 B5
Clevelândia do Norte,
  Brazil 121 C7
Clew B., *Ireland* 15 C2
Clewiston, *U.S.A.* 105 M5
Clifden, *Ireland* 15 C1
Clifden, *N.Z.* 87 M1
Cliffdell, *U.S.A.* 112 D5
Clifton, *Australia* 91 D5
Clifton, *Ariz., U.S.A.* . 111 K9
Clifton, *Tex., U.S.A.* .. 109 K6
Clifton Beach, *Australia* . 90 B4
Clifton Forge, *U.S.A.* .. 104 G6
Clifton Hills, *Australia* . 91 D2
Climax, *Canada* 101 D7
Clinch →, *U.S.A.* 105 H3
Clingmans Dome, *U.S.A.* . 105 H4
Clint, *U.S.A.* 111 L10
Clinton, *B.C., Canada* .. 100 C4
Clinton, *Ont., Canada* .. 98 D3
Clinton, *N.Z.* 87 M2
Clinton, *Ark., U.S.A.* .. 109 H8
Clinton, *Ill., U.S.A.* .. 108 E10
Clinton, *Ind., U.S.A.* .. 104 F2
Clinton, *Iowa, U.S.A.* .. 108 E9

Clinton, *Mass., U.S.A.* .. 107 D13
Clinton, *Mo., U.S.A.* ... 108 F8
Clinton, *N.C., U.S.A.* .. 105 H6
Clinton, *Okla., U.S.A.* . 109 H5
Clinton, *S.C., U.S.A.* .. 105 H5
Clinton, *Tenn., U.S.A.* . 105 G3
Clinton, *Wash., U.S.A.* . 112 C4
Clinton C., *Australia* .. 90 C5
Clinton Colden L., *Canada* 96 B9
Clintonville, *U.S.A.* ... 108 C10
Clipperton, I., *Pac. Oc.* . 93 F17
Clisson, *France* 24 E5
Clive L., *Canada* 100 A5
Cliza, *Bolivia* 125 D4
Cloates, Pt., *Australia* . 88 D1
Clocolan, *S. Africa* 85 D4
Clodomira, *Argentina* ... 126 B3
Clonakilty, *Ireland* 15 E3
Clonakilty B., *Ireland* . 15 E3
Cloncurry, *Australia* ... 90 C3
Cloncurry →, *Australia* . 90 B3
Clones, *Ireland* 15 B4
Clonmel, *Ireland* 15 D4
Cloppenburg, *Germany* ... 18 C4
Cloquet, *U.S.A.* 108 B8
Clorinda, *Argentina* 126 B4
Cloud Peak, *U.S.A.* 110 D10
Cloudcroft, *U.S.A.* 111 K11
Cloverdale, *U.S.A.* 112 G4
Clovis, *Calif., U.S.A.* . 111 H4
Clovis, *N. Mex., U.S.A.* . 109 H3
Cloyes-sur-le-Loir, *France* 24 E8
Cluj-Napoca, *Romania* ... 38 C6
Clunes, *Australia* 91 F3
Cluny, *France* 27 B8
Cluses, *France* 27 B10
Clusone, *Italy* 32 C6
Clutha →, *N.Z.* 87 M2
Clwyd □, *U.K.* 12 D4
Clwyd →, *U.K.* 12 D4
Clyde, *N.Z.* 87 L2
Clyde, *U.S.A.* 106 C8
Clyde →, *U.K.* 14 F4
Clyde, Firth of, *U.K.* .. 14 F4
Clyde River, *Canada* 97 A13
Clydebank, *U.K.* 14 F4
Clymer, *U.S.A.* 106 D5
Côa →, *Portugal* 30 D3
Coachella, *U.S.A.* 113 M10
Coachella Canal, *U.S.A.* . 113 N12
Coahoma, *U.S.A.* 109 J4
Coahuayana →, *Mexico* ... 114 D4
Coahuayutla, *Mexico* 114 D4
Coahuila □, *Mexico* 114 B4
Coal →, *Canada* 100 B3
Coalane, *Mozam.* 83 F4
Coalcomán, *Mexico* 114 D4
Coaldale, *Canada* 100 D6
Coalgate, *U.S.A.* 109 H6
Coalinga, *U.S.A.* 111 H3
Coalville, *U.K.* 12 E6
Coalville, *U.S.A.* 110 F8
Coaraci, *Brazil* 123 D4
Coari, *Brazil* 121 D5
Coari →, *Brazil* 121 D5
Coari, L. de, *Brazil* ... 121 D5
Coast □, *Kenya* 82 C4
Coast Mts., *Canada* 100 C3
Coast Ranges, *U.S.A.* ... 112 E4
Coatbridge, *U.K.* 14 F4
Coatepec, *Mexico* 115 D5
Coatepeque, *Guatemala* .. 116 D1
Coatesville, *U.S.A.* 104 F8
Coaticook, *Canada* 99 C5
Coats I., *Canada* 97 B11
Coats Land, *Antarctica* . 5 D1
Coatzacoalcos, *Mexico* .. 115 D6
Cobalt, *Canada* 98 C4
Cobán, *Guatemala* 116 C1
Cobar, *Australia* 91 E4
Cobh, *Ireland* 15 E3
Cobham, *Australia* 91 E3
Cobija, *Bolivia* 124 C4
Cobleskill, *U.S.A.* 107 D10
Coboconk, *Canada* 106 B6
Cobourg, *Canada* 98 D4
Cobourg Pen., *Australia* . 88 B5
Cobram, *Australia* 91 F4
Cobre, *U.S.A.* 110 F6
Cóbué, *Mozam.* 83 E3
Coburg, *Germany* 19 E6
Coca, *Spain* 30 D6
Coca →, *Ecuador* 120 D2
Cocachacra, *Peru* 124 D3
Cocal, *Brazil* 122 B3
Cocanada = Kakinada,
  India 61 L13
Cocentaina, *Spain* 29 G4
Cochabamba, *Bolivia* 125 D4
Coche, I., *Venezuela* ... 121 A5
Cochem, *Germany* 19 E3
Cochemane, *Mozam.* 83 F3
Cochin, *India* 60 Q10
Cochin China = Nam-
  Phan, *Vietnam* 59 G6
Cochise, *U.S.A.* 111 K9
Cochran, *U.S.A.* 105 J4
Cochrane, *Alta., Canada* . 100 C6
Cochrane, *Ont., Canada* . 98 C3
Cochrane →, *Canada* 101 B8
Cochrane, L., *Chile* 128 C2
Cockburn, *Australia* 91 E3
Cockburn, Canal, *Chile* . 128 D2
Cockburn I., *Canada* 98 C3
Cockburn Ra., *Australia* . 88 C4

Cocklebiddy Motel,
  Australia 89 F4
Coco →, *Cent. Amer.* 116 D3
Coco, Pta., *Colombia* ... 120 C2
Cocoa, *U.S.A.* 105 L5
Cocobeach, *Gabon* 80 D1
Côcos, *Brazil* 123 D3
Côcos →, *Brazil* 123 D3
Cocos, I. del, *Pac. Oc.* . 93 G19
Cocos Is., *Ind. Oc.* 92 J1
Cod, C., *U.S.A.* 103 B13
Codajás, *Brazil* 121 D5
Codera, C., *Venezuela* .. 120 A4
Coderre, *Canada* 101 C7
Codigoro, *Italy* 33 D9
Codó, *Brazil* 122 B3
Codogno, *Italy* 32 C6
Codpa, *Chile* 124 D4
Codróipo, *Italy* 33 C10
Cody, *U.S.A.* 110 D9
Coe Hill, *Canada* 98 D4
Coelemu, *Chile* 126 D1
Coelho Neto, *Brazil* 122 B3
Coen, *Australia* 90 A3
Coeroeni →, *Surinam* 121 C6
Coesfeld, *Germany* 18 D3
Cœur d'Alene, *U.S.A.* ... 110 C5
Cœur d'Alene L., *U.S.A.* . 110 C5
Coevorden, *Neths.* 16 C9
Cofete, *Canary Is.* 36 F5
Coffeyville, *U.S.A.* 109 G7
Coffin B., *Australia* ... 91 E2
Coffin Bay Peninsula,
  Australia 91 E2
Coffs Harbour, *Australia* . 91 E5
Cofrentes, *Spain* 29 F3
Cogealac, *Romania* 38 E11
Coghinas →, *Italy* 34 B1
Coghinas, L. di, *Italy* . 34 B2
Cognac, *France* 26 C3
Cogne, *Italy* 32 C4
Cogolludo, *Spain* 28 E1
Cohagen, *U.S.A.* 110 C10
Cohoes, *U.S.A.* 107 D11
Cohuna, *Australia* 91 F3
Coiba, I., *Panama* 116 E3
Coig →, *Argentina* 128 D3
Coihaique, *Chile* 128 C2
Coimbatore, *India* 60 P10
Coimbra, *Brazil* 125 D6
Coimbra, *Portugal* 30 E2
Coimbra □, *Portugal* 30 E2
Coín, *Spain* 31 J6
Coipasa, L. de, *Bolivia* . 124 D4
Coipasa, Salar de, *Bolivia* 124 D4
Cojata, *Peru* 124 D4
Cojedes □, *Venezuela* ... 120 B4
Cojedes →, *Venezuela* ... 120 B4
Cojimíes, *Ecuador* 120 C1
Cojocna, *Romania* 38 C6
Cojutepequé, *El Salv.* .. 116 D2
Cokeville, *U.S.A.* 110 E8
Colac, *Australia* 91 F3
Colares, *Portugal* 31 G1
Colatina, *Brazil* 123 E3
Colbeck, C., *Antarctica* . 5 D13
Colbinabbin, *Australia* . 91 F3
Colborne, *Canada* 106 B7
Colby, *U.S.A.* 108 F4
Colchagua □, *Chile* 126 C1
Colchester, *U.K.* 13 F8
Coldstream, *U.K.* 14 F6
Coldwater, *Canada* 106 B5
Coldwater, *U.S.A.* 109 G5
Colebrook, *Australia* ... 90 G4
Colebrook, *U.S.A.* 107 B13
Coleman, *Canada* 100 D6
Coleman, *U.S.A.* 109 K5
Coleman →, *Australia* ... 90 B3
Colenso, *S. Africa* 85 D4
Coleraine, *Australia* ... 91 F3
Coleraine, *U.K.* 15 A5
Coleraine □, *U.K.* 15 A5
Coleridge, L., *N.Z.* 87 K3
Colesberg, *S. Africa* ... 84 E4
Coleville, *U.S.A.* 112 G7
Colfax, *Calif., U.S.A.* . 112 F6
Colfax, *La., U.S.A.* 109 K8
Colfax, *Wash., U.S.A.* .. 110 C5
Colhué Huapí, L.,
  Argentina 128 C3
Cólico, *Italy* 32 B6
Coligny, *France* 27 B9
Coligny, *S. Africa* 85 D4
Colima, *Mexico* 114 D4
Colima □, *Mexico* 114 D4
Colima, Nevado de, *Mexico* 114 D4
Colina, *Chile* 126 C1
Colina do Norte,
  Guinea-Biss. 78 C2
Colinas, *Goiás, Brazil* . 123 D2
Colinas, *Maranhão, Brazil* 122 C3
Coll, *U.K.* 14 E2
Collaguasi, *Chile* 126 A2
Collarada, Peña, *Spain* . 28 C4
Collarenebri, *Australia* . 91 D4
Collbran, *U.S.A.* 111 G10
Colle di Val d'Elsa, *Italy* 33 E8
Colle Salvetti, *Italy* .. 32 E7
Colle Sannita, *Italy* ... 35 A7
Collécchio, *Italy* 32 D7
Colleen Bawn, *Zimbabwe* . 83 G2
College Park, *U.S.A.* ... 105 J3
Collette, *Canada* 99 C6
Collie, *Australia* 89 F2

Collier B., Australia 88 C3
Collier Ra., Australia 88 D2
Colline Metallifere, Italy .. 32 E7
Collingwood, Canada 98 D3
Collingwood, N.Z. 87 J4
Collins, Canada 98 B2
Collinsville, Australia 90 C4
Collipulli, Chile 126 D1
Collo, Algeria 75 A6
Collonges, France 27 B9
Collooney, Ireland 15 B3
Colmar, France 25 D14
Colmars, France 27 D10
Colmenar, Spain 31 J6
Colmenar de Oreja, Spain .. 28 E1
Colmenar Viejo, Spain 30 E7
Colne, U.K. 12 D5
Colo →, Australia 91 E5
Cologna Véneta, Italy 33 C8
Cologne = Köln, Germany .. 18 E2
Colom, I., Spain 36 B11
Coloma, U.S.A. 112 G6
Colomb-Béchar = Béchar,
  Algeria 75 B4
Colombey-les-Belles,
  France 25 D12
Colombey-les-Deux-Églises,
  France 25 D11
Colômbia, Brazil 123 F2
Colombia ■, S. Amer. .. 120 C3
Colombier, Switz. 22 C3
Colombo, Sri Lanka 60 R11
Colome, U.S.A. 108 D5
Colón, Argentina 126 C4
Colón, Cuba 116 B3
Colón, Panama 116 E4
Colón, Peru 124 A1
Colona, Australia 89 F5
Colonella, Italy 33 F10
Colonia, Uruguay 126 C4
Colonia de San Jordi, Spain 36 B9
Colonia Dora, Argentina .. 126 B3
Colonial Heights, U.S.A. .. 104 G7
Colonna, C. delle, Italy .. 35 C10
Colonsay, Canada 101 C7
Colonsay, U.K. 14 E2
Colorado □, U.S.A. 111 G10
Colorado →, Argentina .. 128 A4
Colorado →, N. Amer. .. 111 L6
Colorado →, U.S.A. 109 L7
Colorado City, U.S.A. .. 109 J4
Colorado Desert, U.S.A. .. 102 D3
Colorado Plateau, U.S.A. . 111 H8
Colorado River Aqueduct,
  U.S.A. 113 L12
Colorado Springs, U.S.A. . 108 F2
Colorno, Italy 32 D7
Colotlán, Mexico 114 C4
Colquechaca, Bolivia 125 D4
Colton, Calif., U.S.A. 113 L9
Colton, N.Y., U.S.A. 107 B10
Colton, Wash., U.S.A. .. 110 C5
Columbia, La., U.S.A. .. 109 J8
Columbia, Miss., U.S.A. . 109 K10
Columbia, Mo., U.S.A. .. 108 F8
Columbia, Pa., U.S.A. .. 107 F8
Columbia, S.C., U.S.A. .. 105 H5
Columbia, Tenn., U.S.A. . 105 H2
Columbia →, U.S.A. 110 C1
Columbia, C., Canada 4 A4
Columbia, District of □,
  U.S.A. 104 F7
Columbia, Mt., Canada .. 100 C5
Columbia Basin, U.S.A. .. 110 C4
Columbia Falls, U.S.A. .. 110 B6
Columbia Heights, U.S.A. . 108 C8
Columbiana, U.S.A. 106 F4
Columbretes, Is., Spain .. 28 E5
Columbus, Ga., U.S.A. .. 105 J3
Columbus, Ind., U.S.A. .. 104 F3
Columbus, Kans., U.S.A. . 109 G7
Columbus, Miss., U.S.A. . 105 J1
Columbus, Mont., U.S.A. . 110 D9
Columbus, N. Dak.,
  U.S.A. 108 A3
Columbus, N. Mex.,
  U.S.A. 111 L10
Columbus, Nebr., U.S.A. . 108 E6
Columbus, Ohio, U.S.A. .. 104 F4
Columbus, Tex., U.S.A. .. 109 L6
Columbus, Wis., U.S.A. .. 108 D10
Colunga, Spain 30 B5
Colusa, U.S.A. 112 F4
Colville, U.S.A. 110 B5
Colville →, U.S.A. 96 A4
Colville, C., N.Z. 87 G5
Colwyn Bay, U.K. 12 D4
Coma, Ethiopia 77 F4
Comácchio, Italy 33 D9
Comalcalco, Mexico 115 D6
Comallo, Argentina 128 B2
Comanche, Okla., U.S.A. . 109 H6
Comanche, Tex., U.S.A. .. 109 K5
Comandante Luis
  Piedrabuena, Argentina . 128 C3
Comăneşti, Romania 38 C9
Comarapa, Bolivia 125 D5
Comayagua, Honduras .. 116 D2
Combahee →, U.S.A. .. 105 J5
Combeaufontaine, France . 25 E12
Comber, Canada 106 D2
Comblain-au-Pont, Belgium 17 H7
Combles, France 25 B9
Combourg, France 24 D5
Combronde, France 26 C7

Comeragh Mts., Ireland .. 15 D4
Comet, Australia 90 C4
Comilla, Bangla. 61 H17
Comines, Belgium 17 G1
Comino, Malta 37 C1
Comino, C., Italy 34 B2
Cómiso, Italy 35 F7
Comitán, Mexico 115 D6
Commentry, France 26 B6
Commerce, Ga., U.S.A. .. 105 H4
Commerce, Tex., U.S.A. .. 109 J7
Commercy, France 25 D12
Commewijne □, Surinam . 121 B7
Committee B., Canada .. 97 B11
Commonwealth B.,
  Antarctica 5 C10
Commonwealth of
  Independent States ■,
  Eurasia 45 D11
Commoron Cr. →,
  Australia 91 D5
Communism Pk. =
  Kommunizma, Pik,
  Tajikistan 44 F8
Como, Italy 32 C6
Como, L. di, Italy 32 B6
Comodoro Rivadavia,
  Argentina 128 C3
Comorin, C., India 60 Q10
Comoro Is. = Comoros ■,
  Ind. Oc. 71 H8
Comoros ■, Ind. Oc. .. 71 H8
Comox, Canada 100 D4
Compiègne, France 25 C9
Comporta, Portugal 31 G2
Compostela, Mexico 114 C4
Comprida, I., Brazil 127 A6
Compton, U.S.A. 113 M8
Compton Downs, Australia 91 E4
Con Cuong, Vietnam 58 C5
Con Son, Is., Vietnam .. 59 H6
Cona Niyeu, Argentina .. 128 B3
Conakry, Guinea 78 D2
Conara Junction, Australia 90 G4
Conceição, Brazil 122 C4
Conceição, Mozam. 83 F4
Conceição da Barra, Brazil 123 E4
Conceição do Araguaia,
  Brazil 122 C2
Conceição do Canindé,
  Brazil 122 C3
Concepción, Argentina .. 126 B2
Concepción, Bolivia 125 D5
Concepción, Chile 126 D1
Concepción, Mexico 115 D6
Concepción, Paraguay .. 126 A4
Concepción, Peru 124 C2
Concepción □, Chile 126 D1
Concepción →, Mexico .. 114 A2
Concepción, Est. de, Chile 128 D2
Concepción, L., Bolivia .. 125 D5
Concepción, Punta, Mexico 114 B2
Concepción del Oro,
  Mexico 114 C4
Concepción del Uruguay,
  Argentina 126 C4
Conception, Pt., U.S.A. .. 113 L6
Conception B., Namibia .. 84 C1
Conception I., Bahamas .. 117 B4
Concession, Zimbabwe .. 83 F3
Conchas Dam, U.S.A. .. 109 H2
Conche, Canada 99 B8
Concho, U.S.A. 111 J9
Concho →, U.S.A. 109 K5
Conchos →, Chihuahua,
  Mexico 114 B4
Conchos →, Tamaulipas,
  Mexico 115 B5
Concord, Calif., U.S.A. .. 112 H4
Concord, N.C., U.S.A. .. 105 H5
Concord, N.H., U.S.A. .. 107 C13
Concordia, Argentina .. 126 C4
Concórdia, Brazil 120 D4
Concordia, Mexico 114 C3
Concordia, U.S.A. 108 F6
Concots, France 26 D5
Concrete, U.S.A. 110 B3
Condamine, Australia .. 91 D5
Condat, France 26 C6
Conde, Brazil 123 D4
Conde, U.S.A. 108 C5
Condé-sur-l'Escaut, France 25 B10
Condé-sur-Noireau, France 24 D6
Condeúba, Brazil 123 D3
Condobolin, Australia .. 91 E4
Condom, France 26 E4
Condon, U.S.A. 110 D3
Condove, Italy 32 C4
Conegliano, Italy 33 C9
Conejera, I., Spain 36 B9
Conejos, Mexico 114 B4
Conflans-en-Jarnisy, France 25 C12
Confolens, France 26 B4
Confuso →, Paraguay .. 126 B4
Congjiang, China 52 E7
Congleton, U.K. 12 D5
Congo = Zaïre →, Africa 80 F2
Congo, Brazil 122 C4
Congo (Kinshasa) =
  Zaïre ■, Africa 80 E4
Congo ■, Africa 80 E3
Congo Basin, Africa 70 G6
Congonhas, Brazil 123 F3
Congress, U.S.A. 111 J7

Conil, Spain 31 J4
Coniston, Canada 98 C3
Conjeeveram =
  Kanchipuram, India 60 N11
Conjuboy, Australia 90 B3
Conklin, Canada 101 B6
Conlea, Australia 91 E3
Conn, L., Ireland 15 B2
Connacht, Ireland 15 C3
Conneaut, U.S.A. 106 E4
Connecticut □, U.S.A. .. 107 E12
Connecticut →, U.S.A. .. 107 E12
Connell, U.S.A. 110 C4
Connellsville, U.S.A. 106 F5
Connemara, Ireland 15 C2
Connemaugh →, U.S.A. .. 106 F5
Connerré, France 24 D7
Connersville, U.S.A. 104 F3
Connors Ra., Australia .. 90 C4
Conoble, Australia 91 E3
Cononaco →, Ecuador .. 120 D2
Cononbridge, U.K. 14 D4
Conquest, Canada 101 C7
Conrad, U.S.A. 110 B8
Conran, C., Australia .. 91 F4
Conroe, U.S.A. 109 K7
Conselheiro Lafaiete,
  Brazil 123 F3
Conselheiro Pena, Brazil . 123 E3
Consort, Canada 101 C6
Constance = Konstanz,
  Germany 19 H5
Constance, L. = Bodensee,
  Europe 23 A8
Constanţa, Romania 38 E11
Constantina, Spain 31 H5
Constantine, Algeria 75 A6
Constitución, Chile 126 D1
Constitución, Uruguay .. 126 C4
Consuegra, Spain 31 F7
Consul, Canada 101 D7
Contact, U.S.A. 110 F6
Contai, India 63 J12
Contamana, Peru 124 B3
Contarina, Italy 33 C9
Contas →, Brazil 123 D4
Contes, France 27 E11
Contoocook →, U.S.A. .. 107 C13
Contra Costa, Mozam. .. 85 D5
Contres, France 24 E8
Contrexéville, France .. 25 D12
Contumaza, Peru 124 B2
Convención, Colombia .. 120 B3
Conversano, Italy 35 B10
Conway = Conwy, U.K. .. 12 D4
Conway = Conwy →,
  U.K. 12 D4
Conway, Ark., U.S.A. .. 109 H8
Conway, N.H., U.S.A. ... 107 C13
Conway, S.C., U.S.A. .. 105 J6
Conway, L., Australia .. 91 D2
Conwy, U.K. 12 D4
Conwy →, U.K. 12 D4
Coober Pedy, Australia ... 91 D1
Cooch Behar = Koch
  Bihar, India 61 F16
Coodardy, Australia 89 E2
Cook, Australia 89 F5
Cook, U.S.A. 108 B8
Cook, B., Chile 128 E2
Cook, Mt., N.Z. 87 K3
Cook Inlet, U.S.A. 96 C4
Cook Is., Pac. Oc. 93 J11
Cook Strait, N.Z. 87 J5
Cookeville, U.S.A. 105 G3
Cookhouse, S. Africa .. 84 E4
Cookshire, Canada 107 A13
Cookstown, U.K. 15 B5
Cookstown □, U.K. 15 B5
Cooksville, Canada 106 C5
Cooktown, Australia 90 B4
Coolabah, Australia 91 E4
Cooladdi, Australia 91 D4
Coolah, Australia 91 E4
Coolamon, Australia 91 E4
Coolangatta, Australia .. 91 D5
Coolgardie, Australia .. 89 F3
Coolibah, Australia 88 C5
Coolidge, U.S.A. 111 K8
Coolidge Dam, U.S.A. .. 111 K8
Cooma, Australia 91 F4
Coonabarabran, Australia . 91 E4
Coonamble, Australia .. 91 E4
Coonana, Australia 89 F3
Coondapoor, India 60 N9
Coongie, Australia 91 D3
Coongoola, Australia .. 91 D4
Cooninie, L., Australia .. 91 D2
Cooper, U.S.A. 109 J7
Cooper →, U.S.A. 105 J6
Cooper Cr. →, Australia . 91 D2
Cooperstown, N. Dak.,
  U.S.A. 108 B5
Cooperstown, N.Y., U.S.A. 107 D10
Coorabie, Australia 91 F5
Coorabulka, Australia .. 90 C3
Coorow, Australia 89 E2
Cooroy, Australia 91 D5
Coos Bay, U.S.A. 110 E1
Cootamundra, Australia . 91 E4
Cootehill, Ireland 15 B4
Cooyar, Australia 91 D5
Cooyeana, Australia 90 C2
Copahue Paso, Argentina . 126 D1

Copainalá, Mexico 115 D6
Copán, Honduras 116 D2
Copatana, Brazil 120 D4
Cope, U.S.A. 108 F3
Cope, C., Spain 29 H3
Copenhagen = København,
  Denmark 11 J6
Copertino, Italy 35 B11
Copiapó, Chile 126 B1
Copiapó →, Chile 126 B1
Copley, Australia 91 E2
Copp L., Canada 100 A6
Copparo, Italy 33 D8
Coppename →, Surinam . 121 B6
Copper Center, U.S.A. .. 96 B5
Copper Cliff, Canada .. 98 C3
Copper Harbor, U.S.A. .. 104 B2
Copper Queen, Zimbabwe 83 F2
Copperbelt □, Zambia .. 83 E2
Coppermine, Canada .. 96 B8
Coppermine →, Canada . 96 B8
Copperopolis, U.S.A. .. 112 H6
Coquet →, U.K. 12 B6
Coquilhatville =
  Mbandaka, Zaïre 80 D3
Coquille, U.S.A. 110 E1
Coquimbo, Chile 126 B1
Coquimbo □, Chile 126 C1
Corabia, Romania 38 F7
Coração de Jesus, Brazil . 123 E3
Coracora, Peru 124 D3
Coradi, Is., Italy 35 B10
Coral Gables, U.S.A. .. 105 N5
Coral Harbour, Canada . 97 B11
Coral Sea, Pac. Oc. 92 J7
Corato, Italy 35 A9
Corbeil-Essonnes, France . 25 D9
Corbie, France 25 C9
Corbières, France 26 F6
Corbigny, France 25 E10
Corbin, U.S.A. 104 G3
Corbion, Belgium 17 J6
Corbones →, Spain 31 H5
Corby, U.K. 13 E7
Corby Glen, U.K. 13 E7
Corcoles →, Spain 29 F1
Corcoran, U.S.A. 111 H4
Corcubión, Spain 30 C1
Corcyra = Kérkira, Greece 37 A3
Cordele, U.S.A. 105 K4
Cordell, U.S.A. 109 H5
Cordenons, Italy 33 C9
Cordes, France 26 D5
Cordisburgo, Brazil 123 E3
Córdoba, Argentina 126 C3
Córdoba, Mexico 115 D5
Córdoba, Spain 31 H6
Córdoba □, Argentina .. 126 C3
Córdoba □, Colombia .. 120 B2
Córdoba, Sierra de,
  Argentina 126 C3
Cordon, Phil. 55 C4
Cordova, Ala., U.S.A. .. 105 J2
Cordova, Alaska, U.S.A. .. 96 B5
Corella, Spain 28 C3
Corella →, Australia .. 90 B3
Coremas, Brazil 122 C4
Corentyne →, Guyana .. 121 B6
Corfield, Australia 90 C3
Corfu = Kérkira, Greece 37 A3
Corfu, Str of, Greece .. 37 A4
Corgo, Spain 30 C3
Corguinho, Brazil 125 D7
Cori, Italy 34 A5
Coria, Spain 30 F4
Coria del Río, Spain 31 H4
Corigliano Cálabro, Italy . 35 C9
Coringa Is., Australia .. 90 B4
Corinna, Australia 90 G4
Corinth = Kórinthos,
  Greece 39 M5
Corinth, Miss., U.S.A. .. 105 H1
Corinth, N.Y., U.S.A. .. 107 C11
Corinth, G. of =
  Korinthiakós Kólpos,
  Greece 39 L5
Corinth Canal, Greece .. 39 M6
Corinto, Brazil 123 E3
Corinto, Nic. 116 D2
Cork, Ireland 15 E3
Cork □, Ireland 15 E3
Cork Harbour, Ireland .. 15 E3
Corlay, France 24 D3
Corleone, Italy 34 E6
Corleto Perticara, Italy .. 35 B9
Çorlu, Turkey 39 H10
Cormack L., Canada 100 A4
Cormóns, Italy 33 C10
Cormorant, Canada 101 C8
Cormorant L., Canada .. 101 C8
Corn Is. = Maíz, Is. del,
  Nic. 116 D3
Cornélio Procópio, Brazil . 127 A5
Cornell, U.S.A. 108 C9
Corner Brook, Canada .. 99 C8
Corníglio, Italy 32 D7
Corning, Ark., U.S.A. .. 109 G9
Corning, Calif., U.S.A. .. 110 G2
Corning, Iowa, U.S.A. .. 108 E7
Corning, N.Y., U.S.A. .. 106 D7
Corno, Monte, Italy 33 F10
Cornwall, Canada 98 C5
Cornwall □, U.K. 13 G3
Corny Pt., Australia 91 E2

Coro, Venezuela 120 A4
Coroaci, Brazil 123 E3
Coroatá, Brazil 122 B3
Corocoro, Bolivia 124 D4
Corocoro, I., Venezuela . 121 B5
Coroico, Bolivia 124 D4
Coromandel, Brazil 123 E2
Coromandel, N.Z. 87 G5
Coromandel Coast, India . 60 N12
Corona, Australia 91 E3
Corona, Calif., U.S.A. .. 113 M9
Corona, N. Mex., U.S.A. . 111 J11
Coronado, U.S.A. 113 N9
Coronado, B. de,
  Costa Rica 116 E3
Coronados, G. de los, Chile 128 B2
Coronados, Is. los, U.S.A. 113 N9
Coronation, Canada 100 C6
Coronation Gulf, Canada . 96 B8
Coronation I., Antarctica . 5 C18
Coronation I., U.S.A. .. 100 B2
Coronation Is., Australia . 88 B3
Coronda, Argentina 126 C3
Coronel, Chile 126 D1
Coronel Bogado, Paraguay 126 B4
Coronel Dorrego,
  Argentina 126 D3
Coronel Fabriciano, Brazil 123 E3
Coronel Murta, Brazil .. 123 E3
Coronel Oviedo, Paraguay 126 B4
Coronel Ponce, Brazil .. 125 D6
Coronel Pringles, Argentina 126 D3
Coronel Suárez, Argentina 126 D3
Coronel Vidal, Argentina . 126 D4
Corongo, Peru 124 B2
Coronie □, Surinam 121 B6
Coropuna, Nevado, Peru . 124 D3
Çorovoda, Albania 39 J3
Corowa, Australia 91 F4
Corozal, Belize 115 D7
Corozal, Colombia 120 B2
Corps, France 27 D9
Corpus, Argentina 127 B4
Corpus Christi, U.S.A. .. 109 M6
Corpus Christi, L., U.S.A. 109 L6
Corque, Bolivia 124 D4
Corral, Chile 128 A2
Corral de Almaguer, Spain 28 F1
Corralejo, Canary Is. .. 36 F6
Corréggio, Italy 32 D7
Corrente, Brazil 122 D2
Corrente →, Brazil 123 D3
Correntes →, Brazil 125 D6
Correntes, C. das, Mozam. 85 C6
Correntina, Brazil 123 D3
Corrèze □, France 26 C5
Corrèze →, France 26 C5
Corrib, L., Ireland 15 C2
Corrientes, Argentina .. 126 B4
Corrientes □, Argentina . 126 B4
Corrientes →, Argentina . 126 C4
Corrientes →, Peru 120 D3
Corrientes, C., Colombia . 120 B2
Corrientes, C., Cuba .. 116 B3
Corrientes, C., Mexico .. 114 C3
Corrigan, U.S.A. 109 K7
Corrigin, Australia 89 F2
Corry, U.S.A. 106 E5
Corse, France 27 F13
Corse, C., France 27 E13
Corse-du-Sud □, France . 27 G13
Corsica = Corse, France . 27 F13
Corsicana, U.S.A. 109 J6
Corte, France 27 F13
Corte do Pinto, Portugal . 31 H3
Cortegana, Spain 31 H4
Cortez, U.S.A. 111 H9
Cortina d'Ampezzo, Italy . 33 B9
Cortland, U.S.A. 107 D8
Cortona, Italy 33 E8
Coruche, Portugal 31 G2
Çoruh →, Turkey 67 C9
Çorum, Turkey 66 C6
Çorum □, Turkey 66 C6
Corumbá, Brazil 125 D6
Corumbá →, Brazil 123 E2
Corumbá de Goiás, Brazil 123 E2
Corumbaíba, Brazil 123 E2
Corunna = La Coruña,
  Spain 30 B2
Corvallis, U.S.A. 110 D2
Corvette, L. de la, Canada 98 B5
Corydon, U.S.A. 108 E8
Cosalá, Mexico 114 C3
Cosamaloapan, Mexico .. 115 D5
Cosenza, Italy 35 C9
Coshocton, U.S.A. 106 F3
Cosmo Newberry, Australia 89 E3
Cosne-sur-Loire, France . 25 E9
Coso Junction, U.S.A. .. 113 J9
Coso Pk., U.S.A. 113 J9
Cospeito, Spain 30 B3
Cosquín, Argentina 126 C3
Cossato, Italy 32 C5
Cossé-le-Vivien, France . 24 E6
Cosson →, France 24 E8
Costa Blanca, Spain 29 G4
Costa Brava, Spain 28 D8
Costa del Sol, Spain 31 J6
Costa Dorada, Spain 28 E6
Costa Mesa, U.S.A. 113 M9
Costa Rica ■, Cent. Amer. 116 D3
Costa Smeralda, Italy .. 34 A2
Costigliole d'Asti, Italy . 32 D5
Costilla, U.S.A. 111 H11

Cosumnes →, *U.S.A.* 112 G5
Coswig, *Germany* 18 D8
Cotabato, *Phil.* 55 H6
Cotacajes →, *Bolivia* ... 124 D4
Cotagaita, *Bolivia* 126 A2
Cotahuasi, *Peru* 124 D3
Côte d'Azur, *France* 27 E11
Côte-d'Ivoire ■ = Ivory
  Coast ■, *Africa* 78 D3
Côte d'Or, *France* 25 E11
Côte-d'Or □, *France* 25 E11
Coteau des Prairies, *U.S.A.* 108 C6
Coteau du Missouri, *U.S.A.* 108 B4
Coteau Landing, *Canada* . 107 A10
Cotegipe, *Brazil* 123 D3
Cotentin, *France* 24 C5
Côtes-d'Armor □, *France* . 24 D4
Côtes de Meuse, *France* .. 25 C12
Côtes-du-Nord = Côtes-
  d'Armor □, *France* 24 D4
Cotiella, *Spain* 28 C5
Cotillo, *Canary Is.* 36 F5
Cotina →, *Bos.-H.* 21 M8
Cotoca, *Bolivia* 125 D5
Cotonou, *Benin* 79 D5
Cotopaxi, *Ecuador* 120 D2
Cotopaxi □, *Ecuador* 120 D2
Cotronei, *Italy* 35 C9
Cotswold Hills, *U.K.* 13 F5
Cottage Grove, *U.S.A.* ... 110 E2
Cottbus, *Germany* 18 D10
Cottingham, *U.K.* 12 C5
Cottonwood, *U.S.A.* 111 J7
Cotulla, *U.S.A.* 109 L5
Coubre, Pte. de la, *France* 26 C2
Couches, *France* 25 F11
Couço, *Portugal* 31 G2
Coudersport, *U.S.A.* 106 E6
Couedic, C. du, *Australia* . 91 F2
Couëron, *France* 24 E5
Couesnon →, *France* 24 D5
Couhé, *France* 26 B4
Coulanges-sur-Yonne,
  France 25 E10
Coulee City, *U.S.A.* 110 C4
Coulman I., *Antarctica* .. 5 D11
Coulommiers, *France* 25 D10
Coulonge →, *Canada* 98 C4
Coulonges-sur-l'Autize,
  France 26 B3
Coulterville, *U.S.A.* 112 H6
Council, Alaska, *U.S.A.* .. 96 B3
Council, Idaho, *U.S.A.* ... 110 D5
Council Bluffs, *U.S.A.* .. 108 E7
Council Grove, *U.S.A.* ... 108 F6
Coupeville, *U.S.A.* 112 B4
Courantyne →, *S. Amer.* 121 B6
Courcelles, *Belgium* 17 H4
Courçon, *France* 26 B3
Couronne, C., *France* 27 E9
Cours-la-Ville, *France* ... 27 B8
Coursan, *France* 26 E7
Courseulles-sur-Mer,
  France 24 C6
Court-St.-Etienne, *Belgium* 17 G5
Courtenay, *Canada* 100 D3
Courtland, *U.S.A.* 112 G5
Courtrai = Kortrijk,
  Belgium 17 G2
Courtright, *Canada* 106 D2
Courville-sur-Eure, *France* 24 D8
Coushatta, *U.S.A.* 109 J8
Coutances, *France* 24 C5
Couterne, *France* 24 D6
Coutras, *France* 26 C3
Coutts, *Canada* 100 D6
Couvet, *Switz.* 22 C3
Couvin, *Belgium* 17 H4
Covarrubias, *Spain* 28 C1
Coveñas, *Colombia* 120 B2
Coventry, *U.K.* 13 E6
Coventry L., *Canada* 101 A7
Covilhã, *Portugal* 30 E3
Covington, Ga., *U.S.A.* .. 105 J4
Covington, Ky., *U.S.A.* .. 104 F3
Covington, Okla., *U.S.A.* 109 G6
Covington, Tenn., *U.S.A.* 109 H10
Cowal, L., *Australia* 91 E4
Cowan, *Canada* 101 C8
Cowan, L., *Australia* 89 F3
Cowan L., *Canada* 101 C7
Cowangie, *Australia* 91 F3
Cowansville, *Canada* 107 A12
Cowarie, *Australia* 91 D2
Cowcowing Lakes,
  Australia 89 F2
Cowdenbeath, *U.K.* 14 E5
Cowell, *Australia* 91 E2
Cowes, *U.K.* 13 G6
Cowlitz →, *U.S.A.* 112 D4
Cowra, *Australia* 91 E4
Coxilha Grande, *Brazil* .. 127 B5
Coxim, *Brazil* 125 D7
Coxim →, *Brazil* 125 D7
Cox's Bazar, *Bangla.* 61 J17
Cox's Cove, *Canada* 99 C8
Coyame, *Mexico* 114 B3
Coyote Wells, *U.S.A.* ... 113 N11
Coyuca de Benítez, *Mexico* 115 D4
Coyuca de Catalan, *Mexico* 114 D4
Cozad, *U.S.A.* 108 E5
Cozumel, *Mexico* 115 C7
Cozumel, I. de, *Mexico* .. 115 C7
Craboon, *Australia* 91 E4
Cracow = Kraków, *Poland* 20 E9

Cracow, *Australia* 91 D5
Cradock, S. *Africa* 84 E4
Craig, Alaska, *U.S.A.* ... 100 B2
Craig, Colo., *U.S.A.* 110 F10
Craigavon = Lurgan, *U.K.* 15 B5
Craigmore, *Zimbabwe* ... 83 G3
Crailsheim, *Germany* 19 F6
Craiova, *Romania* 38 E6
Cramsie, *Australia* 90 C3
Cranberry Portage, *Canada* 101 C8
Cranbrook, *Tas., Australia* 90 G4
Cranbrook, W. Austral.,
  Australia 89 F2
Cranbrook, *Canada* 100 D5
Crandon, *U.S.A.* 108 C10
Crane, Oreg., *U.S.A.* 110 E4
Crane, Tex., *U.S.A.* 109 K3
Cranston, *U.S.A.* 107 E13
Craon, *France* 24 E6
Craonne, *France* 25 C10
Craponne-sur-Arzon,
  France 26 C7
Crasna, *Romania* 38 C10
Crater L., *U.S.A.* 110 E2
Crateús, *Brazil* 122 C3
Crati →, *Italy* 35 C9
Crato, *Brazil* 122 C4
Crato, *Portugal* 31 F3
Cravo Norte, *Colombia* .. 120 B3
Cravo Norte →, *Colombia* 120 B3
Crawford, *U.S.A.* 108 D3
Crawfordsville, *U.S.A.* .. 104 E2
Crawley, *U.K.* 13 F7
Crazy Mts., *U.S.A.* 110 C8
Crean L., *Canada* 101 C7
Crécy-en-Brie, *France* .. 25 D9
Crécy-en-Ponthieu, *France* 25 B8
Crediton, *Canada* 106 C3
Credo, *Australia* 89 F3
Cree →, *Canada* 101 B7
Cree →, *U.K.* 14 G4
Cree L., *Canada* 101 B7
Creede, *U.S.A.* 111 H10
Creel, *Mexico* 114 B3
Creighton, *U.S.A.* 108 D6
Creil, *France* 25 C9
Crema, *Italy* 32 C6
Cremona, *Italy* 32 C7
Crepori →, *Brazil* 125 B6
Crépy, *France* 25 C10
Crépy-en-Valois, *France* . 25 C9
Cres, *Croatia* 33 D11
Cresbard, *U.S.A.* 108 C5
Crescent, Okla., *U.S.A.* . 109 H6
Crescent, Oreg., *U.S.A.* . 110 E3
Crescent City, *U.S.A.* ... 110 F1
Crescentino, *Italy* 32 C5
Crespino, *Italy* 33 D8
Crespo, *Argentina* 126 C3
Cressy, *Australia* 91 F3
Crest, *France* 27 D9
Cresta, Mt., *Phil.* 55 C5
Crested Butte, *U.S.A.* ... 111 G10
Crestline, Calif., *U.S.A.* . 113 L9
Crestline, Ohio, *U.S.A.* .. 106 F2
Creston, *Canada* 100 D5
Creston, Calif., *U.S.A.* .. 112 K6
Creston, Iowa, *U.S.A.* ... 108 E7
Creston, Wash., *U.S.A.* .. 110 C4
Crestview, Calif., *U.S.A.* 112 H8
Crestview, Fla., *U.S.A.* .. 105 K2
Crete = Kríti, *Greece* 37 D7
Crete, *U.S.A.* 108 E6
Crete, Sea of, *Greece* ... 39 N8
Creus, C., *Spain* 28 C8
Creuse □, *France* 26 B6
Creuse →, *France* 26 B4
Creuzburg, *Germany* 18 D6
Crevalcore, *Italy* 33 D8
Crèvecœur-le-Grand,
  France 25 C9
Crevillente, *Spain* 29 G4
Crewe, *U.K.* 12 D5
Crewkerne, *U.K.* 13 G5
Criciúma, *Brazil* 127 B6
Crieff, *U.K.* 14 E5
Crikvenica, *Croatia* 33 C11
Crimea = Krymskiy
  Poluostrov, *Ukraine* .. 42 C5
Crimmitschau, *Germany* . 18 E8
Cristalândia, *Brazil* 122 D2
Cristino Castro, *Brazil* .. 122 C3
Crişul Alb →, *Romania* .. 38 C4
Crişul Negru →, *Romania* 38 C4
Crişul Repede →,
  Romania 38 C3
Crivitz, *Germany* 18 B7
Crixás, *Brazil* 123 D2
Crna Gora =
  Montenegro □,
  Montenegro 21 N9
Crni Drim →, *Macedonia* 39 H3
Črnomelj, *Slovenia* 33 C12
Croaghpatrick, *Ireland* .. 15 C2
Croatia ■, *Europe* 33 C13
Crocker, Banjaran,
  Malaysia 56 C5
Crockett, *U.S.A.* 109 K7
Crocodile = Krokodil →,
  Mozam. 85 D5
Crocodile Is., *Australia* .. 90 A1
Crocq, *France* 26 C6
Croisette, C., *France* 27 E9
Croisic, Pte. du, *France* . 24 E4
Croix, L. La, *Canada* 98 C1
Croker, C., *Australia* 88 B5

Croker I., *Australia* 88 B5
Cromarty, *Canada* 101 B10
Cromarty, *U.K.* 14 D4
Cromer, *U.K.* 12 E9
Cromwell, *N.Z.* 87 L2
Cronat, *France* 25 F10
Cronulla, *Australia* 91 E5
Crooked →, *Canada* 100 C4
Crooked →, *U.S.A.* 110 D3
Crooked I., *Bahamas* 117 B5
Crooked Island Passage,
  Bahamas 117 B5
Crookston, Minn., *U.S.A.* 108 B6
Crookston, Nebr., *U.S.A.* 108 D4
Crooksville, *U.S.A.* 104 F4
Crookwell, *Australia* 91 E4
Crosby, Minn., *U.S.A.* ... 108 B8
Crosby, N. Dak., *U.S.A.* . 101 D8
Crosby, Pa., *U.S.A.* 106 E6
Crosbyton, *U.S.A.* 109 J4
Cross →, *Nigeria* 79 E6
Cross City, *U.S.A.* 105 L4
Cross Fell, *U.K.* 12 C5
Cross L., *Canada* 101 C9
Cross Plains, *U.S.A.* 109 J5
Cross River □, *Nigeria* .. 79 D6
Cross Sound, *U.S.A.* 96 C6
Crossett, *U.S.A.* 109 J9
Crossfield, *Canada* 100 C6
Crosshaven, *Ireland* 15 E3
Croton-on-Hudson, *U.S.A.* 107 E11
Crotone, *Italy* 35 C10
Crow →, *Canada* 100 B4
Crow Agency, *U.S.A.* 110 D10
Crow Hd., *Ireland* 15 E1
Crowell, *U.S.A.* 109 J5
Crowley, *U.S.A.* 109 K8
Crowley, L., *U.S.A.* 112 H8
Crown Point, *U.S.A.* 104 E2
Crows Landing, *U.S.A.* .. 112 H5
Crows Nest, *Australia* .. 91 D5
Crowsnest Pass, *Canada* . 100 D6
Croydon, *Australia* 90 B3
Croydon, *U.K.* 13 F7
Crozet Is., *Ind. Oc.* 3 G12
Crozon, *France* 24 D2
Cruz, C., *Cuba* 116 C4
Cruz Alta, *Brazil* 127 B5
Cruz das Almas, *Brazil* .. 123 D4
Cruz de Malta, *Brazil* ... 122 C3
Cruz del Eje, *Argentina* . 126 C3
Cruzeiro, *Brazil* 123 F2
Cruzeiro do Oeste, *Brazil* 127 A5
Cruzeiro do Sul, *Brazil* .. 124 B3
Cry L., *Canada* 100 B3
Crystal Bay, *U.S.A.* 112 F7
Crystal Brook, *Australia* . 91 E2
Crystal City, Mo., *U.S.A.* 108 F9
Crystal City, Tex., *U.S.A.* 109 L5
Crystal Falls, *U.S.A.* 104 B1
Crystal River, *U.S.A.* ... 105 L4
Crystal Springs, *U.S.A.* . 109 K9
Csongrád, *Hungary* 21 J10
Csorna, *Hungary* 21 H7
Csurgo, *Hungary* 21 J7
Cu Lao Hon, *Vietnam* .. 59 G7
Cua Rao, *Vietnam* 58 C5
Cuácua →, *Mozam.* 83 F4
Cuamato, *Angola* 84 B2
Cuamba, *Mozam.* 83 E4
Cuando →, *Angola* 81 H4
Cuando Cubango □,
  Angola 84 B3
Cuangar, *Angola* 84 B2
Cuanza →, *Angola* 70 G5
Cuarto →, *Argentina* 126 C3
Cuatrociénegas, *Mexico* . 114 B4
Cuauhtémoc, *Mexico* 114 B3
Cuba, *Portugal* 31 G3
Cuba, N. Mex., *U.S.A.* .. 111 J10
Cuba, N.Y., *U.S.A.* 106 D6
Cuba ■, *W. Indies* 116 B4
Cubango →, *Africa* 84 B3
Cuballing, *Australia* 89 F2
Cubuk, *Turkey* 66 C5
Cucamonga, *U.S.A.* 113 L9
Cuchi, *Angola* 81 G3
Cuchillo-Có, *Argentina* .. 128 A4
Cuchivero →, *Venezuela* . 120 B4
Cuchumatanes, Sierra de
  los, *Guatemala* 116 C1
Cucuí, *Brazil* 120 C4
Cucurpe, *Mexico* 114 A2
Cucurrupí, *Colombia* 120 C2
Cúcuta, *Colombia* 120 B3
Cudahy, *U.S.A.* 104 D2
Cudalbi, *Romania* 38 D10
Cuddalore, *Australia* 60 P11
Cuddapah, *India* 60 M11
Cuddapan, L., *Australia* . 90 D3
Cudgewa, *Australia* 91 F4
Cudillero, *Spain* 30 B4
Cue, *Australia* 89 E2
Cuéllar, *Spain* 30 D6
Cuenca, *Ecuador* 120 D2
Cuenca, *Spain* 28 E2
Cuenca □, *Spain* 28 F2
Cuenca, Serranía de, *Spain* 28 F3
Cuerdo del Pozo, Pantano
  de la, *Spain* 28 D2
Cuernavaca, *Mexico* 115 D5
Cuero, *U.S.A.* 109 L6
Cuers, *France* 27 E10
Cuervo, *U.S.A.* 109 H2
Cuesmes, *Belgium* 17 H3

Cuevas, Cerro, *Bolivia* ... 125 E4
Cuevas del Almanzora,
  Spain 29 H3
Cuevo, *Bolivia* 125 E5
Cuiabá, *Brazil* 125 D6
Cuiabá →, *Brazil* 125 D6
Cuilco, *Guatemala* 116 C1
Cuillin Hills, *U.K.* 14 D2
Cuillin Sd., *U.K.* 14 D2
Cuima, *Angola* 81 G3
Cuiseaux, *France* 27 B9
Cuité, *Brazil* 122 C4
Cuiuni →, *Brazil* 121 D5
Cukai, *Malaysia* 59 K4
Culan, *France* 26 B6
Culbertson, *U.S.A.* 108 A2
Culcairn, *Australia* 91 F4
Culebra, Sierra de la, *Spain* 30 D4
Culemborg, *Neths.* 16 E6
Culgoa →, *Australia* 91 D4
Culiacán, *Mexico* 114 C3
Culiacán →, *Mexico* 114 C3
Culion, *Phil.* 55 F4
Cullarin Ra., *Australia* .. 91 E4
Cullen, *U.K.* 14 D6
Cullen Pt., *Australia* 90 A3
Cullera, *Spain* 29 F4
Cullman, *U.S.A.* 105 H2
Culloden Moor, *U.K.* 14 D4
Culoz, *France* 27 C9
Culpeper, *U.S.A.* 104 F7
Culuene →, *Brazil* 125 C7
Culver, Pt., *Australia* ... 89 F3
Culverden, *N.Z.* 87 K4
Cumaná, *Venezuela* 121 A5
Cumare, *Colombia* 120 C3
Cumari, *Brazil* 123 E2
Cumberland, *Canada* 100 D3
Cumberland, Md., *U.S.A.* 104 F6
Cumberland, Wis., *U.S.A.* 108 C8
Cumberland →, *U.S.A.* .. 105 G2
Cumberland I., *U.S.A.* .. 105 K5
Cumberland Is., *Australia* . 90 C4
Cumberland L., *Canada* .. 101 C8
Cumberland Pen., *Canada* 97 B13
Cumberland Plateau,
  U.S.A. 105 H3
Cumberland Sd., *Canada* . 97 B13
Cumborah, *Australia* 91 D4
Cumbres Mayores, *Spain* . 31 G4
Cumbria □, *U.K.* 12 C5
Cumbrian Mts., *U.K.* 12 C4
Cumbum, *India* 60 M11
Cuminá →, *Brazil* 121 D6
Cuminapanema →, *Brazil* 121 D7
Cummings Mt., *U.S.A.* .. 113 K8
Cummins, *Australia* 91 E2
Cumnock, *Australia* 91 E4
Cumnock, *U.K.* 14 F4
Cumpas, *Mexico* 114 A3
Cumplida, Pta., *Canary Is.* 36 F2
Cúneo, *Italy* 32 D4
Cunillera, I., *Spain* 36 C7
Cunlhat, *France* 26 C7
Cunnamulla, *Australia* .. 91 D4
Cuorgnè, *Italy* 32 C4
Cupar, *Canada* 101 C8
Cupar, *U.K.* 14 E5
Cupica, G. de, *Colombia* . 120 B2
Čuprija, *Serbia* 21 M11
Curaçá, *Brazil* 122 C4
Curaçao, Neth. Ant. 117 D6
Curacautín, *Chile* 128 A2
Curahuara de Carangas,
  Bolivia 124 D4
Curanilahue, *Chile* 126 D1
Curaray →, *Peru* 120 D3
Curatabaca, *Venezuela* .. 121 B5
Cure →, *France* 25 E10
Curepto, *Chile* 126 D1
Curiapo, *Venezuela* 121 B5
Curicó, *Chile* 126 C1
Curicó □, *Chile* 126 C1
Curicuriari →, *Brazil* 120 D4
Curimatá, *Brazil* 122 D3
Curiplaya, *Colombia* 120 C3
Curitiba, *Brazil* 127 B6
Currabubula, *Australia* .. 91 E5
Currais Novos, *Brazil* ... 122 C4
Curralinho, *Brazil* 122 B2
Currant, *U.S.A.* 110 G6
Curraweena, *Australia* .. 91 E4
Currawilla, *Australia* 90 D3
Current →, *U.S.A.* 109 G9
Currie, *Australia* 90 F3
Currie, *U.S.A.* 110 F6
Currie, Mt., S. *Africa* ... 85 E4
Currituck Sd., *U.S.A.* ... 105 G8
Curtea de Argeş, *Romania* 38 D7
Curtis, *Spain* 30 B2
Curtis, *U.S.A.* 108 E4
Curtis Group, *Australia* .. 90 F4
Curtis I., *Australia* 90 C5
Curuá →, Pará, *Brazil* .. 121 D7
Curuá →, Pará, *Brazil* .. 125 B7

Curuá, I., *Brazil* 122 A1
Curuaés →, *Brazil* 125 B7
Curuápanema →, *Brazil* . 121 D6
Curuçá, *Brazil* 122 B2
Curuguaty, *Paraguay* 127 A4
Curup, *Indonesia* 56 E2
Curupira, Serra, S. *Amer.* 121 C5
Cururu →, *Brazil* 125 B6
Cururupu, *Brazil* 122 B3
Curuzú Cuatiá, *Argentina* . 126 B4
Curvelo, *Brazil* 123 E3
Cushing, *U.S.A.* 109 H6
Cushing, Mt., *Canada* ... 100 B3
Cusihuiriáchic, *Mexico* .. 114 B3
Cusna, Monte, *Italy* 32 D7
Cusset, *France* 26 B7
Custer, *U.S.A.* 108 D3
Cut Bank, *U.S.A.* 110 B7
Cuthbert, *U.S.A.* 105 K3
Cutler, *U.S.A.* 112 J7
Cutral-Có, *Argentina* 128 A3
Cutro, *Italy* 35 C9
Cuttaburra →, *Australia* . 91 D3
Cuttack, *India* 61 J14
Cuvier, C., *Australia* 89 D1
Cuvier I., *N.Z.* 87 G5
Cuxhaven, *Germany* 18 B4
Cuyabeno, *Ecuador* 120 D2
Cuyahoga Falls, *U.S.A.* .. 106 E3
Cuyapo, *Phil.* 55 D4
Cuyo, *Phil.* 55 F4
Cuyo East Pass, *Phil.* ... 55 F4
Cuyo West Pass, *Phil.* ... 55 F4
Cuyuni →, *Guyana* 121 B6
Cuzco, *Bolivia* 124 E4
Cuzco, *Peru* 124 C3
Cuzco □, *Peru* 124 C3
Cwmbran, *U.K.* 13 F4
Cyangugu, *Rwanda* 82 C2
Cyclades = Kikládhes,
  Greece 39 M7
Cygnet, *Australia* 90 G4
Cynthiana, *U.S.A.* 104 F3
Cypress Hills, *Canada* ... 101 D7
Cyprus ■, *Asia* 37 E12
Cyrenaica, *Libya* 70 C6
Cyrene = Shaḥḥāt, *Libya* . 73 B9
Czar, *Canada* 101 C6
Czarne, *Poland* 20 B6
Czech Rep. ■, *Europe* ... 20 F4
Czersk, *Poland* 20 B7
Częstochowa, *Poland* 20 E9

D

Da →, *Vietnam* 58 B5
Da Hinggan Ling, *China* .. 54 B7
Da Lat, *Vietnam* 59 G7
Da Nang, *Vietnam* 58 D7
Da Qaidam, *China* 54 C4
Da Yunhe →, *China* 51 G11
Da'an, *China* 51 B13
Daarlerveen, *Neths.* 16 D9
Dab'a, Râs el, *Egypt* 76 H6
Daba Shan, *China* 52 B7
Dabai, *Nigeria* 79 C6
Dabajuro, *Venezuela* 120 A3
Dabakala, *Ivory C.* 78 D4
Dabeiba, *Colombia* 120 B2
Dabhoi, *India* 62 H5
Dąbie, *Poland* 20 B4
Dabie Shan, *China* 53 B10
Dabo, *Indonesia* 56 E2
Dabola, *Guinea* 78 C2
Dabou, *Ivory C.* 78 D4
Daboya, *Ghana* 79 D4
Dabrowa Tarnówska,
  Poland 20 E10
Dabu, *China* 53 E11
Dabung, *Malaysia* 59 K4
Dabus →, *Ethiopia* 77 E4
Dacato →, *Ethiopia* 77 F5
Dacca = Dhaka, *Bangla.* . 63 H14
Dacca = Dhaka □, *Bangla.* 63 G14
Dachau, *Germany* 19 G7
Dadanawa, *Guyana* 121 C6
Daday, *Turkey* 42 F5
Dade City, *U.S.A.* 105 L4
Dades, Oued →, *Morocco* 74 B3
Dadiya, *Nigeria* 79 D7
Dadra and Nagar Haveli □,
  India 60 J8
Dadri = Charkhi Dadri,
  India 62 E7
Dadu, *Pakistan* 62 F2
Dadu He →, *China* 52 C4
Dǎeni, *Romania* 38 E11
Daet, *Phil.* 55 D5
Dafang, *China* 52 D5
Dagana, *Senegal* 78 B1
Dagash, *Sudan* 76 D3
Dagestanskiye Ogni, *Russia* 43 E13
Dagestan Republic □,
  Russia 43 E12
Daghfeli, *Sudan* 76 D3
Dagö = Hiiumaa, *Estonia* . 40 B3
Dagu, *China* 51 E9
Daguan, *China* 52 D4
Dagupan, *Phil.* 55 C4
Dahab, *Egypt* 76 B3

Dahlak Kebir, Eritrea	68	D3
Dahlenburg, Germany	18	B6
Dahlonega, U.S.A.	105	H4
Dahme, Germany	18	D9
Dahod, India	62	H6
Dahomey = Benin ■, Africa	79	D5
Dahong Shan, China	53	B9
Dahra, Senegal	78	B1
Dahra, Massif de, Algeria	75	A5
Dai Hao, Vietnam	58	C6
Dai-Sen, Japan	49	G6
Dai Shan, China	53	B14
Dai Xian, China	50	E7
Daicheng, China	50	E9
Daimiel, Spain	29	F1
Daingean, Ireland	15	C4
Dainkog, China	52	A1
Daintree, Australia	90	B4
Daiō-Misaki, Japan	49	G8
Dairût, Egypt	76	B3
Daisetsu-Zan, Japan	48	C11
Dajarra, Australia	90	C2
Dajia, Taiwan	53	E13
Dajin Chuan →, China	52	B3
Dak Dam, Cambodia	58	F6
Dak Nhe, Vietnam	58	E6
Dak Pek, Vietnam	58	E6
Dak Song, Vietnam	59	F6
Dak Sui, Vietnam	58	E6
Dakar, Senegal	78	C1
Dakhla, W. Sahara	74	D1
Dakhla, El Wâhât el-, Egypt	76	B2
Dakhovskaya, Russia	43	D9
Dakingari, Nigeria	79	C5
Dakor, India	62	H5
Dakoro, Niger	79	C6
Dakota City, U.S.A.	108	D6
Đakovica, Serbia	21	N10
Đakovo, Croatia	21	K8
Dalaba, Guinea	78	C2
Dalachi, China	50	F3
Dalai Nur, China	50	C9
Dālakī, Iran	65	D6
Dalälven, Sweden	9	F14
Dalaman, Turkey	66	E3
Dalaman →, Turkey	66	E3
Dalandzadgad, Mongolia	50	C3
Dalarö, Sweden	9	G15
Dālbandīn, Pakistan	60	E4
Dalbeattie, U.K.	14	G5
Dalbosjön, Sweden	11	F6
Dalby, Australia	91	D5
Dalby, Sweden	11	J7
Dalen, Neths.	16	C9
Dalen, Norway	10	E2
Dalfsen, Neths.	16	C8
Dalga, Egypt	76	B3
Dalgán, Iran	65	E8
Dalhart, U.S.A.	109	G3
Dalhousie, Canada	99	C6
Dalhousie, India	62	C6
Dali, Shaanxi, China	50	G5
Dali, Yunnan, China	52	E3
Dalian, China	51	E11
Daliang Shan, China	52	D4
Dalias, Spain	29	J2
Daling He →, China	51	D11
Dāliyat el Karmel, Israel	69	C4
Dalkeith, U.K.	14	F5
Dall I., U.S.A.	100	C2
Dallarnil, Australia	91	D5
Dallas, Oreg., U.S.A.	110	D2
Dallas, Tex., U.S.A.	109	J6
Dallol, Ethiopia	77	E5
Dalmacija = Dalmatia □, Croatia	21	M7
Dalmatia □, Croatia	21	M7
Dalmellington, U.K.	14	F4
Dalnegorsk, Russia	45	E14
Dalnerechensk, Russia	45	E14
Daloa, Ivory C.	78	D3
Dalou Shan, China	52	C6
Dalsjöfors, Sweden	11	G7
Dalskog, Sweden	11	F6
Daltenganj, India	63	G11
Dalton, Canada	98	C3
Dalton, Ga., U.S.A.	105	H3
Dalton, Mass., U.S.A.	107	D11
Dalton, Nebr., U.S.A.	108	E3
Dalton Iceberg Tongue, Antarctica	5	C9
Dalupiri I., Phil.	55	B4
Dalvík, Iceland	8	D4
Daly →, Australia	88	B5
Daly City, U.S.A.	112	H4
Daly L., Canada	101	B7
Daly Waters, Australia	90	B1
Dam Doi, Vietnam	59	H5
Dam Ha, Vietnam	58	B6
Daman, India	60	J8
Dāmaneh, Iran	65	C6
Damanhûr, Egypt	76	H7
Damanzhuang, China	50	E9
Damar, Indonesia	57	F7
Damaraland, Namibia	84	C2
Damascus = Dimashq, Syria	69	B5
Damaturu, Nigeria	79	C7
Damāvand, Iran	65	C7
Damāvand, Qolleh-ye, Iran	65	C7
Damba, Angola	80	F3
Dame Marie, Haiti	117	C5
Dāmghān, Iran	65	B7
Dămienesti, Romania	38	C10
Damietta = Dumyât, Egypt	76	H7
Daming, China	50	F8
Damīr Qābū, Syria	64	B4
Dammam = Ad Dammām, Si. Arabia	65	E6
Dammarie, France	24	D8
Dammartin-en-Goële, France	25	C9
Dammastock, Switz.	23	C6
Damme, Germany	18	C4
Damodar →, India	63	H12
Damoh, India	63	H8
Damous, Algeria	75	A5
Dampier, Australia	88	D2
Dampier, Selat, Indonesia	57	E8
Dampier Arch., Australia	88	D2
Damrei, Chuor Phnum, Cambodia	59	G4
Damville, France	24	D8
Damvillers, France	25	C12
Dan-Gulbi, Nigeria	79	C6
Dana, Indonesia	57	F6
Dana, L., Canada	98	B4
Dana, Mt., U.S.A.	112	H7
Danakil Depression, Ethiopia	77	E5
Danao, Phil.	55	F6
Danbury, U.S.A.	107	E11
Danby L., U.S.A.	111	J6
Dand, Afghan.	62	D1
Dandaragan, Australia	89	F2
Dandeldhura, Nepal	63	E9
Dandeli, India	60	M9
Dandenong, Australia	91	F4
Dandong, China	51	D13
Danfeng, China	50	H6
Danforth, U.S.A.	99	C6
Dangan Liedao, China	53	F10
Danger Is. = Pukapuka, Cook Is.	93	J11
Danger Pt., S. Africa	84	E2
Dangla, Ethiopia	77	E4
Dangora, Nigeria	79	C6
Dangrek, Phnom, Thailand	58	E5
Dangriga, Belize	115	D7
Dangshan, China	50	G9
Dangtu, China	53	B12
Dangyang, China	53	B8
Daniel, U.S.A.	110	E8
Daniel's Harbour, Canada	99	B8
Danielskuil, S. Africa	84	D3
Danielson, U.S.A.	107	E13
Danilov, Russia	41	B12
Danilovka, Russia	41	F14
Daning, China	50	F6
Danissa, Kenya	82	B5
Danja, Nigeria	79	C6
Dankalwa, Nigeria	79	C7
Dankama, Nigeria	79	C6
Dankhar Gompa, India	60	C11
Dankov, Russia	41	E11
Danleng, China	52	B4
Danlí, Honduras	116	D2
Dannemora, Sweden	9	F14
Dannemora, U.S.A.	107	B11
Dannenberg, Germany	18	B7
Dannevirke, N.Z.	87	J6
Dannhauser, S. Africa	85	D5
Danshui, Taiwan	53	E13
Dansville, U.S.A.	106	D7
Dantan, India	63	J12
Dante, Somali Rep.	68	E5
Danvers, U.S.A.	107	D14
Danville, Ill., U.S.A.	104	E2
Danville, Ky., U.S.A.	104	G3
Danville, Va., U.S.A.	105	G6
Danyang, China	53	B12
Danzhai, China	52	D6
Danzig = Gdańsk, Poland	20	A8
Dao, Phil.	57	B6
Dão →, Portugal	30	E2
Dao Xian, China	53	E8
Daocheng, China	52	C3
Daora, W. Sahara	74	C2
Daoud = Aïn Beïda, Algeria	75	A6
Daoulas, France	24	D2
Dapitan, Phil.	55	G5
Dapong, Togo	79	C5
Daqing Shan, China	50	D6
Daqu Shan, China	53	B14
Dar es Salaam, Tanzania	82	D4
Dar Mazār, Iran	65	D8
Dar'ā, Syria	69	C5
Dar'ā □, Syria	69	C5
Dārāb, Iran	65	D7
Daraj, Libya	75	B7
Dārān, Iran	65	C6
Daravica, Serbia	21	N10
Daraw, Egypt	76	C3
Dārayyā, Syria	69	B5
Darazo, Nigeria	79	C7
Darband, Pakistan	62	B5
Darband, Kūh-e, Iran	65	D8
Darbhanga, India	63	F11
Darby, U.S.A.	110	C6
Dardanelle, Ark., U.S.A.	109	H8
Dardanelle, Calif., U.S.A.	112	G7
Dardanelles = Çanakkale Boğazı, Turkey	66	C2
Darende, Turkey	66	D7
Dārestān, Iran	65	D8
Darfo, Italy	32	C7
Dârfûr, Sudan	70	E6
Dargai, Pakistan	62	B4
Dargan Ata, Uzbekistan	44	E7
Dargaville, N.Z.	87	F4
Darhan Muminggan Lianheqi, China	50	D6
Dari, Sudan	77	F3
Darién, G. del, Colombia	120	B2
Darién, Serranía del, Colombia	120	B2
Dariganga, Mongolia	50	B7
Darjeeling = Darjiling, India	63	F13
Darjiling, India	63	F13
Dark Cove, Canada	99	C9
Darkan, Australia	89	F2
Darkhazīneh, Iran	65	D6
Darkot Pass, Pakistan	63	A5
Darling →, Australia	91	E3
Darling Downs, Australia	91	D5
Darling Ra., Australia	89	F2
Darlington, U.K.	12	C6
Darlington, S.C., U.S.A.	105	H6
Darlington, Wis., U.S.A.	108	D9
Darlot, L., Australia	89	E3
Darłowo, Poland	20	A6
Darmstadt, Germany	19	F4
Darnah, Libya	73	B9
Darnall, S. Africa	85	D5
Darnétal, France	24	C8
Darney, France	25	D13
Darnley, C., Antarctica	5	C6
Darnley B., Canada	96	B7
Daroca, Spain	28	D3
Darr, Australia	90	C3
Darr →, Australia	90	C3
Darrington, U.S.A.	110	B3
Darsser Ort, Germany	18	A8
Dart →, U.K.	13	G4
Dart, C., Antarctica	5	D14
Dartmoor, Australia	90	C3
Dartmouth, Canada	99	D7
Dartmouth, U.K.	13	G4
Dartmouth, L., Australia	91	D4
Dartuch, C., Spain	36	B10
Darvaza, Turkmenistan	44	E6
Darvel, Teluk, Malaysia	57	D5
Darwha, India	60	J10
Darwin, Australia	88	B5
Darwin, U.S.A.	113	J9
Darwin, Mt., Chile	128	D3
Darwin River, Australia	88	B5
Daryoi Amu = Amudarya →, Uzbekistan	44	E6
Dās, U.A.E.	65	E7
Dashetai, China	50	D5
Dashkesan, Azerbaijan	43	F12
Dasht, Iran	65	B8
Dasht →, Pakistan	60	G2
Dasht-e Mārgow, Afghan.	60	D3
Dasht-i-Nawar, Afghan.	62	C3
Daska, Pakistan	62	C6
Dassa-Zoume, Benin	79	D5
Dasseneiland, S. Africa	84	E2
Datça, Turkey	66	E2
Datia, India	63	G8
Datian, China	53	E11
Datong, Anhui, China	53	B11
Datong, Shanxi, China	50	D7
Datu, Tanjung, Indonesia	56	D3
Datu Piang, Phil.	55	H6
Daugava →, Latvia	40	C4
Daugavpils, Latvia	40	D5
Daule, Ecuador	120	D2
Daule →, Ecuador	120	D2
Daulpur, India	62	F7
Daun, Germany	19	E2
Dauphin, Canada	101	C8
Dauphin I., U.S.A.	105	K1
Dauphin L., Canada	101	C9
Dauphiné, France	27	C9
Daura, Borno, Nigeria	79	C7
Daura, Kaduna, Nigeria	79	C6
Dausa, India	62	F7
Davangere, India	60	M9
Davao, Phil.	55	H6
Davao, G. of, Phil.	55	H6
Dāvar Panāh, Iran	65	E9
Davenport, Calif., U.S.A.	112	H4
Davenport, Iowa, U.S.A.	108	E9
Davenport, Wash., U.S.A.	110	C4
Davenport Downs, Australia	90	C3
Davenport Ra., Australia	90	C1
David, Panama	116	E3
David City, U.S.A.	108	E6
David Gorodok, Belorussia	40	E5
Davidson, Canada	101	C7
Davis, U.S.A.	112	G5
Davis Dam, U.S.A.	113	K12
Davis Inlet, Canada	99	A7
Davis Mts., U.S.A.	109	K2
Davis Sea, Antarctica	5	C7
Davis Str., N. Amer.	97	B14
Davos, Switz.	23	C9
Davy L., Canada	101	B7
Dawa →, Ethiopia	77	G5
Dawaki, Bauchi, Nigeria	79	C6
Dawaki, Kano, Nigeria	79	C6
Dawes Ra., Australia	90	C5
Dawson, Canada	96	B6
Dawson, Ga., U.S.A.	105	K3
Dawson, N. Dak., U.S.A.	108	B5
Dawson, I., Chile	128	D2
Dawson Creek, Canada	100	B4
Dawson Inlet, Canada	101	A10
Dawson Ra., Australia	90	C4
Dawu, China	52	B3
Dax, France	26	E2
Daxian, China	52	B6
Daxin, China	52	F6
Daxindian, China	51	F11
Daxinggou, China	51	C15
Daxue Shan, Sichuan, China	52	B3
Daxue Shan, Yunnan, China	52	F2
Dayao, China	52	E3
Daye, China	53	C8
Dayi, China	52	B4
Daylesford, Australia	91	F3
Dayong, China	53	C8
Dayr az Zawr, Syria	64	C4
Daysland, Canada	100	C6
Dayton, Nev., U.S.A.	112	F7
Dayton, Ohio, U.S.A.	104	F3
Dayton, Pa., U.S.A.	106	F5
Dayton, Tenn., U.S.A.	105	H3
Dayton, Wash., U.S.A.	110	C4
Daytona Beach, U.S.A.	105	L5
Dayu, China	53	E10
Dayville, U.S.A.	110	D4
Dazhu, China	52	B6
Dazu, China	52	C5
De Aar, S. Africa	84	E3
De Bilt, Neths.	16	D6
De Funiak Springs, U.S.A.	105	K2
De Grey, Australia	88	D2
De Grey →, Australia	88	D2
De Kalb, U.S.A.	108	E10
De Koog, Neths.	16	B5
De Land, U.S.A.	105	L5
De Leon, U.S.A.	109	J5
De Panne, Belgium	17	F1
De Pere, U.S.A.	104	C1
De Queen, U.S.A.	109	H7
De Quincy, U.S.A.	109	K8
De Ridder, U.S.A.	109	K8
De Rijp, Neths.	16	C5
De Smet, U.S.A.	108	C6
De Soto, U.S.A.	108	F9
De Tour Village, U.S.A.	104	C4
De Witt, U.S.A.	109	H9
Dead Sea, Asia	69	D4
Deadwood, U.S.A.	108	C3
Deadwood L., Canada	100	B3
Deakin, Australia	89	F4
Deal, U.K.	13	F9
Deal I., Australia	90	F4
Dealesville, S. Africa	84	D4
De'an, China	53	C10
Dean, Forest of, U.K.	13	F5
Dearborn, U.S.A.	98	D3
Dease →, Canada	100	B3
Dease L., Canada	100	B2
Dease Lake, Canada	100	B2
Death Valley, U.S.A.	113	J10
Death Valley Junction, U.S.A.	113	J10
Death Valley National Monument, U.S.A.	113	J10
Deauville, France	24	C7
Deba Habe, Nigeria	79	C7
Debaltsevo, Ukraine	42	B8
Debao, China	52	F6
Debar, Macedonia	39	H3
Debden, Canada	101	C7
Debdou, Morocco	75	B4
Dębica, Poland	20	E11
Dęblin, Poland	20	D11
Débo, L., Mali	78	B4
Debolt, Canada	100	B5
Deborah East, L., Australia	89	F2
Deborah West, L., Australia	89	F2
Debre Birhan, Ethiopia	77	F4
Debre Markos, Ethiopia	77	E4
Debre May, Ethiopia	77	E4
Debre Sina, Ethiopia	77	F4
Debre Tabor, Ethiopia	77	E4
Debre Zebit, Ethiopia	77	E4
Debrecen, Hungary	21	H11
Dečani, Serbia	21	N10
Decatur, Ala., U.S.A.	105	H2
Decatur, Ga., U.S.A.	105	J3
Decatur, Ill., U.S.A.	108	F10
Decatur, Ind., U.S.A.	104	E3
Decatur, Tex., U.S.A.	109	J6
Decazeville, France	26	D6
Deccan, India	60	M10
Dechang, China	52	D4
Děčín, Czech.	20	E4
Decize, France	25	F10
Deckerville, U.S.A.	106	C2
Decollatura, Italy	35	C9
Decorah, U.S.A.	108	D9
Dedéagach = Alexandroúpolis, Greece	39	J8
Dedegöl Dağları, Turkey	66	E4
Dedemsvaart, Neths.	16	C8
Dedham, U.S.A.	107	D13
Dedilovo, Russia	41	E10
Dédougou, Burkina Faso	78	C4
Dedza, Malawi	83	E3
Dee →, Clwyd, U.K.	12	D4
Dee →, Gramp., U.K.	14	D6
Deep B., Canada	100	A5
Deep Well, Australia	90	C1
Deepwater, Australia	91	D5
Deer →, Canada	101	B10
Deer Lake, Nfld., Canada	99	C8
Deer Lake, Ont., Canada	101	C10
Deer Lodge, U.S.A.	110	C7
Deer Park, U.S.A.	110	C5
Deer River, U.S.A.	108	B8
Deeral, Australia	90	B4
Deerdepoort, S. Africa	84	C4
Deerlijk, Belgium	17	G2
Deferiet, U.S.A.	107	B9
Defiance, U.S.A.	104	E3
Dêgê, China	52	B2
Degebe →, Portugal	31	G3
Degeh Bur, Ethiopia	68	F3
Degema, Nigeria	79	E6
Degersheim, Switz.	23	B8
Deggendorf, Germany	19	G8
Deh Bīd, Iran	65	D7
Deh-e Shīr, Iran	65	D7
Dehaj, Iran	65	D7
Dehdez, Iran	65	D6
Dehestān, Iran	65	D7
Dehgolān, Iran	64	C5
Dehi Titan, Afghan.	60	C3
Dehibat, Tunisia	75	B7
Dehlorān, Iran	64	C5
Dehra Dun, India	62	D8
Dehri, India	63	G11
Dehua, China	53	E12
Dehui, China	51	B13
Deinze, Belgium	17	G3
Dej, Romania	38	B6
Dejiang, China	52	C7
Dekemhare, Eritrea	77	D4
Dekese, Zaïre	80	E4
Del Mar, U.S.A.	113	N9
Del Norte, U.S.A.	111	H10
Del Rio, U.S.A.	109	L4
Delai, Sudan	76	D4
Delano, U.S.A.	113	K7
Delareyville, S. Africa	84	D4
Delavan, U.S.A.	108	D10
Delaware, U.S.A.	104	E4
Delaware □, U.S.A.	104	F8
Delaware →, U.S.A.	104	F8
Delaware B., U.S.A.	103	C12
Delegate, Australia	91	F4
Delémont, Switz.	22	B4
Delft, Neths.	16	D4
Delfzijl, Neths.	16	B9
Delgado, C., Mozam.	83	E5
Delgerhet, Mongolia	50	B6
Delgo, Sudan	76	C3
Delhi, Canada	106	D4
Delhi, India	62	E7
Delhi, U.S.A.	107	D10
Delia, Canada	100	C6
Delice, Turkey	66	D6
Delice →, Turkey	66	D6
Delicias, Mexico	114	B3
Delījān, Iran	65	C6
Delitzsch, Germany	18	D8
Dell City, U.S.A.	111	L11
Dell Rapids, U.S.A.	108	D6
Delle, France	25	E14
Dellys, Algeria	75	A5
Delmar, U.S.A.	107	D11
Delmenhorst, Germany	18	B4
Delmiro Gouveia, Brazil	122	C4
Delnice, Croatia	33	C11
Delong, Ostrova, Russia	45	B15
Deloraine, Australia	90	G4
Deloraine, Canada	101	D8
Delphi, U.S.A.	104	E2
Delphos, U.S.A.	104	E3
Delportshoop, S. Africa	84	D3
Delray Beach, U.S.A.	105	M5
Delsbo, Sweden	10	C10
Delta, Colo., U.S.A.	111	G9
Delta, Utah, U.S.A.	110	G7
Delta □, Nigeria	79	D6
Delta Amacuro □, Venezuela	121	B5
Delungra, Australia	91	D5
Delvina, Albania	39	K3
Delvinákion, Greece	39	K3
Demanda, Sierra de la, Spain	28	C1
Demavend = Damāvand, Iran	65	C7
Demba, Zaïre	80	F4
Dembecha, Ethiopia	77	E4
Dembi, Ethiopia	77	F4
Dembia, Zaïre	82	B2
Dembidolo, Ethiopia	77	F3
Demer →, Belgium	17	G5
Demidov, Russia	40	E6
Deming, N. Mex., U.S.A.	111	K10
Deming, Wash., U.S.A.	112	B4
Demini →, Brazil	121	D5
Demirci, Turkey	66	D3
Demirköy, Turkey	66	C2
Demmin, Germany	18	B9
Demnate, Morocco	74	B3
Demonte, Italy	32	D4
Demopolis, U.S.A.	105	J2
Dempo, Indonesia	56	E2
Demyansk, Russia	40	C8
Den Burg, Neths.	16	B5
Den Chai, Thailand	58	D3
Den Dungen, Neths.	17	E6

Den Haag = 's-
Gravenhage, *Neths.* 16 D4
Den Ham, *Neths.* 16 D8
Den Helder, *Neths.* 16 C5
Den Hulst, *Neths.* 16 C8
Den Oever, *Neths.* 16 C6
Denain, *France* 25 B10
Denair, *U.S.A.* 112 H6
Denau, *Uzbekistan* 44 F7
Denbigh, *U.K.* 12 D4
Dendang, *Indonesia* 56 E3
Dender →, *Belgium* 17 F4
Denderhoutem, *Belgium* .. 17 G4
Denderleeuw, *Belgium* ... 17 G4
Dendermonde, *Belgium* ... 17 F4
Deneba, *Ethiopia* 77 F4
Denekamp, *Neths.* 16 D10
Deng Xian, *China* 53 A9
Dengchuan, *China* 52 E3
Denge, *Nigeria* 79 C6
Dengfeng, *China* 50 G7
Dengi, *Nigeria* 79 D6
Dengkou, *China* 50 D4
Denham, *Australia* 89 E1
Denham Ra., *Australia* ... 90 C4
Denham Sd., *Australia* ... 89 E1
Denia, *Spain* 29 G5
Denial B., *Australia* 91 E1
Deniliquin, *Australia* ... 91 F3
Denison, *Iowa, U.S.A.* ... 108 D7
Denison, *Tex., U.S.A.* ... 109 J6
Denison Plains, *Australia* 88 C4
Denizli, *Turkey* 66 E3
Denizli □, *Turkey* 66 E3
Denman Glacier, *Antarctica* 5 C7
Denmark, *Australia* 89 F2
Denmark ■, *Europe* 11 J3
Denmark Str., *Atl. Oc.* .. 4 C6
Dennison, *U.S.A.* 106 F3
Denpasar, *Indonesia* 56 F5
Denton, *Mont., U.S.A.* ... 110 C9
Denton, *Tex., U.S.A.* 109 J6
D'Entrecasteaux, Pt.,
Australia 89 F2
Dents du Midi, *Switz.* 22 D3
Denu, *Ghana* 79 D5
Denver, *U.S.A.* 108 F2
Denver City, *U.S.A.* 109 J3
Deoband, *India* 62 E7
Deoghar, *India* 63 G12
Deolali, *India* 60 K8
Deoli = Devli, *India* 62 G6
Deoria, *India* 63 F10
Deosai Mts., *Pakistan* ... 63 B6
Deping, *China* 51 F9
Deposit, *U.S.A.* 107 D9
Depot Springs, *Australia* .. 89 E3
Deputatskiy, *Russia* 45 C14
Dêqên, *China* 52 C2
Deqing, *China* 53 F8
Dera Ghazi Khan, *Pakistan* 62 D4
Dera Ismail Khan, *Pakistan* 62 D4
Derbent, *Russia* 43 E13
Derby, *Australia* 88 C3
Derby, *U.K.* 12 E6
Derby, *Conn., U.S.A.* 107 E11
Derby, *N.Y., U.S.A.* 106 D6
Derbyshire □, *U.K.* 12 E6
Dereli, *Turkey* 67 C8
Derg →, *U.K.* 15 B4
Derg, L., *Ireland* 15 D3
Dergachi, *Ukraine* 42 A7
Dergaon, *India* 61 F19
Derik, *Turkey* 67 E9
Derinkuyu, *Turkey* 66 D6
Dernieres, Isles, *U.S.A.* . 109 L9
Dêrong, *China* 52 C2
Derry = Londonderry,
U.K. 15 B4
Derryveagh Mts., *Ireland* . 15 B3
Derudub, *Sudan* 76 D4
Derval, *France* 24 E5
Derwent, *Canada* 101 C6
Derwent →, *Derby, U.K.* .. 12 E6
Derwent →, *N. Yorks.,
U.K.* 12 D7
Derwent Water, *U.K.* 12 C4
Des Moines, *Iowa, U.S.A.* 108 E8
Des Moines, *N. Mex.,
U.S.A.* 109 G3
Des Moines →, *U.S.A.* ... 108 E9
Desaguadero →, *Argentina* 126 C2
Desaguadero →, *Bolivia* . 124 D4
Descanso, Pta., *Mexico* . 113 N9
Descartes, *France* 26 B4
Deschaillons, *Canada* 99 C5
Descharme →, *Canada* ... 101 B7
Deschutes →, *U.S.A.* 110 D3
Dese, *Ethiopia* 68 E2
Deseado, C., *Chile* 128 D2
Desenzano del Gardo, *Italy* 32 C7
Desert Center, *U.S.A.* 113 M11
Desert Hot Springs, *U.S.A.* 113 M10
Désirade, I., *Guadeloupe* . 117 C7
Deskenatlata L., *Canada* . 100 A6
Desna →, *Ukraine* 40 F7
Desnãtui →, *Romania* 38 E6
Desolación, I., *Chile* 128 D2
Despeñaperros, Paso, *Spain* 29 G1
Despotovac, *Serbia* 21 L11
Dessau, *Germany* 18 D8
Dessel, *Belgium* 17 F6
Dessye = Dese, *Ethiopia* . 68 E2
D'Estrees B., *Australia* ... 91 F2

Desuri, *India* 62 G5
Desvres, *France* 25 B8
Det Udom, *Thailand* 58 E5
Dete, *Zimbabwe* 83 F2
Detinja →, *Serbia* 21 M9
Detmold, *Germany* 18 D4
Detour, Pt., *U.S.A.* 104 C2
Detroit, *Mich., U.S.A.* ... 98 D3
Detroit, *Tex., U.S.A.* 109 J7
Detroit Lakes, *U.S.A.* 108 B7
Deurne, *Belgium* 17 F4
Deurne, *Neths.* 17 F7
Deutsche Bucht, *Germany* . 18 A4
Deutschlandsberg, *Austria* 21 J5
Deux-Sèvres □, *France* .. 24 F6
Deva, *Romania* 38 D5
Devakottai, *India* 60 Q11
Devaprayag, *India* 63 D8
Dévaványa, *Hungary* 21 H10
Deveci Daği, *Turkey* 42 F7
Deveci Dağları, *Turkey* .. 66 C6
Develi, *Turkey* 66 D6
Deventer, *Neths.* 16 D8
Deveron →, *U.K.* 14 D6
Devgadh Bariya, *India* ... 62 H5
Devils Den, *U.S.A.* 112 K7
Devils Lake, *U.S.A.* 108 A5
Devils Paw, *Canada* 100 B2
Devizes, *U.K.* 13 F6
Devli, *India* 62 G6
Devnya, *Bulgaria* 38 F10
Devolii →, *Albania* 39 J3
Devon, *Canada* 100 C6
Devon □, *U.K.* 13 G4
Devon I., *Canada* 4 B3
Devonport, *Australia* 90 G4
Devonport, *N.Z.* 87 G5
Devonport, *U.K.* 13 G3
Devrek, *Turkey* 66 C4
Devrekâni, *Turkey* 66 C5
Devrez →, *Turkey* 66 C6
Dewas, *India* 62 H7
Dewetsdorp, *S. Africa* 84 D4
Dewsbury, *U.K.* 12 D6
Dexing, *China* 53 C11
Dexter, *Mo., U.S.A.* 109 G9
Dexter, *N. Mex., U.S.A.* .. 109 J2
Dey-Dey, L., *Australia* ... 89 E5
Deyang, *China* 52 B5
Deyhūk, *Iran* 65 C8
Deyyer, *Iran* 65 E6
Dezadeash L., *Canada* 100 A1
Dezfūl, *Iran* 65 C6
Dezhneva, Mys, *Russia* ... 45 C19
Dezhou, *China* 50 F9
Dháfni, *Greece* 37 D7
Dhahaban, *Si. Arabia* 76 C4
Dhahiriya = Aẓ Ẓāhirīyah,
Jordan 69 D3
Dhahran = Aẓ Ẓahrān,
Si. Arabia 65 E6
Dhaka, *Bangla.* 63 H14
Dhaka □, *Bangla.* 63 G14
Dhali, *Cyprus* 37 D12
Dhamar, *Yemen* 68 E3
Dhamási, *Greece* 39 K5
Dhampur, *India* 63 E8
Dhamtari, *India* 61 J12
Dhanbad, *India* 63 H12
Dhangarhi, *Nepal* 61 E12
Dhankuta, *Nepal* 63 F12
Dhar, *India* 62 H6
Dharampur, *India* 62 H6
Dharamsala = Dharmsala,
India 62 C7
Dharmapuri, *India* 60 N11
Dharmsala, *India* 62 C7
Dharwad, *India* 60 M9
Dharwar, *India* 60 M9
Dhaulagiri, *Nepal* 63 E10
Dhebar, L., *India* 62 G6
Dheftera, *Cyprus* 37 D12
Dhenkanal, *India* 61 J14
Dhenoúsa, *Greece* 39 M8
Dherinia, *Cyprus* 37 D12
Dheskáti, *Greece* 39 K4
Dhespotikó, *Greece* 39 N7
Dhestina, *Greece* 39 L5
Dhiarrizos →, *Cyprus* ... 37 E11
Dhībān, *Jordan* 69 D4
Dhíkti Óros, *Greece* 37 D7
Dhimitsána, *Greece* 39 M5
Dhírfis, *Greece* 39 L6
Dhodhekánisos, *Greece* ... 39 N10
Dholiana, *Greece* 39 K3
Dholka, *India* 62 H5
Dhoraji, *India* 62 J4
Dhoxáton, *Greece* 39 H7
Dhráhstis, Ákra, *Greece* . 37 A3
Dhrápanon, Ákra, *Greece* . 37 D6
Dhrol, *India* 62 H4
Dhuburi, *India* 61 F16
Dhule, *India* 60 J9
Dhut →, *Somali Rep.* 68 E5
Di Linh, *Vietnam* 59 G7
Di Linh, Cao Nguyen,
Vietnam 59 G7
Día, *Greece* 37 D7
Diablo, Mt., *U.S.A.* 112 H5
Diablo Range, *U.S.A.* 112 J5
Diafarabé, *Mali* 78 C4
Diala, *Mali* 78 C3
Dialakoro, *Mali* 78 C3
Diallassagou, *Mali* 78 C4

Diamante, *Argentina* 126 C3
Diamante →, *Argentina* .. 126 C2
Diamantina, *Brazil* 123 E3
Diamantina →, *Australia* . 91 D2
Diamantino, *Brazil* 125 C6
Diamond Harbour, *India* .. 63 H13
Diamond Is., *Australia* ... 90 B5
Diamond Mts., *U.S.A.* 110 G6
Diamond Springs, *U.S.A.* . 112 G6
Diamondville, *U.S.A.* 110 F8
Dianbai, *China* 53 G8
Diancheng, *China* 53 G8
Diano Marina, *Italy* 32 E5
Dianópolis, *Brazil* 123 D2
Dianra, *Ivory C.* 78 D3
Diapaga, *Burkina Faso* ... 79 C5
Diapangou, *Burkina Faso* . 79 C5
Diariguila, *Guinea* 78 C2
Dībā, *Oman* 65 E8
Dibaya, *Zaïre* 80 F4
Dibaya-Lubue, *Zaïre* 80 E3
Dibbi, *Ethiopia* 68 G3
Dibete, *Botswana* 84 C4
Dibrugarh, *India* 61 F19
Dickinson, *U.S.A.* 108 B3
Dickson, *U.S.A.* 105 G2
Dickson City, *U.S.A.* 107 E9
Dicomano, *Italy* 33 E8
Didam, *Neths.* 16 E8
Didesa, W. →, *Ethiopia* . 77 E4
Didiéni, *Mali* 78 C3
Didsbury, *Canada* 100 C6
Didwana, *India* 62 F6
Die, *France* 27 D9
Diébougou, *Burkina Faso* . 78 C4
Diefenbaker L., *Canada* .. 101 C7
Diego Garcia, *Ind. Oc.* .. 3 E13
Diekirch, *Lux.* 17 J8
Diélette, *France* 24 C5
Diéma, *Mali* 78 C3
Diémbéring, *Senegal* 78 C1
Diemen, *Neths.* 16 D5
Dien Ban, *Vietnam* 58 E7
Dien Bien, *Vietnam* 58 B4
Dien Khanh, *Vietnam* 59 F7
Diepenbeek, *Belgium* 17 G6
Diepenheim, *Neths.* 16 D9
Diepenveen, *Neths.* 16 D8
Diepholz, *Germany* 18 C4
Diepoldsau, *Switz.* 23 B9
Dieppe, *France* 24 C8
Dieren, *Neths.* 16 D8
Dierks, *U.S.A.* 109 H7
Diessen, *Neths.* 17 F6
Diessenhofen, *Switz.* 23 A7
Diest, *Belgium* 17 G6
Dietikon, *Switz.* 23 B6
Dieulefit, *France* 25 D13
Dieuze, *France* 25 D13
Diever, *Neths.* 16 C8
Differdange, *Lux.* 17 J7
Dig, *India* 62 F7
Digba, *Zaïre* 82 B2
Digby, *Canada* 99 D6
Digges, *Canada* 101 B10
Digges Is., *Canada* 97 B12
Dighinala, *Bangla.* 61 H18
Dighton, *U.S.A.* 108 F4
Digne, *France* 27 D10
Digoin, *France* 26 B7
Digor, *Turkey* 67 C10
Digos, *Phil.* 55 H6
Digranes, *Iceland* 8 C6
Digul →, *Indonesia* 57 F9
Dihang →, *India* 61 F19
Dīhōk, *Iraq* 64 B3
Dijlah, Nahr →, *Asia* 64 D5
Dijle →, *Belgium* 17 G5
Dijon, *France* 25 E12
Dikala, *Sudan* 77 G3
Dikkil, *Djibouti* 77 E5
Dikomu di Kai, *Botswana* . 84 C3
Diksmuide, *Belgium* 17 F1
Dikson, *Russia* 44 B9
Dikwa, *Nigeria* 79 C7
Dila, *Ethiopia* 77 F4
Dilbeek, *Belgium* 17 G4
Dili, *Indonesia* 57 F7
Dilizhan, *Armenia* 43 F11
Dillenburg, *Germany* 18 E4
Dilley, *U.S.A.* 109 L5
Dilling, *Sudan* 77 E2
Dillingen, *Germany* 19 G6
Dillingham, *U.S.A.* 96 C4
Dillon, *Canada* 101 B7
Dillon, *Mont., U.S.A.* ... 110 D7
Dillon, *S.C., U.S.A.* 105 H6
Dillon →, *Canada* 101 B7
Dilolo, *Zaïre* 80 G4
Dilsen, *Belgium* 17 F7
Dilston, *Australia* 90 G4
Dimas, *Mexico* 114 C3
Dimashq, *Syria* 69 B5
Dimashq □, *Syria* 69 B5
Dimbaza, *S. Africa* 85 E4
Dimbokro, *Ivory C.* 78 D4
Dimboola, *Australia* 91 F3
Dîmbovița →, *Romania* .. 38 E9
Dîmbovnic →, *Romania* .. 38 E8
Dimbulah, *Australia* 90 B4
Dimitrovgrad, *Bulgaria* . 39 G8
Dimitrovgrad, *Russia* 41 D16
Dimitrovgrad, *Serbia* ... 21 M12
Dimitrovo = Pernik,
Bulgaria 38 G6

Dimmitt, *U.S.A.* 109 H3
Dimo, *Sudan* 77 F2
Dimona, *Israel* 69 D4
Dimovo, *Bulgaria* 38 F5
Dinagat, *Phil.* 55 F6
Dinajpur, *Bangla.* 61 G16
Dinan, *France* 24 D4
Dīnān Āb, *Iran* 65 C8
Dinant, *Belgium* 17 H5
Dinapur, *India* 63 G11
Dinar, *Turkey* 66 D4
Dinara Planina, *Croatia* . 33 E13
Dinard, *France* 24 D4
Dinaric Alps = Dinara
Planina, *Croatia* ... 33 E13
Dinder, Nahr ed →, *Sudan* 77 E3
Dindigul, *India* 60 P11
Dingalan, *Phil.* 55 D4
Dingbian, *China* 50 F4
Dingelstädt, *Germany* ... 18 D6
Dinghai, *China* 53 B14
Dingle, *Ireland* 15 D1
Dingle B., *Ireland* 15 D1
Dingmans Ferry, *U.S.A.* . 107 E10
Dingnan, *China* 53 E10
Dingo, *Australia* 90 C4
Dingolfing, *Germany* 19 G8
Dingqiao, *China* 50 G8
Dingtao, *China* 50 G8
Dinguiraye, *Guinea* 78 C2
Dingwall, *U.K.* 14 D4
Dingxi, *China* 50 G3
Dingxiang, *China* 50 E7
Dingyuan, *China* 53 A11
Dinh, Mui, *Vietnam* 59 G7
Dinh Lap, *Vietnam* 58 B6
Dinkel →, *Neths.* 16 D9
Dinkelsbühl, *Germany* ... 19 F6
Dinokwe, *Botswana* 84 C4
Dinosaur National
Monument, *U.S.A.* 110 F9
Dinslaken, *Germany* 17 E9
Dintel →, *Neths.* 17 E4
Dinteloord, *Neths.* 17 E4
Dinuba, *U.S.A.* 111 H4
Dinxperlo, *Neths.* 16 E9
Diósgyőr, *Hungary* 21 G10
Diourbel, *Senegal* 78 C1
Diplo, *Pakistan* 62 G3
Dipolog, *Phil.* 55 G5
Dipşa, *Romania* 38 C7
Dir, *Pakistan* 60 B7
Diré, *Mali* 78 B4
Dire Dawa, *Ethiopia* 68 F3
Diriamba, *Nic.* 116 D2
Dirico, *Angola* 81 H4
Dirk Hartog I., *Australia* . 89 E1
Dirranbandi, *Australia* .. 91 D4
Disa, *India* 62 G5
Disa, *Sudan* 77 E3
Disappointment, C.,
U.S.A. 110 C1
Disappointment, L.,
Australia 88 D3
Disaster B., *Australia* ... 91 F4
Discovery B., *Australia* .. 91 F3
Disentis, *Switz.* 23 C7
Dishna, *Egypt* 76 B3
Disina, *Nigeria* 79 C6
Disko, *Greenland* 4 C5
Disko Bugt, *Greenland* ... 4 C5
Disna →, *Belorussia* 40 D6
Dison, *Belgium* 17 G7
Disteghil Sar, *Pakistan* . 63 A6
Distrito Federal □, *Brazil* 123 E2
Distrito Federal □,
Venezuela 120 A4
Disūq, *Egypt* 76 H7
Diu, *India* 62 J4
Dīvāndarreh, *Iran* 64 C5
Dives →, *France* 24 C6
Dives-sur-Mer, *France* ... 24 C6
Divichi, *Azerbaijan* 43 F13
Divide, *U.S.A.* 110 D7
Dividing Ra., *Australia* .. 89 E2
Divinópolis, *Brazil* 123 F3
Divisões, Serra dos, *Brazil* 123 E1
Divnoye, *Russia* 43 D10
Divo, *Ivory C.* 78 D3
Divriği, *Turkey* 67 D8
Diwāl Kol, *Afghan.* 62 B2
Dixie Mt., *U.S.A.* 112 F6
Dixon, *Calif., U.S.A.* ... 112 G5
Dixon, *Ill., U.S.A.* 108 E10
Dixon, *Mont., U.S.A.* 110 C6
Dixon, *N. Mex., U.S.A.* .. 111 H11
Dixon Entrance, *U.S.A.* .. 100 C2
Dixonville, *Canada* 100 B5
Diyadin, *Turkey* 67 D10
Diyarbakir, *Turkey* 67 E9
Diyarbakir □, *Turkey* 67 E9
Djado, *Niger* 73 D7
Djakarta = Jakarta,
Indonesia 57 G12
Djamâa, *Algeria* 75 B6
Djamba, *Angola* 84 B1
Djambala, *Congo* 80 E2
Djanet, *Algeria* 75 D6
Djawa = Jawa, *Indonesia* . 57 G14
Djebiniana, *Tunisia* 75 A7
Djelfa, *Algeria* 75 B5
Djema, *C.A.R.* 82 A2
Djendel, *Algeria* 75 A5
Djeneïene, *Tunisia* 75 B7
Djenné, *Mali* 78 C4
Djenoun, Garet el, *Algeria* 75 C6

Djerba, *Tunisia* 75 B7
Djerba, I. de, *Tunisia* .. 73 B7
Djerid, Chott, *Tunisia* .. 75 B6
Djibo, *Burkina Faso* 79 C4
Djibouti, *Djibouti* 68 E3
Djibouti ■, *Africa* 68 E3
Djolu, *Zaïre* 80 D4
Djougou, *Benin* 79 D5
Djoum, *Cameroon* 80 D2
Djourab, *Chad* 73 E8
Djugu, *Zaïre* 82 B3
Djúpivogur, *Iceland* 8 D6
Djursholm, *Sweden* 10 E12
Djursland, *Denmark* 11 H4
Dmitriev-Lgovskiy, *Russia* 40 E9
Dmitriya Lapteva, Proliv,
Russia 45 B15
Dmitrov, *Russia* 41 C10
Dmitrovsk-Orlovskiy,
Russia 40 E9
Dnepr →, *Ukraine* 42 C5
Dneprodzerzhinsk, *Ukraine* 42 B6
Dneprodzerzhinskoye
Vdkhr., *Ukraine* 42 B6
Dnepropetrovsk, *Ukraine* . 42 B6
Dneprorudnoye, *Ukraine* . 42 C6
Dnestr →, *Europe* 42 C4
Dnestrovski = Belgorod,
Russia 41 F10
Dnieper = Dnepr →,
Ukraine 42 C5
Dniester = Dnestr →,
Europe 42 C4
Dnipro = Dnepr →,
Ukraine 42 C5
Dniprodzerzhynsk =
Dneprodzerzhinsk,
Ukraine 42 B6
Dnipropetrovsk =
Dnepropetrovsk, *Ukraine* 42 B6
Dno, *Russia* 40 C6
Dnyapro = Dnepr →,
Ukraine 42 C5
Doan Hung, *Vietnam* 58 B5
Doba, *Chad* 73 G8
Dobbiaco, *Italy* 33 B9
Dobbyn, *Australia* 90 B3
Döbeln, *Germany* 18 D9
Doberai, Jazirah, *Indonesia* 57 E8
Dobiegniew, *Poland* 20 C5
Doblas, *Argentina* 126 D3
Dobo, *Indonesia* 57 F8
Doboj, *Bos.-H.* 21 L8
Dobra, Dîmbovita,
Romania 38 E8
Dobra, Hunedoara,
Romania 38 D5
Dobreta-Turnu-Severin,
Romania 38 E5
Dobrinishta, *Bulgaria* .. 39 H6
Dobrodzień, *Poland* 20 E8
Dobropole, *Ukraine* 42 B7
Dobruja, *Romania* 38 E11
Dobrush, *Belorussia* 40 E7
Dobtong, *Sudan* 77 F3
Doc, Mui, *Vietnam* 58 D6
Doce →, *Brazil* 123 E4
Doda, *India* 63 C6
Dodecanese =
Dhodhekánisos, *Greece* . 39 N10
Dodewaard, *Neths.* 16 E7
Dodge Center, *U.S.A.* 108 C8
Dodge City, *U.S.A.* 109 G5
Dodge L., *Canada* 101 B7
Dodgeville, *U.S.A.* 108 D9
Dodo, *Sudan* 77 F2
Dodola, *Ethiopia* 77 F4
Dodoma, *Tanzania* 82 D4
Dodoma □, *Tanzania* 82 D4
Dodsland, *Canada* 101 C7
Dodson, *U.S.A.* 110 B9
Doesburg, *Neths.* 16 D8
Doetinchem, *Neths.* 16 E8
Dog Creek, *Canada* 100 C4
Dog L., *Man., Canada* ... 101 C9
Dog L., *Ont., Canada* 98 C2
Doğanşehir, *Turkey* 67 D7
Dogger Bank, *N. Sea* 6 E6
Dogi, *Afghan.* 60 C3
Dogliani, *Italy* 32 D4
Dogondoutci, *Niger* 79 C5
Dogran, *Pakistan* 62 D5
Doğubayazıt, *Turkey* 67 D11
Doguéraoua, *Niger* 79 C6
Doha = Ad Dawhah, *Qatar* 65 E6
Dohazari, *Bangla.* 61 H18
Doi, *Indonesia* 57 D7
Doi Luang, *Thailand* 58 C3
Doi Saket, *Thailand* 58 C2
Doig →, *Canada* 100 B4
Dois Irmãos, Sa., *Brazil* . 122 C3
Dokka, *Norway* 9 F11
Dokka →, *Norway* 10 D4
Dokkum, *Neths.* 16 B7
Dokkumer Ee →, *Neths.* . 16 B7
Dokri, *Pakistan* 62 F3
Dol-de-Bretagne, *France* . 24 D5
Doland, *U.S.A.* 108 C5
Dolbeau, *Canada* 99 C5
Dole, *France* 25 E12
Doleib, Wadi →, *Sudan* . 77 E3
Dolgellau, *U.K.* 12 E4
Dolgelley = Dolgellau,
U.K. 12 E4
Dolginovo, *Belorussia* ... 40 D5

Dolianova, Italy	34 C2	Dongmen, China	52 F6
Dolinskaya, Ukraine	42 B5	Dongning, China	51 B16
Dollart, Neths.	16 B10	Dongnyi, China	52 C3
Dolna Banya, Bulgaria	38 G6	Dongola, Sudan	76 D3
Dolni Dŭbnik, Bulgaria	38 F7	Dongou, Congo	80 D3
Dolo, Ethiopia	77 G5	Dongping, China	50 G9
Dolo, Italy	33 C9	Dongshan, China	53 F11
Dolomites = Dolomiti, Italy	33 B8	Dongsheng, China	50 E6
Dolomiti, Italy	33 B8	Dongshi, Taiwan	53 E13
Dolores, Argentina	126 D4	Dongtai, China	51 H11
Dolores, Uruguay	126 C4	Dongting Hu, China	53 C9
Dolores, U.S.A.	111 H9	Dongxiang, China	53 C11
Dolores →, U.S.A.	111 G9	Dongxing, China	52 G7
Dolphin, C., Falk. Is.	128 D5	Dongyang, China	53 C13
Dolphin and Union Str., Canada	96 B8	Dongzhi, China	53 B11
Dom, Switz.	22 D5	Donington, C., Australia	91 E2
Dom Joaquim, Brazil	123 E3	Doniphan, U.S.A.	109 G9
Dom Pedrito, Brazil	127 C5	Donja Stubica, Croatia	33 C13
Dom Pedro, Brazil	122 B3	Donji Dušnik, Serbia	21 M12
Doma, Nigeria	79 D6	Donji Miholjac, Croatia	21 K8
Domaniç, Turkey	66 D3	Donji Milanovac, Serbia	21 L12
Domasi, Malawi	83 F4	Donji Vakuf, Bos.-H.	21 L7
Domat Ems, Switz.	23 C8	Dønna, Norway	8 C12
Domažlice, Czech.	20 F2	Donna, U.S.A.	109 M5
Dombarovskiy, Russia	44 D6	Donnaconna, Canada	99 C5
Dombås, Norway	9 E10	Donnelly's Crossing, N.Z.	87 F4
Dombasle-sur-Meurthe, France	25 D13	Donnybrook, Australia	89 F2
Dombes, France	27 B8	Donnybrook, S. Africa	85 D4
Dombóvár, Hungary	21 J8	Donora, U.S.A.	106 F5
Domburg, Neths.	17 E3	Donor's Hill, Australia	90 B3
Domérat, France	26 B6	Donostia = San Sebastián, Spain	28 B3
Domeyko, Chile	126 B1	Donskoy, Russia	41 E11
Domeyko, Cordillera, Chile	126 A2	Donsol, Phil.	55 E5
Domfront, France	24 D6	Donya Lendava, Slovenia	33 B13
Dominador, Chile	126 A2	Donzère, France	27 D8
Dominica ■, W. Indies	117 C7	Donzère-Mondragon, Barr. de, France	27 D8
Dominica Passage, W. Indies	117 C7	Donzy, France	25 E10
Dominican Rep. ■, W. Indies	117 C5	Doon →, U.K.	14 F4
Dömitz, Germany	18 B7	Doorn, Neths.	16 D6
Domme, France	26 D5	Dora, L., Australia	88 D3
Dommel →, Neths.	17 E6	Dora Báltea →, Italy	32 C5
Domo, Ethiopia	68 F4	Dora Riparia →, Italy	32 C4
Domodóssola, Italy	32 B5	Doran L., Canada	101 A7
Dompaire, France	25 D13	Dorchester, U.K.	13 G5
Dompierre-sur-Besbre, France	26 B7	Dorchester, C., Canada	97 B12
Dompim, Ghana	78 D4	Dordogne □, France	26 C4
Domrémy-la-Pucelle, France	25 D12	Dordogne →, France	26 C3
Domsjö, Sweden	10 A12	Dordrecht, Neths.	16 E5
Domville, Mt., Australia	91 D5	Dordrecht, S. Africa	84 E4
Domvraína, Greece	39 L5	Dore →, France	26 C7
Domžale, Slovenia	33 B11	Dore, Mts., France	26 C6
Don →, Russia	43 C8	Doré L., Canada	101 C7
Don →, Gramp., U.K.	14 D6	Doré Lake, Canada	101 C7
Don →, S. Yorks., U.K.	12 D7	Dores do Indaiá, Brazil	123 E2
Don, C., Australia	88 B5	Dorfen, Germany	19 G8
Don Benito, Spain	31 G5	Dorgali, Italy	34 B2
Don Duong, Vietnam	59 G7	Dori, Burkina Faso	79 C4
Don Martín, Presa de, Mexico	114 B4	Doring →, S. Africa	84 E2
Dona Ana = Nhamaabué, Mozam.	83 F4	Doringbos, S. Africa	84 E2
Donaghadee, U.K.	15 B6	Dorion, Canada	98 C5
Donald, Australia	91 F3	Dormaa-Ahenkro, Ghana	78 D4
Donalda, Canada	100 C6	Dormo, Ras, Eritrea	77 E5
Donaldsonville, U.S.A.	109 K9	Dornach, Switz.	22 B5
Donalsonville, U.S.A.	105 K3	Dornberg, Slovenia	33 C10
Donau →, Austria	21 G7	Dornbirn, Austria	19 H5
Donaueschingen, Germany	19 H4	Dornes, France	25 F10
Donauwörth, Germany	19 G6	Dornoch, U.K.	14 D4
Doncaster, U.K.	12 D6	Dornoch Firth, U.K.	14 D4
Dondo, Angola	80 F2	Dornogovĭ □, Mongolia	50 B6
Dondo, Mozam.	83 F3	Doro, Mali	79 B4
Dondo, Teluk, Indonesia	57 D6	Dorogobuzh, Russia	40 D8
Dondra Head, Sri Lanka	60 S12	Dorohoi, Romania	38 B9
Donegal, Ireland	15 B3	Döröö Nuur, Mongolia	54 B4
Donegal □, Ireland	15 B4	Dorr, Iran	65 C6
Donegal B., Ireland	15 B3	Dorre I., Australia	89 E1
Donets →, Russia	43 C9	Dorrigo, Australia	91 E5
Donetsk, Ukraine	42 C7	Dorris, U.S.A.	110 F3
Dong Ba Thin, Vietnam	59 F7	Dorset, Canada	106 A6
Dong Dang, Vietnam	58 B6	Dorset, U.S.A.	106 E4
Dong Giam, Vietnam	58 C5	Dorset □, U.K.	13 G5
Dong Ha, Vietnam	58 D6	Dorsten, Germany	18 D2
Dong Hene, Laos	58 D5	Dortmund, Germany	18 D3
Dong Hoi, Vietnam	58 D6	Dörtyol, Turkey	66 E7
Dong Jiang →, China	53 F10	Dorum, Germany	18 B4
Dong Khe, Vietnam	58 A6	Doruma, Zaïre	82 B2
Dong Van, Vietnam	58 A5	Dorüneh, Iran	65 C8
Dong Xoai, Vietnam	59 G6	Dos Bahías, C., Argentina	128 B3
Donga, Nigeria	79 D7	Dos Hermanas, Spain	31 H5
Dong'an, China	53 D8	Dos Palos, U.S.A.	112 J6
Dongara, Australia	89 E1	Dosso, Niger	79 C5
Dongbei, China	51 D13	Dothan, U.S.A.	105 K3
Dongchuan, China	52 D4	Dottignies, Belgium	17 G2
Dongen, Neths.	17 E5	Doty, U.S.A.	112 D3
Donges, France	24 E4	Douai, France	25 B10
Dongfang, China	58 C7	Douala, Cameroon	79 E6
Dongfeng, China	51 C13	Douarnenez, France	24 D2
Donggala, Indonesia	57 E5	Double Island Pt., Australia	91 D5
Donggou, China	51 E13	Doubrava →, Czech.	20 F5
Dongguan, China	53 F9	Doubs □, France	25 E13
Dongguang, China	50 F9	Doubs →, France	25 F12
Donghai Dao, China	53 G8	Doubtful Sd., N.Z.	87 L1
Dongjingcheng, China	51 B15	Doubtless B., N.Z.	87 F4
Donglan, China	52 E6	Doudeville, France	24 C7
Dongliu, China	53 B11	Doué-la-Fontaine, France	24 E6
		Douentza, Mali	78 C4
		Douglas, S. Africa	84 D3
		Douglas, U.K.	12 C3
		Douglas, Alaska, U.S.A.	100 B2
		Douglas, Ariz., U.S.A.	111 L9
		Douglas, Ga., U.S.A.	105 K4
		Douglas, Wyo., U.S.A.	108 D2
		Douglastown, Canada	99 C7
		Douglasville, U.S.A.	105 J3

Douirat, Morocco	74 B4	Drumbo, Canada	106 C4
Doukáton, Ákra, Greece	39 L3	Drumheller, Canada	100 C6
Doulevant-le-Château, France	25 D11	Drummond, U.S.A.	110 C7
Doullens, France	25 B9	Drummond I., U.S.A.	98 C3
Doumé, Cameroon	80 D2	Drummond Pt., Australia	91 E2
Douna, Mali	78 C4	Drummond Ra., Australia	90 C4
Dounan, Taiwan	53 F13	Drummondville, Canada	98 C5
Dounreay, U.K.	14 C5	Drumright, U.S.A.	109 H6
Dour, Belgium	17 H3	Drunen, Neths.	17 E6
Dourada, Serra, Brazil	123 D2	Druskininkai, Lithuania	40 D3
Dourados, Brazil	127 A5	Drut →, Belorussia	40 E7
Dourados →, Brazil	127 A5	Druten, Neths.	16 E7
Dourdan, France	25 D9	Druya, Latvia	40 D5
Douro →, Europe	30 D2	Druzhina, Russia	45 C15
Douvaine, France	27 B10	Drvar, Bos.-H.	33 D13
Douz, Tunisia	75 B6	Drvenik, Croatia	33 E13
Douze →, France	26 E3	Dry Tortugas, U.S.A.	116 B3
Dove →, U.K.	12 E6	Dryanovo, Bulgaria	38 G8
Dove Creek, U.S.A.	111 H9	Dryden, Canada	101 D10
Dover, Australia	90 G4	Dryden, U.S.A.	109 K3
Dover, U.K.	13 F9	Drygalski I., Antarctica	5 C7
Dover, Del., U.S.A.	104 F8	Drysdale →, Australia	88 B4
Dover, N.H., U.S.A.	107 C14	Drysdale I., Australia	90 A2
Dover, N.J., U.S.A.	107 F10	Dschang, Cameroon	79 D7
Dover, Ohio, U.S.A.	106 F3	Du Bois, U.S.A.	106 E6
Dover, Pt., Australia	89 F4	Du Quoin, U.S.A.	108 G10
Dover, Str. of, Europe	24 B8	Duaringa, Australia	90 C4
Dover-Foxcroft, U.S.A.	99 C6	Dubā, Si. Arabia	64 E2
Dover Plains, U.S.A.	107 E11	Dubai = Dubayy, U.A.E.	65 E7
Dovey = Dyfi →, U.K.	13 E4	Dubawnt →, Canada	101 A8
Dovrefjell, Norway	10 B3	Dubawnt, L., Canada	101 A8
Dow Rūd, Iran	65 C6	Dubbeldam, Neths.	16 E5
Dowa, Malawi	83 E3	Dubbo, Australia	91 E4
Dowagiac, U.S.A.	104 E2	Dubele, Zaïre	82 B2
Dowgha'i, Iran	65 B8	Dübendorf, Switz.	23 B7
Dowlatābād, Iran	65 D8	Dubica, Croatia	33 C13
Down □, U.K.	15 B6	Dublin, Ireland	15 C5
Downey, Calif., U.S.A.	113 M8	Dublin, Ga., U.S.A.	105 J4
Downey, Idaho, U.S.A.	110 E7	Dublin, Tex., U.S.A.	109 J5
Downham Market, U.K.	13 E8	Dublin □, Ireland	15 C5
Downieville, U.S.A.	112 F6	Dublin B., Ireland	15 C5
Downpatrick, U.K.	15 B6	Dubna, Russia	41 C10
Downpatrick Hd., Ireland	15 B2	Dubna, Russia	41 D10
Dowsārī, Iran	65 D8	Dubno, Ukraine	40 F4
Doyle, U.S.A.	112 E6	Dubois, U.S.A.	110 D7
Doylestown, U.S.A.	107 F9	Dubossary, Moldavia	42 C3
Draa, C., Morocco	74 C2	Dubossary Vdkhr., Moldavia	42 C3
Draa, Oued →, Morocco	74 C2	Dubovka, Russia	43 B11
Drac →, France	27 C9	Dubovskoye, Russia	43 C10
Drachten, Neths.	16 B8	Dubrajpur, India	63 H12
Drăgănești, Romania	38 E7	Dubréka, Guinea	78 D2
Drăgănești-Viașca, Romania	38 E8	Dubrovitsa, Ukraine	40 F5
Dragaš, Serbia	21 N10	Dubrovnik, Croatia	21 N8
Drăgășani, Romania	38 E7	Dubrovskoye, Russia	45 D12
Dragonera, I., Spain	36 B9	Dubuque, U.S.A.	108 D9
Draguignan, France	27 E10	Duchang, China	53 C11
Drain, U.S.A.	110 E2	Duchesne, U.S.A.	110 F8
Drake, Australia	91 D5	Duchess, Australia	90 C2
Drake, U.S.A.	108 B4	Ducie I., Pac. Oc.	93 K15
Drake Passage, S. Ocean	5 B17	Duck Cr. →, Australia	88 D2
Drakensberg, S. Africa	85 E4	Duck Lake, Canada	101 C7
Dráma, Greece	39 H7	Duck Mountain Prov. Park, Canada	101 C8
Drammen, Norway	10 E4	Duckwall, Mt., U.S.A.	112 H6
Drangajökull, Iceland	8 C2	Düdelange, Lux.	17 K8
Drangedal, Norway	10 E3	Duderstadt, Germany	18 D6
Dranov, Ostrov, Romania	38 E12	Dudhi, India	61 G13
Dras, India	63 B6	Düdingen, Switz.	22 C4
Drau = Drava →, Croatia	21 K8	Dudinka, Russia	45 C9
Drava →, Croatia	21 K8	Dudley, U.K.	13 E5
Draveil, France	25 D9	Dueñas, Spain	30 D6
Dravograd, Slovenia	33 B12	Dueré, Brazil	123 D2
Drawa →, Poland	20 C5	Duero = Douro →, Europe	30 D2
Drawno, Poland	20 B5	Duffel, Belgium	17 F5
Drayton Valley, Canada	100 C6	Dufftown, U.K.	14 D5
Dreibergen, Neths.	16 D6	Dufourspitz, Switz.	22 E5
Drenthe □, Neths.	16 C9	Dugi Otok, Croatia	33 E12
Drentsche Hoofdvaart, Neths.	16 C8	Dugo Selo, Croatia	33 C13
Drepanum, C., Cyprus	37 E11	Duifken Pt., Australia	90 A3
Dresden, Canada	106 D2	Duisburg, Germany	18 D2
Dresden, Germany	18 D9	Duitama, Colombia	120 B3
Dreux, France	24 D8	Duiveland, Neths.	17 E4
Driel, Neths.	16 E7	Duiwelskloof, S. Africa	85 C5
Driffield = Great Driffield, U.K.	12 C7	Dūkdamīn, Iran	65 C8
Driftwood, U.S.A.	106 E6	Duke I., U.S.A.	100 C2
Driggs, U.S.A.	110 E8	Dukhān, Qatar	65 E6
Drin i zi →, Albania	39 H3	Dukhovshchina, Russia	40 D8
Drina →, Bos.-H.	21 L9	Duki, Pakistan	60 D6
Drincea →, Romania	38 E5	Duku, Bauchi, Nigeria	79 C7
Drini →, Albania	38 G3	Duku, Sokoto, Nigeria	79 C5
Drinjača →, Bos.-H.	21 L9	Dulag, Phil.	55 F6
Drissa = Verkhnedvinsk, Belorussia	40 D5	Dulce →, Argentina	126 C3
Drivstua, Norway	10 B3	Dulce, G., Costa Rica	116 E3
Drniš, Croatia	33 E13	Dulf, Iraq	64 C5
Drøbak, Norway	10 E4	Dŭlgopol, Bulgaria	38 F10
Drogheda, Ireland	15 C5	Dulit, Banjaran, Malaysia	56 D4
Drogichin, Belorussia	40 E4	Duliu, China	50 E9
Drogobych, Ukraine	40 G3	Dullewala, Pakistan	62 D4
Drohobych = Drogobych, Ukraine	40 G3	Dülmen, Germany	18 D3
Droichead Nua, Ireland	15 C5	Dulovo, Bulgaria	38 F10
Droitwich, U.K.	13 E5	Dulq Maghār, Syria	64 B3
Drôme □, France	27 D9	Dululu, Australia	90 C5
Drôme →, France	27 D8	Duluth, U.S.A.	108 B8
Dromedary, C., Australia	91 F5	Dum Dum, India	63 H13
Dronero, Italy	32 D4	Dum Duma, India	61 F19
Dronfield, Australia	90 C3	Dum Hadjer, Chad	73 F8
Dronne →, France	26 C3	Dūmā, Lebanon	69 A4
Dronninglund, Denmark	11 G4	Dūmā, Syria	69 B5
Dronrijp, Neths.	16 B7	Dumaguete, Phil.	55 G5
Dropt →, France	26 D3	Dumai, Indonesia	56 D2
		Dumaran, Phil.	55 F3

Dumas, Ark., U.S.A.	109 J9
Dumas, Tex., U.S.A.	109 H4
Dumbarton, U.K.	14 F4
Dumbleyung, Australia	89 F2
Dumfries, U.K.	14 F5
Dumfries & Galloway □, U.K.	14 F5
Dumka, India	63 G12
Dümmersee, Germany	18 C4
Dumoine →, Canada	98 C4
Dumoine L., Canada	98 C4
Dumraon, India	63 G11
Dumyât, Egypt	76 H7
Dumyât, Masabb, Egypt	76 H7
Dun Laoghaire, Ireland	15 C5
Dun-le-Palestel, France	26 B5
Dun-sur-Auron, France	25 F9
Duna →, Hungary	21 K8
Dunaföldvár, Hungary	21 J8
Dunaj →, Slovak Rep.	21 H8
Dunajec →, Poland	20 E10
Dunajska Streda, Slovak Rep.	21 H7
Dunapatai, Hungary	21 J9
Dunărea →, Romania	38 D12
Dunaújváros, Hungary	21 J8
Dunav →, Serbia	21 L11
Dunback, N.Z.	87 L3
Dunbar, Australia	90 B3
Dunbar, U.K.	14 E6
Dunblane, U.K.	14 E5
Duncan, Canada	100 D4
Duncan, Ariz., U.S.A.	111 K9
Duncan, Okla., U.S.A.	109 H6
Duncan, L., Canada	98 B4
Duncan L., Canada	100 A6
Duncan Town, Bahamas	116 B4
Duncannon, U.S.A.	106 F7
Dundalk, Canada	106 B4
Dundalk, Ireland	15 B5
Dundalk Bay, Ireland	15 C5
Dundas, Canada	98 D4
Dundas, L., Australia	89 F3
Dundas I., Canada	100 C2
Dundas Str., Australia	88 B5
Dundee, S. Africa	85 D5
Dundee, U.K.	14 E6
Dundgovĭ □, Mongolia	50 B4
Dundoo, Australia	91 D3
Dundrum, U.K.	15 B6
Dundrum B., U.K.	15 B6
Dundwara, India	63 F8
Dunedin, N.Z.	87 L3
Dunedin, U.S.A.	105 L4
Dunedin →, Canada	100 B4
Dunfermline, U.K.	14 E5
Dungannon, Canada	106 C3
Dungannon, U.K.	15 B5
Dungannon □, U.K.	15 B5
Dungarpur, India	62 H5
Dungarvan, Ireland	15 D4
Dungarvan Bay, Ireland	15 D4
Dungeness, U.K.	13 G8
Dungo, L. do, Angola	84 B2
Dungog, Australia	91 E5
Dungu, Zaïre	82 B2
Dungunâb, Sudan	76 C4
Dungunâb, Khalij, Sudan	76 C4
Dunhua, China	51 C15
Dunhuang, China	54 B4
Dunières, France	27 C8
Dunk I., Australia	90 B4
Dunkeld, U.K.	14 E5
Dunkerque, France	25 A9
Dunkery Beacon, U.K.	13 F4
Dunkirk = Dunkerque, France	25 A9
Dunkirk, U.S.A.	106 D5
Dunkuj, Sudan	77 E3
Dunkwa, Central, Ghana	78 D4
Dunkwa, Central, Ghana	79 D4
Dunlap, U.S.A.	108 E7
Dúnleary = Dun Laoghaire, Ireland	15 C5
Dunmanus B., Ireland	15 E2
Dunmara, Australia	90 B1
Dunmore, U.S.A.	107 E9
Dunmore Hd., Ireland	15 D1
Dunmore Town, Bahamas	116 A4
Dunn, U.S.A.	105 H6
Dunnellon, U.S.A.	105 L4
Dunnet Hd., U.K.	14 C5
Dunning, U.S.A.	108 E4
Dunnville, Canada	106 D5
Dunolly, Australia	91 F3
Dunoon, U.K.	14 F4
Dunqul, Egypt	76 C3
Duns, U.K.	14 F6
Dunseith, U.S.A.	108 A4
Dunsmuir, U.S.A.	110 F2
Dunstable, U.K.	13 F7
Dunstan Mts., N.Z.	87 L2
Dunster, U.K.	13 F4
Duntou, China	100 C5
Dunvegan L., Canada	101 A7
Duolun, China	50 C9
Duong Dong, Vietnam	59 G4
Dupree, U.S.A.	108 C4
Dupuyer, U.S.A.	110 B7
Duque de Caxias, Brazil	123 F3
Duque de York, I., Chile	128 D1
Durack →, Australia	88 C4
Durack Ra., Australia	88 C4
Durağan, Turkey	66 C6
Durance →, France	27 E8

Durand

Durand, *U.S.A.* 104 **D4**
Durango = Victoria de Durango, *Mexico* 114 **C4**
Durango, *Spain* 28 **B2**
Durango, *U.S.A.* 111 **H10**
Durango □, *Mexico* 114 **C4**
Duranillin, *Australia* 89 **F2**
Durant, *U.S.A.* 109 **J6**
Duratón →, *Spain* 30 **D6**
Durazno, *Uruguay* 126 **C4**
Durazzo = Durrësi, *Albania* 39 **H2**
Durban, *France* 26 **F6**
Durban, *S. Africa* 85 **D5**
Dúrcal, *Spain* 31 **J7**
Düren, *Germany* 18 **E2**
Durg, *India* 61 **J12**
Durgapur, *India* 63 **H12**
Durham, *Canada* 98 **D3**
Durham, *U.K.* 12 **C6**
Durham, *Calif., U.S.A.* 112 **F5**
Durham, *N.C., U.S.A.* 105 **G6**
Durham □, *U.K.* 12 **C6**
Durham Downs, *Australia* 91 **D4**
Durmitor, *Montenegro* 21 **M9**
Durness, *U.K.* 14 **C4**
Durrësi, *Albania* 39 **H2**
Durrie, *Australia* 90 **D3**
Dursunbey, *Turkey* 66 **D3**
Durtal, *France* 24 **E6**
Duru, *Zaïre* 82 **B2**
D'Urville, Tanjung, *Indonesia* 57 **E9**
D'Urville I., *N.Z.* 87 **J4**
Duryea, *U.S.A.* 107 **E9**
Dusa Mareb, *Somali Rep.* 68 **F4**
Dûsh, *Egypt* 76 **C3**
Dushak, *Turkmenistan* 44 **F7**
Dushan, *China* 52 **E6**
Dushanbe, *Tajikistan* 44 **F7**
Dusheti, *Georgia* 43 **E11**
Dusky Sd., *N.Z.* 87 **L1**
Dussejour, C., *Australia* 88 **B4**
Düsseldorf, *Germany* 18 **D2**
Dussen, *Neths.* 16 **E5**
Dutch Harbor, *U.S.A.* 96 **C3**
Dutlwe, *Botswana* 84 **C3**
Dutsan Wai, *Nigeria* 79 **C6**
Dutton, *Canada* 106 **D3**
Dutton →, *Australia* 90 **C3**
Duved, *Sweden* 10 **A6**
Duvno, *Bos.-H.* 21 **M7**
Duyun, *China* 52 **D6**
Düzce, *Turkey* 66 **C4**
Duzdab = Zāhedān, *Iran* 65 **D9**
Dvina, Sev. →, *Russia* 44 **C5**
Dvinsk = Daugavpils, *Latvia* 40 **D5**
Dvor, *Croatia* 33 **C13**
Dwarka, *India* 62 **H3**
Dwellingup, *Australia* 89 **F2**
Dwight, *Canada* 106 **A5**
Dwight, *U.S.A.* 104 **E1**
Dyakovskoya, *Russia* 41 **A12**
Dyatkovo, *Russia* 40 **E9**
Dyatlovo, *Belorussia* 40 **E4**
Dyer, C., *Canada* 97 **B13**
Dyer Plateau, *Antarctica* 5 **D17**
Dyersburg, *U.S.A.* 109 **G10**
Dyfed □, *U.K.* 13 **E3**
Dyfi →, *U.K.* 13 **E4**
Dyje →, *Czech.* 20 **G6**
Dyle →, *Belgium* 17 **G5**
Dynevor Downs, *Australia* 91 **D3**
Dynów, *Poland* 20 **F12**
Dysart, *Canada* 101 **C8**
Dzamin Üüd, *Mongolia* 50 **C6**
Dzerzhinsk, *Belorussia* 40 **E5**
Dzerzhinsk, *Russia* 41 **C13**
Dzhalinda, *Russia* 45 **D13**
Dzhambeyty, *Kazakhstan* 43 **A15**
Dzhambul, *Kazakhstan* 44 **E8**
Dzhankoi, *Ukraine* 42 **D6**
Dzhanybek, *Kazakhstan* 43 **B12**
Dzhardzhan, *Russia* 45 **C13**
Dzhelinde, *Russia* 45 **C12**
Dzhetygara, *Kazakhstan* 44 **D7**
Dzhezkazgan, *Kazakhstan* 44 **E7**
Dzhikimde, *Russia* 45 **D13**
Dzhizak, *Uzbekistan* 44 **E7**
Dzhugdzur, Khrebet, *Russia* 45 **D14**
Dzhvari, *Georgia* 43 **E10**
Działdowo, *Poland* 20 **B10**
Działoszyn, *Poland* 20 **D8**
Dzierzgoń, *Poland* 20 **B9**
Dzierzoniów, *Poland* 20 **E6**
Dzilam de Bravo, *Mexico* 115 **C7**
Dzioua, *Algeria* 75 **B6**
Dzungaria = Junggar Pendi, *China* 54 **B3**
Dzungarian Gate = Alataw Shankou, *China* 54 **B3**
Dzuumod, *Mongolia* 54 **B5**

E

Eabamet, L., *Canada* 98 **B2**
Eads, *U.S.A.* 108 **F3**
Eagle, *U.S.A.* 110 **G10**
Eagle →, *Canada* 99 **B8**
Eagle Butte, *U.S.A.* 108 **C4**
Eagle Grove, *U.S.A.* 108 **D8**
Eagle L., *Calif., U.S.A.* 110 **F3**
Eagle L., *Maine, U.S.A.* 99 **C6**
Eagle Lake, *U.S.A.* 109 **L6**
Eagle Mountain, *U.S.A.* 113 **M11**
Eagle Nest, *U.S.A.* 111 **H11**
Eagle Pass, *U.S.A.* 109 **L4**
Eagle Pk., *U.S.A.* 112 **G7**
Eagle Pt., *Australia* 88 **C3**
Eagle River, *U.S.A.* 108 **C10**
Ealing, *U.K.* 13 **F7**
Earaheedy, *Australia* 89 **E3**
Earl Grey, *Canada* 101 **C8**
Earle, *U.S.A.* 109 **H9**
Earlimart, *U.S.A.* 113 **K7**
Earn →, *U.K.* 14 **E5**
Earn, L., *U.K.* 14 **E4**
Earnslaw, Mt., *N.Z.* 87 **L2**
Earth, *U.S.A.* 109 **H3**
Easley, *U.S.A.* 105 **H4**
East Angus, *Canada* 99 **C5**
East Aurora, *U.S.A.* 106 **D6**
East B., *U.S.A.* 109 **L10**
East Bengal, *Bangla.* 61 **G17**
East Beskids = Vychodné Beskydy, *Europe* 20 **F11**
East Brady, *U.S.A.* 106 **F5**
East C., *N.Z.* 87 **G7**
East Chicago, *U.S.A.* 104 **E2**
East China Sea, *Asia* 54 **C7**
East Coulee, *Canada* 100 **C6**
East Falkland, *Falk. Is.* 128 **D5**
East Grand Forks, *U.S.A.* 108 **B6**
East Greenwich, *U.S.A.* 107 **E13**
East Hartford, *U.S.A.* 107 **E12**
East Helena, *U.S.A.* 110 **C8**
East Indies, *Asia* 57 **E6**
East Jordan, *U.S.A.* 104 **C3**
East Lansing, *U.S.A.* 104 **D3**
East Liverpool, *U.S.A.* 106 **F4**
East London, *S. Africa* 85 **E4**
East Main = Eastmain, *Canada* 98 **B4**
East Orange, *U.S.A.* 107 **F10**
East Pacific Ridge, *Pac. Oc.* 93 **J17**
East Pakistan = Bangladesh ■, *Asia* 61 **H17**
East Palestine, *U.S.A.* 106 **F4**
East Pine, *Canada* 100 **B4**
East Pt., *Canada* 99 **C7**
East Point, *U.S.A.* 105 **J3**
East Providence, *U.S.A.* 107 **E13**
East Retford, *U.K.* 12 **D7**
East St. Louis, *U.S.A.* 108 **F9**
East Schelde → = Oosterschelde, *Neths.* 17 **E4**
East Siberian Sea, *Russia* 45 **B17**
East Stroudsburg, *U.S.A.* 107 **E9**
East Sussex □, *U.K.* 13 **G8**
East Tawas, *U.S.A.* 104 **C4**
East Toorale, *Australia* 91 **E4**
East Walker →, *U.S.A.* 112 **G7**
Eastbourne, *N.Z.* 87 **J5**
Eastbourne, *U.K.* 13 **G8**
Eastend, *Canada* 101 **D7**
Easter Dal = Österdalälven →, *Sweden* 9 **F12**
Easter Islands = Pascua, I. de, *Pac. Oc.* 93 **K17**
Eastern □, *Kenya* 82 **B4**
Eastern □, *Uganda* 82 **B3**
Eastern Cr. →, *Australia* 90 **C3**
Eastern Ghats, *India* 60 **N11**
Eastern Group = Lau Group, *Fiji* 87 **C9**
Eastern Group, *Australia* 89 **F3**
Eastern Province □, *S. Leone* 78 **D2**
Easterville, *Canada* 101 **C9**
Easthampton, *U.S.A.* 107 **D12**
Eastland, *U.S.A.* 109 **J5**
Eastleigh, *U.K.* 13 **G6**
Eastmain, *Canada* 98 **B4**
Eastmain →, *Canada* 98 **B4**
Eastman, *Canada* 107 **A12**
Eastman, *U.S.A.* 105 **J4**
Easton, *Md., U.S.A.* 104 **F7**
Easton, *Pa., U.S.A.* 107 **F9**
Easton, *Wash., U.S.A.* 112 **C5**
Eastport, *U.S.A.* 99 **D6**
Eastsound, *U.S.A.* 112 **B4**
Eaton, *U.S.A.* 108 **E2**
Eatonia, *Canada* 101 **C7**
Eatonton, *U.S.A.* 105 **J4**
Eatontown, *U.S.A.* 107 **F10**
Eatonville, *U.S.A.* 112 **D4**
Eau Claire, *Fr. Guiana* 121 **C7**
Eau Claire, *U.S.A.* 108 **C9**
Eauze, *France* 26 **E4**
Ebagoola, *Australia* 90 **A3**
Eban, *Nigeria* 79 **D5**
Ebbw Vale, *U.K.* 13 **F4**
Ebeggui, *Algeria* 75 **C6**
Ebeltoft, *Denmark* 9 **H11**
Ebensburg, *U.S.A.* 106 **F6**
Ebensee, *Austria* 21 **H3**
Eber Gölü, *Turkey* 66 **D4**
Eberbach, *Germany* 19 **F4**
Eberswalde, *Germany* 18 **C9**
Ebetsu, *Japan* 48 **C10**
Ebian, *China* 52 **C4**
Ebikon, *Switz.* 23 **B6**
Ebingen, *Germany* 19 **G5**
Ebnat-Kappel, *Switz.* 23 **B8**
Eboli, *Italy* 35 **B8**
Ebolowa, *Cameroon* 79 **E7**
Ebrach, *Germany* 19 **F6**
Ébrié, Lagune, *Ivory C.* 78 **D4**
Ebro →, *Spain* 28 **E5**
Ebro, Pantano del, *Spain* 30 **B7**
Ebstorf, *Germany* 18 **B6**
Ecaussines-d' Enghien, *Belgium* 17 **G4**
Eceabat, *Turkey* 66 **C2**
Ech Cheliff, *Algeria* 75 **A5**
Echallens, *Switz.* 22 **C3**
Echeng, *China* 53 **B10**
Echigo-Sammyaku, *Japan* 49 **F9**
Echizen-Misaki, *Japan* 49 **G7**
Echmiadzin, *Armenia* 43 **F11**
Echo Bay, *N.W.T., Canada* 96 **B8**
Echo Bay, *Ont., Canada* 98 **C3**
Echoing →, *Canada* 101 **B10**
Echt, *Neths.* 17 **F7**
Echternach, *Lux.* 17 **J8**
Echuca, *Australia* 91 **F3**
Ecija, *Spain* 31 **H5**
Eckernförde, *Germany* 18 **A5**
Eclipse Is., *Australia* 88 **B4**
Écommoy, *France* 24 **E7**
Ecoporanga, *Brazil* 123 **E3**
Écos, *France* 25 **C8**
Écouché, *France* 24 **D6**
Ecuador ■, *S. Amer.* 120 **D2**
Écueillé, *France* 24 **E8**
Ed, *Sweden* 11 **F5**
Ed Dabbura, *Sudan* 76 **D3**
Ed Dâmer, *Sudan* 76 **D3**
Ed Debba, *Sudan* 76 **D3**
Ed-Déffa, *Egypt* 76 **A2**
Ed Deim, *Sudan* 77 **E2**
Ed Dueim, *Sudan* 77 **E3**
Edah, *Australia* 89 **E2**
Edam, *Canada* 101 **C7**
Edam, *Neths.* 16 **C6**
Eday, *U.K.* 14 **B6**
Edd, *Eritrea* 68 **E3**
Eddrachillis B., *U.K.* 14 **C3**
Eddystone, *U.K.* 13 **G3**
Eddystone Pt., *Australia* 90 **G4**
Ede, *Neths.* 16 **D7**
Ede, *Nigeria* 79 **D5**
Édea, *Cameroon* 79 **E7**
Edegem, *Belgium* 17 **F4**
Edehon L., *Canada* 101 **A9**
Edekel, Adrar, *Algeria* 75 **D6**
Eden, *Australia* 91 **F4**
Eden, *N.C., U.S.A.* 105 **G6**
Eden, *N.Y., U.S.A.* 106 **D6**
Eden, *Tex., U.S.A.* 109 **K5**
Eden, *Wyo., U.S.A.* 110 **E9**
Eden →, *U.K.* 12 **C4**
Eden L., *Canada* 101 **B8**
Edenburg, *S. Africa* 84 **D4**
Edendale, *S. Africa* 85 **D5**
Edenderry, *Ireland* 15 **C4**
Edenton, *U.S.A.* 105 **G7**
Edenville, *S. Africa* 85 **D4**
Eder →, *Germany* 18 **D5**
Ederstausee, *Germany* 18 **D4**
Edgar, *U.S.A.* 108 **E5**
Edgartown, *U.S.A.* 107 **E14**
Edge Hill, *U.K.* 13 **E6**
Edgefield, *U.S.A.* 105 **J5**
Edgeley, *U.S.A.* 108 **B5**
Edgemont, *U.S.A.* 108 **D3**
Edgeøya, *Svalbard* 4 **B9**
Edhessa, *Greece* 39 **J5**
Edievale, *N.Z.* 87 **L2**
Edina, *Liberia* 78 **D2**
Edina, *U.S.A.* 108 **E8**
Edinburg, *U.S.A.* 109 **M5**
Edinburgh, *U.K.* 14 **F5**
Edirne, *Turkey* 39 **H9**
Edirne □, *Turkey* 66 **C2**
Edison, *U.S.A.* 112 **B4**
Edithburgh, *Australia* 91 **F2**
Edjeleh, *Algeria* 75 **C6**
Edjudina, *Australia* 89 **E3**
Edmeston, *U.S.A.* 107 **D9**
Edmond, *U.S.A.* 109 **H6**
Edmonds, *U.S.A.* 112 **C4**
Edmonton, *Australia* 90 **B4**
Edmonton, *Canada* 100 **C6**
Edmund L., *Canada* 101 **C10**
Edmundston, *Canada* 99 **C6**
Edna, *U.S.A.* 109 **L6**
Edna Bay, *U.S.A.* 100 **B2**
Edo □, *Nigeria* 79 **D6**
Edolo, *Italy* 32 **B7**
Edremit, *Turkey* 66 **D2**
Edremit Körfezi, *Turkey* 66 **D2**
Edsbyn, *Sweden* 10 **C9**
Edsele, *Sweden* 10 **A10**
Edson, *Canada* 100 **C5**
Eduardo Castex, *Argentina* 126 **D3**
Edward →, *Australia* 91 **F3**
Edward, L., *Africa* 82 **C2**
Edward I., *Canada* 98 **C2**
Edward River, *Australia* 90 **A3**
Edward VII Land, *Antarctica* 5 **E13**
Edwards, *U.S.A.* 113 **L9**
Edwards Plateau, *U.S.A.* 109 **K4**
Edwardsville, *U.S.A.* 107 **E9**
Edzo, *Canada* 100 **A5**
Eefde, *Neths.* 16 **D8**
Eekloo, *Belgium* 17 **F3**
Eelde, *Neths.* 16 **B9**
Eem →, *Neths.* 16 **D6**
Eems →, *Neths.* 16 **B9**
Eems Kanaal, *Neths.* 16 **B9**
Eenrum, *Neths.* 16 **B8**
Eernegem, *Belgium* 17 **F2**
Eerste Valthermond, *Neths.* 16 **C9**
Efferi, *Algeria* 75 **D6**
Effingham, *U.S.A.* 104 **F1**
Effretikon, *Switz.* 23 **B7**
Eforie Sud, *Romania* 38 **E11**
Ega →, *Spain* 28 **C3**
Égadi, Ísole, *Italy* 34 **E5**
Eganville, *Canada* 98 **C4**
Egeland, *U.S.A.* 108 **A5**
Egenolf L., *Canada* 101 **B9**
Eger = Cheb, *Czech.* 20 **E2**
Eger, *Hungary* 21 **H10**
Eger →, *Hungary* 21 **H10**
Egersund, *Norway* 9 **G9**
Egg L., *Canada* 101 **B7**
Eggenburg, *Austria* 20 **G5**
Eggenfelden, *Germany* 19 **G8**
Eggiwil, *Switz.* 22 **C5**
Éghezée, *Belgium* 17 **G5**
Eginbah, *Australia* 88 **D2**
Égletons, *France* 26 **C6**
Eglisau, *Switz.* 23 **A7**
Egmond-aan-Zee, *Neths.* 16 **C5**
Egmont, C., *N.Z.* 87 **H4**
Egmont, Mt., *N.Z.* 87 **H5**
Eğridir, *Turkey* 66 **E4**
Eğridir Gölü, *Turkey* 66 **E4**
Egtved, *Denmark* 11 **J3**
Éguas →, *Brazil* 123 **D3**
Egume, *Nigeria* 79 **D6**
Éguzon, *France* 26 **B5**
Egvekinot, *Russia* 45 **C19**
Egypt ■, *Africa* 76 **J7**
Eha Amufu, *Nigeria* 79 **D6**
Ehime □, *Japan* 49 **H6**
Ehingen, *Germany* 19 **G5**
Ehrenberg, *U.S.A.* 113 **M12**
Ehrwald, *Austria* 19 **H6**
Eibar, *Spain* 28 **B2**
Eibergen, *Neths.* 16 **D9**
Eichstatt, *Germany* 19 **G7**
Eider →, *Germany* 18 **A4**
Eidsvold, *Australia* 91 **D5**
Eidsvoll, *Norway* 9 **F11**
Eifel, *Germany* 19 **E2**
Eiffel Flats, *Zimbabwe* 83 **F3**
Eigg, *U.K.* 14 **E2**
Eighty Mile Beach, *Australia* 88 **C3**
Eil, *Somali Rep.* 68 **F4**
Eil, L., *U.K.* 14 **E3**
Eildon, L., *Australia* 91 **F4**
Eileen L., *Canada* 101 **A7**
Eilenburg, *Germany* 18 **D8**
Ein el Luweiqa, *Sudan* 77 **E3**
Einasleigh, *Australia* 90 **B3**
Einasleigh →, *Australia* 90 **B3**
Einbeck, *Germany* 18 **D5**
Eindhoven, *Neths.* 17 **F6**
Einsiedeln, *Switz.* 23 **B7**
Eire ■ = Ireland ■, *Europe* 15 **D4**
Eiríksjökull, *Iceland* 8 **D3**
Eirlandsche Gat, *Neths.* 16 **B5**
Eirunepé, *Brazil* 124 **B4**
Eisden, *Belgium* 17 **G7**
Eisenach, *Germany* 18 **E6**
Eisenberg, *Germany* 18 **E7**
Eisenerz, *Austria* 21 **H4**
Eisenhüttenstadt, *Germany* 18 **C10**
Eisenstadt, *Austria* 21 **H6**
Eiserfeld, *Germany* 18 **E3**
Eisfeld, *Germany* 18 **E6**
Eisleben, *Germany* 18 **D7**
Eivissa = Ibiza, *Spain* 36 **C7**
Ejby, *Denmark* 11 **J3**
Eje, Sierra del, *Spain* 30 **C4**
Ejea de los Caballeros, *Spain* 28 **C3**
Ejutla, *Mexico* 115 **D5**
Ekalaka, *U.S.A.* 108 **C2**
Ekeren, *Belgium* 17 **F4**
Eket, *Nigeria* 79 **E6**
Eketahuna, *N.Z.* 87 **J5**
Ekhínos, *Greece* 39 **H8**
Ekibastuz, *Kazakhstan* 44 **D8**
Ekimchan, *Russia* 45 **D14**
Ekoli, *Zaïre* 82 **C1**
Eksel, *Belgium* 17 **F6**
Ekwan →, *Canada* 98 **B3**
Ekwan Pt., *Canada* 98 **B3**
El Aaiún, *W. Sahara* 74 **C2**
El Aargub, *Mauritania* 74 **D1**
El Abiodh-Sidi-Cheikh, *Algeria* 75 **B5**
El 'Agrûd, *Egypt* 69 **E3**
El Aïoun, *Morocco* 75 **B4**
El 'Aiyat, *Egypt* 76 **J7**
El Alamein, *Egypt* 76 **H6**
El Alto, *Peru* 124 **A1**
El 'Aqaba, W. →, *Egypt* 69 **E2**
El 'Arag, *Egypt* 76 **B2**
El Arahal, *Spain* 31 **H5**
El Arenal, *Spain* 36 **B9**
El Aricha, *Algeria* 75 **B4**
El Arīhā, *Jordan* 69 **D4**
El Arish, *Australia* 90 **B4**
El 'Arîsh, *Egypt* 69 **D2**
El 'Arîsh, W. →, *Egypt* 69 **D2**
El Arrouch, *Algeria* 75 **A6**
El Asnam = Ech Cheliff, *Algeria* 75 **A5**
El Astillero, *Spain* 30 **B7**
El Badâri, *Egypt* 76 **B3**
El Bahrein, *Egypt* 76 **B2**
El Ballâs, *Egypt* 76 **B3**
El Balyana, *Egypt* 76 **B3**
El Banco, *Colombia* 120 **B3**
El Baqeir, *Sudan* 76 **D3**
El Barco de Ávila, *Spain* 30 **E5**
El Barco de Valdeorras, *Spain* 30 **C4**
El Bauga, *Sudan* 76 **D3**
El Baúl, *Venezuela* 120 **B4**
El Bawiti, *Egypt* 76 **J6**
El Bayadh, *Algeria* 75 **B5**
El Bierzo, *Spain* 30 **C4**
El Bluff, *Nic.* 116 **D3**
El Bolsón, *Argentina* 128 **B2**
El Bonillo, *Spain* 29 **G2**
El Brûk, W. →, *Egypt* 69 **E2**
El Buheirat □, *Sudan* 77 **F2**
El Caín, *Argentina* 128 **B3**
El Cajon, *U.S.A.* 113 **N10**
El Callao, *Venezuela* 121 **B5**
El Camp, *Spain* 28 **D6**
El Campo, *U.S.A.* 109 **L6**
El Carmen, *Bolivia* 125 **C5**
El Carmen, *Venezuela* 120 **C4**
El Castillo, *Spain* 31 **H4**
El Centro, *U.S.A.* 113 **N11**
El Cerro, *Bolivia* 125 **D5**
El Cerro, *Spain* 31 **H4**
El Cocuy, *Colombia* 120 **B3**
El Compadre, *Mexico* 113 **N10**
El Corcovado, *Argentina* 128 **B2**
El Coronil, *Spain* 31 **H5**
El Cuy, *Argentina* 128 **A3**
El Cuyo, *Mexico* 115 **C7**
El Dab'a, *Egypt* 76 **H6**
El Daheir, *Egypt* 69 **D3**
El Deir, *Egypt* 76 **B3**
El Dere, *Somali Rep.* 68 **G4**
El Descanso, *Mexico* 113 **N10**
El Desemboque, *Mexico* 114 **A2**
El Dilingat, *Egypt* 76 **H7**
El Diviso, *Colombia* 120 **C2**
El Djem, *Tunisia* 75 **A7**
El Djouf, *Mauritania* 70 **D3**
El Dorado, *Ark., U.S.A.* 109 **J8**
El Dorado, *Kans., U.S.A.* 109 **G6**
El Dorado, *Venezuela* 121 **B5**
El Eglab, *Algeria* 74 **C4**
El Escorial, *Spain* 30 **E6**
El Eulma, *Algeria* 75 **A6**
El Faiyûm, *Egypt* 76 **J7**
El Fâsher, *Sudan* 77 **E2**
El Fashn, *Egypt* 76 **J7**
El Ferrol, *Spain* 30 **B2**
El Fifi, *Sudan* 77 **E1**
El Fuerte, *Mexico* 114 **B3**
El Gal, *Somali Rep.* 68 **E5**
El Gebir, *Sudan* 77 **E2**
El Gedida, *Egypt* 76 **B2**
El Geteina, *Sudan* 77 **E3**
El Gezira □, *Sudan* 77 **E3**
El Gîza, *Egypt* 76 **H7**
El Goléa, *Algeria* 75 **B5**
El Guettar, *Algeria* 75 **B5**
El Hadeb, *W. Sahara* 74 **C2**
El Hadjira, *Algeria* 75 **B6**
El Hagiz, *Sudan* 77 **D4**
El Hajeb, *Morocco* 74 **B3**
El Hammam, *Egypt* 76 **H6**
El Hammâmi, *Mauritania* 74 **D2**
El Hank, *Mauritania* 74 **D3**
El Harrach, *Algeria* 75 **A5**
El Hasian, *W. Sahara* 74 **C2**
El Hawata, *Sudan* 77 **E3**
El Heiz, *Egypt* 76 **B2**
El 'Idisât, *Egypt* 76 **B3**
El Iskandarîya, *Egypt* 76 **H6**
El Jadida, *Morocco* 74 **B3**
El Jebelein, *Sudan* 77 **E3**
El Kab, *Sudan* 76 **D3**
El Kabrît, G., *Egypt* 69 **F2**
El Kala, *Algeria* 75 **A6**
El Kalâa, *Morocco* 74 **B3**
El Kamlin, *Sudan* 77 **D3**
El Kantara, *Algeria* 75 **A6**
El Kantara, *Tunisia* 75 **B7**
El Karaba, *Sudan* 76 **D3**
El Kef, *Tunisia* 75 **A6**
El Khandaq, *Sudan* 76 **D3**
El Khârga, *Egypt* 76 **B3**
El Khartûm, *Sudan* 77 **D3**
El Khartûm □, *Sudan* 77 **D3**
El Khartûm Bahrî, *Sudan* 77 **D3**
El Khroub, *Algeria* 75 **A6**
El Kseur, *Algeria* 75 **A5**
El Ksiba, *Morocco* 74 **B3**
El Kuntilla, *Egypt* 69 **E3**
El Laqâwa, *Sudan* 77 **E2**
El Laqeita, *Egypt* 76 **B3**
El Leiya, *Sudan* 77 **D4**
El Mafâza, *Sudan* 77 **E3**
El Mahalla el Kubra, *Egypt* 76 **H7**
El Mahârîq, *Egypt* 76 **B3**
El Mahmûdîya, *Egypt* 76 **H7**
El Maitén, *Argentina* 128 **B2**
El Maiz, *Algeria* 75 **C4**
El-Maks el-Bahari, *Egypt* 76 **C3**
El Manshâh, *Egypt* 76 **B3**
El Mansour, *Algeria* 75 **C4**
El Mansûra, *Egypt* 76 **H7**

El Mantico, Venezuela	121	B5
El Manzala, Egypt	76	H7
El Marâgha, Egypt	76	B3
El Masid, Sudan	77	D3
El Matariya, Egypt	76	H8
El Medano, Canary Is.	36	F3
El Meghaier, Algeria	75	B6
El Meraguen, Algeria	75	C4
El Metemma, Sudan	77	D3
El Miamo, Venezuela	121	B5
El Milagro, Argentina	126	C2
El Milia, Algeria	75	A6
El Minyâ, Egypt	76	J7
El Molar, Spain	28	E1
El Mreyye, Mauritania	78	B3
El Obeid, Sudan	77	E3
El Odaiya, Sudan	77	E2
El Oro, Mexico	115	D4
El Oro □, Ecuador	120	D2
El Oued, Algeria	75	B6
El Palmar, Bolivia	125	D5
El Palmar, Venezuela	121	B5
El Palmito, Presa, Mexico	114	B3
El Panadés, Spain	28	D6
El Pardo, Spain	30	E7
El Paso, U.S.A.	111	L10
El Paso Robles, U.S.A.	112	K6
El Pedernoso, Spain	29	F2
El Pedroso, Spain	31	H5
El Pobo de Dueñas, Spain	28	E3
El Portal, U.S.A.	111	H4
El Porvenir, Mexico	114	A3
El Prat de Llobregat, Spain	28	D7
El Progreso, Honduras	116	C2
El Provencío, Spain	29	F2
El Pueblito, Mexico	114	B3
El Pueblo, Canary Is.	36	F2
El Qâhira, Egypt	76	H7
El Qantara, Egypt	69	E1
El Quseima, Egypt	69	E3
El Qusîya, Egypt	76	B3
El Râshda, Egypt	76	B2
El Reno, U.S.A.	109	H6
El Ribero, Spain	30	C2
El Rîdisiya, Egypt	76	C3
El Rio, U.S.A.	113	L7
El Ronquillo, Spain	31	H4
El Roque, Pta., Canary Is.	36	F4
El Rosarito, Mexico	114	B2
El Rubio, Spain	31	H5
El Saff, Egypt	76	J7
El Saheira, W. →, Egypt	69	E2
El Salado, Mexico	114	C3
El Salto, Mexico	114	C3
El Salvador ■, Cent. Amer.	116	D2
El Sancejo, Spain	31	H5
El Sauce, Nic.	116	D2
El Shallal, Egypt	76	C3
El Simbillawein, Egypt	76	H7
El Sombrero, Venezuela	120	B4
El Suweis, Egypt	76	J8
El Tamarâni, W. →, Egypt	69	E3
El Thamad, Egypt	69	F3
El Tigre, Venezuela	121	B5
El Tîh, G., Egypt	69	F2
El Tîna, Khalîg, Egypt	69	D1
El Tocuyo, Venezuela	120	B4
El Tofo, Chile	126	B1
El Tránsito, Chile	126	B1
El Tûr, Egypt	76	J8
El Turbio, Argentina	128	D2
El Uqsur, Egypt	76	B3
El Vado, Spain	28	D1
El Vallés, Spain	28	D7
El Venado, Mexico	114	C4
El Vigía, Venezuela	120	B3
El Wabeira, Egypt	69	F2
El Wak, Kenya	82	B5
El Waqf, Egypt	76	B3
El Wâsta, Egypt	76	J7
El Weguet, Ethiopia	77	F5
El Wuz, Sudan	77	D3
Elafónisos, Greece	39	N5
Elandsvlei, S. Africa	84	E2
Élassa, Greece	39	P9
Elassón, Greece	39	K5
Elat, Israel	69	F3
Elâzığ, Turkey	67	D8
Elâzığ □, Turkey	67	D8
Elba, Italy	32	F7
Elba, U.S.A.	105	K2
Elbasani, Albania	39	H3
Elbe, U.S.A.	112	D4
Elbe →, Europe	18	B4
Elbe-Seiten Kanal, Germany	18	C6
Elbert, Mt., U.S.A.	111	G10
Elberta, U.S.A.	104	C2
Elberton, U.S.A.	105	H4
Elbeuf, France	24	C4
Elbing = Elbląg, Poland	20	A9
Elbląg, Poland	20	A9
Elbow, Canada	101	C7
Elbrus, Asia	43	E10
Elburg, Neths.	16	D7
Elburz Mts. = Alborz, Reshteh-ye Kūhhā-ye, Iran	65	C7
Elche, Spain	29	G4
Elche de la Sierra, Spain	29	G2
Elcho I., Australia	90	A2
Elda, Spain	29	G4
Eldon, Mo., U.S.A.	108	F8
Eldon, Wash., U.S.A.	112	C3
Eldora, U.S.A.	108	D8
Eldorado, Argentina	127	B5
Eldorado, Canada	101	B7
Eldorado, Mexico	114	C3
Eldorado, Ill., U.S.A.	104	G1
Eldorado, Tex., U.S.A.	109	K4
Eldorado Springs, U.S.A.	109	G8
Eldoret, Kenya	82	B4
Eldred, U.S.A.	106	E6
Elea, C., Cyprus	37	D13
Electra, U.S.A.	109	H5
Elefantes →, Mozam.	85	C5
Elefantes, G., Chile	128	C2
Elektrogorsk, Russia	41	D11
Elektrostal, Russia	41	D11
Elele, Nigeria	79	D6
Elephant Butte Reservoir, U.S.A.	111	K10
Elephant I., Antarctica	5	C18
Elesbão Veloso, Brazil	122	C3
Eleşkirt, Turkey	67	D10
Eleuthera, Bahamas	116	A4
Elgepiggen, Norway	10	B5
Elgeyo-Marakwet □, Kenya	82	B4
Elgg, Switz.	23	B7
Elgin, N.B., Canada	99	C6
Elgin, Ont., Canada	107	B8
Elgin, U.K.	14	D5
Elgin, Ill., U.S.A.	104	D1
Elgin, N. Dak., U.S.A.	108	B4
Elgin, Nebr., U.S.A.	108	E5
Elgin, Nev., U.S.A.	111	H6
Elgin, Oreg., U.S.A.	110	D5
Elgin, Tex., U.S.A.	109	K6
Elgon, Mt., Africa	82	B3
Eliase, Indonesia	57	F8
Elida, U.S.A.	109	J3
Elikón, Greece	39	L5
Elim, S. Africa	84	E2
Elisabethville = Lubumbashi, Zaïre	83	E2
Eliseu Martins, Brazil	122	C3
Elista, Russia	43	C11
Elizabeth, Australia	91	E2
Elizabeth, U.S.A.	107	F10
Elizabeth City, U.S.A.	105	G7
Elizabethton, U.S.A.	105	G4
Elizabethtown, Ky., U.S.A.	104	G3
Elizabethtown, N.Y., U.S.A.	107	B11
Elizabethtown, Pa., U.S.A.	107	F8
Elizondo, Spain	28	B3
Elk, Poland	20	B12
Elk City, U.S.A.	109	H5
Elk Creek, U.S.A.	112	F4
Elk Grove, U.S.A.	112	G5
Elk Island Nat. Park, Canada	100	C6
Elk Lake, Canada	98	C3
Elk Point, Canada	101	C6
Elk River, Idaho, U.S.A.	110	C5
Elk River, Minn., U.S.A.	108	C8
Elkedra, Australia	90	C2
Elkedra →, Australia	90	C2
Elkhart, Ind., U.S.A.	104	E3
Elkhart, Kans., U.S.A.	109	G4
Elkhorn, Canada	101	D8
Elkhorn →, U.S.A.	108	E6
Elkhotovo, Russia	43	E11
Elkhovo, Bulgaria	38	G9
Elkin, U.S.A.	105	G5
Elkins, U.S.A.	104	F6
Elko, Canada	100	D5
Elko, U.S.A.	110	F6
Ell, L., Australia	89	E4
Ellecom, Neths.	16	D8
Ellendale, Australia	88	C3
Ellendale, U.S.A.	108	B5
Ellenville, U.S.A.	107	E10
Ellery, Mt., Australia	91	F4
Ellesmere, Mt., N.Z.	87	M4
Ellesmere I., Canada	4	B4
Ellesmere Port, U.K.	12	D5
Ellezelles, Belgium	17	G3
Ellice Is. = Tuvalu ■, Pac. Oc.	92	H9
Ellinwood, U.S.A.	108	F5
Elliot, Australia	90	B1
Elliot, S. Africa	85	E4
Elliot Lake, Canada	98	C3
Elliotdale = Xhora, S. Africa	85	E4
Ellis, U.S.A.	108	F5
Elliston, Australia	91	E1
Ellon, U.K.	14	D6
Ellore = Eluru, India	61	L12
Ells →, Canada	100	B6
Ellsworth, U.S.A.	108	F5
Ellsworth Land, Antarctica	5	D16
Ellsworth Mts., Antarctica	5	D16
Ellwangen, Germany	19	G6
Ellwood City, U.S.A.	106	F4
Elm, Switz.	23	C8
Elma, Canada	101	D9
Elma, U.S.A.	112	D3
Elmadağ, Turkey	66	D5
Elmalı, Turkey	66	E3
Elmhurst, U.S.A.	104	E2
Elmina, Ghana	79	D4
Elmira, Canada	106	C4
Elmira, U.S.A.	106	D8
Elmore, Australia	91	F3
Elmore, U.S.A.	113	M11
Elmshorn, Germany	18	B5
Elmvale, Canada	106	B5
Elne, France	26	F6
Elora, Canada	106	C4
Elorza, Venezuela	120	B4
Eloúnda, Greece	37	D7
Eloy, U.S.A.	111	K8
Éloyes, France	25	D13
Elrose, Canada	101	C7
Elsas, Canada	98	C3
Elsie, U.S.A.	112	E3
Elsinore = Helsingør, Denmark	11	H6
Elsinore, U.S.A.	111	G7
Elspe, Germany	18	D4
Elspeet, Neths.	16	D7
Elst, Neths.	16	E7
Elster →, Germany	18	D7
Elsterwerda, Germany	18	D9
Elten, Neths.	16	E8
Eltham, N.Z.	87	H5
Elton, Russia	43	B12
Eluanbi, Taiwan	53	G13
Eluru, India	61	L12
Elvas, Portugal	31	G3
Elven, France	24	E4
Elverum, Norway	10	D5
Elvire →, Australia	88	C4
Elvo →, Italy	32	C5
Elvran, Norway	10	A5
Elwood, Ind., U.S.A.	104	E3
Elwood, Nebr., U.S.A.	108	E5
Elx = Elche, Spain	29	G4
Ely, U.K.	13	E8
Ely, Minn., U.S.A.	108	B9
Ely, Nev., U.S.A.	110	G6
Elyria, U.S.A.	106	E2
Elz →, Germany	19	G3
Emāmrūd, Iran	65	B7
Emba, Kazakhstan	44	E6
Emba →, Kazakhstan	44	E6
Embarcación, Argentina	126	A3
Embarras Portage, Canada	101	B6
Embetsu, Japan	48	B10
Embira →, Brazil	124	B3
Embóna, Greece	37	C9
Embrach, Switz.	23	A7
Embrun, France	27	D10
Embu, Kenya	82	C4
Embu □, Kenya	82	C4
Emden, Germany	18	B3
Emerald, Australia	90	C4
Emerson, Canada	101	D9
Emery, U.S.A.	111	G8
Emet, Turkey	66	D3
Emi Koussi, Chad	73	E8
Emilia-Romagna □, Italy	32	D7
Emilius, Mte., Italy	32	C4
Eminabad, Pakistan	62	C6
Emirdağ, Turkey	66	D4
Emlenton, U.S.A.	106	E5
Emlichheim, Germany	18	C2
Emme →, Switz.	22	B5
Emmeloord, Neths.	16	C7
Emmen, Neths.	16	C9
Emmendingen, Germany	19	G3
Emmental, Switz.	22	C4
Emmer-Compascuum, Neths.	16	C10
Emmerich, Germany	18	D2
Emmet, Australia	90	C3
Emmetsburg, U.S.A.	108	D7
Emmett, U.S.A.	110	E5
Empalme, Mexico	114	B2
Empangeni, S. Africa	85	D5
Empedrado, Argentina	126	B4
Emperor Seamount Chain, Pac. Oc.	92	D9
Empoli, Italy	32	E7
Emporia, Kans., U.S.A.	108	F6
Emporia, Va., U.S.A.	105	G7
Emporium, U.S.A.	106	E6
Empress, Canada	101	C6
Emptinne, Belgium	17	H6
Empty Quarter = Rub' al Khali, Si. Arabia	68	D4
Ems →, Germany	18	B3
Emsdale, Canada	106	A5
Emsdetten, Germany	18	C3
Emu, China	51	C15
Emu Park, Australia	90	C5
'En 'Avrona, Israel	69	F3
En Nahud, Sudan	77	E2
Ena, Japan	49	G8
Enafors, Sweden	10	A6
Enambú, Colombia	120	C3
Enana, Namibia	84	B2
Enånger, Sweden	10	C11
Enaratoli, Indonesia	57	E9
Enard B., U.K.	14	C3
Enare = Inarijärvi, Finland	8	B19
Encantadas, Serra, Brazil	127	C5
Encanto, C., Phil.	57	A6
Encarnación, Paraguay	127	B4
Encarnación de Diaz, Mexico	114	C4
Enchi, Ghana	78	D4
Encinal, U.S.A.	109	L5
Encinitas, U.S.A.	113	M9
Encino, U.S.A.	111	J11
Encontrados, Venezuela	120	B3
Encruzilhada, Brazil	123	E3
Ende, Indonesia	57	F6
Endeavour, Canada	101	C8
Endeavour Str., Australia	90	A3
Endelave, Denmark	11	J4
Enderbury I., Kiribati	92	H10
Enderby, Canada	100	C5
Enderby I., Australia	88	D2
Enderby Land, Antarctica	5	C5
Enderlin, U.S.A.	108	B6
Endicott, N.Y., U.S.A.	107	D8
Endicott, Wash., U.S.A.	110	C5
Endimari →, Brazil	124	B4
Endyalgout I., Australia	88	B5
Ene →, Peru	124	C3
Enewetak Atoll, Pac. Oc.	92	F8
Enez, Turkey	66	C2
Enfida, Tunisia	75	A7
Enfield, U.K.	13	F7
Engadin, Switz.	19	J6
Engaño, C., Dom. Rep.	117	C6
Engaño, C., Phil.	57	A6
Engcobo, S. Africa	85	E4
Engelberg, Switz.	23	C6
Engels = Pokrovsk, Russia	41	F15
Engemann L., Canada	101	B7
Enger, Norway	10	D4
Enggano, Indonesia	56	F2
Enghien, Belgium	17	G4
Engil, Morocco	74	B4
Engkilili, Malaysia	56	D4
England, U.S.A.	109	H9
England □, U.K.	7	E5
Englee, Canada	99	B8
Englehart, Canada	98	C4
Engler L., Canada	101	B7
Englewood, Colo., U.S.A.	108	F2
Englewood, Kans., U.S.A.	109	G5
English →, Canada	101	C10
English Bazar = Ingraj Bazar, India	63	G13
English Channel, Europe	13	G6
English River, Canada	98	C1
Enid, U.S.A.	109	G6
Enipévs →, Greece	39	K5
Enkhuizen, Neths.	16	C6
Enköping, Sweden	10	E11
Enle, China	52	E3
Enna, Italy	35	E7
Ennadai, Canada	101	A8
Ennadai L., Canada	101	A8
Ennedi, Chad	73	E9
Enngonia, Australia	91	D4
Ennis, Ireland	15	D3
Ennis, Mont., U.S.A.	110	D8
Ennis, Tex., U.S.A.	109	J6
Enniscorthy, Ireland	15	D5
Enniskillen, U.K.	15	B4
Ennistimon, Ireland	15	D2
Enns →, Austria	21	G4
Enontekiö, Finland	8	B17
Enping, China	53	F9
Enriquillo, L., Dom. Rep.	117	C5
Ens, Neths.	16	C7
Enschede, Neths.	16	D9
Ensenada, Argentina	126	C4
Ensenada, Mexico	114	A1
Enshi, China	52	B7
Ensiola, Pta., Spain	36	B9
Ensisheim, France	25	E14
Entebbe, Uganda	82	B3
Enter, Neths.	16	D9
Enterprise, Canada	100	A5
Enterprise, Oreg., U.S.A.	110	D5
Enterprise, Utah, U.S.A.	111	H7
Entlebuch, Switz.	22	C6
Entre Ríos, Bolivia	126	A3
Entre Rios, Bahia, Brazil	123	D4
Entre Rios, Pará, Brazil	125	B7
Entre Ríos □, Argentina	126	C4
Entrepeñas, Pantano de, Spain	28	E2
Enugu, Nigeria	79	D6
Enugu □, Nigeria	79	D6
Enugu Ezike, Nigeria	79	D6
Enumclaw, U.S.A.	112	C5
Envermeu, France	24	C8
Envigado, Colombia	120	B2
Envira, Brazil	124	B3
Enz →, Germany	19	F5
Enza →, Italy	32	D7
Eólie, Is., Italy	35	D7
Epanomí, Greece	39	J5
Epe, Neths.	16	D7
Epe, Nigeria	79	D5
Épernay, France	25	C10
Épernon, France	25	D8
Ephesus, Turkey	66	E2
Ephraim, U.S.A.	110	G8
Ephrata, U.S.A.	110	C4
Epila, Spain	28	D3
Épinac-les-Mines, France	25	F11
Épinal, France	25	D13
Epira, Guyana	121	B6
Episkopi, Cyprus	37	E11
Episkopí, Greece	37	D6
Episkopi Bay, Cyprus	37	E11
Epping, U.K.	13	F8
Epukiro, Namibia	84	C2
Equatorial Guinea ■, Africa	80	D1
Equeipa, Venezuela	121	B5
Er Rahad, Sudan	77	E3
Er Rif, Morocco	75	A4
Er Roseires, Sudan	77	E3
Erāwadī Myit = Irrawaddy →, Burma	61	M19
Erba, Italy	32	C6
Erba, Sudan	76	D4
Erbaa, Turkey	66	C7
Erbil = Arbīl, Iraq	64	B5
Erçek Gölü, Turkey	67	D10
Ercha, Russia	45	C15
Erçis, Turkey	67	D10
Erciyaş Dağı, Turkey	66	D6
Erdao Jiang →, China	51	C14
Erdek, Turkey	66	C2
Erdemli, Turkey	66	E6
Erdene, Mongolia	50	B6
Erding, Germany	19	G7
Erdre →, France	24	E5
Erebato →, Venezuela	121	B5
Erebus, Mt., Antarctica	5	D11
Erechim, Brazil	127	B5
Ereğli, Konya, Turkey	66	E6
Ereğli, Zonguldak, Turkey	66	C4
Erei, Monti, Italy	35	E7
Erembodegem, Belgium	17	G4
Erenhot, China	50	C7
Eresma →, Spain	30	D6
Erewadi Myitwanya, Burma	61	M19
Erfenisdam, S. Africa	84	D4
Erfoud, Morocco	74	B4
Erft →, Germany	18	D2
Erfurt, Germany	18	E7
Ergani, Turkey	67	D8
Ergeni Vozvyshennost, Russia	43	C11
Ērgļi, Latvia	40	C4
Eria →, Spain	30	C5
Eriba, Sudan	77	D4
Eribol, L., U.K.	14	C4
Erica, Neths.	16	C9
Érice, Italy	34	D5
Erie, U.S.A.	106	D4
Erie, L., N. Amer.	106	D3
Erie Canal, U.S.A.	106	C6
Erieau, Canada	106	D3
Erigavo, Somali Rep.	68	E4
Erikoúsa, Greece	37	A3
Eriksdale, Canada	101	C9
Erikslund, Sweden	10	B9
Erímanthos, Greece	39	M4
Erimo-misaki, Japan	48	D11
Eriswil, Switz.	22	B5
Erithraí, Greece	39	L6
Eritrea ■, Africa	77	E4
Erjas →, Portugal	31	F3
Erlangen, Germany	19	F7
Erldunda, Australia	90	D1
Erlin, Taiwan	53	F13
Ermelo, Neths.	16	D7
Ermelo, S. Africa	85	D4
Ermenak, Turkey	66	E5
Ermióni, Greece	39	M6
Ermones, Greece	37	A3
Ermoúpolis = Síros, Greece	39	M7
Ernakulam = Cochin, India	60	Q10
Erne →, Ireland	15	B3
Erne, Lower L., U.K.	15	B4
Erne, Upper L., U.K.	15	B4
Ernée, France	24	D6
Ernest Giles Ra., Australia	89	E3
Ernstberg, Germany	19	E2
Erode, India	60	P10
Eromanga, Australia	91	D3
Erongo, Namibia	84	C2
Erp, Neths.	17	E7
Erquelinnes, Belgium	17	H4
Erquy, France	24	D4
Erquy, C. d', France	24	D4
Err, Piz d', Switz.	23	C9
Errabiddy, Australia	89	E2
Erramala Hills, India	60	M11
Errer →, Ethiopia	77	F5
Errigal, Ireland	15	A3
Erris Hd., Ireland	15	B1
Erseka, Albania	39	J3
Erskine, U.S.A.	108	B7
Erstein, France	25	D14
Erstfeld, Switz.	23	C7
Ertil, Russia	41	F12
Ertis = Irtysh →, Russia	44	C7
Ertvelde, Belgium	17	F3
Eruh, Turkey	67	E10
Eruwa, Nigeria	79	D5
Ervy-le-Châtel, France	25	D10
Erwin, U.S.A.	105	G4
Eryuan, China	52	D2
Erzgebirge, Germany	18	E9
Erzin, Russia	45	D10
Erzincan, Turkey	67	D8
Erzincan □, Turkey	67	D8
Erzurum, Turkey	67	D9
Erzurum □, Turkey	67	D9
Es Caló, Spain	36	C8
Es Caná, Spain	36	B8
Es Sahrâ' Esh Sharqîya, Egypt	76	B3
Es Sînâ', Egypt	76	J8
Es Sûkî, Sudan	77	E3
Esambo, Zaïre	82	C1
Esan-Misaki, Japan	48	D10
Esashi, Hokkaidō, Japan	48	B11
Esashi, Hokkaidō, Japan	48	D10
Esbjerg, Denmark	11	J2
Escada, Brazil	122	C4
Escalante, U.S.A.	111	H8
Escalante →, U.S.A.	111	H8
Escalón, Mexico	114	B4
Escalona, Spain	30	E6
Escambia →, U.S.A.	105	K2

Escanaba, *U.S.A.* 104 C2
Escaut →, *Belgium* 17 F3
Esch-sur-Alzette, *Lux.* ... 17 J7
Eschede, *Germany* 18 C6
Escholzmatt, *Switz.* 22 C5
Eschwege, *Germany* 18 D6
Eschweiler, *Germany* 18 E2
Escoma, *Bolivia* 124 D4
Escondido, *U.S.A.* 113 M9
Escuinapa, *Mexico* 114 C3
Escuintla, *Guatemala* ... 116 D1
Eséka, *Cameroon* 79 E7
Esens, *Germany* 18 B3
Esera →, *Spain* 28 C5
Esfahān, *Iran* 65 C6
Esfīdeh, *Iran* 65 C8
Esgueva →, *Spain* 30 D6
Esh Sham = Dimashq,
 Syria 69 B5
Esh Shamâlîya □, *Sudan* . 76 D2
Eshan, *China* 52 E4
Eshowe, *S. Africa* 85 D5
Esiama, *Ghana* 78 K4
Esil = Ishim →, *Russia* .. 44 D8
Esino →, *Italy* 33 E10
Esk →, *Dumf. & Gall.*,
 U.K. 14 G5
Esk →, *N. Yorks.*, *U.K.* . 12 C7
Eskifjörður, *Iceland* 8 D7
Eskilstuna, *Sweden* 10 E10
Eskimalatya, *Turkey* 67 D8
Eskimo Pt., *Canada* 101 A10
Eskişehir, *Turkey* 66 D4
Eskişehir □, *Turkey* 66 D4
Esla →, *Spain* 30 D4
Esla, Pantano del, *Spain* . 30 D4
Eslāmābād-e Gharb, *Iran* . 64 C5
Eslöv, *Sweden* 11 J7
Eşme, *Turkey* 66 D3
Esmeralda, I., *Chile* 128 C1
Esmeraldas, *Ecuador* 120 C2
Esmeraldas □, *Ecuador* .. 120 C2
Esmeraldas →, *Ecuador* . 120 C2
Esneux, *Belgium* 17 G7
Espada, Pta., *Colombia* .. 120 A3
Espalion, *France* 26 D6
Espalmador, I., *Spain* 36 C7
Espanola, *Canada* 98 C3
Espardell, I. del, *Spain* ... 36 C7
Esparraguera, *Spain* 28 D6
Esparta, *Costa Rica* 116 E3
Espejo, *Spain* 31 H6
Esperança, *Brazil* 122 C4
Esperance, *Australia* 89 F3
Esperance B., *Australia* .. 89 F3
Esperantinópolis, *Brazil* . 122 B3
Esperanza, *Santa Cruz*,
 Argentina 128 D2
Esperanza, *Santa Fe*,
 Argentina 126 C3
Esperanza, *Phil.* 55 G6
Espéraza, *France* 26 F6
Espichel, C., *Portugal* ... 31 G1
Espiel, *Spain* 31 G5
Espigão, Serra do, *Brazil* . 127 B5
Espinal, *Colombia* 120 C3
Espinar, *Peru* 124 C3
Espinazo, Sierra del =
 Espinhaço, Serra do,
 Brazil 123 E3
Espinhaço, Serra do, *Brazil* 123 E3
Espinho, *Portugal* 30 D2
Espinilho, Serra do, *Brazil* 127 B5
Espino, *Venezuela* 120 B4
Espinosa de los Monteros,
 Spain 30 B7
Espírito Santo □, *Brazil* . 123 F3
Espíritu Santo, B. del,
 Mexico 115 D7
Espíritu Santo, I., *Mexico* 114 C2
Espita, *Mexico* 115 C7
Espiye, *Turkey* 67 C8
Esplanada, *Brazil* 123 D4
Espluga de Francolí, *Spain* 28 D6
Espuña, Sierra, *Spain* 29 H3
Espungabera, *Mozam.* 85 C5
Esquel, *Argentina* 128 B2
Esquina, *Argentina* 126 C4
Essaouira, *Morocco* 74 B3
Essebie, *Zaïre* 82 B3
Essen, *Belgium* 17 F4
Essen, *Germany* 18 D2
Essendon, Mt., *Australia* . 89 E3
Essequibo →, *Guyana* ... 121 B6
Essex, *Canada* 106 D2
Essex, *Calif.*, *U.S.A.* 113 L11
Essex, *N.Y.*, *U.S.A.* 107 B11
Essex □, *U.K.* 13 F8
Esslingen, *Germany* 19 G5
Essonne □, *France* 25 D9
Essvik, *Sweden* 10 B11
Estaca, Pta. del, *Spain* ... 30 B3
Estadilla, *Spain* 28 C5
Estados, I. de Los,
 Argentina 128 D4
Estagel, *France* 26 F6
Eşṭahbānāt, *Iran* 65 D7
Estallenchs, *Spain* 36 B9
Estância, *Brazil* 122 D4
Estancia, *U.S.A.* 111 J10
Estārm, *Iran* 65 D8
Estarreja, *Portugal* 30 E2
Estats, Pic d', *Spain* 28 C6
Estavayer-le-Lac, *Switz.* .. 22 C3
Estcourt, *S. Africa* 85 D4

Este, *Italy* 33 C8
Esteban, *Spain* 30 B4
Estelí, *Nic.* 116 D2
Estella, *Spain* 28 C2
Estelline, *S. Dak.*, *U.S.A.* 108 C6
Estelline, *Tex.*, *U.S.A.* .. 109 H4
Estena →, *Spain* 31 F6
Estepa, *Spain* 31 H6
Estepona, *Spain* 31 J5
Esterhazy, *Canada* 101 C8
Esternay, *France* 25 D10
Esterri de Aneu, *Spain* ... 28 C6
Estevan, *Canada* 101 D8
Estevan Group, *Canada* .. 100 C3
Estherville, *U.S.A.* 108 D7
Estissac, *France* 25 D10
Eston, *Canada* 101 C7
Estonia ■, *Europe* 40 B4
Estoril, *Portugal* 31 G1
Estouk, *Mali* 79 B5
Estrêla, Serra da, *Portugal* 30 E3
Estrella, *Spain* 29 G1
Estremoz, *France* 31 G3
Estremoz, *Portugal* 31 G3
Estrondo, Serra do, *Brazil* 122 C2
Esztergom, *Hungary* 21 H8
Et Tîdra, *Mauritania* 78 B1
Étables-sur-Mer, *France* .. 24 D4
Etadunna, *Australia* 91 D2
Etah, *India* 63 F8
Étain, *France* 25 C12
Étalle, *Belgium* 17 J7
Etamamu, *Canada* 99 B8
Étampes, *France* 25 D9
Étang-sur-Arroux, *France* . 27 B8
Etanga, *Namibia* 84 B1
Étaples, *France* 25 B8
Etawah, *India* 63 F8
Etawah →, *U.S.A.* 105 H3
Etawney L., *Canada* 101 B9
Ete, *Nigeria* 79 D6
Éthe, *Belgium* 17 J7
Ethel, *U.S.A.* 112 D4
Ethel, Oued el →, *Algeria* 74 C4
Ethel Creek, *Australia* ... 88 D3
Ethelbert, *Canada* 101 C8
Ethiopia ■, *Africa* 68 F3
Ethiopian Highlands,
 Ethiopia 70 E7
Etive, L., *U.K.* 14 E3
Etna, *Italy* 35 E8
Etoile, *Zaïre* 83 E2
Etolin I., *U.S.A.* 100 B2
Etosha Pan, *Namibia* 84 B2
Etowah, *U.S.A.* 105 H3
Étrépagny, *France* 25 C8
Étretat, *France* 24 C7
Ettelbruck, *Lux.* 17 J8
Etten, *Neths.* 17 E5
Ettlingen, *Germany* 19 G4
Ettrick Water →, *U.K.* ... 14 F6
Etuku, *Zaïre* 82 C2
Etzatlán, *Mexico* 114 C4
Eu, *France* 24 B8
Euboea = Évvoia, *Greece* . 39 L7
Eucla Motel, *Australia* ... 89 F4
Euclid, *U.S.A.* 106 E3
Euclides da Cunha, *Brazil* 122 D4
Eucumbene, L., *Australia* . 91 F4
Eudora, *U.S.A.* 109 J9
Eufaula, *Ala.*, *U.S.A.* 105 K3
Eufaula, *Okla.*, *U.S.A.* .. 109 H7
Eufaula L., *U.S.A.* 109 H7
Eugene, *U.S.A.* 110 E2
Eugowra, *Australia* 91 E4
Eulo, *Australia* 91 D4
Eunice, *La.*, *U.S.A.* 109 K8
Eunice, *N. Mex.*, *U.S.A.* . 109 J3
Eupen, *Belgium* 17 G8
Euphrates = Furāt, Nahr
 al →, *Asia* 64 D5
Eure □, *France* 24 C8
Eure →, *France* 24 C8
Eure-et-Loir □, *France* ... 24 D8
Eureka, *Canada* 4 B3
Eureka, *Calif.*, *U.S.A.* ... 110 F1
Eureka, *Kans.*, *U.S.A.* ... 109 G6
Eureka, *Mont.*, *U.S.A.* .. 110 B6
Eureka, *Nev.*, *U.S.A.* ... 110 G5
Eureka, *S. Dak.*, *U.S.A.* . 108 C5
Eureka, *Utah*, *U.S.A.* ... 110 G7
Eureka, Mt., *Australia* ... 89 E3
Euroa, *Australia* 91 F4
Europa, I., *Ind. Oc.* 81 J8
Europa, Picos de, *Spain* .. 30 B6
Europa, Pta. de, *Gib.* 31 J5
Europa Pt. = Europa, Pta.
 de, *Gib.* 31 J5
Europe 6 F10
Europoort, *Neths.* 16 E4
Euskirchen, *Germany* 18 E2
Eustis, *U.S.A.* 105 L5
Eutin, *Germany* 18 A6
Eutsuk L., *Canada* 100 C3
Eva, *Brazil* 121 D6
Eva Downs, *Australia* 90 B1
Evale, *Angola* 84 B2
Evans, *U.S.A.* 108 E2
Evans Head, *Australia* ... 91 D5
Evans L., *Canada* 98 B4
Evans Mills, *U.S.A.* 107 B9
Evanston, *Ill.*, *U.S.A.* ... 104 D2
Evanston, *Wyo.*, *U.S.A.* . 110 F8
Evansville, *Ind.*, *U.S.A.* . 104 F2
Evansville, *Wis.*, *U.S.A.* . 108 D10
Évaux-les-Bains, *France* .. 26 B6

Evaz, *Iran* 65 E7
Eveleth, *U.S.A.* 108 B8
Evensk, *Russia* 45 C16
Evenstad, *Norway* 10 C5
Everard, L., *Australia* 91 E1
Everard Park, *Australia* .. 89 E5
Everard Ras., *Australia* .. 89 E5
Evere, *Belgium* 17 G4
Everest, Mt., *Nepal* 63 E12
Everett, *Pa.*, *U.S.A.* 106 F6
Everett, *Wash.*, *U.S.A.* .. 112 C4
Evergem, *Belgium* 17 F3
Everglades, The, *U.S.A.* .. 105 N5
Everglades City, *U.S.A.* .. 105 N5
Everglades National Park,
 U.S.A. 105 N5
Evergreen, *U.S.A.* 105 K2
Everson, *U.S.A.* 110 B2
Evesham, *U.K.* 13 E6
Évian-les-Bains, *France* .. 27 B10
Evinayong, *Eq. Guin.* 80 D2
Évinos →, *Greece* 39 L4
Évisa, *France* 27 F12
Évora, *Portugal* 31 G3
Évora □, *Portugal* 31 G3
Evowghlī, *Iran* 64 B5
Évreux, *France* 24 C8
Évron, *France* 24 D6
Evrótas →, *Greece* 39 N5
Évvoia, *Greece* 39 L7
Évvoia □, *Greece* 39 L6
Ewe, L., *U.K.* 14 D3
Ewing, *U.S.A.* 108 D5
Ewo, *Congo* 80 E2
Exaltación, *Bolivia* 125 C4
Excelsior Springs, *U.S.A.* . 108 F7
Excideuil, *France* 26 C5
Exe →, *U.K.* 13 G4
Exeter, *Canada* 106 C3
Exeter, *U.K.* 13 G4
Exeter, *Calif.*, *U.S.A.* ... 111 H4
Exeter, *N.H.*, *U.S.A.* ... 107 D14
Exeter, *Nebr.*, *U.S.A.* ... 108 E6
Exloo, *Neths.* 16 C9
Exmes, *France* 24 D7
Exmoor, *U.K.* 13 F4
Exmouth, *Australia* 88 D1
Exmouth, *U.K.* 13 G4
Exmouth G., *Australia* ... 88 D1
Expedition Ra., *Australia* . 90 C4
Extremadura □, *Spain* ... 31 F4
Exuma Sound, *Bahamas* . 116 B4
Eyasi, L., *Tanzania* 82 C4
Eyeberry L., *Canada* 101 A8
Eyemouth, *U.K.* 14 F6
Eygurande, *France* 26 C6
Eyjafjörður, *Iceland* 8 C4
Eymet, *France* 26 D4
Eymoutiers, *France* 26 C5
Eynesil, *Turkey* 67 C8
Eyrarbakki, *Iceland* 8 E3
Eyre, *Australia* 89 F4
Eyre (North), L., *Australia* 91 D2
Eyre (South), L., *Australia* 91 D2
Eyre Cr. →, *Australia* ... 91 D2
Eyre Mts., *N.Z.* 87 L2
Eyre Pen., *Australia* 91 E2
Eyvānkī, *Iran* 65 C6
Ez Zeidab, *Sudan* 76 D3
Ezcaray, *Spain* 28 C2
Ezine, *Turkey* 66 D2
Ezmul, *Mauritania* 74 D1
Ezouza →, *Cyprus* 37 E11

F

Fabens, *U.S.A.* 111 L10
Fåborg, *Denmark* 11 J4
Fabriano, *Italy* 33 E9
Făcăeni, *Romania* 38 E10
Facatativá, *Colombia* 120 C3
Fachi, *Niger* 72 E7
Facture, *France* 26 D3
Fada, *Chad* 73 E9
Fada-n-Gourma,
 Burkina Faso 79 C5
Faddeyevskiy, Ostrov,
 Russia 45 B15
Fadghāmī, *Syria* 64 C4
Fadlab, *Sudan* 76 D3
Faenza, *Italy* 33 D8
Fafa, *Mali* 79 B5
Fafe, *Portugal* 30 D2
Fagam, *Nigeria* 79 C7
Făgăraş, *Romania* 38 D7
Făgăraş, Munţii, *Romania* 38 D7
Fågelsjö, *Sweden* 10 C8
Fagernes, *Norway* 9 F10
Fagersta, *Sweden* 9 F13
Făget, *Romania* 38 D5
Fagnano, L., *Argentina* .. 128 D3
Fagnano Castello, *Italy* ... 35 C9
Fagnières, *France* 25 D11
Fahlīān, *Iran* 65 D6
Fahraj, *Kermān*, *Iran* ... 65 D8
Fahraj, *Yazd*, *Iran* 65 D7
Faial, *Madeira* 36 D3
Faido, *Switz.* 23 D7
Fair Hd., *U.K.* 15 A5
Fair Oaks, *U.S.A.* 112 G5
Fairbank, *U.S.A.* 111 L8
Fairbanks, *U.S.A.* 96 B5

Fairbury, *U.S.A.* 108 E6
Fairfax, *U.S.A.* 109 G6
Fairfield, *Ala.*, *U.S.A.* ... 105 J2
Fairfield, *Calif.*, *U.S.A.* .. 112 G4
Fairfield, *Conn.*, *U.S.A.* . 107 E11
Fairfield, *Idaho*, *U.S.A.* .. 110 E6
Fairfield, *Ill.*, *U.S.A.* 104 F1
Fairfield, *Iowa*, *U.S.A.* .. 108 E9
Fairfield, *Mont.*, *U.S.A.* . 110 C8
Fairfield, *Tex.*, *U.S.A.* ... 109 K7
Fairford, *Canada* 101 C9
Fairhope, *U.S.A.* 105 K2
Fairlie, *N.Z.* 87 L3
Fairmead, *U.S.A.* 112 H6
Fairmont, *Minn.*, *U.S.A.* 108 D7
Fairmont, *W. Va.*, *U.S.A.* 104 F5
Fairmount, *U.S.A.* 113 L8
Fairplay, *U.S.A.* 111 G11
Fairport, *U.S.A.* 106 C7
Fairport Harbor, *U.S.A.* .. 106 E3
Fairview, *Australia* 90 B3
Fairview, *Canada* 100 B5
Fairview, *Mont.*, *U.S.A.* . 108 B2
Fairview, *Okla.*, *U.S.A.* .. 109 G5
Fairview, *Utah*, *U.S.A.* .. 110 G8
Fairweather, Mt., *U.S.A.* . 96 C6
Faisalabad, *Pakistan* 62 D5
Faith, *U.S.A.* 108 C3
Faizabad, *India* 63 F10
Fajardo, *Puerto Rico* 117 C6
Fakak, *Indonesia* 57 E8
Fakenham, *U.K.* 12 E8
Fakfak, *Indonesia* 57 E8
Fakobli, *Ivory C.* 78 D3
Fakse, *Denmark* 11 J6
Fakse B., *Denmark* 11 J6
Fakse Ladeplads, *Denmark* 11 J6
Faku, *China* 51 C12
Falaise, *France* 24 D6
Falaise, Mui, *Vietnam* ... 58 C5
Falam, *Burma* 61 H18
Falces, *Spain* 28 C3
Fălciu, *Romania* 38 C11
Falcón □, *Venezuela* 120 A4
Falcón, C., *Spain* 36 C7
Falcon, C., *Algeria* 75 A4
Falcon Dam, *U.S.A.* 109 M5
Falconara Marittima, *Italy* 33 E10
Falconer, *U.S.A.* 106 D5
Faléa, *Mali* 78 C2
Falenki, *Russia* 41 B17
Faleshty, *Moldavia* 42 C2
Falfurrias, *U.S.A.* 109 M5
Falher, *Canada* 100 B5
Falirakí, *Greece* 37 C10
Falkenberg, *Germany* ... 18 D9
Falkenberg, *Sweden* 11 H6
Falkensee, *Germany* 18 C9
Falkenstein, *Germany* ... 18 E8
Falkirk, *U.K.* 14 F5
Falkland, East, I., *Falk. Is.* 128 D5
Falkland, West, I., *Falk. Is.* 128 D4
Falkland Is. ■, *Atl. Oc.* .. 128 D5
Falkland Is.
 Dependency □, *Atl. Oc.* 5 B1
Falkland Sd., *Falk. Is.* ... 128 D5
Falköping, *Sweden* 11 F7
Fall River, *U.S.A.* 107 E13
Fall River Mills, *U.S.A.* .. 110 F3
Fallbrook, *U.S.A.* 111 K5
Fallbrook, *Calif.*, *U.S.A.* . 113 M9
Fallon, *Mont.*, *U.S.A.* .. 108 B2
Fallon, *Nev.*, *U.S.A.* 110 G4
Falls City, *Nebr.*, *U.S.A.* 108 E7
Falls City, *Oreg.*, *U.S.A.* 110 D2
Falls Creek, *U.S.A.* 106 E6
Falmouth, *Jamaica* 116 C4
Falmouth, *U.K.* 13 G2
Falmouth, *U.S.A.* 104 F3
False B., *S. Africa* 84 E2
Falset, *Spain* 28 D5
Falso, C., *Honduras* 116 C3
Falster, *Denmark* 11 K5
Falsterbo, *Sweden* 11 J6
Fălticeni, *Romania* 38 B9
Falun, *Sweden* 9 F13
Famagusta, *Cyprus* 37 D12
Famagusta Bay, *Cyprus* .. 37 D13
Famatina, Sierra de,
 Argentina 126 B2
Family L., *Canada* 101 C9
Famoso, *U.S.A.* 113 K7
Fan Xian, *China* 50 G8
Fana, *Mali* 78 C3
Fandriana, *Madag.* 85 C8
Fang, *Thailand* 58 C2
Fang Xian, *China* 53 A8
Fangchang, *China* 53 B12
Fangcheng,
 Guangxi Zhuangzu,
 China 52 G7
Fangcheng, *Henan*, *China* 50 H7
Fangliao, *Taiwan* 53 F13
Fangshan, *China* 50 E6
Fangzi, *China* 51 F10
Fani i Madh →, *Albania* . 39 H3
Fanjiatun, *China* 51 C13
Fannich, L., *U.K.* 14 D4
Fannūj, *Iran* 65 E8
Fanny Bay, *Canada* 100 D4
Fanø, *Denmark* 11 J2
Fano, *Italy* 33 E10
Fanshaw, *U.S.A.* 100 B2
Fanshi, *China* 50 E7
Fao = Al Fāw, *Iraq* 65 D6
Faqirwali, *Pakistan* 62 E5
Fara in Sabina, *Italy* 33 F9

Faradje, *Zaïre* 82 B2
Farafangana, *Madag.* 85 C8
Farâfra, El Wâhât el-,
 Egypt 76 B2
Farāh, *Afghan.* 60 C3
Farāh □, *Afghan.* 60 C3
Farahalana, *Madag.* 85 A9
Faraid, Gebel, *Egypt* 76 C4
Faramana, *Burkina Faso* . 78 C4
Faranah, *Guinea* 78 C2
Farasān, Jazā'ir, *Si. Arabia* 68 D3
Farasan Is. = Farasān,
 Jazā'ir, *Si. Arabia* 68 D3
Faratsiho, *Madag.* 85 B8
Fardes →, *Spain* 29 H1
Fareham, *U.K.* 13 G6
Farewell, C., *N.Z.* 87 J4
Farewell C. = Farvel, Kap,
 Greenland 4 D5
Farghona = Fergana,
 Uzbekistan 44 E8
Fargo, *U.S.A.* 108 B6
Fari'a →, *Jordan* 69 C4
Faribault, *U.S.A.* 108 C8
Faridkot, *India* 62 D6
Faridpur, *Bangla.* 63 H13
Färila, *Sweden* 10 C9
Farim, *Guinea-Biss.* 78 C1
Farina, *Australia* 91 E2
Farinha →, *Brazil* 122 C2
Fariones, Pta., *Canary Is.* . 36 E6
Fâriskûr, *Egypt* 76 H7
Farmerville, *U.S.A.* 109 J8
Farmington, *Calif.*, *U.S.A.* 112 H6
Farmington, *N.H.*, *U.S.A.* 107 C13
Farmington, *N. Mex.*,
 U.S.A. 111 H9
Farmington, *Utah*, *U.S.A.* 110 F8
Farmington →, *U.S.A.* .. 107 E12
Farmville, *U.S.A.* 104 G6
Farnborough, *U.K.* 13 F7
Farne Is., *U.K.* 12 B6
Farnham, *Canada* 107 A12
Faro, *Brazil* 121 D6
Faro, *Portugal* 31 H3
Fårö, *Sweden* 9 H15
Faro □, *Portugal* 31 H2
Faroe Is. = Føroyar,
 Atl. Oc. 7 C4
Farquhar, C., *Australia* .. 89 D1
Farrars Cr. →, *Australia* . 90 D3
Farrāshband, *Iran* 65 D7
Farrell, *U.S.A.* 106 E4
Farrell Flat, *Australia* ... 91 E2
Farrokhī, *Iran* 65 C8
Farruch, C., *Spain* 36 B10
Farrukhabad-cum-
 Fatehgarh, *India* 63 F8
Fārs □, *Iran* 65 D7
Fársala, *Greece* 39 K5
Farsø, *Denmark* 11 H3
Farsund, *Norway* 9 G9
Fartak, Râs, *Si. Arabia* ... 64 D2
Fartura, Serra da, *Brazil* . 127 B5
Faru, *Nigeria* 79 C6
Fārūj, *Iran* 65 B8
Farum, *Denmark* 11 J6
Farvel, Kap, *Greenland* .. 4 D5
Farwell, *U.S.A.* 109 H3
Fasā, *Iran* 65 D7
Fasano, *Italy* 35 B10
Fashoda, *Sudan* 77 F3
Fastnet Rock, *Ireland* ... 15 E2
Fastov, *Ukraine* 40 F6
Fatagar, Tanjung, *Indonesia* 57 E8
Fatehgarh, *India* 63 F8
Fatehpur, *Raj.*, *India* ... 62 F6
Fatehpur, *Ut. P.*, *India* .. 63 G9
Fatesh, *Russia* 41 E9
Fatick, *Senegal* 78 C1
Fatima, *Canada* 99 C7
Fátima, *Portugal* 31 F2
Fatoya, *Guinea* 78 C3
Faucille, Col de la, *France* 27 B10
Faulkton, *U.S.A.* 108 C5
Faulquemont, *France* ... 25 C13
Fauquembergues, *France* . 25 B9
Faure I., *Australia* 89 E1
Fāureh, *Romania* 38 D10
Fauresmith, *S. Africa* 84 D4
Fauske, *Norway* 8 C13
Fauvillers, *Belgium* 17 J7
Favara, *Italy* 34 E6
Favaritx, C., *Spain* 36 A11
Favignana, *Italy* 34 E5
Favignana, I., *Italy* 34 E5
Favourable Lake, *Canada* . 98 B1
Fawn →, *Canada* 98 A2
Fawnskin, *U.S.A.* 113 L10
Faxaflói, *Iceland* 8 D2
Faya-Largeau, *Chad* 73 E8
Fayd, *Si. Arabia* 64 E4
Fayence, *France* 27 E10
Fayette, *Ala.*, *U.S.A.* 105 J2
Fayette, *Mo.*, *U.S.A.* 108 F8
Fayetteville, *Ark.*, *U.S.A.* 109 G7
Fayetteville, *N.C.*, *U.S.A.* 105 H6
Fayetteville, *Tenn.*, *U.S.A.* 105 H2
Fayón, *Spain* 28 D5
Fazenda Nova, *Brazil* 123 E1
Fazilka, *India* 62 D6
Fazilpur, *Pakistan* 62 E4
Fdérik, *Mauritania* 74 D2
Feale →, *Ireland* 15 D2

Fear, C., U.S.A. 105 J7
Feather →, U.S.A. 110 G3
Feather Falls, U.S.A. 112 F5
Featherston, N.Z. 87 J5
Featherstone, Zimbabwe .. 83 F3
Fécamp, France 24 C7
Fedala = Mohammedia,
  Morocco 74 B3
Federación, Argentina 126 C4
Fedeshkūh, Iran 65 D7
Fedjadj, Chott el, Tunisia . 75 B6
Fehmarn, Germany 18 A7
Fehmarn Bælt, Denmark . 18 A7
Fei Xian, China 51 G9
Feilding, N.Z. 87 J5
Feijó, Brazil 124 B3
Feira de Santana, Brazil .. 123 D4
Feixiang, China 50 F8
Fejø, Denmark 11 K5
Feke, Turkey 66 E6
Felanitx, Spain 36 B10
Feldberg, Baden-W.,
  Germany 19 H3
Feldberg,
  Mecklenburg-Vorpommern,
  Germany 18 B9
Feldkirch, Austria 19 H5
Felipe Carrillo Puerto,
  Mexico 115 D7
Felixlândia, Brazil 123 E3
Felixstowe, U.K. 13 F9
Felletin, France 26 C6
Felton, U.K. 12 B6
Felton, U.S.A. 112 H4
Feltre, Italy 33 B8
Femø, Denmark 11 K5
Femunden, Norway 10 B5
Fen He →, China 50 G6
Fenelon Falls, Canada 106 B6
Feneroa, Ethiopia 77 E4
Feng Xian, Jiangsu, China 50 G9
Feng Xian, Shaanxi, China 50 H4
Fengári, Greece 39 J8
Fengcheng, Jiangxi, China 53 C10
Fengcheng, Liaoning,
  China 51 D13
Fengdu, China 52 C6
Fengfeng, China 50 F8
Fenggang, China 52 D6
Fenghua, China 53 C13
Fenghuang, China 52 D7
Fenghuangzui, China 52 A7
Fengjie, China 52 B7
Fengkai, China 53 F8
Fengle, China 53 B9
Fengning, China 50 D9
Fengqing, China 52 E2
Fengqiu, China 50 G8
Fengrun, China 51 E10
Fengshan,
  Guangxi Zhuangzu,
  China 52 E7
Fengshan,
  Guangxi Zhuangzu,
  China 52 E6
Fengtai, Anhui, China 53 A11
Fengtai, Beijing, China ... 50 E9
Fengxian, China 53 B13
Fengxiang, China 50 G4
Fengxin, China 53 C10
Fengyang, China 51 H9
Fengyi, China 52 E3
Fengzhen, China 50 D7
Fenit, Ireland 15 D2
Fennimore, U.S.A. 108 D9
Feno, C. de, France 27 G12
Fenoarivo Afovoany,
  Madag. 85 B8
Fenoarivo Atsinanana,
  Madag. 85 B8
Fens, The, U.K. 12 E7
Fenton, U.S.A. 104 D4
Fenxi, China 50 F6
Fenyang, China 54 C6
Fenyang, Shanxi, China .. 50 F6
Fenyi, China 53 D10
Feodosiya, Ukraine 42 D6
Fer, C. de, Algeria 75 A6
Ferdows, Iran 65 C8
Fère-Champenoise, France 25 D10
Fère-en-Tardenois, France 25 C10
Ferentino, Italy 34 A6
Ferfer, Somali Rep. 68 F4
Fergana, Uzbekistan 44 E8
Fergus, Canada 98 D3
Fergus Falls, U.S.A. 108 B6
Fériana, Tunisia 75 B6
Feričanci, Croatia 21 K8
Ferkane, Algeria 75 B6
Ferkéssédougou, Ivory C. . 78 D3
Ferlach, Austria 21 J4
Ferland, Canada 98 B2
Ferlo, Vallée du, Senegal . 78 B2
Fermanagh □, U.K. 15 B4
Fermo, Italy 33 E10
Fermoselle, Spain 30 D4
Fermoy, Ireland 15 D3
Fernán Nuñéz, Spain 31 H6
Fernández, Argentina 126 B3
Fernandina Beach, U.S.A. 105 K5
Fernando de Noronha,
  Brazil 122 B5
Fernando Póo = Bioko,
  Eq. Guin. 79 E6
Fernandópolis, Brazil 123 F1

Ferndale, Calif., U.S.A. .. 110 F1
Ferndale, Wash., U.S.A. .. 112 B4
Fernie, Canada 100 D5
Fernlees, Australia 90 C4
Fernley, U.S.A. 110 G4
Ferozepore = Firozpur,
  India 62 D6
Férrai, Greece 39 J9
Ferrandina, Italy 35 B9
Ferrara, Italy 33 D8
Ferrato, C., Italy 34 C2
Ferreira do Alentejo,
  Portugal 31 G2
Ferreñafe, Peru 124 B2
Ferrerías, Spain 36 B11
Ferret, C., France 26 D2
Ferrette, France 25 E14
Ferriday, U.S.A. 109 K9
Ferrières, France 25 D9
Ferriete, Italy 32 D6
Ferrol = El Ferrol, Spain . 30 B2
Ferrol, Pen. de, Peru 124 B2
Ferron, U.S.A. 111 G8
Ferros, Brazil 123 E3
Ferryland, Canada 99 C9
Fertile, U.S.A. 108 B6
Fertília, Italy 34 B1
Fès, Morocco 74 B4
Feschaux, Belgium 17 H5
Feshi, Zaïre 80 F3
Fessenden, U.S.A. 108 B5
Fetești, Romania 38 E10
Fethiye, Turkey 66 E3
Fetlar, U.K. 14 A8
Feuerthalen, Switz. 23 A7
Feuilles →, Canada 97 C12
Feurs, France 27 C8
Fezzan, Libya 70 D5
Ffestiniog, U.K. 12 E4
Fiambalá, Argentina 126 B2
Fianarantsoa, Madag. 85 C8
Fianarantsoa □, Madag. .. 85 B8
Fianga, Cameroon 73 G8
Fichtelgebirge, Germany .. 19 E7
Ficksburg, S. Africa 85 D4
Fiditi, Nigeria 79 D5
Field, Canada 98 C3
Field →, Australia 90 C2
Field I., Australia 88 B5
Fieri, Albania 39 J2
Fiesch, Switz. 22 D6
Fife □, U.K. 14 E5
Fife Ness, U.K. 14 E6
Fifth Cataract, Sudan 76 D3
Figeac, France 26 D6
Figline Valdarno, Italy ... 33 E8
Figtree, Zimbabwe 83 G2
Figueira Castelo Rodrigo,
  Portugal 30 E4
Figueira da Foz, Portugal . 30 E2
Figueiró dos Vinhos,
  Portugal 30 F2
Figueras, Spain 28 C7
Figuig, Morocco 75 B4
Fihaonana, Madag. 85 B8
Fiherenana, Madag. 85 C8
Fiherenana →, Madag. ... 85 C7
Fiji ■, Pac. Oc. 87 C8
Fika, Nigeria 79 C7
Filabres, Sierra de los,
  Spain 29 H2
Filadelfia, Bolivia 124 C4
Filadélfia, Brazil 122 C2
Filadélfia, Italy 35 D9
Filer, U.S.A. 110 E6
Filey, U.K. 12 C7
Filfla, Malta 37 D1
Filiași, Romania 38 E6
Filiátes, Greece 39 K3
Filiatrá, Greece 39 M4
Filicudi, Italy 35 D7
Filiouri →, Greece 39 H8
Filipstad, Sweden 9 G13
Fillmore, Canada 101 D8
Fillmore, Calif., U.S.A. ... 113 L8
Fillmore, Utah, U.S.A. ... 111 G7
Filottrano, Italy 33 E10
Filyos, Turkey 42 F5
Finale Lígure, Italy 32 D5
Finale nell' Emília, Italy .. 33 D8
Fiñana, Spain 29 H2
Finch, Canada 107 A9
Findhorn →, U.K. 14 D5
Findlay, U.S.A. 104 E4
Finger L., Canada 101 C10
Fíngõe, Mozam. 83 E3
Finike, Turkey 66 E4
Finistère □, France 24 D2
Finisterre, Spain 30 C1
Finisterre, C., Spain 30 C1
Finke, Australia 90 D1
Finke →, Australia 91 D2
Finland ■, Europe 9 E19
Finland, G. of, Europe ... 9 G19
Finlay →, Canada 100 B3
Finley, Australia 91 F4
Finley, U.S.A. 108 B6
Finn →, Ireland 15 B4
Finnigan, Mt., Australia . 90 B4
Finniss, C., Australia 91 E1
Finnmark fylke □, Norway 8 B18
Finsteraarhorn, Switz. ... 22 C6
Finsterwalde, Germany .. 18 D9

Finsterwolde, Neths. 16 B10
Fiora →, Italy 33 F8
Fiorenzuola d'Arda, Italy . 32 D6
Fiq, Syria 69 C4
Firat = Furāt, Nahr al →,
  Asia 64 D5
Fire River, Canada 98 C3
Firebag →, Canada 101 B6
Firebaugh, U.S.A. 112 J6
Firedrake L., Canada 101 A8
Firenze, Italy 33 E8
Firk →, Iraq 64 D5
Firmi, France 26 D6
Firminy, France 27 C8
Firozabad, India 63 F8
Firozpur, India 62 D6
Firūzābād, Iran 65 D7
Firūzkūh, Iran 65 C7
Firvale, Canada 100 C3
Fish →, Namibia 84 D2
Fish →, S. Africa 84 E3
Fisher, Australia 89 F5
Fisher B., Canada 101 C9
Fishguard, U.K. 13 F3
Fishing L., Canada 101 C9
Fismes, France 25 C10
Fitchburg, U.S.A. 107 D13
Fitero, Spain 28 C3
Fitri, L., Chad 73 F8
Fitz Roy, Argentina 128 C3
Fitzgerald, Canada 100 B6
Fitzgerald, U.S.A. 105 K4
Fitzmaurice →, Australia 88 B5
Fitzroy →, Queens.,
  Australia 90 C5
Fitzroy →, W. Austral.,
  Australia 88 C3
Fitzroy Crossing, Australia 88 C4
Fitzwilliam I., Canada ... 106 A3
Fiume = Rijeka, Croatia . 33 C11
Fiumefreddo Brúzio, Italy 35 C9
Five Points, U.S.A. 112 J6
Fivizzano, Italy 32 D7
Fizi, Zaïre 82 C2
Fjellerup, Denmark 11 H4
Fjerritslev, Denmark 11 G3
Fkih ben Salah, Morocco . 74 B3
Flå, Norway 10 A4
Flagler, U.S.A. 108 F3
Flagstaff, U.S.A. 111 J8
Flaherty I., Canada 98 A4
Flåm, Norway 9 F9
Flambeau →, U.S.A. 108 C9
Flamborough Hd., U.K. .. 12 C7
Flaming Gorge Dam,
  U.S.A. 110 F9
Flaming Gorge Reservoir,
  U.S.A. 110 F9
Flamingo, Teluk, Indonesia 57 F9
Flanders = West-
  Vlaanderen □, Belgium 17 G2
Flandre Occidentale □,
  West-Vlaanderen □,
  Belgium 17 G2
Flandre Orientale = Oost-
  Vlaanderen □, Belgium 17 F3
Flandreau, U.S.A. 108 C6
Flanigan, U.S.A. 112 E7
Flannan Is., U.K. 14 C1
Flåsjön, Sweden 8 D13
Flat →, Canada 100 A3
Flat River, U.S.A. 109 G9
Flatey, Barðastrandarsýsla,
  Iceland 8 C5
Flatey,
  Suður-þingeyjarsýsla,
  Iceland 8 D2
Flathead L., U.S.A. 110 C6
Flattery, C., U.S.A. 112 B2
Flattery, C., Australia 90 A4
Flavy-le-Martel, France .. 25 C10
Flawil, Switz. 23 B8
Flaxton, U.S.A. 108 A3
Fleetwood, U.K. 12 D4
Flekkefjord, Norway 9 G9
Flémalle, Belgium 17 G6
Flemington, U.S.A. 106 E7
Flensborg Fjord, Germany 11 K3
Flensburg, Germany 18 A5
Flers, France 24 D6
Flesherton, Canada 106 B4
Flesko, Tanjung, Indonesia 57 D6
Fleurance, France 26 E4
Fleurier, Switz. 22 C3
Fleurus, Belgium 17 H5
Flevoland □, Neths. 16 C7
Flims, Switz. 23 C8
Flin Flon, Canada 101 C8
Flinders →, Australia ... 90 B3
Flinders B., Australia 89 F2
Flinders Group, Australia . 90 A3
Flinders I., Australia 90 F4
Flinders Ras., Australia .. 91 E2
Flinders Reefs, Australia . 90 B4
Flint, U.K. 12 D4
Flint, U.S.A. 104 D4
Flint →, U.S.A. 105 K3
Flint I., Kiribati 93 J12
Flinton, Australia 91 D4
Flix, Spain 28 D5
Flixecourt, France 25 B9
Flobecq, Belgium 17 G3
Flodden, U.K. 12 B5
Floodwood, U.S.A. 108 B8
Flora, Norway 10 A5

Flora, U.S.A. 104 F1
Florac, France 26 D7
Florala, U.S.A. 105 K2
Florânia, Brazil 122 C4
Floreffe, Belgium 17 H5
Florence = Firenze, Italy . 33 E8
Florence, Ala., U.S.A. 105 H2
Florence, Ariz., U.S.A. ... 111 K8
Florence, Colo., U.S.A. .. 108 F2
Florence, Oreg., U.S.A. .. 110 E1
Florence, S.C., U.S.A. ... 105 H6
Florence, L., Australia ... 91 D2
Florennes, Belgium 17 H5
Florensac, France 26 E7
Florenville, Belgium 17 J6
Flores, Brazil 122 C4
Flores, Guatemala 116 C2
Flores, Indonesia 57 F6
Flores I., Canada 100 D3
Flores Sea, Indonesia 57 F6
Floresta, Brazil 122 C4
Floresville, U.S.A. 109 L5
Floriano, Brazil 122 C3
Florianópolis, Brazil 127 B6
Florida, Cuba 116 B4
Florida, Uruguay 127 C4
Florida □, U.S.A. 105 L5
Florida B., U.S.A. 116 A3
Florida, Straits of, U.S.A. 116 B3
Florida Keys, U.S.A. 103 F10
Florídia, Italy 35 E8
Floridsdorf, Austria 21 G6
Flórina, Greece 39 J4
Florø, Norway 9 F8
Flower Station, Canada .. 107 A8
Flower's Cove, Canada ... 99 B8
Floydada, U.S.A. 109 J4
Fluk, Indonesia 57 E7
Flumen →, Spain 28 D4
Flumendosa →, Italy 34 C2
Fluminimaggiore, Italy ... 34 C1
Flushing = Vlissingen,
  Neths. 17 F3
Fluviá →, Spain 28 C8
Flying Fish, C., Antarctica 5 D15
Foam Lake, Canada 101 C8
Foča, Bos.-H. 21 M8
Foça, Turkey 66 D2
Focșani, Romania 38 D10
Fogang, China 53 F9
Foggaret el Arab, Algeria . 75 C5
Foggaret ez Zoua, Algeria 75 C5
Fóggia, Italy 35 A8
Foggo, Nigeria 79 C6
Foglia →, Italy 33 E9
Fogo, Canada 99 C9
Fogo I., Canada 99 C9
Fohnsdorf, Austria 21 H4
Föhr, Germany 18 A4
Foia, Portugal 31 H2
Foix, France 26 F5
Fokino, Russia 40 E9
Folda, Nord-Trøndelag,
  Norway 8 D11
Folda, Nordland, Norway . 8 C13
Foleyet, Canada 98 C3
Folgefonn, Norway 9 F9
Foligno, Italy 33 F9
Folkestone, U.K. 13 F9
Folkston, U.S.A. 105 K5
Follett, U.S.A. 109 G4
Follónica, Italy 32 F7
Follónica, G. di, Italy 32 F7
Folsom Res., U.S.A. 112 G5
Fond-du-Lac, Canada 101 B7
Fond du Lac, U.S.A. 108 D10
Fond-du-Lac →, Canada . 101 B7
Fonda, U.S.A. 107 D10
Fondi, Italy 34 A6
Fonfría, Spain 30 D4
Fongen, Norway 10 A5
Fonni, Italy 34 B2
Fonsagrada, Spain 30 B3
Fonseca, G. de,
  Cent. Amer. 116 D2
Fontaine-Française, France 25 E12
Fontainebleau, France ... 25 D9
Fontana, L., Argentina ... 128 B2
Fontas →, Canada 100 B4
Fonte Boa, Brazil 120 D4
Fontem, Cameroon 79 D6
Fontenay-le-Comte, France 26 B3
Fontur, Iceland 8 C6
Fonyód, Hungary 21 J7
Foochow = Fuzhou, China 53 D12
Foping, China 50 H4
Foppiano, Italy 32 B5
Forbach, France 25 C13
Forbes, Australia 91 E4
Forbesganj, India 63 F12
Forcados, Nigeria 79 D6
Forcados →, Nigeria 79 D6
Forcall →, Spain 28 E4
Forcalquier, France 27 E9
Forchheim, Germany 19 F7
Forclaz, Col de la, Switz. . 22 D4
Ford City, Calif., U.S.A. . 113 K7
Ford City, Pa., U.S.A. ... 106 F5
Ford's Bridge, Australia .. 91 D4
Fordyce, U.S.A. 109 J8
Forécariah, Guinea 78 D2
Forel, Mt., Greenland 4 C6
Foremost, Canada 100 D6
Forenza, Italy 35 B8
Forest, Belgium 17 G4

Forest, Canada 106 C3
Forest, U.S.A. 109 J10
Forest City, Iowa, U.S.A. . 108 D8
Forest City, N.C., U.S.A. . 105 H5
Forest City, Pa., U.S.A. .. 107 E9
Forest Grove, U.S.A. 112 E3
Forestburg, Canada 100 C6
Foresthill, U.S.A. 112 F6
Forestier Pen., Australia . 90 G4
Forestville, Canada 99 C6
Forestville, Calif., U.S.A. . 112 G4
Forestville, Wis., U.S.A. .. 104 C2
Forez, Mts. du, France ... 26 C7
Forfar, U.K. 14 E6
Forges-les-Eaux, France .. 25 C8
Forks, U.S.A. 112 C2
Forlì, Italy 33 D9
Forman, U.S.A. 108 B6
Formazza, Italy 32 B5
Formby Pt., U.K. 12 D4
Formentera, Spain 36 C7
Formentor, C. de, Spain . 36 B10
Fórmia, Italy 34 A6
Formiga, Brazil 123 F2
Formigine, Italy 32 D7
Formiguères, France 26 F6
Formosa = Taiwan ■, Asia 53 F13
Formosa, Argentina 126 B4
Formosa, Brazil 123 E2
Formosa □, Argentina ... 126 B3
Formosa, Serra, Brazil ... 125 C6
Formosa Bay, Kenya 82 C5
Formosa Strait, Asia 53 E12
Formoso →, Brazil 123 D2
Fornells, Spain 36 A11
Fornos de Algodres,
  Portugal 30 E3
Fornovo di Taro, Italy 32 D7
Føroyar, Atl. Oc. 7 C4
Forres, U.K. 14 D5
Forrest, Vic., Australia ... 91 F3
Forrest, W. Austral.,
  Australia 89 F4
Forrest, Mt., Australia ... 89 D4
Forrest City, U.S.A. 109 H9
Forrières, Belgium 17 H6
Forsa, Sweden 10 C11
Forsayth, Australia 90 B3
Forsmo, Sweden 10 A11
Forst, Germany 18 D10
Forster, Australia 91 E5
Forsyth, Ga., U.S.A. 105 J4
Forsyth, Mont., U.S.A. .. 110 C10
Fort Albany, Canada 98 B3
Fort Apache, U.S.A. 111 K9
Fort Assiniboine, Canada . 100 C6
Fort Augustus, U.K. 14 D4
Fort Beaufort, S. Africa .. 84 E4
Fort Benton, U.S.A. 110 C8
Fort Bragg, U.S.A. 110 G2
Fort Bridger, U.S.A. 110 F8
Fort Chipewyan, Canada . 101 B6
Fort Collins, U.S.A. 108 E2
Fort-Coulonge, Canada .. 98 C4
Fort Davis, U.S.A. 109 K3
Fort-de-France, Martinique 117 D7
Fort de Possel = Possel,
  C.A.R. 80 C3
Fort Defiance, U.S.A. 111 J9
Fort Dodge, U.S.A. 108 D7
Fort Edward, U.S.A. 107 C11
Fort Frances, Canada 101 D10
Fort Franklin, Canada ... 96 B7
Fort Garland, U.S.A. 111 H11
Fort George, Canada 98 B4
Fort Good-Hope, Canada . 96 B7
Fort Hertz = Putao, Burma 61 F20
Fort Hope, Canada 98 B2
Fort Irwin, U.S.A. 113 K10
Fort Jameson = Chipata,
  Zambia 83 E3
Fort Kent, U.S.A. 99 C6
Fort Klamath, U.S.A. 110 E3
Fort Lallemand, Algeria .. 75 B6
Fort-Lamy = Ndjamena,
  Chad 73 F7
Fort Laramie, U.S.A. 108 D2
Fort Lauderdale, U.S.A. .. 105 M5
Fort Liard, Canada 100 A4
Fort Liberté, Haiti 117 C5
Fort Lupton, U.S.A. 108 E2
Fort Mackay, Canada 100 B6
Fort McKenzie, Canada .. 99 A6
Fort Macleod, Canada ... 100 D6
Fort MacMahon, Algeria . 75 C5
Fort McMurray, Canada .. 100 B6
Fort McPherson, Canada . 96 B6
Fort Madison, U.S.A. 108 E9
Fort Meade, U.S.A. 105 M5
Fort Miribel, Algeria 75 C5
Fort Morgan, U.S.A. 108 E3
Fort Myers, U.S.A. 105 M5
Fort Nelson, Canada 100 B4
Fort Nelson →, Canada . 100 B4
Fort Norman, Canada ... 96 B7
Fort Payne, U.S.A. 105 H3
Fort Peck, U.S.A. 110 B10
Fort Peck Dam, U.S.A. .. 110 C10
Fort Peck L., U.S.A. 110 C10
Fort Pierce, U.S.A. 105 M5
Fort Pierre, U.S.A. 108 C4
Fort Pierre Bordes = Ti-n-
  Zaouâtene, Algeria .. 75 E5
Fort Plain, U.S.A. 107 D10

Fort Portal, *Uganda* 82 B3
Fort Providence, *Canada* . 100 A5
Fort Qu'Appelle, *Canada* . 101 C8
Fort Resolution, *Canada* . 100 A6
Fort Rixon, *Zimbabwe* ... 83 G2
Fort Rosebery = Mansa, *Zambia* 83 E2
Fort Ross, *U.S.A.* 112 G3
Fort Rupert, *Canada* 98 B4
Fort Saint, *Tunisia* 75 B6
Fort St. James, *Canada* ... 100 C4
Fort St. John, *Canada* ... 100 B4
Fort Sandeman, *Pakistan* . 62 D3
Fort Saskatchewan, *Canada* 100 C6
Fort Scott, *U.S.A.* 109 G7
Fort Severn, *Canada* 98 A2
Fort Shevchenko, *Kazakhstan* 43 E14
Fort-Sibut, *C.A.R.* 73 G8
Fort Simpson, *Canada* ... 100 A4
Fort Smith, *Canada* 100 B6
Fort Smith, *U.S.A.* 109 H7
Fort Stanton, *U.S.A.* 111 K11
Fort Stockton, *U.S.A.* ... 109 K3
Fort Sumner, *U.S.A.* 109 H2
Fort Trinquet = Bir Mogrein, *Mauritania* ... 74 C2
Fort Valley, *U.S.A.* 105 J4
Fort Vermilion, *Canada* .. 100 B5
Fort Walton Beach, *U.S.A.* 105 K2
Fort Wayne, *U.S.A.* 104 E3
Fort William, *U.K.* 14 E3
Fort Worth, *U.S.A.* 109 J6
Fort Yates, *U.S.A.* 108 B4
Fort Yukon, *U.S.A.* 96 B5
Fortaleza, *Bolivia* 124 C4
Fortaleza, *Brazil* 122 B4
Forteau, *Canada* 99 B8
Forth →, *U.K.* 14 E5
Forth, Firth of, *U.K.* 14 E6
Forthassa Rharbia, *Algeria* 75 B4
Fortín Coronel Eugenio Garay, *Paraguay* 125 E5
Fortín Garrapatal, *Paraguay* 125 E5
Fortín General Pando, *Paraguay* 125 D6
Fortín Madrejón, *Paraguay* 125 E6
Fortín Uno, *Argentina* .. 128 A3
Fortore →, *Italy* 33 G12
Fortrose, *U.K.* 14 D4
Fortuna, *Spain* 29 G3
Fortuna, *Calif., U.S.A.* .. 110 F1
Fortuna, *N. Dak., U.S.A.* 108 A3
Fortune B., *Canada* 99 C8
Fos-sur-Mer, *France* 27 E8
Foshan, *China* 53 F9
Fossacesia, *Italy* 33 F11
Fossano, *Italy* 32 D4
Fosses-la-Ville, *Belgium* .. 17 H5
Fossil, *U.S.A.* 110 D3
Fossilbrook, *Australia* ... 90 B3
Fossombrone, *Italy* 33 E9
Fosston, *U.S.A.* 108 B7
Foster, *Canada* 107 A12
Foster →, *Canada* 101 B8
Fosters Ra., *Australia* ... 90 C1
Fostoria, *U.S.A.* 104 E4
Fougamou, *Gabon* 80 E2
Fougères, *France* 24 D5
Foul Pt., *Sri Lanka* 60 Q12
Foula, *U.K.* 14 A6
Foulness I., *U.K.* 13 F8
Foulpointe, *Madag.* 85 B8
Foum Assaka, *Morocco* .. 74 C2
Foum Zguid, *Morocco* ... 74 B3
Foumban, *Cameroon* 79 D7
Foundiougne, *Senegal* ... 78 C1
Fountain, *Colo., U.S.A.* .. 108 F2
Fountain, *Utah, U.S.A.* .. 110 G8
Fountain Springs, *U.S.A.* 113 K8
Fourchambault, *France* .. 25 E10
Fourchu, *Canada* 99 C7
Fouriesburg, *S. Africa* ... 84 D4
Fourmies, *France* 25 B11
Foúrnoi, *Greece* 39 M9
Fours, *France* 25 F10
Fouta Djalon, *Guinea* ... 78 C2
Foux, Cap-à-, *Haiti* 117 C5
Foveaux Str., *N.Z.* 87 M2
Fowey, *U.K.* 13 G3
Fowler, *Calif., U.S.A.* ... 111 H4
Fowler, *Colo., U.S.A.* ... 108 F2
Fowler, *Kans., U.S.A.* ... 109 G4
Fowlers B., *Australia* ... 89 F5
Fowlerton, *U.S.A.* 109 L5
Fox →, *Canada* 101 B10
Fox Valley, *Canada* 101 C7
Foxe Basin, *Canada* 97 B12
Foxe Chan., *Canada* 97 B11
Foxe Pen., *Canada* 97 B12
Foxhol, *Neths.* 16 B9
Foxpark, *U.S.A.* 110 F10
Foxton, *N.Z.* 87 J5
Foyle, Lough, *U.K.* 15 A4
Foynes, *Ireland* 15 D2
Foz, *Spain* 30 B3
Fóz do Cunene, *Angola* .. 84 B1
Foz do Gregório, *Brazil* .. 124 B3
Foz do Iguaçu, *Brazil* ... 127 B5
Foz do Riosinho, *Brazil* .. 124 B3
Frackville, *U.S.A.* 107 F8
Fraga, *Spain* 28 D5
Fraire, *Belgium* 17 H5
Frameries, *Belgium* 17 H3

Framingham, *U.S.A.* 107 D13
Franca, *Brazil* 123 F2
Francavilla al Mare, *Italy* . 33 F11
Francavilla Fontana, *Italy* . 35 B10
France ■, *Europe* 7 F6
Frances, *Australia* 91 F3
Frances →, *Canada* 100 A3
Frances L., *Canada* 100 A3
Francés Viejo, C., *Dom. Rep.* 117 C6
Franceville, *Gabon* 80 E2
Franche-Comté, *France* . 25 F12
Franches Montagnes, *Switz.* 22 B4
Francisco de Orellana, *Ecuador* 120 D2
Francisco I. Madero, *Coahuila, Mexico* 114 B4
Francisco I. Madero, *Durango, Mexico* 114 C4
Francisco Sá, *Brazil* 123 E3
Francistown, *Botswana* .. 85 C4
Francofonte, *Italy* 35 E7
François, *Canada* 99 C8
François L., *Canada* 100 C3
Francorchamps, *Belgium* . 17 H7
Franeker, *Neths.* 16 B7
Frankado, *Djibouti* 77 E5
Frankenberg, *Germany* .. 18 D4
Frankenthal, *Germany* ... 19 F4
Frankenwald, *Germany* .. 19 E7
Frankfort, *S. Africa* 85 D4
Frankfort, *Ind., U.S.A.* .. 104 E2
Frankfort, *Kans., U.S.A.* . 108 F6
Frankfort, *Ky., U.S.A.* ... 104 F3
Frankfort, *Mich., U.S.A.* . 104 C2
Frankfurt am Main, *Germany* 19 E4
Frankfurt an der Oder, *Germany* 18 C10
Fränkische Alb, *Germany* . 19 F7
Fränkische Rezal →, *Germany* 19 F7
Fränkische Saale →, *Germany* 19 E5
Fränkische Schweiz, *Germany* 19 F7
Frankland →, *Australia* . 89 G2
Franklin, *Ky., U.S.A.* 105 G2
Franklin, *La., U.S.A.* 109 L9
Franklin, *Mass., U.S.A.* .. 107 D13
Franklin, *N.H., U.S.A.* ... 107 C13
Franklin, *Nebr., U.S.A.* .. 108 E5
Franklin, *Pa., U.S.A.* 106 E5
Franklin, *Tenn., U.S.A.* .. 105 H2
Franklin, *Va., U.S.A.* 105 G7
Franklin, *W. Va., U.S.A.* . 104 F6
Franklin B., *Canada* 96 B7
Franklin D. Roosevelt L., *U.S.A.* 110 B4
Franklin I., *Antarctica* .. 5 D11
Franklin L., *U.S.A.* 110 F6
Franklin Mts., *Canada* ... 96 B7
Franklin Str., *Canada* ... 96 A10
Franklinton, *U.S.A.* 109 K9
Franklinville, *U.S.A.* 106 D6
Franks Pk., *U.S.A.* 110 E9
Frankston, *Australia* 91 F4
Fränsta, *Sweden* 10 B10
Frantsa Iosifa, Zemlya, *Russia* 44 A6
Franz, *Canada* 98 C3
Franz Josef Land = Frantsa Iosifa, Zemlya, *Russia* .. 44 A6
Franzburg, *Germany* 18 A8
Frascati, *Italy* 34 A5
Fraser →, *B.C., Canada* . 100 D4
Fraser →, *Nfld., Canada* . 99 A7
Fraser I., *Australia* 91 D5
Fraser Lake, *Canada* 100 C4
Fraserburg, *S. Africa* 84 E3
Fraserburgh, *U.K.* 14 D6
Fraserdale, *Canada* 98 C3
Frasne, *France* 25 F13
Frauenfeld, *Switz.* 23 A7
Fray Bentos, *Uruguay* ... 126 C4
Frazier Downs, *Australia* . 88 C3
Frechilla, *Spain* 30 C6
Fredericia, *Denmark* 11 J3
Frederick, *Md., U.S.A.* .. 104 F7
Frederick, *Okla., U.S.A.* . 109 H5
Frederick, *S. Dak., U.S.A.* 108 C5
Frederick Sd., *U.S.A.* ... 100 B2
Fredericksburg, *Tex., U.S.A.* 109 K5
Fredericksburg, *Va., U.S.A.* 104 F7
Fredericktown, *U.S.A.* .. 109 G9
Frederico I. Madero, Presa, *Mexico* 114 B3
Fredericton, *Canada* 99 C6
Fredericton Junc., *Canada* 99 C6
Frederikshåb, *Greenland* . 4 C5
Frederikshavn, *Denmark* . 11 G4
Frederikssund, *Denmark* . 11 J6
Frederiksted, *Virgin Is.* .. 117 C7
Fredonia, *Ariz., U.S.A.* .. 111 H7
Fredonia, *Kans., U.S.A.* . 109 G7
Fredonia, *N.Y., U.S.A.* .. 106 D5
Fredrikstad, *Norway* 10 E4
Freehold, *U.S.A.* 107 F10
Freel Peak, *U.S.A.* 112 G7
Freeland, *U.S.A.* 107 E9
Freels, C., *Canada* 99 C9
Freeman, *Calif., U.S.A.* .. 113 K9

Freeman, *S. Dak., U.S.A.* 108 D6
Freeport, *Bahamas* 116 A4
Freeport, *Canada* 99 D6
Freeport, *Ill., U.S.A.* 108 D10
Freeport, *N.Y., U.S.A.* ... 107 F11
Freeport, *Tex., U.S.A.* ... 109 L7
Freetown, *S. Leone* 78 D2
Frégate, L., *Canada* 98 B5
Fregenal de la Sierra, *Spain* 31 G4
Fregene, *Italy* 34 A5
Fréhel, C., *France* 24 D4
Freiberg, *Germany* 18 E9
Freibourg = Fribourg, *Switz.* 22 C4
Freiburg, *Baden-W., Germany* 19 H3
Freiburg, *Niedersachsen, Germany* 18 B5
Freiburger Alpen, *Switz.* . 22 C4
Freire, *Chile* 128 A2
Freirina, *Chile* 126 B1
Freising, *Germany* 19 G7
Freistadt, *Austria* 20 G4
Freital, *Germany* 18 E9
Fréjus, *France* 27 E10
Fremantle, *Australia* 89 F2
Fremont, *Calif., U.S.A.* .. 111 H2
Fremont, *Mich., U.S.A.* .. 104 D3
Fremont, *Nebr., U.S.A.* .. 108 E6
Fremont, *Ohio, U.S.A.* .. 104 E4
Fremont →, *U.S.A.* 111 G8
Fremont L., *U.S.A.* 110 E9
French Camp, *U.S.A.* ... 112 H5
French Creek →, *U.S.A.* . 106 E5
French Guiana ■, *S. Amer.* 121 C7
French Pass, *N.Z.* 87 J4
French Polynesia ■, *Pac. Oc.* 93 J13
French Terr. of Afars & Issas = Djibouti ■, *Africa* 68 E3
Frenchglen, *U.S.A.* 110 E4
Frenchman Butte, *Canada* 101 C7
Frenchman Cr. →, *Mont., U.S.A.* 110 B10
Frenchman Cr. →, *Nebr., U.S.A.* 108 E4
Frenda, *Algeria* 75 A5
Fresco →, *Brazil* 125 B7
Freshfield, C., *Antarctica* . 5 C10
Fresnay-sur-Sarthe, *France* 24 D7
Fresnillo, *Mexico* 114 C4
Fresno, *U.S.A.* 111 H4
Fresno Alhandiga, *Spain* . 30 E5
Fresno Reservoir, *U.S.A.* . 110 B9
Freudenstadt, *Germany* .. 19 G4
Freux, *Belgium* 17 J6
Frévent, *France* 25 B9
Frew →, *Australia* 90 C2
Frewena, *Australia* 90 B2
Freycinet Pen., *Australia* . 90 G4
Freyming-Merlebach, *France* 25 C13
Freyung, *Germany* 19 G9
Fria, *Guinea* 78 C2
Fria, C., *Namibia* 84 B1
Friant, *U.S.A.* 112 J7
Frías, *Argentina* 126 B2
Fribourg, *Switz.* 22 C4
Fribourg □, *Switz.* 22 C4
Frick, *Switz.* 22 A6
Friday Harbor, *U.S.A.* .. 112 B3
Friedberg, *Bayern, Germany* 19 G6
Friedberg, *Hessen, Germany* 19 E4
Friedland, *Germany* 18 B9
Friedrichshafen, *Germany* 19 H5
Friedrichskoog, *Germany* 18 A4
Friedrichstadt, *Germany* . 18 A5
Friendly Is. = Tonga ■, *Pac. Oc.* 87 D11
Friesack, *Germany* 18 C8
Friesche Wad, *Neths.* ... 16 B7
Friesland □, *Neths.* 16 B7
Friesoythe, *Germany* 18 B3
Frillesås, *Sweden* 11 G6
Frio →, *U.S.A.* 109 L5
Friona, *U.S.A.* 109 H3
Frisian Is., *Europe* 18 B2
Fristad, *Sweden* 11 G7
Fritch, *U.S.A.* 109 H4
Fritsla, *Sweden* 11 G6
Fritzlar, *Germany* 18 D5
Friuli-Venezia Giulia □, *Italy* 33 B10
Frobisher B., *Canada* ... 97 B13
Frobisher Bay = Iqaluit, *Canada* 97 B13
Frobisher L., *Canada* ... 101 B7
Frohavet, *Norway* 8 E10
Froid, *U.S.A.* 108 A2
Froid-Chapelle, *Belgium* . 17 H4
Frolovo, *Russia* 43 B10
Fromberg, *U.S.A.* 110 D9
Frome, *U.K.* 13 F5
Frome, L., *Australia* 91 E2
Frome Downs, *Australia* . 91 E2
Frómista, *Spain* 30 C6
Front Range, *U.S.A.* 110 G11
Front Royal, *U.S.A.* 104 F6
Fronteira, *Portugal* 31 F3
Fronteiras, *Brazil* 122 C3
Frontera, *Canary Is.* 36 G2
Frontera, *Mexico* 115 D6

Frontignan, *France* 26 E7
Frosinone, *Italy* 34 A6
Frosolone, *Italy* 35 A7
Frostburg, *U.S.A.* 104 F6
Frostisen, *Norway* 8 B14
Frouard, *France* 25 D13
Frøya, *Norway* 8 E10
Fruges, *France* 25 B9
Frumoasa, *Romania* 38 C8
Frunze = Bishkek, *Kirghizia* 44 E8
Frutal, *Brazil* 123 F2
Frutigen, *Switz.* 22 C5
Frýdek-Místek, *Czech.* .. 20 F8
Frýdlant, *Czech.* 20 E5
Fu Jiang →, *China* 52 C6
Fu Xian, *Liaoning, China* 51 E11
Fu Xian, *Shaanxi, China* . 50 F5
Fu'an, *China* 53 D12
Fubian, *China* 52 B4
Fucécchio, *Italy* 32 E7
Fucheng, *China* 50 F9
Fuchou = Fuzhou, *China* . 53 D12
Fuchū, *Japan* 49 G6
Fuchuan, *China* 53 E8
Fuchun Jiang →, *China* . 53 B13
Fúcino, Conca del, *Italy* . 33 F10
Fuding, *China* 53 D13
Fuencaliente, *Canary Is.* . 36 F2
Fuencaliente, *Spain* 31 G6
Fuencaliente, Pta., *Canary Is.* 36 F2
Fuengirola, *Spain* 31 J6
Fuente Alamo, *Albacete, Spain* 29 G3
Fuente Álamo, *Murcia, Spain* 29 H3
Fuente de Cantos, *Spain* . 31 G4
Fuente del Maestre, *Spain* 31 G4
Fuente el Fresno, *Spain* .. 31 F7
Fuente Ovejuna, *Spain* .. 31 G5
Fuentes de Andalucía, *Spain* 31 H5
Fuentes de Ebro, *Spain* .. 28 D4
Fuentes de León, *Spain* .. 31 G4
Fuentes de Oñoro, *Spain* . 30 E4
Fuentesaúco, *Spain* 30 D5
Fuerte →, *Mexico* 114 B3
Fuerte Olimpo, *Paraguay* 126 A4
Fuerteventura, *Canary Is.* 36 F6
Fufeng, *China* 50 G4
Fuga I., *Phil.* 55 B4
Fugløysund, *Norway* 8 A16
Fugong, *China* 52 D2
Fugou, *China* 50 G8
Fugu, *China* 50 E6
Fuhai, *China* 54 B3
Fuḥaymī, *Iraq* 64 C4
Fuji, *Japan* 49 G9
Fuji-San, *Japan* 49 G9
Fuji-yoshida, *Japan* 49 G9
Fujian □, *China* 53 E12
Fujinomiya, *Japan* 49 G9
Fujisawa, *Japan* 49 G9
Fukien = Fujian □, *China* 53 E12
Fukuchiyama, *Japan* 49 G7
Fukue-Shima, *Japan* 49 H4
Fukui, *Japan* 49 F8
Fukui □, *Japan* 49 G8
Fukuoka, *Japan* 49 H5
Fukuoka □, *Japan* 49 H5
Fukushima, *Japan* 48 F10
Fukushima □, *Japan* 48 F10
Fukuyama, *Japan* 49 G6
Fulda, *Germany* 18 E5
Fulda →, *Germany* 18 D5
Fuling, *China* 52 C6
Fullerton, *Calif., U.S.A.* . 113 M9
Fullerton, *Nebr., U.S.A.* . 108 E5
Fulongquan, *China* 51 B13
Fulton, *Mo., U.S.A.* 108 F9
Fulton, *N.Y., U.S.A.* 107 C8
Fulton, *Tenn., U.S.A.* ... 105 G1
Fuluälven →, *Sweden* ... 10 C7
Fulufjället, *Sweden* 10 C6
Fumay, *France* 25 C11
Fumel, *France* 26 D4
Fumin, *China* 52 E4
Funabashi, *Japan* 49 G10
Funchal, *Madeira* 36 D3
Fundación, *Colombia* ... 120 A3
Fundão, *Brazil* 123 E3
Fundão, *Portugal* 30 E3
Fundy, B. of, *Canada* ... 99 D6
Funing, *Hebei, China* ... 51 E10
Funing, *Jiangsu, China* .. 51 H10
Funing, *Yunnan, China* . 52 F5
Funiu Shan, *China* 50 H7
Funsi, *Ghana* 78 C4
Funtua, *Nigeria* 79 C6
Fuping, *Hebei, China* ... 50 E8
Fuping, *Shaanxi, China* . 50 G5
Fuqing, *China* 53 E12
Fuquan, *China* 52 D6
Fur, *Denmark* 11 H3
Furano, *Japan* 48 C11
Furāt, Nahr al →, *Asia* .. 64 D5
Fürg, *Iran* 65 D7
Furkapass, *Switz.* 23 C7
Furmanov, *Russia* 41 C12
Furmanovo, *Kazakhstan* . 43 B13
Furnás, *Spain* 36 B8
Furnas, Reprêsa de, *Brazil* 123 F2
Furneaux Group, *Australia* 90 G4
Furness, *U.K.* 12 C4

Furqlus, *Syria* 69 A6
Fürstenau, *Germany* 18 C3
Fürstenberg, *Germany* ... 18 B9
Fürstenfeld, *Austria* 21 H6
Fürstenfeldbruck, *Germany* 19 G7
Fürstenwalde, *Germany* . 18 C10
Fürth, *Germany* 19 F6
Furth im Wald, *Germany* . 19 F8
Furtwangen, *Germany* ... 19 G4
Furukawa, *Japan* 48 E10
Furusund, *Sweden* 10 E12
Fury and Hecla Str., *Canada* 97 B11
Fusagasuga, *Colombia* .. 120 C3
Fuscaldo, *Italy* 35 C9
Fushan, *Shandong, China* 51 F11
Fushan, *Shanxi, China* .. 50 G6
Fushun, *Liaoning, China* 51 D12
Fushun, *Sichuan, China* . 52 C5
Fusio, *Switz.* 23 D7
Fusong, *China* 51 C14
Füssen, *Germany* 19 H6
Fusui, *China* 52 F6
Futrono, *Chile* 128 B2
Futuna, *Wall. & F. Is.* ... 87 B8
Fuwa, *Egypt* 76 H7
Fuxin, *China* 51 C11
Fuyang, *Anhui, China* .. 50 H8
Fuyang, *Zhejiang, China* . 53 B12
Fuyang He →, *China* 50 E9
Fuying Dao, *China* 53 D13
Fuyu, *China* 51 B13
Fuyuan, *Heilongjiang, China* 54 B8
Fuyuan, *Yunnan, China* . 52 E5
Fuzhou, *China* 53 D12
Fylde, *U.K.* 12 D5
Fyn, *Denmark* 11 J4
Fyne, L., *U.K.* 14 F3
Fyns Amtskommune □, *Denmark* 11 J4
Fyresvatn, *Norway* 10 E2

G

Gaanda, *Nigeria* 79 C7
Gabarin, *Nigeria* 79 C7
Gabas →, *France* 26 E3
Gabela, *Angola* 80 G2
Gabès, *Tunisia* 75 B7
Gabès, G. de, *Tunisia* ... 75 B7
Gabgaba, W. →, *Egypt* .. 76 C3
Gabon ■, *Africa* 80 E2
Gaborone, *Botswana* ... 84 C4
Gabriels, *U.S.A.* 107 B10
Gābrīk, *Iran* 65 E8
Gabrovo, *Bulgaria* 38 G8
Gacé, *France* 24 D7
Gāch Sār, *Iran* 65 B6
Gachsārān, *Iran* 65 D6
Gacko, *Bos.-H.* 21 M9
Gadag, *India* 60 M9
Gadamai, *Sudan* 77 D4
Gadap, *Pakistan* 62 G2
Gadarwara, *India* 63 H8
Gadebusch, *Germany* ... 18 B6
Gadein, *Sudan* 77 F2
Gadhada, *India* 62 J4
Gadmen, *Switz.* 23 C6
Gádor, Sierra de, *Spain* . 29 J2
Gadsden, *Ala., U.S.A.* .. 105 H2
Gadsden, *Ariz., U.S.A.* .. 111 K6
Gadwal, *India* 60 L10
Gadyach, *Ukraine* 40 F9
Găeşti, *Romania* 38 E8
Gaeta, *Italy* 34 A6
Gaeta, G. di, *Italy* 34 A6
Gaffney, *U.S.A.* 105 H5
Gafsa, *Tunisia* 75 B6
Gagarin = Gzhatsk, *Russia* 40 D9
Gagetown, *Canada* 99 C6
Gagino, *Russia* 41 D14
Gagliano del Capo, *Italy* . 35 C11
Gagnoa, *Ivory C.* 78 D3
Gagnon, *Canada* 99 B6
Gagnon, L., *Canada* 101 A6
Gagra, *Georgia* 43 E9
Gahini, *Rwanda* 82 C3
Gahmar, *India* 63 G10
Gai Xian, *China* 51 D12
Gaïdhouronísi, *Greece* .. 37 E7
Gail, *U.S.A.* 109 J4
Gail →, *Austria* 21 J3
Gaillac, *France* 26 E5
Gaillon, *France* 24 C8
Gaimán, *Argentina* 128 B3
Gaines, *U.S.A.* 106 E7
Gainesville, *Fla., U.S.A.* . 105 L4
Gainesville, *Ga., U.S.A.* . 105 H4
Gainesville, *Mo., U.S.A.* . 109 G8
Gainesville, *Tex., U.S.A.* . 109 J6
Gainsborough, *U.K.* 12 D7
Gairdner, L., *Australia* .. 91 E2
Gairloch, L., *U.K.* 14 D3
Gais, *Switz.* 23 B8
Gakuch, *Pakistan* 63 A5
Galán, Cerro, *Argentina* . 126 B2
Galana →, *Kenya* 82 C5
Galangue, *Angola* 81 G3
Galápagos, *Pac. Oc.* 93 H18
Galashiels, *U.K.* 14 F6
Galaţi, *Romania* 38 D11

Galatia, Turkey 66 D5
Galatina, Italy 35 B11
Galátone, Italy 35 B11
Galax, U.S.A. 105 G5
Galaxídhion, Greece 39 L5
Galbraith, Australia 90 B3
Galcaio, Somali Rep. 68 F4
Galela, Indonesia 57 D7
Galera, Spain 29 H2
Galera, Pta., Chile 128 A2
Galera Point, Trin. & Tob. 117 D7
Galesburg, U.S.A. 108 E9
Galeton, U.S.A. 106 E7
Galheirão →, Brazil 123 D2
Galheiros, Brazil 123 D2
Gali, Georgia 43 E9
Galich, Russia 41 B13
Galiche, Bulgaria 38 F6
Galicia □, Spain 30 C3
Galilee = Hagalil, Israel . 69 C4
Galilee, L., Australia 90 C4
Galilee, Sea of = Yam
  Kinneret, Israel 69 C4
Galinoporni, Cyprus 37 D13
Galion, U.S.A. 106 F2
Galite, Is. de la, Tunisia . 75 A6
Galiuro Mts., U.S.A. 111 K8
Gallabat, Sudan 77 E4
Gallardon, France 25 D8
Gallarate, Italy 32 C5
Gallatin, U.S.A. 105 G2
Galle, Sri Lanka 60 R12
Gállego →, Spain 28 D4
Gallegos →, Argentina .. 128 D3
Galley Hd., Ireland 15 E3
Galliate, Italy 32 C5
Gallinas, Pta., Colombia . 120 A3
Gallipoli = Gelibolu,
  Turkey 39 J9
Gallípoli, Italy 35 B11
Gallipolis, U.S.A. 104 F4
Gällivare, Sweden 8 C16
Gallo, C., Italy 34 D6
Gallocanta, L. de, Spain . 28 E3
Galloway, U.K. 14 G4
Galloway, Mull of, U.K. . 14 G4
Gallup, U.S.A. 111 J9
Gallur, Spain 28 D3
Galong, Australia 91 E4
Galoya, Sri Lanka 60 Q12
Galt, U.S.A. 112 G5
Galtström, Sweden 10 B11
Galtür, Austria 19 J6
Galty Mts., Ireland 15 D3
Galtymore, Ireland 15 D3
Galva, U.S.A. 108 E9
Galvarino, Chile 128 A2
Galve de Sorbe, Spain .. 28 D1
Galveston, U.S.A. 109 L7
Galveston B., U.S.A. ... 109 L7
Gálvez, Argentina 126 C3
Gálvez, Spain 31 F6
Galway, Ireland 15 C2
Galway □, Ireland 15 C2
Galway B., Ireland 15 C2
Gam →, Vietnam 58 B5
Gamagori, Japan 49 G8
Gamari, L., Ethiopia ... 77 E5
Gamawa, Nigeria 79 C7
Gamay, Phil. 55 E6
Gambaga, Ghana 79 C4
Gambat, Pakistan 62 F3
Gambela, Ethiopia 77 F3
Gambia ■, W. Afr. 78 C1
Gambia →, W. Afr. 78 C1
Gambier, C., Australia . 88 B5
Gambier Is., Australia .. 91 F2
Gamboli, Pakistan 62 E3
Gamboma, Congo 80 E3
Gamerco, U.S.A. 111 J9
Gamlakarleby = Kokkola,
  Finland 8 E17
Gammon →, Canada .. 101 C9
Gammouda, Tunisia ... 75 A6
Gamu-Gofa □, Ethiopia . 77 F4
Gan, France 26 E3
Gan Gan, Argentina ... 128 B3
Gan Goriama, Mts.,
  Cameroon 79 D7
Gan Jiang →, China ... 53 C10
Ganado, Ariz., U.S.A. . 111 J9
Ganado, Tex., U.S.A. .. 109 L6
Gananoque, Canada ... 98 D4
Ganaveh, Iran 65 D6
Gäncä = Gyandzha,
  Azerbaijan 43 F12
Gand = Gent, Belgium . 17 F3
Ganda, Angola 81 G2
Gandak →, India 63 G11
Gandava, Pakistan 62 E2
Gander, Canada 99 C9
Gander L., Canada 99 C9
Ganderowe Falls,
  Zimbabwe 83 F2
Gandesa, Spain 28 D5
Gandhi Sagar, India .. 62 G6
Gandi, Nigeria 79 C6
Gandía, Spain 29 G4
Gandino, Italy 32 C6
Gando, Pta., Canary Is. . 36 G4
Gandole, Nigeria 79 D7
Gandu, Brazil 123 D4
Ganedidalem = Gani,
  Indonesia 57 E7

Ganetti, Sudan 76 D3
Ganga →, India 63 H14
Ganga, Mouths of the,
  India 63 J13
Ganganagar, India ... 62 E5
Gangapur, India 62 F7
Gangara, Niger 79 C6
Gangaw, Burma 61 H19
Gangdisê Shan, China . 61 D12
Ganges = Ganga →, India 63 H14
Ganges, France 26 E7
Gangoh, India 62 E7
Gangtok, India 61 F16
Gangu, China 50 G3
Gangyao, China 51 B14
Gani, Indonesia 57 E7
Ganj, India 63 F8
Gannat, France 26 B7
Gannett Peak, U.S.A. . 110 E9
Gannvalley, U.S.A. .. 108 C5
Ganquan, China 50 F5
Gänserdorf, Austria .. 21 G6
Ganshui, China 52 C6
Gansu □, China 50 G3
Ganta, Liberia 78 D3
Gantheaume, C., Australia 91 F2
Gantheaume B., Australia 89 E1
Gantsevichi, Belorussia .. 40 E5
Ganyem, Indonesia .. 57 E10
Ganyu, China 51 G10
Ganyushkino, Kazakhstan 43 C13
Ganzhou, China 53 E10
Gao, Mali 79 B5
Gao Xian, China ... 52 C5
Gao'an, China 53 C10
Gaohe, China 53 F9
Gaohebu, China 53 B11
Gaokeng, China 53 D9
Gaolan Dao, China . 53 G9
Gaoligong Shan, China 52 E2
Gaomi, China 51 F10
Gaoping, China 50 G7
Gaoua, Burkina Faso . 78 C4
Gaoual, Guinea 78 C2
Gaoxiong, Taiwan .. 53 F13
Gaoyang, China 50 E8
Gaoyou, China 53 A12
Gaoyou Hu, China .. 51 H10
Gaoyuan, China 51 F9
Gaozhou, China 53 G8
Gap, France 27 D10
Gapan, Phil. 55 D4
Gar, China 54 C2
Garabogazköl Aylagy =
  Kara Bogaz Gol, Zaliv,
  Turkmenistan 44 E6
Garachico, Canary Is. . 36 F3
Garachiné, Panama .. 116 E4
Garafia, Canary Is. .. 36 F2
Garajonay, Canary Is. . 36 F2
Garanhuns, Brazil ... 122 C4
Garawe, Liberia 78 E3
Garba Tula, Kenya .. 82 B4
Garber, U.S.A. 109 G6
Garberville, U.S.A. . 110 F2
Garça, Brazil 123 F2
Garças →, Mato Grosso,
  Brazil 125 D7
Garças →, Pernambuco,
  Brazil 122 C4
Garcias, Brazil 125 E7
Gard, Somali Rep. .. 68 F4
Gard □, France 27 D8
Gard →, France 27 E8
Garda, L. di, Italy .. 32 C7
Gardanne, France ... 27 E9
Garde L., Canada ... 101 A7
Gardelegen, Germany . 18 C7
Garden City, Kans., U.S.A. 109 G4
Garden City, Tex., U.S.A. 109 K4
Garden Grove, U.S.A. 113 M9
Gardêz, Afghan. 62 C3
Gardiner, U.S.A. 110 D8
Gardiners I., U.S.A. . 107 E12
Gardner, U.S.A. 107 D13
Gardner Canal, Canada 100 C3
Gardnerville, U.S.A. . 112 G7
Gare Tigre, Fr. Guiana 121 C7
Garéssio, Italy 32 D5
Garey, U.S.A. 113 L6
Garfield, U.S.A. 110 C5
Gargan, Mt., France . 26 C5
Gargano, Mte., Italy . 35 A8
Gargouna, Mali 79 B5
Garhshankar, India . 62 D7
Garibaldi Prov. Park,
  Canada 100 D4
Garies, S. Africa ... 84 E2
Garigliano →, Italy . 34 A6
Garissa, Kenya 82 C4
Garissa □, Kenya .. 82 C5
Garkida, Nigeria ... 79 C7
Garko, Nigeria 79 C6
Garland, U.S.A. 110 F7
Garlasco, Italy 32 C5
Garm, Tajikistan ... 44 F8
Garmāb, Iran 65 C8
Garmisch-Partenkirchen,
  Germany 19 H7
Garmsär, Iran 65 C7
Garner, U.S.A. 108 D8
Garnett, U.S.A. 108 F7
Garo Hills, India ... 63 G14
Garoe, Somali Rep. . 68 F4

Garonne →, France .. 26 C3
Garonne, Canal Latéral à
  la →, France 26 D4
Garoua, Cameroon .. 79 D7
Garrel, Germany 18 C3
Garrigue, France ... 26 E7
Garrison, Mont., U.S.A. . 110 C7
Garrison, N. Dak., U.S.A. 108 B4
Garrison, Tex., U.S.A. 109 K7
Garrison Res. =
  Sakakawea, L., U.S.A. 108 B3
Garrovillas, Spain .. 31 F4
Garrucha, Spain 29 H3
Garry →, U.K. 14 E5
Garry, L., Canada .. 96 B9
Garsen, Kenya 82 C5
Garson L., Canada . 101 B6
Gartempe →, France 26 B4
Gartz, Germany 18 B10
Garu, Ghana 79 C4
Garub, Namibia 84 D2
Garut, Indonesia ... 57 G12
Garvão, Portugal ... 31 H2
Garvie Mts., N.Z. .. 87 L2
Garwa = Garoua,
  Cameroon 79 D7
Garwa, India 63 G10
Garwolin, Poland .. 20 D11
Gary, U.S.A. 104 E2
Garz, Germany 18 A9
Garzê, China 52 B3
Garzón, Colombia .. 120 C2
Gas-San, Japan 48 E10
Gasan Kuli, Turkmenistan 44 F6
Gascogne, France .. 26 E4
Gascogne, G. de, Europe . 28 B2
Gascony = Gascogne,
  France 26 E4
Gascoyne →, Australia 89 D1
Gascoyne Junc. T.O.,
  Australia 89 E2
Gascueña, Spain ... 28 E2
Gash, Wadi →, Ethiopia 77 D4
Gashaka, Nigeria .. 79 D7
Gasherbrum, Pakistan 63 B7
Gashua, Nigeria ... 79 C7
Gaspé, Canada 99 C7
Gaspé, C. de, Canada 99 C7
Gaspé, Pén. de, Canada 99 C6
Gaspésie, Parc Prov. de la,
  Canada 99 C6
Gassaway, U.S.A. .. 104 F5
Gasselte, Neths. ... 16 C9
Gasselternijveen, Neths. 16 C9
Gássino Torinese, Italy 32 C4
Gassol, Nigeria 79 D7
Gasteiz = Vitoria, Spain 28 C2
Gastonia, U.S.A. ... 105 H5
Gastoúni, Greece .. 39 M4
Gastoúri, Greece .. 39 K2
Gastre, Argentina .. 128 B3
Gata, C., Cyprus ... 37 E12
Gata, C. de, Spain . 29 J2
Gata, Sierra de, Spain 30 E4
Gataga →, Canada . 100 B3
Gătaia, Romania ... 38 D4
Gatchina, Russia ... 40 B7
Gates, U.S.A. 106 C7
Gateshead, U.K. ... 12 C6
Gatesville, U.S.A. . 109 K6
Gaths, Zimbabwe .. 83 G3
Gatico, Chile 126 A1
Gâtinais, France ... 25 D9
Gâtine, Hauteurs de,
  France 26 B3
Gatineau →, Canada 98 C4
Gatineau, Parc de la,
  Canada 98 C4
Gattaran, Phil. 55 B4
Gattinara, Italy ... 32 C5
Gatun, L., Panama . 116 E4
Gatyana, S. Africa . 85 E4
Gau, Fiji 87 D8
Gaucín, Spain 31 J5
Gauer L., Canada . 101 B9
Gauhati, India 63 F14
Gauja →, Latvia .. 40 C4
Gaula →, Norway . 8 E11
Gaurain-Ramecroix,
  Belgium 17 G3
Gausta, Norway .. 10 E2
Gāv Koshī, Iran .. 65 D8
Gavà, Spain 28 D6
Gāvakān, Iran 65 D7
Gavarnie, France .. 26 F3
Gavàter, Iran 65 E9
Gāvbandī, Iran ... 65 E7
Gavdhopoúla, Greece 37 E6
Gávdhos, Greece . 37 E6
Gavere, Belgium . 17 G3
Gavião, Portugal . 31 F3
Gaviota, U.S.A. .. 113 L6
Gävleborgs län □, Sweden 10 C10
Gavorrano, Italy . 32 F7
Gavray, France .. 24 D5
Gavrilov Yam, Russia 41 C11
Gawachab, Namibia 84 D2
Gawilgarh Hills, India 60 J10
Gawler, Australia . 91 E2
Gaxun Nur, China 54 B5
Gaya, India 63 G11
Gaya, Niger 79 C5
Gaya, Nigeria 79 C6
Gaylord, U.S.A. .. 104 C3
Gayndah, Australia 91 D5

Gaysin, Ukraine 42 B3
Gayvoron, Ukraine 42 B3
Gaza, Egypt 69 D3
Gaza □, Mozam. 85 C5
Gaza Strip, Egypt .. 69 D3
Gazaoua, Niger 79 C6
Găzbor, Iran 65 D8
Gazi, Zaïre 82 B1
Gaziantep, Turkey .. 66 E7
Gaziantep □, Turkey 66 E7
Gazipaşa, Turkey ... 66 E5
Gazli, Uzbekistan ... 44 E7
Gbarnga, Liberia ... 78 D3
Gbekebo, Nigeria .. 79 D5
Gboko, Nigeria 79 D6
Gbongan, Nigeria .. 79 D5
Gcuwa, S. Africa .. 85 E4
Gdańsk, Poland 20 A8
Gdańska, Zatoka, Poland . 20 A9
Gdov, Russia 40 B5
Gdynia, Poland 20 A8
Gebe, Indonesia ... 57 D7
Gebeit Mine, Sudan 76 C4
Gebel Mûsa, Egypt 76 J8
Gebze, Turkey 66 C3
Gecha, Ethiopia ... 77 F4
Gedaref, Sudan 77 E4
Gede, Tanjung, Indonesia 56 F3
Gedinne, Belgium .. 17 J5
Gediz, Turkey 66 D3
Gediz →, Turkey .. 66 D2
Gedo, Ethiopia 77 F4
Gédre, France 26 F4
Gedser, Denmark .. 11 K5
Gedser Odde, Denmark 11 K5
Geegully Cr. →, Australia 88 C3
Geel, Belgium 17 F5
Geelong, Australia . 91 F3
Geelvink Chan., Australia 89 E1
Geer →, Belgium .. 17 G7
Geesthacht, Germany 18 B6
Geffen, Neths. 16 E6
Geidam, Nigeria ... 79 C7
Geikie →, Canada . 101 B8
Geili, Sudan 77 D3
Geilo, Norway 10 D2
Geisingen, Germany 19 H4
Geislingen, Germany 19 G5
Geita, Tanzania ... 82 C3
Geita □, Tanzania . 82 C3
Gejiu, China 52 F4
Gel →, Sudan 77 F2
Gel River, Sudan .. 77 F2
Gela, Italy 35 E7
Gela, G. di, Italy .. 35 F7
Geladi, Ethiopia ... 68 F4
Gelderland □, Neths. 16 D8
Geldermalsen, Neths. 16 E6
Geldern, Germany . 18 D2
Geldrop, Neths. ... 17 F7
Geleen, Neths. 17 G7
Gelehun, S. Leone . 78 D2
Gelendost, Turkey . 66 D4
Gelendzhik, Russia 42 D8
Gelibolu, Turkey .. 39 J9
Gelidonya Burnu, Turkey . 66 E4
Gelnhausen, Germany 19 E5
Gelsenkirchen, Germany 18 D3
Gelting, Germany . 18 A5
Gemas, Malaysia .. 59 L4
Gembloux, Belgium 17 G5
Gemena, Zaïre 80 D3
Gemerek, Turkey .. 66 D7
Gemert, Neths. 17 E7
Gemlik, Turkey ... 66 C3
Gemona del Friuli, Italy 33 B10
Gemsa, Egypt 76 B3
Gemünden, Germany 19 E5
Genale, Ethiopia .. 77 F4
Genappe, Belgium . 17 G4
Gençvatan, Belgium 17 G4
Genç, Turkey 67 D9
Gençay, France ... 26 B4
Gendringen, Neths. 16 E8
Gendt, Neths. 16 E7
Geneina, Gebel, Egypt 76 J8
Genemuiden, Neths. 16 C8
General Acha, Argentina . 126 D3
General Alvear,
  Buenos Aires, Argentina 126 D3
General Alvear, Mendoza,
  Argentina 126 D2
General Artigas, Paraguay 126 B4
General Belgrano,
  Argentina 126 D4
General Cabrera, Argentina 126 C3
General Carrera, L., Chile 128 C2
General Cepeda, Mexico . 114 B4
General Conesa, Argentina 128 B4
General Guido, Argentina 126 D4
General Juan Madariaga,
  Argentina 126 D4
General La Madrid,
  Argentina 126 D3
General Lorenzo Vintter,
  Argentina 128 B4
General MacArthur, Phil. 55 F6
General Martin Miguel de
  Güemes, Argentina 126 A3
General Paz, Argentina . 126 B4
General Pico, Argentina . 126 D3
General Pinedo, Argentina 126 B3
General Pinto, Argentina 126 C3
General Sampaio, Brazil 122 B4
General Santos, Phil. . 55 H6
General Toshevo, Bulgaria 38 F11

General Trevino, Mexico . 115 B5
General Trías, Mexico 114 B3
General Viamonte,
  Argentina 126 D3
General Villegas, Argentina 126 D3
General Vintter, L.,
  Argentina 128 B2
Generoso, Mte., Switz. .. 23 E8
Genesee, Idaho, U.S.A. . 110 C5
Genesee, Pa., U.S.A. .. 106 E7
Genesee →, U.S.A. .. 106 C7
Geneseo, Ill., U.S.A. .. 108 E9
Geneseo, Kans., U.S.A. 108 F5
Geneseo, N.Y., U.S.A. . 106 D7
Geneva = Genève, Switz. 22 D2
Geneva, Ala., U.S.A. .. 105 K3
Geneva, N.Y., U.S.A. .. 106 D7
Geneva, Nebr., U.S.A. . 108 E6
Geneva, Ohio, U.S.A. . 106 E4
Geneva, L. = Léman, Lac,
  Switz. 22 D3
Geneva, L., U.S.A. .. 104 D1
Genève, Switz. 22 D2
Genève □, Switz. ... 22 D2
Gengenbach, Germany 19 G4
Gengma, China 52 F2
Genichesk, Ukraine 42 C6
Genil →, Spain 31 H5
Génissiat, Barr. de, France 27 B9
Genk, Belgium 17 G7
Genlis, France 25 E12
Gennargentu, Mti. del,
  Italy 34 C2
Gennep, Neths. ... 17 E7
Gennes, France ... 24 E6
Genoa = Génova, Italy 32 D5
Genoa, Australia .. 91 F4
Genoa, N.Y., U.S.A. . 107 D8
Genoa, Nebr., U.S.A. 108 E6
Genoa, Nev., U.S.A. 112 F7
Génova, G. di, Italy 32 E6
Gent, Belgium 17 F3
Genthin, Germany . 18 C8
Gentio do Ouro, Brazil 122 D3
Geographe B., Australia 89 F2
Geographe Chan., Australia 89 D1
Geokchay, Azerbaijan 43 F12
Georga, Zemlya, Russia . 44 A5
George, S. Africa ... 84 E3
George →, Canada . 99 A6
George, L., N.S.W.,
  Australia 91 F4
George, L., S. Austral.,
  Australia 91 F3
George, L., W. Austral.,
  Australia 88 D3
George, L., Uganda . 82 B3
George, L., Fla., U.S.A. . 105 L5
George, L., N.Y., U.S.A. 107 C11
George Gill Ra., Australia 88 D5
George River = Port
  Nouveau-Québec,
  Canada 97 C13
George Sound, N.Z. . 87 L1
George Town, Bahamas . 116 B4
George Town, Malaysia . 59 K3
George V Land, Antarctica 5 C10
George VI Sound,
  Antarctica 5 D17
George West, U.S.A. .. 109 L5
Georgetown, Australia . 90 B3
Georgetown, Ont., Canada 98 D4
Georgetown, P.E.I.,
  Canada 99 C7
Georgetown, Cayman Is. 116 C3
Georgetown, Gambia . 78 C2
Georgetown, Guyana . 121 B6
Georgetown, Calif., U.S.A. 112 G6
Georgetown, Colo., U.S.A. 110 G11
Georgetown, Ky., U.S.A. 104 F3
Georgetown, S.C., U.S.A. 105 J6
Georgetown, Tex., U.S.A. 109 K6
Georgia □, U.S.A. .. 105 J4
Georgia ■, Asia 43 E10
Georgia, Str. of, Canada 100 D4
Georgian B., Canada . 98 C3
Georgievsk, Russia . 43 D10
Georgina →, Australia 90 C2
Georgina Downs, Australia 90 C2
Georgiu-Dezh = Liski,
  Russia 41 F11
Gera, Germany 18 E8
Geraardsbergen, Belgium 17 G3
Geral, Serra, Bahia, Brazil 123 D3
Geral, Serra, Goiás, Brazil 122 D2
Geral, Serra, Sta. Catarina,
  Brazil 127 B6
Geral de Goiás, Serra,
  Brazil 123 D2
Geral do Paraná, Serra,
  Brazil 123 E2
Geraldine, U.S.A. .. 110 C8
Geraldton, Australia . 89 E1
Geraldton, Canada . 98 C2
Gérardmer, France . 25 D13
Gerçüş, Turkey 67 E9
Gerede, Turkey 42 F5
Gereshk, Afghan. .. 60 D4
Gérgal, Spain 29 H2
Gerik, Malaysia ... 59 K3
Gering, U.S.A. 108 E3
Gerlach, U.S.A. 110 F4

Gerlachovka, *Slovak Rep.* 20 F10
Gerlogubi, *Ethiopia* 68 F4
Germansen Landing, *Canada* 100 B4
Germany ■, *Europe* 18 E6
Germersheim, *Germany* 19 F4
Germiston, *S. Africa* 85 D4
Gernsheim, *Germany* 19 F4
Gero, *Japan* 49 G8
Gerolstein, *Germany* 19 E2
Gerolzhofen, *Germany* 19 F4
Gerona, *Spain* 28 D7
Gerona □, *Spain* 28 C7
Gérouville, *Belgium* 17 J6
Gerrard, *Canada* 100 C5
Gers □, *France* 26 E4
Gers →, *France* 26 D4
Gersfeld, *Germany* 18 E5
Gerze, *Turkey* 66 C6
Geseke, *Germany* 18 D4
Geser, *Indonesia* 57 E8
Gesso →, *Italy* 32 D4
Gestro, Wabi →, *Ethiopia* 77 G5
Gesves, *Belgium* 17 H6
Getafe, *Spain* 30 E7
Gethsémani, *Canada* 99 B7
Gettysburg, *Pa., U.S.A.* 104 F7
Gettysburg, *S. Dak., U.S.A.* 108 C5
Getz Ice Shelf, *Antarctica* 5 D14
Geul →, *Neths.* 17 G7
Gevaş, *Turkey* 67 D10
Gévaudan, *France* 26 D7
Gevgelija, *Macedonia* 39 H5
Gévora →, *Spain* 31 G4
Gex, *France* 27 B10
Geyser, *U.S.A.* 110 C8
Geyserville, *U.S.A.* 112 G4
Geysir, *Iceland* 8 D3
Geyve, *Turkey* 66 C4
Ghâbat el Arab = Wang Kai, *Sudan* 77 F2
Ghaghara →, *India* 63 G11
Ghalla, Wadi el →, *Sudan* 77 E2
Ghallamane, *Mauritania* 74 D3
Ghana ■, *W. Afr.* 79 D4
Ghansor, *India* 63 H9
Ghanzi, *Botswana* 84 C3
Ghanzi □, *Botswana* 84 C3
Gharb el Istiwa'iya □, *Sudan* 77 F2
Gharbîya, Es Sahrâ el, *Egypt* 76 B2
Ghard Abû Muharik, *Egypt* 76 B2
Ghardaïa, *Algeria* 75 B5
Ghârib, G., *Egypt* 76 J8
Ghârib, Râs, *Egypt* 76 J8
Gharyãn, *Libya* 75 B7
Gharyān □, *Libya* 75 B7
Ghat, *Libya* 75 D7
Ghatal, *India* 63 H12
Ghatampur, *India* 63 F9
Ghaṭṭī, *Si. Arabia* 64 D3
Ghawdex = Gozo, *Malta* 37 C1
Ghazal, Bahr el →, *Chad* 73 F8
Ghazâl, Bahr el →, *Sudan* 77 F3
Ghazaouet, *Algeria* 75 A4
Ghaziabad, *India* 62 E7
Ghazipur, *India* 63 G10
Ghaznī, *Afghan.* 62 C3
Ghaznī □, *Afghan.* 60 C6
Ghedi, *Italy* 32 C7
Ghèlinsor, *Somali Rep.* 68 F4
Ghent = Gent, *Belgium* 17 F3
Gheorghe Gheorghiu-Dej, *Romania* 38 C9
Gheorgheni, *Romania* 38 C8
Ghergani, *Romania* 38 E8
Gherla, *Romania* 38 B6
Ghilarza, *Italy* 34 B1
Ghisonaccia, *France* 27 F13
Ghisoni, *France* 27 F13
Ghizao, *Afghan.* 62 C1
Ghizar →, *Pakistan* 63 A5
Ghogha, *India* 62 J5
Ghot Ogrein, *Egypt* 76 A2
Ghotaru, *India* 62 F4
Ghotki, *Pakistan* 62 E3
Ghowr □, *Afghan.* 60 C4
Ghudaf, W. al →, *Iraq* 64 C4
Ghudāmis, *Libya* 75 B6
Ghughri, *India* 63 H9
Ghugus, *India* 60 K11
Ghulam Mohammad Barrage, *Pakistan* 62 G3
Ghūriān, *Afghan.* 60 B2
Gia Dinh, *Vietnam* 59 G6
Gia Lai = Pleiku, *Vietnam* 58 F7
Gia Nghia, *Vietnam* 59 G6
Gia Ngoc, *Vietnam* 58 E7
Gia Vuc, *Vietnam* 58 E7
Gian, *Phil.* 57 C7
Giannutri, *Italy* 32 F8
Giant Forest, *U.S.A.* 112 J8
Giant Mts. = Krkonoše, *Czech.* 20 E5
Giants Causeway, *U.K.* 15 A5
Giarabub = Al Jaghbūb, *Libya* 73 C9
Giarre, *Italy* 35 E8
Giaveno, *Italy* 32 C4
Gibara, *Cuba* 116 B4
Gibb River, *Australia* 88 C4
Gibbon, *U.S.A.* 108 E5
Gibe →, *Ethiopia* 77 F4

Gibellina, *Italy* 34 E6
Gibraléon, *Spain* 31 H4
Gibraltar ■, *Europe* 31 J5
Gibraltar, Str. of, *Medit. S.* 31 K5
Gibson Desert, *Australia* 88 D4
Gibsons, *Canada* 100 D4
Gibsonville, *U.S.A.* 112 F6
Giddings, *U.S.A.* 109 K6
Gidole, *Ethiopia* 77 F4
Gien, *France* 25 E9
Giessen, *Germany* 18 E4
Gieten, *Neths.* 16 B9
Gifãn, *Iran* 65 B8
Gifatin, Geziret, *Egypt* 76 B3
Gifford Creek, *Australia* 88 D2
Gifhorn, *Germany* 18 C6
Gifu, *Japan* 49 G8
Gifu □, *Japan* 49 G8
Gigant, *Russia* 43 C9
Giganta, Sa. de la, *Mexico* 114 B2
Gigen, *Bulgaria* 38 F7
Gigha, *U.K.* 14 F3
Giglio, *Italy* 32 F7
Gignac, *France* 26 E7
Gigüela →, *Spain* 29 F1
Gijón, *Spain* 30 B5
Gil I., *Canada* 100 C3
Gila →, *U.S.A.* 111 K6
Gila Bend, *U.S.A.* 111 K7
Gila Bend Mts., *U.S.A.* 111 K7
Gīlãn □, *Iran* 65 B6
Gilbert →, *Australia* 90 B3
Gilbert Is., *Kiribati* 92 G9
Gilbert Plains, *Canada* 101 C8
Gilbert River, *Australia* 90 B3
Gilberton, *Australia* 90 B3
Gilbués, *Brazil* 122 C2
Gilf el Kebîr, Hadabat el, *Egypt* 76 C2
Gilford I., *Canada* 100 C3
Gilgandra, *Australia* 91 E4
Gilgil, *Kenya* 82 C4
Gilgit, *India* 63 B6
Gilgit →, *Pakistan* 63 B6
Giljeva Planina, *Serbia* 21 M10
Gillam, *Canada* 101 B10
Gilleleje, *Denmark* 11 H6
Gillen, L., *Australia* 89 E3
Gilles, L., *Australia* 91 E2
Gillette, *U.S.A.* 108 C2
Gilliat, *Australia* 90 C3
Gillingham, *U.K.* 13 F8
Gilly, *Belgium* 17 H4
Gilmer, *U.S.A.* 109 J7
Gilmore, *Australia* 91 F4
Gilmore, L., *Australia* 89 F3
Gilmour, *Canada* 98 D4
Gilo →, *Ethiopia* 77 F3
Gilort →, *Romania* 38 E6
Gilroy, *U.S.A.* 111 H3
Gilze, *Neths.* 17 E5
Gimbi, *Ethiopia* 77 F4
Gimigliano, *Italy* 35 D9
Gimli, *Canada* 101 C9
Gimone →, *France* 26 E5
Gimont, *France* 26 E4
Gin Gin, *Australia* 91 D5
Gînâh, *Egypt* 76 B3
Gindie, *Australia* 90 C4
Gingin, *Australia* 89 F2
Gîngiova, *Romania* 38 F6
Ginir, *Ethiopia* 68 F3
Ginosa, *Italy* 35 B9
Ginzo de Limia, *Spain* 30 C3
Giohar, *Somali Rep.* 68 G4
Gióia, G. di, *Italy* 35 D8
Gióia del Colle, *Italy* 35 B9
Gióia Táuro, *Italy* 35 D8
Gioiosa Iónica, *Italy* 35 D9
Gióna, Óros, *Greece* 39 L5
Giovi, Passo dei, *Italy* 32 D5
Giovinazzo, *Italy* 35 A9
Gir Hills, *India* 62 J4
Girab, *India* 62 F4
Girâfi, W. →, *Egypt* 69 F3
Giraltovce, *Slovak Rep.* 20 F11
Girard, *Kans., U.S.A.* 109 G7
Girard, *Ohio, U.S.A.* 106 E4
Girard, *Pa., U.S.A.* 106 D4
Girardot, *Colombia* 120 C3
Girdle Ness, *U.K.* 14 D6
Giresun, *Turkey* 67 C8
Giresun □, *Turkey* 67 C8
Girga, *Egypt* 76 B3
Giridih, *India* 63 G12
Girifalco, *Italy* 35 D9
Girilambone, *Australia* 91 E4
Giro, *Nigeria* 79 C5
Giromagny, *France* 25 E13
Girona = Gerona, *Spain* 28 D7
Gironde □, *France* 26 D3
Gironde →, *France* 26 C2
Gironella, *Spain* 28 C6
Giru, *Australia* 90 B4
Girvan, *U.K.* 14 F4
Gisborne, *N.Z.* 87 H7
Gisenyi, *Rwanda* 82 C2
Gisors, *France* 25 C8
Gistel, *Belgium* 17 F1
Giswil, *Switz.* 22 C6
Gitega, *Burundi* 82 C2
Gits, *Belgium* 17 F2
Giuba →, *Somali Rep.* 68 G3
Giubiasco, *Switz.* 23 D8
Giugliano in Campania, *Italy* 35 B7

Giulianova, *Italy* 33 F10
Giurgeni, *Romania* 38 E10
Giurgiu, *Romania* 38 F8
Give, *Denmark* 11 J3
Givet, *France* 25 B11
Givors, *France* 27 C8
Givry, *Belgium* 17 H4
Givry, *France* 25 F11
Giyon, *Ethiopia* 77 F4
Giza = El Gîza, *Egypt* 76 H7
Gizhiga, *Russia* 45 C17
Gizhiginskaya Guba, *Russia* 45 C16
Giżycko, *Poland* 20 A11
Gizzeria, *Italy* 35 D9
Gjegjan, *Albania* 39 H3
Gjerstad, *Norway* 10 F3
Gjirokastra, *Albania* 39 J3
Gjoa Haven, *Canada* 96 B10
Gjøl, *Denmark* 11 G3
Gjøvik, *Norway* 10 D4
Glace Bay, *Canada* 99 C8
Glacier Bay, *U.S.A.* 100 B1
Glacier Nat. Park, *Canada* 100 C5
Glacier Park, *U.S.A.* 110 B7
Glacier Peak, *U.S.A.* 110 B3
Gladewater, *U.S.A.* 109 J7
Gladstone, *Queens., Australia* 90 C5
Gladstone, *S. Austral., Australia* 91 E2
Gladstone, *W. Austral., Australia* 89 E1
Gladstone, *Canada* 101 C9
Gladstone, *U.S.A.* 104 C2
Gladwin, *U.S.A.* 104 D3
Gladys L., *Canada* 100 B2
Glåma, *Iceland* 8 D2
Glåma →, *Norway* 10 E4
Glamis, *U.S.A.* 113 N11
Glåma →, *Norway* 10 E4
Glamoč, *Bos.-H.* 33 D13
Glan, *Sweden* 11 F10
Glanerbrug, *Neths.* 16 D9
Glarner Alpen, *Switz.* 23 C8
Glärnisch, *Switz.* 23 C7
Glarus, *Switz.* 23 B8
Glarus □, *Switz.* 23 C8
Glasco, *Kans., U.S.A.* 108 F6
Glasco, *N.Y., U.S.A.* 107 D11
Glasgow, *U.K.* 14 F4
Glasgow, *Ky., U.S.A.* 104 G3
Glasgow, *Mont., U.S.A.* 110 B10
Glastonbury, *U.K.* 13 F5
Glastonbury, *U.S.A.* 107 E12
Glatt →, *Switz.* 23 B7
Glattfelden, *Switz.* 23 A7
Glauchau, *Germany* 18 E8
Glazov, *Russia* 41 B18
Gleiwitz = Gliwice, *Poland* 20 E8
Glen, *U.S.A.* 107 B13
Glen Affric, *U.K.* 14 D4
Glen Canyon Dam, *U.S.A.* 111 H8
Glen Canyon National Recreation Area, *U.S.A.* 111 H8
Glen Coe, *U.K.* 14 E4
Glen Cove, *U.S.A.* 107 F11
Glen Garry, *U.K.* 14 D3
Glen Innes, *Australia* 91 D5
Glen Lyon, *U.S.A.* 107 E8
Glen Mor, *U.K.* 14 D4
Glen Moriston, *U.K.* 14 D4
Glen Orchy, *U.K.* 14 E4
Glen Spean, *U.K.* 14 E4
Glen Ullin, *U.S.A.* 108 B4
Glénan, Is. de, *France* 24 E2
Glenburgh, *Australia* 89 E2
Glencoe, *Canada* 106 D3
Glencoe, *S. Africa* 85 D5
Glencoe, *U.S.A.* 108 C7
Glendale, *Ariz., U.S.A.* 111 K7
Glendale, *Calif., U.S.A.* 113 L8
Glendale, *Oreg., U.S.A.* 110 E2
Glendale, *Zimbabwe* 83 F3
Glendive, *U.S.A.* 108 B2
Glendo, *U.S.A.* 108 D2
Glenelg, *Australia* 91 E2
Glenelg →, *Australia* 91 F3
Glenflorrie, *Australia* 88 D2
Glengarriff, *Ireland* 15 E2
Glengyle, *Australia* 90 C2
Glenmora, *U.S.A.* 109 K8
Glenmorgan, *Australia* 91 D4
Glenn, *U.S.A.* 112 F4
Glenns Ferry, *U.S.A.* 110 E6
Glenorchy, *Australia* 90 G4
Glenore, *Australia* 90 B3
Glenormiston, *Australia* 90 C2
Glenreagh, *Australia* 91 E5
Glenrock, *U.S.A.* 110 E11
Glenrothes, *U.K.* 14 E5
Glens Falls, *U.S.A.* 107 C11
Glenties, *Ireland* 15 B3
Glenville, *U.S.A.* 104 F5
Glenwood, *Alta., Canada* 100 D6
Glenwood, *Nfld., Canada* 99 C9
Glenwood, *Ark., U.S.A.* 109 H8
Glenwood, *Hawaii, U.S.A.* 102 J17
Glenwood, *Iowa, U.S.A.* 108 E7
Glenwood, *Minn., U.S.A.* 108 C7
Glenwood, *Wash., U.S.A.* 112 D5
Glenwood Springs, *U.S.A.* 110 G10
Gletsch, *Switz.* 22 C6
Glina, *Croatia* 33 C13
Glittertind, *Norway* 10 C2
Gliwice, *Poland* 20 E8
Globe, *U.S.A.* 111 K8

Glödnitz, *Austria* 21 J4
Głogów, *Poland* 20 D6
Glorieuses, Is., *Ind. Oc.* 85 A8
Glossop, *U.K.* 12 D6
Gloucester, *Australia* 91 E5
Gloucester, *U.K.* 13 F5
Gloucester, *U.S.A.* 107 D14
Gloucester I., *Australia* 90 B4
Gloucestershire □, *U.K.* 13 F5
Gloversville, *U.S.A.* 107 C10
Glovertown, *Canada* 99 C9
Główno, *Poland* 20 D9
Głubczyce, *Poland* 20 E7
Glubokiy, *Russia* 43 B9
Glubokoye, *Belorussia* 40 D5
Głuchołazy, *Poland* 20 E7
Glukhov, *Ukraine* 40 F8
Glussk, *Belorussia* 40 E6
Gmünd, *Kärnten, Austria* 21 J3
Gmünd, *Niederösterreich, Austria* 20 G5
Gnarp, *Sweden* 10 B11
Gnesta, *Sweden* 10 E11
Gniew, *Poland* 20 B8
Gniezno, *Poland* 20 C7
Gnoien, *Germany* 18 B8
Gnowangerup, *Australia* 89 F2
Go Cong, *Vietnam* 59 G6
Gō-no-ura, *Japan* 49 H4
Go Quao, *Vietnam* 59 H5
Goa, *India* 60 M8
Goa □, *India* 60 M8
Goalen Hd., *Australia* 91 F5
Goalpara, *India* 61 F17
Goalundo Ghat, *Bangla.* 63 H13
Goaso, *Ghana* 78 D4
Goat Fell, *U.K.* 14 F3
Goba, *Ethiopia* 68 F2
Goba, *Mozam.* 85 D5
Gobabis, *Namibia* 84 C2
Gobernador Gregores, *Argentina* 128 C2
Gobi, *Asia* 50 C5
Gobō, *Japan* 49 H7
Gobo, *Sudan* 77 F3
Gochas, *Namibia* 84 C2
Goch, *Germany* 18 D2
Godavari →, *India* 61 L13
Godavari Point, *India* 61 L13
Godbout, *Canada* 99 C6
Godda, *India* 63 G12
Godegård, *Sweden* 11 F9
Goderich, *Canada* 98 D3
Goderville, *France* 24 C7
Godhavn, *Greenland* 4 C5
Godhra, *India* 62 H5
Gödöllő, *Hungary* 21 H9
Godoy Cruz, *Argentina* 126 C2
Gods →, *Canada* 101 B10
Gods L., *Canada* 101 C10
Godthåb, *Greenland* 97 B14
Godwin Austen = K2, Mt., *Pakistan* 63 B7
Goeie Hoop, Kaap die = Good Hope, C. of, *S. Africa* 84 E2
Goéland, L. au, *Canada* 98 C4
Goeree, *Neths.* 16 E4
Goes, *Neths.* 17 F3
Gogama, *Canada* 98 C3
Gogango, *Australia* 90 C5
Gogebic, L., *U.S.A.* 108 B10
Gogra = Ghaghara →, *India* 63 G11
Gogriâl, *Sudan* 77 F2
Goiana, *Brazil* 122 C5
Goianésia, *Brazil* 123 E2
Goiânia, *Brazil* 123 E2
Goiás, *Brazil* 123 E1
Goiás □, *Brazil* 122 D2
Goiatuba, *Brazil* 123 E2
Goio-Ere, *Brazil* 127 A5
Goioerê, *Brazil* 127 A5
Goirle, *Neths.* 17 E6
Góis, *Portugal* 30 E2
Gojam □, *Ethiopia* 77 E4
Gojeb, Wabi →, *Ethiopia* 77 F4
Gojō, *Japan* 49 G7
Gojra, *Pakistan* 62 D5
Gokarannath, *India* 63 F9
Gökçeada, *Turkey* 39 J8
Gökirmak →, *Turkey* 66 C6
Göksu →, *Turkey* 66 E6
Göksun, *Turkey* 66 D7
Gokteik, *Burma* 61 H20
Gokurt, *Pakistan* 62 E2
Gola, *India* 63 E9
Golakganj, *India* 63 F13
Golan Heights = Hagolan, *Syria* 69 B4
Goläshkerd, *Iran* 65 E8
Golaya Pristen, *Ukraine* 42 C5
Gölbaşı, *Adiyaman, Turkey* 67 D8
Gölbaşı, *Ankara, Turkey* 66 D5
Golchikha, *Russia* 4 B12
Golconda, *U.S.A.* 110 F5
Gölcük, *Kocaeli, Turkey* 66 C3
Gölcük, *Niğde, Turkey* 66 D6
Gold Beach, *U.S.A.* 110 E1
Gold Coast, *Australia* 91 D5
Gold Coast, *W. Afr.* 79 E5
Gold Hill, *U.S.A.* 110 E2
Goldach, *Switz.* 23 B8

Goldau, *Switz.* 23 B7
Goldberg, *Germany* 18 B8
Golden, *Canada* 100 C5
Golden, *U.S.A.* 108 F2
Golden B., *N.Z.* 87 J4
Golden Gate, *U.S.A.* 110 H2
Golden Hinde, *Canada* 100 D3
Golden Lake, *Canada* 106 A7
Golden Prairie, *Canada* 101 C7
Golden Vale, *Ireland* 15 D3
Goldendale, *U.S.A.* 110 D3
Goldfield, *U.S.A.* 111 H5
Goldfields, *Canada* 101 B7
Goldsand L., *Canada* 101 B8
Goldsboro, *U.S.A.* 105 H7
Goldsmith, *U.S.A.* 109 K3
Goldsworthy, *Australia* 88 D2
Goldthwaite, *U.S.A.* 109 K5
Golegã, *Portugal* 31 F2
Golęniów, *Poland* 20 B4
Golestānak, *Iran* 65 D7
Goleta, *U.S.A.* 113 L7
Golfito, *Costa Rica* 116 E3
Golfo Aranci, *Italy* 34 B2
Gölgeli Dağları, *Turkey* 66 E3
Goliad, *U.S.A.* 109 L6
Golija, *Serbia* 21 M10
Gölköy, *Turkey* 67 C7
Golo →, *France* 27 F13
Golovanevsk, *Ukraine* 42 B4
Golpâyegân, *Iran* 65 C6
Gölpazarı, *Turkey* 66 C4
Golra, *Pakistan* 62 C5
Golspie, *U.K.* 14 D5
Golyama Kamchiya →, *Bulgaria* 38 F10
Goma, *Rwanda* 82 C2
Goma, *Zaïre* 82 C2
Gomati →, *India* 63 G10
Gombari, *Zaïre* 82 B2
Gombe, *Nigeria* 79 C7
Gombe →, *Tanzania* 82 C3
Gombi, *Nigeria* 79 C7
Gomel, *Belorussia* 40 E7
Gomera, *Canary Is.* 36 F2
Gómez Palacio, *Mexico* 114 B4
Gomîshān, *Iran* 65 B7
Gommern, *Germany* 18 C7
Gomogomo, *Indonesia* 57 F8
Gomoh, *India* 61 H15
Gompa = Ganta, *Liberia* 78 D3
Goms, *Switz.* 22 C6
Gonābād, *Iran* 65 C8
Gonaïves, *Haiti* 117 C5
Gonâve, G. de la, *Haiti* 117 C5
Gonâve, I. de la, *Haiti* 117 C5
Gonbab-e Kāvūs, *Iran* 65 B7
Gonda, *India* 63 F9
Gondal, *India* 62 J4
Gonder, *Ethiopia* 77 E4
Gonder □, *Ethiopia* 77 E4
Gondia, *India* 60 J12
Gondola, *Mozam.* 83 F3
Gondomar, *Portugal* 30 D2
Gondomar, *Spain* 30 C2
Gondrecourt-le-Château, *France* 25 D12
Gönen, *Turkey* 66 C2
Gong Xian, *China* 52 C5
Gong'an, *China* 53 B9
Gongcheng, *China* 53 E8
Gongguan, *China* 54 C7
Gongga Shan, *China* 52 C3
Gongguan, *China* 52 G7
Gonghe, *China* 54 C5
Gongola →, *Nigeria* 79 D7
Gongolgon, *Australia* 91 E4
Gongshan, *China* 52 D2
Gongtan, *China* 52 C7
Goniadz, *Poland* 20 B12
Goniri, *Nigeria* 79 C7
Gonjo, *China* 52 B2
Gonnesa, *Italy* 34 C1
Gónnos, *Greece* 39 K5
Gonnosfanadiga, *Italy* 34 C1
Gonzaga, *Phil.* 55 B5
Gonzales, *Calif., U.S.A.* 111 H3
Gonzales, *Tex., U.S.A.* 109 L6
González Chaves, *Argentina* 126 D3
Good Hope, C. of, *S. Africa* 84 E2
Gooderham, *Canada* 98 D4
Goodeve, *Canada* 101 C8
Gooding, *U.S.A.* 110 E6
Goodland, *U.S.A.* 108 F4
Goodnight, *U.S.A.* 109 H4
Goodooga, *Australia* 91 D4
Goodsoil, *Canada* 101 C7
Goodsprings, *U.S.A.* 111 J6
Goole, *U.K.* 12 D7
Goolgowi, *Australia* 91 E4
Goomalling, *Australia* 89 F2
Goombalie, *Australia* 91 D4
Goonda, *Mozam.* 83 F3
Goondiwindi, *Australia* 91 D5
Goongarrie, L., *Australia* 89 F3
Goonyella, *Australia* 90 C4
Goor, *Neths.* 16 D9
Gooray, *Australia* 91 D5
Goose →, *Canada* 99 B7
Goose L., *U.S.A.* 110 F3
Gop, *India* 60 H6
Gopalganj, *India* 63 F11
Goppenstein, *Switz.* 22 D5
Göppingen, *Germany* 19 G5

Gresham

Gor, *Spain* 29 H2
Góra, *Poland* 20 D6
Gorakhpur, *India* 63 F10
Gorbatov, *Russia* 41 C13
Gorbea, Peña, *Spain* 28 B2
Gorda, *U.S.A.* 112 K5
Gorda, Pta., *Nic.* 116 D3
Gorda, Pta., *Canary Is.* 36 F2
Gordan B., *Australia* 88 B5
Gordon, *U.S.A.* 108 D3
Gordon →, *Australia* 90 G4
Gordon, I., *Chile* 128 D3
Gordon Downs, *Australia* 88 C4
Gordon L., *Alta., Canada* 101 B6
Gordon L., *N.W.T., Canada* 100 A6
Gordonia, *S. Africa* 84 D3
Gordonvale, *Australia* 90 B4
Gore, *Australia* 91 D5
Goré, *Chad* 73 G8
Gore, *Ethiopia* 77 F4
Gore, *N.Z.* 87 M2
Gore Bay, *Canada* 98 C3
Görele, *Turkey* 67 C8
Gorey, *Ireland* 15 D5
Gorg, *Iran* 65 D8
Gorgān, *Iran* 65 B7
Gorgona, *Italy* 32 E6
Gorgora, *Ethiopia* 77 E4
Gorham, *U.S.A.* 107 B13
Gori, *Georgia* 43 E11
Gorinchem, *Neths.* 16 E5
Gorinhatã, *Brazil* 123 E2
Goritsy, *Russia* 41 C10
Gorízia, *Italy* 33 C10
Gorki = Nizhniy Novgorod, *Russia* 41 C14
Gorki, *Belorussia* 40 D7
Gorkiy = Nizhniy Novgorod, *Russia* 41 C14
Gorkovskoye Vdkhr., *Russia* 41 C13
Gørlev, *Denmark* 11 J5
Gorlice, *Poland* 20 F11
Görlitz, *Germany* 18 D10
Gorlovka, *Ukraine* 42 B8
Gorman, *Calif., U.S.A.* 113 L8
Gorman, *Tex., U.S.A.* 109 J5
Gorna Dzhumayo = Blagoevgrad, *Bulgaria* 39 G6
Gorna Oryakhovitsa, *Bulgaria* 38 F8
Gornja Radgona, *Slovenia* 33 B13
Gornja Tuzla, *Bos.-H.* 21 L8
Gornji Grad, *Slovenia* 33 B11
Gornji Milanovac, *Serbia* 21 M10
Gornji Vakuf, *Bos.-H.* 21 M7
Gorno-Altaysk, *Russia* 44 D9
Gorno Slinkino, *Russia* 44 C8
Gornyi, *Russia* 48 B6
Gornyy, *Russia* 41 F16
Gorodenka, *Ukraine* 42 B1
Gorodets, *Russia* 41 C13
Gorodishche, *Russia* 41 E14
Gorodishche, *Ukraine* 42 B4
Gorodnitsa, *Ukraine* 40 F5
Gorodnya, *Ukraine* 40 F7
Gorodok, *Belorussia* 40 D7
Gorodok, *Ukraine* 40 G3
Gorokhov, *Ukraine* 40 F4
Gorokhovets, *Russia* 41 C13
Gorom Gorom, *Burkina Faso* 79 C4
Goromonzi, *Zimbabwe* 83 F3
Gorongose →, *Mozam.* 85 C5
Gorongoza, *Mozam.* 83 F3
Gorongoza, Sa. da, *Mozam.* 83 F3
Gorontalo, *Indonesia* 57 D6
Goronyo, *Nigeria* 79 C6
Gorredijk, *Neths.* 16 C8
Gorron, *France* 24 D6
Gorssel, *Neths.* 16 D8
Gort, *Ireland* 15 C3
Gortis, *Greece* 37 D6
Gorzkowice, *Poland* 20 D9
Gorzów Śląski, *Poland* 20 D8
Gorzów Wielkopolski, *Poland* 20 C5
Göschenen, *Switz.* 23 C7
Gosford, *Australia* 91 E5
Goshen, *Calif., U.S.A.* 112 J7
Goshen, *Ind., U.S.A.* 104 E3
Goshen, *N.Y., U.S.A.* 107 E10
Goshogawara, *Japan* 48 D10
Goslar, *Germany* 18 D6
Gospič, *Croatia* 33 D12
Gosport, *U.K.* 13 G6
Gossau, *Switz.* 23 B8
Gosse →, *Australia* 90 B1
Gostivar, *Macedonia* 39 H3
Gostyń, *Poland* 20 D7
Gostynin, *Poland* 20 C9
Göta älv →, *Sweden* 11 G5
Göta kanal, *Sweden* 9 G12
Göteborg, *Sweden* 11 G5
Göteborgs och Bohus län □, *Sweden* 9 G11
Götene, *Sweden* 11 F7
Gotha, *Germany* 18 E6
Gothenburg, *U.S.A.* 108 E4
Gotland, *Sweden* 9 H15
Gotse Delchev, *Bulgaria* 39 H6
Gotska Sandön, *Sweden* 9 G15
Gōtsu, *Japan* 49 G6
Göttingen, *Germany* 18 D5
Gottwald = Zmiyev, *Ukraine* 42 B7
Gottwaldov = Zlin, *Czech.* 20 F7
Goubangzi, *China* 51 D11
Gouda, *Neths.* 16 D5
Goúdhoura, Ákra, *Greece* 37 E8
Goudiry, *Senegal* 78 C2
Gough I., *Atl. Oc.* 2 G9
Gouin, Rés., *Canada* 98 C5
Gouitafla, *Ivory C.* 78 D3
Goulburn, *Australia* 91 E4
Goulburn Is., *Australia* 90 A1
Goulia, *Ivory C.* 78 C3
Goulimine, *Morocco* 74 C3
Goulmina, *Morocco* 74 B4
Gounou-Gaya, *Chad* 73 G8
Goúra, *Greece* 39 M5
Gouraya, *Algeria* 75 A5
Gourdon, *France* 26 D5
Gouré, *Niger* 79 C7
Gouri, *Chad* 73 E8
Gourits →, *S. Africa* 84 E3
Gourma Rharous, *Mali* 79 B4
Goúrnais, *Greece* 37 D7
Gournay-en-Bray, *France* 25 C8
Gourock Ra., *Australia* 91 F4
Goursi, *Burkina Faso* 78 C4
Gouvêa, *Brazil* 123 E3
Gouverneur, *U.S.A.* 107 B9
Gouviá, *Greece* 37 A3
Gouzon, *France* 26 B6
Govan, *Canada* 101 C8
Governador Valadares, *Brazil* 123 E3
Governor's Harbour, *Bahamas* 116 A4
Gowan Ra., *Australia* 90 C4
Gowanda, *U.S.A.* 106 D6
Gowd-e Zirreh, *Afghan.* 60 E3
Gower, *U.K.* 13 F3
Gowna, L., *Ireland* 15 C4
Goya, *Argentina* 126 B4
Goyder Lagoon, *Australia* 91 D2
Goyllarisquisga, *Peru* 124 C2
Göynük, *Turkey* 66 C4
Goz Beïda, *Chad* 73 F9
Goz Regeb, *Sudan* 77 D4
Gozo, *Malta* 37 C1
Graaff-Reinet, *S. Africa* 84 E3
Grabow, *Germany* 18 B7
Grabs, *Switz.* 23 B8
Gračac, *Croatia* 33 D12
Gračanica, *Bos.-H.* 21 L8
Graçay, *France* 25 E8
Grace, *U.S.A.* 110 E8
Graceville, *U.S.A.* 108 C6
Gracias a Dios, C., *Honduras* 116 C3
Graciosa, I., *Canary Is.* 36 E6
Gradaús, *Brazil* 122 C1
Gradaús, Serra dos, *Brazil* 122 C1
Gradets, *Bulgaria* 38 G9
Grado, *Italy* 33 C10
Grado, *Spain* 30 B4
Gradule, *Australia* 91 D4
Grady, *U.S.A.* 109 H3
Graeca, Lacul, *Romania* 38 E9
Graénalon, L., *Iceland* 8 D5
Grafenau, *Germany* 19 G9
Gräfenberg, *Germany* 19 F7
Grafton, *Australia* 91 D5
Grafton, *U.S.A.* 108 A6
Gragnano, *Italy* 35 B7
Graham, *Canada* 98 C1
Graham, *N.C., U.S.A.* 105 G6
Graham, *Tex., U.S.A.* 109 J5
Graham →, *Canada* 100 B4
Graham, Mt., *U.S.A.* 111 K9
Graham Bell, Os., *Russia* 44 A7
Graham I., *Canada* 100 C2
Graham Land, *Antarctica* 5 C17
Grahamdale, *Canada* 101 C9
Grahamstown, *S. Africa* 84 E4
Graïba, *Tunisia* 75 B7
Graide, *Belgium* 17 J6
Graie, Alpi, *Europe* 32 C4
Grain Coast, *W. Afr.* 70 F2
Grajaú, *Brazil* 122 C2
Grajaú →, *Brazil* 122 B3
Grajewo, *Poland* 20 B12
Gramada, *Bulgaria* 38 F5
Gramat, *France* 26 D5
Grammichele, *Italy* 35 E7
Grampian □, *U.K.* 14 D6
Grampian Highlands = Grampian Mts., *U.K.* 14 E5
Grampian Mts., *U.K.* 14 E5
Gran →, *Surinam* 121 C6
Gran Altiplanicie Central, *Argentina* 128 C3
Gran Canaria, *Canary Is.* 36 F4
Gran Chaco, *S. Amer.* 126 B3
Gran Paradiso, *Italy* 32 C4
Gran Sasso d'Italia, *Italy* 33 F10
Granada, *Nic.* 116 D2
Granada, *Spain* 29 H1
Granada, *U.S.A.* 109 F3
Granada □, *Spain* 31 H7
Granadilla de Abona, *Canary Is.* 36 F3
Granard, *Ireland* 15 C4
Granbury, *U.S.A.* 109 J6
Granby, *Canada* 98 C5
Grand →, *Mo., U.S.A.* 108 F8
Grand →, *S. Dak., U.S.A.* 108 C4
Grand Bahama, *Bahamas* 116 A4
Grand Bank, *Canada* 99 C8
Grand Bassam, *Ivory C.* 78 D4
Grand Béréby, *Ivory C.* 78 E3
Grand-Bourg, *Guadeloupe* 117 C7
Grand Canal = Yun Ho →, *China* 51 E9
Grand Canyon, *U.S.A.* 111 H7
Grand Canyon National Park, *U.S.A.* 111 H7
Grand Cayman, *Cayman Is.* 116 C3
Grand Cess, *Liberia* 78 E3
Grand Coulee, *U.S.A.* 110 C4
Grand Coulee Dam, *U.S.A.* 110 C4
Grand Erg Occidental, *Algeria* 75 B5
Grand Erg Oriental, *Algeria* 75 C6
Grand Falls, *Canada* 99 C8
Grand Forks, *Canada* 100 D5
Grand Forks, *U.S.A.* 108 B6
Grand-Fougeray, *France* 24 E5
Grand Haven, *U.S.A.* 104 D2
Grand I., *U.S.A.* 104 B2
Grand Island, *U.S.A.* 108 E5
Grand Isle, *U.S.A.* 109 L10
Grand Junction, *U.S.A.* 111 G9
Grand L., *U.S.A.* 109 L8
Grand Lac Victoria, *Canada* 98 C4
Grand Lahou, *Ivory C.* 78 D3
Grand L., *N.B., Canada* 99 C6
Grand L., *Nfld., Canada* 99 C8
Grand L., *Nfld., Canada* 99 B7
Grand Lake, *U.S.A.* 110 F11
Grand-Leez, *Belgium* 17 G5
Grand-Lieu, L. de, *France* 24 E5
Grand Manan I., *Canada* 99 D6
Grand Marais, *Canada* 108 B9
Grand Marais, *U.S.A.* 104 B3
Grand-Mère, *Canada* 98 C5
Grand Popo, *Benin* 79 D5
Grand Portage, *U.S.A.* 98 C2
Grand Rapids, *Canada* 101 C9
Grand Rapids, *Mich., U.S.A.* 104 D2
Grand Rapids, *Minn., U.S.A.* 108 B8
Grand St-Bernard, Col du, *Switz.* 22 E4
Grand Santi, *Fr. Guiana* 121 C7
Grand Teton, *U.S.A.* 110 E8
Grand Valley, *U.S.A.* 110 G9
Grand View, *Canada* 101 C8
Grandas de Salime, *Spain* 30 B4
Grande →, *Jujuy, Argentina* 126 A2
Grande →, *Mendoza, Argentina* 126 D2
Grande →, *Bolivia* 125 D5
Grande →, *Bahia, Brazil* 122 D3
Grande →, *Minas Gerais, Brazil* 123 F1
Grande →, *Spain* 29 F4
Grande →, *Venezuela* 121 B5
Grande, B., *Argentina* 128 D3
Grande, I., *Brazil* 123 F3
Grande, Rio →, *U.S.A.* 109 N6
Grande, Serra, *Goiás, Brazil* 122 D2
Grande, Serra, *Piauí, Brazil* 122 C2
Grande Baie, *Canada* 99 C5
Grande Baleine, R. de la →, *Canada* 98 A4
Grande Cache, *Canada* 100 C5
Grande de Santiago →, *Mexico* 114 C3
Grande Dixence, Barr. de la, *Switz.* 22 D4
Grande-Entrée, *Canada* 99 C7
Grande Prairie, *Canada* 100 B5
Grande-Rivière, *Canada* 99 C7
Grande Sauldre →, *France* 25 E9
Grande-Vallée, *Canada* 99 C6
Grandes-Bergeronnes, *Canada* 99 C6
Grandfalls, *U.S.A.* 109 K3
Grandoe Mines, *Canada* 100 B3
Grândola, *Portugal* 31 G2
Grandpré, *France* 25 C11
Grandson, *Switz.* 22 C3
Grandview, *U.S.A.* 110 C4
Grandvilliers, *France* 25 C8
Graneros, *Chile* 126 C1
Grangemouth, *U.K.* 14 E5
Granger, *Wash., U.S.A.* 110 C3
Granger, *Wyo., U.S.A.* 110 F9
Grangeville, *U.S.A.* 110 D5
Granite City, *U.S.A.* 108 F9
Granite Falls, *U.S.A.* 108 C7
Granite Mt., *U.S.A.* 113 M10
Granite Peak, *Australia* 89 E3
Granite Peak, *U.S.A.* 110 D9
Granity, *N.Z.* 87 J3
Granja, *Brazil* 122 B3
Granja de Moreruela, *Spain* 30 D5
Granja de Torrehermosa, *Spain* 31 G5
Granollers, *Spain* 28 D7
Gransee, *Germany* 18 B9
Grant, *U.S.A.* 108 E4
Grant, Mt., *U.S.A.* 110 G4
Grant City, *U.S.A.* 108 E7
Grant I., *Australia* 88 B5
Grant Range, *U.S.A.* 111 G6
Grantham, *U.K.* 12 E7
Grantown-on-Spey, *U.K.* 14 D5
Grants, *U.S.A.* 111 J10
Grants Pass, *U.S.A.* 110 E2
Grantsburg, *U.S.A.* 108 C8
Grantsville, *U.S.A.* 110 F7
Granville, *France* 24 D5
Granville, *N. Dak., U.S.A.* 108 A4
Granville, *N.Y., U.S.A.* 104 D9
Granville L., *Canada* 101 B8
Grao de Gandía, *Spain* 29 F4
Grapeland, *U.S.A.* 109 K7
Gras, L. de, *Canada* 96 B8
Graskop, *S. Africa* 85 C5
Grass →, *Canada* 101 B9
Grass Range, *U.S.A.* 110 C9
Grass River Prov. Park, *Canada* 101 C8
Grass Valley, *Calif., U.S.A.* 112 F6
Grass Valley, *Oreg., U.S.A.* 110 D3
Grassano, *Italy* 35 B9
Grasse, *France* 27 E10
Grassmere, *Australia* 91 E3
Graubünden □, *Switz.* 23 C9
Graulhet, *France* 26 E5
Graus, *Spain* 28 C5
Gravatá, *Brazil* 122 C4
Grave, *Neths.* 16 E7
Grave, Pte. de, *France* 26 C2
's-Graveland, *Neths.* 16 D6
Gravelbourg, *Canada* 101 D7
Gravelines, *France* 25 B9
's-Gravendeel, *Neths.* 16 E5
's-Gravenhage, *Neths.* 16 D4
Gravenhurst, *Canada* 106 B5
's-Gravenpolder, *Neths.* 17 F3
's-Gravensande, *Neths.* 16 D4
Gravesend, *Australia* 91 D5
Gravesend, *U.K.* 13 F8
Gravina di Púglia, *Italy* 35 B9
Gravois, Pointe-à-, *Haiti* 117 C5
Gravone →, *France* 27 G12
Gray, *France* 25 E12
Grayling, *U.S.A.* 104 C3
Grayling →, *Canada* 100 B3
Grays Harbor, *U.S.A.* 110 C1
Grays L., *U.S.A.* 110 E8
Grays River, *U.S.A.* 112 D3
Grayson, *Canada* 101 C8
Graz, *Austria* 21 H5
Grazalema, *Spain* 31 J5
Greasy L., *Canada* 100 A4
Great Abaco I., *Bahamas* 116 A4
Great Artesian Basin, *Australia* 90 C3
Great Australian Bight, *Australia* 89 F5
Great Bahama Bank, *Bahamas* 116 B4
Great Barrier I., *N.Z.* 87 G5
Great Barrier Reef, *Australia* 90 B4
Great Barrington, *U.S.A.* 107 D11
Great Basin, *U.S.A.* 110 G5
Great Bear →, *Canada* 96 B7
Great Bear L., *Canada* 96 B7
Great Belt = Store Bælt, *Denmark* 11 J5
Great Bend, *Kans., U.S.A.* 108 F5
Great Bend, *Pa., U.S.A.* 107 E9
Great Blasket I., *Ireland* 15 D1
Great Britain, *Europe* 6 E5
Great Central, *Canada* 100 D3
Great Dividing Ra., *Australia* 90 C4
Great Driffield, *U.K.* 12 C7
Great Exuma I., *Bahamas* 116 B4
Great Falls, *Canada* 101 C9
Great Falls, *U.S.A.* 110 C8
Great Fish = Groot Vis →, *S. Africa* 84 E4
Great Guana Cay, *Bahamas* 116 B4
Great Harbour Deep, *Canada* 99 B8
Great Inagua I., *Bahamas* 117 B5
Great Indian Desert = Thar Desert, *India* 62 F4
Great I., *Canada* 101 B9
Great Karoo, *S. Africa* 84 E3
Great Lake, *Australia* 90 G4
Great Ormes Head, *U.K.* 12 D4
Great Ouse →, *U.K.* 12 E8
Great Palm I., *Australia* 90 B4
Great Plains, *N. Amer.* 102 A6
Great Ruaha →, *Tanzania* 82 D4
Great Saint Bernard P. = Grand St-Bernard, Col du, *Switz.* 22 E4
Great Salt L., *U.S.A.* 110 F7
Great Salt Lake Desert, *U.S.A.* 110 F7
Great Salt Plains L., *U.S.A.* 109 G5
Great Sandy Desert, *Australia* 88 D3
Great Sangi = Sangihe, P., *Indonesia* 57 D7
Great Scarcies →, *S. Leone* 78 D2
Great Slave L., *Canada* 100 A5
Great Smoky Mts. Nat. Pk., *U.S.A.* 105 H4
Great Stour = Stour →, *U.K.* 13 F9
Great Victoria Desert, *Australia* 89 E4
Great Wall, *China* 50 E5
Great Whernside, *U.K.* 12 C6
Great Yarmouth, *U.K.* 12 E9
Greater Antilles, *W. Indies* 117 C5
Greater London □, *U.K.* 13 F7
Greater Manchester □, *U.K.* 12 D5
Greater Sunda Is., *Indonesia* 56 F4
Grebbestad, *Sweden* 11 F5
Grebenka, *Ukraine* 40 F8
Greco, C., *Cyprus* 37 E13
Greco, Mte., *Italy* 34 A6
Gredos, Sierra de, *Spain* 30 E5
Greece, *U.S.A.* 106 C7
Greece ■, *Europe* 39 K6
Greeley, *Colo., U.S.A.* 108 E2
Greeley, *Nebr., U.S.A.* 108 E5
Green →, *Ky., U.S.A.* 104 G2
Green →, *Utah, U.S.A.* 111 G9
Green B., *U.S.A.* 104 C2
Green Bay, *U.S.A.* 104 C2
Green C., *Australia* 91 F5
Green Cove Springs, *U.S.A.* 105 L5
Green River, *U.S.A.* 111 G8
Greenbank, *U.S.A.* 112 B4
Greenbush, *Mich., U.S.A.* 106 B1
Greenbush, *Minn., U.S.A.* 108 A6
Greencastle, *U.S.A.* 104 F2
Greene, *U.S.A.* 107 D9
Greenfield, *Calif., U.S.A.* 112 J5
Greenfield, *Calif., U.S.A.* 113 K8
Greenfield, *Ind., U.S.A.* 104 F3
Greenfield, *Iowa, U.S.A.* 108 E7
Greenfield, *Mass., U.S.A.* 107 D12
Greenfield, *Mo., U.S.A.* 109 G8
Greenfield Park, *Canada* 107 A11
Greenland ■, *N. Amer.* 4 C5
Greenland Sea, *Arctic* 4 B7
Greenock, *U.K.* 14 F4
Greenore, *Ireland* 15 B5
Greenore Pt., *Ireland* 15 D5
Greenough →, *Australia* 89 E1
Greenport, *U.S.A.* 107 E12
Greensboro, *Ga., U.S.A.* 105 J4
Greensboro, *N.C., U.S.A.* 105 G6
Greensburg, *Ind., U.S.A.* 104 F3
Greensburg, *Kans., U.S.A.* 109 G5
Greensburg, *Pa., U.S.A.* 106 F5
Greenville, *Liberia* 78 D3
Greenville, *Ala., U.S.A.* 105 K2
Greenville, *Calif., U.S.A.* 112 E6
Greenville, *Ill., U.S.A.* 108 F10
Greenville, *Maine, U.S.A.* 99 C6
Greenville, *Mich., U.S.A.* 104 D3
Greenville, *Miss., U.S.A.* 109 J9
Greenville, *N.C., U.S.A.* 105 H7
Greenville, *Ohio, U.S.A.* 104 E3
Greenville, *Pa., U.S.A.* 106 E4
Greenville, *S.C., U.S.A.* 105 H4
Greenville, *Tenn., U.S.A.* 105 G4
Greenville, *Tex., U.S.A.* 109 J6
Greenwater Lake Prov. Park, *Canada* 101 C8
Greenwich, *U.K.* 13 F8
Greenwich, *Conn., U.S.A.* 107 E11
Greenwich, *N.Y., U.S.A.* 107 C11
Greenwich, *Ohio, U.S.A.* 106 E2
Greenwood, *Canada* 100 D5
Greenwood, *Miss., U.S.A.* 109 J9
Greenwood, *S.C., U.S.A.* 105 H4
Greenwood, Mt., *Australia* 88 B5
Gregório →, *Brazil* 124 B3
Gregory, *U.S.A.* 108 D5
Gregory →, *Australia* 90 B2
Gregory, L., *S. Austral., Australia* 91 D2
Gregory, L., *W. Austral., Australia* 89 E2
Gregory Downs, *Australia* 90 B2
Gregory L., *Australia* 88 D4
Gregory Ra., *Queens., Australia* 90 B3
Gregory Ra., *W. Austral., Australia* 88 D3
Greiffenberg, *Germany* 18 B9
Greifswald, *Germany* 18 A9
Greifswalder Bodden, *Germany* 18 A9
Grein, *Austria* 21 G4
Greiz, *Germany* 18 E8
Gremikha, *Russia* 44 C4
Grenå, *Denmark* 11 H4
Grenada, *U.S.A.* 109 J10
Grenada ■, *W. Indies* 117 D7
Grenade, *France* 26 E5
Grenadines, *W. Indies* 117 D7
Grenchen, *Switz.* 22 B4
Grenen, *Denmark* 11 G4
Grenfell, *Australia* 91 E4
Grenfell, *Canada* 101 C8
Grenoble, *France* 27 C9
Grenora, *U.S.A.* 108 A3
Grenville, C., *Australia* 90 A3
Grenville Chan., *Canada* 100 C3
Gréoux-les-Bains, *France* 27 E9
Gresham, *U.S.A.* 112 E4

Gresik, *Indonesia* 57 G15
Gréssoney St. Jean, *Italy* . 32 C4
Gretna Green, *U.K.* 14 F5
Grevelingen Krammer,
  Neths. 16 E4
Greven, *Germany* 18 C3
Grevená, *Greece* 39 J4
Grevenbroich, *Germany* .. 18 D2
Grevenmacher, *Lux.* 17 J8
Grevesmühlen, *Germany* .. 18 B7
Grevie, *Sweden* 11 H6
Grey →, *N.Z.* 87 K3
Grey, C., *Australia* 90 A2
Grey Ra., *Australia* 91 D3
Grey Res., *Canada* 99 C8
Greybull, *U.S.A.* 110 D9
Greymouth, *N.Z.* 87 K3
Greytown, *N.Z.* 87 J5
Greytown, *S. Africa* 85 D5
Gribanovskiy, *Russia* ... 41 F12
Gribbell I., *Canada* 100 C3
Gridley, *U.S.A.* 112 F5
Griekwastad, *S. Africa* ... 84 D3
Griffin, *U.S.A.* 105 J3
Griffith, *Australia* 91 E4
Grijpskerk, *Neths.* 16 B8
Grillby, *Sweden* 10 E11
Grimari, *C.A.R.* 73 G9
Grimaylov, *Ukraine* 40 G5
Grimbergen, *Belgium* ... 17 G4
Grimes, *U.S.A.* 112 F5
Grimma, *Germany* 18 D8
Grimmen, *Germany* 18 A9
Grimsby, *Canada* 106 C5
Grimsby, *U.K.* 12 D7
Grimselpass, *Switz.* 23 C6
Grímsey, *Iceland* 8 C5
Grimshaw, *Canada* 100 B5
Grimstad, *Norway* 11 F2
Grindelwald, *Switz.* 22 C6
Grindsted, *Denmark* ... 11 J2
Grindu, *Romania* 38 E9
Grinnell, *U.S.A.* 108 E8
Griñón, *Spain* 30 E7
Grintavec, *Slovenia* 33 B11
Grip, *Norway* 10 A1
Gris-Nez, C., *France* ... 25 B8
Grisolles, *France* 26 E5
Grisons = Graubünden □,
  Switz. 23 C9
Grivegnée, *Belgium* 17 G7
Grmeč Planina, *Bos.-H.* . 33 D13
Groais I., *Canada* 99 B8
Groblersdal, *S. Africa* ... 85 D4
Grobming, *Austria* 21 H3
Grodno, *Belorussia* 40 E3
Grodzisk Mázowiecki,
  Poland 20 C10
Grodzisk Wielkopolski,
  Poland 20 C6
Grodzyanka, *Belorussia* .. 40 E6
Groenlo, *Neths.* 16 D9
Groesbeck, *U.S.A.* 109 K6
Groesbeek, *Neths.* 16 E7
Groix, *France* 24 E3
Groix, I. de, *France* 24 E3
Grójec, *Poland* 20 D10
Grolloo, *Neths.* 16 C9
Gronau, *Niedersachsen,*
  Germany 18 C5
Gronau,
  Nordrhein-Westfalen,
  Germany 18 C3
Grong, *Norway* 8 D12
Groningen, *Neths.* 16 B9
Groningen, *Surinam* ... 121 B6
Groningen □, *Neths.* ... 16 B9
Groninger Wad, *Neths.* .. 16 B9
Gronsveld, *Neths.* 17 G7
Groom, *U.S.A.* 109 H4
Groot →, *S. Africa* 84 E3
Groot Berg →, *S. Africa* .. 84 E2
Groot-Brakrivier, *S. Africa* 84 E3
Groot-Kei →, *S. Africa* .. 85 E4
Groot Vis →, *S. Africa* .. 84 E4
Groote Eylandt, *Australia* 90 A2
Grootebroek, *Neths.* 16 C6
Grootfontein, *Namibia* .. 84 B2
Grootlaagte →, *Africa* ... 84 C3
Grootvloer, *S. Africa* ... 84 E3
Gros C., *Canada* 100 A6
Grosa, Pta., *Spain* 36 B8
Grósio, *Italy* 32 B7
Grosne →, *France* 27 B8
Gross Glockner, *Austria* .. 21 H2
Grossenbrode, *Germany* .. 18 A7
Grossenhain, *Germany* .. 18 D9
Grosseto, *Italy* 32 F8
Groswater B., *Canada* ... 99 B8
Grote Gette →, *Neths.* .. 17 G6
Grote Nete →, *Belgium* .. 17 F5
Groton, *Conn., U.S.A.* .. 107 E12
Groton, *S. Dak., U.S.A.* . 108 C5
Grottáglie, *Italy* 35 B10
Grottaminarda, *Italy* 35 A8
Grottammare, *Italy* 33 F10
Grouard Mission, *Canada* . 100 B5
Grouin, Pte. du, *France* .. 24 D5
Groundhog →, *Canada* .. 98 C3
Grouse Creek, *U.S.A.* ... 110 F7
Grouw, *Neths.* 16 B7
Grove City, *U.S.A.* 106 E4
Groveland, *U.S.A.* 112 H6
Grover City, *U.S.A.* 113 K6
Groveton, *N.H., U.S.A.* .. 107 B13

Groveton, *Tex., U.S.A.* .. 109 K7
Grožnjan, *Croatia* 33 C10
Groznyy, *Russia* 43 E11
Grubbenvorst, *Neths.* ... 17 F8
Gruissan, *France* 26 E7
Grumo Áppula, *Italy* ... 35 A9
Grünberg, *Germany* 18 E4
Grundy Center, *U.S.A.* .. 108 D8
Gruver, *U.S.A.* 109 G4
Gruyères, *Switz.* 22 C4
Gryazi, *Russia* 41 E11
Gryazovets, *Russia* 41 B12
Gstaad, *Switz.* 22 D4
Gua, *India* 61 H14
Gua Musang, *Malaysia* .. 59 K3
Guacanayabo, G. de, *Cuba* 116 B4
Guacara, *Venezuela* 120 A4
Guachípas →, *Argentina* . 126 B2
Guachiría →, *Colombia* .. 120 B3
Guadajoz →, *Spain* 31 H6
Guadalajara, *Mexico* 114 C4
Guadalajara, *Spain* 28 E1
Guadalajara □, *Spain* ... 28 E2
Guadalcanal, *Solomon Is.* . 92 H8
Guadalcanal, *Spain* 31 G5
Guadalén →, *Spain* 31 G7
Guadales, *Argentina* 126 C2
Guadalete →, *Spain* 31 J4
Guadalhorce →, *Spain* ... 31 J6
Guadalimar →, *Spain* ... 29 G1
Guadalmena →, *Spain* ... 29 G2
Guadalmez →, *Spain* ... 31 G5
Guadalope →, *Spain* 28 D4
Guadalquivir →, *Spain* .. 31 J4
Guadalupe =
  Guadeloupe ■, *W. Indies* 117 C7
Guadalupe, *Brazil* 122 C2
Guadalupe, *Mexico* 113 N10
Guadalupe, *Spain* 31 F5
Guadalupe, *U.S.A.* 113 L6
Guadalupe →, *Mexico* ... 113 N10
Guadalupe →, *U.S.A.* ... 109 L6
Guadalupe, Sierra de,
  Spain 31 F5
Guadalupe Bravos, *Mexico* 114 A3
Guadalupe Peak, *U.S.A.* . 111 L11
Guadalupe y Calvo, *Mexico* 114 B3
Guadarrama, Sierra de,
  Spain 30 E6
Guadeloupe ■, *W. Indies* 117 C7
Guadeloupe Passage,
  W. Indies 117 C7
Guadiamar →, *Spain* ... 31 J4
Guadiana →, *Portugal* ... 31 H3
Guadiana Menor →, *Spain* 29 H1
Guadiaro →, *Spain* 31 J5
Guadiato →, *Spain* 31 H5
Guadiela →, *Spain* 28 E2
Guadix, *Spain* 29 H1
Guafo, Boca del, *Chile* ... 128 B2
Guafo, I., *Chile* 128 B2
Guainía □, *Colombia* ... 120 C4
Guainía →, *Colombia* ... 120 C4
Guaíra, *Brazil* 127 A5
Guaitecas, Is., *Chile* 128 B2
Guajará-Mirim, *Brazil* ... 125 C4
Guajira □, *Colombia* ... 120 A3
Guajira, Pen. de la,
  Colombia 120 A3
Gualaceo, *Ecuador* 120 D2
Gualán, *Guatemala* 116 C2
Gualdo Tadino, *Italy* 33 E9
Gualeguay, *Argentina* ... 126 C4
Gualeguaychú, *Argentina* . 126 C4
Gualicho, Salina, *Argentina* 128 B3
Gualjaina, *Argentina* 128 B2
Guam ■, *Pac. Oc.* 92 F6
Guamá, *Brazil* 122 B2
Guamá →, *Brazil* 122 B2
Guamblin, I., *Chile* 128 B1
Guaminí, *Argentina* 126 D3
Guamote, *Ecuador* 120 D2
Guampí, Sierra de,
  Venezuela 121 B4
Guamúchil, *Mexico* 114 B3
Guan Xian, *China* 52 B4
Guanabacoa, *Cuba* 116 B3
Guanacaste, Cordillera del,
  Costa Rica 116 D2
Guanacevi, *Mexico* 114 B3
Guanahani = San Salvador,
  Bahamas 117 B5
Guanajay, *Cuba* 116 B3
Guanajuato, *Mexico* 114 C4
Guanajuato □, *Mexico* .. 114 C4
Guanambi, *Brazil* 123 D3
Guanare, *Venezuela* 120 B4
Guanare →, *Venezuela* .. 120 B4
Guandacol, *Argentina* ... 126 B2
Guane, *Cuba* 116 B3
Guang'an, *China* 52 B6
Guangchang, *China* 53 D11
Guangde, *China* 53 B12
Guangdong □, *China* ... 53 F9
Guangfeng, *China* 53 C12
Guanghan, *China* 52 B5
Guanghua, *China* 53 A8
Guangji, *China* 53 C10
Guangling, *China* 50 E8
Guangning, *China* 53 F9
Guangrao, *China* 51 F10
Guangshun, *China* 52 D6
Guangwu, *China* 50 F3
Guangxi Zhuangzu
  Zizhiqu □, *China* 52 E7

Guangyuan, *China* 52 A5
Guangze, *China* 53 D11
Guangzhou, *China* 53 F9
Guanhães, *Brazil* 123 E3
Guanipa →, *Venezuela* .. 121 B5
Guanling, *China* 52 E5
Guannan, *China* 51 G10
Guanta, *Venezuela* 121 A5
Guantánamo, *Cuba* 117 B4
Guantao, *China* 50 F8
Guanyang, *China* 53 E8
Guanyun, *China* 51 G10
Guapí, *Colombia* 120 C2
Guápiles, *Costa Rica* 116 D3
Guaporé →, *Brazil* 125 C4
Guara, Sierra de, *Spain* .. 28 C4
Guarabira, *Brazil* 122 C4
Guaranda, *Ecuador* 120 D2
Guarapari, *Brazil* 123 F3
Guarapuava, *Brazil* 123 G1
Guaratinguetá, *Brazil* ... 127 A6
Guaratuba, *Brazil* 127 B6
Guarda, *Portugal* 30 E3
Guarda □, *Portugal* 30 E3
Guardafui, C. = Asir, Ras,
  Somali Rep. 68 E5
Guardamar del Segura,
  Spain 29 G4
Guardavalle, *Italy* 35 D9
Guardiagrele, *Italy* 33 F11
Guardo, *Spain* 30 C6
Guareña, *Spain* 31 G4
Guareña →, *Spain* 30 D5
Guaria □, *Paraguay* 126 B4
Guárico □, *Venezuela* ... 120 B4
Guarrojo →, *Colombia* .. 120 C3
Guarujá, *Brazil* 127 A6
Guarus, *Brazil* 123 F3
Guasave, *Mexico* 114 B3
Guascama, Pta., *Colombia* 120 C2
Guasdualito, *Venezuela* .. 120 B3
Guasipati, *Venezuela* 121 B5
Guastalla, *Italy* 32 D7
Guatemala, *Guatemala* .. 116 D1
Guatemala ■, *Cent. Amer.* 116 C1
Guatire, *Venezuela* 120 A4
Guaviare □, *Colombia* .. 120 C3
Guaviare →, *Colombia* .. 120 C4
Guaxupé, *Brazil* 127 A6
Guayabero →, *Colombia* . 120 C3
Guayama, *Puerto Rico* .. 117 C6
Guayaneco, Arch., *Chile* . 128 C1
Guayaquil, *Ecuador* 120 D2
Guayaquil, G. de, *Ecuador* 120 D1
Guayaramerín, *Bolivia* ... 125 C4
Guayas □, *Ecuador* 120 D2
Guaymas, *Mexico* 114 B2
Guazhou, *China* 53 A12
Guba, *Zaïre* 83 E2
Gûbâl, Madîq, *Egypt* ... 76 B3
Gubat, *Phil.* 55 E6
Gúbbio, *Italy* 33 E9
Gubin, *Nigeria* 79 C7
Gubkin, *Russia* 41 F10
Gudata, *Georgia* 43 E9
Gudbrandsdalen, *Norway* . 9 F10
Guddu Barrage, *Pakistan* . 60 E6
Gudenå →, *Denmark* ... 11 H3
Gudermes, *Russia* 43 E12
Gudivada, *India* 61 L12
Gudur, *India* 60 M11
Guebwiller, *France* 25 E14
Guecho, *Spain* 28 B2
Guékédou, *Guinea* 78 D2
Guelma, *Algeria* 75 A6
Guelph, *Canada* 98 D3
Guelt es Stel, *Algeria* ... 75 A5
Gueltara, *Algeria* 75 C4
Guemar, *Algeria* 75 B6
Guéméné-Penfao, *France* . 24 E5
Guéméné-sur-Scorff, *France* 24 D3
Guéné, *Benin* 79 C5
Güepi, *Peru* 120 D2
Guer, *France* 24 E4
Güer Aike, *Argentina* ... 128 D3
Guérande, *France* 24 E4
Guercif, *Morocco* 75 B4
Guéréda, *Chad* 73 F9
Guéret, *France* 26 B5
Guérigny, *France* 25 E10
Guerneville, *U.S.A.* 112 G4
Guernica, *Spain* 28 B2
Guernsey, *U.K.* 13 H5
Guernsey, *U.S.A.* 108 D2
Guerrara, Oasis, *Algeria* . 75 B5
Guerrara, Saoura, *Algeria* . 75 C4
Guerrero □, *Mexico* 115 D5
Guerzim, *Algeria* 75 C4
Gueugnon, *France* 27 B8
Gúgher, *Iran* 65 D8
Guglionesi, *Italy* 35 A7
Gui Jiang →, *China* 53 F8
Gui Xian, *China* 52 F7
Guia, *Canary Is.* 36 F4
Guia de Isora, *Canary Is.* . 36 F3
Guia Lopes da Laguna,
  Brazil 127 A4
Guichi, *China* 53 B11
Guider, *Cameroon* 79 D7
Guidimouni, *Niger* 79 C6
Guiding, *China* 52 D6
Guidong, *China* 53 D9
Guidonia, *China* 34 A5
Guiglo, *Ivory C.* 78 D3

Guijá, *Mozam.* 85 C5
Guijo de Coria, *Spain* ... 30 E4
Guildford, *U.K.* 13 F7
Guilford, *U.S.A.* 99 C6
Guilin, *China* 53 E8
Guillaumes, *France* 27 D10
Guillestre, *France* 27 D10
Guilvinec, *France* 24 E2
Güímar, *Canary Is.* 36 F3
Guimarães, *Brazil* 122 B3
Guimarães, *Portugal* 30 D2
Guimaras, *Phil.* 55 F5
Guinda, *U.S.A.* 112 G4
Guinea ■, *W. Afr.* 78 C2
Guinea, Gulf of, *Atl. Oc.* . 70 F3
Guinea-Bissau ■, *Africa* . 78 C2
Güines, *Cuba* 116 B3
Guingamp, *France* 24 D3
Guipavas, *France* 24 D2
Guiping, *China* 53 F8
Guipúzcoa □, *Spain* 28 B2
Güir, O. →, *Algeria* 75 B4
Guiratinga, *Brazil* 125 D7
Güiria, *Venezuela* 121 A5
Guiscard, *France* 25 C10
Guise, *France* 25 C10
Guitiriz, *Spain* 30 B3
Guiuan, *Phil.* 55 F6
Guixi, *China* 53 C11
Guiyang, *Guizhou, China* . 52 D6
Guiyang, *Hunan, China* .. 53 E9
Guizhou □, *China* 52 D6
Gujan-Mestras, *France* ... 26 D2
Gujarat □, *India* 62 H4
Gujiang, *China* 53 D10
Gujranwala, *Pakistan* 62 C6
Gujrat, *Pakistan* 62 C6
Gukovo, *Russia* 43 B8
Gulbarga, *India* 60 L10
Gulbene, *Latvia* 40 C5
Gulf, The, *Asia* 65 E6
Gulfport, *U.S.A.* 109 K10
Gulgong, *Australia* 91 E4
Gulin, *China* 52 C5
Gulistan, *Pakistan* 62 D2
Gull Lake, *Canada* 101 C7
Gullegem, *Belgium* 17 G2
Güllük, *Turkey* 66 E2
Gulma, *Nigeria* 79 C5
Gulmarg, *India* 63 B6
Gülnar, *Turkey* 66 E5
Gulpen, *Neths.* 17 G7
Gülşehir, *Turkey* 66 D6
Gulshad, *Kazakhstan* 44 E8
Gulsvik, *Norway* 10 D3
Gulu, *Uganda* 82 B3
Gulwe, *Tanzania* 82 D4
Gulyaypole, *Ukraine* 42 C7
Gum Lake, *Australia* 91 E3
Gumal →, *Pakistan* 62 D4
Gumbaz, *Pakistan* 62 D3
Gumel, *Nigeria* 79 C6
Gumiel de Hizán, *Spain* . 28 D1
Gumlu, *Australia* 90 B4
Gumma □, *Japan* 49 F9
Gummersbach, *Germany* . 18 D3
Gummi, *Nigeria* 79 C6
Gümüshacıköy, *Turkey* .. 42 F6
Gümüshane, *Turkey* 67 C8
Gümüshane □, *Turkey* .. 67 C8
Gumzai, *Indonesia* 57 F8
Guna, *Ethiopia* 77 E4
Guna, *India* 62 G7
Gundagai, *Australia* 91 F4
Gundelfingen, *Germany* .. 19 G6
Gundih, *Indonesia* 57 G14
Guneydogu Toroslar,
  Turkey 67 D9
Gungu, *Zaïre* 80 F3
Gunisao →, *Canada* 101 C9
Gunisao L., *Canada* 101 C9
Gunnbjørn Fjeld,
  Greenland 4 C6
Gunnedah, *Australia* 91 E5
Gunningbar Cr. →,
  Australia 91 E4
Gunnison, *Colo., U.S.A.* . 111 G10
Gunnison, *Utah, U.S.A.* . 110 G8
Gunnison →, *U.S.A.* ... 111 G9
Gunpowder, *Australia* ... 90 B2
Guntakal, *India* 60 M10
Guntersville, *U.S.A.* 105 H2
Guntong, *Malaysia* 59 K3
Guntur, *India* 61 L12
Gunungapi, *Indonesia* ... 57 F7
Gunungsitoli, *Indonesia* .. 56 D1
Günz →, *Germany* 19 G6
Gunza, *Angola* 80 G2
Günzburg, *Germany* 19 G6
Gunzenhausen, *Germany* . 19 F6
Guo He →, *China* 51 H9
Guoyang, *China* 50 H9
Gupis, *Pakistan* 63 A5
Gura Humorului, *Romania* 38 B8
Gurag, *Ethiopia* 77 F4
Gurdaspur, *India* 62 C6
Gurdon, *U.S.A.* 109 J8
Gurdzhaani, *Georgia* 43 F11
Gurgaon, *India* 62 E7
Gurgueia →, *Brazil* 122 C3
Gürgentepe, *Turkey* 67 C8
Gurha, *India* 62 G4
Gurk →, *Austria* 21 J4

Gurkha, *Nepal* 63 E11
Gurley, *Australia* 91 D4
Gurué, *Mozam.* 83 F4
Gurun, *Malaysia* 59 K3
Gürün, *Turkey* 66 D7
Gurupá, *Brazil* 121 D7
Gurupá, I. Grande de,
  Brazil 121 D7
Gurupi, *Brazil* 123 D7
Gurupi →, *Brazil* 122 B2
Gurupi, Serra da, *Brazil* . 122 C2
Guryev = Atyrau,
  Kazakhstan 43 C14
Gus-Khrustalnyy, *Russia* . 41 D12
Gusau, *Nigeria* 79 C6
Gusev, *Russia* 40 D3
Gushan, *China* 51 E12
Gushi, *China* 53 A10
Gushiago, *Ghana* 79 D4
Gusinje, *Montenegro* 21 N9
Gusinoozersk, *Russia* ... 45 D11
Gúspini, *Italy* 34 C1
Gustanj, *Slovenia* 33 B11
Gustine, *U.S.A.* 111 H3
Güstrow, *Germany* 18 B8
Gusum, *Sweden* 11 F10
Guta = Kalárovo,
  Slovak Rep. 21 H7
Gütersloh, *Germany* 18 D4
Gutha, *Australia* 89 E2
Guthalongra, *Australia* .. 90 B4
Guthrie, *U.S.A.* 109 H6
Gutian, *China* 53 D12
Gutiérrez, *Bolivia* 125 D5
Guttannen, *Switz.* 23 C6
Guttenberg, *U.S.A.* 108 D9
Guyana ■, *S. Amer.* 121 B6
Guyane française ■ =
  French Guiana ■,
  S. Amer. 121 C7
Guyang, *China* 50 D6
Guyenne, *France* 26 D4
Guymon, *U.S.A.* 109 G4
Guyra, *Australia* 91 E5
Guyuan, *Hebei, China* .. 50 D8
Guyuan, *Ningxia Huizu,*
  China 50 F4
Guzhang, *China* 52 C7
Guzhen, *China* 51 H9
Guzmán, L. de, *Mexico* . 114 A3
Gwa, *Burma* 61 L19
Gwaai, *Zimbabwe* 83 F2
Gwabegar, *Australia* 91 E4
Gwadabawa, *Nigeria* 79 C6
Gwádar, *Pakistan* 60 G3
Gwagwada, *Nigeria* 79 C6
Gwalia, *Australia* 89 E3
Gwalior, *India* 62 F8
Gwanda, *Zimbabwe* 83 G2
Gwandu, *Nigeria* 79 C5
Gwane, *Zaïre* 82 B2
Gwaram, *Nigeria* 79 C7
Gwarzo, *Nigeria* 79 C6
Gweebarra B., *Ireland* ... 15 B3
Gweedore, *Ireland* 15 A3
Gwent □, *U.K.* 13 F5
Gweru, *Zimbabwe* 83 F2
Gwi, *Nigeria* 79 D6
Gwinn, *U.S.A.* 104 B2
Gwio Kura, *Nigeria* 79 C7
Gwol, *Ghana* 78 C4
Gwoza, *Nigeria* 79 C7
Gwydir →, *Australia* 91 D4
Gwynedd □, *U.K.* 12 E4
Gyandzha, *Azerbaijan* ... 43 F12
Gyaring Hu, *China* 54 C4
Gydanskiy P-ov., *Russia* . 44 C8
Gympie, *Australia* 91 D5
Gyoma, *Hungary* 21 J10
Gyöngyös, *Hungary* 21 H9
Györ, *Hungary* 21 H7
Gypsum Pt., *Canada* 100 A6
Gypsumville, *Canada* ... 101 C9
Gyula, *Hungary* 21 J11
Gyumri = Kumayri,
  Armenia 43 F10
Gzhatsk, *Russia* 40 D9

H

Ha 'Arava →, *Israel* 69 E4
Ha Coi, *Vietnam* 58 B6
Ha Dong, *Vietnam* 58 B5
Ha Giang, *Vietnam* 58 A5
Ha Tien, *Vietnam* 59 G5
Ha Tinh, *Vietnam* 58 C5
Ha Trung, *Vietnam* 58 C5
Haacht, *Belgium* 17 G5
Haag, *Germany* 19 G8
Haaksbergen, *Neths.* 16 D9
Haaltert, *Belgium* 17 G4
Haamstede, *Neths.* 17 E3
Haapamäki, *Finland* 8 E18
Haapsalu, *Estonia* 40 B3
Haarlem, *Neths.* 16 D5
Haast →, *N.Z.* 87 K2
Haast Bluff, *Australia* ... 88 D5
Haastrecht, *Neths.* 16 E5
Hab Nadi Chauki, *Pakistan* 62 G2
Habaswein, *Kenya* 82 B4
Habay, *Canada* 100 B5
Habay-la-Neuve, *Belgium* . 17 J7

Habbānīyah, Iraq 64 C4
Haboro, Japan 48 B10
Haccourt, Belgium 17 G7
Hachenburg, Germany ... 18 E3
Hachijō-Jima, Japan 49 H9
Hachinohe, Japan 48 D10
Hachiōji, Japan 49 G9
Hachŏn, N. Korea 51 D15
Hachy, Belgium 17 J7
Hacıbektaş, Turkey 66 D6
Hacılar, Turkey 66 D6
Hackensack, U.S.A. 107 F10
Haçli Gölü, Turkey 67 D10
Hadali, Pakistan 62 C5
Hadarba, Ras, Sudan 76 C4
Hadarom □, Israel 69 E3
Haddington, U.K. 14 F6
Hadejia, Nigeria 79 C7
Hadejia →, Nigeria 79 C7
Haden, Australia 91 D5
Hadera, Israel 69 C3
Hadera, N. →, Israel 69 C3
Haderslev, Denmark 11 J3
Hadhramaut =
  Hadramawt, Yemen 68 D4
Hadım, Turkey 66 E5
Hadjeb El Aïoun, Tunisia .. 75 A6
Hadong, S. Korea 51 G14
Hadramawt, Yemen 68 D4
Hadrian's Wall, U.K. 12 C5
Hadsten, Denmark 11 H4
Hadsund, Denmark 11 H4
Haeju, N. Korea 51 E13
Haenam, S. Korea 51 G14
Haerhpin = Harbin, China .. 51 B14
Hafik, Turkey 66 D7
Ḥafīrat al 'Aydā, Si. Arabia .. 64 E3
Hafizabad, Pakistan 62 C5
Haflong, India 61 G18
Hafnarfjörður, Iceland 8 D3
Hafun, Ras, Somali Rep. 68 E5
Hagalil, Israel 69 C4
Hagen, Germany 18 D3
Hagenow, Germany 18 B7
Hagerman, U.S.A. 109 J2
Hagerstown, U.S.A. 104 F7
Hagetmau, France 26 E3
Hagfors, Sweden 9 F12
Häggenås, Sweden 10 A8
Hagi, Iceland 8 D2
Hagi, Japan 49 G5
Hagolan, Syria 69 B4
Hagondange-Briey, France .. 25 C13
Hags Hd., Ireland 15 D2
Hague, C. de la, France 24 C5
Hague, The = 's-
  Gravenhage, Neths. 16 D4
Haguenau, France 25 D14
Hai □, Tanzania 82 C4
Hai Duong, Vietnam 58 B6
Hai'an, Guangdong, China .. 53 G8
Hai'an, Jiangsu, China ... 53 A13
Haicheng, Fujian, China .. 53 E11
Haicheng, Liaoning, China .. 51 D12
Haidar Khel, Afghan. 62 C3
Haifa = Ḥefa, Israel 69 C3
Haifeng, China 53 F10
Haig, Australia 89 F4
Haiger, Germany 18 E4
Haikang, China 53 G8
Haikou, China 54 D6
Ḥā'il, Si. Arabia 64 E4
Hailar, China 54 B6
Hailey, U.S.A. 110 E6
Haileybury, Canada 98 C4
Hailin, China 51 B15
Hailing Dao, China 53 G8
Hailong, China 51 C13
Hailun, China 54 B7
Hailuoto, Finland 8 D18
Haimen, Guangdong,
  China 53 F11
Haimen, Jiangsu, China .. 53 B13
Haimen, Zhejiang, China . 53 E5
Hainan □, China 54 E5
Hainaut □, Belgium 17 H4
Haines, U.S.A. 110 D5
Haines City, U.S.A. 105 L5
Haines Junction, Canada . 100 A1
Haining, China 53 B13
Haiphong, Vietnam 54 D5
Haiti ■, W. Indies 117 C5
Haiya Junction, Sudan 76 D4
Haiyan, China 53 B13
Haiyang, China 51 F11
Haiyuan,
  Guangxi Zhuangzu,
  China 52 F6
Haiyuan, Ningxia Huizu,
  China 50 F3
Haizhou, China 51 G10
Haizhou Wan, China 51 G10
Haja, Indonesia 57 E7
Hajar Bangar, Sudan 73 F9
Hajdúböszörmény, Hungary 21 H11
Hajdúszoboszló, Hungary . 21 H11
Hajipur, India 63 G11
Ḥājjī Muḥsin, Iraq 64 C5
Ḥājjīābād, Eşfahan, Iran .. 65 C7
Ḥājjīābād, Hormozgan,
  Iran 65 D7
Hakansson, Mts., Zaïre 83 D2
Håkantorp, Sweden 11 F6

Hakkâri, Turkey 67 E10
Hakkâri □, Turkey 67 E10
Hakkâri Dağları, Turkey .. 67 E10
Hakken-Zan, Japan 49 G7
Hakodate, Japan 48 D10
Haku-San, Japan 49 F8
Hakui, Japan 49 F8
Hala, Pakistan 60 G6
Ḥalab, Syria 64 B3
Ḥalabjah, Iraq 64 C5
Halaib, Sudan 76 C4
Halanzy, Belgium 17 J7
Ḥālat 'Ammār, Si. Arabia .. 64 D3
Halbā, Lebanon 69 A5
Halberstadt, Germany 18 D7
Halcombe, N.Z. 87 J5
Halcon, Mt., Phil. 57 B6
Halden, Norway 10 E5
Haldensleben, Germany 18 C7
Haldia, India 61 H16
Haldwani, India 63 E8
Hale →, Australia 90 C2
Haleakala Crater, U.S.A. . 102 H16
Halen, Belgium 17 G6
Haleyville, U.S.A. 105 H2
Half Assini, Ghana 78 D4
Halfway →, Canada 100 B4
Haliburton, Canada 98 C4
Halifax, Australia 90 B4
Halifax, Canada 99 D7
Halifax, U.K. 12 D6
Halifax B., Australia 90 B4
Halifax I., Namibia 84 D2
Halīl →, Iran 65 E8
Hall, Austria 19 H7
Hall Beach, Canada 97 B11
Hall Pt., Australia 88 C3
Hallands län □, Sweden 11 H6
Hallands Väderö, Sweden . 11 H6
Hallandsås, Sweden 11 H7
Halle, Belgium 17 G4
Halle, Nordrhein-Westfalen,
  Germany 18 C4
Halle, Sachsen-Anhalt,
  Germany 18 D7
Hällefors, Sweden 9 G13
Hallein, Austria 21 H3
Hällekis, Sweden 11 F7
Hallett, Australia 91 E2
Hallettsville, U.S.A. 109 L6
Hällevadsholm, Sweden 11 F5
Halliday, U.S.A. 108 B3
Halliday L., Canada 101 A7
Hallim, S. Korea 51 H14
Hallingdal →, Norway ... 9 F10
Hällnäs, Sweden 8 D15
Hallock, U.S.A. 101 D9
Halls Creek, Australia 88 C4
Hallstahammar, Sweden 10 E10
Hallstead, U.S.A. 107 E9
Halmahera, Indonesia 57 D7
Halmeu, Romania 38 B6
Halmstad, Sweden 11 H6
Halq el Oued, Tunisia 75 A7
Hals, Denmark 11 H4
Halsafjorden, Norway 10 A2
Hälsingborg = Helsingborg,
  Sweden 11 H6
Halstad, U.S.A. 108 B6
Haltdalen, Norway 10 B5
Haltern, Germany 18 D3
Halul, Qatar 65 E7
Ḥalvān, Iran 65 C8
Ham, France 25 C10
Ham Tan, Vietnam 59 G6
Ham Yen, Vietnam 58 A5
Hamab, Namibia 84 D2
Hamad, Sudan 77 D3
Hamada, Japan 49 G6
Hamadān, Iran 65 C6
Hamadān □, Iran 65 C6
Hamadia, Algeria 75 A5
Hamāh, Syria 64 C3
Hamamatsu, Japan 49 G8
Hamar, Norway 10 D5
Hamarøy, Norway 8 B13
Hamâta, Gebel, Egypt 76 C3
Hambantota, Sri Lanka 60 R12
Hamber Prov. Park,
  Canada 100 C5
Hamburg, Germany 18 B5
Hamburg, Ark., U.S.A. 109 J9
Hamburg, Iowa, U.S.A. 108 E7
Hamburg, N.Y., U.S.A. 106 D6
Hamburg, Pa., U.S.A. 107 F9
Hamburg □, Germany 18 B6
Ḥamd, W. al →,
  Si. Arabia 64 E3
Hamden, U.S.A. 107 E12
Hame □ = Hämeen
  lääni □, Finland 9 F18
Hämeen lääni □, Finland . 9 F18
Hämeenlinna, Finland 9 F18
Hamélé, Ghana 78 C4
Hamelin Pool, Australia .. 89 E1
Hameln, Germany 18 C5
Hamer Koke, Ethiopia 77 F4
Hamerkaz □, Israel 69 C3
Hamersley Ra., Australia . 88 D2
Hamhung, N. Korea 51 E14
Hami, China 54 B4
Hamilton, Australia 91 F3
Hamilton, Canada 98 D4
Hamilton, N.Z. 87 G5
Hamilton, U.K. 14 F4

Hamilton, Mo., U.S.A. ... 108 F8
Hamilton, Mont., U.S.A. . 110 C6
Hamilton, N.Y., U.S.A. ... 107 D9
Hamilton, Ohio, U.S.A. ... 104 F3
Hamilton, Tex., U.S.A. .. 109 K5
Hamilton →, Australia ... 90 C2
Hamilton City, U.S.A. ... 112 F4
Hamilton Hotel, Australia . 90 C3
Hamilton Inlet, Canada ... 99 B8
Hamiota, Canada 101 C8
Hamlet, U.S.A. 105 H6
Hamley Bridge, Australia . 91 E2
Hamlin = Hameln,
  Germany 18 C5
Hamlin, N.Y., U.S.A. .. 106 C7
Hamlin, Tex., U.S.A. .. 109 J4
Hamm, Germany 18 D3
Hammam Bouhadjar,
  Algeria 75 A4
Hammamet, Tunisia 75 A7
Hammamet, G. de, Tunisia 75 A7
Hammarstrand, Sweden 10 A10
Hamme, Belgium 17 F4
Hamme-Mille, Belgium 17 G5
Hammel, Denmark 11 H3
Hammelburg, Germany 19 E5
Hammerfest, Norway 8 A17
Hammond, Ind., U.S.A. ... 104 E2
Hammond, La., U.S.A. .. 109 K9
Hammonton, U.S.A. 104 F8
Hamoir, Belgium 17 H7
Hamont, Belgium 17 F7
Hamoyet, Jebel, Sudan .. 76 D4
Hampden, N.Z. 87 L3
Hampshire □, U.K. 13 F6
Hampshire Downs, U.K. .. 13 F6
Hampton, Ark., U.S.A. .. 109 J8
Hampton, Iowa, U.S.A. .. 108 D8
Hampton, N.H., U.S.A. . 107 D14
Hampton, S.C., U.S.A. .. 105 J5
Hampton, Va., U.S.A. .. 104 G7
Hampton Tableland,
  Australia 89 F4
Hamrat esh Sheykh, Sudan 77 E2
Hamur, Turkey 67 D10
Hamyang, S. Korea 51 G14
Han Jiang →, China 53 F11
Han Shui →, China 53 B10
Hana, U.S.A. 102 H17
Hanak, Si. Arabia 64 E3
Hanamaki, Japan 48 E10
Hanang, Tanzania 82 C4
Hanau, Germany 19 E4
Hanbogd, Mongolia 50 C4
Hancheng, China 50 G6
Hanchuan, China 53 B9
Hancock, Mich., U.S.A. .. 108 B10
Hancock, Minn., U.S.A. .. 108 C7
Hancock, N.Y., U.S.A. ... 107 E9
Handa, Japan 49 G8
Handa, Somali Rep. 68 E5
Handan, China 50 F8
Handen, Sweden 10 E12
Handeni, Tanzania 82 D4
Handeni □, Tanzania ... 82 D4
Handub, Sudan 76 D4
Handwara, India 63 B6
Handzame, Belgium 17 F2
Hanegev, Israel 69 E3
Haney, Canada 100 D4
Hanford, U.S.A. 111 H4
Hang Chat, Thailand 58 C2
Hang Dong, Thailand 58 C2
Hangang →, S. Korea .. 51 F14
Hangayn Nuruu, Mongolia 54 B4
Hangchou = Hangzhou,
  China 53 B13
Hanggin Houqi, China ... 50 D4
Hanggin Qi, China 50 E5
Hangö, Finland 9 G17
Hangu, China 51 E9
Hangu, Pakistan 62 C4
Hangzhou, China 53 B13
Hangzhou Wan, China 53 B13
Hanhongor, Mongolia 50 C3
Ḥanīdh, Si. Arabia 65 E6
Ḥanīsh, Yemen 68 E3
Hanjiang, China 53 E12
Hankinson, U.S.A. 108 B6
Hanko = Hangö, Finland . 9 G17
Hanko, Finland 9 G17
Hankou, China 53 B10
Hanksville, U.S.A. 111 G8
Hanle, India 63 C8
Hanmer Springs, N.Z. ... 87 K4
Hann →, Australia 88 C4
Hann, Mt., Australia ... 88 C4
Hanna, Canada 100 C6
Hannaford, U.S.A. 108 B5
Hannah, U.S.A. 108 A5
Hannah B., Canada 98 B4
Hannibal, U.S.A. 108 F9
Hannik, Sudan 76 D3
Hannover, Germany 18 C5
Hannut, Belgium 17 G6
Hanoi, Vietnam 54 D5
Hanover = Hannover,
  Germany 18 C5
Hanover, Canada 106 B3
Hanover, S. Africa 84 E3
Hanover, N.H., U.S.A. . 107 C12
Hanover, Ohio, U.S.A. .. 106 F2
Hanover, Pa., U.S.A. .. 104 F7
Hanover, I., Chile 128 D2
Hanshou, China 53 C8
Hansi, India 62 E6

Hanson, L., Australia 91 E2
Hanyang, China 53 B10
Hanyin, China 52 A7
Hanyuan, China 52 C4
Hanzhong, China 50 H4
Hanzhuang, China 51 G9
Haora, India 63 H13
Hapert, Neths. 17 F6
Happy, U.S.A. 109 H4
Happy Camp, U.S.A. 110 F2
Happy Valley-Goose Bay,
  Canada 99 B7
Hapsu, N. Korea 51 D15
Hapur, India 62 E7
Ḥaql, Si. Arabia 69 F3
Haquira, Peru 124 C3
Har, Indonesia 57 F8
Har-Ayrag, Mongolia 50 B5
Har Hu, China 54 C4
Har Us Nuur, Mongolia .. 54 B4
Har Yehuda, Israel 69 D3
Ḥaraḍ, Si. Arabia 68 C4
Haranomachi, Japan 48 F10
Harardera, Somali Rep. .. 68 G4
Harare, Zimbabwe 83 F3
Harat, Eritrea 77 D4
Harazé, Chad 73 F8
Harbin, China 51 B14
Harbiye, Turkey 66 E7
Harboør, Denmark 11 H2
Harbor Beach, U.S.A. ... 104 D4
Harbor Springs, U.S.A. .. 104 C3
Harbour Breton, Canada . 99 C8
Harbour Grace, Canada .. 99 C9
Harburg, Germany 18 B5
Hårby, Denmark 11 J4
Harda, India 62 H7
Hardangerfjorden, Norway 9 F8
Hardap Dam, Namibia 84 C2
Hardegarijp, Neths. 16 B7
Hardenberg, Neths. 16 C9
Harderwijk, Neths. 16 D7
Hardey →, Australia ... 88 D2
Hardin, U.S.A. 110 D10
Harding, S. Africa 85 E4
Harding Ra., Australia .. 88 C3
Hardisty, Canada 100 C6
Hardman, U.S.A. 110 D4
Hardoi, India 63 F9
Hardwar = Haridwar, India 62 E8
Hardwick, U.S.A. 107 B12
Hardy, U.S.A. 109 G9
Hardy, Pen., Chile 128 E3
Hare B., Canada 99 B8
Harelbeke, Belgium 17 G2
Haren, Germany 18 C3
Haren, Neths. 16 B9
Harer, Ethiopia 68 F3
Harerge □, Ethiopia ... 77 F5
Hareto, Ethiopia 77 F4
Harfleur, France 24 C7
Hargeisa, Somali Rep. .. 68 F3
Hargshamn, Sweden 9 F15
Hari →, Indonesia 56 E2
Haria, Canary Is. 36 E6
Haricha, Hamada el, Mali 74 D4
Haridwar, India 62 E8
Haringhata →, Bangla. . 61 J16
Haringvliet, Neths. 16 E4
Harīrūd →, Asia 60 A2
Harlan, Iowa, U.S.A. .. 108 E7
Harlan, Ky., U.S.A. ... 105 G4
Harlech, U.K. 12 E3
Harlem, U.S.A. 110 B9
Harlingen, Neths. 16 B6
Harlingen, U.S.A. 109 M6
Harlowton, U.S.A. 110 C9
Harmånger, Sweden 10 C11
Harmil, Eritrea 77 D5
Harney Basin, U.S.A. .. 110 E4
Harney L., U.S.A. 110 E4
Harney Peak, U.S.A. .. 108 D3
Härnön, Sweden 10 B12
Härnösand, Sweden 10 B11
Haro, Spain 28 C2
Harp L., Canada 99 A7
Harper, Liberia 78 E3
Harplinge, Sweden 11 H6
Harrand, Pakistan 62 E4
Harriman, U.S.A. 105 H3
Harrington Harbour,
  Canada 99 B8
Harris, U.K. 14 D2
Harris, Sd. of, U.K. .. 14 D1
Harris L., Australia ... 91 E2
Harrisburg, Ill., U.S.A. . 109 G10
Harrisburg, Nebr., U.S.A. 108 E3
Harrisburg, Oreg., U.S.A. 110 D2
Harrisburg, Pa., U.S.A. . 106 F8
Harrismith, S. Africa ... 85 D4
Harrison, Ark., U.S.A. . 109 G8
Harrison, Idaho, U.S.A. . 110 C5
Harrison, Nebr., U.S.A. . 108 D3
Harrison, C., Canada ... 99 B8
Harrison Bay, U.S.A. ... 96 A4
Harrison L., Canada 100 D4
Harrisonburg, U.S.A. ... 104 F6
Harrisonville, U.S.A. ... 108 F7
Harriston, Canada 98 D3
Harrisville, U.S.A. 106 B1
Harrogate, U.K. 12 D6
Harrow, U.K. 13 F7
Harsefeld, Germany 18 B5

Harsīn, Iran 64 C5
Harskamp, Neths. 16 D7
Harstad, Norway 8 B14
Hart, L., Australia 91 E2
Hartbees →, S. Africa . 84 D3
Hartberg, Austria 21 H5
Hartford, Conn., U.S.A. . 107 E12
Hartford, Ky., U.S.A. .. 104 G2
Hartford, S. Dak., U.S.A. 108 D6
Hartford, Wis., U.S.A. . 108 D10
Hartford City, U.S.A. .. 104 E3
Hartland, Canada 99 C6
Hartland Pt., U.K. 13 F3
Hartlepool, U.K. 12 C6
Hartley Bay, Canada ... 100 C3
Hartmannberge, Namibia . 84 B1
Hartney, Canada 101 D8
Harts →, S. Africa ... 84 D3
Hartselle, U.S.A. 105 H2
Hartshorne, U.S.A. 109 H7
Hartsville, U.S.A. 105 H5
Hartwell, U.S.A. 105 H4
Harunabad, Pakistan 62 E5
Harvand, Iran 65 D7
Harvey, Australia 89 F2
Harvey, Ill., U.S.A. ... 104 E2
Harvey, N. Dak., U.S.A. . 108 B5
Harwich, U.K. 13 F9
Haryana □, India 62 E7
Harz, Germany 18 D6
Harzé, Belgium 17 H7
Harzgerode, Germany 18 D7
Hasaheisa, Sudan 77 E3
Hasan Kīādeh, Iran ... 65 B6
Ḥasanābād, Iran 65 C7
Hasanpur, India 62 E8
Haselünne, Germany 18 C3
Hashimoto, Japan 49 G7
Hashtjerd, Iran 65 C6
Håsjö, Sweden 10 A10
Haskell, Okla., U.S.A. . 109 H7
Haskell, Tex., U.S.A. . 109 J5
Haslach, Germany 19 G4
Haslev, Denmark 11 J5
Hasparren, France 26 E2
Hassa, Turkey 66 E7
Hasselt, Belgium 17 G6
Hasselt, Neths. 16 C8
Hassene, Adrar, Algeria . 75 D5
Hassfurt, Germany 19 E6
Hassi Berrekrem, Algeria 75 B6
Hassi bou Khelala, Algeria 75 B4
Hassi Djafou, Algeria ... 75 B5
Hassi el Abiod, Algeria . 75 B5
Hassi el Biod, Algeria .. 75 C6
Hassi el Gassi, Algeria . 75 B6
Hassi el Hadjar, Algeria . 75 B5
Hassi er Rmel, Algeria .. 75 B5
Hassi Imoulaye, Algeria . 75 C5
Hassi Inifel, Algeria ... 75 C5
Hassi Messaoud, Algeria . 75 B6
Hassi Rhénami, Algeria .. 75 B6
Hassi Tartrat, Algeria .. 75 B6
Hassi Zerzour, Morocco .. 74 B4
Hastière-Lavaux, Belgium 17 H5
Hastings, N.Z. 87 H6
Hastings, U.K. 13 G8
Hastings, Mich., U.S.A. . 104 D3
Hastings, Minn., U.S.A. . 108 C8
Hastings, Nebr., U.S.A. . 108 E5
Hastings Ra., Australia . 91 E5
Hat Yai, Thailand 59 J3
Hatanbulag, Mongolia ... 50 C5
Hatay = Antalya, Turkey . 66 E4
Hatay □, Turkey 66 E7
Hatch, U.S.A. 111 K10
Hatches Creek, Australia . 90 C2
Hatchet L., Canada 101 B8
Hațeg, Romania 38 D5
Hațeg, Mții., Romania .. 38 D6
Hatert, Neths. 16 E7
Hateruma-Shima, Japan .. 49 M1
Hatfield P.O., Australia . 91 E3
Hatgal, Mongolia 54 A9
Hathras, India 62 F8
Hatia, Bangla. 61 H17
Hato de Corozal, Colombia 120 B3
Hato Mayor, Dom. Rep. . 117 C6
Hattah, Australia 91 E3
Hattem, Neths. 16 D8
Hatteras, C., U.S.A. ... 105 H8
Hattiesburg, U.S.A. ... 109 K10
Hatvan, Hungary 21 H9
Hau Bon = Cheo Reo,
  Vietnam 58 F7
Hau Duc, Vietnam 58 E7
Haug, Norway 10 D4
Haugastøl, Norway 10 D1
Haugesund, Norway 9 G8
Haulerwijk, Neths. 16 B8
Haultain →, Canada ... 101 B7
Hauraki G., N.Z. 87 G5
Haut Atlas, Morocco 74 B3
Haut-Rhin □, France ... 25 E14
Haut Zaïre □, Zaïre ... 82 B2
Haute-Corse □, France .. 27 F13
Haute-Garonne □, France 26 E5
Haute-Loire □, France .. 26 C7
Haute-Marne □, France .. 25 D12
Haute-Saône □, France .. 25 E13
Haute-Savoie □, France . 27 C10
Haute-Vienne □, France . 26 C5
Hauterive, Canada 99 C6

Hautes-Alpes □, France .. 27 D10
Hautes Fagnes = Hohe
  Venn, Belgium 17 H8
Hautes Fagnes, Belgium .. 17 G8
Hautes-Pyrénées □, France 26 F4
Hauteville-Lompnès,
  France 27 C9
Hautmont, France 25 B10
Hautrage, Belgium 17 H3
Hauts-de-Seine □, France . 25 D9
Hauts Plateaux, Algeria .. 75 B4
Hauzenberg, Germany 19 G9
Havana = La Habana,
  Cuba 116 B3
Havana, U.S.A. 108 E9
Havant, U.K. 13 G7
Havasu, L., U.S.A. 113 L12
Havel →, Germany 18 C8
Havelange, Belgium 17 H6
Havelian, Pakistan 62 B5
Havelock, N.B., Canada .. 99 C6
Havelock, Ont., Canada .. 98 D4
Havelock, N.Z. 87 J4
Havelte, Neths. 16 C8
Haverfordwest, U.K. 13 F3
Haverhill, U.S.A. 107 D13
Havering, U.K. 13 F8
Haverstraw, U.S.A. 107 E11
Håverud, Sweden 11 F6
Havlíčkův Brod, Czech. .. 20 F5
Havneby, Denmark 11 J2
Havre, U.S.A. 110 B9
Havre-Aubert, Canada ... 99 C7
Havre-St.-Pierre, Canada . 99 B7
Havza, Turkey 66 C6
Haw →, U.S.A. 105 H6
Hawaii □, U.S.A. 102 H16
Hawaii I., Pac. Oc. 102 J17
Hawaiian Is., Pac. Oc. .. 102 H17
Hawaiian Ridge, Pac. Oc. 93 E11
Hawarden, Canada 101 C7
Hawarden, U.S.A. 108 D6
Hawea, L., N.Z. 87 L2
Hawera, N.Z. 87 H5
Hawick, U.K. 14 F6
Hawk Junction, Canada .. 98 C3
Hawke B., N.Z. 87 H6
Hawker, Australia 91 E2
Hawkesbury, Canada ... 98 C5
Hawkesbury I., Canada .. 100 C3
Hawkesbury Pt., Australia . 90 A1
Hawkinsville, U.S.A. ... 105 J4
Hawkwood, Australia ... 91 D5
Hawley, U.S.A. 108 B6
Hawrān, Syria 69 C5
Hawsh Mūssá, Lebanon .. 69 B4
Hawthorne, U.S.A. 110 G4
Hawzen, Ethiopia 77 E4
Haxtun, U.S.A. 108 E3
Hay, Australia 91 E3
Hay →, Australia 90 C2
Hay →, Canada 100 A5
Hay, C., Australia 88 B4
Hay L., Canada 100 B5
Hay Lakes, Canada 100 C6
Hay-on-Wye, U.K. 13 E4
Hay River, Canada 100 A5
Hay Springs, U.S.A. ... 108 D3
Hayachine-San, Japan .. 48 E10
Hayange, France 25 C13
Hayden, Ariz., U.S.A. .. 111 K8
Hayden, Colo., U.S.A. .. 110 F10
Haydon, Australia 90 B3
Hayes, U.S.A. 108 C4
Hayes →, Canada 101 B10
Haymana, Turkey 66 D5
Haynesville, U.S.A. ... 109 J8
Hayrabolu, Turkey 66 C2
Hays, Canada 100 C6
Hays, U.S.A. 108 F5
Hayward, Calif., U.S.A. . 112 H4
Hayward, Wis., U.S.A. . 108 B9
Haywards Heath, U.K. .. 13 F7
Hazafon □, Israel 69 C4
Hazar Gölü, Turkey 67 D8
Hazarām, Kūh-e, Iran .. 65 D8
Hazard, U.S.A. 104 G4
Hazaribag, India 63 H11
Hazaribag Road, India .. 63 G11
Hazebrouck, France 25 B9
Hazelton, Canada 100 B3
Hazelton, N. Dak., U.S.A. 108 B4
Hazelton, Pa., U.S.A. .. 107 F9
Hazen, N. Dak., U.S.A. . 108 B4
Hazen, Nev., U.S.A. ... 110 G4
Hazerswoude, Neths. ... 16 D5
Hazlehurst, Ga., U.S.A. . 105 K4
Hazlehurst, Miss., U.S.A. 109 K9
Hazleton, U.S.A. 107 F9
Hazlett, L., Australia .. 88 D4
Hazor, Israel 69 B4
He Xian, Anhui, China .. 53 B12
He Xian,
  Guangxi Zhuangzu,
  China 53 E8
Head of Bight, Australia . 89 F5
Headlands, Zimbabwe .. 83 F3
Healdsburg, U.S.A. 112 G4
Healdton, U.S.A. 109 H6
Healesville, Australia .. 91 F4
Heanor, U.K. 12 D6
Heard I., Ind. Oc. 3 G13
Hearne, U.S.A. 109 K6
Hearne B., Canada 101 A9
Hearne L., Canada 100 A6
Hearst, Canada 98 C3

Heart →, U.S.A. 108 B4
Heart's Content, Canada . 99 C9
Heath →, Bolivia 124 C4
Heath Pt., Canada 99 C7
Heath Steele, Canada .. 99 C6
Heavener, U.S.A. 109 H7
Hebbronville, U.S.A. ... 109 M5
Hebei □, China 50 E9
Hebel, Australia 91 D4
Heber, U.S.A. 113 N11
Heber Springs, U.S.A. .. 109 H9
Hebert, Canada 101 C7
Hebgen L., U.S.A. 110 D8
Hebi, China 50 G8
Hebrides, U.K. 14 D1
Hebron = Al Khalīl,
  Jordan 69 D4
Hebron, Canada 97 C13
Hebron, N. Dak., U.S.A. . 108 B3
Hebron, Nebr., U.S.A. .. 108 E6
Hecate Str., Canada ... 100 C2
Hechi, China 52 E7
Hechingen, Germany ... 19 G4
Hechtel, Belgium 17 F6
Hechuan, China 52 B6
Hecla, U.S.A. 108 C5
Hecla I., Canada 101 C9
Heddal, Norway 10 E3
Hédé, France 24 D5
Hede, Sweden 10 B7
Hedemora, Sweden ... 9 F13
Hedley, U.S.A. 109 H4
Hedmark fylke □, Norway 10 C5
Hedrum, Norway 10 E4
Heeg, Neths. 16 C7
Heegermeer, Neths. ... 16 C7
Heemskerk, Neths. 16 C5
Heemstede, Neths. 16 D5
Heer, Neths. 17 G7
Heerde, Neths. 16 D8
's Heerenburg, Neths. .. 16 E8
Heerenveen, Neths. ... 16 C7
Heerhugowaard, Neths. . 16 C5
Heerlen, Neths. 17 G7
Heers, Belgium 17 G6
Heesch, Neths. 16 E7
Heestert, Belgium 17 G2
Heeze, Neths. 17 F7
Hefa, Israel 69 C3
Hefa □, Israel 69 C4
Hefei, China 53 B11
Hegang, China 54 B8
Hegyalja, Hungary 21 G11
Heichengzhen, China .. 50 F4
Heide, Germany 18 A5
Heidelberg, Germany .. 19 F4
Heidelberg, C. Prov.,
  S. Africa 84 E3
Heidelberg, Trans.,
  S. Africa 85 D4
Heidenheim, Germany . 19 G6
Heijing, China 52 E3
Heilbron, S. Africa 85 D4
Heilbronn, Germany ... 19 F5
Heiligenblut, Austria ... 21 H2
Heiligenhafen, Germany . 18 A6
Heiligenstadt, Germany . 18 D6
Heilongjiang □, China .. 51 B14
Heilunkiang =
  Heilongjiang □, China . 51 B14
Heino, Neths. 16 D8
Heinola, Finland 9 F19
Heinsch, Belgium 17 J7
Heinze Is., Burma 61 M20
Heishan, China 51 D12
Heishui, Liaoning, China 51 C10
Heishui, Sichuan, China . 52 A4
Heist, Belgium 17 F2
Heist-op-den-Berg, Belgium 17 F5
Hejaz = Al Ḥijāz,
  Si. Arabia 68 B2
Hejian, China 50 E9
Hejiang, China 52 C5
Hejin, China 50 G6
Hekelgem, Belgium ... 17 G4
Hekimhan, Turkey 67 D7
Hekla, Iceland 8 E4
Hekou, Gansu, China .. 50 F2
Hekou, Guangdong, China 53 F9
Hekou, Yunnan, China .. 54 D5
Helagsfjället, Sweden .. 10 B6
Helan Shan, China 50 E3
Helchteren, Belgium ... 17 F6
Helden, Neths. 17 F7
Helechosa, Spain 31 F6
Helena, Ark., U.S.A. .. 109 H9
Helena, Mont., U.S.A. . 110 C7
Helendale, U.S.A. 113 L9
Helensburgh, U.K. 14 E4
Helensville, N.Z. 87 G5
Helgeroa, Norway 10 F3
Helgoland, Germany .. 18 A3
Heligoland = Helgoland,
  Germany 18 A3
Heligoland B. = Deutsche
  Bucht, Germany 18 A4
Heliopolis, Egypt 76 H7
Hellebæk, Denmark ... 11 H6
Hellendoorn, Neths. ... 16 D8
Hellevoetsluis, Neths. .. 16 E4
Hellín, Spain 29 G3
Helmand □, Afghan. ... 60 D4
Helmand →, Afghan. .. 60 D2
Helme →, Germany ... 18 D7
Helmond, Neths. 17 F7

Helmsdale, U.K. 14 C5
Helmstedt, Germany .. 18 C7
Helnæs, Denmark 11 J4
Helong, China 51 C15
Helper, U.S.A. 110 G8
Helsingborg, Sweden .. 11 H6
Helsinge, Denmark ... 11 H6
Helsingfors, Finland ... 9 F18
Helsingør, Denmark ... 11 H6
Helsinki, Finland 9 F18
Helston, U.K. 13 G2
Helvellyn, U.K. 12 C4
Helvoirt, Neths. 17 E6
Helwân, Egypt 76 J7
Hemet, U.S.A. 113 M10
Hemingford, U.S.A. ... 108 D3
Hemphill, U.S.A. 109 K8
Hempstead, U.S.A. ... 109 K6
Hemse, Sweden 9 H15
Hemsö, Sweden 10 B12
Henan □, China 50 G8
Henares →, Spain 28 E1
Henashi-Misaki, Japan .. 48 D9
Hendaye, France 26 E2
Hendek, Turkey 66 C4
Henderson, Argentina .. 126 D3
Henderson, Ky., U.S.A. . 104 G2
Henderson, N.C., U.S.A. 105 G6
Henderson, Nev., U.S.A. 113 J12
Henderson, Tenn., U.S.A. 105 H1
Henderson, Tex., U.S.A. 109 J7
Hendersonville, U.S.A. . 105 H4
Hendījān, Iran 65 D6
Hendon, Australia 91 D5
Heng Xian, China 52 F7
Hengcheng, China 50 E4
Hengdaohezi, China ... 51 B15
Hengelo, Gelderland,
  Neths. 16 D8
Hengelo, Overijssel, Neths. 16 D9
Hengfeng, China 53 C10
Hengshan, Hunan, China 53 D9
Hengshan, Shaanxi, China 50 F5
Hengshui, China 50 F8
Hengyang, Hunan, China . 53 D9
Hengyang, Hunan, China . 53 D9
Hénin-Beaumont, France 25 B9
Henlopen, C., U.S.A. .. 104 F8
Hennan, Sweden 10 B9
Hennebont, France ... 24 E3
Hennenman, S. Africa .. 84 D4
Hennessey, U.S.A. 109 G6
Hennigsdorf, Germany . 18 C9
Henrichemont, France . 25 E9
Henrietta, U.S.A. 109 J5
Henrietta, Ostrov, Russia 45 B16
Henrietta Maria C.,
  Canada 98 A3
Henry, U.S.A. 108 E10
Henryetta, U.S.A. 109 H6
Hensall, Canada 106 C3
Hentiyn Nuruu, Mongolia 54 B5
Henty, Australia 91 F4
Henzada, Burma 61 L19
Heping, China 53 E10
Heppner, U.S.A. 110 D4
Hepu, China 52 G7
Hepworth, Canada ... 106 B3
Heqing, China 52 D3
Hequ, China 50 E6
Héraðsflói, Iceland ... 8 D6
Héraðsvötn →, Iceland . 8 D4
Herald Cays, Australia . 90 B4
Herāt, Afghan. 60 B3
Herāt □, Afghan. 60 B3
Hérault □, France 26 E7
Hérault →, France 26 E7
Herbault, France 24 E8
Herbert →, Australia .. 90 B4
Herberton, Australia .. 90 B4
Herbignac, France ... 24 E4
Herborn, Germany ... 18 E4
Herby, Poland 20 E8
Hercegnovi, Montenegro 21 N8
Herðubreið, Iceland ... 8 D5
Hereford, U.K. 13 E5
Hereford, U.S.A. 109 H3
Hereford and Worcester □,
  U.K. 13 E5
Herefoss, Norway 11 F2
Herent, Belgium 17 G5
Herentals, Belgium ... 17 F5
Herenthout, Belgium .. 17 F5
Herfølge, Denmark ... 11 J6
Herford, Germany 18 C4
Herington, U.S.A. 108 F6
Herisau, Switz. 23 B8
Hérisson, France 26 B6
Herjehogna, Norway .. 9 F12
Herk →, Belgium 17 G6
Herkenbosch, Neths. .. 17 F8
Herkimer, U.S.A. 107 D10
Herlong, U.S.A. 112 E6
Herm, Chan. Is. 24 C4
Hermagor-Pressegger See,
  Austria 21 J3
Herman, U.S.A. 108 C6
Hermann, U.S.A. 108 F9
Hermannsburg, Germany 18 C6
Hermannsburg Mission,
  Australia 88 D5
Hermanus, S. Africa ... 84 E2
Herment, France 26 C6

Hermidale, Australia ... 91 E4
Hermiston, U.S.A. 110 D4
Hermitage, N.Z. 87 K3
Hermite, I., Chile 128 E3
Hermon, Mt. = Ash
  Shaykh, J., Lebanon .. 69 B4
Hermosillo, Mexico ... 114 B2
Hernád →, Hungary .. 21 H11
Hernandarias, Paraguay . 127 B5
Hernandez, U.S.A. 112 J6
Hernando, Argentina .. 126 C3
Hernando, U.S.A. 109 H10
Herne, Belgium 17 G4
Herne, Germany 17 E10
Herne Bay, U.K. 13 F9
Herning, Denmark ... 11 H2
Heroica = Caborca, Mexico 114 A2
Heroica Nogales =
  Nogales, Mexico ... 114 A2
Heron Bay, Canada ... 98 C2
Herradura, Pta. de la,
  Canary Is. 36 F5
Herreid, U.S.A. 108 C4
Herrera, Spain 31 H6
Herrera de Alcántar, Spain 31 F3
Herrera de Pisuerga, Spain 30 C6
Herrera del Duque, Spain 31 F5
Herrick, Australia 90 G4
Herrin, U.S.A. 109 G10
Herrljunga, Sweden .. 11 F7
Hersbruck, Germany .. 19 F7
Herseaux, Belgium ... 17 G2
Herselt, Belgium 17 F5
Herstal, Belgium 17 G7
Hertford, U.K. 13 F7
Hertfordshire □, U.K. . 13 F7
's-Hertogenbosch, Neths. 17 E6
Hertzogville, S. Africa . 84 D4
Hervás, Spain 30 E5
Herve, Belgium 17 G7
Herwijnen, Neths. ... 16 E6
Herzberg, Brandenburg,
  Germany 18 D9
Herzberg, Niedersachsen,
  Germany 18 D6
Herzele, Belgium 17 G3
Herzliyya, Israel 69 C3
Herzogenbuchsee, Switz. 22 B5
Heşār, Fārs, Iran 65 D6
Heşār, Markazī, Iran .. 65 C6
Hesdin, France 25 B9
Hesel, Germany 18 B3
Heshui, China 50 G5
Heshun, China 50 F7
Hesperange, Lux. 17 J8
Hesperia, U.S.A. 113 L9
Hesse = Hessen □,
  Germany 18 E5
Hessen □, Germany .. 18 E5
Hetch Hetchy Aqueduct,
  U.S.A. 112 H5
Hettinger, U.S.A. 108 C3
Hettstedt, Germany .. 18 D7
Heugem, Neths. 17 G7
Heule, Belgium 17 G2
Heusden, Belgium ... 17 F6
Heusden, Neths. 16 E6
Hève, C. de la, France . 24 C7
Heverlee, Belgium ... 17 G5
Hewett, C., Canada .. 97 A13
Hexham, U.K. 12 C5
Hexi, Yunnan, China .. 52 E4
Hexi, Zhejiang, China . 53 D12
Hexigten Qi, China ... 51 C9
Hexrivier, S. Africa ... 84 E2
Ḥeydarābād, Iran 65 D7
Heyfield, Australia ... 91 F4
Heysham, U.K. 12 C5
Heythuysen, Neths. .. 17 F7
Heyuan, China 53 F10
Heywood, Australia .. 91 F3
Heze, China 50 G8
Hezhang, China 52 D5
Hi Vista, U.S.A. 113 L9
Hialeah, U.S.A. 105 N5
Hiawatha, Kans., U.S.A. 108 F7
Hiawatha, Utah, U.S.A. 110 G8
Hibbing, U.S.A. 108 B8
Hibbs B., Australia ... 90 G4
Hibernia Reef, Australia 88 B3
Hickory, U.S.A. 105 H5
Hicks, Pt., Australia .. 91 F4
Hicksville, U.S.A. 107 F11
Hida, Romania 38 B6
Hida-Gawa →, Japan . 49 G8
Hida-Sammyaku, Japan 49 F8
Hidaka-Sammyaku, Japan 48 C11
Hidalgo, Mexico 115 C5
Hidalgo □, Mexico ... 115 C5
Hidalgo, Presa M., Mexico 114 B3
Hidalgo, Pta. del,
  Canary Is. 36 F3
Hidalgo del Parral, Mexico 114 B3
Hiddensee, Germany .. 18 A9
Hidrolândia, Brazil ... 123 E2
Hieflau, Austria 21 H4
Hiendelaencina, Spain . 28 D1
Hierapolis, Turkey ... 66 E3
Hierro, Canary Is. 36 G1
Higashiajima-San, Japan 49 F10
Higashiōsaka, Japan .. 49 G7
Higgins, U.S.A. 109 G4
Higgins Corner, U.S.A. 112 F5
Higginsville, Australia . 89 F3

High Atlas = Haut Atlas,
  Morocco 74 B3
High I., Canada 99 A7
High Island, U.S.A. ... 109 L7
High Level, Canada ... 100 B5
High Point, U.S.A. ... 105 H6
High Prairie, Canada .. 100 B5
High River, Canada ... 100 C6
High Springs, U.S.A. .. 105 L4
High Tatra = Tatry,
  Slovak Rep. 20 F9
High Wycombe, U.K. .. 13 F7
Highbury, Australia ... 90 B3
Highland □, U.K. 14 D4
Highland Park, U.S.A. . 104 D2
Highmore, U.S.A. 108 C5
Highrock L., Canada .. 101 B7
Higüay, Dom. Rep. ... 117 C6
Hihya, Egypt 76 H7
Hiiumaa, Estonia 40 B3
Híjar, Spain 28 D4
Ḥijāz □, Si. Arabia ... 68 C2
Hijken, Neths. 16 C8
Hijo = Tagum, Phil. .. 55 H6
Hikari, Japan 49 H5
Hiko, U.S.A. 111 H6
Hikone, Japan 49 G8
Hikurangi, N.Z. 87 F5
Hikurangi, Mt., N.Z. .. 87 H6
Hildburghausen, Germany 19 E6
Hildesheim, Germany . 18 C5
Hill →, Australia 89 F2
Hill City, Idaho, U.S.A. 110 E6
Hill City, Kans., U.S.A. 108 F5
Hill City, Minn., U.S.A. 108 B8
Hill City, S. Dak., U.S.A. 108 D3
Hill Island L., Canada . 101 A7
Hillared, Sweden 11 G7
Hillcrest Center, U.S.A. 113 K8
Hillegom, Neths. 16 D5
Hillerød, Denmark ... 11 J6
Hillingdon, U.K. 13 F7
Hillman, U.S.A. 104 C4
Hillmond, Canada ... 101 C7
Hillsboro, Kans., U.S.A. 108 F6
Hillsboro, N. Dak., U.S.A. 108 B6
Hillsboro, N.H., U.S.A. 107 C13
Hillsboro, N. Mex., U.S.A. 111 K10
Hillsboro, Oreg., U.S.A. 112 E4
Hillsboro, Tex., U.S.A. 109 J6
Hillsborough, Grenada . 117 D7
Hillsdale, Mich., U.S.A. 104 E3
Hillsdale, N.Y., U.S.A. 107 D11
Hillside, Australia 88 D2
Hillston, Australia ... 91 E4
Hillsport, Canada 98 C2
Hillston, Australia ... 91 E4
Hilo, U.S.A. 102 J17
Hilton, U.S.A. 106 C7
Hilvan, Turkey 67 D8
Hilvarenbeek, Neths. . 17 F6
Hilversum, Neths. 16 D6
Himachal Pradesh □, India 62 D7
Himalaya, Asia 63 E11
Himamaylan, Phil. ... 55 F5
Himara, Albania 39 J2
Himatnagar, India ... 60 H8
Himeji, Japan 49 G7
Himi, Japan 49 F8
Himmerland, Denmark 11 H3
Ḥimṣ, Syria 69 A5
Ḥimṣ □, Syria 69 A5
Hinche, Haiti 117 C5
Hinchinbrook I., Australia 90 B4
Hinckley, U.K. 13 E6
Hinckley, U.S.A. 110 G7
Hindås, Sweden 11 G6
Hindaun, India 62 F7
Hindmarsh, L., Australia 91 F3
Hindsholm, Denmark . 11 J4
Hindu Bagh, Pakistan . 62 D2
Hindu Kush, Asia 60 B7
Hindubagh, Pakistan .. 60 D5
Hindupur, India 60 N10
Hines Creek, Canada .. 100 B5
Hinganghat, India 60 J11
Hingeon, Belgium ... 17 G5
Hingham, U.S.A. 110 B8
Hingoli, India 60 K10
Hinigaran, Phil. 55 F5
Hinis, Turkey 67 D9
Hinna = Imi, Ethiopia . 68 F3
Hinna, Nigeria 79 C7
Hinojosa del Duque, Spain 31 G5
Hinsdale, U.S.A. 110 B10
Hinterrhein →, Switz. . 23 C8
Hinton, Canada 100 C5
Hinton, U.S.A. 104 G5
Hinwil, Switz. 23 B7
Hnzir Burnu, Turkey .. 66 C6
Hippolytushoef, Neths. 16 C5
Hirado, Japan 49 H4
Hirakud Dam, India .. 61 J13
Hiratsuka, Japan 49 G9
Hirfanlı Baraji, Turkey . 66 D5
Hirhafok, Algeria 75 D6
Hîrlău, Romania 38 B9
Hiroo, Japan 48 C11
Hirosaki, Japan 48 D10
Hiroshima, Japan 49 G6
Hiroshima □, Japan .. 49 G6
Hirsholmene, Denmark 11 G4
Hirson, France 25 C11
Hîrșova, Romania 38 E10
Hirtshals, Denmark .. 11 G3
Hisar, India 62 E6

Huebra

Hisb →, Iraq 64 D5
Ḩismá, Si. Arabia 64 D3
Hispaniola, W. Indies 117 C5
Hīt, Iraq 64 C4
Hita, Japan 49 H5
Hitachi, Japan 49 F10
Hitchin, U.K. 13 F7
Hitoyoshi, Japan 49 H5
Hitra, Norway 8 E10
Hitzacker, Germany 18 B7
Ḩiyyon, N. →, Israel 69 E4
Hjalmar L., Canada 101 A7
Hjälmare kanal, Sweden 10 E9
Hjälmaren, Sweden 10 E9
Hjartdal, Norway 10 E2
Hjerkinn, Norway 10 B3
Hjørring, Denmark 11 G3
Hjortkvarn, Sweden 11 F9
Hlinsko, Czech. 20 F5
Hluhluwe, S. Africa 85 D5
Ho, Ghana 79 D5
Ho Chi Minh City = Phanh Bho Ho Chi Minh, Vietnam 59 G6
Ho Thuong, Vietnam 58 C5
Hoa Binh, Vietnam 58 B5
Hoa Da, Vietnam 59 G7
Hoa Hiep, Vietnam 59 G5
Hoai Nhon, Vietnam 58 E7
Hoare B., Canada 97 B13
Hobart, Australia 90 G4
Hobart, U.S.A. 109 H5
Hobbs, U.S.A. 109 J3
Hobbs Coast, Antarctica 5 D14
Hobo, Colombia 120 C2
Hoboken, Belgium 17 F4
Hoboken, U.S.A. 107 F10
Hobro, Denmark 11 H3
Hobscheid, Lux. 17 J7
Hoburgen, Sweden 9 H15
Hochdorf, Switz. 23 B6
Hochschwab, Austria 21 H5
Höchstadt, Germany 19 F6
Hockenheim, Germany 19 F4
Hodaka-Dake, Japan 49 F8
Hodgson, Canada 101 C9
Hódmezövásárhely, Hungary 21 J10
Hodna, Chott el, Algeria 75 A5
Hodna, Monts du, Algeria 75 A5
Hodonín, Czech. 20 G7
Hoeamdong, N. Korea 51 C16
Hœdic, I. de, France 24 E4
Hoegaarden, Belgium 17 G5
Hoek van Holland, Neths. 16 E4
Hoeksche Waard, Neths. 16 E4
Hoenderloo, Neths. 16 D7
Hoengsŏng, S. Korea 51 F14
Hoensbroek, Neths. 17 G7
Hoeryong, N. Korea 51 C15
Hoeselt, Belgium 17 G6
Hoeven, Neths. 17 E5
Hoeyang, N. Korea 51 E14
Hof, Germany 19 E7
Hof, Iceland 8 D6
Höfðakaupstaður, Iceland 8 D3
Hofgeismar, Germany 18 D5
Hofmeyr, S. Africa 84 E4
Hofsjökull, Iceland 8 D4
Hofsós, Iceland 8 D4
Hōfu, Japan 49 G5
Hogan Group, Australia 90 F4
Hogansville, U.S.A. 105 J3
Hogeland, U.S.A. 110 B9
Hoggar = Ahaggar, Algeria 75 D6
Högsäter, Sweden 11 F6
Hogsty Reef, Bahamas 117 B5
Hoh →, U.S.A. 112 C2
Hoh Xil Shan, China 54 C3
Hohe Rhön, Germany 19 E5
Hohe Tauern, Austria 21 H2
Hohe Venn, Belgium 17 H8
Hohenau, Austria 20 G6
Hohenems, Austria 19 H5
Hohenstein-Ernstthal, Germany 18 E8
Hohenwald, U.S.A. 105 H2
Hohenwestedt, Germany 18 A5
Hohhot, China 50 D6
Hóhlakas, Greece 37 D9
Hohoe, Ghana 79 D5
Hoi An, Vietnam 58 E7
Hoi Xuan, Vietnam 58 B5
Hoisington, U.S.A. 108 F5
Højer, Denmark 11 K2
Hōjō, Japan 49 H6
Hökerum, Sweden 11 G7
Hokianga Harbour, N.Z. 87 F4
Hokitika, N.Z. 87 K3
Hokkaidō □, Japan 48 C11
Hokksund, Norway 10 E3
Hol-Hol, Djibouti 77 E5
Holbæk, Denmark 11 J5
Holbrook, Australia 91 F4
Holbrook, U.S.A. 111 J8
Holden, Canada 100 C6
Holden, U.S.A. 110 G7
Holdenville, U.S.A. 109 H6
Holderness, U.K. 12 D7
Holdfast, Canada 101 C7
Holdich, Argentina 128 C3
Holdrege, U.S.A. 108 E5
Holguín, Cuba 116 B4
Hollabrunn, Austria 20 G6
Hollams Bird I., Namibia 84 C1
Holland, U.S.A. 104 D2
Hollandia = Jayapura, Indonesia 57 E10
Hollandsch Diep, Neths. 17 E5
Hollandsch IJssel →, Neths. 16 E5
Hollfeld, Germany 19 F7
Hollidaysburg, U.S.A. 106 F6
Hollis, U.S.A. 109 H5
Hollister, Calif., U.S.A. 111 H3
Hollister, Idaho, U.S.A. 110 E6
Hollum, Neths. 16 B7
Holly, U.S.A. 108 F3
Holly Hill, U.S.A. 105 L5
Holly Springs, U.S.A. 109 H10
Hollywood, Calif., U.S.A. 111 J4
Hollywood, Fla., U.S.A. 105 N5
Holm, Sweden 10 B10
Holman Island, Canada 96 A8
Hólmavík, Iceland 8 D3
Holmes Reefs, Australia 90 B4
Holmestrand, Norway 10 E4
Holmsbu, Norway 10 E4
Holmsjön, Sweden 10 B9
Holmsland Klit, Denmark 11 J2
Holmsund, Sweden 8 E16
Holroyd →, Australia 90 A3
Holstebro, Denmark 11 H2
Holsworthy, U.K. 13 G3
Holt, Iceland 8 E4
Holte, Denmark 11 J6
Holten, Neths. 16 D8
Holton, Canada 99 B8
Holton, U.S.A. 108 F7
Holtville, U.S.A. 113 N11
Holwerd, Neths. 16 B7
Holy Cross, U.S.A. 96 B4
Holy I., Gwynedd, U.K. 12 D3
Holy I., Northumb., U.K. 12 B6
Holyhead, U.K. 12 D3
Holyoke, Colo., U.S.A. 108 E3
Holyoke, Mass., U.S.A. 107 D12
Holyrood, Canada 99 C9
Holzkirchen, Germany 19 H7
Holzminden, Germany 18 D5
Homa Bay, Kenya 82 C3
Homa Bay □, Kenya 82 C3
Homalin, Burma 61 G19
Homand, Iran 65 C8
Homberg, Germany 18 D5
Hombori, Mali 79 B4
Homburg, Germany 19 F3
Home B., Canada 97 B13
Home Hill, Australia 90 B4
Homedale, U.S.A. 110 E5
Homer, Alaska, U.S.A. 96 C4
Homer, La., U.S.A. 109 J8
Homestead, Australia 90 C4
Homestead, Fla., U.S.A. 105 N5
Homestead, Oreg., U.S.A. 110 D5
Homewood, U.S.A. 112 F6
Hominy, U.S.A. 109 G6
Homoine, Mozam. 85 C6
Homoljske Planina, Serbia 21 L11
Homorod, Romania 38 C8
Homs = Ḩimş, Syria 69 A5
Homyel = Gomel, Belorussia 40 E7
Hon Chong, Vietnam 59 G5
Hon Me, Vietnam 58 C5
Hon Quan, Vietnam 59 G6
Honan = Henan □, China 50 G8
Honbetsu, Japan 48 C11
Honcut, U.S.A. 112 F5
Honda, Colombia 120 B3
Honda Bay, Phil. 55 G3
Hondeklipbaai, S. Africa 84 E2
Hondo, Japan 49 H5
Hondo, U.S.A. 109 L5
Hondo →, Belize 115 D7
Honduras ■, Cent. Amer. 116 D2
Honduras, G. de, Caribbean 116 C2
Hønefoss, Norway 9 F11
Honesdale, U.S.A. 107 E9
Honey L., U.S.A. 112 E6
Honfleur, France 24 C7
Hong Gai, Vietnam 58 B6
Hong He →, China 50 H8
Hong Kong ■, Asia 53 F10
Hong'an, China 53 B10
Hongchŏn, S. Korea 51 F14
Honghai Wan, China 53 F10
Honghu, China 53 C9
Hongjiang, China 52 D7
Hongliu He →, China 50 F5
Hongor, Mongolia 50 B7
Hongsa, Laos 58 C3
Hongshui He →, China 52 F7
Hongsŏng, S. Korea 51 F14
Hongtong, China 50 F6
Honguedo, Détroit d', Canada 99 C7
Hongwon, N. Korea 51 E14
Hongya, China 52 C4
Hongyuan, China 52 A4
Hongze Hu, China 51 H10
Honiara, Solomon Is. 92 H7
Honiton, U.K. 13 G4
Honjō, Japan 48 E10
Honkorâb, Ras, Egypt 76 C4
Honolulu, U.S.A. 102 H16
Honshū, Japan 49 G9
Hontoria del Pinar, Spain 28 D1
Hood, Mt., U.S.A. 110 D3
Hood, Pt., Australia 89 F2
Hood River, U.S.A. 110 D3
Hoodsport, U.S.A. 112 C3
Hooge, Germany 18 A4
Hoogerheide, Neths. 17 F4
Hoogeveen, Neths. 16 C8
Hoogeveensche Vaart, Neths. 16 C8
Hoogezand, Neths. 16 B9
Hooghly → = Hughli →, India 63 J13
Hooghly-Chinsura = Chunchura, India 63 H13
Hoogkerk, Neths. 16 B9
Hooglede, Belgium 17 G2
Hoogstraten, Belgium 17 F5
Hoogvliet, Neths. 16 E4
Hook Hd., Ireland 15 D5
Hook I., Australia 90 C4
Hook of Holland = Hoek van Holland, Neths. 16 E4
Hooker, U.S.A. 109 G4
Hooker Creek, Australia 88 C5
Hoopeston, U.S.A. 104 E2
Hoopstad, S. Africa 84 D4
Hoorn, Neths. 16 C6
Hoover Dam, U.S.A. 113 K12
Hooversville, U.S.A. 106 F6
Hop Bottom, U.S.A. 107 E9
Hopa, Turkey 43 F9
Hope, Canada 100 D4
Hope, Ariz., U.S.A. 113 M13
Hope, Ark., U.S.A. 109 J8
Hope, N. Dak., U.S.A. 108 B6
Hope, L., Australia 91 D2
Hope, Pt., U.S.A. 96 B3
Hope Town, Bahamas 116 A4
Hopedale, Canada 99 A7
Hopefield, S. Africa 84 E2
Hopei = Hebei □, China 50 E9
Hopelchén, Mexico 115 D7
Hopetoun, Vic., Australia 91 F3
Hopetoun, W. Austral., Australia 89 F3
Hopetown, S. Africa 84 D3
Hopkins, U.S.A. 108 E7
Hopkins, L., Australia 88 D4
Hopkinsville, U.S.A. 105 G2
Hopland, U.S.A. 112 G3
Hoptrup, Denmark 11 J3
Hoquiam, U.S.A. 112 D3
Horasan, Turkey 67 C10
Horcajo de Santiago, Spain 28 F1
Hordaland fylke □, Norway 9 F9
Horden Hills, Australia 88 D5
Horezu, Romania 38 D6
Horgen, Switz. 23 B7
Horinger, China 50 D6
Horlick Mts., Antarctica 5 E15
Horlivka = Gorlovka, Ukraine 42 B8
Hormoz, Iran 65 E7
Hormoz, Jaz. ye, Iran 65 E8
Hormuz Str. of, The Gulf 65 E8
Horn, Ísafjarðarsýsla, Iceland 8 C2
Horn, Suður-Múlasýsla, Iceland 8 D7
Horn, Neths. 17 F7
Horn →, Canada 100 A5
Horn, Cape = Hornos, C. de, Chile 128 E3
Horn Head, Ireland 15 A3
Horn I., Australia 90 A3
Horn I., U.S.A. 105 K1
Horn Mts., Canada 100 A5
Hornachuelos, Spain 31 H5
Hornavan, Sweden 8 C14
Hornbæk, Denmark 11 H6
Hornbeck, U.S.A. 109 K8
Hornbrook, U.S.A. 110 F2
Hornburg, Germany 18 C6
Horncastle, U.K. 12 D7
Hornell, U.S.A. 106 D7
Hornell L., Canada 100 A5
Hornepayne, Canada 98 C3
Hornitos, U.S.A. 112 H6
Hornos, C. de, Chile 128 E3
Hornoy, France 25 C8
Hornsby, Australia 91 E5
Hornsea, U.K. 12 D7
Hornslandet, Sweden 10 C11
Hornslet, Denmark 11 H4
Hornu, Belgium 17 H3
Hörnum, Germany 18 A4
Horobetsu, Japan 48 C10
Horqin Youyi Qianqi, China 51 A12
Horqueta, Paraguay 126 A4
Horred, Sweden 11 G6
Horse Creek, U.S.A. 108 E3
Horse Is., Canada 99 B8
Horsefly L., Canada 100 C4
Horsens, Denmark 11 J3
Horsens Fjord, Denmark 11 J4
Horsham, Australia 91 F3
Horsham, U.K. 13 F7
Horst, Neths. 17 F8
Horten, Norway 10 E4
Hortobágy →, Hungary 21 H11
Horton, U.S.A. 108 F7
Horton →, Canada 96 B7
Horw, Switz. 23 B6
Horwood, L., Canada 98 C3
Hosaina, Ethiopia 77 F4
Hose, Gunung-Gunung, Malaysia 56 D4
Ḩoseynābād, Khuzestān, Iran 65 C6
Ḩoseynābād, Kordestān, Iran 64 C5
Hoshangabad, India 62 H7
Hoshiarpur, India 62 D6
Hosingen, Lux. 17 H8
Hosmer, U.S.A. 108 C5
Hospental, Switz. 23 C7
Hospet, India 60 M10
Hospitalet de Llobregat, Spain 28 D7
Hoste, I., Chile 128 E3
Hostens, France 26 D3
Hot, Thailand 58 C2
Hot Creek Range, U.S.A. 110 G5
Hot Springs, Ark., U.S.A. 109 H8
Hot Springs, S. Dak., U.S.A. 108 D3
Hotagen, Sweden 8 E13
Hotan, China 54 C2
Hotazel, S. Africa 84 D3
Hotchkiss, U.S.A. 111 G10
Hotham, C., Australia 88 B5
Hoting, Sweden 8 D14
Hotte, Massif de la, Haiti 117 C5
Hottentotsbaai, Namibia 84 D1
Hotton, Belgium 17 H6
Houat, I. de, France 24 E4
Houck, U.S.A. 111 J9
Houdan, France 25 D8
Houdeng-Goegnies, Belgium 17 H4
Houei Sai, Laos 58 B3
Houffalize, Belgium 17 H7
Houghton, U.S.A. 108 B10
Houghton L., U.S.A. 104 C3
Houghton-le-Spring, U.K. 12 C6
Houhora Heads, N.Z. 87 F4
Houille →, Belgium 17 H5
Houlton, U.S.A. 99 C6
Houma, U.S.A. 109 L9
Houndé, Burkina Faso 78 C4
Hourtin, France 26 C2
Hourtin-Carcans, Étang d', France 26 C2
Houston, Canada 100 C3
Houston, Mo., U.S.A. 109 G9
Houston, Tex., U.S.A. 109 L7
Houten, Neths. 16 D6
Houthalen, Belgium 17 F6
Houthem, Belgium 17 G1
Houthulst, Belgium 17 G2
Houtman Abrolhos, Australia 89 E1
Houyet, Belgium 17 H6
Hov, Denmark 11 J4
Hova, Sweden 11 F8
Høvåg, Norway 11 F2
Hovd, Mongolia 54 B4
Hove, U.K. 13 G7
Hoveyzeh, Iran 65 D6
Hövsgöl, Mongolia 50 C5
Hövsgöl Nuur, Mongolia 54 A5
Howakil, Eritrea 77 D5
Howar, Wadi →, Sudan 77 D2
Howard, Australia 91 D5
Howard, Kans., U.S.A. 109 G6
Howard, Pa., U.S.A. 106 E7
Howard, S. Dak., U.S.A. 108 C6
Howard I., Australia 90 A2
Howard L., Canada 101 A7
Howe, U.S.A. 110 E7
Howe, C., Australia 91 F5
Howell, U.S.A. 104 D4
Howick, Canada 107 A11
Howick, S. Africa 85 D5
Howick Group, Australia 90 A4
Howitt, L., Australia 91 D2
Howley, Canada 99 C8
Howrah = Haora, India 63 H13
Howth Hd., Ireland 15 C5
Höxter, Germany 18 D5
Hoy, U.K. 14 C5
Hoya, Germany 18 C5
Høyanger, Norway 9 F9
Hoyerswerda, Germany 18 D10
Hoyos, Spain 30 E4
Hpungan Pass, Burma 61 F20
Hradec Králové, Czech. 20 E5
Hranice, Czech. 20 F7
Hrodna = Grodno, Belorussia 40 E3
Hron →, Slovak Rep. 21 H8
Hrubieszów, Poland 20 E13
Hrvatska = Croatia ■, Europe 33 C13
Hsenwi, Burma 61 H20
Hsiamen = Xiamen, China 53 E12
Hsian = Xi'an, China 50 G5
Hsinhailien = Lianyungang, China 51 G10
Hsisha Chuntao, Pac. Oc. 56 A4
Hsüchou = Xuzhou, China 51 G9
Hu Xian, China 50 G5
Hua Hin, Thailand 58 F2
Hua Xian, Henan, China 50 G8
Hua Xian, Shaanxi, China 50 G5
Hua'an, China 53 E11
Huacaya, Bolivia 125 E5
Huacheng, China 53 E10
Huachinera, Mexico 114 A3
Huacho, Peru 124 C2
Huachón, Peru 124 C2
Huade, China 50 D7
Huadian, China 51 C14
Huai He →, China 53 A12
Huai Yot, Thailand 59 J2
Huai'an, Hebei, China 50 D8
Huai'an, Jiangsu, China 51 H10
Huaide, China 51 C13
Huaidezhen, China 51 C13
Huaihua, China 52 D7
Huaiji, China 53 F9
Huainan, China 53 A11
Huaining, China 53 B11
Huairen, China 50 E7
Huairou, China 50 D9
Huaiyang, China 50 H8
Huaiyin, Anhui, China 51 H9
Huaiyuan, Guangxi Zhuangzu, China 52 E7
Huajianzi, China 51 D13
Huajuapan de Leon, Mexico 115 D5
Hualapai Peak, U.S.A. 111 J7
Hualian, Taiwan 53 F13
Huallaga →, Peru 124 B2
Huallanca, Peru 124 B2
Huamachuco, Peru 124 B2
Huambo, Angola 81 G3
Huan Jiang →, China 50 G5
Huan Xian, China 50 F4
Huancabamba, Peru 124 B2
Huancane, Peru 124 D4
Huancapi, Peru 124 C3
Huancavelica, Peru 124 C2
Huancavelica □, Peru 124 C3
Huancayo, Peru 124 C2
Huanchaca, Bolivia 124 E4
Huanchaca, Serranía de, Bolivia 125 C5
Huang Hai = Yellow Sea, China 51 G12
Huang He →, China 51 F10
Huang Xian, China 51 F11
Huangchuan, China 53 A10
Huanggang, China 53 B10
Huangling, China 50 G5
Huangliu, China 54 E5
Huanglong, China 50 G5
Huanglongtan, China 53 A8
Huangmei, China 53 B10
Huangpi, China 53 B10
Huangping, China 52 D6
Huangshi, China 53 B10
Huangsongdian, China 51 C14
Huangyan, China 53 C13
Huangyangsi, China 53 D8
Huaning, China 52 E4
Huanjiang, China 52 E7
Huanta, Peru 124 C3
Huantai, China 51 F9
Huánuco, Peru 124 B2
Huánuco □, Peru 124 B2
Huanuni, Bolivia 124 D4
Huanzo, Cordillera de, Peru 124 C3
Huaping, China 52 D3
Huaral, Peru 124 C2
Huaraz, Peru 124 B2
Huari, Peru 124 B2
Huarmey, Peru 124 C2
Huarochiri, Peru 124 C2
Huarocondo, Peru 124 C3
Huarong, China 53 C9
Huascarán, Peru 124 B2
Huascarán, Nevado, Peru 124 B2
Huasco, Chile 126 B1
Huasco →, Chile 126 B1
Huasna, U.S.A. 113 K6
Huatabampo, Mexico 114 B3
Huauchinango, Mexico 115 C5
Huautla de Jiménez, Mexico 115 D5
Huaxi, China 52 D6
Huay Namota, Mexico 114 C4
Huayin, China 50 G6
Huayllay, Peru 124 C2
Huayuan, China 52 C7
Huazhou, China 53 G8
Hubbard, U.S.A. 109 K6
Hubbart Pt., Canada 101 B10
Hubei □, China 53 B9
Hubli-Dharwad = Dharwad, India 60 M9
Huchang, N. Korea 51 D14
Hückelhoven, Germany 18 D2
Huddersfield, U.K. 12 D6
Hudi, Sudan 76 D3
Hudiksvall, Sweden 10 C11
Hudson, Canada 101 C10
Hudson, Mass., U.S.A. 107 D13
Hudson, Mich., U.S.A. 104 E3
Hudson, N.Y., U.S.A. 107 D11
Hudson, Wis., U.S.A. 108 C8
Hudson, Wyo., U.S.A. 110 E9
Hudson →, U.S.A. 107 F10
Hudson Bay, N.W.T., Canada 97 C11
Hudson Bay, Sask., Canada 101 C8
Hudson Falls, U.S.A. 107 C11
Hudson Mts., Antarctica 5 D16
Hudson Str., Canada 97 B13
Hudson's Hope, Canada 100 B4
Hue, Vietnam 58 D6
Huebra →, Spain 30 D4

Huechucuicui, Pta., Chile . 128 B2
Huedin, Romania 38 C6
Huehuetenango, Guatemala 116 C1
Huejúcar, Mexico 114 C4
Huelgoat, France 24 D3
Huelma, Spain 29 H1
Huelva, Spain 31 H4
Huelva □, Spain 31 H4
Huelva →, Spain 31 H5
Huentelauquén, Chile .. 126 C1
Huércal Overa, Spain ... 29 H3
Huerta, Sa. de la, Argentina 126 C2
Huertas, C. de las, Spain . 29 G4
Huerva →, Spain 28 D4
Huesca, Spain 28 C4
Huesca □, Spain 28 C5
Huéscar, Spain 29 H2
Huetamo, Mexico 114 D4
Huete, Spain 28 E2
Hugh →, Australia 90 D1
Hughenden, Australia .. 90 C3
Hughes, Australia 89 F13
Hughli →, India 63 J13
Hugo, U.S.A. 108 F3
Hugoton, U.S.A. 109 G4
Hui Xian, Gansu, China .. 50 H4
Hui Xian, Henan, China .. 50 G7
Hui'an, China 53 E12
Hui'anbu, China 50 F4
Huichang, China 53 E10
Huichapán, Mexico 115 C5
Huidong, China 52 D4
Huifa He →, China 51 C14
Huila □, Colombia 120 C2
Huila, Nevado del, Colombia 120 C2
Huilai, China 53 F11
Huili, China 52 D4
Huimin, China 51 F9
Huinan, China 51 C14
Huinca Renancó, Argentina 126 C3
Huining, China 50 G3
Huinong, China 50 E4
Huise, Belgium 17 G3
Huishui, China 52 D6
Huisne →, France 24 E7
Huissen, Neths. 16 E7
Huiting, China 50 G9
Huitong, China 52 D7
Huixtla, Mexico 115 D6
Huize, China 52 D4
Huizen, Neths. 16 D6
Huizhou, China 53 F10
Hukawng Valley, Burma . 61 F20
Hukou, China 53 C11
Hukuntsi, Botswana 84 C3
Hula, Ethiopia 77 F4
Hulan, China 54 B7
Hulayfā', Si. Arabia ... 64 E4
Huld, Mongolia 50 B3
Hulin He →, China 51 B12
Hull = Kingston upon Hull, U.K. 12 D7
Hull, Canada 98 C4
Hull →, U.K. 12 D7
Hulst, Neths. 17 F4
Hulun Nur, China 54 B6
Humahuaca, Argentina .. 126 A2
Humaitá, Brazil 125 B5
Humaitá, Paraguay 126 B4
Humansdorp, S. Africa .. 84 E3
Humbe, Angola 84 B1
Humber →, U.K. 12 D7
Humberside □, U.K. 12 D7
Humbert River, Australia . 88 C3
Humble, U.S.A. 109 L8
Humboldt, Canada 101 C7
Humboldt, Iowa, U.S.A. . 108 D7
Humboldt, Tenn., U.S.A. 109 H10
Humboldt →, U.S.A. ... 110 F4
Humboldt Gletscher, Greenland 4 B4
Hume, U.S.A. 112 J8
Hume, L., Australia 91 F4
Humenné, Slovak Rep. .. 20 G11
Humphreys, Mt., U.S.A. 112 H8
Humphreys Peak, U.S.A. 111 J8
Humpolec, Czech. 20 F5
Humptulips, U.S.A. 112 C3
Hūn, Libya 73 C8
Hun Jiang →, China ... 51 D13
Húnaflói, Iceland 8 D3
Hunan □, China 53 D9
Hunchun, China 51 C16
Hundested, Denmark ... 11 J5
Hundred Mile House, Canada 100 C4
Hunedoara, Romania ... 38 D5
Hünfeld, Germany 18 E5
Hung Yen, Vietnam 58 B6
Hungary ■, Europe 21 H9
Hungary, Plain of, Europe 6 F9
Hungerford, Australia .. 91 D3
Hungnam, N. Korea 51 E14
Huni Valley, Ghana 78 D4
Hunsberge, Namibia 84 D2
Hunsrück, Germany 19 F3
Hunstanton, U.K. 12 E8
Hunte →, Germany 18 C4
Hunter, N. Dak., U.S.A. . 108 B6
Hunter, N.Y., U.S.A. ... 107 D10
Hunter I., Australia 90 G3
Hunter I., Canada 100 C3
Hunter Ra., Australia ... 91 E5

Hunters Road, Zimbabwe 83 F2
Hunterville, N.Z. 87 H5
Huntingburg, U.S.A. ... 104 F2
Huntingdon, Canada ... 98 C5
Huntingdon, U.K. 13 E7
Huntingdon, U.S.A. ... 106 F6
Huntington, Ind., U.S.A. 104 E3
Huntington, N.Y., U.S.A. 107 F11
Huntington, Oreg., U.S.A. 110 D5
Huntington, Utah, U.S.A. 110 G8
Huntington, W. Va., U.S.A. 104 F4
Huntington Beach, U.S.A. 113 M8
Huntington Park, U.S.A. 111 K4
Huntly, N.Z. 87 G5
Huntly, U.K. 14 D6
Huntsville, Canada 98 C4
Huntsville, Ala., U.S.A. . 105 H2
Huntsville, Tex., U.S.A. . 109 K7
Hunyuan, China 50 E7
Hunza →, India 63 B6
Huo Xian, China 50 F6
Huong Hoa, Vietnam ... 58 D6
Huong Khe, Vietnam ... 58 C5
Huonville, Australia ... 90 G4
Huoqiu, China 53 A11
Huoshan, Anhui, China . 53 A12
Huoshan, Anhui, China . 53 B11
Huoshao Dao, Taiwan .. 53 F13
Hupeh = Hubei □, China 53 B9
Hūr, Iran 65 D8
Hure Qi, China 51 C11
Hurezani, Romania 38 E6
Hurghada, Egypt 76 B3
Hurley, N. Mex., U.S.A. . 111 K9
Hurley, Wis., U.S.A. ... 108 B9
Huron, Calif., U.S.A. ... 112 J6
Huron, Ohio, U.S.A. ... 106 E2
Huron, S. Dak., U.S.A. . 108 C5
Huron, L., U.S.A. 106 B2
Hurricane, U.S.A. 111 H7
Hurso, Ethiopia 77 F5
Hurum, Norway 10 C2
Hurunui →, N.Z. 87 K4
Hurup, Denmark 11 H2
Húsavík, Iceland 8 C5
Huși, Romania 38 C11
Huskvarna, Sweden ... 9 H13
Hussar, Canada 100 C6
Husum, Germany 18 A5
Husum, Sweden 10 A13
Hutchinson, Kans., U.S.A. 109 F6
Hutchinson, Minn., U.S.A. 108 C7
Huttig, U.S.A. 109 J8
Hutton, Mt., Australia .. 91 D4
Huttwil, Switz. 22 B5
Huwun, Ethiopia 77 G5
Huy, Belgium 17 G6
Hvammur, Iceland 8 D3
Hvar, Croatia 33 E13
Hvarski Kanal, Croatia .. 33 E13
Hvítá, Iceland 8 D3
Hvítá →, Iceland 8 D3
Hvítárvatn, Iceland ... 8 D4
Hwachon-chosuji, S. Korea 51 E14
Hwang Ho = Huang He →, China 51 F10
Hwange, Zimbabwe 83 F2
Hwange Nat. Park, Zimbabwe 84 B4
Hyannis, U.S.A. 108 E4
Hyargas Nuur, Mongolia 54 B4
Hybo, Sweden 10 C10
Hyde Park, Guyana 121 B6
Hyden, Australia 89 F2
Hyderabad, India 60 L11
Hyderabad, Pakistan ... 62 G3
Hyères, France 27 E10
Hyères, Is. d', France .. 27 F10
Hyesan, N. Korea 51 D15
Hyland →, Canada 100 B3
Hyltebruk, Sweden 11 H7
Hymia, India 63 C8
Hyndman Peak, U.S.A. . 110 E6
Hyōgo □, Japan 49 G7
Hyrum, U.S.A. 110 F8
Hysham, U.S.A. 110 C10
Hythe, U.K. 13 F9
Hyūga, Japan 49 H5
Hyvinge = Hyvinkää, Finland 9 F18
Hyvinkää, Finland 9 F18

I

I-n-Échaï, Mali 74 D4
I-n-Gall, Niger 79 B6
Iabès, Erg, Algeria 75 C4
Iaco →, Brazil 124 B4
Iaçu, Brazil 123 D3
Iakora, Madag. 85 C8
Ialomița →, Romania .. 38 B10
Iași, Romania 38 B10
Iauaretê, Colombia 120 C4
Iba, Phil. 55 D3
Ibadan, Nigeria 79 D5
Ibagué, Colombia 120 C2
Ibaiti, Brazil 123 F1
Iballja, Albania 38 G3
Ibănești, Romania 38 C7
Ibar →, Serbia 21 M10
Ibaraki □, Japan 49 F10

Ibarra, Ecuador 120 C2
Ibba, Sudan 77 G2
Ibba, Bahr el →, Sudan . 77 F2
Ibbenbüren, Germany .. 18 C3
Ibembo, Zaïre 82 B1
Ibera, L., Argentina ... 126 B4
Iberian Peninsula, Europe 6 G5
Iberico, Sistema, Spain . 28 E2
Iberville, Canada 98 C5
Iberville, Lac d', Canada . 98 A5
Ibi, Nigeria 79 D6
Ibiá, Brazil 123 E2
Ibicaraí, Brazil 123 D4
Ibicuí, Brazil 123 D4
Ibicuy, Argentina 126 C4
Ibioapaba, Sa. da, Brazil 122 B3
Ibipetuba, Brazil 122 D3
Ibitiara, Brazil 123 D3
Ibiza, Spain 36 C7
Iblei, Monti, Italy 35 E7
Ibo, Mozam. 83 E5
Ibonma, Indonesia 57 E8
Ibotirama, Brazil 123 D3
Ibrāhīm →, Lebanon .. 69 A4
Ibshawâi, Egypt 76 J7
Ibu, Indonesia 57 D7
Iburg, Germany 18 C4
Ibusuki, Japan 49 J5
Icá, Peru 124 C2
Ica □, Peru 124 C2
Içá →, Brazil 124 A4
Icabarú, Venezuela ... 121 C5
Icabarú →, Venezuela . 121 C5
Içana, Brazil 120 C4
Içana →, Brazil 120 C4
Icatu, Brazil 122 B3
İçel = Mersin, Turkey .. 66 E6
İçel □, Turkey 66 E6
Iceland ■, Europe 8 D4
Icha, Russia 45 D16
Ich'ang = Yichang, China 53 B8
Ichchapuram, India ... 61 K14
Ichihara, Japan 49 G10
Ichikawa, Japan 49 G9
Ichilo →, Bolivia 125 D5
Ichinohe, Japan 48 D10
Ichinomiya, Japan 49 G8
Ichinoseki, Japan 48 E10
Ichnya, Ukraine 40 F8
Ichŏn, S. Korea 51 F14
Icht, Morocco 74 C3
Ichtegem, Belgium ... 17 F2
Icó, Brazil 122 C4
Icod, Canary Is. 36 F3
Icoraci, Brazil 122 B2
Icy Str., U.S.A. 100 B1
Ida Grove, U.S.A. 108 D7
Ida Valley, Australia .. 89 E3
Idabel, U.S.A. 109 J7
Idaga Hamus, Ethiopia . 77 E4
Idah, Nigeria 79 D6
Idaho □, U.S.A. 110 D6
Idaho City, U.S.A. 110 E6
Idaho Falls, U.S.A. ... 110 E7
Idaho Springs, U.S.A. . 110 G11
Idanha-a-Nova, Portugal 30 F3
Idar-Oberstein, Germany 19 F3
Idd el Ghanam, Sudan . 73 F9
Iddan, Somali Rep. 68 F4
Idehan, Libya 75 C7
Idehan Marzūq, Libya .. 73 D7
Idelès, Algeria 75 D6
Idfû, Egypt 76 C3
Ídhi Óros, Greece 37 D6
Ídhra, Greece 39 M6
Idi, Indonesia 56 C1
Idiofa, Zaïre 80 E3
Idku, Bahra el, Egypt .. 76 H7
Idlib, Syria 64 C3
Idria, U.S.A. 112 J6
Idrija, Slovenia 33 B11
Idritsa, Russia 40 C6
Idstein, Germany 19 E4
Idutywa, S. Africa 85 E4
Ieper, Belgium 17 G1
Ierápetra, Greece 37 E7
Ierissós, Greece 39 J6
Ierzu, Italy 34 C2
Iesi, Italy 33 E10
Ifach, Punta, Spain ... 29 G5
'Ifāl, W. al →, Si. Arabia 64 D2
Ifanadiana, Madag. ... 85 C8
Ife, Nigeria 79 D5
Iférouâne, Niger 79 B6
Iffley, Australia 90 B3
Ifni, Morocco 74 C2
Ifon, Nigeria 79 D6
Iforas, Adrar des, Mali . 79 B5
Ifould, L., Australia ... 89 F5
Ifrane, Morocco 74 B3
Iganga, Uganda 82 B3
Igara Paraná →, Colombia 120 D3
Igarapava, Brazil 123 F2
Igarapé Açu, Brazil ... 122 B2
Igarapé-Mirim, Brazil . 122 B2
Igarka, Russia 44 C9
Igatimi, Paraguay 127 A4
Igbetti, Nigeria 79 D5
Igbo-Ora, Nigeria 79 D5
Igboho, Nigeria 79 D5
Iğdır, Turkey 67 D11
Iggesund, Sweden 10 C11
Ighil Izane, Algeria ... 75 A5
Iglésias, Italy 34 C1
Igli, Algeria 75 B4

Igloolik, Canada 97 B11
Igma, Gebel el, Egypt .. 76 J8
Ignace, Canada 98 C1
İğneada Burnu, Turkey . 66 C3
Igoshevo, Russia 41 B13
Iguaçu →, Brazil 127 B5
Iguaçu, Cat. del, Brazil . 127 B5
Iguaçu Falls = Iguaçu, Cat. del, Brazil 127 B5
Iguala, Mexico 115 D5
Igualada, Spain 28 D6
Iguape, Brazil 123 F2
Iguassu = Iguaçu →, Brazil 127 B5
Iguatu, Brazil 122 C4
Iguéla, Gabon 80 E1
Igunga □, Tanzania ... 82 C3
Iheya-Shima, Japan ... 49 L3
Ihiala, Nigeria 79 D6
Ihosy, Madag. 85 C8
Ihotry, L., Madag. 85 C7
Ii, Finland 8 D18
Ii-Shima, Japan 49 L3
Iida, Japan 49 G8
Iijoki →, Finland 8 D18
Iisalmi, Finland 8 E19
Iiyama, Japan 49 F9
Iizuka, Japan 49 H5
Ijâfene, Mauritania ... 74 D3
Ijebu-Igbo, Nigeria ... 79 D5
Ijebu-Ode, Nigeria ... 79 D5
IJmuiden, Neths. 16 D5
IJssel →, Neths. 16 C7
IJsselmeer, Neths. 16 C6
IJsselmuiden, Neths. .. 16 C7
IJsselstein, Neths. 16 D6
Ijuí →, Brazil 127 B4
IJzendijke, Neths. 17 F3
IJzer →, Belgium 17 F1
Ikale, Nigeria 79 D6
Ikare, Nigeria 79 D6
Ikaría, Greece 39 M9
Ikast, Denmark 11 H3
Ikeda, Japan 49 G6
Ikeja, Nigeria 79 D5
Ikela, Zaïre 80 E4
Ikerre-Ekiti, Nigeria .. 79 D6
Ikhtiman, Bulgaria ... 38 G6
Iki, Japan 49 H4
Ikimba L., Tanzania .. 82 C3
Ikire, Nigeria 79 D5
İkizdere, Turkey 67 C9
Ikom, Nigeria 79 D6
Ikopa →, Madag. 85 B8
Ikot Ekpene, Nigeria .. 79 D6
Ikungu, Tanzania 82 C3
Ikurun, Nigeria 79 D5
Ila, Nigeria 79 D5
Ilagan, Phil. 55 C4
Ilam, Nepal 63 F12
Īlām, Iran 64 C5
Ilam, Nepal 63 F12
Ilanskiy, Russia 45 D10
Ilanz, Switz. 23 C8
Ilaro, Nigeria 79 D5
Iława, Poland 20 B9
Ilbilbie, Australia 90 C4
Ile-à-la-Crosse, Canada . 101 B7
Ile-à-la-Crosse, Lac, Canada 101 B7
Île-de-France, France .. 25 D9
Ilebo, Zaïre 80 E4
Ileje □, Tanzania 83 D3
Ilek, Russia 44 D6
Ilek →, Russia 44 D6
Ilero, Nigeria 79 D5
Ilesha, Kwara, Nigeria . 79 D5
Ilesha, Oyo, Nigeria .. 79 D5
Ilford, Canada 101 B9
Ilfracombe, Australia .. 90 C3
Ilfracombe, U.K. 13 F3
Ilgaz, Turkey 66 C5
Ilgaz Dağları, Turkey .. 66 C5
Ilgın, Turkey 66 D4
Ilha Grande, Brazil ... 121 D4
Ilha Grande, B. da, Brazil 123 F3
Ílhavo, Portugal 30 E2
Ilhéus, Brazil 123 D4
Ili →, Kazakhstan 44 E8
Iliç, Turkey 67 D8
Ilich, Kazakhstan 44 E7
Iliff, U.S.A. 108 E3
Iligan, Phil. 55 G6
Iligan Bay, Phil. 55 G6
Ilíkí, L., Greece 39 L6
Ilin I., Phil. 55 E4
Iliodhrómia, Greece .. 39 K6
Ilion, U.S.A. 107 D9
Ilirska-Bistrica, Slovenia 33 C11
Ilkeston, U.K. 12 E6
Illampu = Ancohuma, Nevada, Bolivia 124 D4
Illana B., Phil. 55 H5
Illapel, Chile 126 C1
Ille-et-Vilaine □, France 24 D5
Ille-sur-Têt, France ... 26 F6
Iller →, Germany 19 G5
Illescas, Spain 30 E7
Illetas, Spain 36 B9
Illiers-Combray, France 24 D8
Illimani, Bolivia 124 D4
Illinois □, U.S.A. 103 C9
Illinois →, U.S.A. ... 103 C8
Illium = Troy, Turkey .. 66 D2
Illizi, Algeria 75 C6
Illora, Spain 31 H7

Ilm →, Germany 18 D7
Ilmen, Oz., Russia 40 B7
Ilmenau, Germany 18 E6
Ilo, Peru 124 D3
Ilobu, Nigeria 79 D5
Iloilo, Phil. 55 F5
Ilora, Nigeria 79 D5
Ilorin, Nigeria 79 D5
Iloulya, Russia 43 B11
Ilovatka, Russia 41 F14
Ilovlya, Russia 43 B10
Ilubabor □, Ethiopia .. 77 F3
Ilūkste, Latvia 40 D5
Ilva Mică, Romania ... 38 B7
Ilwaco, U.S.A. 112 D2
Ilwaki, Indonesia 57 F7
Ilyichevsk, Ukraine ... 42 C4
Imabari, Japan 49 G6
Imaloto →, Madag. .. 85 C8
İmamoğlu, Turkey ... 66 E6
Imandra, Oz., Russia .. 44 C4
Imari, Japan 49 H4
Imasa, Sudan 76 D4
Imbâbah, Egypt 76 H7
Imbabura □, Ecuador . 120 C2
Imbaimadai, Guyana .. 121 B5
Imbler, U.S.A. 110 D5
Imdahane, Morocco .. 74 B3
imeni 26 Bakinskikh Komissarov, Azerbaijan 67 D13
Imeni Poliny Osipenko, Russia 45 D14
Imeri, Serra, Brazil ... 120 C4
Imerimandroso, Madag. . 85 B8
Imesan, Mauritania .. 74 D1
Imi, Ethiopia 68 F3
Imishly, Azerbaijan ... 43 G13
Imitek, Morocco 74 C3
Imlay, U.S.A. 110 F4
Imlay City, U.S.A. 106 C1
Immenstadt, Germany . 19 H6
Immingham, U.K. 12 D7
Immokalee, U.S.A. ... 105 M5
Imo □, Nigeria 79 D6
Imola, Italy 33 D8
Imotski, Croatia 21 M7
Imperatriz, Amazonas, Brazil 124 B4
Imperatriz, Maranhão, Brazil 122 C2
Impéria, Italy 32 E5
Imperial, Canada 101 C7
Imperial, Peru 124 C2
Imperial, Calif., U.S.A. 113 N11
Imperial, Nebr., U.S.A. 108 E4
Imperial Beach, U.S.A. 113 N9
Imperial Dam, U.S.A. . 113 N12
Imperial Reservoir, U.S.A. 113 N12
Imperial Valley, U.S.A. 113 N11
Imperieuse Reef, Australia 88 C2
Impfondo, Congo 80 D3
Imphal, India 61 G18
Imphy, France 26 B7
Imranlı, Turkey 66 C3
Imranlı, Turkey 67 D8
İmroz = Gökçeada, Turkey 39 J8
Imst, Austria 19 H6
Imuruan B., Phil. 57 B5
In Belbel, Algeria 75 C5
In Delimane, Mali 79 B5
In Rhar, Algeria 75 C5
In Salah, Algeria 75 C5
In Tallak, Mali 79 B5
Ina, Japan 49 G8
Inajá, Brazil 122 C4
Inangahua Junction, N.Z. 87 J3
Inanwatan, Indonesia . 57 E8
Iñapari, Peru 124 C4
Inari, Finland 8 B19
Inarijärvi, Finland ... 8 B19
Inawashiro-Ko, Japan . 48 F10
Inca, Spain 36 B9
Incaguasi, Chile 126 B1
İnce-Burnu, Turkey ... 42 E6
İncekum Burnu, Turkey 66 E5
Inchon, S. Korea 51 F14
Incio, Spain 30 C3
Incomáti →, Mozam. . 85 D5
Inda Silase, Ethiopia .. 77 E4
Indalsälven →, Sweden 10 B11
Indaw, Burma 61 G20
Indbir, Ethiopia 77 F4
Independence, Calif., U.S.A. 111 H4
Independence, Iowa, U.S.A. 108 D9
Independence, Kans., U.S.A. 109 G7
Independence, Mo., U.S.A. 108 F7
Independence, Oreg., U.S.A. 110 D2
Independence Fjord, Greenland 4 A6
Independence Mts., U.S.A. 110 F5
Independência, Brazil . 122 C3
Inderborskiy, Kazakhstan 43 B13
Index, U.S.A. 112 C5
India ■, Asia 60 K11
Indian →, U.S.A. 105 M5
Indian Cabins, Canada . 100 B5
Indian Harbour, Canada 99 B8
Indian Head, Canada .. 101 C8
Indian Ocean 46 K11

Indian Springs, U.S.A. ... 113 J11
Indiana, U.S.A. 106 F5
Indiana □, U.S.A. 104 E3
Indianapolis, U.S.A. 104 F2
Indianola, Iowa, U.S.A. .. 108 E8
Indianola, Miss., U.S.A. . 109 J9
Indiapora, Brazil 123 E1
Indiga, Russia 44 C5
Indigirka →, Russia 45 B15
Inđija, Serbia 21 K10
Indio, U.S.A. 113 M10
Indonesia ■, Asia 56 F5
Indore, India 62 H6
Indramayu, Indonesia ... 57 G13
Indravati →, India 61 K12
Indre □, France 25 F8
Indre →, France 24 E7
Indre-et-Loire □, France . 24 E7
Indus →, Pakistan 62 G2
Indus, Mouth of the,
    Pakistan 62 H2
İnebolu, Turkey 66 C5
İnegöl, Turkey 66 C3
Inés, Mt., Argentina ... 128 C3
Ineu, Romania 38 C4
Inezgane, Morocco 74 B3
Infantes, Spain 29 G1
Infiernillo, Presa del,
    Mexico 114 D4
Infiesto, Spain 30 B5
Ingapirca, Ecuador 120 D2
Ingelmunster, Belgium .. 17 G2
Ingende, Zaïre 80 E3
Ingeniero Jacobacci,
    Argentina 128 B3
Ingenio, Canary Is. 36 G4
Ingenio Santa Ana,
    Argentina 126 B2
Ingersoll, Canada 106 C4
Ingham, Australia 90 B4
Ingleborough, U.K. 12 C5
Inglewood, Queens.,
    Australia 91 D5
Inglewood, Vic., Australia 91 F3
Inglewood, N.Z. 87 H5
Inglewood, U.S.A. 113 M8
Ingólfshöfði, Iceland ... 8 E5
Ingolstadt, Germany ... 19 G7
Ingomar, U.S.A. 110 C10
Ingonish, Canada 99 C7
Ingore, Guinea-Biss. 78 C1
Ingraj Bazar, India 63 G13
Ingrid Christensen Coast,
    Antarctica 5 C6
Ingul →, Ukraine 42 C5
Ingulec, Ukraine 42 C5
Ingulets →, Ukraine ... 42 C5
Inguri →, Georgia 43 E9
Ingwavuma, S. Africa .. 85 D5
Inhaca, I., Mozam. 85 D5
Inhafenga, Mozam. 85 C5
Inhambane, Mozam. 85 C6
Inhambane □, Mozam. .. 85 C5
Inhambupe, Brazil 123 D4
Inhaminga, Mozam. 83 F4
Inharrime, Mozam. 85 C6
Inharrime →, Mozam. .. 85 C6
Inhuma, Brazil 122 C3
Inhumas, Brazil 123 E2
Iniesta, Spain 29 F3
Ining = Yining, China .. 44 E9
Inini □, Fr. Guiana 121 C7
Inírida →, Colombia ... 120 C4
Inishbofin, Ireland 15 C1
Inishmore, Ireland 15 C2
Inishowen, Ireland 15 A4
Injune, Australia 91 D4
Inklin, Canada 100 B2
Inklin →, Canada 100 B2
Inkom, U.S.A. 110 E7
Inle L., Burma 61 J20
Inn →, Austria 19 G9
Innamincka, Australia .. 91 D3
Inner Hebrides, U.K. ... 14 D2
Inner Mongolia = Nei
    Monggol Zizhiqu □,
    China 50 C6
Inner Sound, U.K. 14 D3
Innerkip, Canada 106 C4
Innerkirchen, Switz. ... 22 C6
Innerste →, Germany .. 18 C5
Innetalling I., Canada .. 98 A4
Innisfail, Australia 90 B4
Innisfail, Canada 100 C6
In'no-shima, Japan 49 G6
Innsbruck, Austria 19 H7
Inny →, Ireland 15 C4
Inocência, Brazil 123 E1
Inongo, Zaïre 80 E3
Inoucdjouac, Canada .. 97 C12
Inowrocław, Poland ... 20 C8
Inpundong, N. Korea .. 51 D14
Inquisivi, Bolivia 124 D4
Ins, Switz. 22 B4
Inscription, C., Australia . 89 E1
Insein, Burma 61 L20
Însurăţei, Romania ... 38 E10
Intendente Alvear,
    Argentina 126 D3
Interior, U.S.A. 108 D4
Interlaken, Switz. 25 F14
International Falls, U.S.A. 108 A8
Intiyaco, Argentina ... 126 B3
Intragna, Switz. 23 D7
Intutu, Peru 120 D3

Inútil, B., Chile 128 D2
Inuvik, Canada 96 B6
Inveraray, U.K. 14 E3
Inverbervie, U.K. 14 E6
Invercargill, N.Z. 87 M2
Inverell, Australia 91 D5
Invergordon, U.K. 14 D4
Invermere, Canada 100 C5
Inverness, Canada 99 C7
Inverness, U.K. 14 D4
Inverness, U.S.A. 105 L4
Inverurie, U.K. 14 D6
Inverway, Australia ... 88 C4
Investigator Group,
    Australia 91 E1
Investigator Str., Australia 91 F2
Inya, Russia 44 D9
Inyanga, Zimbabwe ... 83 F3
Inyangani, Zimbabwe .. 83 F3
Inyantue, Zimbabwe ... 83 F2
Inyo Mts., U.S.A. 111 H5
Inyokern, U.S.A. 113 K9
Inza, Russia 41 E15
Inzhavino, Russia 41 E13
Iō-Jima, Japan 49 J5
Ioánnina, Greece 39 K3
Iola, U.S.A. 109 G7
Ion Corvin, Romania .. 38 E10
Iona, U.K. 14 E2
Ione, Calif., U.S.A. ... 112 G6
Ione, Wash., U.S.A. .. 110 B5
Ionia, U.S.A. 104 D3
Ionian Is. = Iónioi Nísoi,
    Greece 39 L3
Ionian Sea, Europe ... 6 H9
Iónioi Nísoi, Greece ... 39 L3
Iori →, Azerbaijan 43 F12
Íos, Greece 39 N8
Iowa □, U.S.A. 108 D8
Iowa City, U.S.A. 108 E9
Iowa Falls, U.S.A. ... 108 D8
Ipala, Tanzania 82 C3
Ipameri, Brazil 123 E2
Iparía, Peru 124 B3
Ipáti, Greece 39 L5
Ipatinga, Brazil 123 E3
Ipatovo, Russia 43 D10
Ipel →, Europe 21 G9
Ipiales, Colombia 120 C2
Ipiaú, Brazil 123 D4
Ipin = Yibin, China .. 52 C5
Ipirá, Brazil 123 D4
Ipiranga, Brazil 120 D4
Ipixuna, Brazil 124 B3
Ipixuna →, Amazonas,
    Brazil 124 B3
Ipixuna →, Amazonas,
    Brazil 125 B5
Ipoh, Malaysia 59 K3
Iporá, Brazil 123 D1
Ippy, C.A.R. 73 G9
Ipsala, Turkey 66 C2
Ipswich, Australia ... 91 D5
Ipswich, U.K. 13 E9
Ipswich, Mass., U.S.A. . 107 D14
Ipswich, S. Dak., U.S.A. 108 C5
Ipu, Brazil 122 B3
Ipueiras, Brazil 122 B3
Ipupiara, Brazil 123 D3
Iput →, Belorussia ... 40 E7
Iqaluit, Canada 97 B13
Iquique, Chile 124 E3
Iquitos, Peru 120 D3
Irabu-Jima, Japan ... 49 M2
Iracoubo, Fr. Guiana . 121 B7
Irafshān, Iran 65 E9
Irahuan, Phil. 55 G3
Iráklia, Greece 39 N8
Iráklion, Greece 37 D7
Iráklion □, Greece ... 37 D7
Irala, Paraguay 127 B5
Iramba □, Tanzania .. 82 C3
Iran ■, Asia 65 C7
Iran, Gunung-Gunung,
    Malaysia 56 D4
Iran Ra. = Iran, Gunung-
    Gunung, Malaysia ... 56 D4
Īrānshahr, Iran 65 E9
Irapa, Venezuela 121 A5
Irapuato, Mexico 114 C4
Iraq ■, Asia 64 C5
Irarrar, O. →, Mali .. 75 D5
Irati, Brazil 127 B5
Irbid, Jordan 69 C4
Irbid □, Jordan 69 C5
Irebu, Zaïre 80 E3
Irecê, Brazil 122 D3
Iregua →, Spain 28 C2
Ireland ■, Europe ... 15 D4
Ireland's Eye, Ireland . 15 C5
Irele, Nigeria 79 D6
Ireng →, Brazil 121 C6
Iret, Russia 45 C16
Irgiz, Bolshaya →, Russia 41 E16
Irharharene, Algeria .. 75 C6
Irharrhar, O. →, Algeria 75 C6
Irherm, Morocco 74 B3
Irhil Mgoun, Morocco . 74 B3
Irhyangdong, N. Korea . 51 D15
Iri, S. Korea 51 G14
Irian Jaya □, Indonesia 57 E9
Irié, Guinea 78 D3
Iriga, Phil. 55 E5
Iringa, Tanzania 82 D4

Iringa □, Tanzania 82 D4
Iriomote-Jima, Japan ... 49 M1
Iriona, Honduras 116 C2
Iriri →, Brazil 121 D7
Iriri Novo →, Brazil ... 125 B7
Irish Republic ■, Europe . 15 D4
Irish Sea, Europe 12 D3
Irkineyeva, Russia 45 D10
Irkutsk, Russia 45 D11
Irma, Canada 101 C6
Iroise, Mer d', France .. 24 D2
Iron Baron, Australia .. 91 E2
Iron Gate = Portile de
    Fier, Europe 38 E5
Iron Knob, Australia ... 91 E2
Iron Mountain, U.S.A. . 104 C1
Iron Ra., Australia 90 A3
Iron River, U.S.A. 108 B10
Ironbridge, U.K. 13 E5
Irondequoit, U.S.A. ... 106 C7
Ironstone Kopje, Botswana 84 D3
Ironton, Mo., U.S.A. .. 109 G9
Ironton, Ohio, U.S.A. .. 104 F4
Ironwood, U.S.A. 108 B9
Iroquois Falls, Canada . 98 C3
Irosin, Phil. 55 E6
Irpen, Ukraine 40 F7
Irrara Cr. →, Australia . 91 D4
Irrawaddy □, Burma .. 61 L19
Irrawaddy →, Burma .. 61 M19
Irsina, Italy 35 B9
Irtysh →, Russia 44 C7
Irumu, Zaïre 82 B2
Irún, Spain 28 B3
Irunea = Pamplona, Spain 28 C3
Irurzun, Spain 28 C3
Irvine, Canada 101 D6
Irvine, U.K. 14 F4
Irvine, Calif., U.S.A. .. 113 M9
Irvine, Ky., U.S.A. ... 104 G4
Irvinestown, U.K. 15 B4
Irving, U.S.A. 109 J6
Irvona, U.S.A. 106 F6
Irwin →, Australia ... 89 E1
Irymple, Australia ... 91 E3
Is-sur-Tille, France ... 25 E12
Isa, Nigeria 79 C6
Isaac →, Australia ... 90 C4
Isabel, U.S.A. 108 C4
Isabela, I., Mexico ... 114 C3
Isabela, Phil. 55 H5
Isabella, Cord., Nic. .. 116 D2
Isabella Ra., Australia . 88 D3
Ísafjarðardjúp, Iceland . 8 C2
Ísafjörður, Iceland ... 8 C2
Isagarh, India 62 G7
Isahaya, Japan 49 H5
Isaka, Tanzania 82 C3
Isana = Içana →, Brazil . 120 C4
Isangi, Zaïre 80 D4
Isar →, Germany 19 G8
Isarco →, Italy 33 B8
Ísari, Greece 39 M5
Isbergues, France ... 25 B9
Iscayachi, Bolivia ... 125 E4
Íschia, Italy 34 B6
Iscuandé, Colombia .. 120 C2
Isdell →, Australia .. 88 C3
Ise, Japan 49 G8
Ise-Wan, Japan 49 G8
Isefjord, Denmark ... 11 J5
Iseltwald, Switz. 22 C5
Isenthal, Switz. 23 C7
Iseo, Italy 32 C7
Iseo, L. d', Italy 32 C7
Iseramagazi, Tanzania . 82 C3
Isère □, France 27 C9
Isère →, France 27 D8
Iserlohn, Germany ... 18 D3
Isérnia, Italy 35 A7
Iseyin, Nigeria 79 D5
Ishigaki-Shima, Japan . 49 M2
Ishikari-Gawa →, Japan . 48 C10
Ishikari-Sammyaku, Japan 48 C11
Ishikari-Wan, Japan .. 48 C10
Ishikawa □, Japan ... 49 F8
Ishim, Russia 44 D7
Ishim →, Russia 44 D8
Ishinomaki, Japan ... 48 E10
Ishioka, Japan 49 F10
Ishkuman, Pakistan .. 63 A5
Ishpeming, U.S.A. ... 104 B2
Isigny-sur-Mer, France . 24 C5
Isil Kul, Russia 44 D8
Isiolo, Kenya 82 B4
Isiolo □, Kenya 82 B4
Isipingo Beach, S. Africa . 85 E5
Isiro, Zaïre 82 B2
Isisford, Australia ... 90 C3
İskederun, Turkey ... 66 E7
İskenderun, Turkey .. 66 E7
İskenderun Körfezi, Turkey 66 E6
İskilip, Turkey 42 F6
Iskůr →, Bulgaria ... 38 F7
Iskut →, Canada 100 B2
Isla →, U.K. 14 E5
Isla Cristina, Spain .. 31 H3
Isla Vista, U.S.A. ... 113 L7
İslâhiye, Turkey 66 E7
Islamabad, Pakistan . 62 C5
Islamkot, Pakistan .. 62 G4
Island →, Canada ... 100 A4
Island Falls, Canada . 98 C3

Island Falls, U.S.A. 99 C6
Island L., Canada 101 C10
Island Lagoon, Australia .. 91 E2
Island Pond, U.S.A. ... 107 B13
Islands, B. of, Canada .. 99 C8
Islay, U.K. 14 F2
Isle →, France 26 D3
Isle aux Morts, Canada .. 99 C8
Isle of Wight □, U.K. ... 13 G6
Isle Royale, U.S.A. ... 108 A10
Isleta, U.S.A. 111 J10
Isleton, U.S.A. 112 G5
Ismail, Ukraine 42 D3
Ismâ'ilîya, Egypt 76 H8
Ismaning, Germany .. 19 G7
Ismay, U.S.A. 108 B2
Isna, Egypt 76 B3
Isogstalo, India 63 B8
Isola del Gran Sasso
    d'Italia, Italy 33 F10
Ísola del Liri, Italy ... 34 A6
Ísola della Scala, Italy . 32 C8
Ísola di Capo Rizzuto, Italy 35 D10
Ísparta, Turkey 66 E4
Ísparta □, Turkey ... 66 E4
Ísperikh, Bulgaria ... 38 F9
Íspica, Italy 35 F7
Íspir, Turkey 43 F9
Israel ■, Asia 69 D3
Issano, Guyana 121 B6
Issia, Ivory C. 78 D3
Issoire, France 26 C7
Issoudun, France ... 25 F8
Issyk-Kul, Ozero, Kirghizia 44 E8
Ist, Croatia 33 D11
Istaihah, U.A.E. 65 F7
İstanbul, Turkey 66 C3
İstanbul □, Turkey .. 66 C3
Istmina, Colombia ... 120 B2
Istok, Serbia 21 N10
Istokpoga, L., U.S.A. . 105 M5
Istra, Croatia 33 C11
Istra, Russia 41 D10
İstranca Dağları, Turkey . 39 H10
Istres, France 27 E8
Istria = Istra, Croatia . 33 C11
Itá, Paraguay 126 B4
Itabaiana, Paraíba, Brazil . 122 C4
Itabaiana, Sergipe, Brazil . 122 D4
Itabaianinha, Brazil .. 122 D4
Itaberaba, Brazil 123 D3
Itaberaí, Brazil 123 E2
Itabira, Brazil 123 E3
Itabirito, Brazil 123 F3
Itaboca, Brazil 121 D5
Itabuna, Brazil 123 D4
Itacajá, Brazil 122 C2
Itacaunas →, Brazil .. 122 C2
Itacoatiara, Brazil ... 121 D6
Itacuaí →, Brazil 124 A3
Itaguaçu, Brazil 123 E3
Itaguari →, Brazil ... 123 D3
Itaguatins, Brazil 122 C2
Itaim →, Brazil 122 C3
Itainópolis, Brazil ... 122 C3
Itaipú Dam, Brazil ... 127 B5
Itaituba, Brazil 121 D6
Itajaí, Brazil 127 B6
Itajubá, Brazil 123 F2
Itajuípe, Brazil 123 D4
Itaka, Tanzania 83 D3
Italy ■, Europe 7 G8
Itamataré, Brazil 122 B2
Itambacuri, Brazil ... 123 E3
Itambé, Brazil 123 E3
Itampolo, Madag. ... 85 C7
Itanhaém, Brazil 127 A6
Itanhauã →, Brazil .. 121 D5
Itanhém, Brazil 123 E3
Itapaci, Brazil 123 D2
Itapagé, Brazil 122 B4
Itaparica, I. de, Brazil . 123 D4
Itapebi, Brazil 123 E4
Itapecuru-Mirim, Brazil . 122 B3
Itapemirim, Brazil ... 123 F3
Itaperuna, Brazil 123 F3
Itapetinga, Brazil 123 E3
Itapetininga, Brazil ... 127 A6
Itapeva, Brazil 127 A6
Itapicuru →, Bahia, Brazil 122 D4
Itapicuru →, Maranhão,
    Brazil 122 B3
Itapinima, Brazil 125 B5
Itapipoca, Brazil 122 B4
Itapiranga, Brazil ... 121 D6
Itapiúna, Brazil 122 B4
Itaporanga, Brazil ... 122 C4
Itapuá □, Paraguay .. 127 B4
Itapuranga, Brazil ... 123 E2
Itaquari, Brazil 123 F3
Itaquatiara, Brazil ... 121 D6
Itaquí, Brazil 126 B4
Itararé, Brazil 127 A6
Itarsi, India 62 H7
Itarumã, Brazil 123 E1
Itatí, Argentina 126 B4
Itatira, Brazil 122 B4
Itatuba, Brazil 125 B5
Itatup, Brazil 121 D7
Itaueira, Brazil 122 C3
Itaueira →, Brazil ... 122 C3
Itaúna, Brazil 123 F3
Itbayat, Phil. 55 A5
Itchen →, U.K. 13 G6
Ite, Peru 124 D3
Itezhi Tezhi, L., Zambia . 83 F2
Ithaca = Itháki, Greece . 39 L3

Ithaca, U.S.A. 107 D8
Itháki, Greece 39 L3
Itinga, Brazil 123 E3
Itiquira, Brazil 125 D7
Itiquira →, Brazil ... 125 D6
Itirucu, Brazil 123 D3
Itiúba, Brazil 122 D4
Ito, Japan 49 G9
Itoigawa, Japan 49 F8
Iton →, France 24 C8
Itonamas →, Bolivia . 125 C5
Itsa, Egypt 76 J7
Íttiri, Italy 34 B1
Ittoqqortoormiit =
    Scoresbysund, Greenland . 4 B6
Itu □, Brazil 127 A6
Itu, Nigeria 79 D6
Ituaçu, Brazil 123 D3
Ituango, Colombia .. 120 B2
Ituiutaba, Brazil 123 E2
Itumbiara, Brazil ... 123 E2
Ituna, Canada 101 C8
Itunge Port, Tanzania . 83 D3
Ituni, Guyana 121 B6
Itupiranga, Brazil ... 122 C2
Iturama, Brazil 123 E1
Iturbe, Argentina ... 126 A2
Ituri →, Zaïre 82 B2
Iturup, Ostrov, Russia . 45 E15
Ituverava, Brazil ... 123 F2
Ituxi →, Brazil 125 B5
Ituyuro →, Argentina . 126 A3
Itzehoe, Germany .. 18 B5
Ivaí →, Brazil 127 A5
Ivalo, Finland 8 B19
Ivalojoki →, Finland . 8 B19
Ivangorod, Russia .. 40 B6
Ivanhoe, N.S.W., Australia 91 E3
Ivanhoe, W. Austral.,
    Australia 88 C4
Ivanhoe, U.S.A. 112 J7
Ivanhoe L., Canada .. 101 A7
Ivanić Grad, Croatia .. 33 C13
Ivanjica, Serbia 21 M10
Ivanjščice, Croatia .. 33 B13
Ivankoyskoye Vdkhr.,
    Russia 41 C10
Ivano-Frankivsk = Ivano-
    Frankovsk, Ukraine ... 40 G4
Ivano-Frankovsk, Ukraine . 40 G4
Ivanovo, Belorussia .. 40 E4
Ivanovo, Russia 41 C12
Ivato, Madag. 85 C8
Ivaylovgrad, Bulgaria . 39 H9
Ivinheima →, Brazil .. 127 A5
Iviza = Ibiza, Spain .. 36 C7
Ivohibe, Madag. 85 C8
Ivolândia, Brazil 123 E1
Ivory Coast ■, Africa . 78 D3
Ivrea, Italy 32 C4
Ivugivik, Canada 97 B12
Iwahig, Phil. 56 C5
Iwaizumi, Japan 48 E10
Iwaki, Japan 49 F10
Iwakuni, Japan 49 G6
Iwamizawa, Japan .. 48 C10
Iwanai, Japan 48 C10
Iwata, Japan 49 G8
Iwate □, Japan 48 E10
Iwate-San, Japan ... 48 E10
Iwo, Nigeria 79 D5
Ixiamas, Bolivia 124 C4
Ixopo, S. Africa 85 E5
Ixtepec, Mexico 115 D5
Ixtlán del Río, Mexico . 114 C4
Iyo, Japan 49 H6
Izabal, L. de, Guatemala . 116 C2
Izamal, Mexico 115 C7
Izberbash, Russia ... 43 E12
Izegem, Belgium ... 17 G2
Izena-Shima, Japan .. 49 L3
Izhevsk, Russia 44 D6
Izmayil = Ismail, Ukraine . 42 D3
İzmir, Turkey 66 D2
İzmir □, Turkey 66 D2
İzmit, Turkey 66 C3
Iznajar, Spain 31 H6
Iznalloz, Spain 29 H1
İznik Gölü, Turkey .. 66 C3
Izobil'nyy, Russia .. 43 D9
Izola, Slovenia 33 C10
Izozog, Bañados de, Bolivia 125 D5
Izra, Syria 69 C5
Iztochni Rodopi, Bulgaria . 39 H8
Izu-Shotō, Japan ... 49 G10
Izumi-sano, Japan .. 49 G7
Izumo, Japan 49 G6
Izyaslav, Ukraine ... 40 F5
Izyum, Ukraine 42 B7

J

J.F. Rodrigues, Brazil ... 122 B1
Jaba, Ethiopia 77 F4
Jabal el Awlîya, Sudan ... 77 D3
Jabal Lubnān, Lebanon . 69 B4
Jabalón →, Spain ... 31 G6
Jabalpur, India 63 H8
Jabbūl, Syria 64 B3
Jablah, Syria 64 C3
Jablanac, Croatia ... 33 D11
Jablonec, Czech. 20 E5

Jabłonowo, Poland 20 B9
Jaboatão, Brazil 122 C4
Jaboticabal, Brazil 127 A6
Jaburu, Brazil 125 B5
Jaca, Spain 28 C4
Jacaré →, Brazil 122 D3
Jacareí, Brazil 127 A6
Jacarèzinho, Brazil 127 A6
Jaciara, Brazil 125 D7
Jacinto, Brazil 123 E3
Jaciparaná, Brazil 125 B5
Jackman, U.S.A. 99 C5
Jackson, Australia 91 D4
Jackson, Ala., U.S.A. 105 K2
Jackson, Calif., U.S.A. 112 G6
Jackson, Ky., U.S.A. 104 G4
Jackson, Mich., U.S.A. 104 D3
Jackson, Minn., U.S.A. 108 D7
Jackson, Miss., U.S.A. 109 J9
Jackson, Mo., U.S.A. 109 G10
Jackson, Ohio, U.S.A. 104 F4
Jackson, Tenn., U.S.A. 105 H1
Jackson, Wyo., U.S.A. 110 E8
Jackson B., N.Z. 87 K2
Jackson L., U.S.A. 110 E8
Jacksons, N.Z. 87 K3
Jacksonville, Ala., U.S.A. 105 J3
Jacksonville, Calif., U.S.A. 112 H6
Jacksonville, Fla., U.S.A. 105 K5
Jacksonville, Ill., U.S.A. 108 F9
Jacksonville, N.C., U.S.A. 105 H7
Jacksonville, Oreg., U.S.A. 110 E2
Jacksonville, Tex., U.S.A. 109 K7
Jacksonville Beach, U.S.A. 105 K5
Jacmel, Haiti 117 C5
Jacob Lake, U.S.A. 111 H7
Jacobabad, Pakistan 62 E3
Jacobina, Brazil 122 D3
Jacques-Cartier, Mt., Canada 99 C6
Jacqueville, Ivory C. 78 D4
Jacuí →, Brazil 127 C5
Jacumba, U.S.A. 113 N10
Jacundá →, Brazil 122 B1
Jade, Germany 18 B4
Jadebusen, Germany 18 B4
Jadoigne, Belgium 17 G5
Jadotville = Likasi, Zaïre 83 E2
Jadraque, Spain 28 E2
Jādū, Libya 75 B7
Jaén, Peru 124 B2
Jaén, Spain 31 H1
Jaén □, Spain 31 H7
Jafène, Africa 74 D3
Jaffa = Tel Aviv-Yafo, Israel 69 C3
Jaffa, C., Australia 91 F2
Jaffna, Sri Lanka 60 Q12
Jagadhri, India 62 D7
Jagadishpur, India 63 G11
Jagdalpur, India 61 K12
Jagersfontein, S. Africa 84 D4
Jagraon, India 60 D9
Jagst →, Germany 19 F5
Jagtial, India 60 K11
Jaguaquara, Brazil 123 D4
Jaguariaíva, Brazil 127 A6
Jaguaribe, Brazil 122 C4
Jaguaribe →, Brazil 122 B4
Jaguaruana, Brazil 122 B4
Jagüey Grande, Cuba 116 B3
Jahangirabad, India 62 E8
Jahrom, Iran 65 D7
Jaicós, Brazil 122 C3
Jailolo, Indonesia 57 D7
Jailolo, Selat, Indonesia 57 D7
Jaipur, India 62 F6
Jājarm, Iran 65 B8
Jajce, Bos.-H. 21 L7
Jakarta, Indonesia 57 G12
Jakobstad, Finland 8 E17
Jakupica, Macedonia 39 H4
Jal, U.S.A. 109 J3
Jalalabad, Afghan. 62 B4
Jalalabad, India 63 F8
Jalalpur Jattan, Pakistan 62 C6
Jalama, U.S.A. 113 L6
Jalapa, Guatemala 116 D2
Jalapa Enríquez, Mexico 115 D5
Jalaun, India 63 F8
Jales, Brazil 123 F1
Jaleswar, Nepal 63 F11
Jalgaon, Maharashtra, India 60 J10
Jalgaon, Maharashtra, India 60 J9
Jalhay, Belgium 17 G7
Jalībah, Iraq 64 D5
Jalingo, Nigeria 79 D7
Jalisco □, Mexico 114 C4
Jalkot, Pakistan 63 B5
Jallas →, Spain 30 C1
Jalna, India 60 K9
Jalón →, Spain 28 D3
Jalpa, Mexico 114 C4
Jalpaiguri, India 61 F16
Jaluit I., Pac. Oc. 92 G8
Jalūlā, Iraq 64 C5
Jamaari, Nigeria 79 C6
Jamaica ■, W. Indies 116 C4
Jamalpur, Bangla. 61 G16
Jamalpur, India 63 G12
Jamalpurganj, India 63 H13
Jamanxim →, Brazil 125 A6
Jamari, Brazil 125 B5
Jamari →, Brazil 125 B5

Jambe, Indonesia 57 E8
Jambes, Belgium 17 H5
Jambi, Indonesia 56 E2
Jambi □, Indonesia 56 E2
Jambusar, India 62 H5
James →, U.S.A. 108 D6
James B., Canada 97 C11
James Ras., Australia 88 D5
James Ross I., Antarctica 5 C18
Jamestown, Australia 91 E2
Jamestown, S. Africa 84 E4
Jamestown, Ky., U.S.A. 104 G3
Jamestown, N. Dak., U.S.A. 108 B5
Jamestown, N.Y., U.S.A. 106 D5
Jamestown, Pa., U.S.A. 106 E4
Jamestown, Tenn., U.S.A. 105 G3
Jamīlābād, Iran 65 C6
Jamiltepec, Mexico 115 D5
Jamkhandi, India 60 L9
Jammerbugt, Denmark 11 G3
Jammu, India 62 C6
Jammu & Kashmir □, India 63 B7
Jamnagar, India 62 H4
Jampur, Pakistan 62 E4
Jamrud, Pakistan 62 C4
Jamshedpur, India 63 H12
Jamtara, India 63 H12
Jämtlands län □, Sweden 10 B7
Jan Kempdorp, S. Africa 84 D3
Jan L., Canada 101 C8
Jan Mayen, Arctic 4 B7
Janaúba, Brazil 123 E3
Janaucu, I., Brazil 122 A1
Jand, Pakistan 62 C5
Janda, L. de la, Spain 31 J5
Jandaia, Brazil 123 E1
Jandaq, Iran 65 C7
Jandia, Canary Is. 36 F5
Jandia, Pta. de, Canary Is. 36 F5
Jandiatuba →, Brazil 120 D4
Jandola, Pakistan 62 C4
Jandowae, Australia 91 D5
Jandrain-Jandrenouilles, Belgium 17 G5
Jándula →, Spain 31 G6
Janesville, U.S.A. 108 D10
Janga, Ghana 79 C4
Jango, Brazil 125 E6
Janīn, Jordan 69 C4
Janjina, Croatia 21 N7
Janos, Mexico 114 A3
Jánosháza, Hungary 21 H7
Janów Podlaski, Poland 20 C13
Januária, Brazil 123 E3
Janub Dârfûr □, Sudan 77 E2
Janub Kordofân □, Sudan 77 E3
Janubio, Canary Is. 36 F6
Janville, France 25 D8
Janzé, France 24 E5
Jaora, India 62 H6
Japan ■, Asia 49 G8
Japan, Sea of, Asia 48 E7
Japan Trench, Pac. Oc. 92 D6
Japen = Yapen, Indonesia 57 E9
Japurá →, Brazil 120 D4
Jaque, Panama 120 B2
Jarābulus, Syria 64 B3
Jaraguá, Brazil 123 E2
Jaraguari, Brazil 125 E7
Jaraicejo, Spain 31 F5
Jaraiz, Spain 30 E5
Jarama →, Spain 28 E1
Jaramillo, Argentina 128 C3
Jarandilla, Spain 30 E5
Jaranwala, Pakistan 62 D5
Jarash, Jordan 69 C4
Jarauçu →, Brazil 121 D7
Jardim, Brazil 126 A4
Jardín →, Spain 29 G2
Jardines de la Reina, Is., Cuba 116 B4
Jargalang, China 51 C12
Jargalant = Hovd, Mongolia 54 B4
Jargeau, France 25 E9
Jari →, Brazil 121 D7
Jarmen, Germany 18 B9
Jarnac, France 26 C3
Jarny, France 25 C12
Jarocin, Poland 20 D7
Jarosław, Poland 20 E12
Järpås, Sweden 11 F6
Järpen, Sweden 10 A7
Jarrahdale, Australia 89 F2
Jarres, Plaine des, Laos 58 C4
Jarso, Ethiopia 77 F4
Jartai, China 50 E3
Jaru, Brazil 125 C5
Jaru →, Brazil 125 C5
Jarud Qi, China 51 B11
Jarvis, Canada 106 D4
Jarvis I., Pac. Oc. 93 H12
Jarwa, India 63 F10
Jaša Tomić, Serbia 21 K10
Jāsimīyah, Iraq 64 C5
Jasin, Malaysia 59 L4
Jāsk, Iran 65 E8
Jasło, Poland 20 F11
Jason, Is., Falk. Is. 128 D4
Jasper, Alta., Canada 100 C5
Jasper, Ont., Canada 107 B9
Jasper, Ala., U.S.A. 105 J2

Jasper, Fla., U.S.A. 105 K4
Jasper, Minn., U.S.A. 108 D6
Jasper, Tex., U.S.A. 109 K8
Jasper Nat. Park, Canada 100 C5
Jassy = Iași, Romania 38 B10
Jastrebarsko, Croatia 33 C12
Jastrzębie Zdrój, Poland 20 F8
Jászárokszállás, Hungary 21 H10
Jászberény, Hungary 21 H9
Jászladány, Hungary 21 H10
Jataí, Brazil 123 E1
Jatapu →, Brazil 121 D6
Jati, Pakistan 62 G3
Jatibarang, Indonesia 57 G13
Jatinegara, Indonesia 57 G12
Játiva, Spain 29 G4
Jatobal, Brazil 122 B2
Jaú, Brazil 127 A6
Jaú →, Brazil 121 D5
Jauaperí →, Brazil 121 D5
Jauche, Belgium 17 G5
Jauja, Peru 124 C2
Jaunjelgava, Latvia 40 C4
Jaunpur, India 63 G10
Jauru →, Brazil 125 D6
Java = Jawa, Indonesia 57 G14
Java Sea, Indonesia 56 E3
Java Trench, Ind. Oc. 92 H2
Jávea, Spain 29 G5
Javhlant = Ulyasutay, Mongolia 54 B4
Javier, I., Chile 128 C2
Javron, France 24 D6
Jawa, Indonesia 57 G14
Jawor, Poland 20 D6
Jaworzno, Poland 20 E9
Jay, U.S.A. 109 G7
Jaya, Puncak, Indonesia 57 E9
Jayanca, Peru 124 B2
Jayanti, India 61 F16
Jayapura, Indonesia 57 E10
Jayawijaya, Pegunungan, Indonesia 57 E9
Jaynagar, India 61 F15
Jayrūd, Syria 64 C3
Jayton, U.S.A. 109 J4
Jazīreh-ye Shīf, Iran 65 D6
Jazminal, Mexico 114 C4
Jazzīn, Lebanon 69 B4
Jean, U.S.A. 113 K11
Jean Marie River, Canada 100 A4
Jean Rabel, Haiti 117 C5
Jeanerette, U.S.A. 109 L9
Jeanette, Ostrov, Russia 45 B16
Jeannette, U.S.A. 106 F5
Jebba, Morocco 74 A4
Jebba, Nigeria 79 D5
Jebel, Bahr el →, Sudan 77 F3
Jebel Qerri, Sudan 77 D3
Jeberos, Peru 124 B2
Jedburgh, U.K. 14 F6
Jedda = Jiddah, Si. Arabia 68 C2
Jędrzejów, Poland 20 E10
Jedway, Canada 100 C2
Jeetzel →, Germany 18 B7
Jefferson, Iowa, U.S.A. 108 D7
Jefferson, Ohio, U.S.A. 106 E4
Jefferson, Tex., U.S.A. 109 J7
Jefferson, Wis., U.S.A. 108 D10
Jefferson, Mt., Nev., U.S.A. 110 G5
Jefferson, Mt., Oreg., U.S.A. 110 D3
Jefferson City, Mo., U.S.A. 108 F8
Jefferson City, Tenn., U.S.A. 105 G4
Jeffersonville, U.S.A. 104 F3
Jega, Nigeria 79 C5
Jēkabpils, Latvia 40 C4
Jelenia Góra, Poland 20 E5
Jelgava, Latvia 9 H17
Jelli, Sudan 77 F3
Jellicoe, Canada 98 C2
Jemaja, Indonesia 56 D3
Jemaluang, Malaysia 59 L4
Jemappes, Belgium 17 H3
Jember, Indonesia 57 H15
Jembongan, Malaysia 56 C5
Jemeppe, Belgium 17 G7
Jemnice, Czech. 20 F5
Jena, Germany 18 E7
Jena, U.S.A. 109 K8
Jendouba, Tunisia 75 A6
Jenkins, U.S.A. 104 G4
Jenner, U.S.A. 112 G3
Jennings, U.S.A. 109 K8
Jennings →, Canada 100 B2
Jeparit, Australia 91 F3
Jequié, Brazil 123 D3
Jequitaí, Brazil 123 E3
Jequitinhonha, Brazil 123 E3
Jequitinhonha →, Brazil 123 E4
Jerada, Morocco 75 B4
Jerantut, Malaysia 59 L4
Jérémie, Haiti 117 C5
Jeremoabo, Brazil 122 D4
Jerez, Punta, Mexico 115 C5
Jerez de García Salinas, Mexico 114 C4
Jerez de la Frontera, Spain 31 J4
Jerez de los Caballeros, Spain 31 G4
Jericho = Arīḥā, Syria 64 C3
Jericho = El Arīḥā, Jordan 69 D4
Jericho, Australia 90 C4

Jerichow, Germany 18 C8
Jerilderie, Australia 91 F4
Jermyn, U.S.A. 107 E9
Jerome, U.S.A. 111 J8
Jersey, Chan. Is. 13 H5
Jersey City, U.S.A. 107 F10
Jersey Shore, U.S.A. 106 E7
Jerseyville, U.S.A. 108 F9
Jerusalem, Israel 69 D4
Jervis B., Australia 91 F5
Jesenice, Slovenia 33 B11
Jesenké, Slovak Rep. 21 G10
Jesselton = Kota Kinabalu, Malaysia 56 C5
Jessnitz, Germany 18 D8
Jessore, Bangla. 61 H16
Jesup, U.S.A. 105 K5
Jesús, Peru 124 B2
Jesús Carranza, Mexico 115 D5
Jesús María, Argentina 126 C3
Jetmore, U.S.A. 109 F5
Jetpur, India 62 J4
Jette, Belgium 17 G4
Jevnaker, Norway 10 D4
Jewett, Ohio, U.S.A. 106 F3
Jewett, Tex., U.S.A. 109 K6
Jewett City, U.S.A. 107 E13
Jeypore, India 61 K13
Jeziorany, Poland 20 B10
Jhajjar, India 62 E7
Jhal Jhao, Pakistan 60 F4
Jhalawar, India 62 G7
Jhang Maghiana, Pakistan 62 D5
Jhansi, India 63 G8
Jharia, India 63 H12
Jharsaguda, India 61 J14
Jhelum, Pakistan 62 C5
Jhelum →, Pakistan 62 D5
Jhunjhunu, India 62 E6
Ji Xian, Hebei, China 50 F8
Ji Xian, Henan, China 50 G8
Ji Xian, Shanxi, China 50 F6
Jia Xian, Henan, China 50 H7
Jia Xian, Shaanxi, China 50 E6
Jiading, China 53 B13
Jiahe, China 53 E9
Jiali, Taiwan 53 F13
Jialing Jiang →, China 52 C6
Jiamusi, China 54 B8
Ji'an, Jiangxi, China 53 D10
Ji'an, Jilin, China 51 D14
Jianchang, China 51 D11
Jianchangying, China 51 D10
Jianchuan, China 52 D2
Jiande, China 53 C12
Jiangbei, China 52 C6
Jiangcheng, China 52 F3
Jiangdi, China 52 D4
Jiange, China 52 A5
Jiangjin, China 52 C6
Jiangkou, China 52 D7
Jiangle, China 53 D11
Jiangling, China 53 B9
Jiangmen, China 53 F9
Jiangshan, China 53 C12
Jiangsu □, China 51 H10
Jiangxi □, China 53 D10
Jiangyin, China 53 B13
Jiangyong, China 53 E8
Jiangyou, China 52 B5
Jianhe, China 52 D7
Jianli, China 53 C9
Jianning, China 53 D11
Jian'ou, China 53 D12
Jianshi, China 52 B7
Jianshui, China 52 F4
Jianyang, Fujian, China 53 D12
Jianyang, Sichuan, China 52 B5
Jiao Xian, China 51 F11
Jiaohe, Hebei, China 50 E9
Jiaohe, Jilin, China 51 C14
Jiaoling, China 53 E11
Jiaozhou Wan, China 51 F11
Jiaozuo, China 50 G7
Jiashan, China 53 A11
Jiawang, China 51 G9
Jiaxiang, China 50 G9
Jiaxing, China 53 B13
Jiayi, Taiwan 53 F13
Jiayu, China 53 C9
Jibão, Serra do, Brazil 123 D3
Jibiya, Nigeria 79 C6
Jibou, Romania 38 B6
Jibuti = Djibouti ■, Africa 68 E3
Jicarón, I., Panama 116 E3
Jičín, Czech. 20 E5
Jiddah, Si. Arabia 68 C2
Jido, India 61 E19
Jieshou, China 50 H8
Jiexiu, China 50 F6
Jieyang, China 53 F11
Jigawa □, Nigeria 79 C6
Jiggalong, Australia 88 D3
Jihlava, Czech. 20 F5
Jihlava →, Czech. 20 G6
Jijel, Algeria 75 A6
Jijiga, Ethiopia 68 F3
Jijona, Spain 29 G4
Jikamshi, Nigeria 79 C6
Jilin, China 51 C14
Jilin □, China 51 C13
Jiloca →, Spain 28 D3
Jilong, Taiwan 53 E13
Jima, Ethiopia 77 F4
Jimbolia, Romania 38 D3

Jimena de la Frontera, Spain 31 J5
Jiménez, Mexico 114 B4
Jimo, China 51 F11
Jin Jiang →, China 53 C10
Jin Xian, Hebei, China 50 E8
Jin Xian, Liaoning, China 51 E11
Jinan, China 50 F9
Jincheng, China 50 G7
Jinchuan, China 52 B4
Jind, India 62 E7
Jindabyne, Australia 91 F4
Jindrichuv Hradeç, Czech. 20 F5
Jing He →, China 50 G5
Jing Shan, China 53 B8
Jing Xian, Anhui, China 53 B12
Jing Xian, Hunan, China 52 D7
Jing'an, China 53 C10
Jingbian, China 50 F5
Jingchuan, China 50 G4
Jingde, China 53 B12
Jingdezhen, China 53 C11
Jingdong, China 52 E3
Jinggu, China 52 F3
Jinghai, China 50 E9
Jinghong, China 52 F3
Jingjiang, China 53 A13
Jingle, China 50 E6
Jingmen, China 53 B9
Jingning, China 50 G3
Jingpo Hu, China 51 C15
Jingshan, China 53 B9
Jingtai, China 50 F3
Jingxi, China 52 F6
Jingxing, China 50 E8
Jingyang, China 50 G5
Jingyu, China 51 C14
Jingyuan, China 50 F3
Jingziguan, China 50 H6
Jinhua, China 53 C12
Jining, Nei Mongol Zizhiqu, China 50 D7
Jining, Shandong, China 50 G9
Jinja, Uganda 82 B3
Jinjang, Malaysia 59 L3
Jinji, China 50 F4
Jinjiang, Fujian, China 53 E12
Jinjiang, Yunnan, China 52 D3
Jinjie, China 52 F6
Jinjini, Ghana 78 D4
Jinkou, China 53 B10
Jinmen Dao, China 53 E12
Jinning, China 52 E4
Jinotega, Nic. 116 D2
Jinotepe, Nic. 116 D2
Jinping, Guizhou, China 52 D7
Jinping, Yunnan, China 52 F5
Jinsha, China 52 D6
Jinsha Jiang →, China 52 C5
Jinshan, China 53 B13
Jinshi, China 53 C8
Jintan, China 53 B12
Jinxi, Jiangxi, China 53 D11
Jinxi, Liaoning, China 51 D11
Jinxian, China 53 C11
Jinxiang, China 50 G9
Jinyun, China 53 C13
Jinzhai, China 53 B10
Jinzhou, China 51 D11
Jiparaná →, Brazil 125 B5
Jipijapa, Ecuador 120 D1
Jiquilpan, Mexico 114 D4
Jishan, China 50 G6
Jishou, China 52 C7
Jishui, China 53 D10
Jisr ash Shughūr, Syria 64 C3
Jitarning, Australia 89 F2
Jitra, Malaysia 59 J3
Jiu →, Romania 38 F6
Jiudengkou, China 50 E5
Jiujiang, Guangdong, China 53 F9
Jiujiang, Jiangxi, China 53 C10
Jiuling Shan, China 52 C3
Jiulong, China 54 C4
Jiuquan, China 51 B13
Jiutai, China 50 H8
Jiuxiangcheng, China 50 H8
Jiuxincheng, China 50 E8
Jiuyuhang, China 53 B12
Jixi, Anhui, China 53 B12
Jixi, Heilongjiang, China 51 B16
Jiyang, China 50 F9
Jīzān, Si. Arabia 68 D3
Jize, China 50 F8
Jizera →, Czech. 20 E4
Jizō-Zaki, Japan 49 G6
Joaçaba, Brazil 127 B5
Joaíma, Brazil 123 E3
João, Brazil 122 B1
João Amaro, Brazil 123 D3
João Câmara, Brazil 122 C4
João Pessoa, Brazil 122 C5
João Pinheiro, Brazil 123 E2
Joaquim Távora, Brazil 123 F2
Joaquín V. González, Argentina 126 B3
Jobourg, Nez de, France 24 C5
Jódar, Spain 29 H1
Jodhpur, India 62 F5
Jœuf, France 25 C13
Jofane, Mozam. 85 C5
Joggins, Canada 99 C7
Jogjakarta = Yogyakarta, Indonesia 57 G14

Johannesburg, *S. Africa* .. 85 D4
Johannesburg, *U.S.A.* 113 K9
John Day, *U.S.A.* 110 D4
John Day →, *U.S.A.* 110 D3
John H. Kerr Reservoir,
  U.S.A. 105 G6
John o' Groats, *U.K.* 14 C5
Johnnie, *U.S.A.* 113 J10
John's Ra., *Australia* 90 C1
Johnson, *U.S.A.* 109 G4
Johnson City, *N.Y., U.S.A.* 107 D9
Johnson City, *Tenn.,*
  U.S.A. 105 G4
Johnson City, *Tex., U.S.A.* 109 K5
Johnsonburg, *U.S.A.* 106 E6
Johnsondale, *U.S.A.* 113 K8
Johnson's Crossing, *Canada* 100 A2
Johnston, L., *Australia* ... 89 F3
Johnston Falls =
  Mambilima Falls, *Zambia* 83 E2
Johnston I., *Pac. Oc.* 93 F11
Johnstone Str., *Canada* ... 100 C3
Johnstown, *N.Y., U.S.A.* .. 107 C10
Johnstown, *Pa., U.S.A.* ... 106 F6
Johor Baharu, *Malaysia* .. 59 M4
Joigny, *France* 25 E10
Joinvile, *Brazil* 127 B6
Joinville, *France* 25 D12
Joinville I., *Antarctica* ... 5 C18
Jojutla, *Mexico* 115 D5
Jokkmokk, *Sweden* 8 C15
Jökulså á Bru →, *Iceland* 8 D6
Jökulså á Fjöllum →,
  Iceland 8 C5
Jolfã, *Āzarbāyjān-e Sharqī,*
  Iran 64 B5
Jolfã, *Eşfahan, Iran* 65 C6
Joliet, *U.S.A.* 104 E1
Joliette, *Canada* 98 C5
Jolo, *Phil.* 55 J4
Jolon, *U.S.A.* 112 K5
Jomalig, *Phil.* 55 D5
Jombang, *Indonesia* 57 G15
Jomda, *China* 52 B2
Jome, *Indonesia* 57 E7
Jomfruland, *Norway* 11 F3
Jönåker, *Sweden* 11 F10
Jonava, *Lithuania* 40 D4
Jones Sound, *Canada* 4 B3
Jonesboro, *Ark., U.S.A.* . 109 H9
Jonesboro, *Ill., U.S.A.* .. 109 G10
Jonesboro, *La., U.S.A.* .. 109 J8
Jonesport, *U.S.A.* 99 D6
Jonglei, *Sudan* 77 F3
Jonglei □, *Sudan* 77 F3
Joniškis, *Lithuania* 40 C3
Jönköping, *Sweden* 9 H13
Jönköpings län □, *Sweden* 9 H13
Jonquière, *Canada* 99 C5
Jonsberg, *Sweden* 11 F10
Jonsered, *Sweden* 11 G6
Jonzac, *France* 26 C3
Joplin, *U.S.A.* 109 G7
Jordan, *U.S.A.* 110 C10
Jordan ■, *Asia* 69 E5
Jordan →, *Asia* 69 D4
Jordan Valley, *U.S.A.* 110 E5
Jordânia, *Brazil* 123 E3
Jorge, C., *Chile* 128 D1
Jorhat, *India* 61 F19
Jörn, *Sweden* 8 D16
Jorong, *Indonesia* 56 E4
Jorquera →, *Chile* 126 B2
Jos, *Nigeria* 79 D6
José Batlle y Ordóñez,
  Uruguay 127 C4
José de San Martín,
  Argentina 128 B2
Joseph, *U.S.A.* 110 D5
Joseph, L., *Nfld., Canada* 99 B6
Joseph, L., *Ont., Canada* . 106 A5
Joseph Bonaparte G.,
  Australia 88 B4
Joseph City, *U.S.A.* 111 J8
Joshua Tree, *U.S.A.* 113 L10
Joshua Tree National
  Monument, *U.S.A.* 113 M10
Josselin, *France* 24 E4
Jostedal, *Norway* 9 F9
Jotunheimen, *Norway* 10 C2
Jourdanton, *U.S.A.* 109 L5
Joure, *Neths.* 16 C7
Joussard, *Canada* 100 B5
Jovellanos, *Cuba* 116 B3
Joyeuse, *France* 27 D8
Józefów, *Poland* 20 C11
Ju Xian, *China* 51 F10
Juan Aldama, *Mexico* 114 C4
Juan Bautista Alberdi,
  Argentina 126 C3
Juan de Fuca Str., *Canada* 112 B2
Juan de Nova, *Ind. Oc.* .. 85 B7
Juan Fernández, Arch. de,
  Pac. Oc. 93 L20
Juan José Castelli,
  Argentina 126 B3
Juan L. Lacaze, *Uruguay* . 126 C4
Juanjuí, *Peru* 124 B2
Juárez, *Argentina* 126 D4
Juárez, *Mexico* 113 N11
Juárez, Sierra de, *Mexico* 114 A1
Juatinga, Ponta de, *Brazil* 123 F3
Jubà →, *Brazil* 122 C3
Juàzeiro, *Brazil* 122 C4
Juàzeiro do Norte, *Brazil* . 122 C4
Jubayl, *Lebanon* 69 A4

Jubbah, *Si. Arabia* 64 D4
Jubbulpore = Jabalpur,
  India 63 H8
Jübek, *Germany* 18 A5
Jubga, *Russia* 43 D8
Jubilee L., *Australia* 89 E4
Juby, C., *Morocco* 72 C2
Júcar →, *Spain* 29 F4
Júcaro, *Cuba* 116 B4
Juchitán, *Mexico* 115 D5
Judaea = Har Yehuda,
  Israel 69 D3
Judenburg, *Austria* 21 H4
Judith →, *U.S.A.* 110 C9
Judith, Pt., *U.S.A.* 107 E13
Judith Gap, *U.S.A.* 110 C9
Jufari →, *Brazil* 121 D5
Jugoslavia = Yugoslavia ■,
  Europe 21 M10
Juigalpa, *Nic.* 116 D2
Juillac, *France* 26 C5
Juist, *Germany* 18 B2
Juiz de Fora, *Brazil* 123 F3
Jujuy, *Argentina* 126 A2
Jujuy □, *Argentina* 126 A2
Julesburg, *U.S.A.* 108 E3
Juli, *Peru* 124 D4
Julia Cr. →, *Australia* 90 C3
Julia Creek, *Australia* 90 C3
Juliaca, *Peru* 124 D3
Julian, *U.S.A.* 113 M10
Julian Alps = Julijske
  Alpe, *Slovenia* 33 B11
Julianakanaal, *Neths.* 17 F7
Julianatop, *Surinam* 121 C6
Julianehåb, *Greenland* ... 4 C5
Jülich, *Germany* 18 E2
Julierpass, *Switz.* 23 D9
Julijske Alpe, *Slovenia* ... 33 B11
Julimes, *Mexico* 114 B3
Jullundur, *India* 62 D6
Julu, *China* 50 F8
Jumbo, *Zimbabwe* 83 F3
Jumbo Pk., *U.S.A.* 113 J12
Jumentos Cays, *Bahamas* . 117 B4
Jumet, *Belgium* 17 H4
Jumilla, *Spain* 29 G3
Jumla, *Nepal* 63 E10
Jumna = Yamuna →,
  India 63 G9
Junagadh, *India* 62 J4
Junction, *Tex., U.S.A.* ... 109 K5
Junction, *Utah, U.S.A.* ... 111 G7
Junction B., *Australia* 90 A1
Junction City, *Kans.,*
  U.S.A. 108 F6
Junction City, *Oreg.,*
  U.S.A. 110 D2
Junction Pt., *Australia* ... 90 A1
Jundah, *Australia* 90 C3
Jundiaí, *Brazil* 127 A6
Juneau, *U.S.A.* 96 C6
Junee, *Australia* 91 E4
Jungfrau, *Switz.* 22 C5
Junggar Pendi, *China* 54 B3
Junglinster, *Lux.* 17 J8
Jungshahi, *Pakistan* 62 G2
Juniata →, *U.S.A.* 106 F7
Junín, *Argentina* 126 C3
Junín, *Peru* 124 C2
Junín □, *Peru* 124 C3
Junín de los Andes,
  Argentina 128 A2
Jūniyah, *Lebanon* 69 B4
Juntura, *U.S.A.* 110 E4
Juparanã, L., *Brazil* 123 E3
Jupiter →, *Canada* 99 C7
Juquiá, *Brazil* 123 F2
Jur, Nahr el →, *Sudan* ... 77 F2
Jura = Jura, Mts. du,
  Europe 27 B10
Jura = Schwäbische Alb,
  Germany 19 G5
Jura, *Europe* 25 F13
Jura, *U.K.* 14 F3
Jura □, *France* 25 F12
Jura, Mts. du, *Europe* 27 B10
Jura, Sd. of, *U.K.* 14 F3
Jura Suisse, *Switz.* 22 B3
Jurado, *Colombia* 120 B2
Jurong, *China* 53 B12
Juruá →, *Brazil* 120 D4
Juruena, *Brazil* 125 C6
Juruena →, *Brazil* 125 B6
Juruti, *Brazil* 121 D6
Jussey, *France* 25 E12
Justo Daract, *Argentina* .. 126 C2
Jutaí, *Brazil* 124 B4
Jutaí →, *Brazil* 120 D4
Juticalpa, *Honduras* 116 D2
Jutland = Jylland,
  Denmark 11 H3
Jutphaas, *Neths.* 16 D6
Juventud, I. de la, *Cuba* . 116 B3
Juvigny-sous-Andaine,
  France 24 D6
Juvisy-sur-Orge, *France* .. 25 D9
Juwain, *Afghan.* 60 D2
Jūy Zar, *Iran* 64 C5
Juye, *China* 50 G9
Juzennecourt, *France* 25 D11
Jylland, *Denmark* 11 H3
Jyväskylä, *Finland* 8 E18

K

K2, Mt., *Pakistan* 63 B7
Kaap Plateau, *S. Africa* .. 84 D3
Kaapkruis, *Namibia* 84 C1
Kaapstad = Cape Town,
  S. Africa 84 E2
Kaatsheuvel, *Neths.* 17 E6
Kabaena, *Indonesia* 57 F6
Kabala, *S. Leone* 78 D2
Kabale, *Uganda* 82 C3
Kabalo, *Zaïre* 82 D2
Kabambare, *Zaïre* 82 C2
Kabango, *Zaïre* 83 D2
Kabanjahe, *Indonesia* 56 D1
Kabankalan, *Phil.* 55 G5
Kabara, *Mali* 78 B4
Kabardinka, *Russia* 42 D7
Kabardino-Balkar
  Republic □, *Russia* 43 E10
Kabare, *Indonesia* 57 E8
Kabarega Falls, *Uganda* . 82 B3
Kabasalan, *Phil.* 55 H5
Kabin Buri, *Thailand* 58 F3
Kabinakagami L., *Canada* 98 C3
Kabīr, Zab al →, *Iraq* 64 C4
Kabkabīyah, *Sudan* 73 F9
Kabna, *Sudan* 76 D3
Kabompo, *Zambia* 83 E1
Kabompo →, *Zambia* 81 G4
Kabondo, *Zaïre* 83 D2
Kabongo, *Zaïre* 82 D2
Kabou, *Togo* 79 D5
Kaboudia, Rass, *Tunisia* . 75 A7
Kabra, *Australia* 90 C5
Kabūd Gonbad, *Iran* 65 B8
Kabugao, *Phil.* 55 B4
Kābul, *Afghan.* 62 B3
Kābul □, *Afghan.* 60 B6
Kabul →, *Pakistan* 62 C5
Kabunga, *Zaïre* 82 C2
Kaburuang, *Indonesia* 57 D7
Kabushiya, *Sudan* 77 D3
Kabwe, *Zambia* 83 E2
Kačanik, *Serbia* 21 N11
Kachanovo, *Russia* 40 C5
Kachchh, Gulf of, *India* .. 62 H3
Kachchh, Rann of, *India* . 62 G4
Kachebera, *Zambia* 83 E3
Kachin □, *Burma* 61 F20
Kachira, L., *Uganda* 82 C3
Kachiry, *Kazakhstan* 44 D8
Kachisi, *Ethiopia* 77 F4
Kachot, *Cambodia* 59 G4
Kackar, *Turkey* 43 F9
Kadan Kyun, *Burma* 56 B1
Kadanai →, *Afghan.* 62 D1
Kadarkút, *Hungary* 21 J7
Kade, *Ghana* 79 D4
Kadi, *India* 62 H5
Kadina, *Australia* 91 E2
Kadınhanı, *Turkey* 66 D5
Kadirli, *Turkey* 66 E7
Kadiyevka, *Ukraine* 43 B8
Kadoka, *U.S.A.* 108 D4
Kadom, *Russia* 41 D13
Kadoma, *Zimbabwe* 83 F2
Kâdugli, *Sudan* 77 E2
Kaduna, *Nigeria* 79 C6
Kaduna □, *Nigeria* 79 C6
Kaédi, *Mauritania* 78 B2
Kaélé, *Cameroon* 79 C7
Kaeng Khoï, *Thailand* 58 E3
Kaesŏng, *N. Korea* 51 F14
Kāf, *Si. Arabia* 64 D3
Kafakumba, *Zaïre* 80 F4
Kafan, *Armenia* 67 D12
Kafanchan, *Nigeria* 79 D6
Kafareti, *Nigeria* 79 C7
Kaffrine, *Senegal* 78 C1
Kafia Kingi, *Sudan* 73 G9
Kafinda, *Zambia* 83 E3
Kafirévs, Ákra, *Greece* ... 39 L7
Kafr el Dauwâr, *Egypt* ... 76 H7
Kafr el Sheikh, *Egypt* 76 H7
Kafue, *Zambia* 83 F2
Kafue →, *Zambia* 81 H5
Kafue Flats, *Zambia* 83 F2
Kafue Nat. Park, *Zambia* . 83 F2
Kafulwe, *Zambia* 83 D2
Kaga, *Japan* 62 B4
Kaga Bandoro, *C.A.R.* ... 73 G8
Kagan, *Uzbekistan* 44 F7
Kagawa □, *Japan* 49 G6
Kagera □, *Tanzania* 82 C3
Kagera →, *Uganda* 82 C3
Kağızman, *Turkey* 67 C10
Kagoshima, *Japan* 49 J5
Kagoshima □, *Japan* 49 J5
Kagul, *Moldavia* 42 D3
Kahak, *Iran* 65 B6
Kahama, *Tanzania* 82 C3
Kahama □, *Tanzania* 82 C3
Kahang, *Malaysia* 59 L4
Kahayan →, *Indonesia* ... 56 E4
Kahe, *Tanzania* 82 C4
Kahemba, *Zaïre* 80 F3
Kahil, Djebel bou, *Algeria* 75 B5
Kahniah →, *Canada* 100 B4
Kahnūj, *Iran* 65 E8
Kahoka, *U.S.A.* 108 E9
Kahoolawe, *U.S.A.* 102 H16
Kahramanmaraş, *Turkey* . 66 E7

Kahramanmaraş □, *Turkey* 66 E7
Kâhta, *Turkey* 67 E8
Kahuta, *Pakistan* 62 C5
Kai, Kepulauan, *Indonesia* 57 F8
Kai Besar, *Indonesia* 57 F8
Kai Is. = Kai, Kepulauan,
  Indonesia 57 F8
Kai-Ketil, *Indonesia* 57 F8
Kai Xian, *China* 52 B7
Kaiama, *Nigeria* 79 D5
Kaiapoi, *N.Z.* 87 K4
Kaieteur Falls, *Guyana* .. 121 B6
Kaifeng, *China* 50 G8
Kaihua, *China* 53 C12
Kaikohe, *N.Z.* 87 F4
Kaikoura, *N.Z.* 87 K4
Kaikoura Ra., *N.Z.* 87 J4
Kailahun, *S. Leone* 78 D2
Kaili, *China* 52 D6
Kailu, *China* 51 C11
Kailua Kona, *U.S.A.* 102 J17
Kaimana, *Indonesia* 57 E8
Kaimanawa Mts., *N.Z.* ... 87 H5
Kaimganj, *India* 63 F8
Kaimur Hills, *India* 63 G9
Kaingaroa Forest, *N.Z.* ... 87 H6
Kainji Res., *Nigeria* 79 C5
Kaipara Harbour, *N.Z.* ... 87 G5
Kaiping, *China* 53 F9
Kaipokok B., *Canada* 99 B8
Kairana, *India* 62 E7
Kaironi, *Indonesia* 57 E8
Kairouan, *Tunisia* 75 A7
Kaiserslautern, *Germany* . 19 F3
Kaitaia, *N.Z.* 87 F4
Kaitangata, *N.Z.* 87 M2
Kaithal, *India* 62 E7
Kaitu →, *Pakistan* 62 C4
Kaiwi Channel, *U.S.A.* ... 102 H16
Kaiyang, *China* 52 D6
Kaiyuan, Liaoning, *China* 51 C13
Kaiyuan, Yunnan, *China* . 52 F4
Kajaani, *Finland* 8 D19
Kajabbi, *Australia* 90 B3
Kajana = Kajaani, *Finland* 8 D19
Kajang, *Malaysia* 59 L3
Kajiado, *Kenya* 82 C4
Kajiado □, *Kenya* 82 C4
Kajo Kaji, *Sudan* 77 G3
Kaka, *Sudan* 77 E3
Kakabeka Falls, *Canada* . 98 C2
Kakamas, *S. Africa* 84 D3
Kakamega, *Kenya* 82 B3
Kakamega □, *Kenya* 82 B3
Kakanj, *Bos.-H.* 21 L8
Kakanui Mts., *N.Z.* 87 L3
Kake, *Japan* 49 G6
Kakegawa, *Japan* 49 G9
Kakeroma-Jima, *Japan* ... 49 K4
Kakhib, *Russia* 43 E12
Kakhovka, *Ukraine* 42 C5
Kakhovskoye Vdkhr.,
  Ukraine 42 C6
Kakinada, *India* 61 L13
Kakisa →, *Canada* 100 A5
Kakisa L., *Canada* 100 A5
Kakogawa, *Japan* 49 G7
Kakwa →, *Canada* 100 C5
Kāl Gūsheh, *Iran* 65 D8
Kal Safīd, *Iran* 64 C5
Kala, *Nigeria* 79 C7
Kala, *Sri Lanka* 60 R11
Kalaa-Kebira, *Tunisia* 75 A7
Kalabagh, *Pakistan* 62 C4
Kalabahi, *Indonesia* 57 F6
Kalabáka, *Greece* 39 K4
Kalabo, *Zambia* 81 G4
Kalach, *Russia* 41 F12
Kalach na Donu, *Russia* . 43 B10
Kaladan →, *Burma* 61 J18
Kaladar, *Canada* 106 B7
Kalahari, *Africa* 84 C3
Kalahari Gemsbok Nat.
  Park, *S. Africa* 84 D3
Kalak, *Iran* 65 E8
Kalakamati, *Botswana* ... 85 C4
Kalakan, *Russia* 45 D12
Kalakh, *Syria* 64 C3
K'alak'unlun Shank'ou,
  Pakistan 63 B7
Kalam, *Pakistan* 63 B5
Kalama, *U.S.A.* 112 D4
Kalama, *Zaïre* 82 C2
Kalamariá, *Greece* 39 J5
Kalamata, *Greece* 39 M5
Kalamazoo, *U.S.A.* 104 D3
Kalamazoo →, *U.S.A.* ... 104 D2
Kalambo Falls, *Tanzania* . 83 D3
Kálamos, *Greece* 39 L3
Kalannie, *Australia* 89 F2
Kalāntarī, *Iran* 65 C7
Kalao, *Indonesia* 57 F6
Kalaotoa, *Indonesia* 57 F6
Kälarne, *Sweden* 10 B10
Kalárovo, *Slovak Rep.* ... 21 H7
Kalasin, *Thailand* 58 D4
Kalat, *Pakistan* 60 E5
Kalāteh, *Iran* 65 B7
Kalāteh-ye-Ganj, *Iran* 65 E8
Kálathos, *Greece* 39 N11
Kalaus →, *Russia* 43 D11
Kalávrita, *Greece* 39 L5
Kalbarri, *Australia* 89 E1

Kalehe, *Zaïre* 82 C2
Kalema, *Tanzania* 82 C3
Kalemie, *Zaïre* 82 D2
Kalety, *Poland* 20 E8
Kalewa, *Burma* 61 H19
Kálfafellsstaður, *Iceland* .. 8 D6
Kalgan = Zhangjiakou,
  China 50 D8
Kalgoorlie-Boulder,
  Australia 89 F3
Kaliakra, Nos, *Bulgaria* .. 38 F11
Kalianda, *Indonesia* 56 F3
Kaliganj, *Bangla.* 63 H13
Kalibo, *Phil.* 55 F5
Kalima, *Zaïre* 82 C2
Kalimantan, *Indonesia* ... 56 E4
Kalimantan Barat □,
  Indonesia 56 E4
Kalimantan Selatan □,
  Indonesia 56 E5
Kalimantan Tengah □,
  Indonesia 56 E4
Kalimantan Timur □,
  Indonesia 56 D5
Kálimnos, *Greece* 39 N10
Kalimpong, *India* 63 F13
Kalinin = Tver, *Russia* ... 41 C9
Kaliningrad, *Russia* 40 D2
Kalinkavichy =
  Kalinkovichi, *Belorussia* 40 E6
Kalinkovichi, *Belorussia* . 40 E6
Kalinovik, *Bos.-H.* 21 M8
Kalipetrovo, *Bulgaria* 38 E10
Kaliro, *Uganda* 82 B3
Kalispell, *U.S.A.* 110 B6
Kalisz, *Poland* 20 D8
Kaliua, *Tanzania* 82 D3
Kalix →, *Sweden* 8 D17
Kalka, *India* 62 D7
Kalkan, *Turkey* 66 E3
Kalkaska, *U.S.A.* 104 C3
Kalkfeld, *Namibia* 84 C2
Kalkrand, *Namibia* 84 C2
Kállandsö, *Sweden* 11 F7
Kallithéa, *Greece* 39 M6
Kallonís, Kólpos, *Greece* . 39 K9
Kallsjön, *Sweden* 8 E12
Kalmalo, *Nigeria* 79 C6
Kalmar, *Sweden* 9 H14
Kalmthout, *Belgium* 17 F4
Kalmyk Republic □, *Russia* 43 C12
Kalmykovo, *Kazakhstan* . 43 B14
Kalna, *India* 63 H13
Kalocsa, *Hungary* 21 J9
Kalokhorio, *Cyprus* 37 E12
Kaloko, *Zaïre* 82 D2
Kalol, *Gujarat, India* 62 H5
Kalol, *Gujarat, India* 62 H5
Kalolímnos, *Greece* 39 M10
Kalomo, *Zambia* 83 F2
Kalpi, *India* 63 F8
Kaltbrunn, *Switz.* 23 B8
Kaltungo, *Nigeria* 79 D7
Kalu →, *Pakistan* 62 G2
Kaluga, *Russia* 41 D10
Kalulushi, *Zambia* 83 E2
Kalundborg, *Denmark* ... 11 J5
Kalush, *Ukraine* 40 G4
Kałuszyn, *Poland* 20 C11
Kalutara, *Sri Lanka* 60 R11
Kalyazin, *Russia* 41 C10
Kama, *Zaïre* 82 C2
Kama →, *Russia* 44 D6
Kamachumu, *Tanzania* .. 82 C3
Kamaishi, *Japan* 48 E10
Kamalia, *Pakistan* 62 D5
Kamapanda, *Zambia* 83 E1
Kamaran, *Yemen* 68 D3
Kamativi, *Zimbabwe* 83 F2
Kamba, *Nigeria* 79 C5
Kambalda, *Australia* 89 F3
Kambar, *Pakistan* 62 F3
Kambia, *S. Leone* 78 D2
Kambolé, *Zambia* 83 D3
Kambos, *Cyprus* 37 D11
Kambove, *Zaïre* 83 E2
Kamchatka, P-ov., *Russia* 45 D16
Kamchatka Pen. =
  Kamchatka, P-ov., *Russia* 45 D16
Kamen, *Russia* 44 D9
Kamen Kashirskiy, *Ukraine* 40 F4
Kamen-Rybolov, *Russia* .. 48 B6
Kamenets-Podolskiy,
  Ukraine 42 B2
Kamenjak, Rt., *Croatia* ... 33 D10
Kamenka, *Russia* 41 E14
Kamenka, *Russia* 41 F11
Kamenka, *Ukraine* 42 B5
Kamenka Bugskaya,
  Ukraine 40 F4
Kamenka Dneprovskaya,
  Ukraine 42 C6
Kamenolomni, *Russia* ... 43 C9
Kamensk-Shakhtinskiy,
  Russia 43 B9
Kamensk Uralskiy, *Russia* 44 D7
Kamenskiy, *Russia* 41 F14
Kamenskiy, *Russia* 43 B9
Kamenskoye, *Russia* 45 C17
Kamenyak, *Bulgaria* 38 F9
Kamenz, *Germany* 18 D10
Kameoka, *Japan* 49 G7
Kamiah, *U.S.A.* 110 C5
Kamień Pomorski, *Poland* 20 B4

Kamieskroon, *S. Africa* ... 84 E2
Kamilukuak, L., *Canada* . 101 A8
Kamina, *Zaïre* 83 D1
Kaminak L., *Canada* 101 A9
Kaminoyama, *Japan* 48 E10
Kamiros, *Greece* 37 C9
Kamituga, *Zaïre* 82 C2
Kamloops, *Canada* 100 C4
Kamnik, *Slovenia* 33 B11
Kamo, *Armenia* 43 F11
Kamo, *Japan* 48 F9
Kamoa Mts., *Guyana* ... 121 C6
Kamoke, *Pakistan* 62 C6
Kamp →, *Austria* 21 G5
Kampala, *Uganda* 82 B3
Kampar, *Malaysia* 59 K3
Kampar →, *Indonesia* .. 56 D2
Kampen, *Neths.* 16 C7
Kamperland, *Neths.* 17 E3
Kamphaeng Phet, *Thailand* 58 D2
Kampolombo, L., *Zambia* 83 E2
Kampong To, *Thailand* . 59 J3
Kampot, *Cambodia* 59 G5
Kampti, *Burkina Faso* .. 78 C4
Kampuchea = Cambodia ■, *Asia* ... 58 F5
Kampung →, *Indonesia* . 57 F9
Kampung Air Putih, *Malaysia* 59 K4
Kampung Jerangau, *Malaysia* 59 K4
Kampung Raja, *Malaysia* . 59 K4
Kampungbaru = Tolitoli, *Indonesia* 57 D6
Kamrau, Teluk, *Indonesia* 57 E8
Kamsack, *Canada* 101 C8
Kamskoye Ustye, *Russia* . 41 D16
Kamuchawie L., *Canada* . 101 B8
Kamui-Misaki, *Japan* ... 48 C10
Kamyanets-Podilskyy = Kamenets-Podolskiy, *Ukraine* 42 B2
Kāmyārān, *Iran* 64 C5
Kamyshin, *Russia* 41 F14
Kamyzyak, *Russia* 43 C13
Kanaaupscow, *Canada* . 98 B4
Kanab, *U.S.A.* 111 H7
Kanab →, *U.S.A.* 111 H7
Kanagi, *Japan* 48 D10
Kanairiktok →, *Canada* . 99 A7
Kanália, *Greece* 39 K5
Kananga, *Zaïre* 80 F4
Kanarraville, *U.S.A.* ... 111 H7
Kanash, *Russia* 41 D15
Kanaskat, *U.S.A.* 112 C5
Kanawha →, *U.S.A.* ... 104 F4
Kanazawa, *Japan* 49 F8
Kanchanaburi, *Thailand* . 58 E2
Kanchenjunga, *Nepal* ... 63 F13
Kanchipuram, *India* 60 N11
Kanda Kanda, *Zaïre* ... 80 F4
Kandahar = Qandahār, *Afghan.* 60 D4
Kandalaksha, *Russia* ... 44 C4
Kandalu, *Afghan.* 60 E3
Kandangan, *Indonesia* . 56 E5
Kandanos, *Greece* 37 D5
Kander →, *Switz.* 22 C5
Kandersteg, *Switz.* 22 D5
Kandhíla, *Greece* 39 M5
Kandhkot, *Pakistan* ... 62 E3
Kandhla, *India* 62 E7
Kandi, *Benin* 79 C5
Kandi, *India* 63 H13
Kandıra, *Turkey* 66 C4
Kandla, *India* 62 H4
Kandos, *Australia* 91 E4
Kandy, *Sri Lanka* 60 R12
Kane, *U.S.A.* 106 E6
Kane Basin, *Greenland* .. 4 B4
Kanevskaya, *Russia* ... 43 C8
Kanfanar, *Croatia* 33 C10
Kangaba, *Mali* 78 C3
Kangal, *Turkey* 66 D7
Kangān, *Fārs, Iran* 65 E7
Kangān, *Hormozgān, Iran* 65 E8
Kangar, *Malaysia* 59 J3
Kangaroo I., *Australia* . 91 F2
Kangavar, *Iran* 65 C6
Kangding, *China* 52 B3
Kangdong, *N. Korea* ... 51 E14
Kangean, Kepulauan, *Indonesia* 56 F5
Kangean Is. = Kangean, Kepulauan, *Indonesia* . 56 F5
Kanggye, *N. Korea* 51 D14
Kanggyŏng, *S. Korea* .. 51 F14
Kanghwa, *S. Korea* ... 51 F14
Kangnŭng, *S. Korea* ... 51 F15
Kango, *Gabon* 80 D2
Kangping, *China* 51 C12
Kangto, *India* 61 F18
Kani, *Ivory C.* 78 D3
Kaniama, *Zaïre* 82 D1
Kaniapiskau →, *Canada* . 99 A6
Kaniapiskau L., *Canada* . 99 B6
Kanin, P-ov., *Russia* ... 44 C5
Kanin Nos, Mys, *Russia* . 44 C5
Kanin Pen. = Kanin, P-ov., *Russia* 44 C5
Kaniva, *Australia* 91 F3
Kanjiža, *Serbia* 21 J10
Kanjut Sar, *Pakistan* ... 63 A6
Kankakee, *U.S.A.* 104 E2
Kankakee →, *U.S.A.* .. 104 E1

Kankan, *Guinea* 78 C3
Kanker, *India* 61 J12
Kankunskiy, *Russia* ... 45 D13
Kannapolis, *U.S.A.* ... 105 H5
Kannauj, *India* 63 F8
Kannod, *India* 60 H10
Kano, *Nigeria* 79 C6
Kano □, *Nigeria* 79 C6
Kan'onji, *Japan* 49 G6
Kanoroba, *Ivory C.* ... 78 D3
Kanowit, *Malaysia* ... 56 D4
Kanowna, *Australia* ... 89 F3
Kanoya, *Japan* 49 J5
Kanpetlet, *Burma* 61 J18
Kanpur, *India* 63 F9
Kansas □, *U.S.A.* 108 F6
Kansas →, *U.S.A.* 108 F7
Kansas City, *Kans., U.S.A.* 108 F7
Kansas City, *Mo., U.S.A.* 108 F7
Kansenia, *Zaïre* 83 E2
Kansk, *Russia* 45 D10
Kansŏng, *S. Korea* ... 51 E15
Kansu = Gansu □, *China* 50 G3
Kantang, *Thailand* ... 59 J2
Kantché, *Niger* 79 C6
Kanté, *Togo* 79 D5
Kantemirovka, *Russia* . 43 B8
Kantharalak, *Thailand* . 58 E5
Kantō □, *Japan* 49 F9
Kantō-Sanchi, *Japan* .. 49 G9
Kanturk, *Ireland* 15 D3
Kanuma, *Japan* 49 F9
Kanus, *Namibia* 84 D2
Kanye, *Botswana* 84 C4
Kanzenze, *Zaïre* 83 E2
Kanzi, Ras, *Tanzania* .. 82 D4
Kaohsiung = Gaoxiong, *Taiwan* 53 F13
Kaokoveld, *Namibia* ... 84 B1
Kaolack, *Senegal* 78 C1
Kaoshan, *China* 51 B13
Kapadvanj, *India* 62 H5
Kapanga, *Zaïre* 80 F4
Kapchagai, *Kazakhstan* . 44 E8
Kapellen, *Belgium* 17 F4
Kapéllo, Ákra, *Greece* . 39 N6
Kapema, *Zaïre* 83 E2
Kapfenberg, *Austria* .. 21 H5
Kapiri Mposhi, *Zambia* . 83 E2
Kapiskau →, *Canada* .. 98 B3
Kapit, *Malaysia* 56 D4
Kapiti I., *N.Z.* 87 J5
Kaplice, *Czech.* 20 G4
Kapoe, *Thailand* 59 H2
Kapos →, *Hungary* ... 21 J8
Kaposvár, *Hungary* ... 21 J7
Kapowsin, *U.S.A.* 112 C4
Kappeln, *Germany* ... 18 A5
Kapps, *Namibia* 84 C2
Kaprije, *Croatia* 33 E12
Kaprijke, *Belgium* 17 F3
Kapsan, *N. Korea* 51 D15
Kapsukas = Mariyampol, *Lithuania* 40 D3
Kapuas →, *Indonesia* . 56 E3
Kapuas Hulu, Pegunungan, *Malaysia* 56 D4
Kapuas Hulu Ra. = Kapuas Hulu, Pegunungan, *Malaysia* . 56 D4
Kapulo, *Zaïre* 83 D2
Kapunda, *Australia* ... 91 E2
Kapuni, *N.Z.* 87 H5
Kapurthala, *India* 62 D6
Kapuskasing, *Canada* . 98 C3
Kapuskasing →, *Canada* . 98 C3
Kapustin Yar, *Russia* .. 43 B11
Kaputar, *Australia* ... 91 E5
Kaputir, *Kenya* 82 B4
Kapuvár, *Hungary* ... 21 H7
Kara, *Russia* 44 C7
Kara Bogaz Gol, Zaliv, *Turkmenistan* 44 E6
Kara Kalpak Republic □, *Uzbekistan* 44 E6
Kara Kum = Karakum, Peski, *Turkmenistan* .. 44 F6
Kara Sea, *Russia* 44 B7
Karabük, *Turkey* 42 F5
Karaburun, *Turkey* ... 66 D2
Karaburuni, *Albania* .. 39 J2
Karabutak, *Kazakhstan* . 44 E7
Karacabey, *Turkey* ... 66 C3
Karacasu, *Turkey* 66 E3
Karachala, *Azerbaijan* . 43 G13
Karachayevsk, *Russia* . 43 E9
Karachev, *Russia* 40 E9
Karachi, *Pakistan* 62 G2
Karad, *India* 60 L9
Karadeniz Boğazı, *Turkey* 66 C3
Karaga, *Ghana* 79 D4
Karaganda, *Kazakhstan* . 44 E8
Karagayly, *Kazakhstan* . 44 E8
Karaginskiy, Ostrov, *Russia* 45 D17
Karagüney Dağları, *Turkey* 66 C6
Karagwe □, *Tanzania* . 82 C3
Karaikal, *India* 60 P11
Karaikkudi, *India* 60 P11
Karaisalı, *Turkey* 66 E6
Karaj, *Iran* 65 C6
Karak, *Malaysia* 59 L4
Karakas, *Kazakhstan* .. 44 E9
Karakitang, *Indonesia* . 57 D7
Karaklis, *Armenia* 43 F11

Karakoçan, *Turkey* 67 D9
Karakoram Pass, *Pakistan* 63 B7
Karakoram Ra., *Pakistan* . 63 B7
Karakum, Peski, *Turkmenistan* 44 F6
Karakurt, *Turkey* 67 C10
Karalon, *Russia* 45 D12
Karaman, *Turkey* 66 E5
Karamay, *China* 54 B3
Karambu, *Indonesia* .. 56 E5
Karamea Bight, *N.Z.* .. 87 J3
Karamoja □, *Uganda* . 82 B3
Karamsad, *India* 62 H5
Karand, *Iran* 64 C5
Karanganyar, *Indonesia* . 57 G13
Karapınar, *Turkey* 66 E5
Karasburg, *Namibia* .. 84 D2
Karasino, *Russia* 44 C9
Karasjok, *Norway* 8 B18
Karasu, *Turkey* 66 C4
Karasu →, *Turkey* 67 D8
Karasuk, *Russia* 44 D8
Karasuyama, *Japan* .. 49 F10
Karataş Burnu, *Turkey* . 66 E6
Karatau, *Kazakhstan* .. 44 E8
Karatau, Khrebet, *Kazakhstan* 44 E7
Karatepe, *Turkey* 66 E7
Karauli, *India* 62 F7
Karavostasi, *Cyprus* .. 37 D11
Karawang, *Indonesia* .. 57 G12
Karawanken, *Europe* .. 21 J4
Karayazar, *Turkey* ... 67 D10
Karazhal, *Kazakhstan* . 44 E8
Karbalā, *Iraq* 64 C5
Kårböle, *Sweden* 10 C9
Karcag, *Hungary* 21 H10
Karcha →, *Pakistan* .. 63 B7
Karda, *Russia* 45 D11
Kardhámila, *Greece* .. 39 L9
Kardhítsa, *Greece* ... 39 K4
Kärdla, *Estonia* 40 B3
Kareeberge, *S. Africa* . 84 E3
Kareima, *Sudan* 76 D3
Karelian Republic □, *Russia* 44 C4
Kārevāndar, *Iran* 65 E9
Kargasok, *Russia* 44 D9
Kargat, *Russia* 44 D9
Kargı, *Turkey* 42 F6
Kargil, *India* 63 B7
Karguéri, *Niger* 79 C7
Karia ba Mohammed, *Morocco* 74 B3
Kariān, *Iran* 65 E8
Kariba, *Zimbabwe* ... 83 F2
Kariba, L., *Zimbabwe* . 83 F2
Kariba Dam, *Zimbabwe* . 83 F2
Kariba Gorge, *Zambia* . 83 F2
Karibib, *Namibia* 84 C2
Karimata, Kepulauan, *Indonesia* 56 E3
Karimata, Selat, *Indonesia* 56 E3
Karimata Is. = Karimata, Kepulauan, *Indonesia* . 56 E3
Karimnagar, *India* ... 60 K11
Karimunjawa, Kepulauan, *Indonesia* 56 F4
Karin, *Somali Rep.* ... 68 E4
Karīt, *Iran* 65 C8
Kariya, *Japan* 49 G8
Karkaralinsk, *Kazakhstan* 44 E8
Karkinitsky Zaliv, *Ukraine* 42 D5
Karkur Tohl, *Egypt* ... 76 C2
Karl Libknekht, *Russia* . 40 F9
Karl-Marx-Stadt = Chemnitz, *Germany* 18 E8
Karla, L. = Voiviïs Límni, *Greece* 39 K5
Karlobag, *Croatia* ... 33 D12
Karlovac, *Croatia* ... 33 C12
Karlovka, *Ukraine* ... 42 B6
Karlovy Vary, *Czech.* . 20 E2
Karlsbad = Karlovy Vary, *Czech.* 20 E2
Karlsborg, *Sweden* ... 11 F8
Karlshamn, *Sweden* .. 9 H13
Karlskoga, *Sweden* ... 9 G13
Karlskrona, *Sweden* .. 9 H13
Karlsruhe, *Germany* .. 19 F4
Karlstad, *Sweden* 9 G12
Karlstad, *U.S.A.* 108 A6
Karlstadt, *Germany* .. 19 F5
Karnal, *India* 62 E7
Karnali →, *Nepal* 63 E9
Karnaphuli Res., *Bangla.* . 61 H18
Karnataka □, *India* ... 60 N10
Karnes City, *U.S.A.* .. 109 L6
Karnische Alpen, *Europe* 21 J3
Karo, *Mali* 78 C4
Karoi, *Zimbabwe* 83 F2
Karonga, *Malawi* 83 D3
Karoonda, *Australia* .. 91 F2
Karora, *Sudan* 76 D4
Káros, *Greece* 39 N8
Karousádhes, *Greece* . 39 K2
Karpasia □, *Cyprus* .. 37 D13
Kárpathos, *Greece* ... 39 P10
Kárpathos, Stenón, *Greece* 39 P10
Kárrebæk, *Denmark* .. 11 J5
Kars, *Turkey* 43 F10
Kars □, *Turkey* 67 C10
Karsakpay, *Kazakhstan* . 44 E7
Karsha, *Kazakhstan* .. 43 B14
Karshi, *Uzbekistan* ... 44 F7

Karsiyang, *India* 63 F13
Karst, *Croatia* 33 C11
Karsun, *Russia* 41 D15
Kartaly, *Russia* 44 D7
Karthaus, *U.S.A.* 106 E6
Kartapur, *India* 62 D6
Kartuzy, *Poland* 20 A8
Karufa, *Indonesia* ... 57 E8
Karumba, *Australia* .. 90 B3
Karumo, *Tanzania* ... 82 C3
Karumwa, *Tanzania* .. 82 C3
Karungu, *Kenya* 82 C3
Karup, *Denmark* 11 H3
Karviná, *Czech.* 20 F8
Karwar, *India* 60 M9
Karwi, *India* 63 G9
Kasache, *Malawi* 83 E3
Kasai →, *Zaïre* 80 E3
Kasai Oriental □, *Zaïre* . 82 C1
Kasaji, *Zaïre* 83 E1
Kasama, *Zambia* 83 E3
Kasan-dong, *N. Korea* . 51 D14
Kasane, *Namibia* 84 B3
Kasanga, *Tanzania* ... 83 D3
Kasangulu, *Zaïre* 80 E3
Kasaragod, *India* 60 N9
Kasba L., *Canada* 101 A8
Kasba Tadla, *Morocco* . 74 B3
Kāseh Garān, *Iran* ... 64 C5
Kasempa, *Zambia* 83 E2
Kasenga, *Zaïre* 83 E2
Kasese, *Uganda* 82 B3
Kasewa, *Zambia* 83 E2
Kasganj, *India* 63 F8
Kashabowie, *Canada* . 98 C1
Kāshān, *Iran* 65 C6
Kashi, *China* 54 C2
Kashimbo, *Zaïre* 83 E2
Kashin, *Russia* 41 C10
Kashipur, *India* 63 E8
Kashira, *Russia* 41 D11
Kashiwazaki, *Japan* .. 49 F9
Kashk-e Kohneh, *Afghan.* 60 B3
Kāshmar, *Iran* 65 C8
Kashmir, *Asia* 63 C7
Kashmor, *Pakistan* ... 62 E3
Kashpirovka, *Russia* .. 41 E16
Kashun Noerh = Gaxun Nur, *China* 54 B9
Kasimov, *Russia* 41 D12
Kasinge, *Zaïre* 82 D2
Kasiruta, *Indonesia* .. 57 E7
Kaskaskia →, *U.S.A.* . 108 G10
Kaskattama →, *Canada* . 101 B10
Kaskinen, *Finland* ... 8 E16
Kaskö, *Finland* 8 E16
Kaslo, *Canada* 100 D5
Kasmere L., *Canada* .. 101 B8
Kasongo, *Zaïre* 82 C2
Kasongo Lunda, *Zaïre* . 80 F3
Kásos, *Greece* 39 P9
Kásos, Stenón, *Greece* . 39 P9
Kaspi, *Georgia* 43 F11
Kaspiysk, *Russia* 43 E12
Kaspiyskiy, *Russia* ... 43 D12
Kassab ed Doleib, *Sudan* . 77 E3
Kassaba, *Egypt* 76 C2
Kassala, *Sudan* 77 D4
Kassalâ □, *Sudan* ... 77 D4
Kassel, *Germany* 18 D5
Kassinger, *Sudan* 76 D3
Kassiópi, *Greece* 37 A3
Kassue, *Indonesia* ... 57 F9
Kastamonu, *Turkey* .. 66 C5
Kastamonu □, *Turkey* . 66 C5
Kastav, *Croatia* 33 C11
Kastélli, *Greece* 37 D5
Kastéllion, *Greece* ... 37 D7
Kastellou, Ákra, *Greece* 39 P10
Kasterlee, *Belgium* ... 17 F5
Kastóri, *Greece* 39 M5
Kastoría, *Greece* 39 J4
Kastornoye, *Russia* .. 41 F11
Kástron, *Greece* 39 K8
Kasulu, *Tanzania* 82 C3
Kasulu □, *Tanzania* .. 82 C3
Kasumi, *Japan* 49 G7
Kasumkent, *Azerbaijan* . 43 F13
Kasungu, *Malawi* 83 E3
Kasur, *Pakistan* 62 D6
Kata, *Russia* 45 D11
Kataba, *Zambia* 83 F2
Katako Kombe, *Zaïre* . 82 C1
Katákolon, *Greece* ... 39 M4
Katale, *Tanzania* 82 C3
Katamatite, *Australia* . 91 F4
Katanda, *Kivu, Zaïre* . 82 C2
Katanda, *Shaba, Zaïre* . 82 D1
Katangi, *India* 60 J11
Katangli, *Russia* 45 D15
Katavi Swamp, *Tanzania* 82 D3
Katerini, *Greece* 39 J5
Katha, *Burma* 61 G20
Katherîna, Gebel, *Egypt* 76 J8
Katherine, *Australia* .. 88 B5
Kathiawar, *India* 62 H4
Kathikas, *Cyprus* 37 E11
Kati, *Mali* 78 C3
Katihar, *India* 63 G12
Katima Mulilo, *Zambia* . 84 B3
Katimbira, *Malawi* ... 83 E3
Katingan = Mendawai →, *Indonesia* 56 E4
Katiola, *Ivory C.* 78 D3

Katmandu, *Nepal* 63 F11
Kato Akhaïa, *Greece* . 39 L4
Káto Arkhánai, *Greece* . 37 D7
Káto Khorió, *Greece* .. 37 D7
Kato Pyrgos, *Cyprus* .. 37 D11
Káto Stavros, *Greece* .. 39 J6
Katompe, *Zaïre* 82 D2
Katonga →, *Uganda* .. 82 B3
Katoomba, *Australia* .. 91 E5
Katowice, *Poland* 20 E9
Katrine, L., *U.K.* 14 E4
Katrineholm, *Sweden* . 10 E11
Katsepe, *Madag.* 85 B8
Katsina, *Nigeria* 79 C6
Katsina □, *Nigeria* ... 79 C6
Katsina Ala →, *Nigeria* . 79 D6
Katsumoto, *Japan* ... 49 H4
Katsuura, *Japan* 49 G10
Katsuyama, *Japan* ... 49 F8
Kattaviá, *Greece* 37 D9
Kattegatt, *Denmark* .. 11 H5
Katumba, *Zaïre* 82 D2
Katungu, *Kenya* 82 C5
Katwa, *India* 63 H13
Katwijk-aan-Zee, *Neths.* . 16 D4
Kauai, *U.S.A.* 102 H15
Kauai Channel, *U.S.A.* . 102 H15
Kaub, *Germany* 19 E3
Kaufbeuren, *Germany* . 19 H6
Kaufman, *U.S.A.* 109 J6
Kaukauna, *U.S.A.* ... 104 C1
Kaukauveld, *Namibia* . 84 C3
Kaukonen, *Finland* ... 8 C18
Kauliranta, *Finland* .. 8 C17
Kaunas, *Lithuania* ... 40 D3
Kaura Namoda, *Nigeria* . 79 C6
Kautokeino, *Norway* .. 8 B17
Kavacha, *Russia* 45 C17
Kavaja, *Albania* 39 H2
Kavak, *Turkey* 66 C7
Kavalerovo, *Russia* ... 48 B7
Kavali, *India* 60 M12
Kavála, *Greece* 39 J7
Kavār, *Iran* 65 D7
Kavarna, *Bulgaria* ... 38 F11
Kavos, *Greece* 37 B4
Kaw, *Fr. Guiana* 121 C7
Kawa, *Sudan* 77 D3
Kawagama L., *Canada* . 106 A6
Kawagoe, *Japan* 49 G9
Kawaguchi, *Japan* ... 49 G9
Kawaihae, *U.S.A.* ... 102 H17
Kawambwa, *Zambia* .. 83 D2
Kawanoe, *Japan* 49 G6
Kawardha, *India* 63 J9
Kawasaki, *Japan* 49 G9
Kawene, *Canada* 98 C1
Kawerau, *N.Z.* 87 H6
Kawhia Harbour, *N.Z.* . 87 H5
Kawio, Kepulauan, *Indonesia* 57 D7
Kawnro, *Burma* 61 H21
Kawthoolei = Kawthule □, *Burma* 61 L20
Kawthule □, *Burma* ... 61 L20
Kaya, *Burkina Faso* .. 79 C4
Kayah □, *Burma* 61 K20
Kayan →, *Indonesia* .. 56 D5
Kaycee, *U.S.A.* 110 E10
Kayeli, *Indonesia* 57 E7
Kayenta, *U.S.A.* 111 H8
Kayes, *Mali* 78 C2
Kayima, *S. Leone* ... 78 D2
Kayl, *Lux.* 17 K8
Kayoa, *Indonesia* 57 D7
Kayomba, *Zambia* ... 83 E1
Kayoro, *Ghana* 79 C4
Kayrunnera, *Australia* . 91 E3
Kaysatskoye, *Russia* .. 43 B12
Kayseri, *Turkey* 66 C6
Kayseri □, *Turkey* ... 66 C6
Kaysville, *U.S.A.* 110 F8
Kayuagung, *Indonesia* . 56 E2
Kazachinskoye, *Russia* . 45 D11
Kazachye, *Russia* 45 B14
Kazakhstan ■, *Asia* .. 44 E7
Kazan, *Russia* 41 D16
Kazan-Rettō, *Pac. Oc.* . 92 E6
Kazanlúk, *Bulgaria* .. 38 G8
Kazanskaya, *Russia* .. 43 B9
Kazatin, *Ukraine* 42 B3
Kazbek, *Georgia* 43 E11
Kāzerūn, *Iran* 65 D6
Kazi Magomed, *Azerbaijan* 43 F13
Kazincbarcika, *Hungary* . 21 G10
Kaztalovka, *Kazakhstan* . 43 B13
Kazumba, *Zaïre* 80 F4
Kazuno, *Japan* 48 D10
Kazym →, *Russia* 44 C7
Kcynia, *Poland* 20 C7
Ké-Macina, *Mali* 78 C3
Kéa, *Greece* 39 M7
Keams Canyon, *U.S.A.* . 111 J8
Kearney, *U.S.A.* 108 E5
Keban, *Turkey* 67 D8
Keban Baraji, *Turkey* . 67 D8
Kebbje □, *Nigeria* ... 79 C6
Kébi, *Ivory C.* 78 D3
Kebili, *Tunisia* 75 B6
Kebnekaise, *Sweden* .. 8 C15
Kebri Dehar, *Ethiopia* . 68 F3
Kebumen, *Indonesia* . 57 G13
Kecel, *Hungary* 21 J9
Kechika →, *Canada* .. 100 B3

Kimamba

Kecskemét, *Hungary* 21 J9
Kedada, *Ethiopia* 77 F4
Kedgwick, *Canada* 99 C6
Kédhros Óros, *Greece* 37 D6
Kedia Hill, *Botswana* 84 C3
Kediniai, *Lithuania* 40 D4
Kediri, *Indonesia* 57 G15
Kédougou, *Senegal* 78 C2
Kedzierzyn, *Poland* 20 E8
Keeler, *U.S.A.* 112 J9
Keeley L., *Canada* 101 C7
Keeling Is. = Cocos Is., *Ind. Oc.* 92 J1
Keene, *Calif., U.S.A.* 113 K8
Keene, *N.H., U.S.A.* 107 D12
Keeper Hill, *Ireland* 15 D3
Keer-Weer, C., *Australia* 90 A3
Keerbergen, *Belgium* 17 F5
Keeseville, *U.S.A.* 107 B11
Keeten Mastgat, *Neths.* 17 E4
Keetmanshoop, *Namibia* 84 D2
Keewatin, *U.S.A.* 108 B8
Keewatin □, *Canada* 101 A9
Keewatin →, *Canada* 101 B8
Kefa □, *Ethiopia* 77 F4
Kefallinía, *Greece* 39 L3
Kefamenanu, *Indonesia* 57 F6
Keffi, *Nigeria* 79 D6
Kefken, *Turkey* 66 C4
Keflavík, *Iceland* 8 D2
Keg River, *Canada* 100 B5
Kegaska, *Canada* 99 B7
Kehl, *Germany* 19 G3
Keighley, *U.K.* 12 D6
Keimoes, *S. Africa* 84 D3
Keita, *Niger* 79 C6
Keith, *Australia* 91 F3
Keith, *U.K.* 14 D6
Keith Arm, *Canada* 96 B7
Kejser Franz Joseph Fjord = Kong Franz Joseph Fd., *Greenland* 4 B6
Kekri, *India* 62 G6
Kël, *Russia* 45 C13
Kelamet, *Eritrea* 77 D4
Kelan, *China* 50 E6
Kelang, *Malaysia* 59 L3
Kelantan →, *Malaysia* 59 J4
Kelheim, *Germany* 19 G7
Kelibia, *Tunisia* 75 A7
Kelkit, *Turkey* 67 C8
Kelkit →, *Turkey* 66 C7
Kellé, *Congo* 80 E2
Keller, *U.S.A.* 110 B4
Kellerberrin, *Australia* 89 F2
Kellett, C., *Canada* 4 B1
Kelleys I., *U.S.A.* 106 E2
Kellogg, *U.S.A.* 110 C5
Kelloselkä, *Finland* 8 C20
Kells = Ceanannus Mor, *Ireland* 15 C5
Kélo, *Chad* 73 G8
Kelokedhara, *Cyprus* 37 E11
Kelowna, *Canada* 100 D5
Kelsey Bay, *Canada* 100 C3
Kelseyville, *U.S.A.* 112 G4
Kelso, *N.Z.* 87 L2
Kelso, *U.K.* 14 F6
Kelso, *U.S.A.* 112 D4
Keluang, *Malaysia* 59 L4
Kelvington, *Canada* 101 C8
Kem, *Russia* 44 C4
Kem-Kem, *Morocco* 74 B4
Kema, *Indonesia* 57 D7
Kemah, *Turkey* 67 D8
Kemaliye, *Turkey* 67 D8
Kemano, *Canada* 100 C3
Kemasik, *Malaysia* 59 K4
Kembolcha, *Ethiopia* 77 E4
Kemer, *Turkey* 66 E4
Kemerovo, *Russia* 44 D9
Kemi, *Finland* 8 D18
Kemi älv = Kemijoki →, *Finland* 8 D18
Kemijärvi, *Finland* 8 C19
Kemijoki →, *Finland* 8 D18
Kemmel, *Belgium* 17 G1
Kemmerer, *U.S.A.* 110 F8
Kemmuna = Comino, *Malta* 37 C1
Kemp, L., *U.S.A.* 109 J5
Kemp Land, *Antarctica* 5 C5
Kempsey, *Australia* 91 E5
Kempt, L., *Canada* 98 C5
Kempten, *Germany* 19 H6
Kemptville, *Canada* 98 C4
Kenadsa, *Algeria* 75 B4
Kendal, *Indonesia* 56 F4
Kendal, *U.K.* 12 C5
Kendall, *Australia* 91 E5
Kendall →, *Australia* 90 A3
Kendallville, *U.S.A.* 104 E3
Kendari, *Indonesia* 57 E6
Kendawangan, *Indonesia* 56 E4
Kende, *Nigeria* 79 C5
Kendenup, *Australia* 89 F2
Kendrapara, *India* 61 J15
Kendrew, *S. Africa* 84 E3
Kendrick, *U.S.A.* 110 C5
Kene Thao, *Laos* 58 D3
Kenedy, *U.S.A.* 109 L6
Kenema, *S. Leone* 78 D2
Keng Kok, *Laos* 58 D5
Keng Tawng, *Burma* 61 J21
Keng Tung, *Burma* 61 J21
Kenge, *Zaïre* 80 E3
Kengeja, *Tanzania* 82 D4
Kenhardt, *S. Africa* 84 D3
Kenitra, *Morocco* 74 B3
Kenli, *China* 51 F10
Kenmare, *Ireland* 15 E2
Kenmare, *U.S.A.* 108 A3
Kenmare →, *Ireland* 15 E2
Kennebec, *U.S.A.* 108 D5
Kennedy, *Zimbabwe* 83 F2
Kennedy Ra., *Australia* 89 D2
Kennedy Taungdeik, *Burma* 61 H18
Kennet →, *U.K.* 13 F7
Kenneth Ra., *Australia* 88 D2
Kennett, *U.S.A.* 109 G9
Kennewick, *U.S.A.* 110 C4
Kénogami, *Canada* 99 C5
Kenogami →, *Canada* 98 B3
Kenora, *Canada* 101 D10
Kenosha, *U.S.A.* 104 D2
Kensington, *Canada* 99 C7
Kensington, *U.S.A.* 108 F5
Kensington Downs, *Australia* 90 C3
Kent, *Ohio, U.S.A.* 106 E3
Kent, *Oreg., U.S.A.* 110 D3
Kent, *Tex., U.S.A.* 109 K2
Kent, *Wash., U.S.A.* 112 C4
Kent □, *U.K.* 13 F8
Kent Group, *Australia* 90 F4
Kent Pen., *Canada* 96 B9
Kentau, *Kazakhstan* 44 E7
Kentland, *U.S.A.* 104 E2
Kenton, *U.S.A.* 104 E4
Kentucky □, *U.S.A.* 104 G3
Kentucky →, *U.S.A.* 104 F3
Kentucky L., *U.S.A.* 105 G2
Kentville, *Canada* 99 C7
Kentwood, *La., U.S.A.* 109 K9
Kentwood, *La., U.S.A.* 109 K9
Kenya ■, *Africa* 82 B4
Kenya, Mt., *Kenya* 82 C4
Keo Neua, Deo, *Vietnam* 58 C5
Keokuk, *U.S.A.* 108 E9
Kep, *Cambodia* 59 G5
Kep, *Vietnam* 58 B6
Kepi, *Indonesia* 57 F9
Kępno, *Poland* 20 D7
Kepsut, *Turkey* 66 D3
Kerala □, *India* 60 P10
Kerama-Rettō, *Japan* 49 L3
Keran, *Pakistan* 63 B5
Kerang, *Australia* 91 F3
Keraudren, C., *Australia* 88 C2
Kerch, *Ukraine* 42 D7
Kerchenskiy Proliv, *Black Sea* 42 D7
Kerchoual, *Mali* 79 B5
Kerempe Burnu, *Turkey* 66 B5
Keren, *Eritrea* 77 D4
Kerewan, *Gambia* 78 C1
Kerguelen, *Ind. Oc.* 3 G13
Keri Kera, *Sudan* 77 E3
Kericho, *Kenya* 82 C4
Kericho □, *Kenya* 82 C4
Kerinci, *Indonesia* 56 E2
Kerkdriel, *Neths.* 16 E6
Kerkenna, Is., *Tunisia* 75 B7
Kerki, *Turkmenistan* 44 F7
Kérkira, *Greece* 37 A3
Kerkrade, *Neths.* 17 G8
Kerma, *Sudan* 76 D3
Kermadec Is., *Pac. Oc.* 92 K10
Kermadec Trench, *Pac. Oc.* 92 L10
Kermān, *Iran* 65 D8
Kerman, *U.S.A.* 112 J6
Kermān □, *Iran* 65 D8
Kermānshāh = Bākhtarān, *Iran* 64 C5
Kerme Körfezi, *Turkey* 66 E2
Kermit, *U.S.A.* 109 K3
Kern →, *U.S.A.* 113 K7
Kerns, *Switz.* 23 C6
Kernville, *U.S.A.* 113 K8
Keroh, *Malaysia* 59 K3
Kerrobert, *Canada* 101 C7
Kerrville, *U.S.A.* 109 K5
Kerry □, *Ireland* 15 D2
Kerry Hd., *Ireland* 15 D2
Kersa, *Ethiopia* 77 F5
Kerteminde, *Denmark* 11 J4
Kertosono, *Indonesia* 57 G15
Kerulen →, *Asia* 54 B6
Kerzaz, *Algeria* 75 C4
Kerzers, *Switz.* 22 C4
Kesagami →, *Canada* 98 B4
Kesagami L., *Canada* 98 B3
Keşan, *Turkey* 66 C2
Kesch, Piz, *Switz.* 23 C9
Kesennuma, *Japan* 48 E10
Keshit, *Iran* 65 D8
Keşiş Dağ, *Turkey* 67 D8
Keski-Suomen lääni □, *Finland* 8 E18
Keskin, *Turkey* 66 D5
Kessel, *Belgium* 17 F5
Kessel, *Neths.* 17 F8
Kessel-Lo, *Belgium* 17 G5
Kestell, *S. Africa* 85 D4
Kestenga, *Russia* 44 C4
Kesteren, *Neths.* 16 E7
Keswick, *U.K.* 12 C4
Keszthely, *Hungary* 21 J7
Ket →, *Russia* 44 D9
Keta, *Ghana* 79 D5
Ketapang, *Indonesia* 56 E4
Ketchikan, *U.S.A.* 96 C6
Ketchum, *U.S.A.* 110 E6
Kete Krachi, *Ghana* 79 D4
Ketef, Khalîg Umm el, *Egypt* 76 C4
Ketelmeer, *Neths.* 16 C7
Keti Bandar, *Pakistan* 62 G2
Ketri, *India* 62 E6
Kętrzyn, *Poland* 20 A11
Kettering, *U.K.* 13 E7
Kettle →, *Canada* 101 B11
Kettle Falls, *U.S.A.* 110 B4
Kettleman City, *U.S.A.* 112 J7
Kevin, *U.S.A.* 110 B8
Kewanee, *U.S.A.* 108 E10
Kewaunee, *U.S.A.* 104 C2
Keweenaw B., *U.S.A.* 104 B1
Keweenaw Pen., *U.S.A.* 104 B2
Keweenaw Pt., *U.S.A.* 104 B2
Key Harbour, *Canada* 98 C3
Key West, *U.S.A.* 103 F10
Keyser, *U.S.A.* 104 F6
Keystone, *U.S.A.* 108 D3
Kezhma, *Russia* 45 D11
Kežmarok, *Slovak Rep.* 20 F10
Khabarovo, *Russia* 44 C7
Khabarovsk, *Russia* 45 E14
Khabr, *Iran* 65 D8
Khābūr →, *Syria* 64 C4
Khachmas, *Azerbaijan* 43 F13
Khachrod, *India* 62 H6
Khadari, W. el →, *Sudan* 77 E2
Khadro, *Pakistan* 62 F3
Khadyzhensk, *Russia* 43 D8
Khadzhilyangar, *India* 63 B8
Khagaria, *India* 63 G12
Khaipur, *Bahawalpur, Pakistan* 62 E5
Khaipur, *Hyderabad, Pakistan* 62 F3
Khair, *India* 62 F7
Khairabad, *India* 63 F9
Khairagarh, *India* 63 J9
Khairpur, *Pakistan* 60 F6
Khakhea, *Botswana* 84 C3
Khalafābād, *Iran* 65 D6
Khalfallah, *Algeria* 75 B5
Khalilabad, *India* 63 F10
Khalīlī, *Iran* 65 E7
Khalkhāl, *Iran* 65 B6
Khálki, *Greece* 39 K5
Khalkís, *Greece* 39 L6
Khalmer-Sede = Tazovskiy, *Russia* 44 C8
Khalmer Yu, *Russia* 44 C7
Khalturin, *Russia* 41 B16
Khalūf, *Oman* 68 C6
Kham Keut, *Laos* 58 C5
Khamas Country, *Botswana* 84 C4
Khambat, G. of, *India* 62 J5
Khambhaliya, *India* 62 H3
Khambhat, *India* 62 H5
Khamilonísion, *Greece* 39 P9
Khamīr, *Iran* 65 E7
Khamir, *Yemen* 68 D3
Khamsa, *Egypt* 69 E1
Khān Abū Shāmat, *Syria* 69 B5
Khān Azād, *Iraq* 64 C5
Khān Mujiddah, *Iraq* 64 C4
Khān Shaykhūn, *Syria* 64 C3
Khān Yūnis, *Egypt* 69 D3
Khānaqīn, *Iraq* 64 C5
Khānbāghī, *Iran* 65 B7
Khandrá, *Greece* 39 P9
Khandwa, *India* 60 J10
Khandyga, *Russia* 45 C14
Khāneh, *Iran* 64 B5
Khanewal, *Pakistan* 62 D4
Khanh Duong, *Vietnam* 58 F7
Khaniá, *Greece* 37 D6
Khaniá □, *Greece* 37 D6
Khaníon, Kólpos, *Greece* 37 D5
Khanka, Ozero, *Asia* 45 E14
Khankendy, *Azerbaijan* 67 D12
Khanna, *India* 62 D7
Khanpur, *Pakistan* 62 E4
Khanty-Mansiysk, *Russia* 44 C7
Khapalu, *Pakistan* 63 B7
Khapcheranga, *Russia* 45 E12
Kharagpur, *India* 63 H12
Khárakas, *Greece* 37 D7
Kharan Kalat, *Pakistan* 60 E4
Kharānaq, *Iran* 65 C7
Kharda, *India* 60 K9
Khardung La, *India* 63 B7
Khârga, El Wâhât el, *Egypt* 76 B3
Khargon, *India* 60 J9
Khârit, Wadi el →, *Egypt* 76 C3
Khārk, Jazīreh, *Iran* 65 D6
Kharkiv = Kharkov, *Ukraine* 42 B7
Kharkov, *Ukraine* 42 B7
Kharmanli, *Bulgaria* 39 H8
Kharovsk, *Russia* 41 B12
Khartoum = El Khartûm, *Sudan* 77 D3
Khasan, *Russia* 48 C5
Khasavyurt, *Russia* 43 E12
Khāsh, *Iran* 60 E2
Khashm el Girba, *Sudan* 77 E4
Khashuri, *Georgia* 43 F10
Khaskovo, *Bulgaria* 39 H8
Khatanga, *Russia* 45 B11
Khatanga →, *Russia* 45 B11
Khatauli, *India* 62 E7
Khātūnābād, *Iran* 65 C6
Khatyrka, *Russia* 45 C18
Khaybar, Harrat, *Si. Arabia* 64 E4
Khāzimiyah, *Iraq* 64 C4
Khazzân Jabal el Awliyâ, *Sudan* 77 D3
Khe Bo, *Vietnam* 58 C5
Khe Long, *Vietnam* 58 B5
Khed Brahma, *India* 60 G8
Khekra, *India* 62 E7
Khemarak Phouminville, *Cambodia* 59 G4
Khemelnik, *Ukraine* 42 B2
Khemis Miliana, *Algeria* 75 A5
Khemissèt, *Morocco* 74 B3
Khemmarat, *Thailand* 58 D5
Khenāmān, *Iran* 65 D8
Khenchela, *Algeria* 75 A6
Khenifra, *Morocco* 74 B3
Kherrata, *Algeria* 75 A6
Kherson, *Ukraine* 42 C5
Khersónisos Akrotíri, *Greece* 37 D6
Kheta →, *Russia* 45 B11
Khilok, *Russia* 45 D12
Khimki, *Russia* 41 D10
Khíos, *Greece* 39 L9
Khirbat Qanāfār, *Lebanon* 69 B4
Khiuma = Hiiumaa, *Estonia* 40 B3
Khiva, *Uzbekistan* 44 E7
Khīyāv, *Iran* 64 B5
Khlong Khlung, *Thailand* 58 D2
Khmelnitskiy, *Ukraine* 40 G5
Khmelnytskyy = Khmelnitskiy, *Ukraine* 40 G5
Khmer Rep. = Cambodia ■, *Asia* 58 F5
Khoai, Hon, *Vietnam* 59 H5
Khodzent, *Tajikistan* 44 E7
Khojak P., *Afghan.* 60 D5
Khok Kloi, *Thailand* 59 H2
Khok Pho, *Thailand* 59 J3
Khokholskiy, *Russia* 41 F11
Kholm, *Russia* 40 C7
Kholmsk, *Russia* 45 E15
Khomas Hochland, *Namibia* 84 C2
Khomayn, *Iran* 65 C6
Khon Kaen, *Thailand* 58 D4
Khong, *Laos* 58 E5
Khong Sedone, *Laos* 58 E5
Khonu, *Russia* 45 C15
Khoper →, *Russia* 41 G13
Khor el 'Atash, *Sudan* 77 E3
Khóra, *Greece* 39 M4
Khóra Sfakíon, *Greece* 37 D6
Khorāsān □, *Iran* 65 C8
Khorat = Nakhon Ratchasima, *Thailand* 58 E4
Khorat, Cao Nguyen, *Thailand* 58 E4
Khorb el Ethel, *Algeria* 74 C3
Khorixas, *Namibia* 84 C1
Khorog, *Tajikistan* 44 F8
Khorol, *Ukraine* 42 B5
Khorramābād, *Khorāsān, Iran* 65 C8
Khorramābād, *Lorestān, Iran* 65 C6
Khorrāmshahr, *Iran* 65 D6
Khosravī, *Iran* 65 D6
Khosrowābād, *Khuzestān, Iran* 65 D6
Khosrowābād, *Kordestān, Iran* 64 C5
Khosūyeh, *Iran* 65 D7
Khotin, *Ukraine* 42 B2
Khouribga, *Morocco* 74 B3
Khowai, *Bangla.* 61 G17
Khoyniki, *Belorussia* 40 F6
Khrami →, *Azerbaijan* 43 F11
Khrenovoye, *Russia* 41 F12
Khristianá, *Greece* 39 N8
Khrysokhou B., *Cyprus* 37 D11
Khu Khan, *Thailand* 58 E5
Khuff, *Si. Arabia* 64 E5
Khūgīānī, *Afghan.* 62 D1
Khulna, *Bangla.* 61 H16
Khulna □, *Bangla.* 61 H16
Khulo, *Georgia* 43 F10
Khumago, *Botswana* 84 C3
Khūnsorkh, *Iran* 65 E8
Khunzakh, *Russia* 43 E12
Khūr, *Iran* 65 C8
Khurai, *India* 62 G8
Khurayş, *Si. Arabia* 65 E6
Khūrīyā Mūrīyā, Jazā 'ir, *Oman* 68 D6
Khurja, *India* 62 E7
Khūsf, *Iran* 65 C8
Khush, *Afghan.* 60 C3
Khushab, *Pakistan* 62 C5
Khuzdar, *Pakistan* 62 F2
Khūzestān □, *Iran* 65 D6
Khvājeh, *Iran* 64 B5
Khvalynsk, *Russia* 41 E16
Khvānsār, *Iran* 65 D7
Khvatovka, *Russia* 41 E15
Khvor, *Iran* 65 C7
Khvorgū, *Iran* 65 E8
Khvormūj, *Iran* 65 D6
Khvoy, *Iran* 64 B5
Khvoynaya, *Russia* 40 B9
Khyber Pass, *Afghan.* 62 B4
Kiabukwa, *Zaïre* 83 D1
Kiama, *Australia* 91 E5
Kiamba, *Phil.* 55 H6
Kiambi, *Zaïre* 82 D2
Kiambu, *Kenya* 82 C4
Kiangsi = Jiangxi □, *China* 53 D10
Kiangsu = Jiangsu □, *China* 51 H10
Kibæk, *Denmark* 11 H2
Kibanga Port, *Uganda* 82 B3
Kibangou, *Congo* 80 E2
Kibara, *Tanzania* 82 C3
Kibare, Mts., *Zaïre* 82 D2
Kibombo, *Zaïre* 82 C2
Kibondo, *Tanzania* 82 C3
Kibondo □, *Tanzania* 82 C3
Kibumbu, *Burundi* 82 C2
Kibungu, *Rwanda* 82 C3
Kibuye, *Burundi* 82 C2
Kibuye, *Rwanda* 82 C2
Kibwesa, *Tanzania* 82 D2
Kibwezi, *Kenya* 82 C4
Kichiga, *Russia* 45 D17
Kicking Horse Pass, *Canada* 100 C5
Kidal, *Mali* 79 B5
Kidderminster, *U.K.* 13 E5
Kidete, *Tanzania* 82 D4
Kidira, *Senegal* 78 C2
Kidnappers, C., *N.Z.* 87 H6
Kidston, *Australia* 90 B3
Kidugallo, *Tanzania* 82 D4
Kiel, *Germany* 18 A6
Kiel Kanal = Nord-Ostsee Kanal, *Germany* 18 A5
Kielce, *Poland* 20 E10
Kieldrecht, *Belgium* 17 F4
Kieler Bucht, *Germany* 18 A6
Kien Binh, *Vietnam* 59 H5
Kien Tan, *Vietnam* 59 G5
Kienge, *Zaïre* 83 E2
Kiessé, *Niger* 79 C5
Kiev = Kiyev, *Ukraine* 40 F7
Kiffa, *Mauritania* 78 B2
Kifisiá, *Greece* 39 L6
Kifissós →, *Greece* 39 L6
Kifrī, *Iraq* 64 C5
Kigali, *Rwanda* 82 C3
Kigarama, *Tanzania* 82 C3
Kigoma □, *Tanzania* 82 D2
Kigoma-Ujiji, *Tanzania* 82 C2
Kigomasha, Ras, *Tanzania* 82 C4
Kihee, *Australia* 91 D3
Kii-Sanchi, *Japan* 49 G7
Kii-Suidō, *Japan* 49 H7
Kikaiga-Shima, *Japan* 49 K4
Kikinda, *Serbia* 21 K10
Kikládhes, *Greece* 39 M7
Kikwit, *Zaïre* 80 E3
Kílalki, *Greece* 39 N10
Kilauea Crater, *U.S.A.* 102 J17
Kilchberg, *Switz.* 23 B7
Kilcoy, *Australia* 91 D5
Kildare, *Ireland* 15 C5
Kildare □, *Ireland* 15 C5
Kilgore, *U.S.A.* 109 J7
Kilifi, *Kenya* 82 C4
Kilifi □, *Kenya* 82 C4
Kilimanjaro, *Tanzania* 82 C4
Kilimanjaro □, *Tanzania* 82 C4
Kilindini, *Kenya* 82 C4
Kilis, *Turkey* 66 E7
Kiliya, *Ukraine* 42 D3
Kilju, *N. Korea* 51 D15
Kilkee, *Ireland* 15 D2
Kilkenny, *Ireland* 15 D4
Kilkenny □, *Ireland* 15 D4
Kilkieran B., *Ireland* 15 C2
Kilkís, *Greece* 39 J5
Killala, *Ireland* 15 B2
Killala B., *Ireland* 15 B2
Killaloe, *Ireland* 15 D3
Killaloe Sta., *Canada* 106 A7
Killam, *Canada* 100 C6
Killarney, *Australia* 91 D5
Killarney, *Canada* 98 C3
Killarney, *Ireland* 15 D2
Killarney, Lakes of, *Ireland* 15 E2
Killary Harbour, *Ireland* 15 C2
Killdeer, *Canada* 101 D7
Killdeer, *U.S.A.* 108 B3
Killeen, *U.S.A.* 109 K6
Killiecrankie, Pass of, *U.K.* 14 E5
Killin, *U.K.* 14 E4
Killíni, *Ilía, Greece* 39 M4
Killíni, *Korinthía, Greece* 39 M5
Killybegs, *Ireland* 15 B3
Kilmarnock, *U.K.* 14 F4
Kilmez, *Russia* 41 C17
Kilmez →, *Russia* 41 C17
Kilmore, *Australia* 91 F3
Kilondo, *Tanzania* 83 D3
Kilosa, *Tanzania* 82 D4
Kilosa □, *Tanzania* 82 D4
Kilrush, *Ireland* 15 D2
Kilwa □, *Tanzania* 83 D4
Kilwa Kisiwani, *Tanzania* 83 D4
Kilwa Kivinje, *Tanzania* 83 D4
Kilwa Masoko, *Tanzania* 83 D4
Kim, *U.S.A.* 109 G3
Kimaam, *Indonesia* 57 F9
Kimamba, *Tanzania* 82 D4

Kimba

Kimba, Australia 91 E2
Kimball, Nebr., U.S.A. 108 E3
Kimball, S. Dak., U.S.A. 108 D5
Kimberley, Canada 100 D5
Kimberley, S. Africa 84 D3
Kimberley Downs, Australia 88 C3
Kimberly, U.S.A. 110 E6
Kimchaek, N. Korea 51 D15
Kimchŏn, S. Korea 51 F15
Kími, Greece 39 L7
Kimje, S. Korea 51 G14
Kímolos, Greece 39 N7
Kimovsk, Russia 41 D11
Kimparana, Mali 78 C4
Kimry, Russia 41 C10
Kimsquit, Canada 100 C3
Kimstad, Sweden 11 F9
Kinabalu, Gunong, Malaysia 56 C5
Kínaros, Greece 39 N9
Kinaskan L., Canada 100 B2
Kinbasket L., Canada 100 C5
Kincaid, Canada 101 D7
Kincardine, Canada 98 D3
Kinda, Zaïre 83 D2
Kinder Scout, U.K. 12 D6
Kindersley, Canada 101 C7
Kindia, Guinea 78 C2
Kindu, Zaïre 82 C2
Kinel, Russia 41 E17
Kineshma, Russia 41 C13
Kinesi, Tanzania 82 C3
King, L., Australia 89 F2
King, Mt., Australia 90 D4
King City, U.S.A. 111 H3
King Cr. →, Australia 90 C2
King Edward →, Australia 88 B4
King Frederick VI Land = Kong Frederik VI.s Kyst, Greenland 4 C5
King George B., Falk. Is. 128 D4
King George I., Antarctica 5 C18
King George Is., Canada 97 C11
King I. = Kadan Kyun, Burma 56 B1
King I., Australia 90 F3
King I., Canada 100 C3
King Leopold Ras., Australia 88 C4
King Sd., Australia 88 C3
King William I., Canada 96 B10
King William's Town, S. Africa 84 E4
Kingaroy, Australia 91 D5
Kingfisher, U.S.A. 109 H6
Kingirbān, Iraq 64 C5
Kingisepp = Kuressaare, Estonia 40 B3
Kingisepp, Russia 40 B6
Kingman, Ariz., U.S.A. 113 K12
Kingman, Kans., U.S.A. 109 G5
Kingoonya, Australia 91 E2
Kings →, U.S.A. 111 H4
Kings Canyon National Park, U.S.A. 111 H4
King's Lynn, U.K. 12 E8
Kings Mountain, U.S.A. 105 H5
King's Peak, U.S.A. 110 F8
Kingsbridge, U.K. 13 G4
Kingsburg, U.S.A. 111 H4
Kingscote, Australia 91 F2
Kingscourt, Ireland 15 C5
Kingsley, U.S.A. 108 D7
Kingsport, U.S.A. 105 G4
Kingston, Canada 98 D4
Kingston, Jamaica 116 C4
Kingston, N.Z. 87 L2
Kingston, N.Y., U.S.A. 107 E10
Kingston, Pa., U.S.A. 107 E9
Kingston, R.I., U.S.A. 107 E13
Kingston Pk., U.S.A. 113 K11
Kingston South East, Australia 91 F2
Kingston upon Hull, U.K. 12 D7
Kingston-upon-Thames, U.K. 13 F7
Kingstown, St. Vincent 117 D7
Kingstree, U.S.A. 105 J6
Kingsville, Canada 98 D3
Kingsville, U.S.A. 109 M6
Kingussie, U.K. 14 D4
Kinistino, Canada 101 C7
Kinkala, Congo 80 E2
Kinki □, Japan 49 H8
Kinleith, N.Z. 87 H5
Kinmount, Canada 106 B6
Kinna, Sweden 11 G6
Kinnaird, Canada 100 D5
Kinnairds Hd., U.K. 14 D7
Kinnared, Sweden 11 G7
Kinnarodden, Norway 6 A11
Kino, Mexico 114 B2
Kinoje →, Canada 98 B3
Kinomoto, Japan 49 G8
Kinoni, Uganda 82 C3
Kinrooi, Belgium 17 F7
Kinross, U.K. 14 E5
Kinsale, Ireland 15 E3
Kinsale, Old Hd. of, Ireland 15 E3
Kinsha = Chang Jiang →, China 53 B13
Kinshasa, Zaïre 80 E3
Kinsley, U.S.A. 109 G5
Kinston, U.S.A. 105 H7
Kintampo, Ghana 79 D4
Kintap, Indonesia 56 E5
Kintore Ra., Australia 88 D4
Kintyre, U.K. 14 F3
Kintyre, Mull of, U.K. 14 F3
Kinushseo →, Canada 98 A3
Kinuso, Canada 100 B5
Kinyangiri, Tanzania 82 C3
Kinzig →, Germany 19 G3
Kinzua, U.S.A. 106 E6
Kinzua Dam, U.S.A. 106 E5
Kiosk, Canada 98 C4
Kiowa, Kans., U.S.A. 109 G5
Kiowa, Okla., U.S.A. 109 H7
Kipahigan L., Canada 101 B8
Kipanga, Tanzania 82 D4
Kiparissía, Greece 39 M4
Kiparissiakós Kólpos, Greece 39 M4
Kipembawe, Tanzania 82 D3
Kipengere Ra., Tanzania 83 D3
Kipili, Tanzania 82 D3
Kipini, Kenya 82 C5
Kipling, Canada 101 C8
Kippure, Ireland 15 C5
Kipushi, Zaïre 83 E2
Kiratpur, India 62 E8
Kirchberg, Switz. 22 B5
Kirchhain, Germany 18 E4
Kirchheim, Germany 19 G5
Kirchheim-Bolanden, Germany 19 F4
Kirensk, Russia 45 D11
Kirgella Rocks, Australia 89 F3
Kirghizia ■, Asia 44 E8
Kirghizstan = Kirghizia ■, Asia 44 E8
Kirgizia = Kirghizia ■, Asia 44 E8
Kiri, Zaïre 80 E3
Kiribati ■, Pac. Oc. 92 H10
Kırıkhan, Turkey 66 E7
Kırıkkale, Turkey 66 D5
Kirillov, Russia 41 B11
Kirin = Jilin, China 51 C14
Kirin = Jilin □, China 51 C13
Kirishi, Russia 40 B7
Kiritimati, Kiribati 93 G12
Kırka, Turkey 66 D4
Kirkcaldy, U.K. 14 E5
Kirkcudbright, U.K. 14 G4
Kirkee, India 60 K8
Kirkenær, Norway 10 D6
Kirkenes, Norway 8 B21
Kirkintilloch, U.K. 14 F4
Kirkjubæjarklaustur, Iceland 8 E4
Kirkland, U.S.A. 111 J7
Kirkland Lake, Canada 98 C3
Kırklareli, Turkey 39 H10
Kırklareli □, Turkey 66 C2
Kirksville, U.S.A. 108 E8
Kirkūk, Iraq 64 C5
Kirkwall, U.K. 14 C6
Kirkwood, S. Africa 84 E4
Kirn, Germany 19 F3
Kirov = Vyatka, Russia 41 B16
Kirov, Russia 40 D9
Kirovabad = Gyandzha, Azerbaijan 43 F12
Kirovakan = Karaklis, Armenia 43 F11
Kirovo-Chepetsk, Russia 41 B17
Kirovograd, Ukraine 42 B5
Kirovohrad = Kirovograd, Ukraine 42 B5
Kirovsk, Russia 44 C4
Kirovsk, Turkmenistan 44 F7
Kirovsk, Ukraine 43 B8
Kirovski, Russia 43 D13
Kirovskiy, Russia 45 D16
Kirovskiy, Russia 48 B6
Kirriemuir, U.K. 14 E6
Kirsanov, Russia 41 E13
Kırşehir, Turkey 66 D6
Kırşehir □, Turkey 66 D6
Kirstonia, S. Africa 84 D3
Kirtachi, Niger 79 C5
Kirthar Range, Pakistan 62 F2
Kiruna, Sweden 8 C16
Kirundu, Zaïre 82 C2
Kirup, Australia 89 F2
Kirya, Russia 41 D15
Kiryū, Japan 49 F9
Kisaga, Tanzania 82 C3
Kisalaya, Nic. 116 D3
Kisámou, Kólpos, Greece 37 D5
Kisanga, Zaïre 82 B2
Kisangani, Zaïre 82 B2
Kisar, Indonesia 57 F7
Kisaran, Indonesia 56 D1
Kisarawe, Tanzania 82 D4
Kisarawe □, Tanzania 82 D4
Kisarazu, Japan 49 G9
Kisbér, Hungary 21 H8
Kiselevsk, Russia 44 D9
Kishanganga →, Pakistan 63 B5
Kishanganj, India 63 F13
Kishangarh, India 62 F4
Kishi, Nigeria 79 D5
Kishinev, Moldavia 42 C3
Kishiwada, Japan 49 G7
Kishtwar, India 63 C6
Kisii, Kenya 82 C3
Kisii □, Kenya 82 C3
Kisiju, Tanzania 82 D4
Kısır Dağ, Turkey 43 F10
Kisizi, Uganda 82 C2
Kiska I., U.S.A. 96 C1
Kiskatinaw →, Canada 100 B4
Kiskittogisu L., Canada 101 C9
Kiskőrös, Hungary 21 J9
Kiskundorozsma, Hungary 21 J10
Kiskunfélegyháza, Hungary 21 J9
Kiskunhalas, Hungary 21 J9
Kiskunmajsa, Hungary 21 J9
Kislovodsk, Russia 43 E10
Kiso-Gawa →, Japan 49 G8
Kiso-Sammyaku, Japan 49 G8
Kisofukushima, Japan 49 G8
Kisoro, Uganda 82 C2
Kispest, Hungary 21 H9
Kissidougou, Guinea 78 D2
Kissimmee, U.S.A. 105 L5
Kissimmee →, U.S.A. 105 M5
Kississing L., Canada 101 B8
Kissónerga, Cyprus 37 E11
Kistanje, Croatia 33 E12
Kisújszállás, Hungary 21 H10
Kisumu, Kenya 82 C3
Kisvárda, Hungary 21 G12
Kiswani, Tanzania 82 C4
Kiswere, Tanzania 83 D4
Kit Carson, U.S.A. 108 F3
Kita, Mali 78 C3
Kitab, Uzbekistan 44 F7
Kitaibaraki, Japan 49 F10
Kitakami, Japan 48 E10
Kitakami-Gawa →, Japan 48 E10
Kitakami-Sammyaku, Japan 48 E10
Kitakata, Japan 48 F9
Kitakyūshū, Japan 49 H5
Kitale, Kenya 82 B4
Kitami, Japan 48 C11
Kitami-Sammyaku, Japan 48 B11
Kitangiri, L., Tanzania 82 C3
Kitaya, Tanzania 83 E5
Kitchener, Australia 89 F3
Kitchener, Canada 98 D3
Kitega = Gitega, Burundi 82 C2
Kitengo, Zaïre 82 D1
Kiteto □, Tanzania 82 C4
Kitgum, Uganda 82 B3
Kíthira, Greece 39 N7
Kíthnos, Greece 39 M7
Kiti, Cyprus 37 E12
Kiti, C., Cyprus 37 E12
Kitikmeot □, Canada 96 A9
Kitimat, Canada 100 C3
Kitinen →, Finland 8 C19
Kitiyab, Sudan 77 D3
Kítros, Greece 39 J5
Kitsuki, Japan 49 H5
Kittakittaooloo, L., Australia 91 D2
Kittanning, U.S.A. 106 F5
Kittatinny Mts., U.S.A. 107 E10
Kittery, U.S.A. 105 D10
Kitui, Kenya 82 C4
Kitui □, Kenya 82 C4
Kitwe, Zambia 83 E2
Kitzbühel, Austria 19 H8
Kitzingen, Germany 19 F6
Kivalo, Finland 8 C19
Kivarli, India 62 G5
Kividhes, Cyprus 37 E11
Kivu □, Zaïre 82 C2
Kivu, L., Zaïre 82 C2
Kiyev, Ukraine 40 F7
Kiyevskoye Vdkhr., Ukraine 40 F7
Kiziguru, Rwanda 82 C3
Kızıl Irmak →, Turkey 42 F6
Kizil Jilga, India 63 B8
Kizil Yurt, Russia 43 E12
Kızılcahamam, Turkey 42 F5
Kızılhisar, Turkey 66 E3
Kızılırmak, Turkey 66 C5
Kızıltepe, Turkey 67 E9
Kizimkazi, Tanzania 82 D4
Kizlyar, Russia 43 E12
Kizyl-Arvat, Turkmenistan 44 F6
Kjellerup, Denmark 11 H3
Kladanj, Bos.-H. 21 L8
Kladno, Czech. 20 E4
Kladovo, Serbia 21 L12
Klaeng, Thailand 58 F3
Klagenfurt, Austria 21 J4
Klagshamn, Sweden 11 J6
Klagstorp, Sweden 11 J7
Klaipėda, Lithuania 40 D2
Klamath →, U.S.A. 110 F1
Klamath Falls, U.S.A. 110 E3
Klamath Mts., U.S.A. 110 F2
Klanjec, Croatia 33 B12
Klappan →, Canada 100 B3
Klarälven →, Sweden 9 G12
Klaten, Indonesia 57 G14
Klatovy, Czech. 20 F3
Klawer, S. Africa 84 E2
Klawock, U.S.A. 100 B2
Klazienaveen, Neths. 16 C10
Kleczew, Poland 20 C8
Kleena Kleene, Canada 100 C4
Klein, U.S.A. 110 C9
Klein-Karas, Namibia 84 D2
Kleine Gette →, Belgium 17 G6
Kleine Nete →, Belgium 17 F5
Klekovača, Bos.-H. 33 D13
Klenovec, Macedonia 39 H3
Klenovec, Slovak Rep. 20 G9
Klerksdorp, S. Africa 84 D4
Kletnya, Russia 40 E8
Kletsk, Belorussia 40 E5
Kletskiy, Russia 43 B10
Kleve, Germany 18 D2
Klickitat, U.S.A. 110 D3
Klickitat →, U.S.A. 112 E5
Klidhes, Cyprus 37 D13
Klimovichi, Belorussia 40 E8
Klin, Russia 41 C10
Klinaklini →, Canada 100 C3
Klintsey, Russia 40 E8
Klipdale, S. Africa 84 E2
Klipplaat, S. Africa 84 E3
Klitmøller, Denmark 11 G2
Kljajićevo, Serbia 21 K9
Ključ, Bos.-H. 33 D13
Kłobuck, Poland 20 E8
Kłodzko, Poland 20 E6
Kloetinge, Neths. 17 F3
Klondike, Canada 96 B6
Kloosterzande, Neths. 17 F4
Klosterneuburg, Austria 21 G6
Klosters, Switz. 23 C9
Kloten, Switz. 23 B7
Klötze, Germany 18 C7
Klouto, Togo 79 D5
Kluane L., Canada 96 B6
Kluczbork, Poland 20 E8
Klundert, Neths. 17 E5
Klyuchevskaya, Gora, Russia 45 D17
Knaresborough, U.K. 12 C6
Knee L., Man., Canada 101 B10
Knee L., Sask., Canada 101 B7
Kneïss, Is., Tunisia 75 B7
Knesselare, Belgium 17 F2
Knezha, Bulgaria 38 F7
Knić, Serbia 21 M10
Knight Inlet, Canada 100 C3
Knighton, U.K. 13 E4
Knights Ferry, U.S.A. 112 H6
Knights Landing, U.S.A. 112 G5
Knin, Croatia 33 D13
Knittelfeld, Austria 21 H4
Knjaževac, Serbia 21 M12
Knob, C., Australia 89 F2
Knockmealdown Mts., Ireland 15 D4
Knokke, Belgium 17 F2
Knossós, Greece 37 D7
Knox, U.S.A. 104 E2
Knox, C., Canada 100 C2
Knox City, U.S.A. 109 J5
Knox Coast, Antarctica 5 C8
Knoxville, Iowa, U.S.A. 108 E8
Knoxville, Tenn., U.S.A. 105 H4
Knutshø, Norway 10 B3
Knysna, S. Africa 84 E3
Knyszyn, Poland 20 B12
Ko Kha, Thailand 58 C2
Ko Tao, Thailand 59 G2
Koartac, Canada 97 B13
Koba, Aru, Indonesia 57 F8
Koba, Bangka, Indonesia 56 E3
Kobarid, Slovenia 33 B10
Kobayashi, Japan 49 J5
Kobdo = Hovd, Mongolia 54 B4
Kōbe, Japan 49 G7
Kobelyaki, Ukraine 42 B6
København, Denmark 11 J6
Kōbi-Sho, Japan 49 M1
Koblenz, Germany 19 E3
Koblenz, Switz. 22 A6
Kobo, Ethiopia 77 E4
Kobrin, Belorussia 40 E4
Kobroor, Kepulauan, Indonesia 57 F8
Kobuleti, Georgia 43 F9
Kobyłka, Poland 20 C11
Kobylkino, Russia 41 D13
Kobylnik, Belorussia 40 D5
Kocaeli = İzmit, Turkey 66 C3
Kocaeli □, Turkey 66 C3
Kočani, Macedonia 39 H5
Koceljevo, Serbia 21 L9
Kočevje, Slovenia 33 C11
Koch Bihar, India 61 F16
Kochang, S. Korea 51 G14
Kochas, India 63 G10
Kocher →, Germany 19 F5
Kocheya, Russia 45 D13
Kōchi, Japan 49 H6
Kōchi □, Japan 49 H6
Kochiu = Gejiu, China 52 F4
Kodiak, U.S.A. 96 C4
Kodiak I., U.S.A. 96 C4
Kodinar, India 62 J4
Kodori →, Georgia 43 E9
Koekelare, Belgium 17 F1
Koersel, Belgium 17 F6
Koes, Namibia 84 D2
Koffiefontein, S. Africa 84 D4
Kofiau, Indonesia 57 E7
Koforidua, Ghana 79 D4
Kōfu, Japan 49 G9
Koga, Japan 49 F9
Kogaluk →, Canada 99 A7
Kogan, Australia 91 D5
Kogi □, Nigeria 79 D6
Kogin Baba, Nigeria 79 D7
Koh-i-Bābā, Afghan. 60 B5
Koh-i-Khurd, Afghan. 62 C1
Kohat, Pakistan 62 C4
Kohima, India 61 G19
Kohkīlūyeh va Būyer Aḥmadi □, Iran 65 D6
Kohler Ra., Antarctica 5 D15
Kohtla-Järve, Estonia 40 B5
Koin-dong, N. Korea 51 D14
Kojŏ, N. Korea 51 E14
Kojonup, Australia 89 F2
Kojūr, Iran 65 B6
Koka, Sudan 76 C3
Kokand, Uzbekistan 44 E8
Kokanee Glacier Prov. Park, Canada 100 D5
Kokas, Indonesia 57 E8
Kokchetav, Kazakhstan 44 D7
Kokemäenjoki, Finland 9 F16
Kokerite, Guyana 121 B6
Kokhma, Russia 41 C12
Kokkola, Finland 8 E17
Koko, Nigeria 79 C5
Koko Kyunzu, Burma 61 M18
Kokolopozo, Ivory C. 78 D3
Kokomo, U.S.A. 104 E2
Kokonau, Indonesia 57 E9
Kokoro, Niger 79 C5
Koksan, N. Korea 51 E14
Koksoak →, Canada 97 C13
Kokstad, S. Africa 85 E4
Kokubu, Japan 49 J5
Kokuora, Russia 45 B15
Kola, Indonesia 57 F8
Kola, Russia 44 C4
Kola Pen. = Kolskiy Poluostrov, Russia 44 C4
Kolahoi, India 63 B6
Kolahun, Liberia 78 D2
Kolaka, Indonesia 57 E6
Kolar, India 60 N11
Kolar Gold Fields, India 60 N11
Kolari, Finland 8 C17
Kolayat, India 60 F8
Kolby Kås, Denmark 11 J4
Kolchugino = Leninsk-Kuznetskiy, Russia 44 D9
Kolchugino, Russia 41 C11
Kolda, Senegal 78 C2
Kolding, Denmark 11 J3
Kole, Zaïre 80 E4
Koléa, Algeria 75 A5
Kolepom = Yos Sudarso, Pulau, Indonesia 57 F9
Kolguyev, Ostrov, Russia 44 C5
Kolham, Neths. 16 B9
Kolhapur, India 60 L9
Kolia, Ivory C. 78 D3
Kolín, Czech. 20 E5
Kolind, Denmark 11 H4
Kölleda, Germany 18 D7
Kollum, Neths. 16 B8
Kolmanskop, Namibia 84 D2
Köln, Germany 18 E2
Koło, Poland 20 C8
Kołobrzeg, Poland 20 A5
Kologriv, Russia 41 B14
Kolokani, Mali 78 C3
Kolomna, Russia 41 D11
Kolomyya, Ukraine 42 B1
Kolondiéba, Mali 78 C3
Kolonodale, Indonesia 57 E6
Kolosib, India 61 G18
Kolpashevo, Russia 44 D9
Kolpino, Russia 40 B7
Kolpny, Russia 41 E10
Kolskiy Poluostrov, Russia 44 C4
Kolubara →, Serbia 21 L10
Koluszki, Poland 20 D9
Kolwezi, Zaïre 83 E2
Kolyberovo, Russia 41 D11
Kolyma →, Russia 45 C17
Kolymskoye, Okhotsko, Russia 45 C16
Kôm Ombo, Egypt 76 C3
Komandorskiye Is. = Komandorskiye Ostrova, Russia 45 D17
Komandorskiye Ostrova, Russia 45 D17
Komárno, Slovak Rep. 21 H8
Komárom, Hungary 21 H8
Komarovo, Russia 40 B8
Komatipoort, S. Africa 85 D5
Komatou Yialou, Cyprus 37 D13
Komatsu, Japan 49 F8
Komatsujima, Japan 49 H7
Kombissiri, Burkina Faso 79 C4
Kombori, Burkina Faso 78 C4
Komen, Slovenia 33 C10
Komenda, Ghana 79 D4
Komi Republic □, Russia 44 C6
Komiža, Croatia 33 E13
Komló, Hungary 21 J8
Kommunarsk, Ukraine 43 B8
Kommunizma, Pik, Tajikistan 44 F8
Komodo, Indonesia 57 F5
Komoé, Ivory C. 78 D4
Komono, Congo 80 E2
Komoran, Pulau, Indonesia 57 F9
Komoro, Japan 49 F9
Komotini, Greece 39 H8
Kompasberg, S. Africa 84 E3
Kompong Bang, Cambodia 59 F5
Kompong Cham, Cambodia 59 F5
Kompong Chhnang, Cambodia 59 F5

Kompong Chikreng, *Cambodia* ... 58 F5
Kompong Kleang, *Cambodia* ... 58 F5
Kompong Luong, *Cambodia* ... 59 G5
Kompong Pranak, *Cambodia* ... 58 F5
Kompong Som, *Cambodia* 59 G4
Kompong Som, Chhung, *Cambodia* ... 59 G4
Kompong Speu, *Cambodia* 59 G4
Kompong Sralao, *Cambodia* ... 58 E5
Kompong Thom, *Cambodia* 58 F5
Kompong Trabeck, *Cambodia* ... 58 F5
Kompong Trabeck, *Cambodia* ... 59 G5
Kompong Trach, *Cambodia* 59 G5
Kompong Tralach, *Cambodia* ... 59 G5
Komrat, *Moldavia* ... 42 C3
Komsberg, *S. Africa* ... 84 E3
Komsomolets, Ostrov, *Russia* ... 45 A10
Komsomolsk, *Russia* ... 41 C12
Komsomolsk, *Russia* ... 45 D14
Komsomolskiy, *Russia* ... 41 E16
Konakovo, *Russia* ... 41 C10
Konarhá □, *Afghan.* ... 60 B7
Konārī, *Iran* ... 65 D6
Konawa, *U.S.A.* ... 109 H6
Konch, *India* ... 63 G8
Kondakovo, *Russia* ... 45 C16
Konde, *Tanzania* ... 82 C4
Kondinin, *Australia* ... 89 F2
Kondoa, *Tanzania* ... 82 C4
Kondoa □, *Tanzania* ... 82 D4
Kondókali, *Greece* ... 37 A3
Kondratyevo, *Russia* ... 45 D10
Konduga, *Nigeria* ... 79 C7
Kong, *Ivory C.* ... 78 D4
Kong →, *Cambodia* ... 58 F5
Kong, Koh, *Cambodia* ... 59 G4
Kong Christian IX.s Land, *Greenland* ... 4 C6
Kong Christian X.s Land, *Greenland* ... 4 B6
Kong Franz Joseph Fd., *Greenland* ... 4 B6
Kong Frederik IX.s Land, *Greenland* ... 4 C5
Kong Frederik VI.s Kyst, *Greenland* ... 4 C5
Kong Frederik VIII.s Land, *Greenland* ... 4 B6
Kong Oscar Fjord, *Greenland* ... 4 B6
Kongeå →, *Denmark* ... 11 J3
Kongju, *S. Korea* ... 51 F14
Konglu, *Burma* ... 61 F20
Kongolo, Kasai Or., *Zaïre* ... 82 D1
Kongolo, Shaba, *Zaïre* ... 82 D5
Kongor, *Sudan* ... 77 F3
Kongoussi, *Burkina Faso* ... 79 C4
Kongsberg, *Norway* ... 10 E3
Kongsvinger, *Norway* ... 10 D6
Kongwa, *Tanzania* ... 82 D4
Koni, *Zaïre* ... 83 E2
Koni, Mts., *Zaïre* ... 83 E2
Königsberg = Kaliningrad, *Russia* ... 40 D2
Königslutter, *Germany* ... 18 C6
Königswusterhausen, *Germany* ... 18 C9
Konin, *Poland* ... 20 C8
Kónitsa, *Greece* ... 39 J3
Köniz, *Switz.* ... 22 C4
Konjice, *Slovenia* ... 33 B12
Konkiep, *Namibia* ... 84 D2
Konkouré →, *Guinea* ... 78 D2
Könnern, *Germany* ... 18 D7
Kono, *S. Leone* ... 78 D2
Konolfingen, *Switz.* ... 22 C5
Konongo, *Ghana* ... 79 D4
Konosha, *Russia* ... 44 C5
Kōnosu, *Japan* ... 49 F9
Konotop, *Ukraine* ... 40 F8
Konqi He →, *China* ... 54 B4
Końskie, *Poland* ... 20 D10
Konstantinovka, *Ukraine* ... 42 B7
Konstantinovski, *Russia* ... 43 C9
Konstanz, *Germany* ... 19 H5
Kont, *Iran* ... 65 E9
Kontagora, *Nigeria* ... 79 C6
Kontich, *Belgium* ... 17 F4
Kontum, *Vietnam* ... 58 E7
Kontum, Plateau du, *Vietnam* ... 58 E7
Konya, *Turkey* ... 66 E5
Konya □, *Turkey* ... 66 E5
Konya Ovasi, *Turkey* ... 66 D5
Konz, *Germany* ... 19 F2
Konza, *Kenya* ... 82 C4
Kookynie, *Australia* ... 89 E3
Kooline, *Australia* ... 88 D2
Kooloonong, *Australia* ... 91 E3
Koolyanobbing, *Australia* ... 89 F2
Koondrook, *Australia* ... 91 F3
Koonibba, *Australia* ... 91 E1
Koorawatha, *Australia* ... 91 E4
Koorda, *Australia* ... 89 F2
Kooskia, *U.S.A.* ... 110 C6
Kootenai →, *Canada* ... 110 B5

Kootenay L., *Canada* ... 100 D5
Kootenay Nat. Park, *Canada* ... 100 C5
Kootjieskolk, *S. Africa* ... 84 E3
Kopaonik, *Serbia* ... 21 M11
Kopanovka, *Russia* ... 43 C12
Kópavogur, *Iceland* ... 8 D3
Koper, *Slovenia* ... 33 C10
Kopervik, *Norway* ... 9 G8
Kopeysk, *Russia* ... 44 D7
Kopi, *Australia* ... 91 E2
Köping, *Sweden* ... 10 E10
Kopiste, *Croatia* ... 33 F13
Köpmanholmen, *Sweden* ... 10 A12
Koppang, *Norway* ... 10 C5
Kopparberg, *Sweden* ... 9 G13
Kopparbergs län □, *Sweden* ... 9 F13
Kopperå, *Norway* ... 10 A5
Koppies, *S. Africa* ... 85 D4
Koprivnica, *Croatia* ... 33 B13
Kopychintsy, *Ukraine* ... 40 G4
Kopys, *Belorussia* ... 40 D7
Korab, *Macedonia* ... 39 H3
Korakiána, *Greece* ... 37 A3
Korba, *India* ... 63 H10
Korbach, *Germany* ... 18 D4
Korbu, G., *Malaysia* ... 59 K3
Korça, *Albania* ... 39 J3
Korce = Korça, *Albania* ... 39 J3
Korčula, *Croatia* ... 33 F14
Korčulanski Kanal, *Croatia* ... 33 E13
Kord Kūy, *Iran* ... 65 B7
Kord Sheykh, *Iran* ... 65 D7
Kordestān □, *Iran* ... 64 C5
Korea, North ■, *Asia* ... 51 E14
Korea, South ■, *Asia* ... 51 F15
Korea Bay, *Korea* ... 51 E13
Korea Strait, *Asia* ... 51 G15
Korenevo, *Russia* ... 40 F9
Korenovsk, *Russia* ... 43 D8
Korets, *Ukraine* ... 40 F5
Korgan, *Turkey* ... 67 C7
Korgus, *Sudan* ... 76 D3
Korhogo, *Ivory C.* ... 78 D3
Koribundu, *S. Leone* ... 78 D2
Korim, *Indonesia* ... 57 E9
Korinthiakós Kólpos, *Greece* ... 39 L5
Kórinthos, *Greece* ... 39 M5
Korioumé, *Mali* ... 78 B4
Koríssa, Límni, *Greece* ... 37 B3
Kōriyama, *Japan* ... 48 F10
Korkuteli, *Turkey* ... 66 E4
Kormakiti, C., *Cyprus* ... 37 D11
Körmend, *Hungary* ... 21 H6
Kornat, *Croatia* ... 33 E12
Korneshty, *Moldavia* ... 42 C3
Kornsjø, *Norway* ... 10 F5
Kornstad, *Norway* ... 10 B1
Koro, *Fiji* ... 87 C8
Koro, *Ivory C.* ... 78 D3
Koro, *Mali* ... 78 C4
Koro Sea, *Fiji* ... 87 C9
Korocha, *Russia* ... 41 F10
Köroğlu Dağları, *Turkey* ... 66 C4
Korogwe, *Tanzania* ... 82 D4
Korogwe □, *Tanzania* ... 82 D4
Koroit, *Australia* ... 91 F3
Koronadal, *Phil.* ... 55 H6
Koronowo, *Poland* ... 20 B7
Koror, *Pac. Oc.* ... 57 C8
Körös →, *Hungary* ... 21 J10
Korosten, *Ukraine* ... 40 F6
Korotoyak, *Russia* ... 41 F11
Korraraika, Helodranon' i, *Madag.* ... 85 B7
Korsakov, *Russia* ... 45 E15
Korshunovo, *Russia* ... 45 D12
Korsør, *Denmark* ... 9 J11
Korsun Shevchenkovskiy, *Ukraine* ... 42 B4
Korsze, *Poland* ... 20 A11
Kortemark, *Belgium* ... 17 F2
Kortessem, *Belgium* ... 17 G6
Korti, *Sudan* ... 76 D3
Kortrijk, *Belgium* ... 17 G2
Korwai, *India* ... 62 G8
Koryakskiy Khrebet, *Russia* ... 45 C18
Koryŏng, *S. Korea* ... 51 G15
Kos, *Greece* ... 39 N10
Kosa, *Ethiopia* ... 77 F4
Kosaya Gora, *Russia* ... 41 D10
Kościan, *Poland* ... 20 C6
Kościerzyna, *Poland* ... 20 A7
Kosciusko, *U.S.A.* ... 109 J10
Kosciusko, Mt., *Australia* ... 91 F4
Kosciusko I., *U.S.A.* ... 100 B2
Kösély →, *Hungary* ... 21 H11
Kosha, *Sudan* ... 76 C3
Kōshetau = Kokchetav, *Kazakhstan* ... 44 D7
K'oshih = Kashi, *China* ... 54 C2
Koshiki-Rettō, *Japan* ... 49 J4
Kosi, *India* ... 62 F7
Kosi-meer, *S. Africa* ... 85 D5
Košice, *Slovak Rep.* ... 20 G11
Kosjerić, *Serbia* ... 21 M9
Koskhinoú, *Greece* ... 37 C10
Kosŏng, *N. Korea* ... 51 E15
Kosovska-Mitrovica, *Serbia* ... 21 N10
Kostajnica, *Croatia* ... 33 C13
Kostanjevica, *Slovenia* ... 33 C12
Kostelec, *Czech.* ... 20 E6
Koster, *S. Africa* ... 84 D4
Kôstî, *Sudan* ... 77 E3

Kostopol, *Ukraine* ... 40 F5
Kostroma, *Russia* ... 41 C12
Kostromskoye Vdkhr., *Russia* ... 41 C12
Kostyantynivka = Konstantinovka, *Ukraine* ... 42 B7
Kostyukovichi, *Belorussia* ... 40 E8
Koszalin, *Poland* ... 20 A6
Köszeg, *Hungary* ... 21 H6
Kot Addu, *Pakistan* ... 62 D4
Kot Moman, *Pakistan* ... 62 C5
Kota, *India* ... 62 G6
Kota Baharu, *Malaysia* ... 59 J4
Kota Belud, *Malaysia* ... 56 C5
Kota Kinabalu, *Malaysia* ... 56 C5
Kota Tinggi, *Malaysia* ... 59 M4
Kotaagung, *Indonesia* ... 56 F2
Kotabaru, *Indonesia* ... 56 E5
Kotabumi, *Indonesia* ... 56 E2
Kotagede, *Indonesia* ... 57 G14
Kotamobagu, *Indonesia* ... 57 D6
Kotaneelee →, *Canada* ... 100 A4
Kotawaringin, *Indonesia* ... 56 E4
Kotcho L., *Canada* ... 100 B4
Kotelnich, *Russia* ... 41 B16
Kotelnikovo, *Russia* ... 43 C10
Kotelnyy, Ostrov, *Russia* ... 45 B14
Köthen, *Germany* ... 18 D7
Kothi, *India* ... 63 G9
Kotiro, *Pakistan* ... 62 F2
Kotka, *Finland* ... 9 F19
Kotlas, *Russia* ... 44 C5
Kotli, *Pakistan* ... 62 C5
Kotmul, *Pakistan* ... 63 B6
Kotonkoro, *Nigeria* ... 79 C6
Kotor, *Montenegro* ... 21 N8
Kotoriba, *Croatia* ... 33 B13
Kotovo, *Russia* ... 41 F14
Kotovsk, *Ukraine* ... 42 C3
Kotputli, *India* ... 62 F7
Kotri, *Pakistan* ... 62 G3
Kótronas, *Greece* ... 39 N5
Kottayam, *India* ... 60 Q10
Kotturu, *India* ... 60 M10
Kotuy →, *Russia* ... 45 B11
Kotzebue, *U.S.A.* ... 96 B3
Kouango, *C.A.R.* ... 80 C4
Koudekerke, *Neths.* ... 17 F3
Koudougou, *Burkina Faso* ... 78 C4
Koufonísi, *Greece* ... 37 E8
Kougaberge, *S. Africa* ... 84 E3
Kouibli, *Ivory C.* ... 78 D3
Kouilou →, *Congo* ... 80 E2
Kouki, *C.A.R.* ... 80 C3
Koula Moutou, *Gabon* ... 80 E2
Koulen, *Cambodia* ... 58 F5
Koulikoro, *Mali* ... 78 C3
Kouloúra, *Greece* ... 37 A3
Koúm-bournoú, Ákra, *Greece* ... 37 C10
Koumala, *Australia* ... 90 C4
Koumankou, *Mali* ... 78 C3
Koumbia, *Burkina Faso* ... 78 C4
Koumbia, *Guinea* ... 78 C2
Koumboum, *Guinea* ... 78 C2
Koumpenntoum, *Senegal* ... 78 C2
Koumra, *Chad* ... 73 G8
Koundara, *Guinea* ... 78 C2
Kounradskiy, *Kazakhstan* ... 44 E8
Kountze, *U.S.A.* ... 109 K7
Koupéla, *Burkina Faso* ... 79 C4
Kouris →, *Cyprus* ... 37 E11
Kourou, *Fr. Guiana* ... 121 B7
Kouroussa, *Guinea* ... 78 C3
Koussané, *Mali* ... 78 C2
Kousséri, *Cameroon* ... 73 F7
Koutiala, *Mali* ... 78 C3
Kouto, *Ivory C.* ... 78 D3
Kouvé, *Togo* ... 79 D5
Kovačica, *Serbia* ... 21 K10
Kovel, *Ukraine* ... 40 F4
Kovin, *Serbia* ... 21 L10
Kovrov, *Russia* ... 41 C12
Kowanyama, *Australia* ... 90 B3
Kowkash, *Canada* ... 98 B2
Kowloon, *H.K.* ... 53 F10
Kowŏn, *N. Korea* ... 51 E14
Koyabuti, *Indonesia* ... 57 E10
Köyceğiz, *Turkey* ... 66 E3
Koyuk, *U.S.A.* ... 96 B3
Koyukuk →, *U.S.A.* ... 96 B4
Koyulhisar, *Turkey* ... 42 F7
Koza, *Japan* ... 49 L3
Kozan, *Turkey* ... 66 E6
Kozáni, *Greece* ... 39 J4
Kozara, *Bos.-H.* ... 33 D14
Kozarac, *Bos.-H.* ... 33 D13
Kozelsk, *Russia* ... 40 D9
Kozhikode = Calicut, *India* ... 60 P9
Kozje, *Slovenia* ... 33 B12
Kozlovets, *Bulgaria* ... 38 F8
Kozlu, *Turkey* ... 66 C4
Kozluk, *Turkey* ... 67 D9
Koźmin, *Poland* ... 20 D7
Kozmodemyansk, *Russia* ... 41 C15
Kpabia, *Ghana* ... 79 D4
Kpalimé, *Togo* ... 79 D5
Kpandae, *Ghana* ... 79 D4
Kpessi, *Togo* ... 79 D5
Kra, Isthmus of = Kra, Kho Khot, *Thailand* ... 59 G2
Kra, Kho Khot, *Thailand* ... 59 G2
Kra Buri, *Thailand* ... 59 G2
Krabbendijke, *Neths.* ... 17 F4
Krabi, *Thailand* ... 59 H2

Kragan, *Indonesia* ... 57 G14
Kragerø, *Norway* ... 10 F3
Kragujevac, *Serbia* ... 21 L10
Krajina, *Bos.-H.* ... 33 D13
Krakatau = Rakata, Pulau, *Indonesia* ... 56 F3
Krakor, *Cambodia* ... 58 F5
Kraków, *Poland* ... 20 E9
Kraksaan, *Indonesia* ... 57 G15
Kralanh, *Cambodia* ... 58 F4
Kraljevo, *Serbia* ... 21 M10
Kralovice, *Czech.* ... 20 F3
Kralupy, *Czech.* ... 20 E4
Kramatorsk, *Ukraine* ... 42 B7
Kramfors, *Sweden* ... 10 B11
Kramis, C., *Algeria* ... 75 A5
Krångede, *Sweden* ... 10 A10
Kranj, *Slovenia* ... 33 B11
Kranjska Gora, *Slovenia* ... 33 B10
Krankskop, *S. Africa* ... 85 D5
Krapina, *Croatia* ... 33 B12
Krapina →, *Croatia* ... 33 C12
Krapivna, *Russia* ... 41 E10
Krapkowice, *Poland* ... 20 E7
Krasavino, *Russia* ... 45 E14
Krasnaya Gorbatka, *Russia* ... 41 D12
Krasnaya Polyana, *Russia* ... 43 E9
Kraśnik, *Poland* ... 20 E12
Kraśnik Fabryczny, *Poland* ... 20 E12
Krasnoarmeisk, *Ukraine* ... 42 B7
Krasnoarmeysk, *Russia* ... 41 F14
Krasnoarmeysk, *Russia* ... 43 B11
Krasnodar, *Russia* ... 43 D8
Krasnodon, *Ukraine* ... 43 B8
Krasnodonetskaya, *Russia* ... 43 B9
Krasnogorskiy, *Russia* ... 41 C16
Krasnograd, *Ukraine* ... 42 B6
Krasnogvardeyskoye, *Russia* ... 43 D9
Krasnogvardeysk, *Ukraine* ... 42 D6
Krasnokutsk, *Ukraine* ... 40 F9
Krasnoperekopsk, *Ukraine* ... 42 D5
Krasnorechenskiy, *Russia* ... 48 B7
Krasnoselkupsk, *Russia* ... 44 C9
Krasnoslobodsk, *Russia* ... 41 D13
Krasnoslobodsk, *Russia* ... 43 B11
Krasnoturinsk, *Russia* ... 44 D7
Krasnoufimsk, *Russia* ... 44 D6
Krasnouralsk, *Russia* ... 44 D7
Krasnovodsk, *Turkmenistan* ... 44 E6
Krasnoyarsk, *Russia* ... 45 D10
Krasnoye = Krasnyy, *Russia* ... 40 D7
Krasnoye, *Russia* ... 41 B15
Krasnoye, *Russia* ... 43 C11
Krasnozavodsk, *Russia* ... 41 C11
Krasny Liman, *Ukraine* ... 42 B7
Krasny Sulin, *Russia* ... 43 C9
Krasnystaw, *Poland* ... 20 E13
Krasnyy, *Russia* ... 40 D7
Krasnyy Kholm, *Russia* ... 41 B10
Krasnyy Kut, *Russia* ... 41 F15
Krasnyy Luch, *Ukraine* ... 43 B8
Krasnyy Profintern, *Russia* ... 41 C12
Krasnyy Yar, *Russia* ... 41 E17
Krasnyy Yar, *Russia* ... 41 F14
Krasnyy Yar, *Russia* ... 43 C13
Krasnyye Baki, *Russia* ... 41 C14
Krasnyyoskolskoye Vdkhr., *Ukraine* ... 42 B7
Kraszna →, *Hungary* ... 21 G12
Kratie, *Cambodia* ... 58 F6
Krau, *Indonesia* ... 57 E10
Kravanh, Chuor Phnum, *Cambodia* ... 59 G4
Krefeld, *Germany* ... 18 D2
Krémaston, Límni, *Greece* ... 39 L4
Kremenchug, *Ukraine* ... 42 B5
Kremenchugskoye Vdkhr., *Ukraine* ... 42 B5
Kremenchuk = Kremenchug, *Ukraine* ... 42 B5
Kremenets, *Ukraine* ... 42 A1
Kremennaya, *Ukraine* ... 42 B8
Kremges = Svetlovodsk, *Ukraine* ... 40 G8
Kremikovtsi, *Bulgaria* ... 38 G6
Kremmen, *Germany* ... 18 C9
Kremmling, *U.S.A.* ... 110 F10
Krems, *Austria* ... 21 G5
Kremsmünster, *Austria* ... 21 G4
Kretinga, *Lithuania* ... 40 D2
Krettamia, *Algeria* ... 74 C4
Krettsy, *Russia* ... 40 B8
Kreuzberg, *Germany* ... 19 E5
Kreuzlingen, *Switz.* ... 23 A8
Kribi, *Cameroon* ... 79 E6
Krichem, *Bulgaria* ... 38 G7
Krichev, *Belorussia* ... 40 E7
Krim, *Slovenia* ... 33 C11
Krimpen, *Neths.* ... 17 E4
Kriós, Ákra, *Greece* ... 37 D5
Krishna →, *India* ... 61 M12
Krishnanagar, *India* ... 63 H13
Kristiansand, *Norway* ... 9 G10
Kristianstad, *Sweden* ... 9 H13
Kristianstads län □, *Sweden* ... 9 H13
Kristiansund, *Norway* ... 10 A1
Kristiinankaupunki, *Finland* ... 8 E16
Kristinehamn, *Sweden* ... 9 G13
Kristinestad, *Finland* ... 8 E16
Kríti, *Greece* ... 37 D7

Kritsá, *Greece* ... 37 D7
Kriva →, *Macedonia* ... 38 G4
Kriva Palanka, *Macedonia* ... 38 G5
Krivaja →, *Bos.-H.* ... 21 L8
Krivoy Rog, *Ukraine* ... 42 C5
Križevci, *Croatia* ... 33 B13
Krk, *Croatia* ... 33 C11
Krka →, *Slovenia* ... 33 C12
Krkonoše, *Czech.* ... 20 E5
Krnov, *Czech.* ... 20 E7
Krobia, *Poland* ... 20 D6
Krokeaí, *Greece* ... 39 N5
Krokodil →, *Mozam.* ... 85 D5
Krokom, *Sweden* ... 10 A8
Krolevets, *Ukraine* ... 40 F8
Kroměříž, *Czech.* ... 20 F7
Krommenie, *Neths.* ... 16 D5
Kromy, *Russia* ... 40 E9
Kronach, *Germany* ... 19 E7
Kronoberg län □, *Sweden* ... 9 H13
Kronprins Olav Kyst, *Antarctica* ... 5 C5
Kronshtadt, *Russia* ... 40 A6
Kroonstad, *S. Africa* ... 84 D4
Kröpelin, *Germany* ... 18 A7
Kropotkin, *Russia* ... 43 D9
Kropotkin, *Russia* ... 45 D12
Kropp, *Germany* ... 18 A5
Krościenko, *Poland* ... 20 F10
Krosno, *Poland* ... 20 F11
Krosno Odrzańskie, *Poland* ... 20 C5
Krotoszyn, *Poland* ... 20 D7
Kroussón, *Greece* ... 37 D6
Krško, *Slovenia* ... 33 C12
Kruger Nat. Park, *S. Africa* ... 85 C5
Krugersdorp, *S. Africa* ... 85 D4
Kruiningen, *Neths.* ... 17 F4
Kruisfontein, *S. Africa* ... 84 E3
Kruishoutem, *Belgium* ... 17 G3
Kruisland, *Neths.* ... 17 E4
Kruja, *Albania* ... 39 H2
Krulevshchina, *Belorussia* ... 40 D5
Kruma, *Albania* ... 38 G3
Krumbach, *Germany* ... 19 G6
Krung Thep = Bangkok, *Thailand* ... 58 F3
Krupanj, *Serbia* ... 21 L9
Krupinica →, *Slovak Rep.* ... 21 G8
Kruševac, *Serbia* ... 21 M11
Kruzof I., *U.S.A.* ... 100 B1
Krychaw = Krichev, *Belorussia* ... 40 E7
Krymsk Abinsk, *Russia* ... 42 D8
Krymsky Poluostrov, *Ukraine* ... 42 D5
Krynica Morska, *Poland* ... 20 A9
Krynki, *Poland* ... 20 B13
Kryvyy Rih = Krivoy Rog, *Ukraine* ... 42 C5
Krzywiń, *Poland* ... 20 D6
Krzyz, *Poland* ... 20 C6
Ksabi, *Morocco* ... 74 B4
Ksar Chellala, *Algeria* ... 75 A5
Ksar el Boukhari, *Algeria* ... 75 A5
Ksar el Kebir, *Morocco* ... 74 B3
Ksar es Souk = Ar Rachidiya, *Morocco* ... 74 B4
Ksar Rhilane, *Tunisia* ... 75 B6
Ksour, Mts. des, *Algeria* ... 75 B4
Kstovo, *Russia* ... 41 C14
Kuala, *Indonesia* ... 56 D3
Kuala Berang, *Malaysia* ... 59 K4
Kuala Dungun, *Malaysia* ... 59 K4
Kuala Kangsar, *Malaysia* ... 59 K3
Kuala Kelawang, *Malaysia* ... 59 L4
Kuala Kerai, *Malaysia* ... 59 K4
Kuala Kubu Baharu, *Malaysia* ... 59 L3
Kuala Lipis, *Malaysia* ... 59 K4
Kuala Lumpur, *Malaysia* ... 59 L3
Kuala Nerang, *Malaysia* ... 59 J3
Kuala Pilah, *Malaysia* ... 59 L4
Kuala Rompin, *Malaysia* ... 59 L4
Kuala Selangor, *Malaysia* ... 59 L3
Kuala Terengganu, *Malaysia* ... 59 K4
Kualajelai, *Indonesia* ... 56 E4
Kualakapuas, *Indonesia* ... 56 E4
Kualakurun, *Indonesia* ... 56 E4
Kualapembuang, *Indonesia* ... 56 E4
Kualasimpang, *Indonesia* ... 56 D1
Kuancheng, *China* ... 51 D10
Kuandang, *Indonesia* ... 57 D6
Kuandian, *China* ... 51 D13
Kuangchou = Guangzhou, *China* ... 53 F9
Kuantan, *Malaysia* ... 59 L4
Kuba, *Azerbaijan* ... 43 F13
Kuban →, *Russia* ... 42 D8
Kubenskoye, Oz., *Russia* ... 41 B11
Kuberle, *Russia* ... 43 C10
Kubokawa, *Japan* ... 49 H6
Kubrat, *Bulgaria* ... 38 F9
Kučevo, *Serbia* ... 21 L11
Kucha Gompa, *India* ... 63 B7
Kuchaman, *India* ... 62 F6
Kuchino-eruba-Jima, *Japan* ... 49 J5
Kuchino-Shima, *Japan* ... 49 K4
Kuchinotsu, *Japan* ... 49 H5
Kucing, *Malaysia* ... 56 D4
Kuçovë = Qytet Stalin, *Albania* ... 39 J2
Kud →, *Pakistan* ... 62 F2
Kuda, *India* ... 60 H7
Kudat, *Malaysia* ... 56 C5

Kudus, *Indonesia* 57 G14
Kudymkar, *Russia* 44 D6
Kueiyang = Guiyang,
  China 52 D6
Kufstein, *Austria* 19 H8
Kugong I., *Canada* 98 A4
Kūh-e Dīnār, *Iran* 65 D6
Kūh-e-Hazārān, *Iran* 65 D8
Kūhak, *Iran* 60 F3
Kūhbonān, *Iran* 65 D8
Kūhestak, *Iran* 65 E8
Kūhīn, *Iran* 65 C6
Kūhīrī, *Iran* 65 E9
Kuhnsdorf, *Austria* 21 J4
Kūhpāyeh, *Esfahan, Iran* . . 65 C7
Kūhpāyeh, *Kermān, Iran* . . 65 D8
Kui Buri, *Thailand* 59 F2
Kuinre, *Neths.* 16 C7
Kuito, *Angola* 81 G3
Kujang, *N. Korea* 51 E14
Kuji, *Japan* 48 D10
Kujū-San, *Japan* 49 H5
Kukawa, *Nigeria* 79 C7
Kukerin, *Australia* 89 F2
Kukmor, *Russia* 41 C17
Kukup, *Malaysia* 59 M4
Kukvidze, *Russia* 41 F13
Kula, *Serbia* 21 K9
Kulai, *Malaysia* 59 M4
Kulal, Mt., *Kenya* 82 B4
Kulaly, Os., *Kazakhstan* . . 43 D14
Kulasekarappattinam, *India* 60 Q11
Kuldiga, *Latvia* 40 C2
Kuldja = Yining, *China* . . 44 E9
Kuldu, *Sudan* 77 E2
Kulebaki, *Russia* 41 D13
Kulen Vakuf, *Bos.-H.* 33 D13
Kulgam, *India* 63 C6
Kuli, *Russia* 43 E12
Kulim, *Malaysia* 59 K3
Kulin, *Australia* 89 F2
Kulja, *Australia* 89 F2
Kulm, *U.S.A.* 108 B5
Kulmbach, *Germany* 19 E7
Kulp, *Turkey* 67 D9
Kulsary, *Kazakhstan* 44 E6
Kultay, *Kazakhstan* 43 D14
Kulti, *India* 63 H12
Kulu, *Turkey* 66 D5
Kulumbura, *Australia* 88 B4
Kulunda, *Russia* 44 D8
Kulungar, *Afghan.* 62 C3
Kūlvand, *Iran* 65 D7
Kulwin, *Australia* 91 F3
Kulyab, *Tajikistan* 44 F7
Kum Tekei, *Kazakhstan* . . . 44 E8
Kuma →, *Russia* 43 D12
Kumaganum, *Nigeria* 79 C7
Kumagaya, *Japan* 49 F9
Kumai, *Indonesia* 56 E4
Kumamba, Kepulauan,
  Indonesia 57 E9
Kumamoto, *Japan* 49 H5
Kumamoto □, *Japan* 49 H5
Kumanovo, *Macedonia* . . . 38 G4
Kumara, *N.Z.* 87 K3
Kumarl, *Australia* 89 F3
Kumasi, *Ghana* 78 D4
Kumayri, *Armenia* 43 F10
Kumba, *Cameroon* 79 E6
Kumbakonam, *India* 60 P11
Kumbarilla, *Australia* 91 D5
Kumbo, *Cameroon* 79 D7
Kŭmchŏn, *N. Korea* 51 E14
Kumdok, *India* 63 C8
Kume-Shima, *Japan* 49 L3
Kumeny, *Russia* 41 B16
Kŭmhwa, *S. Korea* 51 E14
Kumi, *Uganda* 82 B3
Kumla, *Sweden* 9 G13
Kumluca, *Turkey* 66 E4
Kummerower See,
  Germany 18 B8
Kumo, *Nigeria* 79 C7
Kumon Bum, *Burma* 61 F20
Kumtorkala, *Russia* 43 E12
Kumylzhenskaya, *Russia* . . 43 B10
Kunama, *Australia* 91 F4
Kunashir, Ostrov, *Russia* . . 45 E15
Kunda, *Estonia* 40 B5
Kundla, *India* 62 J4
Kungala, *Australia* 91 D5
Kungälv, *Sweden* 11 G5
Kunghit I., *Canada* 100 C2
Kungrad, *Uzbekistan* 44 E6
Kungsbacka, *Sweden* 11 G6
Kungur, *Russia* 44 D6
Kungurri, *Australia* 90 C4
Kunhar →, *Pakistan* 63 B5
Kunhegyes, *Hungary* 21 H10
Kuningan, *Indonesia* 57 G13
Kunlong, *Burma* 61 H21
Kunlun Shan, *Asia* 54 C3
Kunming, *China* 52 E4
Kunrade, *Neths.* 17 G7
Kunsan, *S. Korea* 51 G14
Kunshan, *China* 53 B13
Kununurra, *Australia* 88 C4
Kunwarara, *Australia* 90 C5
Kunya-Urgench,
  Turkmenistan 44 E6
Künzelsau, *Germany* 19 F5
Kuopio, *Finland* 8 E19
Kuopion lääni □, *Finland* . 8 E19
Kupa →, *Croatia* 33 C13

Kupang, *Indonesia* 57 F6
Kupres, *Bos.-H.* 21 L7
Kupyansk, *Ukraine* 42 B7
Kupyansk-Uzlovoi, *Ukraine* 42 B7
Kuqa, *China* 54 B3
Kuranda, *Australia* 90 B4
Kurashiki, *Japan* 49 G6
Kurayoshi, *Japan* 49 G6
Kurdistan, *Asia* 67 E10
Kure, *Japan* 49 G6
Küre, *Turkey* 66 C5
Küre Dağları, *Turkey* 66 C6
Kuressaare, *Estonia* 40 B3
Kurgaldzhino, *Kazakhstan* . 44 D8
Kurgan, *Russia* 44 D7
Kurganinsk, *Russia* 43 D9
Kurgannaya = Kurganinsk,
  Russia 43 D9
Kuria Maria Is. = Khūrīyā
  Mūrīyā, Jazā 'ir, *Oman* . 68 D6
Kuridala, *Australia* 90 C3
Kurigram, *Bangla.* 61 G16
Kuril Is. = Kurilskiye
  Ostrova, *Russia* 45 E15
Kuril Trench, *Pac. Oc.* 92 C7
Kurilsk, *Russia* 45 E15
Kurilskiye Ostrova, *Russia* . 45 E15
Kuringen, *Belgium* 17 G6
Kurino, *Japan* 49 J5
Kurkur, *Egypt* 76 C3
Kurlovskiy, *Russia* 41 D12
Kurmuk, *Sudan* 77 E3
Kurnool, *India* 60 M10
Kuro-Shima, *Kagoshima,
  Japan* 49 J4
Kuro-Shima, *Okinawa,
  Japan* 49 M2
Kurovskoye, *Russia* 41 D11
Kurow, *N.Z.* 87 L3
Kurrajong, *Australia* 91 E5
Kurram →, *Pakistan* 62 C4
Kurri Kurri, *Australia* 91 E5
Kursavka, *Russia* 43 D10
Kuršėnai, *Lithuania* 40 C3
Kursk, *Russia* 41 F10
Kuršumlija, *Serbia* 21 M11
Kurşunlu, *Turkey* 66 C5
Kurtalan, *Turkey* 67 E9
Kuru, Bahr el →, *Sudan* . . 77 F2
Kurucaşile, *Turkey* 66 C5
Kuruktag, *China* 54 B3
Kuruman, *S. Africa* 84 D3
Kuruman →, *S. Africa* 84 D3
Kurume, *Japan* 49 H5
Kurunegala, *Sri Lanka* . . . 60 R12
Kurupukari, *Guyana* 121 C6
Kurya, *Russia* 45 C11
Kus Gölü, *Turkey* 66 C2
Kuşadası, *Turkey* 66 E2
Kusatsu, *Japan* 49 F9
Kusawa L., *Canada* 100 A1
Kusel, *Germany* 19 F3
Kushchevskaya, *Russia* . . . 43 C8
Kushikino, *Japan* 49 J5
Kushima, *Japan* 49 J5
Kushimoto, *Japan* 49 H7
Kushiro, *Japan* 48 C12
Kushiro →, *Japan* 48 C12
Kūshk, *Iran* 65 D8
Kushka, *Turkmenistan* . . . 44 F7
Kūshkī, Īlām, *Iran* 64 C5
Kūshkī, Khorāsān, *Iran* . . . 65 B8
Kushkū, *Iran* 65 E7
Kushol, *India* 63 C7
Kushtia, *Bangla.* 61 H16
Kushum →, *Kazakhstan* . . 43 B14
Kuskokwim →, *U.S.A.* . . . 96 B3
Kuskokwim B., *U.S.A.* . . . 96 C3
Küsnacht, *Switz.* 23 B7
Kussharo-Ko, *Japan* 48 C12
Küssnacht, *Switz.* 23 B6
Kustanay, *Kazakhstan* 44 D7
Kut, Ko, *Thailand* 59 G4
Kütahya, *Turkey* 66 D4
Kütahya □, *Turkey* 66 D3
Kutaisi, *Georgia* 43 E10
Kutaraja = Banda Aceh,
  Indonesia 56 C1
Kutch, Gulf of = Kachchh,
  Gulf of, *India* 62 H3
Kutch, Rann of =
  Kachchh, Rann of, *India* 62 G4
Kutina, *Croatia* 33 C13
Kutiyana, *India* 62 J4
Kutkashen, *Azerbaijan* . . . 43 F12
Kutná Hora, *Czech.* 20 F5
Kutno, *Poland* 20 C9
Kuttabul, *Australia* 90 C4
Kutu, *Zaïre* 80 E3
Kutum, *Sudan* 77 E1
Kuujjuaq, *Canada* 97 C13
Kŭup-tong, *N. Korea* 51 D14
Kuurne, *Belgium* 17 G2
Kuvshinovo, *Russia* 40 C9
Kuwait = Al Kuwayt,
  Kuwait 64 D5
Kuwait ■, *Asia* 64 D5
Kuwana, *Japan* 49 G8
Kuybyshev = Samara,
  Russia 41 E17
Kuybyshev, *Russia* 44 D8
Kuybyshevo, *Russia* 42 C7
Kuybyshevskoye Vdkhr.,
  Russia 41 D16

Kuye He →, *China* 50 E6
Kūyeh, *Iran* 64 B5
Kūysanjaq, *Iraq* 64 B5
Kuyumba, *Russia* 45 C10
Kuzey Anadolu Dağları,
  Turkey 66 C6
Kuznetsk, *Russia* 41 E15
Kvænangen, *Norway* 8 A16
Kvam, *Norway* 10 C3
Kvareli, *Georgia* 43 F11
Kvarner, *Croatia* 33 D11
Kvarnerič, *Croatia* 33 D11
Kviteseid, *Norway* 10 E2
Kwabhaca, *S. Africa* 85 E4
Kwabhaca, *S. Africa* 85 E4
Kwadacha →, *Canada* 100 B3
Kwakhanai, *Botswana* 84 C3
Kwakoegron, *Surinam* 121 B6
Kwale, *Kenya* 82 C4
Kwale, *Nigeria* 79 D6
Kwale □, *Kenya* 82 C4
KwaMashu, *S. Africa* 85 D5
Kwamouth, *Zaïre* 80 E3
Kwando →, *Africa* 84 B3
Kwangdaeri, *N. Korea* 51 D14
Kwangju, *S. Korea* 51 G14
Kwangsi-Chuang =
  Guangxi Zhuangzu
  Zizhiqu □, *China* 52 E7
Kwangtung =
  Guangdong □, *China* . . 53 F9
Kwara □, *Nigeria* 79 D5
Kwataboahegan →,
  Canada 98 B3
Kwatisore, *Indonesia* 57 E8
Kweichow = Guizhou □,
  China 52 D6
Kwekwe, *Zimbabwe* 83 F2
Kwimba □, *Tanzania* 82 C3
Kwinana New Town,
  Australia 89 F2
Kwoka, *Indonesia* 57 E8
Kyabé, *Chad* 73 G8
Kyabra Cr. →, *Australia* . . 91 D3
Kyabram, *Australia* 91 F4
Kyaikto, *Burma* 58 D1
Kyakhta, *Russia* 45 D11
Kyancutta, *Australia* 91 E2
Kyangin, *Burma* 61 K19
Kyaukpadaung, *Burma* . . . 61 J19
Kyaukpyu, *Burma* 61 K18
Kyaukse, *Burma* 61 J20
Kyburz, *U.S.A.* 112 G6
Kycen, *Russia* 45 D11
Kyenjojo, *Uganda* 82 B3
Kyle Dam, *Zimbabwe* 83 G3
Kyle of Lochalsh, *U.K.* . . . 14 D3
Kyll →, *Germany* 19 F2
Kyllburg, *Germany* 19 E2
Kynuna, *Australia* 90 C3
Kyneton, *Australia* 91 F3
Kyō-ga-Saki, *Japan* 49 G7
Kyoga, L., *Uganda* 82 B3
Kyogle, *Australia* 91 D5
Kyongju, *S. Korea* 51 G15
Kyongpyaw, *Burma* 61 L19
Kyŏngsŏng, *N. Korea* 51 D15
Kyōto, *Japan* 49 G7
Kyōto □, *Japan* 49 G7
Kyparissovouno, *Cyprus* . . 37 D12
Kyperounda, *Cyprus* 37 E11
Kyrenia, *Cyprus* 37 D12
Kyritz, *Germany* 18 C8
Kystatyam, *Russia* 45 C13
Kytal Ktakh, *Russia* 45 C13
Kythréa, *Cyprus* 37 D12
Kyulyunken, *Russia* 45 C13
Kyunhla, *Burma* 61 H19
Kyuquot, *Canada* 100 C3
Kyurdamir, *Azerbaijan* . . . 43 F13
Kyūshū, *Japan* 49 H5
Kyūshū □, *Japan* 49 H5
Kyūshū-Sanchi, *Japan* . . . 49 H5
Kyustendil, *Bulgaria* 38 G5
Kyusyur, *Russia* 45 B13
Kywong, *Australia* 91 E4
Kyyiv = Kiyev, *Ukraine* . . 40 F7
Kyyjärvi, *Finland* 8 E18
Kyzyl, *Russia* 45 D10
Kyzyl-Kiya, *Kirghizia* 44 E8
Kyzylkum, Peski,
  Uzbekistan 44 E7
Kzyl-Orda, *Kazakhstan* . . . 44 E7

L

La Albuera, *Spain* 31 G4
La Alcarria, *Spain* 28 E2
La Algaba, *Spain* 31 H4
La Almarcha, *Spain* 28 F2
La Almunia de Doña
  Godina, *Spain* 28 D3
La Asunción, *Venezuela* . . 121 A5
La Banda, *Argentina* 126 B3
La Bañeza, *Spain* 30 C5
La Barca, *Mexico* 114 C4
La Barge, *U.S.A.* 110 E8
La Bassée, *France* 25 B9
La Bastide-Puylaurent,
  France 26 D7
La Baule, *France* 24 E4
La Belle, *U.S.A.* 105 M5

La Biche →, *Canada* 100 B4
La Bisbal, *Spain* 28 D8
La Blanquilla, *Venezuela* . . 121 A5
La Bomba, *Mexico* 114 A1
La Bresse, *France* 25 D13
La Bureba, *Spain* 28 C1
La Cal →, *Bolivia* 125 D6
La Calera, *Chile* 126 C1
La Campiña, *Spain* 31 H6
La Canal, *Spain* 36 C7
La Cañiza, *Spain* 30 C2
La Capelle, *France* 25 C10
La Carlota, *Argentina* 126 C3
La Carlota, *Phil.* 55 F5
La Carolina, *Spain* 31 G7
La Cavalerie, *France* 26 D7
La Ceiba, *Honduras* 116 C2
La Chaise-Dieu, *France* . . . 26 C7
La Chaize-le-Vicomte,
  France 24 F5
La Chapelle d'Angillon,
  France 25 E9
La Chapelle-Glain, *France* . 24 E5
La Charité-sur-Loire,
  France 25 E10
La Chartre-sur-le-Loir,
  France 24 E7
La Châtaigneraie, *France* . . 26 B3
La Châtre, *France* 26 B5
La Chaux de Fonds, *Switz.* 22 B3
La Chorrera, *Colombia* . . . 120 D3
La Ciotat, *France* 27 E9
La Clayette, *France* 27 B8
La Cocha, *Argentina* 126 B2
La Concepción = Ri-Aba,
  Eq. Guin. 79 E6
La Concepción, *Venezuela* . 120 A3
La Concordia, *Mexico* 115 D6
La Conner, *U.S.A.* 110 B2
La Coruña, *Spain* 30 B2
La Coruña □, *Spain* 30 B2
La Côte, *Switz.* 22 D2
La Côte-St.-André, *France* . 27 C9
La Courtine-le-Trucq,
  France 26 C6
La Crau, *France* 27 E8
La Crete, *Canada* 100 B5
La Crosse, *Kans., U.S.A.* . . 108 F5
La Crosse, *Wis., U.S.A.* . . . 108 D9
La Cruz, *Costa Rica* 116 D2
La Cruz, *Mexico* 114 C3
La Dorada, *Colombia* 120 B3
La Ensenada, *Chile* 128 B2
La Escondida, *Mexico* 114 C5
La Esmeralda, *Paraguay* . . 126 A3
La Esperanza, *Argentina* . . 128 B3
La Esperanza, *Cuba* 116 B3
La Esperanza, *Honduras* . . 116 D2
La Estrada, *Spain* 30 C2
La Fayette, *U.S.A.* 105 H3
La Fé, *Cuba* 116 B3
La Fère, *France* 25 C10
La Ferté-Bernard, *France* . . 24 D7
La Ferté-Macé, *France* . . . 24 D6
La Ferté-St.-Aubin, *France* . 25 E8
La Ferté-sous-Jouarre,
  France 25 D10
La Ferté-Vidame, *France* . . 24 D7
La Flèche, *France* 24 E6
La Follette, *U.S.A.* 105 G3
La Fregeneda, *Spain* 30 E4
La Fría, *Venezuela* 120 B3
La Fuente de San Esteban,
  Spain 30 E4
La Gineta, *Spain* 29 F2
La Gloria, *Colombia* 120 B3
La Gran Sabana, *Venezuela* 121 B5
La Grand-Combe, *France* . . 27 D8
La Grande, *U.S.A.* 110 D4
La Grande-Motte, *France* . . 27 E8
La Grange, *Calif., U.S.A.* . . 112 H6
La Grange, *Ga., U.S.A.* . . . 105 J3
La Grange, *Ky., U.S.A.* . . . 104 F3
La Grange, *Tex., U.S.A.* . . 109 L6
La Grita, *Venezuela* 120 B3
La Guaira, *Venezuela* 120 A4
La Guardia, *Spain* 30 D2
La Gudiña, *Spain* 30 C3
La Güera, *Mauritania* 74 D1
La Guerche-de-Bretagne,
  France 24 E5
La Guerche-sur-l'Aubois,
  France 25 F9
La Habana, *Cuba* 116 B3
La Harpe, *U.S.A.* 108 E9
La Haye-du-Puits, *France* . 24 C5
La Horqueta, *Venezuela* . . 121 B5
La Horra, *Spain* 30 D7
La Independencia, *Mexico* . 115 D6
La Isabela, *Dom. Rep.* . . . 117 C5
La Jara, *U.S.A.* 111 H11
La Joya, *Peru* 124 D3
La Junquera, *Spain* 28 C7
La Junta, *U.S.A.* 109 F3
La Laguna, *Canary Is.* 36 F3
La Libertad, *Guatemala* . . . 116 C1
La Libertad, *Mexico* 114 B2
La Libertad □, *Peru* 124 B2
La Ligua, *Chile* 126 C1
La Línea de la Concepción,
  Spain 31 J5
La Loche, *Canada* 101 B7
La Londe-les-Maures,
  France 27 E10
La Lora, *Spain* 30 C7

La Loupe, *France* 24 D8
La Louvière, *Belgium* 17 H4
La Machine, *France* 25 F10
La Maddalena, *Italy* 34 A2
La Malbaie, *Canada* 99 C5
La Mancha, *Spain* 29 F2
La Mariña, *Spain* 30 B3
La Mesa, *Calif., U.S.A.* . . . 113 N9
La Mesa, *N. Mex., U.S.A.* . 111 K10
La Misión, *Mexico* 114 A1
La Mothe-Achard, *France* . 24 F5
La Motte, *France* 27 D10
La Motte-Chalançon,
  France 27 D9
La Moure, *U.S.A.* 108 B5
La Muela, *Spain* 28 D3
La Mure, *France* 27 D9
La Negra, *Chile* 126 A1
La Neuveville, *Switz.* 22 B4
La Oliva, *Canary Is.* 36 F6
La Oraya, *Peru* 124 C2
La Orotava, *Canary Is.* . . . 36 F3
La Pacaudière, *France* 26 B7
La Palma, *Canary Is.* 36 F2
La Palma, *Panama* 116 E4
La Palma, *Spain* 31 H4
La Paloma, *Chile* 126 C1
La Pampa □, *Argentina* . . 126 D2
La Paragua, *Venezuela* . . . 121 B5
La Paz, *Entre Ríos,
  Argentina* 126 C4
La Paz, *San Luis,
  Argentina* 126 C2
La Paz, *Bolivia* 124 D4
La Paz, *Honduras* 116 D2
La Paz, *Mexico* 114 C2
La Paz, *Phil.* 55 D4
La Paz □, *Bolivia* 124 D4
La Paz Centro, *Nic.* 116 D2
La Pedrera, *Colombia* 120 D4
La Perouse Str., *Asia* 48 B11
La Pesca, *Mexico* 115 C5
La Piedad, *Mexico* 114 C4
La Pine, *U.S.A.* 110 E3
La Plant, *U.S.A.* 108 C4
La Plata, *Argentina* 126 D4
La Plata, *Colombia* 120 C2
La Plata, L., *Argentina* . . . 128 B2
La Pobla de Lillet, *Spain* . . 28 C6
La Pola de Gordón, *Spain* . 30 C5
La Porte, *U.S.A.* 104 E2
La Puebla, *Spain* 28 F8
La Puebla de Cazalla,
  Spain 31 H5
La Puebla de los Infantes,
  Spain 31 H5
La Puebla de Montalbán,
  Spain 30 F6
La Puerta, *Spain* 29 G2
La Punt, *Switz.* 23 C9
La Purísima, *Mexico* 114 B2
La Push, *U.S.A.* 112 C2
La Quiaca, *Argentina* 126 A2
La Rambla, *Spain* 31 H6
La Reine, *Canada* 98 C4
La Réole, *France* 26 D3
La Restinga, *Canary Is.* . . . 36 G2
La Rioja, *Argentina* 126 B2
La Rioja □, *Argentina* 126 B2
La Rioja □, *Spain* 28 C2
La Robla, *Spain* 30 C5
La Roche, *Switz.* 22 C4
La Roche-Bernard, *France* . 24 E4
La Roche-Canillac, *France* . 26 C5
La Roche-en-Ardenne,
  Belgium 17 H7
La Roche-sur-Yon, *France* . 24 F5
La Rochefoucauld, *France* . 26 C4
La Rochelle, *France* 26 B2
La Roda, *Albacete, Spain* . 29 F2
La Roda, *Sevilla, Spain* . . . 31 H5
La Romana, *Dom. Rep.* . . . 117 C6
La Ronge, *Canada* 101 B7
La Rumorosa, *Mexico* 113 N10
La Sabina, *Spain* 36 C7
La Sagra, *Spain* 29 H2
La Salle, *U.S.A.* 108 E10
La Sanabria, *Spain* 30 C4
La Santa, *Canary Is.* 36 E6
La Sarraz, *Switz.* 22 C3
La Sarre, *Canada* 98 C4
La Scie, *Canada* 99 C8
La Selva, *Spain* 28 D7
La Selva Beach, *U.S.A.* . . . 112 J5
La Serena, *Chile* 126 B1
La Serena, *Spain* 31 G5
La Seyne, *France* 27 E9
La Sila, *Italy* 35 C9
La Solana, *Spain* 29 G1
La Souterraine, *France* . . . 26 B5
La Spézia, *Italy* 32 D6
La Suze-sur-Sarthe, *France* 24 E7
La Tagua, *Colombia* 120 C3
La Teste, *France* 26 D2
La Tortuga, *Venezuela* 117 D6
La Tour-du-Pin, *France* . . . 27 C9
La Tranche-sur-Mer,
  France 24 F5
La Tremblade, *France* 26 C2
La Tuque, *Canada* 98 C5
La Unión, *Chile* 128 B2
La Unión, *Colombia* 120 C2
La Unión, *El Salv.* 116 D2
La Unión, *Mexico* 114 D4
La Unión, *Peru* 124 B2

La Unión, Spain 29 H4
La Urbana, Venezuela .. 120 B4
La Vecilla, Spain 30 C5
La Vega, Dom. Rep. 117 C5
La Vega, Peru 124 C2
La Vela, Venezuela 120 A4
La Veleta, Spain 31 H7
La Venta, Mexico 115 D6
La Ventura, Mexico 114 C4
La Venturosa, Colombia 120 B4
La Victoria, Venezuela . 120 A4
La Voulte-sur-Rhône,
   France 27 D8
La Zarza, Spain 31 H4
Laaber →, Germany 19 G8
Laage, Germany 18 B8
Laba →, Russia 43 D8
Labason, Phil. 55 G5
Labastide-Murat, France . 26 D5
Labastide-Rouairoux,
   France 26 E6
Labbézenga, Mali 79 B5
Labe = Elbe →, Europe . 18 B4
Labé, Guinea 78 C2
Laberec →, Slovak Rep. . 20 G11
Laberge, L., Canada ... 100 A1
Labin, Croatia 33 C11
Labinsk, Russia 43 D9
Labis, Malaysia 59 L4
Labo, Phil. 55 D5
Laboe, Germany 18 A6
Labouheyre, France 26 D3
Laboulaye, Argentina .. 126 C3
Labra, Peña, Spain 30 B6
Labrador, Coast of □,
   Canada 99 B7
Labrador City, Canada . 99 B6
Lábrea, Brazil 125 B5
Labrède, France 26 D3
Labuan, Pulau, Malaysia 56 C5
Labuha, Indonesia 57 E7
Labuhan, Indonesia ... 57 G11
Labuhanbajo, Indonesia . 57 F6
Labuissière, Belgium .. 17 H4
Labuk, Telok, Malaysia . 56 C5
Labyrinth, L., Australia . 91 E12
Labytnangi, Russia 44 C7
Lac Allard, Canada 99 B7
Lac Bouchette, Canada . 99 C5
Lac du Flambeau, U.S.A. 108 B10
Lac Édouard, Canada .. 98 C5
Lac La Biche, Canada . 100 C6
Lac la Martre, Canada . 96 B8
Lac-Mégantic, Canada . 99 C5
Lac Seul, Res., Canada . 98 B1
Lac Thien, Vietnam ... 58 F7
Lacanau, France 26 D2
Lacanau, Étang de, France 26 D2
Lacantúm →, Mexico .. 115 D6
Lacara →, Spain 31 G4
Lacaune, France 26 E6
Lacaune, Mts. de, France 26 E6
Laccadive Is. =
   Lakshadweep Is.,
   Ind. Oc. 46 J11
Lacepede B., Australia . 91 F2
Lacepede Is., Australia . 88 C3
Lacerdónia, Mozam. ... 83 F4
Lacey, U.S.A. 112 C4
Lachay, Pta., Peru 124 C2
Lachen, Switz. 23 B7
Lachhmangarh, India .. 62 F6
Lachi, Pakistan 62 C4
Lachine, Canada 98 C5
Lachlan →, Australia . 91 E3
Lachute, Canada 98 C5
Lackawanna, U.S.A. .. 106 D6
Lacolle, Canada 107 A11
Lacombe, Canada 100 C6
Lacona, U.S.A. 107 C8
Láconi, Italy 34 C2
Laconia, U.S.A. 107 C13
Lacq, France 26 E3
Lacrosse, U.S.A. 110 C5
Ladakh Ra., India 63 B8
Ladário, Brazil 125 D6
Ládhon →, Greece 39 M4
Lådik, Turkey 42 F6
Ladismith, S. Africa .. 84 E3
Lādīz, Iran 65 D9
Ladnun, India 62 F6
Ladoga, L. = Ladozhskoye
   Ozero, Russia 44 C4
Ladon, France 25 D9
Ladozhskoye Ozero, Russia 44 C4
Ladrillero, G., Chile .. 128 C1
Lady Grey, S. Africa .. 84 E4
Ladybrand, S. Africa .. 84 D4
Ladysmith, Canada 100 D4
Ladysmith, S. Africa .. 85 D4
Ladysmith, U.S.A. 108 C9
Lae, Papua N. G. 92 H6
Laem Ngop, Thailand . 59 F4
Laem Pho, Thailand ... 59 J3
Læsø, Denmark 11 G4
Læsø Rende, Denmark . 11 G4
Lafayette, Colo., U.S.A. 108 F2
Lafayette, Ind., U.S.A. 104 E2
Lafayette, La., U.S.A. . 109 K9
Lafayette, Tenn., U.S.A. 105 G3
Laferte →, Canada ... 100 A5
Lafia, Nigeria 79 D6
Lafiagi, Nigeria 79 D6
Lafleche, Canada 101 D7
Lafon, Sudan 77 F3

Laforsen, Sweden 10 C9
Lagan →, Sweden 11 H7
Lagan →, U.K. 15 B6
Lagarfljót →, Iceland .. 8 D6
Lagarto, Brazil 122 D4
Lage, Germany 18 D4
Lage, Spain 30 B2
Lage-Mierde, Neths. .. 17 F6
Lågen →, Norway 9 F11
Lägerdorf, Germany ... 18 B5
Laghouat, Algeria 75 B5
Lagnieu, France 27 C9
Lagny, France 25 D9
Lago, Italy 35 C9
Lago Posadas, Argentina 128 C2
Lago Ranco, Chile 128 B2
Lagôa, Portugal 31 H2
Lagoaça, Portugal 30 D4
Lagodekhi, Georgia ... 43 F12
Lagónegro, Italy 35 B8
Lagonoy Gulf, Phil. ... 55 E5
Lagos, Nigeria 79 D5
Lagos, Portugal 31 H2
Lagos de Moreno, Mexico 114 C4
Lagrange, Australia ... 88 C3
Lagrange B., Australia . 88 C3
Laguardia, Spain 28 C2
Laguépie, France 26 D5
Laguna, Brazil 127 B6
Laguna, U.S.A. 111 J10
Laguna Beach, U.S.A. . 113 M9
Laguna de la Janda, Spain 31 J5
Laguna Limpia, Argentina 126 B4
Laguna Madre, U.S.A. . 115 B5
Lagunas, Chile 126 A2
Lagunas, Peru 124 B2
Lagunillas, Bolivia ... 125 D5
Lahad Datu, Malaysia ... 57 C5
Lahan Sai, Thailand .. 58 E4
Lahanam, Laos 58 D5
Laharpur, India 63 F9
Lahat, Indonesia 56 E2
Lahewa, Indonesia 56 D1
Lahiang Lahiang, Phil. . 55 H4
Lahijan, Iran 65 B6
Lahn →, Germany 19 E3
Laholm, Sweden 11 H7
Laholmsbukten, Sweden . 11 H6
Lahontan Reservoir,
   U.S.A. 110 G4
Lahore, Pakistan 62 D6
Lahr, Germany 19 G3
Lahti, Finland 9 F18
Lahtis = Lahti, Finland . 9 F18
Laï, Chad 73 G8
Lai Chau, Vietnam ... 58 A4
Lai'an, China 53 A12
Laibin, China 52 F7
Laidley, Australia 91 D5
Laifeng, China 52 C7
L'Aigle, France 24 D7
Laignes, France 25 E11
L'Aiguillon-sur-Mer, France 26 B2
Laikipia □, Kenya 82 B4
Lairg, U.K. 14 C4
Laishui, China 50 E8
Laiwu, China 51 F9
Laixi, China 51 F11
Laiyang, China 51 F11
Laiyuan, China 50 E8
Laizhou Wan, China .. 51 F10
Laja →, Mexico 114 C4
Lajere, Nigeria 79 C7
Lajes, Rio Grande do N.,
   Brazil 122 C4
Lajes, Sta. Catarina, Brazil 127 B5
Lajinha, Brazil 123 F3
Lajkovac, Serbia 21 L10
Lajosmizse, Hungary .. 21 H9
Lak Sao, Laos 58 C5
Lakaband, Pakistan ... 62 D3
Lakar, Indonesia 57 F7
Lake Alpine, U.S.A. .. 112 G6
Lake Andes, U.S.A. .. 108 D5
Lake Anse, U.S.A. ... 104 B1
Lake Arthur, U.S.A. .. 109 K8
Lake Cargelligo, Australia 91 E4
Lake Charles, U.S.A. . 109 K8
Lake City, Colo., U.S.A. 111 G10
Lake City, Fla., U.S.A. 105 K4
Lake City, Iowa, U.S.A. 108 D7
Lake City, Mich., U.S.A. 104 C3
Lake City, Minn., U.S.A. 108 C8
Lake City, Pa., U.S.A. 106 D4
Lake City, S.C., U.S.A. 105 J6
Lake George, U.S.A. . 107 C11
Lake Grace, Australia . 89 F2
Lake Harbour, Canada . 97 B13
Lake Havasu City, U.S.A. 113 L12
Lake Hughes, U.S.A. . 113 L8
Lake Isabella, U.S.A. . 113 K8
Lake King, Australia .. 89 F2
Lake Lenore, Canada . 101 C8
Lake Louise, Canada .. 100 C5
Lake Mead National
   Recreation Area, U.S.A. 113 K12
Lake Mills, U.S.A. ... 108 D8
Lake Nash, Australia . 90 C2
Lake Providence, U.S.A. 109 J9
Lake River, Canada .. 98 B3
Lake Superior Prov. Park,
   Canada 98 C3
Lake Village, U.S.A. . 109 J9
Lake Wales, U.S.A. .. 105 M5

Lake Worth, U.S.A. ... 105 M5
Lakefield, Canada 98 D4
Lakeland, Australia ... 90 B3
Lakeland, U.S.A. 105 L5
Lakemba, Fiji 87 D9
Lakeport, U.S.A. 112 F4
Lakes Entrance, Australia 91 F4
Lakeside, Ariz., U.S.A. 111 J9
Lakeside, Calif., U.S.A. 113 N10
Lakeside, Nebr., U.S.A. 108 D3
Lakeview, U.S.A. 110 E3
Lakewood, Colo., U.S.A. 108 F2
Lakewood, N.J., U.S.A. 107 F10
Lakewood, Ohio, U.S.A. 106 E3
Lakewood Center, U.S.A. 112 C4
Lakhaniá, Greece 37 D9
Lakhonpheng, Laos ... 58 E5
Lakhpat, India 62 H3
Laki, Iceland 8 D4
Lakin, U.S.A. 109 G4
Lakitusaki →, Canada . 98 B3
Lákkoi, Greece 37 D5
Lakonikós Kólpos, Greece 39 N5
Lakota, Ivory C. 78 D3
Lakota, U.S.A. 108 A5
Laksefjorden, Norway . 8 A19
Lakselv, Norway 8 A18
Lakshadweep Is., Ind. Oc. 46 J11
Lakshmikantapur, India 63 H13
Lala Ghat, India 61 G18
Lala Musa, Pakistan .. 62 C5
Lalago, Tanzania 82 C3
Lalapanzi, Zimbabwe . 83 F3
Lalganj, India 63 G11
Lalibela, Ethiopia 77 E4
Lalin, China 51 B14
Lalín, Spain 30 C2
Lalin He →, China ... 51 B13
Lalinde, France 26 D4
Lalitapur = Patan, Nepal 61 F14
Lalitpur, India 63 G8
Lam, Vietnam 58 B6
Lam Pao Res., Thailand . 58 D4
Lama Kara, Togo 79 D5
Lamaing, Burma 61 M20
Lamar, Colo., U.S.A. . 108 F3
Lamar, Mo., U.S.A. .. 109 G7
Lamarque, Argentina . 128 A3
Lamas, Peru 124 B2
Lamastre, France 27 D8
Lamballe, France 24 D4
Lambaréné, Gabon ... 80 E2
Lambasa, Fiji 87 C8
Lambay I., Ireland ... 15 C5
Lambayeque □, Peru . 124 B2
Lambert, U.S.A. 108 B2
Lambert Glacier, Antarctica 5 D6
Lamberts Bay, S. Africa . 84 E2
Lambesc, France 27 E9
Lámbia, Greece 39 M4
Lambro →, Italy 32 C6
Lame, Nigeria 79 C6
Lame Deer, U.S.A. ... 110 D10
Lamego, Portugal 30 D3
Lamèque, Canada 99 C7
Lameroo, Australia ... 91 F3
Lamesa, U.S.A. 109 J4
Lamía, Greece 39 L5
Lamitan, Phil. 55 H5
Lammermuir Hills, U.K. 14 F6
Lamon Bay, Phil. 55 D5
Lamont, Canada 100 C6
Lamont, U.S.A. 113 K8
Lampa, Peru 124 D3
Lampang, Thailand ... 58 C2
Lampasas, U.S.A. 109 K5
Lampaul, France 24 D1
Lampazos de Naranjo,
   Mexico 114 B4
Lampeter, U.K. 13 E3
Lampione, Medit. S. .. 75 A7
Lampman, Canada 101 D8
Lamprey, Canada 101 B10
Lampung □, Indonesia . 56 F2
Lamu, Kenya 82 C5
Lamu □, Kenya 82 C5
Lamud, Peru 124 B2
Lamy, U.S.A. 111 J11
Lan Xian, China 50 E6
Lan Yu, Taiwan 53 F13
Lanai I., U.S.A. 102 H16
Lanak La, India 63 B8
Lanaken, Belgium 17 G7
Lanak'o Shank'ou = Lanak
   La, India 63 B8
Lanao, L., Phil. 55 H6
Lanark, Canada 107 A8
Lanark, U.K. 14 F5
Lancang, China 52 F2
Lancang Jiang →, China 52 G3
Lancashire □, U.K. .. 12 D5
Lancaster, Canada 107 A10
Lancaster, U.K. 12 C5
Lancaster, Calif., U.S.A. 113 L8
Lancaster, Ky., U.S.A. 104 G3
Lancaster, N.H., U.S.A. 107 B13
Lancaster, N.Y., U.S.A. 106 D6
Lancaster, Pa., U.S.A. 107 F8
Lancaster, S.C., U.S.A. 105 H5
Lancaster, Wis., U.S.A. 108 D9
Lancaster Sd., Canada . 97 A11
Lancer, Canada 101 C7
Lanchow = Lanzhou,
   China 50 F2
Lanciano, Italy 33 F11

Lanco, Chile 128 A2
Lancones, Peru 124 A1
Lancun, China 51 F11
Łancut, Poland 20 E12
Lancy, Switz. 22 D2
Landau, Bayern, Germany 19 G8
Landau, Rhld.-Pfz.,
   Germany 19 F4
Landeck, Austria 19 H6
Landen, Belgium 17 G6
Lander, U.S.A. 110 E9
Lander →, Australia . 88 D5
Landerneau, France .. 24 D2
Landeryd, Sweden 11 G7
Landes, France 26 D3
Landes □, France 26 E3
Landi Kotal, Pakistan . 62 B4
Landivisiau, France .. 24 D2
Landor, Australia 89 E2
Landquart, Switz. 23 C9
Landquart →, Switz. . 23 C9
Landrecies, France ... 25 B10
Land's End, U.K. 13 G2
Landsberg, Germany . 19 G6
Landsborough Cr. →,
   Australia 90 C3
Landshut, Germany ... 19 G8
Landskrona, Sweden .. 11 J6
Landstuhl, Germany .. 19 F3
Landvetter, Sweden .. 11 G6
Laneffe, Belgium 17 H5
Lanesboro, U.S.A. ... 107 E9
Lanett, U.S.A. 105 J3
Lang Bay, Canada 100 D4
Lang Qua, Vietnam .. 58 A5
Lang Shan, China 50 D4
Lang Son, Vietnam ... 58 B6
Lang Suan, Thailand . 59 H2
La'nga Co, China 61 D12
Lángadhás, Greece ... 39 J6
Langádhia, Greece ... 39 M5
Langar, Iran 65 C9
Langara I., Canada ... 100 C2
Langatabbetje, Surinam . 121 C7
Langdai, China 52 D5
Langdon, U.S.A. 108 A5
Langdorp, Belgium ... 17 G5
Langeac, France 26 C7
Langeais, France 24 E7
Langeb Baraka →, Sudan 76 D4
Langeberg, S. Africa .. 84 E3
Langeberge, S. Africa . 84 D3
Langeland, Denmark .. 11 K4
Langemark, Belgium .. 17 G1
Langen, Germany 19 F4
Langenburg, Canada .. 101 C8
Langeness, Germany .. 18 A4
Langenthal, Switz. ... 22 B5
Langeoog, Germany .. 18 B3
Langesund, Norway .. 10 F3
Länghem, Sweden 11 G7
Langhirano, Italy 32 D7
Langholm, U.K. 14 F6
Langhus, Norway 10 E4
Langjökull, Iceland ... 8 D3
Langkawi, P., Malaysia 59 J2
Langklip, S. Africa ... 84 D3
Langkon, Malaysia ... 56 C5
Langlade, St- P. & M. . 99 C8
Langlois, U.S.A. 110 E1
Langnau, Switz. 22 C5
Langogne, France 26 D7
Langon, France 26 D3
Langøya, Norway 8 B13
Langres, France 25 E12
Langres, Plateau de, France 25 E12
Langsa, Indonesia 56 D1
Långsele, Sweden 10 A11
Langtry, U.S.A. 109 L4
Langu, Thailand 59 J2
Languedoc, France ... 26 E7
Langwies, Switz. 23 C9
Langxi, China 53 B12
Langxiangzhen, China 50 E9
Langzhong, China 52 B5
Lanigan, Canada 101 C7
Lankao, China 50 G8
Lannemezan, France . 26 E4
Lannilis, France 24 D2
Lannion, France 24 D3
L'Annonciation, Canada 98 C5
Lanouaille, France ... 26 C5
Lanping, China 52 D2
Lansdale, U.S.A. 107 F9
Lansdowne, Australia . 91 E5
Lansdowne, Canada .. 107 B8
Lansdowne House, Canada 98 B2
L'Anse, U.S.A. 98 C2
L'Anse au Loup, Canada 99 B8
Lansford, U.S.A. 107 F9
Lanshan, China 53 E9
Lansing, U.S.A. 104 D3
Lanslebourg-Mont-Cenis,
   France 27 C10
Lantian, China 50 G5
Lanus, Argentina 126 C4
Lanusei, Italy 34 C2
Lanuza, Phil. 55 G7
Lanxi, China 53 C12
Lanzarote, Canary Is. . 36 E6
Lanzhou, China 50 F2

Lanzo Torinese, Italy .. 32 C4
Lao →, Italy 35 C8
Lao Bao, Laos 58 D6
Lao Cai, Vietnam 58 A4
Laoag, Phil. 55 B4
Laoang, Phil. 55 E6
Laoha He →, China .. 51 C11
Laois □, Ireland 15 D4
Laon, France 25 C10
Laona, U.S.A. 104 C1
Laos ■, Asia 58 D5
Lapa, Brazil 127 B6
Lapalisse, France 26 B7
Laparan, Phil. 57 C6
Lapeer, U.S.A. 104 D4
Lapi □ = Lapin lääni □,
   Finland 8 C19
Lapin lääni □, Finland . 8 C19
Lapithos, Cyprus 37 D12
Lapland = Lappland,
   Europe 8 B18
Laporte, U.S.A. 107 E8
Lapovo, Serbia 21 L11
Lappland, Europe 8 B18
Laprida, Argentina ... 126 D3
Laptev Sea, Russia ... 45 B13
Lăpusul →, Romania . 38 B6
L'Aquila, Italy 33 F10
Lār, Āzarbājān-e Sharqī,
   Iran 64 B5
Lār, Fārs, Iran 65 E7
Lara □, Venezuela ... 120 A4
Larabanga, Ghana ... 78 D4
Laracha, Spain 30 B2
Larache, Morocco 74 A3
Laragne-Montéglin, France 27 D9
Laramie, U.S.A. 108 E2
Laranjeiras, Brazil ... 122 D4
Laranjeiras do Sul, Brazil . 127 B5
Larantuka, Indonesia . 57 F6
Larap, Phil. 55 D5
Larat, Indonesia 57 F8
L'Arbresle, France ... 27 C8
Larde, Mozam. 83 F4
Larder Lake, Canada .. 98 C4
Lardhos, Ákra, Greece . 37 C10
Lardhos, Órmos, Greece 37 C10
Laredo, Spain 28 B1
Laredo, U.S.A. 109 M5
Laredo Sd., Canada .. 100 C3
Laren, Neths. 16 D6
Largentière, France .. 27 D8
L'Argentière-la-Bessée,
   France 27 D10
Largs, U.K. 14 F4
Lari, Italy 32 E7
Lariang, Indonesia ... 57 E5
Larimore, U.S.A. 108 B6
Lārīn, Iran 65 C7
Larino, Italy 35 A7
Lárisa, Greece 39 K5
Larkana, Pakistan ... 62 F3
Larnaca, Cyprus 37 E12
Larnaca Bay, Cyprus . 37 E12
Larne, U.K. 15 B6
Larned, U.S.A. 108 F5
Larochette, Belgium .. 17 J8
Laroquebrou, France . 26 D6
Larrimah, Australia .. 88 C5
Larsen Ice Shelf, Antarctica 5 C17
Larvik, Norway 10 E4
Laryak, Russia 44 C8
Larzac, Causse du, France 26 E7
Las Alpujarras, Spain . 29 J1
Las Animas, U.S.A. .. 108 F3
Las Anod, Somali Rep. . 68 F4
Las Blancos, Spain ... 29 H4
Las Brenãs, Argentina . 126 B3
Las Cabezas de San Juan,
   Spain 31 J5
Las Chimeneas, Mexico . 113 N10
Las Coloradas, Argentina 128 A2
Las Cruces, U.S.A. ... 111 K10
Las Flores, Argentina . 126 D4
Las Heras, Argentina . 126 C2
Las Horquetas, Argentina 128 C2
Las Khoreh, Somali Rep. . 68 E4
Las Lajas, Argentina . 128 A2
Las Lomas, Peru 124 A1
Las Lomitas, Argentina 126 A3
Las Marismas, Spain .. 31 H4
Las Mercedes, Venezuela 120 B4
Las Navas de la
   Concepción, Spain ... 31 H5
Las Navas de Tolosa, Spain 31 G7
Las Navas del Marqués,
   Spain 30 E6
Las Palmas, Argentina . 126 B4
Las Palmas, Canary Is. . 36 F4
Las Palmas →, Mexico . 113 N10
Las Piedras, Uruguay . 127 C4
Las Pipinas, Argentina 126 D4
Las Plumas, Argentina 128 B3
Las Rosas, Argentina . 126 C3
Las Tablas, Panama .. 116 E3
Las Termas, Argentina . 126 B3
Las Truchas, Mexico . 114 D4
Las Varillas, Argentina 126 C3
Las Vegas, N. Mex.,
   U.S.A. 111 J11
Las Vegas, Nev., U.S.A. 113 J11
Lascano, Uruguay 127 C5
Lashburn, Canada 101 C7
Lashio, Burma 61 H20

175

Lashkar, *India* 62 F8
Łasin, *Poland* 20 B9
Lasíthi, *Greece* 37 D7
Lasíthi □, *Greece* 37 D7
Laško, *Slovenia* 33 B12
Lassance, *Brazil* 123 E3
Lassay, *France* 24 D6
Lassen Pk., *U.S.A.* 110 F3
Last Mountain L., *Canada* 101 C7
Lastoursville, *Gabon* 80 E2
Lastovo, *Croatia* 33 F13
Lastovski Kanal, *Croatia* . 33 F13
Lat Yao, *Thailand* 58 E2
Latacunga, *Ecuador* 120 D2
Latakia = Al Lādhiqīyah,
 Syria 64 C2
Latchford, *Canada* 98 C4
Laterza, *Italy* 35 B9
Latham, *Australia* 89 E2
Lathen, *Germany* 18 C3
Lathrop Wells, *U.S.A.* . . . 113 J10
Latiano, *Italy* 35 B10
Latina, *Italy* 34 A5
Latisana, *Italy* 33 C10
Latium = Lazio □, *Italy* . . 33 F9
Laton, *U.S.A.* 112 J7
Latorica →, *Slovak Rep.* . 21 G11
Latouche Treville, C.,
 Australia 88 C3
Latrobe, *Australia* 90 G4
Latrobe, *U.S.A.* 106 F5
Latrónico, *Italy* 35 B9
Latvia ■, *Europe* 40 C3
Lau Group, *Fiji* 87 C9
Lauca →, *Bolivia* 124 D4
Lauchhammer, *Germany* . . 18 D9
Lauenburg, *Germany* 18 B6
Läufelfingen, *Switz.* 22 B5
Laufen, *Switz.* 22 B5
Lauffen, *Germany* 19 F5
Laugarbakki, *Iceland* 8 D3
Laujar, *Spain* 29 J2
Launceston, *Australia* 90 G4
Launceston, *U.K.* 13 G3
Laune →, *Ireland* 15 D2
Laupheim, *Germany* 19 G5
Laura, *Australia* 90 B3
Laureana di Borrello, *Italy* 35 D9
Laurel, *Miss., U.S.A.* 109 K10
Laurel, *Mont., U.S.A.* . . . 110 D9
Laurencekirk, *U.K.* 14 E6
Laurens, *U.S.A.* 105 H4
Laurentian Plateau, *Canada* 99 B6
Laurentides, Parc Prov.
 des, *Canada* 99 C5
Lauria, *Italy* 35 B8
Laurie L., *Canada* 101 B8
Laurinburg, *U.S.A.* 105 H6
Laurium, *U.S.A.* 104 B1
Lausanne, *Switz.* 22 C3
Laut, *Indonesia* 56 D3
Laut Ketil, Kepulauan,
 Indonesia 56 E5
Lautaro, *Chile* 128 A2
Lauterbach, *Germany* 18 E5
Lauterbrunnen, *Switz.* 22 C5
Lauterecken, *Germany* 19 F3
Lautoka, *Fiji* 87 C7
Lauwe, *Belgium* 17 G2
Lauwers, *Neths.* 16 A8
Lauwers Zee, *Neths.* 16 B8
Lauzon, *Canada* 99 C5
Lava Hot Springs, *U.S.A.* 110 E7
Lavadores, *Spain* 30 C2
Lavagna, *Italy* 32 D6
Laval, *France* 24 D6
Lavalle, *Argentina* 126 B2
Lávara, *Greece* 39 H9
Lavardac, *France* 26 D4
Lavaur, *France* 26 E5
Lavaux, *Switz.* 22 D3
Lavelanet, *France* 26 F5
Lavello, *Italy* 35 A8
Laverne, *U.S.A.* 109 G5
Laverton, *Australia* 89 E3
Lavos, *Portugal* 30 E2
Lavre, *Portugal* 31 G2
Lavrentiya, *Russia* 45 C19
Lávrion, *Greece* 39 M7
Lávris, *Greece* 37 D6
Lavumisa, *Swaziland* 85 D5
Lawas, *Malaysia* 56 D5
Lawele, *Indonesia* 57 F6
Lawn Hill, *Australia* 90 B2
Lawng Pit, *Burma* 61 G20
Lawqah, *Si. Arabia* 64 D4
Lawra, *Ghana* 78 C4
Lawrence, *N.Z.* 87 L2
Lawrence, *Kans., U.S.A.* . 108 F7
Lawrence, *Mass., U.S.A.* . 107 D13
Lawrenceburg, *Ind.,
 U.S.A.* 104 F3
Lawrenceburg, *Tenn.,
 U.S.A.* 105 H2
Lawrenceville, *U.S.A.* . . . 105 J4
Laws, *U.S.A.* 112 H8
Lawton, *U.S.A.* 109 H5
Lawu, *Indonesia* 57 G14
Laxford, L., *U.K.* 14 C3
Layla̱n, *Iraq* 64 C5
Layon →, *France* 24 E6
Laysan I., *Pac. Oc.* 93 E11
Laytonville, *U.S.A.* 110 G2

Lazio □, *Italy* 33 F9
Lazo, *Russia* 48 C6
Le Barcarès, *France* 26 F7
Le Beausset, *France* 27 E9
Le Blanc, *France* 26 B5
Le Bleymard, *France* 26 D7
Le Bourgneuf-la-Fôret,
 France 24 D6
Le Bouscat, *France* 26 D3
Le Brassus, *Switz.* 22 C2
Le Bugue, *France* 26 D4
Le Canourgue, *France* 26 D7
Le Cateau, *France* 25 B10
Le Chambon-Feugerolles,
 France 27 C8
Le Château-d'Oléron,
 France 26 C2
Le Châtelard, *Switz.* 22 D3
Le Châtelet, *France* 26 B6
Le Châtelet-en-Brie, *France* 25 D9
Le Chesne, *France* 25 C11
Le Cheylard, *France* 27 D8
Le Conquet, *France* 24 D2
Le Creusot, *France* 25 F11
Le Croisic, *France* 24 E4
Le Donjon, *France* 26 B7
Le Dorat, *France* 26 B5
Le François, *Martinique* . . 117 D7
Le Grand-Lucé, *France* . . . 24 E7
Le Grand-Pressigny, *France* 24 F7
Le Havre, *France* 24 C7
Le Lavandou, *France* 27 E10
Le Lion-d'Angers, *France* . 24 E6
Le Locle, *Switz.* 22 B3
Le Louroux-Béconnais,
 France 24 E6
Le Luc, *France* 27 E10
Le Madonie, *Italy* 34 E6
Le Maire, Est. de,
 Argentina 128 D4
Le Mans, *France* 24 E7
Le Marinel, *Zaïre* 83 E2
Le Mars, *U.S.A.* 108 D6
Le Mêle-sur-Sarthe, *France* 24 D7
Le Merlerault, *France* 24 D7
Le Monastier-sur-Gazeille,
 France 26 D7
Le Monêtier-les-Bains,
 France 27 D10
Le Mont d'Or, *France* 25 F13
Le Mont-Dore, *France* 26 C6
Le Mont-St.-Michel, *France* 24 D5
Le Moule, *Guadeloupe* . . . 117 C7
Le Muy, *France* 27 E10
Le Palais, *France* 24 E3
Le Perthus, *France* 26 F6
Le Pont, *Switz.* 22 C2
Le Pouldu, *France* 24 E3
Le Puy, *France* 26 C7
Le Quesnoy, *France* 25 B10
Le Roy, *U.S.A.* 109 F7
Le Sentier, *Switz.* 22 C2
Le Sueur, *U.S.A.* 108 C8
Le Teil, *France* 27 D8
Le Teilleul, *France* 24 D6
Le Theil, *France* 24 D7
Le Thillot, *France* 25 E13
Le Thuy, *Vietnam* 58 D6
Le Touquet-Paris-Plage,
 France 25 B8
Le Tréport, *France* 24 B8
Le Val-d'Ajol, *France* 25 E13
Le Verdon-sur-Mer, *France* 26 C2
Le Vigan, *France* 26 E7
Lea →, *U.K.* 13 F7
Leach, *Cambodia* 59 F4
Lead, *U.S.A.* 108 C3
Leader, *Canada* 101 C7
Leadhills, *U.K.* 14 F5
Leadville, *U.S.A.* 111 G10
Leaf →, *U.S.A.* 109 K10
Leakey, *U.S.A.* 109 L5
Leamington, *Canada* 98 D3
Leamington, *U.S.A.* 110 G7
Leamington Spa = Royal
 Leamington Spa, *U.K.* . 13 E6
Le'an, *China* 53 D10
Leandro Norte Alem,
 Argentina 127 B4
Learmonth, *Australia* 88 D1
Leask, *Canada* 101 C7
Leavenworth, *Kans.,
 U.S.A.* 108 F7
Leavenworth, *Wash.,
 U.S.A.* 110 C3
Łeba, *Poland* 20 A7
Lebak, *Phil.* 55 H6
Lebam, *U.S.A.* 112 D3
Lebanon, *Ind., U.S.A.* . . . 104 E2
Lebanon, *Kans., U.S.A.* . . 108 F5
Lebanon, *Ky., U.S.A.* . . . 104 G3
Lebanon, *Mo., U.S.A.* . . . 109 G8
Lebanon, *Oreg., U.S.A.* . . 110 D2
Lebanon, *Pa., U.S.A.* 107 F8
Lebanon, *Tenn., U.S.A.* . . 105 G2
Lebanon ■, *Asia* 69 B4
Lebbeke, *Belgium* 17 G4
Lebec, *U.S.A.* 113 L8
Lebedin, *Ukraine* 40 F9
Lebedyan, *Russia* 41 E11
Lebomboberge, *S. Africa* . . 85 C5
Lębork, *Poland* 20 A7
Lebrija, *Spain* 31 J4
Lebu, *Chile* 126 D1
Lecce, *Italy* 35 B11

Lecco, *Italy* 32 C6
Lecco, L. di, *Italy* 32 C6
Lécera, *Spain* 28 D4
Lech, *Austria* 19 H6
Lech →, *Germany* 19 G6
Lechang, *China* 53 E9
Lechtaler Alpen, *Austria* . . 19 H6
Lectoure, *France* 26 E4
Łęczyca, *Poland* 20 C9
Ledbury, *U.K.* 13 E5
Lede, *Belgium* 17 G3
Ledeberg, *Belgium* 17 F3
Ledesma, *Spain* 30 D5
Ledong, *China* 58 C7
Leduc, *Canada* 100 C6
Ledyczek, *Poland* 20 B6
Lee, *U.S.A.* 107 D11
Lee →, *Ireland* 15 E3
Lee Vining, *U.S.A.* 112 H7
Leech L., *U.S.A.* 108 B7
Leedey, *U.S.A.* 109 H5
Leeds, *U.K.* 12 D6
Leeds, *U.S.A.* 105 J2
Leek, *Neths.* 16 B8
Leek, *U.K.* 12 D5
Leende, *Neths.* 17 F7
Leer, *Germany* 18 B3
Leerdam, *Neths.* 16 E6
Leersum, *Neths.* 16 E6
Leesburg, *U.S.A.* 105 L5
Leesville, *U.S.A.* 109 K8
Leeton, *Australia* 91 E4
Leetonia, *U.S.A.* 106 F4
Leeu Gamka, *S. Africa* . . . 84 E3
Leeuwarden, *Neths.* 16 B7
Leeuwin, C., *Australia* 89 F2
Leeward Is., *Atl. Oc.* 117 C7
Lefka, *Cyprus* 37 D11
Lefkoniko, *Cyprus* 37 D12
Lefors, *U.S.A.* 109 H4
Lefroy, L., *Australia* 89 F3
Legal, *Canada* 100 C6
Leganés, *Spain* 30 E7
Legazpi, *Phil.* 55 E5
Legendre I., *Australia* 88 D2
Leghorn = Livorno, *Italy* . 32 E7
Legionowo, *Poland* 20 C10
Léglise, *Belgium* 17 J7
Legnago, *Italy* 33 C8
Legnano, *Italy* 32 C5
Legnica, *Poland* 20 D6
Legrad, *Croatia* 33 B13
Legume, *Australia* 91 D5
Leh, *India* 63 B7
Lehi, *U.S.A.* 110 F8
Lehighton, *U.S.A.* 107 F9
Lehrte, *Germany* 18 C5
Lehututu, *Botswana* 84 C3
Lei Shui →, *China* 53 D9
Leiah, *Pakistan* 62 D4
Leibnitz, *Austria* 21 J5
Leibo, *China* 52 C4
Leicester, *U.K.* 13 E6
Leicestershire □, *U.K.* . . . 13 E6
Leichhardt →, *Australia* . . 90 B2
Leichhardt Ra., *Australia* . 90 C4
Leiden, *Neths.* 16 D5
Leiderdorp, *Neths.* 16 D5
Leidschendam, *Neths.* 16 D4
Leie →, *Belgium* 25 A10
Leignon, *Belgium* 17 H6
Leine →, *Germany* 18 C5
Leinster, *Australia* 89 E3
Leinster □, *Ireland* 15 C4
Leinster, Mt., *Ireland* 15 D5
Leipzig, *Germany* 18 D8
Leiria, *Portugal* 31 F2
Leiria □, *Portugal* 31 F2
Leisler, Mt., *Australia* 88 D4
Leith, *U.K.* 14 F5
Leith Hill, *U.K.* 13 F7
Leitha →, *Europe* 21 H7
Leitrim, *Ireland* 15 B3
Leitrim □, *Ireland* 15 B3
Leiyang, *China* 53 D9
Leiza, *Spain* 28 B3
Leizhou Bandao, *China* . . . 54 D6
Leizhou Wan, *China* 53 G8
Lek →, *Neths.* 16 E5
Leke, *Belgium* 17 F1
Lekkerkerk, *Neths.* 16 E5
Leksula, *Indonesia* 57 E7
Leland, *U.S.A.* 109 J9
Leland Lakes, *Canada* . . . 101 A6
Leleque, *Argentina* 128 B2
Lelystad, *Neths.* 16 D6
Lema, *Nigeria* 79 C5
Léman, Lac, *Switz.* 22 D3
Lemelerveld, *Neths.* 16 D8
Lemera, *Zaïre* 82 C2
Lemery, *Phil.* 55 E4
Lemgo, *Germany* 18 C4
Lemhi Ra., *U.S.A.* 110 D7
Lemmer, *Neths.* 16 C7
Lemmon, *U.S.A.* 108 C3
Lemoore Grove, *U.S.A.* . . 113 N9
Lemoore, *U.S.A.* 111 H4
Lempdes, *France* 26 C7
Lemsid, *W. Sahara* 74 C2
Lemvig, *Denmark* 11 H2
Lena →, *Russia* 45 B13
Lencl0ître, *France* 24 F7
Lençóis, *Brazil* 123 D3
Léndas, *Greece* 37 E6
Lendeh, *Iran* 65 D6

Lendelede, *Belgium* 17 G2
Lendinara, *Italy* 33 C8
Lengerich, *Germany* 18 C3
Lenggong, *Malaysia* 59 K3
Lenggries, *Germany* 19 H7
Lengua de Vaca, Pta.,
 Chile 126 C1
Lenin, *Russia* 43 B9
Leninabad = Khodzent,
 Tajikistan 44 E7
Leninakan = Kumayri,
 Armenia 43 F10
Leningrad = Sankt-
 Peterburg, *Russia* 40 B7
Lenino, *Ukraine* 42 D6
Leninogorsk = Ridder,
 Kazakhstan 44 D9
Leninsk, *Russia* 43 B11
Leninsk, *Russia* 43 C10
Leninsk-Kuznetskiy, *Russia* 44 D9
Leninskaya Sloboda, *Russia* 41 C14
Leninskoye, *Russia* 41 B15
Leninskoye, *Russia* 41 E14
Lenk, *Switz.* 22 D4
Lenkoran, *Azerbaijan* 67 D13
Lenmalu, *Indonesia* 57 E8
Lenne →, *Germany* 18 D3
Lennox, I., *Chile* 128 E3
Lennoxville, *Canada* 107 A13
Leno, *Italy* 32 C7
Lenoir, *U.S.A.* 105 H5
Lenoir City, *U.S.A.* 105 H3
Lenora, *U.S.A.* 108 F4
Lenore L., *Canada* 101 C8
Lenox, *U.S.A.* 107 D11
Lens, *Belgium* 17 G3
Lens St. Remy, *Belgium* . . 17 G6
Lens, *France* 25 B9
Lensk, *Russia* 45 C12
Lenskoye, *Ukraine* 42 D6
Lent, *Neths.* 16 E7
Lentini, *Italy* 35 E8
Lentvaric, *Lithuania* 40 D4
Lenwood, *U.S.A.* 113 L9
Lenzburg, *Switz.* 22 B6
Lenzen, *Germany* 18 B7
Lenzerheide, *Switz.* 23 C9
Léo, *Burkina Faso* 78 C4
Leoben, *Austria* 21 H5
Leola, *U.S.A.* 108 C5
Leominster, *U.K.* 13 E5
Leominster, *U.S.A.* 107 D13
Léon, *France* 26 E2
León, *Mexico* 114 C4
León, *Nic.* 116 D2
León, *Spain* 30 C5
Leon, *U.S.A.* 108 E8
León □, *Spain* 30 C5
León, Montañas de, *Spain* . 30 C4
Leonardtown, *U.S.A.* 104 F7
Leone, Mte., *Switz.* 22 D6
Leonforte, *Italy* 35 E7
Leongatha, *Australia* 91 F4
Leonídhion, *Greece* 39 M5
Leonora, *Australia* 89 E3
Léopold II, Lac = Mai-
 Ndombe, L., *Zaïre* 80 E3
Leopoldina, *Brazil* 123 F3
Leopoldo Bulhões, *Brazil* . 123 E2
Leopoldsburg, *Belgium* . . . 17 F6
Léopoldville = Kinshasa,
 Zaïre 80 E3
Leoti, *U.S.A.* 108 F4
Leoville, *Canada* 101 C7
Lépa, L. do, *Angola* 84 B2
Lepe, *Spain* 31 H3
Lepel, *Belorussia* 40 D6
Lepikha, *Russia* 45 C13
Leping, *China* 53 C11
Lepontine, Alpi, *Italy* 23 D6
Lequeitio, *Spain* 28 B2
Lequila, *Spain* 28 C6
Lercara Friddi, *Italy* 34 E6
Lerdo, *Mexico* 114 B4
Léré, *Chad* 73 G7
Lere, *Nigeria* 79 D6
Leribe, *Lesotho* 85 D4
Lérici, *Italy* 32 D6
Lérida, *Spain* 28 D5
Lérida □, *Spain* 28 C6
Lérins, Is. de, *France* 27 E11
Lerma, *Spain* 30 C7
Léros, *Greece* 39 M9
Lérouville, *France* 25 D12
Lerwick, *U.K.* 14 A7
Les Abrets, *France* 27 C9
Les Andelys, *France* 24 C8
Les Arcs, *France* 27 E10
Les Baux-de-Provence,
 France 27 E8
Les Bois, *Switz.* 22 B3
Les Cayes, *Haiti* 117 C5
Les Diablerets, *Switz.* 22 D4
Les Échelles, *France* 27 C9
Les Essarts, *France* 24 F5
Les Eyzies-de-Tayac-
 Sireuil, *France* 26 D5
Les Herbiers, *France* 24 F5
Les Minquiers, *Chan. Is.* . . 24 D4
Les Ponts-de-Cé, *France* . . 24 E6
Les Riceys, *France* 25 E11
Les Sables-d'Olonne,
 France 26 B2
Les Vans, *France* 27 D8
Les Verrières, *Switz.* 22 C2

Lesbos = Lésvos, *Greece* . 39 K9
Leshan, *China* 52 C4
Lésina, L. di, *Italy* 33 G12
Lesja, *Norway* 10 B2
Lesjaverk, *Norway* 10 B2
Leskov I., *Antarctica* 5 B1
Leskovac, *Serbia* 21 M11
Leslie, *U.S.A.* 109 H8
Lesneven, *France* 24 D2
Lešnica, *Serbia* 21 L9
Lesnoye, *Russia* 40 B9
Lesopilnoye, *Russia* 48 A7
Lesotho ■, *Africa* 85 D4
Lesozavodsk, *Russia* 45 D4
Lesparre-Médoc, *France* . . 26 C3
Lessay, *France* 24 C5
Lesse →, *Belgium* 17 H5
Lesser Antilles, *W. Indies* . 117 C7
Lesser Slave L., *Canada* . . 100 B5
Lesser Sunda Is., *Indonesia* 57 F6
Lessines, *Belgium* 17 G3
Lester, *U.S.A.* 112 C5
Lestock, *Canada* 101 C8
Lesuer I., *Australia* 88 B5
Lésvos, *Greece* 39 K9
Leszno, *Poland* 20 D6
Letchworth, *U.K.* 13 F7
Letea, Ostrov, *Romania* . . 38 D12
Lethbridge, *Canada* 100 D6
Lethem, *Guyana* 121 C6
Leti, Kepulauan, *Indonesia* 57 F7
Leti Is. = Leti, Kepulauan,
 Indonesia 57 F7
Letiahau →, *Botswana* . . . 84 C3
Leticia, *Colombia* 120 D4
Leting, *China* 51 E10
Letjiesbos, *S. Africa* 84 E3
Lethakeng, *Botswana* 84 C3
Letpadan, *Burma* 61 L19
Letpan, *Burma* 61 K19
Letterkenny, *Ireland* 15 B4
Leu, *Romania* 38 E7
Leucadia, *U.S.A.* 113 M9
Leucate, *France* 26 F7
Leucate, Étang de, *France* . 26 F7
Leuk, *Switz.* 22 D5
Leukerbad, *Switz.* 22 D5
Leupegem, *Belgium* 17 G3
Leuser, G., *Indonesia* 56 D1
Leutkirch, *Germany* 19 H6
Leuven, *Belgium* 17 G5
Leuze, *Hainaut, Belgium* . . 17 G3
Leuze, *Namur, Belgium* . . . 17 G5
Lev Tolstoy, *Russia* 41 E11
Levádhia, *Greece* 39 L5
Levan, *U.S.A.* 110 G8
Levanger, *Norway* 8 E11
Levant, I. du, *France* 27 E10
Lévanto, *Italy* 32 D6
Levanzo, *Italy* 34 E5
Levelland, *U.S.A.* 109 J3
Leven, *U.K.* 14 E6
Leven, L., *U.K.* 14 E5
Leven, Toraka, *Madag.* . . . 85 A8
Levens, *France* 27 E11
Leveque C., *Australia* 88 C3
Leverano, *Italy* 35 B10
Leverkusen, *Germany* 18 D2
Levet, *France* 25 F9
Levice, *Slovak Rep.* 21 G8
Levico, *Italy* 33 C8
Levie, *France* 27 G13
Levier, *France* 25 F13
Levin, *N.Z.* 87 J5
Lévis, *Canada* 99 C5
Levis, L., *Canada* 100 A5
Levítha, *Greece* 39 M9
Levittown, *N.Y., U.S.A.* . . 107 F11
Levittown, *Pa., U.S.A.* . . . 107 F10
Lévka Óri, *Greece* 37 D6
Levkás, *Greece* 39 L3
Levkímmi, *Greece* 37 B4
Levkímmi, Ákra, *Greece* . . 37 B4
Levkôsia = Nicosia, *Cyprus* 37 D12
Levoča, *Slovak Rep.* 20 F10
Levroux, *France* 25 F8
Levski, *Bulgaria* 38 F8
Levskigrad, *Bulgaria* 38 G7
Lewellen, *U.S.A.* 108 E3
Lewes, *U.K.* 13 G8
Lewes, *U.S.A.* 104 F8
Lewis, *U.K.* 14 C2
Lewis →, *U.S.A.* 112 E4
Lewis, Butt of, *U.K.* 14 C2
Lewis Ra., *Australia* 88 D4
Lewis Range, *U.S.A.* 110 C7
Lewisburg, *Pa., U.S.A.* . . . 106 F8
Lewisburg, *Tenn., U.S.A.* . 105 H2
Lewisporte, *Canada* 99 C8
Lewiston, *Idaho, U.S.A.* . . 110 C5
Lewiston, *Maine, U.S.A.* . 105 C11
Lewistown, *Mont., U.S.A.* 110 C9
Lewistown, *Pa., U.S.A.* . . 106 F7
Lexington, *Ill., U.S.A.* . . . 108 E10
Lexington, *Ky., U.S.A.* . . . 104 F3
Lexington, *Miss., U.S.A.* . 109 J9
Lexington, *Mo., U.S.A.* . . 108 F8
Lexington, *N.C., U.S.A.* . . 105 H5
Lexington, *Nebr., U.S.A.* . 108 E5
Lexington, *Ohio, U.S.A.* . . 106 F2
Lexington, *Oreg., U.S.A.* . 110 D4
Lexington, *Tenn., U.S.A.* . 105 H1
Lexington Park, *U.S.A.* . . 104 F7
Leye, *China* 52 E6
Leyre →, *France* 26 D2

Leysin, *Switz.* 22 D4
Leyte, *Phil.* 55 F6
Leyte Gulf, *Phil.* 55 F6
Lezay, *France* 26 B4
Lézignan-Corbières, *France* 26 E6
Lezoux, *France* 26 C7
Lgov, *Russia* 40 F9
Lhasa, *China* 54 D4
Lhazê, *China* 54 D3
Lhokkruet, *Indonesia* 56 D1
Lhokseumawe, *Indonesia* . 56 C1
Lhuntsi Dzong, *India* 61 F17
Li, *Thailand* 58 D2
Li Shui →, *China* 53 C9
Li Xian, *Gansu, China* 50 G3
Li Xian, *Hebei, China* 50 E8
Li Xian, *Hunan, China* . . . 53 C8
Li Xian, *Sichuan, China* . . 52 B4
Liádhoi, *Greece* 39 N9
Lian Xian, *China* 53 E9
Liancheng, *China* 53 E11
Lianga, *Phil.* 55 G7
Liangcheng,
Nei Mongol Zizhiqu,
China 50 D7
Liangcheng, *Shandong,*
China 51 G10
Liangdang, *China* 50 H4
Lianghekou, *China* 52 C7
Liangping, *China* 52 B6
Lianhua, *China* 53 D9
Lianjiang, *Fujian, China* . . 53 D12
Lianjiang, *Guangdong,*
China 53 G8
Lianping, *China* 53 E10
Lianshan, *China* 53 E9
Lianshanguan, *China* 51 D12
Lianshui, *China* 51 H10
Lianyuan, *China* 53 D8
Lianyungang, *China* 51 G10
Liao He →, *China* 51 D11
Liaocheng, *China* 50 F8
Liaodong Bandao, *China* . 51 E12
Liaodong Wan, *China* 51 D11
Liaoning □, *China* 54 B7
Liaoning □, *Liaoning,*
China 51 D12
Liaoyang, *China* 51 D12
Liaoyuan, *China* 51 C13
Liaozhong, *China* 51 D12
Liapádhes, *Greece* 39 K2
Liard →, *Canada* 100 A4
Liari, *Pakistan* 62 G2
Líbano, *Colombia* 120 C2
Libau = Liepãja, *Latvia* . . 40 C2
Libby, *U.S.A.* 110 B6
Libenge, *Zaïre* 80 D3
Liberal, *Kans., U.S.A.* . . . 109 G4
Liberal, *Mo., U.S.A.* 109 G7
Liberdade, *Brazil* 124 C3
Liberdade →, *Brazil* 125 B7
Liberec, *Czech.* 20 E5
Liberia, *Costa Rica* 116 D2
Liberia ■, *W. Afr.* 78 D3
Libertad, *Venezuela* 120 B4
Liberty, *Mo., U.S.A.* 108 F7
Liberty, *Tex., U.S.A.* 109 K7
Libin, *Belgium* 17 J6
Libîya, Sahrâ', *Africa* 73 C9
Libo, *China* 52 E6
Libobo, Tanjung, *Indonesia* 57 E7
Libode, *S. Africa* 85 E4
Libonda, *Zambia* 81 G4
Libourne, *France* 26 D3
Libramont, *Belgium* 17 J6
Libreville, *Gabon* 80 D1
Libya ■, *N. Afr.* 73 C8
Libyan Desert = Libîya,
Sahrâ', *Africa* 73 C9
Libyan Plateau = Ed-
Déffa, *Egypt* 76 A2
Licantén, *Chile* 126 D1
Licata, *Italy* 34 E6
Lice, *Turkey* 67 D9
Licheng, *China* 50 F7
Lichfield, *U.K.* 12 E6
Lichinga, *Mozam.* 83 E4
Lichtaart, *Belgium* 17 F5
Lichtenburg, *S. Africa* 84 D4
Lichtenfels, *Germany* 19 E7
Lichtenvoorde, *Neths.* 16 E9
Lichtervelde, *Belgium* 17 F2
Lichuan, *Hubei, China* . . . 52 B7
Lichuan, *Jiangxi, China* . . 53 D11
Licosa, Punta, *Italy* 35 B7
Lida, *Belorussia* 40 E4
Lida, *U.S.A.* 111 H5
Lidingö, *Sweden* 10 E12
Lidköping, *Sweden* 11 F7
Lido, *Italy* 33 C9
Lido, *Niger* 79 C5
Lido di Roma = Óstia,
Lido di, *Italy* 34 A5
Lidzbark Warmiński,
Poland 20 A10
Liebenwalde, *Germany* . . . 18 C9
Lieberose, *Germany* 18 D10
Liebig, Mt., *Australia* 88 D5
Liechtenstein ■, *Europe* . . 23 B9
Liederkerke, *Belgium* 17 G4
Liège, *Belgium* 17 G7
Liège □, *Belgium* 17 G7
Liegnitz = Legnica, *Poland* 20 D6

Liempde, *Neths.* 17 E6
Lienart, *Zaïre* 82 B2
Lienyünchiangshih =
Lianyungang, *China* . . . 51 G10
Lienz, *Austria* 21 J2
Liepãja, *Latvia* 40 C2
Lier, *Belgium* 17 F5
Lierneux, *Belgium* 17 H7
Lieshout, *Neths.* 17 E7
Liestal, *Switz.* 22 B5
Liévin, *France* 25 B9
Lièvre →, *Canada* 98 C4
Liezen, *Austria* 21 H4
Liffey →, *Ireland* 15 C5
Lifford, *Ireland* 15 B4
Liffré, *France* 24 D5
Lifjell, *Norway* 10 E2
Lifudzin, *Russia* 48 B7
Ligao, *Phil.* 55 E5
Lightning Ridge, *Australia* 91 D4
Lignano, *Italy* 33 C10
Ligny-en-Barrois, *France* . 25 D12
Ligny-le-Châtel, *France* . . 25 E10
Ligoúrion, *Greece* 39 M6
Ligueil, *France* 24 E7
Liguria □, *Italy* 32 D6
Ligurian Sea, *Italy* 32 E5
Lihou Reefs and Cays,
Australia 90 B5
Lihue, *U.S.A.* 102 H15
Lijiang, *China* 52 D3
Likasi, *Zaïre* 83 E2
Likati, *Zaïre* 80 D4
Likhoslavl, *Russia* 40 C9
Likhovski, *Russia* 43 B9
Likoma I., *Malawi* 83 E3
Likumburu, *Tanzania* 83 D4
L'Île-Bouchard, *France* . . 24 E7
L'Île-Rousse, *France* 27 F12
Liling, *China* 53 D9
Lille, *Belgium* 17 F5
Lille, *France* 25 B10
Lille Bælt, *Denmark* 11 J3
Lillebonne, *France* 24 C7
Lillehammer, *Norway* 10 C4
Lillers, *France* 25 B9
Lillesand, *Norway* 11 F2
Lilleshall, *U.K.* 13 E5
Lillestrøm, *Norway* 10 E5
Lillian Point, Mt., *Australia* 89 E4
Lillo, *Spain* 28 F1
Lillooet →, *Canada* 100 D4
Lilongwe, *Malawi* 83 E3
Liloy, *Phil.* 57 C6
Lim →, *Bos.-H.* 21 M9
Lima, *Indonesia* 57 E7
Lima, *Peru* 124 C2
Lima, *Mont., U.S.A.* 110 D7
Lima, *Ohio, U.S.A.* 104 E3
Lima □, *Peru* 124 C2
Lima →, *Portugal* 30 D2
Limages, *Canada* 107 A9
Liman, *Russia* 43 D12
Limassol, *Cyprus* 37 E12
Limavady, *U.K.* 15 A5
Limavady □, *U.K.* 15 B5
Limay →, *Argentina* 128 A3
Limay Mahuida, *Argentina* 126 D2
Limbang, *Brunei* 56 D5
Limbara, Monti, *Italy* 34 B2
Limbdi, *India* 62 H4
Limbe, *Cameroon* 79 E6
Limbourg, *Belgium* 17 G7
Limbri, *Australia* 91 E5
Limbunya, *Australia* 88 C4
Limburg, *Germany* 19 E4
Limburg □, *Belgium* 17 F6
Limburg □, *Neths.* 17 F7
Limeira, *Brazil* 127 A6
Limerick, *Ireland* 15 D3
Limerick □, *Ireland* 15 D3
Limestone, *U.S.A.* 106 D6
Limestone →, *Canada* . . . 101 B10
Limfjorden, *Denmark* 11 H3
Limia = Lima →, *Portugal* 30 D2
Limmared, *Sweden* 11 G7
Limmen, *Neths.* 16 C5
Limmen Bight, *Australia* . . 90 A2
Limmen Bight →,
Australia 90 B2
Límni, *Greece* 39 L6
Límnos, *Greece* 39 K8
Limoeiro, *Brazil* 122 C4
Limoeiro do Norte, *Brazil* 122 C4
Limoges, *France* 26 C5
Limón, *Costa Rica* 116 D3
Limon, *U.S.A.* 108 F3
Limone Piemonte, *Italy* . . 32 D4
Limousin, *France* 26 C5
Limousin, Plateau du,
France 26 C5
Limoux, *France* 26 E6
Limpopo →, *Africa* 85 D5
Limuru, *Kenya* 82 C4
Lin Xian, *China* 50 F6
Lin'an, *China* 53 B12
Linapacan I., *Phil.* 55 F3
Linapacan Str., *Phil.* 55 F3
Linares, *Chile* 126 D1
Linares, *Colombia* 120 C2
Linares, *Mexico* 115 C5
Linares, *Spain* 29 G1
Linares □, *Chile* 126 D1
Línas Mte., *Italy* 34 C1

Lincang, *China* 52 F3
Lincheng, *China* 50 F8
Linchuan, *China* 53 D11
Lincoln, *Argentina* 126 C3
Lincoln, *N.Z.* 87 K4
Lincoln, *U.K.* 12 D7
Lincoln, *Calif., U.S.A.* . . . 112 G5
Lincoln, *Ill., U.S.A.* 108 E10
Lincoln, *Kans., U.S.A.* . . . 108 F5
Lincoln, *Maine, U.S.A.* . . . 99 C6
Lincoln, *N.H., U.S.A.* 107 B13
Lincoln, *N. Mex., U.S.A.* . 111 K11
Lincoln, *Nebr., U.S.A.* . . . 108 E6
Lincoln Hav = Lincoln
Sea, *Arctic* 4 A5
Lincoln Sea, *Arctic* 4 A5
Lincoln Wolds, *U.K.* 12 D7
Lincolnshire □, *U.K.* 12 D7
Lincolnton, *U.S.A.* 105 H5
L'Incudine, *France* 27 G13
Lind, *U.S.A.* 110 C4
Linda, *U.S.A.* 112 F5
Lindau, *Germany* 19 H5
Linde →, *Neths.* 16 C7
Linden, *Guyana* 121 B6
Linden, *Calif., U.S.A.* 112 G5
Linden, *Tex., U.S.A.* 109 J7
Lindenheuvel, *Neths.* 17 G7
Lindenhurst, *U.S.A.* 107 F11
Linderöd, *Sweden* 11 J7
Linderödsåsen, *Sweden* . . 11 J7
Lindesnes, *Norway* 6 D7
Líndhos, *Greece* 37 C10
Lindi, *Tanzania* 83 D4
Lindi □, *Tanzania* 83 D4
Lindi →, *Zaïre* 82 B2
Lindoso, *Portugal* 30 D2
Lindow, *Germany* 18 C8
Lindsay, *Canada* 98 D4
Lindsay, *Calif., U.S.A.* . . . 111 H4
Lindsay, *Okla., U.S.A.* . . . 109 H6
Lindsborg, *U.S.A.* 108 F6
Linfen, *China* 50 F6
Ling Xian, *Hunan, China* . 53 D9
Ling Xian, *Shandong,*
China 50 F9
Lingao, *China* 58 C7
Lingayen, *Phil.* 57 A6
Lingayen G., *Phil.* 55 C4
Lingbi, *China* 51 H9
Lingchuan,
Guangxi Zhuangzu,
China 53 E8
Lingchuan, *Shanxi, China* . 50 G7
Lingen, *Germany* 18 C3
Lingga, *Indonesia* 56 E2
Lingga, Kepulauan,
Indonesia 56 E2
Lingga Arch. = Lingga,
Kepulauan, *Indonesia* . . 56 E2
Lingle, *U.S.A.* 108 D2
Lingling, *China* 53 D8
Lingqiu, *China* 50 E8
Lingshan, *China* 52 F7
Lingshi, *China* 50 F6
Lingshou, *China* 50 E8
Lingshui, *China* 58 C8
Lingtai, *China* 50 G4
Linguère, *Senegal* 78 B1
Lingui, *China* 53 E8
Lingyuan, *China* 51 D10
Lingyun, *China* 52 E6
Linh Cam, *Vietnam* 58 C5
Linhai, *China* 53 C13
Linhares, *Brazil* 123 E3
Linhe, *China* 50 D4
Linjiang, *China* 51 D14
Linköping, *Sweden* 11 F9
Linkou, *China* 51 B16
Linli, *China* 53 C8
Linlithgow, *U.K.* 14 F5
Linnhe, L., *U.K.* 14 E3
Linosa, I., *Medit. S.* 75 A7
Linqi, *China* 50 G7
Linqing, *China* 50 F8
Linru, *China* 50 G7
Lins, *Brazil* 127 A6
Linshui, *China* 52 B6
Lintao, *China* 50 G2
Linth →, *Switz.* 19 H5
Linthal, *Switz.* 23 C8
Lintlaw, *Canada* 101 C8
Linton, *Canada* 99 C5
Linton, *Ind., U.S.A.* 104 F2
Linton, *N. Dak., U.S.A.* . . 108 B4
Lintong, *China* 50 G5
Linville, *Australia* 91 D5
Linwood, *Canada* 106 C4
Linwu, *China* 53 E9
Linxi, *China* 51 C10
Linxia, *China* 54 C5
Linxiang, *China* 53 C9
Linyanti →, *Africa* 84 B4
Linyi, *China* 51 G10
Linz, *Austria* 21 G4
Linz, *Germany* 18 E3
Linzhenzhen, *China* 50 F5
Linzi, *China* 51 F10
Lion, G. du, *France* 27 E8
Lionárisso, *Cyprus* 37 D13
Lioni, *Italy* 35 B8
Lions, G. of = Lion, G.
du, *France* 27 E8
Lion's Den, *Zimbabwe* . . . 83 F3

Lion's Head, *Canada* 98 D3
Liozna, *Belorussia* 40 D7
Lipa, *Phil.* 55 E4
Lipali, *Mozam.* 83 F4
Lípari, *Italy* 35 D7
Lípari, Is., *Italy* 35 D7
Lipetsk, *Russia* 41 E11
Liping, *China* 52 D7
Lipkany, *Moldavia* 42 B2
Lipljan, *Serbia* 21 N11
Lipno, *Poland* 20 C9
Lipova, *Romania* 38 C4
Lipovcy Manzovka, *Russia* 48 B6
Lipovets, *Ukraine* 42 B3
Lippe →, *Germany* 18 D2
Lippstadt, *Germany* 18 D4
Lipscomb, *U.S.A.* 109 G4
Lipsko, *Poland* 20 D11
Lipsói, *Greece* 39 M9
Liptovský Svaty Milkuláš,
Slovak Rep. 20 F9
Liptrap C., *Australia* 91 F4
Lipu, *China* 53 E8
Liri →, *Italy* 34 A6
Liria, *Spain* 28 F4
Lisala, *Zaïre* 80 D4
Lisboa, *Portugal* 31 G1
Lisboa □, *Portugal* 31 G1
Lisbon = Lisboa, *Portugal* 31 G1
Lisbon, *N. Dak., U.S.A.* . . 108 B6
Lisbon, *N.H., U.S.A.* 107 B13
Lisbon, *Ohio, U.S.A.* 106 F4
Lisburn, *U.K.* 15 B5
Lisburne, C., *U.S.A.* 96 B3
Liscannor, B., *Ireland* 15 D2
Liscia →, *Italy* 34 A2
Lishe Jiang →, *China* 52 E3
Lishi, *China* 50 F6
Lishu, *China* 51 C13
Lishui, *Jiangsu, China* . . . 53 B12
Lishui, *Zhejiang, China* . . 53 C12
Lisianski I., *Pac. Oc.* 92 E10
Lisichansk, *Ukraine* 42 B8
Lisieux, *France* 24 C7
Liski, *Russia* 41 F11
L'Isle-Adam, *France* 25 C9
L'Isle-Jourdain, *Gers,*
France 26 E5
L'Isle-Jourdain, *Vienne,*
France 26 B4
L'Isle-sur-le-Doubs, *France* 25 E13
Lisle-sur-Tarn, *France* . . . 26 E5
Lismore, *Australia* 91 D5
Lismore, *Ireland* 15 D4
Lisse, *Neths.* 16 D5
List, *Germany* 18 A4
Lista, *Norway* 9 G9
Lista, *Sweden* 9 G14
Lister, Mt., *Antarctica* 5 D11
Liston, *Australia* 91 D5
Listowel, *Canada* 98 D3
Listowel, *Ireland* 15 D2
Lit-et-Mixe, *France* 26 D2
Litang, *Guangxi Zhuangzu,*
China 52 F7
Litang, *Sichuan, China* . . . 52 B3
Litang, *Malaysia* 57 C5
Litang Qu →, *China* 52 C3
Litani →, *Lebanon* 69 B4
Litchfield, *Calif., U.S.A.* . . 112 E6
Litchfield, *Conn., U.S.A.* . 107 E11
Litchfield, *Ill., U.S.A.* 108 F10
Litchfield, *Minn., U.S.A.* . 108 C7
Lithgow, *Australia* 91 E5
Líthinon, Ákra, *Greece* . . . 37 E6
Lithuania ■, *Europe* 40 D3
Litija, *Slovenia* 33 B11
Litókhoron, *Greece* 39 J5
Litoměřice, *Czech.* 20 E4
Little Abaco I., *Bahamas* . 116 A4
Little Barrier I., *N.Z.* 87 G5
Little Belt Mts., *U.S.A.* . . . 110 C8
Little Blue →, *U.S.A.* 108 F6
Little Bushman Land,
S. Africa 84 D2
Little Cadotte →, *Canada* 100 B5
Little Cayman, I.,
Cayman Is. 116 C3
Little Churchill →, *Canada* 101 B9
Little Colorado →, *U.S.A.* 111 H8
Little Current, *Canada* . . . 98 C3
Little Current →, *Canada* . 98 B3
Little Falls, *Minn., U.S.A.* . 108 C7
Little Falls, *N.Y., U.S.A.* . . 107 C10
Little Fork →, *U.S.A.* 108 A8
Little Grand Rapids,
Canada 101 C9
Little Humboldt →,
U.S.A. 110 F5
Little Inagua I., *Bahamas* . 117 B5
Little Karoo, *S. Africa* . . . 84 E3
Little Lake, *U.S.A.* 113 K9
Little Laut Is. = Laut
Ketil, Kepulauan,
Indonesia 56 E5
Little Minch, *U.K.* 14 D2
Little Missouri →, *U.S.A.* . 108 B3
Little Namaqualand,
S. Africa 84 D2
Little Ouse →, *U.K.* 13 E8
Little Rann, *India* 62 H4
Little Red →, *U.S.A.* 109 H9
Little River, *N.Z.* 87 K4
Little Rock, *U.S.A.* 109 H8

Little Ruaha →, *Tanzania* . 82 D4
Little Sable Pt., *U.S.A.* . . . 104 D2
Little Sioux →, *U.S.A.* . . . 108 E6
Little Smoky →, *Canada* . . 100 C5
Little Snake →, *U.S.A.* . . . 110 F9
Little Valley, *U.S.A.* 106 D6
Little Wabash →, *U.S.A.* . 104 G1
Littlefield, *U.S.A.* 109 J3
Littlefork, *U.S.A.* 108 A8
Littlehampton, *U.K.* 13 G7
Littleton, *U.S.A.* 107 B13
Liu He →, *China* 51 D11
Liu Jiang →, *China* 52 F7
Liuba, *China* 50 H4
Liucheng, *China* 52 E7
Liugou, *China* 51 D10
Liuhe, *China* 51 C13
Liuheng Dao, *China* 53 C14
Liukang Tenggaja,
Indonesia 57 F5
Liuli, *Tanzania* 83 E3
Liuwa Plain, *Zambia* 81 G4
Liuyang, *China* 53 C9
Liuzhou, *China* 52 E7
Liuzhuang, *China* 51 H11
Livadherón, *Greece* 39 J4
Livadhia, *Cyprus* 37 E12
Livarot, *France* 24 D7
Live Oak, *Calif., U.S.A.* . . 112 F5
Live Oak, *Fla., U.S.A.* 105 K4
Liveras, *Cyprus* 37 D11
Liveringa, *Australia* 88 C3
Livermore, *U.S.A.* 112 H5
Livermore, Mt., *U.S.A.* . . . 109 K2
Liverpool, *Australia* 91 E5
Liverpool, *Canada* 99 D7
Liverpool, *U.K.* 12 D5
Liverpool Plains, *Australia* 91 E5
Liverpool Ra., *Australia* . . 91 E5
Livingston, *Guatemala* . . . 116 C2
Livingston, *Calif., U.S.A.* . 112 H6
Livingston, *Mont., U.S.A.* 110 D8
Livingston, *Tex., U.S.A.* . . 109 K7
Livingstone, *Zambia* 83 F2
Livingstone Mts., *Tanzania* 83 D3
Livingstonia, *Malawi* 83 E3
Livny, *Russia* 41 E10
Livonia, *U.S.A.* 104 D4
Livorno, *Italy* 32 E7
Livramento, *Brazil* 127 C4
Livramento do Brumado,
Brazil 123 D3
Livron-sur-Drôme, *France* 27 D8
Liwale, *Tanzania* 83 D4
Liwale □, *Tanzania* 83 D4
Lixi, *China* 52 D3
Liyang, *China* 53 B12
Lizard I., *Australia* 90 A4
Lizard Pt., *U.K.* 13 H2
Lizarda, *Brazil* 122 C2
Lizzano, *Italy* 35 B10
Ljubija, *Bos.-H.* 33 D13
Ljubljana, *Slovenia* 33 B11
Ljubno, *Slovenia* 33 B11
Ljubuški, *Bos.-H.* 21 M7
Ljung, *Sweden* 11 F7
Ljungan →, *Sweden* 10 B11
Ljungaverk, *Sweden* 10 B10
Ljungby, *Sweden* 9 H12
Ljusdal, *Sweden* 10 C10
Ljusnan = Ljungan →,
Sweden 10 B11
Ljusnan →, *Sweden* 9 F14
Ljusne, *Sweden* 9 F14
Ljutomer, *Slovenia* 33 B13
Llagostera, *Spain* 28 D7
Llamellín, *Peru* 124 B2
Llancanelo, Salina,
Argentina 126 D2
Llandeilo, *U.K.* 13 F3
Llandovery, *U.K.* 13 F4
Llandrindod Wells, *U.K.* . . 13 E4
Llandudno, *U.K.* 12 D4
Llanelli, *U.K.* 13 F3
Llanes, *Spain* 30 B6
Llangollen, *U.K.* 12 E4
Llanidloes, *U.K.* 13 E4
Llano, *U.S.A.* 109 K5
Llano →, *U.S.A.* 109 K5
Llano Estacado, *U.S.A.* . . 109 J3
Llanos, *S. Amer.* 118 C3
Llanquihue □, *Chile* 128 B2
Llanquihue, L., *Chile* 128 B1
Llebetx, C., *Spain* 36 B9
Lleida = Lérida, *Spain* . . . 28 D5
Llentrisca, C., *Spain* 36 C7
Llera, *Mexico* 115 C5
Llerena, *Spain* 31 G4
Llica, *Bolivia* 124 D4
Llico, *Chile* 126 C1
Llobregat →, *Spain* 28 D7
Lloret de Mar, *Spain* 28 D7
Lloyd B., *Australia* 90 A3
Lloyd L., *Canada* 101 B7
Lloydminster, *Canada* 101 C6
Lluchmayor, *Spain* 36 B9
Llullaillaco, Volcán,
S. Amer. 126 A2
Lo, *Belgium* 17 G1
Lo →, *Vietnam* 58 B5
Loa, *U.S.A.* 111 G8
Loa →, *Chile* 126 A1
Loano, *Italy* 32 D5
Lobatse, *Botswana* 84 D4
Löbau, *Germany* 18 D10

Lobbes

Lobbes, *Belgium* 17 H4
Lobenstein, *Germany* 18 E7
Lobería, *Argentina* ... 126 D4
Lobito, *Angola* 81 G2
Lobón, Canal de, *Spain* . 31 G4
Lobos, *Argentina* 126 D4
Lobos, I., *Mexico* 114 B2
Lobos, Is., *Peru* 118 C1
Lobos, I. de, *Canary Is.* . 36 F6
Lobos de Tierra, I., *Peru* . 124 B1
Loc Binh, *Vietnam* 58 B6
Loc Ninh, *Vietnam* 59 G6
Locarno, *Switz.* 23 D7
Lochaber, *U.K.* 14 E4
Lochcarron, *U.K.* 14 D3
Lochem, *Neths.* 16 D8
Loches, *France* 24 E8
Lochgelly, *U.K.* 14 E5
Lochgilphead, *U.K.* 14 E3
Lochinver, *U.K.* 14 C3
Lochnagar, *Australia* ... 90 C4
Lochnagar, *U.K.* 14 E5
Łochów, *Poland* 20 C11
Lochy →, *U.K.* 14 E3
Lock, *Australia* 91 E2
Lock Haven, *U.S.A.* 106 E7
Lockeford, *U.S.A.* 112 G5
Lockeport, *Canada* 99 D6
Lockerbie, *U.K.* 14 F5
Lockhart, *U.S.A.* 109 L6
Lockhart, L., *Australia* .. 89 F2
Lockney, *U.S.A.* 109 H4
Lockport, *U.S.A.* 106 C6
Locminé, *France* 24 E4
Locri, *Italy* 35 D9
Locronan, *France* 24 D2
Loctudy, *France* 24 E2
Lod, *Israel* 69 D3
Lodève, *France* 26 E7
Lodge Grass, *U.S.A.* ... 110 D10
Lodgepole, *U.S.A.* 108 E3
Lodgepole Cr. →, *U.S.A.* 108 E2
Lodhran, *Pakistan* 62 E4
Lodi, *Italy* 32 C6
Lodi, *U.S.A.* 112 G5
Lodja, *Zaïre* 82 C1
Lodosa, *Spain* 28 C2
Lödöse, *Sweden* 11 F6
Lodwar, *Kenya* 82 B4
Łódź, *Poland* 20 D9
Loei, *Thailand* 58 D3
Loenen, *Neths.* 16 D8
Loengo, *Zaïre* 82 C2
Loeriesfontein, *S. Africa* . 84 E2
Lofoten, *Norway* 8 B13
Lofsdalen, *Sweden* 10 B7
Lofsen →, *Sweden* 10 B7
Logan, *Kans., U.S.A.* ... 108 F5
Logan, *Ohio, U.S.A.* 104 F4
Logan, *Utah, U.S.A.* 110 F8
Logan, *W. Va., U.S.A.* .. 104 G5
Logan, Mt., *Canada* 96 B5
Logan Pass, *U.S.A.* 100 D6
Logandale, *U.S.A.* 113 J12
Logansport, *Ind., U.S.A.* . 104 E2
Logansport, *La., U.S.A.* . 109 K8
Logo, *Sudan* 77 F3
Logone →, *Chad* 73 F8
Logroño, *Spain* 28 C2
Logrosán, *Spain* 31 F5
Løgstør, *Denmark* 11 H3
Lohardaga, *India* 63 H11
Lohr, *Germany* 19 F5
Loi-kaw, *Burma* 61 K20
Loimaa, *Finland* 9 F17
Loir →, *France* 24 E6
Loir-et-Cher □, *France* .. 24 E8
Loire □, *France* 27 C8
Loire →, *France* 24 E4
Loire-Atlantique □, *France* 24 E5
Loiret □, *France* 25 E9
Loitz, *Germany* 18 B9
Loja, *Ecuador* 124 D2
Loja, *Spain* 31 H6
Loja □, *Ecuador* 120 D2
Loji, *Indonesia* 57 E7
Loka, *Sudan* 77 G3
Lokandu, *Zaïre* 82 C2
Løken, *Norway* 10 E5
Lokeren, *Belgium* 17 F3
Lokhvitsa, *Ukraine* 40 F8
Lokichokio, *Kenya* 82 B3
Lokitaung, *Kenya* 82 B4
Lokka, *Finland* 8 C19
Løkken, *Denmark* 11 G3
Løkken Verk, *Norway* ... 10 A3
Loknya, *Russia* 40 C7
Lokoja, *Nigeria* 79 D6
Lokolama, *Zaïre* 80 E3
Lol →, *Sudan* 77 F2
Lola, *Guinea* 78 D3
Lola, Mt., *U.S.A.* 112 F6
Lolibai, Gebel, *Sudan* .. 77 G3
Lolimi, *Sudan* 77 G3
Loliondo, *Tanzania* 82 C4
Lolland, *Denmark* 11 K5
Lollar, *Germany* 18 E4
Lolo, *U.S.A.* 110 C6
Lolodorf, *Cameroon* 79 E7
Lom, *Bulgaria* 38 F6
Lom →, *Bulgaria* 38 F6
Lom Kao, *Thailand* 58 D3
Lom Sak, *Thailand* 58 D3
Loma, *U.S.A.* 110 C8
Loma Linda, *U.S.A.* 113 L9

Lomami →, *Zaïre* 82 B1
Lomas de Zamóra,
  Argentina 126 C4
Lombadina, *Australia* ... 88 C3
Lombardia □, *Italy* 32 C6
Lombardy = Lombardia □,
  Italy 32 C6
Lombez, *France* 26 E4
Lomblen, *Indonesia* 57 F6
Lombok, *Indonesia* 56 F5
Lomé, *Togo* 79 D5
Lomela, *Zaïre* 80 E4
Lomela →, *Zaïre* 80 E4
Lomello, *Italy* 32 C5
Lometa, *U.S.A.* 109 K5
Lomié, *Cameroon* 80 D2
Lomma, *Sweden* 11 J7
Lomme →, *Belgium* 17 H6
Lommel, *Belgium* 17 F6
Lomond, *Canada* 100 C6
Lomond, L., *U.K.* 14 E4
Lomonosov, *Russia* 40 B6
Lomphat, *Cambodia* 58 F6
Lompobatang, *Indonesia* . 57 F5
Lompoc, *U.S.A.* 113 L6
Lomsegga, *Norway* 10 C2
Łomza, *Poland* 20 B12
Loncoche, *Chile* 128 A2
Loncopuè, *Argentina* ... 128 A2
Londa, *India* 60 M9
Londerzeel, *Belgium* 17 G4
Londiani, *Kenya* 82 C4
Londinières, *France* 24 C8
London, *Canada* 98 D3
London, *U.K.* 13 F7
London, *Ky., U.S.A.* ... 104 G3
London, *Ohio, U.S.A.* .. 104 F4
London, Greater □, *U.K.* 13 F7
Londonderry, *U.K.* 15 B4
Londonderry □, *U.K.* ... 15 B4
Londonderry, C., *Australia* 88 B4
Londonderry, I., *Chile* .. 128 E2
Londrina, *Brazil* 127 A5
Lone Pine, *U.S.A.* 111 H4
Long Beach, *Calif., U.S.A.* 113 M8
Long Beach, *N.Y., U.S.A.* 107 F11
Long Beach, *Wash., U.S.A.* 112 D2
Long Branch, *U.S.A.* ... 107 F11
Long Creek, *U.S.A.* 110 D4
Long Eaton, *U.K.* 12 E6
Long I., *Australia* 90 C4
Long I., *Bahamas* 117 B4
Long I., *U.S.A.* 107 F11
Long Island Sd., *U.S.A.* . 107 E12
Long L., *Canada* 98 C2
Long Lake, *U.S.A.* 107 C10
Long Pine, *U.S.A.* 108 D5
Long Pt., *Nfld., Canada* . 99 C8
Long Pt., *Ont., Canada* . 106 D4
Long Point B., *Canada* .. 106 D4
Long Range Mts., *Canada* 99 C8
Long Reef, *Australia* ... 88 B4
Long Str. = Longa, Proliv,
  Russia 4 C16
Long Thanh, *Vietnam* ... 59 G6
Long Xian, *China* 50 G4
Long Xuyen, *Vietnam* ... 59 G5
Longá, *Greece* 39 N4
Longa, Proliv, *Russia* ... 4 C16
Long'an, *China* 52 F6
Longarone, *Italy* 33 B9
Longchang, *China* 52 C5
Longchi, *China* 52 C4
Longchuan, *Guangdong,
  China* 53 E10
Longchuan, *Yunnan, China* 50 G4
Longde, *China* 50 G4
Longeau, *France* 25 E12
Longford, *Australia* 90 G4
Longford, *Ireland* 15 C4
Longford □, *Ireland* ... 15 C4
Longguan, *China* 50 D8
Longhua, *China* 51 D9
Longhui, *China* 53 D8
Longido, *Tanzania* 82 C4
Longiram, *Indonesia* ... 56 E5
Longkou, *Jiangxi, China* . 53 D10
Longkou, *Shandong, China* 51 F11
Longlac, *Canada* 98 C2
Longli, *China* 52 D6
Longlier, *Belgium* 17 J6
Longlin, *China* 52 E5
Longling, *China* 52 E2
Longmen, *China* 53 F10
Longming, *China* 52 F6
Longmont, *U.S.A.* 108 E2
Longnan, *China* 53 E10
Longnawan, *Indonesia* .. 56 D4
Longobucco, *Italy* 35 C9
Longquan, *China* 53 C12
Longreach, *Australia* ... 90 C3
Longshan, *China* 52 C7
Longsheng, *China* 53 E8
Longton, *Australia* 90 C4
Longtown, *U.K.* 13 F5
Longué-Jumelles, *France* . 24 E6
Longueau, *France* 25 C9
Longueuil, *Canada* 107 A11
Longuyon, *France* 25 C12
Longview, *Canada* 100 C6
Longview, *Tex., U.S.A.* . 109 J7
Longview, *Wash., U.S.A.* 112 D4
Longvilly, *Belgium* 17 H7
Longwy, *France* 25 C12
Longxi, *China* 50 G3

Longyou, *China* 53 C12
Longzhou, *China* 52 F6
Lonigo, *Italy* 33 C8
Löningen, *Germany* 18 C3
Lonja →, *Croatia* 33 C13
Lonoke, *U.S.A.* 109 H9
Lonquimay, *Chile* 128 A2
Lons-le-Saunier, *France* . 25 F12
Lønstrup, *Denmark* 11 G3
Lookout, C., *U.S.A.* 105 H7
Lookout, C., *Canada* ... 98 A3
Loolmalasin, *Tanzania* .. 82 C4
Loon →, *Alta., Canada* . 100 B5
Loon →, *Man., Canada* . 101 B8
Loon Lake, *Canada* 101 C7
Loon-op-Zand, *Neths.* .. 17 E6
Loongana, *Australia* 89 F4
Loop Hd., *Ireland* 15 D2
Loosduinen, *Neths.* 16 D4
Lop Buri, *Thailand* 58 E3
Lop Nor = Lop Nur, *China* 54 B4
Lop Nur, *China* 54 B4
Lopare, *Bos.-H.* 21 L8
Lopatin, *Russia* 43 E12
Lopatina, G., *Russia* ... 45 D15
Lopaye, *Sudan* 77 F3
Lopera, *Spain* 31 H6
Lopez, *Phil.* 55 E5
Lopez, C., *Gabon* 80 E1
Loppersum, *Neths.* 16 B9
Lopphavet, *Norway* 8 A16
Lora →, *Afghan.* 60 D4
Lora, Hamun-i-, *Pakistan* 60 E4
Lora Cr. →, *Australia* .. 91 D2
Lora del Río, *Spain* 31 H5
Lorain, *U.S.A.* 106 E2
Loralai, *Pakistan* 62 D3
Lorca, *Spain* 29 H3
Lord Howe I., *Pac. Oc.* . 92 L7
Lord Howe Ridge,
  Pac. Oc. 92 L8
Lordsburg, *U.S.A.* 111 K9
Loreto, *Bolivia* 125 D5
Loreto, *Brazil* 122 C2
Loreto, *Italy* 33 E10
Loreto, *Mexico* 114 B2
Loreto, *Peru* 120 D3
Loreto Aprutina, *Italy* .. 33 F10
Lorgues, *France* 27 E10
Lorica, *Colombia* 120 B2
Lorient, *France* 24 E3
Lorn, *U.K.* 14 E3
Lorn, Firth of, *U.K.* ... 14 E3
Lorne, *Australia* 91 F3
Lorovouno, *Cyprus* 37 D11
Lörrach, *Germany* 19 H3
Lorraine, *France* 25 D12
Lorrainville, *Canada* ... 98 C4
Los, Îles de, *Guinea* ... 78 D2
Los Alamos, *Calif., U.S.A.* 113 L6
Los Alamos, *N. Mex.,
  U.S.A.* 111 J10
Los Altos, *U.S.A.* 112 H4
Los Andes, *Chile* 126 C1
Los Angeles, *Chile* 126 D1
Los Angeles, *U.S.A.* ... 113 L8
Los Angeles Aqueduct,
  U.S.A. 113 K9
Los Antiguos, *Argentina* 128 C2
Los Banos, *U.S.A.* 111 H3
Los Barrios, *Spain* 31 J5
Los Blancos, *Argentina* . 126 A3
Los Cristianos, *Canary Is.* 36 F3
Los Gatos, *U.S.A.* 112 H5
Los Hermanos, *Venezuela* 117 D7
Los Islotes, *Canary Is.* .. 36 E6
Los Lagos, *Chile* 128 A2
Los Llanos de Aridane,
  Canary Is. 36 F2
Los Lomas, *Peru* 124 A1
Los Lunas, *U.S.A.* 111 J10
Los Menucos, *Argentina* 128 B3
Los Mochis, *Mexico* 114 B3
Los Monegros, *Spain* ... 28 D4
Los Olivos, *U.S.A.* 113 L6
Los Palacios, *Cuba* 116 B3
Los Palacios y Villafranca,
  Spain 31 H5
Los Reyes, *Mexico* 114 D4
Los Ríos □, *Ecuador* .. 120 D2
Los Roques, *Venezuela* . 120 A4
Los Santos de Maimona,
  Spain 31 G4
Los Teques, *Venezuela* . 120 A4
Los Testigos, *Venezuela* 121 A5
Los Vilos, *Chile* 126 C1
Los Yébenes, *Spain* 31 F7
Losada →, *Colombia* ... 120 C3
Loshkalakh, *Russia* 45 C15
Lošinj, *Croatia* 33 D11
Losser, *Neths.* 16 D10
Lossiemouth, *U.K.* 14 D5
Lot □, *France* 26 D5
Lot →, *France* 26 D4
Lot-et-Garonne □, *France* 26 D4
Lota, *Chile* 126 D1
Løten, *Norway* 10 D5
Lotfābād, *Iran* 65 B8
Lothair, *S. Africa* 85 D5
Lothian □, *U.K.* 14 F5
Lothiers, *France* 25 F8
Lötschbergtunnel, *Switz.* 22 D5
Lottefors, *Sweden* 10 C10
Lotzwil, *Switz.* 22 B5

Loubomo, *Congo* 80 E2
Loudéac, *France* 24 D4
Loudi, *China* 53 D8
Loudon, *U.S.A.* 105 H3
Loudonville, *U.S.A.* 106 F2
Loudun, *France* 24 E7
Loué, *France* 24 E6
Loue →, *France* 25 E12
Louga, *Senegal* 78 B1
Loughborough, *U.K.* ... 12 E6
Loughrea, *Ireland* 15 C3
Loughros More B., *Ireland* 15 B3
Louhans, *France* 27 B9
Louis Trichardt, *S. Africa* 85 C4
Louis XIV, Pte., *Canada* . 98 B4
Louisa, *U.S.A.* 104 F4
Louisbourg, *Canada* 99 C8
Louise I., *Canada* 100 C2
Louiseville, *Canada* 98 C5
Louisiade Arch.,
  Papua N. G. 92 J7
Louisiana, *U.S.A.* 108 F9
Louisiana □, *U.S.A.* ... 109 K9
Louisville, *Ky., U.S.A.* . 104 F3
Louisville, *Miss., U.S.A.* 109 J10
Loulay, *France* 26 B3
Loulé, *Portugal* 31 H2
Louny, *Czech.* 20 E3
Loup City, *U.S.A.* 108 E5
Lourdes, *France* 26 E3
Lourdes-du-Blanc-Sablon,
  Canada 99 B8
Lourenço, *Brazil* 121 C7
Lourenço-Marques =
  Maputo, *Mozam.* 85 D5
Loures, *Portugal* 31 G1
Lourinhã, *Portugal* 31 F1
Lousã, *Portugal* 30 E2
Louth, *Australia* 91 E4
Louth, *Ireland* 15 C5
Louth, *U.K.* 12 D7
Louth □, *Ireland* 15 C5
Louvain = Leuven,
  Belgium 17 G5
Louveigné, *Belgium* 17 G7
Louviers, *France* 24 C8
Louwsburg, *S. Africa* ... 85 D5
Lovat →, *Russia* 40 B7
Loveland, *U.S.A.* 108 E2
Lovell, *U.S.A.* 110 D9
Lovelock, *U.S.A.* 110 F4
Lóvere, *Italy* 32 C7
Loviisa = Lovisa, *Finland* 9 F19
Loving, *U.S.A.* 109 J2
Lovington, *U.S.A.* 109 J3
Lovios, *Spain* 30 D2
Lovran, *Croatia* 33 C11
Lovrin, *Romania* 38 C6
Lower Arrow L., *Canada* 100 D5
Lower California = Baja
  California, *Mexico* ... 114 A1
Lower California =
  California, Baja, *Mexico* 114 A1
Lower Hutt, *N.Z.* 87 J5
Lower L., *U.S.A.* 110 F3
Lower Lake, *U.S.A.* 112 G4
Lower Post, *Canada* 100 B3
Lower Red L., *U.S.A.* .. 108 B7
Lower Saxony =
  Niedersachsen □,
  Germany 18 C5
Lower Tunguska =
  Nizhnyaya →, *Russia* . 45 C9
Lowestoft, *U.K.* 13 E9
Lowicz, *Poland* 20 C9
Lowville, *U.S.A.* 107 C9
Loxton, *Australia* 91 E3
Loxton, *S. Africa* 84 E3
Loyalton, *U.S.A.* 112 F6
Loyalty Is. = Loyauté, Is.,
  N. Cal. 92 K8
Loyang = Luoyang, *China* 50 G7
Loyauté, Is., *N. Cal.* ... 92 K8
Loyev, *Belorussia* 40 F7
Loyoro, *Uganda* 82 B3
Lož, *Slovenia* 33 C11
Lozère □, *France* 26 D7
Loznica, *Serbia* 21 L9
Lozova, *Ukraine* 42 B7
Luachimo, *Angola* 80 F4
Luacono, *Angola* 80 G4
Lualaba →, *Zaïre* 82 B5
Luampa, *Zambia* 83 F1
Lu'an, *China* 53 B11
Luan Chau, *Vietnam* ... 58 B4
Luan He →, *China* 51 E10
Luan Xian, *China* 51 E10
Luancheng,
  *Guangxi Zhuangzu,
  China* 52 F7
Luancheng, *Hebei, China* 50 F8
Luanda, *Angola* 80 F2
Luang Prabang, *Laos* ... 58 C4
Luang Thale, *Thailand* .. 59 J3
Luangwa, *Zambia* 83 F3
Luangwa →, *Zambia* ... 83 E3

Luangwa Valley, *Zambia* . 83 E3
Luanne, *China* 51 D9
Luanping, *China* 51 D9
Luanshya, *Zambia* 83 E2
Luapula □, *Zambia* 83 E2
Luapula →, *Africa* 83 D2
Luarca, *Spain* 30 B4
Luashi, *Zaïre* 83 E1
Luau, *Angola* 80 G4
Lubalo, *Angola* 80 F3
Luban, *Poland* 20 D5
Lubana, Ozero, *Latvia* . 40 C5
Lubang, *Phil.* 55 E4
Lubang Is., *Phil.* 57 B6
Lubartów, *Poland* 20 D12
Lubawa, *Poland* 20 B9
Lubbeek, *Belgium* 17 G5
Lübben, *Germany* 18 D9
Lübbenau, *Germany* ... 18 D9
Lubbock, *U.S.A.* 109 J4
Lübeck, *Germany* 18 B6
Lübecker Bucht, *Germany* 18 A7
Lubefu, *Zaïre* 82 C1
Lubefu →, *Zaïre* 82 C1
Lubero = Luofu, *Zaïre* .. 82 C2
Lubicon L., *Canada* ... 100 B5
Lublin, *Poland* 20 D12
Lubliniec, *Poland* 20 E8
Lubnān, J., *Lebanon* ... 69 B4
Lubny, *Ukraine* 40 F8
Lubon, *Poland* 20 C6
Lubongola, *Zaïre* 82 C2
Lubsko, *Poland* 20 D4
Lübtheen, *Germany* 18 B7
Lubuagan, *Phil.* 55 C4
Lubudi, →, *Zaïre* 83 D2
Lubuk Antu, *Malaysia* .. 56 D4
Lubuklinggau, *Indonesia* 56 E2
Lubuksikaping, *Indonesia* 56 D2
Lubumbashi, *Zaïre* 83 E2
Lubunda, *Zaïre* 82 D2
Lubungu, *Zambia* 83 E2
Lubutu, *Zaïre* 82 C2
Luc An Chau, *Vietnam* . 58 A5
Luc-en-Diois, *France* ... 27 D9
Lucan, *Canada* 106 C3
Lucban, *Phil.* 55 E4
Lucca, *Italy* 32 E7
Luce Bay, *U.K.* 14 G4
Lucea, *Jamaica* 116 C4
Lucedale, *U.S.A.* 105 K1
Lucena, *Phil.* 55 E4
Lucena, *Spain* 31 H6
Lucena del Cid, *Spain* .. 28 E4
Lučenec, *Slovak Rep.* .. 21 G9
Lucens, *Switz.* 22 C3
Lucera, *Italy* 35 A8
Lucerne = Luzern, *Switz.* 23 B6
Lucerne, *U.S.A.* 112 F4
Lucerne Valley, *U.S.A.* . 113 L10
Lucero, *Mexico* 114 A3
Luchena →, *Spain* 29 H3
Lucheng, *China* 50 F7
Lucheringo →, *Mozam.* . 83 E4
Lüchow, *Germany* 18 C7
Luchuan, *China* 53 F8
Lucie →, *Surinam* 121 C6
Lucira, *Angola* 81 G2
Luckau, *Germany* 18 D9
Luckenwalde, *Germany* . 18 C9
Lucknow, *India* 63 F9
Luçon, *France* 26 B2
Lüda = Dalian, *China* .. 51 E11
Luda Kamchiya →,
  Bulgaria 38 F10
Ludbreg, *Croatia* 33 B13
Lüdenscheid, *Germany* .. 18 D3
Lüderitz, *Namibia* 84 D2
Ludewe □, *Tanzania* ... 83 D3
Ludhiana, *India* 62 D6
Ludian, *China* 52 D4
Luding Qiao, *China* 52 C4
Lüdinghausen, *Germany* . 18 D3
Ludington, *U.S.A.* 104 D2
Ludlow, *U.K.* 13 E5
Ludlow, *Calif., U.S.A.* . 113 L10
Ludlow, *Vt., U.S.A.* ... 107 C12
Ludus, *Romania* 38 C7
Ludvika, *Sweden* 9 F13
Ludwigsburg, *Germany* . 19 G5
Ludwigshafen, *Germany* 19 F4
Ludwigslust, *Germany* .. 18 B7
Ludza, *Latvia* 40 C5
Luebo, *Zaïre* 80 F4
Lueki, *Zaïre* 82 C2
Luena, *Zaïre* 83 D2
Luena, *Zambia* 83 E3
Luepa, *Venezuela* 121 B5
Lüeyang, *China* 50 G5
Lufeng, *Guangdong, China* 53 F10
Lufeng, *Yunnan, China* . 52 E4
Lufira →, *Zaïre* 83 D2
Lufkin, *U.S.A.* 109 K7
Lufupa, *Zaïre* 83 E1
Luga, *Russia* 40 B6
Luga →, *Russia* 40 B6
Lugang, *Taiwan* 53 E13
Lugano, *Switz.* 23 D7
Lugano, L. di, *Switz.* ... 23 D8
Lugansk, *Ukraine* 43 B8
Lugard's Falls, *Kenya* .. 82 C4
Lugela, *Mozam.* 83 F4
Lugenda →, *Mozam.* ... 83 E4
Lugh Ganana, *Somali Rep.* 68 G3
Lugnaquilla, *Ireland* ... 15 D5

Lugnvik, Sweden 10 B11
Lugo, Italy 33 D8
Lugo, Spain 30 B3
Lugo □, Spain 30 C3
Lugoj, Romania 38 D4
Lugones, Spain 30 B5
Lugovoye, Kazakhstan .. 44 E8
Luhansk = Lugansk,
  Ukraine 43 B8
Luhe, China 53 A12
Luhe →, Germany 18 B6
Luhuo, China 52 B3
Luiana, Angola 84 B3
Luino, Italy 32 C5
Luís Correia, Brazil ... 122 B3
Luís Gonçalves, Brazil . 122 C1
Luitpold Coast, Antarctica 5 D1
Luiza, Zaïre 80 F4
Luizi, Zaïre 82 D2
Luján, Argentina 126 C4
Lujiang, China 53 B11
Lukanga Swamp, Zambia 83 E2
Lukenie →, Zaïre 80 E3
Lukhisaral, India 63 G12
Lŭki, Bulgaria 39 H7
Lukolela, Equateur, Zaïre 80 E3
Lukolela, Kasai Or., Zaïre 82 D1
Lukosi, Zimbabwe 83 F2
Lukovit, Bulgaria 38 F7
Luków, Poland 20 D12
Lukoyanov, Russia 41 D14
Lule älv →, Sweden ... 8 D17
Luleå, Sweden 8 D17
Lüleburgaz, Turkey 39 H10
Luliang, China 52 E4
Luling, U.S.A. 109 L6
Lulong, China 51 E10
Lulonga →, Zaïre 80 D3
Lulua →, Zaïre 80 E4
Luluabourg = Kananga,
  Zaïre 80 F4
Lumai, Angola 81 G4
Lumajang, Indonesia .. 57 H15
Lumbala N'guimbo, Angola 81 G4
Lumberton, Miss., U.S.A. 109 K10
Lumberton, N.C., U.S.A. 105 H6
Lumberton, N. Mex.,
  U.S.A. 111 H10
Lumbres, France 25 B9
Lumbwa, Kenya 82 C4
Lummen, Belgium 17 G6
Lumsden, N.Z. 87 L2
Lumut, Malaysia 59 K3
Lumut, Tg., Indonesia . 56 E3
Luna, Phil. 55 C4
Lunan, China 52 E4
Lunavada, India 62 H5
Lunca, Romania 38 B8
Lund, Sweden 11 J7
Lund, U.S.A. 110 G6
Lundazi, Zambia 83 E3
Lunde, Norway 10 E3
Lunderskov, Denmark . 11 J3
Lundi →, Zimbabwe .. 83 G3
Lundu, Malaysia 56 D3
Lundy, U.K. 13 F3
Lune →, U.K. 12 C5
Lüneburg, Germany ... 18 B6
Lüneburg Heath =
  Lüneburger Heide,
  Germany 18 C6
Lüneburger Heide,
  Germany 18 C6
Lunel, France 27 E8
Lünen, Germany 18 D3
Lunenburg, Canada ... 99 D7
Lunéville, France 25 D13
Lunga →, Zambia 83 E2
Lungern, Switz. 22 C6
Lungi Airport, S. Leone 78 D2
Lunglei, India 61 H18
Luni, India 62 F5
Luni →, India 62 G4
Luninets, Belorussia . 40 E5
Luning, U.S.A. 110 G4
Lunino, Russia 41 E14
Luninyets = Luninets,
  Belorussia 40 E5
Lunner, Norway 10 D4
Lunsemfwa →, Zambia 83 E3
Lunsemfwa Falls, Zambia 83 E2
Lunteren, Neths. 16 D7
Luo He →, China ... 50 G6
Luocheng, China 52 E7
Luochuan, China 50 G5
Luoci, China 52 E4
Luoding, China 53 F8
Luodong, Taiwan ... 53 E13
Luofu, Zaïre 82 C2
Luohe, China 50 H8
Luojiang, China 52 B5
Luonan, China 50 G6
Luoning, China 50 G6
Luoshan, China 53 A10
Luotian, China 53 B10
Luoyang, China 50 G7
Luoyuan, China 53 D12
Luozi, Zaïre 80 E2
Luozigou, China ... 51 C16
Lupeni, Romania .. 38 D6
Lupilichi, Mozam. . 83 E4
Luping, China 52 E6
Luqiao, China 52 E4
Luque, Paraguay .. 126 B4

Luque, Spain 31 H6
Luray, U.S.A. 104 F6
Lure, France 25 E13
Luremo, Angola 80 F3
Lurgan, U.K. 15 B5
Luribay, Bolivia 124 D4
Lurin, Peru 124 C2
Lusaka, Zambia 83 F2
Lusambo, Zaïre 82 C1
Lusangaye, Zaïre 82 C2
Luseland, Canada 101 C7
Lushan, Henan, China .. 50 H7
Lushan, Sichuan, China . 52 B4
Lushi, China 50 G6
Lushnja, Albania 39 J2
Lushoto, Tanzania 82 C4
Lushoto □, Tanzania .. 82 C4
Lushui, China 52 E2
Lüshun, China 51 E11
Lusignan, France 26 B4
Lusigny-sur-Barse, France 25 D11
Lusk, U.S.A. 108 D2
Lussac-les-Châteaux,
  France 26 B4
Lussanvira, Brazil ... 123 F1
Luta = Dalian, China . 51 E11
Luton, U.K. 13 F7
Lutong, Malaysia 56 D4
Lutry, Switz. 22 C3
Lutsk, Ukraine 40 F4
Lützow Holmbukta,
  Antarctica 5 C4
Lutzputs, S. Africa .. 84 D3
Luverne, U.S.A. 108 D6
Luvua, Zaïre 83 D2
Luvua →, Zaïre 82 D2
Luwegu →, Tanzania . 83 D4
Luwuk, Indonesia ... 57 E6
Luxembourg, Lux. ... 17 J8
Luxembourg □, Belgium 17 J7
Luxembourg ■, Europe 17 J8
Luxeuil-les-Bains, France 25 E13
Luxi, Hunan, China .. 53 C8
Luxi, Yunnan, China . 52 E2
Luxi, Yunnan, China . 52 E4
Luxor = El Uqsur, Egypt 76 B3
Luy →, France 26 E2
Luy-de-Béarn →, France 26 E3
Luy-de-France →, France 26 E3
Luyi, China 50 H8
Luyksgestel, Neths. .. 17 F6
Luz-St.-Sauveur, France 26 F4
Luzern, Switz. 23 B6
Luzern □, Switz. 22 B5
Luzhai, China 52 E7
Luzhou, China 52 C5
Luziânia, Brazil 123 E2
Luzilândia, Brazil ... 122 B3
Luzon, Phil. 55 D4
Luzy, France 25 F10
Luzzi, Italy 35 C9
Lviv = Lvov, Ukraine . 40 G4
Lvov, Ukraine 40 G4
Lyakhovichi, Belorussia 40 E5
Lyakhovskiye, Ostrova,
  Russia 45 B15
Lyaki, Azerbaijan ... 43 F12
Lyallpur = Faisalabad,
  Pakistan 62 D5
Lycaonia, Turkey 66 D5
Lychen, Germany 18 B9
Lycia, Turkey 66 E3
Lycksele, Sweden 8 D15
Lydda = Lod, Israel .. 69 D3
Lydenburg, S. Africa . 85 D5
Lydia, Turkey 66 D3
Lyell, N.Z. 87 J4
Lyell I., Canada 100 C2
Lygnern, Sweden 11 G6
Lyman, U.S.A. 110 F8
Lyme Regis, U.K. 13 G5
Lymington, U.K. 13 G6
Lynchburg, U.S.A. .. 104 G6
Lynd →, Australia .. 90 B3
Lynd Ra., Australia . 91 D4
Lynden, Canada 106 C4
Lynden, U.S.A. 112 B4
Lyndhurst, Queens.,
  Australia 90 B3
Lyndhurst, S. Austral.,
  Australia 91 E2
Lyndon →, Australia . 89 D1
Lyndonville, N.Y., U.S.A. 106 C6
Lyndonville, Vt., U.S.A. 107 B12
Lyngdal, Norway 10 E3
Lynher Reef, Australia 88 C3
Lynn, U.S.A. 107 D14
Lynn Canal, U.S.A. .. 100 B1
Lynn Lake, Canada .. 101 B8
Lynnwood, U.S.A. .. 112 C4
Lynton, U.K. 13 F4
Lyntupy, Belorussia . 40 D5
Lynx L., Canada 101 A7
Lyø, Denmark 11 J4
Lyon, France 27 C8
Lyonnais, France ... 27 C8
Lyons = Lyon, France 27 C8
Lyons, Colo., U.S.A. . 108 E2
Lyons, Ga., U.S.A. . 105 J4
Lyons, Kans., U.S.A. 108 F5
Lyons, N.Y., U.S.A. . 106 C8
Lyrestad, Sweden ... 11 F8
Lys = Leie →, Belgium 25 A10
Lysekil, Sweden 11 F5
Lyskovo, Russia 41 D14

Lyss, Switz. 22 B4
Lytle, U.S.A. 109 L5
Lyttelton, N.Z. 87 K4
Lytton, Canada 100 C4
Lyuban, Russia 40 B7
Lyubcha, Belorussia .. 40 E5
Lyubertsy, Russia 41 D10
Lyubim, Russia 41 B12
Lyuboml, Ukraine 40 F4
Lyubotin, Ukraine 42 B6
Lyubytino, Russia 40 B8
Lyudinovo, Russia 40 E9

M

Ma →, Vietnam 58 C5
Ma'adaba, Jordan 69 E4
Maamba, Zambia 84 B4
Ma'ān, Jordan 69 E4
Ma'ān □, Jordan 69 F5
Ma'anshan, China 53 B12
Maarheeze, Neths. ... 17 F7
Maarianhamina, Finland 9 F15
Maarn, Neths. 16 D6
Ma'arrat an Nu'mān, Syria 64 C3
Maarssen, Neths. 16 D6
Maartensdijk, Neths. . 16 D6
Maas →, Neths. 16 E5
Maasbracht, Belgium . 17 F7
Maasbree, Neths. 17 F8
Maasdam, Neths. 16 E5
Maasdijk, Neths. 16 E4
Maaseik, Belgium 17 F7
Maasland, Neths. 16 E4
Maasniel, Neths. 17 F8
Maassluis, Neths. ... 16 E4
Maastricht, Neths. .. 17 G7
Maave, Mozam. 85 C5
Mabaruma, Guyana .. 121 B6
Mabel L., Canada ... 100 C5
Mabenge, Zaïre 82 B1
Mabian, China 52 C4
Mablethorpe, U.K. .. 12 D8
Maboma, Zaïre 82 B2
Mabrouk, Mali 79 B4
Mabton, U.S.A. 110 C3
Mac Bac, Vietnam .. 59 H6
Macachín, Argentina 126 D3
Macaé, Brazil 123 F3
Macaíba, Brazil 122 C4
Macajuba, Brazil ... 123 D3
McAlester, U.S.A. .. 109 H7
McAllen, U.S.A. 109 M5
Macamic, Canada ... 98 C4
Macao = Macau ■, China 53 F9
Macão, Portugal 31 F3
Macapá, Brazil 121 C7
Macará, Ecuador ... 120 D2
Macarani, Brazil ... 123 E3
Macarena, Serranía de la,
  Colombia 120 C3
McArthur →, Australia . 90 B2
McArthur, Port, Australia 90 B2
McArthur River, Australia 90 B2
Macas, Ecuador 120 D2
Macate, Peru 124 B2
Macau, Brazil 122 C4
Macau ■, China 53 F9
Macaúbas, Brazil ... 123 D3
Macaya →, Colombia 120 C3
McBride, Canada ... 100 C4
McCall, U.S.A. 110 D5
McCamey, U.S.A. .. 109 K3
McCammon, U.S.A. 110 E7
McCauley I., Canada 100 C2
McCleary, U.S.A. .. 112 C3
Macclesfield, U.K. .. 12 D5
McClintock, Canada 101 B10
McClintock Ra., Australia 88 C4
McCloud, U.S.A. ... 110 F2
McCluer I., Australia 88 B5
McClure, U.S.A. ... 106 F7
McClure, L., U.S.A. 112 H6
M'Clure Str., Canada 4 B2
McClusky, U.S.A. .. 108 B4
McComb, U.S.A. ... 109 K9
McConaughy, L., U.S.A. 108 E4
McCook, U.S.A. 108 E4
McCullough Mt., U.S.A. 113 K11
McCusker →, Canada 101 B7
McDame, Canada ... 100 B3
McDermitt, U.S.A. .. 110 F5
Macdonald, L., Australia 88 D4
Macdonald Is., Ind. Oc. . 3 G13
Macdonnell Ras., Australia 88 D5
McDouall Peak, Australia 91 D1
Macdougall L., Canada 96 B10
McDowell, L., Canada 98 B1
Macduff, U.K. 14 D6
Macedonia, Europe .. 39 H4
Maceió, Brazil 122 C4
Maceira, Portugal .. 31 F2
Macenta, Guinea ... 78 D3
Macerata, Italy 33 E10
McFarland, U.S.A. . 113 K7
McFarlane →, Canada 101 B7
McGehee, U.S.A. ... 109 J9
McGill, U.S.A. 110 G6
Macgillycuddy's Reeks,
  Ireland 15 D2

MacGregor, Canada .. 101 D9
McGregor, U.S.A. ... 108 D9
McGregor →, Canada 100 B4
McGregor Ra., Australia 91 D3
Mach, Pakistan 60 E5
Māch Kowr, Iran ... 65 E9
Machacalis, Brazil .. 123 E3
Machado = Jiparaná →,
  Brazil 125 B5
Machagai, Argentina 126 B3
Machakos, Kenya ... 82 C4
Machakos □, Kenya . 82 C4
Machala, Ecuador .. 120 D2
Machanga, Mozam. .. 85 C6
Machattie, L., Australia 90 C2
Machava, Mozam. ... 85 D5
Machece, Mozam. ... 83 F4
Machecoul, France .. 24 F5
Machelen, Belgium .. 17 G4
Macheng, China 53 B10
Machevna, Russia ... 45 C18
Machezo, Spain 31 F6
Machias, U.S.A. 99 D6
Machichaco, C., Spain . 28 A2
Machico, Madeira ... 36 D3
Machichi →, Canada 101 B10
Machilipatnam, India 61 L12
Machiques, Venezuela 120 A3
Machupicchu, Peru .. 124 C3
Machynlleth, U.K. .. 13 E4
McIlwraith Ra., Australia 90 A3
Măcin, Romania 38 D11
Macina, Mali 78 C4
McIntosh, U.S.A. .. 108 C4
McIntosh L., Canada 101 B8
Macintosh Ra., Australia 89 E4
Macintyre →, Australia 91 D5
Macizo Galaico, Spain 30 C3
Mackay, Australia .. 90 C4
Mackay, U.S.A. 110 E7
MacKay →, Canada 100 B6
Mackay, L., Australia 88 D4
McKay Ra., Australia 88 D3
McKeesport, U.S.A. 106 F5
McKenna, U.S.A. .. 112 C4
Mackenzie, Canada . 100 B4
Mackenzie, Guyana . 121 B6
McKenzie, U.S.A. .. 105 G1
Mackenzie →, Australia 90 C4
Mackenzie →, Canada 96 B6
McKenzie →, U.S.A. 110 D2
Mackenzie Bay, Canada 4 B1
Mackenzie City = Linden,
  Guyana 121 B6
Mackenzie Highway,
  Canada 100 B5
Mackenzie Mts., Canada 96 B6
Mackinaw City, U.S.A. 104 C3
McKinlay, Australia . 90 C3
McKinlay →, Australia 90 C3
McKinley, Mt., U.S.A. 96 B4
McKinley Sea, Arctic . 4 A7
McKinney, U.S.A. .. 109 J6
Mackinnon Road, Kenya 82 C4
Macksville, Australia 91 E5
McLaughlin, U.S.A. 108 C4
Maclean, Australia . 91 D5
McLean, U.S.A. 109 H4
McLeansboro, U.S.A. 108 F10
Maclear, S. Africa .. 85 E4
Macleay →, Australia 91 E5
McLennan, Canada . 100 B5
MacLeod, B., Canada 101 A7
McLeod, L., Australia 89 D1
MacLeod Lake, Canada 100 C4
M'Clintock Chan., Canada 96 A9
McLoughlin, Mt., U.S.A. 110 E2
McLure, Canada 100 C4
McMechen, U.S.A. .. 106 G4
McMillan, L., U.S.A. 109 J2
McMinnville, Oreg., U.S.A. 110 D2
McMinnville, Tenn.,
  U.S.A. 105 H3
McMorran, Canada . 101 C7
McMurdo Sd., Antarctica 5 D11
McMurray = Fort
  McMurray, Canada . 100 B6
McMurray, U.S.A. .. 112 B4
McNary, U.S.A. 111 J9
MacNutt, Canada ... 101 C8
Macodoene, Mozam. . 85 C6
Macomb, U.S.A. 108 E9
Macomer, Italy 34 B1
Mâcon, France 27 B8
Macon, Ga., U.S.A. . 105 J4
Macon, Miss., U.S.A. 105 J1
Macon, Mo., U.S.A. 108 F8
Macondo, Angola .. 81 G4
Macossa, Mozam. ... 83 F3
Macoun L., Canada . 101 B8
Macovane, Mozam. .. 85 C6
McPherson, U.S.A. . 108 F6
McPherson Ra., Australia 91 D5
Macquarie Harbour,
  Australia 90 G4
Macquarie Is., Pac. Oc. 92 N7
MacRobertson Land,
  Antarctica 5 D6
Macroom, Ireland .. 15 E3
Macroy, Australia .. 88 D2
MacTier, Canada ... 106 A5
Macubela, Mozam. .. 83 F4
Macugnaga, Italy ... 32 C4
Macuira, Mozam. ... 83 F3

Macujer, Colombia 120 C3
Macusani, Peru 124 C3
Macuse, Mozam. 83 F4
Macuspana, Mexico ... 115 D6
Macusse, Angola 84 B3
McVille, U.S.A. 108 B5
Madadeni, S. Africa .. 85 D5
Madagali, Nigeria 79 C7
Madagascar ■, Africa . 85 C8
Madā'in Sālih, Si. Arabia 64 E3
Madama, Niger 73 D7
Madame I., Canada ... 99 C7
Madaoua, Niger 79 C6
Madara, Nigeria 79 C7
Madaripur, Bangla. .. 61 H17
Madauk, Burma 61 L20
Madawaska, Canada .. 106 A7
Madawaska →, Canada 98 C4
Madaya, Burma 61 H20
Madbar, Sudan 77 F3
Maddaloni, Italy 35 A7
Made, Neths. 17 E5
Madeira, Atl. Oc. 36 D3
Madeira →, Brazil .. 121 D6
Madeleine, Is. de la,
  Canada 99 C7
Maden, Turkey 67 D8
Madera, U.S.A. 111 H3
Madha, India 60 L9
Madhubani, India .. 63 F12
Madhya Pradesh □, India . 62 J7
Madian, China 53 A11
Madidi →, Bolivia . 124 C4
Madikeri, India 60 N9
Madill, U.S.A. 109 H6
Madimba, Zaïre ... 80 E3
Ma'din, Syria 64 C3
Madīnat ash Sha'b, Yemen 68 E3
Madingou, Congo .. 80 E2
Madirovalo, Madag. . 85 B8
Madison, Calif., U.S.A. 112 G5
Madison, Fla., U.S.A. 105 K4
Madison, Ind., U.S.A. 104 F3
Madison, Nebr., U.S.A. 108 E6
Madison, Ohio, U.S.A. 106 E3
Madison, S. Dak., U.S.A. 108 D6
Madison, Wis., U.S.A. 108 D10
Madison →, U.S.A. 110 D8
Madisonville, Ky., U.S.A. 104 G2
Madisonville, Tex., U.S.A. 109 K7
Madista, Botswana . 84 C4
Madiun, Indonesia . 57 G14
Madley, U.K. 13 E5
Madol, Sudan 77 F2
Madon →, France . 25 D13
Madona, Latvia ... 40 C5
Madras = Tamil Nadu □,
  India 60 P10
Madras, India 60 N12
Madras, U.S.A. ... 110 D3
Madre, L., Mexico . 115 B5
Madre, Laguna, U.S.A. 109 M6
Madre, Sierra, Phil. . 55 C5
Madre de Dios □, Peru . 124 C3
Madre de Dios →, Bolivia 124 C4
Madre de Dios, I., Chile . 128 D1
Madre del Sur, Sierra,
  Mexico 115 D5
Madre Occidental, Sierra,
  Mexico 114 B3
Madre Oriental, Sierra,
  Mexico 114 C4
Madri, India 62 G5
Madrid, Spain 30 E7
Madrid □, Spain .. 30 E7
Madridejos, Spain . 31 F7
Madrigal de las Altas
  Torres, Spain 30 D6
Madrona, Sierra, Spain 31 G6
Madroñera, Spain . 31 F5
Madu, Sudan 77 E2
Madura, Selat, Indonesia 57 G15
Madura Motel, Australia 89 F4
Madurai, India 60 Q11
Madurantakam, India 60 N11
Madzhalis, Russia . 43 E12
Mae Chan, Thailand 58 B2
Mae Hong Son, Thailand 58 C2
Mae Khlong →, Thailand 58 F3
Mae Phrik, Thailand 58 D2
Mae Ramat, Thailand 58 D2
Mae Rim, Thailand . 58 C2
Mae Sot, Thailand . 58 D2
Mae Suai, Thailand 58 C2
Mae Tha, Thailand . 58 C2
Maebashi, Japan ... 49 F9
Maella, Spain 28 D5
Măeruş, Romania .. 38 D8
Maesteg, U.K. 13 F4
Maestra, Sierra, Cuba 116 B4
Maestrazgo, Mts. del, Spain 28 E4
Maevatanana, Madag. 85 B8
Mafeking = Mafikeng,
  S. Africa 84 D4
Mafeking, Canada .. 101 C8
Maféré, Ivory C. ... 78 D4
Mafeteng, Lesotho . 84 D4
Maffe, Belgium 17 H6
Maffra, Australia .. 91 F4
Mafia I., Tanzania . 82 D4
Mafikeng, S. Africa 84 D4
Mafra, Brazil 127 B6
Mafra, Portugal ... 31 G1
Mafungabusi Plateau,
  Zimbabwe 83 F2

Magadan

Magadan, *Russia* 45 D16
Magadi, *Kenya* 82 C4
Magadi, L., *Kenya* 82 C4
Magaliesburg, *S. Africa* 85 D4
Magallanes □, *Chile* 128 D2
Magallanes, Estrecho de, *Chile* 128 D2
Magangué, *Colombia* 120 B3
Magaria, *Niger* 79 C6
Magburaka, *S. Leone* 78 D2
Magdalen Is. = Madeleine, Is. de la, *Canada* 99 C7
Magdalena, *Argentina* 126 D4
Magdalena, *Bolivia* 125 C5
Magdalena, *Malaysia* 56 D5
Magdalena, *Mexico* 114 A2
Magdalena, *U.S.A.* 111 J10
Magdalena □, *Colombia* 120 A3
Magdalena →, *Colombia* 120 A3
Magdalena →, *Mexico* 114 A2
Magdalena, B., *Mexico* 114 C2
Magdalena, I., *Chile* 128 B2
Magdalena, Llano de la, *Mexico* 114 C2
Magdeburg, *Germany* 18 C7
Magdelaine Cays, *Australia* 90 B5
Magdub, *Sudan* 77 E2
Magee, *U.S.A.* 109 K10
Magee, I., *U.K.* 15 B6
Magelang, *Indonesia* 57 G14
Magellan's Str. = Magallanes, Estrecho de, *Chile* 128 D2
Magenta, *Italy* 32 C5
Magenta, L., *Australia* 89 F2
Maggia, *Switz.* 23 D7
Maggia →, *Switz.* 23 D7
Maggiorasca, Mte., *Italy* 32 D6
Maggiore, L., *Italy* 32 C5
Maghama, *Mauritania* 78 B2
Magherafelt, *U.K.* 15 B5
Maghnia, *Algeria* 75 B4
Magione, *Italy* 33 E9
Magliano in Toscana, *Italy* 33 F8
Máglie, *Italy* 35 B11
Magnac-Laval, *France* 26 B5
Magnetic Pole (North) = North Magnetic Pole, *Canada* 4 B2
Magnetic Pole (South) = South Magnetic Pole, *Antarctica* 5 C9
Magnitogorsk, *Russia* 44 D6
Magnolia, *Ark., U.S.A.* 109 J8
Magnolia, *Miss., U.S.A.* 109 K9
Magnor, *Norway* 10 E6
Magny-en-Vexin, *France* 25 C8
Magog, *Canada* 99 C5
Magoro, *Uganda* 82 B3
Magosa = Famagusta, *Cyprus* 37 D12
Magouládhes, *Greece* 37 A3
Magoye, *Zambia* 83 F2
Magpie L., *Canada* 99 B7
Magrath, *Canada* 100 D6
Magro →, *Spain* 29 F4
Magrur, Wadi →, *Sudan* 77 D2
Magu □, *Tanzania* 82 C3
Maguan, *China* 52 F5
Maguarinho, C., *Brazil* 122 B2
Maguse L., *Canada* 101 A9
Maguse Pt., *Canada* 101 A10
Magwe, *Burma* 61 J19
Maha Sarakham, *Thailand* 58 D4
Mahābād, *Iran* 64 B5
Mahabharat Lekh, *Nepal* 63 E9
Mahabo, *Madag.* 85 C7
Mahadeo Hills, *India* 62 H8
Mahagi, *Zaïre* 82 B3
Mahaicony, *Guyana* 121 B6
Mahajamba →, *Madag.* 85 B8
Mahajamba, Helodranon' i, *Madag.* 85 B8
Mahajan, *India* 62 E5
Mahajanga, *Madag.* 85 B8
Mahajanga □, *Madag.* 85 B8
Mahajilo →, *Madag.* 85 B8
Mahakam →, *Indonesia* 56 E5
Mahalapye, *Botswana* 84 C4
Maḩallāt, *Iran* 65 C6
Māhān, *Iran* 65 D8
Mahanadi →, *India* 61 J15
Mahanoro, *Madag.* 85 B8
Mahanoy City, *U.S.A.* 107 F8
Maharashtra □, *India* 60 J9
Maharès, *Tunisia* 75 B7
Mahari Mts., *Tanzania* 82 D2
Mahasham, W. →, *Egypt* 69 E3
Mahasolo, *Madag.* 85 B8
Mahattat ash Shīdīyah, *Jordan* 69 F4
Mahattat 'Unayzah, *Jordan* 69 E4
Mahaxay, *Laos* 58 D5
Mahbes, *W. Sahara* 74 C3
Mahbubnagar, *India* 60 L10
Maḩḑah, *Oman* 65 E7
Mahdia, *Guyana* 121 B6
Mahdia, *Tunisia* 75 A7
Mahe, *India* 63 C8
Mahenge, *Tanzania* 83 D4
Maheno, *N.Z.* 87 L3
Mahesana, *India* 62 H5
Mahia Pen., *N.Z.* 87 H6
Mahilyow = Mogilev, *Belorussia* 40 E7
Mahirija, *Morocco* 75 B4
Mahmiya, *Sudan* 77 D3
Mahmud Kot, *Pakistan* 62 D4
Mahmudia, *Romania* 38 D12
Mahnomen, *U.S.A.* 108 B7
Mahoba, *India* 63 G8
Mahón, *Spain* 36 B11
Mahone Bay, *Canada* 99 D7
Mahuta, *Nigeria* 79 C5
Mai-Ndombe, L., *Zaïre* 80 E3
Mai-Sai, *Thailand* 58 B2
Maicao, *Colombia* 120 A3
Maîche, *France* 25 E13
Maici →, *Brazil* 125 B5
Maicurú →, *Brazil* 121 D7
Máida, *Italy* 35 D9
Maidan Khula, *Afghan.* 62 C3
Maidenhead, *U.K.* 13 F7
Maidi, *Yemen* 77 D5
Maidstone, *Canada* 101 C7
Maidstone, *U.K.* 13 F8
Maiduguri, *Nigeria* 79 C7
Maignelay, *France* 25 C9
Maigo, *Phil.* 55 G5
Maigualida, Sierra, *Venezuela* 121 B4
Maigudo, *Ethiopia* 77 F4
Maijdi, *Bangla.* 61 H17
Maikala Ra., *India* 61 J12
Mailly-le-Camp, *France* 25 D11
Mailsi, *Pakistan* 62 E5
Main →, *Germany* 19 F4
Main →, *U.K.* 15 B5
Main Centre, *Canada* 101 C7
Mainburg, *Germany* 19 G7
Maine, *France* 24 E6
Maine □, *U.S.A.* 99 C6
Maine →, *Ireland* 15 D2
Maine-et-Loire □, *France* 24 E6
Maïne-Soroa, *Niger* 79 C7
Maingkwan, *Burma* 61 F20
Mainit, L., *Phil.* 55 G6
Mainland, *Orkney, U.K.* 14 C5
Mainland, *Shet., U.K.* 14 A7
Mainpuri, *India* 63 F8
Maintenon, *France* 25 D8
Maintirano, *Madag.* 85 B7
Mainvault, *Belgium* 17 G3
Mainz, *Germany* 19 F4
Maipú, *Argentina* 126 D4
Maiquetía, *Venezuela* 120 A4
Maira →, *Italy* 32 D4
Mairabari, *India* 61 F18
Mairipotaba, *Brazil* 123 E2
Maisí, *Cuba* 117 B5
Maisi, Pta. de, *Cuba* 117 B5
Maisse, *France* 25 D9
Maissin, *Belgium* 17 J6
Maitland, *N.S.W., Australia* 91 E5
Maitland, *S. Austral., Australia* 91 E2
Maitland →, *Canada* 106 C3
Maiyema, *Nigeria* 79 C5
Maiyuan, *China* 53 E11
Maiz, Is. del, *Nic.* 116 D3
Maizuru, *Japan* 49 G7
Majagual, *Colombia* 120 B3
Majalengka, *Indonesia* 57 G13
Majari →, *Brazil* 121 C5
Majene, *Indonesia* 57 E5
Majes →, *Peru* 124 D3
Maji, *Ethiopia* 77 F4
Majiang, *China* 52 D6
Major, *Canada* 101 C7
Majorca = Mallorca, *Spain* 36 B10
Majuriã, *Brazil* 125 B5
Maka, *Senegal* 78 C2
Makak, *Cameroon* 79 E7
Makale, *Indonesia* 57 E5
Makamba, *Burundi* 82 C2
Makari, *Cameroon* 80 B2
Makarikari = Makgadikgadi Salt Pans, *Botswana* 84 C4
Makarovo, *Russia* 45 D11
Makarska, *Croatia* 21 M7
Makaryev, *Russia* 41 C13
Makasar = Ujung Pandang, *Indonesia* 57 F5
Makasar, Selat, *Indonesia* 57 E5
Makasar, Str. of = Makasar, Selat, *Indonesia* 57 E5
Makat, *Kazakhstan* 44 E6
Makedonija = Macedonia ■, *Europe* 39 H4
Makena, *U.S.A.* 102 H16
Makeni, *S. Leone* 78 D2
Makeyevka, *Ukraine* 42 B7
Makgadikgadi Salt Pans, *Botswana* 84 C4
Makhachkala, *Russia* 43 E12
Makhambet, *Kazakhstan* 43 C14
Makharadze = Ozurgety, *Georgia* 43 F10
Makhmūr, *Iraq* 64 C4
Makian, *Indonesia* 57 D7
Makindu, *Kenya* 82 C4
Makinsk, *Kazakhstan* 44 D8
Makiyivka = Makeyevka, *Ukraine* 42 B7
Makkah, *Si. Arabia* 68 C2
Makkovik, *Canada* 99 A8
Makkum, *Neths.* 16 B6
Makó, *Hungary* 21 J10
Makokou, *Gabon* 80 D2
Makongo, *Zaïre* 82 B2
Makoro, *Zaïre* 82 B2
Makoua, *Congo* 80 E3
Makrá, *Greece* 39 N8
Makrai, *India* 60 H10
Makran Coast Range, *Pakistan* 60 G4
Makrana, *India* 62 F6
Makriyialos, *Greece* 37 D7
Maksimkin Yar, *Russia* 44 D9
Maktar, *Tunisia* 75 A6
Mākū, *Iran* 64 B5
Makumbi, *Zaïre* 80 F4
Makunda, *Botswana* 84 C3
Makurazaki, *Japan* 49 J5
Makurdi, *Nigeria* 79 D6
Makūyeh, *Iran* 65 D7
Makwassie, *S. Africa* 84 D4
Mal B., *Ireland* 15 D2
Mal i Nemërçkës, *Albania* 39 J3
Mal i Tomorit, *Albania* 39 J3
Mala, *Peru* 124 C2
Mala, Pta., *Panama* 116 E3
Mala Kapela, *Croatia* 33 D12
Malabang, *Phil.* 55 H6
Malabar Coast, *India* 60 P9
Malabo = Rey Malabo, *Eq. Guin.* 79 E6
Malabon, *Phil.* 55 D4
Malacca, Str. of, *Indonesia* 59 L3
Malacky, *Slovak Rep.* 21 G7
Malad City, *U.S.A.* 110 E7
Maladzyechna = Molodechno, *Belorussia* 40 D5
Málaga, *Colombia* 120 B3
Málaga, *Spain* 31 J6
Malaga, *U.S.A.* 109 J2
Málaga □, *Spain* 31 J6
Malagarasi, *Tanzania* 82 D3
Malagarasi →, *Tanzania* 82 D2
Malagón, *Spain* 31 F7
Malagón →, *Spain* 31 H3
Malaimbandy, *Madag.* 85 C8
Malakâl, *Sudan* 77 F3
Malakand, *Pakistan* 62 B4
Malakoff, *U.S.A.* 109 J7
Malamyzh, *Russia* 45 E14
Malang, *Indonesia* 57 G15
Malanje, *Angola* 80 F3
Mälaren, *Sweden* 10 E11
Malargüe, *Argentina* 126 D2
Malartic, *Canada* 98 C4
Malatya, *Turkey* 67 D8
Malatya □, *Turkey* 67 D8
Malawi ■, *Africa* 83 E3
Malawi, L., *Africa* 83 E3
Malay Pen., *Asia* 59 J3
Malaya Belozërka, *Ukraine* 42 C6
Malaya Vishera, *Russia* 40 B8
Malaya Viska, *Ukraine* 42 B4
Malaybalay, *Phil.* 55 G6
Malāyer, *Iran* 65 C6
Malaysia ■, *Asia* 56 D4
Malazgirt, *Turkey* 67 D10
Malbon, *Australia* 90 C3
Malbooma, *Australia* 91 E1
Malbork, *Poland* 20 A9
Malcésine, *Italy* 32 C7
Malchin, *Germany* 18 B8
Malchow, *Germany* 18 B8
Malcolm, *Australia* 89 E3
Malcolm, Pt., *Australia* 89 F3
Maldegem, *Belgium* 17 F2
Malden, *Mass., U.S.A.* 107 D13
Malden, *Mo., U.S.A.* 109 G10
Malden I., *Kiribati* 93 H12
Maldives ■, *Ind. Oc.* 47 J11
Maldonado, *Uruguay* 127 C5
Maldonado, Punta, *Mexico* 115 D5
Malé, *Italy* 32 B7
Maléa, Ákra, *Greece* 39 N6
Malebo, Pool, *Africa* 70 G5
Malegaon, *India* 60 J9
Malei, *Mozam.* 83 F4
Malek Kandī, *Iran* 64 B5
Malela, *Zaïre* 82 C2
Malema, *Mozam.* 83 E4
Máleme, *Greece* 37 D5
Malerkotla, *India* 62 D6
Máles, *Greece* 37 D7
Malesherbes, *France* 25 D9
Malestroit, *France* 24 E4
Malfa, *Italy* 35 D7
Malgobek, *Russia* 43 E11
Malgomaj, *Sweden* 8 D14
Malgrat, *Spain* 28 D7
Malha, *Sudan* 77 D2
Malheur →, *U.S.A.* 110 D5
Malheur L., *U.S.A.* 110 E4
Mali, *Guinea* 78 C2
Mali ■, *Africa* 78 B4
Mali →, *Burma* 61 G20
Mali Kanal, *Serbia* 21 K9
Malibu, *U.S.A.* 113 L8
Malik, *Indonesia* 57 E6
Malili, *Indonesia* 57 E6
Malimba, Mts., *Zaïre* 82 D2
Malin, *Ukraine* 40 F6
Malin Hd., *Ireland* 15 A4
Malindi, *Kenya* 82 C5
Malines = Mechelen, *Belgium* 17 F4
Maling, *Indonesia* 57 D6
Malinyi, *Tanzania* 83 D4
Malipo, *China* 52 F5
Maliqi, *Albania* 39 J3
Malita, *Phil.* 57 C7
Malkara, *Turkey* 66 C2
Małkinia Górna, *Poland* 20 C12
Malko Tŭrnovo, *Bulgaria* 39 H10
Mallacoota, *Australia* 91 F4
Mallacoota Inlet, *Australia* 91 F4
Mallaig, *U.K.* 14 E3
Mallawan, *India* 63 F9
Mallawi, *Egypt* 76 B3
Malleco □, *Chile* 128 A2
Mallemort, *France* 27 E9
Málles Venosta, *Italy* 32 B7
Mállia, *Greece* 37 D7
Malliόn, Kólpos, *Greece* 37 D7
Mallorca, *Spain* 36 B10
Mallorytown, *Canada* 107 B9
Mallow, *Ireland* 15 D3
Malmberget, *Sweden* 8 C16
Malmédy, *Belgium* 17 H8
Malmesbury, *S. Africa* 84 E2
Malmö, *Sweden* 11 J6
Malmöhus län □, *Sweden* 11 J7
Malmslätt, *Sweden* 11 F9
Malmyzh, *Russia* 41 C17
Maloarkhangelsk, *Russia* 41 E10
Maloca, *Brazil* 121 C6
Maloja, *Switz.* 23 D9
Maloja, P., *Switz.* 23 D9
Malolos, *Phil.* 57 B6
Malombe L., *Malawi* 83 E4
Malone, *U.S.A.* 107 B10
Malong, *China* 52 E4
Malorita, *Belorussia* 40 F4
Maloyaroslovets, *Russia* 41 D10
Malpartida, *Spain* 31 F4
Malpaso, *Canary Is.* 36 G1
Malpica, *Spain* 30 B2
Malta, *Brazil* 122 C4
Malta, *Idaho, U.S.A.* 110 E7
Malta, *Mont., U.S.A.* 110 B10
Malta ■, *Europe* 37 D1
Malta Channel, *Medit. S.* 34 F6
Maltahöhe, *Namibia* 84 C2
Malters, *Switz.* 22 B6
Malton, *Canada* 106 C5
Malton, *U.K.* 12 C7
Maluku, *Indonesia* 57 E7
Maluku □, *Indonesia* 57 E7
Maluku Sea, *Indonesia* 57 E6
Malumfashi, *Nigeria* 79 C6
Malvan, *India* 60 L8
Malvern, *U.S.A.* 109 H8
Malvern Hills, *U.K.* 13 E5
Malvik, *Norway* 10 A4
Malvinas, Is. = Falkland Is. ■, *Atl. Oc.* 128 D5
Malya, *Tanzania* 82 C3
Malyy Lyakhovskiy, Ostrov, *Russia* 45 B15
Mama, *Russia* 45 D12
Mamadysh, *Russia* 41 D17
Mamanguape, *Brazil* 122 C4
Mamasa, *Indonesia* 57 E5
Mambasa, *Zaïre* 82 B2
Mamberamo →, *Indonesia* 57 E9
Mambilima Falls, *Zambia* 83 E2
Mambirima, *Zaïre* 83 E2
Mambo, *Tanzania* 82 C4
Mambrui, *Kenya* 82 C5
Mamburao, *Phil.* 55 E4
Mameigwess L., *Canada* 98 B2
Mamer, *Lux.* 17 J8
Mamers, *France* 24 D7
Mamfe, *Cameroon* 79 D6
Mamiña, *Chile* 124 E4
Mámmola, *Italy* 35 D9
Mammoth, *U.S.A.* 111 K8
Mamoré →, *Bolivia* 125 C4
Mamou, *Guinea* 78 C2
Mampatá, *Guinea-Biss.* 78 C2
Mampong, *Ghana* 79 D4
Mamuil Malal, Paso, *S. Amer.* 128 A2
Mamuju, *Indonesia* 57 E5
Man, *Ivory C.* 78 D3
Man, I. of, *U.K.* 12 C3
Man Na, *Burma* 61 H20
Mana, *Fr. Guiana* 121 B7
Mana →, *Fr. Guiana* 121 B7
Måna →, *Norway* 10 E2
Manaar, G. of = Mannar, G. of, *Asia* 60 Q11
Manabí □, *Ecuador* 120 D1
Manacacías →, *Colombia* 120 C3
Manacapuru, *Brazil* 121 D5
Manacapuru →, *Brazil* 121 D5
Manacor, *Spain* 36 B10
Manado, *Indonesia* 57 D6
Manage, *Belgium* 17 G4
Managua, *Nic.* 116 D2
Managua, L., *Nic.* 116 D2
Manakara, *Madag.* 85 C8
Manama = Al Manāmah, *Bahrain* 65 E6
Manambao →, *Madag.* 85 B7
Manambato, *Madag.* 85 A8
Manambolo →, *Madag.* 85 B7
Manambolosy, *Madag.* 85 B8
Mananara, *Madag.* 85 B8
Mananara →, *Madag.* 85 C8
Mananjary, *Madag.* 85 C8
Manantenina, *Madag.* 85 C8
Manaos = Manaus, *Brazil* 121 D6
Manapire →, *Venezuela* 120 B4
Manapouri, *N.Z.* 87 L1
Manapouri, L., *N.Z.* 87 L1
Manas, *China* 54 B3
Manas →, *India* 61 F17
Manaslu, *Nepal* 63 E11
Manasquan, *U.S.A.* 107 F10
Manassa, *U.S.A.* 111 H11
Manaung, *Burma* 61 K18
Manaus, *Brazil* 121 D6
Manavgat, *Turkey* 66 E4
Manawan L., *Canada* 101 B8
Manay, *Phil.* 55 H7
Manbij, *Syria* 64 B3
Mancelona, *U.S.A.* 104 C3
Mancha Real, *Spain* 31 H7
Manche □, *France* 24 C5
Manchester, *U.K.* 12 D5
Manchester, *Calif., U.S.A.* 112 G3
Manchester, *Conn., U.S.A.* 107 E12
Manchester, *Ga., U.S.A.* 105 J3
Manchester, *Iowa, U.S.A.* 108 D9
Manchester, *Ky., U.S.A.* 104 G4
Manchester, *N.H., U.S.A.* 107 D13
Manchester, *N.Y., U.S.A.* 106 D7
Manchester, *Vt., U.S.A.* 107 C11
Manchester L., *Canada* 101 A7
Manchuria = Dongbei, *China* 51 D13
Manciano, *Italy* 33 F8
Mancifa, *Ethiopia* 77 F5
Mancora, Pta., *Peru* 124 A1
Mand →, *Iran* 65 D7
Manda, *Chunya, Tanzania* 82 D3
Manda, *Ludewe, Tanzania* 83 E3
Mandabé, *Madag.* 85 C7
Mandaguari, *Brazil* 127 A5
Mandah, *Mongolia* 50 B5
Mandal, *Norway* 9 G9
Mandalay, *Burma* 61 J20
Mandale = Mandalay, *Burma* 61 J20
Mandalgovi, *Mongolia* 50 B4
Mandalī, *Iraq* 64 C5
Mandan, *U.S.A.* 108 B4
Mandaon, *Phil.* 55 E5
Mandar, Teluk, *Indonesia* 57 E5
Mandas, *Italy* 34 C2
Mandasor = Mandsaur, *India* 62 G6
Mandaue, *Phil.* 55 F5
Mandelieu-la-Napoule, *France* 27 E10
Mandera, *Kenya* 82 B5
Mandera □, *Kenya* 82 B5
Manderfeld, *Belgium* 17 H8
Mandi, *India* 62 D7
Mandimba, *Mozam.* 83 E4
Mandioli, *Indonesia* 57 E7
Mandioré, L., *S. Amer.* 125 D6
Mandla, *India* 63 H9
Mandø, *Denmark* 11 J2
Mandoto, *Madag.* 85 B8
Mandoúdhion, *Greece* 39 L6
Mandra, *Pakistan* 62 C5
Mandrare →, *Madag.* 85 D8
Mandritsara, *Madag.* 85 B8
Mandsaur, *India* 62 G6
Mandurah, *Australia* 89 F2
Mandúria, *Italy* 35 B10
Mandvi, *India* 62 H3
Mandya, *India* 60 N10
Mandzai, *Pakistan* 62 D2
Mané, *Burkina Faso* 79 C4
Maneh, *Iran* 65 B8
Manenguoba, Mts., *Cameroon* 79 D6
Maneroo, *Australia* 90 C3
Maneroo Cr. →, *Australia* 90 C3
Manfalût, *Egypt* 76 B3
Manfred, *Australia* 91 E3
Manfredónia, *Italy* 35 A8
Manfredónia, G. di, *Italy* 35 A9
Manga, *Brazil* 123 D3
Manga, *Burkina Faso* 79 C4
Manga, *Niger* 79 C7
Mangabeiras, Chapada das, *Brazil* 122 D2
Mangalia, *Romania* 38 F11
Mangalore, *India* 60 N9
Manganeses, *Spain* 30 D5
Mangaweka, *N.Z.* 87 H5
Manggar, *Indonesia* 56 E3
Manggawitu, *Indonesia* 57 E8
Mangkalihat, Tanjung, *Indonesia* 57 D5
Mangla Dam, *Pakistan* 63 C5
Manglares, C., *Colombia* 120 C2
Manglaur, *India* 62 E7
Mangnai, *China* 54 C4
Mango, *Togo* 79 C5
Mangoche, *Malawi* 83 E4
Mangoky →, *Madag.* 85 C7
Mangole, *Indonesia* 57 E7
Mangombe, *Zaïre* 82 C2
Mangonui, *N.Z.* 87 F4
Mangualde, *Portugal* 30 E3
Mangueigne, *Chad* 73 F9
Mangueira, L. da, *Brazil* 127 C5
Manguéni, Hamada, *Niger* 75 D7
Mangum, *U.S.A.* 109 H5
Mangyshlak Poluostrov, *Kazakhstan* 43 D15
Mangyshlakskiy Zaliv, *Kazakhstan* 43 D14
Manhattan, *U.S.A.* 108 F6

Manhiça, *Mozam.* 85 D5
Manhuaçu, *Brazil* 123 F3
Manhumirim, *Brazil* 123 F3
Maní, *Colombia* 120 C3
Mania →, *Madag.* 85 B8
Maniago, *Italy* 33 B9
Manica, *Mozam.* 85 B5
Manica e Sofala □,
  Mozam. 85 B5
Manicaland □, *Zimbabwe* 83 F3
Manicoré, *Brazil* 125 B5
Manicoré →, *Brazil* 125 B5
Manicouagan →, *Canada* 99 C6
Manīfah, *Si. Arabia* ... 65 E6
Manifold, *Australia* 90 C5
Manifold, C., *Australia* .. 90 C5
Maniganggo, *China* 52 B2
Manigotagan, *Canada* .. 101 C9
Manihiki, *Cook Is.* 93 J11
Manika, Plateau de la,
  Zaïre 83 E2
Manila, *Phil.* 55 D4
Manila, *U.S.A.* 110 F9
Manila B., *Phil.* 55 D4
Manilla, *Australia* 91 E5
Manimpé, *Mali* 78 C3
Maningrida, *Australia* .. 90 A1
Manipur □, *India* 61 G18
Manipur →, *Burma* 61 H19
Manisa, *Turkey* 66 D2
Manisa □, *Turkey* 66 D2
Manistee, *U.S.A.* 104 C2
Manistee →, *U.S.A.* ... 104 C2
Manistique, *U.S.A.* 104 C2
Manito L., *Canada* 101 C7
Manitoba □, *Canada* ... 101 B9
Manitoba, L., *Canada* .. 101 C9
Manitou, *Canada* 101 D9
Manitou, *U.S.A.* 98 C2
Manitou Is., *U.S.A.* 104 C2
Manitou L., *Canada* 99 B6
Manitou Springs, *U.S.A.* 108 F2
Manitoulin I., *Canada* .. 98 C3
Manitowaning, *Canada* . 98 C3
Manitowoc, *U.S.A.* 104 C2
Manitsauá-Missu →, *Brazil* 125 C7
Manizales, *Colombia* ... 120 B2
Manja, *Madag.* 85 C7
Manjacaze, *Mozam.* 85 C5
Manjhand, *Pakistan* 62 G3
Manjil, *Iran* 65 B6
Manjimup, *Australia* ... 89 F2
Manjra →, *India* 60 K10
Mankato, *Kans., U.S.A.* . 108 F5
Mankato, *Minn., U.S.A.* . 108 C8
Mankayane, *Swaziland* .. 85 D5
Mankono, *Ivory C.* 78 D3
Mankota, *Canada* 101 D7
Manlay, *Mongolia* 50 B4
Manlleu, *Spain* 28 C7
Manly, *Australia* 91 E5
Manmad, *India* 60 J9
Mann Ras., *Australia* ... 89 E5
Manna, *Indonesia* 56 E2
Mannahill, *Australia* ... 91 E3
Mannar, *Sri Lanka* 60 Q11
Mannar, G. of, *Asia* ... 60 Q11
Mannar I., *Sri Lanka* ... 60 Q11
Männedorf, *Switz.* 23 B7
Mannheim, *Germany* ... 19 F4
Manning, *Canada* 100 B5
Manning, *Oreg., U.S.A.* . 112 E3
Manning, *S.C., U.S.A.* .. 105 J5
Manning Prov. Park,
  Canada 100 D4
Mannington, *U.S.A.* 104 F5
Mannu →, *Italy* 34 C2
Mannu, C., *Italy* 34 B1
Mannum, *Australia* 91 E2
Mano, *S. Leone* 78 D2
Manoa, *Bolivia* 125 B4
Manokwari, *Indonesia* .. 57 E8
Manombo, *Madag.* 85 C7
Manono, *Zaïre* 82 D2
Manosque, *France* 27 E9
Manouane, L., *Canada* .. 99 B5
Manpojin, *N. Korea* ... 51 D14
Manresa, *Spain* 28 D6
Mansa, *Gujarat, India* .. 62 H5
Mansa, *Punjab, India* .. 62 E6
Mansa, *Zambia* 83 E2
Mansehra, *Pakistan* 62 B5
Mansel I., *Canada* 97 B11
Mansfield, *Australia* 91 F4
Mansfield, *U.K.* 12 D6
Mansfield, *La., U.S.A.* .. 109 J8
Mansfield, *Mass., U.S.A.* 107 D13
Mansfield, *Ohio, U.S.A.* . 106 F2
Mansfield, *Pa., U.S.A.* .. 106 E7
Mansfield, *Wash., U.S.A.* 110 C4
Mansidão, *Brazil* 122 D3
Mansilla de las Mulas,
  Spain 30 C5
Mansle, *France* 26 C4
Manso →, *Brazil* 123 D2
Mansoa, *Guinea-Biss.* .. 78 C1
Manson Creek, *Canada* . 100 B4
Mansoura, *Algeria* 75 A5
Manta, *Ecuador* 120 D1
Manta, B. de, *Ecuador* .. 120 D1
Mantalingajan, Mt., *Phil.* 55 G2
Mantare, *Tanzania* 82 C3
Manteca, *U.S.A.* 111 H3
Mantecal, *Venezuela* ... 120 B4

Mantena, *Brazil* 123 E3
Manteo, *U.S.A.* 105 H8
Mantes-la-Jolie, *France* .. 25 D8
Manthani, *India* 60 K11
Manthelan, *France* 24 E7
Manti, *U.S.A.* 110 G8
Mantiqueira, Serra da,
  Brazil 123 F3
Manton, *U.S.A.* 104 C3
Mantorp, *Sweden* 11 F9
Mántova, *Italy* 32 C7
Mänttä, *Finland* 8 E18
Mantua = Mántova, *Italy* 32 C7
Manturovo, *Russia* 41 B14
Manu, *Peru* 124 C3
Manu →, *Peru* 124 C3
Manua Is., *Amer. Samoa* 87 B14
Manuae, *Cook Is.* 93 J12
Manuel Alves →, *Brazil* . 123 D2
Manuel Alves Grande →,
  Brazil 122 C2
Manuel Urbano, *Brazil* .. 124 B4
Manui, *Indonesia* 57 E6
Manuripi →, *Bolivia* 124 C4
Many, *U.S.A.* 109 K8
Manyara, L., *Tanzania* .. 82 C4
Manyas, *Turkey* 66 D2
Manyoni, *Tanzania* 82 D3
Manyoni □, *Tanzania* ... 82 D3
Manzai, *Pakistan* 62 C4
Manzala, Bahra el, *Egypt* 76 H7
Manzanares, *Spain* 29 F1
Manzaneda, Cabeza de,
  Spain 30 C3
Manzanillo, *Cuba* 116 B4
Manzanillo, *Mexico* 114 D4
Manzanillo, Pta., *Panama* 116 E4
Manzano Mts., *U.S.A.* .. 111 J10
Manzarīyeh, *Iran* 65 C6
Manzhouli, *China* 54 B6
Manzini, *Swaziland* 85 D5
Mao, *Chad* 73 F8
Maoke, Pegunungan,
  Indonesia 57 E9
Maolin, *China* 51 C12
Maoming, *China* 53 G8
Maowen, *China* 52 B4
Maoxing, *China* 51 B13
Mapam Yumco, *China* .. 54 C3
Mapastepec, *Mexico* ... 115 D6
Mapia, Kepulauan,
  Indonesia 57 D8
Mapimí, *Mexico* 114 B4
Mapimí, Bolsón de, *Mexico* 114 B4
Maping, *China* 53 D9
Mapinga, *Tanzania* 82 D4
Mapinhane, *Mozam.* ... 85 C6
Mapire, *Venezuela* 121 B5
Maple Creek, *Canada* ... 101 D7
Maple Valley, *U.S.A.* ... 112 C4
Mapleton, *U.S.A.* 110 D2
Mapuera →, *Brazil* 121 D6
Maputo, *Mozam.* 85 D5
Maputo, B. de, *Mozam.* . 85 D5
Maqiaohe, *China* 51 B16
Maqnā, *Si. Arabia* 64 D2
Maqteïr, *Mauritania* 74 D2
Maquela do Zombo,
  Angola 80 F3
Maquinchao, *Argentina* .. 128 B3
Maquoketa, *U.S.A.* 108 D9
Mar, Serra do, *Brazil* ... 127 B6
Mar Chiquita, L.,
  Argentina 126 C3
Mar del Plata, *Argentina* . 126 D4
Mar Menor, L., *Spain* ... 29 H4
Mara, *Guyana* 121 B6
Mara, *Tanzania* 82 C3
Mara □, *Tanzania* 82 C3
Maraã, *Brazil* 120 D4
Marabá, *Brazil* 122 C2
Maracá, I. de, *Brazil* ... 121 C7
Maracaibo, *Venezuela* .. 120 A3
Maracaibo, L. de,
  Venezuela 120 B3
Maracaju, *Brazil* 127 A4
Maracaju, Serra de, *Brazil* 125 E6
Maracanã, *Brazil* 122 B2
Maracás, *Brazil* 123 D3
Maracay, *Venezuela* 120 A4
Marādah, *Libya* 73 C8
Maradi, *Niger* 79 C6
Maradun, *Nigeria* 79 C6
Marāgheh, *Iran* 64 B5
Maragogipe, *Brazil* 123 D4
Marāh, *Si. Arabia* 64 E5
Marajó, B. de, *Brazil* ... 122 B2
Marajó, I. de, *Brazil* ... 122 B2
Marākand, *Iran* 64 B5
Maralal, *Kenya* 82 B4
Maralinga, *Australia* 89 F5
Marama, *Australia* 91 F3
Marampa, *S. Leone* 78 D2
Maran, *Malaysia* 59 L4
Marana, *U.S.A.* 111 K8
Maranboy, *Australia* 88 B5
Maranchón, *Spain* 28 D2
Marand, *Iran* 64 B5
Marang, *Malaysia* 59 K4
Maranguape, *Brazil* 122 B4
Maranhão = São Luís,
  Brazil 122 B3

Maranhão □, *Brazil* 122 B2
Marano, L. di, *Italy* 33 C10
Maranoa →, *Australia* .. 91 D4
Marañón →, *Peru* 124 A3
Marão, *Mozam.* 85 C5
Marapi →, *Brazil* 121 C6
Marari, *Brazil* 124 B4
Maraş = Kahramanmaraş,
  Turkey 66 E7
Mărăşeşti, *Romania* 38 D10
Maratea, *Italy* 35 C8
Marateca, *Portugal* 31 G2
Marathasa □, *Cyprus* ... 37 E11
Marathókambos, *Greece* . 39 M9
Marathon, *Australia* 90 C3
Marathon, *Canada* 98 C2
Marathón, *Greece* 39 L6
Marathon, *N.Y., U.S.A.* . 107 D8
Marathon, *Tex., U.S.A.* . 109 K3
Marathóvouno, *Cyprus* .. 37 D12
Maratua, *Indonesia* 57 D5
Maraú, *Brazil* 123 D4
Maravatío, *Mexico* 114 D4
Marawi City, *Phil.* 55 G6
Marāwih, *U.A.E.* 65 E7
Marbella, *Spain* 31 J6
Marble Bar, *Australia* ... 88 D2
Marble Falls, *U.S.A.* 109 K5
Marblehead, *U.S.A.* 107 D14
Marburg, *Germany* 18 E4
Marby, *Sweden* 10 A8
Marcal →, *Hungary* 21 H7
Marcapata, *Peru* 124 C3
Marcaria, *Italy* 32 C7
March, *U.K.* 13 E8
Marchand = Rommani,
  Morocco 74 B3
Marche, *France* 26 B5
Marche □, *Italy* 33 E10
Marche-en-Famenne,
  Belgium 17 H6
Marchena, *Spain* 31 H5
Marches = Marche □, *Italy* 33 E10
Marchiana Marina, *Italy* . 32 F7
Marcianise, *Italy* 35 A7
Marcigny, *France* 27 B8
Marcillat-en-Combraille,
  France 26 B6
Marcinelle, *Belgium* 17 H4
Marck, *France* 25 B8
Marckolsheim, *France* .. 25 D14
Marcona, *Peru* 124 D2
Marcos Juárez, *Argentina* . 126 C3
Marcus I. = Minami-Tori-
  Shima, *Pac. Oc.* 92 E7
Marcus Necker Ridge,
  Pac. Oc. 92 F9
Marcy, Mt., *U.S.A.* 107 B11
Mardan, *Pakistan* 62 B5
Mardie, *Australia* 88 D2
Mardin, *Turkey* 67 E9
Maree L., *U.K.* 14 D3
Mareeba, *Australia* 90 B4
Marek = Stanke Dimitrov,
  Bulgaria 38 G6
Marek, *Indonesia* 57 E6
Maremma, *Italy* 32 F8
Maréna, *Mali* 78 C3
Marenberg, *Slovenia* ... 33 B12
Marengo, *U.S.A.* 108 E8
Marennes, *France* 26 C2
Marenyi, *Kenya* 82 C4
Marerano, *Madag.* 85 C7
Maréttimo, *Italy* 34 E5
Mareuil-sur-Lay, *France* . 26 B2
Marfa, *U.S.A.* 109 K2
Marfa Pt., *Malta* 37 D1
Marganets, *Ukraine* 42 C6
Margaret →, *Australia* .. 88 C4
Margaret Bay, *Canada* .. 100 C3
Margaret L., *Canada* ... 100 B5
Margaret River, *Australia* . 88 C4
Margarita, I. de, *Venezuela* 121 A5
Margarítion, *Greece* 39 K3
Margaritovo, *Russia* 48 C7
Margate, *S. Africa* 85 E5
Margate, *U.K.* 13 F9
Margelan, *Uzbekistan* ... 44 E8
Margeride, Mts. de la,
  France 26 D7
Margherita di Savola, *Italy* 35 A9
Margosatubig, *Phil.* 55 H5
Marguerite, *Canada* 100 C4
Marhoum, *Algeria* 75 B4
Mari Republic □, *Russia* . 41 C16
María Elena, *Chile* 126 A2
María Grande, *Argentina* . 126 C4
Maria I., *N. Terr.,*
  Australia 90 A2
Maria I., *Tas., Australia* . 90 G4
Maria van Diemen, C.,
  N.Z. 87 F4
Mariager, *Denmark* 11 H4
Mariager Fjord, *Denmark* . 11 H4
Mariakani, *Kenya* 82 C4
Marian L., *Canada* 100 A5
Mariana Trench, *Pac. Oc.* 92 F6
Marianao, *Cuba* 116 B3
Marianna, *Ark., U.S.A.* . 109 H9
Marianna, *Fla., U.S.A.* .. 105 K3
Mariánské Lázně, *Czech.* . 20 F2
Marias →, *U.S.A.* 110 C8
Mariato, Punta, *Panama* . 116 E3

Ma'rib, *Yemen* 68 D4
Maribo, *Denmark* 11 K5
Maribor, *Slovenia* 33 B12
Marico →, *Africa* 84 C4
Maricopa, *Ariz., U.S.A.* . 111 K7
Maricopa, *Calif., U.S.A.* . 113 K7
Maricourt, *Canada* 97 C12
Marīdī, *Sudan* 77 G2
Maridi, Wadi →, *Sudan* . 77 F2
Marié →, *Brazil* 120 D4
Marie Byrd Land,
  Antarctica 5 D14
Marie-Galante, *Guadeloupe* 117 C7
Mariecourt, *Canada* 97 B12
Mariefred, *Sweden* 10 E11
Mariehamn, *Finland* 9 F15
Marienbad = Mariánské
  Lázně, *Czech.* 20 F2
Marienberg, *Germany* .. 18 E9
Marienberg, *Neths.* 16 D9
Marienbourg, *Belgium* .. 17 H5
Mariental, *Namibia* 84 C2
Marienville, *U.S.A.* 106 E5
Mariestad, *Sweden* 11 F7
Marietta, *Ga., U.S.A.* .. 105 J3
Marietta, *Ohio, U.S.A.* . 104 F5
Marieville, *Canada* 107 A11
Marignane, *France* 27 E9
Marihatag, *Phil.* 55 G7
Mariinsk, *Russia* 44 D9
Mariinskiy Posad, *Russia* . 41 C15
Marília, *Brazil* 127 A5
Marillana, *Australia* 88 D2
Marín, *Spain* 30 C2
Marina, *U.S.A.* 112 J5
Marina di Cirò, *Italy* ... 35 C10
Marina Plains, *Australia* . 90 A3
Marineo, *Italy* 34 E6
Marinette, *U.S.A.* 104 C2
Maringá, *Brazil* 127 A5
Marinha Grande, *Portugal* 31 F2
Marion, *Ala., U.S.A.* ... 105 J2
Marion, *Ill., U.S.A.* 109 G10
Marion, *Ind., U.S.A.* ... 104 E3
Marion, *Iowa, U.S.A.* .. 108 D9
Marion, *Kans., U.S.A.* .. 108 F6
Marion, *Mich., U.S.A.* .. 104 C3
Marion, *N.C., U.S.A.* .. 105 H4
Marion, *Ohio, U.S.A.* .. 104 E4
Marion, *S.C., U.S.A.* ... 105 H6
Marion, *Va., U.S.A.* ... 105 G5
Marion, L., *U.S.A.* 105 J5
Maripa, *Venezuela* 121 B4
Maripasoula, *Fr. Guiana* . 121 C7
Mariposa, *U.S.A.* 111 H4
Mariscal Estigarribia,
  Paraguay 126 A3
Maritime Alps =
  Maritimes, Alpes,
  Europe 27 D11
Maritimes, Alpes, *Europe* 27 D11
Maritsa, *Greece* 37 C10
Mariupol, *Ukraine* 42 C7
Marīvān, *Iran* 64 C5
Mariyampol, *Lithuania* .. 40 D3
Markam, *China* 52 C2
Markazī □, *Iran* 65 C6
Markdale, *Canada* 106 B4
Marke, *Belgium* 17 G2
Marked Tree, *U.S.A.* ... 109 H9
Markelsdorfer Huk,
  Germany 18 A6
Marken, *Neths.* 16 D6
Markermeer, *Neths.* 16 C6
Market Drayton, *U.K.* .. 12 E5
Market Harborough, *U.K.* 13 E7
Markham, *Canada* 106 C5
Markham, Mt., *Antarctica* 5 E11
Markham L., *Canada* ... 101 A8
Marki, *Poland* 20 C11
Markleeville, *U.S.A.* 112 G7
Markoupoulon, *Greece* .. 39 M6
Markovo, *Russia* 45 C17
Markoye, *Burkina Faso* .. 79 C5
Marks, *Russia* 41 F15
Marksville, *U.S.A.* 109 K8
Markt Schwaben, *Germany* 19 G7
Markt Uzbekistan, *Germany* 44 E8
Marktredwitz, *Germany* . 19 F7
Marla, *Australia* 91 D1
Marlboro, *U.S.A.* 107 D13
Marlborough, *Australia* .. 90 C4
Marlborough Downs, *U.K.* 13 F6
Marle, *France* 25 C10
Marlin, *U.S.A.* 109 K6
Marlow, *Germany* 18 A8
Marlow, *U.S.A.* 109 H6
Marly-le-Grand, *Switz.* .. 22 C4
Marmagao, *India* 60 M8
Marmande, *France* 26 D4
Marmara, *Turkey* 42 F2
Marmara, Sea of =
  Marmara Denizi, *Turkey* 66 C3
Marmara Denizi, *Turkey* . 66 C3
Marmara Gölü, *Turkey* .. 66 D3
Marmaris, *Turkey* 66 D3
Marmarth, *U.S.A.* 108 B3
Marmelos →, *Brazil* ... 125 B5
Marmion, Mt., *Australia* . 89 E2
Marmion L., *Canada* ... 98 C1
Marmolada, Mte., *Italy* . 33 B8
Marmolejo, *Spain* 31 G6
Marmora, *Canada* 98 D4
Marnay, *France* 25 E12

Marne, *Germany* 18 B5
Marne □, *France* 25 D11
Marne →, *France* 25 D9
Marneuli, *Georgia* 43 F11
Maroa, *Venezuela* 120 C4
Maroala, *Madag.* 85 B8
Maroantsetra, *Madag.* .. 85 B8
Maromandia, *Madag.* .. 85 A8
Marondera, *Zimbabwe* .. 83 F3
Maroni →, *Fr. Guiana* .. 121 B7
Maronne →, *France* 26 C5
Maroochydore, *Australia* . 91 D5
Maroona, *Australia* 91 F3
Maros →, *Hungary* 21 J10
Marosakoa, *Madag.* 85 B8
Marostica, *Italy* 33 C8
Maroua, *Cameroon* 79 C7
Marovoay, *Madag.* 85 B8
Marowijne →, *Surinam* .. 121 C7
Marowijne □, *Surinam* .. 121 C7
Marquard, *S. Africa* 84 D4
Marqueira, *Portugal* 31 G1
Marquesas Is. = Marquises,
  Is., Pac. Oc. 93 H14
Marquette, *U.S.A.* 104 B2
Marquise, *France* 25 B8
Marquises, Is., *Pac. Oc.* . 93 H14
Marra, Gebel, *Sudan* ... 77 F2
Marracuene, *Mozam.* .. 85 D5
Marradi, *Italy* 33 D8
Marrakech, *Morocco* ... 74 B3
Marrawah, *Australia* ... 90 G3
Marrecas, Serra das, *Brazil* 122 C3
Marree, *Australia* 91 D2
Marrilla, *Australia* 88 D1
Marrimane, *Mozam.* ... 85 C5
Marromeu, *Mozam.* 85 B6
Marroquí, Punta, *Spain* .. 31 K5
Marrowie Cr. →, *Australia* 91 E4
Marrubane, *Mozam.* ... 83 F4
Marrum, *Neths.* 16 B7
Marrupa, *Mozam.* 83 E4
Marsá Matrûh, *Egypt* ... 76 A2
Marsá Susah, *Libya* 73 B9
Marsabit, *Kenya* 82 B4
Marsabit □, *Kenya* 82 B4
Marsala, *Italy* 34 E5
Marsalforn, *Malta* 37 C1
Marsberg, *Germany* 18 D4
Marsciano, *Italy* 33 F9
Marsden, *Australia* 91 E4
Marsdiep, *Neths.* 16 C5
Marseillan, *France* 26 E7
Marseille, *France* 27 E9
Marseilles = Marseille,
  France 27 E9
Marsh I., *U.S.A.* 109 L9
Marsh L., *U.S.A.* 108 C6
Marshall, *Liberia* 78 D2
Marshall, *Ark., U.S.A.* .. 109 H8
Marshall, *Mich., U.S.A.* . 104 D3
Marshall, *Minn., U.S.A.* . 108 C7
Marshall, *Mo., U.S.A.* .. 108 F8
Marshall, *Tex., U.S.A.* .. 109 J7
Marshall →, *Australia* .. 90 C2
Marshall Is. ■, *Pac. Oc.* . 92 G9
Marshalltown, *U.S.A.* ... 108 D8
Marshfield, *Mo., U.S.A.* . 109 G8
Marshfield, *Wis., U.S.A.* . 108 C9
Marshūn, *Iran* 65 B6
Mársico Nuovo, *Italy* ... 35 B8
Märsta, *Sweden* 10 E11
Marstal, *Denmark* 11 K4
Marstrand, *Sweden* 11 G5
Mart, *U.S.A.* 109 K6
Marta →, *Italy* 33 F8
Martaban, *Burma* 61 L20
Martaban, G. of, *Burma* . 61 L20
Martano, *Italy* 35 B11
Martapura, *Kalimantan,*
  Indonesia 56 E4
Martapura, *Sumatera,*
  Indonesia 56 E2
Marte, *Nigeria* 79 C7
Martel, *France* 26 D5
Martelange, *Belgium* ... 17 J7
Martés, Sierra, *Spain* ... 29 F4
Martha's Vineyard, *U.S.A.* 107 E14
Martigné-Ferchaud, *France* 24 E5
Martigny, *Switz.* 22 D4
Martigues, *France* 27 E9
Martil, *Morocco* 74 A3
Martin, *Slovak Rep.* 20 F8
Martin, *S. Dak., U.S.A.* . 108 D4
Martin, *Tenn., U.S.A.* .. 109 G10
Martín →, *Spain* 28 D4
Martin L., *U.S.A.* 105 J3
Martina, *Switz.* 23 C10
Martina Franca, *Italy* ... 35 B10
Martinborough, *N.Z.* ... 87 J5
Martinez, *U.S.A.* 112 G4
Martinho Campos, *Brazil* . 123 E2
Martinique ■, *W. Indies* . 117 D7
Martinique Passage,
  W. Indies 117 C7
Martínon, *Greece* 39 L6
Martinópolis, *Brazil* 127 A5
Martins Ferry, *U.S.A.* ... 106 F4
Martinsburg, *Pa., U.S.A.* . 106 F6
Martinsburg, *W. Va.,*
  U.S.A. 104 F7
Martinsville, *Ind., U.S.A.* . 104 F2
Martinsville, *Va., U.S.A.* . 105 G6
Marton, *N.Z.* 87 J5
Martorell, *Spain* 28 D6
Martos, *Spain* 31 H7

Martuni, *Armenia* 43 F11
Maru, *Nigeria* 79 C6
Marudi, *Malaysia* 56 D4
Ma'ruf, *Afghan.* 60 D5
Marugame, *Japan* 49 G6
Marúggio, *Italy* 35 B10
Maruim, *Brazil* 122 D4
Marum, *Neths.* 16 B8
Marunga, *Angola* 84 B3
Marungu, Mts., *Zaïre* 82 D2
Marvast, *Iran* 65 D7
Marvejols, *France* 26 D7
Marwar, *India* 62 G5
Mary, *Turkmenistan* 44 F7
Mary Frances L., *Canada* . 101 A7
Mary Kathleen, *Australia* . 90 C2
Maryborough = Port
  Laoise, *Ireland* 15 C4
Maryborough, *Queens.,*
  Australia 91 D5
Maryborough, *Vic.,*
  Australia 91 F3
Maryfield, *Canada* 101 D8
Maryland □, *U.S.A.* 104 F7
Maryland Junction,
  Zimbabwe 83 F3
Maryport, *U.K.* 12 C4
Mary's Harbour, *Canada* . 99 B8
Marystown, *Canada* 99 C8
Marysvale, *U.S.A.* 111 G7
Marysville, *Canada* 100 D5
Marysville, *Calif., U.S.A.* 112 F5
Marysville, *Kans., U.S.A.* 108 F6
Marysville, *Mich., U.S.A.* 106 D2
Marysville, *Ohio, U.S.A.* 104 E4
Marysville, *Wash., U.S.A.* 112 B4
Maryvale, *Australia* 91 D5
Maryville, *U.S.A.* 105 H4
Marzo, Punta, *Colombia* . 120 B2
Marzûq, *Libya* 73 C7
Masahunga, *Tanzania* 82 C3
Masai, *Malaysia* 59 M4
Masai Steppe, *Tanzania* .. 82 C4
Masaka, *Uganda* 82 C3
Masalembo, Kepulauan,
  Indonesia 56 F4
Masalima, Kepulauan,
  Indonesia 56 F5
Masamba, *Indonesia* 57 E6
Masan, *S. Korea* 51 G15
Masanasa, *Spain* 29 F4
Masasi, *Tanzania* 83 E4
Masasi □, *Tanzania* 83 E4
Masaya, *Nic.* 116 D2
Masba, *Nigeria* 79 C7
Masbate, *Phil.* 55 E5
Mascara, *Algeria* 75 A5
Mascota, *Mexico* 114 C4
Masela, *Indonesia* 57 F7
Maseru, *Lesotho* 84 D4
Mashaba, *Zimbabwe* 83 G3
Mashābih, *Si. Arabia* 64 E3
Mashan, *China* 52 F7
Masherbrum, *Pakistan* 63 B7
Mashhad, *Iran* 65 B8
Mashi, *Nigeria* 79 C6
Mashīz, *Iran* 65 D8
Mashkel, Hamun-i-,
  Pakistan 60 E3
Mashki Chāh, *Pakistan* .. 60 E3
Mashonaland Central □,
  Zimbabwe 85 B5
Mashonaland East □,
  Zimbabwe 85 B5
Mashonaland West □,
  Zimbabwe 85 B4
Mashtaga, *Azerbaijan* ... 43 F13
Masi, *Norway* 8 B17
Masi Manimba, *Zaïre* 80 E3
Masindi, *Uganda* 82 B3
Masindi Port, *Uganda* 82 B3
Masisea, *Peru* 124 B3
Masisi, *Zaïre* 82 C2
Masjed Soleyman, *Iran* ... 65 D6
Mask, L., *Ireland* 15 C2
Maslinica, *Croatia* 33 E13
Masnou, *Spain* 28 D7
Masoala, Tanjon' i, *Madag.* 85 B9
Masoarivo, *Madag.* 85 B7
Masohi, *Indonesia* 57 E7
Masomeloka, *Madag.* 85 C8
Mason, *Nev., U.S.A.* 112 G7
Mason, *Tex., U.S.A.* 109 K5
Mason City, *U.S.A.* 108 D8
Maspalomas, *Canary Is.* . 36 G4
Maspalomas, Pta.,
  Canary Is. 36 G4
Masqat, *Oman* 68 C6
Massa, *Italy* 32 D7
Massa, O. →, *Morocco* .. 74 B3
Massa Maríttima, *Italy* .. 32 E7
Massachusetts □, *U.S.A.* 107 D12
Massachusetts B., *U.S.A.* 107 D14
Massafra, *Italy* 35 B10
Massaguet, *Chad* 73 F8
Massakory, *Chad* 73 F8
Massanella, *Spain* 36 B9
Massangena, *Mozam.* 85 C5
Massapê, *Brazil* 122 B3
Massarosa, *Italy* 32 E7
Massat, *France* 26 F5
Massawa = Mitsiwa,
  Eritrea 77 D4
Massena, *U.S.A.* 107 B10
Massénya, *Chad* 73 F8

Masset, *Canada* 100 C2
Massiac, *France* 26 C7
Massif Central, *France* ... 26 D7
Massillon, *U.S.A.* 106 F3
Massinga, *Mozam.* 85 C6
Masson, *Canada* 107 A9
Masson I., *Antarctica* 5 C7
Mastanli = Momchilgrad,
  Bulgaria 39 H8
Masterton, *N.Z.* 87 J5
Mástikho, Ákra, *Greece* .. 39 L9
Mastuj, *Pakistan* 63 A5
Mastung, *Pakistan* 60 E5
Mastūrah, *Si. Arabia* 76 C4
Masuda, *Japan* 49 G5
Masvingo, *Zimbabwe* 83 G3
Masvingo □, *Zimbabwe* .. 83 G3
Maswa □, *Tanzania* 82 C3
Maşyāf, *Syria* 64 C3
Mata de São João, *Brazil* . 123 D4
Matabeleland North □,
  Zimbabwe 83 F2
Matabeleland South □,
  Zimbabwe 83 G2
Mataboor, *Indonesia* 57 E9
Matachel →, *Spain* 31 G4
Matachewan, *Canada* 98 C3
Matacuni →, *Venezuela* . 121 C4
Matad, *Mongolia* 54 B6
Matadi, *Zaïre* 80 F2
Matagalpa, *Nic.* 116 D2
Matagami, *Canada* 98 C4
Matagami, L., *Canada* 98 C4
Matagorda, *U.S.A.* 109 L7
Matagorda B., *U.S.A.* 109 L6
Matagorda I., *U.S.A.* 109 L6
Matak, P., *Indonesia* 59 L6
Matakana, *Australia* 91 E4
Mátala, *Greece* 37 E6
Matalaque, *Peru* 124 D3
Matam, *Senegal* 78 B2
Matameye, *Niger* 79 C6
Matamoros, *Campeche,*
  Mexico 115 D6
Matamoros, *Coahuila,*
  Mexico 114 B4
Matamoros, *Puebla, Mexico* 115 D5
Matamoros, *Tamaulipas,*
  Mexico 115 B5
Ma'ţan as Sarra, *Libya* ... 73 D9
Matandu →, *Tanzania* .. 83 D3
Matane, *Canada* 99 C6
Matang, *China* 52 F5
Matankari, *Niger* 79 C5
Matanzas, *Cuba* 116 B3
Matapan, C. = Taínaron,
  Ákra, *Greece* 39 N5
Matapédia, *Canada* 99 C6
Matara, *Sri Lanka* 60 S12
Mataram, *Indonesia* 56 F5
Matarani, *Peru* 124 D3
Mataranka, *Australia* 88 B5
Matarma, Râs, *Egypt* 69 E1
Mataró, *Spain* 28 D7
Matarraña →, *Spain* 28 D5
Matatiele, *S. Africa* 85 E4
Mataura, *N.Z.* 87 M2
Mategua, *Bolivia* 125 C5
Matehuala, *Mexico* 114 C4
Mateira, *Brazil* 123 E1
Mateke Hills, *Zimbabwe* . 83 G3
Matélica, *Italy* 33 E10
Matera, *Italy* 35 B9
Mátészalka, *Hungary* 21 H12
Matetsi, *Zimbabwe* 83 F2
Mateur, *Tunisia* 75 A6
Matfors, *Sweden* 10 B11
Matha, *France* 26 C3
Matheson Island, *Canada* . 101 C9
Mathis, *U.S.A.* 109 L6
Mathura, *India* 62 F7
Mati, *Phil.* 55 H7
Mati →, *Albania* 39 H2
Matías Romero, *Mexico* .. 115 D5
Matibane, *Mozam.* 83 E5
Matima, *Botswana* 84 C3
Matiri Ra., *N.Z.* 87 J4
Matlock, *U.K.* 12 D6
Matmata, *Tunisia* 75 B6
Matna, *Sudan* 77 E4
Mato →, *Venezuela* 121 B4
Mato, Serranía de,
  Venezuela 120 B4
Mato Grosso □, *Brazil* .. 125 C6
Mato Grosso, Planalto do,
  Brazil 125 C7
Mato Grosso do Sul □,
  Brazil 125 D7
Matochkin Shar, *Russia* . 44 B6
Matopo Hills, *Zimbabwe* . 83 G2
Matopos, *Zimbabwe* 83 G2
Matosinhos, *Portugal* 30 D2
Matour, *France* 27 B8
Matsena, *Nigeria* 79 C7
Matsesta, *Russia* 43 E8
Matsue, *Japan* 49 G6
Matsumae, *Japan* 48 D10
Matsumoto, *Japan* 49 F9
Matsusaka, *Japan* 49 G8
Matsuura, *Japan* 49 H4
Matsuyama, *Japan* 49 H6
Mattagami →, *Canada* .. 98 B3
Mattancheri, *India* 60 Q10
Mattawa, *Canada* 98 C4
Mattawamkeag, *U.S.A.* .. 99 C6
Matterhorn, *Switz.* 22 E5

Matthew Town, *Bahamas* . 117 B5
Matthew's Ridge, *Guyana* 121 B5
Mattice, *Canada* 98 C3
Mattituck, *U.S.A.* 107 F12
Mattmar, *Sweden* 10 A7
Matuba, *Mozam.* 85 C5
Matucana, *Peru* 124 C2
Matun, *Afghan.* 62 C3
Maturín, *Venezuela* 121 B5
Mau, *India* 63 G10
Mau Escarpment, *Kenya* . 82 C4
Mau Ranipur, *India* 63 G8
Maubeuge, *France* 25 B10
Maubourguet, *France* 26 E4
Maud, Pt., *Australia* 88 D1
Maude, *Australia* 91 E3
Maudin Sun, *Burma* 61 M19
Maués, *Brazil* 121 D6
Mauganj, *India* 61 G12
Maui, *U.S.A.* 102 H16
Maulamyaing = Moulmein,
  Burma 61 L20
Maule □, *Chile* 126 D1
Mauléon-Licharre, *France* 26 E3
Maullín, *Chile* 128 B2
Maumee, *U.S.A.* 104 E4
Maumee →, *U.S.A.* 104 E4
Maumere, *Indonesia* 57 F6
Maun, *Botswana* 84 B3
Mauna Kea, *U.S.A.* 102 J17
Mauna Loa, *U.S.A.* 102 J17
Maungmagan Kyunzu,
  Burma 61 M20
Maupin, *U.S.A.* 110 D3
Maure-de-Bretagne, *France* 24 E5
Maurepas, L., *U.S.A.* 109 K9
Maures, *France* 27 E10
Mauriac, *France* 26 C6
Maurice, L., *Australia* 89 E5
Mauritania ■, *Africa* 74 D3
Mauritius ■, *Ind. Oc.* .. 71 J9
Mauron, *France* 24 D4
Maurs, *France* 26 D6
Mauston, *U.S.A.* 108 D9
Mauterndorf, *Austria* 21 H3
Mauvezin, *France* 26 E4
Mauzé-sur-le-Mignon,
  France 26 B3
Mavaca →, *Venezuela* . 121 C4
Mavinga, *Angola* 81 H4
Mavli, *India* 62 G5
Mavrova, *Albania* 39 J2
Mavuradonha Mts.,
  Zimbabwe 83 F3
Mawa, *Zaïre* 82 B2
Mawana, *India* 62 E7
Mawand, *Pakistan* 62 E3
Mawk Mai, *Burma* 61 J20
Mawlaik, *Burma* 61 H19
Mawquq, *Si. Arabia* 64 E4
Mawson Coast, *Antarctica* 5 C6
Max, *U.S.A.* 108 B4
Maxcanú, *Mexico* 115 C6
Maxesibeni, *S. Africa* 85 E4
Maxhamish L., *Canada* .. 100 B4
Maxixe, *Mozam.* 85 C6
Maxville, *Canada* 107 A10
Maxwell, *U.S.A.* 112 F4
Maxwelton, *Australia* 90 C3
May Downs, *Australia* .. 90 C4
May Pen, *Jamaica* 116 C4
Maya, *Spain* 28 B3
Maya →, *Russia* 45 D14
Maya Mts., *Belize* 115 D7
Mayaguana, *Bahamas* .. 117 B5
Mayagüez, *Puerto Rico* .. 117 C6
Mayahi, *Niger* 79 C6
Mayals, *Spain* 28 D5
Mayāmey, *Iran* 65 B7
Mayang, *China* 52 D7
Mayarí, *Cuba* 117 B4
Maybell, *U.S.A.* 110 F9
Maychew, *Ethiopia* 77 E4
Maydan, *Iraq* 64 C5
Maydena, *Australia* 90 G4
Mayen, *Germany* 19 E3
Mayenne, *France* 24 D6
Mayenne □, *France* 24 D6
Mayenne →, *France* 24 E6
Mayer, *U.S.A.* 111 J7
Mayerthorpe, *Canada* .. 100 C5
Mayfield, *U.S.A.* 105 G1
Mayhill, *U.S.A.* 111 K11
Maykop, *Russia* 43 D9
Maymyo, *Burma* 58 A1
Maynard, *U.S.A.* 112 C4
Maynard Hills, *Australia* . 89 E2
Mayne →, *Australia* 90 C3
Maynooth, *Ireland* 15 C5
Mayo, *Canada* 96 B6
Mayo □, *Ireland* 15 C2
Mayo →, *Argentina* 128 C3
Mayo →, *Peru* 124 B2
Mayo L., *Canada* 96 B6
Mayon Volcano, *Phil.* .. 55 E5
Mayor I., *N.Z.* 87 G6
Mayorga, *Spain* 30 C5
Mayraira Pt., *Phil.* 55 B4
Mayskiy, *Russia* 43 E11
Mayson L., *Canada* 101 B7
Maysville, *U.S.A.* 104 F4
Mayu, *Indonesia* 57 D7
Mayville, *N. Dak., U.S.A.* 108 B6
Mayville, *N.Y., U.S.A.* .. 106 D5
Mayya, *Russia* 45 C14

Mazabuka, *Zambia* 83 F2
Mazagán = El Jadida,
  Morocco 74 B3
Mazagão, *Brazil* 121 D7
Mazamet, *France* 26 E6
Mazán, *Peru* 120 D3
Māzandarān □, *Iran* 65 B7
Mazapil, *Mexico* 114 C4
Mazar, O. →, *Algeria* .. 75 B5
Mazara del Vallo, *Italy* .. 34 E5
Mazarredo, *Argentina* .. 128 C3
Mazarrón, *Spain* 29 H3
Mazarrón, G. de, *Spain* . 29 H3
Mazaruni →, *Guyana* .. 121 B6
Mazatán, *Mexico* 114 B2
Mazatenango, *Guatemala* 116 D1
Mazatlán, *Mexico* 114 C3
Mažeikiai, *Lithuania* 40 C3
Māzhān, *Iran* 65 C8
Mazīnān, *Iran* 65 B8
Mazoe, *Mozam.* 83 F3
Mazoe →, *Mozam.* 83 F3
Mazowe, *Zimbabwe* 83 F3
Mazrûb, *Sudan* 77 E2
Mazu Dao, *China* 53 D12
Mazurian Lakes =
  Mazurski, Pojezierze,
  Poland 20 B10
Mazurski, Pojezierze,
  Poland 20 B10
Mazzarino, *Italy* 35 E7
Mbaba, *Senegal* 78 C1
Mbabane, *Swaziland* 85 D5
Mbagne, *Mauritania* 78 B2
M'bahiakro, *Ivory C.* 78 D4
Mbaïki, *C.A.R.* 80 D3
Mbala, *Zambia* 83 D3
Mbale, *Uganda* 82 B3
Mbalmayo, *Cameroon* .. 79 E7
Mbamba Bay, *Tanzania* . 83 E3
Mbandaka, *Zaïre* 80 D3
Mbanga, *Cameroon* 79 E6
Mbanza Congo, *Angola* . 80 F2
Mbanza Ngungu, *Zaïre* . 80 F2
Mbarara, *Uganda* 82 C3
Mbashe →, *S. Africa* .. 85 E4
Mbatto, *Ivory C.* 78 D4
Mbenkuru →, *Tanzania* . 83 D4
Mberengwa, *Zimbabwe* . 83 G2
Mberengwa, Mt.,
  Zimbabwe 83 G2
Mberubu, *Nigeria* 79 D6
Mbesuma, *Zambia* 83 D3
Mbeya, *Tanzania* 83 D3
Mbeya □, *Tanzania* 82 D3
Mbinga, *Tanzania* 83 E4
Mbinga □, *Tanzania* 83 E3
Mbini □, *Eq. Guin.* 80 D2
Mboki, *C.A.R.* 77 F2
Mboro, *Senegal* 78 B1
Mboune, *Senegal* 78 C2
Mbour, *Senegal* 78 C1
Mbout, *Mauritania* 78 B2
Mbozi □, *Tanzania* 83 D3
Mbuji-Mayi, *Zaïre* 82 D1
Mbulu, *Tanzania* 82 C4
Mbulu □, *Tanzania* 82 C4
Mburucuyá, *Argentina* .. 126 B4
Mcherrah, *Algeria* 74 C4
Mchinja, *Tanzania* 83 D4
Mchinji, *Malawi* 83 E3
Mdennah, *Mauritania* .. 74 D3
Mead, L., *U.S.A.* 113 J12
Meade, *U.S.A.* 109 G4
Meadow, *Australia* 89 E1
Meadow Lake, *Canada* .. 101 C7
Meadow Lake Prov. Park,
  Canada 101 C7
Meadow Valley Wash →,
  U.S.A. 113 J12
Meadville, *U.S.A.* 106 E4
Meaford, *Canada* 98 D3
Mealhada, *Portugal* 30 E2
Mealy Mts., *Canada* 99 B8
Meander River, *Canada* . 100 B5
Meares, C., *U.S.A.* 110 D2
Mearim →, *Brazil* 122 B3
Meath □, *Ireland* 15 C5
Meath Park, *Canada* 101 C7
Meaulne, *France* 26 B6
Meaux, *France* 25 D9
Mebechi-Gawa →, *Japan* 48 D10
Mecanhelas, *Mozam.* .. 83 F4
Mecaya →, *Colombia* .. 120 C2
Mecca = Makkah,
  Si. Arabia 68 C2
Mecca, *U.S.A.* 113 M10
Mechanicsburg, *U.S.A.* . 106 F8
Mechanicville, *U.S.A.* .. 107 D11
Mechara, *Ethiopia* 77 F5
Mechelen, *Antwerpen,*
  Belgium 17 F4
Mechelen, *Limburg,*
  Belgium 17 G7
Mecheria, *Algeria* 75 B4
Mechernich, *Germany* .. 18 E2
Mechetinskaya, *Russia* .. 43 C9
Mechra Benâbbou,
  Morocco 74 B3
Mecitözü, *Turkey* 42 F6
Mecklenburg-
  Vorpommern □,
  Germany 18 B8
Mecklenburger Bucht,
  Germany 18 A7

Meconta, *Mozam.* 83 E4
Meda, *Australia* 88 C3
Meda, *Portugal* 30 E3
Medan, *Indonesia* 56 D1
Médanos, *Argentina* 128 A4
Medanosa, Pta., *Argentina* 128 C3
Medéa, *Algeria* 75 A5
Medeiros Neto, *Brazil* .. 123 E3
Medel, Pic, *Switz.* 23 C7
Medellín, *Colombia* 120 B2
Medemblik, *Neths.* 16 C6
Mederdra, *Mauritania* .. 78 B1
Medford, *Mass., U.S.A.* 107 D13
Medford, *Oreg., U.S.A.* . 110 E2
Medford, *Wis., U.S.A.* .. 108 C9
Medgidia, *Romania* 38 E11
Medi, *Sudan* 77 F3
Media Agua, *Argentina* . 126 C2
Media Luna, *Argentina* . 126 C2
Mediaş, *Romania* 38 C7
Medical Lake, *U.S.A.* .. 110 C5
Medicina, *Italy* 33 D8
Medicine Bow, *U.S.A.* .. 110 F10
Medicine Bow Pk., *U.S.A.* 110 F10
Medicine Bow Ra., *U.S.A.* 110 F10
Medicine Hat, *Canada* .. 101 D6
Medicine Lake, *U.S.A.* .. 108 A2
Medicine Lodge, *U.S.A.* . 109 G5
Medina = Al Madīnah,
  Si. Arabia 64 E3
Medina, *Brazil* 123 E3
Medina, *Colombia* 120 C3
Medina, *N. Dak., U.S.A.* 108 B5
Medina, *N.Y., U.S.A.* .. 106 C6
Medina, *Ohio, U.S.A.* .. 106 E3
Medina →, *U.S.A.* 109 L5
Medina de Ríoseco, *Spain* 30 D5
Medina del Campo, *Spain* 30 D6
Medina L., *U.S.A.* 109 L5
Medina-Sidonia, *Spain* .. 31 J5
Medinaceli, *Spain* 28 D2
Medinipur, *India* 63 H12
Mediterranean Sea, *Europe* 70 C5
Medjerda, O. →, *Tunisia* 75 A7
Medley, *Canada* 101 C6
Médoc, *France* 26 C3
Medstead, *Canada* 101 C7
Medulin, *Croatia* 33 D10
Medveda, *Serbia* 21 N11
Medveditsa →, *Russia* . 41 G13
Medveditsa →, *Russia* . 41 C10
Medvedok, *Russia* 41 C17
Medvezhi, Ostrava, *Russia* 45 B17
Medvezhyegorsk, *Russia* . 44 C4
Medway →, *U.K.* 13 F8
Medyn, *Russia* 41 D9
Medzilaborce, *Slovak Rep.* 20 F11
Meeberrie, *Australia* 89 E2
Meekatharra, *Australia* .. 89 E2
Meeker, *U.S.A.* 110 F10
Meer, *Belgium* 17 F5
Meerane, *Germany* 18 E8
Meerbeke, *Belgium* 17 G4
Meerhout, *Belgium* 17 F6
Meerle, *Belgium* 17 F5
Meersburg, *Germany* .. 19 H5
Meerssen, *Neths.* 17 G7
Meerut, *India* 62 E7
Meeteetse, *U.S.A.* 110 D9
Meeuwen, *Belgium* 17 F7
Mega, *Ethiopia* 77 G4
Megálo Petalí, *Greece* .. 39 M7
Megalópolis, *Greece* 39 M5
Meganísi, *Greece* 39 L3
Mégara, *Greece* 39 M6
Megarine, *Algeria* 75 B6
Megève, *France* 27 C10
Meghalaya □, *India* 61 G17
Meghezez, *Ethiopia* 77 F4
Mégiscane, L., *Canada* . 98 C4
Mehadia, *Romania* 38 E5
Mehaigne →, *Belgium* . 17 G6
Mehaïguene, O. →,
  Algeria 75 B5
Meheisa, *Sudan* 76 D3
Mehndawal, *India* 63 F10
Mehr Jān, *Iran* 65 C7
Mehrābād, *Iran* 64 C5
Mehrān, *Iran* 64 C5
Mehrīz, *Iran* 65 D7
Mehun-sur-Yèvre, *France* 25 E9
Mei Jiang →, *China* 53 E11
Mei Xian, *Guangdong,*
  China 53 E11
Mei Xian, *Shaanxi, China* 50 G4
Meia Ponte →, *Brazil* .. 123 E2
Meichengzhen, *China* .. 53 C12
Meichengzhen, *China* .. 53 C8
Meichuan, *China* 53 B10
Meiganga, *Cameroon* .. 80 C2
Meijel, *Neths.* 17 F7
Meiktila, *Burma* 61 J19
Meilen, *Switz.* 23 B7
Meiningen, *Germany* .. 18 E6
Meio →, *Brazil* 123 D3
Meira, Sierra de, *Spain* . 30 B3
Meiringen, *Switz.* 22 C6
Meishan, *China* 52 B4
Meissen, *Germany* 18 D9
Meissner, *Germany* 18 D5
Meitan, *China* 52 D6
Mejillones, *Chile* 126 A1
Meka, *Australia* 89 E2
Mékambo, *Gabon* 80 D2

Millingen

Mekdela, *Ethiopia* 77 E4
Mekele, *Ethiopia* 77 E4
Mekhtar, *Pakistan* 60 D6
Meknès, *Morocco* 74 B3
Meko, *Nigeria* 79 D5
Mekong →, *Asia* 59 H6
Mekongga, *Indonesia* 57 E6
Melagiri Hills, *India* 60 N10
Melah, Sebkhet el, *Algeria* 75 C4
Melaka, *Malaysia* 59 L4
Melalap, *Malaysia* 56 C5
Mélambes, *Greece* 37 D6
Melanesia, *Pac. Oc.* 92 H7
Melbourne, *Australia* 91 F3
Melbourne, *U.S.A.* 105 L5
Melchor Múzquiz, *Mexico* 114 B4
Melchor Ocampo, *Mexico* 114 C4
Méldola, *Italy* 33 D9
Meldorf, *Germany* 18 A5
Melegnano, *Italy* 32 C6
Melenci, *Serbia* 21 K10
Melenki, *Russia* 41 D12
Mélèzes →, *Canada* 97 C12
Melfi, *Chad* 73 F8
Melfi, *Italy* 35 B8
Melfort, *Canada* 101 C8
Melfort, *Zimbabwe* 83 F3
Melgaço, *Madeira* 30 C2
Melgar de Fernamental, *Spain* 30 C6
Melhus, *Norway* 10 A4
Melick, *Neths.* 17 F8
Melide, *Switz.* 23 E7
Meligalá, *Greece* 39 M4
Melilla, *Morocco* 75 A4
Melipilla, *Chile* 126 C1
Mélissa, Ákra, *Greece* 37 D6
Melita, *Canada* 101 D8
Mélito di Porto Salvo, *Italy* 35 E8
Melitopol, *Ukraine* 42 C6
Melk, *Austria* 21 G5
Mellansel, *Sweden* 8 E15
Melle, *Belgium* 17 G3
Melle, *France* 26 B3
Melle, *Germany* 18 C4
Mellégue, O. →, *Tunisia* 75 A6
Mellen, *U.S.A.* 108 B9
Mellerud, *Sweden* 11 F6
Mellette, *U.S.A.* 108 C5
Mellid, *Spain* 30 C2
Mellieha, *Malta* 37 D1
Mellit, *Sudan* 77 E2
Mellizo Sur, Cerro, *Chile* 128 C2
Mellrichstadt, *Germany* 19 E6
Melnik, *Bulgaria* 39 H6
Mělník, *Czech.* 20 E4
Melo, *Uruguay* 127 C5
Melolo, *Indonesia* 57 F6
Melouprey, *Cambodia* 58 F5
Melovoye, *Ukraine* 43 B9
Melrhir, Chott, *Algeria* 75 B6
Melrose, *N.S.W., Australia* 91 E4
Melrose, *W. Austral., Australia* 89 E3
Melrose, *U.K.* 14 F6
Melrose, *U.S.A.* 109 H3
Mels, *Switz.* 23 B8
Melsele, *Belgium* 17 F4
Melstone, *U.S.A.* 110 C10
Melsungen, *Germany* 18 D5
Melton Mowbray, *U.K.* 12 E7
Melun, *France* 25 D9
Melut, *Sudan* 77 E3
Melville, *Canada* 101 C8
Melville, C., *Australia* 90 A3
Melville, L., *Canada* 99 B8
Melville B., *Australia* 90 A2
Melville I., *Australia* 88 B5
Melville I., *Canada* 4 B2
Melville Pen., *Canada* 97 B11
Melvin →, *Canada* 100 B5
Memaliaj, *Albania* 39 J2
Memba, *Mozam.* 83 E5
Memboro, *Indonesia* 57 F5
Membrilla, *Spain* 29 G1
Memel = Klaìpéda, *Lithuania* 40 D2
Memel, *S. Africa* 85 D4
Memmingen, *Germany* 19 H6
Mempawah, *Indonesia* 56 D3
Memphis, *Tenn., U.S.A.* 109 H10
Memphis, *Tex., U.S.A.* 109 H4
Mena, *U.S.A.* 109 H7
Mena →, *Ethiopia* 77 F5
Menai Strait, *U.K.* 12 D3
Ménaka, *Mali* 79 B5
Menaldum, *Neths.* 16 B7
Menan = Chao Phraya →, *Thailand* 58 F3
Menarandra →, *Madag.* 85 D7
Menard, *U.S.A.* 109 K5
Menasha, *U.S.A.* 104 C1
Menate, *Indonesia* 56 E4
Mendawai →, *Indonesia* 56 E4
Mende, *France* 26 D7
Mendebo, *Ethiopia* 77 F4
Mendez, *Mexico* 115 B5
Mendhar, *India* 63 C6
Mendi, *Ethiopia* 77 F4
Mendip Hills, *U.K.* 13 F5
Mendocino, *U.S.A.* 110 G2
Mendocino, C., *U.S.A.* 110 F1
Mendota, *Calif., U.S.A.* 111 H3
Mendota, *Ill., U.S.A.* 108 E10
Mendoza, *Argentina* 126 C2
Mendoza □, *Argentina* 126 C2
Mendrisio, *Switz.* 23 E7
Mene Grande, *Venezuela* 120 B3
Menemen, *Turkey* 66 D2
Menen, *Belgium* 17 G2
Menéndez, L., *Argentina* 128 B2
Menfi, *Italy* 34 E5
Mengcheng, *China* 53 A11
Mengdingjie, *China* 52 F2
Mengeš, *Slovenia* 33 B11
Menggala, *Indonesia* 56 E3
Menghai, *China* 52 G3
Mengíbar, *Spain* 31 H7
Mengjin, *China* 50 G7
Mengla, *China* 52 G3
Menglian, *China* 52 F2
Mengoub, *Algeria* 74 C3
Mengshan, *China* 53 E8
Mengyin, *China* 51 G9
Mengzhe, *China* 52 F3
Mengzi, *China* 52 F4
Menihek L., *Canada* 99 B6
Menin = Menen, *Belgium* 17 G2
Menindee, *Australia* 91 E3
Menindee L., *Australia* 91 E3
Meningie, *Australia* 91 F2
Menlo Park, *U.S.A.* 112 H4
Menominee, *U.S.A.* 104 C2
Menominee →, *U.S.A.* 104 C2
Menomonie, *U.S.A.* 108 C9
Menongue, *Angola* 81 G3
Menorca, *Spain* 36 B11
Mentakab, *Malaysia* 59 L4
Mentawai, Kepulauan, *Indonesia* 56 E1
Menton, *France* 27 E11
Mentor, *U.S.A.* 106 E3
Mentz Dam, *S. Africa* 84 E4
Menzel-Bourguiba, *Tunisia* 75 A6
Menzel Chaker, *Tunisia* 75 B7
Menzel-Temime, *Tunisia* 75 A7
Menzies, *Australia* 89 E3
Me'ona, *Israel* 69 B4
Meoqui, *Mexico* 114 B3
Mepaco, *Mozam.* 83 F3
Meppel, *Neths.* 16 C8
Meppen, *Germany* 18 C3
Mequinenza, *Spain* 28 D5
Mer Rouge, *U.S.A.* 109 J9
Merabéllou, Kólpos, *Greece* 37 D7
Meramangye, L., *Australia* 89 E5
Meran = Merano, *Italy* 33 B8
Merano, *Italy* 33 B8
Merate, *Italy* 32 C6
Merauke, *Indonesia* 57 F10
Merbabu, *Indonesia* 57 G14
Merbein, *Australia* 91 E3
Merca, *Somali Rep.* 68 G3
Mercadal, *Spain* 36 B11
Mercato Saraceno, *Italy* 33 E9
Merced, *U.S.A.* 111 H3
Merced Pk., *U.S.A.* 112 H7
Mercedes, *Buenos Aires, Argentina* 126 C4
Mercedes, *Corrientes, Argentina* 126 B4
Mercedes, *San Luis, Argentina* 126 C2
Mercedes, *Uruguay* 126 C4
Merceditas, *Chile* 126 B1
Mercer, *N.Z.* 87 G5
Mercer, *U.S.A.* 106 E4
Merchtem, *Belgium* 17 G4
Mercier, *Bolivia* 124 C4
Mercury, *U.S.A.* 113 J11
Mercy C., *Canada* 97 B13
Merdrignac, *France* 24 D4
Mere, *Belgium* 17 G3
Meredith, C., *Falk. Is.* 128 D4
Meredith, L., *U.S.A.* 109 H4
Merelbeke, *Belgium* 17 G3
Méréville, *France* 25 D9
Merga = Nukheila, *Sudan* 76 D2
Mergenevsky, *Kazakhstan* 43 B14
Mergui Arch. = Myeik Kyunzu, *Burma* 59 G1
Mérida, *Mexico* 115 C7
Mérida, *Spain* 31 G4
Mérida, *Venezuela* 120 B3
Mérida □, *Venezuela* 120 B3
Mérida, Cord. de, *Venezuela* 118 B2
Meriden, *U.S.A.* 107 E12
Meridian, *Calif., U.S.A.* 112 F5
Meridian, *Idaho, U.S.A.* 110 E5
Meridian, *Miss., U.S.A.* 105 J1
Meridian, *Tex., U.S.A.* 109 K6
Mering, *Germany* 19 G7
Meriruma, *Brazil* 121 C7
Merkel, *U.S.A.* 109 J4
Merksem, *Belgium* 17 F4
Merksplas, *Belgium* 17 F5
Mermaid Reef, *Australia* 88 C2
Mern, *Denmark* 11 J6
Merowe, *Sudan* 76 D3
Merredin, *Australia* 89 F2
Merrick, *U.K.* 14 F4
Merrickville, *Canada* 107 B9
Merrill, *Oreg., U.S.A.* 110 E3
Merrill, *Wis., U.S.A.* 108 C10
Merriman, *U.S.A.* 108 D4
Merritt, *Canada* 100 C4
Merriwa, *Australia* 91 E5
Merriwagga, *Australia* 91 E4
Merry I., *Canada* 98 A4
Merrygoen, *Australia* 91 E4
Merryville, *U.S.A.* 109 K8
Mersa Fatma, *Eritrea* 68 E3
Mersch, *Lux.* 17 J8
Merseburg, *Germany* 18 D7
Mersey →, *U.K.* 12 D5
Merseyside □, *U.K.* 12 D5
Mersin, *Turkey* 66 E6
Mersing, *Malaysia* 59 L4
Merta, *India* 62 F6
Mertert, *Lux.* 17 J8
Merthyr Tydfil, *U.K.* 13 F4
Mértola, *Portugal* 31 H3
Mertzig, *Lux.* 17 J8
Mertzon, *U.S.A.* 109 K4
Méru, *France* 25 C9
Meru, *Kenya* 82 B4
Meru, *Tanzania* 82 C4
Meru □, *Kenya* 82 B4
Merville, *France* 25 B9
Méry-sur-Seine, *France* 25 D10
Merzifon, *Turkey* 42 F6
Merzig, *Germany* 19 F2
Merzouga, Erg Tin, *Algeria* 75 D7
Mesa, *U.S.A.* 111 K8
Mesach Mellet, *Libya* 75 D7
Mesagne, *Italy* 35 B10
Mesanagrós, *Greece* 37 C9
Mesaoría □, *Cyprus* 37 D12
Mesarás, Kólpos, *Greece* 37 D6
Meschede, *Germany* 18 D4
Mesfinto, *Ethiopia* 77 E4
Mesgouez, L., *Canada* 98 B4
Meshchovsk, *Russia* 40 D9
Meshed = Mashhad, *Iran* 65 B8
Meshoppen, *U.S.A.* 107 E8
Meshra er Req, *Sudan* 77 F2
Mesick, *U.S.A.* 104 C3
Mesilinka →, *Canada* 100 B4
Mesilla, *U.S.A.* 111 K10
Meslay-du-Maine, *France* 24 E6
Mesocco, *Switz.* 23 D8
Mesolóngion, *Greece* 39 L4
Mesopotamia = Al Jazirah, *Iraq* 64 C5
Mesoraca, *Italy* 35 C9
Mesquite, *U.S.A.* 111 H6
Mess Cr. →, *Canada* 100 B2
Messac, *France* 24 E5
Messad, *Algeria* 75 B5
Messalo →, *Mozam.* 83 E4
Méssaména, *Cameroon* 79 E7
Messancy, *Belgium* 17 J7
Messier, Canal, *Chile* 128 C2
Messina, *Italy* 35 D8
Messina, *S. Africa* 85 C5
Messina, Str. di, *Italy* 35 D8
Messíni, *Greece* 39 M5
Messiniakós Kólpos, *Greece* 39 N5
Messkirch, *Germany* 19 H5
Messonghi, *Greece* 37 B3
Mesta →, *Bulgaria* 39 H7
Mestanza, *Spain* 31 G6
Mestre, *Italy* 33 C9
Mestre, Espigão, *Brazil* 123 D2
Městys Zelezná Ruda, *Czech.* 20 F3
Meta □, *Colombia* 120 C3
Meta →, *S. Amer.* 120 B4
Metairie, *U.S.A.* 109 L9
Metaline Falls, *U.S.A.* 110 B5
Metán, *Argentina* 126 B3
Metangula, *Mozam.* 83 E3
Metauro →, *Italy* 33 E10
Metema, *Ethiopia* 77 E4
Metengobalame, *Mozam.* 83 E3
Méthana, *Greece* 39 M6
Methven, *N.Z.* 87 K3
Methy L., *Canada* 101 B7
Metil, *Mozam.* 83 F4
Metlakatla, *U.S.A.* 100 B2
Metlaoui, *Tunisia* 75 B6
Metlika, *Slovenia* 33 C12
Metropolis, *U.S.A.* 109 G10
Mettet, *Belgium* 17 H5
Mettur Dam, *India* 60 P10
Metz, *France* 25 C13
Meulaboh, *Indonesia* 56 D1
Meulan, *France* 25 C8
Meung-sur-Loire, *France* 25 E8
Meureudu, *Indonesia* 56 C1
Meurthe →, *France* 25 D13
Meurthe-et-Moselle □, *France* 25 D13
Meuse □, *France* 25 C12
Meuse →, *Europe* 17 G7
Meuselwitz, *Germany* 18 D8
Mexborough, *U.K.* 12 D6
Mexia, *U.S.A.* 109 K6
Mexiana, I., *Brazil* 122 A2
Mexicali, *Mexico* 114 A1
México, *Mexico* 115 D5
Mexico, *Maine, U.S.A.* 107 B14
Mexico, *Mo., U.S.A.* 108 F9
México □, *Mexico* 114 D5
Mexico ■, *Cent. Amer.* 114 C4
Mexico, G. of, *Cent. Amer.* 115 C7
Meyenburg, *Germany* 18 B8
Meymac, *France* 26 C6
Meymaneh, *Afghan.* 60 B4
Meyrargues, *France* 27 E9
Meyrueis, *France* 26 D7
Meyssac, *France* 26 C5
Mezdra, *Bulgaria* 38 F6
Mèze, *France* 26 E7
Mezen, *Russia* 44 C5
Mezen →, *Russia* 44 C5
Mézenc, Mt., *France* 27 D8
Mezha →, *Russia* 40 D7
Mézidon, *France* 24 C6
Mézilhac, *France* 27 D8
Mézin, *France* 26 D4
Mezöberény, *Hungary* 21 J11
Mezökövácsháza, *Hungary* 21 J10
Mezökövesd, *Hungary* 21 H10
Mézos, *France* 26 D2
Mezötúr, *Hungary* 21 J10
Mezquital, *Mexico* 114 C4
Mezzolombardo, *Italy* 32 B8
Mgeta, *Tanzania* 83 D4
Mglin, *Russia* 40 E8
Mhlaba Hills, *Zimbabwe* 83 F3
Mhow, *India* 62 H6
Miahuatlán, *Mexico* 115 D5
Miajadas, *Spain* 31 F5
Miallo, *Australia* 90 B4
Miami, *Ariz., U.S.A.* 111 K8
Miami, *Fla., U.S.A.* 105 N5
Miami, *Tex., U.S.A.* 109 H4
Miami →, *U.S.A.* 104 F3
Miami Beach, *U.S.A.* 105 N5
Miamisburg, *U.S.A.* 104 F3
Mian Xian, *China* 50 H4
Mianchi, *China* 50 G6
Mīāndowāb, *Iran* 64 B5
Miandrivazo, *Madag.* 85 B8
Mīāneh, *Iran* 64 B5
Mianning, *China* 52 C4
Mianwali, *Pakistan* 62 C4
Mianyang, *Hubei, China* 53 B9
Mianyang, *Sichuan, China* 52 B5
Mianzhu, *China* 52 B5
Miaoli, *Taiwan* 53 E13
Miarinarivo, *Madag.* 85 B8
Miass, *Russia* 44 D7
Miastko, *Poland* 20 A6
Michelstadt, *Germany* 19 F5
Michigan □, *U.S.A.* 104 C3
Michigan, L., *U.S.A.* 104 C2
Michigan City, *U.S.A.* 104 E2
Michikamau L., *Canada* 99 B7
Michipicoten, *Canada* 98 C3
Michipicoten I., *Canada* 98 C2
Michoacan □, *Mexico* 114 D4
Michurin, *Bulgaria* 38 G10
Michurinsk, *Russia* 41 E12
Miclere, *Australia* 90 C4
Mico, Pta., *Nic.* 116 D3
Micronesia, Federated States of ■, *Pac. Oc.* 92 G7
Mid Glamorgan □, *U.K.* 13 F4
Midai, P., *Indonesia* 59 L6
Midale, *Canada* 101 D8
Middagsfjället, *Sweden* 10 A6
Middelbeers, *Neths.* 17 F6
Middelburg, *Neths.* 17 F3
Middelburg, *C. Prov., S. Africa* 84 E3
Middelburg, *Trans., S. Africa* 85 D4
Middelfart, *Denmark* 11 J3
Middelharnis, *Neths.* 16 E4
Middelkerke, *Belgium* 17 F1
Middelrode, *Neths.* 17 E6
Middelwit, *S. Africa* 84 C4
Middle Alkali L., *U.S.A.* 110 F3
Middle Fork Feather →, *U.S.A.* 112 F5
Middle I., *Australia* 89 F3
Middle Loup →, *U.S.A.* 108 E5
Middleboro, *U.S.A.* 107 E14
Middleburg, *N.Y., U.S.A.* 107 D10
Middleburg, *Pa., U.S.A.* 106 F7
Middlebury, *U.S.A.* 107 B11
Middleport, *U.S.A.* 104 F4
Middlesboro, *Ky., U.S.A.* 103 C10
Middlesboro, *Ky., U.S.A.* 105 G4
Middlesbrough, *U.K.* 12 C6
Middlesex, *Belize* 116 C2
Middlesex, *U.S.A.* 107 F10
Middleton, *Australia* 90 C3
Middleton, *Canada* 99 D6
Middletown, *Calif., U.S.A.* 112 G4
Middletown, *Conn., U.S.A.* 107 E12
Middletown, *N.Y., U.S.A.* 107 E10
Middletown, *Ohio, U.S.A.* 104 F3
Middletown, *Pa., U.S.A.* 107 F8
Midelt, *Morocco* 74 B4
Midi, Canal du →, *France* 26 E5
Midi d'Ossau, Pic du, *France* 26 F3
Midland, *Canada* 98 D4
Midland, *Calif., U.S.A.* 113 M12
Midland, *Mich., U.S.A.* 104 D3
Midland, *Pa., U.S.A.* 106 F4
Midland, *Tex., U.S.A.* 109 K3
Midlands □, *Zimbabwe* 83 F2
Midleton, *Ireland* 15 E3
Midlothian, *U.S.A.* 109 J6
Midongy, Tangorombohitr' i, *Madag.* 85 C8
Midongy Atsimo, *Madag.* 85 C8
Midou →, *France* 26 E3
Midouze →, *France* 26 E3
Midsayap, *Phil.* 55 H6
Midu, *China* 52 E3
Midway Is., *Pac. Oc.* 92 E10
Midway Wells, *U.S.A.* 113 N11
Midwest, *U.S.A.* 103 B9
Midwest, *Wyo., U.S.A.* 110 E10
Midwolda, *Neths.* 16 B9
Midyat, *Turkey* 67 E9
Mie □, *Japan* 49 G8
Miechów, *Poland* 20 E10
Międzychód, *Poland* 20 C5
Międzyrzec Podlaski, *Poland* 20 D12
Międzyrzecz, *Poland* 20 C5
Miélan, *France* 26 E4
Mielec, *Poland* 20 E11
Mienga, *Angola* 84 B2
Miercurea Ciuc, *Romania* 38 C8
Mieres, *Spain* 30 B5
Mierlo, *Neths.* 17 F7
Mieso, *Ethiopia* 77 F5
Mifflintown, *U.S.A.* 106 F7
Mifraz Ḥefa, *Israel* 69 C4
Migdāl, *Israel* 69 C4
Migennes, *France* 25 E10
Migliarino, *Italy* 33 D8
Miguel Alemán, Presa, *Mexico* 115 D5
Miguel Alves, *Brazil* 122 B3
Miguel Calmon, *Brazil* 122 D3
Mihaliççik, *Turkey* 66 D4
Mihara, *Japan* 49 G6
Mijares →, *Spain* 28 F4
Mijas, *Spain* 31 J6
Mikese, *Tanzania* 82 D4
Mikha-Tskhakaya = Senaki, *Georgia* 43 E10
Mikhailovka, *Ukraine* 42 C6
Mikhaylovgrad, *Bulgaria* 38 F6
Mikhaylovka, *Azerbaijan* 43 F13
Mikhaylovka, *Russia* 41 D11
Mikhaylovka, *Russia* 41 F13
Mikhnevo, *Russia* 41 D10
Mikínai, *Greece* 39 M5
Mikkeli, *Finland* 9 F19
Mikkeli □ = Mikkelin lääni □, *Finland* 8 F20
Mikkelin lääni □, *Finland* 8 F20
Mikkwa →, *Canada* 100 B6
Mikniya, *Sudan* 77 D3
Mikołajki, *Poland* 20 B11
Míkonos, *Greece* 39 M8
Mikrón Dhérion, *Greece* 39 H9
Mikulov, *Czech.* 20 G6
Mikumi, *Tanzania* 82 D4
Milaca, *U.S.A.* 108 C8
Milagro, *Ecuador* 120 D2
Milagros, *Phil.* 55 E5
Milan = Milano, *Italy* 32 C6
Milan, *Mo., U.S.A.* 108 E8
Milan, *Tenn., U.S.A.* 105 H1
Milang, *Australia* 91 E2
Milange, *Mozam.* 83 F4
Milano, *Italy* 32 C6
Milâs, *Turkey* 66 E2
Mílatos, *Greece* 37 D7
Milazzo, *Italy* 35 D8
Milbank, *U.S.A.* 108 C6
Milden, *Canada* 101 C7
Mildmay, *Canada* 106 B3
Mildura, *Australia* 91 E3
Mile, *China* 52 E4
Miléai, *Greece* 39 K6
Mileh Tharthār, *Iraq* 64 C4
Miles, *Australia* 91 D5
Miles, *U.S.A.* 109 K4
Miles City, *U.S.A.* 108 B2
Milestone, *Canada* 101 D8
Mileto, *Italy* 35 D9
Miletto, Mte., *Italy* 35 A7
Miletus, *Turkey* 66 E2
Mileura, *Australia* 89 E2
Milford, *Calif., U.S.A.* 112 E6
Milford, *Conn., U.S.A.* 107 E11
Milford, *Del., U.S.A.* 104 F8
Milford, *Mass., U.S.A.* 107 D13
Milford, *Pa., U.S.A.* 107 E10
Milford, *Utah, U.S.A.* 111 G7
Milford Haven, *U.K.* 13 F2
Milford Sd., *N.Z.* 87 L1
Milgun, *Australia* 89 D2
Milḥ, Baḥr al, *Iraq* 64 C4
Miliana, *Aïn Salah, Algeria* 75 C5
Miliana, *Médéa, Algeria* 75 A5
Miling, *Australia* 89 F2
Militello in Val di Catánia, *Italy* 35 E7
Milk →, *U.S.A.* 110 B10
Milk, Wadi el →, *Sudan* 76 D3
Milk River, *Canada* 100 D6
Mill, *Neths.* 17 E7
Mill City, *U.S.A.* 110 D2
Mill I., *Antarctica* 5 C8
Mill Valley, *U.S.A.* 112 H4
Millau, *France* 26 D7
Millbridge, *Canada* 106 B7
Millbrook, *Canada* 106 B6
Mille Lacs, L. des, *Canada* 98 C1
Mille Lacs L., *U.S.A.* 108 B8
Milledgeville, *U.S.A.* 105 J4
Millen, *U.S.A.* 105 J5
Miller, *U.S.A.* 108 C5
Millerovo, *Russia* 43 B9
Millersburg, *Ohio, U.S.A.* 106 F3
Millersburg, *Pa., U.S.A.* 106 F8
Millerton, *U.S.A.* 107 E11
Millerton L., *U.S.A.* 112 J7
Millevaches, Plateau de, *France* 26 C6
Millicent, *Australia* 91 F3
Millingen, *Neths.* 16 E8

Millinocket

Millinocket, *U.S.A.* 99 C6
Millmerran, *Australia* 91 D5
Mills L., *Canada* 100 A5
Millsboro, *U.S.A.* 106 G4
Milltown Malbay, *Ireland* 15 D2
Millville, *U.S.A.* 104 F8
Millwood L., *U.S.A.* 109 J8
Milly-la-Forêt, *France* 25 D9
Milna, *Croatia* 33 E13
Milne →, *Australia* 90 C2
Milne Inlet, *Canada* 97 A11
Milnor, *U.S.A.* 108 B6
Milo, *Canada* 100 C6
Mílos, *Greece* 39 N7
Miloševo, *Serbia* 21 K10
Milparinka P.O., *Australia* 91 D3
Miltenberg, *Germany* 19 F5
Milton, *Canada* 106 C5
Milton, *N.Z.* 87 M2
Milton, *U.K.* 14 D4
Milton, *Calif., U.S.A.* 112 G6
Milton, *Fla., U.S.A.* 105 K2
Milton, *Pa., U.S.A.* 106 F8
Milton-Freewater, *U.S.A.* 110 D4
Milton Keynes, *U.K.* 13 E7
Miltou, *Chad* 73 F8
Milverton, *Canada* 106 C4
Milwaukee, *U.S.A.* 104 D2
Milwaukee Deep, *Atl. Oc.* 117 C6
Milwaukie, *U.S.A.* 112 E4
Mim, *Ghana* 78 D4
Mimizan, *France* 26 D2
Mimoso, *Brazil* 123 E2
Min Chiang →, *China* 53 E12
Min Jiang →, *China* 52 C5
Min Xian, *China* 50 G3
Mina, *U.S.A.* 111 G4
Mina Pirquitas, *Argentina* 126 A2
Mīnā Su'ud, *Si. Arabia* 65 D6
Mīnā'al Aḥmadī, *Kuwait* 65 D6
Mīnāb, *Iran* 65 E8
Minago →, *Canada* 101 C9
Minaki, *Canada* 101 D10
Minamata, *Japan* 49 H5
Minami-Tori-Shima, *Pac. Oc.* 92 E7
Minas, *Uruguay* 127 C4
Minas, Sierra de las, *Guatemala* 116 C2
Minas Basin, *Canada* 99 C7
Minas de Rio Tinto, *Spain* 31 H4
Minas de San Quintín, *Spain* 31 G6
Minas Gerais □, *Brazil* 123 E2
Minas Novas, *Brazil* 123 E3
Minatitlán, *Mexico* 115 D6
Minbu, *Burma* 61 J19
Mincio →, *Italy* 32 C7
Mindanao, *Phil.* 55 H6
Mindanao Sea = Bohol Sea, *Phil.* 57 C6
Mindanao Trench, *Pac. Oc.* 55 F7
Mindel →, *Germany* 19 G6
Mindelheim, *Germany* 19 G6
Minden, *Canada* 106 B6
Minden, *Germany* 18 C4
Minden, *La., U.S.A.* 109 J8
Minden, *Nev., U.S.A.* 112 G7
Mindiptana, *Indonesia* 57 F10
Mindoro, *Phil.* 55 E4
Mindoro Str., *Phil.* 55 E4
Mindouli, *Congo* 80 E2
Mine, *Japan* 49 G5
Minehead, *U.K.* 13 F4
Mineiros, *Brazil* 125 D7
Mineola, *U.S.A.* 109 J7
Mineral King, *U.S.A.* 112 J8
Mineral Wells, *U.S.A.* 109 J5
Mineralnyye Vody, *Russia* 43 D10
Minersville, *Pa., U.S.A.* 107 F8
Minersville, *Utah, U.S.A.* 111 G7
Minerva, *U.S.A.* 106 F3
Minervino Murge, *Italy* 35 A9
Minetto, *U.S.A.* 107 C8
Mingan, *Canada* 99 B7
Mingechaur, *Azerbaijan* 43 F12
Mingechaurskoye Vdkhr., *Azerbaijan* 43 F12
Mingela, *Australia* 90 B4
Mingenew, *Australia* 89 E2
Mingera Cr. →, *Australia* 90 C2
Minggang, *China* 53 A10
Mingin, *Burma* 61 H19
Minglanilla, *Spain* 28 F3
Minglun, *China* 52 E7
Mingorria, *Spain* 30 E6
Mingt'iehkaitafan = Mintaka Pass, *Pakistan* 63 A6
Mingxi, *China* 53 D11
Mingyuegue, *China* 51 C15
Minhou, *China* 53 E12
Minićevo, *Serbia* 21 M12
Minidoka, *U.S.A.* 110 E7
Minigwal, L., *Australia* 89 E3
Minilya, *Australia* 89 D1
Minilya →, *Australia* 89 D1
Minipi, L., *Canada* 99 B7
Mink L., *Canada* 100 A5
Minna, *Nigeria* 79 D6
Minneapolis, *Kans., U.S.A.* 108 F6
Minneapolis, *Minn., U.S.A.* 108 C8
Minnedosa, *Canada* 101 C9
Minnesota □, *U.S.A.* 108 B7
Minnesund, *Norway* 10 D5
Minnie Creek, *Australia* 89 D2
Minnipa, *Australia* 91 E2
Minnitaki L., *Canada* 98 C1
Mino, *Japan* 49 G8
Miño →, *Spain* 30 D2
Minorca = Menorca, *Spain* 36 B11
Minore, *Australia* 91 E4
Minot, *U.S.A.* 108 A4
Minqin, *China* 50 E2
Minqing, *China* 53 D12
Minsen, *Germany* 18 B3
Minsk, *Belorussia* 40 E5
Mińsk Mazowiecki, *Poland* 20 C11
Mintaka Pass, *Pakistan* 63 A6
Minto, *U.S.A.* 96 B5
Minton, *Canada* 101 D8
Minturn, *U.S.A.* 110 G10
Minturno, *Italy* 34 A6
Minûf, *Egypt* 76 H7
Minusinsk, *Russia* 45 D10
Minutang, *India* 61 E20
Minvoul, *Gabon* 80 D2
Minya el Qamh, *Egypt* 76 H7
Mionica, *Serbia* 21 L10
Mir, *Niger* 79 C7
Mir-Bashir, *Azerbaijan* 43 F12
Mīr Kūh, *Iran* 65 E8
Mīr Shahdād, *Iran* 65 E8
Mira, *Italy* 33 C9
Mira, *Portugal* 30 E2
Mira →, *Colombia* 120 C2
Mira →, *Portugal* 31 H2
Mira por vos Cay, *Bahamas* 117 B5
Mirabella Eclano, *Italy* 35 A7
Miracema do Norte, *Brazil* 122 C2
Mirador, *Brazil* 122 C3
Miraflores, *Colombia* 120 C3
Miraj, *India* 60 L9
Miram Shah, *Pakistan* 62 C4
Miramar, *Argentina* 126 D4
Miramar, *Mozam.* 85 C6
Miramas, *France* 27 E8
Mirambeau, *France* 26 C3
Miramichi B., *Canada* 99 C7
Miramont-de-Guyenne, *France* 26 D4
Miranda, *Brazil* 125 E6
Miranda □, *Venezuela* 120 A4
Miranda →, *Brazil* 125 D6
Miranda de Ebro, *Spain* 28 C2
Miranda do Corvo, *Spain* 30 E2
Miranda do Douro, *Portugal* 30 D4
Mirande, *France* 26 E4
Mirandela, *Portugal* 30 D3
Mirando City, *U.S.A.* 109 M5
Mirandola, *Italy* 32 D8
Mirandópolis, *Brazil* 127 A5
Mirango, *Malawi* 83 E3
Mirani, *Australia* 90 C4
Mirano, *Italy* 33 C9
Mirassol, *Brazil* 127 A6
Mirbāṭ, *Oman* 68 D5
Mirear, *Egypt* 76 C4
Mirebeau, *Côte-d'Or, France* 25 E12
Mirebeau, *Vienne, France* 24 F7
Mirecourt, *France* 25 D13
Mirgorod, *Ukraine* 40 G8
Miri, *Malaysia* 56 D4
Miriam Vale, *Australia* 90 C5
Mirim, L., *S. Amer.* 127 C5
Mirimire, *Venezuela* 120 A4
Miriti, *Brazil* 125 B6
Mirnyy, *Russia* 45 C12
Mirond L., *Canada* 101 B8
Mirpur, *Pakistan* 63 C5
Mirpur Bibiwari, *Pakistan* 62 E2
Mirpur Khas, *Pakistan* 62 G3
Mirpur Sakro, *Pakistan* 62 G2
Mirria, *Niger* 79 C6
Mirror, *Canada* 100 C6
Mîrşani, *Romania* 38 E6
Miryang, *S. Korea* 51 G15
Mirzaani, *Georgia* 43 F12
Mirzapur, *India* 63 G10
Mirzapur-cum-Vindhyachal = Mirzapur, *India* 63 G10
Misantla, *Mexico* 115 D5
Misawa, *Japan* 48 D10
Miscou I., *Canada* 99 C7
Mish'āb, Ra'as al, *Si. Arabia* 65 D6
Mishagua →, *Peru* 124 C3
Mishan, *China* 54 B8
Mishawaka, *U.S.A.* 104 E2
Mishbih, Gebel, *Egypt* 76 C3
Mishima, *Japan* 49 G9
Misilmeri, *Italy* 34 D6
Misión, *Mexico* 113 N10
Misión Fagnano, *Argentina* 128 D3
Misiones □, *Argentina* 127 B5
Misiones □, *Paraguay* 126 B4
Miskah, *Si. Arabia* 64 E4
Miskitos, Cayos, *Nic.* 116 D3
Miskolc, *Hungary* 21 G10
Misoke, *Zaïre* 82 C2
Misool, *Indonesia* 57 E8
Misrātah, *Libya* 73 B8
Missanabie, *Canada* 98 C3
Missão Velha, *Brazil* 122 C4
Missinaibi →, *Canada* 98 B3
Missinaibi L., *Canada* 98 C3
Mission, *S. Dak., U.S.A.* 108 D4
Mission, *Tex., U.S.A.* 109 M5
Mission City, *Canada* 100 D4
Mission Viejo, *U.S.A.* 113 M9
Missisa L., *Canada* 98 B2
Mississagi →, *Canada* 98 C3
Mississippi □, *U.S.A.* 109 J10
Mississippi →, *U.S.A.* 109 L10
Mississippi L., *Canada* 107 A8
Mississippi River Delta, *U.S.A.* 109 L9
Mississippi Sd., *U.S.A.* 109 K10
Missoula, *U.S.A.* 110 C6
Missour, *Morocco* 74 B4
Missouri □, *U.S.A.* 108 F8
Missouri →, *U.S.A.* 108 F9
Missouri Valley, *U.S.A.* 108 E7
Mist, *U.S.A.* 112 E3
Mistake B., *Canada* 101 A10
Mistassini →, *Canada* 99 C5
Mistassini L., *Canada* 98 B5
Mistastin L., *Canada* 99 A7
Mistatim, *Canada* 101 C8
Mistelbach, *Austria* 20 G6
Misterbianco, *Italy* 35 E8
Mistretta, *Italy* 35 E7
Misty L., *Canada* 101 B8
Misurata = Misrātah, *Libya* 73 B8
Mît Ghamr, *Egypt* 76 H7
Mitatib, *Sudan* 77 D4
Mitchell, *Australia* 91 D4
Mitchell, *Canada* 106 C3
Mitchell, *Ind., U.S.A.* 104 F2
Mitchell, *Nebr., U.S.A.* 108 E3
Mitchell, *Oreg., U.S.A.* 110 D3
Mitchell, *S. Dak., U.S.A.* 108 D5
Mitchell →, *Australia* 90 B3
Mitchell, Mt., *U.S.A.* 105 H4
Mitchell Ras., *Australia* 90 A2
Mitchelstown, *Ireland* 15 D3
Mitha Tiwana, *Pakistan* 62 C5
Mitilíni, *Greece* 39 K9
Mito, *Japan* 49 F10
Mitsinjo, *Madag.* 85 B8
Mitsiwa, *Eritrea* 77 D4
Mitsiwa Channel, *Eritrea* 77 D5
Mitsukaidō, *Japan* 49 F9
Mittagong, *Australia* 91 E5
Mittelland, *Switz.* 22 C4
Mittelland Kanal, *Germany* 18 C3
Mittenwalde, *Germany* 18 C9
Mitterteich, *Germany* 19 F8
Mittweida, *Germany* 18 E8
Mitú, *Colombia* 120 C3
Mituas, *Colombia* 120 C4
Mitumba, *Tanzania* 82 D3
Mitumba, Chaîne des, *Zaïre* 82 D2
Mitumba Mts. = Mitumba, Chaîne des, *Zaïre* 82 D2
Mitwaba, *Zaïre* 83 D2
Mityana, *Uganda* 82 B3
Mitzic, *Gabon* 80 D2
Mixteco →, *Mexico* 115 D5
Miyagi □, *Japan* 48 E10
Miyâh, W. el →, *Egypt* 76 B3
Miyah, W. el →, *Syria* 64 C3
Miyake-Jima, *Japan* 49 G9
Miyako, *Japan* 48 E10
Miyako-Jima, *Japan* 49 M2
Miyako-Rettō, *Japan* 49 M2
Miyakonojō, *Japan* 49 J5
Miyanoura-Dake, *Japan* 49 J5
Miyazaki, *Japan* 49 J5
Miyazaki □, *Japan* 49 H5
Miyazu, *Japan* 49 G7
Miyet, Bahr el = Dead Sea, *Asia* 69 D4
Miyi, *China* 52 D4
Miyoshi, *Japan* 49 G6
Miyun, *China* 50 D9
Miyun Shuiku, *China* 51 D9
Mizamis = Ozamiz, *Phil.* 55 G5
Mizdah, *Libya* 75 B7
Mizen Hd., *Cork, Ireland* 15 E2
Mizen Hd., *Wick., Ireland* 15 D5
Mizhi, *China* 50 F6
Mizil, *Romania* 38 E9
Mizoram □, *India* 61 H18
Mizpe Ramon, *Israel* 69 E3
Mizusawa, *Japan* 48 E10
Mjöbäck, *Sweden* 11 G6
Mjölby, *Sweden* 11 F9
Mjörn, *Sweden* 11 G6
Mjøsa, *Norway* 10 D5
Mkata, *Tanzania* 82 D4
Mkokotoni, *Tanzania* 82 D4
Mkomazi, *Tanzania* 82 C4
Mkomazi →, *S. Africa* 85 E5
Mkulwe, *Tanzania* 83 D3
Mkumbi, Ras, *Tanzania* 82 D4
Mkushi, *Zambia* 83 E2
Mkushi River, *Zambia* 83 E2
Mkuze, *S. Africa* 85 D5
Mkuze →, *S. Africa* 85 D5
Mladá Boleslav, *Czech.* 20 E4
Mladenovac, *Serbia* 21 L10
Mlala Hills, *Tanzania* 82 D3
Mlange, *Malawi* 83 F4
Mlava →, *Serbia* 21 L11
Mława, *Poland* 20 B10
Mlinište, *Bos.-H.* 33 D13
Mljet, *Croatia* 21 N7
Młynąry, *Poland* 20 A9
Mmabatho, *S. Africa* 84 D4
Mme, *Cameroon* 79 D7
Mo i Rana, *Norway* 8 C13
Moa, *Indonesia* 57 F7
Moa →, *S. Leone* 78 D2
Moab, *U.S.A.* 111 G9
Moabi, *Gabon* 80 E2
Moaco →, *Brazil* 124 B4
Moala, *Fiji* 87 D8
Moalie Park, *Australia* 91 D3
Moaña, *Spain* 30 C2
Moba, *Zaïre* 82 D2
Mobārakābād, *Iran* 65 D7
Mobārakīyeh, *Iran* 65 C6
Mobaye, *C.A.R.* 80 D4
Mobayi, *Zaïre* 80 D4
Moberly, *U.S.A.* 108 F8
Moberly →, *Canada* 100 B4
Mobile, *U.S.A.* 105 K1
Mobile B., *U.S.A.* 105 K2
Mobridge, *U.S.A.* 108 C4
Mobutu Sese Seko, L., *Africa* 82 B3
Moc Chau, *Vietnam* 58 B5
Moc Hoa, *Vietnam* 59 G5
Mocabe Kasari, *Zaïre* 83 D2
Mocajuba, *Brazil* 122 B2
Moçambique, *Mozam.* 83 F5
Moçâmedes = Namibe, *Angola* 81 H2
Mocapra →, *Venezuela* 120 B4
Mocha, I., *Chile* 128 A2
Mochudi, *Botswana* 84 C4
Mocimboa da Praia, *Mozam.* 83 E5
Moclips, *U.S.A.* 112 C2
Mocoa, *Colombia* 120 C2
Mococa, *Brazil* 127 A6
Mocorito, *Mexico* 114 B3
Moctezuma, *Mexico* 114 B3
Moctezuma →, *Mexico* 115 C5
Mocuba, *Mozam.* 83 F4
Mocúzari, Presa, *Mexico* 114 B3
Modane, *France* 27 C10
Modasa, *India* 62 H5
Modave, *Belgium* 17 H6
Modder →, *S. Africa* 84 D3
Modderrivier, *S. Africa* 84 D3
Módena, *Italy* 32 D7
Modena, *U.S.A.* 111 H7
Modesto, *U.S.A.* 111 H3
Módica, *Italy* 35 F7
Modigliana, *Italy* 33 D8
Modo, *Sudan* 77 F3
Modra, *Slovak Rep.* 21 G7
Moe, *Australia* 91 F4
Moebase, *Mozam.* 83 F4
Moëlan-sur-Mer, *France* 24 E3
Moengo, *Surinam* 121 B7
Moergestel, *Neths.* 17 E6
Moers, *Germany* 17 F9
Moësa →, *Switz.* 23 D8
Moffat, *U.K.* 14 F5
Moga, *India* 62 D6
Mogadishu = Muqdisho, *Somali Rep.* 68 G4
Mogador = Essaouira, *Morocco* 74 B3
Mogadouro, *Portugal* 30 D4
Mogalakwena →, *S. Africa* 85 C4
Mogami →, *Japan* 48 E10
Mogán, *Canary Is.* 36 G4
Mogaung, *Burma* 61 G20
Møgeltønder, *Denmark* 11 K2
Mogente, *Spain* 29 G4
Mogho, *Ethiopia* 77 G5
Mogi das Cruzes, *Brazil* 127 A6
Mogi-Guaçu →, *Brazil* 127 A6
Mogi-Mirim, *Brazil* 127 A6
Mogielnica, *Poland* 20 D10
Mogilev, *Belorussia* 40 E7
Mogilev-Podolskiy, *Moldavia* 42 B2
Mogilno, *Poland* 20 C7
Mogincual, *Mozam.* 83 F5
Mogliano Véneto, *Italy* 33 C9
Mogocha, *Russia* 45 D12
Mogoi, *Indonesia* 57 E8
Mogok, *Burma* 61 H20
Moguer, *Spain* 31 H4
Mogumber, *Australia* 89 F2
Mohács, *Hungary* 21 K8
Mohales Hoek, *Lesotho* 84 E4
Mohall, *U.S.A.* 108 A4
Moḥammadābād, *Iran* 65 B8
Mohammadia, *Algeria* 75 A5
Mohammedia, *Morocco* 74 B3
Mohave, L., *U.S.A.* 113 K12
Mohawk →, *U.S.A.* 107 D11
Möhne →, *Germany* 18 D3
Moholm, *Sweden* 11 F8
Mohoro, *Tanzania* 82 D4
Moia, *Sudan* 77 F2
Moidart, L., *U.K.* 14 E3
Moineşti, *Romania* 38 C9
Mointy, *Kazakhstan* 44 E8
Moirans, *France* 27 C9
Moirans-en-Montagne, *France* 27 B9
Moíres, *Greece* 37 D6
Moisaküla, *Estonia* 40 B4
Moisie, *Canada* 99 B6
Moisie →, *Canada* 99 B6
Moissac, *France* 26 D5
Moïssala, *Chad* 73 G8
Moita, *Portugal* 31 G2
Mojácar, *Spain* 29 H3
Mojados, *Spain* 30 D6
Mojave, *U.S.A.* 113 K8
Mojave Desert, *U.S.A.* 113 L10
Mojiang, *China* 52 F3
Mojo, *Bolivia* 126 A2
Mojo, *Ethiopia* 77 F4
Mojokerto, *Indonesia* 57 G15
Mojos, Llanos de, *Bolivia* 125 D5
Moju →, *Brazil* 122 B2
Mokai, *N.Z.* 87 H5
Mokambo, *Zaïre* 83 E2
Mokameh, *India* 63 G11
Mokelumne →, *U.S.A.* 112 G5
Mokelumne Hill, *U.S.A.* 112 G6
Mokhós, *Greece* 37 D7
Mokhotlong, *Lesotho* 85 D4
Moknine, *Tunisia* 75 A7
Mokokchung, *India* 61 F19
Mokra Gora, *Serbia* 21 N10
Mokronog, *Slovenia* 33 C12
Moksha →, *Russia* 41 D12
Mokshan, *Russia* 41 E14
Mol, *Belgium* 17 F6
Mola, C. de la, *Spain* 28 F9
Mola di Bari, *Italy* 35 A10
Moláoi, *Greece* 39 N5
Molat, *Croatia* 33 D11
Molchanovo, *Russia* 44 D9
Mold, *U.K.* 12 D4
Moldavia = Moldova, *Romania* 38 C10
Moldavia ■, *Europe* 42 C3
Molde, *Norway* 8 E9
Moldova, *Romania* 38 C10
Moldova ■ = Moldavia ■, *Europe* 42 C3
Moldova Nouă, *Romania* 38 E4
Moldoveanu, *Romania* 38 D7
Molepolole, *Botswana* 84 C4
Moléson, *Switz.* 22 C4
Molfetta, *Italy* 35 A9
Molina de Aragón, *Spain* 28 E3
Moline, *U.S.A.* 108 E9
Molinella, *Italy* 33 D8
Molinos, *Argentina* 126 B2
Moliro, *Zaïre* 82 D3
Molise □, *Italy* 33 G11
Moliterno, *Italy* 35 B8
Mollahat, *Bangla.* 63 H13
Mölle, *Sweden* 11 H6
Molledo, *Spain* 30 B6
Mollendo, *Peru* 124 D3
Mollerin, L., *Australia* 89 F2
Mollerusa, *Spain* 28 D5
Mollina, *Spain* 31 H6
Mölln, *Germany* 18 B6
Mölltorp, *Sweden* 11 F8
Mölndal, *Sweden* 11 G6
Molochansk, *Ukraine* 42 C6
Molochnaya →, *Ukraine* 42 C6
Molodechno, *Belorussia* 40 D5
Molokai, *U.S.A.* 102 H16
Moloma →, *Russia* 41 B16
Molong, *Australia* 91 E4
Molopo →, *Africa* 84 D3
Mólos, *Greece* 39 L5
Molotov = Perm, *Russia* 44 D6
Moloundou, *Cameroon* 80 D3
Molsheim, *France* 25 D14
Molson L., *Canada* 101 C9
Molteno, *S. Africa* 84 E4
Molu, *Indonesia* 57 F8
Molucca Sea = Maluku Sea, *Indonesia* 57 E6
Moluccas = Maluku, *Indonesia* 57 E7
Moma, *Mozam.* 83 F4
Moma, *Zaïre* 82 C1
Mombaça, *Brazil* 122 C4
Mombasa, *Kenya* 82 C4
Mombetsu, *Japan* 48 B11
Mombuey, *Spain* 30 C4
Momchilgrad, *Bulgaria* 39 H8
Momi, *Zaïre* 82 C2
Momignies, *Belgium* 17 H4
Mompós, *Colombia* 120 B3
Møn, *Denmark* 11 K6
Mon →, *Burma* 61 J19
Mona, Canal de la, *W. Indies* 117 C6
Mona, Isla, *Puerto Rico* 117 C6
Mona, Pta., *Costa Rica* 116 E3
Mona, Pta., *Spain* 31 J7
Monach Is., *U.K.* 14 D1
Monaco ■, *Europe* 27 E11
Monadhliath Mts., *U.K.* 14 D4
Monagas □, *Venezuela* 121 B5
Monaghan, *Ireland* 15 B5
Monaghan □, *Ireland* 15 B5
Monahans, *U.S.A.* 109 K3
Monapo, *Mozam.* 83 E5
Monarch Mt., *Canada* 100 C3
Monastir = Bitola, *Macedonia* 39 H4
Monastir, *Tunisia* 75 A7
Monastyriska, *Ukraine* 40 G4
Moncada, *Phil.* 55 D4
Moncada, *Spain* 28 F4
Moncalieri, *Italy* 32 D4
Moncalvo, *Italy* 32 C5
Moncão, *Portugal* 30 C2
Moncarapacho, *Portugal* 31 H3
Moncayo, Sierra del, *Spain* 28 D3
Mönchengladbach, *Germany* 18 D2
Monchique, *Portugal* 31 H2

Moskenesøya

Monclova, *Mexico* 114 B4
Moncontour, *France* 24 D4
Moncoutant, *France* 26 B3
Moncton, *Canada* 99 C7
Mondego →, *Portugal* 30 E2
Mondego, C., *Portugal* 30 E2
Mondeodo, *Indonesia* 57 E6
Mondolfo, *Italy* 33 E10
Mondoñedo, *Spain* 30 B3
Mondoví, *Italy* 32 D4
Mondovi, *U.S.A.* 108 C9
Mondragon, *France* 27 D8
Mondragon, *Phil.* 55 E6
Mondragone, *Italy* 34 A6
Mondrain I., *Australia* 89 F3
Monduli □, *Tanzania* 82 C4
Monemvasía, *Greece* 39 N6
Monessen, *U.S.A.* 106 F5
Monesterio, *Spain* 31 G4
Monestier-de-Clermont, *France* 27 D9
Monett, *U.S.A.* 109 G8
Monfalcone, *Italy* 33 C10
Monflanquin, *France* 26 D4
Monforte, *Portugal* 31 F3
Monforte de Lemos, *Spain* 30 C3
Mong Hsu, *Burma* 61 J21
Mong Kung, *Burma* 61 J20
Mong Nai, *Burma* 61 J20
Mong Pawk, *Burma* 61 H21
Mong Ton, *Burma* 61 J21
Mong Wa, *Burma* 61 J22
Mong Yai, *Burma* 61 H21
Mongalla, *Sudan* 77 F3
Mongers, L., *Australia* 89 E2
Monghyr = Munger, *India* 63 G12
Mongo, *Chad* 73 F8
Mongolia ■, *Asia* 45 E10
Mongonu, *Nigeria* 79 C7
Mongororo, *Chad* 73 F9
Mongu, *Zambia* 81 H4
Môngua, *Angola* 84 B2
Monistrol-d'Allier, *France* 26 D7
Monistrol-sur-Loire, *France* 27 C8
Monkey Bay, *Malawi* 83 E4
Monkey River, *Belize* 115 D7
Monkira, *Australia* 90 C3
Monkoto, *Zaïre* 80 E4
Monmouth, *U.K.* 13 F5
Monmouth, *U.S.A.* 108 E9
Mono L., *U.S.A.* 111 H4
Monolith, *U.S.A.* 113 K8
Monólithos, *Greece* 37 C9
Monongahela, *U.S.A.* 106 F5
Monópoli, *Italy* 35 B10
Monor, *Hungary* 21 H9
Monóvar, *Spain* 29 G4
Monqoumba, *C.A.R.* 80 D3
Monreal del Campo, *Spain* 28 E3
Monreale, *Italy* 34 D6
Monroe, *Ga., U.S.A.* 105 J4
Monroe, *La., U.S.A.* 109 J8
Monroe, *Mich., U.S.A.* 104 E4
Monroe, *N.C., U.S.A.* 105 H5
Monroe, *N.Y., U.S.A.* 107 E10
Monroe, *Utah, U.S.A.* 111 G7
Monroe, *Wash., U.S.A.* 112 C5
Monroe, *Wis., U.S.A.* 108 D10
Monroe City, *U.S.A.* 108 F9
Monroeville, *Ala., U.S.A.* 105 K2
Monroeville, *Pa., U.S.A.* 106 F5
Monrovia, *Liberia* 78 D2
Monrovia, *U.S.A.* 111 J4
Mons, *Belgium* 17 H3
Monsaraz, *Portugal* 31 G3
Monse, *Indonesia* 57 E6
Monsefú, *Peru* 124 B2
Monségur, *France* 26 D4
Monsélice, *Italy* 33 C8
Monster, *Neths.* 16 D4
Mont Cenis, Col du, *France* 27 C10
Mont-de-Marsan, *France* 26 E3
Mont-Joli, *Canada* 99 C6
Mont-Laurier, *Canada* 98 C4
Mont-St.-Michel, Le = Le Mont-St.-Michel, *France* 24 D5
Mont-sous-Vaudrey, *France* 25 F12
Mont-sur-Marchienne, *Belgium* 17 H4
Mont Tremblant Prov. Park, *Canada* 98 C5
Montabaur, *Germany* 18 E3
Montagnac, *France* 26 E7
Montagnana, *Italy* 33 C8
Montagu, *S. Africa* 84 E3
Montagu I., *Antarctica* 5 B1
Montague, *Canada* 99 C7
Montague, *U.S.A.* 110 F2
Montague, I., *Mexico* 114 A2
Montague Ra., *Australia* 89 E2
Montague Sd., *Australia* 88 B4
Montaigu, *France* 24 F5
Montalbán, *Spain* 28 E4
Montalbano di Elicona, *Italy* 35 D8
Montalbano Iónico, *Italy* 35 B9
Montalbo, *Spain* 28 F2
Montalcino, *Italy* 33 E8
Montalegre, *Portugal* 30 D3
Montalto di Castro, *Italy* 33 F8
Montalto Uffugo, *Italy* 35 C9
Montalvo, *U.S.A.* 113 L7
Montamarta, *Spain* 30 D5
Montaña, *Peru* 124 B3
Montana, *Switz.* 22 D4
Montana □, *U.S.A.* 110 C9
Montaña Clara, I., *Canary Is.* 36 E6
Montánchez, *Spain* 31 F4
Montañita, *Colombia* 120 C2
Montargis, *France* 25 E9
Montauban, *France* 26 D5
Montauk, *U.S.A.* 107 E13
Montauk Pt., *U.S.A.* 107 E13
Montbard, *France* 25 E11
Montbéliard, *France* 25 E13
Montblanch, *Spain* 28 D6
Montbrison, *France* 27 C8
Montcalm, Pic de, *France* 26 F5
Montceau-les-Mines, *France* 25 F11
Montchanin, *France* 27 B8
Montclair, *U.S.A.* 107 F10
Montcornet, *France* 25 C11
Montcuq, *France* 26 D5
Montdidier, *France* 25 C9
Monte Albán, *Mexico* 115 D5
Monte Alegre, *Brazil* 121 D7
Monte Alegre de Goiás, *Brazil* 123 D2
Monte Alegre de Minas, *Brazil* 123 E2
Monte Azul, *Brazil* 123 E3
Monte Bello Is., *Australia* 88 D2
Monte-Carlo, *Monaco* 27 E11
Monte Carmelo, *Brazil* 123 E2
Monte Caseros, *Argentina* 126 C4
Monte Comán, *Argentina* 126 C2
Monte Cristi, *Dom. Rep.* 117 C5
Monte Dinero, *Argentina* 128 D3
Monte Lindo →, *Paraguay* 126 A4
Monte Quemado, *Argentina* 126 B3
Monte Redondo, *Portugal* 30 F2
Monte Rio, *U.S.A.* 112 G4
Monte San Giovanni, *Italy* 34 A6
Monte San Savino, *Italy* 33 E8
Monte Sant' Ángelo, *Italy* 35 A8
Monte Santu, C. di, *Italy* 34 B2
Monte Vista, *U.S.A.* 111 H10
Monteagudo, *Argentina* 127 B5
Monteagudo, *Bolivia* 125 D5
Montealegre, *Spain* 29 G3
Montebello, *Canada* 98 C5
Montebelluna, *Italy* 33 C9
Montebourg, *France* 24 C5
Montecastrilli, *Italy* 33 F9
Montecatini Terme, *Italy* 32 E7
Montecito, *U.S.A.* 113 L7
Montecristi, *Ecuador* 120 D1
Montecristo, *Italy* 32 F7
Montefalco, *Italy* 33 F9
Montefiascone, *Italy* 33 F9
Montefrío, *Spain* 31 H6
Montegnée, *Belgium* 17 G7
Montego Bay, *Jamaica* 116 C4
Montegranaro, *Italy* 33 E10
Monteiro, *Brazil* 122 C4
Montejicar, *Spain* 29 H1
Montejinnie, *Australia* 88 C5
Montelíbano, *Colombia* 120 B2
Montélimar, *France* 27 D8
Montella, *Italy* 35 B8
Montellano, *Spain* 31 J5
Montello, *U.S.A.* 108 D10
Montelupo Fiorentino, *Italy* 32 E8
Montemor-o-Novo, *Portugal* 31 G2
Montemor-o-Velho, *Portugal* 30 E2
Montemorelos, *Mexico* 115 B5
Montendre, *France* 26 C3
Montenegro, *Brazil* 127 B5
Montenegro □, *Montenegro* 21 N9
Montenero di Bisaccia, *Italy* 33 G11
Montepuez, *Mozam.* 83 E4
Montepuez →, *Mozam.* 83 E5
Montepulciano, *Italy* 33 E8
Montereale, *Italy* 33 F10
Montereau-Fault-Yonne, *France* 25 D9
Monterey, *U.S.A.* 111 H3
Monterey B., *U.S.A.* 112 J5
Montería, *Colombia* 120 B2
Montero, *Bolivia* 125 D5
Monteros, *Argentina* 126 B2
Monterotondo, *Italy* 33 F9
Monterrey, *Mexico* 114 B4
Montes Altos, *Brazil* 122 C2
Montes Claros, *Brazil* 123 E3
Montesano, *U.S.A.* 112 D3
Montesárchio, *Italy* 35 A7
Montescaglioso, *Italy* 35 B9
Montesilvano, *Italy* 33 F11
Montevarchi, *Italy* 33 E8
Montevideo, *Uruguay* 127 C4
Montevideo, *U.S.A.* 108 C7
Montezuma, *U.S.A.* 108 E8
Montfaucon, *France* 25 C12
Montfaucon-en-Velay, *France* 27 C8
Montfort, *France* 24 D5
Montfort, *Neths.* 17 F7
Montfort-l'Amaury, *France* 25 D8
Montgenèvre, *France* 27 D10
Montgomery = Sahiwal, *Pakistan* 62 D5
Montgomery, *U.K.* 13 E4
Montgomery, *Ala., U.S.A.* 105 J2
Montgomery, *W. Va., U.S.A.* 104 F5
Montguyon, *France* 26 C3
Monthey, *Switz.* 22 D3
Monticelli d'Ongina, *Italy* 32 C6
Monticello, *Ark., U.S.A.* 109 J9
Monticello, *Fla., U.S.A.* 105 K4
Monticello, *Ind., U.S.A.* 104 E2
Monticello, *Iowa, U.S.A.* 108 D9
Monticello, *Ky., U.S.A.* 105 G3
Monticello, *Minn., U.S.A.* 108 C8
Monticello, *Miss., U.S.A.* 109 K9
Monticello, *N.Y., U.S.A.* 107 E10
Monticello, *Utah, U.S.A.* 111 H9
Montichiari, *Italy* 32 C7
Montier-en-Der, *France* 25 D11
Montignac, *France* 26 C5
Montignies-sur-Sambre, *Belgium* 17 H4
Montigny, *France* 25 C13
Montigny-sur-Aube, *France* 25 E11
Montijo, *Spain* 31 G4
Montijo, Presa de, *Spain* 31 G4
Montilla, *Spain* 31 H6
Montlhéry, *France* 25 D9
Montluçon, *France* 26 B6
Montmagny, *Canada* 99 C5
Montmarault, *France* 26 B6
Montmartre, *Canada* 101 C8
Montmédy, *France* 25 C12
Montmélian, *France* 27 C10
Montmirail, *France* 25 D10
Montmoreau-St.-Cybard, *France* 26 C4
Montmorency, *Canada* 99 C5
Montmorillon, *France* 26 B4
Montmort, *France* 25 D10
Monto, *Australia* 90 C5
Montoir-sur-le-Loir, *France* 24 E7
Montório al Vomano, *Italy* 33 F10
Montoro, *Spain* 31 G6
Montour Falls, *U.S.A.* 106 D8
Montpelier, *Idaho, U.S.A.* 110 E8
Montpelier, *Ohio, U.S.A.* 104 E3
Montpelier, *Vt., U.S.A.* 107 B12
Montpellier, *France* 26 E7
Montpezat-de-Quercy, *France* 26 D5
Montpon-Ménestérol, *France* 26 D4
Montréal, *Canada* 98 C5
Montréal, *France* 26 E6
Montreal L., *Canada* 101 C7
Montreal Lake, *Canada* 101 C7
Montredon-Labessonnié, *France* 26 E6
Montréjeau, *France* 26 E4
Montrésor, *France* 24 E8
Montreuil, *France* 25 B8
Montreuil-Bellay, *France* 24 E6
Montreux, *Switz.* 22 D3
Montrevault, *France* 24 E5
Montrevel-en-Bresse, *France* 27 B9
Montrichard, *France* 24 E8
Montrose, *U.K.* 14 E6
Montrose, *Colo., U.S.A.* 111 G10
Montrose, *Pa., U.S.A.* 107 E9
Monts, Pte. des, *Canada* 99 C6
Monts-sur-Guesnes, *France* 24 F7
Montsalvy, *France* 26 D6
Montsant, Sierra de, *Spain* 28 D5
Montsauche, *France* 25 E11
Montsech, Sierra del, *Spain* 28 C5
Montseny, *Spain* 28 D2
Montserrat, *Spain* 28 D6
Montserrat ■, *W. Indies* 117 C7
Montuenga, *Spain* 30 D6
Montuiri, *Spain* 36 B9
Monveda, *Zaïre* 80 D4
Monywa, *Burma* 61 H19
Monza, *Italy* 32 C6
Monze, *Zambia* 83 F2
Monze, C., *Pakistan* 62 G2
Monzón, *Spain* 28 D5
Mooi River, *S. Africa* 85 D4
Mook, *Neths.* 16 E7
Moolawatana, *Australia* 91 D2
Mooliabeenee, *Australia* 89 F2
Mooloogool, *Australia* 89 E2
Moomin Cr. →, *Australia* 91 D4
Moonah →, *Australia* 90 C2
Moonbeam, *Canada* 98 C3
Moonda, L., *Australia* 90 D3
Moonie, *Australia* 91 D5
Moonie →, *Australia* 91 D4
Moonta, *Australia* 91 E2
Moora, *Australia* 89 F2
Mooraberree, *Australia* 90 D3
Moorarie, *Australia* 89 E2
Moorcroft, *U.S.A.* 108 C2
Moore →, *Australia* 89 F2
Moore, L., *Australia* 89 E2
Moore Reefs, *Australia* 90 B4
Moorefield, *U.S.A.* 104 F6
Moores Res., *U.S.A.* 107 B13
Mooresville, *U.S.A.* 105 H5
Moorfoot Hills, *U.K.* 14 F5
Moorhead, *U.S.A.* 108 B6
Mooroopna, *Australia* 91 F4
Moorpark, *U.S.A.* 113 L8
Moorreesburg, *S. Africa* 84 E2
Moorslede, *Belgium* 17 G2
Moosburg, *Germany* 19 G7
Moose →, *Canada* 98 B3
Moose Factory, *Canada* 98 B3
Moose I., *Canada* 101 C9
Moose Jaw, *Canada* 101 C7
Moose Jaw →, *Canada* 101 C7
Moose Lake, *Canada* 101 C8
Moose Lake, *U.S.A.* 108 B8
Moose Mountain Cr. →, *Canada* 101 D8
Moose Mountain Prov. Park, *Canada* 101 D8
Moose River, *Canada* 98 B3
Moosehead L., *U.S.A.* 99 C6
Moosomin, *Canada* 101 C8
Moosonee, *Canada* 98 B3
Moosup, *U.S.A.* 107 E13
Mopeia Velha, *Mozam.* 83 F4
Mopipi, *Botswana* 84 C3
Mopoi, *C.A.R.* 82 A2
Mopti, *Mali* 78 C4
Moqatta, *Sudan* 77 E4
Moquegua, *Peru* 124 D3
Moquegua □, *Peru* 124 D3
Mór, *Hungary* 21 H8
Móra, *Portugal* 31 G2
Mora, *Sweden* 9 F13
Mora, *Minn., U.S.A.* 108 C8
Mora, *N. Mex., U.S.A.* 111 J11
Mora de Ebro, *Spain* 28 D5
Mora de Rubielos, *Spain* 28 E4
Mora la Nueva, *Spain* 28 D5
Morača →, *Montenegro* 21 N9
Morada Nova, *Brazil* 122 C4
Morada Nova de Minas, *Brazil* 123 E2
Moradabad, *India* 63 E8
Morafenobe, *Madag.* 85 B7
Morąg, *Poland* 20 B9
Moral de Calatrava, *Spain* 29 G1
Moraleja, *Spain* 30 E4
Morales, *Colombia* 120 C2
Moramanga, *Madag.* 85 B8
Moran, *Kans., U.S.A.* 109 G7
Moran, *Wyo., U.S.A.* 110 E8
Moranbah, *Australia* 90 C4
Morano Cálabro, *Italy* 35 C9
Morant Cays, *Jamaica* 116 C4
Morant Pt., *Jamaica* 116 C4
Morar, L., *U.K.* 14 E3
Moratalla, *Spain* 29 G3
Moratuwa, *Sri Lanka* 60 R11
Morava →, *Europe* 20 G6
Moravia, *U.S.A.* 108 E8
Moravian Hts. = Ceskomoravská Vrchovina, *Czech.* 20 F5
Moravica →, *Serbia* 21 M10
Moravice →, *Czech.* 20 F7
Moraviţa, *Romania* 21 K11
Moravská Třebová, *Czech.* 20 F6
Morawa, *Australia* 89 E2
Morawhanna, *Guyana* 121 B6
Moray Firth, *U.K.* 14 D5
Morbach, *Germany* 19 F3
Morbegno, *Italy* 32 B6
Morbi, *India* 62 H4
Morbihan □, *France* 24 E4
Morcenx, *France* 26 D3
Mordelles, *France* 24 D5
Morden, *Canada* 101 D9
Mordovian Republic □, *Russia* 41 D14
Mordovo, *Russia* 41 E12
Mordvinia = Mordovian Republic □, *Russia* 41 D14
Møre og Romsdal fylke □, *Norway* 10 B2
Morea, *Australia* 91 F3
Morea, *Greece* 6 H10
Moreau →, *U.S.A.* 108 C4
Morecambe, *U.K.* 12 C5
Morecambe B., *U.K.* 12 C5
Moree, *Australia* 91 D4
Morehead, *U.S.A.* 104 F4
Morehead City, *U.S.A.* 105 H7
Morelia, *Mexico* 114 D4
Morella, *Australia* 90 C3
Morella, *Spain* 28 E4
Morelos, *Mexico* 114 B3
Morelos □, *Mexico* 115 D5
Morena, Sierra, *Spain* 31 G7
Morenci, *U.S.A.* 111 K9
Moreni, *Romania* 38 E8
Morero, *Bolivia* 125 C4
Moreru →, *Brazil* 125 C6
Moresby I., *Canada* 100 C2
Morestel, *France* 27 C9
Moret-sur-Loing, *France* 25 D9
Moreton, *Australia* 90 A3
Moreton I., *Australia* 91 D5
Moreuil, *France* 25 C9
Morey, *Spain* 36 B10
Morez, *France* 27 B10
Morgan, *Australia* 91 E2
Morgan, *U.S.A.* 110 F8
Morgan City, *U.S.A.* 109 L9
Morgan Hill, *U.S.A.* 112 H5
Morganfield, *U.S.A.* 104 G2
Morganton, *U.S.A.* 105 H5
Morgantown, *U.S.A.* 104 F6
Morgat, *France* 24 D2
Morgenzon, *S. Africa* 85 D4
Morges, *Switz.* 22 C2
Morghak, *Iran* 65 D8
Morhange, *France* 25 D13
Mori, *Italy* 32 C7
Morialmée, *Belgium* 17 H5
Morice L., *Canada* 100 C3
Morichal, *Colombia* 120 C3
Morichal Largo →, *Venezuela* 121 B5
Moriki, *Nigeria* 79 C6
Morinville, *Canada* 100 C6
Morioka, *Japan* 48 E10
Moris, *Mexico* 114 B3
Morlaàs, *France* 26 E3
Morlaix, *France* 24 D3
Morlanwelz, *Belgium* 17 H4
Mormanno, *Italy* 35 C8
Mormant, *France* 25 D9
Mornington, *Vic., Australia* 91 F4
Mornington, *W. Austral., Australia* 88 C4
Mornington, I., *Chile* 128 C1
Mornington I., *Australia* 90 B2
Mórnos →, *Greece* 39 L4
Moro, *Sudan* 77 E3
Moro G., *Phil.* 55 H5
Morocco ■, *N. Afr.* 74 B3
Morococha, *Peru* 124 C2
Morogoro, *Tanzania* 82 D4
Morogoro □, *Tanzania* 82 D4
Moroleón, *Mexico* 114 C4
Morombe, *Madag.* 85 C7
Moron, *Argentina* 126 C4
Morón, *Cuba* 116 B4
Mörön →, *Mongolia* 54 B6
Morón de Almazán, *Spain* 28 D2
Morón de la Frontera, *Spain* 31 H5
Morona →, *Peru* 120 D2
Morona-Santiago □, *Ecuador* 120 D2
Morondava, *Madag.* 85 C7
Morondo, *Ivory C.* 78 D3
Morongo Valley, *U.S.A.* 113 L10
Moronou, *Ivory C.* 78 D4
Morotai, *Indonesia* 57 D7
Moroto, *Uganda* 82 B3
Moroto Summit, *Kenya* 82 B3
Morozovsk, *Russia* 43 B9
Morpeth, *U.K.* 12 B6
Morphou, *Cyprus* 37 D11
Morphou Bay, *Cyprus* 37 D11
Morrilton, *U.S.A.* 109 H8
Morrinhos, *Ceara, Brazil* 122 B3
Morrinhos, *Minas Gerais, Brazil* 123 E2
Morrinsville, *N.Z.* 87 G5
Morris, *Canada* 101 D9
Morris, *Ill., U.S.A.* 104 E1
Morris, *Minn., U.S.A.* 108 C7
Morris, Mt., *Australia* 89 E5
Morrisburg, *Canada* 98 D4
Morrison, *U.S.A.* 108 E10
Morristown, *Ariz., U.S.A.* 111 K7
Morristown, *N.J., U.S.A.* 107 F10
Morristown, *S. Dak., U.S.A.* 108 C4
Morristown, *Tenn., U.S.A.* 105 G4
Morro, Pta., *Chile* 126 B1
Morro Bay, *U.S.A.* 111 J3
Morro del Jable, *Canary Is.* 36 F5
Morro do Chapéu, *Brazil* 123 D3
Morro Jable, Pta. de, *Canary Is.* 36 F5
Morros, *Brazil* 122 B3
Morrosquillo, G. de, *Colombia* 116 E4
Morrumbene, *Mozam.* 85 C6
Mors, *Denmark* 11 H2
Morshansk, *Russia* 41 E12
Mörsil, *Sweden* 10 A7
Mortagne →, *France* 25 D13
Mortagne-au-Perche, *France* 24 D7
Mortagne-sur-Gironde, *France* 26 C3
Mortagne-sur-Sèvre, *France* 24 F6
Mortain, *France* 24 D6
Mortara, *Italy* 32 C5
Morteau, *France* 25 E13
Morteros, *Argentina* 126 C3
Mortes, R. das →, *Brazil* 123 D1
Mortlake, *Australia* 91 F3
Morton, *Tex., U.S.A.* 109 J3
Morton, *Wash., U.S.A.* 112 D4
Mortsel, *Belgium* 17 F4
Morundah, *Australia* 91 E4
Moruya, *Australia* 91 F5
Morvan, *France* 25 E11
Morven, *Australia* 91 D4
Morvern, *U.K.* 14 E3
Morwell, *Australia* 91 F4
Mosalsk, *Russia* 40 D9
Mosbach, *Germany* 19 F5
Mošćenice, *Croatia* 33 C11
Mosciano Sant' Ángelo, *Italy* 33 F10
Moscos Is., *Burma* 58 E1
Moscow = Moskva, *Russia* 41 D10
Moscow, *U.S.A.* 110 C5
Mosel →, *Europe* 19 E3
Moselle = Mosel →, *Europe* 19 E3
Moselle □, *France* 25 D13
Moses Lake, *U.S.A.* 110 C4
Mosgiel, *N.Z.* 87 L3
Moshi, *Tanzania* 82 C4
Moshi □, *Tanzania* 82 C4
Moshupa, *Botswana* 84 C4
Mosjøen, *Norway* 8 D12
Moskenesøya, *Norway* 8 C12

Moskenstraumen, *Norway*　8　C12
Moskva, *Russia* ....　41　D10
Moskva →, *Russia* ......　41　D11
Moslavačka Gora, *Croatia*　33　C13
Mosomane, *Botswana* ....　84　C4
Mosonmagyaróvár,
　Hungary ....　21　H7
Mospino, *Ukraine* ....　42　C7
Mosquera, *Colombia* ....　120　C2
Mosquero, *U.S.A.* ......　109　H3
Mosqueruela, *Spain* ....　28　E4
Mosquitia, *Honduras* ...　116　C3
Mosquitos, G. de los,
　Panama ....　116　E3
Moss, *Norway* ....　10　E4
Moss Vale, *Australia* ....　91　E5
Mossaka, *Congo* ....　80　E3
Mossâmedes, *Brazil* ....　123　E1
Mossbank, *Canada* ....　101　D7
Mossburn, *N.Z.* ....　87　L2
Mosselbaai, *S. Africa* ...　84　E3
Mossendjo, *Congo* .....　80　E2
Mosses, Col des, *Switz.* ...　22　D4
Mossgiel, *Australia* ....　91　E3
Mossman, *Australia* ...　90　B4
Mossoró, *Brazil* ......　122　C4
Mossuril, *Mozam.* ....　83　E5
Mossy →, *Canada* .....　101　C8
Most, *Czech.* ....　20　E3
Mosta, *Malta* ....　37　D1
Moṣṭafáábād, *Iran* ....　65　C7
Mostaganem, *Algeria* ....　75　A5
Mostar, *Bos.-H.* ......　21　M7
Mostardas, *Brazil* ....　127　C5
Mostefa, Rass, *Tunisia* ...　75　A7
Mostiska, *Ukraine* .....　40　G3
Móstoles, *Spain* ....　30　E7
Mosty, *Belorussia* ......　40　E4
Mosul = Al Mawṣil, *Iraq* ..　64　B4
Mosulpo, *S. Korea* .....　51　H14
Mota del Cuervo, *Spain* ..　28　F2
Mota del Marqués, *Spain* ..　30　D5
Motagua →, *Guatemala* .　116　C2
Motala, *Sweden* ......　11　F9
Motherwell, *U.K.* .....　14　F5
Motihari, *India* ....　63　F11
Motilla del Palancar, *Spain*　28　F3
Motnik, *Slovenia* ......　33　B11
Motocurunya, *Venezuela* .　121　C5
Motovun, *Croatia* .....　33　C10
Motozintla de Mendoza,
　Mexico ....　115　D6
Motril, *Spain* ....　29　J1
Motru →, *Romania* ...　38　E6
Mott, *U.S.A.* ....　108　B3
Móttola, *Italy* ....　35　B10
Motueka, *N.Z.* ....　87　J4
Motueka →, *N.Z.* .....　87　J4
Motul, *Mexico* ....　115　C7
Mouanda, *Gabon* .....　80　E2
Mouchalagane →, *Canada*　99　B6
Mouding, *China* ....　52　E3
Moudjeria, *Mauritania* ...　78　B2
Moudon, *Switz.* ....　22　C3
Mouila, *Gabon* ....　80　E2
Moulamein, *Australia* ..　91　F3
Moulianá, *Greece* .....　37　D7
Moulins, *France* ......　26　B7
Moulmein, *Burma* ....　61　L20
Moulouya, O. →, *Morocco*　75　A4
Moulton, *U.S.A.* .....　109　L6
Moultrie, *U.S.A.* .....　105　K4
Moultrie, L., *U.S.A.* ...　105　J5
Mound City, *Mo., U.S.A.*　108　E7
Mound City, *S. Dak.,*
　U.S.A. ....　108　C4
Moúnda, Ákra, *Greece* ..　39　L3
Moundou, *Chad* ......　73　G8
Moundsville, *U.S.A.* ...　106　G4
Moung, *Cambodia* .....　58　F4
Mount Airy, *U.S.A.* ...　105　G5
Mount Albert, *Canada* ..　106　B5
Mount Amherst, *Australia*　88　C4
Mount Angel, *U.S.A.* ..　110　D2
Mount Augustus, *Australia*　88　D2
Mount Barker, *S. Austral.,*
　Australia ....　91　F2
Mount Barker, *W. Austral.,*
　Australia ....　89　F2
Mount Carmel, *U.S.A.* ..　104　F2
Mount Clemens, *U.S.A.* ..　98　D3
Mount Coolon, *Australia* .　90　C4
Mount Darwin, *Zimbabwe*　83　F3
Mount Desert I., *U.S.A.* .　99　D6
Mount Dora, *U.S.A.* ...　105　L5
Mount Douglas, *Australia* .　90　C4
Mount Eba, *Australia* ..　91　E2
Mount Edgecumbe, *U.S.A.*　100　B1
Mount Elizabeth, *Australia*　88　C4
Mount Fletcher, *S. Africa* .　85　E4
Mount Forest, *Canada* ..　98　D3
Mount Gambier, *Australia*　91　F3
Mount Garnet, *Australia* .　90　B4
Mount Hope, *N.S.W.,*
　Australia ....　91　E4
Mount Hope, *S. Austral.,*
　Australia ....　91　E2
Mount Hope, *U.S.A.* ...　104　G5
Mount Horeb, *U.S.A.* ..　108　D10
Mount Howitt, *Australia* .　91　D3
Mount Isa, *Australia* ...　90　C2
Mount Keith, *Australia* ..　89　E3
Mount Laguna, *U.S.A.* ..　113　N10
Mount Larcom, *Australia* .　90　C5
Mount Lofty Ra., *Australia*　91　E2

Mount McKinley National
　Park, *U.S.A.* ....　96　B5
Mount Magnet, *Australia* .　89　E2
Mount Margaret, *Australia*　91　D3
Mount Maunganui, *N.Z.* .　87　G6
Mount Molloy, *Australia* ..　90　B4
Mount Monger, *Australia* .　89　F3
Mount Morgan, *Australia* .　90　C5
Mount Morris, *U.S.A.* ....　106　D7
Mount Mulligan, *Australia*　90　B3
Mount Narryer, *Australia* .　89　E2
Mount Olympus = Uludağ,
　Turkey ....　66　C3
Mount Oxide Mine,
　Australia ....　90　B2
Mount Pearl, *Canada* ....　99　C9
Mount Perry, *Australia* ..　91　D5
Mount Phillips, *Australia* .　88　D2
Mount Pleasant, *Iowa,*
　U.S.A. ....　108　E9
Mount Pleasant, *Mich.,*
　U.S.A. ....　104　D3
Mount Pleasant, *Pa.,*
　U.S.A. ....　106　F5
Mount Pleasant, *S.C.,*
　U.S.A. ....　105　J6
Mount Pleasant, *Tenn.,*
　U.S.A. ....　105　H2
Mount Pleasant, *Tex.,*
　U.S.A. ....　109　J7
Mount Pleasant, *Utah,*
　U.S.A. ....　110　G8
Mount Pocono, *U.S.A.* ...　107　E9
Mount Rainier National
　Park, *U.S.A.* ....　112　D5
Mount Revelstoke Nat.
　Park, *Canada* ....　100　C5
Mount Robson Prov. Park,
　Canada ....　100　C5
Mount Sandiman, *Australia*　89　D2
Mount Shasta, *U.S.A.* ...　110　F2
Mount Signal, *U.S.A.* ...　113　N11
Mount Sterling, *Ill., U.S.A.*　108　F9
Mount Sterling, *Ky.,*
　U.S.A. ....　104　F4
Mount Surprise, *Australia* .　90　B3
Mount Union, *U.S.A.* ...　106　F7
Mount Vernon, *Australia* .　88　D2
Mount Vernon, *Ind.,*
　U.S.A. ....　108　F10
Mount Vernon, *N.Y.,*
　U.S.A. ....　107　F11
Mount Vernon, *Ohio,*
　U.S.A. ....　106　F2
Mount Vernon, *Wash.,*
　U.S.A. ....　112　B4
Mountain Center, *U.S.A.* .　113　M10
Mountain City, *Nev.,*
　U.S.A. ....　110　F6
Mountain City, *Tenn.,*
　U.S.A. ....　105　G5
Mountain Grove, *U.S.A.* .　109　G8
Mountain Home, *Ark.,*
　U.S.A. ....　109　G8
Mountain Home, *Idaho,*
　U.S.A. ....　110　E6
Mountain Iron, *U.S.A.* ..　108　B8
Mountain Park, *Canada* ..　100　C5
Mountain Pass, *U.S.A.* ..　113　K11
Mountain View, *Ark.,*
　U.S.A. ....　109　H8
Mountain View, *Calif.,*
　U.S.A. ....　111　H2
Mountainair, *U.S.A.* ...　111　J10
Mountmellick, *Ireland* ...　15　C4
Moura, *Australia* ......　90　C4
Moura, *Brazil* ....　121　D5
Moura, *Portugal* ......　31　G3
Mourão, *Portugal* .....　31　G3
Mourdi, Dépression du,
　Chad ....　73　E9
Mourdiah, *Mali* ....　78　C3
Mourenx-Ville-Nouvelle,
　France ....　26　E3
Mouri, *Ghana* ....　79　D4
Mourne →, *U.K.* ......　15　B4
Mourne Mts., *U.K.* ....　15　B5
Mournies, *Greece* .....　37　D6
Mouscron, *Belgium* ...　17　G2
Moussoro, *Chad* ......　73　F8
Mouthe, *France* ......　25　F13
Moutier, *Switz.* ......　22　B4
Moûtiers, *France* .....　27　C10
Moutohara, *N.Z.* .....　87　H6
Moutong, *Indonesia* ...　57　D6
Mouy, *France* ....　25　C9
Mouzáki, *Greece* .....　39　K4
Movas, *Mexico* ....　114　B3
Moville, *Ireland* ......　15　A4
Moxhe, *Belgium* ......　17　G6
Moxotó →, *Brazil* ....　122　C4
Moy →, *Ireland* ......　15　B3
Moyale, *Kenya* ....　68　G2
Moyamba, *S. Leone* ...　78　D2
Moyen Atlas, *Morocco* ..　74　B3
Moyle □, *U.K.* ....　15　A5
Moyo, *Indonesia* .....　56　F5
Moyobamba, *Peru* ....　124　B2
Moyyero →, *Russia* ...　45　C11
Mozambique =
　Moçambique, *Mozam.*　83　F5
Mozambique ■, *Africa*　83　F4

Mozambique Chan., *Africa*　85　B7
Mozdok, *Russia* ....　43　E11
Mozdūrān, *Iran* ....　65　B9
Mozhaysk, *Russia* .....　41　D10
Mozhga, *Russia* ....　41　C18
Mozhnābād, *Iran* .....　65　C9
Mozirje, *Slovenia* .....　33　B11
Mozyr, *Belorussia* .....　40　E6
Mpanda, *Tanzania* ....　82　D3
Mpanda □, *Tanzania* ..　82　D3
Mpésoba, *Mali* ....　78　C3
Mpika, *Zambia* ....　83　E3
Mpulungu, *Zambia* ....　83　D3
Mpumalanga, *S. Africa*　85　D5
Mpwapwa, *Tanzania* ..　82　D4
Mpwapwa □, *Tanzania* ..　82　D4
Mrągowo, *Poland* ....　20　B11
Mramor, *Serbia* ....　21　M11
Mrimina, *Morocco* ....　74　C3
Mrkonjić Grad, *Bos.-H.* .　21　L7
Mrkopalj, *Croatia* .....　33　C11
Msab, Oued en →, *Algeria*　75　B6
Msaken, *Tunisia* ......　75　A7
Msambansovu, *Zimbabwe*　83　F3
Msoro, *Zambia* ....　83　E3
M'sila, *Algeria* ......　75　A5
Msta →, *Russia* ......　40　B7
Mstislavl, *Belorussia* ...　40　E7
Mtama, *Tanzania* .....　83　E4
Mtilikwe →, *Zimbabwe* .　83　G3
Mtsensk, *Russia* ......　41　E10
Mtskheta, *Georgia* ....　43　F11
Mtubatuba, *S. Africa* ..　85　D5
Mtwara-Mikindani,
　Tanzania ....　83　E5
Mu Gia, Deo, *Vietnam* ..　58　D5
Mu Us Shamo, *China* ..　50　E5
Muaná, *Brazil* ....　122　B2
Muang Chiang Rai,
　Thailand ....　58　C2
Muang Lamphun, *Thailand*　58　C2
Muang Pak Beng, *Laos* ..　58　C3
Muar, *Malaysia* ....　59　L4
Muarabungo, *Indonesia* ..　56　E2
Muaraenim, *Indonesia* ..　56　E2
Muarajuloi, *Indonesia* ..　56　E4
Muarakaman, *Indonesia* .　56　E5
Muaratebo, *Indonesia* ..　56　E2
Muaratembesi, *Indonesia* .　56　E2
Muaratewe, *Indonesia* ..　56　E4
Mubarakpur, *India* ....　63　F10
Mubarraz = Al Mubarraz,
　Si. Arabia ....　65　E6
Mubende, *Uganda* ....　82　B3
Mubi, *Nigeria* ....　79　C7
Mubur, P., *Indonesia* ..　59　L6
Mucajaí, *Brazil* ......　121　C5
Mucajaí, Serra do, *Brazil* .　121　C5
Muchachos, Roque de los,
　Canary Is. ....　36　F2
Müncheln, *Germany* ...　18　D7
Muchinga Mts., *Zambia* .　83　E3
Muchkapskiy, *Russia* ..　41　F13
Muck, *U.K.* ....　14　E2
Muckadilla, *Australia* ..　91　D4
Muco →, *Colombia* ...　120　C3
Muconda, *Angola* .....　80　G4
Mucum →, *Brazil* ....　125　B5
Mucura, *Brazil* ....　121　D5
Mucuri, *Brazil* ....　123　E4
Mucurici, *Brazil* .....　123　E3
Mucusso, *Angola* .....　84　B3
Muda, *Canary Is.* .....　36　F6
Mudan Jiang →, *China* ..　51　A15
Mudanjiang, *China* ...　51　B15
Mudanya, *Turkey* .....　66　C4
Muddy Cr. →, *U.S.A.* ..　111　H8
Mudgee, *Australia* ....　91　E4
Mudjatik →, *Canada* ..　101　B7
Mudurnu, *Turkey* .....　66　C4
Muecate, *Mozam.* .....　83　E4
Mueda, *Mozam.* ......　83　E4
Mueller Ra., *Australia* ..　88　C4
Muende, *Mozam.* .....　83　E3
Muerto, Mar, *Mexico* ..　115　D6
Muertos, Punta de los,
　Spain ....　29　J3
Mufindi □, *Tanzania* ..　83　D4
Mufu Shan, *China* ....　53　C10
Mufulira, *Zambia* .....　83　E2
Mufumbiro Range, *Africa*　82　C2
Mugardos, *Spain* .....　30　B2
Muge, *Portugal* ......　31　F2
Muge →, *Portugal* ....　31　F2
Múggia, *Italy* ....　33　C10
Mughayrā', *Si. Arabia* ..　64　D3
Mugi, *Japan* ....　49　H7
Mugia, *Spain* ....　30　B1
Mugila, Mts., *Zaïre* ...　82　D2
Muğla, *Turkey* ....　66　E3
Muğla □, *Turkey* .....　66　E3
Müğlizh, *Bulgaria* ....　38　G8
Mugu, *Nepal* ....　63　E10
Muhammad, Râs, *Egypt* .　76　B3
Muhammad Qol, *Sudan* .　76　C4
Muhammadabad, *India* ..　63　F10
Muhesi →, *Tanzania* ...　82　D4
Muheza □, *Tanzania* ...　82　C4
Mühldorf, *Germany* ...　19　G8
Mühlhausen, *Germany* ..　18　D6
Mühlig Hofmann fjella,
　Antarctica ....　5　D3
Muhutwe, *Tanzania* ...　82　C3
Muiden, *Neths.* ......　16　D6

Muikamachi, *Japan* ...　49　F9
Muine Bheag, *Ireland* ...　15　D5
Muiños, *Spain* ....　30　D3
Muir, L., *Australia* ....　89　F2
Mukachevo, *Ukraine* ..　40　G3
Mukah, *Malaysia* .....　56　D4
Mukawwa, Geziret, *Egypt*　76　C4
Mukdahan, *Thailand* ..　58　D5
Mukden = Shenyang,
　China ....　51　D12
Mukhtolovo, *Russia* ...　41　D13
Mukhtuya = Lensk, *Russia*　45　C12
Mukinbudin, *Australia* ..　89　F2
Mukishi, *Zaïre* ....　83　D1
Mukomuko, *Indonesia* ..　56　E2
Mukomwenze, *Zaïre* ..　82　D2
Muktsar, *India* ....　62　D6
Mukur, *Afghan.* ......　62　C2
Mukutawa →, *Canada* ..　101　C9
Mukwela, *Zambia* ....　83　F2
Mula, *Spain* ....　29　G3
Mulange, *Zaïre* ....　82　C2
Mulchén, *Chile* ......　126　D1
Mulde →, *Germany* ...　18　D8
Mule Creek, *U.S.A.* ...　108　D2
Muleba, *Tanzania* ....　82　C3
Muleba □, *Tanzania* ..　82　C3
Mulegns, *Switz.* ......　23　C9
Muleshoe, *U.S.A.* ....　109　H3
Mulgathing, *Australia* ..　91　E1
Mulgrave, *Canada* ...　99　C7
Mulhacén, *Spain* .....　29　H1
Mülheim, *Germany* ...　18　D2
Mulhouse, *France* ....　25　E14
Muli, *China* ....　52　D3
Muling, *China* ....　51　B16
Mull, *U.K.* ....　14　E3
Mullaittivu, *Sri Lanka* ..　60　Q12
Mullen, *U.S.A.* ....　108　D4
Mullengudgery, *Australia* .　91　E4
Mullens, *U.S.A.* .....　104　G5
Muller, Pegunungan,
　Indonesia ....　56　D4
Mullet Pen., *Ireland* ...　15　B1
Mullewa, *Australia* ...　89　E2
Müllheim, *Germany* ..　19　H3
Mulligan →, *Australia* .　90　C2
Mullin, *U.S.A.* ....　109　K5
Mullingar, *Ireland* ...　15　C4
Mullins, *U.S.A.* ......　105　H6
Mullumbimby, *Australia* .　91　D5
Mulobezi, *Zambia* ....　83　F2
Multan, *Pakistan* .....　62　D4
Multrå, *Sweden* ......　10　A11
Mulvane, *U.S.A.* .....　109　G6
Mulwad, *Sudan* ......　76　D3
Mulwala, *Australia* ...　91　F4
Mumbwa, *Zambia* ....　83　E2
Mumra, *Russia* ....　43　D12
Mun →, *Thailand* ....　58　E5
Muna, *Indonesia* .....　57　F6
Munamagi, *Estonia* ...　40　C5
Münchberg, *Germany* ..　19　E7
Müncheberg, *Germany* .　18　C10
München, *Germany* ...　19　G7
Munchen-Gladbach =
　Mönchengladbach,
　Germany ....　18　D2
Muncho Lake, *Canada* ..　100　B3
Munchŏn, *N. Korea* ...　51　E14
Münchwilen, *Switz.* ...　23　B7
Muncie, *U.S.A.* ......　104　E3
Muncoonie, L., *Australia* .　90　D2
Mundala, *Indonesia* ...　57　E10
Mundare, *Canada* ....　100　C6
Munday, *U.S.A.* ......　109　J5
Münden, *Germany* ...　18　D5
Mundiwindi, *Australia* ..　88　D3
Mundo →, *Spain* .....　29　G2
Mundo Novo, *Brazil* ..　123　D3
Mundra, *India* ....　62　H3
Mundrabilla, *Australia* ..　89　F4
Munducurus, *Brazil* ...　121　D6
Munera, *Spain* ....　29　F2
Mungallala, *Australia* ..　91　D4
Mungallala Cr. →,
　Australia ....　91　D4
Mungana, *Australia* ...　90　B4
Mungaoli, *India* ......　62　G8
Mungari, *Mozam.* .....　83　F3
Mungbere, *Zaïre* .....　82　B2
Munger, *India* ....　63　G12
Mungindi, *Australia* ...　91　D4
Munhango, *Angola* ...　81　G3
Munich = München,
　Germany ....　19　G7
Munising, *U.S.A.* .....　104　B2
Munka-Ljungby, *Sweden*　11　H6
Munkedal, *Sweden* ...　11　F5
Munku-Sardyk, *Russia* ..　45　D11
Münnerstadt, *Germany* ..　19　E6
Munoz Gamero, Pen.,
　Chile ....　128　D2
Munroe L., *Canada* ...　101　B9
Munsan, *S. Korea* ....　51　F14
Münsingen, *Switz.* ....　22　C5
Munster, *France* .....　25　D14
Munster, *Niedersachsen,*
　Germany ....　18　C6
Münster,
　Nordrhein-Westfalen,
　Germany ....　18　D3
Münster, *Switz.* ......　23　D6

Munster □, *Ireland* ...　15　D3
Muntadgin, *Australia* ..　89　F2
Muntele Mare, *Romania* .　38　C6
Muntok, *Indonesia* ...　56　E3
Munyak, *Uzbekistan* ..　44　E6
Munyama, *Zambia* ....　83　F2
Muong Beng, *Laos* ....　58　B3
Muong Boum, *Vietnam* ..　58　A4
Muong Et, *Laos* ......　58　B5
Muong Hai, *Laos* .....　58　B3
Muong Hiem, *Laos* ...　58　B4
Muong Houn, *Laos* ...　58　B3
Muong Hung, *Vietnam* .　58　B4
Muong Kau, *Laos* .....　58　E5
Muong Khao, *Laos* ...　58　C4
Muong Khoua, *Laos* ..　58　B4
Muong Liep, *Laos* ....　58　C3
Muong May, *Laos* ....　58　E6
Muong Ngeun, *Laos* ..　58　B3
Muong Ngoi, *Laos* ...　58　B4
Muong Nhie, *Vietnam* ..　58　A4
Muong Nong, *Laos* ...　58　D6
Muong Ou Tay, *Laos* ..　58　A3
Muong Oua, *Laos* ....　58　C3
Muong Peun, *Laos* ...　58　B4
Muong Phalane, *Laos* ..　58　D5
Muong Phieng, *Laos* ..　58　C3
Muong Phine, *Laos* ...　58　D6
Muong Sai, *Laos* .....　58　B3
Muong Saiapoun, *Laos* ..　58　C3
Muong Sen, *Vietnam* ..　58　C5
Muong Sing, *Laos* ....　58　A3
Muong Son, *Laos* ....　58　B4
Muong Soui, *Laos* ...　58　C4
Muong Va, *Laos* .....　58　B4
Muong Xia, *Vietnam* :...　58　B5
Muonio, *Finland* .....　8　C17
Muotathal, *Switz.* ....　23　C7
Mupa, *Angola* ....　81　H3
Muping, *China* ....　51　F11
Muqaddam, Wadi →,
　Sudan ....　76　D3
Muqdisho, Somali Rep. ..　68　G4
Mur-de-Bretagne, *France* .　24　D4
Mura →, *Slovenia* ....　33　B13
Muradiye, *Turkey* ....　67　D10
Murakami, *Japan* .....　48　E9
Murallón, Cuerro, *Chile* .　128　C2
Muralto, *Switz.* ......　23　D7
Muranda, *Rwanda* ....　82　C2
Murang'a, *Kenya* .....　82　C4
Murashi, *Russia* ......　41　B16
Murat, *France* ....　26　C6
Murat →, *Turkey* ....　67　D8
Muratlı, *Turkey* ......　66　C2
Muravera, *Italy* ......　34　C2
Murayama, *Japan* ....　48　E10
Murban, *U.A.E.* ......　65　F7
Murça, *Portugal* .....　30　D3
Murchison →, *Australia* .　89　E1
Murchison, Mt., *Antarctica*　5　D11
Murchison Falls =
　Kabarega Falls, *Uganda*　82　B3
Murchison House, *Australia*　89　E1
Murchison Ra., *Australia* .　90　C1
Murchison Rapids, *Malawi*　83　F3
Murcia, *Spain* ....　29　H3
Murcia □, *Spain* ......　29　H3
Murdo, *U.S.A.* ....　108　D4
Murdoch Pt., *Australia* ..　90　A3
Mureş →, *Romania* ...　38　C3
Mureşul = Mureş →,
　Romania ....　38　C3
Muret, *France* ....　26　E5
Murfatlar, *Romania* ...　38　E11
Murfreesboro, *U.S.A.* ..　105　H2
Murg, *Switz.* ....　23　B8
Murg →, *Germany* ...　19　G4
Murgab, *Tajikistan* ...　44　F8
Murgenthal, *Switz.* ...　22　B5
Murgon, *Australia* ...　91　D5
Murgoo, *Australia* ...　89　E2
Muri, *Switz.* ....　23　B6
Muria, *Indonesia* .....　57　G14
Muriaé, *Brazil* ....　123　F3
Murias de Paredes, *Spain* .　30　C4
Murici, *Brazil* ....　122　C4
Muriel Mine, *Zimbabwe* .　83　F3
Müritz See, *Germany* ..　18　B8
Murka, *Kenya* ....　82　C4
Murmansk, *Russia* ...　44　C4
Murmerwoude, *Neths.* ..　16　B8
Murnau, *Germany* ....　19　H7
Muro, *France* ....　27　F12
Muro, *Spain* ....　36　B10
Muro, C. de, *France* ...　27　G12
Muro Lucano, *Italy* ...　35　B8
Murom, *Russia* ......　41　D13
Muroran, *Japan* ......　48　C10
Muros, *Spain* ....　30　C1
Muros y de Noya, Ría de,
　Spain ....　30　C2
Muroto, *Japan* ....　49　H7
Muroto-Misaki, *Japan* ..　49　H7
Murphy, *U.S.A.* ......　110　E5
Murphys, *U.S.A.* .....　112　G6
Murphysboro, *U.S.A.* ..　109　G10
Murrat, *Sudan* ....　76　D2
Murray, *Ky., U.S.A.* ...　105　G1
Murray, *Utah, U.S.A.* ..　110　F8
Murray →, *Australia* ..　91　F2
Murray →, *Canada* ...　100　B4
Murray, L., *U.S.A.* ...　105　H5
Murray Bridge, *Australia* .　91　F2
Murray Downs, *Australia* .　90　C1

Murray Harbour, Canada . 99 C7
Murraysburg, S. Africa ... 84 E3
Murree, Pakistan 62 C5
Murrieta, U.S.A. 113 M9
Murrin Murrin, Australia . 89 E3
Murrumbidgee →,
  Australia 91 E3
Murrumburrah, Australia . 91 E4
Murrurundi, Australia ... 91 E5
Mursala, Indonesia 56 D1
Murshid, Sudan 76 C3
Murshidabad, India 63 G13
Murska Sobota, Slovenia . 33 B13
Murten, Switz. 22 C4
Murtensee, Switz. 22 C4
Murtle L., Canada 100 C5
Murtoa, Australia 91 F3
Murtosa, Portugal 30 E2
Muru →, Brazil 124 B3
Murungu, Tanzania 82 C3
Murwara, India 63 H9
Murwillumbah, Australia . 91 D5
Mürz →, Austria 21 H5
Mürzzuschlag, Austria ... 21 H5
Muş, Turkey 67 D9
Muş □, Turkey 67 D9
Mûsa, G., Egypt 76 J8
Musa Khel, Pakistan 62 D3
Mûsá Qal'eh, Afghan. ... 60 C4
Musaffargarh, Pakistan .. 60 D7
Musala, Bulgaria 38 G6
Musan, N. Korea 51 C15
Musangu, Zaïre 83 E1
Musasa, Tanzania 82 C3
Musay'īd, Qatar 65 E6
Muscat = Masqaṭ, Oman . 68 C6
Muscat & Oman =
  Oman ■, Asia 68 C6
Muscatine, U.S.A. 108 E9
Musel, Spain 30 B5
Musgrave, Australia 90 A3
Musgrave Ras., Australia . 89 E5
Mushie, Zaïre 80 E3
Mushin, Nigeria 79 D5
Musi →, Indonesia 56 E2
Muskeg →, Canada 100 A4
Muskegon, U.S.A. 104 D2
Muskegon →, U.S.A. .. 104 D2
Muskegon Heights, U.S.A. 104 D2
Muskogee, U.S.A. 109 H7
Muskwa →, Canada ... 100 B4
Muslīmiyah, Syria 64 B3
Musmar, Sudan 76 D4
Musofu, Zambia 83 E2
Musoma, Tanzania 82 C3
Musoma □, Tanzania ... 82 C3
Musquaro, L., Canada .. 99 B7
Musquodoboit Harbour,
  Canada 99 D7
Musselburgh, U.K. 14 F5
Musselkanaal, Neths. ... 16 C10
Musselshell →, U.S.A. . 110 C10
Mussidan, France 26 C4
Mussomeli, Italy 34 E6
Musson, Belgium 17 J7
Mussoorie, India 62 D8
Mussuco, Angola 84 B2
Mustafakemalpaşa, Turkey 66 C3
Mustang, Nepal 63 E10
Musters, L., Argentina .. 128 C3
Musudan, N. Korea 51 D15
Muswellbrook, Australia . 91 E5
Mût, Egypt 76 B2
Mut, Turkey 66 E5
Mutanda, Mozam. 85 C5
Mutanda, Zambia 83 E2
Mutaray, Russia 45 C11
Mutare, Zimbabwe 83 F3
Muting, Indonesia 57 F10
Mutshatsha, Zaïre 83 E1
Mutsu, Japan 48 D10
Mutsu-Wan, Japan 48 D10
Muttaburra, Australia .. 90 C3
Mutuáli, Mozam. 83 E4
Mutunópolis, Brazil 123 D2
Muweilih, Egypt 69 E3
Muxima, Angola 80 F2
Muy Muy, Nic. 116 D2
Muya, Russia 45 D12
Muyinga, Burundi 82 C3
Muzaffarabad, Pakistan . 63 B5
Muzaffargarh, Pakistan . 62 D4
Muzaffarnagar, India ... 62 E7
Muzaffarpur, India 63 F11
Muzhi, Russia 44 C7
Muzillac, France 24 E4
Muzon, C., U.S.A. 100 C2
Muztag, China 54 C3
Mvôlô, Sudan 77 F2
Mvuma, Zimbabwe 83 F3
Mvurwi, Zimbabwe 83 F3
Mwadui, Tanzania 82 C3
Mwambo, Tanzania 83 E5
Mwandi, Zambia 83 F1
Mwanza, Tanzania 82 C3
Mwanza, Zaïre 82 D2
Mwanza, Zambia 83 F1
Mwanza □, Tanzania ... 82 C3
Mwaya, Tanzania 83 D3
Mweelrea, Ireland 15 C2
Mweka, Zaïre 80 E4
Mwenezi, Zimbabwe ... 83 G3
Mwenezi →, Mozam. ... 83 G3
Mwenga, Zaïre 82 C2
Mweru, L., Zambia 83 D2

Mweza Range, Zimbabwe 83 G3
Mwilambwe, Zaïre 82 D5
Mwimbi, Tanzania 83 D3
Mwinilunga, Zambia ... 83 E1
My Tho, Vietnam 59 G6
Mya, O. →, Algeria ... 75 B5
Myajlar, India 62 F4
Myanaung, Burma 61 K19
Myanmar = Burma ■, Asia 61 J20
Myaungmya, Burma 61 L19
Mycenae = Mikínai, Greece 39 M5
Myeik Kyunzu, Burma .. 59 G1
Myerstown, U.S.A. 107 F8
Myingyan, Burma 61 J19
Myitkyina, Burma 61 G20
Myjava, Slovak Rep. ... 20 G7
Mykolayiv = Nikolayev,
  Ukraine 42 C4
Mymensingh, Bangla. .. 61 G17
Mynydd Du, U.K. 13 F4
Mýrdalsjökull, Iceland .. 8 E4
Myroodah, Australia ... 88 C3
Myrtle Beach, U.S.A. .. 105 J6
Myrtle Creek, U.S.A. .. 110 E2
Myrtle Point, U.S.A. ... 110 E1
Myrtou, Cyprus 37 D12
Mysen, Norway 10 E5
Mysia, Turkey 66 D2
Myslenice, Poland 20 F9
Myślibórz, Poland 20 C4
Mysłowice, Poland ... 20 E9
Mysore = Karnataka □,
  India 60 N10
Mysore, India 60 N10
Mystic, U.S.A. 107 E13
Myszków, Poland 20 E9
Mythen, Switz. 23 B7
Mytishchi, Russia 41 D10
Myton, U.S.A. 110 F8
Mývatn, Iceland 8 D5
Mzimba, Malawi 83 E3
Mzimkulu →, S. Africa . 85 E5
Mzimvubu →, S. Africa . 85 E4
Mzuzu, Malawi 83 E3

N

N' Dioum, Senegal 78 B2
Na Noi, Thailand 58 C3
Na Phao, Laos 58 D5
Na Sam, Vietnam 58 A6
Na San, Vietnam 58 B5
Naab →, Germany 19 F8
Naaldwijk, Neths. 16 E4
Na'am, Sudan 77 F2
Naantali, Finland 9 F17
Naarden, Neths. 16 D6
Naas, Ireland 15 C5
Nababiep, S. Africa ... 84 D2
Nabadwip = Navadwip,
  India 63 H13
Nabari, Japan 49 G8
Nabawa, Australia 89 E1
Nabberu, L., Australia . 89 E3
Nabburg, Germany 19 F8
Naberezhnyye Chelny,
  Russia 44 D6
Nabeul, Tunisia 75 A7
Nabha, India 62 D7
Nabīd, Iran 65 D8
Nabire, Indonesia 57 E9
Nabisar, Pakistan 62 G3
Nabisipi →, Canada .. 99 B7
Nabiswera, Uganda ... 82 B3
Nablus = Nābulus, Jordan 69 C4
Naboomspruit, S. Africa . 85 C4
Nabua, Phil. 55 E5
Nābulus, Jordan 69 C4
Nābulus □, Jordan 69 C4
Nacala, Mozam. 83 E5
Nacala-Velha, Mozam. . 83 E5
Nacaome, Honduras ... 116 D2
Nacaroa, Mozam. 83 E4
Naches, U.S.A. 110 C3
Naches →, U.S.A. ... 112 D6
Nachingwea, Tanzania . 83 E4
Nachingwea □, Tanzania . 83 E4
Nachna, India 62 F4
Náchod, Czech. 20 E6
Nacimiento Reservoir,
  U.S.A. 112 K6
Nacka, Sweden 10 E12
Nackara, Australia ... 91 E2
Naco, Mexico 114 A3
Naco, U.S.A. 111 L9
Nacogdoches, U.S.A. . 109 K7
Nácori Chico, Mexico . 114 B3
Nacozari, Mexico 114 A3
Nadi, Sudan 76 D3
Nadiad, India 62 H5
Nădlac, Romania 38 C3
Nador, Morocco 75 A4
Nadur, Malta 37 C1
Nadūshan, Iran 65 C7
Nadvornaya, Ukraine . 42 B1
Nadym, Russia 44 C8
Nadym →, Russia ... 44 C8
Næstved, Denmark ... 11 J5
Nafada, Nigeria 79 C7
Näfels, Switz. 23 B8
Naftshahr, Iran 64 C5
Nafud Desert = An Nafūd,
  Si. Arabia 64 D4

Nafūsah, Jabal, Libya 75 B7
Nag Hammâdi, Egypt 76 B3
Naga, Phil. 55 E5
Naga, Kreb en, Africa ... 74 D3
Nagagami →, Canada ... 98 C3
Nagahama, Japan 49 G8
Nagai, Japan 48 E10
Nagaland □, India 61 F19
Nagano, Japan 49 F9
Nagano □, Japan 49 F9
Nagaoka, Japan 49 F9
Nagappattinam, India ... 60 P11
Nagar Parkar, Pakistan .. 62 G4
Nagasaki, Japan 49 H4
Nagasaki □, Japan 49 H4
Nagato, Japan 49 G5
Nagercoil, India 60 Q10
Nagina, India 63 E8
Nagīneh, Iran 65 C8
Nagir, Pakistan 63 A6
Nagold, Germany 19 G4
Nagold →, Germany ... 19 G4
Nagoorin, Australia ... 90 C5
Nagornyy, Russia 45 D13
Nagorsk, Russia 41 B17
Nagoya, Japan 49 G8
Nagpur, India 60 J11
Nagua, Dom. Rep. 117 C6
Nagykanizsa, Hungary . 21 J7
Nagykörös, Hungary ... 21 H9
Nagyléta, Hungary 21 H11
Naha, Japan 49 L3
Nahanni Butte, Canada . 100 A4
Nahanni Nat. Park, Canada 100 A3
Nahariyya, Israel 64 C2
Nahāvand, Iran 65 C6
Nahe →, Germany ... 19 F3
Nahîya, Wadi →, Egypt . 76 J7
Nahlin, Canada 100 B2
Nahuel Huapí, L.,
  Argentina 128 B2
Naicá, Mexico 114 B3
Naicam, Canada 101 C8
Na'ifah, Si. Arabia ... 68 D5
Naila, Germany 19 E7
Nain, Canada 99 A7
Na'īn, Iran 65 C7
Naini Tal, India 63 E8
Nainpur, India 60 H12
Naintré, France 24 F7
Naipu, Romania 38 E8
Naira, Indonesia 57 E7
Nairn, U.K. 14 D5
Nairobi, Kenya 82 C4
Naivasha, Kenya 82 C4
Naivasha, L., Kenya .. 82 C4
Najac, France 26 D5
Najafābād, Iran 65 C6
Nájera, Spain 28 C2
Najerilla →, Spain .. 28 C2
Najibabad, India 62 E8
Najin, N. Korea 51 C16
Najmah, Si. Arabia .. 65 E6
Naju, S. Korea 51 G14
Nakadōri-Shima, Japan . 49 H4
Nakalagba, Zaïre 82 B2
Nakaminato, Japan ... 49 F10
Nakamura, Japan 49 H6
Nakano, Japan 49 F9
Nakano-Shima, Japan . 49 K4
Nakashibetsu, Japan .. 48 C12
Nakfa, Eritrea 77 D4
Nakhichevan, Azerbaijan . 67 D11
Nakhichevan Republic □,
  Azerbaijan 44 F5
Nakhl, Egypt 69 F2
Nakhl-e Taqī, Iran ... 65 E7
Nakhodka, Russia ... 45 E14
Nakhon Nayok, Thailand 58 E3
Nakhon Pathom, Thailand 58 F3
Nakhon Phanom, Thailand 58 D5
Nakhon Ratchasima,
  Thailand 58 E4
Nakhon Sawan, Thailand 58 E3
Nakhon Si Thammarat,
  Thailand 59 H3
Nakhon Thai, Thailand .. 58 D3
Nakina, B.C., Canada .. 100 B2
Nakina, Ont., Canada .. 98 B2
Nakło nad Notecią, Poland 20 B7
Nakodar, India 62 D6
Nakskov, Denmark .. 11 K5
Näkten, Sweden 10 B8
Naktong →, S. Korea . 51 G15
Nakuru, Kenya 82 C4
Nakuru □, Kenya ... 82 C4
Nakuru, L., Kenya .. 82 C4
Nakusp, Canada 100 C5
Nal →, Pakistan ... 62 G1
Nalchik, Russia 43 E10
Nälden, Sweden 10 A8
Näldsjön, Sweden .. 10 A8
Nalgonda, India 60 L11
Nalhati, India 63 G12
Nallamalai Hills, India . 60 M11
Nallıhan, Turkey ... 66 C4
Nalón →, Spain ... 30 B4
Nālūt, Libya 75 B7
Nam Can, Vietnam .. 59 H5
Nam Co, China 54 C4
Nam Dinh, Vietnam . 58 B6
Nam Du, Hon, Vietnam . 59 H5

Nam Ngum Dam, Laos ... 58 C4
Nam-Phan, Vietnam 59 G6
Nam Phong, Thailand ... 58 D4
Nam Tha, Laos 58 B3
Nam Tok, Thailand 58 E2
Namacunde, Angola 84 B2
Namacurra, Mozam. 85 B6
Namak, Daryācheh-ye, Iran 65 C7
Namak, Kavir-e, Iran ... 65 C8
Namaland, Namibia 84 C2
Namapa, Mozam. 83 E4
Namaqualand, S. Africa . 84 D2
Namasagali, Uganda ... 82 B3
Namber, Indonesia 57 E8
Nambour, Australia ... 91 D5
Nambucca Heads, Australia 91 E5
Namche Bazar, Nepal .. 63 F12
Namchonjŏm, N. Korea . 51 E14
Namèche, Belgium 17 H6
Namecunda, Mozam. ... 83 E4
Nameh, Indonesia 56 D5
Nameponda, Mozam. .. 83 F4
Nametil, Mozam. 83 F4
Namew L., Canada 101 C8
Namib Desert =
  Namibwoestyn, Namibia 84 C2
Namibe, Angola 81 H2
Namibe □, Angola 84 B1
Namibia ■, Africa 84 C2
Namibwoestyn, Namibia . 84 C2
Namlea, Indonesia 57 E7
Namoi →, Australia ... 91 E4
Namous, O. en →, Algeria 75 B4
Nampa, U.S.A. 110 E5
Nampō-Shotō, Japan ... 49 J10
Nampula, Mozam. 83 F4
Namrole, Indonesia ... 57 E7
Namse Shankou, China . 61 E13
Namsen →, Norway .. 8 D11
Namsos, Norway 8 D11
Namtay, Russia 45 C13
Namtu, Burma 61 H20
Namtumbo, Tanzania . 83 E4
Namu, Canada 100 C3
Namur, Belgium 17 H5
Namur □, Belgium ... 17 H6
Namutoni, Namibia .. 84 B2
Namwala, Zambia ... 83 F2
Namwŏn, S. Korea .. 51 G14
Namysłów, Poland .. 20 D7
Nan, Thailand 58 C3
Nan →, Thailand .. 58 E3
Nan Xian, China ... 53 C9
Nanaimo, Canada .. 100 D4
Nanam, N. Korea .. 51 D15
Nanan, China 53 E12
Nanango, Australia . 91 D5
Nan'an, China 53 F11
Nanao, Japan 49 F8
Nanbu, China 52 B6
Nanchang, China .. 53 C10
Nancheng, China .. 53 D11
Nanchong, China .. 52 B6
Nanchuan, China .. 52 C6
Nancy, France 25 D13
Nanda Devi, India . 63 D8
Nandan, China 52 E6
Nandan, Japan 49 G7
Nanded, India 60 K10
Nandewar Ra., Australia 91 E5
Nandi, Fiji 87 C7
Nandi □, Kenya ... 82 B4
Nandurbar, India .. 60 J9
Nandyal, India ... 60 M11
Nanfeng, Guangdong,
  China 53 F8
Nanfeng, Jiangxi, China 53 D11
Nanga, Australia .. 89 E1
Nanga-Eboko, Cameroon 79 E7
Nanga Parbat, Pakistan 63 B6
Nangade, Mozam. .. 83 E4
Nangapinoh, Indonesia 56 E4
Nangarhár □, Afghan. . 60 B7
Nangatayap, Indonesia 56 E4
Nangeya Mts., Uganda 82 B3
Nangis, France 25 D10
Nangong, China ... 50 F8
Nanhua, China 52 E3
Nanhui, China 53 B13
Nanji Shan, China .. 53 D13
Nanjian, China 52 E3
Nanjiang, China ... 52 A6
Nanjing, Fujian, China 53 E12
Nanjing, Jiangsu, China 53 A12
Nanjirinji, Tanzania . 83 D4
Nankana Sahib, Pakistan 62 D5
Nankang, China ... 53 E10
Nanking = Nanjing, China 53 A12
Nankoku, Japan ... 49 H6
Nanling, China 53 B12
Nanning, China ... 52 F7
Nannup, Australia .. 89 F2
Nanpan Jiang →, China 52 E6
Nanpara, India 63 F9
Nanpi, China 50 E9
Nanping, Fujian, China 53 D12
Nanping, Henan, China 53 C9
Nanri Dao, China .. 53 E12
Nanripe, Mozam. .. 83 E4
Nansei-Shotō = Ryūkyū-
  rettō, Japan 49 M2

Nansen Sd., Canada 4 A3
Nansio, Tanzania 82 C3
Nant, France 26 D7
Nantes, France 24 E5
Nanteuil-le-Haudouin,
  France 25 C9
Nantiat, France 26 B5
Nanticoke, U.S.A. 107 E8
Nanton, Canada 100 C6
Nantong, China 53 A13
Nantua, France 27 B9
Nantucket I., U.S.A. .. 94 E12
Nanuque, Brazil 123 E3
Nanutarra, Australia . 88 D2
Nanxiong, China 53 E10
Nanyang, China 50 H7
Nanyi Hu, China 53 B12
Nanyuan, China 50 E9
Nanyuki, Kenya 82 B4
Nanzhang, China ... 53 B8
Nāo, C. de la, Spain . 29 G5
Naococane L., Canada . 99 B5
Naoetsu, Japan 49 F9
Náousa, Greece 39 J5
Naozhou Dao, China . 53 G8
Napa, U.S.A. 112 G4
Napa →, U.S.A. ... 112 G4
Napanee, Canada ... 98 D4
Napanoch, U.S.A. .. 107 E10
Nape, Laos 58 C5
Nape Pass = Keo Neua,
  Deo, Vietnam 58 C5
Napf, Switz. 22 B5
Napier, N.Z. 87 H6
Napier Broome B.,
  Australia 88 B4
Napier Downs, Australia . 88 C3
Napier Pen., Australia . 90 A2
Naples = Nápoli, Italy . 35 B7
Naples, U.S.A. 105 M5
Napo, China 52 F5
Napo □, Ecuador ... 120 D2
Napo →, Peru 120 D3
Napoleon, N. Dak., U.S.A. 108 B5
Napoleon, Ohio, U.S.A. . 104 E3
Nápoli, Italy 35 B7
Nápoli, G. di, Italy .. 35 B7
Napopo, Zaïre 82 B2
Nappa Merrie, Australia . 91 D3
Naqâda, Egypt 76 B3
Naqqāsh, Iran 65 C6
Nara, Japan 49 G7
Nara, Mali 78 B3
Nara □, Japan 49 G8
Nara Canal, Pakistan . 62 G3
Nara Visa, U.S.A. .. 109 H3
Naracoorte, Australia . 91 F3
Naradhan, Australia . 91 E4
Narasapur, India ... 61 L12
Narathiwat, Thailand . 59 J3
Narayanganj, Bangla. . 61 H17
Narayanpet, India .. 60 L10
Narbonne, France .. 26 E7
Narcea →, Spain .. 30 B4
Nardìn, Iran 65 B7
Nardò, Italy 35 B11
Narembeen, Australia . 89 F2
Nares Str., Arctic ... 94 B13
Naretha, Australia .. 89 F3
Narew →, Poland .. 20 C10
Nari →, Pakistan .. 62 E2
Narin, Afghan. 60 A6
Narindra, Helodranon' i,
  Madag. 85 A8
Nariño □, Colombia . 120 C2
Narita, Japan 49 G10
Narmada →, India . 62 J5
Narman, Turkey ... 67 C9
Narnaul, India 62 E7
Narni, Italy 33 F9
Naro, Ghana 78 C4
Naro, Italy 34 E6
Naro Fominsk, Russia . 41 D10
Narodnaya, Russia . 6 B17
Narok, Kenya 82 C4
Narok □, Kenya ... 82 C4
Narón, Spain 30 B2
Narooma, Australia . 91 F5
Narowal, Pakistan . 62 C6
Narrabri, Australia . 91 E4
Narran →, Australia . 91 D4
Narrandera, Australia . 91 E4
Narraway →, Canada . 100 B5
Narrogin, Australia . 89 F2
Narromine, Australia . 91 E4
Narsimhapur, India . 63 H8
Nartkala, Russia ... 43 E10
Naruto, Japan 49 G7
Narva, Estonia 40 B6
Narva →, Russia .. 40 B6
Narvik, Norway ... 8 B14
Narvskoye Vdkhr., Russia 40 B6
Narwana, India ... 62 E7
Naryan-Mar, Russia . 44 C6
Naryilco, Australia . 91 D3
Narym, Russia 44 D9
Narymskoye, Kazakhstan 44 E9
Naryn, Kirghizia .. 44 E8
Nasa, Norway 8 C13
Nasarawa, Nigeria . 79 D6
Năsăud, Romania .. 38 B7
Naseby, N.Z. 87 L3
Naselle, U.S.A. ... 112 D3
Naser, Buheirat en, Egypt 76 C3
Nashua, Iowa, U.S.A. . 108 D8

Nashua, Mont., U.S.A. 110 B10
Nashua, N.H., U.S.A. 107 D13
Nashville, Ark., U.S.A. .. 109 J8
Nashville, Ga., U.S.A. ... 105 K4
Nashville, Tenn., U.S.A. . 105 G2
Našice, Croatia 21 K8
Nasielsk, Poland 20 C10
Nasik, India 60 K8
Nasipit, Phil. 55 G6
Nasirabad, India 62 F6
Naskaupi →, Canada 99 B7
Naso, Italy 35 D7
Nasriān-e Pā'īn, Iran 64 C5
Nass →, Canada 100 B3
Nassau, Bahamas 116 A4
Nassau, U.S.A. 107 D11
Nassau, B., Chile 128 E3
Nasser, L. = Naser,
 Buheirat en, Egypt 76 C3
Nasser City = Kôm Ombo,
 Egypt 76 C3
Nassian, Ivory C. 78 D4
Nässjö, Sweden 9 H13
Nasugbu, Phil. 55 D4
Näsviken, Sweden 10 C10
Nat Kyizin, Burma 61 M20
Nata, Botswana 84 C4
Natagaima, Colombia ... 120 C2
Natal, Brazil 122 C4
Natal, Canada 100 D6
Natal, Indonesia 56 D1
Natal □, S. Africa 85 D5
Natalinci, Serbia 21 L10
Naṭanz, Iran 65 C6
Natashquan, Canada 99 B7
Natashquan →, Canada .. 99 B7
Natchez, U.S.A. 109 K9
Natchitoches, U.S.A. ... 109 K8
Naters, Switz. 22 D5
Nathalia, Australia 91 F4
Nathdwara, India 62 G5
Nati, Pta., Spain 36 A10
Natimuk, Australia 91 F3
Nation →, Canada 100 B4
National City, U.S.A. .. 113 N9
Natitingou, Benin 79 C5
Natividad, I., Mexico .. 114 B2
Natoma, U.S.A. 108 F5
Natron, L., Tanzania .. 82 C4
Natrona Heights, U.S.A. 106 F5
Natrûn, W. el →, Egypt . 76 H7
Natuna Besar, Kepulauan,
 Indonesia 59 L7
Natuna Is. = Natuna
 Besar, Kepulauan,
 Indonesia 59 L7
Natuna Selatan,
 Kepulauan, Indonesia . 59 L7
Natural Bridge, U.S.A. . 107 B9
Naturaliste, C., Australia . 90 G4
Nau Qala, Afghan. 62 B3
Naubinway, U.S.A. 98 C2
Naucelle, France 26 D6
Nauders, Austria 19 J6
Nauen, Germany 18 C8
Naugatuck, U.S.A. 107 E11
Naujoji Vilnia, Lithuania . 40 D4
Naumburg, Germany ... 18 D7
Nā'ūr at Tunayb, Jordan . 69 D4
Nauru ■, Pac. Oc. 92 H8
Naushahra = Nowshera,
 Pakistan 60 B8
Nauta, Peru 120 D3
Nautanwa, India 61 F13
Nautla, Mexico 115 C5
Nava, Mexico 114 B4
Nava del Rey, Spain ... 30 D5
Navacerrada, Puerto de,
 Spain 30 E7
Navadwip, India 63 H13
Navahermosa, Spain ... 31 F6
Navajo Reservoir, U.S.A. 111 H10
Navalcarnero, Spain ... 30 E6
Navalmoral de la Mata,
 Spain 30 F5
Navalvillar de Pela, Spain . 31 F5
Navan = An Uaimh,
 Ireland 15 C5
Navarino, Chile 128 E3
Navarra □, Spain 28 C3
Navarre →, U.S.A. 106 F3
Navarrenx, France 26 E3
Navarro →, U.S.A. 112 F3
Navasota, U.S.A. 109 K6
Navassa, W. Indies 117 C5
Nave, Italy 32 C7
Naver →, U.K. 14 C4
Navia, Spain 30 B4
Navia →, Spain 30 B4
Navia de Suarna, Spain . 30 C4
Navidad, Chile 126 C1
Navlya, Russia 40 E9
Navoi, Uzbekistan 44 E7
Navojoa, Mexico 114 B3
Navolato, Mexico 114 C3
Návpaktos, Greece 39 L4
Návplion, Greece 39 M5
Navrongo, Ghana 79 C4
Navsari, India 60 J8
Nawa Kot, Pakistan ... 62 E4
Nawabganj, Ut. P., India . 63 F9
Nawabganj, Ut. P., India . 63 E8
Nawabshah, Pakistan .. 62 F3
Nawada, India 63 G11
Nawakot, Nepal 63 F11

Nawalgarh, India 62 F6
Nawanshahr, India 63 C6
Nawi, Sudan 76 D3
Náxos, Greece 39 M8
Nay, France 26 E3
Nāy Band, Iran 65 E7
Naya →, Colombia 120 C2
Nayakhan, Russia 45 C16
Nayarit □, Mexico 114 C4
Nayé, Senegal 78 C2
Nayong, China 52 D5
Nayoro, Japan 48 B11
Nayyāl, W. →, Si. Arabia 64 D3
Nazaré, Bahia, Brazil .. 123 D4
Nazaré, Goiás, Brazil .. 122 C2
Nazaré, Pará, Brazil ... 125 B7
Nazaré, Portugal 31 F1
Nazareth = Nazerat, Israel 69 C4
Nazas, Mexico 114 B4
Nazas →, Mexico 114 B4
Naze, The, U.K. 13 F9
Nazerat, Israel 69 C4
Nāzik, Iran 64 B5
Nazik Gölü, Turkey ... 67 D10
Nazilli, Turkey 66 E3
Nazir Hat, Bangla. ... 61 H17
Nazko, Canada 100 C4
Nazko →, Canada 100 C4
Nazret, Ethiopia 77 F4
Nchanga, Zambia 83 E2
Ncheu, Malawi 83 E3
Ndala, Tanzania 82 C3
Ndalatando, Angola .. 80 F2
Ndali, Benin 79 D5
Ndareda, Tanzania ... 82 C4
Ndélé, C.A.R. 73 G9
Ndendé, Gabon 80 E2
Ndjamena, Chad 73 F7
Ndjolé, Gabon 80 E2
Ndola, Zambia 83 E2
Ndoto Mts., Kenya .. 82 B4
Nduguti, Tanzania .. 82 C3
Nea →, Norway 10 A5
Néa Flippiás, Greece . 39 K3
Neagh, Lough, U.K. .. 15 B5
Neah Bay, U.S.A. ... 112 B2
Neale, L., Australia .. 88 D5
Neápolis, Kozan, Greece 39 J4
Neápolis, Kríti, Greece 37 D7
Neápolis, Lakonia, Greece 39 N6
Near Is., U.S.A. 96 C1
Neath, U.K. 13 F4
Nebbou, Burkina Faso 79 C4
Nebine Cr. →, Australia 91 D4
Nebit Dag, Turkmenistan . 44 F6
Nebolchy, Russia 40 B8
Nebraska □, U.S.A. .. 108 E5
Nebraska City, U.S.A. . 108 E7
Nébrodi, Monti, Italy . 35 E7
Necedah, U.S.A. 108 C9
Nechako →, Canada .. 100 C4
Neches →, U.S.A. ... 109 L8
Neckar →, Germany .. 19 F4
Necochea, Argentina .. 126 D4
Nedelišće, Croatia 33 B13
Neder Rijn →, Neths. .. 16 E8
Nederbrakel, Belgium . 17 G3
Nederweert, Neths. ... 17 F7
Nédha →, Greece 39 M4
Nedroma, Algeria 75 A4
Neede, Neths. 16 D9
Needles, U.S.A. 113 L12
Needles, The, U.K. ... 13 G6
Neembucú □, Paraguay 126 B4
Neemuch = Nimach, India 62 G6
Neenah, U.S.A. 104 C1
Neepawa, Canada ... 101 C9
Neer, Neths. 17 F7
Neerpelt, Belgium ... 17 F6
Neft-chala = imeni 26
 Bakinskikh Komissarov,
 Azerbaijan 67 D13
Nefta, Tunisia 75 B6
Neftah Sidi Boubekeur,
 Algeria 75 A5
Neftegorsk, Russia ... 43 D8
Neftekumsk, Russia .. 43 D11
Neftenbach, Switz. ... 23 A7
Negapatam =
 Nagappattinam, India . 60 P11
Negaunee, U.S.A. ... 104 B2
Negele, Ethiopia 68 F2
Negev Desert = Hanegev,
 Israel 69 E3
Negombo, Sri Lanka .. 60 R11
Negotin, Serbia 21 L12
Negra, Peña, Spain .. 30 C4
Negra, Pta., Mauritania 74 D1
Negra, Pta., Peru 124 B1
Negra Pt., Phil. 57 A6
Negrais, C. = Maudin Sun,
 Burma 61 M19
Negreira, Spain 30 C2
Négrine, Algeria 75 B6
Negro →, Bolivia 125 C5
Negro →, Brazil 121 D6
Negro →, Uruguay ... 127 C4
Negros, Phil. 55 G5
Nehalem →, U.S.A. .. 112 E3
Nehāvand, Iran 65 C6
Nehbandān, Iran 65 D9
Neheim, Germany ... 18 D4
Nehoiaşu, Romania .. 38 D9
Nei Monggol Zizhiqu □,
 China 50 C6

Neidpath, Canada 101 C7
Neihart, U.S.A. 110 C8
Neijiang, China 52 C5
Neilton, U.S.A. 110 C2
Neiqiu, China 50 F8
Neira de Jusá, Spain ... 30 C3
Neiva, Colombia 120 C2
Neixiang, China 50 H6
Nejanilini L., Canada .. 101 B9
Nejo, Ethiopia 77 F4
Nekā, Iran 65 B7
Nekemte, Ethiopia 77 F4
Nêkheb, Egypt 76 B3
Neksø, Denmark 9 J13
Nelas, Portugal 30 E3
Nelia, Australia 90 C3
Nelidovo, Russia 40 C8
Neligh, U.S.A. 108 D5
Nelkan, Russia 45 D14
Nellore, India 60 M11
Nelma, Russia 45 E14
Nelson, Canada 100 D5
Nelson, N.Z. 87 J4
Nelson, U.K. 12 D5
Nelson, U.S.A. 111 J7
Nelson →, Canada 101 C9
Nelson, C., Australia .. 91 F3
Nelson, Estrecho, Chile . 128 D2
Nelson Forks, Canada .. 100 B4
Nelson House, Canada .. 101 B9
Nelson L., Canada 101 B8
Nelspoort, S. Africa ... 84 E3
Nelspruit, S. Africa ... 85 D5
Néma, Mauritania 78 B3
Neman →, Lithuania .. 40 D2
Nemeiben L., Canada .. 101 B7
Nemira, Romania 38 C9
Nemours, France 25 D9
Nemunas = Neman →,
 Lithuania 40 D2
Nemuro, Japan 48 C12
Nemuro-Kaikyō, Japan . 48 C12
Nemuy, Russia 45 D14
Nen Jiang →, China ... 51 B13
Nenagh, Ireland 15 D3
Nenana, U.S.A. 96 B5
Nenasi, Malaysia 59 L4
Nene →, U.K. 12 E8
Nenjiang, China 54 B7
Neno, Malawi 83 F3
Nenusa, Kepulauan,
 Indonesia 57 D7
Neodesha, U.S.A. 109 G7
Neópolis, Brazil 122 D4
Neosho, U.S.A. 109 G7
Neosho →, U.S.A. ... 109 H7
Nepal ■, Asia 63 F11
Nepalganj, Nepal 63 E9
Nephi, U.S.A. 110 G8
Nephin, Ireland 15 B2
Neptune, U.S.A. 107 F10
Néra →, Romania 38 E4
Nérac, France 26 D4
Nerchinsk, Russia 45 D12
Nerchinskiy Zavod, Russia 45 D12
Nereju, Romania 38 D9
Nerekhta, Russia 41 C12
Néret L., Canada 99 B5
Neringa, Lithuania ... 40 D2
Nerja, Spain 31 J7
Nerl →, Russia 41 C12
Nerpio, Spain 29 G2
Nerva, Spain 31 H4
Nes, Iceland 8 D5
Nes, Neths. 16 B7
Nesbyen, Norway 10 D3
Nesebŭr, Bulgaria 38 G10
Neskaupstaður, Iceland . 8 D7
Nesland, Norway 10 E1
Neslandsvatn, Norway . 10 F3
Nesle, France 25 C9
Nesodden, Norway ... 10 E4
Nesque →, France ... 27 E8
Ness, L., U.K. 14 D4
Nesselwang, Germany . 19 H6
Nesttun, Norway 9 F8
Néstos →, Greece 39 H7
Nesvizh, Belorussia .. 40 E5
Netanya, Israel 69 C3
Nète →, Belgium 17 F4
Netherdale, Australia . 90 C4
Netherlands ■, Europe 16 E6
Netherlands Antilles ■,
 W. Indies 120 A4
Neto →, Italy 35 C10
Nettancourt, France .. 25 D11
Nettilling L., Canada . 97 B12
Nettuno, Italy 34 A5
Netzahualcoyotl, Presa,
 Mexico 115 D6
Neu-Isenburg, Germany . 19 E4
Neu-Ulm, Germany .. 19 G6
Neubrandenburg, Germany 18 B9
Neubukow, Germany . 18 A7
Neuburg, Germany ... 19 G7
Neuchâtel, Switz. 22 C3
Neuchâtel □, Switz. .. 22 C3
Neuchâtel, Lac de, Switz. 22 C3
Neudau, Austria 21 H6
Neuenegg, Switz. 22 C4
Neuenhaus, Germany . 18 C2
Neuf-Brisach, France . 25 D14
Neufahrn, Germany .. 19 G8
Neufchâteau, Belgium . 17 J6
Neufchâteau, France .. 25 D12

Neufchâtel-en-Bray, France 24 C8
Neufchâtel-sur-Aisne,
 France 25 C11
Neuhaus, Germany 18 B6
Neuhausen, Switz. 23 A7
Neuillé-Pont-Pierre, France 24 E7
Neuilly-St.-Front, France . 25 C10
Neukalen, Germany 18 B8
Neumarkt, Germany ... 19 F7
Neumünster, Germany . 18 A5
Neung-sur-Beuvron, France 25 E8
Neunkirchen, Austria .. 21 H6
Neunkirchen, Germany . 19 F3
Neuquén, Argentina ... 128 A3
Neuquén □, Argentina .. 126 D2
Neuquén →, Argentina . 128 A3
Neuruppin, Germany .. 18 C8
Neuse →, U.S.A. 105 H7
Neusiedler See, Austria . 21 H6
Neuss, Germany 17 F9
Neussargues-Moissac,
 France 26 C7
Neustadt, Baden-W.,
 Germany 19 H4
Neustadt, Bayern, Germany 19 F8
Neustadt, Bayern, Germany 19 G7
Neustadt, Bayern, Germany 19 F6
Neustadt, Bayern, Germany 19 E7
Neustadt, Brandenburg,
 Germany 18 C8
Neustadt, Hessen, Germany 18 E5
Neustadt, Niedersachsen,
 Germany 18 C5
Neustadt, Rhld.-Pfz.,
 Germany 19 F4
Neustadt,
 Schleswig-Holstein,
 Germany 18 A6
Neustadt, Thüringen,
 Germany 18 E7
Neustrelitz, Germany .. 18 B9
Neuvic, France 26 C6
Neuville, Belgium 17 H5
Neuville-aux-Bois, France . 25 D9
Neuville-de-Poitou, France 26 B4
Neuville-sur-Saône, France 27 C8
Neuvy-le-Roi, France .. 24 E7
Neuvy-St.-Sépulchre,
 France 26 B5
Neuvy-sur-Barangeon,
 France 25 E9
Neuwerk, Germany 18 B4
Neuwied, Germany 18 E3
Neva →, Russia 6 D12
Nevada, U.S.A. 109 G7
Nevada □, U.S.A. 110 G5
Nevada, Sierra, Spain .. 29 H1
Nevada, Sierra, U.S.A. .. 110 G3
Nevada City, U.S.A. .. 112 F6
Nevado, Cerro, Argentina 126 D2
Nevanka, Russia 45 D10
Nevel, Russia 40 D6
Nevele, Belgium 17 F3
Nevers, France 25 F10
Nevertire, Australia .. 91 E4
Neville, Canada 101 D7
Nevinnomyssk, Russia . 43 D9
Nevis, W. Indies 117 C7
Nevrokop = Gotse
 Delchev, Bulgaria ... 39 H6
Nevşehir, Turkey 66 D6
Nevşehir □, Turkey .. 66 D6
New →, Guyana 121 C6
New Albany, Ind., U.S.A. 104 F3
New Albany, Miss., U.S.A. 109 H10
New Albany, Pa., U.S.A. 107 E8
New Amsterdam, Guyana 121 B6
New Angledool, Australia 91 D4
New Bedford, U.S.A. .. 107 E14
New Bern, U.S.A. 105 H7
New Bethlehem, U.S.A. 106 F5
New Bloomfield, U.S.A. 106 F7
New Boston, U.S.A. .. 109 J7
New Braunfels, U.S.A. . 109 L5
New Brighton, N.Z. ... 87 K4
New Brighton, U.S.A. . 106 F4
New Britain, Papua N. G. 92 H7
New Britain, U.S.A. .. 107 E12
New Brunswick, U.S.A. 107 F10
New Brunswick □, Canada 99 C6
New Bussa, Nigeria .. 79 D5
New Caledonia, Pac. Oc. 92 K8
New Castile = Castilla La
 Mancha □, Spain ... 31 F7
New Castle, Ind., U.S.A. 104 F3
New Castle, Pa., U.S.A. 106 F4
New City, U.S.A. 107 E11
New Cumberland, U.S.A. 106 F4
New Cuyama, U.S.A. . 113 L7
New Delhi, India 62 E7
New Denver, Canada .. 100 D5
New Don Pedro Reservoir,
 U.S.A. 112 H6
New England, U.S.A. . 108 B3
New England Ra.,
 Australia 91 E5
New Forest, U.K. 13 G6
New Glasgow, Canada . 99 C7
New Guinea, Oceania . 92 H5
New Hamburg, Canada . 106 C4
New Hampshire □, U.S.A. 107 C13
New Hampton, U.S.A. . 108 D8
New Hanover, S. Africa . 85 D5

New Haven, Conn., U.S.A. 107 E12
New Haven, Mich., U.S.A. 106 D2
New Hazelton, Canada ... 100 B3
New Hebrides =
 Vanuatu ■, Pac. Oc. ... 92 J8
New Iberia, U.S.A. 109 K9
New Ireland, Papua N. G. 92 H7
New Jersey □, U.S.A. .. 107 F10
New Kensington, U.S.A. . 106 F5
New Lexington, U.S.A. . 104 F4
New Liskeard, Canada .. 98 C4
New London, Conn.,
 U.S.A. 107 E12
New London, Minn.,
 U.S.A. 108 C7
New London, Ohio, U.S.A. 106 E2
New London, Wis., U.S.A. 108 C10
New Madrid, U.S.A. ... 109 G10
New Meadows, U.S.A. .. 110 D5
New Melones L., U.S.A. . 112 H6
New Mexico □, U.S.A. . 111 J10
New Milford, Conn.,
 U.S.A. 107 E11
New Milford, Pa., U.S.A. 107 E9
New Norcia, Australia ... 89 F2
New Norfolk, Australia .. 90 G4
New Orleans, U.S.A. ... 109 K9
New Philadelphia, U.S.A. 106 F3
New Plymouth, N.Z. ... 87 H5
New Plymouth, U.S.A. .. 110 E5
New Providence, Bahamas 116 A4
New Radnor, U.K. 13 E4
New Richmond, U.S.A. . 108 C8
New Roads, U.S.A. ... 109 K9
New Rochelle, U.S.A. .. 107 F11
New Rockford, U.S.A. .. 108 B5
New Ross, Ireland 15 D5
New Scone, U.K. 14 E5
New Siberian Is. = Novaya
 Sibir, Ostrov, Russia .. 45 B16
New Siberian Is. =
 Novosibirskiye Ostrova,
 Russia 45 B15
New Smyrna Beach, U.S.A. 105 L5
New South Wales □,
 Australia 91 E4
New Springs, Australia .. 89 E3
New Town, U.S.A. 108 A3
New Ulm, U.S.A. 108 C7
New Waterford, Canada . 99 C7
New Westminster, Canada 100 D4
New York □, U.S.A. ... 107 D9
New York City, U.S.A. . 107 F11
New Zealand ■, Oceania . 87 J5
Newala, Tanzania 83 E4
Newala □, Tanzania ... 83 E4
Newark, Del., U.S.A. .. 104 F8
Newark, N.J., U.S.A. .. 107 F10
Newark, N.Y., U.S.A. .. 106 C7
Newark, Ohio, U.S.A. .. 106 F2
Newark-on-Trent, U.K. . 12 D7
Newaygo, U.S.A. 104 D3
Newberg, U.S.A. 110 D2
Newberry, Mich., U.S.A. 98 C2
Newberry, S.C., U.S.A. . 105 H5
Newberry Springs, U.S.A. 113 L10
Newbrook, Canada ... 100 C6
Newburgh, U.S.A. 107 E10
Newbury, U.K. 13 F6
Newbury, U.S.A. 107 B12
Newburyport, U.S.A. .. 107 D14
Newcastle, Australia .. 91 E5
Newcastle, Canada ... 99 C6
Newcastle, S. Africa .. 85 D4
Newcastle, U.K. 15 B6
Newcastle, Calif., U.S.A. 112 G5
Newcastle, Wyo., U.S.A. 108 D2
Newcastle Emlyn, U.K. . 13 E3
Newcastle Ra., Australia 88 C5
Newcastle-under-Lyme,
 U.K. 12 D5
Newcastle-upon-Tyne, U.K. 12 C6
Newcastle Waters, Australia 90 B1
Newdegate, Australia .. 89 F2
Newell, U.S.A. 108 C3
Newfoundland □, Canada 99 B8
Newhalem, U.S.A. 100 D4
Newhall, U.S.A. 113 L8
Newham, U.K. 13 F8
Newhaven, U.K. 13 G8
Newkirk, U.S.A. 109 G6
Newman, Australia ... 88 D2
Newman, U.S.A. 112 H5
Newmarket, Canada .. 106 B5
Newmarket, Ireland .. 15 D3
Newmarket, U.K. 13 E8
Newmarket, U.S.A. .. 107 C14
Newnan, U.S.A. 105 J3
Newport, I. of W., U.K. . 13 G6
Newport, Gwent, U.K. . 13 F5
Newport, Shrops., U.K. . 13 E5
Newport, Ark., U.S.A. . 109 H9
Newport, Ky., U.S.A. . 104 F3
Newport, N.H., U.S.A. . 107 C12
Newport, Oreg., U.S.A. . 110 D1
Newport, Pa., U.S.A. .. 106 F7
Newport, R.I., U.S.A. .. 107 E13
Newport, Tenn., U.S.A. . 105 H4
Newport, Vt., U.S.A. .. 107 B12
Newport, Wash., U.S.A. . 110 B5
Newport Beach, U.S.A. . 113 M9
Newport News, U.S.A. . 104 G7
Newquay, U.K. 13 G2
Newry, U.K. 15 B5

Newry & Mourne □, U.K.   15 B5
Newton, Iowa, U.S.A.   108 E8
Newton, Mass., U.S.A.   107 D13
Newton, Miss., U.S.A.   109 J10
Newton, N.C., U.S.A.   105 H5
Newton, N.J., U.S.A.   107 E10
Newton, Tex., U.S.A.   109 K8
Newton Abbot, U.K.   13 G4
Newton Boyd, Australia   91 D5
Newton Stewart, U.K.   14 G4
Newtonmore, U.K.   14 D4
Newtown, U.K.   13 E4
Newtownabbey □, U.K.   15 B6
Newtownards, U.K.   15 B6
Newville, U.S.A.   106 F7
Nexon, France   26 C5
Neya, Russia   41 B13
Neyrīz, Iran   65 D7
Neyshābūr, Iran   65 B8
Nezhin, Ukraine   40 F7
Nezperce, U.S.A.   110 C5
Ngabang, Indonesia   56 D3
Ngabordamlu, Tanjung, Indonesia   57 F8
Ngambé, Cameroon   79 D7
Ngami Depression, Botswana   84 C3
Ngamo, Zimbabwe   83 F2
Nganglong Kangri, China   61 C12
Nganjuk, Indonesia   57 G14
Ngao, Thailand   58 C2
Ngaoundéré, Cameroon   80 C2
Ngapara, N.Z.   87 L3
Ngara, Tanzania   82 C3
Ngara □, Tanzania   82 C3
Ngawi, Indonesia   57 G14
Nghia Lo, Vietnam   58 B5
Ngoma, Malawi   83 E3
Ngomahura, Zimbabwe   83 G3
Ngomba, Tanzania   83 D3
Ngop, Sudan   77 F3
Ngoring Hu, China   54 C4
Ngorkou, Mali   78 B4
Ngorongoro, Tanzania   82 C4
Ngozi, Burundi   82 C2
Ngudu, Tanzania   82 C3
Nguigmi, Niger   73 F7
Ngukurr, Australia   90 A1
Ngunga, Tanzania   82 C3
Nguru, Nigeria   79 C7
Nguru Mts., Tanzania   82 D4
Nguyen Binh, Vietnam   58 A5
Nha Trang, Vietnam   59 F7
Nhacoongo, Mozam.   85 C6
Nhamaabué, Mozam.   83 F4
Nhambiquara, Brazil   125 C6
Nhamundá, Brazil   121 D6
Nhamundá →, Brazil   121 D6
Nhangutazi, L., Mozam.   85 C5
Nhecolândia, Brazil   125 D6
Nhill, Australia   91 F3
Nho Quan, Vietnam   58 B5
Nhulunbuy, Australia   90 A2
Nia-nia, Zaïre   82 B2
Niafounké, Mali   78 B4
Niagara, U.S.A.   104 C1
Niagara Falls, Canada   98 D4
Niagara Falls, U.S.A.   106 C6
Niagara-on-the-Lake, Canada   106 C5
Niah, Malaysia   56 D4
Niamey, Niger   79 C5
Nianforando, Guinea   78 D2
Nianfors, Sweden   10 C10
Niangara, Zaïre   82 B2
Nias, Indonesia   56 D1
Niassa □, Mozam.   83 E4
Nibbiano, Italy   32 D6
Nibe, Denmark   11 H3
Nicaragua ■, Cent. Amer.   116 D2
Nicaragua, L. de, Nic.   116 D2
Nicastro, Italy   35 D9
Nice, France   27 E11
Niceville, U.S.A.   105 K2
Nichinan, Japan   49 J5
Nicholás, Canal, W. Indies   116 B3
Nicholasville, U.S.A.   104 G3
Nichols, U.S.A.   107 D8
Nicholson, Australia   88 C4
Nicholson, U.S.A.   107 E9
Nicholson →, Australia   90 B2
Nicholson Ra., Australia   89 E2
Nickerie □, Surinam   121 C6
Nickerie →, Surinam   121 B6
Nicobar Is., Ind. Oc.   46 J13
Nicoclí, Colombia   120 B2
Nicola, Canada   100 C4
Nicolet, Canada   98 C5
Nicolls Town, Bahamas   116 A4
Nicosia, Cyprus   37 D12
Nicosia, Italy   35 E7
Nicótera, Italy   35 D8
Nicoya, Costa Rica   116 D2
Nicoya, G. de, Costa Rica   116 E3
Nicoya, Pen. de, Costa Rica   116 E2
Nidau, Switz.   22 B4
Nidd →, U.K.   12 C6
Nidda, Germany   18 E5
Nidda →, Germany   19 E4
Nidwalden □, Switz.   23 C6
Nidzica, Poland   20 B10
Niebüll, Germany   18 A4
Nied →, Germany   25 C13
Niederaula, Germany   18 E5
Niederbipp, Switz.   22 B5

Niederbronn-les-Bains, France   25 D14
Niedere Tauern, Austria   21 H4
Niedersachsen □, Germany   18 C5
Niekerkshoop, S. Africa   84 D3
Niel, Belgium   17 F4
Niellé, Ivory C.   78 C3
Niemba, Zaïre   82 D2
Niemen = Neman →, Lithuania   40 D2
Nienburg, Germany   18 C5
Niers →, Germany   18 D2
Niesen, Switz.   22 C5
Niesky, Germany   18 D10
Nieu Bethesda, S. Africa   84 E3
Nieu-Amsterdam, Neths.   16 C9
Nieuw Amsterdam, Surinam   121 B6
Nieuw Beijerland, Neths.   16 E4
Nieuw-Dordrecht, Neths.   16 C9
Nieuw Loosdrecht, Neths.   16 D6
Nieuw Nickerie, Surinam   121 B6
Nieuw-Schoonebeek, Neths.   16 C10
Nieuw-Vennep, Neths.   16 D5
Nieuw-Vossemeer, Neths.   17 E4
Nieuwe-Niedorp, Neths.   16 C5
Nieuwe-Pekela, Neths.   16 B9
Nieuwe-Schans, Neths.   16 B10
Nieuwendijk, Neths.   16 E5
Nieuwerkerken, Belgium   17 G6
Nieuwkoop, Neths.   16 D5
Nieuwleusen, Neths.   16 C8
Nieuwnamen, Neths.   17 F4
Nieuwolda, Neths.   16 B9
Nieuwoudtville, S. Africa   84 E2
Nieuwpoort, Belgium   17 F1
Nieuwveen, Neths.   16 D5
Nieves, Spain   30 C2
Nieves, Pico de las, Canary Is.   36 G4
Nièvre □, France   25 E10
Niğde, Turkey   66 E6
Niğde □, Turkey   66 E6
Nigel, S. Africa   85 D4
Niger □, Nigeria   79 C6
Niger ■, W. Afr.   79 B6
Niger →, W. Afr.   79 D6
Nigeria ■, W. Afr.   79 D6
Nightcaps, N.Z.   87 L2
Nigríta, Greece   39 J6
Nihtaur, India   63 E8
Nii-Jima, Japan   49 G9
Niigata, Japan   48 F9
Niigata □, Japan   49 F9
Niihama, Japan   49 H6
Niihau, U.S.A.   102 H14
Niimi, Japan   49 G6
Niitsu, Japan   48 F9
Níjar, Spain   29 J2
Nijil, Jordan   69 E4
Nijkerk, Neths.   16 D7
Nijlen, Belgium   17 F5
Nijmegen, Neths.   16 E7
Nijverdal, Neths.   16 D8
Nīk Pey, Iran   65 B6
Nike, Nigeria   79 D6
Nikel, Russia   8 B21
Nikiniki, Indonesia   57 F6
Nikki, Benin   79 D5
Nikkō, Japan   49 F9
Nikolayev, Ukraine   42 C4
Nikolayevsk, Russia   41 G14
Nikolayevsk-na-Amur, Russia   45 D15
Nikolsk, Russia   41 B14
Nikolskoye, Russia   45 D17
Nikopol, Bulgaria   38 F7
Nikopol, Ukraine   42 C6
Niksar, Turkey   42 F7
Nīkshahr, Iran   65 E9
Nikšić, Montenegro   21 N8
Nîl, Nahr en →, Africa   76 H7
Nîl el Abyad →, Sudan   77 D3
Nîl el Azraq →, Sudan   77 D3
Niland, U.S.A.   113 M11
Nile = Nîl, Nahr en →, Africa   76 H7
Nile □, Uganda   82 B3
Nile Delta, Egypt   76 H7
Niles, U.S.A.   106 E4
Nilo Peçanha, Brazil   123 D4
Nimach, India   62 G6
Nimbahera, India   62 G6
Nîmes, France   27 E8
Nimfaíon, Ákra-, Greece   39 J7
Nimmitabel, Australia   91 F4
Nimneryskiy, Russia   45 D13
Nimule, Sudan   77 G3
Nin, Croatia   33 D12
Nīnawá, Iraq   64 B4
Nindigully, Australia   91 D4
Ninemile, U.S.A.   100 B2
Nineveh = Nīnawá, Iraq   64 B4
Ning Xian, China   50 G4
Ning'an, China   51 B15
Ningaloo, Australia   88 D1
Ningbo, China   53 C13
Ningcheng, China   51 D10
Ningde, China   53 D12
Ningdu, China   53 D10
Ninggang, China   53 D9
Ningguo, China   53 B12
Ninghai, China   53 C13
Ninghua, China   53 D11
Ningjin, China   50 F8

Ningjing Shan, China   52 B2
Ninglang, China   52 D3
Ningling, China   50 G8
Ningming, China   52 F6
Ningnan, China   52 D4
Ningpo = Ningbo, China   53 C13
Ningqiang, China   50 H4
Ningshan, China   50 H5
Ningsia Hui A.R. = Ningxia Huizu Zizhiqu □, China   50 E3
Ningwu, China   50 E7
Ningxia Huizu Zizhiqu □, China   50 E3
Ningxiang, China   53 C9
Ningyang, China   50 G9
Ningyuan, China   53 E8
Ninh Binh, Vietnam   58 B5
Ninh Giang, Vietnam   58 B6
Ninh Hoa, Vietnam   58 F7
Ninh Ma, Vietnam   58 F7
Ninove, Belgium   17 G4
Nioaque, Brazil   127 A4
Niobrara, U.S.A.   108 D6
Niobrara →, U.S.A.   108 D6
Nioro du Rip, Senegal   78 C1
Nioro du Sahel, Mali   78 B3
Niort, France   26 B3
Nipawin, Canada   101 C8
Nipawin Prov. Park, Canada   101 C8
Nipigon, Canada   98 C2
Nipigon, L., Canada   98 C2
Nipin →, Canada   101 B7
Nipishish L., Canada   99 B7
Nipissing L., Canada   98 C4
Nipomo, U.S.A.   113 K6
Nipton, U.S.A.   113 K11
Niquelândia, Brazil   123 D2
Nīr, Iran   64 B5
Nirasaki, Japan   49 G9
Nirmal, India   60 K11
Nirmali, India   63 F12
Niš, Serbia   21 M11
Nisa, Portugal   31 F3
Nişāb, Yemen   68 E4
Niscemi, Italy   35 E7
Nishinomiya, Japan   49 G7
Nishin'omote, Japan   49 J5
Nishiwaki, Japan   49 G7
Nísíros, Greece   39 N10
Niskibi →, Canada   98 A2
Nispen, Neths.   17 F4
Nisqually →, U.S.A.   112 C4
Nissáki, Greece   37 A3
Nissan →, Sweden   11 H6
Nissedal, Norway   10 E2
Nisser, Norway   10 E2
Nissum Fjord, Denmark   11 H2
Nistelrode, Neths.   17 E7
Nisutlin →, Canada   100 A2
Nitchequon, Canada   99 B5
Niterói, Brazil   123 F3
Nith →, U.K.   14 F5
Nitra, Slovak Rep.   21 G8
Nitra →, Slovak Rep.   21 H8
Nittedal, Norway   10 D4
Nittendau, Germany   19 F8
Niuafo'ou, Tonga   87 B11
Niue, Cook Is.   93 J11
Niulan Jiang →, China   52 D4
Niut, Indonesia   56 D4
Niutou Shan, China   53 C13
Niuzhuang, China   51 D12
Nivelles, Belgium   17 G4
Nivernais, France   25 E10
Nixon, U.S.A.   109 L6
Nizamabad, India   60 K11
Nizamghat, India   61 E19
Nizhne Kolymsk, Russia   45 C17
Nizhne-Vartovsk, Russia   44 C8
Nizhneangarsk, Russia   45 D11
Nizhnegorskiy, Ukraine   42 D6
Nizhnekamsk, Russia   41 D17
Nizhnekolymsk, Russia   45 D10
Nizhneyansk, Russia   45 B14
Nizhniy Lomov, Russia   41 E13
Nizhniy Novgorod, Russia   41 C14
Nizhniy Tagil, Russia   44 D6
Nizip, Turkey   67 E7
Nizké Tatry, Slovak Rep.   20 G9
Nizza Monferrato, Italy   32 D5
Njakwa, Malawi   83 E3
Njanji, Zambia   83 E3
Njinjo, Tanzania   83 D4
Njombe, Tanzania   83 D3
Njombe □, Tanzania   83 D3
Njombe →, Tanzania   82 D4
Nkambe, Cameroon   79 D7
Nkana, Zambia   83 E2
Nkawkaw, Ghana   79 D4
Nkayi, Zimbabwe   83 F2
Nkhata Bay, Malawi   80 G6
Nkhota Kota, Malawi   83 E3
Nkongsamba, Cameroon   79 E6
Nkurenkuru, Namibia   84 B2
Nkwanta, Ghana   78 D4
Nmai →, Burma   61 G20
Noakhali = Maijdi, Bangla.   61 H17
Noatak, U.S.A.   96 B3
Nobel, Canada   106 A4
Nobeoka, Japan   49 H5
Noblejas, Spain   28 F1
Noblesville, U.S.A.   104 E3

Noce →, Italy   32 B8
Nocera Inferiore, Italy   35 B7
Nocera Terinese, Italy   35 C9
Nocera Umbra, Italy   33 E9
Noci, Italy   35 B10
Nocona, U.S.A.   109 J6
Noda, Japan   49 G9
Noel, U.S.A.   109 G7
Nogales, Mexico   114 A2
Nogales, U.S.A.   111 L8
Nōgata, Japan   49 H5
Nogent-en-Bassigny, France   25 D12
Nogent-le-Rotrou, France   24 D7
Nogent-sur-Seine, France   25 D10
Noggerup, Australia   89 F2
Noginsk, Russia   41 D11
Noginsk, Sib., Russia   45 C10
Nogoa →, Australia   90 C4
Nogoyá, Argentina   126 C4
Nogueira de Ramuín, Spain   30 C3
Noguera Pallaresa →, Spain   28 D5
Noguera Ribagorzana →, Spain   28 D5
Nohar, India   62 E6
Noire, Mt., France   24 D3
Noirétable, France   26 C7
Noirmoutier, I. de, France   24 F4
Noirmoutier-en-l'Ile, France   24 F4
Nojane, Botswana   84 C3
Nojima-Zaki, Japan   49 G9
Nok Kundi, Pakistan   60 E3
Nokaneng, Botswana   84 B3
Nokhtuysk, Russia   45 C12
Nokomis, Canada   101 C8
Nokomis L., Canada   101 B8
Nol, Sweden   11 G6
Nola, C.A.R.   80 D3
Nola, Italy   35 B7
Nolay, France   25 F11
Noli, C. di, Italy   32 D5
Nolinsk, Russia   41 C16
Noma Omuramba →, Namibia   84 B3
Noman L., Canada   101 A7
Nombre de Dios, Panama   116 E4
Nome, U.S.A.   96 B3
Nomo-Zaki, Japan   49 H4
Nonacho L., Canada   101 A7
Nonancourt, France   24 D8
Nonant-le-Pin, France   24 D7
Nonda, Australia   90 C3
Nong Chang, Thailand   58 E2
Nong Het, Laos   58 C4
Nong Khai, Thailand   58 D4
Nong'an, China   51 B13
Nongoma, S. Africa   85 D5
Nonoava, Mexico   114 B3
Nonthaburi, Thailand   58 F3
Nontron, France   26 C4
Nonza, France   27 F13
Noonamah, Australia   88 B5
Noonan, U.S.A.   108 A3
Noondoo, Australia   91 D4
Noonkanbah, Australia   88 C3
Noord-Bergum, Neths.   16 B8
Noord Brabant □, Neths.   17 E6
Noord Holland □, Neths.   16 D5
Noordbeveland, Neths.   17 E3
Noordeloos, Neths.   16 E5
Noordhorn, Neths.   16 B8
Noordoostpolder, Neths.   16 C7
Noordwijk aan Zee, Neths.   16 D4
Noordwijk-Binnen, Neths.   16 D4
Noordwijkerhout, Neths.   16 D5
Noordzee Kanaal, Neths.   16 D5
Noorwolde, Neths.   16 C8
Nootka, Canada   100 D3
Nootka I., Canada   100 D3
Nóqui, Angola   80 F2
Nora, Eritrea   77 D5
Noranda, Canada   98 C4
Nórcia, Italy   33 F10
Norco, U.S.A.   113 M9
Nord □, France   25 B10
Nord-Ostsee Kanal, Germany   18 A5
Nord-Trøndelag fylke □, Norway   8 D12
Nordagutu, Norway   10 E3
Nordaustlandet, Svalbard   4 B9
Nordborg, Denmark   11 J3
Nordby, Århus, Denmark   11 J4
Nordby, Ribe, Denmark   11 J2
Nordeich, Germany   18 B3
Nordegg, Canada   100 C5
Norden, Germany   18 B3
Nordenham, Germany   18 B4
Norderhov, Norway   10 D4
Norderney, Germany   18 B3
Nordfriesische Inseln, Germany   18 A4
Nordhausen, Germany   18 D6
Nordhorn, Germany   18 C3
Nordjyllands Amtskommune □, Denmark   11 H4
Nordkapp, Norway   8 A18
Nordkapp, Svalbard   4 A9
Nordkinn = Kinnarodden, Norway   6 A11
Nordland fylke □, Norway   8 D12

Nördlingen, Germany   19 G6
Nordrhein-Westfalen □, Germany   18 D3
Nordstrand, Germany   18 A4
Nordvik, Russia   45 B12
Nore, Norway   10 D3
Norefjell, Norway   10 D3
Norembega, Canada   98 C3
Noresund, Norway   10 D3
Norfolk, Nebr., U.S.A.   108 D6
Norfolk, Va., U.S.A.   104 G7
Norfolk □, U.K.   12 E9
Norfolk Broads, U.K.   12 E9
Norfolk I., Pac. Oc.   92 K8
Norfork Res., U.S.A.   109 G8
Norg, Neths.   16 B8
Norilsk, Russia   45 C9
Norley, Australia   91 D3
Norma, Mt., Australia   90 C3
Normal, U.S.A.   108 E10
Norman, U.S.A.   109 H6
Norman →, Australia   90 B3
Norman Wells, Canada   96 B7
Normanby →, Australia   90 A3
Normandie, France   24 D7
Normandie, Collines de, France   24 D6
Normandin, Canada   98 C5
Normandy = Normandie, France   24 D7
Normanhurst, Mt., Australia   89 E3
Normanton, Australia   90 B3
Norquay, Canada   101 C8
Norquinco, Argentina   128 B2
Norrbotten □, Sweden   8 C17
Norrby, Sweden   8 D15
Nørre Åby, Denmark   11 J3
Nørre Nebel, Denmark   11 J2
Nørresundby, Denmark   11 G3
Norris, U.S.A.   110 D8
Norristown, U.S.A.   107 F9
Norrköping, Sweden   11 F10
Norrland, Sweden   8 E13
Norrtälje, Sweden   10 E12
Norseman, Australia   89 F3
Norsholm, Sweden   11 F9
Norsk, Russia   45 D14
Norte, Pta., Argentina   128 B4
Norte, Pta. del, Canary Is.   36 G2
Norte de Santander □, Colombia   120 B3
Nortelândia, Brazil   125 C6
North Adams, U.S.A.   107 D11
North America   94 F10
North Battleford, Canada   101 C7
North Bay, Canada   98 C4
North Belcher Is., Canada   98 A4
North Bend, Canada   100 D4
North Bend, Oreg., U.S.A.   110 E1
North Bend, Pa., U.S.A.   106 E7
North Bend, Wash., U.S.A.   112 C5
North Berwick, U.K.   14 E6
North Berwick, U.S.A.   107 C14
North Buganda □, Uganda   82 B3
North Canadian →, U.S.A.   109 H7
North Cape = Nordkapp, Norway   8 A18
North Cape = Nordkapp, Svalbard   4 A9
North C., U.S.A.   99 C7
North C., N.Z.   87 F4
North Caribou L., Canada   98 B1
North Carolina □, U.S.A.   105 H5
North Channel, Canada   98 C3
North Channel, U.K.   14 G3
North Chicago, U.S.A.   104 D2
North Dakota □, U.S.A.   108 B5
North Dandalup, Australia   89 F2
North Down □, U.K.   15 B6
North Downs, U.K.   13 F8
North East, U.S.A.   106 D5
North East Frontier Agency = Arunachal Pradesh □, India   61 E19
North East Providence Chan., W. Indies   116 A4
North Eastern □, Kenya   82 B5
North Esk →, U.K.   14 E6
North European Plain, Europe   6 D11
North Foreland, U.K.   13 F9
North Fork, U.S.A.   112 H7
North Fork American →, U.S.A.   112 G5
North Fork Feather →, U.S.A.   112 F5
North Frisian Is. = Nordfriesische Inseln, Germany   18 A4
North Henik L., Canada   101 A9
North Highlands, U.S.A.   112 G5
North Horr, Kenya   82 B4
North I., Kenya   82 B3
North I., N.Z.   87 H5
North Kingsville, U.S.A.   106 E4
North Knife →, Canada   101 B10
North Koel →, India   63 G10
North Korea ■, Asia   51 E14
North Lakhimpur, India   61 F19
North Las Vegas, U.S.A.   113 J11
North Loup →, U.S.A.   108 E5
North Magnetic Pole, Canada   4 B2

North Minch, *U.K.* 14 C3
North Nahanni →, *Canada* 100 A4
North Olmsted, *U.S.A.* .. 106 E3
North Ossetian Republic □,
Russia 43 E11
North Pagai, I. = Pagai
Utara, *Indonesia* 56 E2
North Palisade, *U.S.A.* ... 111 H4
North Platte, *U.S.A.* 108 E4
North Platte →, *U.S.A.* .. 108 E4
North Pt., *Canada* 99 C7
North Pole, *Arctic* ...... 4 A
North Portal, *Canada* ... 101 D8
North Powder, *U.S.A.* ... 110 D5
North Rhine
Westphalia □ =
Nordrhein-Westfalen □,
Germany 18 D3
North Ronaldsay, *U.K.* .. 14 B6
North Saskatchewan →,
Canada 101 C7
North Sea, *Europe* 6 D6
North Sporades = Voríai
Sporádhes, *Greece* 39 K6
North Sydney, *Canada* .. 99 C7
North Taranaki Bight, *N.Z.* 87 H5
North Thompson →,
Canada 100 C4
North Tonawanda, *U.S.A.* 106 C6
North Troy, *U.S.A.* 107 B12
North Truchas Pk., *U.S.A.* 111 J11
North Twin I., *Canada* .. 98 B3
North Tyne →, *U.K.* 12 C5
North Uist, *U.K.* 14 D1
North Vancouver, *Canada* 100 D4
North Vernon, *U.S.A.* ... 104 F3
North Wabasca L., *Canada* 100 B6
North Walsham, *U.K.* 12 E9
North West C., *Australia* 88 D1
North West Christmas I.
Ridge, *Pac. Oc.* 93 G11
North West Frontier □,
Pakistan 62 C4
North West Highlands,
U.K. 14 D3
North West Providence
Channel, *W. Indies* .. 116 A4
North West River, *Canada* 99 B7
North West Territories □,
Canada 96 B9
North Western □, *Zambia* 83 E2
North York Moors, *U.K.* . 12 C7
North Yorkshire □, *U.K.* . 12 C6
Northallerton, *U.K.* 12 C6
Northam, *S. Africa* 84 C4
Northam, *Australia* 89 E1
Northampton, *U.K.* 13 E7
Northampton, *Mass.*,
U.S.A. 107 D12
Northampton, *Pa.*, *U.S.A.* 107 F9
Northampton Downs,
Australia 90 C4
Northamptonshire □, *U.K.* 13 E7
Northbridge, *U.S.A.* 107 D13
Northcliffe, *Australia* ... 89 F2
Northeim, *Germany* 18 D6
Northern □, *Malawi* 83 E3
Northern □, *Uganda* 82 B3
Northern □, *Zambia* 83 E3
Northern Circars, *India* . 61 L13
Northern Indian L.,
Canada 101 B9
Northern Ireland □, *U.K.* 15 B5
Northern Light, L., *Canada* 98 C1
Northern Marianas ■,
Pac. Oc. 92 F6
Northern Province □,
S. Leone 78 D2
Northern Territory □,
Australia 88 D5
Northfield, *U.S.A.* 108 C8
Northland □, *N.Z.* 87 F4
Northome, *U.S.A.* 108 B7
Northport, *Ala.*, *U.S.A.* . 105 J2
Northport, *Mich.*, *U.S.A.* 104 C3
Northport, *Wash.*, *U.S.A.* 110 B5
Northumberland □, *U.K.* . 12 B5
Northumberland, C.,
Australia 91 F3
Northumberland Is.,
Australia 90 C4
Northumberland Str.,
Canada 99 C7
Northwich, *U.K.* 12 D5
Northwood, *Iowa*, *U.S.A.* 108 D8
Northwood, *N. Dak.*,
U.S.A. 108 B6
Norton, *U.S.A.* 108 F5
Norton, *Zimbabwe* 83 F3
Norton Sd., *U.S.A.* 96 B3
Nortorf, *Germany* 18 A5
Norwalk, *Calif.*, *U.S.A.* . 113 M8
Norwalk, *Conn.*, *U.S.A.* 107 E11
Norwalk, *Ohio*, *U.S.A.* .. 106 E2
Norway, *U.S.A.* 104 C2
Norway ■, *Europe* 8 E11
Norway House, *Canada* .. 101 C9
Norwegian Sea, *Atl. Oc.* . 4 C8
Norwich, *Canada* 106 D4
Norwich, *U.K.* 12 E9
Norwich, *Conn.*, *U.S.A.* 107 E12
Norwood, *Canada* 106 B7
Noshiro, *Japan* 48 D10
Nosok, *Russia* 44 B9
Nosovka, *Ukraine* 40 F7

Noss Hd., *U.K.* 14 C5
Nossa Senhora da Glória,
Brazil 122 D4
Nossa Senhora das Dores,
Brazil 122 D4
Nossa Senhora do
Livramento, *Brazil* ... 125 D6
Nossebro, *Sweden* 11 F6
Nossob →, *S. Africa* ... 84 D3
Nosy Bé, *Madag.* 81 G9
Nosy Boraha, *Madag.* ... 85 B8
Nosy Mitsio, *Madag.* 81 G9
Nosy Varika, *Madag.* 85 C8
Noteć →, *Poland* 20 C5
Notikewin →, *Canada* .. 100 B5
Notios Evvoïkos Kólpos,
Greece 39 L7
Noto, *Italy* 35 F8
Noto, G. di, *Italy* 35 F8
Notodden, *Norway* 10 E3
Notre-Dame, *Canada* ... 99 C7
Notre Dame B., *Canada* .. 99 C8
Notre Dame de Koartac =
Koartac, *Canada* 97 B13
Notre Dame d'Ivugivic =
Ivugivik, *Canada* 97 B12
Notsé, *Togo* 79 D5
Nottawa →, *Canada* 98 B4
Nøtterøy, *Norway* 10 E4
Nottingham, *U.K.* 12 E6
Nottinghamshire □, *U.K.* . 12 D7
Nottoway →, *U.S.A.* ... 104 G7
Notwane →, *Botswana* . 84 C4
Nouâdhibou, *Mauritania* 74 D1
Nouâdhibou, Ras,
Mauritania 74 D1
Nouakchott, *Mauritania* . 78 B1
Nouméa, *N. Cal.* 92 K8
Noupoort, *S. Africa* 84 E3
Nouveau Comptoir, *Canada* 98 B4
Nouvelle-Calédonie = New
Caledonia, *Pac. Oc.* .. 92 K8
Nouzonville, *France* 25 C11
Nová Baňa, *Slovak Rep.* . 21 G8
Nová Bystřice, *Czech.* ... 20 F5
Nova Casa Nova, *Brazil* . 122 C3
Nova Cruz, *Brazil* 122 C4
Nova Era, *Brazil* 123 E3
Nova Esperança, *Brazil* . 127 A5
Nova Friburgo, *Brazil* .. 123 F3
Nova Gaia = Cambundi-
Catembo, *Angola* 80 G3
Nova Gradiška, *Croatia* .. 21 K7
Nova Granada, *Brazil* ... 123 F2
Nova Iguaçu, *Brazil* 123 F3
Nova Iorque, *Brazil* 122 C3
Nova Lamego, *Guinea-Biss.* 78 C2
Nova Lima, *Brazil* 127 A7
Nova Lisboa = Huambo,
Angola 81 G3
Nova Lusitânia, *Mozam.* . 83 F3
Nova Mambone, *Mozam.* 85 C6
Nova Mesto, *Slovenia* ... 33 C12
Nova Ponte, *Brazil* 123 E2
Nova Scotia □, *Canada* .. 99 C7
Nova Sofala, *Mozam.* 85 C5
Nova Venécia, *Brazil* 123 E3
Nova Vida, *Brazil* 125 C5
Nova Zagora, *Bulgaria* .. 38 G8
Novaleksandrovskaya,
Russia 43 D9
Novannenskiy, *Russia* ... 41 F13
Novara, *Italy* 32 C5
Novato, *U.S.A.* 112 G4
Novaya Kakhovka, *Ukraine* 42 C5
Novaya Lyalya, *Russia* .. 44 D7
Novaya Síbir, Ostrov,
Russia 45 B16
Novaya Zemlya, *Russia* .. 44 B6
Novelda, *Spain* 29 G4
Novellara, *Italy* 32 D7
Noventa Vicentina, *Italy* . 33 C8
Novgorod, *Russia* 40 B7
Novgorod-Severskiy,
Ukraine 40 E8
Novi Bečej, *Serbia* 21 K10
Novi Grad, *Croatia* 33 C10
Novi Krichim, *Bulgaria* . 38 G7
Novi Lígure, *Italy* 32 D5
Novi Pazar, *Bulgaria* ... 38 F10
Novi Pazar, *Serbia* 21 M10
Novi Sad, *Serbia* 21 K9
Novi Vinodolski, *Croatia* . 33 C11
Novigrad, *Croatia* 33 D12
Noville, *Belgium* 17 H7
Novo Acôrdo, *Brazil* 122 D2
Novo Aripuanã, *Brazil* .. 121 E5
Nôvo Cruzeiro, *Brazil* .. 123 E3
Nôvo Hamburgo, *Brazil* . 127 B5
Novo Horizonte, *Brazil* . 123 F2
Novo Remanso, *Brazil* .. 122 C3
Novo-Zavidovskiy, *Russia* 41 C10
Novoakrainka, *Ukraine* .. 42 B4
Novoataysk, *Russia* 44 D9
Novoazovsk, *Ukraine* ... 42 C8
Novobelitsa, *Belorussia* . 40 E7
Novobogatinskoye,
Kazakhstan 43 C14
Novocherkassk, *Russia* .. 43 C9
Novodevichye, *Russia* ... 41 E16
Novograd-Volynskiy,
Ukraine 40 F5
Novogrudok, *Belorussia* . 40 E4
Novokachalinsk, *Russia* . 48 B6
Novokayakent, *Russia* ... 43 E12

Novokazalinsk, *Kazakhstan* 44 E7
Novokhopersk, *Russia* ... 41 F12
Novokuybyshevsk, *Russia* 41 E16
Novokuznetsk, *Russia* ... 44 D9
Novomirgorod, *Ukraine* . 42 B4
Novomoskovsk, *Russia* .. 41 D11
Novomoskovsk, *Ukraine* . 42 B6
Novopolotsk, *Belorussia* . 40 D6
Novorossiysk, *Russia* ... 42 D7
Novorybnoye, *Russia* ... 45 B11
Novorzhev, *Russia* 40 C6
Novoselitsa, *Ukraine* 42 B2
Novoshakhtinsk, *Russia* . 43 C8
Novosibirsk, *Russia* 44 D9
Novosibirskiye Ostrova,
Russia 45 B15
Novosil, *Russia* 41 E10
Novosokolniki, *Russia* ... 40 C7
Novotroitsk, *Russia* 44 D6
Novotulskiy, *Russia* 41 D10
Novouzensk, *Russia* 41 F16
Novovolynsk, *Ukraine* ... 40 F4
Novovyatsk, *Russia* 41 B16
Novozybkov, *Russia* 40 E8
Novska, *Croatia* 21 K6
Novvy Port, *Russia* 44 C8
Novy Bug, *Ukraine* 42 C5
Nový Bydzov, *Czech.* 20 E5
Novy Dwór Mazowiecki,
Poland 20 C10
Novyy Afon, *Georgia* 43 E9
Novyy Oskol, *Russia* 41 F10
Now Shahr, *Iran* 65 B6
Nowa Deba, *Poland* 20 E11
Nowa Ruda, *Poland* 20 E6
Nowa Sól, *Poland* 20 D5
Nowbarān, *Iran* 65 C6
Nowe, *Poland* 20 B8
Nowghāb, *Iran* 65 C8
Nowgong, *India* 61 F18
Nowogard, *Poland* 20 B5
Nowogród, *Poland* 20 B11
Nowra, *Australia* 91 E5
Nowshera, *Pakistan* 60 B8
Nowy Korczyn, *Poland* .. 20 E10
Nowy Sącz, *Poland* 20 F10
Noxen, *U.S.A.* 107 E8
Noxon, *U.S.A.* 110 C6
Noya, *Spain* 30 C2
Noyant, *France* 24 E7
Noyers, *France* 25 E10
Noyes I., *U.S.A.* 100 B2
Noyon, *France* 25 C9
Noyon, *Mongolia* 50 C2
Nozay, *France* 24 E5
Nsa O. en →, *Algeria* ... 75 B6
Nsanje, *Malawi* 83 F4
Nsawam, *Ghana* 79 D4
Nsomba, *Zambia* 83 E2
Nsukka, *Nigeria* 79 D6
Nu Jiang →, *China* 52 C1
Nu Shan, *China* 52 D2
Nuba Mts. = Nubah,
Jibalan, *Sudan* 77 E3
Nubah, Jibalan, *Sudan* .. 77 E3
Nubian Desert = Nûbíya,
Es Sahrâ En, *Sudan* ... 76 C3
Nûbíya, Es Sahrâ En,
Sudan 76 C3
Nuble →, *Chile* 126 D1
Nuboai, *Indonesia* 57 E9
Nubra →, *India* 63 B7
Nueces →, *U.S.A.* 109 M6
Nueltin L., *Canada* 101 A9
Nuenen, *Neths.* 17 F7
Nueva, I., *Chile* 128 E3
Nueva Antioquia,
Colombia 120 B4
Nueva Asunción □,
Paraguay 126 A3
Nueva Esparta □,
Venezuela 121 A5
Nueva Gerona, *Cuba* ... 116 B3
Nueva Imperial, *Chile* ... 128 A2
Nueva Palmira, *Uruguay* . 126 C4
Nueva Rosita, *Mexico* ... 114 B4
Nueva San Salvador,
El Salv. 116 D2
Nuéve de Julio, *Argentina* 126 D3
Nuevitas, *Cuba* 116 B4
Nuevo, G., *Argentina* ... 128 B4
Nuevo Guerrero, *Mexico* 115 B5
Nuevo Laredo, *Mexico* .. 115 B5
Nuevo León □, *Mexico* .. 114 C4
Nuevo Mundo, Cerro,
Bolivia 124 E4
Nuevo Rocafuerte, *Ecuador* 120 D3
Nugget Pt., *N.Z.* 87 M2
Nugrus, Gebel, *Egypt* ... 76 C3
Nuhaka, *N.Z.* 87 H6
Nuits-St.-Georges, *France* 25 E11
Nukey Bluff, *Australia* ... 91 E2
Nukheila, *Sudan* 76 D2
Nuku'alofa, *Tonga* 87 E11
Nukus, *Uzbekistan* 44 E6
Nuland, *Neths.* 16 E6
Nulato, *U.S.A.* 96 B4
Nules, *Spain* 28 F4
Nullagine →, *Australia* .. 88 D3
Nullarbor, *Australia* 89 F5
Nullarbor Plain, *Australia* . 89 F4
Numalla, L., *Australia* 91 D3
Numan, *Nigeria* 79 D7
Numansdorp, *Neths.* 16 E4
Numata, *Japan* 49 F9
Numatinna →, *Sudan* ... 77 F2

Numazu, *Japan* 49 G9
Numbulwar, *Australia* ... 90 A2
Numfoor, *Indonesia* 57 E8
Numurkah, *Australia* 91 F4
Nunaksaluk I., *Canada* .. 99 A7
Nuneaton, *U.K.* 13 E6
Nungo, *Mozam.* 83 E4
Nungwe, *Tanzania* 82 C3
Nunivak I., *U.S.A.* 96 B3
Nunkun, *India* 63 C7
Nunspeet, *Neths.* 16 D7
Nuoro, *Italy* 34 B2
Nuquí, *Colombia* 120 B2
Nūrābād, *Iran* 65 E8
Nure →, *Italy* 32 C6
Nuremberg = Nürnberg,
Germany 19 F7
Nuri, *Mexico* 114 B3
Nurina, *Australia* 89 F4
Nuriootpa, *Australia* 91 E2
Nurlat, *Russia* 41 D17
Nürnberg, *Germany* 19 F7
Nurran, L. = Terewah, L.,
Australia 91 D4
Nurrari Lakes, *Australia* . 89 E5
Nurri, *Italy* 34 C2
Nusa Barung, *Indonesia* . 57 H15
Nusa Kambangan,
Indonesia 57 G13
Nusa Tenggara Barat □,
Indonesia 56 F5
Nusa Tenggara Timur □,
Indonesia 57 F6
Nushki, *Pakistan* 62 E2
Nutak, *Canada* 97 C13
Nuth, *Neths.* 17 G7
Nutwood Downs, *Australia* 90 B1
Nuuk = Godthåb,
Greenland 97 B14
Nuwakot, *Nepal* 63 E10
Nuweiba', *Egypt* 76 B3
Nuweveldberge, *S. Africa* . 84 E3
Nuyts, C., *Australia* 89 F5
Nuyts Arch., *Australia* ... 91 E1
Nxau-Nxau, *Botswana* ... 84 B3
Nyaake, *Liberia* 78 E3
Nyack, *U.S.A.* 107 E11
Nyadal, *Sweden* 10 B11
Nyah West, *Australia* 91 F3
Nyahanga, *Tanzania* 82 C3
Nyahua, *Tanzania* 82 D3
Nyahururu, *Kenya* 82 B4
Nyaingentanglha Shan,
China 54 C4
Nyakanazi, *Tanzania* 82 C3
Nyakrom, *Ghana* 79 D4
Nyâlâ, *Sudan* 77 E1
Nyamandhlovu, *Zimbabwe* 83 F2
Nyambiti, *Tanzania* 82 C3
Nyamwaga, *Tanzania* 82 C3
Nyandekwa, *Tanzania* ... 82 C3
Nyanding →, *Sudan* 77 F3
Nyangana, *Namibia* 84 B3
Nyanguge, *Tanzania* 82 C3
Nyankpala, *Ghana* 79 D4
Nyanza, *Burundi* 82 C2
Nyanza, *Rwanda* 82 C2
Nyanza □, *Kenya* 82 C3
Nyarling →, *Canada* 100 A6
Nyasa, L. = Malawi, L.,
Africa 83 E3
Nyazura, *Zimbabwe* 83 F3
Nyazwidzi →, *Zimbabwe* . 83 F3
Nyborg, *Denmark* 11 J4
Nybro, *Sweden* 9 H13
Nyda, *Russia* 44 C8
Nyda →, *Russia* 44 C8
Nyeri, *Kenya* 82 C4
Nyerol, *Sudan* 77 F3
Nyhem, *Sweden* 10 B9
Nyiel, *Sudan* 77 F3
Nyinahin, *Ghana* 78 D4
Nyirbátor, *Hungary* 21 H12
Nyíregyháza, *Hungary* ... 21 H11
Nykarleby, *Finland* 8 E17
Nykøbing, Sjælland,
Denmark 11 J5
Nykøbing, Storstrøm,
Denmark 11 K5
Nykøbing, Viborg,
Denmark 11 H2
Nyköping, *Sweden* 11 F11
Nykvarn, *Sweden* 10 E11
Nyland, *Sweden* 10 A11
Nylstroom, *S. Africa* 85 C4
Nymagee, *Australia* 91 E4
Nymburk, *Czech.* 20 E5
Nynäshamn, *Sweden* 10 F11
Nyngan, *Australia* 91 E4
Nyon, *Switz.* 22 D2
Nyong →, *Cameroon* ... 79 E6
Nyons, *France* 27 D9
Nyord, *Denmark* 11 J6
Nyou, *Burkina Faso* 79 C4
Nysa, *Poland* 20 E7
Nysa →, *Europe* 18 C10
Nyssa, *U.S.A.* 110 E5
Nysted, *Denmark* 11 K5
Nyunzu, *Zaïre* 82 D2
Nyurba, *Russia* 45 C12
Nzega, *Tanzania* 82 C3
Nzega □, *Tanzania* 82 C3
N'Zérékoré, *Guinea* 78 D3
Nzeto, *Angola* 80 F2
Nzilo, Chutes de, *Zaïre* .. 83 E2
Nzubuka, *Tanzania* 82 C3

O

Ō-Shima, *Nagasaki, Japan* 49 G4
Ō-Shima, *Shizuoka, Japan* 49 G9
Oacoma, *U.S.A.* 108 D5
Oahe, L., *U.S.A.* 108 C4
Oahe Dam, *U.S.A.* 108 C4
Oahu, *U.S.A.* 102 H16
Oak Creek, *U.S.A.* 110 F10
Oak Harbor, *U.S.A.* 112 B4
Oak Hill, *U.S.A.* 104 G5
Oak Park, *U.S.A.* 104 E2
Oak Ridge, *U.S.A.* 105 G3
Oak View, *U.S.A.* 113 L7
Oakan-Dake, *Japan* 48 C12
Oakbank, *Australia* 91 E3
Oakdale, *Calif.*, *U.S.A.* . 111 H3
Oakdale, *La.*, *U.S.A.* ... 109 K8
Oakengates, *U.K.* 12 E5
Oakes, *U.S.A.* 108 B5
Oakesdale, *U.S.A.* 110 C5
Oakey, *Australia* 91 D5
Oakham, *U.K.* 12 E7
Oakhurst, *U.S.A.* 112 H7
Oakland, *Calif.*, *U.S.A.* . 111 H2
Oakland, *Oreg.*, *U.S.A.* . 110 E2
Oakland City, *U.S.A.* 104 F2
Oakley, *Idaho*, *U.S.A.* . 110 E7
Oakley, *Kans.*, *U.S.A.* .. 108 F4
Oakover →, *Australia* ... 88 D3
Oakridge, *U.S.A.* 110 E2
Oakville, *U.S.A.* 112 D3
Oamaru, *N.Z.* 87 L3
Oasis, *Calif.*, *U.S.A.* ... 113 M10
Oasis, *Nev.*, *U.S.A.* 112 H9
Oates Land, *Antarctica* .. 5 C11
Oatman, *U.S.A.* 113 K12
Oaxaca, *Mexico* 115 D5
Oaxaca □, *Mexico* 115 D5
Ob →, *Russia* 44 C7
Oba, *Canada* 98 C3
Obala, *Cameroon* 79 E7
Obama, *Japan* 49 G7
Oban, *U.K.* 14 E3
Obbia, *Somali Rep.* 68 F4
Obdam, *Neths.* 16 C5
Obed, *Canada* 100 C5
Ober-Aagau, *Switz.* 22 B5
Obera, *Argentina* 127 B4
Oberalppass, *Switz.* 23 C7
Oberalpstock, *Switz.* 23 C7
Oberammergau, *Germany* 19 H7
Oberdrauburg, *Austria* .. 21 J2
Oberengadin, *Switz.* 23 C9
Oberentfelden, *Switz.* ... 22 B6
Oberhausen, *Germany* ... 18 D2
Oberkirch, *Germany* 19 G4
Oberland, *Switz.* 22 C5
Oberlin, *Kans.*, *U.S.A.* . 108 F4
Oberlin, *La.*, *U.S.A.* ... 109 K8
Oberlin, *Ohio*, *U.S.A.* .. 106 E2
Obernai, *France* 25 D14
Oberndorf, *Germany* 19 G4
Oberon, *Australia* 91 E4
Oberpfälzer Wald,
Germany 19 F8
Obersiggenthal, *Switz.* ... 23 B6
Oberstdorf, *Germany* 19 H6
Oberwil, *Switz.* 22 A5
Obi, Kepulauan, *Indonesia* 57 E7
Obi Is. = Obi, Kepulauan,
Indonesia 57 E7
Obiaruku, *Nigeria* 79 D6
Óbidos, *Brazil* 121 D6
Óbidos, *Portugal* 31 F1
Obihiro, *Japan* 48 C11
Obilatu, *Indonesia* 57 E7
Obilnoye, *Russia* 43 C11
Obing, *Germany* 19 H8
Öbisfelde, *Germany* 18 C6
Objat, *France* 26 C5
Obluchye, *Russia* 45 E14
Obninsk, *Russia* 41 D10
Obo, *C.A.R.* 82 A2
Obo, *Ethiopia* 77 G4
Oboa, Mt., *Uganda* 82 B3
Obock, *Djibouti* 77 E5
Oborniki, *Poland* 20 C6
Oboyan, *Russia* 41 F10
Obozerskaya, *Russia* 44 C5
Obrovac, *Croatia* 33 D12
Obruk, *Turkey* 66 D5
Observatory Inlet, *Canada* 100 B3
Obshchi Syrt, *Kazakhstan* 6 E16
Obskaya Guba, *Russia* ... 44 C8
Obuasi, *Ghana* 79 D4
Obubra, *Nigeria* 79 D6
Obwalden □, *Switz.* 22 C6
Obzor, *Bulgaria* 38 G10
Ocala, *U.S.A.* 105 L4
Ocamo →, *Venezuela* ... 121 C5
Ocampo, *Mexico* 114 B3
Ocaña, *Colombia* 120 B3
Ocaña, *Spain* 28 F1
Ocanomowoc, *U.S.A.* ... 108 D10
Ocate, *U.S.A.* 109 G2
Occidental, Cordillera,
Colombia 120 C3
Occidental, Cordillera,
Peru 124 C3
Ocean City, *N.J.*, *U.S.A.* 104 F8
Ocean City, *Wash.*, *U.S.A.* 112 C2
Ocean I. = Banaba,
Kiribati 92 H8

Ocean Park, U.S.A. 112 D2
Oceano, U.S.A. 113 K6
Oceanport, U.S.A. 107 F10
Oceanside, U.S.A. 113 M9
Ochagavia, Spain 28 C3
Ochamchire, Georgia 43 E9
Ochamps, Belgium 17 J6
Ochil Hills, U.K. 14 E5
Ochre River, Canada 101 C9
Ochsenfurt, Germany 19 F6
Ochsenhausen, Germany 19 G5
Ocilla, U.S.A. 105 K4
Ocmulgee →, U.S.A. 105 K4
Ocna Sibiului, Romania 38 D7
Ocoña, Peru 124 D3
Ocoña →, Peru 124 D3
Oconee →, U.S.A. 105 K4
Oconto, U.S.A. 104 C2
Oconto Falls, U.S.A. 104 C1
Ocosingo, Mexico 115 D6
Ocotal, Nic. 116 D2
Ocotlán, Mexico 114 C4
Ocquier, Belgium 17 H6
Ocreza →, Portugal 31 F5
Octave, U.S.A. 111 J7
Octeville, France 24 C5
Ocumare del Tuy, Venezuela 120 A4
Ocuri, Bolivia 125 D4
Oda, Ghana 79 D4
Ōda, Japan 49 G6
Oda, J., Sudan 76 C4
Ódáðahraun, Iceland 8 D5
Ódákra, Sweden 11 H6
Odate, Japan 48 D10
Odawara, Japan 49 G9
Odda, Norway 9 F9
Odder, Denmark 11 J4
Oddur, Somali Rep. 68 G3
Odei →, Canada 101 B9
Odemira, Portugal 31 H2
Ödemiş, Turkey 66 D3
Odendaalsrus, S. Africa 84 D4
Odense, Denmark 11 J4
Odenwald, Germany 19 F5
Oder →, Germany 18 B10
Oderzo, Italy 33 C9
Odesa = Odessa, Ukraine 42 C4
Odessa, Canada 107 B8
Odessa, Ukraine 42 C4
Odessa, Tex., U.S.A. 109 K3
Odessa, Wash., U.S.A. 110 C4
Odiakwe, Botswana 84 C4
Odiel →, Spain 31 H4
Odienné, Ivory C. 78 D3
Odintsovo, Russia 41 D10
Odiongan, Phil. 55 E4
Odobeşti, Romania 38 D10
O'Donnell, U.S.A. 109 J4
Odoorn, Neths. 16 C9
Odorheiu Secuiesc, Romania 38 C8
Odoyevo, Russia 41 E10
Odra →, Poland 20 B4
Odra →, Spain 30 C6
Odžaci, Serbia 21 K9
Odzi, Zimbabwe 85 B5
Oedelem, Belgium 17 F2
Oegstgeest, Neths. 16 D4
Oeiras, Brazil 122 C3
Oeiras, Portugal 31 G1
Oelrichs, U.S.A. 108 D3
Oelsnitz, Germany 18 E8
Oelwein, U.S.A. 108 D9
Oenpelli, Australia 88 B5
Of, Turkey 67 C9
Ofanto →, Italy 35 A9
Offa, Nigeria 79 D5
Offaly □, Ireland 15 C4
Offenbach, Germany 19 E4
Offenburg, Germany 19 G3
Offerdal, Sweden 10 A8
Offida, Italy 33 F10
Offranville, France 24 C8
Ofidhousa, Greece 39 N9
Ofotfjorden, Norway 8 B14
Ōfunato, Japan 48 E10
Oga, Japan 48 E9
Oga-Hantō, Japan 48 E9
Ogahalla, Canada 98 B2
Ōgaki, Japan 49 G8
Ogallala, U.S.A. 108 E4
Ogasawara Gunto, Pac. Oc. 92 G4
Ogbomosho, Nigeria 79 D5
Ogden, Iowa, U.S.A. 108 D8
Ogden, Utah, U.S.A. 110 F7
Ogdensburg, U.S.A. 107 B9
Ogeechee →, U.S.A. 105 K5
Ogilby, U.S.A. 113 N12
Oglio →, Italy 32 C7
Ogmore, Australia 90 C4
Ognon →, France 25 E12
Ogoja, Nigeria 79 D6
Ogoki, Canada 98 B2
Ogoki L., Canada 98 B2
Ogoki Res., Canada 98 B2
Ogooué →, Gabon 80 E1
Ogosta →, Bulgaria 38 F6
Ogowe = Ogooué →, Gabon 80 E1
Ogr = Sharafa, Sudan 77 E2
Ogrein, Sudan 76 D3
Ogulin, Croatia 33 C12

Ogun □, Nigeria 79 D5
Oguta, Nigeria 79 D6
Ogwashi-Uku, Nigeria 79 D6
Ogwe, Nigeria 79 E6
Ohai, N.Z. 87 L2
Ohakune, N.Z. 87 H5
Ohanet, Algeria 75 C6
Ohata, Japan 48 D10
Ohau, L., N.Z. 87 L2
Ohey, Belgium 17 H6
Ohio □, U.S.A. 104 E3
Ohio →, U.S.A. 104 G1
Ohre →, Czech. 20 E4
Ohre →, Germany 18 C7
Ohrid, Macedonia 39 H3
Ohridsko, Jezero, Macedonia 39 H3
Ohrigstad, S. Africa 85 C5
Öhringen, Germany 19 F5
Oiapoque →, Brazil 121 C7
Oikou, China 51 E9
Oil City, U.S.A. 106 E5
Oildale, U.S.A. 113 K7
Oirschot, Neths. 17 E6
Oise □, France 25 C9
Oise →, France 25 D9
Oisterwijk, Neths. 17 E6
Ōita, Japan 49 H5
Ōita □, Japan 49 H5
Oiticica, Brazil 122 C3
Ojai, U.S.A. 113 L7
Ojinaga, Mexico 114 B4
Ojiya, Japan 49 F9
Ojos del Salado, Cerro, Argentina 126 B2
Oka →, Russia 41 C13
Okaba, Indonesia 57 F9
Okahandja, Namibia 84 C2
Okahukura, N.Z. 87 H5
Okanagan L., Canada 100 C5
Okandja, Gabon 80 E2
Okanogan, U.S.A. 110 B4
Okanogan →, U.S.A. 110 B4
Okaputa, Namibia 84 C2
Okara, Pakistan 62 D5
Okarito, N.Z. 87 K3
Okaukuejo, Namibia 84 B2
Okavango Swamps, Botswana 84 B3
Okaya, Japan 49 F9
Okayama, Japan 49 G6
Okayama □, Japan 49 G6
Okazaki, Japan 49 G8
Oke-Iho, Nigeria 79 D5
Okeechobee, U.S.A. 105 M5
Okeechobee, L., U.S.A. 105 M5
Okefenokee Swamp, U.S.A. 105 K4
Okehampton, U.K. 13 G3
Okene, Nigeria 79 D6
Oker →, Germany 18 C6
Okha, Russia 45 D15
Ókhi Óros, Greece 39 L7
Okhotsk, Russia 45 D15
Okhotsk, Sea of, Asia 45 D15
Okhotskiy Perevoz, Russia 45 C14
Okhotsko Kolymskoye, Russia 45 C16
Oki-Shotō, Japan 49 F6
Okiep, S. Africa 84 D2
Okigwi, Nigeria 79 D6
Okija, Nigeria 79 D6
Okinawa □, Japan 49 L3
Okinawa-Guntō, Japan 49 L3
Okinawa-Jima, Japan 49 L4
Okino-erabu-Shima, Japan 49 L4
Okitipupa, Nigeria 79 D5
Oklahoma □, U.S.A. 109 H6
Oklahoma City, U.S.A. 109 H6
Okmulgee, U.S.A. 109 H7
Oknitsa, Ukraine 42 B2
Okolo, Uganda 82 B3
Okolona, U.S.A. 109 H10
Okrika, Nigeria 79 E6
Oktabrsk, Kazakhstan 44 E6
Oktyabrsk, Russia 41 E16
Oktyabrskiy, Belorussia 40 E6
Oktyabrskoy Revolyutsii, Os., Russia 45 B10
Oktyabrskoye = Zhovtnevoye, Ukraine 42 C5
Oktyabrskoye, Russia 44 C7
Okulovka, Russia 40 B8
Okuru, N.Z. 87 K2
Okushiri-Tō, Japan 48 C9
Okuta, Nigeria 79 D5
Okwa →, Botswana 84 C3
Ola, U.S.A. 109 H8
Ólafsfjörður, Iceland 8 C4
Ólafsvík, Iceland 8 D2
Olancha, U.S.A. 113 J8
Olancha Pk., U.S.A. 113 J8
Olanchito, Honduras 116 C2
Öland, Sweden 9 H14
Olargues, France 26 E6
Olary, Australia 91 E3
Olascoaga, Argentina 126 D3
Olathe, U.S.A. 108 F7
Olavarría, Argentina 126 D3
Oława, Poland 20 E7
Ólbia, Italy 34 B2
Ólbia, G. di, Italy 34 B2
Old Bahama Chan. = Bahama, Canal Viejo de, W. Indies 116 B4

Old Baldy Pk. = San Antonio, Mt., U.S.A. 113 L9
Old Castile = Castilla y Leon □, Spain 30 D6
Old Castle, Ireland 15 C4
Old Cork, Australia 90 C3
Old Crow, Canada 96 B6
Old Dale, U.S.A. 113 L11
Old Dongola, Sudan 76 D3
Old Fletton, U.K. 13 E7
Old Forge, N.Y., U.S.A. 107 C10
Old Forge, Pa., U.S.A. 107 E9
Old Fort →, Canada 101 B6
Old Shinyanga, Tanzania 82 C3
Old Speck Mt., U.S.A. 107 B14
Old Town, U.S.A. 99 D6
Old Wives L., Canada 101 C7
Oldbury, U.K. 13 F5
Oldeani, Tanzania 82 C4
Oldenburg, Niedersachsen, Germany 18 B4
Oldenburg, Schleswig-Holstein, Germany 18 A6
Oldenzaal, Neths. 16 D9
Oldham, U.K. 12 D5
Oldman →, Canada 100 D6
Olds, Canada 100 C6
Olean, U.S.A. 106 D6
Oléggio, Italy 32 C5
Oleiros, Portugal 30 F3
Olekma →, Russia 45 C13
Olekminsk, Russia 45 C13
Olema, U.S.A. 112 G4
Olen, Belgium 17 F5
Olenek, Russia 45 C12
Olenek →, Russia 45 B13
Olenino, Russia 40 C8
Oléron, I. d', France 26 C2
Oleśnica, Poland 20 D7
Olesno, Poland 20 E8
Olevsk, Ukraine 40 F5
Olga, Russia 45 E14
Olga, L., Canada 98 C4
Olga, Mt., Australia 89 E5
Ølgod, Denmark 11 J2
Olhão, Portugal 31 H3
Olib, Croatia 33 D11
Oliena, Italy 34 B2
Oliete, Spain 28 D4
Olifants →, Africa 85 C5
Olifantshoek, S. Africa 84 D3
Olimbos, Greece 39 P10
Ólimbos, Óros, Greece 39 J5
Olímpia, Brazil 127 A6
Olinda, Brazil 122 C5
Olindiná, Brazil 122 D4
Olite, Spain 28 C3
Oliva, Argentina 126 C3
Oliva, Spain 29 G4
Oliva, Punta del, Spain 30 B5
Oliva de la Frontera, Spain 31 G4
Olivares, Spain 28 F2
Olivehurst, U.S.A. 112 F5
Oliveira, Brazil 123 F3
Oliveira de Azemeis, Portugal 30 E2
Oliveira dos Brejinhos, Brazil 123 D3
Olivenza, Spain 31 G3
Oliver, Canada 100 D5
Oliver L., Canada 101 B8
Olivone, Switz. 23 C7
Olkhovka, Russia 43 B11
Olkusz, Poland 20 E9
Ollagüe, Chile 126 A2
Olloy, Belgium 17 H5
Olmedo, Spain 30 D6
Olmos, Peru 124 B2
Olney, Ill., U.S.A. 104 F1
Olney, Tex., U.S.A. 109 J5
Oloma, Cameroon 79 E7
Olomane →, Canada 99 B7
Olomouc, Czech. 20 F7
Olonets, Russia 40 B8
Olongapo, Phil. 55 D4
Oloron, Gave d' →, France 26 E2
Oloron-Ste.-Marie, France 26 E3
Olot, Spain 28 C7
Olovo, Bos.-H. 21 L8
Olovyannaya, Russia 45 D12
Oloy →, Russia 45 C16
Olpe, Germany 18 D3
Olshanka, Ukraine 42 B4
Olshany, Ukraine 42 A6
Olst, Neths. 16 D8
Olsztyn, Poland 20 B10
Olt □, Romania 38 F7
Olt →, Romania 38 E9
Oltenița, Romania 38 E9
Olton, U.S.A. 109 H3
Oltu, Turkey 67 C9
Olur, Turkey 67 C10
Olutanga, Phil. 55 H5
Olvega, Spain 28 D3
Olvera, Spain 31 J5
Olymbos, Cyprus 37 D12
Olympia, Greece 39 M4
Olympia, U.S.A. 112 D4
Olympic Mts., U.S.A. 112 C3
Olympic Nat. Park, U.S.A. 112 C3
Olympus, Cyprus 37 E11
Olympus, Mt. = Ólimbos, Óros, Greece 39 J5
Olympus, Mt., U.S.A. 112 C3

Olyphant, U.S.A. 107 E9
Om →, Russia 44 D8
Om Hajer, Eritrea 77 E4
Om Koi, Thailand 58 D2
Ōma, Japan 48 D10
Ōmachi, Japan 49 F8
Omae-Zaki, Japan 49 G9
Ōmagari, Japan 48 E10
Omagh, U.K. 15 B4
Omagh □, U.K. 15 B4
Omaha, U.S.A. 108 E7
Omak, U.S.A. 110 B4
Omalos, Greece 37 D5
Oman ■, Asia 68 C6
Oman, G. of, Asia 65 E8
Omaruru, Namibia 84 C2
Omaruru →, Namibia 84 C1
Omate, Peru 124 D3
Ombai, Selat, Indonesia 57 F6
Omboué, Gabon 80 E1
Ombrone →, Italy 32 F8
Omdurmân, Sudan 77 D3
Omega, Italy 32 C5
Omeonga, Zaïre 82 C1
Ometepe, I. de, Nic. 116 D2
Ometepec, Mexico 115 D5
Ominato, Japan 48 D10
Omineca →, Canada 100 B4
Omiš, Croatia 33 E13
Omišalj, Croatia 33 C11
Omitara, Namibia 84 C2
Ōmiya, Japan 49 G9
Omme Å →, Denmark 11 J2
Ommen, Neths. 16 C8
Ömnögovĭ □, Mongolia 50 C3
Omo →, Ethiopia 77 F4
Omodhos, Cyprus 37 E11
Omolon →, Russia 45 C16
Omono-Gawa →, Japan 48 E10
Omsk, Russia 44 D8
Omsukchan, Russia 45 C16
Ōmu, Japan 48 B11
Omul, Vf., Romania 38 D8
Ōmura, Japan 49 H4
Omuramba Omatako →, Namibia 81 H4
Omurtag, Bulgaria 38 F9
Ōmuta, Japan 49 H5
Omutninsk, Russia 41 B18
On, Belgium 17 H6
Oña, Spain 28 C1
Onaga, U.S.A. 108 F6
Onalaska, U.S.A. 108 D9
Onamia, U.S.A. 108 B8
Onancock, U.S.A. 104 G8
Onang, Indonesia 57 E5
Onaping L., Canada 98 C3
Oñate, Spain 28 B2
Onavas, Mexico 114 B3
Onawa, U.S.A. 108 D6
Onaway, U.S.A. 104 C3
Oncócua, Angola 84 B1
Onda, Spain 28 F4
Ondaejin, N. Korea 51 D15
Ondangua, Namibia 84 B2
Ondárroa, Spain 28 B2
Ondas →, Brazil 123 D3
Ondava →, Slovak Rep. 20 G11
Onderdijk, Neths. 16 C6
Ondjiva, Angola 84 B2
Ondo, Nigeria 79 D5
Ondo □, Nigeria 79 D5
Öndörhaan, Mongolia 54 B6
Öndörshil, Mongolia 50 B5
Öndverðarnes, Iceland 8 D1
Onega, Russia 44 C4
Onega →, Russia 6 C13
Onega, G. of = Onezhskaya Guba, Russia 44 C4
Onega, L. = Onezhskoye Ozero, Russia 44 C4
Onehunga, N.Z. 87 G5
Oneida, U.S.A. 107 C9
Oneida L., U.S.A. 107 C9
O'Neill, U.S.A. 108 D5
Onekotan, Ostrov, Russia 45 E16
Onema, Zaïre 82 C1
Oneonta, Ala., U.S.A. 105 J2
Oneonta, N.Y., U.S.A. 107 D9
Onezhskaya Guba, Russia 44 C4
Onezhskoye Ozero, Russia 44 C4
Ongarue, N.Z. 87 H5
Ongerup, Australia 89 F2
Ongjin, N. Korea 51 F13
Ongkharak, Thailand 58 E3
Ongniud Qi, China 51 C10
Ongoka, Zaïre 82 C2
Ongole, India 60 M12
Ongon, Mongolia 50 B7
Onguren, Russia 45 D11
Onhaye, Belgium 17 H5
Oni, Georgia 43 E10
Onida, U.S.A. 108 C4
Onilahy →, Madag. 85 C7
Onitsha, Nigeria 79 D6
Onoda, Japan 49 G5
Onpyŏng-ni, S. Korea 51 H14
Onsala, Sweden 11 G6
Onslow, Australia 88 D2
Onslow B., U.S.A. 105 H7
Onstwedde, Neths. 16 B10
Ontake-San, Japan 49 G8

Ontario, Calif., U.S.A. 113 L9
Ontario, Oreg., U.S.A. 110 D5
Ontario □, Canada 98 B2
Ontario, L., Canada 98 D4
Onteniente, Spain 29 G4
Ontonagon, U.S.A. 108 B10
Ontur, Spain 29 G3
Onyx, U.S.A. 113 K8
Oodnadatta, Australia 91 D2
Ooldea, Australia 89 F5
Ooltgensplaat, Neths. 17 E4
Oombulgurri, Australia 88 C4
Oona River, Canada 100 C2
Oordegem, Belgium 17 G3
Oorindi, Australia 90 C3
Oost-Vlaanderen □, Belgium 17 F3
Oost-Vlieland, Neths. 16 B6
Oostakker, Belgium 17 F3
Oostburg, Neths. 17 F3
Oostduinkerke, Belgium 17 F1
Oostelijk-Flevoland, Neths. 16 C7
Oostende, Belgium 17 F1
Oosterbeek, Neths. 16 E7
Oosterdijk, Neths. 16 C6
Oosterend, Friesland, Neths. 16 B6
Oosterend, Noord-Holland, Neths. 16 B5
Oosterhout, Noord-Brabant, Neths. 17 E7
Oosterhout, Noord-Brabant, Neths. 17 E5
Oosterschelde, Neths. 17 E4
Oosterwolde, Neths. 16 B8
Oosterzele, Belgium 17 G3
Oostkamp, Belgium 17 F2
Oostmalle, Belgium 17 F5
Oostrozebeke, Belgium 17 G2
Oostvleteven, Belgium 17 G1
Oostvoorne, Neths. 16 E4
Oostzaan, Neths. 16 D5
Ootacamund, India 60 P10
Ootmarsum, Neths. 16 D9
Ootsa L., Canada 100 C3
Opala, Russia 45 D16
Opala, Zaïre 82 C1
Opanake, Sri Lanka 60 R12
Opasatika, Canada 98 C3
Opasquia, Canada 101 C10
Opatija, Croatia 33 C11
Opava, Czech. 20 F7
Opeinde, Neths. 16 B8
Opelousas, U.S.A. 109 K8
Opémisca, L., Canada 98 C5
Opglabbeek, Belgium 17 F7
Opheim, U.S.A. 110 B10
Ophthalmia Ra., Australia 88 D2
Opi, Nigeria 79 D6
Opinaca →, Canada 98 B4
Opinaca L., Canada 98 B4
Opiskotish, L., Canada 99 B6
Oploo, Neths. 17 E7
Opmeer, Neths. 16 C5
Opobo, Nigeria 79 E6
Opochka, Russia 40 C6
Opoczno, Poland 20 D10
Opol, Phil. 55 G6
Opole, Poland 20 E7
Oporto = Porto, Portugal 30 D2
Opotiki, N.Z. 87 H6
Opp, U.S.A. 105 K2
Oppenheim, Germany 19 F4
Opperdoes, Neths. 16 C6
Óppido Mamertina, Italy 35 D8
Oppland fylke □, Norway 10 C3
Oppstad, Norway 10 D5
Oprtalj, Croatia 33 C10
Opua, N.Z. 87 F5
Opunake, N.Z. 87 H4
Opuzen, Croatia 21 M7
Ora, Cyprus 37 E12
Ora, Italy 33 B8
Ora Banda, Australia 89 F3
Oracle, U.S.A. 111 K8
Oradea, Romania 38 B4
Öræfajökull, Iceland 8 D5
Orahovac, Serbia 21 N10
Orai, India 63 G8
Oraison, France 27 E9
Oral = Ural →, Kazakhstan 43 C14
Oral = Uralsk, Kazakhstan 44 D6
Oran, Algeria 75 A4
Oran, Argentina 126 A3
Orange = Oranje →, S. Africa 84 D2
Orange, Australia 91 E4
Orange, France 27 D8
Orange, Calif., U.S.A. 113 M9
Orange, Mass., U.S.A. 107 D12
Orange, Tex., U.S.A. 109 K8
Orange, Va., U.S.A. 104 F6
Orange, C., Brazil 121 C7
Orange Cove, U.S.A. 112 J7
Orange Free State □, S. Africa 84 D4
Orange Grove, U.S.A. 109 M6
Orange Walk, Belize 115 D7
Orangeburg, U.S.A. 105 J5
Orangeville, Canada 98 D3
Orani, Phil. 55 D4
Oranienburg, Germany 18 C9
Oranje →, S. Africa 84 D2
Oranje Vrystaat = Orange Free State □, S. Africa 84 D4

Oranjemund, *Namibia*	84	D2
Oranjerivier, *S. Africa*	84	D3
Oras, *Phil.*	55	E6
Orăştie, *Romania*	38	D6
Oraşul Stalin = Braşov, *Romania*	38	D8
Orava →, *Slovak Rep.*	20	F9
Oravita, *Romania*	38	D4
Orb →, *France*	26	E7
Orba →, *Italy*	32	D5
Ørbæk, *Denmark*	11	J4
Orbe, *Switz.*	22	C3
Orbec, *France*	24	C7
Orbetello, *Italy*	33	F8
Órbigo →, *Spain*	30	C5
Orbost, *Australia*	91	F4
Orce, *Spain*	29	H2
Orce →, *Spain*	29	H2
Orchies, *France*	25	B10
Orchila, I., *Venezuela*	120	A4
Orco →, *Italy*	32	C4
Orcopampa, *Peru*	124	D3
Orcutt, *U.S.A.*	113	L6
Ord →, *Australia*	88	C4
Ord, Mt., *Australia*	88	C4
Ordenes, *Spain*	30	B2
Orderville, *U.S.A.*	111	H7
Ording, *Germany*	18	A4
Ordos = Mu Us Shamo, *China*	50	E5
Ordu, *Turkey*	67	C7
Ordu □, *Turkey*	67	C7
Orduña, *Álava, Spain*	28	C7
Orduña, *Granada, Spain*	29	H1
Ordway, *U.S.A.*	108	F3
Ordzhonikidze = Vladikavkaz, *Russia*	43	E11
Ordzhonikidze, *Ukraine*	42	C6
Ore, *Zaïre*	82	B2
Ore Mts. = Erzgebirge, *Germany*	18	E9
Orealla, *Guyana*	121	B6
Örebro, *Sweden*	9	G13
Örebro län □, *Sweden*	9	G13
Oregon, *U.S.A.*	108	D10
Oregon □, *U.S.A.*	110	E3
Oregon City, *U.S.A.*	112	E4
Orekhov, *Ukraine*	42	C6
Orekhovo-Zuyevo, *Russia*	41	D11
Orel, *Russia*	41	E10
Orel →, *Ukraine*	42	B6
Orellana, Canal de, *Spain*	31	F5
Orellana, Pantano de, *Spain*	31	F5
Orellana la Vieja, *Spain*	31	F5
Orem, *U.S.A.*	110	F8
Ören, *Turkey*	66	E2
Orenburg, *Russia*	44	D6
Orense, *Spain*	30	C3
Orense □, *Spain*	30	C3
Orepuki, *N.Z.*	87	M1
Orestiás, *Greece*	39	H9
Øresund, *Europe*	11	J6
Orford Ness, *U.K.*	13	E9
Orgaña, *Spain*	28	C6
Organos, Pta. de los, *Canary Is.*	36	F2
Orgaz, *Spain*	31	F7
Orgeyev, *Moldavia*	42	C3
Orgon, *France*	27	E9
Orhaneli, *Turkey*	66	D3
Orhangazi, *Turkey*	66	C3
Orhon Gol →, *Mongolia*	54	A5
Óría, *Italy*	35	B10
Orient, *Australia*	91	D3
Oriental, Cordillera, *Bolivia*	125	D4
Oriental, Cordillera, *Colombia*	120	B3
Oriente, *Argentina*	126	D3
Origny-Ste.-Benoîte, *France*	25	C10
Orihuela, *Spain*	29	G4
Orihuela del Tremedal, *Spain*	28	E3
Oriku, *Albania*	39	J2
Orinduik, *Guyana*	121	C5
Orinoco →, *Venezuela*	121	B5
Orissa □, *India*	61	K14
Oristano, *Italy*	34	C1
Oristano, G. di, *Italy*	34	C1
Orituco →, *Venezuela*	120	B4
Orizaba, *Mexico*	115	D5
Orizona, *Brazil*	123	E2
Orjen, *Bos.-H.*	21	N8
Orjiva, *Spain*	29	J1
Orkanger, *Norway*	10	A3
Örkelljunga, *Sweden*	11	H7
Örkény, *Hungary*	21	H9
Orkla →, *Norway*	10	A3
Orkney, *S. Africa*	84	D4
Orkney □, *U.K.*	14	C6
Orkney Is., *U.K.*	14	C6
Orland, *U.S.A.*	112	F4
Orlando, *U.S.A.*	105	L5
Orlando, C. d', *Italy*	35	D7
Orléanais, *France*	25	E9
Orléans, *France*	25	E8
Orleans, *U.S.A.*	107	B12
Orléans, I. d', *Canada*	99	C5
Orlice →, *Czech.*	20	E6
Orlice, *Slovak Rep.*	20	F10
Orlov Gay, *Russia*	41	F16
Ormara, *Pakistan*	60	G4
Ormea, *Italy*	32	D4

Ormília, *Greece*	39	J6
Ormoc, *Phil.*	55	F6
Ormond, *N.Z.*	87	H6
Ormond Beach, *U.S.A.*	105	L5
Ormož, *Slovenia*	33	B13
Ormstown, *Canada*	107	A11
Ornans, *France*	25	E13
Orne □, *France*	24	D7
Orne →, *France*	24	C6
Ørnhøj, *Denmark*	11	H2
Ornö, *Sweden*	10	E12
Örnsköldsvik, *Sweden*	10	A12
Oro, *N. Korea*	51	D14
Oro →, *Mexico*	114	B3
Oro Grande, *U.S.A.*	113	L9
Orobie, Alpi, *Italy*	32	B6
Orocué, *Colombia*	120	C3
Orodo, *Nigeria*	79	D6
Orogrande, *U.S.A.*	111	K10
Orol, *Spain*	30	B3
Oromocto, *Canada*	99	C6
Oron, *Nigeria*	79	E6
Oron, *Switz.*	22	C3
Orono, *Canada*	106	C6
Oropesa, *Spain*	30	F5
Oroquieta, *Phil.*	55	G5
Orós, *Brazil*	122	C4
Orosei, G. di, *Italy*	34	B2
Orosháza, *Hungary*	21	J10
Orotukan, *Russia*	45	C16
Oroville, *Calif., U.S.A.*	112	F5
Oroville, *Wash., U.S.A.*	110	B4
Oroville, L., *U.S.A.*	112	F5
Ororoo, *Australia*	91	E2
Orrville, *U.S.A.*	106	F3
Orsara di Púglia, *Italy*	35	A8
Orsha, *Belorussia*	40	D7
Orsk, *Russia*	44	D6
Ørslev, *Denmark*	11	J5
Orsogna, *Italy*	33	F11
Orşova, *Romania*	38	E5
Ørsted, *Denmark*	11	H4
Orta, L. d', *Italy*	32	C5
Orta Nova, *Italy*	35	A8
Ortaca, *Turkey*	66	E3
Ortaköy, *Çorum, Turkey*	66	C6
Ortaköy, *Niğde, Turkey*	66	D6
Orte, *Italy*	33	F9
Ortegal, C., *Spain*	30	B3
Orteguaza →, *Colombia*	120	C2
Orthez, *France*	26	E3
Ortho, *Belgium*	17	H7
Ortigueira, *Spain*	30	B3
Orting, *U.S.A.*	112	C4
Ortles, *Italy*	32	B7
Ortón →, *Bolivia*	124	C4
Ortona, *Italy*	33	F11
Orūmīyeh, *Iran*	64	B5
Orūmīyeh, Daryācheh-ye, *Iran*	64	B5
Orune, *Italy*	34	B2
Oruro, *Bolivia*	124	D4
Oruro □, *Bolivia*	124	D4
Orust, *Sweden*	11	F5
Oruzgān □, *Afghan.*	60	C5
Orvault, *France*	24	E5
Orvieto, *Italy*	33	F9
Orwell, *U.S.A.*	106	E4
Orwell →, *U.K.*	13	E9
Oryakhovo, *Bulgaria*	38	F6
Orzinuovi, *Italy*	32	C6
Orzysz, *Poland*	20	B11
Osa, Pen. de, *Costa Rica*	116	E3
Osage, *Iowa, U.S.A.*	108	D8
Osage, *Wyo., U.S.A.*	108	D2
Osage →, *U.S.A.*	108	F9
Osage City, *U.S.A.*	108	F7
Ōsaka, *Japan*	49	G7
Osan, *S. Korea*	51	F14
Osawatomie, *U.S.A.*	108	F7
Osborne, *U.S.A.*	108	F5
Osceola, *Ark., U.S.A.*	109	H10
Osceola, *Iowa, U.S.A.*	108	E8
Oschatz, *Germany*	18	D9
Oschersleben, *Germany*	18	C7
Óschiri, *Italy*	34	B2
Oscoda, *U.S.A.*	106	B1
Ösel = Saaremaa, *Estonia*	40	B1
Osëry, *Russia*	41	D11
Osh, *Kirghizia*	44	E8
Oshawa, *Canada*	98	D4
Oshkosh, *Nebr., U.S.A.*	108	E3
Oshkosh, *Wis., U.S.A.*	108	C10
Oshmyany, *Belorussia*	40	D4
Oshnovīyeh, *Iran*	64	B5
Oshogbo, *Nigeria*	79	D5
Oshtorīnān, *Iran*	65	C6
Oshwe, *Zaïre*	80	E3
Osijek, *Croatia*	21	K8
Ósilo, *Italy*	34	B1
Ósimo, *Italy*	33	E10
Osintorf, *Belorussia*	40	D7
Osipenko = Berdyansk, *Ukraine*	42	C7
Osipovichi, *Belorussia*	40	E6
Osizweni, *S. Africa*	85	D5
Oskaloosa, *U.S.A.*	108	E8
Oskarshamn, *Sweden*	9	H14
Oskélanéo, *Canada*	98	C4
Öskemen = Ust-Kamenogorsk, *Kazakhstan*	44	E9
Oskol →, *Ukraine*	41	G10
Oslo, *Norway*	10	E4

Oslob, *Phil.*	55	G5
Oslofjorden, *Norway*	10	E4
Osmanabad, *India*	60	K10
Osmancık, *Turkey*	42	F6
Osmaniye, *Turkey*	66	E7
Ösmo, *Sweden*	10	F11
Osnabrück, *Germany*	18	C4
Osor, *Italy*	33	D11
Osorio, *Brazil*	127	B5
Osorno, *Chile*	128	B2
Osorno, *Spain*	30	C6
Osorno □, *Chile*	128	B2
Osorno, Vol., *Chile*	128	B2
Osoyoos, *Canada*	100	D5
Ospika →, *Canada*	100	B4
Osprey Reef, *Australia*	90	A4
Oss, *Neths.*	16	E7
Ossa, Mt., *Australia*	90	G4
Óssa, Óros, *Greece*	39	K5
Ossa de Montiel, *Spain*	29	G2
Ossabaw I., *U.S.A.*	105	K5
Osse →, *France*	26	D4
Ossendrecht, *Neths.*	17	F4
Ossining, *U.S.A.*	107	E11
Ossipee, *U.S.A.*	107	C13
Ossokmanuan L., *Canada*	99	B7
Ossora, *Russia*	45	D17
Ostashkov, *Russia*	40	C8
Oste →, *Germany*	18	B5
Ostend = Oostende, *Belgium*	17	F1
Oster, *Ukraine*	40	F7
Osterburg, *Germany*	18	C7
Osterburken, *Germany*	19	F5
Österdälven →, *Sweden*	9	F12
Östergötlands län □, *Sweden*	11	F9
Osterholz-Scharmbeck, *Germany*	18	B4
Østerild, *Denmark*	11	G2
Ostermundigen, *Switz.*	22	C4
Östersund, *Sweden*	10	A8
Østfold fylke □, *Norway*	10	E5
Ostfriesische Inseln, *Germany*	18	B3
Ostfriesland, *Germany*	18	B3
Óstia, Lido di, *Italy*	34	A5
Ostíglia, *Italy*	33	C8
Ostra, *Italy*	33	E10
Ostrava, *Czech.*	20	F8
Ostróda, *Poland*	20	B9
Ostrog, *Ukraine*	40	F5
Ostrogozhsk, *Russia*	41	F11
Ostrołęka, *Poland*	20	B11
Ostrov, *Bulgaria*	38	F7
Ostrov, *Romania*	38	E10
Ostrov, *Russia*	40	C6
Ostrów Mazowiecka, *Poland*	20	C11
Ostrów Wielkopolski, *Poland*	20	D7
Ostrowiec-Świętokrzyski, *Poland*	20	E11
Ostrzeszów, *Poland*	20	D7
Ostseebad-Kühlungsborn, *Germany*	18	A7
Ostuni, *Italy*	35	B10
Osum →, *Bulgaria*	38	F7
Osumi →, *Albania*	39	J3
Ōsumi-Kaikyō, *Japan*	49	J5
Ōsumi-Shotō, *Japan*	49	J5
Osun □, *Nigeria*	79	D5
Osuna, *Spain*	31	H5
Oswego, *U.S.A.*	107	C8
Oswestry, *U.K.*	12	E4
Oświecim, *Poland*	20	E9
Otago □, *N.Z.*	87	L2
Otago Harbour, *N.Z.*	87	L3
Ōtake, *Japan*	49	G6
Otaki, *N.Z.*	87	J5
Otaru, *Japan*	48	C10
Otaru-Wan = Ishikari-Wan, *Japan*	48	C10
Otava, *Czech.*	20	F4
Otavalo, *Ecuador*	120	C2
Otavi, *Namibia*	84	B2
Otchinjau, *Angola*	84	B1
Otelec, *Romania*	38	D3
Otero de Rey, *Spain*	30	B3
Othello, *U.S.A.*	110	C4
Othonoí, *Greece*	39	K2
Óthris, Óros, *Greece*	39	K5
Otira Gorge, *N.Z.*	87	K3
Otis, *U.S.A.*	108	E3
Otjiwarongo, *Namibia*	84	C2
Otočac, *Croatia*	33	D12
Otoineppu, *Japan*	48	B11
Otorohanga, *N.Z.*	87	H5
Otoskwin →, *Canada*	98	B2
Otosquen, *Canada*	101	C8
Otranto, *Italy*	35	B11
Otranto, C. d', *Italy*	35	B11
Otranto, Str. of, *Italy*	35	B11
Otse, *S. Africa*	84	D4
Ōtsu, *Japan*	49	G7
Ōtsuki, *Japan*	49	G9
Otta, *Norway*	10	C3
Ottawa = Outaouais →, *Canada*	98	C5
Ottawa, *Canada*	98	C4
Ottawa, *Ill., U.S.A.*	108	E10
Ottawa, *Kans., U.S.A.*	108	F7
Ottawa Is., *Canada*	97	C11

Ottélé, *Cameroon*	79	E7
Otter L., *Canada*	101	B8
Otter Rapids, *Ont., Canada*	98	B3
Otter Rapids, *Sask., Canada*	101	B8
Otterndorf, *Germany*	18	B4
Otterup, *Denmark*	11	J4
Otterville, *Canada*	106	D4
Ottignies, *Belgium*	17	G5
Otto Beit Bridge, *Zimbabwe*	83	F2
Ottosdal, *S. Africa*	84	D4
Ottoshoop, *S. Africa*	84	D4
Ottsjön, *Sweden*	10	A7
Ottumwa, *U.S.A.*	108	E8
Otu, *Nigeria*	79	D5
Otukpa, *Nigeria*	79	D6
Oturkpo, *Nigeria*	79	D6
Otway, B., *Chile*	128	D2
Otway, C., *Australia*	91	F3
Otwock, *Poland*	20	C11
Ötz, *Austria*	19	H6
Ötz →, *Austria*	19	H6
Ötztaler Alpen, *Austria*	19	J7
Ou →, *Laos*	58	B4
Ou Neua, *Laos*	58	A3
Ou-Sammyaku, *Japan*	48	E10
Ouachita →, *U.S.A.*	109	K9
Ouachita, L., *U.S.A.*	109	H8
Ouachita Mts., *U.S.A.*	109	H7
Ouâdane, *Mauritania*	74	D2
Ouadda, *C.A.R.*	73	G9
Ouagadougou, *Burkina Faso*	79	C4
Ouahigouya, *Burkina Faso*	78	C4
Ouahila, *Algeria*	74	C3
Ouahran = Oran, *Algeria*	75	A4
Oualâta, *Mauritania*	78	B3
Ouallene, *Algeria*	75	D5
Ouanda Djallé, *C.A.R.*	73	G9
Ouango, *C.A.R.*	80	D4
Ouarâne, *Mauritania*	74	D2
Ouargla, *Algeria*	75	B6
Ouarkziz, Djebel, *Algeria*	74	C3
Ouarzazate, *Morocco*	74	B3
Ouatagouna, *Mali*	79	B5
Oubangi →, *Zaïre*	80	E3
Oubarakaï, O. →, *Algeria*	75	C6
Ouche →, *France*	25	E12
Oud-Beijerland, *Neths.*	16	E4
Oud-Gastel, *Neths.*	17	E4
Oud Turnhout, *Belgium*	17	F6
Ouddorp, *Neths.*	16	E3
Oude-Pekela, *Neths.*	16	B10
Oude Rijn →, *Neths.*	16	D4
Oudega, *Neths.*	16	B8
Oudenaarde, *Belgium*	17	G3
Oudenbosch, *Neths.*	17	E5
Oudenburg, *Belgium*	17	F2
Ouderkerk, *Utrecht, Neths.*	16	D5
Ouderkerk, *Zuid-Holland, Neths.*	16	E5
Oudeschild, *Neths.*	16	B5
Oudewater, *Neths.*	16	D5
Oudkarspel, *Neths.*	16	C5
Oudon, *France*	24	E5
Oudtshoorn, *S. Africa*	84	E3
Oued Zem, *Morocco*	74	B3
Ouellé, *Ivory C.*	78	D4
Ouenza, *Algeria*	75	A6
Ouessa, *Burkina Faso*	78	C4
Ouessant, I. d', *France*	24	D1
Ouesso, *Congo*	80	D3
Ouest, Pte., *Canada*	99	C7
Ouezzane, *Morocco*	74	B3
Ouffet, *Belgium*	17	H6
Ouidah, *Benin*	79	D5
Ouistreham, *France*	24	C6
Oujda, *Morocco*	75	B4
Oujeft, *Mauritania*	74	D2
Ould Yenjé, *Mauritania*	78	B2
Ouled Djellal, *Algeria*	75	B6
Ouled Naïl, Mts. des, *Algeria*	75	B5
Oulmès, *Morocco*	74	B3
Oulu, *Finland*	8	D18
Oulu □ = Oulun lääni □, *Finland*	8	D19
Oulujärvi, *Finland*	8	D19
Oulujoki →, *Finland*	8	D18
Oulun lääni □, *Finland*	8	D19
Oulx, *Italy*	32	C3
Oum Chalouba, *Chad*	73	E9
Oum-el-Bouaghi, *Algeria*	75	A6
Oum el Ksi, *Algeria*	74	C3
Oum-er-Rbia, O. →, *Morocco*	74	B3
Oumè, *Ivory C.*	78	D3
Ounane, Dj., *Algeria*	75	C6
Ounguati, *Namibia*	84	C2
Ounianga-Kébir, *Chad*	73	E9
Ounianga Sérir, *Chad*	73	E9
Our →, *Lux.*	17	J8
Ouray, *U.S.A.*	111	G10
Ourcq →, *France*	25	C10
Oureg, Oued el →, *Algeria*	75	B5
Ourém, *Brazil*	122	B2
Ourense = Orense, *Spain*	30	C3
Ouricuri, *Brazil*	122	C3
Ourinhos, *Brazil*	127	A6
Ourique, *Portugal*	31	H2
Ouro Fino, *Brazil*	127	A6
Ouro Prêto, *Brazil*	123	F3
Ouro Sogui, *Senegal*	78	B2
Oursi, *Burkina Faso*	79	C4
Ourthe →, *Belgium*	17	H7

Ouse, *Australia*	90	G4
Ouse →, *E. Susx., U.K.*	13	G8
Ouse →, *N. Yorks., U.K.*	12	C8
Oust, *France*	26	F5
Oust →, *France*	24	E4
Outaouais →, *Canada*	98	C5
Outardes →, *Canada*	99	C6
Outat Oulad el Haj, *Morocco*	75	B4
Outer Hebrides, *U.K.*	14	D1
Outer I., *Canada*	99	B8
Outes, *Spain*	30	C2
Outjo, *Namibia*	84	C2
Outlook, *Canada*	101	C7
Outlook, *U.S.A.*	108	A2
Outreau, *France*	25	B8
Ouvèze →, *France*	27	E8
Ouyen, *Australia*	91	F3
Ouzouer-le-Marché, *France*	25	E8
Ovada, *Italy*	32	D5
Ovalau, *Fiji*	87	C8
Ovalle, *Chile*	126	C1
Ovar, *Portugal*	30	E2
Ovejas, *Colombia*	120	B2
Overdinkel, *Neths.*	16	D10
Overflakkee, *Neths.*	16	E4
Overijse, *Belgium*	17	G5
Overijssel □, *Neths.*	16	D9
Overijsselsch Kanaal →, *Neths.*	16	C8
Overpelt, *Belgium*	17	F7
Overton, *U.S.A.*	113	J12
Övertorneå, *Sweden*	8	C17
Ovid, *U.S.A.*	108	E3
Ovidiopol, *Ukraine*	42	C4
Oviedo, *Spain*	30	B5
Oviedo □, *Spain*	30	B5
Oviken, *Sweden*	10	A8
Oviksfjällen, *Sweden*	10	B7
Övör Hangay □, *Mongolia*	50	B2
Ovoro, *Nigeria*	79	D6
Ovruch, *Ukraine*	40	F6
Owaka, *N.Z.*	87	M2
Owase, *Japan*	49	G8
Owatonna, *U.S.A.*	108	C8
Owbeh, *Afghan.*	60	B3
Owego, *U.S.A.*	107	D8
Owen Falls, *Uganda*	82	B3
Owen Sound, *Canada*	98	D3
Owendo, *Gabon*	80	D1
Owens →, *U.S.A.*	112	J9
Owens L., *U.S.A.*	113	J9
Owensboro, *U.S.A.*	104	G2
Owensville, *U.S.A.*	108	F9
Owerri, *Nigeria*	79	D6
Owl →, *Canada*	101	B10
Owo, *Nigeria*	79	D6
Owosso, *U.S.A.*	104	D3
Owyhee, *U.S.A.*	110	F5
Owyhee →, *U.S.A.*	110	E5
Owyhee, L., *U.S.A.*	110	E5
Ox Mts., *Ireland*	15	B3
Oxapampa, *Peru*	124	C2
Oxelösund, *Sweden*	11	F11
Oxford, *N.Z.*	87	K4
Oxford, *U.K.*	13	F6
Oxford, *Miss., U.S.A.*	109	H10
Oxford, *N.C., U.S.A.*	105	G6
Oxford, *Ohio, U.S.A.*	104	F3
Oxford L., *Canada*	101	C9
Oxfordshire □, *U.K.*	13	F6
Oxley, *Australia*	91	E3
Oxnard, *U.S.A.*	113	L7
Oxus = Amudarya →, *Uzbekistan*	44	E6
Oya, *Malaysia*	56	D4
Oyama, *Japan*	49	F9
Oyapock →, *Fr. Guiana*	121	C7
Oyem, *Gabon*	80	D2
Oyen, *Canada*	101	C6
Øyeren, *Norway*	10	E5
Oykel →, *U.K.*	14	D4
Oymyakon, *Russia*	45	C15
Oyo, *Nigeria*	79	D5
Oyo □, *Nigeria*	79	D5
Oyón, *Peru*	124	C2
Oyonnax, *France*	27	B9
Oyster Bay, *U.S.A.*	107	F11
Ōyūbari, *Japan*	48	C11
Ozalp, *Turkey*	67	D10
Ozamiz, *Phil.*	55	G5
Ozark, *Ala., U.S.A.*	105	K3
Ozark, *Ark., U.S.A.*	109	H8
Ozark, *Mo., U.S.A.*	109	G8
Ozark Plateau, *U.S.A.*	109	G9
Ozarks, L. of the, *U.S.A.*	108	F8
Ózd, *Hungary*	21	G10
Ozette, *U.S.A.*	112	B2
Ozieri, *Italy*	34	B2
Ozona, *U.S.A.*	109	K4
Ozorków, *Poland*	20	D9
Ozuluama, *Mexico*	115	C5
Ozurgety, *Georgia*	43	F10

P

P.K. le Roux Dam, *S. Africa*	84	E3
Pa, *Burkina Faso*	78	C4
Pa-an, *Burma*	61	L20
Pa Mong Dam, *Thailand*	58	D4
Paal, *Belgium*	17	F6

Paamiut = Frederikshåb,
  Greenland 4 C5
Paar, Germany 19 G6
Paarl, S. Africa 84 E2
Paatsi →, Russia 8 B20
Paauilo, U.S.A. 102 H17
Pab Hills, Pakistan ... 62 F2
Pabianice, Poland 20 D9
Pabna, Bangla. 61 G16
Pabo, Uganda 82 B3
Pacaás Novos, Serra dos,
  Brazil 125 C5
Pacaipampa, Peru 124 B2
Pacaja →, Brazil 122 B1
Pacajus, Brazil 122 B4
Pacaraima, Sierra,
  Venezuela 121 C5
Pacarán, Peru 124 C2
Pacaraos, Peru 124 C2
Pacasmayo, Peru 124 B2
Paceco, Italy 34 E5
Pachacamac, Peru 124 C2
Pachhar, India 62 G7
Pachino, Italy 35 F8
Pachitea →, Peru 124 B3
Pachiza, Peru 124 B2
Pacho, Colombia 120 B3
Pachpadra, India 60 G8
Pachuca, Mexico 115 C5
Pacific, Canada 100 C3
Pacific-Antarctic Ridge,
  Pac. Oc. 93 M16
Pacific Grove, U.S.A. . 111 H3
Pacific Ocean, Pac. Oc. 93 G14
Pacifica, U.S.A. 112 H4
Pacitan, Indonesia ... 57 H14
Packwood, U.S.A. 112 D5
Pacuí →, Brazil 123 E2
Padaido, Kepulauan,
  Indonesia 57 E9
Padang, Indonesia ... 56 E2
Padangpanjang, Indonesia 56 E2
Padangsidempuan,
  Indonesia 56 D1
Padauari →, Brazil ... 121 D5
Padborg, Denmark 11 K3
Padcaya, Bolivia 125 E5
Paddockwood, Canada . 101 C7
Paderborn, Germany .. 18 D5
Padilla, Bolivia 125 D5
Padloping Island, Canada 97 B13
Pádova, Italy 33 C8
Padra, India 62 H5
Padrauna, India 63 F10
Padre I., U.S.A. 109 M6
Padro, Mte., France .. 27 F12
Padrón, Spain 30 C2
Padstow, U.K. 13 G3
Padua = Pádova, Italy 33 C8
Paducah, Ky., U.S.A. . 104 G1
Paducah, Tex., U.S.A. 109 H4
Padul, Spain 31 H7
Padula, Italy 35 B8
Paengnyong-do, S. Korea 51 F13
Paeroa, N.Z. 87 G5
Paesana, Italy 32 D4
Pafúri, Mozam. 85 C5
Pag, Croatia 33 D11
Paga, Ghana 79 C4
Pagadian, Phil. 55 H5
Pagai Selatan, P., Indonesia 56 E2
Pagai Utara, Indonesia 56 E2
Pagalu = Annobón,
  Atl. Oc. 71 G4
Pagastikós Kólpos, Greece 39 K6
Pagatan, Indonesia ... 56 E5
Page, Ariz., U.S.A. ... 111 H8
Page, N. Dak., U.S.A. 108 B6
Páglieta, Italy 33 F11
Pagny-sur-Moselle, France 25 D13
Pago Pago, Amer. Samoa 87 B13
Pagosa Springs, U.S.A. 111 H10
Pagwa River, Canada . 98 B2
Pahala, U.S.A. 102 J17
Pahang →, Malaysia .. 59 L4
Pahiatua, N.Z. 87 J5
Pahrump, U.S.A. 113 J11
Pahute Mesa, U.S.A. . 112 H10
Pai, Thailand 58 C2
Paia, U.S.A. 102 H16
Paicines, U.S.A. 112 J5
Paide, Estonia 40 B4
Paignton, U.K. 13 G4
Paiján, Peru 124 B2
Päijänne, Finland 9 F18
Paimbœuf, France ... 24 E4
Paimpol, France 24 D3
Painan, Indonesia ... 56 E2
Painesville, U.S.A. ... 106 E3
Paint Hills = Nouveau
  Comptoir, Canada .. 98 B4
Paint L., Canada 101 B9
Paint Rock, U.S.A. ... 109 K5
Painted Desert, U.S.A. 111 J8
Paintsville, U.S.A. ... 104 G4
País Vasco □, Spain .. 28 C2
Paisley, Canada 106 B3
Paisley, U.K. 14 F4
Paisley, U.S.A. 110 E3
Paita, Peru 124 B1
Paiva →, Portugal ... 30 D2
Paizhou, China 53 D9
Pajares, Spain 30 B5
Pajares, Puerto de, Spain 30 C5

Pak Lay, Laos 58 C3
Pak Phanang, Thailand 59 H3
Pak Sane, Laos 58 C4
Pak Song, Laos 58 E6
Pak Suong, Laos 58 C4
Pakaraima Mts., Guyana 121 B5
Pákhnes, Greece 37 D6
Pakistan ■, Asia 62 E3
Pakistan, East =
  Bangladesh ■, Asia . 61 H17
Pakkading, Laos 58 C4
Pakokku, Burma 61 J19
Pakpattan, Pakistan .. 62 D5
Pakrac, Croatia 21 K7
Paks, Hungary 21 J8
Pakse, Laos 58 E5
Paktiā □, Afghan. ... 60 C6
Pakwach, Uganda 82 B3
Pala, Chad 73 G8
Pala, U.S.A. 113 M9
Pala, Zaïre 82 D2
Palabek, Uganda 82 B3
Palacios, U.S.A. 109 L6
Palafrugell, Spain ... 28 D8
Palagiano, Italy 35 B10
Palagonía, Italy 35 E7
Palagruža, Croatia ... 33 F13
Palaiókastron, Greece . 37 D8
Palaiokhóra, Greece .. 37 D5
Palam, India 60 K10
Palamás, Greece 39 K5
Palamós, Spain 28 D8
Palampur, India 62 C7
Palana, Australia 90 F4
Palana, Russia 45 D16
Palanan, Phil. 55 C5
Palanan Pt., Phil. ... 55 C5
Palandri, Pakistan ... 63 C5
Palangkaraya, Indonesia 56 E4
Palani Hills, India ... 60 P10
Palanpur, India 62 G5
Palapye, Botswana ... 84 C4
Palas, Pakistan 63 B5
Palatka, Russia 45 C16
Palatka, U.S.A. 105 L5
Palau = Belau ■, Pac. Oc. 92 G5
Palawan, Phil. 55 G3
Palayankottai, India .. 60 Q10
Palazzo, Pte., France . 27 F12
Palazzo San Gervásio, Italy 35 B8
Palazzolo Acreide, Italy 35 E7
Palca, Chile 124 D4
Paldiski, Estonia 40 B4
Paleleh, Indonesia ... 57 D6
Palembang, Indonesia 56 E2
Palena →, Chile 128 B2
Palena, L., Chile 128 B2
Palencia, Spain 30 C6
Palencia □, Spain 30 C6
Paleokastrítsa, Greece 37 A3
Paleometokho, Cyprus 37 D12
Palermo, Colombia ... 120 C2
Palermo, Italy 34 D6
Palermo, U.S.A. 110 G3
Palestine, Asia 69 D4
Palestine, U.S.A. 109 K7
Palestrina, Italy 34 A5
Paletwa, Burma 61 J18
Palghat, India 60 P10
Palgrave, Mt., Australia 88 D2
Pali, India 62 G5
Palinuro, C., Italy ... 35 B8
Palisade, U.S.A. 108 E4
Paliseul, Belgium 17 J6
Palitana, India 62 J4
Palizada, Mexico 115 D6
Palizzi, Italy 35 E8
Palk Bay, Asia 60 Q11
Palk Strait, Asia 60 Q11
Palkānah, Iraq 64 C5
Palla Road = Dinokwe,
  Botswana 84 C4
Pallanza = Verbánia, Italy 32 C5
Pallasovka, Russia ... 41 F15
Pallisa, Uganda 82 B3
Pallu, India 62 E6
Palm Beach, U.S.A. .. 105 M6
Palm Desert, U.S.A. . 113 M10
Palm Is., Australia ... 90 B4
Palm Springs, U.S.A. . 113 M10
Palma, Mozam. 83 E5
Palma →, Brazil 123 D2
Palma, B. de, Spain .. 36 B9
Palma de Mallorca, Spain 36 B9
Palma del Río, Spain . 31 H5
Palma di Montechiaro, Italy 34 E6
Palma Soriano, Cuba . 116 B4
Palmanova, Italy 33 C10
Palmares, Brazil 122 C4
Palmarito, Venezuela . 120 B3
Palmarola, Italy 34 B5
Palmas, Brazil 127 B5
Palmas, C., Liberia ... 78 E3
Pálmas, G. di, Italy .. 34 C1
Palmas de Monte Alto,
  Brazil 123 D3
Palmdale, U.S.A. 113 L8
Palmeira, Brazil 123 G2
Palmeira dos Índios, Brazil 122 C4
Palmeirais, Brazil 122 C3
Palmeiras →, Brazil .. 123 D2
Palmeirinhas, Pta. das,
  Angola 80 F2
Palmelo, Brazil 123 E2

Palmer, U.S.A. 96 B5
Palmer →, Australia .. 90 B3
Palmer Arch., Antarctica 5 C17
Palmer Land, U.S.A. . 108 F7
Palmer Land, Antarctica 5 D18
Palmerston, Canada .. 106 C4
Palmerston, N.Z. 87 L3
Palmerston North, N.Z. 87 J5
Palmerton, U.S.A. ... 107 F9
Palmetto, U.S.A. 105 M4
Palmi, Italy 35 D8
Palmira, Argentina ... 126 C2
Palmira, Colombia ... 120 C2
Palmyra = Tudmur, Syria 64 C3
Palmyra, Mo., U.S.A. 108 F9
Palmyra, N.Y., U.S.A. 106 C7
Palmyra Is., Pac. Oc. . 93 G11
Palo Alto, U.S.A. 111 H2
Palo del Colle, Italy .. 35 A9
Palo Verde, U.S.A. ... 113 M12
Palombara Sabina, Italy 33 F9
Palompon, Phil. 55 F6
Palopo, Indonesia ... 57 E6
Palos, C. de, Spain ... 29 H4
Palos Verdes, U.S.A. . 113 M8
Palos Verdes, Pt., U.S.A. 113 M8
Palouse, U.S.A. 110 C5
Palpa, Peru 124 C2
Palparara, Australia .. 90 C3
Palu, Indonesia 57 E5
Paluan, Phil. 55 B6
Palwal, India 62 E7
Pama, Burkina Faso .. 79 C5
Pamanukan, Indonesia 57 G12
Pamekasan, Indonesia 57 G15
Pamiers, France 26 E5
Pamirs, Tajikistan ... 44 F8
Pamlico →, U.S.A. ... 105 H7
Pamlico Sd., U.S.A. .. 105 H8
Pampa, U.S.A. 109 H4
Pampa de Agma, Argentina 128 B3
Pampa de las Salinas,
  Argentina 126 C2
Pampa Grande, Bolivia 125 D5
Pampa Hermosa, Peru 124 B2
Pampanua, Indonesia 57 E6
Pamparato, Italy 32 D4
Pampas, Argentina ... 126 D3
Pampas, Peru 124 C3
Pampas →, Peru 124 C3
Pamphylia, Turkey ... 66 E4
Pamplona, Colombia . 120 B3
Pamplona, Spain 28 C3
Pampoenpoort, S. Africa 84 E3
Pamukkale, Turkey .. 66 E3
Pan Xian, China 52 E5
Pana, U.S.A. 108 F10
Panabo, Phil. 55 H6
Panaca, U.S.A. 111 H6
Panagyurishte, Bulgaria 38 G7
Panaitan, Indonesia .. 57 G11
Panaji, India 60 M8
Panamá, Panama 116 E4
Panama ■, Cent. Amer. 116 E4
Panamá, G. de, Panama 116 E4
Panama Canal, Panama 116 E4
Panama City, U.S.A. . 105 K3
Panamint Range, U.S.A. 113 J9
Panamint Springs, U.S.A. 113 J9
Panão, Peru 124 B2
Panaon I., Phil. 55 F6
Panare, Thailand 59 J3
Panarea, Italy 35 D8
Panaro →, Italy 32 D8
Panarukan, Indonesia 57 G15
Panay, Phil. 55 F5
Panay, G., Phil. 55 F5
Pancake Range, U.S.A. 111 G6
Pančevo, Serbia 21 L10
Pancorbo, Paso, Spain 28 C1
Pandan, Antique, Phil. 55 F5
Pandan, Catanduanes, Phil. 55 D6
Pandegelang, Indonesia 57 G12
Pandharpur, India ... 60 L9
Pandilla, Spain 28 D1
Pando, Uruguay 127 C4
Pando □, Bolivia 124 C4
Pando, L. = Hope, L.,
  Australia 91 D2
Pandokrátor, Greece . 37 A3
Pandora, Costa Rica .. 116 E3
Pandora, Lithuania .. 40 D4
Panevėžys, Lithuania 40 D4
Panfilov, Kazakhstan . 44 E8
Panfilovo, Russia 41 F13
Pang-Long, Burma ... 61 H21
Pang-Yang, Burma ... 61 H21
Panga, Zaïre 82 B2
Pangalanes, Canal des,
  Madag. 85 C8
Pangani, Tanzania ... 82 D4
Pangani □, Tanzania . 82 D4
Pangani →, Tanzania 82 D4
Pangfou = Bengbu, China 51 H9
Pangil, Zaïre 82 C2
Pangkah, Tanjung,
  Indonesia 57 G15
Pangkajene, Indonesia 57 E5
Pangkalanbrandan,
  Indonesia 56 D1
Pangkalanbuun, Indonesia 56 E4
Pangkalansusu, Indonesia 56 D1
Pangkalpinang, Indonesia 56 E3
Pangkoh, Indonesia .. 56 E4
Pangnirtung, Canada . 97 B13

Pangrango, Indonesia . 57 G12
Panguipulli, Chile 128 A2
Panguitch, U.S.A. 111 H7
Pangutaran Group, Phil. 55 H4
Panhandle, U.S.A. ... 109 H4
Pani Mines, India 62 H5
Pania-Mutombo, Zaïre 82 D1
Panipat, India 62 E7
Panjal Range, India .. 62 C7
Panjgur, Pakistan ... 60 F4
Panjim = Panaji, India 60 M8
Panjinad Barrage, Pakistan 60 E7
Panjwai, Afghan. 62 D1
Pankshin, Nigeria ... 79 D6
Panna, India 63 G9
Panna Hills, India ... 63 G9
Pano Lefkara, Cyprus . 37 E12
Pano Panayia, Cyprus 37 E11
Panorama, Brazil 127 A5
Pánormon, Greece ... 37 D6
Panshan, China 51 D12
Panshi, China 51 C14
Pantar, Indonesia ... 57 F6
Pante Macassar, Indonesia 57 F6
Pantelleria, Italy 34 F5
Pantón, Spain 30 C3
Pánuco, Mexico 115 C5
Panyam, Nigeria 79 D6
Panyu, China 53 F9
Pao →, Anzoátegui,
  Venezuela 121 B5
Pao →, Apure, Venezuela 120 B4
Páola, Italy 35 C9
Paola, Malta 37 D2
Paola, U.S.A. 108 F7
Paonia, U.S.A. 111 G10
Paoting = Baoding, China 50 E8
Paot'ou = Baotou, China 50 D6
Paoua, C.A.R. 73 G8
Pápa, Hungary 21 H7
Papagayo →, Mexico . 115 D5
Papagayo, G. de,
  Costa Rica 116 D2
Papakura, N.Z. 87 G5
Papantla, Mexico 115 C5
Papar, Malaysia 56 C5
Pápas, Ákra, Greece .. 39 L4
Papenburg, Germany . 18 B3
Paphlagonia, Turkey . 66 C5
Paphos, Cyprus 37 E11
Papien Chiang = Da →,
  Vietnam 58 B5
Papigochic →, Mexico 114 B3
Paposo, Chile 126 B1
Papoutsa, Cyprus 37 E12
Papua New Guinea ■,
  Oceania 92 H6
Papuča, Croatia 33 D12
Papudo, Chile 126 C1
Papuk, Croatia 21 K7
Papun, Burma 61 K20
Papunya, Australia .. 88 D5
Pará = Belém, Brazil . 122 B2
Pará □, Brazil 125 A7
Pará □, Surinam 121 B6
Parábita, Italy 35 B11
Paraburdoo, Australia 88 D2
Paracale, Phil. 55 D5
Paracas, Pen., Peru .. 124 C2
Paracatu, Brazil 123 E2
Paracatu →, Brazil ... 123 E2
Paracel Is. = Hsisha
  Chuntao, Pac. Oc. .. 56 A4
Parachilna, Australia . 91 E2
Parachinar, Pakistan . 62 C4
Paraćin, Serbia 21 M11
Paracuru, Brazil 122 B4
Parada, Punta, Peru .. 124 D2
Paradas, Spain 31 H5
Paradela, Spain 30 C3
Paradhísi, Greece 37 C10
Paradip, India 61 J15
Paradise, Calif., U.S.A. 112 F5
Paradise, Mont., U.S.A. 110 C6
Paradise, Nev., U.S.A. 113 J11
Paradise →, Canada .. 99 B8
Paradise Valley, U.S.A. 110 F5
Parado, Indonesia ... 57 F5
Paragould, U.S.A. ... 109 G9
Paraguá →, Bolivia .. 125 C5
Paragua →, Venezuela 121 B5
Paraguaçu →, Brazil . 123 D4
Paraguaçu Paulista, Brazil 127 A5
Paraguaipoa, Venezuela 120 A3
Paraguaná, Pen. de,
  Venezuela 120 A3
Paraguarí, Paraguay .. 126 B4
Paraguarí □, Paraguay 126 B4
Paraguay ■, S. Amer. . 126 A4
Paraguay →, Paraguay 126 B4
Paraíba = João Pessoa,
  Brazil 122 C5
Paraíba □, Brazil 122 C4
Paraíba do Sul →, Brazil 123 F3
Parainen, Finland ... 9 F17
Paraíso, Mexico 115 D6
Parak, Iran 65 E7
Parakhino Paddubye,
  Russia 40 B8
Parakou, Benin 79 D5
Paralimni, Cyprus ... 37 D12
Paramaribo, Surinam . 121 B6
Parambu, Brazil 122 C3
Paramillo, Nudo del,
  Colombia 120 B2

Paramirim, Brazil 123 D3
Paramirim →, Brazil . 123 D3
Paramithiá, Greece .. 39 K3
Paramushir, Ostrov, Russia 45 D16
Paran →, Israel 69 E4
Paraná, Argentina ... 126 C3
Paraná, Brazil 123 D2
Paraná □, Brazil 127 A5
Paraná →, Argentina . 126 C4
Paranaguá, Brazil 127 B6
Paranaíba →, Brazil .. 123 F1
Paranaíba →, Brazil .. 127 A5
Paranapanema →,
  Brazil 127 A6
Paranapiacaba, Serra do,
  Brazil 127 A5
Paranavaí, Brazil 127 A5
Parang, Jolo, Phil. ... 55 J4
Parang, Mindanao, Phil. 57 C6
Parangaba, Brazil 122 B4
Parapóla, Greece 39 N6
Paraspóri, Ákra, Greece 39 P10
Paratinga, Brazil 123 D3
Paratoo, Australia ... 91 E2
Parattah, Australia .. 90 G4
Paraúna, Brazil 123 E1
Paray-le-Monial, France 27 B8
Parbati →, India 62 G7
Parbhani, India 60 K10
Parchim, Germany ... 18 B7
Parczew, Poland 20 D12
Pardes Hanna, Israel . 69 C3
Pardilla, Spain 30 D7
Pardo →, Bahia, Brazil 123 E4
Pardo →, Mato Grosso,
  Brazil 127 A5
Pardo →, Minas Gerais,
  Brazil 123 E3
Pardo →, São Paulo,
  Brazil 123 F2
Pardubice, Czech. ... 20 E5
Pare, Indonesia 57 G15
Pare □, Tanzania 82 C4
Pare Mts., Tanzania .. 82 C4
Parecis, Serra dos, Brazil 125 C6
Paredes de Nava, Spain 30 C6
Pareh, Iran 64 B5
Parelhas, Brazil 122 C4
Paren, Russia 45 C17
Parent, Canada 98 C5
Parent, L., Canada ... 98 C4
Parentis-en-Born, France 26 D2
Parepare, Indonesia .. 57 E5
Parfino, Russia 40 C7
Pargo, Pta. do, Madeira 36 D2
Paria, G. de, Venezuela 121 A5
Paria, Pen. de, Venezuela 121 A5
Pariaguán, Venezuela 121 B5
Pariaman, Indonesia . 56 E2
Paricatuba, Brazil ... 121 D5
Paricutín, Cerro, Mexico 114 D4
Parigi, Java, Indonesia 57 G13
Parigi, Sulawesi, Indonesia 57 E6
Parika, Guyana 121 B6
Parima, Serra, Brazil . 121 C5
Parinari, Peru 124 A3
Paring, Romania 38 D6
Parintins, Brazil 121 D6
Pariparit Kyun, Burma 61 M18
Paris, Canada 98 D3
Paris, France 25 D9
Paris, Idaho, U.S.A. .. 110 E8
Paris, Ky., U.S.A. ... 104 F3
Paris, Tenn., U.S.A. .. 105 G1
Paris, Tex., U.S.A. ... 109 J7
Paris, Ville de □, France 25 D9
Parish, U.S.A. 107 C8
Pariti, Indonesia 57 F6
Park City, U.S.A. 112 B4
Park City, U.S.A. 110 F8
Park Falls, U.S.A. ... 108 C9
Park Range, U.S.A. .. 110 G10
Park Rapids, U.S.A. .. 108 B7
Park River, U.S.A. ... 108 A6
Park Rynie, S. Africa . 85 E5
Parkā Bandar, Iran .. 65 E8
Parker, Ariz., U.S.A. . 113 L12
Parker, S. Dak., U.S.A. 108 D6
Parker Dam, U.S.A. .. 113 L12
Parkersburg, U.S.A. .. 104 F5
Parkerview, Canada .. 101 C8
Parkes, Australia 91 E4
Parkfield, U.S.A. 112 K6
Parkland, U.S.A. 112 C4
Parkside, Canada 101 C7
Parkston, U.S.A. 108 D5
Parksville, Canada ... 100 D4
Parma, Italy 32 D7
Parma, Idaho, U.S.A. 110 E5
Parma, Ohio, U.S.A. . 106 E3
Parma →, Italy 32 D7
Parnaguá, Brazil 122 D3
Parnaíba, Piauí, Brazil 122 B3
Parnaíba, São Paulo, Brazil 125 D7
Parnaíba →, Brazil .. 122 B3
Parnamirim, Brazil .. 122 C4
Parnarama, Brazil ... 122 C3
Parnassós, Greece ... 39 L5
Párnis, Greece 39 L6
Párnon Óros, Greece . 39 M5
Pärnu, Estonia 40 B4
Paroo →, Australia .. 91 E3
Páros, Greece 39 M8
Parowan, U.S.A. 111 H7
Parpaillon, France ... 27 D10
Parral, Chile 126 D1
Parramatta, Australia . 91 E5

Parras, *Mexico* 114 B4
Parrett →, *U.K.* 13 F5
Parris I., *U.S.A.* 105 J5
Parrsboro, *Canada* 99 C7
Parry Is., *Canada* 4 B2
Parry Sound, *Canada* 98 C3
Parsberg, *Germany* 19 F7
Parshall, *U.S.A.* 108 B3
Parsnip →, *Canada* 100 B4
Parsons, *U.S.A.* 109 G7
Parsons Ra., *Australia* ... 90 A2
Partanna, *Italy* 34 E5
Parthenay, *France* 24 F6
Partinico, *Italy* 34 D6
Paru →, *Brazil* 121 D7
Parú →, *Venezuela* 120 C4
Paru de Oeste →, *Brazil* . 121 C6
Parucito →, *Venezuela* ... 120 B4
Paruro, *Peru* 124 C3
Parván □, *Afghan.* 60 B6
Parvatipuram, *India* 61 K13
Parys, *S. Africa* 84 D4
Pas-de-Calais □, *France* .. 25 B9
Pasadena, *Calif., U.S.A.* . 113 L8
Pasadena, *Tex., U.S.A.* .. 109 L7
Pasaje, *Ecuador* 120 D2
Pasaje →, *Argentina* 126 B3
Pasay, *Phil.* 55 D4
Pascagoula, *U.S.A.* 109 K10
Pascagoula →, *U.S.A.* ... 109 K10
Paşcani, *Romania* 38 B9
Pasco, *U.S.A.* 110 C4
Pasco □, *Peru* 124 C2
Pasco, Cerro de, *Peru* ... 124 C2
Pascua, I. de, *Pac. Oc.* .. 93 K17
Pasewalk, *Germany* 18 B10
Pasfield L., *Canada* 101 B7
Pasha →, *Russia* 40 B8
Pashiwari, *Pakistan* 63 B6
Pashmakli = Smolyan,
   Bulgaria 39 H7
Pasinler, *Turkey* 67 D9
Pasirian, *Indonesia* 57 H15
Paskūh, *Iran* 65 E9
Pasley, C., *Australia* 89 F3
Pašman, *Croatia* 33 E12
Pasni, *Pakistan* 60 G3
Paso Cantinela, *Mexico* ... 113 N11
Paso de Indios, *Argentina* . 128 B3
Paso de los Libres,
   Argentina 126 B4
Paso de los Toros, *Uruguay* 126 C4
Paso Flores, *Argentina* ... 128 B2
Paso Robles, *U.S.A.* 111 J3
Pasorapa, *Bolivia* 125 D5
Paspébiac, *Canada* 99 C6
Pasrur, *Pakistan* 62 C6
Passage West, *Ireland* 15 E3
Passaic, *U.S.A.* 107 F10
Passau, *Germany* 19 G9
Passendale, *Belgium* 17 G2
Passero, C., *Italy* 35 F8
Passo Fundo, *Brazil* 127 B5
Passos, *Brazil* 123 F2
Passow, *Germany* 18 B10
Passwang, *Switz.* 22 B5
Passy, *France* 27 C10
Pastaza □, *Ecuador* 120 D2
Pastaza →, *Peru* 120 D2
Pastęk, *Poland* 20 A9
Pasto, *Colombia* 120 C2
Pastos Bons, *Brazil* 122 C3
Pastrana, *Spain* 28 E2
Pasuruan, *Indonesia* 57 G15
Patagonia, *Argentina* 128 C2
Patagonia, *U.S.A.* 111 L8
Patambar, *Iran* 65 D9
Patan, *India* 60 H8
Patan, *Maharashtra, India* 62 H5
Patan, *Nepal* 61 F14
Patani, *Indonesia* 57 D7
Pataudi, *India* 62 E7
Patay, *France* 25 D8
Patchewollock, *Australia* . 91 F3
Patchogue, *U.S.A.* 107 F11
Patea, *N.Z.* 87 H5
Pategi, *Nigeria* 79 D6
Patensie, *S. Africa* 84 E3
Paternò, *Italy* 35 E7
Pateros, *U.S.A.* 110 B4
Paterson, *U.S.A.* 107 F10
Paterson Ra., *Australia* ... 88 D3
Paterswolde, *Neths.* 16 B9
Pathankot, *India* 62 C6
Pathfinder Reservoir,
   U.S.A. 110 E10
Pathiu, *Thailand* 59 G2
Pathum Thani, *Thailand* .. 58 E3
Pati, *Indonesia* 57 G14
Patía, *Colombia* 120 C2
Patía →, *Colombia* 120 C2
Patiala, *India* 62 D7
Patine Kouka, *Senegal* 78 C2
Pativilca, *Peru* 124 C2
Patkai Bum, *India* 61 F19
Pátmos, *Greece* 39 M9
Patna, *India* 63 G11
Patnos, *Turkey* 67 D10
Patonga, *Uganda* 82 B3
Patos, *Brazil* 122 C4
Patos, L. dos, *Brazil* 127 C5
Patos de Minas, *Brazil* 123 E2
Patquía, *Argentina* 126 C2
Pátrai, *Greece* 39 L4
Pátraïkós Kólpos, *Greece* . 39 L4

Patricio Lynch, I., *Chile* .. 128 C1
Patrocínio, *Brazil* 123 E2
Patta, *Kenya* 82 C5
Pattada, *Italy* 34 B2
Pattani, *Thailand* 59 J3
Patten, *U.S.A.* 99 C6
Patterson, *Calif., U.S.A.* . 111 H3
Patterson, *La., U.S.A.* 109 L9
Patterson, Mt., *U.S.A.* ... 112 G7
Patti, *India* 62 D6
Patti, *Italy* 35 D7
Pattoki, *Pakistan* 62 D5
Patton, *U.S.A.* 106 F6
Patu, *Brazil* 122 C4
Patuakhali, *Bangla.* 61 H17
Patuca →, *Honduras* 116 C3
Patuca, Punta, *Honduras* . 116 C3
Pâturages, *Belgium* 17 H3
Pátzcuaro, *Mexico* 114 D4
Pau, *France* 26 E3
Pau, Gave de →, *France* . 26 E2
Pau d' Arco, *Brazil* 122 C2
Pau dos Ferros, *Brazil* 122 C4
Paucartambo, *Peru* 124 C3
Pauillac, *France* 26 C3
Pauini, *Brazil* 124 B4
Pauini →, *Brazil* 121 D5
Pauk, *Burma* 61 J19
Paul I., *Canada* 99 A7
Paul Isnard, *Fr. Guiana* .. 121 C7
Paulhan, *France* 26 E7
Paulís = Isiro, *Zaïre* 82 B2
Paulista, *Brazil* 122 C5
Paulistana, *Brazil* 122 C3
Paullina, *U.S.A.* 108 D7
Paulo Afonso, *Brazil* 122 C4
Paulo de Faria, *Brazil* 123 F2
Paulpietersburg, *S. Africa* . 85 D5
Pauls Valley, *U.S.A.* 109 H6
Pauma Valley, *U.S.A.* 113 M10
Pausa, *Peru* 124 D3
Pauto →, *Colombia* 120 B3
Pāveh, *Iran* 64 C5
Pavelets, *Russia* 41 E11
Pavia, *Italy* 32 C6
Pavlikeni, *Bulgaria* 38 F8
Pavlodar, *Kazakhstan* 44 D8
Pavlograd, *Ukraine* 42 B6
Pavlovo, *Russia* 41 D13
Pavlovo, *Russia* 45 C12
Pavlovsk, *Russia* 41 F12
Pavlovskaya, *Russia* 43 C8
Pavlovskiy-Posad, *Russia* . 41 D11
Pavullo nel Frignano, *Italy* 32 D7
Pawhuska, *U.S.A.* 109 G6
Pawling, *U.S.A.* 107 E11
Pawnee, *U.S.A.* 109 G6
Pawnee City, *U.S.A.* 108 E6
Pawtucket, *U.S.A.* 107 E13
Paximádhia, *Greece* 37 D6
Paxoí, *Greece* 39 K3
Paxton, *Ill., U.S.A.* 104 E1
Paxton, *Nebr., U.S.A.* ... 108 E4
Payakumbuh, *Indonesia* .. 56 E2
Payerne, *Switz.* 22 C3
Payette, *U.S.A.* 110 D5
Paymogo, *Spain* 31 H3
Payne Bay = Bellin,
   Canada 97 B13
Payne L., *Canada* 97 C12
Paynes Find, *Australia* 89 E2
Paynesville, *Liberia* 78 D2
Paynesville, *U.S.A.* 108 C7
Paysandú, *Uruguay* 126 C4
Payson, *Ariz., U.S.A.* 111 J8
Payson, *Utah, U.S.A.* 110 F8
Paz →, *Guatemala* 116 D1
Paz, B. la, *Mexico* 114 C2
Pāzanān, *Iran* 65 D6
Pazar, *Turkey* 67 C9
Pazarcık, *Turkey* 66 E7
Pazardzhik, *Bulgaria* 38 G7
Pazin, *Croatia* 33 C10
Pazña, *Bolivia* 124 D4
Pčinja →, *Macedonia* 39 H4
Pe Ell, *U.S.A.* 112 D3
Peabody, *U.S.A.* 107 D14
Peace →, *Canada* 100 B6
Peace Point, *Canada* 100 B6
Peace River, *Canada* 100 B5
Peach Springs, *U.S.A.* 111 J7
Peak, The = Kinder Scout,
   U.K. 12 D6
Peak Downs, *Australia* ... 90 C4
Peak Downs Mine,
   Australia 90 C4
Peak Hill, *N.S.W.,
   Australia* 91 E4
Peak Hill, *W. Austral.,
   Australia* 89 E2
Peak Ra., *Australia* 90 C4
Peake, *Australia* 91 F2
Peake Cr. →, *Australia* ... 91 D2
Peale, Mt., *U.S.A.* 111 G9
Pearblossom, *U.S.A.* 113 L9
Pearl →, *U.S.A.* 109 K10
Pearl City, *U.S.A.* 102 H16
Pearsall, *U.S.A.* 109 L5
Pearse I., *Canada* 100 C2
Peary Land, *Greenland* ... 4 A6
Pease →, *U.S.A.* 109 H5
Pebane, *Mozam.* 83 F4
Pebas, *Peru* 120 D3
Pebble, I., *Falk. Is.* 128 D5
Pebble Beach, *U.S.A.* 112 J5

Peč, *Serbia* 21 N10
Peçanha, *Brazil* 123 E3
Péccioli, *Italy* 32 E7
Pechea, *Romania* 38 D10
Pechenezhin, *Ukraine* 42 B1
Pechenga, *Russia* 44 C4
Pechiguera, Pta.,
   Canary Is. 36 F6
Pechnezhskoye Vdkhr.,
   Ukraine 42 A7
Pechora →, *Russia* 44 C6
Pechorskaya Guba, *Russia* 44 C6
Pecica, *Romania* 38 C4
Pečka, *Serbia* 21 L9
Pécora, C., *Italy* 34 C1
Pečory, *Russia* 40 C5
Pecos, *U.S.A.* 109 K3
Pecos →, *U.S.A.* 109 L3
Pécs, *Hungary* 21 J8
Pedder, L., *Australia* 90 G4
Peddie, *S. Africa* 85 E4
Pédernales, *Dom. Rep.* ... 117 C5
Pedieos →, *Cyprus* 37 D12
Pedirka, *Australia* 91 D2
Pedra Azul, *Brazil* 123 E3
Pedra Grande, Recifes de,
   Brazil 123 E4
Pedras Negras, *Brazil* 125 C5
Pedreiras, *Brazil* 122 B3
Pedro Afonso, *Brazil* 122 C2
Pedro Cays, *Jamaica* 116 C4
Pedro Chico, *Colombia* ... 120 C3
Pedro de Valdivia, *Chile* . 126 A2
Pedro Juan Caballero,
   Paraguay 127 A4
Pedro Muñoz, *Spain* 29 F2
Pedrógão Grande, *Portugal* 30 F2
Peebinga, *Australia* 91 E3
Peebles, *U.K.* 14 F5
Peekskill, *U.S.A.* 107 E11
Peel →, *U.K.* 12 C3
Peel →, *Australia* 91 E5
Peel →, *Canada* 96 B6
Peene →, *Germany* 18 A9
Peera Peera Poolanna L.,
   Australia 91 D2
Peers, *Canada* 100 C5
Pegasus Bay, *N.Z.* 87 K4
Pegnitz, *Germany* 19 F7
Pegnitz →, *Germany* 19 F6
Pego, *Spain* 29 G4
Pegu, *Burma* 61 L20
Pegu Yoma, *Burma* 61 K19
Pehuajó, *Argentina* 126 D3
Pei Xian, *China* 50 G9
Peine, *Chile* 126 A2
Peine, *Germany* 18 C6
Peip'ing = Beijing, *China* . 50 E9
Peissenberg, *Germany* 19 H7
Peitz, *Germany* 18 D10
Peixe, *Brazil* 123 D2
Peixe →, *Brazil* 123 F1
Peixoto de Azeredo →,
   Brazil 125 C6
Peize, *Neths.* 16 B8
Pek →, *Serbia* 21 L11
Pekalongan, *Indonesia* ... 57 G13
Pekan, *Malaysia* 59 L4
Pekanbaru, *Indonesia* 56 D2
Pekin, *U.S.A.* 108 E10
Peking = Beijing, *China* .. 50 E9
Pelabuhan Kelang,
   Malaysia 59 L3
Pelabuhan Ratu, Teluk,
   Indonesia 57 G12
Pelabuhanratu, *Indonesia* . 57 G12
Pélagos, *Greece* 39 K7
Pelaihari, *Indonesia* 56 E4
Pelat, Mt., *France* 27 D10
Peleaga, *Romania* 38 D5
Pelechuco, *Bolivia* 124 C4
Pelée, Mt., *Martinique* ... 117 D7
Pelée, Pt., *Canada* 98 D3
Pelee I., *Canada* 98 D3
Pelejo, *Peru* 124 B2
Pelekech, *Kenya* 82 B4
Peleng, *Indonesia* 57 E6
Pelham, *U.S.A.* 105 K3
Pelhřimov, *Czech.* 20 F5
Pelican L., *Canada* 101 C8
Pelican Narrows, *Canada* . 101 B8
Pelican Rapids, *Canada* ... 101 C8
Pelkosenniemi, *Finland* ... 8 C19
Pella, *S. Africa* 84 D2
Pella, *U.S.A.* 108 E8
Péllaro, *Italy* 35 D8
Pellworm, *Germany* 18 A4
Pelly →, *Canada* 96 B6
Pelly Bay, *Canada* 97 B11
Pelly L., *Canada* 96 B9

Pemberton, *Canada* 100 C4
Pembina, *N. Dak., U.S.A.* 101 D9
Pembina, *N. Dak., U.S.A.* 108 A6
Pembina →, *U.S.A.* 101 D9
Pembine, *U.S.A.* 104 C2
Pembroke, *Canada* 98 C4
Pembroke, *U.K.* 13 F3
Pembroke, *U.S.A.* 105 J5
Pen-y-Ghent, *U.K.* 12 C5
Peña, Sierra de la, *Spain* . 28 C4
Peña de Francia, Sierra de,
   Spain 30 E4
Peñafiel, *Portugal* 30 D2
Peñafiel, *Spain* 30 D6
Peñaflor, *Spain* 31 H5
Peñalara, Pico, *Spain* 30 E7
Penalva, *Brazil* 122 B2
Penamacôr, *Portugal* 30 E3
Penang = Pinang, *Malaysia* 59 K3
Penápolis, *Brazil* 127 A6
Peñaranda de Bracamonte,
   Spain 30 E5
Peñarroya-Pueblonuevo,
   Spain 31 G5
Peñas, C. de, *Spain* 30 B5
Penas, G. de, *Chile* 128 C2
Peñas, Pta., *Venezuela* ... 121 A5
Peñas de San Pedro, *Spain* 29 G2
Peñas del Chache,
   Canary Is. 36 E6
Peñausende, *Spain* 30 D5
Pench'i = Benxi, *China* .. 51 D12
Pend Oreille →, *U.S.A.* .. 110 B5
Pend Oreille L., *U.S.A.* .. 110 C5
Pendembu, *S. Leone* 78 D2
Pendências, *Brazil* 122 C4
Pender B., *Australia* 88 C3
Pendleton, *Calif., U.S.A.* . 113 M9
Pendleton, *Oreg., U.S.A.* . 110 D4
Penedo, *Brazil* 122 D4
Penetanguishene, *Canada* . 98 D4
Peng Xian, *China* 52 B4
Pengalengan, *Indonesia* .. 57 G12
Penge, *Kasai Or., Zaïre* .. 82 D1
Penge, *Kivu, Zaïre* 82 C2
Penglai, *China* 51 F11
Pengshui, *China* 52 C7
Penguin, *Australia* 90 G4
Pengxi, *China* 52 B5
Pengze, *China* 53 C11
Penhalonga, *Zimbabwe* ... 83 F3
Peniche, *Portugal* 31 F1
Penicuik, *U.K.* 14 F5
Penida, *Indonesia* 56 F5
Peninsular Malaysia □,
   Malaysia 59 L4
Peñíscola, *Spain* 28 E5
Penitente, Serra dos, *Brazil* 122 C2
Penmarch, *France* 24 E2
Penmarch, Pte. de, *France* 24 E2
Penn Hills, *U.S.A.* 106 F5
Penn Yan, *U.S.A.* 106 D7
Pennabilli, *Italy* 33 E9
Pennant, *Canada* 101 C7
Penne, *Italy* 33 F10
Penner →, *India* 60 M12
Pennine, Alpi, *Alps* 32 B4
Pennines, *U.K.* 12 C5
Pennington, *U.S.A.* 112 F5
Pennino, Mte., *Italy* 33 E9
Pennsylvania □, *U.S.A.* .. 104 E6
Penny, *Canada* 100 C4
Peno, *Russia* 40 C8
Penola, *Australia* 91 F3
Penong, *Australia* 89 F5
Penonomé, *Panama* 116 E3
Penrith, *Australia* 91 E5
Penrith, *U.K.* 12 C5
Pensacola, *U.S.A.* 105 K2
Pensacola Mts., *Antarctica* 5 E1
Pense, *Canada* 101 C8
Penshurst, *Australia* 91 F3
Pentecoste, *Brazil* 122 B4
Penticton, *Canada* 100 D5
Pentland, *Australia* 90 C4
Pentland Firth, *U.K.* 14 C5
Pentland Hills, *U.K.* 14 F5
Penylan L., *Canada* 101 A7
Penza, *Russia* 41 E14
Penzance, *U.K.* 13 G2
Penzberg, *Germany* 19 H7
Penzhino, *Russia* 45 C17
Penzhinskaya Guba, *Russia* 45 C17
Penzlin, *Germany* 18 B9
Peoria, *Ariz., U.S.A.* 111 K7
Peoria, *Ill., U.S.A.* 108 E10
Pepingen, *Belgium* 17 G4
Pepinster, *Belgium* 17 G7
Pera Hd., *Australia* 90 A3
Perabumilih, *Indonesia* ... 56 E2
Perakhóra, *Greece* 39 L5
Perales de Alfambra, *Spain* 28 E4
Perales del Puerto, *Spain* . 30 E4
Peralta, *Spain* 28 C3
Pérama, *Kérkira, Greece* .. 37 A3
Pérama, *Kríti, Greece* 37 D6
Percé, *Canada* 99 C7
Perche, *France* 24 D8
Perche, Collines du, *France* 24 D7
Percival Lakes, *Australia* . 88 D4
Percy, *France* 24 D5
Percy Is., *Australia* 90 C5
Perdido →, *Argentina* 128 B3
Perdido, Mte., *Spain* 26 F4
Perdu, Mt. = Perdido,
   Mte., *Spain* 26 F4

Pereira, *Colombia* 120 C2
Pereira Barreto, *Brazil* ... 123 F1
Perekerten, *Australia* 91 E3
Perené →, *Peru* 124 C3
Perenjori, *Australia* 89 E2
Pereslav Khmelnitskiy,
   Ukraine 41 C11
Pereyaslav Khmelnitskiy,
   Ukraine 40 F7
Pérez, I., *Mexico* 115 C7
Pergamino, *Argentina* 126 C3
Pérgine Valsugano, *Italy* .. 33 B8
Pérgola, *Italy* 33 E9
Perham, *U.S.A.* 108 B7
Perhentian, Kepulauan,
   Malaysia 59 K4
Periam, *Romania* 38 C3
Péribonca →, *Canada* 99 C5
Péribonca, L., *Canada* 99 B5
Perico, *Argentina* 126 A2
Pericos, *Mexico* 114 B3
Périers, *France* 24 C5
Périgord, *France* 26 D4
Périgueux, *France* 26 D4
Perijá, Sierra de, *Colombia* 120 B3
Peristéra, *Greece* 39 K6
Peristerona →, *Cyprus* ... 37 D12
Perito Moreno, *Argentina* . 128 C2
Peritoró, *Brazil* 122 B3
Perković, *Croatia* 33 E13
Perlas, Arch. de las,
   Panama 116 E4
Perlas, Punta de, *Nic.* 116 D3
Perleberg, *Germany* 18 B7
Perlevka, *Russia* 41 F11
Perm, *Russia* 44 D6
Pernambuco = Recife,
   Brazil 122 C5
Pernambuco □, *Brazil* 122 C4
Pernatty Lagoon, *Australia* 91 E2
Pernik, *Bulgaria* 38 G6
Peron, C., *Australia* 89 E1
Peron Is., *Australia* 88 B5
Peron Pen., *Australia* 89 E1
Péronne, *France* 25 C9
Péronnes, *Belgium* 17 H4
Perosa Argentina, *Italy* ... 32 D4
Perow, *Canada* 100 C3
Perpendicular Pt., *Australia* 91 E5
Perpignan, *France* 26 F6
Perris, *U.S.A.* 113 M9
Perros-Guirec, *France* 24 D3
Perry, *Fla., U.S.A.* 105 K4
Perry, *Ga., U.S.A.* 105 J4
Perry, *Iowa, U.S.A.* 108 E7
Perry, *Maine, U.S.A.* 105 C12
Perry, *Okla., U.S.A.* 109 G6
Perryton, *U.S.A.* 109 G4
Perryville, *U.S.A.* 109 G10
Persembe, *Turkey* 67 C8
Perseverancia, *Bolivia* 125 C5
Persia = Iran ■, *Asia* 65 C7
Persian Gulf = Gulf, The,
   Asia 65 E6
Perstorp, *Sweden* 11 H7
Pertek, *Turkey* 67 D8
Perth, *Australia* 89 F2
Perth, *Canada* 98 D4
Perth, *U.K.* 14 E5
Perth Amboy, *U.S.A.* 107 F10
Pertuis, *France* 27 E9
Peru, *Ill., U.S.A.* 108 E10
Peru, *Ind., U.S.A.* 104 E2
Peru ■, *S. Amer.* 120 D2
Peru-Chile Trench,
   Pac. Oc. 93 K20
Perúgia, *Italy* 33 E9
Perušić, *Croatia* 33 D12
Péruwelz, *Belgium* 17 G3
Pervomaysk, *Russia* 41 D13
Pervomaysk, *Ukraine* 42 B4
Pervouralsk, *Russia* 44 D6
Perwez, *Belgium* 17 G5
Pes, Pta. del, *Spain* 36 C7
Pésaro, *Italy* 33 E9
Pescara, *Italy* 33 F11
Pescara →, *Italy* 33 F11
Peschanokopskoye, *Russia* 43 C9
Péscia, *Italy* 32 E7
Pescina, *Italy* 33 G10
Peseux, *Switz.* 22 C3
Peshawar, *Pakistan* 62 B4
Peshtigo, *U.S.A.* 104 C2
Peski, *Russia* 41 F13
Peskovka, *Russia* 41 B17
Pesqueira, *Brazil* 122 C4
Pessac, *France* 26 D3
Pessoux, *Belgium* 17 H6
Pestovo, *Russia* 40 C9
Pestravka, *Russia* 41 E16
Petah Tiqwa, *Israel* 69 C3
Petaling Jaya, *Malaysia* ... 59 L3
Petaloudhes, *Greece* 37 C10
Petaluma, *U.S.A.* 112 G4
Petange, *Lux.* 17 J7
Petatlán, *Mexico* 114 D4
Petauke, *Zambia* 83 E3
Petawawa, *Canada* 98 C4
Petegem, *Belgium* 17 G3
Petén Itzá, L., *Guatemala* . 116 C2
Peter I.s Øy, *Antarctica* .. 5 C16
Peter Pond L., *Canada* ... 101 B7
Peterbell, *Canada* 98 C3
Peterborough, *Australia* .. 91 E2
Peterborough, *Canada* 97 D12

Peterborough, *U.K.* 13 E7
Peterborough, *U.S.A.* .. 107 D13
Peterhead, *U.K.* 14 D7
Petermann Bjerg,
  Greenland 94 B17
Peter's Mine, *Guyana* ... 121 B6
Petersburg, *Alaska, U.S.A.* 100 B2
Petersburg, *Ind., U.S.A.* .. 104 F2
Petersburg, *Va., U.S.A.* .. 104 G7
Petersburg, *W. Va., U.S.A.* 104 F6
Petford, *Australia* 90 B3
Petília Policastro, *Italy* .. 35 C9
Petit Bois I., *U.S.A.* 105 K1
Petit-Cap, *Canada* 99 C7
Petit Goâve, *Haiti* 117 C5
Petit Lac Manicouagan,
  Canada 99 B6
Petit Saint Bernard, Col
  du, *Italy* 32 C3
Petitcodiac, *Canada* 99 C6
Petite Baleine →, *Canada* 98 A4
Petite Saguenay, *Canada* . 99 C5
Petitsikapau, L., *Canada* . 99 B6
Petlad, *India* 62 H5
Peto, *Mexico* 115 C7
Petone, *N.Z.* 87 J5
Petoskey, *U.S.A.* 104 C3
Petra, *Jordan* 69 E4
Petra, *Spain* 36 B10
Petra, Ostrova, *Russia* ... 4 B13
Petra Velikogo, Zaliv,
  Russia 48 C5
Petralia, *Italy* 35 E7
Petrel, *Spain* 29 G4
Petreto-Bicchisano, *France* 27 G12
Petrich, *Bulgaria* 39 H6
Petrijanec, *Croatia* 33 B13
Petrikov, *Belorussia* 40 E6
Petrinja, *Croatia* 33 C13
Petrograd = Sankt-
  Peterburg, *Russia* 40 B7
Petrolândia, *Brazil* 122 C4
Petrolia, *Canada* 98 D3
Petrolina, *Brazil* 122 C3
Petropavlovsk, *Kazakhstan* 44 D7
Petropavlovsk-
  Kamchatskiy, *Russia* ... 45 D16
Petropavlovsk-
  Akhtubinsk, *Russia* =
  43 B12
Petrópolis, *Brazil* 123 F3
Petroşeni, *Romania* 38 D6
Petrova Gora, *Croatia* ... 33 C12
Petrovac, *Montenegro* ... 21 N8
Petrovsk, *Russia* 41 E14
Petrovsk-Zabaykalskiy,
  Russia 45 D11
Petrovskoye = Svetlograd,
  Russia 43 D10
Petrozavodsk, *Russia* 44 C4
Petrus Steyn, *S. Africa* .. 85 D4
Petrusburg, *S. Africa* 84 D4
Petukhovka, *Belorussia* ... 40 E7
Peumo, *Chile* 126 C1
Peureulak, *Indonesia* 56 D1
Pevek, *Russia* 45 C18
Peveragno, *Italy* 32 D4
Peyrehorade, *France* 26 E2
Peyruis, *France* 27 D9
Pézenas, *France* 26 E7
Pfaffenhofen, *Germany* ... 19 G7
Pfäffikon, *Switz.* 23 B7
Pfarrkirchen, *Germany* ... 19 G8
Pfeffenhausen, *Germany* .. 19 G7
Pforzheim, *Germany* 19 G4
Pfullendorf, *Germany* 19 H5
Pfungstadt, *Germany* 19 F4
Phagwara, *India* 60 D9
Phaistós, *Greece* 37 D6
Phala, *Botswana* 84 C4
Phalera = Phulera, *India* . 62 F6
Phalodi, *India* 62 F5
Phalsbourg, *France* 25 D14
Phan, *Thailand* 58 C2
Phan Rang, *Vietnam* 59 G7
Phan Ri = Hoa Da,
  Vietnam 59 G7
Phan Thiet, *Vietnam* 59 G7
Phanat Nikhom, *Thailand* . 58 F3
Phangnga, *Thailand* 59 H2
Phanh Bho Ho Chi Minh,
  Vietnam 59 G6
Phanom Sarakham,
  Thailand 58 F3
Pharenda, *India* 63 F10
Phatthalung, *Thailand* ... 59 J3
Phayao, *Thailand* 58 C2
Phelps, *N.Y., U.S.A.* 106 D7
Phelps, *Wis., U.S.A.* 108 B10
Phelps L., *Canada* 101 B8
Phenix City, *U.S.A.* 105 J3
Phet Buri, *Thailand* 58 F2
Phetchabun, *Thailand* ... 58 D3
Phetchabun, Thiu Khao,
  Thailand 58 E3
Phetchaburi = Phet Buri,
  Thailand 58 F2
Phi Phi, Ko, *Thailand* ... 59 J2
Phiafay, *Laos* 58 E6
Phibun Mangsahan,
  Thailand 58 E5
Phichai, *Thailand* 58 D3
Phichit, *Thailand* 58 D3
Philadelphia, *Miss., U.S.A.* 109 J10
Philadelphia, *N.Y., U.S.A.* 107 B9

Philadelphia, *Pa., U.S.A.* . 107 F9
Philip, *U.S.A.* 108 C4
Philippeville, *Belgium* ... 17 H5
Philippi L., *Australia* 90 C2
Philippines ■, *Asia* 55 F5
Philippolis, *S. Africa* 84 E4
Philippopolis = Plovdiv,
  Bulgaria 38 G7
Philipsburg, *Mont., U.S.A.* 110 C7
Philipsburg, *Pa., U.S.A.* .. 106 F6
Philipstown, *S. Africa* 84 E3
Phillip I., *Australia* 91 F4
Phillips, *Tex., U.S.A.* 109 H4
Phillips, *Wis., U.S.A.* 108 C9
Phillipsburg, *Kans., U.S.A.* 108 F5
Phillipsburg, *N.J., U.S.A.* . 107 F9
Phillott, *Australia* 91 D4
Philmont, *U.S.A.* 107 D11
Philomath, *U.S.A.* 110 D2
Phimai, *Thailand* 58 E4
Phitsanulok, *Thailand* ... 58 D3
Phnom Dangrek, *Thailand* 58 E5
Phnom Penh, *Cambodia* . 59 G5
Phoenix, *Ariz., U.S.A.* ... 111 K7
Phoenix, *N.Y., U.S.A.* ... 107 C8
Phoenix Is., *Kiribati* 92 H10
Phoenixville, *U.S.A.* 107 F9
Phon, *Thailand* 58 E4
Phon Tiou, *Laos* 58 D5
Phong →, *Thailand* 58 D4
Phong Saly, *Laos* 58 B4
Phong Tho, *Vietnam* 58 A4
Phonhong, *Laos* 58 C4
Phonum, *Thailand* 59 H2
Phosphate Hill, *Australia* . 90 C2
Photharam, *Thailand* 58 F2
Phra Chedi Sam Ong,
  Thailand 58 E2
Phra Nakhon Si Ayutthaya,
  Thailand 58 E3
Phra Thong, Ko, *Thailand* 59 H2
Phrae, *Thailand* 58 C3
Phrom Phiram, *Thailand* . 58 D3
Phrygia, *Turkey* 66 D3
Phu Dien, *Vietnam* 58 C5
Phu Loi, *Laos* 58 B4
Phu Ly, *Vietnam* 58 B5
Phu Tho, *Vietnam* 58 B5
Phuc Yen, *Vietnam* 58 B5
Phuket, *Thailand* 59 J2
Phuket, Ko, *Thailand* 59 J2
Phulera, *India* 62 F6
Phumiphon, Khuan,
  Thailand 58 D2
Phun Phin, *Thailand* 59 H2
Piacá, *Brazil* 122 C2
Piacenza, *Italy* 32 C6
Piaçabuçu, *Brazil* 122 D4
Piádena, *Italy* 32 C7
Pialba, *Australia* 91 D5
Pian Cr. →, *Australia* ... 91 E4
Piana, *France* 27 F12
Pianella, *Italy* 33 F11
Pianoro, *Italy* 33 D8
Pianosa, *Puglia, Italy* ... 33 F12
Pianosa, *Toscana, Italy* .. 32 F7
Piapot, *Canada* 101 D7
Piare →, *Italy* 33 C9
Pias, *Portugal* 31 G3
Piaseczno, *Poland* 20 C11
Piatã, *Brazil* 123 D3
Piatra, *Romania* 38 F8
Piatra Neamţ, *Romania* .. 38 C9
Piauí □, *Brazil* 122 C3
Piauí →, *Brazil* 122 C3
Piave →, *Italy* 33 C9
Piazza Armerina, *Italy* ... 35 E7
Pibor →, *Sudan* 77 F3
Pibor Post, *Sudan* 77 F3
Pica, *Chile* 124 E4
Picardie, *France* 25 C9
Picardie, Plaine de, *France* 25 C9
Picardy = Picardie, *France* 25 C9
Picayune, *U.S.A.* 109 K10
Picerno, *Italy* 35 B8
Pichilemu, *Chile* 126 C1
Pichincha, □, *Ecuador* ... 120 D2
Pickerel L., *Canada* 98 C1
Pickle Lake, *Canada* 98 B1
Pico Truncado, *Argentina* 128 C3
Picos, *Brazil* 122 C3
Picos Ancares, Sierra de,
  Spain 30 C4
Picota, *Peru* 124 B2
Picquigny, *France* 25 C9
Picton, *Australia* 91 E5
Picton, *Canada* 98 D4
Picton, *N.Z.* 87 J5
Picton, I., *Chile* 128 E3
Pictou, *Canada* 99 C7
Picture Butte, *Canada* ... 100 D6
Picuí, *Brazil* 122 C4
Picún Leufú, *Argentina* .. 128 A3
Pidurutalagala, *Sri Lanka* . 60 R12
Piedecuesta, *Colombia* ... 120 B3
Piedicavallo, *Italy* 32 C4
Piedmont = Piemonte □,
  Italy 32 D4
Piedmont, *U.S.A.* 105 J3
Piedmont Plateau, *U.S.A.* . 105 J5
Piedmonte d'Alife, *Italy* .. 35 A7
Piedra →, *Spain* 28 D3
Piedra del Anguila,
  Argentina 128 B2
Piedra Lais, *Venezuela* ... 120 C4

Piedrabuena, *Spain* 31 F6
Piedrahita, *Spain* 30 E5
Piedras, R. de las →, *Peru* 124 C4
Piedras Negras, *Mexico* .. 114 B4
Piemonte □, *Italy* 32 D4
Pierce, *U.S.A.* 110 C6
Piercefield, *U.S.A.* 107 B10
Pierre, *U.S.A.* 108 C4
Pierre Bénite, Barrage de
  la, *France* 27 C8
Pierre-de-Bresse, *France* . 27 B9
Pierrefeu-du-Var, *France* . 27 E10
Pierrefonds, *France* 25 C9
Pierrefontaine-les-Varans,
  France 25 E13
Pierrefort, *France* 26 D6
Pierrelatte, *France* 27 D8
Pieštany, *Slovak Rep.* ... 20 G7
Piesting →, *Austria* 21 G6
Piet Retief, *S. Africa* 85 D5
Pietarsaari = Jakobstad,
  Finland 8 E17
Pietermaritzburg, *S. Africa* 85 D5
Pietersburg, *S. Africa* 85 C4
Pietraperzia, *Italy* 35 E7
Pietrasanta, *Italy* 32 E7
Pietrosu, *Romania* 38 B8
Pietrosul, *Romania* 38 B7
Pieve di Cadore, *Italy* ... 33 B9
Pieve di Teco, *Italy* 32 D4
Pievepélago, *Italy* 32 D7
Pigádhia, *Greece* 39 P10
Pigeon, *U.S.A.* 104 D4
Piggott, *U.S.A.* 109 G9
Pigna, *Italy* 32 E4
Pigüe, *Argentina* 126 D3
Pihani, *India* 63 F9
Pijnacker, *Neths.* 16 D4
Pikalevo, *Russia* 40 B9
Pikes Peak, *U.S.A.* 108 F2
Piketberg, *S. Africa* 84 E2
Pikeville, *U.S.A.* 104 G4
Pikou, *China* 51 E12
Pikwitonei, *Canada* 101 B9
Piła, *Poland* 20 B6
Pila, *Spain* 29 G3
Pilani, *India* 62 E6
Pilar, *Brazil* 122 C4
Pilar, *Paraguay* 126 B4
Pilas Group, *Phil.* 57 C6
Pilaya →, *Bolivia* 125 E5
Pilcomayo →, *Paraguay* .. 126 B4
Pilibhit, *India* 63 E8
Pilica →, *Poland* 20 D11
Pilkhawa, *India* 62 E7
Pillaro, *Ecuador* 120 D2
Pílos, *Greece* 39 N4
Pilot Mound, *Canada* 101 D9
Pilot Point, *U.S.A.* 109 J6
Pilot Rock, *U.S.A.* 110 D4
Pilsen = Plzeň, *Czech.* ... 20 F3
Pilštanj, *Slovenia* 33 B12
Pima, *U.S.A.* 111 K9
Pimba, *Australia* 91 E2
Pimenta Bueno, *Brazil* ... 125 C5
Pimentel, *Peru* 124 B2
Pina, *Spain* 28 D4
Pinamalayan, *Phil.* 55 E4
Pinang, *Malaysia* 59 K3
Pinar, C. del, *Spain* 36 B10
Pinar del Río, *Cuba* 116 B3
Pinarbaşi, *Turkey* 66 D7
Pinchang, *China* 52 B6
Pincher Creek, *Canada* ... 100 D6
Pinchi L., *Canada* 100 C4
Pinckneyville, *U.S.A.* ... 108 F10
Píncota, *Romania* 38 C4
Pind Dadan Khan, *Pakistan* 62 C5
Pindar, *Australia* 89 E2
Pindaré →, *Brazil* 122 B3
Pindaré Mirim, *Brazil* ... 122 B2
Pindi Gheb, *Pakistan* 62 C5
Pindiga, *Nigeria* 79 D7
Pindobal, *Brazil* 122 B2
Pindos Óros, *Greece* 39 K4
Pindus Mts. = Pindos
  Óros, *Greece* 39 K4
Pine, *U.S.A.* 111 J8
Pine →, *Canada* 101 B7
Pine, C., *Canada* 99 C9
Pine Bluff, *U.S.A.* 109 H8
Pine City, *U.S.A.* 108 C8
Pine Falls, *Canada* 101 C9
Pine Flat L., *U.S.A.* 112 J7
Pine Pass, *Canada* 100 B4
Pine Point, *Canada* 100 A6
Pine Ridge, *U.S.A.* 108 D3
Pine River, *Canada* 101 C8
Pine River, *U.S.A.* 108 B7
Pine Valley, *U.S.A.* 113 N10
Pinecrest, *U.S.A.* 112 G6
Pinedale, *U.S.A.* 112 J7
Pinega →, *Russia* 44 C5
Pinehill, *Australia* 90 C4
Pinerolo, *Italy* 32 D4
Pineto, *Italy* 33 F11
Pinetop, *U.S.A.* 111 J9
Pinetown, *S. Africa* 85 D5
Pinetree, *U.S.A.* 110 E11
Pineville, *Ky., U.S.A.* ... 105 G4
Pineville, *La., U.S.A.* ... 109 K8
Piney, *France* 25 D11
Ping →, *Thailand* 58 E3
Pingaring, *Australia* 89 F2
Pingba, *China* 52 D6

Pingchuan, *China* 52 D3
Pingding, *China* 50 F7
Pingdingshan, *China* 50 H7
Pingdong, *Taiwan* 53 F13
Pingdu, *China* 51 F10
Pingelly, *Australia* 89 F2
Pingguo, *China* 52 F6
Pinghe, *China* 53 E11
Pinghu, *China* 53 B13
Pingjiang, *China* 53 C9
Pingle, *China* 53 E8
Pingli, *China* 52 A7
Pingliang, *China* 50 G4
Pinglu, *China* 50 E7
Pingluo, *China* 50 E4
Pingnan, *Fujian, China* .. 53 D12
Pingnan,
  *Guangxi Zhuangzu,
  China* 53 F8
Pingquan, *China* 51 D10
Pingrup, *Australia* 89 F2
Pingtan, *China* 53 E12
Pingtang, *China* 52 E6
Pingwu, *China* 50 H3
Pingxiang,
  *Guangxi Zhuangzu,
  China* 52 F6
Pingxiang, *Jiangxi, China* . 53 D9
Pingyao, *China* 50 F7
Pingyi, *China* 51 G9
Pingyin, *China* 50 F9
Pingyuan, *Guangdong,
  China* 53 E10
Pingyuan, *Shandong, China* 50 F9
Pingyuanjie, *China* 52 F4
Pinhal, *Brazil* 127 A6
Pinheiro, *Brazil* 122 B2
Pinhel, *Portugal* 30 E3
Pinhuá →, *Brazil* 125 B4
Pini, *Indonesia* 56 D1
Piniós →, *Ilía, Greece* ... 39 M4
Piniós →, *Trikkala, Greece* 39 K5
Pinjarra, *Australia* 89 F2
Pink →, *Canada* 101 B8
Pinnacles, *Australia* 89 E3
Pinnacles, *U.S.A.* 112 J5
Pinnaroo, *Australia* 91 F3
Pinneberg, *Germany* 18 B5
Pino Hachado, Paso,
  S. Amer. 128 A2
Pinon Hills, *U.S.A.* 113 L9
Pinos, *Mexico* 114 C4
Pinos, Mt., *U.S.A.* 113 L7
Pinos Pt., *U.S.A.* 111 H3
Pinos Puente, *Spain* 31 H7
Pinotepa Nacional, *Mexico* 115 D5
Pinrang, *Indonesia* 57 E5
Pinsk, *Belorussia* 40 E5
Pintados, *Chile* 124 E4
Pintumba, *Australia* 89 F5
Pinyang, *China* 53 D13
Pinyug, *Russia* 44 C5
Pinzolo, *Italy* 32 B7
Pio XII, *Brazil* 122 B2
Pioche, *U.S.A.* 111 H6
Piombino, *Italy* 32 F7
Piombino, Canale di, *Italy* 32 F7
Pioner, Os., *Russia* 45 B10
Pionki, *Poland* 20 D11
Piorini →, *Brazil* 121 D5
Piorini, L., *Brazil* 121 D5
Piotrków Trybunalski,
  Poland 20 D9
Piove di Sacco, *Italy* 33 C9
Pīp, *Iran* 65 E9
Pipar, *India* 62 F5
Piparia, *India* 62 H8
Pipestone, *U.S.A.* 108 D6
Pipestone →, *Canada* ... 98 B2
Pipestone Cr. →, *Canada* 101 D8
Pipmuacan, Rés., *Canada* . 99 C5
Pippingarra, *Australia* ... 88 D2
Pipriac, *France* 24 E5
Piqua, *U.S.A.* 104 E3
Piquet Carneiro, *Brazil* .. 122 C4
Piquiri →, *Brazil* 127 A5
Piracanjuba, *Brazil* 123 E2
Piracicaba, *Brazil* 127 A6
Piracuruca, *Brazil* 122 B3
Piræus = Piraiévs, *Greece* 39 M6
Piraiévs, *Greece* 39 M6
Pirâino, *Italy* 35 D7
Pirajuí, *Brazil* 127 A6
Piran, *Slovenia* 33 C10
Pirané, *Argentina* 126 B4
Piranhas, *Brazil* 122 C4
Pirano = Piran, *Slovenia* . 33 C10
Pirapemas, *Brazil* 122 B3
Pirapora, *Brazil* 123 E3
Piray →, *Bolivia* 125 D5
Pires do Rio, *Brazil* 123 E2
Pírgos, *Ilía, Greece* 39 M4
Pírgos, *Messinia, Greece* . 39 N5
Pirgovo, *Bulgaria* 38 F8
Piriac-sur-Mer, *France* ... 24 E4
Piribebuy, *Paraguay* 126 B4
Pirin Planina, *Bulgaria* .. 39 H6
Pirineos, *Spain* 28 C6
Piripiri, *Brazil* 122 B3
Piritu, *Venezuela* 120 B4
Pirmasens, *Germany* 19 F3
Pirna, *Germany* 18 E9
Pirot, *Serbia* 21 M12
Piru, *Indonesia* 57 E7

Piru, *U.S.A.* 113 L8
Piryatin, *Ukraine* 40 F8
Pisa, *Italy* 32 E7
Pisac, *Peru* 124 C3
Pisagua, *Chile* 124 D3
Pisarovina, *Croatia* 33 C12
Pisciotta, *Italy* 35 B8
Pisco, *Peru* 124 C2
Písek, *Czech.* 20 F4
Pishan, *China* 54 C2
Pishin Lora →, *Pakistan* . 62 E1
Pisidia, *Turkey* 66 E4
Pising, *Indonesia* 57 F6
Pismo Beach, *U.S.A.* 113 K6
Pissos, *France* 26 D3
Pissouri, *Cyprus* 37 E11
Pisticci, *Italy* 35 B9
Pistóia, *Italy* 32 E7
Pistol B., *Canada* 101 A10
Pisuerga →, *Spain* 30 D6
Pisz, *Poland* 20 B11
Pitalito, *Colombia* 120 C2
Pitanga, *Brazil* 123 F1
Pitangui, *Brazil* 123 E3
Pitarpunga, L., *Australia* . 91 E3
Pitcairn I., *Pac. Oc.* 93 K14
Pite älv →, *Sweden* 8 D16
Piteå, *Sweden* 8 D16
Piterka, *Russia* 41 F15
Piteşti, *Romania* 38 E7
Pithapuram, *India* 61 L13
Pithara, *Australia* 89 F2
Píthion, *Greece* 39 H9
Pithiviers, *France* 25 D9
Pitigliano, *Italy* 33 F8
Pitlochry, *U.K.* 14 E5
Pitrufquén, *Chile* 128 A2
Pitsilia □, *Cyprus* 37 E12
Pitt I., *Canada* 100 C3
Pittem, *Belgium* 17 F2
Pittsburg, *Kans., U.S.A.* . 109 G7
Pittsburg, *Tex., U.S.A.* .. 109 J7
Pittsburgh, *U.S.A.* 106 F5
Pittsfield, *Ill., U.S.A.* ... 108 F9
Pittsfield, *Mass., U.S.A.* . 107 D11
Pittsfield, *N.H., U.S.A.* .. 107 C13
Pittston, *U.S.A.* 107 E9
Pittsworth, *Australia* 91 D5
Pituri →, *Australia* 90 C2
Piuí, *Brazil* 123 F2
Pium, *Brazil* 122 D2
Piura, *Peru* 124 B1
Piura □, *Peru* 124 A2
Pivijay, *Colombia* 120 A3
Pixley, *U.S.A.* 112 K7
Piyai, *Greece* 39 K4
Pizarro, *Colombia* 120 C2
Pizol, *Switz.* 23 C8
Pizzo, *Italy* 35 D9
Placentia, *Canada* 99 C9
Placentia B., *Canada* 99 C9
Placer, *Phil.* 55 F5
Placerville, *U.S.A.* 112 G6
Placetas, *Cuba* 116 B4
Plaffeien, *Switz.* 22 C4
Plain Dealing, *U.S.A.* ... 109 J8
Plainfield, *U.S.A.* 107 F10
Plains, *Kans., U.S.A.* ... 109 G4
Plains, *Mont., U.S.A.* ... 110 C6
Plains, *Tex., U.S.A.* 109 J3
Plainview, *Nebr., U.S.A.* . 108 D6
Plainview, *Tex., U.S.A.* .. 109 H4
Plainville, *U.S.A.* 108 F5
Plainwell, *U.S.A.* 104 D3
Plaisance, *France* 26 E4
Pláka, *Greece* 39 J8
Pláka, Ákra, *Greece* 37 D8
Plakhino, *Russia* 44 C9
Plana Cays, *Bahamas* ... 117 B5
Planada, *U.S.A.* 112 H6
Plancoët, *France* 24 D4
Planeta Rica, *Colombia* .. 120 B2
Planina, *Slovenia* 33 B12
Planina, *Slovenia* 33 C11
Plankinton, *U.S.A.* 108 D5
Plano, *U.S.A.* 109 J6
Plant City, *U.S.A.* 105 L4
Plaquemine, *U.S.A.* 109 K9
Plasencia, *Spain* 30 E4
Plaški, *Croatia* 33 C12
Plaster City, *U.S.A.* 113 N11
Plaster Rock, *Canada* ... 99 C6
Plastun, *Russia* 48 B8
Plata, Río de la, *S. Amer.* 126 C4
Platani →, *Italy* 34 E6
Plátanos, *Greece* 37 D5
Plateau □, *Nigeria* 79 D6
Plateau du Coteau du
  Missouri, *U.S.A.* 108 B4
Plato, *Colombia* 120 B3
Platte, Piz, *Switz.* 23 D9
Platte, *U.S.A.* 108 D5
Platte →, *U.S.A.* 108 F7
Platteville, *U.S.A.* 108 E2
Plattling, *Germany* 19 G8
Plattsburgh, *U.S.A.* 107 B11
Plattsmouth, *U.S.A.* 108 E7
Plau, *Germany* 18 B8
Plauen, *Germany* 18 E8
Plavinas, *Latvia* 40 C4
Plavnica, *Montenegro* ... 21 N9
Plavsk, *Russia* 41 E10
Playa Blanca, *Canary Is.* . 36 F6
Playa Blanca Sur,
  Canary Is. 36 F6

Playa de las Americas,
  Canary Is. 36 F3
Playa de Mogán, *Canary Is.* 36 G4
Playa del Inglés, *Canary Is.* 36 G4
Playa Esmerelda,
  Canary Is. 36 F5
Playgreen L., *Canada* 101 C9
Pleasant Bay, *Canada* 99 C7
Pleasant Hill, *Calif.,*
  U.S.A. 112 H4
Pleasant Hill, *Mo., U.S.A.* 108 F7
Pleasanton, *U.S.A.* 109 L5
Pleasantville, *U.S.A.* 104 F8
Pléaux, *France* 26 C6
Pleiku, *Vietnam* 58 F7
Plélan-le-Grand, *France* .. 24 D4
Plémet-la-Pierre, *France* . 24 D4
Pléneuf-Val-André, *France* 24 D4
Plenița, *Romania* 38 E6
Plenty →, *Australia* 90 C2
Plenty, B. of, *N.Z.* 87 G6
Plentywood, *U.S.A.* 108 A2
Plessisville, *Canada* 99 C5
Plestin-les-Grèves, *France* . 24 D3
Pleszew, *Poland* 20 D7
Pleternica, *Croatia* 21 K7
Pletipi L., *Canada* 99 B5
Pleven, *Bulgaria* 38 F7
Plevlja, *Montenegro* 21 M9
Płock, *Poland* 20 C9
Plöcken Passo, *Italy* 33 B9
Ploegsteert, *Belgium* 17 G1
Ploemeur, *France* 24 E3
Ploërmel, *France* 24 E4
Ploiești, *Romania* 38 E9
Plombières-les-Bains,
  France 25 E13
Plomin, *Croatia* 33 C11
Plön, *Germany* 18 A6
Plöner See, *Germany* 18 A6
Plonge, Lac la, *Canada* ... 101 B7
Płońsk, *Poland* 20 C10
Płoty, *Poland* 20 B5
Plouaret, *France* 24 D3
Plouay, *France* 24 E3
Ploudalmézeau, *France* ... 24 D2
Plougasnou, *France* 24 D3
Plouha, *France* 24 D4
Plouhinec, *France* 24 E2
Plovdiv, *Bulgaria* 38 G7
Plum, *U.S.A.* 106 F5
Plum I., *U.S.A.* 107 E12
Plummer, *U.S.A.* 110 C5
Plumtree, *Zimbabwe* 83 G2
Plunge, *Lithuania* 40 D2
Pluvigner, *France* 24 E3
Plymouth, *U.K.* 13 G3
Plymouth, *Calif., U.S.A.* . 112 G6
Plymouth, *Ind., U.S.A.* .. 104 E2
Plymouth, *Mass., U.S.A.* . 107 E14
Plymouth, *N.C., U.S.A.* .. 105 H7
Plymouth, *N.H., U.S.A.* .. 107 C13
Plymouth, *Pa., U.S.A.* ... 107 E9
Plymouth, *Wis., U.S.A.* .. 104 D2
Plynlimon = Pumlumon
  Fawr, *U.K.* 13 E4
Plyussa, *Russia* 40 B6
Plyussa →, *Russia* 40 B6
Plzeň, *Czech.* 20 F3
Pniewy, *Poland* 20 C6
Pô, *Burkina Faso* 79 C4
Po →, *Italy* 33 D9
Po, Foci del, *Italy* 33 D9
Po Hai = Bo Hai, *China* . 51 E10
Pobé, *Benin* 79 D5
Pobeda, *Russia* 45 C15
Pobedino, *Russia* 45 E15
Pobedy Pik, *Kirghizia* ... 44 E8
Pobiedziska, *Poland* 20 C7
Pobla de Segur, *Spain* ... 28 C5
Pobla de Valle, *Spain* ... 30 C5
Pocahontas, *Ark., U.S.A.* 109 G9
Pocahontas, *Iowa, U.S.A.* 108 D7
Pocatello, *U.S.A.* 110 E7
Pochep, *Russia* 40 E8
Pochinki, *Russia* 41 D14
Pochinok, *Russia* 40 D8
Pochutla, *Mexico* 115 D5
Poci, *Venezuela* 121 B5
Pocinhos, *Brazil* 122 C4
Poções, *Brazil* 123 D3
Pocomoke City, *U.S.A.* .. 104 F8
Poconé, *Brazil* 125 D6
Poços de Caldas, *Brazil* .. 127 A6
Poddebice, *Poland* 20 D8
Poděbrady, *Czech.* 20 E5
Podensac, *France* 26 D3
Podgorica, *Montenegro* .. 21 N9
Podkamennaya
  Tunguska →, *Russia* .. 45 C10
Podlapac, *Croatia* 33 D12
Podolsk, *Russia* 41 D10
Podor, *Senegal* 78 B1
Podravska Slatina, *Croatia* 21 K7
Podujevo, *Serbia* 21 N11
Poel, *Germany* 18 B7
Pofadder, *S. Africa* 84 D2
Pogamasing, *Canada* 98 C3
Poggiardo, *Italy* 35 B11
Poggibonsi, *Italy* 33 E8
Pogoanele, *Romania* 38 E9
Pogradeci, *Albania* 39 J3
Pogranitšnyi, *Russia* 48 B5

Poh, *Indonesia* 57 E6
Pohang, *S. Korea* 51 F15
Pohnpei, *Pac. Oc.* 92 G7
Pohorelá, *Slovak Rep.* ... 20 G10
Pohorje, *Slovenia* 33 B12
Poiana Mare, *Romania* .. 38 F6
Poinsett, C., *Antarctica* . 5 C8
Point Edward, *Canada* ... 98 D3
Point Pedro, *Sri Lanka* .. 60 Q12
Point Pleasant, *N.J.,*
  U.S.A. 107 F10
Point Pleasant, *W. Va.,*
  U.S.A. 104 F4
Pointe-à-la Hache, *U.S.A.* 109 L10
Pointe-à-Pitre, *Guadeloupe* 117 C7
Pointe Noire, *Congo* 80 E2
Poirino, *Italy* 32 D4
Poisonbush Ra., *Australia* 88 D3
Poissy, *France* 25 D9
Poitiers, *France* 24 F7
Poitou, *France* 26 B3
Poitou, Seuil du, *France* . 26 B4
Poix de Picardie, *France* . 25 C8
Poix-Terron, *France* 25 C11
Pojoaque Valley, *U.S.A.* . 111 J11
Pokaran, *India* 60 F7
Pokataroo, *Australia* 91 D4
Poko, *Sudan* 77 F3
Poko, *Zaïre* 82 B2
Pokrov, *Russia* 41 D11
Pokrovsk, *Russia* 41 F15
Pokrovsk, *Russia* 45 C13
Pol, *Spain* 30 B3
Pola = Pula, *Croatia* 33 D10
Pola de Allande, *Spain* .. 30 B4
Pola de Lena, *Spain* 30 B5
Pola de Siero, *Spain* 30 B5
Pola de Somiedo, *Spain* .. 30 B4
Polacca, *U.S.A.* 111 J8
Polan, *Iran* 65 E9
Poland ■, *Europe* 20 C9
Polanów, *Poland* 20 A6
Polatsk = Polotsk,
  Belorussia 40 D6
Polcura, *Chile* 126 D1
Polden Hills, *U.K.* 13 F5
Polessk, *Russia* 40 D2
Polesye, *Belorussia* 40 E6
Polewali, *Indonesia* 57 E5
Polgar, *Hungary* 21 H11
Põlgyo-ri, *S. Korea* 51 G14
Poli, *Cameroon* 80 C2
Políaigos, *Greece* 39 N7
Policastro, G. di, *Italy* ... 35 C8
Police, *Poland* 20 B4
Polignano a Mare, *Italy* . 35 B10
Poligny, *France* 25 F12
Políkhnitas, *Greece* 39 K9
Polillo Is., *Phil.* 55 D4
Polillo Strait, *Phil.* 55 D4
Polis, *Cyprus* 37 D11
Polístena, *Italy* 35 D9
Políyiros, *Greece* 39 J6
Polk, *U.S.A.* 106 E5
Polla, *Italy* 35 B8
Pollachi, *India* 60 P10
Pollensa, *Spain* 36 B10
Pollensa, B. de, *Spain* ... 36 B10
Póllica, *Italy* 35 B8
Pollino, Mte., *Italy* 35 C9
Pollock, *U.S.A.* 108 C4
Polna, *Russia* 40 B6
Polnovat, *Russia* 44 C7
Polo, *U.S.A.* 108 E10
Pologi, *Ukraine* 42 C7
Polonnoye, *Ukraine* 40 F5
Polotsk, *Belorussia* 40 D6
Polson, *U.S.A.* 110 C6
Poltava, *Ukraine* 42 B6
Polunochnoye, *Russia* ... 44 C7
Polynesia, *Pac. Oc.* 93 H11
Polynésie française □ =
  French Polynesia ■,
  Pac. Oc. 93 J13
Pomarance, *Italy* 32 E7
Pomárico, *Italy* 35 B9
Pomaro, *Mexico* 114 D4
Pombal, *Brazil* 122 C4
Pombal, *Portugal* 30 F2
Pómbia, *Greece* 37 D6
Pomeroy, *Ohio, U.S.A.* .. 104 F4
Pomeroy, *Wash., U.S.A.* . 110 C5
Pomona, *U.S.A.* 113 L9
Pomorie, *Bulgaria* 38 G10
Pomos, *Cyprus* 37 D11
Pomos, C., *Cyprus* 37 D11
Pomoshnaya, *Ukraine* ... 42 B4
Pompano Beach, *U.S.A.* . 105 M5
Pompei, *Italy* 35 B7
Pompey, *France* 25 D13
Pompeys Pillar, *U.S.A.* .. 110 D10
Ponape = Pohnpei,
  Pac. Oc. 92 G7
Ponask, L., *Canada* 98 B1
Ponass L., *Canada* 101 C8
Ponca, *U.S.A.* 108 D6
Ponca City, *U.S.A.* 109 G6
Ponce, *Puerto Rico* 117 C6
Ponchatoula, *U.S.A.* 109 K9
Poncheville, L., *Canada* . 98 B4
Poncin, *France* 27 B9
Pond, *U.S.A.* 113 K7
Pond Inlet, *Canada* 97 A12
Pondicherry, *India* 60 P11
Pondrôme, *Belgium* 17 H6

Ponds, I. of, *Canada* 99 B8
Ponferrada, *Spain* 30 C4
Pongo, Wadi →, *Sudan* .. 77 F2
Poniatowa, *Poland* 20 D12
Ponikva, *Slovenia* 33 B12
Ponnani, *India* 60 P9
Ponnyadaung, *Burma* ... 61 J19
Ponoi →, *Russia* 44 C5
Ponoka, *Canada* 100 C6
Ponorogo, *Indonesia* 57 G14
Pons, *France* 26 C3
Pons, *Spain* 28 D6
Ponsul →, *Portugal* 31 F3
Pont-à-Celles, *Belgium* .. 17 G4
Pont-à-Mousson, *France* . 25 D13
Pont-Audemer, *France* .. 24 C7
Pont-Aven, *France* 24 E3
Pont Canavese, *Italy* 32 C4
Pont-de-Roide, *France* .. 25 E13
Pont-de-Salars, *France* .. 26 D6
Pont-de-Vaux, *France* ... 25 F11
Pont-de-Veyle, *France* ... 27 B8
Pont-l'Abbé, *France* 24 E2
Pont-l'Évêque, *France* ... 24 C7
Pont-St.-Esprit, *France* .. 27 D8
Pont-sur-Yonne, *France* . 25 D10
Ponta de Pedras, *Brazil* . 122 B2
Ponta do Sol, *Madeira* .. 36 D2
Ponta Grossa, *Brazil* 127 B5
Ponta Pora, *Brazil* 127 A4
Pontacq, *France* 26 E3
Pontailler-sur-Saône,
  France 25 E12
Pontal →, *Brazil* 122 C3
Pontalina, *Brazil* 123 E2
Pontarlier, *France* 25 F13
Pontassieve, *Italy* 33 E8
Pontaubault, *France* 24 D5
Pontaumur, *France* 26 C6
Pontcharra, *France* 27 C10
Pontchartrain L., *U.S.A.* . 109 K9
Pontchâteau, *France* 24 E4
Ponte Alta, Serra do,
  Brazil 123 E2
Ponte Alta do Norte, *Brazil* 122 D2
Ponte Branca, *Brazil* 125 D7
Ponte da Barca, *Portugal* . 30 D2
Ponte de Sor, *Portugal* .. 31 F3
Ponte dell 'Olio, *Italy* ... 32 D6
Ponte di Legno, *Italy* 32 B7
Ponte do Pungué, *Mozam.* 83 F3
Ponte-Leccia, *France* 27 F13
Ponte Nova, *Brazil* 123 F3
Ponte San Martino, *Italy* . 32 C4
Ponte San Pietro, *Italy* .. 32 C6
Pontebba, *Italy* 33 B10
Pontecorvo, *Italy* 34 A6
Pontedera, *Italy* 32 E7
Pontefract, *U.K.* 12 D6
Ponteix, *Canada* 101 D7
Pontelandolfo, *Italy* 35 A7
Pontevedra, *Spain* 30 C2
Pontevedra □, *Spain* 30 C2
Pontevedra, R. de →,
  Spain 30 C2
Pontevico, *Italy* 32 C7
Pontiac, *Ill., U.S.A.* 108 E10
Pontiac, *Mich., U.S.A.* .. 104 D4
Pontian Kecil, *Malaysia* . 59 M4
Pontianak, *Indonesia* 56 E3
Pontic Mts. = Kuzey
  Anadolu Dağları, *Turkey* 66 C6
Pontine Is. = Ponziane,
  Isole, *Italy* 34 B5
Pontine Mts. = Kuzey
  Anadolu Dağları, *Turkey* 66 C6
Pontínia, *Italy* 34 A6
Pontivy, *France* 24 D4
Pontoise, *France* 25 C9
Ponton →, *Canada* 100 B5
Pontorson, *France* 24 D5
Pontrémoli, *Italy* 32 D6
Pontresina, *Switz.* 23 D9
Pontrieux, *France* 24 D3
Pontypool, *Canada* 106 B6
Pontypool, *U.K.* 13 F4
Pontypridd, *U.K.* 13 F4
Ponza, *Italy* 34 B5
Ponziane, Isole, *Italy* 34 B5
Poochera, *Australia* 91 E1
Poole, *U.K.* 13 G6
Pooley I., *Canada* 100 C3
Poona = Pune, *India* 60 K8
Pooncarie, *Australia* 91 E3
Poopelloe L., *Australia* .. 91 E3
Poopó, *Bolivia* 124 D4
Poopó, L. de, *Bolivia* 124 D4
Popanyinning, *Australia* . 89 F2
Popayán, *Colombia* 120 C2
Poperinge, *Belgium* 17 G1
Popigay, *Russia* 45 B12
Popilta, L., *Australia* 91 E3
Popio L., *Australia* 91 E3
Poplar, *U.S.A.* 108 A2
Poplar →, *Man., Canada* 101 C9
Poplar →, *N.W.T.,*
  Canada 100 A4
Poplar Bluff, *U.S.A.* 109 G9
Poplarville, *U.S.A.* 109 K10
Popocatepetl, *Mexico* ... 115 D5
Popokabaka, *Zaïre* 80 F3
Pópoli, *Italy* 33 F10
Popovača, *Croatia* 33 C13

Popovo, *Bulgaria* 38 F9
Poppel, *Belgium* 17 F6
Poprád, *Slovak Rep.* 20 F10
Poprád →, *Slovak Rep.* .. 20 F10
Porali →, *Pakistan* 62 G2
Porangaba, *Brazil* 124 B3
Porangatu, *Brazil* 123 D2
Porbandar, *India* 62 J3
Porce →, *Colombia* 120 B3
Porcher I., *Canada* 100 C2
Porco, *Bolivia* 125 D4
Porcos →, *Brazil* 123 D2
Porcuna, *Spain* 31 H6
Porcupine →, *Canada* ... 101 B8
Porcupine →, *U.S.A.* 96 B5
Pordenone, *Italy* 33 C9
Poreč, *Croatia* 33 C10
Porecatu, *Brazil* 123 F1
Poretskoye, *Russia* 41 D15
Pori, *Finland* 9 F16
Porjus, *Sweden* 8 C15
Porkhov, *Russia* 40 C6
Porkkala, *Finland* 9 G18
Porlamar, *Venezuela* 121 A5
Porlezza, *Italy* 32 B6
Porma →, *Spain* 30 C5
Pornic, *France* 24 E4
Poronaysk, *Russia* 45 E15
Póros, *Greece* 39 M6
Poroshiri-Dake, *Japan* .. 48 C11
Poroto Mts., *Tanzania* .. 83 D3
Porpoise B., *Antarctica* . 5 C9
Porquerolles, I. de, *France* 27 F10
Porrentruy, *Switz.* 22 B4
Porreras, *Spain* 36 B10
Porretta, Passo di, *Italy* . 32 D7
Porsangen, *Norway* 8 A18
Porsgrunn, *Norway* 10 E3
Port Adelaide, *Australia* . 91 E2
Port Alberni, *Canada* 100 D4
Port Alfred, *Canada* 99 C5
Port Alfred, *S. Africa* ... 84 E4
Port Alice, *Canada* 100 C3
Port Allegany, *U.S.A.* ... 106 E6
Port Allen, *U.S.A.* 109 K9
Port Alma, *Australia* 90 C5
Port Angeles, *U.S.A.* 112 B3
Port Antonio, *Jamaica* .. 116 C4
Port Aransas, *U.S.A.* 109 M6
Port Arthur = Lüshun,
  China 51 E11
Port Arthur, *Australia* ... 90 G4
Port Arthur, *U.S.A.* 109 L8
Port au Port B., *Canada* . 99 C8
Port-au-Prince, *Haiti* 117 C5
Port Augusta, *Australia* . 91 E2
Port Augusta West,
  Australia 91 E2
Port Austin, *U.S.A.* 98 D3
Port Bell, *Uganda* 82 B3
Port Bergé Vaovao,
  Madag. 85 B8
Port Blandford, *Canada* . 99 C9
Port Bou, *Spain* 28 C8
Port Bouët, *Ivory C.* 78 D4
Port Bradshaw, *Australia* 90 A2
Port Broughton, *Australia* 91 E2
Port Burwell, *Canada* ... 98 D3
Port Canning, *India* 63 H13
Port-Cartier, *Canada* 99 B6
Port Chalmers, *N.Z.* 87 L3
Port Chester, *U.S.A.* 107 F11
Port Clements, *Canada* .. 100 C2
Port Clinton, *U.S.A.* 104 E4
Port Colborne, *Canada* .. 98 D4
Port Coquitlam, *Canada* . 100 D4
Port Credit, *Canada* 106 C5
Port Curtis, *Australia* 90 C5
Port Dalhousie, *Canada* . 106 C5
Port Darwin, *Australia* .. 88 B5
Port Darwin, *Falk. Is.* ... 128 D5
Port Davey, *Australia* 90 G4
Port Dickson, *Malaysia* .. 59 L3
Port Douglas, *Australia* .. 90 B4
Port Dover, *Canada* 106 D4
Port Edward, *Canada* 100 C2
Port Elgin, *Canada* 98 D3
Port Elizabeth, *S. Africa* . 84 E4
Port Ellen, *U.K.* 14 F2
Port-en-Bessin, *France* .. 24 C6
Port Erin, *I. of Man* 12 C3
Port Essington, *Australia* . 88 B5
Port Etienne =
  Nouâdhibou, *Mauritania* 74 D1
Port Fairy, *Australia* 91 F3
Port Fouâd = Bûr Fuad,
  Egypt 76 H8
Port Gamble, *U.S.A.* 112 C4
Port-Gentil, *Gabon* 80 E1
Port Gibson, *U.S.A.* 109 K9
Port Glasgow, *U.K.* 14 F4
Port Harcourt, *Nigeria* .. 79 E6
Port Hardy, *Canada* 100 C3
Port Harrison =
  Inoucdjouac, *Canada* . 97 C12
Port Hawkesbury, *Canada* 99 C7
Port Hedland, *Australia* . 88 D2
Port Henry, *U.S.A.* 107 B11
Port Hood, *Canada* 99 C7
Port Hope, *Canada* 98 D4
Port Hueneme, *U.S.A.* .. 113 L7
Port Huron, *U.S.A.* 104 D4
Port Isabel, *U.S.A.* 109 M6

Port Jefferson, *U.S.A.* ... 107 F11
Port Jervis, *U.S.A.* 107 E10
Port-Joinville, *France* 24 F4
Port Katon, *Russia* 43 C8
Port Kelang = Pelabuhan
  Kelang, *Malaysia* 59 L3
Port Kembla, *Australia* .. 91 E5
Port Kenny, *Australia* ... 91 E1
Port-la-Nouvelle, *France* . 26 E7
Port Laoise, *Ireland* 15 C4
Port Lavaca, *U.S.A.* 109 L6
Port-Leucate, *France* 26 F7
Port Lincoln, *Australia* .. 91 E2
Port Loko, *S. Leone* 78 D2
Port Louis, *France* 24 E3
Port Lyautey = Kenitra,
  Morocco 74 B3
Port MacDonnell, *Australia* 91 F3
Port Macquarie, *Australia* . 91 E5
Port Maria, *Jamaica* 116 C4
Port Mellon, *Canada* 100 D4
Port-Menier, *Canada* 99 C7
Port Morant, *Jamaica* ... 116 C4
Port Moresby, *Papua N. G.* 92 H6
Port Mourant, *Guyana* .. 121 B6
Port Mouton, *Canada* ... 99 D7
Port Musgrave, *Australia* . 90 A3
Port-Navalo, *France* 24 E4
Port Nelson, *Canada* 101 B10
Port Nolloth, *S. Africa* .. 84 D2
Port Nouveau-Québec,
  Canada 97 C13
Port O'Connor, *U.S.A.* .. 109 L6
Port of Spain, *Trin. & Tob.* 117 D7
Port Orchard, *U.S.A.* 112 C4
Port Orford, *U.S.A.* 110 E1
Port Pegasus, *N.Z.* 87 M1
Port Perry, *Canada* 98 D4
Port Phillip B., *Australia* . 91 F3
Port Pirie, *Australia* 91 E2
Port Radium = Echo Bay,
  Canada 96 B8
Port Renfrew, *Canada* ... 100 D4
Port Roper, *Australia* 90 A2
Port Rowan, *Canada* 98 D3
Port Safaga = Bûr Safâga,
  Egypt 76 B3
Port Said = Bûr Sa'îd,
  Egypt 76 H8
Port St. Joe, *U.S.A.* 105 L3
Port St. Johns, *S. Africa* . 85 E4
Port-St.-Louis-du-Rhône,
  France 27 E8
Port San Vicente, *Phil.* .. 55 B5
Port Sanilac, *U.S.A.* 98 D3
Port Saunders, *Canada* .. 99 B8
Port Severn, *Canada* 106 B5
Port Shepstone, *S. Africa* . 85 E5
Port Simpson, *Canada* ... 100 C2
Port Stanley = Stanley,
  Falk. Is. 128 D5
Port Stanley, *Canada* 98 D3
Port Sudan = Bûr Sûdân,
  Sudan 76 D4
Port-sur-Saône, *France* .. 25 E13
Port Talbot, *U.K.* 13 F4
Port Taufiq = Bûr Taufiq,
  Egypt 76 J8
Port Townsend, *U.S.A.* .. 112 B4
Port-Vendres, *France* 26 F7
Port Wakefield, *Australia* . 91 E2
Port Washington, *U.S.A.* 104 D2
Port Weld, *Malaysia* 59 K3
Portachuelo, *Bolivia* 125 D5
Portadown, *U.K.* 15 B5
Portage, *U.S.A.* 108 D10
Portage La Prairie, *Canada* 101 D9
Portageville, *U.S.A.* 109 G10
Portalegre, *Portugal* 31 F3
Portalegre □, *Portugal* ... 31 F3
Portales, *U.S.A.* 109 H3
Portarlington, *Ireland* 15 C4
Porteirinha, *Brazil* 123 E3
Portel, *Brazil* 122 B1
Portel, *Portugal* 31 G3
Porter L., *N.W.T., Canada* 101 A7
Porter L., *Sask., Canada* . 101 B7
Porterville, *S. Africa* 84 E2
Porterville, *U.S.A.* 111 H4
Porthcawl, *U.K.* 13 F4
Porthill, *U.S.A.* 110 B5
Portile de Fier, *Europe* ... 38 E5
Portimão, *Portugal* 31 H2
Portland, *N.S.W., Australia* 91 E4
Portland, *Vic., Australia* . 91 F3
Portland, *Canada* 107 C8
Portland, *Conn., U.S.A.* . 107 E12
Portland, *Maine, U.S.A.* . 99 D5
Portland, *Mich., U.S.A.* . 104 D3
Portland, *Oreg., U.S.A.* . 112 E4
Portland, I. of, *U.K.* 13 G5
Portland B., *Australia* 91 F3
Portland Bill, *U.K.* 13 G5
Portland Prom., *Canada* . 97 C12
Portlands Roads, *Australia* 90 A3
Portneuf, *Canada* 99 C5
Pôrto, *Brazil* 122 B3
Porto, *France* 27 F12
Porto, *Portugal* 30 D2
Porto □, *Portugal* 30 D2
Porto, G. de, *France* 27 F12
Pôrto Acre, *Brazil* 124 B4
Pôrto Alegre, *Pará, Brazil* 121 D7
Pôrto Alegre,
  Rio Grande do S., Brazil 127 C5

Porto Amboim = Gunza, Angola ... 80 G2
Porto Argentera, Italy ... 32 D4
Porto Azzurro, Italy ... 32 F7
Porto Botte, Italy ... 34 C1
Pôrto Cajueiro, Brazil ... 125 C6
Porto Civitanova, Italy ... 33 E10
Porto Cristo, Spain ... 36 B10
Pôrto da Fôlha, Brazil ... 122 C4
Pôrto de Móz, Brazil ... 121 D7
Pôrto de Pedras, Brazil ... 122 C4
Pôrto des Meinacos, Brazil ... 125 C7
Porto Empédocle, Italy ... 34 E6
Pôrto Esperança, Brazil ... 125 D6
Pôrto Esperidão, Brazil ... 125 D6
Pôrto Franco, Brazil ... 122 C2
Porto Garibaldi, Italy ... 33 D9
Porto Grande, Brazil ... 121 C7
Pôrto Jofre, Brazil ... 125 D6
Pôrto Lágo, Greece ... 39 J8
Porto Mendes, Brazil ... 127 A5
Porto Moniz, Madeira ... 36 D2
Pôrto Murtinho, Brazil ... 125 E6
Pôrto Nacional, Brazil ... 122 D2
Porto Novo, Benin ... 79 D5
Porto Petro, Spain ... 36 B10
Porto Recanati, Italy ... 33 E10
Porto San Giórgio, Italy ... 33 E10
Pôrto Santana, Brazil ... 121 D7
Porto Santo, Madeira ... 72 B1
Porto Santo Stefano, Italy ... 32 F8
Pôrto São José, Brazil ... 127 A5
Pôrto Seguro, Brazil ... 123 E4
Porto Tolle, Italy ... 33 D9
Porto Tórres, Italy ... 34 B1
Pôrto União, Brazil ... 127 B5
Porto-Vecchio, France ... 27 G13
Pôrto Velho, Brazil ... 125 B5
Portobelo, Panama ... 116 E4
Portoferráio, Italy ... 32 F7
Portogruaro, Italy ... 33 C9
Portola, U.S.A. ... 112 F6
Portomaggiore, Italy ... 33 D8
Portoscuso, Italy ... 34 C1
Portovénere, Italy ... 32 D6
Portoviejo, Ecuador ... 120 D1
Portpatrick, U.K. ... 14 G3
Portree, U.K. ... 14 D2
Portrush, U.K. ... 15 A5
Portsall, France ... 24 D2
Portsmouth, Domin. ... 117 C7
Portsmouth, N.H., U.S.A. ... 107 C14
Portsmouth, Ohio, U.S.A. ... 104 F4
Portsmouth, R.I., U.S.A. ... 107 E13
Portsmouth, Va., U.S.A. ... 104 G7
Portsoy, U.K. ... 14 D6
Porttipahta, Finland ... 8 B19
Portugal ■, Europe ... 30 F3
Portugalete, Spain ... 28 B1
Portuguesa □, Venezuela ... 120 B4
Portuguese-Guinea = Guinea-Bissau ■, Africa ... 78 C2
Portumna, Ireland ... 15 C3
Portville, U.S.A. ... 106 D6
Porvenir, Bolivia ... 124 C4
Porvenir, Chile ... 128 D2
Porvoo = Borgå, Finland ... 9 F18
Porzuna, Spain ... 31 F6
Posada →, Italy ... 34 B2
Posadas, Argentina ... 127 B4
Posadas, Spain ... 31 H5
Poschiavo, Switz. ... 23 D10
Posets, Spain ... 28 C5
Poshan = Boshan, China ... 51 F9
Posht-e-Badam, Iran ... 65 C7
Posídhion, Ákra, Greece ... 39 K6
Poso, Indonesia ... 57 E6
Posoegroenoe, Surinam ... 121 C6
Posong, S. Korea ... 51 G14
Posse, Brazil ... 123 D2
Possel, C.A.R. ... 80 C3
Possession I., Antarctica ... 5 D11
Pössneck, Germany ... 18 E7
Post, U.S.A. ... 109 J4
Post Falls, U.S.A. ... 110 C5
Postavy, Belorussia ... 40 D5
Poste Maurice Cortier, Algeria ... 75 D5
Postmasburg, S. Africa ... 84 D3
Postojna, Slovenia ... 33 C11
Poston, U.S.A. ... 113 M12
Potchefstroom, S. Africa ... 84 D4
Poté, Brazil ... 123 E3
Poteau, U.S.A. ... 109 H7
Poteet, U.S.A. ... 109 L5
Potelu, Lacul, Romania ... 38 F7
Potenza, Italy ... 35 B8
Potenza →, Italy ... 33 E10
Potenza Picena, Italy ... 33 E10
Poteriteri, L., N.Z. ... 87 M1
Potes, Spain ... 30 B6
Potgietersrus, S. Africa ... 85 C4
Poti, Georgia ... 43 E9
Potiraguá, Brazil ... 123 E4
Potiskum, Nigeria ... 79 C7
Potomac →, U.S.A. ... 104 F7
Potosí, Bolivia ... 125 D4
Potosi □, Bolivia ... 124 E4
Potosi Mt., U.S.A. ... 113 K11
Pototan, Phil. ... 55 F5
Potrerillos, Chile ... 126 B2
Potsdam, Germany ... 18 C9
Potsdam, U.S.A. ... 107 B10

Pottenstein, Germany ... 19 F7
Potter, U.S.A. ... 108 E3
Pottery Hill = Abû Ballas, Egypt ... 76 C2
Pottstown, U.S.A. ... 107 F9
Pottsville, U.S.A. ... 107 F8
Pottuvil, Sri Lanka ... 60 R12
Pouancé, France ... 24 E5
Pouce Coupé, Canada ... 100 B4
Poughkeepsie, U.S.A. ... 107 E11
Pouilly-sur-Loire, France ... 25 E9
Poulaphouca Res., Ireland ... 15 C5
Poulsbo, U.S.A. ... 112 C4
Pourri, Mt., France ... 27 C10
Pouso Alegre, Mato Grosso, Brazil ... 125 C6
Pouso Alegre, Minas Gerais, Brazil ... 127 A6
Pouzauges, France ... 24 F6
Povenets, Russia ... 44 C4
Poverty B., N.Z. ... 87 H7
Póvoa de Lanhosa, Portugal ... 30 D2
Póvoa de Varzim, Portugal ... 30 D2
Povorino, Russia ... 41 F13
Powassan, Canada ... 98 C4
Powder →, U.S.A. ... 108 B2
Powder River, U.S.A. ... 110 E10
Powell, U.S.A. ... 110 D9
Powell L., U.S.A. ... 111 H8
Powell River, Canada ... 100 D4
Powers, Mich., U.S.A. ... 104 C2
Powers, Oreg., U.S.A. ... 110 E1
Powers Lake, U.S.A. ... 108 A3
Powys □, U.K. ... 13 E4
Poxoreu, Brazil ... 125 D7
Poyang Hu, China ... 53 C11
Poyarkovo, Russia ... 45 E13
Poza de la Sal, Spain ... 28 C1
Poza Rica, Mexico ... 115 C5
Pozanti, Turkey ... 66 E6
Požarevac, Serbia ... 21 L11
Pozi, Taiwan ... 53 F13
Poznań, Poland ... 20 C6
Pozo, U.S.A. ... 113 K6
Pozo Alcón, Spain ... 29 H2
Pozo Almonte, Chile ... 124 E4
Pozo Colorado, Paraguay ... 126 A4
Pozo del Dátil, Mexico ... 114 B2
Pozoblanco, Spain ... 31 G6
Pozuzo, Peru ... 124 C2
Pozzallo, Italy ... 35 F7
Pozzuoli, Italy ... 35 B7
Pra →, Ghana ... 79 D4
Prachin Buri, Thailand ... 58 E3
Prachuap Khiri Khan, Thailand ... 59 G2
Pradelles, France ... 26 D7
Pradera, Colombia ... 120 C2
Prades, France ... 26 F6
Prado, Brazil ... 123 E4
Prado del Rey, Spain ... 31 J5
Præstø, Denmark ... 11 J6
Pragersko, Slovenia ... 33 B12
Prague = Praha, Czech. ... 20 E4
Praha, Czech. ... 20 E4
Prahecq, France ... 26 B3
Prahova →, Romania ... 38 E8
Prahovo, Serbia ... 21 L12
Praid, Romania ... 38 C8
Prainha, Amazonas, Brazil ... 125 B5
Prainha, Pará, Brazil ... 121 D7
Prairie, Australia ... 90 C3
Prairie →, U.S.A. ... 109 H5
Prairie City, U.S.A. ... 110 D4
Prairie du Chien, U.S.A. ... 108 D9
Prairies, Canada ... 96 C9
Pramánda, Greece ... 39 K4
Pran Buri, Thailand ... 58 F2
Prang, Ghana ... 79 D4
Prapat, Indonesia ... 56 D1
Prasonísi, Ákra, Greece ... 37 D9
Prata, Brazil ... 123 E2
Pratápgarh, India ... 62 G6
Prática di Mare, Italy ... 34 A5
Prätigau, Switz. ... 23 C9
Prato, Italy ... 32 E8
Prátola Peligna, Italy ... 33 F10
Pratovécchio, Italy ... 33 E8
Prats-de-Mollo-la-Preste, France ... 26 F6
Pratt, U.S.A. ... 109 G5
Pratteln, Switz. ... 22 A5
Prattville, U.S.A. ... 105 J2
Pravdinsk, Russia ... 41 C13
Pravia, Spain ... 30 B4
Praya, Indonesia ... 56 F5
Pré-en-Pail, France ... 24 D6
Pré St. Didier, Italy ... 32 C4
Precordillera, Argentina ... 126 C2
Predáppio, Italy ... 33 D8
Predazzo, Italy ... 33 B8
Predejane, Serbia ... 21 N12
Preeceville, Canada ... 101 C8
Préfailles, France ... 24 E4
Pregonero, Venezuela ... 120 B3
Pregrada, Croatia ... 33 B12
Preko, Croatia ... 33 D12
Prelate, Canada ... 101 C7
Prelog, Croatia ... 33 B13
Premier, Canada ... 100 B3
Premont, U.S.A. ... 109 M5
Premuda, Croatia ... 33 D11
Prenjasi, Albania ... 39 H3

Prentice, U.S.A. ... 108 C9
Prenzlau, Germany ... 18 B9
Preobrazheniye, Russia ... 48 C6
Prepansko Jezero, Macedonia ... 39 J4
Preparis North Channel, Ind. Oc. ... 61 M18
Preparis South Channel, Ind. Oc. ... 61 M18
Přerov, Czech. ... 20 F7
Presanella, Italy ... 32 B7
Prescott, Canada ... 98 D4
Prescott, Ariz., U.S.A. ... 111 J7
Prescott, Ark., U.S.A. ... 109 J8
Preservation Inlet, N.Z. ... 87 M1
Preševo, Serbia ... 21 N11
Presho, U.S.A. ... 108 D4
Presicce, Italy ... 35 C11
Presidencia de la Plaza, Argentina ... 126 B4
Presidencia Roque Saenz Peña, Argentina ... 126 B3
Presidente Epitácio, Brazil ... 123 F1
Presidente Hayes □, Paraguay ... 126 A4
Presidente Hermes, Brazil ... 125 C5
Presidente Prudente, Brazil ... 127 A5
Presidio, Mexico ... 114 B4
Presidio, U.S.A. ... 109 L2
Preslav, Bulgaria ... 38 F9
Prešov, Slovak Rep. ... 20 F11
Prespa, L. = Prepansko Jezero, Macedonia ... 39 J4
Presque Isle, U.S.A. ... 99 C6
Prestbury, U.K. ... 13 F5
Prestea, Ghana ... 78 D4
Presteigne, U.K. ... 13 E5
Presto, Bolivia ... 125 D5
Preston, Canada ... 106 C4
Preston, U.K. ... 12 D5
Preston, Idaho, U.S.A. ... 110 E8
Preston, Minn., U.S.A. ... 108 D8
Preston, Nev., U.S.A. ... 110 G6
Preston, C., Australia ... 88 D2
Prestonpans, U.K. ... 14 F6
Prestwick, U.K. ... 14 F4
Prêto →, Amazonas, Brazil ... 121 D5
Prêto →, Bahia, Brazil ... 122 D3
Prêto do Igapó-Açu →, Brazil ... 121 D6
Pretoria, S. Africa ... 85 D4
Preuilly-sur-Claise, France ... 24 F7
Préveza, Greece ... 39 L3
Priazovskoye, Ukraine ... 42 C6
Pribilof Is., Bering S. ... 4 D17
Priboj, Serbia ... 21 M9
Příbram, Czech. ... 20 F4
Price, U.S.A. ... 110 G8
Price I., Canada ... 100 C3
Prichalnaya, Russia ... 43 B11
Prichard, U.S.A. ... 105 K1
Priego, Spain ... 28 E2
Priego de Córdoba, Spain ... 31 H6
Priekule, Latvia ... 40 C2
Prien, Germany ... 19 H8
Prieska, S. Africa ... 84 D3
Priest →, U.S.A. ... 110 B5
Priest L., U.S.A. ... 110 B5
Priest Valley, U.S.A. ... 112 J6
Priestly, Canada ... 100 C3
Prievidza, Slovak Rep. ... 20 G8
Prijedor, Bos.-H. ... 33 D13
Prikaspiyskaya Nizmennost, Asia ... 43 C13
Prilep, Macedonia ... 39 H4
Priluki, Ukraine ... 40 F8
Prime Seal I., Australia ... 90 G4
Primeira Cruz, Brazil ... 122 B3
Primorsko-Akhtarsk, Russia ... 42 C8
Primorskoye, Ukraine ... 42 C7
Primrose L., Canada ... 101 C7
Prince Albert, Canada ... 101 C7
Prince Albert, S. Africa ... 84 E3
Prince Albert Mts., Antarctica ... 5 D11
Prince Albert Nat. Park, Canada ... 101 C7
Prince Albert Pen., Canada ... 96 A8
Prince Albert Sd., Canada ... 96 A8
Prince Alfred, C., Canada ... 4 B1
Prince Charles I., Canada ... 97 B12
Prince Charles Mts., Antarctica ... 5 D6
Prince Edward I. □, Canada ... 99 C7
Prince Edward Is., Ind. Oc. ... 3 G11
Prince George, Canada ... 100 C4
Prince of Wales, C., U.S.A. ... 94 C3
Prince of Wales I., Australia ... 90 A3
Prince of Wales I., Canada ... 96 A10
Prince of Wales I., U.S.A. ... 100 B2
Prince Patrick I., Canada ... 4 B2
Prince Regent Inlet, Canada ... 4 B3
Prince Rupert, Canada ... 100 C2
Princenhage, Neths. ... 17 F5
Princesa Isabel, Brazil ... 122 C4
Princess Charlotte B., Australia ... 90 A3
Princess May Ras., Australia ... 88 C4
Princess Royal I., Canada ... 100 C3
Princeton, Canada ... 100 D4

Princeton, Calif., U.S.A. ... 112 F4
Princeton, Ill., U.S.A. ... 108 E10
Princeton, Ind., U.S.A. ... 104 F2
Princeton, Ky., U.S.A. ... 104 G2
Princeton, Mo., U.S.A. ... 108 E8
Princeton, N.J., U.S.A. ... 107 F10
Princeton, W. Va., U.S.A. ... 104 G5
Principe, I. de, Atl. Oc. ... 70 F4
Principe Chan., Canada ... 100 C2
Principe da Beira, Brazil ... 125 C5
Prineville, U.S.A. ... 110 D3
Prins Harald Kyst, Antarctica ... 5 D4
Prinsesse Astrid Kyst, Antarctica ... 5 D3
Prinsesse Ragnhild Kyst, Antarctica ... 5 D4
Prinzapolca, Nic. ... 116 D3
Prior, C., Spain ... 30 B2
Pripet = Pripyat →, Europe ... 40 F7
Pripet Marshes = Polesye, Belorussia ... 40 E6
Pripyat →, Europe ... 40 F7
Pripyat Marshes = Polesye, Belorussia ... 40 E6
Prislop, Pasul, Romania ... 38 B8
Pristen, Russia ... 41 F10
Priština, Serbia ... 21 N11
Pritzwalk, Germany ... 18 B8
Privas, France ... 27 D8
Priverno, Italy ... 34 A6
Privolzhsk, Russia ... 41 C12
Privolzhskaya Vozvyshennost, Russia ... 41 F15
Privolzhskiy, Russia ... 41 F15
Privolzhye, Russia ... 41 E16
Priyutnoye, Russia ... 43 C10
Prizren, Serbia ... 21 N10
Prizzi, Italy ... 34 E6
Prnjavor, Bos.-H. ... 21 L7
Probolinggo, Indonesia ... 57 G15
Procida, Italy ... 35 B7
Proddatur, India ... 60 M11
Prodhromos, Cyprus ... 37 E11
Profondeville, Belgium ... 17 H5
Progreso, Mexico ... 115 C7
Prokhladnyy, Russia ... 43 E11
Prokletije, Albania ... 38 G2
Prokopyevsk, Russia ... 44 D9
Prokuplje, Serbia ... 21 M11
Proletarskaya, Russia ... 43 C9
Prome = Pyè, Burma ... 61 K19
Prophet →, Canada ... 100 B4
Propriá, Brazil ... 122 D4
Propriano, France ... 27 G12
Proserpine, Australia ... 90 C4
Prosser, U.S.A. ... 110 C4
Prostějov, Czech. ... 20 F7
Proston, Australia ... 91 D5
Protection, U.S.A. ... 109 G5
Próti, Greece ... 39 M4
Provadiya, Bulgaria ... 38 F10
Proven, Belgium ... 17 G1
Provence, France ... 27 E9
Providence, Ky., U.S.A. ... 104 G2
Providence, R.I., U.S.A. ... 107 E13
Providence Bay, Canada ... 98 C3
Providence Mts., U.S.A. ... 111 J6
Providencia, Ecuador ... 120 D2
Providencia, I. de, Colombia ... 116 D3
Provideniya, Russia ... 45 C19
Provins, France ... 25 D10
Provo, U.S.A. ... 110 F8
Provost, Canada ... 101 C6
Prozor, Bos.-H. ... 21 M7
Prudentópolis, Brazil ... 123 G1
Prud'homme, Canada ... 101 C7
Prudnik, Poland ... 20 E7
Prüm, Germany ... 19 E2
Pruszcz Gdański, Poland ... 20 A8
Pruszków, Poland ... 20 C10
Prut →, Romania ... 38 D11
Pruzhany, Belorussia ... 40 E4
Prvić, Croatia ... 33 D11
Prydz B., Antarctica ... 5 C6
Pryluky = Priluki, Ukraine ... 40 F8
Pryor, U.S.A. ... 109 G7
Przasnysz, Poland ... 20 B10
Przedbórz, Poland ... 20 D9
Przemyśl, Poland ... 20 F12
Przeworsk, Poland ... 20 E12
Przewóz, Poland ... 20 D4
Przhevalsk, Kirghizia ... 44 E8
Przysuchla, Poland ... 20 D10
Psakhná, Greece ... 39 L6
Psará, Greece ... 39 L8
Psel →, Ukraine ... 42 B5
Pserimos, Greece ... 39 N10
Psíra, Greece ... 37 D7
Pskov, Russia ... 40 C5
Psunj, Croatia ... 21 K7
Ptcah →, Belorussia ... 40 E6
Ptolemaís, Greece ... 39 J4
Ptuj, Slovenia ... 33 B12
Ptujska Gora, Slovenia ... 33 B12
Pu Xian, China ... 50 F6
Pua, Thailand ... 58 C3

Puán, Argentina ... 126 D3
Pu'an, China ... 52 E5
Puan, S. Korea ... 51 G14
Pubei, China ... 52 F7
Pucacuro →, Peru ... 120 D3
Pucallpa, Peru ... 124 B3
Pucará, Bolivia ... 125 D5
Pucará, Peru ... 124 D3
Pucarani, Bolivia ... 124 D4
Pucheng, China ... 53 D12
Pučišče, Croatia ... 33 E13
Pucka, Zatoka, Poland ... 20 A8
Puding, China ... 52 D5
Pudukkottai, India ... 60 P11
Puebla, Mexico ... 115 D5
Puebla □, Mexico ... 115 D5
Puebla de Alcocer, Spain ... 31 G5
Puebla de Don Fadrique, Spain ... 29 H2
Puebla de Don Rodrigo, Spain ... 31 F6
Puebla de Guzmán, Spain ... 31 H3
Puebla de Sanabria, Spain ... 30 C4
Puebla de Trives, Spain ... 30 C3
Puebla del Caramiñal, Spain ... 30 C2
Pueblo, U.S.A. ... 108 F2
Pueblo Hundido, Chile ... 126 B1
Pueblo Nuevo, Venezuela ... 120 B3
Puelches, Argentina ... 126 D2
Puelén, Argentina ... 126 D2
Puente Alto, Chile ... 126 C1
Puente del Arzobispo, Spain ... 30 F5
Puente-Genil, Spain ... 31 H6
Puente la Reina, Spain ... 28 C3
Puenteareas, Spain ... 30 C2
Puentedeume, Spain ... 30 B2
Puentes de Garcia Rodriguez, Spain ... 30 B3
Pu'er, China ... 52 F3
Puerco →, U.S.A. ... 111 J10
Puerto, Canary Is. ... 36 F2
Puerto Acosta, Bolivia ... 124 D4
Puerto Aisén, Chile ... 128 C2
Puerto Ángel, Mexico ... 115 D5
Puerto Arista, Mexico ... 115 D5
Puerto Armuelles, Panama ... 116 E3
Puerto Ayacucho, Venezuela ... 120 B4
Puerto Barrios, Guatemala ... 116 C2
Puerto Bermejo, Argentina ... 126 B4
Puerto Bermúdez, Peru ... 124 C3
Puerto Bolívar, Ecuador ... 120 D2
Puerto Cabello, Venezuela ... 120 A4
Puerto Cabezas, Nic. ... 116 D3
Puerto Cabo Gracias á Dios, Nic. ... 116 D3
Puerto Capaz = Jebba, Morocco ... 74 A4
Puerto Carreño, Colombia ... 120 B4
Puerto Castilla, Honduras ... 116 C2
Puerto Chicama, Peru ... 124 B2
Puerto Coig, Argentina ... 128 D3
Puerto Cortes, Costa Rica ... 116 E3
Puerto Cortés, Honduras ... 116 C2
Puerto Cumarebo, Venezuela ... 120 A4
Puerto de Alcudia, Spain ... 36 B10
Puerto de Andraitx, Spain ... 36 B9
Puerto de Cabrera, Spain ... 36 B9
Puerto de Gran Tarajal, Canary Is. ... 36 F5
Puerto de la Cruz, Canary Is. ... 36 F3
Puerto de Pozo Negro, Canary Is. ... 36 F6
Puerto de Santa María, Spain ... 31 J4
Puerto de Sóller, Spain ... 36 B9
Pto. del Carmen, Canary Is. ... 36 F6
Puerto del Rosario, Canary Is. ... 36 F6
Puerto Deseado, Argentina ... 128 C3
Puerto Guaraní, Paraguay ... 125 E6
Puerto Heath, Bolivia ... 124 C4
Puerto Huitoto, Colombia ... 120 C3
Puerto Inca, Peru ... 124 B3
Puerto Juárez, Mexico ... 115 C7
Puerto La Cruz, Venezuela ... 121 A5
Puerto Leguízamo, Colombia ... 120 D3
Puerto Límon, Colombia ... 120 C3
Puerto Lobos, Argentina ... 128 B3
Puerto López, Colombia ... 120 C3
Puerto Lumbreras, Spain ... 29 H3
Puerto Madryn, Argentina ... 128 B3
Puerto Maldonado, Peru ... 124 C4
Puerto Manotí, Cuba ... 116 B4
Puerto Mazarrón, Spain ... 29 H3
Puerto Mercedes, Colombia ... 120 C3
Puerto Miraña, Colombia ... 120 D3
Puerto Montt, Chile ... 128 B2
Puerto Morelos, Mexico ... 115 C7
Puerto Nariño, Colombia ... 120 C4
Puerto Natales, Chile ... 128 D2
Puerto Nuevo, Colombia ... 120 B4
Puerto Nutrias, Venezuela ... 120 B4
Puerto Ordaz, Venezuela ... 121 B5
Puerto Padre, Cuba ... 116 B4
Puerto Páez, Venezuela ... 120 B4
Puerto Peñasco, Mexico ... 114 A2
Puerto Pinasco, Paraguay ... 126 A4
Puerto Pirámides, Argentina ... 128 B4

Puerto Plata, *Dom. Rep.* . 117 C5
Puerto Pollensa, *Spain* ... 36 B10
Puerto Portillo, *Peru* 124 B3
Puerto Princesa, *Phil.* ... 55 G3
Puerto Quellón, *Chile* 128 B2
Puerto Quepos, *Costa Rica* 116 E3
Puerto Real, *Spain* 31 J4
Puerto Rico, *Bolivia* 124 C4
Puerto Rico, *Canary Is.* .. 36 G4
Puerto Rico ■, *W. Indies* . 117 C6
Puerto Rico Trench,
    Atl. Oc. 117 C6
Puerto Saavedra, *Chile* ... 128 A2
Puerto Sastre, *Paraguay* .. 126 A4
Puerto Siles, *Bolivia* 125 C4
Puerto Suárez, *Bolivia* ... 125 D6
Puerto Tejada, *Colombia* .. 120 C2
Puerto Umbría, *Colombia* .. 120 C2
Puerto Vallarta, *Mexico* .. 114 C3
Puerto Varas, *Chile* 128 B2
Puerto Villazón, *Bolivia* .. 125 C5
Puerto Wilches, *Colombia* . 120 B3
Puertollano, *Spain* 31 G6
Puertomarin, *Spain* 30 C3
Puesto Cunambo, *Peru* 120 D2
Pueyrredón, L., *Argentina* . 128 C2
Pugachev, *Kazakhstan* 41 F16
Puge, *China* 52 D4
Puge, *Tanzania* 82 C3
Puget Sound, *U.S.A.* 110 C2
Puget-Théniers, *France* ... 27 E10
Púglia □, *Italy* 35 B9
Pugōdong, *N. Korea* 51 C16
Pugu, *Tanzania* 82 D4
Pūgūnzī, *Iran* 65 E8
Pui, *Romania* 38 D6
Puica, *Peru* 124 C3
Puig Mayor, *Spain* 36 B9
Puigcerdá, *Spain* 28 C6
Puigmal, *Spain* 28 C7
Puigpuñent, *Spain* 36 B9
Puisaye, Collines de la,
    France 25 E10
Puiseaux, *France* 25 D9
Pujilí, *Ecuador* 120 D2
Pujon-chosuji, *N. Korea* .. 51 D14
Puka, *Albania* 38 G2
Pukaki L., *N.Z.* 87 L3
Pukapuka, *Cook Is.* 93 J11
Pukatawagan, *Canada* ... 101 B8
Pukchin, *N. Korea* 51 D13
Pukchŏng, *N. Korea* 51 D15
Pukekohe, *N.Z.* 87 G5
Pukou, *China* 53 A12
Pula, *Croatia* 33 D10
Pula, *Italy* 34 D2
Pulacayo, *Bolivia* 124 E4
Pulaski, *N.Y., U.S.A.* 107 C8
Pulaski, *Tenn., U.S.A.* ... 105 H2
Pulaski, *Va., U.S.A.* 104 G5
Pulawy, *Poland* 20 D11
Pulga, *U.S.A.* 112 F5
Pulicat, L., *India* 60 N12
Pullman, *U.S.A.* 110 C5
Pulog, *Phil.* 55 C4
Pułtusk, *Poland* 20 C11
Pülüinür, *Turkey* 67 D8
Pumlumon Fawr, *U.K.* ... 13 E4
Puna, *Bolivia* 125 D4
Puná, I., *Ecuador* 120 D1
Punakha, *Bhutan* 61 F16
Punasar, *India* 62 F5
Punata, *Bolivia* 125 D4
Punch, *India* 63 C6
Pune, *India* 60 K8
Pungsan, *N. Korea* 51 D15
Pungue, Ponte de, *Mozam.* 83 F3
Puning, *China* 53 F11
Punjab □, *India* 62 D6
Punjab □, *Pakistan* 62 E6
Puno, *Peru* 124 D3
Punta Alta, *Argentina* ... 128 A4
Punta Arenas, *Chile* 128 D2
Punta Cardón, *Venezuela* . 120 A3
Punta Coles, *Peru* 124 D3
Punta de Bombón, *Peru* .. 124 D3
Punta de Díaz, *Chile* 126 B1
Punta Delgada, *Argentina* 128 B4
Punta Gorda, *Belize* 115 D7
Punta Gorda, *U.S.A.* 105 M5
Punta Prieta, *Mexico* ... 114 B2
Punta Prima, *Spain* 36 B11
Puntabie, *Australia* 91 E1
Puntarenas, *Costa Rica* .. 116 E3
Punto Fijo, *Venezuela* ... 120 A3
Punxsatawney, *U.S.A.* ... 106 F5
Puqi, *China* 53 C9
Puquio, *Peru* 124 C3
Pur →, *Russia* 44 C8
Purace, Vol., *Colombia* .. 120 C2
Puralia = Puruliya, *India* . 63 H12
Purbeck, Isle of, *U.K.* ... 13 G4
Purcell, *U.S.A.* 109 H6
Purchena Tetica, *Spain* .. 29 H2
Puri, *India* 61 K14
Purificación, *Colombia* .. 120 C3
Purmerend, *Neths.* 16 C5
Purnia, *India* 63 G12
Purukcahu, *Indonesia* ... 56 E4
Puruliya, *India* 63 H12
Purus →, *Brazil* 121 D5
Pŭrvomay, *Bulgaria* 38 G8
Purwakarta, *Indonesia* ... 57 G12
Purwodadi, *Jawa, Indonesia* 57 G14
Purwodadi, *Jawa, Indonesia* 57 G13

Purwokerto, *Indonesia* ... 57 G13
Purworejo, *Indonesia* 57 G14
Puryŏng, *N. Korea* 51 C15
Pusan, *S. Korea* 51 G15
Pushchino, *Russia* 45 D16
Pushkin, *Russia* 40 B7
Pushkino, *Russia* 41 F15
Pushkino, *Russia* 41 C10
Püspökladány, *Hungary* .. 21 H11
Pustoshka, *Russia* 40 C6
Putahow L., *Canada* 101 B8
Putararu, *N.Z.* 87 H5
Putao, *Burma* 61 F20
Putaruru, *N.Z.* 87 H5
Putbus, *Germany* 18 A9
Puthein Myit →, *Burma* . 61 M19
Putian, *China* 53 E12
Putignano, *Italy* 35 B10
Putina, *Peru* 124 C4
Puting, Tanjung, *Indonesia* 56 E4
Putna →, *Romania* 38 D10
Putnam, *U.S.A.* 107 E13
Putorana, Gory, *Russia* .. 45 C10
Putre, *Chile* 124 D4
Puttalam, *Sri Lanka* 60 Q11
Putte, *Neths.* 17 F4
Putten, *Neths.* 16 D7
Puttgarden, *Germany* ... 18 A7
Putumayo →, *S. Amer.* . 120 D4
Putuo, *China* 53 C14
Putussibau, *Indonesia* ... 56 D4
Puurs, *Belgium* 17 F4
Puy-de-Dôme, *France* ... 26 C6
Puy-de-Dôme □, *France* . 26 C7
Puy-Guillaume, *France* .. 26 C7
Puy-l'Évêque, *France* 26 D5
Puyallup, *U.S.A.* 112 C4
Puyang, *China* 50 G8
Puyehue, *Chile* 128 B2
Puylaurens, *France* 26 E6
Puyo, *Ecuador* 120 D2
Pūzeh Rīg, *Iran* 65 E8
Pwani □, *Tanzania* 82 D4
Pweto, *Zaïre* 83 D2
Pwllheli, *U.K.* 12 E3
Pyana →, *Russia* 41 D15
Pyapon, *Burma* 61 L19
Pyasina →, *Russia* 45 B9
Pyatigorsk, *Russia* 43 D10
Pyatikhatki, *Ukraine* 42 B5
Pyè, *Burma* 61 K19
Pyinmana, *Burma* 61 K20
Pyla, C., *Cyprus* 37 E12
Pyŏktong, *N. Korea* 51 D13
Pyŏnggang, *N. Korea* ... 51 E14
Pyŏngtaek, *S. Korea* 51 F14
P'yŏngyang, *N. Korea* ... 51 E13
Pyote, *U.S.A.* 109 K3
Pyramid L., *U.S.A.* 110 G4
Pyramid Pk., *U.S.A.* 113 J10
Pyramids, *Egypt* 76 J7
Pyrénées, *Europe* 26 F4
Pyrénées-Atlantiques □,
    France 26 E3
Pyrénées-Orientales □,
    France 26 F6
Pyrzyce, *Poland* 20 B4
Pyshchug, *Russia* 41 B14
Pytalovo, *Russia* 40 C5
Pyttegga, *Norway* 10 B1
Pyu, *Burma* 61 K20

Q

Qaanaaq = Thule,
    Greenland 4 B4
Qachasnek, *S. Africa* 85 E4
Qādib, *Yemen* 68 E5
Qa'el Jafr, *Jordan* 69 E5
Qa'emābād, *Iran* 65 D9
Qā'emshahr, *Iran* 65 B7
Qagan Nur, *China* 50 C8
Qahar Youyi Zhongqi,
    China 50 D7
Qahremānshahr =
    Bākhtarān, *Iran* 64 C5
Qaidam Pendi, *China* ... 54 C4
Qajarīyeh, *Iran* 65 D6
Qala, Ras il, *Malta* 37 C1
Qala-i-Jadid, *Afghan.* ... 62 D2
Qala Yangi, *Afghan.* 62 B2
Qal'at al Akhḍar,
    Si. Arabia 64 E3
Qal'at Sukkar, *Iraq* 64 D5
Qal'eh Darreh, *Iran* 64 B5
Qal'eh Shaharak, *Afghan.* 60 B4
Qalyûb, *Egypt* 76 H7
Qamar, Ghubbat al, *Yemen* 68 D5
Qamdo, *China* 52 B1
Qamruddin Karez, *Pakistan* 62 D3
Qandahār, *Afghan.* 60 D4
Qandahār □, *Afghan.* ... 60 D4
Qapān, *Iran* 65 B7
Qaqortoq = Julianehåb,
    Greenland 4 C5
Qâra, *Egypt* 76 B2
Qara Qash →, *India* 63 B8
Qaraghandy = Karaganda,
    Kazakhstan 44 E8
Qārah, *Si. Arabia* 64 D4
Qardud, *Sudan* 77 E2
Qareh →, *Iran* 64 B5

Qareh Tekān, *Iran* 65 B6
Qarqan, *China* 54 C3
Qarqan He →, *China* ... 54 C3
Qarrasa, *Sudan* 77 E3
Qarshi = Karshi,
    Uzbekistan 44 F7
Qartabā, *Lebanon* 69 A4
Qaryat al Gharab, *Iraq* .. 64 D5
Qaryat al 'Ulyā, *Si. Arabia* 64 E5
Qasr 'Amra, *Jordan* 64 D3
Qaşr-e Qand, *Iran* 65 E9
Qasr Farâfra, *Egypt* 76 B2
Qatanā, *Syria* 69 B5
Qatar ■, *Asia* 65 E6
Qatlīsh, *Iran* 65 B8
Qattâra, *Egypt* 76 A2
Qattâra, Munkhafed el,
    Egypt 76 B2
Qattâra Depression =
    Qattâra, Munkhafed el,
    Egypt 76 B2
Qawām al Ḥamzah, *Iraq* . 64 D5
Qāyen, *Iran* 65 C8
Qazaqstan =
    Kazakhstan ■, *Asia* ... 44 E7
Qazvin, *Iran* 65 B6
Qena, *Egypt* 76 B3
Qena, Wadi →, *Egypt* .. 76 B3
Qeqertarsuaq = Disko,
    Greenland 4 C5
Qeqertarsuaq = Godhavn,
    Greenland 4 C5
Qeshlāq, *Iran* 64 C5
Qeshm, *Iran* 65 E8
Qezi'ot, *Israel* 69 E3
Qi Xian, *China* 50 G8
Qian Gorlos, *China* 51 B13
Qian Xian, *China* 50 G5
Qiancheng, *China* 52 D7
Qianjiang,
    *Guangxi Zhuangzu,
    China* 52 F7
Qianjiang, *Hubei, China* . 53 B9
Qianjiang, *Sichuan, China* 52 C7
Qianshan, *China* 53 B11
Qianwei, *China* 52 C4
Qianxi, *China* 52 D6
Qianyang, *Hunan, China* . 53 D8
Qianyang, *Shaanxi, China* 50 G4
Qianyang, *Zhejiang, China* 53 B12
Qiaojia, *China* 52 D4
Qibā', *Si. Arabia* 64 E5
Qichun, *China* 53 B10
Qidong, *Hunan, China* .. 53 D9
Qidong, *Jiangsu, China* .. 53 B13
Qijiang, *China* 52 C6
Qila Safed, *Pakistan* 60 E2
Qila Saifullāh, *Pakistan* . 62 D3
Qilian Shan, *China* 54 C4
Qimen, *China* 53 C11
Qin He →, *China* 50 G7
Qin Jiang →, *China* 53 D10
Qin Ling = Qinling Shandi,
    China 50 H5
Qin'an, *China* 50 G3
Qing Xian, *China* 50 E9
Qingcheng, *China* 51 F9
Qingdao, *China* 51 F11
Qingfeng, *China* 50 G8
Qinghai □, *China* 54 C4
Qinghai Hu, *China* 54 C5
Qinghecheng, *China* 51 D13
Qinghemen, *China* 51 D11
Qingjian, *China* 50 F6
Qingjiang, *Jiangsu, China* . 51 H10
Qingjiang, *Jiangxi, China* . 53 C10
Qingliu, *China* 53 D11
Qinglong, *China* 52 E5
Qingping, *China* 52 D6
Qingpu, *China* 53 B13
Qingshui, *China* 50 G4
Qingshuihe, *China* 50 E6
Qingtian, *China* 53 C13
Qingtongxia Shuiku, *China* 50 F3
Qingxi, *China* 52 D7
Qingxu, *China* 50 F7
Qingyang, *Anhui, China* . 53 B11
Qingyang, *Gansu, China* . 50 F4
Qingyi Jiang →, *China* .. 52 C4
Qingyuan, *Guangdong,
    China* 53 F9
Qingyuan, *Liaoning, China* 51 C13
Qingyuan, *Zhejiang, China* 53 D12
Qingyun, *China* 51 F9
Qingzhen, *China* 52 D6
Qinhuangdao, *China* ... 51 E10
Qinling Shandi, *China* ... 50 H5
Qinshui, *China* 50 G7
Qinyang, *China* 50 G7
Qinyuan, *China* 50 F7
Qinzhou, *China* 52 G7
Qionghai, *China* 58 C8
Qionglai, *China* 52 B4
Qionglai Shan, *China* ... 52 B4
Qiongshan, *China* 58 C8
Qiongzhou Haixia, *China* . 58 B8
Qiqihar, *China* 45 E13
Qiraîya, W. →, *Egypt* .. 69 E3
Qiryat Ata, *Israel* 69 C4
Qiryat Gat, *Israel* 69 D3
Qiryat Mal'akhi, *Israel* .. 69 D3
Qiryat Shemona, *Israel* .. 69 B4
Qiryat Yam, *Israel* 69 C4
Qishan, *China* 50 G4
Qishan, *Taiwan* 53 F13

Qitai, *China* 54 B3
Qiubei, *China* 52 E5
Qixia, *China* 51 F11
Qiyang, *China* 53 D8
Qojūr, *Iran* 64 B5
Qom, *Iran* 65 C6
Qomsheh, *Iran* 65 D6
Qostanay = Kustanay,
    Kazakhstan 44 D7
Qu Jiang →, *China* 52 B6
Qu Xian, *Sichuan, China* . 52 B6
Qu Xian, *Zhejiang, China* 53 C12
Quackenbrück, *Germany* . 18 C3
Quairading, *Australia* ... 89 F2
Qualeup, *Australia* 89 F2
Quambatook, *Australia* .. 91 F3
Quambone, *Australia* ... 91 E4
Quamby, *Australia* 90 C3
Quan Long, *Vietnam* ... 59 H5
Quanah, *U.S.A.* 109 H5
Quandialla, *Australia* ... 91 E4
Quang Ngai, *Vietnam* ... 58 E7
Quang Yen, *Vietnam* ... 58 B6
Quannan, *China* 53 E10
Quantock Hills, *U.K.* ... 13 F4
Quanzhou, *Fujian, China* . 53 E12
Quanzhou,
    *Guangxi Zhuangzu,
    China* 53 E8
Quaraí, *Brazil* 126 C4
Quarré-les-Tombes, *France* 25 E10
Quartu Sant' Elena, *Italy* . 34 C2
Quartzsite, *U.S.A.* 113 M12
Quatsino, *Canada* 100 C3
Quatsino Sd., *Canada* ... 100 C3
Qūchān, *Iran* 65 B8
Queanbeyan, *Australia* .. 91 F4
Québec, *Canada* 99 C5
Québec □, *Canada* 99 B6
Quedlinburg, *Germany* .. 18 D7
Queen Alexandra Ra.,
    Antarctica 5 E11
Queen Charlotte, *Canada* . 100 C2
Queen Charlotte Bay,
    Falk. Is. 128 D4
Queen Charlotte Is.,
    Canada 100 C2
Queen Charlotte Str.,
    Canada 100 C3
Queen Elizabeth Is.,
    Canada 94 B10
Queen Elizabeth Nat. Park,
    Uganda 82 C3
Queen Mary Land,
    Antarctica 5 D7
Queen Maud G., *Canada* . 96 B9
Queen Maud Land,
    Antarctica 5 D3
Queen Maud Mts.,
    Antarctica 5 E13
Queens Chan., *Australia* .. 88 C4
Queenscliff, *Australia* ... 91 F3
Queensland □, *Australia* . 90 C3
Queenstown, *Australia* .. 90 G4
Queenstown, *N.Z.* 87 L2
Queenstown, *S. Africa* .. 84 E4
Queets, *U.S.A.* 112 C2
Queguay Grande →,
    Uruguay 126 C4
Queimadas, *Brazil* 122 D4
Quela, *Angola* 80 F3
Quelimane, *Mozam.* 83 F4
Quelpart = Cheju Do,
    S. Korea 51 H14
Quemado, *N. Mex., U.S.A.* 111 J9
Quemado, *Tex., U.S.A.* .. 109 L4
Quemú-Quemú, *Argentina* 126 D3
Quequén, *Argentina* 126 D4
Querco, *Peru* 124 C3
Querétaro, *Mexico* 114 C4
Querétaro □, *Mexico* ... 114 C5
Querfurt, *Germany* 18 D7
Quesada, *Spain* 29 H1
Queshan, *China* 50 H8
Quesnel, *Canada* 100 C4
Quesnel →, *Canada* 100 C4
Quesnel L., *Canada* 100 C4
Questa, *U.S.A.* 111 H11
Questembert, *France* 24 E4
Quetena, *Bolivia* 124 E4
Quetico Prov. Park,
    Canada 98 C1
Quetrequile, *Argentina* .. 128 B3
Quetta, *Pakistan* 62 D2
Quevedo, *Ecuador* 120 D2
Quezaltenango, *Guatemala* 116 D1
Quezon City, *Phil.* 55 D4
Qufār, *Si. Arabia* 64 E4
Qui Nhon, *Vietnam* 58 F7
Quibaxe, *Angola* 80 F2
Quibdo, *Colombia* 120 B2
Quiberon, *France* 24 E3
Quibor, *Venezuela* 120 B3
Quick, *Canada* 100 C3
Quickborn, *Germany* ... 18 B5
Quiet L., *Canada* 100 A2
Quiévrain, *Belgium* 17 H3
Quiindy, *Paraguay* 126 B4
Quila, *Mexico* 114 C3
Quilán, C., *Chile* 128 B2
Quilcene, *U.S.A.* 112 C4
Quilengues, *Angola* 81 G2
Quilimarí, *Chile* 126 C1
Quilino, *Argentina* 126 C3

Quillabamba, *Peru* 124 C3
Quillacollo, *Bolivia* 124 D4
Quillagua, *Chile* 126 A2
Quillaicillo, *Chile* 126 C1
Quillan, *France* 26 F6
Quillebeuf-sur-Seine,
    France 24 C7
Quillota, *Chile* 126 C1
Quilmes, *Argentina* 126 C4
Quilon, *India* 60 Q10
Quilpie, *Australia* 91 D3
Quilpué, *Chile* 126 C1
Quilua, *Mozam.* 83 F4
Quime, *Bolivia* 124 D4
Quimilí, *Argentina* 126 B3
Quimper, *France* 24 D2
Quimperlé, *France* 24 E3
Quinault →, *U.S.A.* 112 C2
Quincemil, *Peru* 124 C3
Quincy, *Calif., U.S.A.* .. 112 F6
Quincy, *Fla., U.S.A.* ... 105 K3
Quincy, *Ill., U.S.A.* 108 F9
Quincy, *Mass., U.S.A.* .. 107 D14
Quincy, *Wash., U.S.A.* .. 110 C4
Quines, *Argentina* 126 C2
Quinga, *Mozam.* 83 F5
Quingey, *France* 25 E12
Quintana de la Serena,
    Spain 31 G5
Quintana Roo □, *Mexico* . 115 D7
Quintanar de la Orden,
    Spain 28 F1
Quintanar de la Sierra,
    Spain 28 D2
Quintanar del Rey, *Spain* . 29 F3
Quintero, *Chile* 126 C1
Quintin, *France* 24 D4
Quinto, *Spain* 28 D4
Quinyambie, *Australia* .. 91 E3
Quípar →, *Spain* 29 G3
Quipungo, *Angola* 81 G2
Quirihue, *Chile* 126 D1
Quirindi, *Australia* 91 E5
Quiroga, *Spain* 30 C3
Quiruvilca, *Peru* 124 B2
Quissac, *France* 27 E8
Quissanga, *Mozam.* 83 E5
Quitilipi, *Argentina* 126 B3
Quitman, *Ga., U.S.A.* ... 105 K4
Quitman, *Miss., U.S.A.* . 105 J1
Quitman, *Tex., U.S.A.* .. 109 J7
Quito, *Ecuador* 120 D2
Quixadá, *Brazil* 122 B4
Quixaxe, *Mozam.* 83 F5
Quixeramobim, *Brazil* .. 122 C4
Qujing, *China* 52 E4
Qul'ân, Jazā'ir, *Egypt* ... 76 C4
Qumbu, *S. Africa* 85 E4
Quneitra, *Syria* 69 B4
Quoin I., *Australia* 88 B4
Quoin Pt., *S. Africa* 84 E2
Quondong, *Australia* ... 91 E3
Quorn, *Australia* 91 E2
Quqon = Kokand,
    Uzbekistan 44 E8
Qurein, *Sudan* 77 E3
Qurnat as Sawdā', *Lebanon* 69 A5
Qûs, *Egypt* 76 B3
Qusaybah, *Iraq* 64 C4
Quseir, *Egypt* 76 B3
Qūshchī, *Iran* 64 B5
Quthing, *Lesotho* 85 E4
Qūţīābād, *Iran* 65 C6
Quwo, *China* 50 G6
Quyang, *China* 50 E8
Quynh Nhai, *Vietnam* .. 58 B4
Quzi, *China* 50 F4
Qytet Stalin, *Albania* ... 39 J2
Qyzylorda = Kzyl-Orda,
    Kazakhstan 44 E7

R

Ra, Ko, *Thailand* 59 H2
Råå, *Sweden* 11 J6
Raahe, *Finland* 8 D18
Raalte, *Neths.* 16 D8
Raamsdonksveer, *Neths.* . 17 E5
Raasay, *U.K.* 14 D2
Raasay, Sd. of, *U.K.* ... 14 D2
Rab, *Croatia* 33 D11
Raba, *Indonesia* 57 F5
Rába →, *Hungary* 21 H7
Rabaçal →, *Portugal* ... 30 D3
Rabah, *Nigeria* 79 C6
Rabai, *Kenya* 82 C4
Rabastens, *France* 26 E5
Rabastens-de-Bigorre,
    France 26 E4
Rabat, *Malta* 37 D1
Rabat, *Morocco* 74 B3
Rabaul, *Papua N. G.* ... 92 H7
Rabbit →, *Canada* 100 B3
Rabbit Lake, *Canada* ... 101 C7
Rabbitskin →, *Canada* .. 100 A4
Rabka, *Poland* 20 F9
Râbor, *Iran* 65 D8
Rácale, *Italy* 35 C11
Racalmuto, *Italy* 34 E6
Racconigi, *Italy* 32 D4
Race, C., *Canada* 99 C9
Rach Gia, *Vietnam* 59 G5

Raciąż, Poland ... 20 C10
Racibórz, Poland ... 20 E8
Racine, U.S.A. ... 104 D2
Rackerby, U.S.A. ... 112 F5
Radama, Nosy, Madag. ... 85 A8
Radama, Saikanosy, Madag. ... 85 A8
Rădăuţi, Romania ... 38 B8
Radbuza →, Czech. ... 20 F3
Radeburg, Germany ... 18 D9
Radeče, Slovenia ... 33 B12
Radekhov, Ukraine ... 40 F4
Radford, U.S.A. ... 104 G5
Radhanpur, India ... 62 H4
Radiska →, Macedonia ... 39 H3
Radisson, Canada ... 101 C7
Radium Hot Springs, Canada ... 100 C5
Radna, Romania ... 38 C4
Radnor Forest, U.K. ... 13 E4
Radolfzell, Germany ... 19 H4
Radom, Poland ... 20 D11
Radomir, Bulgaria ... 38 G6
Radomsko, Poland ... 20 D9
Radomyshl, Ukraine ... 40 F6
Radoviš, Macedonia ... 39 H5
Radovljica, Slovenia ... 33 B11
Radstock, U.K. ... 13 F5
Radstock, C., Australia ... 91 E1
Răducăneni, Romania ... 38 C10
Radviliškis, Lithuania ... 40 D3
Radville, Canada ... 101 D8
Rae, Canada ... 100 A5
Rae Bareli, India ... 63 F9
Rae Isthmus, Canada ... 97 B11
Raeren, Belgium ... 17 G8
Raeside, L., Australia ... 89 E3
Raetihi, N.Z. ... 87 H5
Rafaela, Argentina ... 126 C3
Rafah, Egypt ... 69 D3
Rafai, C.A.R. ... 82 B1
Raffadali, Italy ... 34 E6
Rafhā, Si. Arabia ... 64 D4
Rafsanjan, Iran ... 65 D8
Raft Pt., Australia ... 88 C3
Ragag, Sudan ... 77 E1
Ragama, Sri Lanka ... 60 R11
Ragged, Mt., Australia ... 89 F3
Raglan, Australia ... 90 C5
Raglan, N.Z. ... 87 G5
Ragunda, Sweden ... 10 A10
Ragusa, Italy ... 35 F7
Raha, Indonesia ... 57 E6
Rahad, Nahr ed →, Sudan ... 77 E3
Rahad al Bardī, Sudan ... 73 F9
Rahaeng = Tak, Thailand ... 58 D2
Rahden, Germany ... 18 C4
Raheita, Eritrea ... 77 E5
Raḥīmah, Si. Arabia ... 65 E6
Rahimyar Khan, Pakistan ... 62 E4
Rāhjerd, Iran ... 65 C6
Raichur, India ... 60 L10
Raiganj, India ... 63 G13
Raigarh, India ... 61 J13
Raijua, Indonesia ... 57 F6
Railton, Australia ... 90 G4
Rainbow Lake, Canada ... 100 B5
Rainier, U.S.A. ... 112 D4
Rainier, Mt., U.S.A. ... 112 D5
Rainy L., Canada ... 101 D10
Rainy River, Canada ... 101 D10
Raipur, India ... 61 J12
Raj Nandgaon, India ... 61 J12
Raja, Ujung, Indonesia ... 56 D1
Raja Ampat, Kepulauan, Indonesia ... 57 E7
Rajahmundry, India ... 61 L12
Rajapalaiyam, India ... 60 Q10
Rajasthan □, India ... 62 F5
Rajasthan Canal, India ... 62 E5
Rajauri, India ... 63 C6
Rajgarh, Mad. P., India ... 62 G7
Rajgarh, Raj., India ... 62 E6
Rajhenburg, Slovenia ... 33 B12
Rajkot, India ... 62 H4
Rajmahal Hills, India ... 63 G12
Rajpipla, India ... 60 J8
Rajpura, India ... 62 D7
Rajshahi, Bangla. ... 61 G16
Rajshahi □, Bangla. ... 63 G13
Rakaia, N.Z. ... 87 K4
Rakaia →, N.Z. ... 87 K4
Rakan, Ra's, Qatar ... 65 E6
Rakaposhi, Pakistan ... 63 A6
Rakata, Pulau, Indonesia ... 56 F3
Rakhni, Pakistan ... 62 D3
Rakitnoye, Russia ... 48 B7
Rakops, Botswana ... 84 C3
Rákospalota, Hungary ... 21 H9
Rakov, Belorussia ... 40 E5
Rakovica, Croatia ... 33 D12
Rakovník, Czech. ... 20 E3
Rakovski, Bulgaria ... 38 G7
Rakvere, Estonia ... 40 B5
Raleigh, U.S.A. ... 105 H6
Raleigh B., U.S.A. ... 105 H7
Ralja, Serbia ... 21 L10
Ralls, U.S.A. ... 109 J4
Ram →, Canada ... 100 A4
Rām Allāh, Jordan ... 69 D4
Ram Hd., Australia ... 91 F4
Rama, Nic. ... 116 D3

Ramacca, Italy ... 35 E7
Ramales de la Victoria, Spain ... 28 B1
Ramalho, Serra do, Brazil ... 123 D3
Raman, Thailand ... 59 J3
Ramanathapuram, India ... 60 Q11
Ramanetaka, B. de, Madag. ... 85 A8
Ramat Gan, Israel ... 69 C3
Ramatlhabama, S. Africa ... 84 D4
Ramban, India ... 63 C6
Rambervillers, France ... 25 D13
Rambipuji, Indonesia ... 57 H15
Rambouillet, France ... 25 D8
Ramea, Canada ... 99 C8
Ramechhap, Nepal ... 63 F12
Ramelau, Indonesia ... 57 F7
Ramenskoye, Russia ... 41 D11
Ramgarh, Bihar, India ... 63 H11
Ramgarh, Raj., India ... 62 F6
Ramgarh, Raj., India ... 62 F4
Rāmhormoz, Iran ... 65 D6
Ramīān, Iran ... 65 B7
Ramingining, Australia ... 90 A2
Ramla, Israel ... 69 D3
Ramlu, Eritrea ... 77 E5
Ramme, Denmark ... 11 H2
Ramnad = Ramanathapuram, India ... 60 Q11
Ramnagar, India ... 63 C6
Ramnäs, Sweden ... 10 E10
Ramon, Russia ... 41 F11
Ramona, U.S.A. ... 113 M10
Ramore, Canada ... 98 C3
Ramotswa, Botswana ... 84 C4
Rampur, H.P., India ... 62 D7
Rampur, Mad. P., India ... 62 H5
Rampur, Ut. P., India ... 63 E8
Rampur Hat, India ... 63 G12
Rampura, India ... 62 G6
Ramree I. = Ramree Kyun, Burma ... 61 K18
Ramree Kyun, Burma ... 61 K18
Rāmsar, Iran ... 65 B6
Ramsel, Belgium ... 17 F5
Ramsey, Canada ... 98 C3
Ramsey, U.K. ... 12 C3
Ramsgate, U.K. ... 13 F9
Ramsjö, Sweden ... 10 B9
Ramtek, India ... 60 J11
Ramvik, Sweden ... 10 B11
Ranaghat, India ... 63 H13
Ranahu, Pakistan ... 62 G3
Ranau, Malaysia ... 56 C5
Rancagua, Chile ... 126 C1
Rance, Belgium ... 17 H4
Rance →, France ... 24 D5
Rance, Barrage de la, France ... 24 D4
Rancharia, Brazil ... 123 F1
Rancheria →, Canada ... 100 A3
Ranchester, U.S.A. ... 110 D10
Ranchi, India ... 63 H11
Ranco, L., Chile ... 128 B2
Randan, France ... 26 B7
Randazzo, Italy ... 35 E7
Randers, Denmark ... 11 H4
Randers Fjord, Denmark ... 11 H4
Randfontein, S. Africa ... 85 D4
Randle, U.S.A. ... 112 D5
Randolph, Mass., U.S.A. ... 107 D13
Randolph, N.Y., U.S.A. ... 106 D6
Randolph, Utah, U.S.A. ... 110 F8
Randolph, Vt., U.S.A. ... 107 C12
Randsfjord, Norway ... 10 D4
Råne älv →, Sweden ... 8 D17
Rangae, Thailand ... 59 J3
Rangaunu B., N.Z. ... 87 F4
Rångedala, Sweden ... 11 G7
Rangia, India ... 61 F17
Rangiora, N.Z. ... 87 K4
Rangitaiki →, N.Z. ... 87 G6
Rangitata →, N.Z. ... 87 K3
Rangkasbitung, Indonesia ... 57 G12
Rangon →, Burma ... 61 L20
Rangoon, Burma ... 61 L20
Rangpur, Bangla. ... 61 G16
Rangsit, Thailand ... 58 F3
Ranibennur, India ... 60 M9
Raniganj, India ... 63 H12
Raniwara, India ... 60 G8
Ranken →, Australia ... 90 C2
Rankin, U.S.A. ... 109 K4
Rankin Inlet, Canada ... 96 B10
Rankins Springs, Australia ... 91 E4
Rannoch, L., U.K. ... 14 E4
Rannoch Moor, U.K. ... 14 E4
Ranobe, Helodranon' i, Madag. ... 85 C7
Ranohira, Madag. ... 85 C8
Ranomafana, Toamasina, Madag. ... 85 B8
Ranomafana, Toliara, Madag. ... 85 C8
Ranong, Thailand ... 59 H2
Rānsa, Iran ... 65 C6
Ransiki, Indonesia ... 57 E8
Rantau, Indonesia ... 56 E5
Rantauprapat, Indonesia ... 56 D1
Rantekombola, Indonesia ... 57 E5
Rantoul, U.S.A. ... 104 E1

Ranum, Denmark ... 11 H3
Raon l'Étape, France ... 25 D13
Raoui, Erg er, Algeria ... 75 C4
Raoyang, China ... 50 E8
Rapa, Pac. Oc. ... 93 K13
Rapallo, Italy ... 32 D6
Rāpch, Iran ... 65 E8
Rapid →, Canada ... 100 B3
Rapid City, U.S.A. ... 108 D3
Rapid River, U.S.A. ... 104 C2
Rapides des Joachims, Canada ... 98 C4
Rapla, Estonia ... 40 B4
Rapperswil, Switz. ... 23 B7
Rapu Rapu I., Phil. ... 55 E6
Rarotonga, Cook Is. ... 93 K12
Ra's al' Ayn, Syria ... 64 B4
Ra's al Khaymah, U.A.E. ... 65 E8
Ra's al-Unuf, Libya ... 73 B8
Ra's an Naqb, Jordan ... 69 F4
Ras Bânâs, Egypt ... 76 C4
Ras Dashen, Ethiopia ... 77 E4
Ras el Ma, Algeria ... 75 B4
Ras Mallap, Egypt ... 76 J8
Ras Timirist, Mauritania ... 78 B1
Rasa, Punta, Argentina ... 128 B4
Rasca, Pta. de la, Canary Is. ... 36 G3
Raseiniai, Lithuania ... 40 D3
Rashad, Sudan ... 77 E3
Rashîd, Egypt ... 76 H7
Rashîd, Masabb, Egypt ... 76 H7
Rasht, Iran ... 65 B6
Rasi Salai, Thailand ... 58 E5
Raška, Serbia ... 21 M10
Rason L., Australia ... 89 E3
Raşova, Romania ... 38 E10
Rasra, India ... 63 G10
Rass el Oued, Algeria ... 75 A6
Rasskazovo, Russia ... 41 E12
Rastatt, Germany ... 19 G4
Rat Buri, Thailand ... 58 F2
Rat Islands, U.S.A. ... 96 C1
Rat River, Canada ... 100 A6
Ratangarh, India ... 62 E6
Raţāwī, Iraq ... 64 D5
Rath, India ... 63 G8
Rath Luirc, Ireland ... 15 D3
Rathdrum, Ireland ... 15 D5
Rathenow, Germany ... 18 C8
Rathkeale, Ireland ... 15 D3
Rathlin, U.K. ... 15 A5
Rathlin O'Birne I., Ireland ... 15 B3
Ratibor = Racibórz, Poland ... 20 E8
Ratlam, India ... 62 H6
Ratnagiri, India ... 60 L8
Raton, U.S.A. ... 109 G2
Rattaphum, Thailand ... 59 J3
Rattray Hd., U.K. ... 14 D7
Ratz, Mt., Canada ... 100 B2
Ratzeburg, Germany ... 18 B6
Raub, Malaysia ... 59 L3
Rauch, Argentina ... 126 D4
Raufarhöfn, Iceland ... 8 C6
Raufoss, Norway ... 10 D4
Raukumara Ra., N.Z. ... 87 H6
Rauland, Norway ... 10 E2
Rauma, Finland ... 9 F16
Rauma →, Norway ... 10 B1
Raurkela, India ... 63 H11
Rausu-Dake, Japan ... 48 B12
Rava Russkaya, Ukraine ... 40 F3
Ravānsar, Iran ... 64 C5
Ravanusa, Italy ... 34 E6
Rāvar, Iran ... 65 D8
Ravels, Belgium ... 17 F6
Ravena, U.S.A. ... 107 D11
Ravenna, Italy ... 33 D9
Ravenna, Nebr., U.S.A. ... 108 E5
Ravenna, Ohio, U.S.A. ... 106 E3
Ravensburg, Germany ... 19 H5
Ravenshoe, Australia ... 90 B4
Ravenstein, Neths. ... 16 E7
Ravensthorpe, Australia ... 89 F3
Ravenswood, Australia ... 90 C4
Ravenswood, U.S.A. ... 104 F5
Ravi →, Pakistan ... 62 D4
Ravna Gora, Croatia ... 33 C11
Rawa Mazowiecka, Poland ... 20 D10
Rawalpindi, Pakistan ... 62 C5
Rawāndūz, Iraq ... 64 B5
Rawang, Malaysia ... 59 L3
Rawdon, Canada ... 98 C5
Rawene, N.Z. ... 87 F4
Rawicz, Poland ... 20 D6
Rawlinna, Australia ... 89 F4
Rawlins, U.S.A. ... 110 F10
Rawlinson Ra., Australia ... 89 D4
Rawson, Argentina ... 128 B3
Ray, U.S.A. ... 108 A3
Ray, C., Canada ... 99 C8
Rayadurg, India ... 60 M10
Rayagada, India ... 61 K13
Raychikhinsk, Russia ... 45 E13
Rāyen, Iran ... 65 D8
Raymond, Canada ... 100 D6
Raymond, Calif., U.S.A. ... 112 H7
Raymond, Wash., U.S.A. ... 112 D3
Raymondville, U.S.A. ... 109 M6
Raymore, Canada ... 101 C8
Rayne, U.S.A. ... 109 K8
Rayón, Mexico ... 114 B2
Rayong, Thailand ... 58 F3

Rayville, U.S.A. ... 109 J9
Raz, Pte. du, France ... 24 D2
Razan, Iran ... 65 C6
Răzana, Serbia ... 21 L9
Ražanj, Serbia ... 21 M11
Razdel'naya, Ukraine ... 42 C4
Razdolnoye, Russia ... 48 C5
Razdolnoye, Ukraine ... 42 D5
Razeh, Iran ... 65 C6
Razelm, Lacul, Romania ... 38 E12
Razgrad, Bulgaria ... 38 F9
Razmak, Pakistan ... 62 C3
Ré, I. de, France ... 26 B2
Reading, U.K. ... 13 F7
Reading, U.S.A. ... 107 F9
Real, Cordillera, Bolivia ... 124 D4
Realicó, Argentina ... 126 D3
Réalmont, France ... 26 E6
Reata, Mexico ... 114 B4
Rebais, France ... 25 D10
Rebecca, L., Australia ... 89 F3
Rebi, Indonesia ... 57 F8
Rebiana, Libya ... 73 D9
Rebun-Tō, Japan ... 48 B10
Recanati, Italy ... 33 E10
Recaş, Romania ... 38 D4
Recherche, Arch. of the, Australia ... 89 F3
Rechitsa, Belorussia ... 40 E7
Recht, Belgium ... 17 H8
Recife, Brazil ... 122 C5
Recklinghausen, Germany ... 17 E10
Reconquista, Argentina ... 126 B4
Recreio, Brazil ... 125 B6
Recreo, Argentina ... 126 B2
Recuay, Peru ... 124 B2
Red →, La., U.S.A. ... 109 K9
Red →, N. Dak., U.S.A. ... 108 A6
Red Bank, U.S.A. ... 107 F10
Red Bay, Canada ... 99 B8
Red Bluff, U.S.A. ... 110 F2
Red Bluff L., U.S.A. ... 109 K3
Red Cliffs, Australia ... 91 E3
Red Cloud, U.S.A. ... 108 E5
Red Deer, Canada ... 100 C6
Red Deer →, Alta., Canada ... 101 C6
Red Deer →, Man., Canada ... 101 C8
Red Deer L., Canada ... 101 C8
Red Indian L., Canada ... 99 C8
Red Lake, Canada ... 101 C10
Red Lake Falls, U.S.A. ... 108 B6
Red Lodge, U.S.A. ... 110 D9
Red Mountain, U.S.A. ... 113 K9
Red Oak, U.S.A. ... 108 E7
Red Rock, Canada ... 98 C2
Red Rock, L., U.S.A. ... 108 E8
Red Rocks Pt., Australia ... 89 F4
Red Sea, Asia ... 68 C2
Red Slate Mt., U.S.A. ... 112 H8
Red Sucker L., Canada ... 101 C10
Red Tower Pass = Turnu Roşu Pasul, Romania ... 38 D7
Red Wing, U.S.A. ... 108 C8
Redange, Lux. ... 17 J7
Redbridge, U.K. ... 13 F8
Redcar, U.K. ... 12 C6
Redcliff, Canada ... 101 C6
Redcliffe, Australia ... 91 D5
Redcliffe, Mt., Australia ... 89 E3
Reddersburg, S. Africa ... 84 D4
Redding, U.S.A. ... 110 F2
Redditch, U.K. ... 13 E6
Redenção, Brazil ... 122 B4
Redfield, U.S.A. ... 108 C5
Redknife →, Canada ... 100 A5
Redlands, U.S.A. ... 113 M9
Redmond, Australia ... 89 F2
Redmond, Oreg., U.S.A. ... 110 D3
Redmond, Wash., U.S.A. ... 112 C4
Redon, France ... 24 E4
Redonda, Antigua ... 117 C7
Redondela, Spain ... 30 C2
Redondo, Portugal ... 31 G3
Redondo Beach, U.S.A. ... 113 M8
Redrock Pt., Canada ... 100 A5
Redruth, U.K. ... 13 G2
Redvers, Canada ... 101 D8
Redwater, Canada ... 100 C6
Redwood, U.S.A. ... 107 B9
Redwood City, U.S.A. ... 111 H2
Redwood Falls, U.S.A. ... 108 C7
Ree, L., Ireland ... 15 C4
Reed, L., Canada ... 101 C8
Reed City, U.S.A. ... 104 D3
Reeder, U.S.A. ... 108 B3
Reedley, U.S.A. ... 111 H4
Reedsburg, U.S.A. ... 108 D9
Reedsport, U.S.A. ... 110 E1
Reefton, N.Z. ... 87 K3
Refahiye, Turkey ... 67 D8
Refugio, U.S.A. ... 109 L6
Rega →, Poland ... 20 A5
Regalbuto, Italy ... 35 E7
Regen, Germany ... 19 G9
Regen →, Germany ... 19 F8
Regeneração, Brazil ... 122 C3
Regensburg, Germany ... 19 F8
Regensdorf, Switz. ... 23 B6
Réggio di Calábria, Italy ... 35 D8
Réggio nell' Emilia, Italy ... 32 D7
Regina, Canada ... 101 C8
Régina, Fr. Guiana ... 121 C7
Registro, Brazil ... 127 A6

Reguengos de Monsaraz, Portugal ... 31 G3
Rehar →, India ... 63 H10
Rehoboth, Namibia ... 84 C2
Rehovot, Israel ... 69 D3
Rei-Bouba, Cameroon ... 73 G7
Reichenbach, Germany ... 18 E8
Reichenbach, Switz. ... 22 C5
Reid, Australia ... 89 F4
Reid River, Australia ... 90 B4
Reiden, Switz. ... 22 B5
Reidsville, U.S.A. ... 105 G6
Reigate, U.K. ... 13 F7
Reillo, Spain ... 28 F3
Reims, France ... 25 C11
Reina Adelaida, Arch., Chile ... 128 D2
Reinach, Aargau, Switz. ... 22 B6
Reinach, Basel, Switz. ... 22 B5
Reinbeck, U.S.A. ... 108 D8
Reindeer →, Canada ... 101 B8
Reindeer I., Canada ... 101 C9
Reindeer L., Canada ... 101 B8
Reinga, C., N.Z. ... 87 F4
Reinosa, Spain ... 30 B6
Reinosa, Paso, Spain ... 30 C6
Reitdiep, Neths. ... 16 B9
Reitz, S. Africa ... 85 D4
Reivilo, S. Africa ... 84 D3
Rejmyre, Sweden ... 11 F9
Reka →, Slovenia ... 33 C11
Rekinniki, Russia ... 45 C17
Reliance, Canada ... 101 A7
Remad, Oued →, Algeria ... 75 B4
Rémalard, France ... 24 D7
Remarkable, Mt., Australia ... 91 E2
Rembang, Indonesia ... 57 G14
Remchi, Algeria ... 75 A4
Remedios, Colombia ... 120 B3
Remedios, Panama ... 116 E3
Remeshk, Iran ... 65 E8
Remich, Lux. ... 17 J8
Rémire, Fr. Guiana ... 121 C7
Remiremont, France ... 25 D13
Remo, Ethiopia ... 77 F5
Remontnoye, Russia ... 43 C10
Remoulins, France ... 27 E8
Remscheid, Germany ... 18 D3
Ren Xian, China ... 50 F8
Renascença, Brazil ... 120 D4
Rende, Italy ... 35 C9
Rendeux, Belgium ... 17 H7
Rendína, Greece ... 39 K4
Rendsburg, Germany ... 18 A5
Rene, Russia ... 45 C19
Renfrew, Canada ... 98 C4
Renfrew, U.K. ... 14 F4
Rengat, Indonesia ... 56 E2
Rengo, Chile ... 126 C1
Renhua, China ... 53 E9
Renhuai, China ... 52 D6
Reni, Moldavia ... 42 D3
Renk, Sudan ... 77 E3
Renkum, Neths. ... 16 E7
Renmark, Australia ... 91 E3
Rennell Sd., Canada ... 100 C2
Renner Springs T.O., Australia ... 90 B1
Rennes, France ... 24 D5
Rennes, Bassin de, France ... 24 D5
Reno, U.S.A. ... 112 F7
Reno →, Italy ... 33 D9
Renovo, U.S.A. ... 106 E7
Renqiu, China ... 50 E9
Rensselaer, Ind., U.S.A. ... 104 E2
Rensselaer, N.Y., U.S.A. ... 107 D11
Rentería, Spain ... 28 B3
Renton, U.S.A. ... 112 C4
Réo, Burkina Faso ... 78 C4
Reotipur, India ... 63 G10
Republic, Mich., U.S.A. ... 104 B2
Republic, Wash., U.S.A. ... 110 B4
Republican →, U.S.A. ... 108 F6
Republican City, U.S.A. ... 108 E5
Republiek, Surinam ... 121 B6
Repulse Bay, Canada ... 97 B11
Requena, Peru ... 124 B3
Requena, Spain ... 29 F3
Resadiye = Datça, Turkey ... 66 E2
Reşadiye, Turkey ... 66 C7
Resele, Sweden ... 10 A11
Reserve, Canada ... 101 C8
Reserve, U.S.A. ... 111 K9
Resht = Rasht, Iran ... 65 B6
Resistencia, Argentina ... 126 B4
Reşiţa, Romania ... 38 D4
Resolution I., Canada ... 97 B13
Resolution I., N.Z. ... 87 L1
Resplandes, Brazil ... 122 C2
Resplendor, Brazil ... 123 E3
Ressano Garcia, Mozam. ... 85 D5
Reston, Canada ... 101 D8
Retalhuleu, Guatemala ... 116 D1
Reteag, Romania ... 38 B7
Retenue, L. de, Zaïre ... 83 E2
Rethel, France ... 25 C11
Rethem, Germany ... 18 C5
Réthímnon, Greece ... 37 D6
Réthímnon □, Greece ... 37 D6
Retiche, Alpi, Switz. ... 23 D10
Retie, Belgium ... 17 F6
Retiers, France ... 24 E5
Retortillo, Spain ... 30 E4
Reuland, Belgium ... 17 H8
Réunion ■, Ind. Oc. ... 71 J9

Reus, *Spain*	28	D6
Reusel, *Neths.*	17	F6
Reuss →, *Switz.*	23	B6
Reutlingen, *Germany*	19	G5
Reutte, *Austria*	19	H6
Reuver, *Neths.*	17	F8
Reval = Tallinn, *Estonia*	40	B4
Revel, *France*	26	E6
Revelganj, *India*	63	G11
Revelstoke, *Canada*	100	C5
Reventazón, *Peru*	124	B1
Revigny-sur-Ornain, *France*	25	D11
Revilla Gigedo, Is., *Pac. Oc.*	93	F16
Revillagigedo I., *U.S.A.*	100	B2
Revin, *France*	25	C11
Revuè →, *Mozam.*	83	F3
Rewa, *India*	63	G9
Rewa →, *Guyana*	121	C6
Rewari, *India*	62	E7
Rexburg, *U.S.A.*	110	E8
Rey, *Iran*	65	C6
Rey, Rio del →, *Nigeria*	79	E6
Rey Malabo, *Eq. Guin.*	79	E6
Reyes, *Bolivia*	124	C4
Reyes, Pt., *U.S.A.*	112	H3
Reykjahlið, *Iceland*	8	D5
Reykjanes, *Iceland*	8	E2
Reykjavík, *Iceland*	8	D3
Reynolds, *Canada*	101	D9
Reynolds Ra., *Australia*	88	D5
Reynoldsville, *U.S.A.*	106	E6
Reynosa, *Mexico*	115	B5
Rēzekne, *Latvia*	40	C5
Rezvān, *Iran*	65	E8
Rharis, O. →, *Algeria*	75	C6
Rhayader, *U.K.*	13	E4
Rheden, *Neths.*	16	D8
Rhein, *Canada*	101	C8
Rhein →, *Europe*	16	E8
Rhein-Main-Donau-Kanal, *Germany*	19	F7
Rheinbach, *Germany*	18	E2
Rheine, *Germany*	18	C3
Rheineck, *Switz.*	23	B9
Rheinfelden, *Switz.*	22	A5
Rheinland-Pfalz □, *Germany*	19	E2
Rheinsberg, *Germany*	18	B8
Rheinwaldhorn, *Switz.*	23	D8
Rhenen, *Neths.*	16	E7
Rheriss, Oued →, *Morocco*	74	B4
Rheydt, *Germany*	18	D2
Rhin = Rhein →, *Europe*	16	E8
Rhinau, *France*	25	D14
Rhine = Rhein →, *Europe*	16	E8
Rhineland-Palatinate □ = Rheinland-Pfalz □, *Germany*	19	E2
Rhinelander, *U.S.A.*	108	C10
Rhino Camp, *Uganda*	82	B3
Rhir, Cap, *Morocco*	74	B3
Rhisnes, *Belgium*	17	G5
Rho, *Italy*	32	C6
Rhode Island □, *U.S.A.*	107	E13
Rhodes = Ródhos, *Greece*	37	C10
Rhodesia = Zimbabwe ■, *Africa*	83	F2
Rhodope Mts. = Rhodopi Planina, *Bulgaria*	39	H7
Rhodopi Planina, *Bulgaria*	39	H7
Rhön = Hohe Rhön, *Germany*	19	E5
Rhondda, *U.K.*	13	F4
Rhône □, *France*	27	C8
Rhône →, *France*	27	E8
Rhum, *U.K.*	14	E2
Rhyl, *U.K.*	12	D4
Rhymney, *U.K.*	13	F4
Ri-Aba, *Eq. Guin.*	79	E6
Riachão, *Brazil*	122	C2
Riacho de Santana, *Brazil*	123	D3
Rialma, *Brazil*	123	E2
Riaño, *Spain*	30	C5
Rians, *France*	27	E9
Riansares →, *Spain*	28	F1
Riasi, *India*	63	C6
Riau □, *Indonesia*	56	D2
Riau, Kepulauan, *Indonesia*	56	D2
Riau Arch. = Riau, Kepulauan, *Indonesia*	56	D2
Riaza, *Spain*	28	D1
Riaza →, *Spain*	28	D1
Riba de Saelices, *Spain*	28	E2
Ribadavia, *Spain*	30	C2
Ribadeo, *Spain*	30	B3
Ribadesella, *Spain*	30	B5
Ribamar, *Brazil*	122	B3
Ribas, *Spain*	28	C7
Ribas do Rio Pardo, *Brazil*	125	E7
Ribble →, *U.K.*	12	C5
Ribe, *Denmark*	11	J2
Ribeauvillé, *France*	25	D14
Ribécourt, *France*	25	C9
Ribeira, *Spain*	30	C2
Ribeira Brava, *Madeira*	36	D2
Ribeira do Pombal, *Brazil*	122	D4
Ribeirão Prêto, *Brazil*	127	A6
Ribeiro Gonçalves, *Brazil*	122	C2
Ribemont, *France*	25	C10
Ribera, *Italy*	34	E6
Ribérac, *France*	26	C4
Riberalta, *Bolivia*	125	C4
Ribnica, *Slovenia*	33	C11
Ribnitz-Damgarten, *Germany*	18	A8
Riccarton, *N.Z.*	87	K4
Riccia, *Italy*	35	A7
Riccione, *Italy*	33	D9
Rice, *U.S.A.*	113	L12
Rice L., *Canada*	106	B6
Rice Lake, *U.S.A.*	108	C9
Rich, *Morocco*	74	B4
Rich Hill, *U.S.A.*	109	F7
Richards Bay, *S. Africa*	85	D5
Richards L., *Canada*	101	B7
Richardson →, *Canada*	101	B6
Richardson Springs, *U.S.A.*	112	F5
Richardton, *U.S.A.*	108	B3
Riche, C., *Australia*	89	F2
Richelieu, *France*	24	E7
Richey, *U.S.A.*	108	B2
Richfield, *Idaho, U.S.A.*	110	E6
Richfield, *Utah, U.S.A.*	111	G8
Richford, *U.S.A.*	107	B12
Richibucto, *Canada*	99	C7
Richland, *Ga., U.S.A.*	105	J3
Richland, *Oreg., U.S.A.*	110	D5
Richland, *Wash., U.S.A.*	110	C4
Richland Center, *U.S.A.*	108	D9
Richlands, *U.S.A.*	104	G5
Richmond, *N.S.W., Australia*	91	E5
Richmond, *Queens., Australia*	90	C3
Richmond, *N.Z.*	87	J4
Richmond, *S. Africa*	85	D5
Richmond, *U.K.*	12	C6
Richmond, *Calif., U.S.A.*	112	H4
Richmond, *Ind., U.S.A.*	104	F3
Richmond, *Ky., U.S.A.*	104	G3
Richmond, *Mich., U.S.A.*	106	D2
Richmond, *Mo., U.S.A.*	108	F8
Richmond, *Tex., U.S.A.*	109	L7
Richmond, *Utah, U.S.A.*	110	F8
Richmond, *Va., U.S.A.*	104	G7
Richmond Ra., *Australia*	91	D5
Richmond-upon-Thames, *U.K.*	13	F7
Richterswil, *Switz.*	23	B7
Richton, *U.S.A.*	105	K1
Richwood, *U.S.A.*	104	F5
Ricla, *Spain*	28	D3
Ridder, *Kazakhstan*	44	D9
Ridderkerk, *Neths.*	16	E5
Riddes, *Switz.*	22	D4
Ridgecrest, *U.S.A.*	113	K9
Ridgedale, *Canada*	101	C8
Ridgefield, *U.S.A.*	112	E4
Ridgeland, *U.S.A.*	105	J5
Ridgelands, *Australia*	90	C5
Ridgetown, *Canada*	98	D3
Ridgewood, *U.S.A.*	107	F10
Ridgway, *U.S.A.*	106	E6
Riding Mountain Nat. Park, *Canada*	101	C8
Ridley, Mt., *Australia*	89	F3
Ried, *Austria*	21	G3
Riedlingen, *Germany*	19	G5
Riel, *Neths.*	17	E6
Rienza →, *Italy*	33	B8
Riesa, *Germany*	18	D9
Riesco, I., *Chile*	128	D2
Riesi, *Italy*	35	E7
Rieti, *Italy*	33	F9
Rieupeyroux, *France*	26	D6
Riez, *France*	27	E10
Riffe L., *U.S.A.*	112	D4
Rifle, *U.S.A.*	110	G10
Rifstangi, *Iceland*	8	C5
Rift Valley →, *Kenya*	82	B4
Rig Rig, *Chad*	73	F7
Riga, *Latvia*	40	C4
Riga, G. of = Rīgas Jūras Līcis, *Latvia*	40	C3
Rīgān, *Iran*	65	D8
Rīgas Jūras Līcis, *Latvia*	40	C3
Rigaud, *Canada*	107	A10
Rigby, *U.S.A.*	110	E8
Rigestān □, *Afghan.*	60	D4
Riggins, *U.S.A.*	110	D5
Rignac, *France*	26	D6
Rigolet, *Canada*	99	B8
Riihimäki, *Finland*	9	F18
Riiser-Larsen-halvøya, *Antarctica*	5	C4
Rijau, *Nigeria*	79	C6
Rijeka, *Croatia*	33	C11
Rijen, *Neths.*	17	E5
Rijkevorsel, *Belgium*	17	F5
Rijn →, *Neths.*	16	D4
Rijnsberg, *Neths.*	16	D4
Rijssen, *Neths.*	16	D9
Rijswijk, *Neths.*	16	D4
Rike, *Ethiopia*	77	E4
Rikuzentakada, *Japan*	48	E10
Rila Planina, *Bulgaria*	38	G6
Riley, *U.S.A.*	110	E4
Rima →, *Nigeria*	79	C6
Rimah, Wadi ar →, *Si. Arabia*	64	E4
Rimavská Sobota, *Slovak Rep.*	21	G10
Rimbey, *Canada*	100	C6
Rimbo, *Sweden*	10	E12
Rimi, *Nigeria*	79	C6
Rímini, *Italy*	33	D9
Rîmnicu Sărat, *Romania*	38	D10
Rîmnicu Vîlcea, *Romania*	38	D7
Rimouski, *Canada*	99	C6
Rimrock, *U.S.A.*	112	D5
Rinca, *Indonesia*	57	F5
Rincón de Romos, *Mexico*	114	C4
Rinconada, *Argentina*	126	A2
Ringarum, *Sweden*	11	F10
Ringe, *Denmark*	11	J4
Ringim, *Nigeria*	79	C6
Ringkøbing, *Denmark*	11	H2
Ringling, *U.S.A.*	110	C8
Ringsaker, *Norway*	10	D4
Ringsted, *Denmark*	11	J5
Ringvassøy, *Norway*	8	B15
Rinjani, *Indonesia*	56	F5
Rinteln, *Germany*	18	C5
Río, Punta del, *Spain*	29	J2
Rio Branco, *Brazil*	124	B4
Río Branco, *Uruguay*	127	C5
Rio Brilhante, *Brazil*	127	A5
Río Bueno, *Chile*	128	B2
Río Chico, *Venezuela*	120	A4
Rio Claro, *Brazil*	127	A6
Rio Claro, *Trin. & Tob.*	117	D7
Río Colorado, *Argentina*	128	A4
Río Cuarto, *Argentina*	126	C3
Rio das Pedras, *Mozam.*	85	C6
Rio de Contas, *Brazil*	123	D3
Rio de Janeiro, *Brazil*	123	F3
Rio de Janeiro □, *Brazil*	123	F3
Rio do Prado, *Brazil*	123	E3
Rio do Sul, *Brazil*	127	B6
Río Gallegos, *Argentina*	128	D3
Río Grande, *Argentina*	128	D3
Rio Grande, *Bolivia*	124	E4
Rio Grande, *Brazil*	127	C5
Río Grande, *Mexico*	114	C4
Río Grande, *Nic.*	116	D3
Río Grande →, *U.S.A.*	109	N6
Rio Grande City, *U.S.A.*	109	M5
Río Grande del Norte →, *N. Amer.*	103	E7
Rio Grande do Norte □, *Brazil*	122	C4
Rio Grande do Sul □, *Brazil*	127	C5
Río Hato, *Panama*	116	E3
Rio Lagartos, *Mexico*	115	C7
Rio Largo, *Brazil*	122	C4
Rio Maior, *Portugal*	31	F2
Rio Marina, *Italy*	32	F7
Río Mayo, *Argentina*	128	C2
Río Mulatos, *Bolivia*	124	D4
Río Muni = Mbini □, *Eq. Guin.*	80	D2
Rio Negro, *Brazil*	127	B6
Río Negro, *Chile*	128	B2
Rio Negro, Pantanal do, *Brazil*	125	D6
Rio Pardo, *Brazil*	127	C5
Río Pico, *Argentina*	128	B2
Río Real, *Brazil*	123	D4
Río Segundo, *Argentina*	126	C3
Río Tercero, *Argentina*	126	C3
Rio Tinto, *Brazil*	122	C4
Rio Tinto, *Portugal*	30	D2
Río Verde, *Brazil*	123	E1
Río Verde, *Mexico*	115	C5
Rio Verde de Mato Grosso, *Brazil*	125	D7
Rio Vista, *U.S.A.*	112	G5
Ríobamba, *Ecuador*	120	D2
Ríohacha, *Colombia*	120	A3
Rioja, *Peru*	124	B2
Riom, *France*	26	C7
Riom-ès-Montagnes, *France*	26	C6
Rion-des-Landes, *France*	26	E3
Rionegro, *Colombia*	120	B2
Rionero in Vúlture, *Italy*	35	B8
Rioni →, *Georgia*	43	E9
Rios, *Spain*	30	D3
Riosucio, *Caldas, Colombia*	120	B2
Riosucio, *Choco, Colombia*	120	B2
Riou L., *Canada*	101	B7
Rioz, *France*	25	E13
Riozinho →, *Brazil*	120	D4
Riparia, Dora →, *Italy*	32	C4
Ripatransone, *Italy*	33	F10
Ripley, *Canada*	106	B3
Ripley, *Calif., U.S.A.*	113	M12
Ripley, *N.Y., U.S.A.*	106	D5
Ripley, *Tenn., U.S.A.*	109	H10
Ripoll, *Spain*	28	C7
Ripon, *U.K.*	12	C6
Ripon, *Calif., U.S.A.*	112	H5
Ripon, *Wis., U.S.A.*	104	D1
Riposto, *Italy*	35	E8
Risalpur, *Pakistan*	62	B4
Risan, *Montenegro*	21	N8
Risaralda □, *Colombia*	120	B2
Riscle, *France*	26	E3
Rishâ, W. ar →, *Si. Arabia*	64	E5
Rishiri-Tō, *Japan*	48	B10
Rishon le Ziyyon, *Israel*	69	D3
Risle →, *France*	24	C7
Rison, *U.S.A.*	109	J8
Risør, *Norway*	11	F3
Rissani, *Morocco*	74	B4
Riti, *Nigeria*	79	D6
Rittman, *U.S.A.*	106	F3
Ritzville, *U.S.A.*	110	C4
Riva Bella, *France*	24	C6
Riva del Garda, *Italy*	32	C7
Rivadavia, *Buenos Aires, Argentina*	126	D3
Rivadavia, *Mendoza, Argentina*	126	C2
Rivadavia, *Salta, Argentina*	126	A3
Rivadavia, *Chile*	126	B1
Rivarolo Canavese, *Italy*	32	C4
Rivas, *Nic.*	116	D2
Rive-de-Gier, *France*	27	C8
River Cess, *Liberia*	78	D3
Rivera, *Uruguay*	127	C4
Riverdale, *U.S.A.*	112	J7
Riverhead, *U.S.A.*	107	F12
Riverhurst, *Canada*	101	C7
Riverina, *Australia*	89	E3
Rivers, *Canada*	101	C8
Rivers □, *Nigeria*	79	E6
Rivers, L. of the, *Canada*	101	D7
Rivers Inlet, *Canada*	100	C3
Riversdale, *S. Africa*	84	E3
Riverside, *Calif., U.S.A.*	113	M9
Riverside, *Wyo., U.S.A.*	110	F10
Riverleigh, *Australia*	90	B2
Riverton, *Australia*	91	E2
Riverton, *Canada*	101	C9
Riverton, *N.Z.*	87	M1
Riverton, *U.S.A.*	110	E9
Riverton Heights, *U.S.A.*	112	C4
Rives, *France*	27	C9
Rivesaltes, *France*	26	F6
Riviera, *Europe*	32	E5
Rivière-à-Pierre, *Canada*	99	C5
Rivière-au-Renard, *Canada*	99	C7
Rivière-du-Loup, *Canada*	99	C6
Rivière-Pentecôte, *Canada*	99	C6
Rivière-Pilote, *Martinique*	117	D7
Rivne = Rovno, *Ukraine*	40	F5
Rívoli, *Italy*	32	C4
Rivoli B., *Australia*	91	F3
Rixensart, *Belgium*	17	G5
Riyadh = Ar Riyāḍ, *Si. Arabia*	64	E5
Rize, *Turkey*	67	C9
Rize □, *Turkey*	67	C9
Rizhao, *China*	51	G10
Rizokarpaso, *Cyprus*	37	D13
Rizzuto, C., *Italy*	35	D10
Rjukan, *Norway*	10	E2
Roa, *Norway*	10	D4
Roa, *Spain*	30	D7
Road Town, *Virgin Is.*	117	C7
Roag, L., *U.K.*	14	C2
Roanne, *France*	27	B8
Roanoke, *Ala., U.S.A.*	105	J3
Roanoke, *Va., U.S.A.*	104	G6
Roanoke →, *U.S.A.*	105	H7
Roanoke I., *U.S.A.*	105	H8
Roanoke Rapids, *U.S.A.*	105	G7
Roatán, *Honduras*	116	C2
Robbins I., *Australia*	90	G4
Robe →, *Australia*	88	D2
Robe →, *Ireland*	15	C2
Röbel, *Germany*	18	B8
Robert Lee, *U.S.A.*	109	K4
Roberts, *U.S.A.*	110	E7
Robertsganj, *India*	63	G10
Robertson, *S. Africa*	84	E2
Robertson I., *Antarctica*	5	C18
Robertson Ra., *Australia*	88	D3
Robertsport, *Liberia*	78	D2
Robertstown, *Australia*	91	E2
Roberval, *Canada*	99	C5
Robeson Chan., *Greenland*	4	A4
Robinson →, *Australia*	90	B2
Robinson Ra., *Australia*	89	E2
Robinson River, *Australia*	90	B2
Robinvale, *Australia*	91	E3
Roblin, *Canada*	101	C8
Roboré, *Bolivia*	125	D6
Robson, Mt., *Canada*	100	C5
Robstown, *U.S.A.*	109	M6
Roca, C. da, *Portugal*	6	H4
Roca Partida, I., *Mexico*	114	D2
Rocas, I., *Brazil*	122	B5
Rocca d'Aspidé, *Italy*	35	B8
Rocca San Casciano, *Italy*	33	D8
Roccalbegna, *Italy*	33	F8
Roccastrada, *Italy*	33	F8
Roccella Iónica, *Italy*	35	D9
Rocha, *Uruguay*	127	C5
Rochdale, *U.K.*	12	D5
Rochechouart, *France*	26	C4
Rochedo, *Brazil*	125	D7
Rochefort, *Belgium*	17	H6
Rochefort, *France*	26	C3
Rochefort-en-Terre, *France*	24	E4
Rochelle, *U.S.A.*	108	E10
Rocher River, *Canada*	100	A6
Rocheservière, *France*	24	F5
Rochester, *Canada*	100	C6
Rochester, *U.K.*	13	F8
Rochester, *Ind., U.S.A.*	104	E2
Rochester, *Minn., U.S.A.*	108	C8
Rochester, *N.H., U.S.A.*	107	C14
Rochester, *N.Y., U.S.A.*	106	C7
Rociana, *Spain*	31	H4
Rociu, *Romania*	38	E8
Rock →, *Canada*	100	A3
Rock Hill, *U.S.A.*	105	H5
Rock Island, *U.S.A.*	108	E9
Rock Rapids, *U.S.A.*	108	D6
Rock River, *U.S.A.*	110	F11
Rock Sound, *Bahamas*	116	B4
Rock Springs, *Mont., U.S.A.*	110	C10
Rock Springs, *Wyo., U.S.A.*	110	F9
Rock Valley, *U.S.A.*	108	D6
Rockall, *Atl. Oc.*	6	D3
Rockanje, *Neths.*	16	E4
Rockdale, *Tex., U.S.A.*	109	K6
Rockdale, *Wash., U.S.A.*	112	C5
Rockefeller Plateau, *Antarctica*	5	E14
Rockford, *U.S.A.*	108	D10
Rockglen, *Canada*	101	D7
Rockhampton, *Australia*	90	C5
Rockhampton Downs, *Australia*	90	B2
Rockingham, *Australia*	89	F2
Rockingham B., *Australia*	90	B4
Rockingham Forest, *U.K.*	13	E7
Rocklake, *U.S.A.*	108	A5
Rockland, *Canada*	107	A9
Rockland, *Idaho, U.S.A.*	110	E7
Rockland, *Maine, U.S.A.*	99	D6
Rockland, *Mich., U.S.A.*	108	B10
Rocklin, *U.S.A.*	112	G5
Rockmart, *U.S.A.*	105	H3
Rockport, *Mo., U.S.A.*	108	E7
Rockport, *Tex., U.S.A.*	109	L6
Rocksprings, *U.S.A.*	109	K4
Rockville, *Conn., U.S.A.*	107	E12
Rockville, *Md., U.S.A.*	104	F7
Rockwall, *U.S.A.*	109	J6
Rockwell City, *U.S.A.*	108	D7
Rockwood, *U.S.A.*	105	H3
Rocky Ford, *U.S.A.*	108	F3
Rocky Gully, *Australia*	89	F2
Rocky Lane, *Canada*	100	B5
Rocky Mount, *U.S.A.*	105	H7
Rocky Mountain House, *Canada*	100	C6
Rocky Mts., *N. Amer.*	100	C4
Rockyford, *Canada*	100	C6
Rocroi, *France*	25	C11
Rod, *Pakistan*	60	E3
Rødberg, *Norway*	10	D2
Rødby, *Denmark*	11	K5
Rødbyhavn, *Denmark*	11	K5
Roddickton, *Canada*	99	B8
Rødding, *Denmark*	11	J3
Rødekro, *Denmark*	11	J3
Roden, *Neths.*	16	B8
Rodenkirchen, *Germany*	18	B4
Roderick I., *Canada*	100	C3
Rodez, *France*	26	D6
Rodholívas, *Greece*	39	J6
Rodhopoú, *Greece*	37	D5
Ródhos, *Greece*	37	C10
Rodi Garganico, *Italy*	35	A8
Rodna, *Romania*	38	B7
Rodney, *Canada*	106	D3
Rodney, C., *N.Z.*	87	G5
Rodniki, *Russia*	41	C12
Rodriguez, *Ind. Oc.*	3	E13
Roe →, *U.K.*	15	A5
Roebling, *U.S.A.*	107	F10
Roebourne, *Australia*	88	D2
Roebuck B., *Australia*	88	C3
Roebuck Plains, *Australia*	88	C3
Roer →, *Neths.*	17	F7
Roermond, *Neths.*	17	F7
Roes Welcome Sd., *Canada*	97	B11
Roeselare, *Belgium*	17	G2
Rœulx, *Belgium*	17	G4
Rogachev, *Belorussia*	40	E7
Rogagua, L., *Bolivia*	124	C4
Rogaland fylke □, *Norway*	9	G9
Rogaška Slatina, *Slovenia*	33	B12
Rogatec, *Slovenia*	33	B12
Rogatin, *Ukraine*	40	G4
Rogdhia, *Greece*	37	D7
Rogers, *U.S.A.*	109	G7
Rogers City, *U.S.A.*	104	C4
Rogerson, *U.S.A.*	110	E6
Rogersville, *U.S.A.*	105	G4
Roggan River, *Canada*	98	B4
Roggel, *Neths.*	17	F7
Roggeveldberge, *S. Africa*	84	E3
Roggiano Gravina, *Italy*	35	C9
Rogliano, *France*	27	F13
Rogliano, *Italy*	35	C9
Rogoaguado, L., *Bolivia*	125	C4
Rogue →, *U.S.A.*	110	E1
Rohan, *France*	24	D4
Róhda, *Greece*	37	A3
Rohnert Park, *U.S.A.*	112	G4
Rohrbach-lès-Bitche, *France*	25	C14
Rohri, *Pakistan*	62	F3
Rohri Canal, *Pakistan*	62	F3
Rohtak, *India*	62	E7
Roi Et, *Thailand*	58	D4
Roisel, *France*	25	C10
Rojas, *Argentina*	126	C3
Rojo, C., *Mexico*	115	C5
Rokan →, *Indonesia*	56	D2
Rokeby, *Australia*	90	A3
Rokiškis, *Lithuania*	40	D4
Rokitno, *Russia*	40	F9
Rolândia, *Brazil*	127	A5
Rolde, *Neths.*	16	C9
Rolette, *U.S.A.*	108	A5
Rolla, *Kans., U.S.A.*	109	G4
Rolla, *Mo., U.S.A.*	109	G9
Rolla, *N. Dak., U.S.A.*	108	A5
Rollag, *Norway*	10	D3
Rolle, *Switz.*	22	D2

Rolleston, *Australia* 90 C4
Rollingstone, *Australia* ... 90 B4
Rom, *Sudan* 77 F3
Roma, *Australia* 91 D4
Roma, *Italy* 34 A5
Roma, *Sweden* 9 H15
Roman, *Romania* 38 C9
Roman, *Russia* 45 C12
Roman-Kosh, Gora,
  Ukraine 42 D6
Romanche →, *France* ... 27 C9
Romang, *Indonesia* 57 F7
Romāni, *Egypt* 69 E1
Romania ■, *Europe* 38 D8
Romano, Cayo, *Cuba* ... 116 B4
Romano di Lombardía,
  Italy 32 C6
Romanovka = Bessarabka,
  Moldavia 42 C3
Romans-sur-Isère, *France* . 27 C9
Romanshorn, *Switz.* 23 A8
Romblon, *Phil.* 55 E5
Rombo □, *Tanzania* 82 C4
Rome = Roma, *Italy* 34 A5
Rome, *Ga., U.S.A.* 105 H3
Rome, *N.Y., U.S.A.* 107 C9
Romeleåsen, *Sweden* 11 J7
Romenay, *France* 27 B9
Romerike, *Norway* 10 D5
Romilly-sur-Seine, *France* . 25 D10
Romîni, *Romania* 38 E7
Rommani, *Morocco* 74 B3
Romney, *U.S.A.* 104 F6
Romney Marsh, *U.K.* ... 13 F8
Romny, *Ukraine* 40 F8
Rømø, *Denmark* 11 J2
Romodan, *Ukraine* 40 G8
Romodanovo, *Russia* ... 41 D14
Romont, *Switz.* 22 C3
Romorantin-Lanthenay,
  France 25 E8
Romsdalen, *Norway* 10 B2
Ron, *Vietnam* 58 D6
Rona, *U.K.* 14 D3
Ronan, *U.S.A.* 110 C6
Roncador, Cayos,
  Caribbean 116 D3
Roncador, Serra do, *Brazil* 123 D1
Roncesvalles, Paso, *Spain* . 28 B3
Ronceverte, *U.S.A.* 104 G5
Ronciglione, *Italy* 33 F9
Ronco →, *Italy* 33 D9
Ronda, *Spain* 31 J5
Ronda, Serranía de, *Spain* 31 J5
Rondane, *Norway* 10 C3
Rondón, *Colombia* 120 B3
Rondônia, *Brazil* 125 C5
Rondônia □, *Brazil* 125 C5
Rondonópolis, *Brazil* ... 125 D7
Rong Jiang →, *China* . 52 E7
Rong Xian,
  Guangxi Zhuangzu,
  China 53 F8
Rong Xian, *Sichuan, China* 52 C5
Rong'an, *China* 52 E7
Rongchang, *China* 52 C5
Ronge, L. la, *Canada* ... 101 B7
Rongjiang, *China* 52 E7
Rongshui, *China* 52 E7
Ronne Ice Shelf, *Antarctica* 5 D18
Ronsard, C., *Australia* .. 89 D1
Ronse, *Belgium* 17 G3
Ronuro →, *Brazil* 125 C7
Roodepoort, *S. Africa* ... 85 D4
Roodeschool, *Neths.* ... 16 B9
Roof Butte, *U.S.A.* ... 111 H9
Roompot, *Neths.* 17 E3
Roorkee, *India* 62 E7
Roosendaal, *Neths.* 17 E4
Roosevelt, *Minn., U.S.A.* . 108 A7
Roosevelt, *Utah, U.S.A.* . 110 F8
Roosevelt →, *Brazil* 125 B5
Roosevelt, Mt., *Canada* . 100 B3
Roosevelt I., *Antarctica* . 5 D12
Roosevelt Res., *U.S.A.* .. 111 K8
Roper →, *Australia* 90 A2
Ropesville, *U.S.A.* 109 J3
Roque Pérez, *Argentina* . 126 D4
Roquefort, *France* 26 D3
Roquemaure, *France* ... 27 D8
Roquetas, *Spain* 28 E5
Roquevaire, *France* 27 E9
Roraima □, *Brazil* 121 C5
Roraima, Mt., *Venezuela* 121 B5
Rorketon, *Canada* 101 C9
Røros, *Norway* 10 B5
Rorschach, *Switz.* 23 B8
Rosa, *Zambia* 83 D3
Rosa, C., *Algeria* 75 A6
Rosa, Monte, *Europe* ... 22 E5
Rosal, *Spain* 30 D2
Rosal de la Frontera, *Spain* 31 H3
Rosalia, *U.S.A.* 110 C5
Rosamond, *U.S.A.* 113 L8
Rosans, *France* 27 D9
Rosário, *Argentina* 126 C3
Rosário, *Brazil* 122 B3
Rosario, *Baja Calif. N.,*
  Mexico 114 A1
Rosario, *Sinaloa, Mexico* . 114 C3
Rosario, *Paraguay* 126 A4
Rosario, Villa del,
  Venezuela 120 A3
Rosario de la Frontera,
  Argentina 126 B3

Rosario de Lerma,
  Argentina 126 A2
Rosario del Tala, *Argentina* 126 C4
Rosário do Sul, *Brazil* .. 127 C5
Rosário Oeste, *Brazil* .. 125 C6
Rosarito, *Mexico* 113 N9
Rosarno, *Italy* 35 D8
Rosas, *Spain* 28 C8
Roscoe, *U.S.A.* 108 C5
Roscoff, *France* 24 D3
Roscommon, *Ireland* ... 15 C3
Roscommon, *U.S.A.* ... 104 C3
Roscommon □, *Ireland* .. 15 C3
Roscrea, *Ireland* 15 D4
Rose →, *Australia* 90 A2
Rose Blanche, *Canada* .. 99 C8
Rose Harbour, *Canada* .. 100 C2
Rose Pt., *Canada* 100 C2
Rose Valley, *Canada* ... 101 C8
Roseau, *Domin.* 117 C7
Roseau, *U.S.A.* 108 A7
Rosebery, *Australia* 90 G4
Rosebud, *U.S.A.* 109 K6
Roseburg, *U.S.A.* 110 E2
Rosedale, *Australia* 90 C5
Rosedale, *U.S.A.* 109 J9
Rosée, *Belgium* 17 H5
Roseland, *U.S.A.* 112 G4
Rosemary, *Canada* 100 C6
Rosenberg, *U.S.A.* 109 L7
Rosendaël, *France* 25 A9
Rosenheim, *Germany* ... 19 H8
Roseto degli Abruzzi, *Italy* 33 F11
Rosetown, *Canada* 101 C7
Rosetta = Rashîd, *Egypt* . 76 H7
Roseville, *U.S.A.* 112 G5
Rosewood, *N. Terr.,*
  Australia 88 C4
Rosewood, *Queens.,*
  Australia 91 D5
Roshkhvār, *Iran* 65 C8
Rosières-en-Santerre,
  France 25 C9
Rosignano Maríttimo, *Italy* 32 E7
Rosignol, *Guyana* 121 B6
Roşiori de Vede, *Romania* 38 E8
Rositsa, *Bulgaria* 38 F10
Rositsa →, *Bulgaria* 38 F8
Roskilde, *Denmark* 11 J6
Roskilde Amtskommune □,
  Denmark 11 J6
Roskilde Fjord, *Denmark* . 11 J6
Roslavl, *Russia* 40 E8
Roslyn, *Australia* 91 E4
Rosmaninhal, *Portugal* .. 31 F3
Rosmead, *S. Africa* 84 E4
Rosolini, *Italy* 35 F7
Rosporden, *France* 24 E3
Ross, *Australia* 90 G4
Ross, *N.Z.* 87 K3
Ross I., *Antarctica* 5 D11
Ross Ice Shelf, *Antarctica* . 5 E12
Ross L., *U.S.A.* 110 B3
Ross-on-Wye, *U.K.* 13 F5
Ross Sea, *Antarctica* ... 5 D11
Rossa, *Switz.* 23 D8
Rossan Pt., *Ireland* 15 B3
Rossano Cálabro, *Italy* .. 35 C9
Rossburn, *Canada* 101 C8
Rosseau, *Canada* 106 A5
Rossignol, L., *Canada* ... 98 B5
Rossignol Res., *Canada* . 99 D6
Rossland, *Canada* 100 D5
Rosslare, *Ireland* 15 D5
Rosslau, *Germany* 18 D8
Rosso, *Mauritania* 78 B1
Rossosh, *Russia* 43 A8
Rossport, *Canada* 98 C2
Rossum, *Neths.* 16 E6
Røssvatnet, *Norway* 8 D13
Rossville, *Australia* 90 B4
Rosthern, *Canada* 101 C7
Rostock, *Germany* 18 A8
Rostov, *Russia* 41 C11
Rostov, *Russia* 43 C8
Rostrenen, *France* 24 D3
Roswell, *U.S.A.* 109 J2
Rosyth, *U.K.* 14 E5
Rota, *Spain* 31 J4
Rotälven →, *Sweden* ... 10 C8
Rotan, *U.S.A.* 109 J4
Rotem, *Belgium* 17 F7
Rotenburg, *Germany* ... 18 B5
Roth, *Germany* 19 F7
Rothaargebirge, *Germany* 18 E4
Rothenburg, *Switz.* 23 B6
Rothenburg ob der Tauber,
  Germany 19 F6
Rother →, *U.K.* 13 G8
Rotherham, *U.K.* 12 D6
Rothes, *U.K.* 14 D5
Rothesay, *Canada* 99 C6
Rothesay, *U.K.* 14 F3
Rothrist, *Switz.* 22 B5
Roti, *Indonesia* 57 F6
Roto, *Australia* 91 E4
Rotondella, *Italy* 35 B9
Rotoroa, L., *N.Z.* 87 J4
Rotorua, *N.Z.* 87 H6
Rotorua, L., *N.Z.* 87 H6
Rotselaar, *Belgium* 17 G5
Rott →, *Germany* 19 G9
Rotten →, *Switz.* 22 D5
Rottenburg, *Germany* ... 19 G4

Rotterdam, *Neths.* 16 E5
Rottnest I., *Australia* ... 89 F2
Rottumeroog, *Neths.* ... 16 A9
Rottweil, *Germany* 19 G4
Rotuma, *Fiji* 92 J9
Roubaix, *France* 25 B10
Rouen, *France* 24 C8
Rouillac, *France* 26 C3
Rouleau, *Canada* 101 C8
Round Mt., *Australia* ... 91 E5
Round Mountain, *U.S.A.* . 110 G5
Roundup, *U.S.A.* 110 C9
Roura, *Fr. Guiana* 121 C7
Rousay, *U.K.* 14 B5
Rouses Point, *U.S.A.* .. 107 B11
Roussillon, *Isère, France* . 27 C8
Roussillon, *Pyrénées-Or.,*
  France 26 F6
Rouveen, *Neths.* 16 C8
Rouxville, *S. Africa* 84 E4
Rouyn, *Canada* 98 C4
Rovaniemi, *Finland* 8 C18
Rovato, *Italy* 32 C7
Rovenki, *Ukraine* 43 B8
Rovereto, *Italy* 32 C8
Rovigo, *Italy* 33 C8
Rovinari, *Romania* 38 E6
Rovinj, *Croatia* 33 C10
Rovira, *Colombia* 120 C2
Rovno, *Ukraine* 40 F5
Rovnoye, *Russia* 41 F15
Rovuma →, *Tanzania* .. 83 E5
Row'ān, *Iran* 65 C6
Rowena, *Australia* 91 D4
Rowley Shoals, *Australia* . 88 C2
Roxa, *Guinea-Biss.* 78 C1
Roxas, *Capiz, Phil.* 55 F5
Roxas, *Isabela, Phil.* ... 55 C4
Roxas, *Mindoro, Phil.* .. 55 E4
Roxboro, *U.S.A.* 105 G6
Roxborough Downs,
  Australia 90 C2
Roxburgh, *N.Z.* 87 L2
Roxen, *Sweden* 11 F9
Roy, *Mont., U.S.A.* 110 C9
Roy, *N. Mex., U.S.A.* ... 109 H2
Roy Hill, *Australia* 88 D2
Roya, Peña, *Spain* 28 E4
Royal Leamington Spa,
  U.K. 13 E6
Royan, *France* 26 C2
Roye, *France* 25 C9
Røyken, *Norway* 10 E4
Rožaj, *Montenegro* 21 N10
Rozay-en-Brie, *France* .. 25 D9
Rozhishche, *Ukraine* ... 40 F4
Rŏžnava, *Slovak Rep.* ... 20 G10
Rozoy-sur-Serre, *France* . 25 C11
Rtishchevo, *Russia* 41 D13
Rúa, *Spain* 30 C3
Ruacaná, *Angola* 84 B1
Ruahine Ra., *N.Z.* 87 H6
Ruapehu, *N.Z.* 87 H5
Ruapuke I., *N.Z.* 87 M2
Ruâq, W. →, *Egypt* ... 69 F2
Rub' al Khali, *Si. Arabia* . 68 D4
Rubeho Mts., *Tanzania* . 82 D4
Rubezhnoye, *Ukraine* .. 42 B8
Rubh a' Mhail, *U.K.* ... 14 F2
Rubha Hunish, *U.K.* ... 14 D2
Rubiataba, *Brazil* 123 E2
Rubicon →, *U.S.A.* ... 112 G5
Rubicone →, *Italy* 33 D9
Rubinéia, *Brazil* 123 F1
Rubino, *Ivory C.* 78 D4
Rubio, *Venezuela* 120 B3
Rubizhne = Rubezhnoye,
  Ukraine 42 B8
Rubtsovsk, *Russia* 44 D9
Ruby L., *U.S.A.* 110 F6
Ruby Mts., *U.S.A.* 110 F6
Rucava, *Latvia* 40 C2
Rucheng, *China* 53 E9
Rud, *Norway* 10 D4
Rūd Sar, *Iran* 65 B6
Ruda Śląska, *Poland* ... 20 E8
Rudall, *Australia* 91 E2
Rudall →, *Australia* ... 88 D3
Ruden, *Germany* 18 A9
Rüdersdorf, *Germany* ... 18 C9
Rudewa, *Tanzania* 83 E3
Rudkøbing, *Denmark* ... 11 K4
Rudnik, *Serbia* 21 L10
Rudnogorsk, *Russia* 45 D11
Rudnya, *Russia* 40 D7
Rudnyy, *Kazakhstan* ... 44 D7
Rudolf, Ostrov, *Russia* . 44 A6
Rudolstadt, *Germany* ... 18 E7
Rudong, *China* 53 A13
Rudozem, *Bulgaria* 39 H7
Rudyard, *U.S.A.* 104 B3
Rue, *France* 25 B8
Ruelle, *France* 26 C4
Rufa'a, *Sudan* 77 E3
Ruffec, *France* 26 B4
Rufiji →, *Tanzania* 82 D4
Rufino, *Argentina* 126 C3
Rufisque, *Senegal* 78 C1
Rufunsa, *Zambia* 83 F2
Rugao, *China* 53 A13
Rugby, *U.K.* 13 E6
Rugby, *U.S.A.* 108 A5
Rügen, *Germany* 18 A9
Rugles, *France* 24 D7

Ruhengeri, *Rwanda* 82 C2
Ruhla, *Germany* 18 E6
Ruhland, *Germany* 18 D9
Ruhr →, *Germany* 18 D2
Ruhuhu →, *Tanzania* .. 83 E3
Rui Barbosa, *Brazil* 123 D3
Rui'an, *China* 53 D13
Ruichang, *China* 53 C10
Ruidosa, *U.S.A.* 109 L2
Ruidoso, *U.S.A.* 111 K11
Ruili, *China* 52 E1
Ruinen, *Neths.* 16 C8
Ruinerwold, *Neths.* 16 C8
Ruiten A Kanaal →,
  Neths. 16 C10
Ruivo, Pico, *Madeira* ... 36 D3
Rujm Tal'at al Jamā'ah,
  Jordan 69 E4
Ruk, *Pakistan* 62 F3
Rukwa □, *Tanzania* 82 D3
Rukwa L., *Tanzania* 82 D3
Rulhieres, C., *Australia* . 88 B4
Rulles, *Belgium* 17 J7
Rum Cay, *Bahamas* 117 B5
Rum Jungle, *Australia* .. 88 B5
Ruma, *Serbia* 21 K9
Rumāḥ, *Si. Arabia* 64 E5
Rumania = Romania ■,
  Europe 38 D8
Rumaylah, *Iraq* 64 D5
Rumbalara, *Australia* ... 90 D1
Rumbêk, *Sudan* 77 F2
Rumbeke, *Belgium* 17 G2
Rumelange, *Lux.* 17 K8
Rumford, *U.S.A.* 107 B14
Rumilly, *France* 27 C9
Rumoi, *Japan* 48 C10
Rumonge, *Burundi* 82 C2
Rumsey, *Canada* 100 C6
Rumula, *Australia* 90 B4
Rumuruti, *Kenya* 82 B4
Runan, *China* 50 H8
Runanga, *N.Z.* 87 K3
Runaway, C., *N.Z.* 87 G6
Runcorn, *U.K.* 12 D5
Rungwa, *Tanzania* 82 D3
Rungwa →, *Tanzania* .. 82 D3
Rungwe, *Tanzania* 83 D3
Rungwe □, *Tanzania* ... 83 D3
Runka, *Nigeria* 79 C6
Runton Ra., *Australia* .. 88 D3
Ruoqiang, *China* 54 C3
Ruo'qiang, *China* 54 C3
Rupa, *India* 61 F18
Rupar, *India* 62 D7
Rupat, *Indonesia* 56 D2
Rupert →, *Canada* 98 B4
Rupert House = Fort
  Rupert, *Canada* 98 B4
Rupununi →, *Guyana* .. 121 C6
Rur →, *Germany* 18 E2
Rurrenabaque, *Bolivia* .. 124 C4
Rus →, *Spain* 29 F2
Rusambo, *Zimbabwe* ... 83 F3
Rusape, *Zimbabwe* 83 F3
Ruschuk = Ruse, *Bulgaria* 38 F8
Ruse, *Bulgaria* 38 F8
Ruşeţu, *Romania* 38 E10
Rushan, *China* 51 F11
Rushden, *U.K.* 13 E7
Rushford, *U.S.A.* 108 D9
Rushville, *Ill., U.S.A.* .. 108 E9
Rushville, *Ind., U.S.A.* . 104 F3
Rushville, *Nebr., U.S.A.* . 108 D3
Rushworth, *Australia* .. 91 F4
Russas, *Brazil* 122 B4
Russell, *Canada* 101 C8
Russell, *U.S.A.* 108 F5
Russell L., *Man., Canada* . 101 B8
Russell L., *N.W.T.,*
  Canada 100 A5
Russellkonda, *India* 61 K14
Russellville, *Ala., U.S.A.* 105 H2
Russellville, *Ark., U.S.A.* 109 H8
Russellville, *Ky., U.S.A.* . 105 G2
Russi, *Italy* 33 D9
Russia ■, *Eurasia* 45 C11
Russian →, *U.S.A.* 112 G3
Russkaya Polyana,
  Kazakhstan 44 D8
Russkoye Ustie, *Russia* . 4 B15
Rustam, *Pakistan* 62 B5
Rustam Shahr, *Pakistan* . 62 F2
Rustavi, *Georgia* 43 F11
Rustenburg, *S. Africa* .. 84 D4
Ruston, *U.S.A.* 109 J8
Ruswil, *Switz.* 22 B6
Rutana, *Burundi* 82 C2
Rute, *Spain* 31 H6
Ruteng, *Indonesia* 57 F6
Ruth, *Mich., U.S.A.* ... 106 C2
Ruth, *Nev., U.S.A.* 110 G6
Rutherford, *U.S.A.* 112 G4
Rutherglen, *U.K.* 14 F4
Rüti, *Switz.* 23 B7
Rutigliano, *Italy* 35 A10
Rutland Plains, *Australia* . 90 B3
Rutledge →, *Canada* ... 101 A6
Rutledge L., *Canada* ... 101 A6
Rutshuru, *Zaïre* 82 C2
Ruurlo, *Neths.* 16 D8
Ruvo di Púglia, *Italy* ... 35 A9
Ruvu, *Tanzania* 82 D4
Ruvu →, *Tanzania* 82 D4
Ruvuma □, *Tanzania* ... 83 E4
Ruwais, *U.A.E.* 65 E7

Ruwenzori, *Africa* 82 B2
Ruyigi, *Burundi* 82 C3
Ruyuan, *China* 53 E9
Ružayevka, *Russia* 41 D14
Ružomberok, *Slovak Rep.* 20 F9
Rwanda ■, *Africa* 82 C3
Ry, *Denmark* 11 H3
Ryakhovo, *Bulgaria* 38 F9
Ryan, L., *U.K.* 14 G3
Ryazan, *Russia* 41 D11
Ryazhsk, *Russia* 41 E12
Rybache, *Kazakhstan* .. 44 E9
Rybachye, *Russia* 41 B11
Rybinsk, *Russia* 41 B11
Rybinskoye Vdkhr., *Russia* 41 B11
Rybnik, *Poland* 20 E8
Rybnitsa, *Moldova* 42 C3
Rybnoye, *Russia* 41 D11
Rychwał, *Poland* 20 C8
Ryde, *U.K.* 13 G6
Ryderwood, *U.S.A.* 112 D3
Rydöbruk, *Sweden* 11 H7
Rydułtowy, *Poland* 20 E8
Rye, *U.K.* 13 G8
Rye →, *U.K.* 12 C7
Rye Patch Reservoir,
  U.S.A. 110 F4
Ryegate, *U.S.A.* 110 C9
Rylstone, *Australia* 91 E4
Rylsk, *Russia* 40 F9
Ryōthu, *Japan* 48 E9
Rypin, *Poland* 20 B9
Ryūgasaki, *Japan* 49 G10
Ryūkyū Is. = Ryūkyū-
  rettō, *Japan* 49 M2
Ryūkyū-rettō, *Japan* ... 49 M2
Rzeszów, *Poland* ...,.. 20 E11
Rzhev, *Russia* 40 C9

S

Sa, *Thailand* 58 C3
Sa Dec, *Vietnam* 59 G5
Sa'ādatābād, *Fārs, Iran* .. 65 D7
Sa'ādatābād, *Kermān, Iran* 65 D7
Saale →, *Germany* 18 D7
Saaler Bodden, *Germany* . 18 A8
Saalfeld, *Germany* 18 E7
Saane →, *Switz.* 22 B4
Saar →, *Europe* 25 C13
Saarbrücken, *Germany* .. 19 F2
Saarburg, *Germany* 19 F2
Saaremaa, *Estonia* 40 B3
Saariselkä, *Finland* 8 B20
Saarland □, *Germany* ... 25 C13
Saarlouis, *Germany* 19 F2
Saas Fee, *Switz.* 22 D5
Sab 'Bi'ar, *Syria* 64 C3
Saba, *W. Indies* 117 C7
Šabac, *Serbia* 21 L9
Sabadell, *Spain* 28 D7
Sabah □, *Malaysia* 56 C5
Sabak Bernam, *Malaysia* . 59 L3
Sábana de la Mar,
  Dom. Rep. 117 C6
Sábanalarga, *Colombia* .. 120 A3
Sabang, *Indonesia* 56 C1
Sabará, *Brazil* 123 E3
Sabarania, *Indonesia* ... 57 E9
Sabattis, *U.S.A.* 107 B10
Sabáudia, *Italy* 34 A6
Sabaya, *Bolivia* 124 D4
Sabhah, *Libya* 73 C7
Sabie, *S. Africa* 85 D5
Sabinal, *Mexico* 114 A3
Sabinal, *U.S.A.* 109 L5
Sabinal, Punta del, *Spain* . 29 J2
Sabinas, *Mexico* 114 B4
Sabinas →, *Mexico* 114 B4
Sabinas Hidalgo, *Mexico* . 114 B4
Sabine →, *U.S.A.* 109 L8
Sabine L., *U.S.A.* 109 L8
Sabine Pass, *U.S.A.* ... 109 L8
Sabinópolis, *Brazil* 123 E3
Sabinov, *Slovak Rep.* ... 20 F11
Sabirabad, *Azerbaijan* .. 43 F13
Sabkhet el Bardawîl, *Egypt* 69 D2
Sablayan, *Phil.* 55 E4
Sable, C., *U.S.A.* 103 E10
Sable, C., *Canada* 99 D6
Sable I., *Canada* 99 D8
Sablé-sur-Sarthe, *France* . 24 E6
Saboeiro, *Brazil* 122 C4
Sabolev, *Russia* 45 D16
Sabor →, *Portugal* 30 D3
Sabou, *Burkina Faso* ... 78 C4
Sabrātah, *Libya* 75 B7
Sabria, *Tunisia* 75 B6
Sabrina Coast, *Antarctica* 5 C9
Sabugal, *Portugal* 30 E3
Sabulubek, *Indonesia* ... 56 E1
Sabzevār, *Iran* 65 B8
Sabzvārān, *Iran* 65 D8
Sac City, *U.S.A.* 108 D7
Sacedón, *Spain* 28 E2
Sachigo →, *Canada* 98 A2
Sachigo, L., *Canada* 98 B1
Sachkhere, *Georgia* 43 E10
Sachseln, *Switz.* 23 C6
Sachsen □, *Germany* ... 18 E9
Sachsen-Anhalt □,
  Germany 18 D8
Sacile, *Italy* 33 C9

Sackets Harbor, *U.S.A.*	107	C8
Saco, *Maine, U.S.A.*	105	D10
Saco, *Mont., U.S.A.*	110	B10
Sacramento, *Brazil*	123	E2
Sacramento, *U.S.A.*	112	G5
Sacramento →, *U.S.A.*	112	G5
Sacramento Mts., *U.S.A.*	111	K11
Sacramento Valley, *U.S.A.*	112	G5
Sacratif, C., *Spain*	29	J1
Săcueni, *Romania*	38	B5
Sada, *Spain*	30	B2
Sádaba, *Spain*	28	C3
Sadani, *Tanzania*	82	D4
Sadao, *Thailand*	59	J3
Sadd el Aali, *Egypt*	76	C3
Saddle Mt., *U.S.A.*	112	E3
Sade, *Nigeria*	79	C7
Sadimi, *Zaïre*	83	D1
Sado, *Japan*	48	E9
Sado →, *Portugal*	31	G2
Sadon, *Burma*	61	G20
Sadon, *Russia*	43	E10
Sæby, *Denmark*	11	G4
Saegertstown, *U.S.A.*	106	E4
Saelices, *Spain*	28	F2
Safaga, *Egypt*	76	B3
Şafājah, *Si. Arabia*	64	E3
Säffle, *Sweden*	9	G12
Safford, *U.S.A.*	111	K9
Saffron Walden, *U.K.*	13	E8
Safi, *Morocco*	74	B3
Ṣafiābād, *Iran*	65	B8
Ṣafīd Dasht, *Iran*	65	C6
Safīd Kūh, *Afghan.*	60	B3
Safonovo, *Russia*	40	D8
Safranbolu, *Turkey*	42	F5
Safwān, *Iraq*	64	D5
Sag Harbor, *U.S.A.*	107	F12
Saga, *Indonesia*	57	E8
Saga, *Japan*	49	H5
Saga □, *Japan*	49	H5
Sagae, *Japan*	48	E10
Sagala, *Mali*	78	C3
Sagar, *India*	60	M9
Sagara, L., *Tanzania*	82	D3
Sagay, *Phil.*	55	F5
Sagil, *Mongolia*	54	A4
Saginaw, *U.S.A.*	104	D4
Saginaw B., *U.S.A.*	104	D4
Sagīr, Zab as →, *Iraq*	64	C4
Sagleipie, *Liberia*	78	D3
Saglouc, *Canada*	97	B12
Sagô-ri, *S. Korea*	51	G14
Sagone, *France*	27	F12
Sagone, G. de, *France*	27	F12
Sagres, *Portugal*	31	J2
Sagua la Grande, *Cuba*	116	B3
Saguache, *U.S.A.*	111	G10
Saguenay →, *Canada*	99	C5
Sagunto, *Spain*	28	F4
Sahaba, *Sudan*	76	D3
Sahagún, *Colombia*	120	B2
Sahagún, *Spain*	30	C5
Şaḥam al Jawlān, *Syria*	69	C4
Sahand, Kūh-e, *Iran*	64	B5
Sahara, *Africa*	70	D4
Saharan Atlas = Saharien, Atlas, *Algeria*	75	B5
Saharanpur, *India*	62	E7
Saharien, Atlas, *Algeria*	75	B5
Sahasinaka, *Madag.*	85	C8
Sahaswan, *India*	63	E8
Sahel, Canal du, *Mali*	78	C3
Sahibganj, *India*	63	G12
Sahiwal, *Pakistan*	62	D5
Şaḥneh, *Iran*	64	C5
Sahtaneh →, *Canada*	100	B4
Sahuaripa, *Mexico*	114	B3
Sahuarita, *U.S.A.*	111	L8
Sahuayo, *Mexico*	114	C4
Sahy, *Slovak Rep.*	21	G8
Sai Buri, *Thailand*	59	J3
Sai-Cinza, *Brazil*	125	B6
Sa'id Bundas, *Sudan*	73	G9
Saïda, *Algeria*	75	B5
Saīdābād, *Kermān, Iran*	65	D7
Sa'īdābād, *Semnān, Iran*	65	B7
Saïdia, *Morocco*	75	A4
Sa'īdiyeh, *Iran*	65	B6
Saidpur, *Bangla.*	61	G16
Saidu, *Pakistan*	63	B5
Saignelégier, *Switz.*	22	B3
Saignes, *France*	26	C6
Saigon = Phanh Bho Ho Chi Minh, *Vietnam*	59	G6
Saijō, *Japan*	49	H6
Saikhoa Ghat, *India*	61	F19
Saiki, *Japan*	49	H5
Saillans, *France*	27	D9
Sailolof, *Indonesia*	57	E8
Saimbeyli, *Turkey*	66	E7
Şa'in Dezh, *Iran*	64	B5
St. Abb's Head, *U.K.*	14	F6
St. Aegyd, *Austria*	21	H5
St.-Affrique, *France*	26	E6
St.-Agrève, *France*	27	C8
St.-Aignan, *France*	24	E8
St. Alban's, *Canada*	99	C8
St. Albans, *U.K.*	13	F7
St. Albans, *Vt., U.S.A.*	107	B11
St. Albans, *W. Va., U.S.A.*	104	F5
St. Alban's Head, *U.K.*	13	G5
St. Albert, *Canada*	100	C6
St.-Amand-en-Puisaye, *France*	25	E10
St.-Amand-les-Eaux, *France*	25	B10
St.-Amand-Mont-Rond, *France*	26	B6
St.-Amarin, *France*	25	E14
St.-Amour, *France*	27	B9
St.-André-de-Cubzac, *France*	26	D3
St.-André-de-l'Eure, *France*	24	D8
St.-André-les-Alpes, *France*	27	E10
St. Andrew's, *Canada*	99	C8
St. Andrews, *U.K.*	14	E6
St-Anicet, *Canada*	107	A10
St. Ann B., *Canada*	99	C7
St. Anne, *U.K.*	24	C4
St. Ann's Bay, *Jamaica*	116	C4
St. Anthony, *Canada*	99	B8
St. Anthony, *U.S.A.*	110	E8
St.-Antonin-Noble-Val, *France*	26	D5
St. Arnaud, *Australia*	91	F3
St. Arthur, *Canada*	99	C6
St. Asaph, *U.K.*	12	D4
St.-Astier, *France*	26	C4
St.-Aubin, *Switz.*	22	C3
St.-Aubin-du-Cormier, *France*	24	D5
St-Augustin-Saguenay, *Canada*	99	B8
St. Augustine, *U.S.A.*	105	L5
St. Austell, *U.K.*	13	G3
St.-Avold, *France*	25	C13
St.-Barthélemy, I., *W. Indies*	117	C7
St. Bee's Hd., *U.K.*	12	C4
St.-Benoît-du-Sault, *France*	26	B5
St.-Bernard, Col du Grand, *Europe*	22	E4
St.-Bernard, Col du Petit, *France*	27	C10
St.-Blaise, *Switz.*	22	B3
St. Boniface, *Canada*	101	D9
St.-Bonnet, *France*	27	D10
St.-Brévin-les-Pins, *France*	24	E4
St.-Brice-en-Coglès, *France*	24	D5
St. Bride's, *Canada*	99	C9
St. Brides B., *U.K.*	13	F2
St.-Brieuc, *France*	24	D4
St.-Calais, *France*	24	E7
St.-Cast-le-Guildo, *France*	24	D4
St. Catharines, *Canada*	98	D4
St. Catherines I., *U.S.A.*	105	K5
St. Catherine's Pt., *U.K.*	13	G6
St.-Céré, *France*	26	D5
St.-Cergue, *Switz.*	22	D2
St.-Cernin, *France*	26	C6
St.-Chamond, *France*	27	C8
St. Charles, *Ill., U.S.A.*	104	E1
St. Charles, *Mo., U.S.A.*	108	F9
St.-Chély-d'Apcher, *France*	26	D7
St.-Chinian, *France*	26	E6
St. Christopher = St. Kitts, *W. Indies*	117	C7
St. Christopher-Nevis ■, *W. Indies*	117	C7
St.-Ciers-sur-Gironde, *France*	26	C3
St. Clair, *Mich., U.S.A.*	106	D2
St. Clair, *Pa., U.S.A.*	107	F8
St. Clair, L., *Canada*	98	D3
St. Clairsville, *U.S.A.*	106	F4
St.-Claud, *France*	26	C4
St. Claude, *Canada*	101	D9
St.-Claude, *France*	27	B9
St. Cloud, *Fla., U.S.A.*	105	L5
St. Cloud, *Minn., U.S.A.*	108	C7
St-Coeur de Marie, *Canada*	99	C5
St. Cricq, C., *Australia*	89	E1
St. Croix, *Virgin Is.*	117	C7
St. Croix →, *U.S.A.*	108	C8
St. Croix Falls, *U.S.A.*	108	C8
St.-Cyr-sur-Mer, *France*	27	E9
St. David's, *Canada*	99	C8
St. David's, *U.K.*	13	F2
St. David's Head, *U.K.*	13	F2
St.-Denis, *France*	25	D9
St.-Denis-d'Orques, *France*	24	D6
St.-Dié, *France*	25	D13
St.-Dizier, *France*	25	D11
St.-Égrève, *France*	27	C9
St. Elias, Mt., *U.S.A.*	96	B5
St. Elias Mts., *Canada*	100	A1
St.-Élie, *Fr. Guiana*	121	C7
St.-Eloy-les-Mines, *France*	26	B6
St.-Émilion, *France*	26	D3
St.-Étienne, *France*	27	C8
St.-Étienne-de-Tinée. *France*	27	D10
St. Eugène, *Canada*	107	A10
St. Eustatius, *W. Indies*	117	C7
St.-Félicien, *Canada*	98	C5
St.-Florent, *France*	27	F13
St.-Florent-sur-Cher, *France*	25	F9
St.-Florentin, *France*	25	D10
St.-Flour, *France*	26	C7
St.-Fons, *France*	27	C8
St. Francis, *U.S.A.*	108	F4
St. Francis →, *U.S.A.*	109	H9
St. Francis, C., *S. Africa*	84	E3
St. Francisville, *U.S.A.*	109	K9
St-François, L., *Canada*	107	A10
St-Fulgent, *France*	24	F5
St-Gabriel-de-Brandon, *Canada*	98	C5
St. Gallen = Sankt Gallen, *Switz.*	23	B8
St.-Gaudens, *France*	26	E4
St.-Gengoux-le-National, *France*	27	B8
St.-Geniez-d'Olt, *France*	26	D6
St. George, *Australia*	91	D4
St. George, *Canada*	99	C6
St. George, *S.C., U.S.A.*	105	J5
St. George, *Utah, U.S.A.*	111	H7
St. George, C., *Canada*	99	C8
St. George, C., *U.S.A.*	105	L3
St. George Ra., *Australia*	88	C4
St-Georges, *Belgium*	17	G6
St. George's, *Canada*	99	C8
St-Georges, *Canada*	99	C5
St.-Georges, *Fr. Guiana*	121	C7
St. George's, *Grenada*	117	D7
St. George's B., *Canada*	99	C8
St. Georges Basin, *Australia*	88	C4
St. George's Channel, *U.K.*	15	E6
St.-Georges-de-Didonne, *France*	26	C3
St. Georges Hd., *Australia*	91	F5
St.-Gérard, *Belgium*	17	H5
St.-Germain-de-Calberte, *France*	26	D7
St.-Germain-des-Fossés, *France*	26	B7
St.-Germain-du-Plain, *France*	25	F11
St.-Germain-en-Laye, *France*	25	D9
St.-Germain-Laval, *France*	27	C8
St.-Germain-Lembron, *France*	26	C7
St.-Gervais-d'Auvergne, *France*	26	B6
St.-Gervais-les-Bains, *France*	27	C10
St.-Gildas, Pte. de, *France*	24	E4
St.-Gilles, *France*	27	E8
St.-Gilles-Croix-de-Vie, *France*	26	B2
St.-Gingolph, *Switz.*	22	D3
St.-Girons, *France*	26	F5
St. Gotthard P. = San Gottardo, Paso del, *Switz.*	23	C7
St.-Gualtier, *France*	24	F8
St.-Guénolé, *France*	24	E2
St. Helena, *U.S.A.*	110	G2
St. Helena ■, *Atl. Oc.*	2	E9
St. Helena, Mt., *U.S.A.*	112	G4
St. Helena, B., *S. Africa*	84	E2
St. Helens, *Australia*	90	G4
St. Helens, *U.K.*	12	D5
St. Helens, *U.S.A.*	112	E4
St. Helens, Mt., *U.S.A.*	112	D4
St. Helier, *U.K.*	13	H5
St.-Hilaire-du-Harcouët, *France*	24	D5
St.-Hippolyte, *France*	25	E13
St.-Hippolyte-du-Fort, *France*	26	E7
St.-Honoré-les-Bains, *France*	25	F10
St-Hubert, *Belgium*	17	H6
St.-Hyacinthe, *Canada*	98	C5
St. Ignace, *U.S.A.*	104	C3
St. Ignace I., *Canada*	98	C2
St. Ignatius, *U.S.A.*	110	C6
St-Imier, *Switz.*	22	B3
St. Ives, *Cambs., U.K.*	13	E7
St. Ives, *Corn., U.K.*	13	G2
St.-James, *France*	24	D5
St. James, *U.S.A.*	108	D7
St-Jean, *Canada*	98	C5
St-Jean →, *Canada*	99	B7
St-Jean, L., *Canada*	99	C5
St. Jean Baptiste, *Canada*	101	D9
St.-Jean-d'Angély, *France*	26	C3
St.-Jean-de-Bournay, *France*	27	C9
St.-Jean-de-Luz, *France*	26	E2
St.-Jean-de-Maurienne, *France*	27	C10
St.-Jean-de-Monts, *France*	24	F4
St.-Jean-du-Gard, *France*	26	D7
St.-Jean-en-Royans, *France*	27	C9
St-Jean-Port-Joli, *Canada*	99	C5
St-Jérôme, *Qué., Canada*	98	C5
St-Jérôme, *Qué., Canada*	99	C5
St. John, *Canada*	99	C6
St. John, *Kans., U.S.A.*	109	G5
St. John, *N. Dak., U.S.A.*	108	A5
St. John →, *U.S.A.*	99	C6
St. John, C., *Canada*	99	B8
St. John's, *Antigua*	117	C7
St. John's, *Canada*	99	C9
St. Johns, *Ariz., U.S.A.*	111	J9
St. Johns, *Mich., U.S.A.*	104	D3
St. Johns →, *U.S.A.*	105	K5
St. Johnsbury, *U.S.A.*	107	B12
St. Johnsville, *U.S.A.*	107	C10
St. Joseph, *La., U.S.A.*	109	K9
St. Joseph, *Mich., U.S.A.*	104	D2
St. Joseph, *Mo., U.S.A.*	108	F7
St. Joseph →, *U.S.A.*	104	D2
St. Joseph, I., *Canada*	98	C3
St. Joseph, L., *Canada*	98	B1
St-Jovite, *Canada*	98	C5
St.-Juéry, *France*	26	E6
St.-Julien-Chapteuil, *France*	27	C8
St.-Julien-du-Sault, *France*	25	D10
St.-Julien-en-Genevois, *France*	27	B10
St.-Junien, *France*	26	C4
St.-Just-en-Chaussée, *France*	25	C9
St.-Just-en-Chevalet, *France*	26	C7
St.-Justin, *France*	26	E3
St. Kilda, *N.Z.*	87	L3
St. Kitts, *W. Indies*	117	C7
St. Kitts-Nevis = St. Christopher-Nevis ■, *W. Indies*	117	C7
St. Laurent, *Canada*	101	C9
St.-Laurent, *Fr. Guiana*	121	B7
St.-Laurent-du-Pont, *France*	27	C9
St.-Laurent-en-Grandvaux, *France*	27	B9
St. Lawrence, *Australia*	90	C4
St. Lawrence, *Canada*	99	C8
St. Lawrence →, *Canada*	99	C6
St. Lawrence, Gulf of, *Canada*	99	C7
St. Lawrence I., *U.S.A.*	96	B3
St.-Léger, *Belgium*	17	J7
St. Leonard, *Canada*	99	C6
St.-Léonard-de-Noblat, *France*	26	C5
St. Lewis →, *Canada*	99	B8
St.-Lô, *France*	24	C5
St-Louis, *Senegal*	78	B1
St. Louis, *Mich., U.S.A.*	104	D3
St. Louis, *Mo., U.S.A.*	108	F9
St. Louis →, *U.S.A.*	108	B8
St.-Loup-sur-Semouse, *France*	25	E13
St. Lucia ■, *W. Indies*	117	D7
St. Lucia, L., *S. Africa*	85	D5
St. Lucia Channel, *W. Indies*	117	D7
St. Lunaire-Griquet, *Canada*	99	B8
St. Maarten, *W. Indies*	117	C7
St.-Maixent-l'École, *France*	26	B3
St.-Malo, *France*	24	D4
St.-Malo, G. de, *France*	24	D4
St.-Mandrier-sur-Mer, *France*	27	E9
St-Marc, *Haiti*	117	C5
St.-Marcellin, *France*	27	C9
St.-Marcouf, Is., *France*	24	C5
St. Maries, *U.S.A.*	110	C5
St.-Martin, *W. Indies*	117	C7
St. Martin, L., *Canada*	101	C9
St.-Martin-de-Ré, *France*	26	B2
St.-Martin-Vésubie, *France*	27	D11
St. Martins, *Canada*	99	C6
St. Martinville, *U.S.A.*	109	K9
St.-Martory, *France*	26	E4
St. Mary Pk., *Australia*	91	E2
St. Mary's, *Canada*	106	C3
St. Marys, *Australia*	90	G4
St. Marys, *Canada*	106	C3
St. Mary's, *U.K.*	13	H1
St. Marys, *U.S.A.*	106	E6
St. Mary's, C., *Canada*	99	C9
St. Mary's B., *Canada*	99	C9
St. Marys Bay, *Canada*	99	D6
St.-Mathieu, Pte., *France*	24	D2
St. Matthews, I. = Zadetkyi Kyun, *Burma*	59	H2
St.-Maur-des-Fossés, *France*	25	D9
St. Maurice, *Switz.*	22	D4
St.-Maurice →, *Canada*	98	C5
St.-Médard-de-Guizières, *France*	26	C3
St.-Méen-le-Grand, *France*	24	D4
St. Michael's Mount, *U.K.*	13	G2
St.-Michel-de-Maurienne, *France*	27	C10
St.-Mihiel, *France*	25	D12
St.-Nazaire, *France*	24	E4
St. Neots, *U.K.*	13	E7
St.-Nicolas-de-Port, *France*	25	D13
St. Niklass = Sint Niklaas, *Belgium*	17	F4
St. Niklaus, *Switz.*	22	D5
St.-Omer, *France*	25	B9
St-Pacome, *Canada*	99	C6
St.-Palais-sur-Mer, *France*	26	C2
St-Pamphile, *Canada*	99	C6
St.-Pardoux-la-Rivière, *France*	26	C4
St. Pascal, *Canada*	99	C6
St. Paul, *Canada*	100	C6
St. Paul, *Minn., U.S.A.*	108	C8
St. Paul, *Nebr., U.S.A.*	108	E5
St. Paul, I., *Ind. Oc.*	3	F13
St.-Paul-de-Fenouillet, *France*	26	F6
St. Paul I., *Canada*	99	C7
St.-Paul-lès-Dax, *France*	26	E2
St.-Péray, *France*	27	D8
St.-Père-en-Retz, *France*	24	E4
St. Peter, *U.S.A.*	108	C8
St. Peter Port, *Chan. Is.*	13	H5
St. Peters, *N.S., Canada*	99	C7
St. Peters, *P.E.I., Canada*	99	C7
St. Petersburg = Sankt-Peterburg, *Russia*	40	B7
St. Petersburg, *U.S.A.*	105	M4
St.-Philbert-de-Grand-Lieu, *France*	24	E5
St-Pierre, *St- P. & M.*	99	C8
St-Pierre, L., *Canada*	98	C5
St.-Pierre-d'Oléron, *France*	26	C2
St.-Pierre-Église, *France*	24	C5
St.-Pierre-en-Port, *France*	24	C7
St.-Pierre et Miquelon □, *St- P. & M.*	99	C8
St.-Pierre-le-Moûtier, *France*	25	F10
St.-Pierre-sur-Dives, *France*	24	C6
St. Pieters Leew, *Belgium*	17	G4
St.-Pol-de-Léon, *France*	24	D2
St.-Pol-sur-Mer, *France*	25	A9
St.-Pol-sur-Ternoise, *France*	25	B9
St.-Pons, *France*	26	E6
St.-Pourçain-sur-Sioule, *France*	26	B7
St.-Quay-Portrieux, *France*	24	D4
St.-Quentin, *France*	25	C10
St.-Rambert-d'Albon, *France*	27	C8
St.-Raphaël, *France*	27	E10
St. Regis, *U.S.A.*	110	C6
St.-Rémy-de-Provence, *France*	27	E8
St.-Renan, *France*	24	D2
St.-Saëns, *France*	24	C8
St.-Sauveur-en-Puisaye, *France*	25	E10
St.-Sauveur-le-Vicomte, *France*	24	C5
St.-Savin, *France*	26	B4
St.-Savinien, *France*	26	C3
St. Sebastien, Tanjon' i, *Madag.*	85	A8
St.-Seine-l'Abbaye, *France*	25	E11
St.-Sernin-sur-Rance, *France*	26	E6
St.-Servan-sur-Mer, *France*	24	D4
St.-Sever, *France*	26	E3
St.-Sever-Calvados, *France*	24	D5
St.-Siméon, *Canada*	99	C5
St. Stephen, *Canada*	99	C6
St.-Sulpice, *France*	26	E5
St.-Sulpice-Laurière, *France*	26	B5
St.-Syprien, *France*	26	F7
St.-Thégonnec, *France*	24	D3
St. Thomas, *Canada*	98	D3
St. Thomas I., *Virgin Is.*	117	C7
St-Tite, *Canada*	98	C5
St.-Tropez, *France*	27	E10
St. Troud = Sint Truiden, *Belgium*	17	G6
St.-Vaast-la-Hougue, *France*	24	C5
St.-Valéry-en-Caux, *France*	24	C7
St.-Valéry-sur-Somme, *France*	25	B8
St.-Vallier, *France*	27	C8
St.-Vallier-de-Thiey, *France*	27	E10
St.-Varent, *France*	24	F6
St. Vincent, *W. Indies*	117	D7
St. Vincent, G., *Australia*	91	F2
St. Vincent & the Grenadines ■, *W. Indies*	117	D7
St.-Vincent-de-Tyrosse, *France*	26	E2
St. Vincent Passage, *W. Indies*	117	D7
St-Vith, *Belgium*	17	H8
St.-Yrieix-la-Perche, *France*	26	C5
Ste.-Adresse, *France*	24	C7
Ste-Agathe-des-Monts, *Canada*	98	C5
Ste-Anne de Beaupré, *Canada*	99	C5
Ste-Anne-des-Monts, *Canada*	99	C6
Ste-Croix, *Switz.*	22	C3
Ste.-Enimie, *France*	26	D7
Ste.-Foy-la-Grande, *France*	26	D4
Ste. Genevieve, *U.S.A.*	108	G9
Ste.-Hermine, *France*	26	B2
Ste.-Livrade-sur-Lot, *France*	26	D4
Ste-Marguerite →, *Canada*	99	B6
Ste.-Marie, *Martinique*	117	D7
Ste.-Marie-aux-Mines, *France*	25	D14
Ste-Marie de la Madeleine, *Canada*	99	C5
Ste.-Maure-de-Touraine, *France*	24	E7
Ste.-Maxime, *France*	27	E10
Ste.-Menehould, *France*	25	C11
Ste.-Mère-Église, *France*	24	C5
Ste.-Rose, *Guadeloupe*	117	C7
Ste. Rose du Lac, *Canada*	101	C9
Saintes, *France*	26	C3
Saintes, I. des, *Guadeloupe*	117	C7
Stes.-Maries-de-la-Mer, *France*	27	E8
Saintonge, *France*	26	C3
Saipan, *Pac. Oc.*	92	F6
Sairang, *India*	61	H18
Sairecábur, Cerro, *Bolivia*	126	A2
Saitama □, *Japan*	49	F9
Sajama, *Bolivia*	124	D4
Sajó →, *S. Africa*	84	E3
Sak →, *S. Africa*	84	E3
Sakai, *Japan*	49	G7
Sakaide, *Japan*	49	G6
Sakaiminato, *Japan*	49	G6
Sakākah, *Si. Arabia*	64	D4
Sakakawea, L., *U.S.A.*	108	B3
Sakami, L., *Canada*	98	B4
Sâkâne, 'Erg i-n, *Mali*	74	D4
Sakania, *Zaïre*	83	E2

Sakarya = Adapazarı, Turkey ... 66 C4
Sakarya □, Turkey ... 66 C4
Sakarya →, Turkey ... 42 F4
Sakashima-Guntō, Japan . 49 M2
Sakata, Japan ... 48 E9
Sakchu, N. Korea ... 51 D13
Sakeny →, Madag. ... 85 C8
Sakété, Benin ... 79 D5
Sakha = Yakut Republic □, Russia ... 45 C13
Sakhalin, Russia ... 45 D15
Sakhalinskiy Zaliv, Russia . 45 D15
Saki, Ukraine ... 42 D5
Šakiai, Lithuania ... 40 D3
Sakon Nakhon, Thailand . 58 D5
Sakrand, Pakistan ... 62 F3
Sakrivier, S. Africa ... 84 E3
Sakskøbing, Denmark ... 11 K5
Sakuma, Japan ... 49 G8
Sakurai, Japan ... 49 G7
Sal →, Russia ... 43 C9
Sala, Sweden ... 9 G14
Sala Consilina, Italy ... 35 B8
Sala-y-Gómez, Pac. Oc. .. 93 K17
Salaberry-de-Valleyfield, Canada ... 98 C5
Saladas, Argentina ... 126 B4
Saladillo, Argentina ... 126 D4
Salado →, Buenos Aires, Argentina ... 126 D4
Salado →, La Pampa, Argentina ... 128 A3
Salado →, Río Negro, Argentina ... 128 B3
Salado →, Santa Fe, Argentina ... 126 C3
Salado →, Mexico ... 114 B5
Salaga, Ghana ... 79 D4
Şalah, Syria ... 69 C5
Sálakhos, Greece ... 37 C9
Salala, Liberia ... 78 D2
Salala, Sudan ... 76 C4
Salālah, Oman ... 68 D5
Salamanca, Chile ... 126 C1
Salamanca, Spain ... 30 E5
Salamanca, U.S.A. ... 106 D6
Salamanca □, Spain ... 30 E5
Salamina, Colombia ... 120 B2
Salamis, Cyprus ... 37 D12
Salamis, Greece ... 39 M6
Salar de Atacama, Chile . 126 A2
Salar de Uyuni, Bolivia . 124 E4
Sălard, Romania ... 38 B5
Salas, Spain ... 30 B4
Salas de los Infantes, Spain 28 C1
Salatiga, Indonesia ... 57 G14
Salaverry, Peru ... 124 B2
Salawati, Indonesia ... 57 E8
Salayar, Indonesia ... 57 F6
Salazar →, Spain ... 28 C3
Salbris, France ... 25 E9
Salcombe, U.K. ... 13 G4
Salda Gölü, Turkey ... 66 E3
Saldaña, Spain ... 30 C6
Saldanha, S. Africa ... 84 E2
Saldanha B., S. Africa ... 84 E2
Saldus, Latvia ... 40 C3
Sale, Australia ... 91 F4
Salé, Morocco ... 74 B3
Sale, U.K. ... 12 D5
Salekhard, Russia ... 44 C7
Salem, India ... 60 P11
Salem, Ind., U.S.A. ... 104 F2
Salem, Mass., U.S.A. ... 107 D14
Salem, Mo., U.S.A. ... 109 G9
Salem, N.J., U.S.A. ... 104 F8
Salem, Ohio, U.S.A. ... 106 F4
Salem, Oreg., U.S.A. ... 110 D2
Salem, S. Dak., U.S.A. ... 108 D6
Salem, Va., U.S.A. ... 104 G5
Salemi, Italy ... 34 E5
Salernes, France ... 27 E10
Salerno, Italy ... 35 B7
Salerno, G. di, Italy ... 35 B7
Salford, U.K. ... 12 D5
Salgir →, Ukraine ... 42 D6
Salgótarján, Hungary ... 21 G9
Salgueiro, Brazil ... 122 C4
Salida, U.S.A. ... 102 C5
Salies-de-Béarn, France .. 26 E3
Salihli, Turkey ... 66 D3
Salima, Malawi ... 81 G6
Salina, Italy ... 35 D7
Salina, U.S.A. ... 108 F6
Salina Cruz, Mexico ... 115 D5
Salinas, Brazil ... 123 E3
Salinas, Chile ... 126 A2
Salinas, Ecuador ... 120 D1
Salinas, U.S.A. ... 111 H3
Salinas →, Guatemala ... 115 D6
Salinas →, U.S.A. ... 111 H3
Salinas, B. de, Nic. ... 116 D2
Salinas, C. de, Spain ... 36 B10
Salinas, Pampa de las, Argentina ... 126 C2
Salinas Ambargasta, Argentina ... 126 B3
Salinas de Hidalgo, Mexico 114 C4
Salinas Grandes, Argentina 126 B2
Saline →, Ark., U.S.A. ... 109 J8
Saline →, Kans., U.S.A. .. 108 F6
Salines, Spain ... 36 B10
Salinópolis, Brazil ... 122 B2

Salins-les-Bains, France .. 25 F12
Salir, Portugal ... 31 H2
Salisbury = Harare, Zimbabwe ... 83 F3
Salisbury, Australia ... 91 E2
Salisbury, U.K. ... 13 F6
Salisbury, Md., U.S.A. ... 104 F8
Salisbury, N.C., U.S.A. ... 105 H5
Salisbury Plain, U.K. ... 13 F6
Săliște, Romania ... 38 D6
Salka, Nigeria ... 79 C5
Salkhad, Jordan ... 69 C5
Sallent, Spain ... 28 D6
Salles-Curan, France ... 26 D6
Salling, Denmark ... 11 H2
Sallisaw, U.S.A. ... 109 H7
Sallom Junction, Sudan ... 76 D4
Salmās, Iran ... 64 B5
Salmerón, Spain ... 28 E2
Salmo, Canada ... 100 D5
Salmon, U.S.A. ... 110 D7
Salmon →, Canada ... 100 C4
Salmon →, U.S.A. ... 110 D5
Salmon Arm, Canada ... 100 C5
Salmon Falls, U.S.A. ... 110 E6
Salmon Gums, Australia .. 89 F3
Salmon Res., Canada ... 99 C8
Salmon River Mts., U.S.A. 110 D6
Salo, Finland ... 9 F17
Salò, Italy ... 32 C7
Salobreña, Spain ... 31 J7
Salome, U.S.A. ... 113 M13
Salon-de-Provence, France 27 E9
Salonica = Thessaloníki, Greece ... 39 J5
Salonta, Romania ... 38 C4
Salor →, Spain ... 31 F3
Salou, C., Spain ... 28 D6
Salsacate, Argentina ... 126 C2
Salses, France ... 26 F6
Salso →, Italy ... 34 E6
Salsomaggiore, Italy ... 32 D6
Salt →, Canada ... 100 B6
Salt →, U.S.A. ... 111 K7
Salt Creek, Australia ... 91 F2
Salt Fork Arkansas →, U.S.A. ... 109 G6
Salt Lake City, U.S.A. ... 110 F8
Salt Range, Pakistan ... 62 C5
Salta, Argentina ... 126 A2
Salta □, Argentina ... 126 A2
Saltcoats, U.K. ... 14 F4
Saltee Is., Ireland ... 15 D5
Saltfjorden, Norway ... 8 C13
Saltholm, Denmark ... 11 J6
Salthólmavík, Iceland ... 8 D3
Saltillo, Mexico ... 114 B4
Salto, Argentina ... 126 C3
Salto, Uruguay ... 126 C4
Salto da Divisa, Brazil ... 123 E4
Salton City, U.S.A. ... 113 M11
Salton Sea, U.S.A. ... 113 M11
Saltpond, Ghana ... 79 D4
Saltsjöbaden, Sweden ... 10 E12
Saltville, U.S.A. ... 104 G5
Saluda →, U.S.A. ... 105 H5
Salûm, Egypt ... 76 A2
Salûm, Khâlig el, Egypt .. 76 A2
Salur, India ... 61 K13
Salut, Is. du, Fr. Guiana . 121 B7
Saluzzo, Italy ... 32 D4
Salvación, B., Chile ... 128 D1
Salvador, Brazil ... 123 D4
Salvador, Canada ... 101 C7
Salvador, L., U.S.A. ... 109 L9
Salvaterra, Brazil ... 122 B2
Salvaterra de Magos, Portugal ... 31 F2
Sálvora, I., Spain ... 30 C2
Salween →, Burma ... 61 L20
Salyany, Azerbaijan ... 67 D13
Salyersville, U.S.A. ... 104 G4
Salza →, Austria ... 21 H4
Salzach →, Austria ... 21 G2
Salzburg, Austria ... 21 H3
Salzgitter, Germany ... 18 C6
Salzwedel, Germany ... 18 C7
Sam Neua, Laos ... 58 B5
Sam Ngao, Thailand ... 58 D2
Sam Rayburn Reservoir, U.S.A. ... 109 K7
Sam Son, Vietnam ... 58 C5
Sam Teu, Laos ... 58 C5
Sama, Russia ... 44 C7
Sama de Langreo, Spain .. 30 B5
Samagaltai, Russia ... 45 D10
Samaipata, Bolivia ... 125 D5
Samales Group, Phil. ... 55 J4
Samâlût, Egypt ... 76 J7
Samana, India ... 62 D7
Samana Cay, Bahamas ... 117 B5
Samandağı, Turkey ... 66 E6
Samanga, Tanzania ... 83 D4
Samangwa, Zaïre ... 82 C1
Samani, Japan ... 48 C11
Samar, Phil. ... 55 F6
Samara, Russia ... 41 E17
Samaria = Shōmrōn, Jordan ... 69 C4
Samariá, Greece ... 37 D5
Samarinda, Indonesia ... 56 E5
Samarkand = Samarqand, Uzbekistan ... 44 F7
Samarqand, Uzbekistan ... 44 F7

Sāmarrā, Iraq ... 64 C4
Samastipur, India ... 63 G11
Samatan, France ... 26 E4
Samaúma, Brazil ... 125 B5
Samba, India ... 63 C6
Samba, Zaïre ... 82 C2
Sambaíba, Brazil ... 122 C2
Sambalpur, India ... 61 J14
Sambar, Tanjung, Indonesia 56 E4
Sambas, Indonesia ... 56 D3
Sambava, Madag. ... 85 A9
Sambawizi, Zimbabwe ... 83 F2
Sambhal, India ... 63 E8
Sambhar, India ... 62 F6
Sambiase, Italy ... 35 D9
Sambonifacio, Italy ... 32 C8
Sambor, Cambodia ... 58 F6
Sambor, Ukraine ... 40 G3
Sambre →, Europe ... 17 H5
Sambuca di Sicilia, Italy .. 34 E6
Samburu □, Kenya ... 82 B4
Samchŏk, S. Korea ... 51 F15
Samchonpo, S. Korea ... 51 G15
Same, Tanzania ... 82 C4
Samedan, Switz. ... 23 C9
Samer, France ... 25 B8
Samfya, Zambia ... 83 E2
Sámi, Greece ... 39 L3
Samnah, Si. Arabia ... 64 E3
Samnaun, Switz. ... 23 C10
Samo Alto, Chile ... 126 C1
Samobor, Croatia ... 33 C12
Samoëns, France ... 27 B10
Samokov, Bulgaria ... 38 G6
Samoorombón, B., Argentina ... 126 D4
Samorogouan, Burkina Faso ... 78 C4
Sámos, Greece ... 39 M9
Samoš, Serbia ... 21 K10
Samos, Spain ... 30 C3
Samothráki, Évros, Greece 39 J8
Samothráki, Kérkira, Greece ... 37 A3
Samoylovka, Russia ... 41 F13
Sampa, Ghana ... 78 D4
Sampacho, Argentina ... 126 C3
Sampang, Indonesia ... 57 G15
Samper de Calanda, Spain 28 D4
Sampit, Indonesia ... 56 E4
Sampit, Teluk, Indonesia . 56 E4
Samrée, Belgium ... 17 H7
Samrong, Cambodia ... 58 E4
Samrong, Thailand ... 58 E3
Samsø, Denmark ... 11 J4
Samsø Bælt, Denmark ... 11 J4
Samsun, Turkey ... 66 C7
Samsun □, Turkey ... 66 C7
Samui, Ko, Thailand ... 59 H3
Samur →, Azerbaijan ... 43 F13
Samusole, Zaïre ... 83 E1
Samut Prakan, Thailand .. 58 F3
Samut Sakhon, Thailand . 58 F3
Samut Songkhram →, Thailand ... 58 F3
Samwari, Pakistan ... 62 E2
San, Mali ... 78 C4
San →, Cambodia ... 58 F5
San →, Poland ... 20 E11
San Adrián, C. de, Spain . 30 B2
San Agustín, Colombia ... 120 C2
San Agustin, C., Phil. ... 55 H7
San Agustín de Valle Fértil, Argentina ... 126 C2
San Ambrosio, Pac. Oc. .. 93 K20
San Andreas, U.S.A. ... 112 G6
San Andrés, I. de, Caribbean ... 116 D3
San Andres Mts., U.S.A. . 111 K10
San Andrés Tuxtla, Mexico 115 D5
San Angelo, U.S.A. ... 109 K4
San Anselmo, U.S.A. ... 112 H4
San Antonio, Belize ... 115 D7
San Antonio, Chile ... 126 C1
San Antonio, Phil. ... 55 D4
San Antonio, N. Mex., U.S.A. ... 111 K10
San Antonio, Tex., U.S.A. 109 L5
San Antonio, Venezuela .. 120 C4
San Antonio →, U.S.A. ... 109 L6
San Antonio, C., Argentina 126 D4
San Antonio, C., Cuba ... 116 B3
San Antonio, C. de, Spain 29 G5
San Antonio, Mt., U.S.A. 113 L9
San Antonio Abad, Spain . 36 C7
San Antonio de los Baños, Cuba ... 116 B3
San Antonio de los Cobres, Argentina ... 126 A2
San Antonio Oeste, Argentina ... 128 B4
San Arcángel, Italy ... 35 B9
San Ardo, U.S.A. ... 112 J6
San Augustín, Canary Is. . 36 G4
San Augustine, U.S.A. ... 109 K7
San Bartolomé, Canary Is. 36 F6
San Bartolomé de Tirajana, Canary Is. ... 36 G4
San Bartolomeo in Galdo, Italy ... 35 A8
San Benedetto, Italy ... 32 C7
San Benedetto del Tronto, Italy ... 33 F10
San Benedicto, I., Mexico 114 D2

San Benito, U.S.A. ... 109 M6
San Benito →, U.S.A. ... 112 J5
San Benito Mt., U.S.A. .. 112 J6
San Bernardino, Paso del, Switz. ... 23 D8
San Bernardino Mts., U.S.A. ... 113 L10
San Bernardino Str., Phil. 55 E6
San Bernardo, Chile ... 126 C1
San Bernardo, I. de, Colombia ... 120 B2
San Blas, Mexico ... 114 B3
San Blas, Arch. de, Panama ... 116 E4
San Blas, C., U.S.A. ... 105 L3
San Borja, Bolivia ... 124 C4
San Buenaventura, Bolivia 124 C4
San Buenaventura, Mexico 114 B4
San Carlos = Butuku-Luba, Eq. Guin. ... 79 E6
San Carlos, Argentina ... 126 C2
San Carlos, Bolivia ... 125 D5
San Carlos, Chile ... 126 D1
San Carlos, Mexico ... 114 B4
San Carlos, Nic. ... 116 D3
San Carlos, Negros, Phil. . 55 F5
San Carlos, Pangasinan, Phil. ... 55 D4
San Carlos, Spain ... 36 B8
San Carlos, Uruguay ... 127 C5
San Carlos, U.S.A. ... 111 K8
San Carlos, Amazonas, Venezuela ... 120 C4
San Carlos, Cojedes, Venezuela ... 120 B4
San Carlos de Bariloche, Argentina ... 128 B2
San Carlos de la Rápita, Spain ... 28 E5
San Carlos del Zulia, Venezuela ... 120 B3
San Carlos L., U.S.A. ... 111 K8
San Cataldo, Italy ... 34 E6
San Celoni, Spain ... 28 D7
San Clemente, Chile ... 126 D1
San Clemente, Spain ... 29 F2
San Clemente, U.S.A. ... 113 M9
San Clemente I., U.S.A. .. 113 N8
San Constanzo, Italy ... 33 E10
San Cristóbal, Argentina . 126 C3
San Cristóbal, Colombia . 120 D3
San Cristóbal, Dom. Rep. 117 C5
San Cristóbal, Mexico ... 115 D6
San Cristóbal, Spain ... 36 B11
San Cristóbal, Venezuela . 120 B3
San Damiano d'Asti, Italy 32 D5
San Daniele del Friuli, Italy 33 B10
San Demétrio Corone, Italy 35 C9
San Diego, Calif., U.S.A. . 113 N9
San Diego, Tex., U.S.A. .. 109 M5
San Diego, C., Argentina . 128 D3
San Diego de la Unión, Mexico ... 114 C4
San Dimitri, Ras, Malta .. 37 C1
San Donà di Piave, Italy . 33 C9
San Elpídio a Mare, Italy . 33 E10
San Estanislao, Paraguay . 126 A4
San Esteban de Gormaz, Spain ... 28 D1
San Felice sul Panaro, Italy 32 D8
San Felipe, Chile ... 126 C1
San Felipe, Colombia ... 120 C4
San Felipe, Venezuela ... 120 A4
San Felipe →, U.S.A. ... 113 M11
San Felíu de Guíxols, Spain 28 D8
San Felíu de Llobregat, Spain ... 28 D7
San Félix, Pac. Oc. ... 93 K20
San Fernando, Chile ... 126 C1
San Fernando, Mexico ... 114 B1
San Fernando, La Union, Phil. ... 55 C4
San Fernando, Pampanga, Phil. ... 55 D4
San Fernando, Baleares, Spain ... 36 C7
San Fernando, Cádiz, Spain 31 J4
San Fernando, Trin. & Tob. ... 117 D7
San Fernando, U.S.A. ... 113 L8
San Fernando →, Mexico 114 C5
San Fernando de Apure, Venezuela ... 120 B4
San Fernando de Atabapo, Venezuela ... 120 C4
San Fernando di Púglia, Italy ... 35 A9
San Francisco, Argentina . 126 C3
San Francisco, Bolivia ... 125 D4
San Francisco, U.S.A. ... 111 H2
San Francisco →, U.S.A. . 111 K9
San Francisco, Paso de, S. Amer. ... 126 B2
San Francisco de Macorís, Dom. Rep. ... 117 C5
San Francisco del Monte de Oro, Argentina ... 126 C2
San Francisco del Oro, Mexico ... 114 B3
San Francisco Javier, Spain 36 C7
San Francisco Solano, Pta., Colombia ... 120 B2
San Fratello, Italy ... 35 D7

San Gabriel, Ecuador ... 120 C2
San Gavino Monreale, Italy 34 C1
San Gil, Colombia ... 120 B3
San Gimignano, Italy ... 32 E8
San Giórgio di Nogaro, Italy ... 33 C10
San Giórgio Iónico, Italy . 35 B10
San Giovanni Bianco, Italy 32 C6
San Giovanni in Fiore, Italy 35 C9
San Giovanni in Persiceto, Italy ... 33 D8
San Giovanni Rotondo, Italy ... 35 A8
San Giovanni Valdarno, Italy ... 33 E8
San Giuliano Terme, Italy 32 E7
San Gorgonio Mt., U.S.A. 113 L10
San Gottardo, Paso del, Switz. ... 23 C7
San Gregorio, Uruguay ... 127 C4
San Gregorio, U.S.A. ... 112 H4
San Guiseppe Iato, Italy .. 34 E6
San Ignacio, Belize ... 115 D7
San Ignacio, Bolivia ... 125 D5
San Ignacio, Mexico ... 114 B2
San Ignacio, Paraguay ... 126 B4
San Ignacio, L., Mexico .. 114 B2
San Ildefonso, C., Phil. .. 55 C5
San Isidro, Argentina ... 126 C4
San Jacinto, Colombia ... 120 B2
San Jacinto, U.S.A. ... 113 M10
San Jaime, Spain ... 36 B11
San Javier, Misiones, Argentina ... 127 B4
San Javier, Santa Fe, Argentina ... 126 C4
San Javier, Beni, Bolivia . 125 C5
San Javier, Santa Cruz, Bolivia ... 125 D5
San Javier, Chile ... 126 D1
San Javier, Spain ... 29 H4
San Jerónimo, Sa. de, Colombia ... 120 B2
San Jeronimo Taviche, Mexico ... 115 D5
San Joaquín, Bolivia ... 125 C5
San Joaquin, U.S.A. ... 112 J6
San Joaquín, Venezuela .. 120 A4
San Joaquín →, Bolivia .. 125 C5
San Joaquin →, U.S.A. ... 111 G3
San Joaquin Valley, U.S.A. 112 J6
San Jordi, Spain ... 36 B9
San Jorge, Argentina ... 126 C3
San Jorge, Spain ... 36 C7
San Jorge, B. de, Mexico 114 A2
San Jorge, G., Argentina . 128 C3
San Jorge, G. de, Spain .. 28 E4
San José, Bolivia ... 125 D5
San José, Costa Rica ... 116 E3
San José, Guatemala ... 116 D1
San José, Mexico ... 114 C2
San José, Phil. ... 55 D4
San José, Spain ... 36 C7
San José, U.S.A. ... 111 H3
San Jose →, U.S.A. ... 111 J10
San Jose de Buenovista, Phil. ... 55 E4
San José de Feliciano, Argentina ... 126 C4
San José de Jáchal, Argentina ... 126 C2
San José de Mayo, Uruguay 126 C4
San José de Ocune, Colombia ... 120 C3
San José de Uchapiamonas, Bolivia ... 124 C4
San José del Cabo, Mexico 114 C3
San José del Guaviare, Colombia ... 120 C3
San José do Anauá, Brazil 121 C5
San Juan, Argentina ... 126 C2
San Juan, Colombia ... 120 B2
San Juan, Mexico ... 114 C4
San Juan, Ica, Peru ... 124 D2
San Juan, Puno, Peru ... 124 C4
San Juan, Phil. ... 55 G7
San Juan, Puerto Rico ... 117 C6
San Juan □, Argentina ... 126 C2
San Juan →, Argentina ... 126 C2
San Juan →, Bolivia ... 125 E4
San Juan →, Colombia ... 120 C2
San Juan →, Nic. ... 116 D3
San Juan →, U.S.A. ... 111 H8
San Juan →, Venezuela .. 121 A5
San Juan, C., Eq. Guin. .. 80 D1
San Juan Bautista, Paraguay ... 126 B4
San Juan Bautista, Spain . 36 B8
San Juan Bautista, U.S.A. 111 H3
San Juan Bautista Valle Nacional, Mexico ... 115 D5
San Juan Capistrano, U.S.A. ... 113 M9
San Juan de Guadalupe, Mexico ... 114 C4
San Juan de los Morros, Venezuela ... 120 B4
San Juan del César, Colombia ... 120 A3
San Juan del Norte, Nic. . 116 D3
San Juan del Norte, B. de, Nic. ... 116 D3
San Juan del Puerto, Spain 31 H4
San Juan del Río, Mexico . 115 C5

San Juan del Sur

San Juan del Sur, *Nic.* 116 D2
San Juan I., *U.S.A.* 112 B3
San Juan Mts., *U.S.A.* 111 H10
San Julián, *Argentina* 128 C3
San Just, Sierra de, *Spain* 28 E4
San Justo, *Argentina* 126 C3
San Kamphaeng, *Thailand* 58 C2
San Lázaro, C., *Mexico* 114 C2
San Lázaro, Sa., *Mexico* 114 C3
San Leandro, *U.S.A.* 111 H2
San Leonardo, *Spain* 28 D1
San Lorenzo, *Argentina* 126 C3
San Lorenzo, *Beni, Bolivia* 125 D4
San Lorenzo, *Tarija, Bolivia* 125 E5
San Lorenzo, *Ecuador* 120 C2
San Lorenzo, *Paraguay* 126 B4
San Lorenzo, *Spain* 36 B10
San Lorenzo, *Venezuela* 120 B3
San Lorenzo →, *Mexico* 114 C3
San Lorenzo, I., *Mexico* 114 B2
San Lorenzo, I., *Peru* 124 C2
San Lorenzo, Mt., *Argentina* 128 C2
San Lorenzo de la Parrilla, *Spain* 28 F2
San Lorenzo de Morunys, *Spain* 28 C6
San Lucas, *Bolivia* 125 E4
San Lucas, *Baja Calif. S., Mexico* 114 C3
San Lucas, *Baja Calif. S., Mexico* 114 B2
San Lucas, *U.S.A.* 112 J5
San Lucas, C., *Mexico* 114 C3
San Lúcido, *Italy* 35 C9
San Luis, *Argentina* 126 C2
San Luis, *Cuba* 116 B3
San Luis, *Guatemala* 116 C2
San Luis, *U.S.A.* 111 H11
San Luis □, *Argentina* 126 C2
San Luis, I., *Mexico* 114 B2
San Luis, L. de, *Bolivia* 125 C5
San Luis, Sierra de, *Argentina* 126 C2
San Luis de la Paz, *Mexico* 114 C4
San Luis Obispo, *U.S.A.* 113 K6
San Luis Potosí, *Mexico* 114 C4
San Luis Potosí □, *Mexico* 114 C4
San Luis Reservoir, *U.S.A.* 112 H5
San Luis Río Colorado, *Mexico* 114 A2
San Marco Argentano, *Italy* 35 C9
San Marco dei Cavoti, *Italy* 35 A7
San Marco in Lámis, *Italy* 35 A8
San Marcos, *Colombia* 120 B2
San Marcos, *Guatemala* 116 D1
San Marcos, *Mexico* 114 B2
San Marcos, *U.S.A.* 109 L6
San Marino ■, *Europe* 33 E9
San Martín, *Argentina* 126 C2
San Martín, *Colombia* 120 C3
San Martín →, *Bolivia* 125 C5
San Martín, L., *Argentina* 128 C2
San Martín de los Andes, *Argentina* 128 B2
San Martín de Valdeiglesias, *Spain* 30 E6
San Martino de Calvi, *Italy* 32 C6
San Mateo, *Phil.* 55 C4
San Mateo, *Baleares, Spain* 36 B7
San Mateo, *Valencia, Spain* 28 E5
San Mateo, *U.S.A.* 111 H2
San Matías, *Bolivia* 125 D6
San Matías, G., *Argentina* 128 B4
San Miguel, *El Salv.* 116 D2
San Miguel, *Panama* 116 E4
San Miguel, *Spain* 36 B7
San Miguel, *U.S.A.* 111 J3
San Miguel, *Venezuela* 120 B4
San Miguel →, *Bolivia* 125 C5
San Miguel →, *S. Amer.* 120 C2
San Miguel de Huachi, *Bolivia* 124 D4
San Miguel de Salinas, *Spain* 29 H4
San Miguel de Tucumán, *Argentina* 126 B2
San Miguel del Monte, *Argentina* 126 D4
San Miguel I., *U.S.A.* 113 L6
San Miniato, *Italy* 32 E7
San Narciso, *Phil.* 55 D4
San Nicolás, *Canary Is.* 36 G4
San Nicolas, *Phil.* 55 B4
San Nicolás de los Arroyas, *Argentina* 126 C3
San Nicolas I., *U.S.A.* 113 M7
San Onofre, *Colombia* 120 B2
San Onofre, *U.S.A.* 113 M9
San Pablo, *Bolivia* 126 A2
San Pablo, *Phil.* 55 D4
San Paolo di Civitate, *Italy* 35 A8
San Pedro, *Buenos Aires, Argentina* 127 B5
San Pedro, *Jujuy, Argentina* 126 A3
San Pedro, *Colombia* 120 C3
San-Pédro, *Ivory C.* 78 E3
San Pedro, *Mexico* 114 C2
San Pedro, *Peru* 124 C3
San Pedro □, *Paraguay* 126 A4
San Pedro →, *Chihuahua, Mexico* 114 B3
San Pedro →, *Michoacan, Mexico* 114 D4
San Pedro →, *Nayarit, Mexico* 114 C3
San Pedro →, *U.S.A.* 111 K8
San Pedro, Pta., *Chile* 126 B1
San Pedro, Sierra de, *Spain* 31 F4
San Pedro Channel, *U.S.A.* 113 M8
San Pedro de Arimena, *Colombia* 120 C3
San Pedro de Atacama, *Chile* 126 A2
San Pedro de Jujuy, *Argentina* 126 A3
San Pedro de las Colonias, *Mexico* 114 B4
San Pedro de Lloc, *Peru* 124 B2
San Pedro de Macorís, *Dom. Rep.* 117 C6
San Pedro del Norte, *Nic.* 116 D3
San Pedro del Paraná, *Paraguay* 126 B4
San Pedro del Pinatar, *Spain* 29 H4
San Pedro Mártir, Sierra, *Mexico* 114 A1
San Pedro Mixtepec, *Mexico* 115 D5
San Pedro Ocampo = Melchor Ocampo, *Mexico* 114 C4
San Pedro Sula, *Honduras* 116 C2
San Pietro, I., *Italy* 34 C1
San Pietro Vernótico, *Italy* 35 B11
San Quintín, *Mexico* 114 A1
San Rafael, *Argentina* 126 C2
San Rafael, *Calif., U.S.A.* 112 H4
San Rafael, *N. Mex., U.S.A.* 111 J10
San Rafael, *Venezuela* 120 A3
San Rafael Mt., *U.S.A.* 113 L7
San Rafael Mts., *U.S.A.* 113 L7
San Ramón, *Bolivia* 125 C5
San Ramón, *Peru* 124 C2
San Ramón de la Nueva Orán, *Argentina* 126 A3
San Remo, *Italy* 32 E4
San Román, C., *Venezuela* 120 A3
San Roque, *Argentina* 126 B4
San Roque, *Spain* 31 J5
San Rosendo, *Chile* 126 D1
San Saba, *U.S.A.* 109 K5
San Salvador, *Bahamas* 117 B5
San Salvador, *El Salv.* 116 D2
San Salvador, *Spain* 36 B10
San Salvador de Jujuy, *Argentina* 126 A3
San Salvador I., *Bahamas* 117 B5
San Sebastián, *Argentina* 128 D3
San Sebastián, *Spain* 28 B3
San Sebastián, *Venezuela* 120 B4
San Sebastian de la Gomera, *Canary Is.* 36 F2
San Serra, *Spain* 36 B10
San Serverino Marche, *Italy* 33 E10
San Simeon, *U.S.A.* 112 K5
San Simon, *U.S.A.* 111 K9
San Stéfano di Cadore, *Italy* 33 B9
San Telmo, *Mexico* 114 A1
San Telmo, *Spain* 36 B9
San Tiburcio, *Mexico* 114 C4
San Valentin, Mte., *Chile* 128 C2
San Vicente de Alcántara, *Spain* 31 F3
San Vicente de la Barquera, *Spain* 30 B6
San Vicente del Caguán, *Colombia* 120 C3
San Vincenzo, *Italy* 32 E7
San Vito, *Italy* 34 C2
San Vito, C., *Italy* 34 D5
San Vito al Tagliamento, *Italy* 33 C9
San Vito Chietino, *Italy* 33 F11
San Vito dei Normanni, *Italy* 35 B10
San Yanaro, *Colombia* 120 C4
San Ygnacio, *U.S.A.* 109 M5
Saña, *Peru* 124 B2
Sana', *Yemen* 68 D3
Sana →, *Bos.-H.* 33 C13
Sanaba, *Burkina Faso* 78 C4
Şanāfīr, *Si. Arabia* 76 B3
Sanaga →, *Cameroon* 79 E6
Sanaloa, Presa, *Mexico* 114 C3
Sanana, *Indonesia* 57 E7
Sanand, *India* 62 H5
Sanandaj, *Iran* 64 C5
Sanandita, *Bolivia* 126 A3
Sanary-sur-Mer, *France* 27 E9
Sanawad, *India* 62 H7
Sancellas, *Spain* 36 B9
Sancergues, *France* 25 E9
Sancerre, *France* 25 E9
Sancerrois, Collines du, *France* 25 E9
Sancha He →, *China* 52 D6
Sanchahe, *China* 51 B14
Sánchez, *Dom. Rep.* 117 C6
Sanchor, *India* 62 G4
Sanco Pt., *Phil.* 57 C7
Sancoins, *France* 25 F9
Sancti-Spíritus, *Cuba* 116 B4
Sancy, Puy de, *France* 26 C6
Sand →, *S. Africa* 85 C5
Sand Springs, *U.S.A.* 109 G6
Sanda, *Japan* 49 G7
Sandakan, *Malaysia* 56 C5
Sandan = Sambor, *Cambodia* 58 F6
Sandanski, *Bulgaria* 39 H6
Sandaré, *Mali* 78 C2
Sanday, *U.K.* 14 B6
Sandefjord, *Norway* 10 E4
Sanders, *U.S.A.* 111 J9
Sanderson, *U.S.A.* 109 K3
Sandfly L., *Canada* 101 B7
Sandgate, *Australia* 91 D5
Sandía, *Peru* 124 C4
Sandıklı, *Turkey* 66 D4
Sandnes, *Norway* 9 G8
Sandness, *U.K.* 14 A7
Sandoa, *Zaïre* 80 F4
Sandona, *Colombia* 120 C2
Sandover →, *Australia* 90 C2
Sandoway, *Burma* 61 K19
Sandpoint, *U.S.A.* 110 B5
Sandringham, *U.K.* 12 E8
Sandslån, *Sweden* 10 A11
Sandspit, *Canada* 100 C2
Sandstone, *Australia* 89 E2
Sandu, *China* 52 E6
Sandusky, *Mich., U.S.A.* 98 D3
Sandusky, *Ohio, U.S.A.* 106 E2
Sandvig, *Sweden* 11 J8
Sandviken, *Sweden* 9 F14
Sandwich, C., *Australia* 90 B4
Sandwich B., *Canada* 99 B8
Sandwich B., *Namibia* 84 C1
Sandwip Chan., *Bangla.* 61 H17
Sandy, *Nev., U.S.A.* 113 K11
Sandy, *Oreg., U.S.A.* 112 E4
Sandy Bight, *Australia* 89 F3
Sandy C., *Queens., Australia* 90 C5
Sandy C., *Tas., Australia* 90 G3
Sandy Cay, *Bahamas* 117 B4
Sandy Cr. →, *U.S.A.* 110 F9
Sandy L., *Canada* 98 B1
Sandy Lake, *Canada* 98 B1
Sandy Narrows, *Canada* 101 B8
Sanford, *Fla., U.S.A.* 105 L5
Sanford, *Maine, U.S.A.* 107 C14
Sanford, *N.C., U.S.A.* 105 H6
Sanford →, *Australia* 89 E2
Sanford, Mt., *U.S.A.* 96 B5
Sang-i-Masha, *Afghan.* 62 C2
Sanga, *Mozam.* 83 E4
Sanga →, *Congo* 80 E3
Sanga-Tolon, *Russia* 45 C15
Sangamner, *India* 60 K9
Sangar, *Afghan.* 62 C1
Sangar, *Russia* 45 C13
Sangar Sarai, *Afghan.* 62 B4
Sangasangadalam, *Indonesia* 56 E5
Sangay, *Ecuador* 120 D2
Sange, *Zaïre* 82 D2
Sangeang, *Indonesia* 57 F5
Sanger, *U.S.A.* 111 H4
Sangerhausen, *Germany* 18 D7
Sanggan He →, *China* 50 E9
Sanggau, *Indonesia* 56 D4
Sangihe, Kepulauan, *Indonesia* 57 D7
Sangihe, P., *Indonesia* 57 D7
Sangju, *S. Korea* 51 F15
Sangkapura, *Indonesia* 56 F4
Sangkhla, *Thailand* 58 E2
Sangli, *India* 60 L9
Sangmélina, *Cameroon* 79 E7
Sangonera →, *Spain* 29 H3
Sangre de Cristo Mts., *U.S.A.* 109 G2
Sangro →, *Italy* 33 F11
Sangudo, *Canada* 100 C6
Sangue →, *Brazil* 125 C6
Sangüesa, *Spain* 28 C3
Sanguinaires, Is., *France* 27 G12
Sangzhi, *China* 53 C8
Sanhala, *Ivory C.* 78 C3
Sāniyah, *Iraq* 64 C4
Sanje, *Uganda* 82 C3
Sanjiang, *China* 52 E7
Sanjo, *Japan* 48 F9
Sankt Antönien, *Switz.* 23 C9
Sankt Blasien, *Germany* 19 H4
Sankt Gallen, *Switz.* 23 B8
Sankt Gallen □, *Switz.* 23 B8
Sankt Goar, *Germany* 19 E3
Sankt Ingbert, *Germany* 19 F3
Sankt Margrethen, *Switz.* 23 B9
Sankt Moritz, *Switz.* 23 D9
Sankt-Peterburg, *Russia* 40 B7
Sankt Pölten, *Austria* 21 G5
Sankt Valentin, *Austria* 21 G4
Sankt Veit, *Austria* 21 J4
Sankt Wendel, *Germany* 19 F3
Sankuru →, *Zaïre* 80 E4
Sanlúcar de Barrameda, *Spain* 31 J4
Sanlúcar la Mayor, *Spain* 31 H4
Sanluri, *Italy* 34 C1
Sanmenxia, *China* 50 G6
Sanming, *China* 53 D11
Sannaspos, *S. Africa* 84 D4
Sannicandro Gargánico, *Italy* 35 A8
Sannidal, *Norway* 10 F3
Sannieshof, *S. Africa* 84 D4
Sannīn, J., *Lebanon* 69 B4
Sanok, *Poland* 20 F12
Sanquhar, *U.K.* 14 F5
Sansanding Dam, *Mali* 78 C3
Sansepolcro, *Italy* 33 E9
Sansha, *China* 53 D13
Sanshui, *China* 53 F9
Sanski Most, *Bos.-H.* 33 D13
Sansui, *China* 52 D7
Santa, *Peru* 124 B2
Sant' Ágata de Goti, *Italy* 35 A7
Sant' Ágata di Militello, *Italy* 35 D7
Santa Ana, *Beni, Bolivia* 125 C4
Santa Ana, *Santa Cruz, Bolivia* 125 D6
Santa Ana, *Santa Cruz, Bolivia* 125 D5
Santa Ana, *Ecuador* 120 D1
Santa Ana, *El Salv.* 116 D2
Santa Ana, *Mexico* 114 A2
Santa Ana, *U.S.A.* 113 M9
Santa Ana →, *Venezuela* 120 B3
Sant' Ángelo Lodigiano, *Italy* 32 C6
Sant' Antíoco, *Italy* 34 C1
Sant' Arcángelo di Romagna, *Italy* 33 D9
Santa Bárbara, *Colombia* 120 B2
Santa Bárbara, *Honduras* 116 D2
Santa Bárbara, *Mexico* 114 B3
Santa Bárbara, *Spain* 28 E5
Santa Barbara, *U.S.A.* 113 L7
Santa Bárbara, *Venezuela* 120 B3
Santa Bárbara, Mt., *Spain* 29 H2
Santa Barbara Channel, *U.S.A.* 113 L7
Santa Barbara I., *U.S.A.* 113 M7
Santa Catalina, *Colombia* 120 A2
Santa Catalina, *Mexico* 114 B2
Santa Catalina, Gulf of, *U.S.A.* 113 N9
Santa Catalina I., *U.S.A.* 113 M8
Santa Catarina □, *Brazil* 127 B6
Santa Catarina, I. de, *Brazil* 127 B6
Santa Caterina Villarmosa, *Italy* 35 E7
Santa Cecília, *Brazil* 127 B5
Santa Clara, *Cuba* 116 B4
Santa Clara, *Calif., U.S.A.* 111 H3
Santa Clara, *Utah, U.S.A.* 111 H7
Santa Clara de Olimar, *Uruguay* 127 C5
Santa Clotilde, *Peru* 120 D3
Santa Coloma de Farners, *Spain* 28 D7
Santa Coloma de Gramanet, *Spain* 28 D7
Santa Comba, *Spain* 30 B2
Santa Croce Camerina, *Italy* 35 F7
Santa Croce di Magliano, *Italy* 35 A7
Santa Cruz, *Argentina* 128 D3
Santa Cruz, *Bolivia* 125 D5
Santa Cruz, *Brazil* 122 C4
Santa Cruz, *Chile* 126 C1
Santa Cruz, *Costa Rica* 116 D2
Santa Cruz, *Madeira* 36 D3
Santa Cruz, *Peru* 124 B2
Santa Cruz, *Phil.* 55 D4
Santa Cruz, *U.S.A.* 111 H2
Santa Cruz, *Venezuela* 121 B5
Santa Cruz □, *Argentina* 128 C3
Santa Cruz □, *Bolivia* 125 D5
Santa Cruz →, *Argentina* 128 D3
Santa Cruz Cabrália, *Brazil* 123 E4
Santa Cruz de la Palma, *Canary Is.* 36 F2
Santa Cruz de Mudela, *Spain* 29 G1
Santa Cruz de Tenerife, *Canary Is.* 36 F3
Santa Cruz del Norte, *Cuba* 116 B3
Santa Cruz del Retamar, *Spain* 30 E6
Santa Cruz del Sur, *Cuba* 116 B4
Santa Cruz do Rio Pardo, *Brazil* 127 A6
Santa Cruz do Sul, *Brazil* 127 B5
Santa Cruz I., *Solomon Is.* 92 J8
Santa Cruz I., *U.S.A.* 113 M7
Santa Domingo, Cay, *Bahamas* 116 B4
Santa Elena, *Argentina* 126 C4
Santa Elena, *Ecuador* 120 D1
Santa Elena, C., *Costa Rica* 116 D2
Sant' Eufémia, G. di, *Italy* 35 D9
Santa Eugenia, Pta., *Mexico* 114 B1
Santa Eulalia, *Spain* 36 C8
Santa Fe, *Argentina* 126 C3
Santa Fe, *Spain* 31 H7
Santa Fe, *U.S.A.* 111 J11
Santa Fé □, *Argentina* 126 C3
Santa Filomena, *Brazil* 122 C2
Santa Galdana, *Spain* 36 B10
Santa Gertrudis, *Spain* 36 B7
Santa Helena, *Brazil* 122 B2
Santa Helena de Goiás, *Brazil* 123 E1
Santa Inês, *Brazil* 123 D4
Santa Inés, *Baleares, Spain* 36 B7
Santa Inés, *Extremadura, Spain* 31 G5
Santa Inés, I., *Chile* 128 D2
Santa Isabel = Rey Malabo, *Eq. Guin.* 79 E6
Santa Isabel, *Argentina* 126 D2
Santa Isabel, *Brazil* 123 D1
Santa Isabel, Pico, *Eq. Guin.* 79 E6
Santa Isabel do Araguaia, *Brazil* 122 C2
Santa Isabel do Morro, *Brazil* 123 D1
Santa Lucía, *Corrientes, Argentina* 126 B4
Santa Lucía, *San Juan, Argentina* 126 C2
Santa Lucía, *Spain* 29 H4
Santa Lucía, *Uruguay* 126 C4
Santa Lucia Range, *U.S.A.* 111 J3
Santa Magdalena, I., *Mexico* 114 C2
Santa Margarita, *Argentina* 126 D3
Santa Margarita, *Mexico* 114 C2
Santa Margarita, *Spain* 36 B10
Santa Margarita, *U.S.A.* 112 K6
Santa Margarita →, *U.S.A.* 113 M9
Santa Margherita, *Italy* 32 D6
Santa María, *Argentina* 126 B2
Santa Maria, *Brazil* 127 B5
Santa Maria, *Phil.* 55 C4
Santa Maria, *Spain* 36 B9
Santa Maria, *Switz.* 23 C10
Santa Maria, *U.S.A.* 113 L6
Santa María →, *Mexico* 114 A3
Santa María, B. de, *Mexico* 114 B3
Santa Maria, C. de, *Portugal* 31 J3
Santa Maria Capua Vetere, *Italy* 35 A7
Santa Maria da Vitória, *Brazil* 123 D3
Santa María de Ipire, *Venezuela* 121 B4
Santa Maria di Leuca, C., *Italy* 35 C11
Santa Maria do Suaçuí, *Brazil* 123 E3
Santa Maria dos Marmelos, *Brazil* 125 B5
Santa María la Real de Nieva, *Spain* 30 D6
Santa Marta, *Colombia* 120 A3
Santa Marta, *Spain* 31 G4
Santa Marta, Ría de, *Spain* 30 B3
Santa Marta, Sierra Nevada de, *Colombia* 120 A3
Santa Marta Grande, C., *Brazil* 127 B6
Santa Maura = Levkás, *Greece* 39 L3
Santa Monica, *U.S.A.* 113 M8
Santa Olalla, *Huelva, Spain* 31 H4
Santa Olalla, *Toledo, Spain* 30 E6
Sant' Onofrio, *Italy* 35 D9
Santa Pola, *Spain* 29 G4
Santa Ponsa, *Spain* 36 B9
Santa Quitéria, *Brazil* 122 B3
Santa Rita, *U.S.A.* 111 K10
Santa Rita, *Guarico, Venezuela* 120 B4
Santa Rita, *Zulia, Venezuela* 120 A3
Santa Rita do Araquaia, *Brazil* 125 D7
Santa Rosa, *La Pampa, Argentina* 126 D3
Santa Rosa, *San Luis, Argentina* 126 C2
Santa Rosa, *Bolivia* 124 C4
Santa Rosa, *Brazil* 127 B5
Santa Rosa, *Colombia* 120 C4
Santa Rosa, *Ecuador* 120 D2
Santa Rosa, *Peru* 124 C3
Santa Rosa, *Calif., U.S.A.* 112 G4
Santa Rosa, *N. Mex., U.S.A.* 109 H2
Santa Rosa, *Venezuela* 120 C4
Santa Rosa de Cabal, *Colombia* 120 C2
Santa Rosa de Copán, *Honduras* 116 D2
Santa Rosa de Osos, *Colombia* 120 B2
Santa Rosa de Río Primero, *Argentina* 126 C3
Santa Rosa de Viterbo, *Colombia* 120 B3
Santa Rosa del Palmar, *Bolivia* 125 D5
Santa Rosa I., *Calif., U.S.A.* 113 M6
Santa Rosa I., *Fla., U.S.A.* 105 K2
Santa Rosa Range, *U.S.A.* 110 F5
Santa Rosalía, *Mexico* 114 B2
Santa Sofia, *Italy* 33 E8
Santa Sylvina, *Argentina* 126 B3
Santa Tecla = Nueva San Salvador, *El Salv.* 116 D2
Santa Teresa, *Argentina* 126 C3
Santa Teresa, *Brazil* 123 E3
Santa Teresa, *Mexico* 115 B5
Santa Teresa, *Venezuela* 121 C5
Santa Teresa di Riva, *Italy* 35 E8
Santa Teresa Gallura, *Italy* 34 A2
Santa Vitória, *Brazil* 123 E1

Santa Vitória do Palmar,
  Brazil 127 C5
Santa Ynez →, U.S.A. 113 L6
Santa Ynez Mts., U.S.A. .. 113 L6
Santa Ysabel, U.S.A. 113 M10
Santadi, Italy 34 C1
Santai, China 52 B5
Santaluz, Brazil 122 D4
Santana, Brazil 123 D3
Santana, Madeira 36 D3
Santana, Coxilha de, Brazil 127 C4
Santana do Ipanema, Brazil 122 C4
Santana do Livramento,
  Brazil 127 C4
Santanayi, Spain 36 B10
Santander, Colombia 120 C2
Santander, Spain 30 B7
Santander Jiménez, Mexico 115 C5
Santaquin, U.S.A. 110 G8
Santarém, Brazil 121 D7
Santarém, Portugal 31 F2
Santarém □, Portugal 31 F2
Santaren Channel,
  W. Indies 116 B4
Santee, U.S.A. 113 N10
Santéramo in Colle, Italy . 35 B9
Santerno →, Italy 33 D8
Santhia, Italy 32 C5
Santiago, Bolivia 125 D6
Santiago, Brazil 127 B5
Santiago, Chile 126 C1
Santiago, Panama 116 E3
Santiago, Peru 124 C2
Santiago, Phil. 55 C4
Santiago □, Chile 126 C1
Santiago →, Peru 120 D2
Santiago, C., Chile 128 D1
Santiago, Punta de,
  Eq. Guin. 79 E6
Santiago, Serranía de,
  Bolivia 125 D6
Santiago de Chuco, Peru . 124 B2
Santiago de Compostela,
  Spain 30 C2
Santiago de Cuba, Cuba .. 116 C4
Santiago de los Cabelleros,
  Dom. Rep. 117 C5
Santiago del Estero,
  Argentina 126 B3
Santiago del Estero □,
  Argentina 126 B3
Santiago del Teide,
  Canary Is. 36 F3
Santiago do Cacém,
  Portugal 31 G2
Santiago Ixcuintla, Mexico 114 C3
Santiago Papasquiaro,
  Mexico 114 B3
Santiaguillo, L. de, Mexico 114 C4
Santillana del Mar, Spain . 30 B6
Säntis, Switz. 23 B8
Santisteban del Puerto,
  Spain 29 G1
Santo →, Peru 124 B2
Santo Amaro, Brazil 123 D4
Santo Anastácio, Brazil .. 127 A5
Santo André, Brazil 127 A6
Santo Ângelo, Brazil 127 B5
Santo Antônio, Brazil 125 D6
Santo Antônio de Jesus,
  Brazil 123 D4
Santo Antônio do Içá,
  Brazil 120 D4
Santo Antônio do
  Leverger, Brazil 125 D6
Santo Corazón, Bolivia .. 125 D6
Santo Domingo,
  Dom. Rep. 117 C6
Santo Domingo,
  Baja Calif. N., Mexico . 114 A1
Santo Domingo,
  Baja Calif. S., Mexico . 114 B2
Santo Domingo, Nic. 116 D3
Santo Domingo de la
  Calzada, Spain 28 C2
Santo Domingo de los
  Colorados, Ecuador 120 D2
Santo Stéfano di Camastro,
  Italy 35 D7
Santo Stino di Livenza,
  Italy 33 C9
Santo Tirso, Portugal 30 D2
Santo Tomás, Mexico 114 A1
Santo Tomás, Peru 124 C3
Santo Tomé, Argentina .. 127 B4
Santo Tomé de Guayana =
  Ciudad Guayana,
  Venezuela 121 B5
Santoña, Spain 30 B7
Santos, Brazil 127 A6
Santos, Sierra de los, Spain 31 G5
Santos Dumont, Brazil .. 123 F3
Santpoort, Neths. 16 D5
Sanvignes-les-Mines, France 25 F11
Sanyuan, China 50 G5
Sanza Pombo, Angola 80 F3
São Anastácio, Brazil 127 A5
São Bartolomeu de
  Messines, Portugal 31 H2
São Benedito, Brazil 122 B3
São Bento, Brazil 122 B3
São Bento do Norte, Brazil 122 C4
São Bernado de Campo,
  Brazil 123 F2
São Borja, Brazil 127 B4

São Bras d'Alportel,
  Portugal 31 H3
São Caitano, Brazil 122 C4
São Carlos, Brazil 127 A6
São Cristóvão, Brazil 123 D4
São Domingos, Brazil 123 D2
São Domingos do
  Maranhão, Brazil 122 C3
São Félix, Brazil 123 D1
São Francisco, Brazil 123 E3
São Francisco →, Brazil . 122 D4
São Francisco do
  Maranhão, Brazil 122 C3
São Francisco do Sul,
  Brazil 127 B6
São Gabriel, Brazil 127 C5
São Gabriel da Palha,
  Brazil 123 E3
São Gonçalo, Brazil 123 F3
São Gotardo, Brazil 123 E2
Sao Hill, Tanzania 83 D4
São João da Boa Vista,
  Brazil 127 A6
São João da Pesqueira,
  Portugal 30 D3
São João da Ponte, Brazil 123 E3
São João del Rei, Brazil .. 123 F3
São João do Araguaia,
  Brazil 122 C2
São João do Paraíso, Brazil 123 E3
São João do Piauí, Brazil . 122 C3
São João dos Patos, Brazil 122 C3
São Joaquim da Barra,
  Brazil 123 F2
São Jorge, Pta. de, Madeira 36 D3
São José, B. de, Brazil .. 122 B3
São José da Laje, Brazil .. 122 C4
São José de Mipibu, Brazil 122 C4
São José do Peixe, Brazil . 122 C3
São José do Rio Prêto,
  Brazil 127 A6
São José dos Campos,
  Brazil 127 A6
São Leopoldo, Brazil 127 B5
São Lourenço, Brazil 123 F2
São Lourenço →, Brazil . 125 D6
São Lourenço, Pantanal do,
  Brazil 125 D6
São Lourenço, Pta. de,
  Madeira 36 D3
São Luís, Brazil 122 B3
São Luís do Curu, Brazil . 122 B4
São Luís Gonzaga, Brazil . 127 B5
São Marcos →, Brazil .. 123 E2
São Marcos, B. de, Brazil 122 B3
São Martinho, Portugal ... 30 E2
São Mateus, Brazil 123 E4
São Mateus →, Brazil ... 123 E4
São Miguel do Araguaia,
  Brazil 123 D1
São Miguel dos Campos,
  Brazil 122 C4
São Nicolau →, Brazil .. 122 C3
São Paulo, Brazil 127 A6
São Paulo □, Brazil 127 A6
São Paulo, I., Atl. Oc. ... 2 D8
São Paulo de Olivença,
  Brazil 120 D4
São Pedro do Sul, Portugal 30 E2
São Rafael, Brazil 122 C4
São Raimundo das
  Mangabeiras, Brazil ... 122 C2
São Raimundo Nonato,
  Brazil 122 C3
São Romão, Brazil 123 E2
São Roque, Madeira 36 D3
São Roque, C. de, Brazil . 122 C4
São Sebastião, I. de, Brazil 127 A6
São Sebastião do Paraíso,
  Brazil 127 A6
São Simão, Brazil 123 E1
São Teotónio, Portugal ... 31 H2
São Tomé, Atl. Oc. 70 F4
São Tomé, Brazil 122 C4
São Tomé, C. de, Brazil .. 123 F3
São Tomé & Principe ■,
  Africa 71 F4
São Vicente, Brazil 127 A6
São Vicente, Madeira 36 D2
São Vicente, C. de,
  Portugal 31 H2
Saona, I., Dom. Rep. 117 C6
Saône →, France 27 C8
Saône-et-Loire □, France . 25 F11
Saonek, Indonesia 57 E8
Saoura, O. →, Algeria .. 75 C4
Sapanca, Turkey 66 C4
Sapão →, Brazil 122 D2
Saparua, Indonesia 57 E7
Sapé, Brazil 122 C4
Sapele, Nigeria 79 D6
Sapelo I., U.S.A. 105 K5
Sapiéntza, Greece 39 N4
Sapone, Burkina Faso 79 C4
Saposoa, Peru 124 B2
Sapozhok, Russia 41 E12
Sappemeer, Neths. 16 B9
Sappho, U.S.A. 112 B2
Sapri, Italy 35 B8
Sapudi, Indonesia 57 G16
Sapulpa, U.S.A. 109 G7
Saqqez, Iran 64 B5
Sar Dasht, Iran 65 C6
Sar Gachīneh, Iran 65 D6

Sar Planina, Macedonia ... 38 G4
Sara, Burkina Faso 78 C4
Sara, Phil. 55 F5
Sara Buri, Thailand 58 E3
Sarāb, Iran 64 B5
Sarabadi, Iraq 64 C5
Sarada →, India 61 F12
Saragossa = Zaragoza,
  Spain 28 D4
Saraguro, Ecuador 120 D2
Sarajevo, Bos.-H. 21 M8
Saramacca □, Surinam .. 121 C6
Saramacca →, Surinam .. 121 B6
Saran, G., Indonesia 56 E4
Saranac Lake, U.S.A. 107 B10
Saranda, Tanzania 82 D3
Sarandí del Yi, Uruguay . 127 C4
Sarandí Grande, Uruguay 126 C4
Sarangani →, Phil. 55 J6
Sarangani Is., Phil. 55 J6
Sarangarh, India 61 J13
Saransk, Russia 41 D14
Sarapul, Russia 44 D6
Sarasota, U.S.A. 105 M4
Saratoga, Calif., U.S.A. . 112 H4
Saratoga, Wyo., U.S.A. . 110 F10
Saratoga Springs, U.S.A. . 107 C11
Saratov, Russia 41 F15
Saravane, Laos 58 E6
Sarawak □, Malaysia 56 D4
Saray, Turkey 67 D11
Saraya, Senegal 78 C2
Sarayköy, Turkey 66 E3
Sarayönü, Turkey 66 D5
Sarbāz, Iran 65 E9
Sarbīsheh, Iran 65 C8
Sarca →, Italy 32 C7
Sarda → = Sarada →,
  India 61 F12
Sardalas, Libya 75 C7
Sardarshahr, India 62 E6
Sardegna, Italy 34 B2
Sardhana, India 62 E7
Sardina, Pta., Canary Is. . 36 F4
Sardinata, Colombia 120 B3
Sardinia = Sardegna, Italy 34 B2
Sardis, Turkey 66 D3
Sārdūīyeh = Dar Mazār,
  Iran 65 D8
Saréyamou, Mali 78 B4
Sargent, U.S.A. 108 E5
Sargodha, Pakistan 62 C5
Sarh, Chad 73 G8
Sarhro, Djebel, Morocco . 74 B3
Sārī, Iran 65 B7
Sária, Greece 39 P10
Sarigöl, Turkey 66 D3
Sarikamiş, Turkey 67 C10
Sarikei, Malaysia 56 D4
Sarina, Australia 90 C4
Sariñena, Spain 28 D4
Sarita, U.S.A. 109 M6
Sariwŏn, N. Korea 51 E13
Sark, Chan. Is. 13 H5
Sarkad, Hungary 21 J11
Şarkışla, Turkey 66 D7
Şarköy, Turkey 66 C2
Sarlat-la-Canéda, France . 26 D5
Sarles, U.S.A. 108 A5
Sărmaşu, Romania 38 C7
Sarmi, Indonesia 57 E9
Sarmiento, Argentina 128 C3
Särna, Sweden 10 C7
Sarnano, Italy 33 E10
Sarnen, Switz. 22 C6
Sarnia, Canada 98 D3
Sarno, Italy 35 B7
Sarny, Ukraine 40 F5
Särö, Sweden 11 G5
Sarolangun, Indonesia .. 56 E2
Saronikós Kólpos, Greece . 39 M6
Saronno, Italy 32 C6
Saros Körfezi, Turkey 66 C2
Sárospatak, Hungary 21 G11
Sarova, Russia 41 D13
Sarpsborg, Norway 10 E5
Sarracín, Spain 28 C1
Sarralbe, France 25 D14
Sarre = Saar □, Europe . 25 C13
Sarre-Union, France 25 D14
Sarrebourg, France 25 D14
Sarreguemines, France .. 25 C14
Sarriá, Spain 30 C3
Sarrión, Spain 28 E4
Sarro, Mali 78 C3
Sarstedt, Germany 18 C5
Sartène, France 27 G12
Sarthe □, France 24 E7
Sarthe →, France 24 E6
Sartilly, France 24 D5
Sartynya, Russia 44 C7
Sárvár, Hungary 21 H6
Sarvestān, Iran 65 D7
Särviför →, Hungary 21 J8
Sárvíz →, Hungary 21 J8
Sarzeau, France 24 E4
Sarzana, Italy 32 D6
Sas van Gent, Neths. 17 F3
Sasabeneh, Ethiopia 68 F3
Sasaram, India 63 G11
Sasebo, Japan 49 H4

Saser, India 63 B7
Saskatchewan □, Canada . 101 C7
Saskatchewan →, Canada 101 C8
Saskatoon, Canada 101 C7
Saskylakh, Russia 45 B12
Sasnovka, Russia 41 C17
Sasolburg, S. Africa 85 D4
Sasovo, Russia 41 D12
Sassandra, Ivory C. 78 E3
Sassandra →, Ivory C. .. 78 E3
Sássari, Italy 34 B1
Sassenheim, Neths. 16 D5
Sassnitz, Germany 18 A9
Sasso Marconi, Italy 33 D8
Sassocorvaro, Italy 33 E9
Sassoferrato, Italy 33 E9
Sassuolo, Italy 32 D7
Sástago, Spain 28 D4
Sastown, Liberia 78 E3
Sasumua Dam, Kenya .. 82 C4
Sata-Misaki, Japan 49 J5
Satadougou, Mali 78 C2
Satanta, U.S.A. 109 G4
Satara, India 60 L8
Satilla →, U.S.A. 105 K5
Satipo, Peru 124 C3
Satmala Hills, India 60 J9
Satna, India 63 G9
Sator, Bos.-H. 33 D13
Sátoraljaújhely, Hungary . 21 G11
Satpura Ra., India 62 J7
Satrup, Germany 18 A5
Satsuna-Shotō, Japan .. 49 K5
Sattahip, Thailand 58 F3
Satui, Indonesia 56 E5
Satun, Thailand 59 J3
Saturnina →, Brazil 125 C6
Sauce, Argentina 126 C4
Sauceda, Mexico 114 B4
Saucillo, Mexico 114 B3
Sauda, Norway 9 G9
Saúde, Brazil 122 D3
Sauðarkrókur, Iceland .. 8 D4
Saudi Arabia ■, Asia 68 B3
Sauer →, Germany 17 J9
Saugeen →, Canada 106 B3
Saugerties, U.S.A. 107 D11
Saugues, France 26 D7
Saujon, France 26 C3
Sauk Centre, U.S.A. 108 C7
Sauk Rapids, U.S.A. 108 C7
Saül, Fr. Guiana 121 C7
Saulgau, Germany 19 G5
Saulieu, France 25 E11
Sault, France 27 D9
Sault Ste. Marie, Canada . 98 C3
Sault Ste. Marie, U.S.A. . 104 B3
Saumlaki, Indonesia 57 F8
Saumur, France 24 E6
Saunders C., N.Z. 87 L3
Saunders I., Antarctica .. 5 B1
Saunders Point, Australia . 89 E4
Saurbær,
  Borgarfjarðarsýsla,
  Iceland 8 D3
Saurbær, Eyjafjarðarsýsla,
  Iceland 8 D4
Sauri, Nigeria 79 C6
Saurimo, Angola 80 F4
Sausalito, U.S.A. 112 H4
Sauri, Colombia 120 B2
Sauveterre-de-Béarn,
  France 26 E3
Sauzé-Vaussais, France .. 26 B4
Savá, Honduras 116 C2
Sava →, Serbia 21 L10
Savage, U.S.A. 108 B2
Savage I. = Niue, Cook Is. 93 J11
Savai'i, W. Samoa 87 A12
Savalou, Benin 79 D5
Savane, Mozam. 83 F4
Savanna, U.S.A. 108 D9
Savanna la Mar, Jamaica . 116 C4
Savannah, Ga., U.S.A. .. 105 J5
Savannah, Mo., U.S.A. .. 108 F7
Savannah, Tenn., U.S.A. . 105 H1
Savannah →, U.S.A. 105 J5
Savannakhet, Laos 58 D5
Savant L., Canada 98 B1
Savant Lake, Canada 98 B1
Savanur, India 60 M9
Savé, Benin 79 D5
Save →, France 26 E5
Save →, Mozam. 85 C5
Sāveh, Iran 65 C6
Savelugu, Ghana 79 D4
Savenay, France 24 E5
Saverdun, France 26 E5
Saverne, France 25 D14
Savièse, Switz. 22 D4
Savigliano, Italy 32 D4
Savigny-sur-Braye, France 24 E7
Saviñao, Spain 30 C3
Savio →, Italy 33 D9
Savognin, Switz. 23 C9
Savoie □, France 27 C10
Savona, Italy 32 D5
Sawahlunto, Indonesia .. 56 E2
Sawai, Indonesia 57 E7
Sawai Madhopur, India . 62 F7
Sawang Daen Din,
  Thailand 58 D4
Sawankhalok, Thailand .. 58 D2

Sawara, Japan 49 G10
Sawatch Mts., U.S.A. 111 G10
Sawel, U.K. 15 B4
Sawi, Thailand 59 G2
Sawmills, Zimbabwe 83 F2
Sawu, Indonesia 57 F6
Sawu Sea, Indonesia 57 F6
Saxby →, Australia 90 B3
Saxon, Switz. 22 D4
Saxony, Lower =
  Niedersachsen □,
  Germany 18 C5
Saxton, U.S.A. 106 F6
Say, Niger 79 C5
Saya, Nigeria 79 D5
Sayabec, Canada 99 C6
Sayaboury, Laos 58 C3
Sayán, Peru 124 C2
Sayan, Vostochnyy, Russia 45 D10
Sayan, Zapadnyy, Russia . 45 D10
Sayasan, Russia 43 E12
Saydā, Lebanon 69 B4
Sayhan-Ovoo, Mongolia . 50 B2
Sayhandulaan, Mongolia . 50 B5
Sayhut, Yemen 68 D5
Saynshand, Mongolia .. 50 B6
Sayre, Okla., U.S.A. 109 H5
Sayre, Pa., U.S.A. 107 E8
Sayula, Mexico 114 D4
Sazin, Pakistan 63 B5
Sazlika →, Bulgaria 39 H8
Sbeïtla, Tunisia 75 A6
Scaër, France 24 D3
Scafell Pikes, U.K. 12 C4
Scalea, Italy 35 C8
Scalpay, U.K. 14 D2
Scandia, Canada 100 C6
Scandiano, Italy 32 D7
Scandinavia, Europe 8 E12
Scansano, Italy 33 F8
Scapa Flow, U.K. 14 C5
Scappoose, U.S.A. 112 E4
Scarborough, Trin. & Tob. 117 D7
Scarborough, U.K. 12 C7
Scebeli, Wabi →,
  Somali Rep. 68 G3
Šćedro, Croatia 33 E13
Scenic, U.S.A. 108 D3
Schaal See, Germany .. 18 B6
Schaan, Liech. 23 B9
Schaesberg, Neths. 17 G8
Schaffen, Belgium 17 G6
Schaffhausen, Switz. 23 A7
Schaffhausen □, Switz. .. 23 A7
Schagen, Neths. 16 C5
Schaijk, Neths. 16 E7
Schalkhaar, Neths. 16 D8
Schalkwijk, Neths. 16 E6
Schangnau, Switz. 22 C5
Schänis, Switz. 23 B8
Schärding, Austria 20 G3
Scharhörn, Germany 18 B4
Scharnitz, Austria 19 H7
Scheessel, Germany 18 B5
Schefferville, Canada 99 B6
Schelde →, Belgium 17 F4
Schell Creek Ra., U.S.A. .. 110 G6
Schenectady, U.S.A. 107 D11
Scherfede, Germany 18 D5
Scherpenheuvel, Belgium . 17 G5
Scherpenisse, Neths. 17 E4
Scherpenzeel, Neths. 16 D7
Schesaplana, Switz. 23 B9
Schesslitz, Germany 19 F7
Scheveningen, Neths. 16 D4
Schiedam, Neths. 16 E4
Schiermonnikoog, Neths. . 16 B8
Schiers, Switz. 23 C9
Schifferstadt, Germany .. 19 F4
Schifflange, Lux. 17 K8
Schijndel, Neths. 17 E6
Schiltigheim, France 25 D14
Schio, Italy 33 C8
Schipbeek, Neths. 16 D8
Schipluiden, Neths. 16 E4
Schirmeck, France 25 D14
Schlei →, Germany 18 A5
Schleiden, Germany 18 E2
Schleiz, Germany 18 E7
Schleswig, Germany 18 A5
Schleswig-Holstein □,
  Germany 18 A5
Schlieren, Switz. 23 B6
Schlüchtern, Germany .. 19 E5
Schmalkalden, Germany . 18 E6
Schmölln, Brandenburg,
  Germany 18 B10
Schmölln, Thüringen,
  Germany 18 E8
Schneeberg, Austria 21 H5
Schneeberg, Germany 18 E8
Schoenberg, Belgium 17 H8
Schofield, U.S.A. 108 C10
Scholls, U.S.A. 112 E4
Schönberg,
  Mecklenburg-Vorpommern,
  Germany 18 B6
Schönberg,
  Schleswig-Holstein,
  Germany 18 A6
Schönebeck, Germany .. 18 C7
Schönenwerd, Switz. 22 B5
Schongau, Germany 19 H6
Schöningen, Germany .. 18 C6
Schoondijke, Neths. 17 F3

Schoonebeek, Neths. 16 C9
Schoonhoven, Neths. 16 E5
Schoorl, Neths. 16 C5
Schortens, Germany 18 B3
Schoten, Belgium 17 F5
Schouten I., Australia 90 G4
Schouten Is. = Supriori, Kepulauan, Indonesia . 57 E9
Schouwen, Neths. 17 E3
Schramberg, Germany 19 G4
Schrankogl, Austria 19 H7
Schreckhorn, Switz. 22 C6
Schreiber, Canada 98 C2
Schrobenhausen, Germany 19 G7
Schruns, Austria 19 H5
Schuler, Canada 101 C6
Schuls, Switz. 23 C10
Schumacher, Canada 98 C3
Schüpfen, Switz. 22 B4
Schüpfheim, Switz. 22 C6
Schurz, U.S.A. 110 G4
Schuyler, U.S.A. 108 E6
Schuylkill Haven, U.S.A. . 107 F8
Schwabach, Germany 19 F7
Schwäbisch Gmünd, Germany 19 G5
Schwäbisch Hall, Germany 19 F5
Schwäbische Alb, Germany 19 G5
Schwabmünchen, Germany 19 G6
Schwanden, Switz. 23 C8
Schwandorf, Germany 19 F8
Schwaner, Pegunungan, Indonesia 56 E4
Schwarmstedt, Germany .. 18 C5
Schwärze, Germany 18 C9
Schwarze Elster →, Germany 18 D8
Schwarzenberg, Germany . 18 E8
Schwarzenburg, Switz. ... 22 C4
Schwarzwald, Germany ... 19 H4
Schwaz, Austria 19 H7
Schwedt, Germany 18 B10
Schweinfurt, Germany 19 E6
Schweizer Mittelland, Switz. 22 C4
Schweizer-Reneke, S. Africa 84 D4
Schwenningen, Germany .. 19 G4
Schwerin, Germany 18 B7
Schweriner See, Germany . 18 B7
Schwetzingen, Germany .. 19 F4
Schwyz, Switz. 23 B7
Schwyz □, Switz. 23 B7
Sciacca, Italy 34 E6
Scicli, Italy 35 F7
Scilla, Italy 35 D8
Scilly, Isles of, U.K. 13 H1
Ścinawa, Poland 20 D6
Scioto →, U.S.A. 104 F4
Scobey, U.S.A. 108 A2
Scone, Australia 91 E5
Scordia, Italy 35 E7
Scoresbysund, Greenland . 4 B6
Scorno, Punta dello, Italy . 34 A1
Scotia, Calif., U.S.A. 110 F1
Scotia, N.Y., U.S.A. 107 D11
Scotia Sea, Antarctica ... 5 B18
Scotland, U.S.A. 108 D6
Scotland □, U.K. 14 E5
Scotland Neck, U.S.A. ... 105 G7
Scott, C., Australia 88 B4
Scott City, U.S.A. 108 F4
Scott Glacier, Antarctica . 5 C8
Scott I., Antarctica 5 C11
Scott Inlet, Canada 97 A12
Scott Is., Canada 100 C3
Scott L., Canada 101 B7
Scott Reef, Australia 88 B3
Scottburgh, S. Africa 85 E5
Scottdale, U.S.A. 106 F5
Scottsbluff, U.S.A. 108 E3
Scottsboro, U.S.A. 105 H2
Scottsburg, U.S.A. 104 F3
Scottsdale, Australia 90 G4
Scottsville, Ky., U.S.A. .. 105 G2
Scottsville, N.Y., U.S.A. . 106 C7
Scottville, U.S.A. 104 D2
Scranton, U.S.A. 107 E9
Scugog, L., Canada 106 B6
Scunthorpe, U.K. 12 D7
Scuol, Switz. 23 C10
Scusciuban, Somali Rep. .. 68 E5
Scutari = Üsküdar, Turkey 39 H11
Seabra, Brazil 123 D3
Seabrook, L., Australia ... 89 F2
Seaford, U.S.A. 104 F8
Seaforth, Canada 98 D3
Seagraves, U.S.A. 109 J3
Seal →, Canada 101 B10
Seal Cove, Canada 99 C8
Seal L., Canada 99 B7
Sealy, U.S.A. 109 L6
Searchlight, U.S.A. 113 K12
Searcy, U.S.A. 109 H9
Searles L., U.S.A. 113 K9
Seaside, Calif., U.S.A. ... 112 J5
Seaside, Oreg., U.S.A. ... 112 E3
Seaspray, Australia 91 F4
Seattle, U.S.A. 112 C4
Seaview Ra., Australia ... 90 B4
Sebastián Vizcaíno, B., Mexico 114 B2
Sebastopol = Sevastopol, Ukraine 42 D5
Sebastopol, U.S.A. 112 G4

Sebderat, Eritrea 77 D4
Sebdou, Algeria 75 B4
Seben, Turkey 66 C4
Sebewaing, U.S.A. 104 D4
Sebha = Sabhah, Libya .. 73 C7
Sébi, Mali 78 B4
Şebinkarahisar, Turkey .. 42 F8
Sebiş, Romania 38 C5
Sebkhet Te-n-Dghâmcha, Mauritania 78 B1
Sebkra Azzel Mati, Algeria 75 C5
Sebkra Mekerghene, Algeria 75 C5
Sebnitz, Germany 18 E10
Sebou, Oued →, Morocco . 74 B3
Sebring, Fla., U.S.A. 105 M5
Sebring, Ohio, U.S.A. 106 F3
Sebringville, Canada 106 C3
Sebta = Ceuta, Morocco . 74 A3
Sebuku, Indonesia 56 E5
Sebuku, Teluk, Malaysia . 56 D5
Secchia →, Italy 32 C8
Sechelt, Canada 100 D4
Sechura, Peru 124 B1
Sechura, Desierto de, Peru 124 B1
Seclin, France 25 B10
Secondigny, France 24 F6
Secretary I., N.Z. 87 L1
Secunderabad, India 60 L11
Sécure →, Bolivia 125 D5
Sedalia, U.S.A. 108 F8
Sedan, Australia 91 E2
Sedan, France 25 C11
Sedan, U.S.A. 109 G6
Sedano, Spain 28 C1
Seddon, N.Z. 87 J5
Seddonville, N.Z. 87 J4
Sedeh, Fārs, Iran 65 D7
Sedeh, Khorāsān, Iran ... 65 C8
Séderot, Israel 69 D3
Sedgewick, Canada 100 C6
Sedhiou, Senegal 78 C1
Sedičany, Czech. 20 F4
Sedico, Italy 33 B9
Sedley, Canada 101 C8
Sedova, Pik, Russia 44 B6
Sedrata, Algeria 75 A6
Sedro-Woolley, U.S.A. ... 112 B4
Sedrun, Switz. 23 C7
Šeduva, Lithuania 40 D3
Seebad Ahlbeck, Germany 18 B10
Seehausen, Germany 18 C7
Seeheim, Namibia 84 D2
Seekoei →, S. Africa 84 E4
Seelaw, Germany 18 C10
Sées, France 24 D7
Seesen, Germany 18 D6
Sefadu, S. Leone 78 D2
Seferihisar, Turkey 66 D2
Séfeto, Mali 78 C3
Sefrou, Morocco 74 B4
Sefwi Bekwai, Ghana 78 D4
Segamat, Malaysia 59 L4
Segarcea, Romania 38 E6
Segbwema, S. Leone 78 D2
Seget, Indonesia 57 E8
Seggueur, O. →, Algeria . 75 B5
Segonzac, France 26 C3
Segorbe, Spain 28 F4
Ségou, Mali 78 C3
Segovia = Coco →, Cent. Amer. 116 D3
Segovia, Colombia 120 B3
Segovia, Spain 30 E6
Segovia □, Spain 30 E6
Segré, France 24 E6
Segre →, Spain 28 D5
Séguéla, Ivory C. 78 D3
Seguin, U.S.A. 109 L6
Segundo →, Argentina ... 126 C3
Segura →, Spain 29 G4
Segura, Sierra de, Spain .. 29 G2
Seh Qal'eh, Iran 65 C8
Sehitwa, Botswana 84 C3
Sehore, India 62 H7
Sehwan, Pakistan 62 F2
Şeica Mare, Romania 38 C7
Seiland, Norway 8 A17
Seiling, U.S.A. 109 G5
Seille →, France 27 B8
Seilles, Belgium 17 G6
Sein, I. de, France 24 D2
Seinäjoki →, Finland 8 E17
Seine →, France 24 C7
Seine, B. de la, France ... 24 C6
Seine-et-Marne □, France . 25 D9
Seine-Maritime □, France . 24 C7
Seine-St.-Denis □, France . 25 D9
Seistan, Iran 65 D9
Sejerø, Denmark 11 J5
Sejerø Bugt, Denmark 11 J5
Seka, Ethiopia 77 F4
Sekayu, Indonesia 56 E2
Seke, Tanzania 82 C3
Sekenke, Tanzania 82 C3
Sekken Veøy, Norway 10 B1
Sekondi-Takoradi, Ghana . 78 E4
Sekuma, Botswana 84 C3
Selah, U.S.A. 110 C3
Selama, Malaysia 59 K3
Selárgius, Italy 34 C2
Selaru, Indonesia 57 F8
Selb, Germany 19 E8
Selby, U.K. 12 D6

Selby, U.S.A. 108 C4
Selca, Croatia 33 E13
Selçuk, Turkey 66 E2
Selden, U.S.A. 108 F4
Sele →, Italy 35 B7
Selemdzha →, Russia 45 D13
Selenga = Selenge Mörön →, Asia 54 A5
Selenge Mörön →, Asia .. 54 A5
Selenica, Albania 39 J2
Selenter See, Germany ... 18 A6
Sélestat, France 25 D14
Seletan, Tg., Indonesia .. 56 E4
Seletin, Romania 38 B8
Selfridge, U.S.A. 108 B4
Sélibabi, Mauritania 78 B2
Seliger, Oz., Russia 40 C8
Seligman, U.S.A. 111 J7
Selima, El Wâhât el, Sudan 76 C2
Selinda Spillway, Botswana 84 B3
Selinoús, Greece 39 M4
Selizharovo, Russia 40 C8
Seljord, Norway 10 E2
Selkirk, Canada 101 C9
Selkirk, U.K. 14 F6
Selkirk I., Canada 101 C9
Selkirk Mts., Canada 100 C5
Selles-sur-Cher, France ... 25 E8
Selliá, Greece 37 D6
Sellières, France 25 F12
Sells, U.S.A. 111 L8
Selma, Ala., U.S.A. 105 J2
Selma, Calif., U.S.A. 111 H4
Selma, N.C., U.S.A. 105 H6
Selmer, U.S.A. 105 H1
Selongey, France 25 E12
Selowandoma Falls, Zimbabwe 83 G3
Selpele, Indonesia 57 E8
Selsey Bill, U.K. 13 G7
Seltz, France 25 D15
Selu, Indonesia 57 F8
Sélune →, France 24 D5
Selva, Argentina 126 B3
Selva, Italy 33 B8
Selva, Spain 28 D6
Selvas, Brazil 124 B4
Selwyn, Australia 90 C3
Selwyn L., Canada 101 A8
Selwyn Ra., Australia 90 C3
Seman →, Albania 39 J2
Semara, W. Sahara 74 C2
Semarang, Indonesia 57 G14
Semau, Indonesia 57 F6
Sembabule, Uganda 82 C3
Sémé, Senegal 78 B2
Semeih, Sudan 77 E3
Semenov, Russia 41 C14
Semenovka, Ukraine 40 E8
Semenovka, Ukraine 42 B5
Semeru, Indonesia 57 H15
Semey = Semipalatinsk, Kazakhstan 44 D9
Semiluki, Russia 41 F11
Seminoe Reservoir, U.S.A. 110 E10
Seminole, Okla., U.S.A. .. 109 H6
Seminole, Tex., U.S.A. ... 109 J3
Semiozernoye, Kazakhstan 44 D7
Semipalatinsk, Kazakhstan 44 D9
Semirara Is., Phil. 55 F4
Semisopochnoi I., U.S.A. . 96 C2
Semitau, Indonesia 56 D4
Semiyarskoye, Kazakhstan 44 D8
Semmering Pass, Austria . 21 H5
Semnān, Iran 65 C7
Semnān □, Iran 65 C7
Semois →, Europe 17 J5
Semporna, Malaysia 57 D5
Semuda, Indonesia 56 E4
Semur-en-Auxois, France . 25 E11
Sena, Bolivia 124 C4
Senā, Iran 65 D6
Sena, Mozam. 83 F3
Sena →, Bolivia 124 C4
Sena Madureira, Brazil ... 124 B4
Senador Pompeu, Brazil .. 122 C4
Senaja, Malaysia 56 C5
Senaki, Georgia 43 E10
Senanga, Zambia 84 B3
Senatobia, U.S.A. 109 H10
Sendafa, Ethiopia 77 F4
Sendai, Kagoshima, Japan 49 J5
Sendai, Miyagi, Japan ... 48 E10
Sendai-Wan, Japan 48 E10
Sendenhorst, Germany ... 18 D3
Seneca, Oreg., U.S.A. 110 D4
Seneca, S.C., U.S.A. 105 H4
Seneca Falls, U.S.A. 107 D8
Seneca L., U.S.A. 106 D8
Seneffe, Belgium 17 G4
Senegal ■, W. Afr. 78 C2
Senegal →, W. Afr. 78 B1
Senegambia, Africa 70 E2
Senekal, S. Africa 85 D4
Senftenberg, Germany ... 18 D10
Senga Hill, Zambia 83 D3
Senge Khambab = Indus →, Pakistan 62 G2
Sengerema □, Tanzania .. 82 C3
Sengiley, Russia 41 E16
Sengkang, Indonesia 57 E6
Sengua →, Zimbabwe ... 83 F2
Senguerr →, Argentina .. 128 C3

Senhor-do-Bonfim, Brazil . 122 D3
Senica, Slovak Rep. 20 G7
Senigállia, Italy 33 E10
Senio →, Italy 33 D9
Senirkent, Turkey 66 D4
Senise, Italy 35 B9
Senj, Croatia 33 D11
Senja, Norway 8 B14
Senlis, France 25 C9
Senmonorom, Cambodia . 58 F6
Sennâr, Sudan 77 E3
Senne →, Belgium 17 G4
Senneterre, Canada 98 C4
Senniquelle, Liberia 78 D3
Senno, Belorussia 40 D6
Sennori, Italy 34 B1
Seno, Laos 58 D5
Senonches, France 24 D8
Senorbì, Italy 34 C2
Senožeče, Slovenia 33 C11
Sens, France 25 D10
Senta, Serbia 21 K10
Sentani, Indonesia 57 E10
Sentery, Zaïre 82 D2
Sentinel, U.S.A. 111 K7
Sentolo, Indonesia 57 G14
Senya Beraku, Ghana 79 D4
Seo de Urgel, Spain 28 C6
Seohara, India 63 E8
Seoni, India 63 H8
Seoul = Sŏul, S. Korea .. 51 F14
Separation Point, Canada . 99 B8
Sepīdān, Iran 65 D7
Sepo-ri, N. Korea 51 E14
Sepone, Laos 58 D6
Sept-Îles, Canada 99 B6
Septemvri, Bulgaria 38 G7
Sepúlveda, Spain 30 D7
Sequeros, Spain 30 E4
Sequim, U.S.A. 112 B3
Sequoia National Park, U.S.A. 111 H4
Serafimovich, Russia 43 B10
Seraing, Belgium 17 G7
Seraja, Indonesia 59 L7
Serakhis →, Cyprus 37 D11
Seram, Indonesia 57 E7
Seram Laut, Kepulauan, Indonesia 57 E8
Seram Sea, Indonesia 57 E7
Serang, Indonesia 57 G12
Serasan, Indonesia 59 L7
Seravezza, Italy 32 C7
Serbia □, Yugoslavia ... 21 M11
Serdo, Ethiopia 77 E5
Serdobsk, Russia 41 E14
Serëdka, Russia 40 B6
Sereflikoçhisar, Turkey .. 66 D5
Seregno, Italy 32 C6
Seremban, Malaysia 59 L3
Serengeti □, Tanzania .. 82 C3
Serengeti Plain, Tanzania . 82 C3
Serenje, Zambia 83 E3
Sereth = Siret →, Romania 38 D11
Sergach, Russia 41 D14
Serge →, Spain 28 D5
Sergino, Russia 44 C7
Sergipe □, Brazil 122 D4
Sergiyev Posad, Russia ... 41 C11
Seria, Brunei 56 D4
Serian, Malaysia 56 D4
Seriate, Italy 32 C6
Seribu, Kepulauan, Indonesia 56 F3
Sérifontaine, France 25 C8
Sérifos, Greece 39 M7
Sérignan, France 26 E7
Serik, Turkey 66 E4
Seringapatam Reef, Australia 88 B3
Sermaize-les-Bains, France 25 D11
Sermata, Indonesia 57 F7
Sérmide, Italy 33 C8
Sernovodsk, Russia 41 E17
Serny Zavod, Turkmenistan 44 F6
Serón, Spain 29 H2
Serós, Spain 28 D5
Serov, Russia 44 D7
Serowe, Botswana 84 C4
Serpa, Portugal 31 H3
Serpeddi, Punta, Italy 34 C2
Serpentara, Italy 34 C2
Serpentine, Australia 89 F2
Serpentine Lakes, Australia 89 E4
Serpis →, Spain 29 G4
Serpukhov, Russia 41 D10
Serra do Navio, Brazil ... 121 C7
Serra San Bruno, Italy ... 35 D9
Serra Talhada, Brazil 122 C4
Serracapriola, Italy 35 A8
Serradilla, Spain 30 F4
Sérrai, Greece 39 H6
Serramanna, Italy 34 C1
Serrat, C., Tunisia 75 A6
Serre-Ponçon, L. de, France 27 D10
Serres, France 27 D9
Serrezuela, Argentina 126 C2
Serrinha, Brazil 123 D4
Serrita, Brazil 122 C4
Sersale, Italy 35 C9
Sertã, Portugal 30 F2
Sertânia, Brazil 122 C4
Sertanópolis, Brazil 127 A5
Sêrtar, China 52 A3

Sertig, Switz. 23 C9
Serua, Indonesia 57 F8
Serui, Indonesia 57 E9
Serule, Botswana 84 C4
Sérvia, Greece 39 J4
Sese Is., Uganda 82 C3
Sesepe, Indonesia 57 E7
Sesfontein, Namibia 84 B1
Sesheke, Zambia 84 B3
Sesia →, Italy 32 C5
Sesimbra, Portugal 31 G1
Sessa Aurunca, Italy 34 A6
S'estañol, Spain 36 B9
Sesto San Giovanni, Italy . 32 C6
Sestri Levante, Italy 32 D6
Sestrières, Italy 32 D3
Sestu, Italy 34 C2
Sesvenna, Switz. 23 C10
Setana, Japan 48 C9
Sète, France 26 E7
Sete Lagôas, Brazil 123 E3
Sétif, Algeria 75 A6
Seto, Japan 49 G8
Setonaikai, Japan 49 G6
Settat, Morocco 74 B3
Setté-Cama, Gabon 80 E1
Séttimo Tor, Italy 32 C4
Setting L., Canada 101 B9
Settle, U.K. 12 C5
Settlement Pt., Bahamas . 105 M6
Setto Calende, Italy 32 C5
Setúbal, Portugal 31 G2
Setúbal □, Portugal 31 G2
Setúbal, B. de, Portugal .. 31 G2
Seugne →, France 26 C3
Seulimeum, Indonesia 56 C1
Seuzach, Switz. 23 A7
Sevan, Armenia 43 F11
Sevan, Ozero, Armenia ... 43 F11
Sevastopol, Ukraine 42 D5
Sevelen, Switz. 23 B8
Seven Emu, Australia 90 B2
Seven Sisters, Canada 100 C3
Sevenum, Neths. 17 F8
Sever →, Spain 31 F3
Séverac-le-Château, France 26 D7
Severn →, Canada 98 A2
Severn →, U.K. 13 F5
Severn L., Canada 98 B1
Severnaya Zemlya, Russia 45 B10
Severo-Kurilsk, Russia ... 45 D16
Severo-Yeniseyskiy, Russia 45 C10
Severodonetsk, Ukraine .. 43 B8
Severodvinsk, Russia 44 C4
Sevier, U.S.A. 111 G7
Sevier →, U.S.A. 111 G7
Sevier L., U.S.A. 110 G7
Sevilla, Colombia 120 C2
Sevilla, Spain 31 H5
Sevilla □, Spain 31 H5
Seville = Sevilla, Spain .. 31 H5
Sevnica, Slovenia 33 B12
Sèvre-Nantaise →, France 24 E5
Sèvre-Niortaise →, France 26 B3
Sevsk, Russia 40 E9
Seward, Alaska, U.S.A. .. 96 B5
Seward, Nebr., U.S.A. ... 108 E6
Seward Pen., U.S.A. 96 B3
Sewell, Chile 126 C1
Sewer, Indonesia 57 F8
Sewickley, U.S.A. 106 F4
Sexbierum, Neths. 16 B6
Sexsmith, Canada 100 B5
Seychelles ■, Ind. Oc. ... 47 K9
Seyðisfjörður, Iceland 8 D7
Seydvān, Iran 64 B5
Seyfe Gölü, Turkey 66 D6
Seyhan Barajı, Turkey ... 66 E6
Seyitgazi, Turkey 66 D4
Seym →, Ukraine 40 F8
Seymchan, Russia 45 C16
Seymour, Australia 91 F4
Seymour, S. Africa 85 E4
Seymour, Conn., U.S.A. . 107 E11
Seymour, Ind., U.S.A. ... 104 F3
Seymour, Tex., U.S.A. ... 109 J5
Seymour, Wis., U.S.A. ... 104 C1
Seyne, France 27 D10
Seyssel, France 27 C9
Sézanne, France 25 D10
Sezze, Italy 34 A6
Sfax, Tunisia 75 B7
Sfîntu Gheorghe, Romania 38 E7
Sfîntu Gheorghe, Brațul →, Romania 38 E12
Sha Xi →, China 53 D12
Sha Xian, China 53 D11
Shaanxi □, China 50 G5
Shaba □, Zaïre 82 D2
Shabunda, Zaïre 82 C2
Shache, China 54 C2
Shackleton Ice Shelf, Antarctica 5 C8
Shackleton Inlet, Antarctica 5 E11
Shādegān, Iran 65 D6
Shadi, China 53 D10
Shadi, India 63 C7
Shadrinsk, Russia 44 D7
Shaffa, Nigeria 79 C7
Shafter, Calif., U.S.A. ... 113 K7
Shafter, Tex., U.S.A. 109 L2
Shaftesbury, U.K. 13 F5
Shagamu, Nigeria 79 D5

Shagram, *Pakistan*	63	A5
Shah Bunder, *Pakistan*	62	G2
Shahabad, *Punjab, India*	62	D7
Shahabad, *Raj., India*	62	G7
Shahabad, *Ut. P., India*	63	F8
Shahadpur, *Pakistan*	62	G3
Shahba, *Syria*	69	C5
Shahdād, *Iran*	65	D8
Shahdadkot, *Pakistan*	62	F2
Shahe, *China*	50	F8
Shahganj, *India*	63	F10
Shahgarh, *India*	60	F6
Shaḩḩāt, *Libya*	73	B9
Shahjahanpur, *India*	63	F8
Shahpur, *India*	62	H7
Shahpur, *Pakistan*	62	E3
Shahpura, *India*	63	H9
Shahr Kord, *Iran*	65	C6
Shāhrakht, *Iran*	65	C9
Shahrig, *Pakistan*	62	D2
Shahukou, *China*	50	D7
Shaikhabad, *Afghan.*	62	B3
Shajapur, *India*	62	H7
Shakargarh, *India*	62	C6
Shakawe, *Botswana*	84	B3
Shaker Heights, *U.S.A.*	106	E3
Shakhty, *Russia*	43	C9
Shakhunya, *Russia*	41	C15
Shaki, *Nigeria*	79	D5
Shakopee, *U.S.A.*	108	C8
Shala, L., *Ethiopia*	77	F4
Shallow Lake, *Canada*	106	B3
Shaluli Shan, *China*	52	B2
Shām, *Iran*	65	E8
Shamâl Dârfûr □, *Sudan*	77	D2
Shamâl Kordofân □, *Sudan*	77	D2
Shamattawa, *Canada*	101	B10
Shamattawa →, *Canada*	98	A2
Shambe, *Sudan*	77	F3
Shambu, *Ethiopia*	77	F4
Shamîl, *Iran*	65	E8
Shamkhor, *Azerbaijan*	43	F12
Shāmkūh, *Iran*	65	C8
Shamli, *India*	62	E7
Shamo = Gobi, *Asia*	50	C5
Shamo, L., *Ethiopia*	77	F4
Shamokin, *U.S.A.*	107	F8
Shamrock, *U.S.A.*	109	H4
Shamva, *Zimbabwe*	83	F3
Shan □, *Burma*	61	J21
Shan Xian, *China*	50	G9
Shanan →, *Ethiopia*	77	F5
Shanchengzhen, *China*	51	C13
Shāndak, *Iran*	65	D9
Shandon, *U.S.A.*	112	K6
Shandong □, *China*	51	F10
Shandong Bandao, *China*	51	F11
Shang Xian, *China*	50	H5
Shangalowe, *Zaïre*	83	E2
Shangani →, *Zimbabwe*	83	F2
Shangbancheng, *China*	51	D10
Shangcai, *China*	53	A10
Shangcheng, *China*	53	B10
Shangchuan Dao, *China*	53	G9
Shangdu, *China*	50	D7
Shanggao, *China*	53	C10
Shanghai, *China*	53	B13
Shanghang, *China*	53	E11
Shanghe, *China*	51	F9
Shangjin, *China*	53	A8
Shanglin, *China*	52	F7
Shangnan, *China*	50	H6
Shangqiu, *China*	50	G8
Shangrao, *China*	53	C11
Shangshui, *China*	50	H8
Shangsi, *China*	52	F6
Shangyou, *China*	53	E10
Shangzhi, *China*	51	B14
Shanhetun, *China*	51	B14
Shani, *Nigeria*	79	C7
Shaniko, *U.S.A.*	110	D3
Shannon, *Greenland*	4	B7
Shannon, *N.Z.*	87	J5
Shannon →, *Ireland*	15	D2
Shansi = Shanxi □, *China*	50	F7
Shantar, Ostrov Bolshoy, *Russia*	45	D14
Shantipur, *India*	63	H13
Shantou, *China*	53	F11
Shantung = Shandong □, *China*	51	F10
Shanxi □, *China*	50	F7
Shanyang, *China*	50	H5
Shanyin, *China*	50	E7
Shaoguan, *China*	53	E9
Shaowu, *China*	53	D11
Shaoxing, *China*	53	C13
Shaoyang, *Hunan, China*	53	D8
Shaoyang, *Hunan, China*	53	D8
Shapinsay, *U.K.*	14	B6
Shaqra', *Si. Arabia*	64	E5
Shaqrā', *Yemen*	68	E4
Sharafa, *Sudan*	77	E2
Sharbot Lake, *Canada*	107	B8
Shari, *Japan*	48	C12
Sharjah = Ash Shāriqah, *U.A.E.*	65	E7
Shark B., *Australia*	89	E1
Sharm el Sheikh, *Egypt*	76	B3
Sharon, *Mass., U.S.A.*	107	D13
Sharon, *Pa., U.S.A.*	106	E4
Sharon Springs, *U.S.A.*	108	F4
Sharp Pt., *Australia*	90	A3
Sharpe, L., *Canada*	101	C10
Sharpsville, *U.S.A.*	106	E4
Sharq el Istiwa'iya □, *Sudan*	77	F3
Sharya, *Russia*	41	B14
Shasha, *Ethiopia*	77	F4
Shashemene, *Ethiopia*	77	F4
Shashi, *Botswana*	85	C4
Shashi, *China*	53	B9
Shashi →, *Africa*	83	G2
Shasta, Mt., *U.S.A.*	110	F2
Shasta L., *U.S.A.*	110	F2
Shatsk, *Russia*	41	D12
Shatt al'Arab →, *Iraq*	65	D6
Shattuck, *U.S.A.*	109	G5
Shatura, *Russia*	41	D11
Shaumyani, *Georgia*	43	F11
Shaunavon, *Canada*	101	D7
Shaver L., *U.S.A.*	112	H7
Shaw →, *Australia*	88	D2
Shaw I., *Australia*	90	C4
Shawan, *China*	54	B3
Shawanaga, *Canada*	106	A4
Shawano, *U.S.A.*	104	C1
Shawinigan, *Canada*	98	C5
Shawnee, *U.S.A.*	109	H6
Shaybārā, *Si. Arabia*	64	E3
Shayib el Banat, Gebel, *Egypt*	76	B3
Shaykh Sa'īd, *Iraq*	64	C5
Shchekino, *Russia*	41	D10
Shcherbakov = Rybinsk, *Russia*	41	B11
Shchigri, *Russia*	41	E10
Shchors, *Ukraine*	40	F7
Shchuchiosk, *Kazakhstan*	44	D8
She Xian, *Anhui, China*	53	C12
She Xian, *Hebei, China*	50	F7
Shea, *Guyana*	121	C6
Shebekino, *Russia*	41	F10
Shebele = Scebeli, Wabi →, *Somali Rep.*	68	G3
Sheboygan, *U.S.A.*	104	D2
Shediac, *Canada*	99	C7
Sheelin, L., *Ireland*	15	C4
Sheep Haven, *Ireland*	15	A4
Sheerness, *U.K.*	13	F8
Sheet Harbour, *Canada*	99	D7
Sheffield, *U.K.*	12	D6
Sheffield, *Ala., U.S.A.*	105	H2
Sheffield, *Mass., U.S.A.*	107	D11
Sheffield, *Pa., U.S.A.*	106	E5
Sheffield, *Tex., U.S.A.*	109	K4
Sheho, *Canada*	101	C8
Shehojele, *Ethiopia*	77	E4
Shehong, *China*	52	B5
Shehuen →, *Argentina*	128	C3
Sheikhpura, *India*	63	G11
Shek Hasan, *Ethiopia*	77	E4
Shekhupura, *Pakistan*	62	D5
Sheki, *Azerbaijan*	43	F12
Sheksna →, *Russia*	41	B11
Shelburne, *N.S., Canada*	99	D6
Shelburne, *Ont., Canada*	98	D3
Shelburne, *U.S.A.*	107	B11
Shelburne B., *Australia*	90	A3
Shelburne Falls, *U.S.A.*	107	D12
Shelby, *Mich., U.S.A.*	104	D2
Shelby, *Mont., U.S.A.*	110	B8
Shelby, *N.C., U.S.A.*	105	H5
Shelby, *Ohio, U.S.A.*	106	F2
Shelbyville, *Ill., U.S.A.*	108	F10
Shelbyville, *Ind., U.S.A.*	104	F3
Shelbyville, *Tenn., U.S.A.*	105	H2
Sheldon, *U.S.A.*	108	D7
Sheldrake, *Canada*	99	B7
Shelikhova, Zaliv, *Russia*	45	D16
Shell Lake, *Canada*	101	C7
Shell Lakes, *Australia*	89	E4
Shellbrook, *Canada*	101	C7
Shellharbour, *Australia*	91	E5
Shelling Rocks, *Ireland*	15	E1
Shelon →, *Russia*	40	B7
Shelton, *Conn., U.S.A.*	107	E11
Shelton, *Wash., U.S.A.*	112	C3
Shemakha, *Azerbaijan*	43	F13
Shen Xian, *China*	50	F8
Shenandoah, *Iowa, U.S.A.*	108	E7
Shenandoah, *Pa., U.S.A.*	107	F8
Shenandoah, *Va., U.S.A.*	104	F6
Shenandoah →, *U.S.A.*	104	F7
Shenchi, *China*	50	E7
Shendam, *Nigeria*	79	D6
Shendî, *Sudan*	77	D3
Sheng Xian, *China*	53	C13
Shengfang, *China*	50	E9
Shēngjergji, *Albania*	39	H3
Shëngjini, *Albania*	39	H2
Shenjingzi, *China*	51	B13
Shenmu, *China*	50	E6
Shennongjia, *China*	53	B8
Shenqiu, *China*	50	H8
Shenqiucheng, *China*	50	H8
Shensi = Shaanxi □, *China*	50	G5
Shenyang, *China*	51	D12
Sheopur Kalan, *India*	60	G10
Shepetovka, *Ukraine*	40	F5
Shepparton, *Australia*	91	F4
Sheqi, *China*	50	H7
Sher Qila, *Pakistan*	63	A6
Sherborne, *U.K.*	13	G5
Sherbro I., *S. Leone*	78	D2
Sherbrooke, *Canada*	99	C5
Shereik, *Sudan*	76	D3
Sheridan, *Ark., U.S.A.*	109	H8
Sheridan, *Wyo., U.S.A.*	110	D10
Sherkot, *India*	63	E8
Sherman, *U.S.A.*	109	J6
Sherridon, *Canada*	101	B8
Sherwood, *N. Dak., U.S.A.*	108	A4
Sherwood, *Tex., U.S.A.*	109	K4
Sherwood Forest, *U.K.*	12	D6
Sheslay, *Canada*	100	B2
Sheslay →, *Canada*	100	B2
Shethanei L., *Canada*	101	B9
Shetland □, *U.K.*	14	A7
Shetland Is., *U.K.*	14	A7
Shewa □, *Ethiopia*	77	F4
Shewa Gimira, *Ethiopia*	77	F4
Sheyenne, *U.S.A.*	108	B5
Sheyenne →, *U.S.A.*	108	B6
Shibām, *Yemen*	68	D4
Shibata, *Japan*	48	F9
Shibecha, *Japan*	48	C12
Shibetsu, *Japan*	48	B11
Shibîn el Kôm, *Egypt*	76	H7
Shibîn el Qanâtir, *Egypt*	76	H7
Shibing, *China*	52	D7
Shibogama L., *Canada*	98	B2
Shibushi, *Japan*	49	J5
Shicheng, *China*	53	D11
Shickshock Mts. = Chic-Chocs, Mts., *Canada*	99	C6
Shidao, *China*	51	F12
Shidian, *China*	52	E2
Shido, *Japan*	49	G7
Shiel, L., *U.K.*	14	E3
Shield, C., *Australia*	90	A2
Shiga □, *Japan*	49	G8
Shigaib, *Sudan*	73	E9
Shigu, *China*	52	D2
Shiguaigou, *China*	50	D6
Shihchiachuangi = Shijiazhuang, *China*	50	E8
Shijiazhuang, *China*	50	E8
Shijiu Hu, *China*	53	B12
Shikarpur, *India*	62	E8
Shikarpur, *Pakistan*	62	F3
Shikoku □, *Japan*	49	H6
Shikoku-Sanchi, *Japan*	49	H6
Shilabo, *Ethiopia*	68	F3
Shiliguri, *India*	61	F16
Shilka, *Russia*	45	D12
Shilka →, *Russia*	45	D13
Shillelagh, *Ireland*	15	D5
Shillong, *India*	61	G17
Shilo, *Jordan*	69	C4
Shilong, *China*	53	F9
Shilou, *China*	50	F6
Shilovo, *Russia*	41	D12
Shimabara, *Japan*	49	H5
Shimada, *Japan*	49	G9
Shimane □, *Japan*	49	G6
Shimanovsk, *Russia*	45	D13
Shimen, *China*	53	C8
Shimenjie, *China*	53	C11
Shimizu, *Japan*	49	G9
Shimodate, *Japan*	49	F9
Shimoga, *India*	60	N9
Shimoni, *Kenya*	82	C4
Shimonoseki, *Japan*	49	H5
Shimpuru Rapids, *Angola*	84	B2
Shimsk, *Russia*	40	B7
Shin, L., *U.K.*	14	C4
Shin-Tone →, *Japan*	49	G10
Shinan, *China*	52	F7
Shinano →, *Japan*	49	F9
Shīndand, *Afghan.*	60	C3
Shingleton, *U.S.A.*	98	C2
Shingū, *Japan*	49	H7
Shinjō, *Japan*	48	E10
Shinkafe, *Nigeria*	79	C6
Shinshār, *Syria*	69	A5
Shinyanga, *Tanzania*	82	C3
Shinyanga □, *Tanzania*	82	C3
Shiogama, *Japan*	48	E10
Shiojiri, *Japan*	49	F8
Shiqma, N. →, *Israel*	69	D3
Shiquan, *China*	50	H5
Shīr Kūh, *Iran*	65	D7
Shiragami-Misaki, *Japan*	48	D10
Shirakawa, *Fukushima, Japan*	49	F10
Shirakawa, *Gifu, Japan*	49	F8
Shirane-San, *Gumma, Japan*	49	F9
Shirane-San, *Yamanashi, Japan*	49	G9
Shiraoi, *Japan*	48	C10
Shīrāz, *Iran*	65	D7
Shirbin, *Egypt*	76	H7
Shire →, *Africa*	83	F4
Shiretoko-Misaki, *Japan*	48	B12
Shirinab →, *Pakistan*	62	D2
Shiringushi, *Russia*	41	E13
Shiriya-Zaki, *Japan*	48	D10
Shiroishi, *Japan*	48	E10
Shīrvān, *Iran*	65	B8
Shirwa, L. = Chilwa, L., *Malawi*	83	F4
Shishou, *China*	53	C9
Shitai, *China*	53	B11
Shivpuri, *India*	62	G7
Shixian, *China*	51	C15
Shixing, *China*	53	E10
Shiyan, *China*	53	A8
Shiyata, *Egypt*	76	B2
Shizhu, *China*	52	C7
Shizong, *China*	52	E5
Shizuishan, *China*	50	E4
Shizuoka, *Japan*	49	G9
Shizuoka □, *Japan*	49	G9
Shklov, *Belorussia*	40	D7
Shkoder = Shkodra, *Albania*	38	G2
Shkodra, *Albania*	38	G2
Shkumbini →, *Albania*	39	H2
Shmidta, O., *Russia*	45	A10
Shō-Gawa →, *Japan*	49	F8
Shoal Lake, *Canada*	101	C8
Shōdo-Shima, *Japan*	49	G7
Shoeburyness, *U.K.*	13	F8
Sholapur = Solapur, *India*	60	L9
Shologontsy, *Russia*	45	C12
Shōmrōn, *Jordan*	69	C4
Shoshone, *Calif., U.S.A.*	113	K10
Shoshone, *Idaho, U.S.A.*	110	E6
Shoshone L., *U.S.A.*	110	D8
Shoshone Mts., *U.S.A.*	110	G5
Shoshong, *Botswana*	84	C4
Shoshoni, *U.S.A.*	110	E9
Shou Xian, *China*	53	A11
Shouchang, *China*	53	C12
Shouguang, *China*	51	F10
Shouning, *China*	53	D12
Shouyang, *China*	50	F7
Show Low, *U.S.A.*	111	J9
Shpola, *Ukraine*	42	B4
Shreveport, *U.S.A.*	109	J8
Shrewsbury, *U.K.*	12	E5
Shrirampur, *India*	63	H13
Shropshire □, *U.K.*	13	E5
Shuangcheng, *China*	51	B14
Shuangfeng, *China*	53	D9
Shuanggou, *China*	51	G9
Shuangjiang, *China*	52	F2
Shuangliao, *China*	51	C12
Shuangshanzi, *China*	51	D10
Shuangyang, *China*	51	C13
Shuangyashan, *China*	54	B8
Shucheng, *China*	53	B11
Shuguri Falls, *Tanzania*	83	D4
Shuiye, *China*	50	F8
Shujalpur, *India*	62	H7
Shukpa Kunzang, *India*	63	B8
Shulan, *China*	51	B14
Shule, *China*	54	C2
Shumagin Is., *U.S.A.*	96	C4
Shumerlya, *Russia*	41	D15
Shumikha, *Russia*	44	D7
Shunchang, *China*	53	D11
Shunde, *China*	53	F9
Shungay, *Kazakhstan*	43	B12
Shungnak, *U.S.A.*	96	B4
Shuo Xian, *China*	50	E7
Shūr →, *Iran*	65	D7
Shūr →, *Iran*	65	C6
Shūr Gaz, *Iran*	65	D8
Shūrāb, *Iran*	65	C8
Shūrjestān, *Iran*	65	D7
Shurma, *Russia*	41	C17
Shurugwi, *Zimbabwe*	83	F3
Shūsf, *Iran*	65	D9
Shūshtar, *Iran*	65	D6
Shuswap L., *Canada*	100	C5
Shuya, *Russia*	41	C12
Shuyang, *China*	51	G10
Shūzū, *Iran*	65	D7
Shwebo, *Burma*	61	H19
Shwegu, *Burma*	61	G20
Shweli →, *Burma*	61	H20
Shymkent = Chimkent, *Kazakhstan*	44	E7
Shyok, *India*	63	B8
Shyok →, *Pakistan*	63	B6
Si Chon, *Thailand*	59	H2
Si Kiang = Xi Jiang →, *China*	53	F9
Si-ngan = Xi'an, *China*	50	G5
Si Prachan, *Thailand*	58	E3
Si Racha, *Thailand*	58	F3
Si Xian, *China*	51	H9
Siahan Range, *Pakistan*	60	F4
Siaksrindrapura, *Indonesia*	56	D2
Sialkot, *Pakistan*	62	C6
Siam = Thailand ■, *Asia*	58	E4
Siantan, P., *Indonesia*	56	D3
Siàpo →, *Venezuela*	120	C4
Siārem, *Iran*	65	D9
Siargao, *Phil.*	55	G7
Siari, *Pakistan*	63	B7
Siasi, *Phil.*	57	C6
Siasi I., *Phil.*	55	J4
Siátista, *Greece*	39	J4
Siau, *Indonesia*	57	D7
Siauliai, *Lithuania*	40	D3
Siaya □, *Kenya*	82	B3
Sibâi, Gebel el, *Egypt*	76	B3
Sibari, *Italy*	35	C9
Sibasa, *S. Africa*	85	C5
Sibayi, L., *S. Africa*	85	D5
Šibenik, *Croatia*	33	E12
Siberia, *Russia*	4	D13
Siberut, *Indonesia*	56	E1
Sibi, *Pakistan*	62	E2
Sibil, *Indonesia*	57	E10
Sibiti, *Congo*	80	E2
Sibiu, *Romania*	38	D7
Sibley, *Iowa, U.S.A.*	108	D7
Sibley, *La., U.S.A.*	109	J8
Sibolga, *Indonesia*	56	D1
Sibret, *Belgium*	17	J7
Sibsagar, *India*	61	F19
Sibu, *Malaysia*	56	D4
Sibuco, *Phil.*	55	H5
Sibuguey B., *Phil.*	55	H5
Sibutu, *Phil.*	57	D5
Sibutu Group, *Phil.*	55	J3
Sibutu Passage, *E. Indies*	57	D5
Sibuyan, *Phil.*	55	E5
Sibuyan Sea, *Phil.*	55	E5
Sicamous, *Canada*	100	C5
Sichuan □, *China*	52	B5
Sicilia □, *Italy*	35	E7
Sicilia, *Italy*	35	E7
Sicilia, Canale di, *Italy*	34	E5
Sicilian Channel = Sicilia, Canale di, *Italy*	34	E5
Sicily = Sicilia, *Italy*	35	E7
Sicuani, *Peru*	124	C3
Siculiana, *Italy*	34	E6
Sidamo □, *Ethiopia*	77	G4
Sidaouet, *Niger*	79	B6
Sidári, *Greece*	37	A3
Siddeburen, *Neths.*	16	B9
Siddhapur, *India*	62	H5
Siddipet, *India*	60	K11
Side, *Turkey*	66	E4
Sidéradougou, *Burkina Faso*	78	C4
Siderno Marina, *Italy*	35	D9
Sídheros, Ákra, *Greece*	37	D8
Sidhirókastron, *Greece*	39	H6
Sîdi Abd el Rahmân, *Egypt*	76	H6
Sidi Barrâni, *Egypt*	76	A2
Sidi-bel-Abbès, *Algeria*	75	A4
Sidi Bennour, *Morocco*	74	B3
Sidi Haneish, *Egypt*	76	A2
Sidi Kacem, *Morocco*	74	B3
Sidi Omar, *Egypt*	76	A1
Sidi Slimane, *Morocco*	74	B3
Sidi Smaïl, *Morocco*	74	B3
Sidlaw Hills, *U.K.*	14	E5
Sidley, Mt., *Antarctica*	5	D14
Sidmouth, *U.K.*	13	G4
Sidmouth, C., *Australia*	90	A3
Sidney, *Canada*	100	D4
Sidney, *Mont., U.S.A.*	108	B2
Sidney, *N.Y., U.S.A.*	107	D9
Sidney, *Nebr., U.S.A.*	108	E3
Sidney, *Ohio, U.S.A.*	104	E3
Sidoarjo, *Indonesia*	57	G15
Sidon = Saydā, *Lebanon*	69	B4
Sidra, G. of = Surt, Khalīj, *Libya*	73	B8
Siedlce, *Poland*	20	C12
Sieg →, *Germany*	18	E3
Siegburg, *Germany*	18	E3
Siegen, *Germany*	18	E4
Siem Pang, *Cambodia*	58	E6
Siem Reap, *Cambodia*	58	F4
Siena, *Italy*	33	E8
Sieradz, *Poland*	20	D8
Sierck-les-Bains, *France*	25	C13
Sierpc, *Poland*	20	C9
Sierpe, Bocas de la, *Venezuela*	121	B5
Sierra Blanca, *U.S.A.*	111	L11
Sierra Blanca Peak, *U.S.A.*	111	K11
Sierra City, *U.S.A.*	112	F6
Sierra Colorada, *Argentina*	128	B3
Sierra de Yeguas, *Spain*	31	H6
Sierra Gorda, *Chile*	126	A2
Sierra Grande, *Argentina*	128	B3
Sierra Leone ■, *W. Afr.*	78	D2
Sierra Madre, *Mexico*	115	D6
Sierra Mojada, *Mexico*	114	B4
Sierraville, *U.S.A.*	112	F6
Sierre, *Switz.*	22	D5
Sif Fatima, *Algeria*	75	B6
Sífnos, *Greece*	39	N7
Sifton, *Canada*	101	C8
Sifton Pass, *Canada*	100	B3
Sig, *Algeria*	75	A4
Sigdal, *Norway*	10	D3
Sigean, *France*	26	E6
Sighetu-Marmatiei, *Romania*	38	B6
Sighişoara, *Romania*	38	C7
Sigli, *Indonesia*	56	C1
Siglufjörður, *Iceland*	8	C4
Sigmaringen, *Germany*	19	G5
Signakhi, *Georgia*	43	F12
Signal, *U.S.A.*	113	L13
Signal Pk., *U.S.A.*	113	M12
Signau, *Switz.*	22	C5
Signy-l'Abbaye, *France*	25	C11
Sigsig, *Ecuador*	120	D2
Sigtuna, *Sweden*	10	E11
Sigüenza, *Spain*	28	D2
Siguiri, *Guinea*	78	C3
Sigulda, *Latvia*	40	C4
Sigurd, *U.S.A.*	111	G8
Sihanoukville = Kompong Som, *Cambodia*	59	G4
Sihaus, *Peru*	124	B2
Sihui, *China*	53	F9

Siirt, *Turkey* 67 E9
Siirt □, *Turkey* 67 E9
Sijarira Ra., *Zimbabwe* ... 83 F2
Sikao, *Thailand* 59 J2
Sikar, *India* 62 F6
Sikasso, *Mali* 78 C3
Sikeston, *U.S.A.* 109 G10
Sikhote Alin, Khrebet, *Russia* 45 E14
Sikhote Alin Ra. = Sikhote Alin, Khrebet, *Russia* .. 45 E14
Sikiá., *Greece* 39 J6
Síkinos, *Greece* 39 N8
Sikkani Chief →, *Canada* .. 100 B4
Sikkim □, *India* 61 F16
Sikotu-Ko, *Japan* 48 C10
Sil →, *Spain* 30 C3
Silacayoapan, *Mexico* 115 D5
Silandro, *Italy* 32 B7
Silay, *Phil.* 55 F5
Silba, *Croatia* 33 D11
Silchar, *India* 61 G18
Silcox, *Canada* 101 B10
Şile, *Turkey* 66 C3
Silenrieux, *Belgium* 17 H4
Siler City, *U.S.A.* 105 H6
Silesia = Śląsk, *Poland* .. 20 E6
Silet, *Algeria* 75 D5
Silgarhi Doti, *Nepal* 63 E9
Silghat, *India* 61 F18
Silifke, *Turkey* 66 E5
Siliguri = Shiliguri, *India* . 61 F16
Siling Co, *China* 54 C3
Silíqua, *Italy* 34 C1
Silistra, *Bulgaria* 38 E10
Silivri, *Turkey* 66 C3
Siljan, *Sweden* 9 F13
Silkeborg, *Denmark* 11 H3
Sillajhuay, Cordillera, *Chile* 124 D4
Sillé-le-Guillaume, *France* . 24 D6
Sillustani, *Peru* 124 D3
Siloam Springs, *U.S.A.* ... 109 G7
Silopi, *Turkey* 67 E10
Silsbee, *U.S.A.* 109 K7
Šilute, *Lithuania* 40 D2
Silva Porto = Kuito, *Angola* 81 G3
Silvan, *Turkey* 67 D9
Silvaplana, *Switz.* 23 D9
Silver City, *N. Mex., U.S.A.* ... 111 K9
Silver City, *Nev., U.S.A.* .. 110 G4
Silver Cr. →, *U.S.A.* 110 E4
Silver Creek, *U.S.A.* 106 D5
Silver L., *Calif., U.S.A.* . 112 G6
Silver L., *Calif., U.S.A.* . 113 K10
Silver Lake, *U.S.A.* 110 E3
Silver Streams, *S. Africa* . 84 D3
Silverton, *Colo., U.S.A.* .. 111 H10
Silverton, *Tex., U.S.A.* .. 109 H4
Silves, *Portugal* 31 H2
Silvi, *Italy* 33 F11
Silvia, *Colombia* 120 C2
Silvies →, *U.S.A.* 110 E4
Silvolde, *Neths.* 16 E8
Silvretta-Gruppe, *Switz.* . 23 C10
Silwa Bahari, *Egypt* 76 C3
Silz, *Austria* 19 H6
Sim, C., *Morocco* 74 B3
Simanggang, *Malaysia* 56 D4
Simao, *China* 52 F3
Simão Dias, *Brazil* 122 D4
Simard, L., *Canada* 98 C4
Simav, *Turkey* 66 D3
Simba, *Tanzania* 82 C4
Simbach, *Germany* 19 G9
Simbirsk, *Russia* 41 D16
Simbo, *Tanzania* 82 C2
Simcoe, *Canada* 98 D3
Simcoe, L., *Canada* 98 D4
Simenga, *Russia* 45 C11
Simeto →, *Italy* 35 E8
Simeulue, *Indonesia* 56 D1
Simferopol, *Ukraine* 42 D6
Sími, *Greece* 39 N10
Simi Valley, *U.S.A.* 113 L8
Simikot, *Nepal* 63 E9
Simití, *Colombia* 120 B3
Simla, *India* 62 D7
Şimleu-Silvaniei, *Romania* . 38 B5
Simme →, *Switz.* 22 C4
Simmern, *Germany* 19 F3
Simmie, *Canada* 101 D7
Simmler, *U.S.A.* 113 K7
Simões, *Brazil* 122 C3
Simojärvi, *Finland* 8 C19
Simojoki →, *Finland* 8 D18
Simojovel, *Mexico* 115 D6
Simonette →, *Canada* 100 B5
Simonstown, *S. Africa* ... 84 E2
Simplício Mendes, *Brazil* . 122 C3
Simplon, *Switz.* 22 D6
Simplon Pass = Simplonpass, *Switz.* ... 22 D6
Simplon Tunnel, *Switz.* ... 22 D6
Simplonpass, *Switz.* 22 D6
Simpson Desert, *Australia* . 90 D2
Simpungdong, *N. Korea* ... 51 D15
Simunjan, *Malaysia* 56 D4
Simushir, Ostrov, *Russia* .. 45 E16
Sinabang, *Indonesia* 56 D1
Sinadogo, *Somali Rep.* ... 68 F4
Sinai = Es Sînâ', *Egypt* .. 76 J8
Sinai, Mt. = Mûsa, G., *Egypt* 76 J8

Sinai Peninsula, *Egypt* 69 F2
Sinaia, *Romania* 38 D8
Sinaloa □, *Mexico* 114 C3
Sinaloa de Levya, *Mexico* . 114 B3
Sinalunga, *Italy* 33 E8
Sinan, *China* 52 D7
Sinarádhes, *Greece* 37 A3
Sīnāwan, *Libya* 75 B7
Sincé, *Colombia* 120 B2
Sincelejo, *Colombia* 120 B2
Sinchang, *N. Korea* 51 D15
Sinchang-ni, *N. Korea* ... 51 E14
Sinclair, *U.S.A.* 110 F10
Sinclair Mills, *Canada* ... 100 C4
Sincorá, Serra do, *Brazil* . 123 D3
Sind, *Pakistan* 62 G3
Sind □, *Pakistan* 62 F3
Sind →, *India* 63 B6
Sind Sagar Doab, *Pakistan* . 62 D4
Sindal, *Denmark* 11 G4
Sindangan, *Phil.* 55 G5
Sindangbarang, *Indonesia* . 57 G12
Sinde, *Zambia* 83 F2
Sinegorski, *Russia* 43 C9
Sinelnikovo, *Ukraine* 42 B6
Sines, *Portugal* 31 H2
Sines, C. de, *Portugal* ... 31 H2
Sineu, *Spain* 36 B10
Sinfra, *Ivory C.* 78 D3
Sing Buri, *Thailand* 58 E3
Singa, *Sudan* 77 E3
Singapore ■, *Asia* 59 M4
Singapore, Straits of, *Asia* . 59 M5
Singaraja, *Indonesia* 56 F5
Singen, *Germany* 19 H4
Singida, *Tanzania* 82 C3
Singida □, *Tanzania* 82 D3
Singitikós Kólpos, *Greece* . 39 J6
Singkaling Hkamti, *Burma* . 61 G19
Singkawang, *Indonesia* ... 56 D3
Singleton, *Australia* 91 E5
Singleton, Mt., *N. Terr., Australia* ... 88 D5
Singleton, Mt., *W. Austral., Australia* ... 89 E2
Singoli, *India* 62 G6
Singora = Songkhla, *Thailand* 59 J3
Singosan, *N. Korea* 51 E14
Sinhung, *N. Korea* 51 D14
Siní □, *Egypt* 69 F2
Siniscóla, *Italy* 34 B2
Sinj, *Croatia* 33 E13
Sinjai, *Indonesia* 57 F6
Sinjär, *Iraq* 64 B4
Sinkat, *Sudan* 76 D4
Sinkiang Uighur = Xinjiang Uygur Zizhiqu □, *China* . 54 B3
Sinmak, *N. Korea* 51 E14
Sínnai, *Italy* 34 C2
Sinni →, *Italy* 35 B9
Sinnuris, *Egypt* 76 J7
Sinoe, L., *Romania* 38 E11
Sinop, *Turkey* 42 E6
Sinop □, *Turkey* 66 C6
Sinpo, *N. Korea* 51 E15
Sins, *Switz.* 23 B6
Sinskoye, *Russia* 45 C13
Sint-Amandsberg, *Belgium* . 17 F3
Sint Annaland, *Neths.* ... 17 E4
Sint Annaparoch, *Neths.* .. 16 B7
Sint-Denijs, *Belgium* 17 G2
Sint Eustatius, I., *Neth. Ant.* 117 C7
Sint-Genesius-Rode, *Belgium* 17 G4
Sint-Gillis-Waas, *Belgium* . 17 F4
Sint-Huibrechts-Lille, *Belgium* 17 F6
Sint-Katelinje-Waver, *Belgium* 17 F5
Sint-Kruis, *Belgium* 17 F2
Sint-Laureins, *Belgium* ... 17 F3
Sint Maarten, I., *W. Indies* 117 C7
Sint-Michiels, *Belgium* ... 17 F2
Sint Nicolaasga, *Neths.* .. 16 C7
Sint Niklaas, *Belgium* ... 17 F4
Sint Oedenrode, *Neths.* ... 17 E6
Sint Pancras, *Neths.* 16 C5
Sint Philipsland, *Neths.* .. 17 E4
Sint Truiden, *Belgium* ... 17 G6
Sint Willebrord, *Neths.* .. 17 E5
Sîntana, *Romania* 38 C4
Sintang, *Indonesia* 56 D4
Sintjohannesga, *Neths.* ... 16 C7
Sinton, *U.S.A.* 109 L6
Sintra, *Portugal* 31 G1
Sinüiju, *N. Korea* 51 D13
Sinyukha →, *Ukraine* 42 B4
Siocon, *Phil.* 55 H5
Siófok, *Hungary* 21 J8
Sioma, *Zambia* 84 B3
Sion, *Switz.* 22 D4
Sioux City, *U.S.A.* 108 D6
Sioux Falls, *U.S.A.* 108 D6
Sioux Lookout, *Canada* ... 98 B1
Sip Song Chau Thai, *Vietnam* 58 B4
Sipalay, *Phil.* 55 G5
Siping, *China* 51 C13
Sipiwesk L., *Canada* 101 B9
Sipora, *Indonesia* 56 E1
Siquia →, *Nic.* 116 D3
Siquijor, *Phil.* 55 G5
Siquirres, *Costa Rica* ... 116 D3

Siquisique, *Venezuela* 120 A4
Sir Edward Pellew Group, *Australia* 90 B2
Sir Graham Moore Is., *Australia* 88 B4
Siracusa, *Italy* 35 E8
Sirajganj, *Bangla.* 63 G13
Sirakoro, *Mali* 78 C3
Şiran, *Turkey* 67 C8
Sirasso, *Ivory C.* 78 D3
Sīrdān, *Iran* 65 B6
Sirer, *Spain* 36 C7
Siret, *Romania* 38 B9
Siret →, *Romania* 38 D11
Şiria, *Romania* 38 C4
Sirino, Monte, *Italy* 35 B8
Sírna, *Greece* 39 N9
Şirnak, *Turkey* 67 E10
Sirohi, *India* 62 G5
Sironj, *India* 62 G7
Síros, *Greece* 39 M7
Sirretta Pk., *U.S.A.* 113 K8
Sirsa, *India* 62 E6
Siruela, *Spain* 31 G5
Sisak, *Croatia* 33 C13
Sisaket, *Thailand* 58 E5
Sisante, *Spain* 29 F2
Sisargas, Is., *Spain* 30 B2
Sishen, *S. Africa* 84 D3
Sishui, *Henan, China* 50 G7
Sishui, *Shandong, China* . 51 G9
Sisipuk L., *Canada* 101 B8
Sisophon, *Cambodia* 58 F4
Sissach, *Switz.* 22 B5
Sisseton, *U.S.A.* 108 C6
Sissonne, *France* 25 C10
Sīstān va Balūchestān □, *Iran* 65 E9
Sisteron, *France* 27 D9
Sisters, *U.S.A.* 110 D3
Sitamarhi, *India* 63 F11
Sitapur, *India* 63 F9
Siteki, *Swaziland* 85 D5
Sitges, *Spain* 28 D6
Sitía, *Greece* 37 D8
Sítio da Abadia, *Brazil* . 123 D2
Sitka, *U.S.A.* 96 C6
Sitoti, *Botswana* 84 C3
Sitra, *Egypt* 76 B2
Sittang Myit →, *Burma* ... 61 L20
Sittard, *Neths.* 17 G7
Sittensen, *Germany* 18 B5
Sittona, *Eritrea* 77 E4
Sittwe, *Burma* 61 J18
Siuna, *Nic.* 116 D3
Siuri, *India* 63 H12
Sivana, *India* 62 E8
Sīvand, *Iran* 65 D7
Sivas, *Turkey* 66 D7
Sivas □, *Turkey* 66 D7
Siverek, *Turkey* 67 E8
Sivrihisar, *Turkey* 66 D4
Sivry, *Belgium* 17 H4
Sîwa, *Egypt* 76 B2
Sîwa, El Wâhât es, *Egypt* . 76 B2
Siwalik Range, *Nepal* 63 F10
Siwan, *India* 63 F11
Siyâl, Jazâ'ir, *Egypt* ... 76 C4
Sizewell, *U.K.* 13 E9
Siziwang Qi, *China* 50 D6
Sjælland, *Denmark* 11 J5
Sjællands Odde, *Denmark* . 11 J5
Själevad, *Sweden* 10 A12
Sjenica, *Serbia* 21 M10
Sjoa, *Norway* 10 C3
Sjöbo, *Sweden* 11 J7
Sjösa, *Sweden* 11 F11
Sjumen = Šumen, *Bulgaria* . 38 F9
Skadovsk, *Ukraine* 42 C5
Skagafjörður, *Iceland* ... 8 D4
Skagastølstindane, *Norway* . 9 F9
Skagen, *Denmark* 11 G4
Skagerrak, *Denmark* 11 G3
Skagit →, *U.S.A.* 112 B4
Skagway, *U.S.A.* 100 B1
Skaidi, *Norway* 8 A18
Skala Podolskaya, *Ukraine* . 42 B2
Skalat, *Ukraine* 40 G4
Skalni Dol = Kamenyak, *Bulgaria* 38 F9
Skals, *Denmark* 11 H3
Skanderborg, *Denmark* 11 H3
Skanör, *Sweden* 11 J6
Skara, *Sweden* 9 G12
Skaraborgs län □, *Sweden* . 9 G12
Skardu, *Pakistan* 63 B6
Skarrild, *Denmark* 11 J2
Skarzysko Kamienna, *Poland* 20 D10
Skebokvarn, *Sweden* 10 E10
Skeena →, *Canada* 100 C2
Skeena Mts., *Canada* 100 B3
Skegness, *U.K.* 12 D8
Skeldon, *Guyana* 121 B6
Skellefte älv →, *Sweden* .. 8 D16
Skellefteå, *Sweden* 8 D16
Skelleftehamn, *Sweden* ... 8 D16
Skender Vakuf, *Bos.-H.* ... 21 L7
Skene, *Sweden* 11 G6
Skerries, The, *U.K.* 12 D3
Skhoinoúsa, *Greece* 39 N8
Ski, *Norway* 10 E4
Skíathos, *Greece* 39 K6
Skibbereen, *Ireland* 15 E2

Skiddaw, *U.K.* 12 C4
Skien, *Norway* 10 E3
Skierniewice, *Poland* 20 D10
Skikda, *Algeria* 75 A6
Skilloura, *Cyprus* 37 D12
Skínári, Ákra, *Greece* ... 39 M3
Skipton, *Australia* 91 F3
Skipton, *U.K.* 12 D5
Skirmish Pt., *Australia* .. 90 A1
Skíros, *Greece* 39 L7
Skivarp, *Sweden* 11 J7
Skive, *Denmark* 11 H3
Skjálfandafljót →, *Iceland* . 8 D5
Skjálfandi, *Iceland* 8 C5
Skjeberg, *Norway* 10 E5
Skjern, *Denmark* 11 J2
Škofja Loka, *Slovenia* ... 33 B11
Skoghall, *Sweden* 9 G12
Skole, *Ukraine* 40 G3
Skópelos, *Greece* 39 K6
Skopí, *Greece* 37 D8
Skopin, *Russia* 41 E11
Skopje, *Macedonia* 39 G4
Skórcz, *Poland* 20 B8
Skövde, *Sweden* 9 G12
Skovorodino, *Russia* 45 D13
Skowhegan, *U.S.A.* 99 D6
Skownan, *Canada* 101 C9
Skradin, *Croatia* 33 E12
Skreanäs, *Sweden* 11 H6
Skudeneshavn, *Norway* 9 G8
Skull, *Ireland* 15 E2
Skultorp, *Sweden* 11 F7
Skunk →, *U.S.A.* 108 E9
Skuodas, *Lithuania* 40 C2
Skurup, *Sweden* 11 J7
Skutskär, *Sweden* 10 D11
Skvira, *Ukraine* 42 B3
Skwierzyna, *Poland* 20 C5
Skye, *U.K.* 14 D2
Skykomish, *U.S.A.* 110 C3
Skyros = Skíros, *Greece* .. 39 L7
Slagelse, *Denmark* 11 J5
Slagharen, *Neths.* 16 C9
Slamet, *Indonesia* 56 F3
Slaney →, *Ireland* 15 D5
Slangerup, *Denmark* 11 J6
Slano, *Croatia* 21 N7
Slantsy, *Russia* 40 B6
Śląsk, *Poland* 20 E6
Slate Is., *Canada* 98 C2
Slatina, *Romania* 38 E7
Slaton, *U.S.A.* 109 J4
Slave →, *Canada* 100 A6
Slave Coast, *W. Afr.* 70 F4
Slave Lake, *Canada* 100 B6
Slave Pt., *Canada* 100 A5
Slavgorod, *Russia* 44 D8
Slavnoye, *Belorussia* 40 D6
Slavonska Požega, *Croatia* . 21 K7
Slavonski Brod, *Croatia* .. 21 K8
Slavuta, *Ukraine* 40 F5
Slavyanka, *Russia* 48 C5
Slavyansk, *Ukraine* 42 B7
Slavyansk-na-Kubani, *Russia* 42 D8
Sławno, *Poland* 20 A6
Sławoborze, *Poland* 20 B5
Sleaford, *U.K.* 12 E7
Sleaford B., *Australia* ... 91 E2
Sleat, Sd. of, *U.K.* 14 D3
Sleeper Is., *Canada* 97 C11
Sleepy Eye, *U.S.A.* 108 C7
Sleidinge, *Belgium* 17 F3
Sleman, *Indonesia* 57 G14
Slemon L., *Canada* 100 A5
Slidell, *U.S.A.* 109 K10
Sliedrecht, *Neths.* 16 E5
Sliema, *Malta* 37 D2
Slieve Aughty, *Ireland* ... 15 C3
Slieve Bloom, *Ireland* ... 15 C4
Slieve Donard, *U.K.* 15 B6
Slieve Gullion, *U.K.* 15 B5
Slieve Mish, *Ireland* 15 D2
Slievenamon, *Ireland* 15 D4
Sligo, *Ireland* 15 B3
Sligo □, *Ireland* 15 B3
Sligo B., *Ireland* 15 B3
Slijpe, *Belgium* 17 F1
Slikkerveer, *Neths.* 16 E5
Slite, *Sweden* 9 H15
Sliven, *Bulgaria* 38 G9
Slivnitsa, *Bulgaria* 38 G6
Sljeme, *Croatia* 33 C12
Sloan, *U.S.A.* 113 K11
Sloansville, *U.S.A.* 107 D10
Slobodskoy, *Russia* 41 B17
Slobozia, *Romania* 38 E10
Slocan, *Canada* 100 D5
Slochteren, *Neths.* 16 B9
Slöinge, *Sweden* 11 H6
Slonim, *Belorussia* 40 E4
Slotermeer, *Neths.* 16 C7
Slough, *U.K.* 13 F7
Sloughhouse, *U.S.A.* 112 G5
Slovak Rep. ■, *Europe* ... 20 G9
Slovakia = Slovak Rep. ■, *Europe* 20 G9
Slovakian Ore Mts. = Slovenské Rudohorie, *Slovak Rep.* 20 G9
Slovenia ■, *Europe* 33 C11
Slovenija = Slovenia ■, *Europe* 33 C11
Slovenj Gradec, *Slovenia* . 33 B12

Slovenska Bistrica, *Slovenia* 33 B12
Slovenská Republika = Slovak Rep. ■, *Europe* . 20 G9
Slovenské Rudohorie, *Slovak Rep.* 20 G9
Slovyansk = Slavyansk, *Ukraine* 42 B7
Słubice, *Poland* 20 C4
Sluch →, *Ukraine* 40 F5
Sluis, *Neths.* 17 F2
Slunj, *Croatia* 33 C12
Słupca, *Poland* 20 C7
Słupsk, *Poland* 20 A7
Slurry, *S. Africa* 84 D4
Slyne Hd., *Ireland* 15 C1
Slyudyanka, *Russia* 45 D11
Smålandsfarvandet, *Denmark* 11 J5
Smålandsstenar, *Sweden* .. 11 G7
Smalltree L., *Canada* 101 A7
Smara, *Morocco* 72 B3
Smarje, *Slovenia* 33 B12
Smartt Syndicate Dam, *S. Africa* 84 E3
Smartville, *U.S.A.* 112 F5
Smeaton, *Canada* 101 C8
Smederevo, *Serbia* 21 L10
Smederevska Palanka, *Serbia* 21 L10
Smela, *Ukraine* 42 B4
Smethport, *U.S.A.* 106 E6
Smidovich, *Russia* 45 E14
Smilde, *Neths.* 16 C8
Smiley, *Canada* 101 C7
Smith, *Canada* 100 B6
Smith →, *Canada* 100 B3
Smith Arm, *Canada* 96 B7
Smith Center, *U.S.A.* 108 F5
Smith Sund, *Greenland* ... 4 B4
Smithburne →, *Australia* . 90 B3
Smithers, *Canada* 100 C3
Smithfield, *S. Africa* ... 85 E4
Smithfield, *N.C., U.S.A.* . 105 H6
Smithfield, *Utah, U.S.A.* . 110 F8
Smiths Falls, *Canada* 98 D4
Smithton, *Australia* 90 G4
Smithtown, *Australia* 91 E5
Smithville, *Canada* 106 C5
Smithville, *U.S.A.* 109 K6
Smoky →, *Canada* 100 B5
Smoky Bay, *Australia* 91 E1
Smoky Falls, *Canada* 98 B3
Smoky Hill →, *U.S.A.* 108 F6
Smoky Lake, *Canada* 100 C6
Smøla, *Norway* 10 A2
Smolensk, *Russia* 40 D8
Smolikas, Óros, *Greece* .. 39 J3
Smolník, *Slovak Rep.* 20 G10
Smolyan, *Bulgaria* 39 H7
Smooth Rock Falls, *Canada* 98 C3
Smoothstone L., *Canada* . 101 C7
Smorgon, *Belorussia* 40 D5
Smyadovo, *Bulgaria* 38 F10
Smyrna = İzmir, *Turkey* .. 66 D2
Snaefell, *U.K.* 12 C3
Snæfellsjökull, *Iceland* .. 8 D2
Snake →, *U.S.A.* 110 C4
Snake I., *Australia* 91 F4
Snake L., *Canada* 101 B7
Snake Range, *U.S.A.* 110 G6
Snake River Plain, *U.S.A.* 110 E7
Snarum, *Norway* 10 D3
Snedsted, *Denmark* 11 H2
Sneek, *Neths.* 16 B7
Sneeker-meer, *Neths.* 16 B7
Sneeuberge, *S. Africa* ... 84 E3
Snejbjerg, *Denmark* 11 H2
Snelling, *U.S.A.* 112 H6
Sneznhoye, *Ukraine* 43 C8
Snežnik, *Slovenia* 33 C11
Snigirevka, *Ukraine* 42 C5
Snizort, L., *U.K.* 14 D2
Snøhetta, *Norway* 10 B3
Snohomish, *U.S.A.* 112 C4
Snoul, *Cambodia* 59 F6
Snow Hill, *U.S.A.* 104 F8
Snow Lake, *Canada* 101 C8
Snow Mt., *U.S.A.* 112 F4
Snowbird L., *Canada* 101 A8
Snowdon, *U.K.* 12 D3
Snowdrift, *Canada* 101 A6
Snowdrift →, *Canada* 101 A6
Snowflake, *U.S.A.* 111 J8
Snowshoe Pk., *U.S.A.* 110 B6
Snowtown, *Australia* 91 E2
Snowville, *U.S.A.* 110 F7
Snowy →, *Australia* 91 F4
Snowy Mts., *Australia* ... 91 F4
Snug Corner, *Bahamas* 117 B5
Snyatyn, *Ukraine* 42 B2
Snyder, *Okla., U.S.A.* ... 109 H5
Snyder, *Tex., U.S.A.* 109 J4
Soacha, *Colombia* 120 C4
Soahanina, *Madag.* 85 B7
Soalala, *Madag.* 85 B8
Soan →, *Pakistan* 62 C4
Soanierana-Ivongo, *Madag.* 85 B8
Soap Lake, *U.S.A.* 110 C4
Sobat, Nahr →, *Sudan* 77 F3
Sobhapur, *India* 62 H8
Sobinka, *Russia* 41 D12
Sobótka, *Poland* 20 E6
Sobrado, *Spain* 30 C3
Sobral, *Brazil* 122 B3

Sobreira Formosa, *Portugal*	31	F3
Soc Giang, *Vietnam*	58	A6
Soc Trang, *Vietnam*	59	H5
Soča →, *Europe*	33	B10
Sochaczew, *Poland*	20	C10
Soch'e = Shache, *China*	54	C2
Sochi, *Russia*	43	E8
Société, Is. de la, *Pac. Oc.*	93	J12
Society Is. = Société, Is. de la, *Pac. Oc.*	93	J12
Socompa, Portezuelo de, *Chile*	126	A2
Socorro, *Colombia*	120	B3
Socorro, *U.S.A.*	111	J10
Socorro, I., *Mexico*	114	D2
Socotra, *Ind. Oc.*	68	E5
Socuéllmos, *Spain*	29	F2
Soda L., *U.S.A.*	111	J5
Soda Plains, *India*	63	B8
Soda Springs, *U.S.A.*	110	E8
Söderhamn, *Sweden*	9	F14
Söderköping, *Sweden*	9	G14
Södermanlands län □, *Sweden*	10	E10
Södertälje, *Sweden*	10	E11
Sodiri, *Sudan*	77	E2
Sodo, *Ethiopia*	77	F4
Sodražica, *Slovenia*	33	C11
Sodus, *U.S.A.*	106	C7
Soekmekaar, *S. Africa*	85	C4
Soest, *Germany*	18	D4
Soest, *Neths.*	16	D6
Soestdijk, *Neths.*	16	D6
Sofádhes, *Greece*	39	K5
Sofara, *Mali*	78	C4
Sofia = Sofiya, *Bulgaria*	38	G6
Sofia →, *Madag.*	85	B8
Sofievka, *Ukraine*	42	B5
Sofiiski, *Russia*	45	D14
Sofikón, *Greece*	39	M6
Sofiya, *Bulgaria*	38	G6
Sōfu-Gan, *Japan*	49	K10
Sogakofe, *Ghana*	79	D5
Sogamoso, *Colombia*	120	B3
Sogār, *Iran*	65	E8
Sögel, *Germany*	18	C3
Sogn og Fjordane fylke □, *Norway*	9	F9
Sogndalsfjøra, *Norway*	9	F9
Sognefjorden, *Norway*	9	F8
Söğüt, *Turkey*	66	C4
Söğüt Gölü, *Turkey*	66	E13
Sögwi-po, *S. Korea*	51	H14
Soh, *Iran*	65	C6
Sohâg, *Egypt*	76	B3
Sōhori, *N. Korea*	51	D15
Soignies, *Belgium*	17	G4
Soira, *Eritrea*	77	E4
Soissons, *France*	25	C10
Sōja, *Japan*	49	G6
Sojat, *India*	62	G5
Sok →, *Russia*	41	E17
Sokal, *Ukraine*	40	F4
Söke, *Turkey*	66	E12
Sokelo, *Zaïre*	83	D1
Sokhumi = Sukhumi, *Georgia*	43	E9
Sokki, Oued In →, *Algeria*	75	C5
Sokna, *Norway*	10	D3
Soknedal, *Norway*	10	B4
Soko Banja, *Serbia*	21	M11
Sokodé, *Togo*	79	D5
Sokol, *Russia*	41	B12
Sokółka, *Poland*	20	B13
Sokolo, *Mali*	78	C3
Sokołów Małopolski, *Poland*	20	E12
Sokołów Podlaski, *Poland*	20	C12
Sokoto, *Nigeria*	79	C6
Sokoto □, *Nigeria*	79	C6
Sokoto →, *Nigeria*	79	C5
Sol Iletsk, *Russia*	44	D6
Solai, *Kenya*	82	B4
Solano, *Phil.*	55	C4
Solapur, *India*	60	L9
Solares, *Spain*	30	B7
Soléa □, *Cyprus*	37	D12
Solec Kujawski, *Poland*	20	B8
Soledad, *Colombia*	120	A3
Soledad, *U.S.A.*	111	H3
Soledad, *Venezuela*	121	B5
Solent, The, *U.K.*	13	G6
Solenzara, *France*	27	G13
Solesmes, *France*	25	B10
Solfonn, *Norway*	9	F9
Solhan, *Turkey*	67	D9
Soligalich, *Russia*	41	B13
Soligorsk, *Belorussia*	40	E5
Solikamsk, *Russia*	44	D6
Solila, *Madag.*	85	C8
Solimões = Amazonas →, *S. Amer.*	121	D7
Solingen, *Germany*	17	F10
Sollebrunn, *Sweden*	11	F6
Sollefteå, *Sweden*	10	A11
Sollentuna, *Sweden*	10	E11
Sóller, *Spain*	36	B9
Solling, *Germany*	18	D5
Solna, *Sweden*	10	E12
Solnechnogorsk, *Russia*	41	C10
Sologne, *France*	25	E8
Solok, *Indonesia*	56	E2
Sololá, *Guatemala*	116	D1
Solomon, N. Fork →, *U.S.A.*	108	F5
Solomon, S. Fork →, *U.S.A.*	108	F5
Solomon Is. ■, *Pac. Oc.*	92	H7
Solon, *China*	54	B7
Solon Springs, *U.S.A.*	108	B9
Solonópole, *Brazil*	122	C4
Solor, *Indonesia*	57	F6
Solotcha, *Russia*	41	D11
Solothurn, *Switz.*	22	B5
Solothurn □, *Switz.*	22	B5
Solsona, *Spain*	28	D6
Solta, *Croatia*	33	E13
Solțānābād, *Khorāsān, Iran*	65	C8
Solțānābād, *Khorāsān, Iran*	65	B8
Solțānābād, *Markazī, Iran*	65	C6
Soltau, *Germany*	18	C5
Soltsy, *Russia*	40	B7
Solunska Glava, *Macedonia*	39	H4
Solvang, *U.S.A.*	113	L6
Solvay, *U.S.A.*	107	C8
Solway Firth, *U.K.*	12	C4
Solwezi, *Zambia*	83	E2
Sōma, *Japan*	48	F10
Soma, *Turkey*	66	D2
Somali Rep. ■, *Africa*	68	F4
Somalia ■ = Somali Rep. ■, *Africa*	68	F4
Sombernon, *France*	25	E11
Sombor, *Serbia*	21	K9
Sombra, *Canada*	106	D2
Sombrerete, *Mexico*	114	C4
Sombrero, *Anguilla*	117	C7
Someren, *Neths.*	17	F7
Somers, *U.S.A.*	110	B6
Somerset, *Canada*	101	D9
Somerset, *Colo., U.S.A.*	111	G10
Somerset, *Ky., U.S.A.*	104	G3
Somerset, *Mass., U.S.A.*	107	E13
Somerset, *Pa., U.S.A.*	106	F5
Somerset □, *U.K.*	13	F5
Somerset East, *S. Africa*	84	E4
Somerset I., *Canada*	96	A10
Somerset West, *S. Africa*	84	E2
Somerton, *U.S.A.*	111	K6
Somerville, *U.S.A.*	107	F10
Someş →, *Romania*	38	B5
Someşul Mare →, *Romania*	38	B7
Somma Lombardo, *Italy*	32	C5
Somma Vesuviana, *Italy*	35	B7
Sommariva, *Australia*	91	D4
Sommatino, *Italy*	34	E6
Somme □, *France*	25	C9
Somme →, *France*	25	B8
Somme, B. de la, *France*	24	B8
Sommelsdijk, *Neths.*	16	E4
Sommepy-Tahure, *France*	25	C11
Sömmerda, *Germany*	18	D7
Sommières, *France*	27	E8
Somoto, *Nic.*	116	D2
Sompolno, *Poland*	20	C8
Somport, Paso, *Spain*	28	C4
Somport, Puerto de, *Spain*	28	C4
Somuncurá, Meseta de, *Argentina*	128	B3
Son, *Neths.*	17	E6
Son, *Norway*	10	E4
Son, *Spain*	30	C2
Son Ha, *Vietnam*	58	E7
Son Hoa, *Vietnam*	58	F7
Son La, *Vietnam*	58	B4
Son Tay, *Vietnam*	58	B5
Soná, *Panama*	116	E3
Sonamarg, *India*	63	B6
Sonamukhi, *India*	63	H12
Sŏnch'ŏn, *N. Korea*	51	E13
Soncino, *Italy*	32	C6
Sóndalo, *Italy*	32	B7
Sondar, *India*	63	C6
Sønder Omme, *Denmark*	11	J2
Sønder Tornby, *Denmark*	11	G3
Sønderborg, *Denmark*	11	K3
Sønderjyllands Amtskommune □, *Denmark*	11	J3
Sondershausen, *Germany*	18	D6
Søndre Strømfjord, *Greenland*	97	B14
Sóndrio, *Italy*	32	B6
Sone, *Mozam.*	83	F3
Sonepur, *India*	61	J13
Song, *Thailand*	58	C3
Song Cau, *Vietnam*	58	F7
Song Xian, *China*	50	G7
Songch'ŏn, *N. Korea*	51	E14
Songea, *Tanzania*	83	E4
Songea □, *Tanzania*	83	E4
Songeons, *France*	25	C8
Songhua Hu, *China*	51	C14
Songhua Jiang →, *China*	54	B8
Songjiang, *China*	53	B13
Songjin, *China*	51	D15
Songjŏng-ni, *S. Korea*	51	G14
Songkan, *China*	52	C6
Songkhla, *Thailand*	59	J3
Songming, *China*	52	E4
Songnim, *N. Korea*	51	E13
Songpan, *China*	52	A4
Songtao, *China*	52	C7
Songwe, *Zaïre*	82	C2
Songwe →, *Africa*	83	D3
Songxi, *China*	53	D12
Songzi, *China*	53	B8
Sonid Youqi, *China*	50	C7
Sonipat, *India*	62	E7
Sonkovo, *Russia*	41	C10
Sonmiani, *Pakistan*	62	G2
Sonnino, *Italy*	34	A6
Sono →, *Goiás, Brazil*	122	C2
Sono →, *Minas Gerais, Brazil*	123	E2
Sonogno, *Switz.*	23	D7
Sonora, *Calif., U.S.A.*	111	H3
Sonora, *Tex., U.S.A.*	109	K4
Sonora □, *Mexico*	114	B2
Sonora →, *Mexico*	114	B2
Sonora Desert, *U.S.A.*	113	M12
Sonoyta, *Mexico*	114	A2
Sŏnsan, *S. Korea*	51	F15
Sonsonate, *El Salv.*	116	D2
Sonthofen, *Germany*	19	H6
Soochow = Suzhou, *China*	53	B13
Sop Hao, *Laos*	58	B5
Sop Prap, *Thailand*	58	D2
Sopachuy, *Bolivia*	125	D5
Sopi, *Indonesia*	57	D7
Sopo, Nahr →, *Sudan*	77	F2
Sopot, *Poland*	20	A8
Sopotnica, *Macedonia*	39	H4
Sopron, *Hungary*	21	H6
Sop's Arm, *Canada*	99	C8
Sopur, *India*	63	B6
Sør-Rondane, *Antarctica*	5	D4
Sør-Trøndelag fylke □, *Norway*	10	B3
Sora, *Italy*	34	A6
Sorah, *Pakistan*	62	F3
Söråker, *Sweden*	10	B11
Sorano, *Italy*	33	F8
Sorata, *Bolivia*	124	D4
Sorbas, *Spain*	29	H2
Soreq, N. →, *Israel*	69	D3
Soresina, *Italy*	32	C6
Sorgono, *Italy*	34	B2
Sorgues, *France*	27	D8
Sorgun, *Turkey*	66	D6
Soria, *Spain*	28	D2
Soria □, *Spain*	28	D2
Soriano, *Uruguay*	126	C4
Soriano nel Cimino, *Italy*	33	F9
Sorkh, Kuh-e, *Iran*	65	C8
Sorø, *Denmark*	11	J5
Soro, *Guinea*	78	C3
Sorocaba, *Brazil*	127	A6
Soroki, *Moldavia*	42	B3
Soron, *India*	63	F8
Sorong, *Indonesia*	57	E8
Soroní, *Greece*	37	C10
Soroti, *Uganda*	82	B3
Sørøya, *Norway*	8	A17
Sørøysundet, *Norway*	8	A17
Sorraia →, *Portugal*	31	G2
Sorrento, *Australia*	91	F3
Sorrento, *Italy*	35	B7
Sorsele, *Sweden*	8	D14
Sorso, *Italy*	34	B1
Sorsogon, *Phil.*	55	E6
Sortino, *Italy*	35	E8
Sorvizhi, *Russia*	41	C16
Sos, *Spain*	28	C3
Sŏsan, *S. Korea*	51	F14
Soscumica, L., *Canada*	98	B4
Sosna →, *Russia*	41	E11
Sosnovka, *Russia*	41	E12
Sosnovka, *Russia*	45	D11
Sosnowiec, *Poland*	20	E9
Sospel, *France*	27	E11
Sostanj, *Slovenia*	33	B12
Sŏsura, *N. Korea*	51	C16
Soto la Marina →, *Mexico*	115	C5
Soto y Amío, *Spain*	30	C5
Sotteville-lès-Rouen, *France*	24	C8
Sotuta, *Mexico*	115	C7
Souanké, *Congo*	80	D2
Soúdha, *Greece*	37	D6
Soúdhas, Kólpos, *Greece*	37	D6
Sougne-Remouchamps, *Belgium*	17	H7
Souillac, *France*	26	D5
Souk-Ahras, *Algeria*	75	A6
Souk el Arba du Rharb, *Morocco*	74	B3
Soukhouma, *Laos*	58	E5
Soultz-sous-Forêts, *France*	25	D14
Soumagne, *Belgium*	17	G7
Sound, The = Øresund, *Europe*	11	J6
Sound, The, *U.K.*	13	G3
Soúnion, Ákra, *Greece*	39	M7
Sour el Ghozlane, *Algeria*	75	A5
Sources, Mt. aux, *Lesotho*	85	D4
Sourdeval, *France*	24	D6
Soure, *Brazil*	122	B2
Soure, *Portugal*	30	E2
Souris, *Man., Canada*	101	D8
Souris, *P.E.I., Canada*	99	C7
Souris →, *Canada*	108	A5
Sousa, *Brazil*	122	C4
Sousel, *Brazil*	122	B1
Sousel, *Portugal*	31	G3
Souss, O. →, *Morocco*	74	B3
Soustons, *France*	26	E2
South Africa ■, *Africa*	84	E3
South Aulatsivik I., *Canada*	99	A7
South Australia □, *Australia*	91	E2
South Baldy, *U.S.A.*	111	J10
South Bend, *Ind., U.S.A.*	104	E2
South Bend, *Wash., U.S.A.*	112	D3
South Boston, *U.S.A.*	105	G6
South Branch, *Canada*	99	C8
South Brook, *Canada*	99	C8
South Buganda □, *Uganda*	82	C3
South Carolina □, *U.S.A.*	105	J5
South Charleston, *U.S.A.*	104	F5
South China Sea, *Asia*	56	C4
South Dakota □, *U.S.A.*	108	C5
South Downs, *U.K.*	13	G7
South East C., *Australia*	90	G4
South East Is., *Australia*	89	F3
South Esk →, *U.K.*	14	E5
South Foreland, *U.K.*	13	F9
South Fork →, *U.S.A.*	110	C7
South Fork, American →, *U.S.A.*	112	G5
South Fork, Feather →, *U.S.A.*	112	F5
South Georgia, *Antarctica*	5	B1
South Glamorgan □, *U.K.*	13	F4
South Haven, *U.S.A.*	104	D2
South Henik, L., *Canada*	101	A9
South Honshu Ridge, *Pac. Oc.*	92	E6
South Horr, *Kenya*	82	B4
South I., *Kenya*	82	B4
South I., *N.Z.*	87	L3
South Invercargill, *N.Z.*	87	M2
South Knife →, *Canada*	101	B10
South Korea ■, *Asia*	51	F15
South Lake Tahoe, *U.S.A.*	112	G6
South Loup →, *U.S.A.*	108	E5
South Magnetic Pole, *Antarctica*	5	C9
South Milwaukee, *U.S.A.*	104	D2
South Molton, *U.K.*	13	F4
South Nahanni →, *Canada*	100	A4
South Natuna Is. = Natuna Selatan, Kepulauan, *Indonesia*	59	L7
South Negril Pt., *Jamaica*	116	C4
South Orkney Is., *Antarctica*	5	C18
South Pagai, I. = Pagai Selatan, P., *Indonesia*	56	E2
South Pass, *U.S.A.*	110	E9
South Pittsburg, *U.S.A.*	105	H3
South Platte →, *U.S.A.*	108	E4
South Pole, *Antarctica*	5	E
South Porcupine, *Canada*	98	C3
South River, *Canada*	98	C4
South River, *U.S.A.*	107	F10
South Ronaldsay, *U.K.*	14	C6
South Sandwich Is., *Antarctica*	5	B1
South Saskatchewan →, *Canada*	101	C7
South Seal →, *Canada*	101	B9
South Shetland Is., *Antarctica*	5	C18
South Shields, *U.K.*	12	C6
South Sioux City, *U.S.A.*	108	D6
South Taranaki Bight, *N.Z.*	87	H5
South Thompson →, *Canada*	100	C4
South Twin I., *Canada*	98	B4
South Tyne →, *U.K.*	12	C5
South Uist, *U.K.*	14	D1
South West Africa = Namibia ■, *Africa*	84	C2
South West C., *Australia*	90	G4
South Yorkshire □, *U.K.*	12	D6
Southampton, *Canada*	98	D3
Southampton, *U.K.*	13	G6
Southampton, *U.S.A.*	107	F12
Southampton I., *Canada*	97	B11
Southbridge, *N.Z.*	87	K4
Southbridge, *U.S.A.*	107	D12
Southend, *Canada*	101	B8
Southend-on-Sea, *U.K.*	13	F8
Southern □, *Malawi*	83	F4
Southern □, *S. Leone*	78	D2
Southern □, *Zambia*	83	F2
Southern Alps, *N.Z.*	87	K3
Southern Cross, *Australia*	89	F2
Southern Hills, *Australia*	89	F3
Southern Indian L., *Canada*	101	B9
Southern Ocean, *Antarctica*	5	C6
Southern Pines, *U.S.A.*	105	H6
Southern Uplands, *U.K.*	14	F5
Southington, *U.S.A.*	107	E12
Southold, *U.S.A.*	107	E12
Southport, *Australia*	91	D5
Southport, *U.K.*	12	D4
Southport, *U.S.A.*	105	J6
Southwest C., *N.Z.*	87	M1
Southwold, *U.K.*	13	E9
Soutpansberg, *S. Africa*	85	C4
Souvigny, *France*	26	B7
Sovetsk, *Russia*	40	D2
Sovetsk, *Russia*	41	C16
Sovetskaya Gavan, *Russia*	45	E15
Sovicille, *Italy*	33	E8
Soviet Union = Commonwealth of Independent States ■, *Eurasia*	45	D11
Sovra, *Croatia*	21	N7
Soweto, *S. Africa*	85	D4
Sōya-Kaikyō = La Perouse Str., *Asia*	48	B11
Sōya-Misaki, *Japan*	48	B10
Soyo, *Angola*	80	F2
Sozh →, *Belorussia*	40	F7
Sozopol, *Bulgaria*	38	G10
Spa, *Belgium*	17	H7
Spain ■, *Europe*	7	H5
Spakenburg, *Neths.*	16	D6
Spalding, *Australia*	91	E2
Spalding, *U.K.*	12	E7
Spalding, *U.S.A.*	108	E5
Spangler, *U.S.A.*	106	F6
Spaniard's Bay, *Canada*	99	C9
Spanish, *Canada*	98	C3
Spanish Fork, *U.S.A.*	110	F8
Spanish Town, *Jamaica*	116	C4
Sparks, *U.S.A.*	112	F7
Sparta = Spárti, *Greece*	39	M5
Sparta, *Ga., U.S.A.*	105	J4
Sparta, *Wis., U.S.A.*	108	D9
Spartanburg, *U.S.A.*	105	H4
Spartansburg, *U.S.A.*	106	E5
Spartel, C., *Morocco*	74	A3
Spárti, *Greece*	39	M5
Spartivento, C., *Calabria, Italy*	35	E9
Spartivento, C., *Sard., Italy*	34	D1
Spas-Demensk, *Russia*	40	D8
Spas-Klepiki, *Russia*	41	D12
Spassk-Dalniy, *Russia*	45	E14
Spassk-Ryazanskiy, *Russia*	41	D12
Spátha, Ákra, *Greece*	37	D5
Spatsizi →, *Canada*	100	B3
Spearfish, *U.S.A.*	108	C3
Spearman, *U.S.A.*	109	G4
Speer, *Switz.*	23	B8
Speers, *Canada*	101	C7
Speightstown, *Barbados*	117	D8
Speke Gulf, *Tanzania*	82	C3
Spekholzerheide, *Neths.*	17	G8
Spence Bay, *Canada*	96	B10
Spencer, *Idaho, U.S.A.*	110	D7
Spencer, *Iowa, U.S.A.*	108	D7
Spencer, *N.Y., U.S.A.*	107	D8
Spencer, *Nebr., U.S.A.*	108	D5
Spencer, *W. Va., U.S.A.*	104	F5
Spencer, C., *Australia*	91	F2
Spencer B., *Namibia*	84	D1
Spencer G., *Australia*	91	E2
Spencerville, *Canada*	107	B9
Spences Bridge, *Canada*	100	C4
Spenser Mts., *N.Z.*	87	K4
Sperkhiós →, *Greece*	39	L5
Sperrin Mts., *U.K.*	15	B5
Spessart, *Germany*	19	E5
Spétsai, *Greece*	39	M6
Spey →, *U.K.*	14	D5
Speyer, *Germany*	19	F4
Speyer →, *Germany*	19	F4
Spezzano Albanese, *Italy*	35	C9
Spiekeroog, *Germany*	18	B3
Spielfeld, *Austria*	33	B12
Spiez, *Switz.*	22	C5
Spijk, *Neths.*	16	B9
Spijkenisse, *Neths.*	16	E4
Spíli, *Greece*	37	D6
Spilimbergo, *Italy*	33	B9
Spin Baldak = Qala-i-Jadid, *Afghan.*	62	D2
Spinalónga, *Greece*	37	D7
Spinazzola, *Italy*	35	B9
Spirit Lake, *Idaho, U.S.A.*	110	C5
Spirit Lake, *Wash., U.S.A.*	112	D4
Spirit River, *Canada*	100	B5
Spiritwood, *Canada*	101	C7
Spišská Nová Ves, *Slovak Rep.*	20	G10
Spithead, *U.K.*	13	G6
Spittal, *Austria*	21	J3
Spitzbergen = Svalbard, *Arctic*	4	B8
Split, *Croatia*	33	E13
Split L., *Canada*	101	B9
Splitski Kanal, *Croatia*	33	E13
Splügen, *Switz.*	23	C8
Splügenpass, *Switz.*	23	C8
Spofford, *U.S.A.*	109	L4
Spokane, *U.S.A.*	110	C5
Spoleto, *Italy*	33	F9
Spooner, *U.S.A.*	108	C9
Sporyy Navolok, Mys, *Russia*	44	B7
Spragge, *Canada*	98	C3
Sprague, *U.S.A.*	110	C5
Sprague River, *U.S.A.*	110	E3
Spratly I., *S. China Sea*	56	C4
Spray, *U.S.A.*	110	D4
Spree →, *Germany*	18	C9
Spremberg, *Germany*	18	D10
Sprimont, *Belgium*	17	G7
Spring City, *U.S.A.*	110	G8
Spring Garden, *U.S.A.*	112	F6
Spring Mts., *U.S.A.*	111	H6
Spring Valley, *Calif., U.S.A.*	113	N10
Spring Valley, *Minn., U.S.A.*	108	D8
Springbok, *S. Africa*	84	D2
Springdale, *Canada*	99	C8
Springdale, *Ark., U.S.A.*	109	G7
Springdale, *Wash., U.S.A.*	110	B5
Springe, *Germany*	18	C5
Springer, *U.S.A.*	109	G2
Springerville, *U.S.A.*	111	J9
Springfield, *Canada*	106	D4
Springfield, *N.Z.*	87	K3
Springfield, *Colo., U.S.A.*	109	G3

Springfield, Ill., U.S.A. ... 108 F10
Springfield, Mass., U.S.A. 107 D12
Springfield, Mo., U.S.A. 109 G8
Springfield, Ohio, U.S.A. 104 F4
Springfield, Oreg., U.S.A. 110 D2
Springfield, Tenn., U.S.A. 105 G2
Springfield, Vt., U.S.A. 107 C12
Springfontein, S. Africa .. 84 E4
Springhill, Canada 99 C7
Springhouse, Canada 100 C4
Springhurst, Australia ... 91 F4
Springs, S. Africa 85 D4
Springsure, Australia 90 C4
Springvale, Queens., Australia ... 90 C3
Springvale, W. Austral., Australia ... 88 C4
Springvale, U.S.A. 107 C14
Springville, Calif., U.S.A. 112 J8
Springville, N.Y., U.S.A. 106 D6
Springville, Utah, U.S.A. 110 F8
Springwater, Canada 101 C7
Spruce-Creek, U.S.A. ... 106 F6
Spur, U.S.A. 109 J4
Spurn Hd., U.K. 12 D8
Spuž, Montenegro 21 N9
Spuzzum, Canada 100 D4
Squam L., U.S.A. 107 C13
Squamish, Canada 100 D4
Square Islands, Canada ... 99 B8
Squillace, G. di, Italy ... 35 D9
Squinzano, Italy 35 B11
Squires, Mt., Australia ... 89 E4
Sragen, Indonesia 57 G14
Srbac, Bos.-H. 21 K7
Srbija = Serbia □, Yugoslavia ... 21 M11
Srbobran, Serbia 21 K9
Sre Khtum, Cambodia ... 59 F6
Sre Umbell, Cambodia ... 59 G4
Srebrnica, Bos.-H. 21 L9
Sredinny Ra. = Sredinnyy Khrebet, Russia ... 45 D16
Sredinnyy Khrebet, Russia 45 D16
Središče, Slovenia 33 B13
Sredna Gora, Bulgaria .. 38 G7
Sredne Tambovskoye, Russia ... 45 D14
Srednekolymsk, Russia .. 45 C16
Srednevilyuysk, Russia .. 45 C13
Śrem, Poland 20 C7
Sremska Mitrovica, Serbia 21 L9
Srepok →, Cambodia ... 58 F6
Sretensk, Russia 45 D12
Sri Lanka ■, Asia 60 R12
Srikakulam, India 61 K13
Srinagar, India 63 B6
Środa Wielkopolski, Poland 20 C7
Srpska Itabej, Serbia ... 21 K10
Staaten →, Australia ... 90 B3
Staberhuk, Germany 18 A7
Stabroek, Belgium 17 F4
Stad Delden, Neths. 16 D9
Stade, Germany 18 B5
Staden, Belgium 17 G2
Staðarhólskirkja, Iceland .. 8 D3
Städjan, Sweden 10 C6
Stadlandet, Norway 8 E12
Stadskanaal, Neths. 16 B9
Stadthagen, Germany ... 18 C5
Stadtlohn, Germany 18 D2
Stadtroda, Germany 18 E7
Stäfa, Switz. 23 B7
Stafafell, Iceland 8 D6
Staffa, U.K. 14 E2
Stafford, U.K. 12 E5
Stafford, U.S.A. 109 G5
Stafford Springs, U.S.A. 107 E12
Staffordshire □, U.K. ... 12 E5
Stagnone, Italy 34 E5
Staines, U.K. 13 F7
Stakhanov = Kadiyevka, Ukraine ... 43 B8
Stalden, Switz. 22 D5
Stalingrad = Volgograd, Russia ... 43 B11
Staliniri = Tskhinvali, Georgia ... 43 E11
Stalino = Donetsk, Ukraine 42 C7
Stalinogorsk = Novomoskovsk, Russia 41 D11
Stalis, Greece 37 D7
Stalowa Wola, Poland .. 20 E12
Stalybridge, U.K. 12 D5
Stamford, Australia 90 C3
Stamford, U.K. 13 E7
Stamford, Conn., U.S.A. 107 E11
Stamford, Tex., U.S.A. . 109 J5
Stamps, U.S.A. 109 J8
Stanberry, U.S.A. 108 E7
Stančevo = Kalipetrovo, Bulgaria ... 38 E10
Standerton, S. Africa ... 85 D4
Standish, U.S.A. 104 D4
Stanford, U.S.A. 110 C8
Stange, Norway 10 D5
Stanger, S. Africa 85 D5
Stanislaus →, U.S.A. .. 112 H5
Stanislav = Ivano-Frankovsk, Ukraine ... 40 G4
Stanke Dimitrov, Bulgaria 38 G6
Stanley, Australia 90 G4
Stanley, N.B., Canada .. 99 C6
Stanley, Sask., Canada .. 101 B8
Stanley, Falk. Is. 128 D5

Stanley, Idaho, U.S.A. ... 110 D6
Stanley, N. Dak., U.S.A. . 108 A3
Stanley, N.Y., U.S.A. ... 106 D7
Stanley, Ohio, U.S.A. ... 108 C9
Stanovoy Khrebet, Russia . 45 D13
Stanovoy Ra. = Stanovoy Khrebet, Russia ... 45 D13
Stans, Switz. 23 C6
Stansmore Ra., Australia . 88 D4
Stanthorpe, Australia 91 D5
Stanton, U.S.A. 109 J4
Stanwood, U.S.A. 112 B4
Staphorst, Neths. 16 C8
Staples, U.S.A. 108 B7
Stapleton, U.S.A. 108 E4
Star City, Canada 101 C8
Stara-minskaya, Russia .. 43 C8
Stara Moravica, Serbia .. 21 K9
Stara Planina, Bulgaria .. 38 F6
Stara Zagora, Bulgaria ... 38 G8
Starachowice, Poland ... 20 D11
Starashcherbinovskaya, Russia ... 43 C8
Staraya Russa, Russia ... 40 C7
Starbuck I., Kiribati 93 H12
Stargard Szczeciński, Poland ... 20 B5
Stari Trg, Slovenia 33 C12
Staritsa, Russia 40 C9
Starke, U.S.A. 105 K4
Starkville, Colo., U.S.A. . 109 G2
Starkville, Miss., U.S.A. . 105 J1
Starnberg, Germany 19 G7
Starnberger See, Germany 19 H7
Starobelsk, Ukraine 43 B8
Starodub, Russia 40 E8
Starogard, Poland 20 B8
Starokonstantinov, Ukraine 42 B2
Start Pt., U.K. 13 G4
Staryy Biryuzyak, Russia . 43 D12
Staryy Chartoriysk, Ukraine 40 F4
Staryy Kheydzhan, Russia 45 C15
Staryy Krym, Ukraine ... 42 D6
Staryy Oskol, Russia ... 41 F10
Stassfurt, Germany 18 D7
State College, U.S.A. ... 106 F7
Staten, I. = Estados, I. de Los, Argentina ... 128 D4
Staten I., U.S.A. 107 F10
Statesboro, U.S.A. 105 J5
Statesville, U.S.A. 105 H5
Stauffer, U.S.A. 113 L7
Staunton, Ill., U.S.A. ... 108 F10
Staunton, Va., U.S.A. .. 104 F6
Stavanger, Norway 9 G8
Staveley, N.Z. 87 K3
Stavelot, Belgium 17 H7
Stavenhagen, Germany .. 18 B8
Stavenisse, Neths. 17 E4
Staveren, Neths. 16 C6
Stavern, Norway 10 F4
Stavre, Sweden 10 B9
Stavropol, Russia 43 D10
Stavros, Cyprus 37 D11
Stavrós, Greece 37 D6
Stavros, Ákra, Greece ... 37 D6
Stavroúpolis, Greece 39 H7
Stawell, Australia 91 F3
Stawell →, Australia ... 90 C3
Stawiszyn, Poland 20 D8
Stayner, Canada 106 B4
Steamboat Springs, U.S.A. 110 F10
Steckborn, Switz. 23 A7
Steele, U.S.A. 108 B5
Steelton, U.S.A. 106 F8
Steelville, U.S.A. 109 G9
Steen River, Canada ... 100 B5
Steenbergen, Neths. 17 E4
Steenkool = Bintuni, Indonesia ... 57 E8
Steenvoorde, France 25 B9
Steenwijk, Neths. 16 C8
Steep Pt., Australia 89 E1
Steep Rock, Canada ... 101 C9
Ştefăneşti, Romania 38 B10
Stefanie L. = Chew Bahir, Ethiopia ... 77 G4
Stefansson Bay, Antarctica 5 C5
Steffisburg, Switz. 22 C5
Stege, Denmark 11 K6
Steiermark □, Austria .. 21 H5
Steigerwald, Germany .. 19 F6
Steilacoom, U.S.A. 112 C4
Stein, Neths. 17 G7
Steinbach, Canada 101 D9
Steinfort, Lux. 17 J7
Steinfurt, Germany 18 C3
Steinheim, Germany ... 18 D5
Steinhuder Meer, Germany 18 C5
Steinkjer, Norway 8 E11
Steinkopf, S. Africa 84 D2
Stekene, Belgium 17 F4
Stellarton, Canada 99 C7
Stellenbosch, S. Africa .. 84 E2
Stellendam, Neths. 16 E4
Stelvio, Paso dello, Italy .. 23 C10
Stemshaug, Norway 10 A2
Stendal, Germany 18 C7
Stene, Belgium 17 F1
Stensele, Sweden 8 D14
Stenstorp, Sweden 11 F7
Stepanakert = Khankendy, Azerbaijan ... 67 D12
Stephen, U.S.A. 108 A6

Stephens Creek, Australia . 91 E3
Stephens I., Canada 100 C2
Stephenville, Canada 99 C8
Stephenville, U.S.A. 109 J5
Stepnica, Poland 20 B4
Stepnoi = Elista, Russia .. 43 C11
Stepnyak, Kazakhstan ... 44 D8
Steppe, Asia 46 E9
Sterkstroom, S. Africa ... 84 E4
Sterling, Colo., U.S.A. ... 108 E3
Sterling, Ill., U.S.A. 108 E10
Sterling, Kans., U.S.A. .. 108 F5
Sterling City, U.S.A. 109 K4
Sterling Run, U.S.A. 106 E6
Sterlitamak, Russia 44 D6
Sternberg, Germany 18 B7
Šternberk, Czech. 20 F7
Stérnes, Greece 37 D6
Stettin = Szczecin, Poland 20 B4
Stettiner Haff, Germany . 18 B10
Stettler, Canada 100 C6
Steubenville, U.S.A. 106 F4
Stevens Point, U.S.A. ... 108 C10
Stevenson, U.S.A. 112 E5
Stevenson L., Canada ... 101 C9
Stevns Klint, Denmark .. 11 J6
Stewart, B.C., Canada .. 100 B3
Stewart, N.W.T., Canada . 96 B6
Stewart, U.S.A. 112 F7
Stewart, C., Australia ... 90 A1
Stewart, I., Chile 128 D2
Stewart I., N.Z. 87 M1
Stewarts Point, U.S.A. .. 112 G3
Stewiacke, Canada 99 C7
Steynsburg, S. Africa ... 84 E4
Steyr, Austria 21 G4
Steytlerville, S. Africa ... 84 E3
Stia, Italy 33 E8
Stiens, Neths. 16 B7
Stigler, U.S.A. 109 H7
Stigliano, Italy 35 B9
Stigsnæs, Denmark 11 J5
Stigtomta, Sweden 11 F10
Stikine →, Canada 100 B2
Stilfontein, S. Africa 84 D4
Stillís, Greece 39 L5
Stillwater, N.Z. 87 K3
Stillwater, Minn., U.S.A. . 108 C8
Stillwater, N.Y., U.S.A. . 107 D11
Stillwater, Okla., U.S.A. . 109 G6
Stillwater Range, U.S.A. . 110 G4
Stilwell, U.S.A. 109 H7
Štip, Macedonia 39 H5
Stíra, Greece 39 L7
Stirling, Australia 90 B3
Stirling, Canada 100 D6
Stirling, U.K. 14 E5
Stirling Ra., Australia ... 89 F2
Stittsville, Canada 107 A9
Stockach, Germany 19 H5
Stockerau, Austria 21 G6
Stockett, U.S.A. 110 C8
Stockholm, Sweden 10 E12
Stockholms län □, Sweden 10 E12
Stockhorn, Switz. 22 C5
Stockport, U.K. 12 D5
Stockton, Calif., U.S.A. . 111 H3
Stockton, Kans., U.S.A. . 108 F5
Stockton, Mo., U.S.A. .. 109 G8
Stockton-on-Tees, U.K. . 12 C6
Stockvik, Sweden 10 B11
Stöde, Sweden 10 B10
Stogovo, Macedonia ... 39 H3
Stoke on Trent, U.K. ... 12 D5
Stokes Bay, Canada ... 98 C3
Stokes Pt., Australia ... 90 G3
Stokes Ra., Australia ... 88 C5
Stokkseyri, Iceland 8 E3
Stokksnes, Iceland 8 D6
Stolac, Bos.-H. 21 M7
Stolberg, Germany 18 E2
Stolbovaya, Russia 41 D10
Stolbovaya, Russia 45 C16
Stolbovoy, Ostrov, Russia 45 D17
Stolbtsy, Belorussia 40 E5
Stolin, Belorussia 40 F5
Stolwijk, Neths. 16 E5
Stomíon, Greece 37 D5
Ston, Croatia 21 N7
Stonehaven, U.K. 14 E6
Stonehenge, Australia ... 90 C3
Stonewall, Canada 101 C9
Stony L., Man., Canada . 101 B9
Stony L., Ont., Canada . 106 B6
Stony Rapids, Canada .. 101 B7
Stony Tunguska = Podkamennaya Tunguska →, Russia ... 45 C10
Stonyford, U.S.A. 112 F4
Stopnica, Poland 20 E10
Stora Lulevatten, Sweden 8 C15
Stora Sjöfallet, Sweden . 8 C15
Storavan, Sweden 8 D15
Store Bælt, Denmark ... 11 J5
Store Creek, Australia .. 91 E4
Store Heddinge, Denmark 11 J6
Støren, Norway 10 A4
Storlulea = Stora Lulevatten, Sweden ... 8 C15
Storm B., Australia 90 G4
Storm Lake, U.S.A. ... 108 D7
Stormberge, S. Africa ... 84 E4
Stormsrivier, S. Africa .. 84 E3
Stornoway, U.K. 14 C2
Storozhinets, Ukraine ... 42 B1

Storsjö, Sweden 10 B7
Storsjøen, Hedmark, Norway ... 10 D5
Storsjøen, Hedmark, Norway ... 10 C5
Storsjön, Sweden 10 B7
Storstrøms Amt. □, Denmark ... 11 K5
Storuman, Sweden 8 D14
Stoughton, Canada 101 D8
Stour →, Dorset, U.K. . 13 G5
Stour →, Here. & Worcs., U.K. ... 13 E5
Stour →, Kent, U.K. ... 13 F9
Stour →, Suffolk, U.K. . 13 F9
Stourbridge, U.K. 13 E5
Stout, L., Canada 101 C10
Stove Pipe Wells Village, U.S.A. ... 113 J9
Stowmarket, U.K. 13 E9
Strabane, U.K. 15 B4
Strabane □, U.K. 15 B4
Stracin, Macedonia 38 G5
Stradella, Italy 32 C6
Strahan, Australia 90 G4
Strakonice, Czech. 20 F3
Straldzha, Bulgaria 38 G9
Stralsund, Germany 18 A9
Strand, S. Africa 84 E2
Strangford L., U.K. 15 B6
Strängnäs, Sweden 10 E11
Strangsville, U.S.A. 106 E3
Stranraer, U.K. 14 G3
Strasbourg, Canada 101 C8
Strasbourg, France 25 D14
Strasburg, Germany 18 B9
Strasburg, U.S.A. 108 B4
Strassen, Lux. 17 J8
Stratford, Canada 98 D3
Stratford, N.Z. 87 H5
Stratford, Calif., U.S.A. . 111 H4
Stratford, Conn., U.S.A. . 107 E11
Stratford, Tex., U.S.A. .. 109 G3
Stratford-upon-Avon, U.K. 13 E6
Strath Spey, U.K. 14 D5
Strathalbyn, Australia ... 91 F2
Strathclyde □, U.K. ... 14 F4
Strathcona Prov. Park, Canada ... 100 D3
Strathmore, Australia ... 90 B3
Strathmore, Canada 100 C6
Strathmore, U.K. 14 E5
Strathmore, U.S.A. 112 J7
Strathnaver, Canada ... 100 C4
Strathpeffer, U.K. 14 D4
Strathroy, Canada 98 D3
Strathy Pt., U.K. 14 C4
Stratton, U.S.A. 108 F3
Straubing, Germany 19 G8
Straumnes, Iceland 8 C2
Strausberg, Germany ... 18 C9
Strawberry Reservoir, U.S.A. ... 110 F8
Strawn, U.S.A. 109 J5
Streaky B., Australia ... 91 E1
Streaky Bay, Australia .. 91 E1
Streator, U.S.A. 108 E10
Streé, Belgium 17 H4
Streeter, U.S.A. 108 B5
Streetsville, Canada ... 106 C5
Strehaia, Romania 38 E6
Strelcha, Bulgaria 38 G7
Strelka, Russia 45 D10
Streng →, Cambodia ... 58 F4
Strésa, Italy 32 C5
Strezhevoy, Russia 44 C8
Stříbro, Czech. 20 F3
Strijen, Neths. 16 E5
Strimón →, Greece 39 J6
Strimonikós Kólpos, Greece 39 J6
Stroeder, Argentina 128 B4
Strofádhes, Greece 39 M4
Strömbacka, Sweden ... 10 C10
Strómboli, Italy 35 D8
Stromeferry, U.K. 14 D3
Stromness, U.K. 14 C5
Ströms vattudal, Sweden 8 D13
Stromsburg, U.S.A. ... 108 E6
Strömstad, Sweden 9 G11
Strömsund, Sweden ... 8 E13
Stróngoli, Italy 35 C10
Stronsay, U.K. 14 B6
Stroud, U.K. 13 F5
Stroud Road, Australia .. 91 E5
Stroudsburg, U.S.A. ... 107 F9
Stroumbi, Cyprus 37 E11
Struer, Denmark 11 H2
Struga, Macedonia 39 H3
Strugi Krasnyye, Russia . 40 B6
Strumica, Macedonia ... 39 H5
Strumica →, Europe ... 39 H6
Struthers, Canada 98 C2
Struthers, U.S.A. 106 E4
Stryi, Ukraine 40 G3
Stryker, U.S.A. 110 B6
Strzegom, Poland 20 E6
Strzelce Krajeńskie, Poland 20 C5
Strzelecki Cr. →, Australia 91 D2
Strzelin, Poland 20 E7
Strzelno, Poland 20 C8
Strzyzów, Poland 20 F11
Stuart, Fla., U.S.A. 105 M5
Stuart, Nebr., U.S.A. .. 108 D5
Stuart →, Canada 100 C4

Stuart Bluff Ra., Australia 88 D5
Stuart L., Canada 100 C4
Stuart Ra., Australia ... 91 D1
Stubbekøbing, Denmark . 11 K6
Stugun, Sweden 10 A9
Stull, L., Canada 98 B1
Stung Treng, Cambodia . 58 F5
Stupart →, Canada ... 101 B10
Stupino, Russia 41 D11
Sturgeon B., Canada ... 101 C9
Sturgeon Bay, U.S.A. .. 104 C2
Sturgeon Falls, Canada . 98 C4
Sturgeon L., Alta., Canada 100 B5
Sturgeon L., Ont., Canada 106 B6
Sturgeon L., Ont., Canada 98 B1
Sturgis, Mich., U.S.A. .. 104 E3
Sturgis, S. Dak., U.S.A. . 108 C3
Sturt Cr. →, Australia .. 88 C4
Sturt Creek, Australia .. 88 C4
Stutterheim, S. Africa ... 84 E4
Stuttgart, Germany 19 G5
Stuttgart, U.S.A. 109 H9
Stuyvesant, U.S.A. 107 D11
Stykkishólmur, Iceland .. 8 D2
Styr →, Belorussia ... 40 E5
Styria = Steiermark □, Austria ... 21 H5
Su Xian, China 50 H9
Suakin, Sudan 76 D4
Suan, N. Korea 51 E14
Suapure →, Venezuela . 120 B4
Suaqui, Mexico 114 B3
Suatá →, Venezuela ... 121 B4
Subang, Indonesia 57 G12
Subansiri →, India 61 F18
Subayhah, Si. Arabia ... 64 D3
Subi, Indonesia 59 L7
Subiaco, Italy 33 G10
Subotica, Serbia 21 J9
Success, Canada 101 C7
Suceava, Romania 38 B9
Suceava →, Romania .. 38 B9
Sucha-Beskidzka, Poland . 20 F9
Suchan, Poland 20 B5
Suchan, Russia 48 C6
Suchitoto, El Salv. 116 D2
Suchou = Suzhou, China . 53 B13
Süchow = Xuzhou, China 51 G9
Suchowola, Poland 20 B13
Sucio →, Colombia ... 120 B2
Suck →, Ireland 15 C3
Sucre, Bolivia 125 D4
Sucre, Colombia 120 B3
Sucre □, Colombia 120 B2
Sucre □, Venezuela ... 121 A5
Sucuaro, Colombia 120 C4
Sućuraj, Croatia 33 E14
Sucuriju, Brazil 122 A2
Sucuriú →, Brazil 125 E7
Sud, Pte., Canada 99 C7
Sud-Ouest, Pte. du, Canada 99 C7
Suda →, Russia 41 B10
Sudak, Ukraine 42 D6
Sudan, U.S.A. 109 H3
Sudan ■, Africa 77 E3
Suday, Russia 41 B13
Sudbury, Canada 98 C3
Sudbury, U.K. 13 E8
Südd, Sudan 77 F2
Suddie, Guyana 121 B6
Süderbrarup, Germany .. 18 A5
Süderlügum, Germany .. 18 A4
Süderoog-Sand, Germany 18 A4
Sudeten Mts. = Sudety, Europe ... 20 E6
Sudety, Europe 20 E6
Sudi, Tanzania 83 E4
Sudirman, Pegunungan, Indonesia ... 57 E9
Sudogda, Russia 41 D12
Sudr, Egypt 76 J8
Sudzha, Russia 40 F9
Sueca, Spain 29 F4
Suedala, Sweden 11 J7
Suez = El Suweis, Egypt . 76 J8
Suez, G. of = Suweis, Khalig el, Egypt ... 76 J8
Suez Canal = Suweis, Qanâl es, Egypt ... 76 H8
Suffield, Canada 101 C6
Suffolk, U.S.A. 104 G7
Suffolk □, U.K. 13 E9
Sugar City, U.S.A. 108 F3
Suğla Gölü, Turkey 66 E5
Sugluk = Saglouc, Canada 97 B12
Sugny, Belgium 17 J5
Suhaia, L., Romania ... 38 F8
Suhār, Oman 65 E8
Suhbaatar, Mongolia ... 54 A5
Sühbaatar □, Mongolia . 50 B8
Suhl, Germany 18 E6
Suhr, Switz. 22 B5
Şuhut, Turkey 66 E4
Sui Xian, Henan, China . 50 G8
Sui Xian, Henan, China . 53 B9
Suiá Missu →, Brazil .. 125 C7
Suichang, China 53 C12
Suichuan, China 53 D10
Suide, China 50 F6
Suifenhe, China 51 B16
Suihua, China 54 B7
Suijiang, China 52 C4
Suining, Hunan, China .. 53 D8
Suining, Jiangsu, China . 51 H9
Suining, Sichuan, China . 52 B5

Suiping, China	50	H7
Suippes, France	25	C11
Suir →, Ireland	15	D4
Suixi, China	53	G8
Suiyang, Guizhou, China	52	D6
Suiyang, Heilongjiang, China	51	B16
Suizhong, China	51	D11
Sujangarh, India	62	F6
Sukabumi, Indonesia	57	G12
Sukadana, Kalimantan, Indonesia	56	E3
Sukadana, Sumatera, Indonesia	56	F3
Sukagawa, Japan	49	F10
Sukaraja, Indonesia	56	E4
Sukarnapura = Jayapura, Indonesia	57	E10
Sukchŏn, N. Korea	51	E13
Sukhinichi, Russia	40	D9
Sukhona →, Russia	44	D4
Sukhothai, Thailand	58	D2
Sukhumi, Georgia	43	E9
Sukkur, Pakistan	62	F3
Sukkur Barrage, Pakistan	62	F3
Sukumo, Japan	49	H6
Sukunka →, Canada	100	B4
Sul, Canal do, Brazil	122	B2
Sula →, Ukraine	40	G8
Sula, Kepulauan, Indonesia	57	E7
Sulaco →, Honduras	116	C2
Sulaiman Range, Pakistan	62	D3
Sulak →, Russia	43	E12
Sulawesi □, Indonesia	57	E6
Sulawesi Sea, Indonesia	57	D6
Sulechów, Poland	20	C5
Sulejów, Poland	20	D9
Sulgen, Switz.	23	A8
Sulima, S. Leone	78	D2
Sulina, Romania	38	D12
Sulina, Braţul →, Romania	38	D12
Sulingen, Germany	18	C4
Sulitälma, Sweden	8	C14
Sulitjelma, Norway	8	C14
Sullana, Peru	124	A1
Sullivan, Ill., U.S.A.	108	F10
Sullivan, Ind., U.S.A.	104	F2
Sullivan, Mo., U.S.A.	108	F9
Sullivan Bay, Canada	100	C3
Sully-sur-Loire, France	25	E9
Sulmona, Italy	33	F10
Sulphur, La., U.S.A.	109	K8
Sulphur, Okla., U.S.A.	109	H6
Sulphur Pt., Canada	100	A6
Sulphur Springs, U.S.A.	109	J7
Sulphur Springs Draw →, U.S.A.	109	J4
Sultan, Canada	98	C3
Sultan, U.S.A.	112	C5
Sultanpur, India	63	F10
Sulu Arch., Phil.	55	J4
Sulu Sea, E. Indies	55	G4
Sülüklü, Turkey	66	D5
Sulula, Ethiopia	77	F4
Suluova, Turkey	66	C6
Suluq, Libya	73	B9
Sulzbach, Germany	19	F3
Sulzbach-Rosenberg, Germany	19	F7
Sulzberger Ice Shelf, Antarctica	5	D10
Sumalata, Indonesia	57	D6
Sumampa, Argentina	126	B3
Sumatera □, Indonesia	56	D2
Sumatra = Sumatera □, Indonesia	56	D2
Sumatra, U.S.A.	110	C10
Sumba, Indonesia	57	F5
Sumba, Selat, Indonesia	57	F5
Sumbawa, Indonesia	56	F5
Sumbawa Besar, Indonesia	56	F5
Sumbawanga □, Tanzania	82	D3
Sumbe, Angola	80	G2
Sumburgh Hd., U.K.	14	B7
Sumdo, India	63	B8
Sumé, Brazil	122	C4
Sumedang, Indonesia	57	G12
Šumen, Bulgaria	38	F9
Sumenep, Indonesia	57	G15
Sumgait, Azerbaijan	43	F13
Sumiswald, Switz.	22	B5
Summer L., U.S.A.	110	E3
Summerland, Canada	100	D5
Summerside, Canada	99	C7
Summerville, Ga., U.S.A.	105	H3
Summerville, S.C., U.S.A.	105	J5
Summit Lake, Canada	100	C4
Summit Peak, U.S.A.	111	H10
Sumner, Iowa, U.S.A.	108	D8
Sumner, Wash., U.S.A.	112	C4
Sumoto, Japan	49	G7
Sumqayit = Sumgait, Azerbaijan	43	F13
Sumter, U.S.A.	105	J5
Sumy, Ukraine	40	F9
Sun City, Ariz., U.S.A.	111	K7
Sun City, Calif., U.S.A.	113	M9
Sunagawa, Japan	48	C10
Sunan, N. Korea	51	E13
Sunart, L., U.K.	14	E3
Sunburst, U.S.A.	110	B8
Sunbury, Australia	91	F3
Sunbury, U.S.A.	107	F8
Sunchales, Argentina	126	C3
Suncho Corral, Argentina	126	B3
Sunchon, S. Korea	51	G14
Suncook, U.S.A.	107	C13
Sunda, Selat, Indonesia	56	F3
Sunda Is., Indonesia	46	K14
Sunda Str. = Sunda, Selat, Indonesia	56	F3
Sundance, U.S.A.	108	C2
Sundarbans, The, Asia	61	J16
Sundargarh, India	61	H14
Sundays = Sondags →, S. Africa	84	E4
Sundsbyberg, Sweden	10	E11
Sunderland, Canada	106	B5
Sunderland, U.K.	12	C6
Sundre, Canada	100	C6
Sundridge, Canada	98	C4
Sunds, Denmark	11	H3
Sundsjö, Sweden	10	B9
Sundsvall, Sweden	10	B11
Sung Hei, Vietnam	59	G6
Sungai Kolok, Thailand	59	J3
Sungai Lembing, Malaysia	59	L4
Sungai Patani, Malaysia	59	K3
Sungaigerong, Indonesia	56	E2
Sungailiat, Indonesia	56	E3
Sungaipenuh, Indonesia	56	E2
Sungaitiram, Indonesia	56	E5
Sungari = Songhua Jiang →, China	54	B8
Sungguminasa, Indonesia	57	F5
Sunghua Chiang = Songhua Jiang →, China	54	B8
Sungikai, Sudan	77	E2
Sungurlu, Turkey	42	F6
Sunja, Croatia	33	C13
Sunnyside, Utah, U.S.A.	110	G8
Sunnyside, Wash., U.S.A.	110	C3
Sunnyvale, U.S.A.	111	H2
Sunray, U.S.A.	109	G4
Suntar, Russia	45	C12
Sunyani, Ghana	78	D4
Supai, U.S.A.	111	H7
Supamo →, Venezuela	121	B5
Supaul, India	63	F12
Supe, Peru	124	C2
Superior, Ariz., U.S.A.	111	K8
Superior, Mont., U.S.A.	110	C6
Superior, Nebr., U.S.A.	108	E5
Superior, Wis., U.S.A.	108	B8
Superior, L., U.S.A.	98	C2
Supetar, Croatia	33	E13
Suphan Buri, Thailand	58	E3
Suphan Dağı, Turkey	67	D10
Supiori, Kepulauan, Indonesia	57	E9
Supung Sk., China	51	D13
Sūq Suwayq, Si. Arabia	64	E3
Suqian, China	51	H10
Sūr, Lebanon	69	B4
Sur, Pt., U.S.A.	111	H3
Sura →, Russia	41	C15
Surab, Pakistan	62	E2
Surabaja = Surabaya, Indonesia	57	G15
Surabaya, Indonesia	57	G15
Suraia, Romania	38	D10
Surakarta, Indonesia	57	G14
Surakhany, Azerbaijan	43	F14
Surat, Australia	91	D4
Surat, India	60	J8
Surat Thani, Thailand	59	H2
Suratgarh, India	62	E5
Surazh, Belorussia	40	D7
Surazh, Russia	40	E8
Surduc Pasul, Romania	38	D6
Surdulica, Serbia	21	N12
Sûre = Sauer →, Germany	17	J9
Surendranagar, India	62	H4
Surf, U.S.A.	113	L6
Surgères, France	26	B3
Surgut, Russia	44	C8
Surhuisterveen, Neths.	16	B8
Suriapet, India	60	L11
Surigao, Phil.	55	G6
Surigao Strait, Phil.	55	F6
Surin, Thailand	58	E4
Surin Nua, Ko, Thailand	59	H1
Surinam ■, S. Amer.	121	C6
Suriname □ = Surinam ■, S. Amer.	121	C6
Suriname →, Surinam	121	B6
Sürmaq, Iran	65	D7
Sürmene, Turkey	43	F9
Surovikino, Russia	43	B10
Surprise L., Canada	100	B2
Surrey □, U.K.	13	F7
Sursee, Switz.	22	B6
Sursk, Russia	41	E14
Surt, Libya	73	B8
Surt, Khalīj, Libya	73	B8
Surtsey, Iceland	8	E3
Surubim, Brazil	122	C4
Sürüç, Turkey	67	E8
Suruga-Wan, Japan	49	G9
Surumu →, Brazil	121	C5
Susa, Italy	32	C4
Suså →, Denmark	11	J5
Sušac, Croatia	33	F13
Susak, Croatia	33	D11
Susaki, Japan	49	H6
Süsangerd, Iran	65	D6
Susanino, Russia	45	D15
Susanville, U.S.A.	110	F3
Susch, Switz.	23	C10
Suşehri, Turkey	67	C8
Susong, China	53	B11
Susquehanna →, U.S.A.	107	G8
Susquehanna Depot, U.S.A.	107	E9
Susques, Argentina	126	A2
Sussex, Canada	99	C6
Sussex, U.S.A.	107	E10
Sussex, E. □, U.K.	13	G8
Sussex, W. □, U.K.	13	G7
Susteren, Neths.	17	F7
Sustut →, Canada	100	B3
Susuman, Russia	45	C15
Susunu, Indonesia	57	E8
Susurluk, Turkey	66	D3
Susz, Turkey	67	C10
Sütçüler, Turkey	66	E4
Sutherland, S. Africa	84	E3
Sutherland, U.S.A.	108	E4
Sutherland Falls, N.Z.	87	L1
Sutherlin, U.S.A.	110	E2
Sutivan, Croatia	33	E13
Sutlej →, Pakistan	62	E4
Sutter, U.S.A.	112	F5
Sutter Creek, U.S.A.	112	G6
Sutton, Canada	107	A12
Sutton, U.S.A.	108	E6
Sutton →, Australia	90	A3
Sutton in Ashfield, U.K.	12	D6
Suttor →, Australia	90	C4
Suttsu, Japan	48	C10
Suva, Fiji	87	D8
Suva Reka, Serbia	21	N10
Suva Rudište, Serbia	21	M10
Suvorov Is. = Suwarrow Is., Cook Is.	93	J11
Suwałki, Poland	20	A12
Suwannaphum, Thailand	58	E4
Suwannee →, U.S.A.	105	L4
Suwanose-Jima, Japan	49	K4
Suwarrow Is., Cook Is.	93	J11
Suwayq aş Şuqban, Iraq	64	D5
Suweis, Khalîg el, Egypt	76	J8
Suweis, Qanâl es, Egypt	76	H8
Suwŏn, S. Korea	51	F14
Suzdal, Russia	41	C12
Suzhou, China	53	B13
Suzu, Japan	49	F8
Suzu-Misaki, Japan	49	F8
Suzuka, Japan	49	G8
Suzzara, Italy	32	C7
Svalbard, Arctic	4	B8
Svalbarð, Iceland	8	C6
Svalöv, Sweden	11	J7
Svanvik, Norway	8	B21
Svappavaara, Sweden	8	C16
Svarstad, Norway	10	E3
Svartisen, Norway	8	C12
Svartvik, Sweden	10	B11
Svatove, Ukraine	42	B8
Svay Chek, Cambodia	58	F4
Svay Rieng, Cambodia	59	G5
Svealand □, Sweden	9	G13
Sveg, Sweden	9	E13
Svendborg, Denmark	11	J4
Svene, Norway	10	E3
Svenljunga, Sweden	11	G7
Svenstrup, Denmark	11	H3
Sverdlovsk = Yekaterinburg, Russia	44	D7
Sverdlovsk, Ukraine	43	B8
Sverdrup Is., Canada	4	B3
Svetac, Croatia	33	E12
Sveti Ivan Zelina, Croatia	33	C13
Sveti Jurij, Slovenia	33	B12
Sveti Lenart, Slovenia	33	B12
Sveti Nikole, Macedonia	39	H4
Sveti Trojica, Slovenia	33	B12
Svetlaya, Russia	48	A9
Svetlogorsk, Belorussia	40	E6
Svetlograd, Russia	43	D10
Svetlovodsk, Ukraine	40	G8
Svetozarevo, Serbia	21	L11
Svidník, Slovak Rep.	20	F11
Svilaja Planina, Croatia	33	E13
Svilengrad, Bulgaria	39	H9
Svir →, Russia	6	C12
Svishtov, Bulgaria	38	F8
Svisloch, Belorussia	40	E4
Svitava →, Czech.	20	F6
Svitavy, Czech.	20	F6
Svobodnyy, Russia	45	D13
Svolvær, Norway	8	B13
Svratka →, Czech.	20	F6
Svrljig, Serbia	21	M12
Swartruggens, S. Africa	84	D4
Swarzędz, Poland	20	C7
Swastika, Canada	98	C3
Swatow = Shantou, China	53	F11
Swaziland ■, Africa	85	D5
Sweden ■, Europe	9	H13
Swedru, Ghana	79	D4
Sweet Home, U.S.A.	110	D2
Sweetwater, Nev., U.S.A.	112	G7
Sweetwater, Tex., U.S.A.	109	J4
Sweetwater →, U.S.A.	110	E10
Swellendam, S. Africa	84	E3
Świdnica, Poland	20	E6
Świdnik, Poland	20	D12
Świdwin, Poland	20	B5
Świebodzin, Poland	20	C5
Świecie, Poland	20	B8
Świętokrzyskie, Góry, Poland	20	E10
Swift Current, Canada	101	C7
Swiftcurrent →, Canada	101	C7
Swilly, L., Ireland	15	A4
Swindle, I., Canada	100	C3
Swindon, U.K.	13	F6
Swinemünde = Świnoujście, Poland	20	B4
Świnoujście, Poland	20	B4
Switzerland ■, Europe	22	D6
Swords, Ireland	15	C5
Syasstroy, Russia	40	A8
Sychevka, Russia	40	D9
Sydney, Australia	91	E5
Sydney, Canada	99	C7
Sydney Mines, Canada	99	C7
Sydprøven, Greenland	4	C5
Sydra G. of = Surt, Khalīj, Libya	73	B8
Syke, Germany	18	C4
Syktyvkar, Russia	44	C6
Sylacauga, U.S.A.	105	J2
Sylarna, Sweden	8	E12
Sylhet, Bangla.	61	G17
Sylt, Germany	18	A4
Sylvan Lake, Canada	100	C6
Sylvania, U.S.A.	105	J5
Sylvester, U.S.A.	105	K4
Sym, Russia	44	C9
Symón, Mexico	114	C4
Synnott Ra., Australia	88	C4
Syracuse, Kans., U.S.A.	109	F4
Syracuse, N.Y., U.S.A.	107	C8
Syrdarya →, Kazakhstan	44	E7
Syria ■, Asia	64	C3
Syul'dzhyukyor, Russia	45	C12
Syzran, Russia	41	E16
Szaraz →, Hungary	21	J10
Szarvas, Hungary	21	J10
Szczebrzeszyn, Poland	20	E12
Szczecin, Poland	20	B4
Szczecinek, Poland	20	B6
Szczekocimy, Poland	20	E9
Szczytno, Poland	20	B11
Szechwan = Sichuan □, China	52	B5
Szeged, Hungary	21	J10
Szeghalom, Hungary	21	H11
Székesfehérvár, Hungary	21	H8
Szekszárd, Hungary	21	J8
Szendrő, Hungary	21	G10
Szentendre, Hungary	21	H9
Szentes, Hungary	21	J10
Szentgotthárd, Hungary	21	J6
Szentlőrinc, Hungary	21	J8
Szigetvár, Hungary	21	J7
Szolnok, Hungary	21	H10
Szombathely, Hungary	21	H6
Szprotawa, Poland	20	D5
Szydłowiec, Poland	20	D10
Szypliszki, Poland	20	A13

T

't Harde, Neths.	16	D7
't Zandt, Neths.	16	B9
Ta Khli Khok, Thailand	58	E3
Ta Lai, Vietnam	59	G6
Tabacal, Argentina	126	A3
Tabaco, Phil.	55	E5
Tabagné, Ivory C.	78	D4
Tabajara, Brazil	125	B5
Tabalos, Peru	124	B2
Tabarca, I. de, Spain	29	G4
Tabarka, Tunisia	75	A6
Ţabas, Khorāsān, Iran	65	C9
Ţabas, Khorāsān, Iran	65	C8
Tabasará, Serranía de, Panama	116	E3
Tabasco □, Mexico	115	D6
Tabatinga, Serra da, Brazil	122	D3
Tabāzīn, Iran	65	D8
Tabelbala, Kahal de, Algeria	75	C4
Taber, Canada	100	D6
Tabernas, Spain	29	H2
Tabernes de Valldigna, Spain	29	F4
Tabira, Brazil	122	C4
Tablas, Phil.	55	E5
Tablas Strait, Phil.	55	E4
Table B. = Tafelbaai, S. Africa	84	E2
Table B., Canada	99	B8
Table Mt., S. Africa	84	E2
Tableland, Australia	88	C4
Tabletop, Mt., Australia	90	C4
Tábor, Czech.	20	F4
Tabora, Tanzania	82	D3
Tabora □, Tanzania	82	D3
Tabou, Ivory C.	78	E3
Tabrīz, Iran	64	B5
Tabuaeran, Pac. Oc.	93	G12
Tabuelan, Phil.	55	F5
Tabuenca, Spain	28	D3
Tabūk, Si. Arabia	64	D3
Tacámbaro de Codallos, Mexico	114	D4
Tacheng, China	54	B3
Tach'ing Shan = Daqing Shan, China	50	D6
Táchira □, Venezuela	120	B3
Tácina →, Italy	35	D9
Tacloban, Phil.	55	F6
Tacna, Peru	124	D3
Tacna □, Peru	124	D3
Tacoma, U.S.A.	112	C4
Tacuarembó, Uruguay	127	C4
Tacutu →, Brazil	121	C5
Tademaït, Plateau du, Algeria	75	C5
Tadent, O. →, Algeria	75	D6
Tadjerdjeri, O., Algeria	75	C6
Tadjerouna, Algeria	75	B5
Tadjettaret, O. →, Algeria	75	D6
Tadjmout, Oasis, Algeria	75	B5
Tadjmout, Saoura, Algeria	75	C5
Tadjoura, Djibouti	68	E3
Tadjoura, Golfe de, Djibouti	77	E5
Tadmor, N.Z.	87	J4
Tadoule, L., Canada	101	B9
Tadoussac, Canada	99	C6
Tadzhikistan = Tajikistan ■, Asia	44	F8
Taechŏn-ni, S. Korea	51	F14
Taegu, S. Korea	51	G15
Taegwan, N. Korea	51	D13
Taejŏn, S. Korea	51	F14
Tafalla, Spain	28	C3
Tafar, Sudan	77	F2
Tafassasset, O. →, Algeria	75	D6
Tafelbaai, S. Africa	84	E2
Tafelney, C., Morocco	74	B3
Tafermaar, Indonesia	57	F8
Taffermit, Morocco	74	C3
Tafí Viejo, Argentina	126	B2
Tafīhān, Iran	65	D7
Tafiré, Ivory C.	78	D3
Tafnidilt, Morocco	74	C2
Tafraoute, Morocco	74	C3
Taft, Iran	65	D7
Taft, Phil.	55	F6
Taft, Calif., U.S.A.	113	K7
Taft, Tex., U.S.A.	109	M6
Taga Dzong, Bhutan	61	F16
Taganrog, Russia	43	C8
Taganrogskiy Zaliv, Russia	42	C8
Tagânt, Mauritania	78	B2
Tagatay, Phil.	55	D4
Tagbilaran, Phil.	55	G5
Tággia, Italy	32	E4
Taghzout, Morocco	74	B4
Tagish, Canada	100	A2
Tagish L., Canada	100	A2
Tagliacozzo, Italy	33	F10
Tagliamento →, Italy	33	C10
Tagna, Colombia	120	D3
Táglio di Po, Italy	33	D9
Tago, Phil.	55	G7
Tagomago, I. de, Spain	36	B8
Taguatinga, Brazil	123	D3
Tagudin, Phil.	55	C4
Tagum, Phil.	55	H6
Tagus = Tejo →, Europe	31	G1
Tahakopa, N.Z.	87	M2
Tahala, Morocco	74	B4
Tahan, Gunong, Malaysia	59	K4
Tahat, Algeria	75	D6
Tāherī, Iran	65	E7
Tahiti, Pac. Oc.	93	J13
Tahoe, L., U.S.A.	112	G6
Tahoe City, U.S.A.	112	F6
Taholah, U.S.A.	112	C2
Tahoua, Niger	79	C6
Tahta, Egypt	76	B3
Tahtali Dağları, Turkey	66	D6
Tahuamanu →, Bolivia	124	C4
Tahulandang, Indonesia	57	D7
Tahuna, Indonesia	57	D7
Taï, Ivory C.	78	D3
Tai Hu, China	53	B13
Tai Xian, China	53	A13
Tai'an, China	51	F9
Taibei, Taiwan	53	E13
Taibique, Canary Is.	36	G2
Taibus Qi, China	50	D8
T'aichung = Taizhong, Taiwan	53	E13
Taidong, Taiwan	53	F13
Taieri →, N.Z.	87	M3
Taigu, China	50	F7
Taihang Shan, China	50	G7
Taihape, N.Z.	87	H5
Taihe, Anhui, China	50	H8
Taihe, Jiangxi, China	53	D10
Taihu, China	53	B11
Taijiang, China	52	D7
Taikang, China	50	G8

Tailem Bend, *Australia* ... 91 F2
Tailfingen, *Germany* 19 G5
Taimyr Peninsula =
  Taymyr, Poluostrov,
  Russia 45 B11
Tain, *U.K.* 14 D4
Tainan, *Taiwan* 53 F13
Taínaron, Ákra, *Greece* .. 39 N5
Taining, *China* 53 D11
Taintignies, *Belgium* 17 G2
Taiobeiras, *Brazil* 123 E3
T'aipei = Taibei, *Taiwan* . 53 E13
Taiping, *China* 53 B12
Taiping, *Malaysia* 59 K3
Taipingzhen, *China* 50 H6
Taipu, *Brazil* 122 C4
Taishan, *China* 53 F9
Taishun, *China* 53 D12
Taita □, *Kenya* 82 C4
Taita Hills, *Kenya* 82 C4
Taitao, C., *Chile* 128 C1
Taitao, Pen. de, *Chile* . 128 C2
Taivalkoski, *Finland* .. 8 D20
Taiwan ■, *Asia* 53 F13
Taiwan Shan, *Taiwan* .. 53 F13
Taixing, *China* 53 A13
Taïyetos Óros, *Greece* .. 39 N5
Taiyiba, *Israel* 69 C4
Taiyuan, *China* 50 F7
Taizhong, *Taiwan* 53 E13
Taizhou, *China* 53 A12
Taizhou Liedao, *China* .. 53 C13
Ta'izz, *Yemen* 68 E3
Tājābād, *Iran* 65 D7
Tajapuru, Furo do, *Brazil* 122 B1
Tajikistan ■, *Asia* 44 F8
Tajo = Tejo →, *Europe* . 31 G1
Tajrīsh, *Iran* 65 C6
Tājūrā, *Libya* 73 B7
Tak, *Thailand* 58 D2
Takāb, *Iran* 64 B5
Takachiho, *Japan* 49 H5
Takada, *Japan* 49 F9
Takahagi, *Japan* 49 F10
Takaka, *N.Z.* 87 J4
Takamatsu, *Japan* 49 G7
Takaoka, *Japan* 49 F8
Takapuna, *N.Z.* 87 G5
Takasaki, *Japan* 49 F9
Takatsuki, *Japan* 49 G7
Takaungu, *Kenya* 82 C4
Takayama, *Japan* 49 F8
Take-Shima, *Japan* ... 49 J5
Takefu, *Japan* 49 G8
Takengon, *Indonesia* .. 56 D1
Takeo, *Cambodia* 59 G5
Takeo, *Japan* 49 H5
Tåkern, *Sweden* 11 F8
Tākestān, *Iran* 65 C6
Taketa, *Japan* 49 H5
Takh, *India* 63 C7
Takhman, *Cambodia* .. 59 G5
Takikawa, *Japan* 48 C10
Takla L., *Canada* 100 B3
Takla Landing, *Canada* ... 100 B3
Takla Makan =
  Taklamakan Shamo,
  China 54 C3
Taklamakan Shamo, *China* 54 C3
Taku →, *Canada* 100 B2
Takum, *Nigeria* 79 D6
Takutu →, *Guyana* .. 121 C5
Tal Halāl, *Iran* 65 D7
Tala, *Uruguay* 127 C4
Talacogan, *Phil.* 55 G6
Talagante, *Chile* 126 C1
Talaïnt, *Morocco* 74 C3
Talak, *Niger* 79 B6
Talamanca, Cordillera de,
  Cent. Amer. 116 E3
Talara, *Peru* 124 A1
Talas, *Kirghizia* 44 E8
Talas, *Turkey* 66 C6
Talâta, *Egypt* 69 E1
Talata Mafara, *Nigeria* . 79 C6
Talaud, Kepulauan,
  Indonesia 57 D7
Talaud Is. = Talaud,
  Kepulauan, *Indonesia* .. 57 D7
Talavera de la Reina, *Spain* 30 F6
Talawana, *Australia* .. 88 D3
Talayan, *Phil.* 55 H6
Talbert, Sillon de, *France* . 24 D3
Talbot, C., *Australia* .. 88 B4
Talbragar →, *Australia* . 91 E4
Talca, *Chile* 126 D1
Talca □, *Chile* 126 D1
Talcahuano, *Chile* ... 126 D1
Talcher, *India* 61 J14
Talcho, *Niger* 79 C5
Taldy Kurgan, *Kazakhstan* 44 E8
Taldyqorghan = Taldy
  Kurgan, *Kazakhstan* .. 44 E8
Talesh, *Iran* 65 B6
Talesh, Kūhhā-ye, *Iran* . 65 B6
Talguharai, *Sudan* ... 76 D4
Tali Post, *Sudan* 77 F3
Taliabu, *Indonesia* ... 57 E6
Talibon, *Phil.* 57 B6
Talibong, Ko, *Thailand* . 59 J2
Talihina, *U.S.A.* 109 H7
Talisayan, *Phil.* 55 G6
Taliwang, *Indonesia* .. 56 F5
Tall 'Asūr, *Jordan* ... 69 D4
Tall Kalakh, *Syria* ... 69 A5

Talla, *Egypt* 76 J7
Talladega, *U.S.A.* 105 J2
Tallahassee, *U.S.A.* ... 105 K3
Tallangatta, *Australia* . 91 F4
Tallarook, *Australia* .. 91 F4
Tallering Pk., *Australia* . 89 E2
Tallinn, *Estonia* 40 B4
Tallulah, *U.S.A.* 109 J9
Talmest, *Morocco* 74 B3
Talmont, *France* 26 B2
Talnoye, *Ukraine* 42 B4
Talodi, *Sudan* 77 E3
Talovaya, *Russia* 41 F12
Talpa de Allende, *Mexico* 114 C4
Talsi, *Latvia* 40 C3
Talsinnt, *Morocco* ... 75 B4
Taltal, *Chile* 126 B1
Taltson →, *Canada* .. 100 A6
Talwood, *Australia* .. 91 D4
Talyawalka Cr. →,
  Australia 91 E3
Tam Chau, *Vietnam* .. 59 G5
Tam Ky, *Vietnam* 58 E7
Tam Quan, *Vietnam* .. 58 E7
Tama, *U.S.A.* 108 E8
Tamala, *Australia* ... 89 E1
Tamalameque, *Colombia* . 120 B3
Tamale, *Ghana* 79 D4
Taman, *Russia* 42 D7
Tamanar, *Morocco* ... 74 B3
Tamano, *Japan* 49 G6
Tamanrasset, *Algeria* .. 75 D6
Tamanrasset, O. →,
  Algeria 75 D5
Tamaqua, *U.S.A.* 107 F9
Tamar →, *U.K.* 13 G3
Támara, *Colombia* ... 120 B3
Tamarang, *Australia* .. 91 E5
Tamarinda, *Spain* ... 36 B10
Tamarite de Litera, *Spain* . 28 D5
Tamashima, *Japan* ... 49 G6
Tamaské, *Niger* 79 C6
Tamaulipas □, *Mexico* . 115 C5
Tamaulipas, Sierra de,
  Mexico 115 C5
Tamazula, *Mexico* ... 114 C3
Tamazunchale, *Mexico* . 115 C5
Tamba-Dabatou, *Guinea* . 78 C2
Tambacounda, *Senegal* ... 78 C2
Tambelan, Kepulauan,
  Indonesia 56 D3
Tambellup, *Australia* . 89 F2
Tambo, *Australia* 90 C4
Tambo, *Peru* 124 C3
Tambo →, *Peru* 124 C3
Tambo de Mora, *Peru* . 124 C2
Tambobamba, *Peru* ... 124 C3
Tambohorano, *Madag.* . 85 B7
Tambopata →, *Peru* .. 124 C4
Tambora, *Indonesia* .. 56 F5
Tambov, *Russia* 41 E12
Tambre →, *Spain* 30 C2
Tambuku, *Indonesia* .. 57 G15
Tamburâ, *Sudan* 77 F2
Tâmchekket, *Mauritania* . 78 B2
Tame, *Colombia* 120 B3
Tamega →, *Portugal* .. 30 D2
Tamelelt, *Morocco* ... 74 B3
Tamenglong, *India* .. 61 G18
Tamerza, *Tunisia* ... 75 B6
Tamgak, Mts., *Niger* .. 72 E6
Tamiahua, L. de, *Mexico* . 115 C5
Tamil Nadu □, *India* .. 60 P10
Tamines, *Belgium* ... 17 H5
Tamis →, *Serbia* 38 E3
Tamluk, *India* 63 H12
Tammerfors = Tampere,
  Finland 9 F17
Tammisaari, *Finland* .. 9 F17
Tamo Abu, Pegunungan,
  Malaysia 56 D5
Tampa, *U.S.A.* 105 M4
Tampa B., *U.S.A.* 105 M4
Tampere, *Finland* 9 F17
Tampico, *Mexico* 115 C5
Tampin, *Malaysia* 59 L4
Tamri, *Morocco* 74 B3
Tamrida = Qādib, *Yemen* 68 E5
Tamsagbulag, *Mongolia* . 54 B6
Tamsalu, *Estonia* ... 40 B5
Tamu, *Burma* 61 G19
Tamuja →, *Spain* 31 F4
Tamworth, *Australia* . 91 E5
Tamworth, *U.K.* 13 E6
Tamyang, *S. Korea* .. 51 G14
Tan An, *Vietnam* 59 G6
Tan-tan, *Morocco* ... 74 C2
Tana, *Norway* 8 A20
Tana →, *Kenya* 82 C5
Tana →, *Norway* 8 A20
Tana, L., *Ethiopia* ... 77 E4
Tana River, *Kenya* ... 82 C4
Tanabe, *Japan* 49 H7
Tanabi, *Brazil* 123 F2
Tanafjorden, *Norway* . 8 A20
Tanaga, Pta., *Canary Is.* . 36 G1
Tanagro →, *Italy* 35 B8
Tanahbala, *Indonesia* . 56 E1
Tanahgrogot, *Indonesia* . 56 E5
Tanahjampea, *Indonesia* . 57 F6
Tanahmasa, *Indonesia* . 56 E1
Tanahmerah, *Indonesia* . 57 F10
Tanakura, *Japan* 49 F10
Tanami, *Australia* ... 88 C4
Tanami Desert, *Australia* . 88 C5
Tanana, *U.S.A.* 96 B4

Tanana →, *U.S.A.* 96 B4
Tananarive =
  Antananarivo, *Madag.* . 85 B8
Tanannt, *Morocco* ... 74 B3
Tánaro →, *Italy* 32 C5
Tanaunella, *Italy* 34 B2
Tanbar, *Australia* ... 90 D3
Tancarville, *France* .. 24 C7
Tancheng, *China* 51 G10
Tanchŏn, *N. Korea* .. 51 D15
Tanda, Ut. P., *India* .. 63 F10
Tanda, Ut. P., *India* .. 63 E8
Tanda, *Ivory C.* 78 D4
Tandag, *Phil.* 55 G7
Tandaia, *Tanzania* ... 83 D3
Tăndărei, *Romania* .. 38 E10
Tandaué, *Angola* 84 B2
Tandil, *Argentina* ... 126 D4
Tandil, Sa. del, *Argentina* . 126 D4
Tandlianwala, *Pakistan* . 62 D5
Tando Adam, *Pakistan* . 62 G3
Tandou L., *Australia* .. 91 E3
Tandsbyn, *Sweden* ... 10 A8
Tane-ga-Shima, *Japan* . 49 J5
Taneatua, *N.Z.* 87 H6
Tanen Tong Dan, *Burma* . 58 D2
Tanezrouft, *Algeria* .. 75 D5
Tang, Koh, *Cambodia* . 59 G4
Tang Krasang, *Cambodia* . 58 F5
Tanga, *Tanzania* 82 D4
Tanga □, *Tanzania* .. 82 D4
Tanganyika, L., *Africa* . 82 D2
Tanger, *Morocco* 74 A3
Tangerang, *Indonesia* . 57 G12
Tangerhütte, *Germany* . 18 C7
Tangermünde, *Germany* . 18 C7
Tanggu, *China* 51 E9
Tanggula Shan, *China* . 54 C4
Tanghe, *China* 50 H7
Tangier = Tanger,
  Morocco 74 A3
Tangorin P.O., *Australia* . 90 C3
Tangshan, *China* 51 E10
Tangtou, *China* 51 G10
Tanguiéta, *Benin* 79 C5
Tangxi, *China* 53 C12
Tangyan He →, *China* . 52 C7
Tanimbar, Kepulauan,
  Indonesia 57 F8
Tanimbar Is. = Tanimbar,
  Kepulauan, *Indonesia* . 57 F8
Taninges, *France* 27 B10
Tanjay, *Phil.* 55 G5
Tanjong Malim, *Malaysia* . 59 L3
Tanjore = Thanjavur, *India* 60 P11
Tanjung, *Indonesia* .. 56 E5
Tanjungbalai, *Indonesia* . 56 D1
Tanjungbatu, *Indonesia* . 56 D5
Tanjungkarang
  Telukbetung, *Indonesia* . 56 F3
Tanjungpandan, *Indonesia* 56 E3
Tanjungpinang, *Indonesia* . 56 D2
Tanjungpriok, *Indonesia* . 57 G12
Tanjungredeb, *Indonesia* . 56 D5
Tanjungselor, *Indonesia* . 56 D5
Tank, *Pakistan* 62 C4
Tänndalen, *Sweden* .. 10 B6
Tannis Bugt, *Denmark* .. 11 G4
Tannu-Ola, *Russia* ... 45 D10
Tano →, *Ghana* 78 D4
Tanon Str., *Phil.* 55 F5
Tanout, *Niger* 79 C6
Tanquinho, *Brazil* ... 123 D4
Tanta, *Egypt* 76 H7
Tantoyuca, *Mexico* ... 115 C5
Tantung = Dandong, *China* 51 D13
Tanumshede, *Sweden* . 11 F5
Tanunda, *Australia* .. 91 E2
Tanus, *France* 26 D6
Tanyeri, *Turkey* 67 D8
Tanzania ■, *Africa* .. 82 D3
Tanzilla →, *Canada* .. 100 B2
Tao Ko, *Thailand* 59 G2
Tao'an, *China* 51 B12
Tao'er He →, *China* .. 51 B13
Taohua Dao, *China* .. 53 C14
Taolanaro, *Madag.* ... 85 D8
Taole, *China* 50 E4
Taormina, *Italy* 35 E8
Taos, *U.S.A.* 111 H11
Taoudenni, *Mali* 74 D4
Taoudrart, Adrar, *Algeria* . 75 D5
Taounate, *Morocco* .. 74 B4
Taourirt, *Algeria* 75 C5
Taourirt, *Morocco* ... 75 B4
Taouz, *Morocco* 74 B4
Taoyuan, *China* 53 C8
Taoyuan, *Taiwan* 53 E13
Tapa, *Estonia* 40 B4
Tapa Shan = Daba Shan,
  China 52 B7
Tapachula, *Mexico* ... 115 E6
Tapah, *Malaysia* 59 K3
Tapajós →, *Brazil* ... 121 D7
Tapaktuan, *Indonesia* . 56 D1
Tapanahoni →, *Surinam* . 121 C7
Tapanui, *N.Z.* 87 L2
Tapauá, *Brazil* 125 B5
Tapauá →, *Brazil* ... 125 B5
Tapeta, *Liberia* 78 D3
Taphan Hin, *Thailand* . 58 D3
Tapi →, *India* 60 J8
Tapia, *Spain* 30 B4
Tápiószele, *Hungary* . 21 H9
Tapiraí, *Brazil* 123 E2
Tapirapé →, *Brazil* .. 122 D1

Tapirapecó, Serra,
  Venezuela 121 C5
Tapirapuã, *Brazil* 125 C6
Tapoeripa, *Surinam* .. 121 B6
Tapolca, *Hungary* ... 21 J7
Tappahannock, *U.S.A.* . 104 G7
Tapuaenuku, Mt., *N.Z.* . 87 J4
Tapul Group, *Phil.* ... 55 J4
Tapurucuará, *Brazil* .. 121 D4
Taqīābād, *Iran* 65 C8
Taqtaq, *Iraq* 64 C5
Taquara, *Brazil* 127 B5
Taquari →, *Brazil* ... 125 C6
Taquaritinga, *Brazil* .. 123 F2
Tara, *Australia* 91 D5
Tara, *Canada* 106 B3
Tara, *Russia* 44 D8
Tara, *Zambia* 83 F2
Tara →, *Russia* 44 D8
Taraba →, *Nigeria* .. 79 D7
Tarabagatay, Khrebet,
  Kazakhstan 44 E9
Tarabuco, *Bolivia* ... 125 D5
Tarābulus, *Lebanon* .. 69 A4
Tarābulus, *Libya* 75 B7
Tarahouahout, *Algeria* . 75 D6
Tarajalejo, *Canary Is.* . 36 F5
Tarakan, *Indonesia* .. 56 D5
Tarakit, Mt., *Kenya* .. 82 B4
Taralga, *Australia* ... 91 E4
Tarama-Jima, *Japan* . 49 M2
Taranagar, *India* 62 E6
Taranaki □, *N.Z.* 87 H5
Tarancón, *Spain* 28 E1
Taranga, *India* 62 H5
Taranga Hill, *India* .. 62 H5
Táranto, *Italy* 35 B10
Táranto, G. di, *Italy* .. 35 B10
Tarapacá, *Colombia* .. 120 D4
Tarapacá □, *Chile* ... 126 A2
Tarapoto, *Peru* 124 B2
Taraquá, *Brazil* 120 C4
Tarare, *France* 27 C8
Tararua Ra., *N.Z.* ... 87 J5
Tarascon, *France* 27 E8
Tarascon-sur-Ariège,
  France 26 F5
Tarashcha, *Ukraine* .. 42 B4
Tarata, *Peru* 124 D3
Tarauacá, *Brazil* 124 B3
Tarauacá →, *Brazil* .. 124 B4
Taravo →, *France* .. 27 G12
Tarawera, *N.Z.* 87 H6
Tarawera L., *N.Z.* ... 87 H6
Tarazona, *Spain* 28 D3
Tarazona de la Mancha,
  Spain 29 F3
Tarbat Ness, *U.K.* ... 14 D5
Tarbela Dam, *Pakistan* . 62 B5
Tarbert, Strath., *U.K.* . 14 F3
Tarbert, W. Isles, *U.K.* . 14 D2
Tarbes, *France* 26 E4
Tarboro, *U.S.A.* 105 H7
Tarbrax, *Australia* ... 90 C3
Tarcento, *Italy* 33 B10
Tarcoola, *Australia* .. 91 E1
Tarcoon, *Australia* .. 91 E4
Tardets-Sorholus, *France* . 26 E3
Tardoire →, *France* .. 26 C4
Taree, *Australia* 91 E5
Tarentaise, *France* ... 27 C10
Tarf, Ras, *Morocco* .. 74 A3
Tarfa, Wadi el →, *Egypt* . 76 J7
Tarfaya, *Morocco* ... 74 C2
Targon, *France* 26 D3
Targuist, *Morocco* ... 74 B4
Tarhbalt, *Morocco* ... 74 B3
Tarhit, *Algeria* 75 B4
Táriba, *Venezuela* ... 120 B3
Tarifa, *Spain* 31 J5
Tarija, *Bolivia* 126 A3
Tarija □, *Bolivia* 126 A3
Tariku →, *Indonesia* . 57 E9
Tarim Basin = Tarim
  Pendi, *China* 54 C3
Tarim He →, *China* .. 54 C3
Tarim Pendi, *China* .. 54 C3
Tarime □, *Tanzania* .. 82 C3
Taritatu →, *Indonesia* . 57 E9
Tarka →, *S. Africa* .. 84 E4
Tarkastad, *S. Africa* .. 84 E4
Tarkhankut, Mys, *Ukraine* 42 D5
Tarko Sale, *Russia* ... 44 C8
Tarkwa, *Ghana* 78 D4
Tarlac, *Phil.* 55 D4
Tarlton Downs, *Australia* . 90 C2
Tarm, *Denmark* 11 J2
Tarma, *Peru* 124 C2
Tarn □, *France* 26 E6
Tarn →, *France* 26 D5
Tarn-et-Garonne □, *France* 26 D5
Tarna →, *Hungary* .. 21 H9
Tärnaby, *Denmark* ... 11 J6
Tarnobrzeg, *Poland* .. 20 E11
Tarnów, *Poland* 20 F11
Táro →, *Italy* 32 D7
Taroom, *Australia* ... 91 D4
Taroudannt, *Morocco* . 74 B3
Tarp, *Germany* 18 A5
Tarpon Springs, *U.S.A.* . 105 L4
Tarquínia, *Italy* 33 F8
Tarragona, *Spain* ... 28 D6
Tarragona □, *Spain* .. 28 D5
Tarrasa, *Spain* 28 D7
Tárrega, *Spain* 28 D6
Tarrytown, *U.S.A.* ... 107 E11

Tarshiha = Me'ona, *Israel* 69 B4
Tarso Emissi, *Chad* ... 73 D8
Tarsus, *Turkey* 66 E6
Tartagal, *Argentina* .. 126 A3
Tartas, *France* 26 E3
Tartu, *Estonia* 40 B5
Tarumirim, *Brazil* ... 123 E3
Tarumizu, *Japan* 49 J5
Tarussa, *Russia* 41 D10
Tarutao, Ko, *Thailand* . 59 J2
Tarutung, *Indonesia* .. 56 D1
Tarvisio, *Italy* 33 B10
Tarz Ulli, *Libya* 75 C7
Tasāwah, *Libya* 73 C7
Taschereau, *Canada* .. 98 C4
Taseko →, *Canada* .. 100 C4
Tash-Kumyr, *Kirghizia* . 44 E8
Tashauz, *Turkmenistan* ... 44 E6
Tashi Chho Dzong =
  Thimphu, *Bhutan* 61 F16
Tashkent, *Uzbekistan* . 44 E7
Tashtagol, *Russia* ... 44 D9
Tasikmalaya, *Indonesia* ... 57 G13
Tåsjön, *Sweden* 8 D13
Taskan, *Russia* 45 C16
Taşköprü, *Turkey* ... 42 F6
Tasman B., *N.Z.* 87 J4
Tasman Mts., *N.Z.* ... 87 J4
Tasman Pen., *Australia* . 90 G4
Tasman Sea, *Pac. Oc.* . 92 L8
Tasmania □, *Australia* . 90 G4
Tăşnad, *Romania* 38 B5
Tassil Tin-Rerhoh, *Algeria* 75 D5
Tassili n-Ajjer, *Algeria* . 75 C6
Tassili-Oua-n-Ahaggar,
  Algeria 75 D6
Tasu Sd., *Canada* 100 C2
Tata, *Morocco* 74 C3
Tatabánya, *Hungary* .. 21 H8
Tatahouine, *Tunisia* .. 75 B7
Tatar Republic □, *Russia* . 44 D6
Tatarbunary, *Ukraine* . 42 D4
Tatarsk, *Russia* 44 D8
Tateyama, *Japan* 49 G9
Tathlina L., *Canada* .. 100 A5
Tathra, *Australia* 91 F4
Tatinnai L., *Canada* .. 101 A9
Tatnam, C., *Canada* .. 101 B10
Tatra = Tatry, *Slovak Rep.* 20 F9
Tatry, *Slovak Rep.* ... 20 F9
Tatsuno, *Japan* 49 G7
Tatta, *Pakistan* 62 G2
Tatuí, *Brazil* 127 A6
Tatum, *U.S.A.* 109 J3
Tat'ung = Datong, *China* . 50 D7
Tatvan, *Turkey* 67 D10
Tauá, *Brazil* 122 C3
Taubaté, *Brazil* 127 A6
Tauberbischofsheim,
  Germany 19 F5
Taucha, *Germany* ... 18 D8
Taufikia, *Sudan* 77 F3
Taumarunui, *N.Z.* ... 87 H5
Taumaturgo, *Brazil* .. 124 B3
Taung, *S. Africa* 84 D3
Taungdwingyi, *Burma* . 61 J19
Taunggyi, *Burma* 61 J20
Taungup, *Burma* 61 K19
Taungup Pass, *Burma* . 61 K19
Taungup Taunggya, *Burma* 61 K18
Taunsa Barrage, *Pakistan* . 62 D4
Taunton, *U.K.* 13 F4
Taunton, *U.S.A.* 107 E13
Taunus, *Germany* ... 19 E4
Taupo, *N.Z.* 87 H6
Taupo, L., *N.Z.* 87 H5
Taurage, *Lithuania* .. 40 D3
Tauranga, *N.Z.* 87 G6
Tauranga Harb., *N.Z.* . 87 G6
Taurianova, *Italy* 35 D9
Taurus Mts. = Toros
  Dağları, *Turkey* 66 E5
Tauste, *Spain* 28 D3
Tauz, *Azerbaijan* 43 F11
Tavannes, *Switz.* 22 B4
Tavda, *Russia* 44 D7
Tavda →, *Russia* 44 D7
Taverny, *France* 25 C9
Taveta, *Tanzania* 82 C4
Taveuni, *Fiji* 87 C9
Tavignano →, *France* . 27 F13
Tavira, *Portugal* 31 H3
Tavistock, *Canada* ... 106 C4
Tavistock, *U.K.* 13 G3
Tavolara, *Italy* 34 B2
Távora →, *Portugal* .. 30 D3
Tavoy, *Burma* 58 E2
Tavşanlı, *Turkey* 66 D3
Taw →, *U.K.* 13 F3
Tawas City, *U.S.A.* ... 104 C4
Tawau, *Malaysia* 56 D5
Tawitawi, *Phil.* 55 J4
Taxila, *Pakistan* 62 C5
Tay →, *U.K.* 14 E5
Tay, Firth of, *U.K.* ... 14 E5
Tay, L., *Australia* 89 F3
Tay, L., *U.K.* 14 E4
Tay Ninh, *Vietnam* .. 59 G6
Tayabamba, *Peru* ... 124 B2
Tayabas Bay, *Phil.* ... 55 E4

Taylor, Mt., *U.S.A.*	111	J10
Taylorville, *U.S.A.*	108	F10
Taymā, *Si. Arabia*	64	E3
Taymyr, Oz., *Russia*	45	B11
Taymyr, Poluostrov, *Russia*	45	B11
Tayport, *U.K.*	14	E6
Tayshet, *Russia*	45	D10
Tayside □, *U.K.*	14	E5
Taytay, *Phil.*	55	F3
Taz →, *Russia*	44	C8
Taza, *Morocco*	74	B4
Tāzah Khurmātū, *Iraq*	64	C5
Tazawa-Ko, *Japan*	48	E10
Tazin L., *Canada*	101	B7
Tazoult, *Algeria*	75	A6
Tazovskiy, *Russia*	44	C8
Tbilisi, *Georgia*	43	F11
Tchad = Chad ■, *Africa*	73	E8
Tchad, L., *Chad*	73	F7
Tchaourou, *Benin*	79	D5
Tch'eng-tou = Chengdu, *China*	52	B5
Tchentlo L., *Canada*	100	B4
Tchibanga, *Gabon*	80	E2
Tchien, *Liberia*	78	D3
Tchin Tabaraden, *Niger*	79	B6
Tch'ong-k'ing = Chongqing, *China*	52	C6
Tczew, *Poland*	20	A8
Te Anau, L., *N.Z.*	87	L1
Te Aroha, *N.Z.*	87	G5
Te Awamutu, *N.Z.*	87	H5
Te Kuiti, *N.Z.*	87	H5
Te Puke, *N.Z.*	87	G6
Te Waewae B., *N.Z.*	87	M1
Tea →, *Brazil*	120	D4
Tea Tree, *Australia*	90	C1
Teague, *U.S.A.*	109	K6
Teano, *Italy*	35	A7
Teapa, *Mexico*	115	D6
Teba, *Spain*	31	J6
Tebakang, *Malaysia*	56	D4
Teberda, *Russia*	43	E9
Tébessa, *Algeria*	75	A6
Tebicuary →, *Paraguay*	126	B4
Tebingtinggi, *Indonesia*	56	D1
Tébourba, *Tunisia*	75	A6
Téboursouk, *Tunisia*	75	A6
Tebulos, *Russia*	43	E11
Tecate, *Mexico*	113	N10
Tecer Daği, *Turkey*	66	D7
Tech →, *France*	26	F7
Techiman, *Ghana*	78	D4
Tecka, *Argentina*	128	B2
Tecomán, *Mexico*	114	D4
Tecopa, *U.S.A.*	113	K10
Tecoripa, *Mexico*	114	B3
Tecuala, *Mexico*	114	C3
Tecuci, *Romania*	38	D10
Tecumseh, *U.S.A.*	104	D4
Tedzhen, *Turkmenistan*	44	F7
Tees →, *U.K.*	12	C6
Teesside, *U.K.*	12	C6
Teeswater, *Canada*	106	C3
Tefé, *Brazil*	121	D5
Tefé →, *Brazil*	121	D5
Tefenni, *Turkey*	66	E3
Tegal, *Indonesia*	57	G13
Tegelen, *Neths.*	17	F8
Tegernsee, *Germany*	19	H7
Teggiano, *Italy*	35	B8
Teghra, *India*	63	G11
Tegid, L. = Bala, L., *U.K.*	12	E4
Tegina, *Nigeria*	79	C6
Tegucigalpa, *Honduras*	116	D2
Tehachapi, *U.S.A.*	113	K8
Tehachapi Mts., *U.S.A.*	113	L8
Tehamiyam, *Sudan*	76	D4
Tehilla, *Sudan*	76	D4
Téhini, *Ivory C.*	78	D4
Tehrān, *Iran*	65	C6
Tehuacán, *Mexico*	115	D5
Tehuantepec, *Mexico*	115	D5
Tehuantepec, G. de, *Mexico*	115	D5
Tehuantepec, Istmo de, *Mexico*	115	D6
Teide, *Canary Is.*	36	F3
Teifi →, *U.K.*	13	E3
Teign →, *U.K.*	13	G4
Teignmouth, *U.K.*	13	G4
Teixeira, *Brazil*	122	C4
Teixeira Pinto, *Guinea-Biss.*	78	C1
Tejo →, *Europe*	31	G1
Tejon Pass, *U.S.A.*	113	L8
Tekamah, *U.S.A.*	108	E6
Tekapo, L., *N.Z.*	87	K3
Tekax, *Mexico*	115	C7
Tekeli, *Kazakhstan*	44	E8
Tekeze →, *Ethiopia*	77	E4
Tekija, *Serbia*	21	L12
Tekirdağ, *Turkey*	66	C2
Tekirdağ □, *Turkey*	66	C2
Tekkali, *India*	61	K14
Tekke, *Turkey*	66	C7
Tekman, *Turkey*	67	D9
Tekoa, *U.S.A.*	110	C5
Tekouiât, O. →, *Algeria*	75	D6
Tel Aviv-Yafo, *Israel*	69	C3
Tel Lakhish, *Israel*	69	D3
Tel Megiddo, *Israel*	69	C4
Tela, *Honduras*	116	C2
Télagh, *Algeria*	75	B4
Telanaipura = Jambi, *Indonesia*	56	E2
Telavi, *Georgia*	43	F11
Telde, *Canary Is.*	36	G4
Telegraph Creek, *Canada*	100	B2
Telekhany, *Belorussia*	40	E4
Telemark fylke □, *Norway*	10	E2
Telén, *Argentina*	126	D2
Teleng, *Iran*	65	E9
Teleño, *Spain*	30	C4
Teleorman →, *Romania*	38	E8
Teles Pires →, *Brazil*	125	B6
Telescope Pk., *U.S.A.*	113	J9
Teletaye, *Mali*	79	B5
Telford, *U.K.*	12	E5
Telfs, *Austria*	19	H7
Télimélé, *Guinea*	78	C2
Telkwa, *Canada*	100	C3
Tell City, *U.S.A.*	104	G2
Tellicherry, *India*	60	P9
Tellin, *Belgium*	17	H6
Telluride, *U.S.A.*	111	H10
Teloloapán, *Mexico*	115	D5
Telpos Iz, *Russia*	6	C17
Telsen, *Argentina*	128	B3
Telšiai, *Lithuania*	40	D3
Teltow, *Germany*	18	C9
Teluk Anson, *Malaysia*	59	K3
Teluk Betung = Tanjungkarang Telukbetung, *Indonesia*	56	F3
Teluk Intan = Teluk Anson, *Malaysia*	59	K3
Telukbutun, *Indonesia*	59	K7
Telukdalem, *Indonesia*	56	D1
Tema, *Ghana*	79	D5
Temanggung, *Indonesia*	57	G14
Temapache, *Mexico*	115	C5
Temax, *Mexico*	115	C7
Temba, *S. Africa*	85	D4
Tembe, *Zaïre*	82	C2
Temblador, *Venezuela*	121	B5
Tembleque, *Spain*	28	F1
Temblor Range, *U.S.A.*	113	K7
Teme →, *U.K.*	13	E5
Temecula, *U.S.A.*	113	M9
Temerloh, *Malaysia*	59	L4
Temir, *Kazakhstan*	44	E6
Temirtau, *Kazakhstan*	44	D8
Temirtau, *Russia*	44	D9
Témiscaming, *Canada*	98	C4
Temma, *Australia*	90	G3
Temnikov, *Russia*	41	D13
Temo →, *Italy*	34	B1
Temora, *Australia*	91	E4
Temosachic, *Mexico*	114	B3
Tempe, *U.S.A.*	111	K8
Tempe Downs, *Australia*	88	D5
Témpio Pausania, *Italy*	34	B2
Tempiute, *U.S.A.*	112	H11
Temple, *U.S.A.*	109	K6
Temple B., *Australia*	90	A3
Templemore, *Ireland*	15	D4
Templeton, *U.S.A.*	112	K6
Templeton →, *Australia*	90	C2
Templeuve, *Belgium*	17	G2
Templin, *Germany*	18	B9
Tempoal, *Mexico*	115	C5
Temryuk, *Russia*	42	D7
Temse, *Belgium*	17	F4
Temska →, *Serbia*	21	M12
Temuco, *Chile*	128	A2
Temuka, *N.Z.*	87	L3
Ten Boer, *Neths.*	16	B9
Tena, *Ecuador*	120	D2
Tenabo, *Mexico*	115	C6
Tenaha, *U.S.A.*	109	K7
Tenali, *India*	60	L12
Tenancingo, *Mexico*	115	D5
Tenango, *Mexico*	115	D5
Tenasserim, *Burma*	59	F2
Tenasserim □, *Burma*	58	F2
Tenay, *France*	27	C9
Tenby, *U.K.*	13	F3
Tenda, Col di, *France*	27	D11
Tendaho, *Ethiopia*	68	E3
Tende, *France*	27	D11
Tendelti, *Sudan*	77	E3
Tendjedi, Adrar, *Algeria*	75	D6
Tendrara, *Morocco*	75	B4
Tendre, Mt., *Switz.*	22	C2
Teneida, *Egypt*	76	B2
Tenente Marques →, *Brazil*	125	C6
Ténéré, *Niger*	79	B7
Tenerife, *Canary Is.*	36	F3
Tenerife, Pico, *Canary Is.*	36	G1
Ténès, *Algeria*	75	A5
Teng Xian, Guangxi Zhuangzu, *China*	53	F8
Teng Xian, Shandong, *China*	51	G9
Tengah □, *Indonesia*	57	E6
Tengah Kepulauan, *Indonesia*	56	F5
Tengchong, *China*	52	E2
Tengchowfu = Penglai, *China*	51	F11
Tenggara □, *Indonesia*	57	E6
Tenggarong, *Indonesia*	56	E5
Tenggol, P., *Malaysia*	59	K4
Tengiz, Ozero, *Kazakhstan*	44	D7
Tenigerbad, *Switz.*	23	C7
Tenino, *U.S.A.*	112	D4
Tenkasi, *India*	60	Q10
Tenke, Shaba, *Zaïre*	83	E2
Tenke, Shaba, *Zaïre*	83	E2
Tenkodogo, *Burkina Faso*	79	C4
Tenna →, *Italy*	33	E10
Tennant Creek, *Australia*	90	B1
Tennessee □, *U.S.A.*	105	H2
Tennessee →, *U.S.A.*	104	G1
Tenneville, *Belgium*	17	H7
Tennille, *U.S.A.*	105	J4
Tennsift, Oued →, *Morocco*	74	B3
Teno, Pta. de, *Canary Is.*	36	F3
Tenom, *Malaysia*	56	C5
Tenosique, *Mexico*	115	D6
Tenryū-Gawa →, *Japan*	49	G8
Tent L., *Canada*	101	A7
Tenterfield, *Australia*	91	D5
Teófilo Otoni, *Brazil*	123	E3
Teotihuacán, *Mexico*	115	D5
Tepa, *Indonesia*	57	F7
Tepalcatepec →, *Mexico*	114	D4
Tepehuanes, *Mexico*	114	B3
Tepequem, Serra, *Brazil*	121	C5
Tepetongo, *Mexico*	114	C4
Tepic, *Mexico*	114	C4
Tepoca, C., *Mexico*	114	A2
Tequila, *Mexico*	114	C4
Ter →, *Spain*	28	C8
Ter Apel, *Neths.*	16	C10
Téra, *Niger*	79	C5
Tera →, *Spain*	30	D5
Teraina, *Kiribati*	93	G11
Téramo, *Italy*	33	F10
Terang, *Australia*	91	F3
Terborg, *Neths.*	16	E8
Tercan, *Turkey*	67	D9
Tercero →, *Argentina*	126	C3
Terebovlya, *Ukraine*	40	G4
Terek →, *Russia*	43	E12
Terenos, *Brazil*	125	E7
Tereshka →, *Russia*	41	F15
Teresina, *Brazil*	122	C3
Teresinha, *Brazil*	121	C7
Terewah, L., *Australia*	91	D4
Terges →, *Portugal*	31	H3
Tergnier, *France*	25	C10
Terhazza, *Mali*	74	D3
Terheijden, *Neths.*	17	E5
Teridgere Cr. →, *Australia*	91	E4
Terlizzi, *Italy*	35	A9
Terme, *Turkey*	42	F7
Termez, *Uzbekistan*	44	F7
Términi Imerese, *Italy*	34	E6
Términos, L. de, *Mexico*	115	D6
Térmoli, *Italy*	33	F12
Ternate, *Indonesia*	57	D7
Terneuzen, *Neths.*	17	F3
Terney, *Russia*	45	E14
Terni, *Italy*	33	F9
Ternitz, *Austria*	21	H6
Ternopol, *Ukraine*	42	B1
Terowie, N.S.W., *Australia*	91	E4
Terowie, S. Austral., *Australia*	91	E2
Terra Bella, *U.S.A.*	113	K7
Terrace, *Canada*	100	C3
Terrace Bay, *Canada*	98	C2
Terracina, *Italy*	34	A6
Terralba, *Italy*	34	C1
Terranova = Ólbia, *Italy*	34	B2
Terranuova Bracciolini, *Italy*	33	E8
Terrasini Favarotta, *Italy*	34	D6
Terrassa = Tarrasa, *Spain*	28	D7
Terrasson-la-Villedieu, *France*	26	C5
Terre Haute, *U.S.A.*	104	F2
Terrebonne B., *U.S.A.*	109	L9
Terrecht, *Mali*	75	D4
Terrell, *U.S.A.*	109	J6
Terrenceville, *Canada*	99	C9
Terrick Terrick, *Australia*	90	C4
Terry, *U.S.A.*	108	B2
Terschelling, *Neths.*	16	B6
Terter →, *Azerbaijan*	43	F12
Teruel, *Spain*	28	E3
Teruel □, *Spain*	28	E4
Tervel, *Bulgaria*	38	F10
Tervola, *Finland*	8	C18
Teryaweyna L., *Australia*	91	E3
Tešanj, *Bos.-H.*	21	L7
Teseney, *Eritrea*	77	D4
Tesha →, *Russia*	41	D13
Teshio, *Japan*	48	B10
Teshio-Gawa →, *Japan*	48	B10
Tesiyn Gol →, *Mongolia*	54	A4
Teslin, *Canada*	100	A2
Teslin →, *Canada*	100	A2
Teslin L., *Canada*	100	A2
Tesouro, *Brazil*	125	D7
Tessalit, *Mali*	79	A5
Tessaoua, *Niger*	79	C6
Tessenderlo, *Belgium*	17	F6
Tessin, *Germany*	18	A8
Tessit, *Mali*	79	B5
Test →, *U.K.*	13	F6
Testa del Gargano, *Italy*	35	A9
Têt →, *France*	26	F7
Tetachuck L., *Canada*	100	C3
Tetas, Pta., *Chile*	126	A1
Tete, *Mozam.*	83	F3
Tete □, *Mozam.*	83	F3
Teterev →, *Ukraine*	40	F6
Teteringen, *Neths.*	17	E5
Teterow, *Germany*	18	B8
Teteven, *Bulgaria*	38	G7
Tethul →, *Canada*	100	A6
Tetiyev, *Ukraine*	42	B3
Teton →, *U.S.A.*	110	C8
Tétouan, *Morocco*	74	A3
Tetovo, *Macedonia*	38	G4
Tetuán = Tétouan, *Morocco*	74	A3
Tetyukhe Pristan, *Russia*	48	B7
Tetyushi, *Russia*	41	D16
Teuco →, *Argentina*	126	B3
Teufen, *Switz.*	23	B8
Teulada, *Italy*	34	D1
Teulon, *Canada*	101	C9
Teun, *Indonesia*	57	F7
Teutoburger Wald, *Germany*	18	C4
Tevere →, *Italy*	33	G9
Teverya, *Israel*	69	C4
Teviot →, *U.K.*	14	F6
Tewantin, *Australia*	91	D5
Tewkesbury, *U.K.*	13	F5
Texada I., *Canada*	100	D4
Texarkana, Ark., *U.S.A.*	109	J8
Texarkana, Tex., *U.S.A.*	109	J7
Texas, *Australia*	91	D5
Texas □, *U.S.A.*	109	K5
Texas City, *U.S.A.*	109	L7
Texel, *Neths.*	16	B5
Texhoma, *U.S.A.*	109	G4
Texline, *U.S.A.*	109	G3
Texoma, L., *U.S.A.*	109	J6
Teykovo, *Russia*	41	C12
Teza →, *Russia*	41	C12
Tezin, *Afghan.*	62	B3
Teziutlán, *Mexico*	115	D5
Tezpur, *India*	61	F18
Tezzeron L., *Canada*	100	C4
Tha-anne →, *Canada*	101	A10
Tha Deua, *Laos*	58	D4
Tha Deua, *Laos*	58	C3
Tha Pla, *Thailand*	58	D3
Tha Rua, *Thailand*	58	E3
Tha Sala, *Thailand*	59	H2
Tha Song Yang, *Thailand*	58	D1
Thaba Nchu, *S. Africa*	84	D4
Thaba Putsoa, *Lesotho*	85	D4
Thabana Ntlenyana, *Lesotho*	85	D4
Thabazimbi, *S. Africa*	85	C4
Thai Binh, *Vietnam*	58	B6
Thai Hoa, *Vietnam*	58	C5
Thai Muang, *Thailand*	59	H2
Thai Nguyen, *Vietnam*	58	B5
Thailand ■, *Asia*	58	E4
Thailand, G. of, *Asia*	59	G3
Thakhek, *Laos*	58	D5
Thal, *Pakistan*	62	C4
Thal Desert, *Pakistan*	62	D4
Thala, *Tunisia*	75	A6
Thala La, *Burma*	61	E20
Thalabarivat, *Cambodia*	58	F5
Thalkirch, *Switz.*	23	C8
Thallon, *Australia*	91	D4
Thalwil, *Switz.*	23	B7
Thame, *U.K.*	13	F6
Thame →, *U.K.*	13	F6
Thames, *N.Z.*	87	G5
Thames →, *Canada*	98	D3
Thames →, *U.K.*	13	F8
Thames →, *U.S.A.*	107	E12
Thamesford, *Canada*	106	C3
Thamesville, *Canada*	106	D3
Than Uyen, *Vietnam*	58	B4
Thane, *India*	60	K8
Thanesar, *India*	62	D7
Thanet, I. of, *U.K.*	13	F9
Thangoo, *Australia*	88	C3
Thangool, *Australia*	90	C5
Thanh Hoa, *Vietnam*	58	C5
Thanh Hung, *Vietnam*	59	H5
Thanh Pho Ho Chi Minh = Phanh Bho Ho Chi Minh, *Vietnam*	59	G6
Thanh Thuy, *Vietnam*	58	A5
Thanjavur, *India*	60	P11
Thann, *France*	25	E14
Thaon-les-Vosges, *France*	25	D13
Thap Sakae, *Thailand*	59	G2
Thap Than, *Thailand*	58	E2
Thar Desert, *India*	62	F4
Tharad, *India*	62	G4
Thargomindah, *Australia*	91	D3
Tharrawaddy, *Burma*	61	L19
Tharthar, W. →, *Iraq*	64	C4
Thásos, *Greece*	39	J7
That Khe, *Vietnam*	58	A6
Thatcher, Ariz., *U.S.A.*	111	K9
Thatcher, Colo., *U.S.A.*	109	G2
Thaton, *Burma*	61	L20
Thau, Bassin de, *France*	26	E7
Thaungdut, *Burma*	61	G19
Thayer, *U.S.A.*	109	G9
Thayetmyo, *Burma*	61	K19
Thazi, *Burma*	61	J20
The Alberga →, *Australia*	91	D2
The Bight, *Bahamas*	117	B4
The Coorong, *Australia*	91	F2
The Dalles, *U.S.A.*	110	D3
The English Company's Is., *Australia*	90	A2
The Frome →, *Australia*	91	D2
The Grampians, *Australia*	91	F3
The Great Divide = Great Dividing Ra., *Australia*	90	C4
The Hague = 's-Gravenhage, *Neths.*	16	D4
The Hamilton →, *Australia*	91	D2
The Macumba →, *Australia*	91	D2
The Neales →, *Australia*	91	D2
The Officer →, *Australia*	89	E5
The Pas, *Canada*	101	C8
The Range, *Zimbabwe*	83	F3
The Rock, *Australia*	91	F4
The Salt L., *Australia*	91	E3
The Stevenson →, *Australia*	91	D2
The Warburton →, *Australia*	91	D2
Thebes = Thívai, *Greece*	39	L6
Thebes, *Egypt*	76	B3
Thedford, *Canada*	106	C3
Thedford, *U.S.A.*	108	E4
Theebine, *Australia*	91	D5
Thekulthili L., *Canada*	101	A7
Thelon →, *Canada*	101	A8
Thénezay, *France*	24	F6
Thenia, *Algeria*	75	A5
Thenon, *France*	26	C5
Theodore, *Australia*	90	C5
Thepha, *Thailand*	59	J3
Thérain →, *France*	25	C9
Theresa, *U.S.A.*	107	B9
Thermaïkós Kólpos, *Greece*	39	J5
Thermopolis, *U.S.A.*	110	E9
Thermopylae P., *Greece*	39	L5
Thessalía □, *Greece*	39	L4
Thessalon, *Canada*	98	C3
Thessaloníki, *Greece*	39	J5
Thessaloniki, Gulf of = Thermaïkós Kólpos, *Greece*	39	J5
Thessaly = Thessalía □, *Greece*	39	L4
Thetford, *U.K.*	13	E8
Thetford Mines, *Canada*	99	C5
Theun →, *Laos*	58	C5
Theunissen, *S. Africa*	84	D4
Theux, *Belgium*	17	G7
Thevenard, *Australia*	91	E1
Thiámis →, *Greece*	39	K3
Thibodaux, *U.S.A.*	109	L9
Thicket Portage, *Canada*	101	B9
Thief River Falls, *U.S.A.*	108	A6
Thiel Mts., *Antarctica*	5	E16
Thiene, *Italy*	33	C8
Thiérache, *France*	25	C10
Thiers, *France*	26	C7
Thies, *Senegal*	78	C1
Thiet, *Sudan*	77	F2
Thika, *Kenya*	82	C4
Thikombia, *Fiji*	87	B9
Thille-Boubacar, *Senegal*	78	B1
Thimphu, *Bhutan*	61	F16
þingvallavatn, *Iceland*	8	D3
Thionville, *France*	25	C13
Thíra, *Greece*	39	N8
Thirasía, *Greece*	39	N8
Thirsk, *U.K.*	12	C6
Thisted, *Denmark*	9	H10
Thistle I., *Australia*	91	F2
Thívai, *Greece*	39	L6
Thiviers, *France*	26	C4
Thizy, *France*	27	B8
þjórsá, *Iceland*	8	E3
Thlewiaza →, Man., *Canada*	101	B8
Thlewiaza →, N.W.T., *Canada*	101	A10
Thmar Puok, *Cambodia*	58	F4
Tho Vinh, *Vietnam*	58	C5
Thoa →, *Canada*	101	A7
Thoen, *Thailand*	58	D2
Thoeng, *Thailand*	58	C3
Thoissey, *France*	27	B8
Tholdi, *Pakistan*	63	B7
Tholen, *Neths.*	17	E4
Thomas, Okla., *U.S.A.*	109	H5
Thomas, W. Va., *U.S.A.*	104	F6
Thomas, L., *Australia*	91	D2
Thomaston, *U.S.A.*	105	J3
Thomasville, Ala., *U.S.A.*	105	K2
Thomasville, Ga., *U.S.A.*	105	K3
Thomasville, N.C., *U.S.A.*	105	H5
Thommen, *Belgium*	17	H8
Thompson, *Canada*	101	B9
Thompson, *U.S.A.*	111	G9
Thompson →, *Canada*	100	C4
Thompson →, *U.S.A.*	108	F8
Thompson Falls, *U.S.A.*	110	C6
Thompson Landing, *Canada*	101	A7
Thompson Pk., *U.S.A.*	110	F2
Thomson's Falls = Nyahururu, *Kenya*	82	B4
Thon Buri, *Thailand*	59	F3
Thônes, *France*	27	C10
Thonon-les-Bains, *France*	27	B10
Thorez, *Ukraine*	43	B8
þórisvatn, *Iceland*	8	D4
þorlákshöfn, *Iceland*	8	E3
Thornaby on Tees, *U.K.*	12	C6
Thornbury, *Canada*	106	B4
þorold, *Canada*	106	C5
þórshöfn, *Iceland*	8	C6
Thouarcé, *France*	24	E6
Thouars, *France*	24	F6
Thouin, C., *Australia*	88	D2
Thousand Oaks, *U.S.A.*	113	L8

Thrace

Name	Page	Grid
Thrace, *Turkey*	66	C2
Thrakikón Pélagos, *Greece*	39	J8
Three Forks, *U.S.A.*	110	D8
Three Hills, *Canada*	100	C6
Three Hummock I., *Australia*	90	G3
Three Lakes, *U.S.A.*	108	C10
Three Points, C., *Ghana*	78	E4
Three Rivers, *Australia*	89	E2
Three Rivers, *Calif., U.S.A.*	112	J8
Three Rivers, *Tex., U.S.A.*	109	L5
Three Sisters, *U.S.A.*	110	D3
Throssell, L., *Australia*	89	E3
Throssell Ra., *Australia*	88	D3
Thuan Hoa, *Vietnam*	59	H5
Thubun Lakes, *Canada*	101	A6
Thueyts, *France*	27	D8
Thuillies, *Belgium*	17	H4
Thuin, *Belgium*	17	H4
Thuir, *France*	26	F6
Thule, *Greenland*	4	B4
Thun, *Switz.*	22	C5
Thundelarra, *Australia*	89	E2
Thunder B., *U.S.A.*	106	B1
Thunder Bay, *Canada*	98	C2
Thunersee, *Switz.*	22	C5
Thung Song, *Thailand*	59	H2
Thunkar, *Bhutan*	61	F17
Thuong Tra, *Vietnam*	58	D6
Thur →, *Switz.*	23	A8
Thurgau □, *Switz.*	23	A8
Thüringen □, *Germany*	18	E7
Thüringer Wald, *Germany*	18	E7
Thurles, *Ireland*	15	D4
Thurloo Downs, *Australia*	91	D3
Thurn P., *Austria*	19	H8
Thursday I., *Australia*	90	A3
Thurso, *Canada*	98	C4
Thurso, *U.K.*	14	C5
Thurston I., *Antarctica*	5	D16
Thury-Harcourt, *France*	24	D6
Thusis, *Switz.*	23	C8
Thutade L., *Canada*	100	B3
Thyborøn, *Denmark*	11	H2
Thylungra, *Australia*	91	D3
Thyolo, *Malawi*	83	F4
Thysville = Mbanza Ngungu, *Zaïre*	80	F2
Ti-n-Barraouene, O. →, *Africa*	79	B5
Ti-n-Medjerdam, O. →, *Algeria*	75	C5
Ti-n-Tarabine, O. →, *Algeria*	75	D6
Ti-n-Zaouatène, *Algeria*	75	E5
Tia, *Australia*	91	E5
Tiahuanacu, *Bolivia*	124	D4
Tian Shan, *China*	54	B3
Tianchang, *China*	53	A12
Tiandong, *China*	52	F6
Tian'e, *China*	52	E6
Tianguá, *Brazil*	122	B3
Tianhe, *China*	52	E7
Tianjin, *China*	51	E9
Tiankoura, *Burkina Faso*	78	C4
Tianlin, *China*	52	E6
Tianmen, *China*	53	B9
Tianquan, *China*	52	B4
Tianshui, *China*	50	G3
Tiantai, *China*	53	C13
Tianyang, *China*	52	F6
Tianzhen, *China*	50	D8
Tianzhu, *China*	52	D7
Tianzhuangtai, *China*	51	D12
Tiaret, *Algeria*	75	A5
Tiassalé, *Ivory C.*	78	D4
Tibagi, *Brazil*	127	A5
Tibagi →, *Brazil*	127	A5
Tibati, *Cameroon*	79	D7
Tiber = Tevere →, *Italy*	33	G9
Tiber Reservoir, *U.S.A.*	110	B8
Tiberias = Teverya, *Israel*	69	C4
Tiberias = Yam Kinneret, *Israel*	69	C4
Tibesti, *Chad*	73	D8
Tibet = Xizang □, *China*	54	C3
Tibiao, *Phil.*	55	F5
Tibiri, *Niger*	79	C6
Ţibleş, *Romania*	38	B7
Tibnī, *Syria*	64	C3
Tibooburra, *Australia*	91	D3
Tibro, *Sweden*	11	F8
Tibugá, G. de, *Colombia*	120	B2
Tiburón, *Mexico*	114	B2
Ticao I., *Phil.*	55	E5
Tîchît, *Mauritania*	78	B3
Tichla, *Mauritania*	74	D2
Ticho, *Ethiopia*	77	F4
Ticino □, *Switz.*	23	D7
Ticino →, *Italy*	32	C6
Ticonderoga, *U.S.A.*	107	C11
Ticul, *Mexico*	115	C7
Tidaholm, *Sweden*	11	F7
Tiddim, *Burma*	61	H18
Tideridjaouine, Adrar, *Algeria*	75	D5
Tidikelt, *Algeria*	75	C5
Tidjikja, *Mauritania*	78	B2
Tidore, *Indonesia*	57	D7
Tiébissou, *Ivory C.*	78	D3
Tiefencastel, *Switz.*	23	C9
Tiel, *Neths.*	16	E6
Tiel, *Senegal*	78	C1
Tieling, *China*	51	C12
Tielt, *Belgium*	17	F2
Tien Shan, *Asia*	46	E11
Tien-tsin = Tianjin, *China*	51	E9
Tien Yen, *Vietnam*	58	B6
T'ienching = Tianjin, *China*	51	E9
Tienen, *Belgium*	17	G5
Tiénigbé, *Ivory C.*	78	D3
Tientsin = Tianjin, *China*	51	E9
Tierra Amarilla, *Chile*	126	B1
Tierra Amarilla, *U.S.A.*	111	H10
Tierra Colorada, *Mexico*	115	D5
Tierra de Barros, *Spain*	31	G4
Tierra de Campos, *Spain*	30	C6
Tierra del Fuego □, *Argentina*	128	D3
Tierra del Fuego, I. Gr. de, *Argentina*	128	D3
Tierralta, *Colombia*	120	B2
Tiétar →, *Spain*	30	F4
Tieté →, *Brazil*	127	A5
Tieyon, *Australia*	91	D1
Tifarati, *W. Sahara*	74	C2
Tiffin, *U.S.A.*	104	E4
Tiflèt, *Morocco*	74	B3
Tiflis = Tbilisi, *Georgia*	43	F11
Tifton, *U.S.A.*	105	K4
Tifu, *Indonesia*	57	E7
Tigil, *Russia*	45	D16
Tignish, *Canada*	99	C7
Tigray □, *Ethiopia*	77	E4
Tigre →, *Peru*	120	D3
Tigre →, *Venezuela*	121	B5
Tigris = Dijlah, Nahr →, *Asia*	64	D5
Tiguentourine, *Algeria*	75	C6
Tigyaing, *Burma*	61	H20
Tigzerte, O. →, *Morocco*	74	C3
Tîh, Gebel el, *Egypt*	76	J8
Tihodaine, Dunes de, *Algeria*	75	C6
Tijesno, *Croatia*	33	E12
Tijī, *Libya*	75	B7
Tijuana, *Mexico*	113	N9
Tikal, *Guatemala*	116	C2
Tikamgarh, *India*	63	G8
Tikhoretsk, *Russia*	43	D9
Tikhvin, *Russia*	40	C8
Tikkadouine, Adrar, *Algeria*	75	D5
Tiko, *Cameroon*	79	E6
Tikrīt, *Iraq*	64	C4
Tiksi, *Russia*	45	B13
Tilamuta, *Indonesia*	57	D6
Tilburg, *Neths.*	17	E6
Tilbury, *Canada*	98	D3
Tilbury, *U.K.*	13	F8
Tilcara, *Argentina*	126	A2
Tilden, *Nebr., U.S.A.*	108	D6
Tilden, *Tex., U.S.A.*	109	L5
Tilemses, *Niger*	79	B5
Tilemsi, Vallée du, *Mali*	79	B5
Tilhar, *India*	63	F8
Tilia, O. →, *Algeria*	75	C5
Tilichiki, *Russia*	45	C17
Tiligul →, *Ukraine*	42	C4
Tililane, *Algeria*	75	C4
Tílissos, *Greece*	37	D7
Till →, *U.K.*	12	B5
Tillabéri, *Niger*	79	C5
Tillamook, *U.S.A.*	110	D2
Tillberga, *Sweden*	10	E10
Tillia, *Niger*	79	B5
Tillsonburg, *Canada*	98	D3
Tillyeria □, *Cyprus*	37	D11
Tílos, *Greece*	39	N10
Tilpa, *Australia*	91	E3
Tilrhemt, *Algeria*	75	B5
Tilsit = Sovetsk, *Russia*	40	D2
Tilt →, *U.K.*	14	E5
Tilton, *U.S.A.*	107	C13
Timagami L., *Canada*	98	C3
Timaru, *N.Z.*	87	L3
Timashevsk, *Russia*	43	D8
Timau, *Italy*	33	B10
Timau, *Kenya*	82	B4
Timbákion, *Greece*	37	D6
Timbaúba, *Brazil*	122	C4
Timbedgha, *Mauritania*	78	B3
Timber Lake, *U.S.A.*	108	C4
Timber Mt., *U.S.A.*	112	H10
Timbío, *Colombia*	120	C2
Timbiqui, *Colombia*	120	C2
Timboon, *Australia*	91	F3
Timbuktu = Tombouctou, *Mali*	78	B4
Timellouline, *Algeria*	75	C6
Timétrine Montagnes, *Mali*	79	B4
Timfristós, Óros, *Greece*	39	L4
Timhadit, *Morocco*	74	B3
Timi, *Cyprus*	37	E11
Timia, *Niger*	79	B6
Timimoun, *Algeria*	75	C5
Timiş = Tamis →, *Serbia*	38	D4
Timişoara, *Romania*	38	D4
Timmins, *Canada*	98	C3
Timok →, *Serbia*	21	L12
Timon, *Brazil*	122	C3
Timor, *Indonesia*	57	F7
Timor □, *Indonesia*	57	F7
Timor Sea, *Ind. Oc.*	88	B4
Tin Alkoum, *Algeria*	75	D7
Tin Gornai, *Mali*	79	B4
Tin Mt., *U.S.A.*	112	J9
Tina, Khalig el, *Egypt*	76	H8
Tinaca Pt., *Phil.*	55	J6
Tinaco, *Venezuela*	120	B4
Tinafak, O. →, *Algeria*	75	C6
Tinajo, *Canary Is.*	36	E6
Tinaquillo, *Venezuela*	120	B4
Tinca, *Romania*	38	C4
Tinchebray, *France*	24	D6
Tindouf, *Algeria*	74	C3
Tinée →, *France*	27	E11
Tineo, *Spain*	30	B4
Tinerhir, *Morocco*	74	B3
Tinfouchi, *Algeria*	74	C3
Ting Jiang →, *China*	53	E11
Tinggi, Pulau, *Malaysia*	59	L5
Tinglev, *Denmark*	11	K3
Tingo Maria, *Peru*	124	B2
Tinh Bien, *Vietnam*	59	G5
Tinharé, I. de, *Brazil*	123	D4
Tinjoub, *Algeria*	72	C3
Tinkurrin, *Australia*	89	F2
Tinnevelly = Tirunelveli, *India*	60	Q10
Tinnoset, *Norway*	10	E3
Tinnsjø, *Norway*	10	E2
Tinogasta, *Argentina*	126	B2
Tínos, *Greece*	39	M8
Tínoso, C., *Spain*	29	H3
Tinta, *Peru*	124	C3
Tintina, *Argentina*	126	B3
Tintinara, *Australia*	91	F3
Tinto →, *Spain*	31	H4
Tioga, *U.S.A.*	106	E7
Tioman, Pulau, *Malaysia*	59	L5
Tione di Trento, *Italy*	32	B7
Tionesta, *U.S.A.*	106	E5
Tior, *Sudan*	77	F3
Tioulilin, *Algeria*	75	C4
Tipongpani, *India*	61	F19
Tipperary, *Ireland*	15	D3
Tipperary □, *Ireland*	15	D4
Tipton, *U.K.*	13	E5
Tipton, *Calif., U.S.A.*	111	H4
Tipton, *Ind., U.S.A.*	104	E2
Tipton, *Iowa, U.S.A.*	108	E9
Tipton Mt., *U.S.A.*	113	K12
Tiptonville, *U.S.A.*	109	G10
Tiquié →, *Brazil*	120	C4
Tiracambu, Serra do, *Brazil*	122	B2
Tīrān, *Iran*	65	C6
Tīrān, *Si. Arabia*	76	B3
Tirana, *Albania*	39	H2
Tiranë = Tirana, *Albania*	39	H2
Tirano, *Italy*	32	B7
Tiraspol, *Moldova*	42	C3
Tirat Karmel, *Israel*	69	C3
Tiratimine, *Algeria*	75	C5
Tirdout, *Mali*	79	B4
Tire, *Turkey*	66	D2
Tirebolu, *Turkey*	67	C8
Tiree, *U.K.*	14	E2
Tîrgovişte, *Romania*	38	E8
Tîrgu Frumos, *Romania*	38	B10
Tîrgu-Jiu, *Romania*	38	D6
Tîrgu Mureş, *Romania*	38	C7
Tîrgu Neamţ, *Romania*	38	B9
Tîrgu Ocna, *Romania*	38	C9
Tîrgu Secuiesc, *Romania*	38	D9
Tirich Mir, *Pakistan*	60	A7
Tiriola, *Italy*	35	D9
Tiririca, Serra da, *Brazil*	123	E2
Tiris, *W. Sahara*	74	D2
Tîrnava Mare →, *Romania*	38	C7
Tîrnava Mică →, *Romania*	38	C7
Tîrnăveni, *Romania*	38	C7
Tírnavos, *Greece*	39	K5
Tirodi, *India*	60	J11
Tiros, *Brazil*	123	E2
Tirschenreuth, *Germany*	19	F8
Tirso →, *Italy*	34	C1
Tirso, L. del, *Italy*	34	B1
Tiruchchirappalli, *India*	60	P11
Tirunelveli, *India*	60	Q10
Tirupati, *India*	60	N11
Tiruppur, *India*	60	P10
Tiruvannamalai, *India*	60	N11
Tisa →, *Hungary*	21	J10
Tisa →, *Serbia*	21	K10
Tisdale, *Canada*	101	C8
Tishomingo, *U.S.A.*	109	H6
Tisnaren, *Sweden*	10	F9
Tisovec, *Slovak Rep.*	20	G9
Tissemsilt, *Algeria*	75	A5
Tissint, *Morocco*	74	C3
Tissø, *Denmark*	11	J5
Tisza = Tisa →, *Hungary*	21	J10
Tiszafüred, *Hungary*	21	H10
Tiszavasvári, *Hungary*	21	H11
Tit, Ahaggar, *Algeria*	75	D6
Tit, Tademait, *Algeria*	75	C5
Tit-Ary, *Russia*	45	B13
Titaguas, *Spain*	28	F3
Titel, *Serbia*	21	K10
Tithwal, *India*	63	B5
Titicaca, L., *S. Amer.*	124	D4
Titiwa, *Nigeria*	79	C7
Titlis, *Switz.*	23	C6
Titograd = Podgorica, *Montenegro*	21	N9
Titov Veles, *Macedonia*	39	H4
Titova Korenica, *Croatia*	33	D12
Titovo Uzice, *Serbia*	21	M9
Titule, *Zaïre*	82	B2
Titumate, *Colombia*	120	B2
Titusville, *Fla., U.S.A.*	105	L5
Titusville, *Pa., U.S.A.*	106	E5
Tivaouane, *Senegal*	78	C1
Tiveden, *Sweden*	11	F8
Tiverton, *U.K.*	13	G4
Tívoli, *Italy*	33	G9
Tiyo, *Eritrea*	77	E5
Tizga, *Morocco*	74	B3
Ti'zi N'Isli, *Morocco*	74	B3
Tizi-Ouzou, *Algeria*	75	A5
Tizimín, *Mexico*	115	C7
Tiznados →, *Venezuela*	120	B4
Tiznit, *Morocco*	74	C3
Tjeggelvas, *Sweden*	8	C14
Tjeukemeer, *Neths.*	16	C7
Tjirebon = Cirebon, *Indonesia*	57	G13
Tjøme, *Norway*	10	E4
Tjonger Kanaal, *Neths.*	16	C7
Tjörn, *Sweden*	11	G5
Tkibuli, *Georgia*	43	E10
Tkvarcheli, *Georgia*	43	E9
Tlacotalpan, *Mexico*	115	D5
Tlahualilo, *Mexico*	114	B4
Tlaquepaque, *Mexico*	114	C4
Tlaxcala, *Mexico*	115	D5
Tlaxcala □, *Mexico*	115	D5
Tlaxiaco, *Mexico*	115	D5
Tlell, *Canada*	100	C2
Tlemcen, *Algeria*	75	B4
Tleta Sidi Bouguedra, *Morocco*	74	B3
Tlumach, *Ukraine*	42	B1
Tlyarata, *Russia*	43	E12
Tmassah, *Libya*	73	C8
Tnine d'Anglou, *Morocco*	74	C3
To Bong, *Vietnam*	58	F7
Toad →, *Canada*	100	B4
Toamasina, *Madag.*	85	B8
Toamasina □, *Madag.*	85	B8
Toay, *Argentina*	126	D3
Toba, *Japan*	49	G8
Toba Kakar, *Pakistan*	62	D3
Toba Tek Singh, *Pakistan*	62	D5
Tobago, *W. Indies*	117	D7
Tobarra, *Spain*	29	G3
Tobelo, *Indonesia*	57	D7
Tobermorey, *Australia*	90	C2
Tobermory, *Canada*	98	C3
Tobermory, *U.K.*	14	E2
Tobin, *U.S.A.*	112	F5
Tobin, L., *Australia*	88	D4
Tobin L., *Canada*	101	C8
Toboali, *Indonesia*	56	E3
Tobol, *Kazakhstan*	44	D7
Tobol →, *Russia*	44	D7
Toboli, *Indonesia*	57	E6
Tobolsk, *Russia*	44	D7
Tobruk = Tubruq, *Libya*	73	B9
Tobyhanna, *U.S.A.*	107	E9
Tocache Nuevo, *Peru*	124	B2
Tocantínia, *Brazil*	122	C2
Tocantinópolis, *Brazil*	122	C2
Tocantins □, *Brazil*	122	B2
Toccoa, *U.S.A.*	105	H4
Toce →, *Italy*	32	C5
Tochi, *Japan*	49	F9
Tochigi □, *Japan*	49	F9
Tocina, *Spain*	31	H5
Tocopilla, *Chile*	126	A1
Tocumwal, *Australia*	91	F4
Tocuyo →, *Venezuela*	120	A4
Tocuyo de la Costa, *Venezuela*	120	A4
Todd →, *Australia*	90	C2
Todeli, *Indonesia*	57	E6
Todenyang, *Kenya*	82	B4
Todi, *Italy*	33	F9
Tödi, *Switz.*	23	C7
Todos os Santos, B. de, *Brazil*	123	D4
Todos Santos, *Mexico*	114	C2
Todtnau, *Germany*	19	H3
Toecé, *Burkina Faso*	79	C4
Tofield, *Canada*	100	C6
Tofino, *Canada*	100	D3
Töfsingdalens nationalpark, *Sweden*	10	B6
Toftlund, *Denmark*	11	J3
Tofua, *Tonga*	87	D11
Tōgane, *Japan*	49	G10
Togba, *Mauritania*	78	B2
Togian, Kepulauan, *Indonesia*	57	E6
Togliatti, *Russia*	41	E16
Togo ■, *W. Afr.*	79	D5
Togtoh, *China*	50	D6
Tohma →, *Turkey*	67	D8
Tōhoku □, *Japan*	48	E10
Toinya, *Sudan*	77	F2
Tojikiston = Tajikistan ■, *Asia*	44	F8
Tojo, *Indonesia*	57	E6
Tōjō, *Japan*	49	G6
Toka, *Guyana*	121	C6
Tokachi-Dake, *Japan*	48	C11
Tokachi-Gawa →, *Japan*	48	C11
Tokaj, *Hungary*	21	G11
Tokala, *Indonesia*	57	E6
Tōkamachi, *Japan*	49	F9
Tokanui, *N.Z.*	87	M2
Tokar, *Sudan*	76	D4
Tokara-Rettō, *Japan*	49	K4
Tokarahi, *N.Z.*	87	L3
Tokashiki-Shima, *Japan*	49	L3
Tokat, *Turkey*	66	C7
Tokat □, *Turkey*	66	C7
Tŏkch'ŏn, *N. Korea*	51	E14
Tokeland, *U.S.A.*	112	D3
Tokelau Is., *Pac. Oc.*	92	H10
Tokmak, *Kirghizia*	44	E8
Toko Ra., *Australia*	90	C2
Tokoro-Gawa →, *Japan*	48	B12
Tokushima, *Japan*	49	G7
Tokushima □, *Japan*	49	H7
Tokuyama, *Japan*	49	G5
Tōkyō, *Japan*	49	G9
Tolaga Bay, *N.Z.*	87	H7
Tolbukhin = Dobrich, *Bulgaria*	38	F10
Toledo, *Spain*	30	F6
Toledo, *Ohio, U.S.A.*	104	E4
Toledo, *Oreg., U.S.A.*	110	D2
Toledo, *Wash., U.S.A.*	110	C2
Toledo, Montes de, *Spain*	31	F6
Tolentino, *Italy*	33	E10
Tolga, *Algeria*	75	B6
Tolga, *Norway*	10	B5
Toliara, *Madag.*	85	C7
Toliara □, *Madag.*	85	C8
Tolima, *Colombia*	120	C2
Tolima □, *Colombia*	120	C2
Tolitoli, *Indonesia*	57	D6
Tolkamer, *Neths.*	16	E8
Tolleson, *U.S.A.*	111	K7
Tollhouse, *U.S.A.*	112	H7
Tolmachevo, *Russia*	40	B6
Tolmezzo, *Italy*	33	B10
Tolmin, *Slovenia*	33	B10
Tolo, *Zaïre*	80	E3
Tolo, Teluk, *Indonesia*	57	E6
Tolochin, *Belorussia*	40	D6
Tolosa, *Spain*	28	B2
Tolox, *Spain*	31	J6
Toltén, *Chile*	128	A2
Toluca, *Mexico*	115	D5
Tom Burke, *S. Africa*	85	C4
Tom Price, *Australia*	88	D2
Tomah, *U.S.A.*	108	D9
Tomahawk, *U.S.A.*	108	C10
Tomakomai, *Japan*	48	C10
Tomales, *U.S.A.*	112	G4
Tomales B., *U.S.A.*	112	G3
Tomar, *Portugal*	31	F2
Tomarza, *Turkey*	66	D6
Tomás Barrón, *Bolivia*	124	D4
Tomaszów Mazowiecki, *Poland*	20	D9
Tomatlán, *Mexico*	114	D4
Tombador, Serra do, *Brazil*	125	C6
Tombé, *Sudan*	77	F3
Tombigbee →, *U.S.A.*	105	K2
Tombstone, *U.S.A.*	111	L8
Tombua, *Angola*	84	B1
Tomé, *Chile*	126	D1
Tomé-Açu, *Brazil*	122	B2
Tomelilla, *Sweden*	11	J7
Tomelloso, *Spain*	29	F1
Tomingley, *Australia*	91	E4
Tomini, *Indonesia*	57	D6
Tomini, Teluk, *Indonesia*	57	E6
Tominian, *Mali*	78	C4
Tomiño, *Spain*	30	D2
Tomkinson Ras., *Australia*	89	E4
Tommot, *Russia*	45	D13
Tomnavoulin, *U.K.*	14	D5
Tomnop Ta Suos, *Cambodia*	59	G5
Tomo, *Colombia*	120	C4
Tomo →, *Colombia*	120	B4
Toms Place, *U.S.A.*	112	H8
Toms River, *U.S.A.*	107	G10
Tomsk, *Russia*	44	D9
Tonalá, *Mexico*	115	D6
Tonale, Passo del, *Italy*	32	B7
Tonalea, *U.S.A.*	111	H8
Tonantins, *Brazil*	120	D4
Tonasket, *U.S.A.*	110	B4
Tonate, *Fr. Guiana*	121	C7
Tonawanda, *U.S.A.*	106	D6
Tonbridge, *U.K.*	13	F8
Tondano, *Indonesia*	57	D6
Tondela, *Portugal*	30	E2
Tønder, *Denmark*	11	K2
Tondi Kiwindi, *Niger*	79	C5
Tondibi, *Mali*	79	B4
Tonekābon, *Iran*	65	B6
Tong Xian, *China*	50	E9
Tonga ■, *Pac. Oc.*	87	D11
Tonga Trench, *Pac. Oc.*	92	J11
Tongaat, *S. Africa*	85	D5
Tong'an, *China*	53	E12
Tongareva, *Cook Is.*	93	H12
Tongatapu, *Tonga*	87	E11
Tongbai, *China*	53	A9
Tongcheng, *Anhui, China*	53	B11
Tongcheng, *Hubei, China*	53	C9
Tongchŏn-ni, *N. Korea*	51	E14
Tongchuan, *China*	50	G5
Tongdao, *China*	52	D7
Tongeren, *Belgium*	17	G6
Tonggu, *China*	53	C10
Tongguan, *China*	50	G6
Tonghai, *China*	52	E4
Tonghua, *China*	51	D13
Tongjiang, *Heilongjiang, China*	54	B8
Tongjiang, *Sichuan, China*	52	B6
Tongjosŏn Man, *N. Korea*	51	E14
Tongking, G. of = Tonkin, G. of, *Asia*	58	B7
Tongliang, *China*	52	C6
Tongliao, *China*	51	C12
Tongling, *China*	53	B11
Tonglu, *China*	53	C12

Tongnae, *S. Korea* 51 G15
Tongnan, *China* 52 B5
Tongobory, *Madag.* 85 C7
Tongoy, *Chile* 126 C1
Tongren, *China* 52 D7
Tongres = Tongeren,
　Belgium 17 G6
Tongsa Dzong, *Bhutan* . . 61 F17
Tongue, *U.K.* 14 C4
Tongue →, *U.S.A.* 108 B2
Tongwei, *China* 50 G3
Tongxin, *China* 50 F3
Tongyang, *N. Korea* 51 E14
Tongyu, *China* 51 B12
Tongzi, *China* 52 C6
Tonj, *Sudan* 77 F2
Tonk, *India* 62 F6
Tonkawa, *U.S.A.* 109 G6
Tonkin = Bac Phan,
　Vietnam 58 B5
Tonkin, G. of, *Asia* 58 B7
Tonlé Sap, *Cambodia* 58 F4
Tonnay-Charente, *France* . 26 C3
Tonneins, *France* 26 D4
Tonnerre, *France* 25 E10
Tönning, *Germany* 18 A4
Tono, *Japan* 48 E10
Tonopah, *U.S.A.* 111 G5
Tonosí, *Panama* 116 E3
Tønsberg, *Norway* 10 E4
Tooele, *U.S.A.* 110 F7
Toompine, *Australia* 91 D3
Toonpan, *Australia* 90 B4
Toora, *Australia* 91 F4
Toora-Khem, *Russia* 45 D10
Toowoomba, *Australia* . . . 91 D5
Topalu, *Romania* 38 E11
Topaz, *U.S.A.* 112 G4
Topeka, *U.S.A.* 108 F7
Topki, *Russia* 44 D9
Topl'a →, *Slovak Rep.* . . . 20 G11
Topley, *Canada* 100 C3
Toplica →, *Serbia* 21 M11
Topliţa, *Romania* 38 C8
Topocalma, Pta., *Chile* . . 126 C1
Topock, *U.S.A.* 113 L12
Topola, *Serbia* 21 L10
Topol'čany, *Slovak Rep.* . . 20 G8
Topoli, *Kazakhstan* 43 C14
Topolnitsa →, *Bulgaria* . . 38 G7
Topolobampo, *Mexico* . . . 114 B3
Topolovgrad, *Bulgaria* . . . 38 G9
Toppenish, *U.S.A.* 110 C3
Topusko, *Croatia* 33 C12
Toquepala, *Peru* 124 D3
Torá, *Spain* 28 D6
Tora Kit, *Sudan* 77 E3
Toraka Vestale, *Madag.* . . 85 B7
Torata, *Peru* 124 D3
Torbalı, *Turkey* 66 D2
Torbay, *Canada* 99 C9
Torbay, *U.K.* 13 G4
Tørdal, *Norway* 10 E2
Tordesillas, *Spain* 30 D6
Tordoya, *Spain* 30 B2
Töreboda, *Sweden* 11 F8
Torfajökull, *Iceland* 8 E4
Torgau, *Germany* 18 D8
Torgelow, *Germany* 18 B9
Torhout, *Belgium* 17 F2
Tori, *Ethiopia* 77 F3
Tori-Shima, *Japan* 49 J10
Torija, *Spain* 28 E1
Torin, *Mexico* 114 B2
Toriñana, C., *Spain* 30 B1
Torino, *Italy* 32 C4
Torit, *Sudan* 77 G3
Torkovichi, *Russia* 40 B7
Tormes →, *Spain* 30 D4
Tornado Mt., *Canada* 100 D6
Torne älv →, *Sweden* 8 D18
Torneå = Tornio, *Finland* . 8 D18
Torneträsk, *Sweden* 8 B15
Tornio, *Finland* 8 D18
Tornionjoki →, *Finland* . . 8 D18
Tornquist, *Argentina* 126 D3
Toro, *Baleares, Spain* 36 B11
Toro, *Zamora, Spain* 30 D5
Torö, *Sweden* 11 F11
Toro, Cerro del, *Chile* . . . 126 B2
Toro Pk., *U.S.A.* 113 M10
Törökszentmiklós, *Hungary* 21 H10
Toronios Kólpos, *Greece* . . 39 J6
Toronto, *Australia* 91 E5
Toronto, *Canada* 98 D4
Toronto, *U.S.A.* 106 F4
Toropets, *Russia* 40 C7
Tororo, *Uganda* 82 B3
Toros Dağları, *Turkey* . . . 66 E5
Torotoro, *Bolivia* 125 D4
Torpshammar, *Sweden* . . . 10 B10
Torquay, *Canada* 101 D8
Torquay, *U.K.* 13 G4
Torquemada, *Spain* 30 C6
Torralba de Calatrava,
　Spain 31 F7
Torrance, *U.S.A.* 113 M8
Torrão, *Portugal* 31 G2
Torre Annunziata, *Italy* . . 35 B7
Tôrre de Moncorvo,
　Portugal 30 D3
Torre del Greco, *Italy* 35 B7
Torre del Mar, *Spain* 31 J6
Torre-Pacheco, *Spain* 29 H4
Torre Pellice, *Italy* 32 D4

Torreblanca, *Spain* 28 E5
Torrecampo, *Spain* 31 G6
Torrecilla en Cameros,
　Spain 28 C2
Torredembarra, *Spain* 28 D6
Torredonjimeno, *Spain* . . . 31 H7
Torrejoncillo, *Spain* 30 F4
Torrelaguna, *Spain* 28 E1
Torrelavega, *Spain* 30 B6
Torremaggiore, *Italy* 35 A8
Torremolinos, *Spain* 31 J6
Torrens, L., *Australia* 91 E2
Torrens Cr. →, *Australia* . 90 C4
Torrens Creek, *Australia* . . 90 C4
Torrente, *Spain* 29 F4
Torrenueva, *Spain* 29 G1
Torréon, *Mexico* 114 B4
Torreperogil, *Spain* 29 G1
Torres, *Mexico* 114 B2
Torres Novas, *Portugal* . . . 31 F2
Torres Strait, *Australia* . . . 92 H6
Torres Vedras, *Portugal* . . 31 F1
Torrevieja, *Spain* 29 H4
Torrey, *U.S.A.* 111 G8
Torridge →, *U.K.* 13 G3
Torridon, L., *U.K.* 14 D3
Torrijos, *Spain* 30 F6
Torrington, *Conn., U.S.A.* . 107 E11
Torrington, *Wyo., U.S.A.* . 108 D2
Torroella de Montgri, *Spain* 28 C8
Torrox, *Spain* 31 J7
Torsö, *Sweden* 11 F7
Tortola, *Virgin Is.* 117 C7
Tórtoles de Esgueva, *Spain* 30 D6
Tortona, *Italy* 32 D5
Tortoreto, *Italy* 33 F10
Tortorici, *Italy* 35 D7
Tortosa, *Spain* 28 E5
Tortosa, C., *Spain* 28 E5
Tortosendo, *Portugal* 30 E3
Tortue, I. de la, *Haiti* . . . 117 B5
Tortum, *Turkey* 67 C9
Toruğd, *Iran* 65 C7
Torul, *Turkey* 67 C8
Toruń, *Poland* 20 B8
Torup, *Denmark* 11 G3
Torup, *Sweden* 11 H7
Tory I., *Ireland* 15 A3
Torysa →, *Slovak Rep.* . . . 20 G11
Torzhok, *Russia* 40 C9
Tosa, *Japan* 49 H6
Tosa-Shimizu, *Japan* 49 H6
Tosa-Wan, *Japan* 49 H6
Toscana, *Italy* 32 E8
Toscano, Arcipelago, *Italy* 32 F7
Toshkent = Tashkent,
　Uzbekistan 44 E7
Tosno, *Russia* 40 B7
Tossa, *Spain* 28 D7
Tostado, *Argentina* 126 B3
Tostedt, *Germany* 18 B5
Tostón, Pta. de, *Canary Is.* 36 F5
Tosu, *Japan* 49 H5
Tosya, *Turkey* 66 C6
Totana, *Spain* 29 H3
Toten, *Norway* 10 D4
Toteng, *Botswana* 84 C3
Tôtes, *France* 24 C8
Tótkomlós, *Hungary* 21 J10
Totma, *Russia* 41 B13
Totnes, *U.K.* 13 G4
Totness, *Surinam* 121 B6
Totonicapán, *Guatemala* . . 116 D1
Totora, *Bolivia* 125 D4
Totten Glacier, *Antarctica* . 5 C8
Tottenham, *Australia* 91 E4
Tottenham, *Canada* 106 B5
Tottori, *Japan* 49 G7
Tottori □, *Japan* 49 G7
Touat, *Algeria* 75 C5
Touba, *Ivory C.* 78 D3
Toubkal, Djebel, *Morocco* . 74 B3
Toucy, *France* 25 E10
Tougan, *Burkina Faso* 78 C4
Touggourt, *Algeria* 75 B6
Tougué, *Guinea* 78 C2
Toukmatine, *Algeria* 75 D6
Toul, *France* 25 D12
Toulepleu, *Ivory C.* 78 D3
Toulon, *France* 27 E9
Toulouse, *France* 26 E5
Toummo, *Niger* 73 D7
Toumodi, *Ivory C.* 78 D3
Tounassine, Hamada,
　Algeria 74 C3
Toungoo, *Burma* 61 K20
Touques →, *France* 24 C7
Touraine, *France* 24 E7
Tourane = Da Nang,
　Vietnam 58 D7
Tourcoing, *France* 25 B10
Tourine, *Mauritania* 74 D2
Tournai, *Belgium* 17 G2
Tournan-en-Brie, *France* . . 25 D9
Tournay, *France* 26 E4
Tournon, *France* 27 C8
Tournon-St.-Martin, *France* 24 F7
Tournus, *France* 27 B8
Touros, *Brazil* 122 C4
Tours, *France* 24 E7
Touwsrivier, *S. Africa* 84 E3
Tovar, *Venezuela* 120 B3
Tovarkovskiy, *Russia* 41 E11
Tovdal, *Norway* 11 F2
Tovdalselva →, *Norway* . . 11 F2
Towada, *Japan* 48 D10

Towada-Ko, *Japan* 48 D10
Towamba, *Australia* 91 F4
Towanda, *U.S.A.* 107 E8
Towang, *India* 61 F17
Tower, *U.S.A.* 108 B8
Towerhill Cr. →, *Australia* 90 C3
Towner, *U.S.A.* 108 A4
Townsend, *U.S.A.* 110 C8
Townshend I., *Australia* . . 90 C5
Townsville, *Australia* 90 B4
Towson, *U.S.A.* 104 F7
Toya-Ko, *Japan* 48 C10
Toyah, *U.S.A.* 109 K3
Toyahvale, *U.S.A.* 109 K3
Toyama, *Japan* 49 F8
Toyama □, *Japan* 49 F8
Toyama-Wan, *Japan* 49 F8
Toyohashi, *Japan* 49 G8
Toyokawa, *Japan* 49 G8
Toyonaka, *Japan* 49 G7
Toyooka, *Japan* 49 G7
Toyota, *Japan* 49 G8
Tozeur, *Tunisia* 75 B6
Tra On, *Vietnam* 59 H5
Trabancos →, *Spain* 30 D5
Traben Trarbach, *Germany* 19 F3
Trabzon, *Turkey* 67 C8
Trabzon □, *Turkey* 67 C8
Tracadie, *Canada* 99 C7
Tracy, *Calif., U.S.A.* 111 H3
Tracy, *Minn., U.S.A.* 108 C7
Tradate, *Italy* 32 C5
Tradovoye, *Russia* 48 C6
Trafalgar, C., *Spain* 31 J4
Traiguén, *Chile* 128 A2
Trail, *Canada* 100 D5
Trainor L., *Canada* 100 A4
Traíra →, *Brazil* 120 D4
Trákhonas, *Cyprus* 37 D12
Tralee, *Ireland* 15 D2
Tralee B., *Ireland* 15 D2
Tramelan, *Switz.* 22 B4
Tramore, *Ireland* 15 D4
Tran Ninh, Cao Nguyen,
　Laos 58 C4
Tranås, *Sweden* 9 G13
Trancas, *Argentina* 126 B2
Trancoso, *Portugal* 30 E3
Tranebjerg, *Denmark* 11 J4
Tranemo, *Sweden* 11 G7
Trang, *Thailand* 59 J2
Trangahy, *Madag.* 85 B7
Trangan, *Indonesia* 57 F8
Trangie, *Australia* 91 E4
Trångsviken, *Sweden* 10 A8
Trani, *Italy* 35 A9
Tranoroa, *Madag.* 85 C8
Tranqueras, *Uruguay* 127 C4
Trans Nzoia □, *Kenya* 82 B3
Transantarctic Mts.,
　Antarctica 5 E12
Transcaucasia =
　Zakavkazye, *Asia* 43 F11
Transcona, *Canada* 101 D9
Transilvania, *Romania* . . . 38 D8
Transkei □, *S. Africa* 85 E4
Transvaal □, *S. Africa* 84 D4
Transylvania =
　Transilvania, *Romania* . . 38 D8
Transylvanian Alps,
　Romania 6 F10
Trápani, *Italy* 34 D5
Trapper Pk., *U.S.A.* 110 D6
Traralgon, *Australia* 91 F4
Trarza, *Mauritania* 78 B2
Trasacco, *Italy* 33 G10
Trǎscǎu, Munţii, *Romania* . 38 C6
Trasimeno, L., *Italy* 33 E9
Trat, *Thailand* 59 F4
Traun, *Austria* 21 G4
Traunstein, *Germany* 19 H8
Tråvad, *Sweden* 11 F7
Traveller's L., *Australia* . . 91 E3
Travemünde, *Germany* . . . 18 B6
Travers, Mt., *N.Z.* 87 K4
Traverse City, *U.S.A.* 104 C3
Travnik, *Bos.-H.* 21 L7
Trayning, *Australia* 89 F2
Trazo, *Spain* 30 B2
Trbovlje, *Slovenia* 33 B12
Trébbia →, *Italy* 32 C6
Trebel →, *Germany* 18 B9
Trebinje, *Bos.-H.* 21 N8
Trebisacce, *Italy* 35 C9
Trebišnica →, *Bos.-H.* . . . 21 N8
Trebišov, *Slovak Rep.* 20 G11
Trebižat →, *Bos.-H.* 21 M7
Trebnje, *Slovenia* 33 C12
Třeboň, *Czech.* 20 G4
Trebujena, *Spain* 31 J4
Trecate, *Italy* 32 C5
Trece Martires, *Phil.* 55 D4
Tredegar, *U.K.* 13 F4
Tregaron, *U.K.* 13 E4
Trégastel-Plage, *France* . . 24 D3
Tregnago, *Italy* 33 C8
Tregrosse Is., *Australia* . . . 90 B5
Tréguier, *France* 24 D3
Tregueza, *France* 24 E4
Treherne, *Canada* 101 D9
Tréia, *Italy* 33 E10
Treignac, *France* 26 C5
Treinta y Tres, *Uruguay* . . 127 C5
Treis, *Germany* 19 E3
Trekveld, *S. Africa* 84 E2
Trelde Næs, *Denmark* 11 J3

Trelew, *Argentina* 128 B3
Trélissac, *France* 26 C4
Trelleborg, *Sweden* 11 J7
Trélon, *France* 25 B11
Tremiti, *Italy* 33 F12
Tremonton, *U.S.A.* 110 F7
Tremp, *Spain* 28 C5
Trenche →, *Canada* 98 C5
Trenčín, *Slovak Rep.* 20 G8
Trenggalek, *Indonesia* 57 H14
Trenque Lauquen,
　Argentina 126 D3
Trent →, *U.K.* 12 D7
Trentino-Alto Adige □,
　Italy 32 B8
Trento, *Italy* 32 B8
Trenton, *Canada* 98 D4
Trenton, *Mo., U.S.A.* 108 E8
Trenton, *N.J., U.S.A.* 107 F10
Trenton, *Nebr., U.S.A.* . . . 108 E4
Trenton, *Tenn., U.S.A.* . . . 109 H10
Trepassey, *Canada* 99 C9
Trepuzzi, *Italy* 35 B11
Tres Arroyos, *Argentina* . . 126 D3
Três Corações, *Brazil* 123 F2
Três Lagoas, *Brazil* 123 F1
Tres Lagos →, *Argentina* . 128 C2
Três Marías, *Mexico* 114 C3
Três Marias, Reprêsa,
　Brazil 123 E2
Tres Montes, C., *Chile* . . . 128 C1
Três Pinos, *U.S.A.* 112 J5
Três Pontas, *Brazil* 123 F2
Tres Puentes, *Chile* 126 B1
Tres Puntas, C., *Argentina* 128 C3
Três Rios, *Brazil* 123 F3
Tres Valles, *Mexico* 115 D5
Treska →, *Macedonia* 39 H4
Trespaderne, *Spain* 28 C1
Trets, *France* 27 E9
Treuchtlingen, *Germany* . . 19 G6
Treuenbrietzen, *Germany* . 18 C8
Treungen, *Norway* 9 G10
Treviglio, *Italy* 32 C6
Trevínca, Peña, *Spain* 30 C4
Treviso, *Italy* 33 C9
Trévoux, *France* 27 C8
Treysa, *Germany* 18 E5
Trgovište, *Serbia* 21 N12
Triabunna, *Australia* 90 G4
Triánda, *Greece* 37 C10
Triang, *Malaysia* 59 L4
Triaucourt-en-Argonne,
　France 25 D12
Tribsees, *Germany* 18 A8
Tribulation, C., *Australia* . 90 B4
Tribune, *U.S.A.* 108 F4
Tricárico, *Italy* 35 B9
Tricase, *Italy* 35 C11
Trichinopoly =
　Tiruchchirappalli, *India* . 60 P11
Trichur, *India* 60 P10
Trida, *Australia* 91 E4
Trier, *Germany* 19 F2
Trieste, *Italy* 33 C10
Trieste, G. di, *Italy* 33 C10
Trieux →, *France* 24 D3
Triggiano, *Italy* 35 A9
Triglav, *Slovenia* 33 B10
Trigno →, *Italy* 33 F11
Trigueros, *Spain* 31 H4
Trikhonis, Límni, *Greece* . 39 L4
Tríkkala, *Greece* 39 K4
Trikomo, *Cyprus* 37 D12
Trikora, Puncak, *Indonesia* 57 E9
Trilj, *Croatia* 33 E13
Trillo, *Spain* 28 E2
Trim, *Ireland* 15 C5
Trincomalee, *Sri Lanka* . . 60 Q12
Trindade, *Brazil* 123 E2
Trindade, I., *Atl. Oc.* 2 F8
Trinidad, *Bolivia* 125 C5
Trinidad, *Colombia* 120 B3
Trinidad, *Cuba* 116 B3
Trinidad, *Uruguay* 126 C4
Trinidad, *U.S.A.* 109 G2
Trinidad, *W. Indies* 117 D7
Trinidad →, *Mexico* 115 D5
Trinidad, G., *Chile* 128 C1
Trinidad, I., *Argentina* . . . 128 A4
Trinidad & Tobago ■,
　W. Indies 117 D7
Trinitápoli, *Italy* 35 A9
Trinity, *Canada* 99 C9
Trinity, *U.S.A.* 109 K7
Trinity →, *Calif., U.S.A.* . 110 F2
Trinity →, *Tex., U.S.A.* . . 109 L7
Trinity B., *Canada* 99 C9
Trinity Range, *U.S.A.* 110 F4
Trinkitat, *Sudan* 76 D4
Trino, *Italy* 32 C5
Trion, *U.S.A.* 105 H3
Trionto, C., *Italy* 35 C9
Triora, *Italy* 32 E4
Tripoli = Tarābulus,
　Lebanon 69 A4
Tripoli = Tarābulus, *Libya* 75 B7
Tripp, *U.S.A.* 108 D6
Tripura □, *India* 61 H17
Tripylos, *Cyprus* 37 E11
Trischen, *Germany* 18 A4
Tristan da Cunha, *Atl. Oc.* . 2 F9
Trivandrum, *India* 60 Q10
Trivento, *Italy* 35 A7
Trnava, *Slovak Rep.* 21 G7
Trochu, *Canada* 100 C6

Trodely I., *Canada* 98 B4
Trogir, *Croatia* 33 E13
Troglav, *Croatia* 33 E13
Trøgstad, *Norway* 10 E5
Tróia, *Italy* 35 A8
Troilus, L., *Canada* 98 B5
Troina, *Italy* 35 E7
Trois Fourches, Cap des,
　Morocco 75 A4
Trois-Pistoles, *Canada* . . . 99 C6
Trois-Rivières, *Canada* . . . 98 C5
Troisvierges, *Belgium* 17 H8
Troitsk, *Russia* 44 D7
Troitsko Pechorsk, *Russia* . 44 C6
Trölladyngja, *Iceland* 8 D5
Trollhättan, *Sweden* 11 F6
Trollheimen, *Norway* 10 B3
Trombetas →, *Brazil* 121 D6
Troms fylke □, *Norway* . . . 8 B15
Tromsø, *Norway* 8 B15
Trona, *U.S.A.* 113 K9
Tronador, *Argentina* 128 B2
Trondheim, *Norway* 10 A4
Trondheimsfjorden,
　Norway 8 E11
Trönninge, *Sweden* 11 H6
Trönö, *Sweden* 10 C10
Tronto →, *Italy* 33 F10
Troodos, *Cyprus* 37 E11
Troon, *U.K.* 14 F4
Tropea, *Italy* 35 D8
Tropic, *U.S.A.* 111 H7
Tropoja, *Albania* 38 G3
Trossachs, The, *U.K.* 14 E4
Trostan, *U.K.* 15 A5
Trostberg, *Germany* 19 G8
Trostyanets, *Ukraine* 40 F9
Trotternish, *U.K.* 14 D2
Troup, *U.S.A.* 109 J7
Trout →, *Canada* 100 A5
Trout L., *N.W.T., Canada* . 100 A4
Trout L., *Ont., Canada* . . . 101 C10
Trout Lake, *Mich., U.S.A.* . 98 C2
Trout Lake, *Wash., U.S.A.* 112 E5
Trout River, *Canada* 99 C8
Trouville-sur-Mer, *France* . 24 C7
Trowbridge, *U.K.* 13 F5
Troy, *Turkey* 66 D2
Troy, *Ala., U.S.A.* 105 K3
Troy, *Idaho, U.S.A.* 110 C5
Troy, *Kans., U.S.A.* 108 F7
Troy, *Mo., U.S.A.* 108 F9
Troy, *Mont., U.S.A.* 110 B6
Troy, *N.Y., U.S.A.* 107 D11
Troy, *Ohio, U.S.A.* 104 E3
Troyan, *Bulgaria* 38 G7
Troyes, *France* 25 D11
Trpanj, *Croatia* 21 M7
Trstena, *Slovak Rep.* 20 F9
Trstenik, *Serbia* 21 M10
Trubchevsk, *Russia* 40 E8
Trucial States = United
　Arab Emirates ■, *Asia* . 65 F7
Truckee, *U.S.A.* 112 F6
Trujillo, *Colombia* 120 C2
Trujillo, *Honduras* 116 C2
Trujillo, *Peru* 124 B2
Trujillo, *Spain* 31 F5
Trujillo, *U.S.A.* 109 H2
Trujillo, *Venezuela* 120 B3
Trujillo □, *Venezuela* 120 B3
Truk, *Pac. Oc.* 92 G7
Trumann, *U.S.A.* 109 H9
Trumbull, Mt., *U.S.A.* . . . 111 H7
Trun, *France* 24 D7
Trun, *Switz.* 23 C7
Trundle, *Australia* 91 E4
Trung-Phan, *Vietnam* 58 E7
Truro, *Canada* 99 C7
Truro, *U.K.* 13 G2
Truslove, *Australia* 89 F3
Trustrup, *Denmark* 11 H4
Truth or Consequences,
　U.S.A. 111 K10
Trutnov, *Czech.* 20 E5
Truyère →, *France* 26 D6
Tryavna, *Bulgaria* 38 G8
Tryon, *U.S.A.* 105 H4
Tryonville, *U.S.A.* 106 E5
Trzcianka, *Poland* 20 B6
Trzciel, *Poland* 20 B4
Trzebiatów, *Poland* 20 A5
Trzebiez, *Poland* 20 B4
Trzebinia-Siersza, *Poland* . 20 E9
Trzebnica, *Poland* 20 D7
Tržič, *Slovenia* 33 B11
Tsageri, *Georgia* 43 E10
Tsaratanana, *Madag.* 85 B8
Tsaratanana, Mt. de,
　Madag. 85 A8
Tsarevo = Michurin,
　Bulgaria 38 G10
Tsarichanka, *Ukraine* 42 B6
Tsau, *Botswana* 84 C3
Tsebrikovo, *Ukraine* 42 C4
Tselinograd, *Kazakhstan* . . 44 D8
Tsetserleg, *Mongolia* 54 B5
Tshabong, *Botswana* 84 D3
Tshane, *Botswana* 84 C3
Tshela, *Zaïre* 80 E2
Tshesebe, *Botswana* 85 C4
Tshibeke, *Zaïre* 82 C2
Tshibinda, *Zaïre* 82 C2
Tshikapa, *Zaïre* 80 F4
Tshilenge, *Zaïre* 82 D1
Tshinsenda, *Zaïre* 83 E2
Tshofa, *Zaïre* 82 D2

Tshwane, *Botswana* 84 C3
Tsigara, *Botswana* 84 C4
Tsihombe, *Madag.* 85 D8
Tsimlyansk, *Russia* 43 C10
Tsimlyansk Res. = Tsimlyanskoye Vdkhr., *Russia* 43 B10
Tsimlyanskoye Vdkhr., *Russia* 43 B10
Tsinan = Jinan, *China* ... 50 F9
Tsineng, *S. Africa* 84 D3
Tsinghai = Qinghai □, *China* ......
Tsingtao = Qingdao, *China* ... 51 F11
Tsinjomitondraka, *Madag.* ... 85 B8
Tsiroanomandidy, *Madag.* ... 85 B8
Tsivilsk, *Russia* 41 D15
Tsivory, *Madag.* 85 C8
Tskhinvali, *Georgia* 43 E11
Tsna →, *Russia* 41 D12
Tso Moriri, L., *India* 63 C8
Tsodilo Hill, *Botswana* 84 B3
Tsogttsetsiy, *Mongolia* 50 C3
Tsolo, *S. Africa* 85 E4
Tsomo, *S. Africa* 85 E4
Tsu, *Japan* 49 G8
Tsu L., *Canada* 100 A6
Tsuchiura, *Japan* 49 F10
Tsugaru-Kaikyō, *Japan* ... 48 D10
Tsumeb, *Namibia* 84 B2
Tsumis, *Namibia* 84 C2
Tsuruga, *Japan* 49 G8
Tsurugi-San, *Japan* 49 H7
Tsuruoka, *Japan* 48 E9
Tsushima, *Gifu, Japan* ... 49 G8
Tsushima, *Nagasaki, Japan* ... 49 G4
Tsvetkovo, *Ukraine* 42 B4
Tua →, *Portugal* 30 D3
Tual, *Indonesia* 57 F8
Tuam, *Ireland* 15 C3
Tuamotu Arch. = Tuamotu Is., *Pac. Oc.* 93 J13
Tuamotu Is., *Pac. Oc.* 93 J13
Tuamotu Ridge, *Pac. Oc.* 93 K14
Tuanfeng, *China* 53 B10
Tuanxi, *China* 52 D6
Tuao, *Phil.* 55 C4
Tuapse, *Russia* 43 D8
Tuatapere, *N.Z.* 87 M1
Tuba City, *U.S.A.* 111 H8
Tuban, *Indonesia* 57 G15
Tubarão, *Brazil* 127 B6
Tūbās, *Jordan* 69 C4
Tubau, *Malaysia* 56 D4
Tubbergen, *Neths.* 16 D9
Tübingen, *Germany* 19 G5
Tubize, *Belgium* 17 G4
Tubruq, *Libya* 73 B9
Tubuai Is., *Pac. Oc.* 93 K12
Tuc Trung, *Vietnam* 59 G6
Tucacas, *Venezuela* 120 A4
Tucano, *Brazil* 122 D4
Tuchang, *Taiwan* 53 E13
Tuchodi →, *Canada* 100 B4
Tuchola, *Poland* 20 B7
Tucson, *U.S.A.* 111 K8
Tucumán □, *Argentina* 126 B2
Tucumcari, *U.S.A.* 109 H3
Tucunaré, *Brazil* 125 B6
Tucupido, *Venezuela* 120 B4
Tucupita, *Venezuela* 121 B5
Tucuruí, *Brazil* 122 B2
Tudela, *Spain* 28 C3
Tudela de Duero, *Spain* ... 30 D6
Tudmur, *Syria* 64 C3
Tudor, L., *Canada* 99 A6
Tudora, *Romania* 38 B9
Tuella →, *Portugal* 30 D3
Tuen, *Australia* 91 D4
Tuéré →, *Brazil* 122 B1
Tugela →, *S. Africa* 85 D5
Tuguegarao, *Phil.* 55 C4
Tugur, *Russia* 45 D14
Tuineje, *Canary Is.* 36 F5
Tukangbesi, Kepulauan, *Indonesia* 57 F6
Tukarak I., *Canada* 98 A4
Tukayyid, *Iraq* 64 D5
Tūkh, *Egypt* 76 H7
Tukobo, *Ghana* 78 D4
Tūkrah, *Libya* 73 B9
Tuktoyaktuk, *Canada* 96 B6
Tukums, *Latvia* 40 C3
Tukuyu, *Tanzania* 83 D3
Tula, *Hidalgo, Mexico* 115 C5
Tula, *Tamaulipas, Mexico* 115 C5
Tula, *Nigeria* 79 D7
Tula, *Russia* 41 D10
Tulancingo, *Mexico* 115 C5
Tulare, *U.S.A.* 111 H4
Tulare Lake Bed, *U.S.A.* ... 111 J4
Tularosa, *U.S.A.* 111 K10
Tulbagh, *S. Africa* 84 E2
Tulcán, *Ecuador* 120 C2
Tulcea, *Romania* 38 D11
Tulchin, *Ukraine* 42 B3
Tŭleh, *Iran* 65 C7
Tulemalu L., *Canada* 101 A9
Tuli, *Indonesia* 57 E6
Tuli, *Zimbabwe* 83 G2
Tulia, *U.S.A.* 109 H4
Tŭlkarm, *Jordan* 69 C4
Tullahoma, *U.S.A.* 105 H2
Tullamore, *Australia* 91 E4
Tullamore, *Ireland* 15 C4
Tulle, *France* 26 C5

Tullibigeal, *Australia* 91 E4
Tullins, *France* 27 C9
Tulln, *Austria* 21 G6
Tullow, *Ireland* 15 D4
Tullus, *Sudan* 77 E1
Tully, *Australia* 90 B4
Tulmaythah, *Libya* 73 B9
Tulmur, *Australia* 90 C3
Tulnici, *Romania* 38 D9
Tulovo, *Bulgaria* 38 G8
Tulsa, *U.S.A.* 109 G7
Tulsequah, *Canada* 100 B2
Tulu Milki, *Ethiopia* 77 F4
Tulu Welel, *Ethiopia* 77 F3
Tulua, *Colombia* 120 C2
Tulun, *Russia* 45 D11
Tulungagung, *Indonesia* ... 56 F4
Tum, *Indonesia* 57 E8
Tuma, *Russia* 41 D12
Tuma →, *Nic.* 116 D3
Tumaco, *Colombia* 120 C2
Tumaco, Ensenada, *Colombia* 120 C2
Tumatumari, *Guyana* 121 B6
Tumba, *Sweden* 10 E11
Tumba, L., *Zaïre* 80 E3
Tumbarumba, *Australia* ... 91 F4
Tumbaya, *Argentina* 126 A2
Túmbes, *Peru* 124 A1
Tumbes □, *Peru* 124 A1
Tumbwe, *Zaïre* 83 E2
Tumby Bay, *Australia* 91 E2
Tumd Youqi, *China* 50 D6
Tumen, *China* 51 C15
Tumen Jiang →, *China* ... 51 C16
Tumeremo, *Venezuela* 121 B5
Tumiritinga, *Brazil* 123 E3
Tumkur, *India* 60 N10
Tummel, L., *U.K.* 14 E5
Tump, *Pakistan* 60 F3
Tumpat, *Malaysia* 59 J4
Tumu, *Ghana* 78 C4
Tumucumaque, Serra, *Brazil* 121 C7
Tumupasa, *Bolivia* 124 C4
Tumut, *Australia* 91 F4
Tumwater, *U.S.A.* 110 C2
Tunas de Zaza, *Cuba* 116 B4
Tunbridge Wells, *U.K.* 13 F8
Tunceli, *Turkey* 67 D8
Tunceli □, *Turkey* 67 D8
Tuncurry, *Australia* 91 E5
Tunduru, *Tanzania* 83 E4
Tunduru □, *Tanzania* 83 E4
Tundzha →, *Bulgaria* 39 H9
Tunga Pass, *India* 61 E19
Tungabhadra →, *India* ... 60 M11
Tungaru, *Sudan* 77 E3
Tungla, *Nic.* 116 D3
Tungnafellsjökull, *Iceland* . 8 D5
Tungsten, *Canada* 100 A3
Tungurahua □, *Ecuador* ... 120 D2
Tunguska, Nizhnyaya →, *Russia* 45 C9
Tunia, *Colombia* 120 C2
Tunica, *U.S.A.* 109 H9
Tunis, *Tunisia* 75 A7
Tunis, Golfe de, *Tunisia* ... 75 A7
Tunisia ■, *Africa* 75 B6
Tunja, *Colombia* 120 B3
Tunkhannock, *U.S.A.* 107 E9
Tunliu, *China* 50 F7
Tunnsjøen, *Norway* 8 D12
Tunungayualok I., *Canada* 99 A7
Tunuyán, *Argentina* 126 C2
Tunuyán →, *Argentina* ... 126 C2
Tunxi, *China* 53 C12
Tuo Jiang →, *China* 52 C5
Tuolumne, *U.S.A.* 111 H3
Tuolumne →, *U.S.A.* 112 H5
Tuoy-Khaya, *Russia* 45 C12
Tūp Āghāj, *Iran* 64 B5
Tupã, *Brazil* 127 A5
Tupaciguara, *Brazil* 123 E2
Tupelo, *U.S.A.* 105 H1
Tupik, *Russia* 40 D8
Tupik, *Russia* 45 D12
Tupinambaranas, *Brazil* ... 121 D6
Tupirama, *Brazil* 122 C2
Tupiratins, *Brazil* 122 C2
Tupiza, *Bolivia* 126 A2
Tupman, *U.S.A.* 113 K7
Tupper, *Canada* 100 B4
Tupper Lake, *U.S.A.* 107 B10
Tupungato, Cerro, *S. Amer.* 126 C2
Tuquan, *China* 51 B11
Túquerres, *Colombia* 120 C2
Tura, *Russia* 45 C11
Turabah, *Si. Arabia* 64 D4
Turagua, Serranía, *Venezuela* 121 B5
Tūrān, *Iran* 65 C8
Turan, *Russia* 45 D10
Turayf, *Si. Arabia* 64 D3
Turbenthal, *Switz.* 23 B7
Turégano, *Spain* 30 D6
Turek, *Poland* 20 C8
Turen, *Venezuela* 120 B4
Turfan = Turpan, *China* ... 54 B3
Turfan Depression = Turpan Hami, *China* 54 B3
Tŭrgovishte, *Bulgaria* 38 F9
Turgutlu, *Turkey* 66 D2
Turhal, *Turkey* 42 F7
Turia →, *Spain* 29 F4

Turiaçu, *Brazil* 122 B2
Turiaçu →, *Brazil* 122 B2
Turin = Torino, *Italy* 32 C4
Turin, *Canada* 100 D6
Turka, *Ukraine* 40 G3
Turkana □, *Kenya* 82 B4
Turkana, L., *Africa* 82 B4
Turkestan, *Kazakhstan* 44 E7
Túrkeve, *Hungary* 21 H10
Turkey ■, *Eurasia* 66 D7
Turkey Creek, *Australia* ... 88 C4
Turki, *Russia* 41 F13
Turkmenistan ■, *Asia* 44 F6
Türkoğlu, *Turkey* 66 E7
Turks & Caicos Is. ■, *W. Indies* 117 B5
Turks Island Passage, *W. Indies* 117 B5
Turku, *Finland* 9 F17
Turkwe →, *Kenya* 82 B4
Turlock, *U.S.A.* 111 H3
Turnagain →, *Canada* 100 B3
Turnagain, C., *N.Z.* 87 J6
Turneffe Is., *Belize* 115 D7
Turner, *Australia* 88 C4
Turner, *U.S.A.* 110 B9
Turner Pt., *Australia* 90 A1
Turner Valley, *Canada* 100 C6
Turners Falls, *U.S.A.* 107 D12
Turnhout, *Belgium* 17 F5
Turnor L., *Canada* 101 B7
Tŭrnovo, *Bulgaria* 38 F8
Turnu Măgurele, *Romania* 38 F7
Turnu Roşu Pasul, *Romania* 38 D7
Turon, *U.S.A.* 109 G5
Turpan, *China* 54 B3
Turpan Hami, *China* 54 B3
Turriff, *U.K.* 14 D6
Tursāq, *Iraq* 64 C5
Tursha, *Russia* 41 C15
Tursi, *Italy* 35 B9
Turtle Head I., *Australia* ... 90 A3
Turtle L., *Canada* 101 C7
Turtle Lake, *N. Dak., U.S.A.* 108 B4
Turtle Lake, *Wis., U.S.A.* 108 C8
Turtleford, *Canada* 101 C7
Turukhansk, *Russia* 45 C9
Turun ja Porin lääni □, *Finland* 9 F17
Turzovka, *Slovak Rep.* 20 F8
Tuscaloosa, *U.S.A.* 105 J2
Tuscánia, *Italy* 33 F8
Tuscany = Toscana, *Italy* 32 E8
Tuscola, *Ill., U.S.A.* 104 F1
Tuscola, *Tex., U.S.A.* 109 J5
Tuscumbia, *U.S.A.* 105 H2
Tuskar Rock, *Ireland* 15 D5
Tuskegee, *U.S.A.* 105 J3
Tustna, *Norway* 10 A2
Tutak, *Turkey* 67 D10
Tutayev, *Russia* 41 C11
Tuticorin, *India* 60 Q11
Tutóia, *Brazil* 122 B3
Tutong, *Brunei* 56 D4
Tutova →, *Romania* 38 C10
Tutrakan, *Bulgaria* 38 E9
Tutshi L., *Canada* 100 B2
Tuttle, *U.S.A.* 108 B5
Tuttlingen, *Germany* 19 H4
Tutuala, *Indonesia* 57 F7
Tutuila, *Amer. Samoa* 87 B13
Tututepec, *Mexico* 115 D5
Tuva Republic □, *Russia* 45 D10
Tuvalu ■, *Pac. Oc.* 92 H9
Tuxpan, *Mexico* 115 C5
Tuxtla Gutiérrez, *Mexico* 115 D6
Tuy, *Spain* 30 C2
Tuy An, *Vietnam* 58 F7
Tuy Duc, *Vietnam* 59 F6
Tuy Hoa, *Vietnam* 58 F7
Tuy Phong, *Vietnam* 59 G7
Tuya L., *Canada* 100 B2
Tuyen Hoa, *Vietnam* 58 D6
Tuyen Quang, *Vietnam* ... 58 B5
Tūysarkān, *Iran* 65 C6
Tūz Khurmātū, *Iraq* 64 C5
Tuzla, *Bos.-H.* 21 L8
Tuzla Gölü, *Turkey* 66 D6
Tuzlov →, *Russia* 43 C8
Tvååker, *Sweden* 11 G6
Tvedestrand, *Norway* 11 F2
Tver, *Russia* 41 C9
Tvŭrditsa, *Bulgaria* 38 G8
Twain, *U.S.A.* 112 E5
Twain Harte, *U.S.A.* 112 G6
Tweed, *Canada* 106 B7
Tweed →, *U.K.* 14 F7
Tweed Heads, *Australia* ... 91 D5
Tweedsmuir Prov. Park, *Canada* 100 C3
Twello, *Neths.* 16 D8
Twentynine Palms, *U.S.A.* 113 L10
Twillingate, *Canada* 99 C9
Twin Bridges, *U.S.A.* 110 D7
Twin Falls, *U.S.A.* 110 E6
Twin Valley, *U.S.A.* 108 B6
Twisp, *U.S.A.* 110 B3
Twistringen, *Germany* 18 C4
Two Harbors, *U.S.A.* 108 B9
Two Hills, *Canada* 100 C6
Two Rivers, *U.S.A.* 104 C2
Twofold B., *Australia* 91 F4

Tychy, *Poland* 20 E8
Tykocin, *Poland* 20 B12
Tyldal, *Norway* 10 B4
Tyler, *U.S.A.* 103 D7
Tyler, *Minn., U.S.A.* 108 C6
Tyler, *Tex., U.S.A.* 109 J7
Týn nad Vltavou, *Czech.* 20 F4
Tynda, *Russia* 45 D13
Tyne →, *U.K.* 12 C6
Tyne & Wear □, *U.K.* 12 C6
Tynemouth, *U.K.* 12 B6
Tynset, *Norway* 10 B4
Tyre = Sūr, *Lebanon* 69 B4
Tyrifjorden, *Norway* 10 D4
Tyringe, *Sweden* 11 H7
Tyristrand, *Norway* 10 D4
Tyrnyauz, *Russia* 43 E10
Tyrone, *U.S.A.* 106 F6
Tyrrell →, *Australia* 91 F3
Tyrrell, L., *Australia* 91 F3
Tyrrell Arm, *Canada* 101 A9
Tyrrell L., *Canada* 101 A7
Tyrrhenian Sea, *Europe* ... 34 B5
Tysfjorden, *Norway* 8 B14
Tystberga, *Sweden* 11 F11
Tyub Karagan, Mys, *Kazakhstan* 43 D14
Tyuleniy, *Russia* 43 D12
Tyumen, *Russia* 44 D7
Tywi →, *U.K.* 13 F3
Tywyn, *U.K.* 13 E3
Tzaneen, *S. Africa* 85 C5
Tzermiádhes, *Greece* 37 D7
Tzermiádhes Neápolis, *Greece* 39 P8
Tzoumérka, Óros, *Greece* . 39 K4
Tzukong = Zigong, *China* 52 C5
Tzummarum, *Neths.* 16 B7

U

U Taphao, *Thailand* 58 F3
U.S.A. = United States of America ■, *N. Amer.* .. 102 C7
Uachadi, Sierra, *Venezuela* 121 C4
Uainambi, *Colombia* 120 C4
Uanda, *Australia* 90 C3
Uarsciek, *Somali Rep.* 68 G4
Uasin □, *Kenya* 82 B4
Uato-Udo, *Indonesia* 57 F7
Uatumã →, *Brazil* 121 D6
Uauá, *Brazil* 122 C4
Uaupés, *Brazil* 120 D4
Uaupés →, *Brazil* 120 C4
Uaxactún, *Guatemala* 116 C2
Ubá, *Brazil* 123 F3
Ubaitaba, *Brazil* 123 D4
Ubangi = Oubangi →, *Zaïre* 80 E3
Ubaté, *Colombia* 120 B3
Ubauro, *Pakistan* 62 E3
Ubaye →, *France* 27 D10
Ube, *Japan* 49 H5
Ubeda, *Spain* 29 G1
Uberaba, *Brazil* 123 E2
Uberaba, L., *Brazil* 125 D6
Uberlândia, *Brazil* 123 E2
Überlingen, *Germany* 19 H5
Ubiaja, *Nigeria* 79 D6
Ubolratna Res., *Thailand* 58 D4
Ubombo, *S. Africa* 85 D5
Ubon Ratchathani, *Thailand* 58 E5
Ubondo, *Zaïre* 82 C2
Ubort →, *Belorussia* 40 E6
Ubrique, *Spain* 31 J5
Ubundu, *Zaïre* 82 C2
Ucayali →, *Peru* 124 A3
Uccle, *Belgium* 17 G4
Uchi Lake, *Canada* 101 C10
Uchiura-Wan, *Japan* 48 C10
Uchiza, *Peru* 124 B2
Uchte, *Germany* 18 C4
Uchur →, *Russia* 45 D14
Ucluelet, *Canada* 100 D3
Uçuriş, *Romania* 38 C4
Uda →, *Russia* 45 D14
Udaipur, *India* 62 G5
Udaipur Garhi, *Nepal* 63 F12
Udbina, *Croatia* 33 D12
Uddel, *Neths.* 16 D7
Uddevalla, *Sweden* 11 F5
Uddjaur, *Sweden* 8 D16
Uden, *Neths.* 17 E7
Udgir, *India* 60 K10
Udhampur, *India* 63 C6
Udi, *Nigeria* 79 D6
Údine, *Italy* 33 B10
Udmurt Republic □, *Russia* 44 D9
Udon Thani, *Thailand* 58 D4
Udupi, *India* 60 N9
Udvoy Balkan, *Bulgaria* ... 38 G9
Udzungwa Range, *Tanzania* 83 D4
Ueckermünde, *Germany* ... 18 B10
Ueda, *Japan* 49 F9
Uedineniya, Os., *Russia* ... 4 B12
Uele →, *Zaïre* 80 D4
Uelen, *Russia* 45 C19
Uelzen, *Germany* 18 C6
Uetendorf, *Switz.* 22 C5
Ufa, *Russia* 44 D6

Uffenheim, *Germany* 19 F6
Ugab →, *Namibia* 84 C1
Ugalla →, *Tanzania* 82 D3
Uganda ■, *Africa* 82 B3
Ugchelen, *Neths.* 16 D7
Ugento, *Italy* 35 C11
Ugep, *Nigeria* 79 D6
Ugie, *S. Africa* 85 E4
Ugijar, *Spain* 29 J1
Ugine, *France* 27 C10
Uglegorsk, *Russia* 45 E15
Uglich, *Russia* 41 C11
Ugljane, *Croatia* 33 E13
Uglyak, *Russia* 45 C13
Ugra →, *Russia* 41 D10
Uğûn Mûsa, *Egypt* 69 F1
Ugûrchin, *Bulgaria* 38 F7
Uh →, *Slovak Rep.* 21 G11
Uherské Hradiště, *Czech.* 21 F7
Uhrichsville, *U.S.A.* 106 F3
Uíge, *Angola* 80 F2
Uijŏngbu, *S. Korea* 51 F14
Uiju, *N. Korea* 51 D13
Uinta Mts., *U.S.A.* 110 F8
Uitenhage, *S. Africa* 84 E4
Uitgeest, *Neths.* 16 C5
Uithoorn, *Neths.* 16 D5
Uithuizen, *Neths.* 16 B9
Uitkerke, *Belgium* 17 F2
Újfehértó, *Hungary* 21 H11
Ujhani, *India* 63 F8
Ujjain, *India* 62 H6
Uji-guntō, *Japan* 49 J4
Ujpest, *Hungary* 21 H9
Ujszász, *Hungary* 21 H10
Ujung Pandang, *Indonesia* 57 F5
Uka, *Russia* 45 D17
Ukara I., *Tanzania* 82 C3
Uke-Shima, *Japan* 49 K4
Ukerewe □, *Tanzania* 82 C3
Ukerewe I., *Tanzania* 82 C3
Ukholovo, *Russia* 41 E12
Ukhrul, *India* 61 G19
Ukhta, *Russia* 44 C6
Ukiah, *U.S.A.* 112 F3
Ukki Fort, *India* 63 C7
Ukmerge, *Lithuania* 40 D4
Ukraine ■, *Europe* 42 B4
Ukwi, *Botswana* 84 C3
Ulaanbaatar, *Mongolia* ... 45 E11
Ulaangom, *Mongolia* 54 A4
Ulamba, *Zaïre* 83 D1
Ulan Bator = Ulaanbaatar, *Mongolia* 45 E11
Ulan Ude, *Russia* 45 D11
Ulanga □, *Tanzania* 83 D4
Ulanów, *Poland* 20 E12
Ulaş, *Turkey* 66 D7
Ulaya, *Morogoro, Tanzania* 82 D4
Ulaya, *Tabora, Tanzania* . 82 C3
Ulcinj, *Montenegro* 39 H2
Ulco, *S. Africa* 84 D3
Ulfborg, *Denmark* 11 H2
Ulft, *Neths.* 16 E8
Ulhasnagar, *India* 60 K8
Uljma, *Serbia* 21 K11
Ulla →, *Spain* 30 C2
Ulladulla, *Australia* 91 F5
Ullånger, *Sweden* 10 B12
Ullapool, *U.K.* 14 D3
Ullared, *Sweden* 11 G6
Ulldecona, *Spain* 28 E5
Ullswater, *U.K.* 12 C5
Ullung-do, *S. Korea* 51 F16
Ulm, *Germany* 19 G5
Ulmarra, *Australia* 91 D5
Ulmeni, *Romania* 38 D9
Ulonguè, *Mozam.* 83 E3
Ulricehamn, *Sweden* 9 H12
Ulsan, *S. Korea* 51 G15
Ulsberg, *Norway* 10 B3
Ulster □, *U.K.* 15 B5
Ulubaria, *India* 63 H13
Ulubat Gölü, *Turkey* 66 C3
Ulubey, *Turkey* 66 D3
Uluborlu, *Turkey* 66 D4
Uludağ, *Turkey* 66 C3
Uludere, *Turkey* 67 E10
Uluguru Mts., *Tanzania* ... 82 D4
Ulukışla, *Turkey* 66 E6
Ulungur He →, *China* 54 B3
Ulutau, *Kazakhstan* 44 E7
Ulverston, *U.K.* 12 C4
Ulverstone, *Australia* 90 G4
Ulya, *Russia* 45 D15
Ulyanovsk = Simbirsk, *Russia* 41 D16
Ulyasutay, *Mongolia* 54 B4
Ulysses, *U.S.A.* 109 G4
Umag, *Croatia* 33 C10
Umala, *Bolivia* 124 D4
Uman, *Ukraine* 42 B4
Umaria, *India* 61 H12
Umarkot, *Pakistan* 60 G6
Umatilla, *U.S.A.* 110 D4
Umba, *Russia* 44 C4
Umbertide, *Italy* 33 E9
Umbra Mts., *N.Z.* 87 L2
Umbria □, *Italy* 33 F9
Ume älv →, *Sweden* 8 E16
Umeå, *Sweden* 8 E16
Umera, *Indonesia* 57 E7
Umfuli →, *Zimbabwe* ... 83 F2

Umgusa, Zimbabwe 83 F2
Umka, Serbia 21 L10
Umkomaas, S. Africa 85 E5
Umm ad Daraj, J., Jordan 69 C4
Umm al Qaywayn, U.A.E. 65 E7
Umm al Qittayn, Jordan 69 C5
Umm Arda, Sudan 77 D3
Umm Bâb, Qatar 65 E6
Umm Bel, Sudan 77 E2
Umm Dubban, Sudan 77 D3
Umm el Fahm, Israel 69 C4
Umm Koweika, Sudan 77 E3
Umm Lajj, Si. Arabia 64 E3
Umm Merwa, Sudan 76 D3
Umm Ruwaba, Sudan 77 E3
Umm Sidr, Sudan 77 E2
Ummanz, Germany 18 A9
Umnak I., U.S.A. 96 C3
Umniati →, Zimbabwe 83 F2
Umpqua →, U.S.A. 110 E1
Umreth, India 62 H5
Umtata, S. Africa 85 E4
Umuahia, Nigeria 79 D6
Umuarama, Brazil 127 A5
Umvukwe Ra., Zimbabwe 83 F3
Umzimvubu = Port St. Johns, S. Africa 85 E4
Umzingwane →, Zimbabwe 83 G2
Umzinto, S. Africa 85 E5
Una, India 62 J4
Una →, Bos.-H. 33 C13
Unac →, Bos.-H. 33 D13
Unadilla, U.S.A. 107 D9
Unalaska, U.S.A. 96 C3
Uncastillo, Spain 28 C3
Uncía, Bolivia 124 D4
Uncompahgre Peak, U.S.A. 111 G10
Unden, Sweden 11 F8
Underberg, S. Africa 85 D4
Underbool, Australia 91 F3
Undersaker, Sweden 10 A7
Undersvik, Sweden 10 C10
Unecha, Russia 40 E8
Uneiuxi →, Brazil 120 D4
Ungarie, Australia 91 E4
Ungarra, Australia 91 E2
Ungava B., Canada 97 C13
Ungava Pen., Canada 97 C12
Ungeny, Moldavia 42 C2
Unggi, N. Korea 51 C16
Ungwatiri, Sudan 77 D4
Uni, Russia 41 C17
União da Vitória, Brazil 127 B5
União dos Palmares, Brazil 122 C4
Unije, Croatia 33 D11
Unimak I., U.S.A. 96 C3
Unini →, Brazil 121 D5
Union, Miss., U.S.A. 109 J10
Union, Mo., U.S.A. 108 F9
Union, S.C., U.S.A. 105 H5
Union, Mt., U.S.A. 111 J7
Union City, Calif., U.S.A. 112 H4
Union City, N.J., U.S.A. 107 F10
Union City, Pa., U.S.A. 106 E5
Union City, Tenn., U.S.A. 109 G10
Union Gap, U.S.A. 110 C3
Union of Soviet Socialist Republics = Commonwealth of Independent States ■, Eurasia 45 D11
Union Springs, U.S.A. 105 J3
Uniondale, S. Africa 84 E3
Uniontown, U.S.A. 104 F6
Unionville, U.S.A. 108 E8
United Arab Emirates ■, Asia 65 F7
United Kingdom ■, Europe 7 E5
United States of America ■, N. Amer. 102 C7
Unity, Canada 101 C7
Universales, Mtes., Spain 28 E3
Unjha, India 62 H5
Unnao, India 63 F9
Uno, Ilha, Guinea-Biss. 78 C1
Unst, U.K. 14 A8
Unstrut →, Germany 18 D7
Unter-engadin, Switz. 23 C10
Unterägeri, Switz. 23 B7
Unterkulm, Switz. 22 B6
Unterseen, Switz. 22 C5
Unterwaldner Alpen, Switz. 23 C6
Unuk →, Canada 100 B2
Ünye, Turkey 42 F7
Unzha, Russia 41 B14
Unzha →, Russia 41 C13
Uors, Switz. 23 C8
Uozu, Japan 49 F8
Upa →, Czech. 20 E6
Upata, Venezuela 121 B5
Upemba, L., Zaïre 83 D2
Upernavik, Greenland 4 B5
Upington, S. Africa 84 D3
Upleta, India 62 J4
Upolu, W. Samoa 87 A13
Upper Alkali Lake, U.S.A. 110 F3
Upper Arrow L., Canada 100 C5
Upper Foster L., Canada 101 B7
Upper Hutt, N.Z. 87 J5
Upper Klamath L., U.S.A. 110 E3
Upper Lake, U.S.A. 112 F4
Upper Musquodoboit, Canada 99 C7
Upper Red L., U.S.A. 108 A7

Upper Sandusky, U.S.A. 104 E4
Upper Volta = Burkina Faso ■, Africa 78 C4
Upphärad, Sweden 11 F6
Uppsala, Sweden 10 E11
Uppsala län □, Sweden 9 G14
Upshi, India 63 C7
Upstart, C., Australia 90 B4
Upton, U.S.A. 108 C2
Ur, Iraq 64 D5
Urabá, G. de, Colombia 120 B2
Uracara, Brazil 121 D6
Urad Qianqi, China 50 D5
Urakawa, Japan 48 C11
Ural, Australia 91 E4
Ural →, Kazakhstan 43 C14
Ural Mts. = Uralskie Gory, Russia 44 D6
Uralla, Australia 91 E5
Uralsk, Kazakhstan 44 D6
Uralskie Gory, Russia 44 D6
Urambo, Tanzania 82 D3
Urambo □, Tanzania 82 D3
Urandangi, Australia 90 C2
Uranium City, Canada 101 B7
Uranquinty, Australia 91 F4
Uraricaá →, Brazil 121 C5
Uraricuera →, Brazil 121 C5
Urawa, Japan 49 G9
Uray, Russia 44 C7
'Uray'irah, Si. Arabia 65 E6
Urbana, Ill., U.S.A. 104 E1
Urbana, Ohio, U.S.A. 104 E4
Urbánia, Italy 33 E9
Urbano Santos, Brazil 122 B3
Urbel →, Spain 28 C1
Urbino, Italy 33 E9
Urbión, Picos de, Spain 28 C2
Urcos, Peru 124 C3
Urda, Kazakhstan 43 B12
Urda, Spain 31 F7
Urdinarrain, Argentina 126 C4
Urdos, France 26 F3
Urdzhar, Kazakhstan 44 E9
Ure →, U.K. 12 C6
Uren, Russia 41 C14
Ures, Mexico 114 B2
Urfa, Turkey 67 E8
Urfa □, Turkey 67 E8
Urfahr, Austria 21 G4
Urganch = Urgench, Uzbekistan 44 E7
Urgench, Uzbekistan 44 E7
Uri, India 63 B6
Uri □, Switz. 23 C7
Uribante →, Venezuela 120 B3
Uribe, Colombia 120 C3
Uribia, Colombia 120 A3
Uriondo, Bolivia 126 A3
Urique, Mexico 114 B3
Urique →, Mexico 114 B3
Urirotstock, Switz. 23 C7
Urk, Neths. 16 C7
Urla, Turkey 66 D2
Urlati, Romania 38 E9
Urmia = Orūmīyeh, Iran 64 B5
Urmia, L. = Orūmīyeh, Daryācheh-ye, Iran 64 B5
Urner Alpen, Switz. 23 C7
Uroševac, Serbia 21 N11
Urrao, Colombia 120 B2
Ursus, Poland 20 C10
Uruaçu, Brazil 123 D2
Uruana, Brazil 123 E2
Uruapan, Mexico 114 D4
Uruará →, Brazil 121 D7
Urubamba, Peru 124 C3
Urubamba →, Peru 124 C3
Urubaxi →, Brazil 121 D5
Urubu →, Brazil 121 D6
Uruçara, Brazil 121 D6
Uruçuí, Brazil 122 C3
Uruçuí, Serra do, Brazil 122 C3
Uruçuí Prêto →, Brazil 122 C3
Urucuia →, Brazil 123 E2
Urucurituba, Brazil 121 D6
Uruguai →, Brazil 127 B5
Uruguaiana, Brazil 126 B4
Uruguay ■, S. Amer. 126 C4
Uruguay →, S. Amer. 126 C4
Urumchi = Ürümqi, China 44 E9
Ürümqi, China 44 E9
Urup →, Russia 43 D9
Urup, Os., Russia 45 E16
Urutaí, Brazil 123 E2
Uryung-Khaya, Russia 45 B12
Uryupinsk, Russia 41 F12
Urzhum, Russia 41 C16
Urziceni, Romania 38 E9
Uşak, Turkey 66 D3
Uşak □, Turkey 66 D3
Usakos, Namibia 84 C2
Usborne, Mt., Falk. Is. 128 D5
Ušče, Serbia 21 M10
Usedom, Germany 18 B9
'Usfān, Si. Arabia 76 C2
Ush-Tobe, Kazakhstan 44 E8
Ushakova, Os., Russia 4 A12
Ushant = Ouessant, I. d', France 24 D1
Ushashi, Tanzania 82 C3
Ushat, Sudan 77 F2
Ushibuka, Japan 49 H5
Ushuaia, Argentina 128 D3
Ushumun, Russia 45 D13
Usk →, U.K. 13 F5

Üsküdar, Turkey 39 H11
Uslar, Germany 18 D5
Usman, Russia 41 E11
Usoke, Tanzania 82 D3
Usolye Sibirskoye, Russia 45 D11
Usoro, Nigeria 79 D6
Uspallata, P. de, Argentina 126 C2
Uspenskiy, Kazakhstan 44 E8
Usquert, Neths. 16 B9
Ussel, France 26 C6
Ussuri →, Asia 48 A7
Ussuriysk, Russia 45 E14
Ussurka, Russia 48 B6
Ust-Aldan = Batamay, Russia 45 C13
Ust Amginskoye = Khandyga, Russia 45 C14
Ust-Bolsheretsk, Russia 45 D16
Ust Buzulukskaya, Russia 41 F13
Ust Chaun, Russia 45 C18
Ust-Donetskiy, Russia 43 C9
Ust'-Ilga, Russia 45 D11
Ust Ilimpeya = Yukti, Russia 45 C11
Ust-Ilimsk, Russia 45 D11
Ust Ishim, Russia 44 D8
Ust-Kamchatsk, Russia 45 D17
Ust-Kamenogorsk, Kazakhstan 44 E9
Ust-Karenga, Russia 45 D12
Ust Khayryuzova, Russia 45 D16
Ust-Kut, Russia 45 D11
Ust Kuyga, Russia 45 B14
Ust-Labinsk, Russia 43 D8
Ust Luga, Russia 40 B6
Ust Maya, Russia 45 C14
Ust-Mil, Russia 45 D14
Ust-Nera, Russia 45 C15
Ust-Nyukzha, Russia 45 D13
Ust Olenek, Russia 45 B12
Ust-Omchug, Russia 45 C15
Ust Port, Russia 44 C9
Ust Tsilma, Russia 44 C6
Ust-Tungir, Russia 45 D13
Ust Urt = Ustyurt, Plato, Kazakhstan 44 E6
Ust Vorkuta, Russia 44 C7
Ustaoset, Norway 10 D2
Ustaritz, France 26 E2
Uste, Russia 41 B11
Uster, Switz. 23 B7
Ústí nad Labem, Czech. 20 E4
Ústí nad Orlicí, Czech. 20 F6
Ustica, Italy 34 D6
Ustinov = Izhevsk, Russia 44 D6
Ustka, Poland 20 A6
Ustrzyki Dolne, Poland 20 F12
Ustye, Russia 45 D10
Ustyurt, Plato, Kazakhstan 44 E6
Ustyuzhna, Russia 41 B10
Usu, China 54 B3
Usuki, Japan 49 H5
Usulután, El Salv. 116 D2
Usumacinta →, Mexico 115 D6
Usumbura = Bujumbura, Burundi 82 C2
Usure, Tanzania 82 C3
Uta, Indonesia 57 E9
Utah □, U.S.A. 110 G8
Utah, L., U.S.A. 110 F8
Ute Creek →, U.S.A. 109 H3
Utena, Lithuania 40 D4
Ütersen, Germany 18 B5
Utete, Tanzania 82 D4
Uthai Thani, Thailand 58 E3
Uthal, Pakistan 62 G2
Utiariti, Brazil 125 C6
Utica, N.Y., U.S.A. 107 C9
Utica, Ohio, U.S.A. 106 F2
Utiel, Spain 28 F3
Utik L., Canada 101 B9
Utikuma L., Canada 100 B5
Utinga, Brazil 123 D3
Utrecht, Neths. 16 D6
Utrecht, S. Africa 85 D5
Utrecht □, Neths. 16 D6
Utrera, Spain 31 H5
Utsjoki, Finland 8 B19
Utsunomiya, Japan 49 F9
Uttar Pradesh □, India 63 F9
Uttaradit, Thailand 58 D3
Uttoxeter, U.K. 12 E6
Ütze, Germany 18 C6
Uudenmaan lääni □, Finland 9 F18
Uusikaarlepyy, Finland 8 E17
Uusikaupunki, Finland 9 F16
Uva, Russia 41 C18
Uvá →, Colombia 120 C3
Uvalde, U.S.A. 109 L5
Uvarovo, Russia 41 F13
Uvat, Russia 44 D7
Uvinza, Tanzania 82 D3
Uvira, Zaïre 82 C2
Uvs Nuur, Mongolia 54 A4
Uwajima, Japan 49 H6
Uweinat, Jebel, Sudan 76 C1
Uxbridge, Canada 106 B5
Uxin Qi, China 50 E5
Uxmal, Mexico 115 C7
Uyandi, Russia 45 C15
Uyo, Nigeria 79 D6
Uyuni, Bolivia 124 E4
Uzbekistan ■, Asia 44 E7
Uzen, Bol. →, Kazakhstan 41 G16
Uzen, Mal. →, Kazakhstan 41 G16

Uzerche, France 26 C5
Uzès, France 27 D8
Uzh →, Ukraine 40 F7
Uzhgorod, Ukraine 40 G3
Uzlovaya, Russia 41 E11
Uzunköprü, Turkey 39 H9
Uzwil, Switz. 23 B8

V

Vaal →, S. Africa 84 D3
Vaal Dam, S. Africa 85 D4
Vaals, Neths. 17 G8
Vaalwater, S. Africa 85 C4
Vaasa, Finland 8 E16
Vaasan lääni □, Finland 8 E17
Vaassen, Neths. 16 D7
Vabre, France 26 E6
Vác, Hungary 21 H9
Vacaria, Brazil 127 B5
Vacaville, U.S.A. 112 G5
Vaccarès, Étang de, France 27 E8
Vach →, Russia 44 C8
Vache, I.-à-, Haiti 117 C5
Vadnagar, India 62 H5
Vadodara, India 62 H5
Vadsø, Norway 8 A20
Vadstena, Sweden 11 F8
Vaduz, Liech. 23 B9
Værøy, Norway 8 C12
Vagnhärad, Sweden 10 F11
Vagos, Portugal 30 E2
Váh →, Slovak Rep. 21 H8
Vahsel B., Antarctica 5 D1
Vái, Greece 37 D8
Vaigach, Russia 44 B6
Vaiges, France 24 D6
Vaihingen, Germany 19 G4
Vailly-sur-Aisne, France 25 C10
Vaison-la-Romaine, France 27 D9
Vakfikebir, Turkey 67 C8
Val-de-Marne □, France 25 D9
Val-d'Oise □, France 25 C9
Val-d'Or, Canada 98 C4
Val Marie, Canada 101 D7
Valadares, Portugal 30 D2
Valahia, Romania 38 E8
Valais □, Switz. 22 D5
Valais, Alpes du, Switz. 22 D5
Valandovo, Macedonia 39 H5
Valcheta, Argentina 128 B3
Valdagno, Italy 33 C8
Valday, Russia 40 C8
Valdayskaya Vozvyshennost, Russia 40 C8
Valdeazogues →, Spain 31 G6
Valdemarsvik, Sweden 11 F10
Valdepeñas, Ciudad Real, Spain 31 G7
Valdepeñas, Jaén, Spain 31 H7
Valderaduey →, Spain 30 D5
Valderrobres, Spain 28 E5
Valdés, Pen., Argentina 128 B4
Valdez, Ecuador 120 C2
Valdez, U.S.A. 96 B5
Valdivia, Chile 128 A2
Valdivia, Colombia 120 B2
Valdivia □, Chile 128 B2
Valdobbiádene, Italy 33 C9
Valdosta, U.S.A. 105 K4
Valdoviño, Spain 30 B2
Valdres, Norway 10 D3
Vale, Georgia 43 F10
Vale, U.S.A. 110 E5
Valea lui Mihai, Romania 38 B5
Valença, Brazil 123 D4
Valença, Portugal 30 C2
Valença do Piauí, Brazil 122 C3
Valençay, France 25 E8
Valence, Drôme, France 27 D8
Valence, Tarn-et-Garonne, France 26 D4
Valencia, Spain 29 F4
Valencia, Venezuela 120 A4
Valencia □, Spain 29 F4
Valencia, Albufera de, Spain 29 F4
Valencia de Alcántara, Spain 31 F3
Valencia de Don Juan, Spain 30 C5
Valencia del Ventoso, Spain 31 G4
Valenciennes, France 25 B10
Valensole, France 27 E9
Valentia Harbour, Ireland 15 E1
Valentia I., Ireland 15 E1
Valentim, Sa. do, Brazil 122 C3
Valentin, Russia 48 C7
Valentine, Nebr., U.S.A. 108 D4
Valentine, Tex., U.S.A. 109 K2
Valenza, Italy 32 C5
Valera, Venezuela 120 B3
Valguarnera Caropepe, Italy 35 E7
Valier, U.S.A. 110 B7
Valinco, G. de, France 27 G12
Valjevo, Serbia 21 L9
Valka, Estonia 40 C5
Valkeakoski, Finland 9 F18
Valkenburg, Neths. 17 G7

Valkenswaard, Neths. 17 F6
Vall de Uxó, Spain 28 F4
Valla, Sweden 10 E10
Valladolid, Mexico 115 C7
Valladolid, Spain 30 D6
Valladolid □, Spain 30 D6
Vallata, Italy 35 A8
Valldemosa, Spain 36 B9
Valle d'Aosta □, Italy 32 C4
Valle de Arán, Spain 28 C5
Valle de Cabuérniga, Spain 30 B6
Valle de la Pascua, Venezuela 120 B4
Valle de las Palmas, Mexico 113 N10
Valle de Santiago, Mexico 114 C4
Valle de Suchil, Mexico 114 C4
Valle de Zaragoza, Mexico 114 B3
Valle del Cauca □, Colombia 120 C2
Valle Fértil, Sierra del, Argentina 126 C2
Valle Hermoso, Mexico 115 B5
Vallecas, Spain 30 E7
Valledupar, Colombia 120 A3
Vallehermoso, Canary Is. 36 F2
Vallejo, U.S.A. 112 G4
Vallenar, Chile 126 B1
Valleraugue, France 26 D7
Vallet, France 24 E5
Valletta, Malta 37 D2
Valley Center, U.S.A. 113 M9
Valley City, U.S.A. 108 B6
Valley Falls, U.S.A. 110 E3
Valley Springs, U.S.A. 112 G6
Valley Wells, U.S.A. 113 K11
Valleyview, U.S.A. 100 B5
Valli di Comácchio, Italy 33 D9
Vallimanca, Arroyo, Argentina 126 D4
Vallo della Lucánia, Italy 35 B8
Vallon-Pont-d'Arc, France 27 D8
Vallorbe, Switz. 22 C2
Valls, Spain 28 D6
Vallsta, Sweden 10 C10
Valmaseda, Spain 28 B1
Valmiera, Latvia 40 C4
Valmont, France 24 C7
Valmontone, Italy 34 A5
Valmy, France 25 C11
Valnera, Mte., Spain 28 B1
Valognes, France 24 C5
Valona = Vlóra, Albania 39 J2
Valongo, Portugal 30 D2
Valpaços, Portugal 30 D3
Valparaíso, Chile 126 C1
Valparaíso, Mexico 114 C4
Valparaiso, U.S.A. 104 E2
Valparaíso □, Chile 126 C1
Valpovo, Croatia 21 K8
Valréas, France 27 D8
Vals, Switz. 23 C8
Vals →, S. Africa 84 D4
Vals, Tanjung, Indonesia 57 F9
Vals-les-Bains, France 27 D8
Valsad, India 60 J8
Valskog, Sweden 10 E9
Válta, Greece 39 J6
Valtellina, Italy 32 B6
Valuyki, Russia 41 F11
Valverde, Canary Is. 36 G2
Valverde del Camino, Spain 31 H4
Valverde del Fresno, Spain 30 E4
Vama, Romania 38 B8
Vámos, Greece 37 D6
Van, Turkey 67 D10
Van □, Turkey 67 D10
Van, L. = Van Gölü, Turkey 67 D10
Van Alstyne, U.S.A. 109 J6
Van Bruyssel, Canada 99 C5
Van Buren, Canada 99 C6
Van Buren, Ark., U.S.A. 109 H7
Van Buren, Maine, U.S.A. 105 B11
Van Buren, Mo., U.S.A. 109 G9
Van Canh, Vietnam 58 F7
Van Diemen, C., N. Terr., Australia 88 B5
Van Diemen, C., Queens., Australia 90 B2
Van Diemen G., Australia 88 B5
Van Gölü, Turkey 67 D10
Van Horn, U.S.A. 109 K2
Van Ninh, Vietnam 58 F7
Van Reenen P., S. Africa 85 D4
Van Rees, Pegunungan, Indonesia 57 E9
Van Tassell, U.S.A. 108 D2
Van Wert, U.S.A. 104 E3
Van Yen, Vietnam 58 B5
Vanavara, Russia 45 C11
Vancouver, Canada 100 D4
Vancouver, U.S.A. 112 E4
Vancouver I., Canada 100 D3
Vandalia, Ill., U.S.A. 108 F10
Vandalia, Mo., U.S.A. 108 F9
Vandenburg, S. Africa 85 D4
Vandenburg, U.S.A. 113 L6
Vandergrift, U.S.A. 106 F5
Vanderhoof, Canada 100 C4
Vanderlin I., Australia 90 B2
Vandyke, Australia 90 C4
Vänern, Sweden 11 F7
Vänersborg, Sweden 11 F6
Vang Vieng, Laos 58 C4

Vanga, *Kenya* 82 C4
Vangaindrano, *Madag.* 85 C8
Vanguard, *Canada* 101 D7
Vanier, *Canada* 98 C4
Vankarem, *Russia* 45 C18
Vankleek Hill, *Canada* ... 98 C5
Vanna, *Norway* 8 A15
Vännäs, *Sweden* 8 E15
Vannes, *France* 24 E4
Vanoise, Massif de la,
  France 27 C10
Vanrhynsdorp, *S. Africa* .. 84 E2
Vanrook, *Australia* 90 B3
Vansbro, *Sweden* 9 F13
Vansittart B., *Australia* ... 88 B4
Vanthli, *India* 62 J4
Vanua Levu, *Fiji* 87 C8
Vanua Mbalavu, *Fiji* 87 C9
Vanuatu ■, *Pac. Oc.* 92 J8
Vanwyksvlei, *S. Africa* ... 84 E3
Vanzylsrus, *S. Africa* 84 D3
Vapnyarka, *Ukraine* 42 B3
Var □, *France* 27 E10
Var →, *France* 27 E11
Vara, *Sweden* 11 F6
Varades, *France* 24 E5
Varaita →, *Italy* 32 D4
Varallo, *Italy* 32 C5
Varanasi, *India* 63 G10
Varangerfjorden, *Norway* . 8 A20
Varaždin, *Croatia* 33 B13
Varazze, *Italy* 32 D5
Varberg, *Sweden* 11 G6
Vardak = Axiós →, *Greece* 39 J5
Varde, *Denmark* 11 J2
Varde Å →, *Denmark* 11 J2
Varel, *Germany* 18 B4
Varella, Mui, *Vietnam* ... 58 F7
Varena, *Lithuania* 40 D4
Varennes-sur-Allier, *France* 26 B7
Vareš, *Bos.-H.* 21 L8
Varese, *Italy* 32 C5
Varese Lígure, *Italy* 32 D6
Vårgårda, *Sweden* 11 F6
Vargem Bonita, *Brazil* ... 123 F2
Vargem Grande, *Brazil* ... 122 B3
Varginha, *Brazil* 127 A6
Vargön, *Sweden* 11 F6
Variadero, *U.S.A.* 109 H2
Varillas, *Chile* 126 A1
Väring, *Sweden* 11 F8
Värmlands län □, *Sweden* 9 G12
Varna, *Bulgaria* 38 F10
Värnamo, *Sweden* 9 H13
Värö, *Sweden* 11 G6
Vars, *Canada* 107 A9
Varsseveld, *Neths.* 16 E8
Varto, *Turkey* 67 D9
Varvarin, *Serbia* 21 M11
Varzaneh, *Iran* 65 C7
Várzea Alegre, *Brazil* 122 C4
Várzea da Palma, *Brazil* .. 123 E3
Várzea Grande, *Brazil* ... 125 D6
Varzi, *Italy* 32 D6
Varzo, *Italy* 32 B5
Varzy, *France* 25 E10
Vasa, *Finland* 8 E16
Vasa Barris →, *Brazil* 122 D4
Vascão →, *Portugal* 31 H3
Vaşcău, *Romania* 38 C5
Vascongadas = País
  Vasco □, *Spain* 28 C2
Vasht = Khāsh, *Iran* 60 E2
Vasilevichi, *Belorussia* ... 40 E6
Vasilikón, *Greece* 39 L6
Vasilkov, *Ukraine* 40 F7
Vaslui, *Romania* 38 C10
Vassar, *Canada* 101 D9
Vassar, *U.S.A.* 104 D4
Västerås, *Sweden* 10 E10
Västerbottens län □,
  Sweden 8 D14
Västernorrlands län □,
  Sweden 10 A11
Västervik, *Sweden* 9 H14
Västmanlands län □,
  Sweden 9 G14
Vasto, *Italy* 33 F11
Vasvár, *Hungary* 21 H6
Vatan, *France* 25 E8
Vathí, *Greece* 39 M10
Váthia, *Greece* 39 N5
Vatican City ■, *Europe* .. 33 G9
Vaticano, C., *Italy* 35 D8
Vatili, *Cyprus* 37 D12
Vatnajökull, *Iceland* 8 D5
Vatnås, *Norway* 10 E3
Vatneyri, *Iceland* 8 D2
Vatoa, *Fiji* 87 D9
Vatólakkos, *Greece* 37 D5
Vatoloha, *Madag.* 85 B8
Vatomandry, *Madag.* 85 B8
Vatra-Dornei, *Romania* .. 38 B8
Vättern, *Sweden* 11 F8
Vättis, *Switz.* 23 C8
Vaucluse □, *France* 27 E9
Vaucouleurs, *France* 25 D12
Vaud □, *Switz.* 22 C2
Vaughn, *Mont., U.S.A.* .. 110 C8
Vaughn, *N. Mex., U.S.A.* 111 J11
Vaulruz, *Switz.* 22 C3
Vaupés = Uaupés →,
  Brazil 120 C4
Vaupes →, *Colombia* ... 120 C3
Vauvert, *France* 27 E8
Vauxhall, *Canada* 100 C6

Vava'u, *Tonga* 87 D11
Vavoua, *Ivory C.* 78 D3
Vaxholm, *Sweden* 10 E12
Växjö, *Sweden* 9 H13
Vaygach, Ostrov, *Russia* .. 44 C6
Váyia, Ákra, *Greece* 37 C10
Veadeiros, *Brazil* 123 D2
Vechta, *Germany* 18 C4
Vechte →, *Neths.* 16 C8
Vecsés, *Hungary* 21 H9
Veddige, *Sweden* 11 G6
Vedea →, *Romania* 38 F8
Vedia, *Argentina* 126 C3
Vedra, I. del, *Spain* 36 C7
Vedrin, *Belgium* 17 G5
Veendam, *Neths.* 16 B9
Veenendaal, *Neths.* 16 D7
Veerle, *Belgium* 17 F5
Vefsna →, *Norway* 8 D12
Vega, *Norway* 8 D11
Vega, *U.S.A.* 109 H3
Vegadeo, *Spain* 30 B3
Vegafjorden, *Norway* 8 D12
Veghel, *Neths.* 17 E7
Vegorritis, Límni, *Greece* . 39 J4
Vegreville, *Canada* 100 C6
Vegusdal, *Norway* 11 F2
Veii, *Italy* 33 F9
Vejen, *Denmark* 11 J3
Vejer de la Frontera, *Spain* 31 J5
Vejle, *Denmark* 11 J3
Vejle Fjord, *Denmark* 11 J3
Vela Luka, *Croatia* 33 F13
Vela, C., *Costa Rica* 116 D2
Velasco, Sierra de,
  Argentina 126 B2
Velay, Mts. du, *France* ... 26 D7
Velddrif, *S. Africa* 84 E2
Veldegem, *Belgium* 17 F2
Velden, *Neths.* 17 F8
Veldhoven, *Neths.* 17 F6
Velebit Planina, *Croatia* .. 33 D12
Velebitski Kanal, *Croatia* . 33 D11
Veleka →, *Bulgaria* 38 G10
Velenje, *Slovenia* 33 B12
Velestínon, *Greece* 39 K5
Vélez, *Colombia* 120 B3
Vélez Blanco, *Spain* 29 H2
Vélez Málaga, *Spain* 31 J6
Vélez Rubio, *Spain* 29 H2
Velhas →, *Brazil* 123 E3
Velika, *Croatia* 21 K7
Velika Gorica, *Croatia* ... 33 C13
Velika Kapela, *Croatia* ... 33 C12
Velika Kladuša, *Bos.-H.* .. 33 C12
Velika Morava →, *Serbia* 21 L11
Velikaya →, *Russia* 40 C6
Velikaya Kema, *Russia* ... 48 B8
Velikaya Lepetikha,
  Ukraine 42 C5
Velike Lašče, *Slovenia* ... 33 C11
Velikiye Luki, *Russia* 40 C7
Velikonda Range, *India* .. 60 M11
Velikoye, Oz., *Russia* 41 D12
Velingrad, *Bulgaria* 39 G6
Velino, Mte., *Italy* 33 F10
Velizh, *Russia* 40 D7
Velke Meziříci, *Czech.* ... 20 F6
Velletri, *Italy* 34 A5
Vellinge, *Sweden* 11 J7
Vellore, *India* 60 N11
Velp, *Neths.* 16 D7
Velsen-Noord, *Neths.* ... 16 D5
Velten, *Germany* 18 C9
Veluwe Meer, *Neths.* 16 D7
Velva, *U.S.A.* 108 A4
Veme, *Norway* 10 D4
Ven, *Sweden* 11 J6
Venaco, *France* 27 F13
Venado Tuerto, *Argentina* 126 C3
Venafro, *Italy* 35 A7
Venarey-les-Laumes,
  France 25 E11
Venaria, *Italy* 32 C4
Venčane, *Serbia* 21 L10
Vence, *France* 27 E11
Venda □, *S. Africa* 85 C5
Vendas Novas, *Portugal* .. 31 G2
Vendée □, *France* 24 F5
Vendée →, *France* 24 F5
Vendéen, Bocage, *France* . 26 B2
Vendeuvre-sur-Barse,
  France 25 D11
Vendôme, *France* 24 E8
Vendrell, *Spain* 28 D6
Vendsyssel, *Denmark* 11 G4
Véneta, L., *Italy* 33 C9
Véneto □, *Italy* 33 C8
Venev, *Russia* 41 D11
Venézia, *Italy* 33 C9
Venézia, G. di, *Italy* 33 C10
Venezuela ■, *S. Amer.* .. 120 B4
Venezuela, G. de,
  Venezuela 120 A3
Vengurla, *India* 60 M8
Venice = Venézia, *Italy* .. 33 C9
Venkatapuram, *India* 61 K12
Venlo, *Neths.* 17 F8
Venraij, *Neths.* 17 E7
Venta de Cardeña, *Spain* . 31 G6
Venta de San Rafael, *Spain* 30 E6
Ventana, Punta de la,
  Mexico 114 C3
Ventana, Sa. de la,
  Argentina 126 D3
Ventersburg, *S. Africa* ... 84 D4

Venterstad, *S. Africa* 84 E4
Ventimíglia, *Italy* 32 E4
Ventnor, *U.K.* 13 G6
Ventotene, *Italy* 34 B6
Ventoux, Mt., *France* 27 D9
Ventspils, *Latvia* 9 H16
Ventuarí →, *Venezuela* .. 120 C4
Ventucopa, *U.S.A.* 113 L7
Ventura, *U.S.A.* 113 L7
Venus B., *Australia* 91 F4
Vera, *Argentina* 126 B3
Vera, *Spain* 29 H3
Veracruz, *Mexico* 115 D5
Veracruz □, *Mexico* 115 D5
Veraval, *India* 62 J4
Verbánia, *Italy* 32 C5
Verbicaro, *Italy* 35 C8
Verbier, *Switz.* 22 D4
Vercelli, *Italy* 32 C5
Verchovcevo, *Ukraine* ... 42 B6
Verdalsøra, *Norway* 8 E11
Verde →, *Argentina* 128 B3
Verde →, *Goiás, Brazil* .. 123 E1
Verde →, *Goiás, Brazil* .. 123 E1
Verde →, *Mato Grosso,
  Brazil* 125 E7
Verde →, *Mato Grosso,
  Brazil* 125 C6
Verde →, *Chihuahua,
  Mexico* 114 B3
Verde →, *Oaxaca, Mexico* 115 D5
Verde →, *Veracruz,
  Mexico* 114 C4
Verde →, *Paraguay* 126 A4
Verde, Cay, *Bahamas* 116 B4
Verde Grande →, *Brazil* . 123 E3
Verde Island Pass, *Phil.* .. 55 E4
Verde Pequeno →, *Brazil* 123 D3
Verden, *Germany* 18 C5
Verdi, *U.S.A.* 112 F7
Verdigre, *U.S.A.* 108 D5
Verdon →, *France* 27 E9
Verdun, *France* 25 C12
Verdun-sur-le-Doubs,
  France 25 C12
Vereeniging, *S. Africa* 85 D4
Vérendrye, Parc Prov. de
  la, *Canada* 98 C4
Verga, C., *Guinea* 78 C2
Vergato, *Italy* 32 D8
Vergemont, *Australia* 90 C3
Vergemont Cr. →,
  Australia 90 C3
Vergennes, *U.S.A.* 107 B11
Vergt, *France* 26 D4
Verín, *Spain* 30 D3
Veriña, *Spain* 30 B5
Verkhnedvinsk, *Belorussia* 40 D5
Verkhnevilyuysk, *Russia* .. 45 C13
Verkhneye Kalinino, *Russia* 45 D11
Verkhniy Baskunchak,
  Russia 43 B12
Verkhovye, *Russia* 41 E10
Verkhoyansk, *Russia* 45 C14
Verkhoyansk Ra. =
  Verkhoyanskiy Khrebet,
  Russia 45 C13
Verkhoyanskiy Khrebet,
  Russia 45 C13
Verlo, *Canada* 101 C7
Verma, *Norway* 10 B2
Vermenton, *France* 25 E10
Vermilion, *Canada* 101 C6
Vermilion →, *Alta.,
  Canada* 101 C6
Vermilion →, *Qué.,
  Canada* 98 C5
Vermilion, B., *U.S.A.* ... 109 L9
Vermilion Bay, *Canada* .. 101 D10
Vermilion Chutes, *Canada* 100 B6
Vermilion L., *U.S.A.* 108 B8
Vermillion, *U.S.A.* 108 D6
Vermont □, *U.S.A.* 107 C12
Vernal, *U.S.A.* 110 F9
Vernalis, *U.S.A.* 112 H5
Vernayaz, *Switz.* 22 D4
Verner, *Canada* 98 C3
Verneuil-sur-Avre, *France* 24 D7
Verneukpan, *S. Africa* ... 84 D3
Vernier, *Switz.* 22 D2
Vernon, *Canada* 100 C5
Vernon, *France* 24 C8
Vernon, *U.S.A.* 109 H5
Vernonia, *U.S.A.* 112 E3
Vero Beach, *U.S.A.* 105 M5
Véroia, *Greece* 39 J5
Verolanuova, *Italy* 32 C7
Véroli, *Italy* 34 A6
Verona, *Italy* 32 C8
Veropol, *Russia* 45 C17
Versailles, *France* 25 D9
Versalles, *Bolivia* 125 C5
Versoix, *Switz.* 22 D2
Vert, C., *Senegal* 78 C1
Vertou, *France* 24 E5
Vertus, *France* 25 D11
Verulam, *S. Africa* 85 D5
Verviers, *Belgium* 17 G7
Vervins, *France* 25 C10
Verzej, *Slovenia* 33 B13
Vescavato, *France* 27 F13
Vesdre →, *Belgium* 17 G7
Veselí nad Lužnicí, *Czech.* 20 F4
Veselovskoye Vdkhr.,
  Russia 43 C9
Veshenskaya, *Russia* 43 B9

Vesle →, *France* 25 C10
Vesoul, *France* 25 E13
Vessigebro, *Sweden* 11 H6
Vest-Agder fylke □,
  Norway 9 G9
Vesterålen, *Norway* 8 B13
Vestersche Veld, *Neths.* .. 16 C8
Vestfjorden, *Norway* 8 C13
Vestfold fylke □, *Norway* . 9 G11
Vestmannaeyjar, *Iceland* . 8 E3
Vestmarka, *Norway* 10 E5
Vestone, *Italy* 32 C7
Vestsjællands
  Amtskommune □,
  Denmark 11 J5
Vestspitsbergen, *Svalbard* . 4 B8
Vestvågøy, *Norway* 8 B12
Vesuvio, *Italy* 35 B7
Vesuvius, Mt. = Vesuvio,
  Italy 35 B7
Vesyegonsk, *Russia* 41 B10
Veszprém, *Hungary* 21 H7
Vésztö, *Hungary* 21 J11
Vetlanda, *Sweden* 9 H13
Vetluga, *Russia* 41 C14
Vetlugu →, *Russia* 41 C15
Vetluzhskiy, *Russia* 41 C14
Vetovo, *Bulgaria* 38 F9
Vetralia, *Italy* 33 F9
Vettore, Monte, *Italy* 33 F10
Veurne, *Belgium* 17 F1
Vevey, *Switz.* 22 D3
Veynes, *France* 27 D9
Veys, *Iran* 65 D6
Vézelise, *France* 25 D13
Vézère →, *France* 26 D4
Vezirköprü, *Turkey* 66 C6
Vi Thanh, *Vietnam* 59 H5
Viacha, *Bolivia* 124 D4
Viadana, *Italy* 32 D7
Viamão, *Brazil* 127 C5
Viana, *Brazil* 122 B3
Viana, *Spain* 28 C2
Viana del Bollo, *Spain* ... 30 C3
Viana do Alentejo,
  Portugal 31 G3
Viana do Castelo, *Portugal* 30 D2
Vianden, *Belgium* 17 J8
Vianen, *Neths.* 16 E6
Vianna do Castelo □,
  Portugal 30 D2
Vianópolis, *Brazil* 123 E2
Viar →, *Spain* 31 H5
Viaréggio, *Italy* 32 E7
Viaur →, *France* 26 D5
Vibank, *Canada* 101 C8
Vibo Valéntia, *Italy* 35 D9
Viborg, *Denmark* 11 H3
Vibraye, *France* 24 D7
Vic-en-Bigorre, *France* ... 26 E4
Vic-Fézensac, *France* 26 E4
Vic-sur-Cère, *France* 26 D6
Vicenza, *Italy* 33 C8
Vich, *Spain* 28 D7
Vichada □, *Colombia* ... 120 C4
Vichada →, *Colombia* ... 120 C4
Vichuga, *Russia* 41 C12
Vichy, *France* 26 B7
Vicksburg, *Ariz., U.S.A.* . 113 M13
Vicksburg, *Mich., U.S.A.* 104 D3
Vicksburg, *Miss., U.S.A.* 109 J9
Vico, L., *Italy* 33 F9
Vico del Gargaro, *Italy* ... 35 A8
Viçosa, *Brazil* 122 C4
Viçosa do Ceará, *Brazil* .. 122 B3
Vicosoprano, *Switz.* 23 D9
Victor, *India* 62 J4
Victor, *Colo., U.S.A.* 108 F2
Victor, *N.Y., U.S.A.* 106 D7
Victor Harbor, *Australia* .. 91 F2
Victoria, *Argentina* 126 C3
Victoria, *Canada* 100 D4
Victoria, *Chile* 128 A2
Victoria, *Guinea* 78 C2
Victoria, *Malaysia* 56 C5
Victoria, *Malta* 37 C1
Victoria, *Phil.* 55 D4
Victoria, *Kans., U.S.A.* .. 108 F5
Victoria, *Tex., U.S.A.* ... 109 L6
Victoria □, *Australia* 91 F3
Victoria →, *Australia* 88 C4
Victoria, Grand L., *Canada* 98 C4
Victoria, L., *Africa* 82 C3
Victoria, L., *Australia* 91 E3
Victoria Beach, *Canada* .. 101 C9
Victoria de Durango,
  Mexico 114 C4
Victoria de las Tunas, *Cuba* 116 B4
Victoria Falls, *Zimbabwe* . 83 F2
Victoria Harbour, *Canada* 98 D4
Victoria I., *Canada* 96 A8
Victoria Ld., *Antarctica* .. 5 D11
Victoria Nile →, *Uganda* . 82 B3
Victoria Res., *Canada* 99 C8
Victoria River Downs,
  Australia 88 C5
Victoria Taungdeik, *Burma* 61 J18
Victoria West, *S. Africa* .. 84 E3
Victorias, *Phil.* 55 F5
Victoriaville, *Canada* 99 C5
Victórica, *Argentina* 126 D2
Victorville, *U.S.A.* 113 L9
Vicuña, *Chile* 126 C1
Vicuña Mackenna,
  Argentina 126 C3
Vidal, *U.S.A.* 113 L12

Vidal Junction, *U.S.A.* ... 113 L12
Vidalia, *U.S.A.* 105 J4
Vidauban, *France* 27 E10
Vídho, *Greece* 37 A3
Vidigueira, *Portugal* 31 G3
Vidin, *Bulgaria* 38 F5
Vidio, C., *Spain* 30 B4
Vidisha, *India* 62 H7
Vidzy, *Belorussia* 40 D5
Viechtach, *Germany* 19 F8
Viedma, *Argentina* 128 B4
Viedma, L., *Argentina* ... 128 C2
Vieira, *Portugal* 30 D2
Viella, *Spain* 28 C5
Vielsalm, *Belgium* 17 H7
Vienenburg, *Germany* ... 18 D6
Vieng Pou Kha, *Laos* 58 B3
Vienna = Wien, *Austria* .. 21 G6
Vienna, *U.S.A.* 109 G10
Vienne, *France* 27 C8
Vienne □, *France* 26 B4
Vienne →, *France* 24 E7
Vientiane, *Laos* 58 D4
Vientos, Paso de los,
  Caribbean 117 C5
Vierlingsbeek, *Neths.* 17 E8
Viersen, *Germany* 18 D2
Vierwaldstättersee, *Switz.* . 23 C7
Vierzon, *France* 25 E9
Vieste, *Italy* 35 A9
Vietnam ■, *Asia* 58 C5
Vieux-Boucau-les-Bains,
  France 26 E2
Vif, *France* 27 C9
Vigan, *Phil.* 55 C4
Vigévano, *Italy* 32 C5
Vigia, *Brazil* 122 B2
Vigía Chico, *Mexico* 115 D7
Víglas, Ákra, *Greece* 37 D9
Vignemale, Pic du, *France* 26 F3
Vigneulles-lès-Hattonchâtel,
  France 25 D12
Vignola, *Italy* 32 D8
Vigo, *Spain* 30 C2
Vigo, Ría de, *Spain* 30 C2
Vihiers, *France* 24 E6
Vijayawada, *India* 61 L12
Vijfhuizen, *Neths.* 16 D5
Viken, *Sweden* 11 F8
Viking, *Canada* 100 C6
Vikna, *Norway* 8 D11
Viksjö, *Sweden* 10 B11
Vikulovo, *Russia* 44 D8
Vila da Maganja, *Mozam.* 83 F4
Vila de João Belo = Xai-
  Xai, *Mozam.* 85 D5
Vila de Rei, *Portugal* 31 F2
Vila do Bispo, *Portugal* .. 31 H2
Vila do Chibuto, *Mozam.* . 85 C5
Vila do Conde, *Portugal* . 30 D2
Vila Franca de Xira,
  Portugal 31 G2
Vila Gamito, *Mozam.* 83 E3
Vila Gomes da Costa,
  Mozam. 85 C5
Vila Machado, *Mozam.* .. 83 F3
Vila Mouzinho, *Mozam.* . 83 E3
Vila Nova de Foscôa,
  Portugal 30 D3
Vila Nova de Ourém,
  Portugal 31 F2
Vila Novo de Gaia,
  Portugal 30 D2
Vila Pouca de Aguiar,
  Portugal 30 D3
Vila Real, *Portugal* 30 D3
Vila Real de Santo
  António, *Portugal* 31 H3
Vila Vasco da Gama,
  Mozam. 83 E3
Vila Velha, *Amapá, Brazil* 121 C7
Vila Velha, *Espírito Santo,
  Brazil* 123 F3
Vila Viçosa, *Portugal* 31 G3
Vilaboa, *Spain* 30 C2
Vilaine →, *France* 24 E4
Vilanandro, Tanjona,
  Madag. 85 B7
Vilanculos, *Mozam.* 85 C6
Vilar Formoso, *Portugal* .. 30 E4
Vilareal □, *Portugal* 30 D3
Vilaseca-Salou, *Spain* 28 D6
Vilcabamba, Cordillera,
  Peru 124 C3
Vilcanchos, *Peru* 124 C3
Vileyka, *Belorussia* 40 D5
Vilhelmina, *Sweden* 8 D14
Vilhena, *Brazil* 125 C5
Viliga, *Russia* 45 C16
Viliya →, *Lithuania* 40 D3
Viljandi, *Estonia* 40 B4
Vilkovo, *Ukraine* 42 D3
Villa Abecia, *Bolivia* 126 A2
Villa Ahumada, *Mexico* .. 114 A3
Villa Ana, *Argentina* 126 B4
Villa Ángela, *Argentina* .. 126 B3
Villa Bella, *Bolivia* 125 C4
Villa Bens = Tarfaya,
  Morocco 74 C2
Villa Cañás, *Argentina* ... 126 C3
Villa Carlos, *Spain* 36 B11
Villa Cisneros = Dakhla,
  W. Sahara 74 D1
Villa Colón, *Argentina* ... 126 C2
Villa Constitución,
  Argentina 126 C3

Villa de Cura, *Venezuela* . 120 A4
Villa de María, *Argentina* . 126 B3
Villa del Rosario, *Venezuela* ... 120 A3
Villa Dolores, *Argentina* .. 126 C2
Villa Frontera, *Mexico* ... 114 B4
Villa Guillermina, *Argentina* ... 126 B4
Villa Hayes, *Paraguay* ... 126 B4
Villa Iris, *Argentina* ... 126 D3
Villa Juárez, *Mexico* ... 114 B4
Villa María, *Argentina* ... 126 C3
Villa Mazán, *Argentina* ... 126 B2
Villa Minozzo, *Italy* ... 32 D7
Villa Montes, *Bolivia* ... 126 A3
Villa Ocampo, *Argentina* ... 126 B4
Villa Ocampo, *Mexico* ... 114 B3
Villa Ojo de Agua, *Argentina* ... 126 B3
Villa San Giovanni, *Italy* . 35 D8
Villa San José, *Argentina* . 126 C4
Villa San Martín, *Argentina* 126 B3
Villa Santina, *Italy* ... 33 B9
Villa Unión, *Mexico* ... 114 C3
Villablino, *Spain* ... 30 C4
Villacañas, *Spain* ... 28 F1
Villacarriedo, *Spain* ... 28 B1
Villacarrillo, *Spain* ... 29 G1
Villacastín, *Spain* ... 30 E6
Villach, *Austria* ... 21 J6
Villaciado, *Italy* ... 34 C1
Villada, *Spain* ... 30 C6
Villadiego, *Spain* ... 30 C6
Villadóssola, *Italy* ... 32 B5
Villafeliche, *Spain* ... 28 D3
Villafranca, *Spain* ... 28 C3
Villafranca de los Barros, *Spain* ... 31 G4
Villafranca de los Caballeros, *Spain* ... 29 F1
Villafranca de los Caballeros, *Spain* ... 36 B10
Villafranca del Bierzo, *Spain* ... 30 C4
Villafranca del Cid, *Spain* . 28 E4
Villafranca del Panadés, *Spain* ... 28 D6
Villafranca di Verona, *Italy* 32 C7
Villagarcía de Arosa, *Spain* 30 C2
Villagrán, *Mexico* ... 115 C5
Villaguay, *Argentina* ... 126 C4
Villaharta, *Spain* ... 31 G6
Villahermosa, *Mexico* ... 115 D6
Villahermosa, *Spain* ... 29 G2
Villaines-la-Juhel, *France* . 24 D6
Villajoyosa, *Spain* ... 29 G4
Villalba, *Spain* ... 30 B3
Villalba de Guardo, *Spain* . 30 C6
Villalcampo, Pantano de, *Spain* ... 30 D4
Villalón de Campos, *Spain* . 30 C5
Villalpando, *Spain* ... 30 D5
Villaluenga, *Spain* ... 30 E7
Villamanán, *Spain* ... 30 C5
Villamartín, *Spain* ... 31 J5
Villamayor, *Spain* ... 28 F2
Villamblard, *France* ... 26 C4
Villanova Monteleone, *Italy* 34 B1
Villanueva, *Colombia* ... 120 A3
Villanueva, *U.S.A.* ... 111 J11
Villanueva de Castellón, *Spain* ... 29 F4
Villanueva de Córdoba, *Spain* ... 31 G6
Villanueva de la Fuente, *Spain* ... 29 G2
Villanueva de la Serena, *Spain* ... 31 G5
Villanueva de la Sierra, *Spain* ... 30 E4
Villanueva de los Castillejos, *Spain* ... 31 H3
Villanueva del Arzobispo, *Spain* ... 29 G1
Villanueva del Duque, *Spain* ... 31 G5
Villanueva del Fresno, *Spain* ... 31 G3
Villanueva y Geltrú, *Spain* . 28 D6
Villaodrid, *Spain* ... 30 B3
Villaputzu, *Italy* ... 34 C2
Villar del Arzobispo, *Spain* 28 F4
Villar del Rey, *Spain* ... 31 F4
Villarcayo, *Spain* ... 28 C1
Villard-Bonnot, *France* ... 27 C9
Villard-de-Lans, *France* ... 27 C9
Villarino de los Aires, *Spain* ... 30 D4
Villarosa, *Italy* ... 35 E7
Villarramiel, *Spain* ... 30 C6
Villarreal, *Spain* ... 28 F4
Villarrica, *Chile* ... 128 A2
Villarrica, *Paraguay* ... 126 B4
Villarrobledo, *Spain* ... 29 F2
Villarroya de la Sierra, *Spain* ... 28 D3
Villarrubia de los Ojos, *Spain* ... 29 F1
Villars-les-Dombes, *France* 27 B9
Villarta de San Juan, *Spain* 29 F1
Villasayas, *Spain* ... 28 D2
Villaseca de los Gamitos, *Spain* ... 30 D4
Villastar, *Spain* ... 28 E3
Villatobas, *Spain* ... 28 F1
Villavicencio, *Argentina* ... 126 C2

Villavicencio, *Colombia* .. 120 C3
Villaviciosa, *Spain* ... 30 B5
Villazón, *Bolivia* ... 126 A2
Ville-Marie, *Canada* ... 98 C4
Ville Platte, *U.S.A.* ... 109 K8
Villedieu-les-Poêlles, *France* ... 24 D5
Villefort, *France* ... 26 D7
Villefranche-de-Lauragais, *France* ... 26 E5
Villefranche-de-Rouergue, *France* ... 26 D6
Villefranche-du-Périgord, *France* ... 26 D5
Villefranche-sur-Cher, *France* ... 25 E8
Villefranche-sur-Saône, *France* ... 27 C8
Villegrande, *Bolivia* ... 125 D5
Villel, *Spain* ... 28 E3
Villemaur-sur-Vanne, *France* ... 25 D10
Villemur-sur-Tarn, *France* . 26 E5
Villena, *Spain* ... 29 G4
Villenauxe-la-Grande, *France* ... 25 D10
Villenave-d'Ornon, *France* . 26 D3
Villeneuve, *Italy* ... 32 C4
Villeneuve, *Switz.* ... 22 D3
Villeneuve-l'Archevêque, *France* ... 25 D10
Villeneuve-lès-Avignon, *France* ... 27 E8
Villeneuve-St.-Georges, *France* ... 25 D9
Villeneuve-sur-Allier, *France* ... 26 B7
Villeneuve-sur-Lot, *France* . 26 D4
Villeréal, *France* ... 26 D4
Villers-Bocage, *France* ... 24 C6
Villers-Bretonneux, *France* . 25 C9
Villers-Cotterêts, *France* ... 25 C10
Villers-le-Bouillet, *Belgium* 17 G6
Villers-le-Gambon, *Belgium* 17 H5
Villers-sur-Mer, *France* ... 24 C6
Villersexel, *France* ... 25 E13
Villerupt, *France* ... 25 C12
Villerville, *France* ... 24 C7
Villiers, *S. Africa* ... 85 D4
Villingen, *Germany* ... 19 G4
Villisca, *U.S.A.* ... 108 E7
Vilna, *Canada* ... 100 C6
Vilnius, *Lithuania* ... 40 D4
Vils →, *Germany* ... 19 G9
Vilsbiburg, *Germany* ... 19 G8
Vilshofen, *Germany* ... 19 G9
Vilskutskogo, Proliv, *Russia* 45 B11
Vilusi, *Montenegro* ... 21 N8
Vilvoorde, *Belgium* ... 17 G4
Vilyuy →, *Russia* ... 45 C13
Vilyuysk, *Russia* ... 45 C13
Vimercate, *Italy* ... 32 C6
Vimioso, *Portugal* ... 30 D4
Vimoutiers, *France* ... 24 D7
Vimperk, *Czech.* ... 20 F3
Viña del Mar, *Chile* ... 126 C1
Vinaroz, *Spain* ... 28 E5
Vincennes, *U.S.A.* ... 104 F2
Vincent, *U.S.A.* ... 113 L8
Vinces, *Ecuador* ... 120 D2
Vinchina, *Argentina* ... 126 B2
Vindel älven →, *Sweden* . 8 E15
Vindeln, *Sweden* ... 8 D15
Vinderup, *Denmark* ... 11 H2
Vindhya Ra., *India* ... 62 H7
Vineland, *U.S.A.* ... 104 F8
Vinga, *Romania* ... 38 D4
Vingnes, *Norway* ... 10 C4
Vinh, *Vietnam* ... 58 C5
Vinh Linh, *Vietnam* ... 58 D6
Vinh Long, *Vietnam* ... 59 G5
Vinh Yen, *Vietnam* ... 58 B5
Vinhais, *Portugal* ... 30 D3
Vinica, *Croatia* ... 33 B13
Vinica, *Slovenia* ... 33 C12
Vinita, *U.S.A.* ... 109 G7
Vinkeveen, *Neths.* ... 16 D5
Vinkovci, *Croatia* ... 21 K8
Vinnitsa, *Ukraine* ... 42 B3
Vinnytsya = Vinnitsa, *Ukraine* ... 42 B3
Vinstra, *Norway* ... 10 C3
Vinton, Calif., *U.S.A.* ... 112 F6
Vinton, Iowa, *U.S.A.* ... 108 D8
Vinton, La., *U.S.A.* ... 109 K8
Vințu de Jos, *Romania* ... 38 D6
Viöl, *Germany* ... 18 A5
Vipava, *Slovenia* ... 33 C10
Vipiteno, *Italy* ... 33 B8
Viqueque, *Indonesia* ... 57 F7
Vir, *Croatia* ... 33 D12
Virac, *Phil.* ... 55 E6
Virachei, *Cambodia* ... 58 F6
Virago Sd., *Canada* ... 100 C2
Viramgam, *India* ... 62 H5
Viranșehir, *Turkey* ... 67 D8
Virden, *Canada* ... 101 D8
Vire, *France* ... 24 D6
Vire →, *France* ... 24 C5
Virgem da Lapa, *Brazil* ... 123 E3
Vírgenes, C., *Argentina* ... 128 D3
Virgin →, *Canada* ... 101 B7
Virgin →, *U.S.A.* ... 111 H6
Virgin Gorda, *Virgin Is.* ... 117 C7
Virgin Is. (British) ■, *W. Indies* ... 117 C7

Virgin Is. (U.S.) ■, *W. Indies* ... 117 C7
Virginia, *S. Africa* ... 84 D4
Virginia, *U.S.A.* ... 108 B8
Virginia □, *U.S.A.* ... 104 G7
Virginia Beach, *U.S.A.* ... 104 G8
Virginia City, Mont., *U.S.A.* ... 110 D8
Virginia City, Nev., *U.S.A.* 112 F7
Virginia Falls, *Canada* ... 100 A3
Virginiatown, *Canada* ... 98 C4
Viroqua, *U.S.A.* ... 108 D9
Virovitica, *Croatia* ... 21 K7
Virton, *Belgium* ... 17 J7
Virtsu, *Estonia* ... 40 B3
Virú, *Peru* ... 124 B2
Virudunagar, *India* ... 60 Q10
Vis, *Croatia* ... 33 E13
Vis Kanal, *Croatia* ... 33 E13
Visalia, *U.S.A.* ... 111 H4
Visayan Sea, *Phil.* ... 55 F5
Visby, *Sweden* ... 9 H15
Viscount Melville Sd., *Canada* ... 4 B2
Visé, *Belgium* ... 17 G7
Višegrad, *Bos.-H.* ... 21 M9
Viseu, *Brazil* ... 122 B2
Viseu, *Portugal* ... 30 E3
Viseu □, *Portugal* ... 30 E3
Vișeu de Sus, *Romania* ... 38 B7
Vishakhapatnam, *India* ... 61 L13
Viskafors, *Sweden* ... 11 G6
Visnagar, *India* ... 62 H5
Višnja Gora, *Slovenia* ... 33 C11
Viso, Mte., *Italy* ... 32 D4
Viso del Marqués, *Spain* .. 29 G1
Visoko, *Bos.-H.* ... 21 M8
Visokoi I., *Antarctica* ... 5 B1
Visp, *Switz.* ... 22 D5
Vispa →, *Switz.* ... 22 D5
Visselhövede, *Germany* ... 18 C5
Vissoie, *Switz.* ... 22 D5
Vista, *U.S.A.* ... 113 M9
Vistula = Wisła →, *Poland* 20 A8
Vit →, *Bulgaria* ... 38 F7
Vitanje, *Slovenia* ... 33 B12
Vitebsk, *Belorussia* ... 40 D7
Viterbo, *Italy* ... 33 F9
Viti Levu, *Fiji* ... 87 C7
Vitigudino, *Spain* ... 30 D4
Vitim, *Russia* ... 45 D12
Vitim →, *Russia* ... 45 D12
Vitória, *Brazil* ... 123 F3
Vitoria, *Spain* ... 28 C2
Vitória da Conquista, *Brazil* ... 123 D3
Vitória de São Antão, *Brazil* ... 122 C4
Vitorino Friere, *Brazil* ... 122 B2
Vitré, *France* ... 24 D5
Vitry-le-François, *France* . 25 D11
Vitsi, Óros, *Greece* ... 39 J4
Vitsyebsk = Vitebsk, *Belorussia* ... 40 D7
Vitteaux, *France* ... 25 E11
Vittel, *France* ... 25 D12
Vittória, *Italy* ... 35 F7
Vittório Véneto, *Italy* ... 33 C9
Vivario, *France* ... 27 F13
Vivegnis, *Belgium* ... 17 G7
Viver, *Spain* ... 28 F4
Vivero, *Spain* ... 30 B3
Viviers, *France* ... 27 D8
Vivonne, *France* ... 26 B4
Vizcaíno, Desierto de, *Mexico* ... 114 B2
Vizcaíno, Sierra, *Mexico* .. 114 B2
Vizcaya □, *Spain* ... 28 B2
Vize, *Turkey* ... 66 C2
Vizianagaram, *India* ... 61 K13
Vizille, *France* ... 27 C9
Viziñada, *Croatia* ... 33 C10
Viziru, *Romania* ... 38 E10
Vizovice, *Czech.* ... 20 F7
Vizzini, *Italy* ... 35 E7
Vlaardingen, *Neths.* ... 16 E4
Vlădeasa, *Romania* ... 38 C5
Vladikavkaz, *Russia* ... 43 E11
Vladimir, *Russia* ... 41 C12
Vladimir Volynskiy, *Ukraine* ... 40 F4
Vladimirovac, *Serbia* ... 21 K10
Vladimirovka, *Russia* ... 43 B12
Vladimirovka, *Russia* ... 43 D11
Vladislavovka, *Ukraine* ... 42 D6
Vladivostok, *Russia* ... 45 E14
Vlamertinge, *Belgium* ... 17 G1
Vlasenica, *Bos.-H.* ... 21 L8
Vlasinsko Jezero, *Serbia* .. 21 N12
Vleuten, *Neths.* ... 16 D6
Vlieland, *Neths.* ... 16 B5
Vliestroom, *Neths.* ... 16 B5
Vlijmen, *Neths.* ... 17 E6
Vlissingen, *Neths.* ... 17 F3
Vlóra, *Albania* ... 39 J2
Vlorës, Gjiri i, *Albania* ... 39 J2
Vltava →, *Czech.* ... 20 E4
Vo Dat, *Vietnam* ... 59 G6
Vobarno, *Italy* ... 32 C7
Voćin, *Croatia* ... 21 K7
Vodice, *Croatia* ... 33 E12
Vodnjan, *Croatia* ... 33 D10
Vogelkop = Doberai, Jazirah, *Indonesia* ... 57 E8
Vogelsberg, *Germany* ... 18 E5

Voghera, *Italy* ... 32 D6
Vohibinany, *Madag.* ... 85 B8
Vohimarina, *Madag.* ... 85 A9
Vohimena, Tanjon' i, *Madag.* ... 85 D8
Vohipeno, *Madag.* ... 85 C8
Voi, *Kenya* ... 82 C4
Void, *France* ... 25 D12
Voiron, *France* ... 27 C9
Voisey B., *Canada* ... 99 A7
Voiviís Límni, *Greece* ... 39 K5
Vojens, *Denmark* ... 11 J3
Vojmsjön, *Sweden* ... 8 D14
Vojnić, *Croatia* ... 33 C12
Vojnik, *Slovenia* ... 33 B12
Volborg, *U.S.A.* ... 108 C2
Volcano Is. = Kazan-Rettō, *Pac. Oc.* ... 92 E6
Volchansk, *Russia* ... 42 A7
Volchayevka, *Russia* ... 45 E14
Volchya →, *Ukraine* ... 42 C7
Volda, *Norway* ... 8 E9
Volendam, *Neths.* ... 16 D6
Volga, *Russia* ... 41 C11
Volga →, *Russia* ... 43 C13
Volga Hts. = Privolzhskaya Vozvyshennost, *Russia* ... 41 F15
Volgodonsk, *Russia* ... 43 C10
Volgograd, *Russia* ... 43 B11
Volgogradskoye Vdkhr., *Russia* ... 41 F14
Volgorechensk, *Russia* ... 41 C12
Volkach, *Germany* ... 19 F6
Volkerak, *Neths.* ... 17 E4
Völkermarkt, *Austria* ... 21 J4
Völklingen, *Germany* ... 19 F2
Volkovysk, *Belorussia* ... 40 E4
Volksrust, *S. Africa* ... 85 D4
Vollenhove, *Neths.* ... 16 C7
Volnovakha, *Ukraine* ... 42 C7
Volochanka, *Russia* ... 45 B10
Volodarsk, *Russia* ... 41 C13
Vologda, *Russia* ... 41 B11
Volokolamsk, *Russia* ... 41 C9
Volokonovka, *Russia* ... 41 F10
Vólos, *Greece* ... 39 K5
Volosovo, *Russia* ... 40 B6
Volozhin, *Belorussia* ... 40 D5
Volsk, *Russia* ... 41 E15
Volta →, *Ghana* ... 70 F4
Volta, L., *Ghana* ... 79 D5
Volta Blanche = White Volta →, *Ghana* ... 79 D4
Volta Redonda, *Brazil* ... 123 F3
Voltaire, C., *Australia* ... 88 B4
Volterra, *Italy* ... 32 E7
Voltri, *Italy* ... 32 D5
Volturara Áppula, *Italy* ... 35 A8
Volturno →, *Italy* ... 34 A6
Volubilis, *Morocco* ... 74 B3
Volvo, *Australia* ... 91 E3
Volzhsk, *Russia* ... 41 D16
Volzhskiy, *Russia* ... 43 B13
Vondrozo, *Madag.* ... 85 C8
Voorburg, *Neths.* ... 16 D4
Voorne Putten, *Neths.* ... 16 E4
Voorst, *Neths.* ... 16 D8
Voorthuizen, *Neths.* ... 16 D7
Vopnafjörður, *Iceland* ... 8 D6
Vóras Óros, *Greece* ... 39 J4
Vorbasse, *Denmark* ... 11 J3
Vorden, *Neths.* ... 16 D8
Vorderrhein →, *Switz.* ... 23 C8
Vordingborg, *Denmark* ... 11 K5
Voreppe, *France* ... 27 C9
Voríai Sporádhes, *Greece* . 39 K6
Vórios Evvoïkós Kólpos, *Greece* ... 39 L6
Vorkuta, *Russia* ... 44 C7
Vorma →, *Norway* ... 10 D5
Vorona →, *Russia* ... 41 F13
Voronezh, *Russia* ... 41 F11
Voronezh, *Ukraine* ... 40 F8
Voronezh →, *Russia* ... 41 F10
Vorontsovo-Aleksandrovskoye = Zelenokumsk, *Russia* ... 43 D10
Voroshilovgrad = Lugansk, *Ukraine* ... 43 B8
Voroshilovsk = Kommunarsk, *Ukraine* . 43 B8
Vorovskoye, *Russia* ... 45 D16
Vorselaar, *Belgium* ... 17 F5
Vorskla →, *Ukraine* ... 42 B6
Võru, *Estonia* ... 40 C5
Vorupør, *Denmark* ... 11 H2
Vosges, *France* ... 25 D14
Vosges □, *France* ... 25 D13
Voskopoja, *Albania* ... 39 J3
Voskresensk, *Russia* ... 41 D11
Voskresenskoye, *Russia* ... 41 C14
Voss, *Norway* ... 9 F9
Vosselaar, *Belgium* ... 17 F5
Vostok I., *Kiribati* ... 93 J12
Vouga →, *Portugal* ... 30 E2
Vouillé, *France* ... 24 F7
Vouvray, *France* ... 24 E7
Vouvry, *Switz.* ... 22 D3
Vóuxa, Ákra, *Greece* ... 37 D5
Vouzela, *Portugal* ... 30 E2

Vouziers, *France* ... 25 C11
Voves, *France* ... 25 D8
Voxna, *Sweden* ... 10 C9
Vozhgaly, *Russia* ... 41 B17
Vozhe, Ostrov, *Russia* ... 45 D10
Voznesensk, *Ukraine* ... 42 C4
Voznesenye, *Russia* ... 44 C4
Vrådal, *Norway* ... 10 E2
Vrakhneíka, *Greece* ... 39 L4
Vrancei, Munții, *Romania* ... 38 D9
Vrangelya, Ostrov, *Russia* ... 45 B19
Vranica, *Bos.-H.* ... 21 M7
Vranje, *Serbia* ... 21 N11
Vransko, *Slovenia* ... 33 B11
Vratsa, *Bulgaria* ... 38 F6
Vrbas, *Serbia* ... 21 K9
Vrbnik, *Croatia* ... 33 C11
Vrbovec, *Croatia* ... 33 C13
Vrbovsko, *Croatia* ... 33 C12
Vrchlabí, *Czech.* ... 20 E5
Vrede, *S. Africa* ... 85 D4
Vredefort, *S. Africa* ... 84 D4
Vredenburg, *S. Africa* ... 84 E2
Vredendal, *S. Africa* ... 84 E2
Vreeswijk, *Neths.* ... 16 D6
Vrena, *Sweden* ... 11 F10
Vrgorac, *Croatia* ... 21 M7
Vrhnika, *Slovenia* ... 33 C11
Vríði, *Ivory C.* ... 78 D4
Vries, *Neths.* ... 16 B9
Vriezenveen, *Neths.* ... 16 D9
Vrindavan, *India* ... 62 F7
Vríses, *Greece* ... 37 D6
Vrnograč, *Bos.-H.* ... 33 C12
Vroomshoop, *Neths.* ... 16 D9
Vršac, *Serbia* ... 21 K11
Vrsacki Kanal, *Serbia* ... 21 K11
Vryburg, *S. Africa* ... 84 D3
Vryheid, *S. Africa* ... 85 D5
Vsetín, *Czech.* ... 20 F8
Vu Liet, *Vietnam* ... 58 C5
Vucha →, *Bulgaria* ... 39 G7
Vught, *Neths.* ... 17 E6
Vukovar, *Croatia* ... 21 K8
Vulcan, *Canada* ... 100 C6
Vulcan, *U.S.A.* ... 104 C2
Vulcano, *Italy* ... 35 D7
Vŭlchedruma, *Bulgaria* ... 38 F6
Vulci, *Italy* ... 33 F8
Vulkaneshty, *Moldavia* ... 42 D3
Vunduzi →, *Mozam.* ... 83 F3
Vung Tau, *Vietnam* ... 59 G6
Vŭrbitsa, *Bulgaria* ... 38 G9
Vyasniki, *Russia* ... 41 C13
Vyatka, *Russia* ... 41 B16
Vyatka →, *Russia* ... 41 C17
Vyatskiye Polyany, *Russia* ... 41 C17
Vyazemskiy, *Russia* ... 45 E14
Vyazma, *Russia* ... 40 D9
Vyborg, *Russia* ... 44 C3
Vychegda →, *Russia* ... 44 C5
Vychodné Beskydy, *Europe* 20 F11
Vyksa, *Russia* ... 41 D13
Vyrnwy, L., *U.K.* ... 12 E4
Vyshniy Volochek, *Russia* ... 40 C9
Vyškov, *Czech.* ... 20 F6
Vysoké Mýto, *Czech.* ... 20 F6
Vysokovsk, *Russia* ... 41 C10
Vysotsk, *Ukraine* ... 40 F5

W

W.A.C. Bennett Dam, *Canada* ... 100 B4
Wa, *Ghana* ... 78 C4
Waal →, *Neths.* ... 16 E6
Waalwijk, *Neths.* ... 17 E6
Waarschoot, *Belgium* ... 17 F3
Waasmunster, *Belgium* ... 17 F4
Wabakimi L., *Canada* ... 98 B2
Wabana, *Canada* ... 99 C9
Wabasca, *Canada* ... 100 B6
Wabash, *U.S.A.* ... 104 E3
Wabash →, *U.S.A.* ... 104 G1
Wabeno, *U.S.A.* ... 104 C1
Wabi →, *Ethiopia* ... 77 F5
Wabigoon L., *Canada* ... 101 D10
Wabowden, *Canada* ... 101 C9
Wąbrzeźno, *Poland* ... 20 B8
Wabu Hu, *China* ... 53 A11
Wabuk Pt., *Canada* ... 98 A2
Wabush, *Canada* ... 99 B6
Wabuska, *U.S.A.* ... 110 G4
Wachtebeke, *Belgium* ... 17 F3
Wächtersbach, *Germany* ... 19 E5
Waco, *U.S.A.* ... 109 K6
Waconichi, L., *Canada* ... 98 B5
Wad Ban Naqa, *Sudan* ... 77 D3
Wad Banda, *Sudan* ... 77 E2
Wad el Haddad, *Sudan* ... 77 E3
Wad en Nau, *Sudan* ... 77 E3
Wad Hamid, *Sudan* ... 77 D3
Wâd Medanî, *Sudan* ... 77 E3
Wad Thana, *Pakistan* ... 62 F2
Wadayama, *Japan* ... 49 G7
Waddeneilanden, *Neths.* ... 16 B6
Waddenzee, *Neths.* ... 16 B6
Wadderin Hill, *Australia* ... 89 F2
Waddington, *U.S.A.* ... 107 B9
Waddington, Mt., *Canada* . 100 C3
Waddinxveen, *Neths.* ... 16 D5
Waddy Pt., *Australia* ... 91 C5

Wadena

Wadena, *Canada* 101 C8
Wadena, *U.S.A.* 108 B7
Wädenswil, *Switz.* 23 B7
Wadesboro, *U.S.A.* 105 H5
Wadhams, *Canada* 100 C3
Wādī as Sīr, *Jordan* 69 D4
Wadi Gemâl, *Egypt* 76 C4
Wadi Halfa, *Sudan* 76 C3
Wadian, *China* 53 A9
Wadowice, *Poland* 20 F9
Wadsworth, *U.S.A.* 110 G4
Waegwan, *S. Korea* 51 G15
Wafrah, *Si. Arabia* 64 D5
Wagenberg, *Neths.* 17 E5
Wageningen, *Neths.* 16 E7
Wageningen, *Surinam* 121 B6
Wager B., *Canada* 97 B11
Wager Bay, *Canada* 97 B10
Wagga Wagga, *Australia* 91 F4
Waghete, *Indonesia* 57 E9
Wagin, *Australia* 89 F2
Wagon Mound, *U.S.A.* 109 G2
Wagoner, *U.S.A.* 109 G7
Wagrowiec, *Poland* 20 C7
Wah, *Pakistan* 62 C5
Wahai, *Indonesia* 57 E7
Wahiawa, *U.S.A.* 102 H15
Wâḥid, *Egypt* 69 E1
Wahnai, *Afghan.* 62 C1
Wahoo, *U.S.A.* 108 E6
Wahpeton, *U.S.A.* 108 B6
Wai, Koh, *Cambodia* 59 H4
Waiau →, *N.Z.* 87 K4
Waibeem, *Indonesia* 57 E8
Waiblingen, *Germany* 19 G5
Waidhofen, *Niederösterreich, Austria* 20 G5
Waidhofen, *Niederösterreich, Austria* 21 H4
Waigeo, *Indonesia* 57 E8
Waihi, *N.Z.* 87 G5
Waihou →, *N.Z.* 87 G5
Waika, *Zaïre* 82 C2
Waikabubak, *Indonesia* 57 F5
Waikari, *N.Z.* 87 K4
Waikato →, *N.Z.* 87 G5
Waikerie, *Australia* 91 E2
Waikokopu, *N.Z.* 87 H6
Waikouaiti, *N.Z.* 87 L3
Waimakariri →, *N.Z.* 87 K4
Waimate, *N.Z.* 87 L3
Waimes, *Belgium* 17 H8
Wainganga →, *India* 60 K11
Waingapu, *Indonesia* 57 F6
Waini →, *Guyana* 121 B6
Wainwright, *Canada* 101 C6
Wainwright, *U.S.A.* 96 A3
Waiouru, *N.Z.* 87 H5
Waipara, *N.Z.* 87 K4
Waipawa, *N.Z.* 87 H6
Waipiro, *N.Z.* 87 H7
Waipu, *N.Z.* 87 F5
Waipukurau, *N.Z.* 87 J6
Wairakei, *N.Z.* 87 H6
Wairarapa, L., *N.Z.* 87 J5
Wairoa, *N.Z.* 87 H6
Waitaki →, *N.Z.* 87 L3
Waitara, *N.Z.* 87 H5
Waitsburg, *U.S.A.* 110 C5
Waiuku, *N.Z.* 87 G5
Wajima, *Japan* 49 F8
Wajir, *Kenya* 82 B5
Wajir □, *Kenya* 82 B5
Wakasa, *Japan* 49 G7
Wakasa-Wan, *Japan* 49 G7
Wakatipu, L., *N.Z.* 87 L2
Wakaw, *Canada* 101 C7
Wakayama, *Japan* 49 G7
Wakayama-ken □, *Japan* 49 H7
Wake Forest, *U.S.A.* 105 H6
Wake I., *Pac. Oc.* 92 F8
Wakefield, *N.Z.* 87 J4
Wakefield, *U.K.* 12 D6
Wakefield, *Mass., U.S.A.* 107 D13
Wakefield, *Mich., U.S.A.* 108 B10
Wakeham Bay = Maricourt, *Canada* 97 C12
Wakema, *Burma* 61 L19
Wakkanai, *Japan* 48 B10
Wakkerstroom, *S. Africa* 85 D5
Wakool, *Australia* 91 F3
Wakool →, *Australia* 91 F3
Wakre, *Indonesia* 57 E8
Wakuach L., *Canada* 99 A6
Walamba, *Zambia* 83 E2
Wałbrzych, *Poland* 20 E6
Walbury Hill, *U.K.* 13 F6
Walcha, *Australia* 91 E5
Walcheren, *Neths.* 17 E3
Walcott, *U.S.A.* 110 F10
Wałcz, *Poland* 20 B6
Wald, *Switz.* 23 B7
Waldbröl, *Germany* 18 E3
Waldburg Ra., *Australia* 88 D2
Waldeck, *Germany* 18 D5
Walden, *Colo., U.S.A.* 110 F10
Walden, *N.Y., U.S.A.* 107 E10
Waldenburg, *Switz.* 22 B5
Waldport, *U.S.A.* 110 D1
Waldron, *U.S.A.* 109 H7
Waldshut, *Germany* 19 H4
Walembele, *Ghana* 78 C4
Walensee, *Switz.* 23 B8
Walenstadt, *Switz.* 23 B8
Wales □, *U.K.* 13 E4
Walewale, *Ghana* 79 C4
Walgett, *Australia* 91 E4
Walgreen Coast, *Antarctica* 5 D15
Walhalla, *Australia* 91 F4
Walhalla, *U.S.A.* 101 D9
Walker, *U.S.A.* 108 B7
Walker L., *Man., Canada* 101 C9
Walker L., *Qué., Canada* 99 B6
Walker L., *U.S.A.* 110 G4
Walkerston, *Australia* 90 C4
Walkerton, *Canada* 106 B3
Wall, *U.S.A.* 108 C3
Walla Walla, *U.S.A.* 110 C4
Wallabadah, *Australia* 90 B3
Wallace, *Idaho, U.S.A.* 110 C6
Wallace, *N.C., U.S.A.* 105 H7
Wallace, *Nebr., U.S.A.* 108 E4
Wallaceburg, *Canada* 98 D3
Wallachia = Valahia, *Romania* 38 E8
Wallal, *Australia* 91 D4
Wallal Downs, *Australia* 88 C3
Wallambin, L., *Australia* 89 F2
Wallaroo, *Australia* 91 E2
Wallasey, *U.K.* 12 D4
Walldürn, *Germany* 19 F5
Wallerawang, *Australia* 91 E5
Wallhallow, *Australia* 90 B2
Wallingford, *U.S.A.* 107 E12
Wallis & Futuna, Is., *Pac. Oc.* 92 J10
Wallisellen, *Switz.* 23 B7
Wallowa, *U.S.A.* 110 D5
Wallowa Mts., *U.S.A.* 110 D5
Wallsend, *Australia* 91 E5
Wallsend, *U.K.* 12 C6
Wallula, *U.S.A.* 110 C4
Wallumbilla, *Australia* 91 D4
Walmsley, L., *Canada* 101 A7
Walney, I. of, *U.K.* 12 C4
Walnut Creek, *U.S.A.* 112 H4
Walnut Ridge, *U.S.A.* 109 G9
Walsall, *U.K.* 13 E6
Walsenburg, *U.S.A.* 109 G2
Walsh, *U.S.A.* 109 G3
Walsh →, *Australia* 90 B3
Walsh P.O., *Australia* 90 B3
Walshoutem, *Belgium* 17 G6
Walsrode, *Germany* 18 C5
Walterboro, *U.S.A.* 105 J5
Walters, *U.S.A.* 109 H5
Waltershausen, *Germany* 18 E6
Waltham, *U.S.A.* 107 D13
Waltham Station, *Canada* 98 C4
Waltman, *U.S.A.* 110 E10
Walton, *U.S.A.* 107 D9
Walvisbaai, *S. Africa* 84 C1
Wamba, *Kenya* 82 B4
Wamba, *Zaïre* 82 B2
Wamego, *U.S.A.* 108 F6
Wamena, *Indonesia* 57 E9
Wamsasi, *Indonesia* 57 E7
Wan Xian, *China* 50 E8
Wana, *Pakistan* 62 C3
Wanaaring, *Australia* 91 D3
Wanaka, *N.Z.* 87 L2
Wanaka L., *N.Z.* 87 L2
Wan'an, *China* 53 D10
Wanapiri, *Indonesia* 57 E9
Wanapitei L., *Canada* 98 C3
Wanbi, *Australia* 91 E3
Wandaik, *Guyana* 121 C6
Wandarrie, *Australia* 89 E2
Wanderer, *Zimbabwe* 83 F3
Wandoan, *Australia* 91 D4
Wandre, *Belgium* 17 G7
Wanfercée-Baulet, *Belgium* 17 H5
Wanfu, *China* 51 D12
Wang →, *Thailand* 58 D2
Wang Kai, *Sudan* 77 F2
Wang Noi, *Thailand* 58 E3
Wang Saphung, *Thailand* 58 D3
Wang Thong, *Thailand* 58 D3
Wanga, *Zaïre* 82 B2
Wangal, *Indonesia* 57 F8
Wanganella, *Australia* 91 F3
Wanganui, *N.Z.* 87 H5
Wangaratta, *Australia* 91 F4
Wangary, *Australia* 91 E2
Wangcang, *China* 52 A6
Wangdu, *China* 50 E8
Wangerooge, *Germany* 18 B3
Wangi, *Kenya* 82 C5
Wangiwangi, *Indonesia* 57 F6
Wangjiang, *China* 53 B11
Wangmo, *China* 52 E6
Wangqing, *China* 51 C15
Wankaner, *India* 62 H4
Wanless, *Canada* 101 C8
Wannian, *China* 53 C11
Wanon Niwat, *Thailand* 58 D4
Wanquan, *China* 50 D8
Wanrong, *China* 50 G6
Wanshan, *China* 52 D7
Wanshengchang, *China* 52 C6
Wanssum, *Neths.* 17 E8
Wanxian, *China* 52 B7
Wanyuan, *China* 52 A7
Wanzai, *China* 53 C10
Wanze, *Belgium* 17 G6
Wapakoneta, *U.S.A.* 104 E3
Wapato, *U.S.A.* 110 C3
Wapawekka L., *Canada* 101 C8
Wapikopa L., *Canada* 98 B2
Wappingers Falls, *U.S.A.* 107 E11
Wapsipinicon →, *U.S.A.* 108 E9
Warangal, *India* 60 L11
Waratah, *Australia* 90 G4
Waratah B., *Australia* 91 F4
Warburg, *Germany* 18 D5
Warburton, *Vic., Australia* 91 F4
Warburton, *W. Austral., Australia* 89 E4
Warburton Ra., *Australia* 89 E4
Ward, *N.Z.* 87 J5
Ward →, *Australia* 91 D4
Ward Cove, *U.S.A.* 100 B2
Ward Mt., *U.S.A.* 112 H8
Warden, *S. Africa* 85 D4
Wardha, *India* 60 J11
Wardha →, *India* 60 K11
Wardlow, *Canada* 100 C6
Ware, *Canada* 100 B3
Ware, *U.S.A.* 107 D12
Waregem, *Belgium* 17 G2
Wareham, *U.S.A.* 107 E14
Waremme, *Belgium* 17 G6
Waren, *Germany* 18 B8
Warendorf, *Germany* 18 D3
Warialda, *Australia* 91 D5
Wariap, *Indonesia* 57 E8
Warin Chamrap, *Thailand* 58 E5
Warkopi, *Indonesia* 57 E8
Warley, *U.K.* 13 E6
Warm Springs, *U.S.A.* 111 G5
Warman, *Canada* 101 C7
Warmbad, *Namibia* 84 D2
Warmbad, *S. Africa* 85 C4
Warmenhuizen, *Neths.* 16 C5
Warmeriville, *France* 25 C11
Warmond, *Neths.* 16 D5
Warnambool Downs, *Australia* 90 C3
Warnemünde, *Germany* 18 A8
Warner, *Canada* 100 D6
Warner Mts., *U.S.A.* 110 F3
Warner Robins, *U.S.A.* 105 J4
Warnes, *Bolivia* 125 D5
Warneton, *Belgium* 17 G1
Warnow →, *Germany* 18 A8
Warnsveld, *Neths.* 16 D8
Waroona, *Australia* 89 F2
Warracknabeal, *Australia* 91 F3
Warragul, *Australia* 91 F4
Warrawagine, *Australia* 88 D3
Warrego →, *Australia* 91 E4
Warrego Ra., *Australia* 90 C4
Warren, *Australia* 91 E4
Warren, *Ark., U.S.A.* 109 J8
Warren, *Mich., U.S.A.* 104 D4
Warren, *Minn., U.S.A.* 108 A6
Warren, *Ohio, U.S.A.* 106 E4
Warren, *Pa., U.S.A.* 106 E5
Warrenpoint, *U.K.* 15 B5
Warrensburg, *U.S.A.* 108 F8
Warrenton, *S. Africa* 84 D3
Warrenton, *U.S.A.* 112 D3
Warrenville, *Australia* 91 D4
Warri, *Nigeria* 79 D6
Warrina, *Australia* 91 D2
Warrington, *U.K.* 12 D5
Warrington, *U.S.A.* 105 K2
Warrnambool, *Australia* 91 F3
Warroad, *U.S.A.* 108 A7
Warsa, *Indonesia* 57 E9
Warsaw = Warszawa, *Poland* 20 C11
Warsaw, *Ind., U.S.A.* 104 E3
Warsaw, *N.Y., U.S.A.* 106 D6
Warsaw, *Ohio, U.S.A.* 106 F2
Warstein, *Germany* 18 D4
Warszawa, *Poland* 20 C11
Warta →, *Poland* 20 C4
Warthe = Warta →, *Poland* 20 C4
Waru, *Indonesia* 57 E8
Warwick, *Australia* 91 D5
Warwick, *U.K.* 13 E6
Warwick, *U.S.A.* 107 E13
Warwickshire □, *U.K.* 13 E6
Wasaga Beach, *Canada* 106 B4
Wasatch Ra., *U.S.A.* 110 F8
Wasbank, *S. Africa* 85 D5
Wasco, *Calif., U.S.A.* 113 K7
Wasco, *Oreg., U.S.A.* 110 D3
Waseca, *U.S.A.* 108 C8
Wasekamio L., *Canada* 101 B7
Wash, The, *U.K.* 12 E8
Washago, *Canada* 106 B5
Washburn, *N. Dak., U.S.A.* 108 B4
Washburn, *Wis., U.S.A.* 108 B9
Washim, *India* 60 J10
Washington, *D.C., U.S.A.* 104 F7
Washington, *Ga., U.S.A.* 105 J4
Washington, *Ind., U.S.A.* 104 F2
Washington, *Iowa, U.S.A.* 108 E9
Washington, *Mo., U.S.A.* 108 F9
Washington, *N.C., U.S.A.* 105 H7
Washington, *N.J., U.S.A.* 107 F10
Washington, *Pa., U.S.A.* 106 F4
Washington, *Utah, U.S.A.* 111 H7
Washington □, *U.S.A.* 110 C3
Washington, Mt., *U.S.A.* 107 B13
Washington I., *U.S.A.* 104 C2
Washougal, *U.S.A.* 112 E4
Wasian, *Indonesia* 57 E8
Wasior, *Indonesia* 57 E8
Waskaiowaka, L., *Canada* 101 B9
Waskesiu Lake, *Canada* 101 C7
Wasmes, *Belgium* 17 H3
Waspik, *Neths.* 17 E5
Wassen, *Switz.* 23 C7
Wassenaar, *Neths.* 16 D4
Wasserburg, *Germany* 19 G8
Wasserkuppe, *Germany* 18 E5
Wassy, *France* 25 D11
Waswanipi, *Canada* 98 C4
Waswanipi, L., *Canada* 98 C4
Watangpone, *Indonesia* 57 E6
Water Park Pt., *Australia* 90 C5
Water Valley, *U.S.A.* 109 H10
Waterberge, *S. Africa* 85 C4
Waterbury, *Conn., U.S.A.* 107 E11
Waterbury, *Vt., U.S.A.* 107 B12
Waterbury L., *Canada* 101 B8
Waterdown, *Canada* 106 C5
Waterford, *Canada* 106 D4
Waterford, *Ireland* 15 D4
Waterford, *U.S.A.* 112 H6
Waterford □, *Ireland* 15 D4
Waterford Harbour, *Ireland* 15 D5
Waterhen L., *Man., Canada* 101 C9
Waterhen L., *Sask., Canada* 101 C7
Wateringen, *Neths.* 16 D4
Waterloo, *Belgium* 17 G4
Waterloo, *Ont., Canada* 98 D3
Waterloo, *Qué., Canada* 107 A12
Waterloo, *S. Leone* 78 D2
Waterloo, *Ill., U.S.A.* 108 F9
Waterloo, *Iowa, U.S.A.* 108 D8
Waterloo, *N.Y., U.S.A.* 106 D8
Watermeal-Boitsford, *Belgium* 17 G4
Watersmeet, *U.S.A.* 108 B10
Waterton-Glacier International Peace Park, *U.S.A.* 110 B7
Watertown, *Conn., U.S.A.* 107 E11
Watertown, *N.Y., U.S.A.* 107 C9
Watertown, *S. Dak., U.S.A.* 108 C6
Watertown, *Wis., U.S.A.* 108 D10
Waterval-Boven, *S. Africa* 85 D5
Waterville, *Canada* 107 A13
Waterville, *Maine, U.S.A.* 99 D6
Waterville, *N.Y., U.S.A.* 107 D9
Waterville, *Pa., U.S.A.* 106 E7
Waterville, *Wash., U.S.A.* 110 C3
Watervliet, *Belgium* 17 F3
Watervliet, *U.S.A.* 107 D11
Wates, *Indonesia* 57 G14
Watford, *Canada* 106 D3
Watford, *U.K.* 13 F7
Watford City, *U.S.A.* 108 B3
Wathaman →, *Canada* 101 B8
Watheroo, *Australia* 89 F2
Wating, *China* 50 G4
Watkins Glen, *U.S.A.* 106 D8
Watling I. = San Salvador, *Bahamas* 117 B5
Watonga, *U.S.A.* 109 H5
Watou, *Belgium* 17 G1
Watrous, *Canada* 101 C7
Watrous, *U.S.A.* 109 H2
Watsa, *Zaïre* 82 B2
Watseka, *U.S.A.* 104 E2
Watson, *Australia* 89 F5
Watson, *Canada* 101 C8
Watson Lake, *Canada* 100 A3
Watsonville, *U.S.A.* 111 H3
Wattenwil, *Switz.* 22 C5
Wattiwarriganna Cr. →, *Australia* 91 D2
Wattwil, *Switz.* 23 B8
Watuata = Batuata, *Indonesia* 57 F6
Watubela, Kepulauan, *Indonesia* 57 E8
Watubela Is. = Watubela, Kepulauan, *Indonesia* 57 E8
Waubach, *Neths.* 17 G8
Waubamik, *Canada* 106 A4
Waubay, *U.S.A.* 108 C6
Waubra, *Australia* 91 F3
Wauchope, *Australia* 91 E5
Wauchula, *U.S.A.* 105 M5
Waugh, *Canada* 101 D9
Waukarlycarly, L., *Australia* 88 D3
Waukegan, *U.S.A.* 104 D2
Waukesha, *U.S.A.* 104 D1
Waukon, *U.S.A.* 108 D9
Wauneta, *U.S.A.* 108 E4
Waupaca, *U.S.A.* 108 C10
Waupun, *U.S.A.* 108 D10
Waurika, *U.S.A.* 109 H6
Wausau, *U.S.A.* 108 C10
Wautoma, *U.S.A.* 108 C10
Wauwatosa, *U.S.A.* 104 D2
Wave Hill, *Australia* 88 C5
Waveney →, *U.K.* 13 E9
Waverley, *N.Z.* 87 H5
Waverly, *Iowa, U.S.A.* 108 D8
Waverly, *N.Y., U.S.A.* 107 D8
Wavre, *Belgium* 17 G5
Wavreille, *Belgium* 17 H6
Wâw, *Sudan* 77 F2
Wāw al Kabīr, *Libya* 73 C8
Wawa, *Canada* 98 C3
Wawa, *Nigeria* 79 D5
Wawa, *Sudan* 76 C3
Wawanesa, *Canada* 101 D9
Wawona, *U.S.A.* 112 H7
Waxahachie, *U.S.A.* 109 J6
Way, L., *Australia* 89 E3
Wayabula Rau, *Indonesia* 57 D7
Wayatinah, *Australia* 90 G4
Waycross, *U.S.A.* 105 K4
Wayi, *Sudan* 77 F3
Wayne, *Nebr., U.S.A.* 108 D6
Wayne, *W. Va., U.S.A.* 104 F4
Waynesboro, *Ga., U.S.A.* 105 J4
Waynesboro, *Miss., U.S.A.* 105 K1
Waynesboro, *Pa., U.S.A.* 104 F7
Waynesboro, *Va., U.S.A.* 104 F6
Waynesburg, *U.S.A.* 104 F5
Waynesville, *U.S.A.* 105 H4
Waynoka, *U.S.A.* 109 G5
Wāzin, *Libya* 75 B7
Wazirabad, *Pakistan* 62 C6
We, *Indonesia* 56 C1
Weald, The, *U.K.* 13 F8
Wear →, *U.K.* 12 C6
Weatherford, *Okla., U.S.A.* 109 H5
Weatherford, *Tex., U.S.A.* 109 J6
Weaverville, *U.S.A.* 110 F2
Webb City, *U.S.A.* 109 G7
Webo = Nyaake, *Liberia* 78 E3
Webster, *Mass., U.S.A.* 107 D13
Webster, *N.Y., U.S.A.* 106 C7
Webster, *S. Dak., U.S.A.* 108 C6
Webster, *Wis., U.S.A.* 108 C8
Webster City, *U.S.A.* 108 D8
Webster Green, *U.S.A.* 108 F9
Webster Springs, *U.S.A.* 104 F5
Weda, *Indonesia* 57 D7
Weda, Teluk, *Indonesia* 57 D7
Weddell I., *Falk. Is.* 128 D4
Weddell Sea, *Antarctica* 5 D1
Wedderburn, *Australia* 91 F3
Wedgeport, *Canada* 99 D6
Wedza, *Zimbabwe* 83 F3
Wee Waa, *Australia* 91 E4
Weed, *U.S.A.* 110 F2
Weed Heights, *U.S.A.* 112 G7
Weedsport, *U.S.A.* 107 C8
Weedville, *U.S.A.* 106 E6
Weemelah, *Australia* 91 D4
Weenen, *S. Africa* 85 D5
Weener, *Germany* 18 B3
Weert, *Neths.* 17 F7
Weesp, *Neths.* 16 D6
Weggis, *Switz.* 23 B6
Wegliniec, *Poland* 20 D5
Węgorzewo, *Poland* 20 A11
Węgrów, *Poland* 20 C12
Wehl, *Neths.* 16 E8
Wei He →, *Hebei, China* 50 F8
Wei He →, *Shaanxi, China* 50 G6
Weichang, *China* 51 D9
Weichuan, *China* 50 G7
Weida, *Germany* 18 E8
Weiden, *Germany* 19 F8
Weifang, *China* 54 C6
Weifang, *Shandong, China* 51 F10
Weihai, *China* 51 F12
Weilburg, *Germany* 18 E4
Weilheim, *Germany* 19 H7
Weimar, *Germany* 18 E7
Weinan, *China* 50 G5
Weinfelden, *Switz.* 23 A8
Weingarten, *Germany* 19 H5
Weinheim, *Germany* 19 F4
Weining, *China* 52 D5
Weipa, *Australia* 90 A3
Weir →, *Australia* 91 D4
Weir →, *Canada* 101 B10
Weir River, *Canada* 101 B10
Weirton, *U.S.A.* 106 F4
Weisen, *Switz.* 23 C9
Weiser, *U.S.A.* 110 D5
Weishan, *Shandong, China* 51 G9
Weishan, *Yunnan, China* 52 E3
Weissenburg, *Germany* 19 F6
Weissenfels, *Germany* 18 D8
Weisshorn, *Switz.* 22 D5
Weissmies, *Switz.* 22 D6
Weisstannen, *Switz.* 23 C8
Weisswasser, *Germany* 18 D10
Weiswampach, *Belgium* 17 H8
Weixi, *China* 52 D2
Weixin, *China* 52 D5
Weiyuan, *China* 50 G3
Weiz, *Austria* 21 H5
Weizhou Dao, *China* 52 G7
Wejherowo, *Poland* 20 A8
Wekusko L., *Canada* 101 C9
Welbourn Hill, *Australia* 91 D1
Welch, *U.S.A.* 104 G5
Weldya, *Ethiopia* 77 E4
Welega □, *Ethiopia* 77 F3
Welkenraedt, *Belgium* 17 G7
Welkite, *Ethiopia* 77 F4
Welkom, *S. Africa* 84 D4
Welland, *Canada* 98 D4
Welland →, *U.K.* 12 E7
Wellen, *Belgium* 17 G6
Wellesley Is., *Australia* 90 B2
Wellin, *Belgium* 17 H6
Wellingborough, *U.K.* 13 E7
Wellington, *Australia* 91 E4
Wellington, *Canada* 98 D4
Wellington, *N.Z.* 87 J5
Wellington, *S. Africa* 84 E2
Wellington, *Shrops., U.K.* 12 E5
Wellington, *Somst., U.K.* 13 G4
Wellington, *Colo., U.S.A.* 108 E2
Wellington, *Kans., U.S.A.* 109 G6
Wellington, *Nev., U.S.A.* 112 G7
Wellington, *Ohio, U.S.A.* 106 E2
Wellington, *Tex., U.S.A.* 109 H4

Wellington, I., Chile 128 C2
Wellington, L., Australia . 91 F4
Wells, Norfolk, U.K. 12 E8
Wells, Somst., U.K. 13 F5
Wells, Maine, U.S.A. ... 107 C14
Wells, Minn., U.S.A. 108 D8
Wells, Nev., U.S.A. 110 F6
Wells, L., Australia 89 E3
Wells Gray Prov. Park,
Canada 100 C4
Wells River, U.S.A. 107 B12
Wellsboro, U.S.A. 106 E7
Wellsburg, U.S.A. 106 F4
Wellsville, Mo., U.S.A. .. 108 F9
Wellsville, N.Y., U.S.A. . 106 D7
Wellsville, Ohio, U.S.A. . 106 F4
Wellsville, Utah, U.S.A. . 110 F8
Wellton, U.S.A. 111 K6
Welmel, Wabi →, Ethiopia 77 F5
Welo □, Ethiopia 77 E4
Wels, Austria 21 G4
Welshpool, U.K. 13 E4
Wem, U.K. 12 E5
Wembere →, Tanzania .. 82 C3
Wemmel, Belgium 17 G4
Wen Xian, Gansu, China . 50 H3
Wen Xian, Henan, China . 50 G7
Wenatchee, U.S.A. 110 C3
Wenchang, China 58 C8
Wencheng, China 53 D13
Wenchi, Ghana 78 D4
Wenchow = Wenzhou,
China 53 C13
Wenchuan, China 52 B4
Wendell, U.S.A. 110 E6
Wenden, U.S.A. 113 M13
Wendeng, China 51 F12
Wendesi, Indonesia 57 E8
Wendo, Ethiopia 77 F4
Wendover, U.S.A. 110 F6
Wenduine, Belgium 17 F2
Weng'an, China 52 D6
Wengcheng, China 53 E9
Wengen, Switz. 22 C5
Wengyuan, China 53 E10
Wenjiang, China 52 B4
Wenling, China 53 C13
Wenlock →, Australia .. 90 A3
Wenshan, China 52 F5
Wenshang, China 50 G9
Wenshui, Guizhou, China 52 C6
Wenshui, Shanxi, China . 50 F7
Wensu, China 54 B3
Wentworth, Australia .. 91 E3
Wenut, Indonesia 57 E8
Wenxi, China 50 G6
Wenzhou, China 53 C13
Weott, U.S.A. 110 F2
Wepener, S. Africa 84 D4
Werbomont, Belgium ... 17 H7
Werda, Botswana 84 D3
Werdau, Germany 18 E8
Werder, Ethiopia 68 F4
Werder, Germany 18 C8
Werdohl, Germany 18 D3
Wereilu, Ethiopia 77 E4
Weri, Indonesia 57 E8
Werkendam, Neths. 16 E5
Werne, Germany 18 D3
Werneck, Germany 19 F6
Wernigerode, Germany . 18 D6
Werra →, Germany 18 D5
Werribee, Australia 91 F3
Werrimull, Australia ... 91 E3
Werris Creek, Australia . 91 E5
Wersar, Indonesia 57 E8
Wertach →, Germany .. 19 G6
Wertheim, Germany 19 F5
Wertingen, Germany ... 19 G6
Wervershoof, Neths. ... 16 C6
Wervik, Belgium 17 G2
Wesel, Germany 18 D2
Weser →, Germany 18 B4
Wesiri, Indonesia 57 F7
Wesley Vale, U.S.A. ... 111 J10
Wesleyville, Canada ... 99 C9
Wesleyville, U.S.A. 106 D4
Wessel, C., Australia ... 90 A2
Wessel Is., Australia ... 90 A2
Wesselburen, Germany . 18 A4
Wessem, Neths. 17 F7
Wessington, U.S.A. 108 C5
Wessington Springs, U.S.A. 108 C5
West, U.S.A. 109 K6
West B., U.S.A. 109 L10
West Baines →, Australia 88 C4
West Bend, U.S.A. 104 D1
West Bengal □, India .. 63 H12
West Beskids = Západné
Beskydy, Europe 20 F9
West Branch, U.S.A. ... 104 C3
West Bromwich, U.K. .. 13 E5
West Cape Howe, Australia 89 G2
West Chazy, U.S.A. 107 B11
West Chester, U.S.A. ... 104 F8
West Columbia, U.S.A. . 109 L7
West Covina, U.S.A. ... 113 L9
West Des Moines, U.S.A. 108 E8
West End, Bahamas 116 A4
West Falkland, Falk. Is. . 128 D4
West Fjord = Vestfjorden,
Norway 8 C13
West Frankfort, U.S.A. . 108 G10
West Glamorgan □, U.K. 13 F4
West Hartford, U.S.A. .. 107 E12
West Haven, U.S.A. 107 E12

West Helena, U.S.A. 109 H9
West Ice Shelf, Antarctica 5 C7
West Indies, Cent. Amer. . 117 C7
West Lorne, Canada ... 106 D3
West Lunga →, Zambia . 83 E1
West Memphis, U.S.A. .. 109 H9
West Midlands □, U.K. . 13 E6
West Mifflin, U.S.A. ... 106 F5
West Monroe, U.S.A. ... 109 J8
West Newton, U.S.A. ... 106 F5
West Nicholson, Zimbabwe 83 G2
West Palm Beach, U.S.A. 105 M5
West Plains, U.S.A. 109 G9
West Pt. = Ouest, Pte.,
Canada 99 C7
West Pt., Australia 91 F2
West Point, Ga., U.S.A. . 105 J3
West Point, Miss., U.S.A. 105 J1
West Point, Nebr., U.S.A. 108 E6
West Point, Va., U.S.A. . 104 G7
West Pokot □, Kenya .. 82 B4
West Road →, Canada . 100 C4
West Rutland, U.S.A. ... 107 C11
West Schelde =
Westerschelde →, Neths. 17 F2
West Seneca, U.S.A. ... 106 D6
West Siberian Plain, Russia 46 C11
West Sussex □, U.K. ... 13 G7
West-Terschelling, Neths. 16 B6
West Virginia □, U.S.A. . 104 F5
West-Vlaanderen □,
Belgium 17 G2
West Walker →, U.S.A. . 112 G7
West Wyalong, Australia 91 E4
West Yellowstone, U.S.A. 110 D8
West Yorkshire □, U.K. . 12 D6
Westall Pt., Australia .. 91 E1
Westbrook, Maine, U.S.A. 105 D10
Westbrook, Tex., U.S.A. 109 J4
Westbury, Australia ... 90 G4
Westby, U.S.A. 108 A2
Westend, U.S.A. 113 K9
Westerbork, Neths. 16 C9
Westerland, Germany .. 18 A4
Western □, Kenya 82 B3
Western □, Uganda 82 B3
Western □, Zambia 83 F1
Western Australia □,
Australia 89 E2
Western Ghats, India .. 60 N9
Western Isles □, U.K. .. 14 D1
Western Sahara ■, Africa 74 D2
Western Samoa ■,
Pac. Oc. 87 A13
Westernport, U.S.A. ... 104 F6
Westerschelde →, Neths. 17 F2
Westerstede, Germany . 18 B3
Westervoort, Neths. ... 16 E7
Westerwald, Germany .. 18 E4
Westfield, Mass., U.S.A. 107 D12
Westfield, N.Y., U.S.A. . 106 D5
Westfield, Pa., U.S.A. .. 106 E7
Westgat, Neths. 17 E3
Westhope, U.S.A. 108 A4
Westkapelle, Belgium .. 17 F2
Westkapelle, Neths. ... 17 E2
Westland Bight, N.Z. ... 87 K3
Westlock, Canada 100 C6
Westmalle, Belgium ... 17 F5
Westmeath □, Ireland .. 15 C4
Westminster, U.S.A. ... 104 F7
Westmorland, U.S.A. .. 111 K6
Weston, Malaysia 56 C5
Weston, Oreg., U.S.A. . 110 D4
Weston, W. Va., U.S.A. . 104 F5
Weston I., Canada 98 B4
Weston-super-Mare, U.K. 13 F5
Westport, Canada 107 B8
Westport, Ireland 15 C2
Westport, N.Z. 87 J3
Westport, Oreg., U.S.A. 112 D3
Westport, Wash., U.S.A. 110 C1
Westray, Canada 101 C8
Westray, U.K. 14 B6
Westree, Canada 98 C3
Westville, Calif., U.S.A. 112 F6
Westville, Ill., U.S.A. .. 104 E2
Westville, Okla., U.S.A. 109 G7
Westwood, U.S.A. 110 F3
Wetar, Indonesia 57 F7
Wetaskiwin, Canada ... 100 C6
Wethersfield, U.S.A. ... 107 E12
Wetteren, Belgium 17 G3
Wettingen, Switz. 23 B6
Wetzikon, Switz. 23 B7
Wetzlar, Germany 18 E4
Wevelgem, Belgium ... 17 G2
Wewoka, U.S.A. 109 H6
Wexford, Ireland 15 D5
Wexford □, Ireland 15 D5
Wexford Harbour, Ireland 15 D5
Weyburn, Canada 101 D8
Weyburn L., Canada ... 100 A5
Weyer, Austria 21 H4
Weyib →, Ethiopia 77 F5
Weymouth, Canada 99 D6
Weymouth, U.K. 13 G5
Weymouth, U.S.A. 107 D14
Weymouth, C., Australia 90 A3
Wezemaal, Belgium ... 17 G5
Wezep, Neths. 16 D7
Whakatane, N.Z. 87 G6
Whale →, Canada 99 A6
Whale Cove, Canada ... 101 A10
Whales, B. of, Antarctica 5 D12
Whalsay, U.K. 14 A7

Whangamomona, N.Z. ... 87 H5
Whangarei, N.Z. 87 F5
Whangarei Harb., N.Z. . 87 F5
Wharfe →, U.K. 12 D6
Wharfedale, U.K. 12 C5
Wharton, N.J., U.S.A. .. 107 F10
Wharton, Pa., U.S.A. .. 106 E6
Wharton, Tex., U.S.A. . 109 L6
Wheatland, Calif., U.S.A. 112 F5
Wheatland, Wyo., U.S.A. 108 D2
Wheatley, Canada 106 D2
Wheaton, U.S.A. 108 C6
Wheelbarrow Pk., U.S.A. 112 H10
Wheeler, Oreg., U.S.A. . 110 D2
Wheeler, Tex., U.S.A. .. 109 H4
Wheeler →, Canada ... 101 B7
Wheeler Pk., N. Mex.,
U.S.A. 111 H11
Wheeler Pk., Nev., U.S.A. 111 G6
Wheeler Ridge, U.S.A. . 113 L8
Wheeling, U.S.A. 106 F4
Whernside, U.K. 12 C5
Whidbey I., U.S.A. 100 D4
Whiskey Gap, Canada .. 100 D6
Whiskey Jack L., Canada . 101 B8
Whistleduck Cr. →,
Australia 90 C2
Whitby, Canada 106 C6
Whitby, U.K. 12 C7
White →, Ark., U.S.A. . 109 J9
White →, Ind., U.S.A. . 104 F2
White →, S. Dak., U.S.A. 108 D5
White →, Utah, U.S.A. . 110 F9
White →, Wash., U.S.A. 112 C4
White, L., Australia 88 D4
White B., Canada 99 B8
White Bear Res., Canada . 99 C8
White Bird, U.S.A. 110 D5
White Butte, U.S.A. ... 108 B3
White City, U.S.A. 108 F6
White Cliffs, Australia . 91 E3
White Deer, U.S.A. 109 H4
White Hall, U.S.A. 108 F9
White Haven, U.S.A. ... 107 E9
White I., N.Z. 87 G6
White L., Canada 107 A8
White L., U.S.A. 109 L8
White Mts., Calif., U.S.A. 111 H4
White Mts., N.H., U.S.A. 107 B13
White Nile = Nîl el
Abyad →, Sudan 77 D3
White Nile Dam =
Khazzân Jabal el Awliyâ,
Sudan 77 D3
White Otter L., Canada . 98 C1
White Pass, Canada ... 100 B1
White Pass, U.S.A. 112 D5
White Plains, U.S.A. ... 107 E11
White River, Canada ... 98 C2
White River, S. Africa .. 85 D5
White River, U.S.A. ... 108 D4
White Russia =
Belorussia ■, Europe .. 40 E5
White Sea = Beloye More,
Russia 44 C4
White Sulphur Springs,
Mont., U.S.A. 110 C8
White Sulphur Springs,
W. Va., U.S.A. 104 G5
White Swan, U.S.A. ... 112 D6
White Volta →, Ghana . 79 D4
Whitecliffs, N.Z. 87 K3
Whitecourt, Canada ... 100 C5
Whiteface, U.S.A. 109 J3
Whitefield, U.S.A. 107 B13
Whitefish, U.S.A. 110 B6
Whitefish L., Canada .. 101 A7
Whitefish Point, U.S.A. 104 B3
Whitegull, L., Canada .. 99 A7
Whitehall, Mich., U.S.A. 104 D2
Whitehall, Mont., U.S.A. 110 D7
Whitehall, N.Y., U.S.A. 107 C11
Whitehall, Wis., U.S.A. 108 C9
Whitehaven, U.K. 12 C4
Whitehorse, Canada ... 100 A1
Whitehorse, Vale of, U.K. 13 F6
Whitemark, Australia .. 90 G4
Whitemouth, Canada .. 101 D9
Whiteplains, Liberia ... 78 D2
Whitesboro, N.Y., U.S.A. 107 C9
Whitesboro, Tex., U.S.A. 109 J6
Whiteshell Prov. Park,
Canada 101 C9
Whiteside, Canal, Chile . 128 D2
Whitetail, U.S.A. 108 A2
Whiteville, U.S.A. 105 H6
Whitewater, U.S.A. 104 D1
Whitewater Baldy, U.S.A. 111 K9
Whitewater L., Canada . 98 B2
Whitewood, Australia .. 90 C3
Whitewood, Canada ... 101 C8
Whitfield, Australia ... 91 F4
Whithorn, U.K. 14 G4
Whitianga, N.Z. 87 G5
Whitman, U.S.A. 107 D14
Whitmire, U.S.A. 105 H5
Whitney, Canada 98 C4
Whitney, Mt., U.S.A. .. 111 H4
Whitney Point, U.S.A. . 107 D9
Whitstable, U.K. 13 F9
Whitsunday I., Australia 90 C4
Whittier, U.S.A. 113 M8
Whittlesea, Australia .. 91 F4
Whitwell, U.S.A. 105 H3
Wholdaia L., Canada .. 101 A8
Whyalla, Australia 91 E2

Whyjonta, Australia ... 91 D3
Wiarton, Canada 98 D3
Wiawso, Ghana 78 D4
Wibaux, U.S.A. 108 B2
Wichabai, Guyana 121 C6
Wichian Buri, Thailand . 58 E3
Wichita, U.S.A. 109 G6
Wichita Falls, U.S.A. .. 109 J5
Wick, U.K. 14 C5
Wickenburg, U.S.A. ... 111 K7
Wickepin, Australia ... 89 F2
Wickham, C., Australia 90 F3
Wickliffe, U.S.A. 106 E3
Wicklow, Ireland 15 D5
Wicklow □, Ireland ... 15 D5
Wicklow Hd., Ireland .. 15 D5
Widgiemooltha, Australia 89 F3
Widnes, U.K. 12 D5
Wiedenbrück, Germany . 18 D4
Wiek, Germany 18 A9
Wielbark, Poland 20 B10
Wieliczka, Poland 20 F10
Wieluń, Poland 20 D8
Wien, Austria 21 G6
Wiener Neustadt, Austria . 21 H6
Wieprz →, Koszalin,
Poland 20 A6
Wieprz →, Lublin, Poland 20 D11
Wierden, Neths. 16 D9
Wiers, Belgium 17 H3
Wiesbaden, Germany .. 19 E4
Wiesental, Germany ... 19 F4
Wigan, U.K. 12 D5
Wiggins, Colo., U.S.A. . 108 E2
Wiggins, Miss., U.S.A. . 109 K10
Wight, I. of □, U.K. ... 13 G6
Wigston, U.K. 13 E6
Wigton, U.K. 12 C4
Wigtown, U.K. 14 G4
Wigtown B., U.K. 14 G4
Wijchen, Neths. 16 E7
Wijhe, Neths. 16 D8
Wijk bij Duurstede, Neths. 16 E6
Wil, Switz. 23 B8
Wilber, U.S.A. 108 E6
Wilberforce, Canada ... 106 A6
Wilberforce, C., Australia 90 A2
Wilburton, U.S.A. 109 H7
Wilcannia, Australia .. 91 E3
Wilcox, U.S.A. 106 E6
Wildbad, Germany 19 G4
Wildeshausen, Germany 18 C4
Wildhorn, Switz. 22 D4
Wildrose, Calif., U.S.A. 113 J9
Wildrose, N. Dak., U.S.A. 108 A3
Wildspitze, Austria ... 19 J6
Wildstrubel, Switz. 22 D5
Wildwood, U.S.A. 104 F8
Wilge →, S. Africa 85 D4
Wilhelm II Coast,
Antarctica 5 C7
Wilhelm-Pieck-Stadt
Guben, Germany 18 D10
Wilhelmina, Geb., Surinam 121 C6
Wilhelmina Kanaal, Neths. 17 E6
Wilhelmsburg, Austria . 21 G5
Wilhelmshaven, Germany 18 B4
Wilhelmstal, Namibia .. 84 C2
Wilkes-Barre, U.S.A. .. 107 E9
Wilkesboro, U.S.A. 105 G5
Wilkie, Canada 101 C7
Wilkinsburg, U.S.A. ... 106 F5
Wilkinson Lakes, Australia 89 E5
Willamina, U.S.A. 110 D2
Willandra Billabong
Creek →, Australia .. 91 E4
Willapa B., U.S.A. 110 C2
Willapa Hills, U.S.A. .. 112 D3
Willard, N. Mex., U.S.A. 111 J10
Willard, Utah, U.S.A. .. 110 F7
Willcox, U.S.A. 111 K9
Willebroek, Belgium ... 17 F4
Willemstad, Neth. Ant. 117 D6
Willeroo, Australia 88 C5
William →, Canada ... 101 B7
William Creek, Australia 91 D2
Williams, Australia 89 F2
Williams, Ariz., U.S.A. 111 J7
Williams, Calif., U.S.A. 112 F4
Williams Lake, Canada . 100 C4
Williamsburg, Ky., U.S.A. 105 G3
Williamsburg, Pa., U.S.A. 106 F6
Williamsburg, Va., U.S.A. 104 G7
Williamson, N.Y., U.S.A. 106 C7
Williamson, W. Va.,
U.S.A. 104 G4
Williamsport, U.S.A. .. 106 E7
Williamston, U.S.A. ... 105 H7
Williamstown, Australia 91 F3
Williamstown, Mass.,
U.S.A. 107 D11
Williamstown, N.Y.,
U.S.A. 107 C9
Williamsville, U.S.A. .. 109 G9
Willimantic, U.S.A. ... 107 E12
Willis Group, Australia 90 B5
Willisau, Switz. 22 B6
Williston, S. Africa 84 E3
Williston, Fla., U.S.A. . 105 L4
Williston, N. Dak., U.S.A. 108 A3
Williston L., Canada .. 100 B4
Willits, U.S.A. 110 G2
Willmar, U.S.A. 108 C7
Willoughby, U.S.A. 106 E3
Willow Bunch, Canada . 101 D7
Willow L., Canada 100 A5

Willow Lake, U.S.A. ... 108 C6
Willow Springs, U.S.A. 109 G8
Willow Wall, The, China . 51 C12
Willowlake →, Canada . 100 A4
Willowmore, S. Africa . 84 E3
Willows, Australia 90 C4
Willows, U.S.A. 112 F4
Willowvale = Gatyana,
S. Africa 85 E4
Wills, L., Australia 88 D4
Wills Cr. →, Australia . 90 C3
Wills Point, U.S.A. 109 J7
Willunga, Australia ... 91 F2
Wilmette, U.S.A. 104 D2
Wilmington, Australia . 91 E2
Wilmington, Del., U.S.A. 104 F8
Wilmington, Ill., U.S.A. 104 E1
Wilmington, N.C., U.S.A. 105 H7
Wilmington, Ohio, U.S.A. 104 F4
Wilpena Cr. →, Australia 91 E2
Wilrijk, Belgium 17 F4
Wilsall, U.S.A. 110 D8
Wilson, U.S.A. 105 H7
Wilson →, Queens.,
Australia 91 D3
Wilson →, W. Austral.,
Australia 88 C4
Wilson Bluff, Australia . 89 F4
Wilsons Promontory,
Australia 91 F4
Wilster, Germany 18 B5
Wilton, U.K. 13 F6
Wilton, U.S.A. 108 B4
Wilton →, Australia ... 90 A1
Wiltshire □, U.K. 13 F6
Wiltz, Lux. 17 J7
Wiluna, Australia 89 E3
Wimereux, France 25 B8
Wimmera →, Australia 91 F3
Winam G., Kenya 82 C3
Winburg, S. Africa 84 D4
Winchendon, U.S.A. ... 107 D12
Winchester, U.K. 13 F6
Winchester, Conn., U.S.A. 107 E11
Winchester, Idaho, U.S.A. 110 C5
Winchester, Ky., U.S.A. 104 G3
Winchester, N.H., U.S.A. 107 D12
Winchester, Nev., U.S.A. 113 J11
Winchester, Tenn., U.S.A. 105 H2
Winchester, Va., U.S.A. 104 F6
Wind →, U.S.A. 110 E9
Wind River Range, U.S.A. 110 E9
Windau = Ventspils, Latvia 9 H16
Windber, U.S.A. 106 F6
Windermere, L., U.K. .. 12 C5
Windfall, Canada 100 C5
Windflower L., Canada . 100 A5
Windhoek, Namibia ... 84 C2
Windom, U.S.A. 108 D7
Windorah, Australia ... 90 D3
Window Rock, U.S.A. . 111 J9
Windrush →, U.K. 13 F6
Windsor, Australia 91 E5
Windsor, N.S., Canada . 99 D7
Windsor, Nfld., Canada . 99 C8
Windsor, Ont., Canada . 98 D3
Windsor, U.K. 13 F7
Windsor, Colo., U.S.A. . 108 E2
Windsor, Conn., U.S.A. 107 E12
Windsor, Mo., U.S.A. . 108 F8
Windsor, N.Y., U.S.A. . 107 D9
Windsor, Vt., U.S.A. .. 107 C12
Windsorton, S. Africa .. 84 D3
Windward Is., W. Indies 117 D7
Windward Passage =
Vientos, Paso de los,
Caribbean 117 C5
Windy L., Canada 101 A8
Winefred L., Canada .. 101 B6
Winejok, Sudan 77 F2
Winfield, U.S.A. 109 G6
Wingate Mts., Australia 88 B5
Wingen, Australia 91 E5
Wingene, Belgium 17 F2
Wingham, Australia ... 91 E5
Wingham, Canada 98 D3
Winifred, U.S.A. 110 C9
Winisk, Canada 98 A2
Winisk →, Canada 98 A2
Winisk L., Canada 98 B2
Wink, U.S.A. 109 K3
Winkler, Canada 101 D9
Winlock, U.S.A. 112 D4
Winneba, Ghana 79 D4
Winnebago, U.S.A. 108 D7
Winnebago, L., U.S.A. . 104 D1
Winnecke Cr. →, Australia 88 C5
Winnemucca, U.S.A. .. 110 F5
Winnemucca L., U.S.A. 110 F4
Winner, U.S.A. 108 D5
Winnett, U.S.A. 110 C9
Winnfield, U.S.A. 109 K8
Winnibigoshish, L., U.S.A. 108 B7
Winning, Australia 88 D1
Winnipeg, Canada 101 D9
Winnipeg, L., Canada .. 101 C9
Winnipeg Beach, Canada 101 C9
Winnipegosis, Canada . 101 C9
Winnipegosis L., Canada 101 C9
Winnipesaukee, L., U.S.A. 107 C13
Winnsboro, La., U.S.A. 109 J9
Winnsboro, S.C., U.S.A. 105 H5
Winnsboro, Tex., U.S.A. 109 J7
Winokapau, L., Canada . 99 B7

Winona, *Minn., U.S.A.* 108 C9
Winona, *Miss., U.S.A.* ... 109 J10
Winooski, *U.S.A.* 107 B11
Winschoten, *Neths.* 16 B10
Winsen, *Germany* 18 B6
Winslow, *Ariz., U.S.A.* ... 111 J8
Winslow, *Wash., U.S.A.* .. 112 C4
Winsted, *U.S.A.* 107 E11
Winston-Salem, *U.S.A.* .. 105 G5
Winter Garden, *U.S.A.* .. 105 L5
Winter Haven, *U.S.A.* ... 105 M5
Winter Park, *U.S.A.* 105 L5
Winterberg, *Germany* ... 18 D4
Winterhaven, *U.S.A.* 113 N12
Winters, *Calif., U.S.A.* .. 112 G5
Winters, *Tex., U.S.A.* ... 109 K5
Winterset, *U.S.A.* 108 E7
Wintersville, *U.S.A.* 106 F4
Winterswijk, *Neths.* 16 E9
Winterthur, *Switz.* 23 B7
Winthrop, *Minn., U.S.A.* . 108 C7
Winthrop, *Wash., U.S.A.* . 110 B3
Winton, *Australia* 90 C3
Winton, *N.Z.* 87 M2
Winton, *U.S.A.* 105 G7
Wintzenheim, *France* 25 D14
Wipper →, *Germany* 18 D7
Wirral, *U.K.* 12 D4
Wirrulla, *Australia* 91 E1
Wisbech, *U.K.* 12 E8
Wisconsin □, *U.S.A.* 108 C10
Wisconsin →, *U.S.A.* 108 D9
Wisconsin Dells, *U.S.A.* . 108 D10
Wisconsin Rapids, *U.S.A.* 108 C10
Wisdom, *U.S.A.* 110 D7
Wishaw, *U.K.* 14 F5
Wishek, *U.S.A.* 108 B5
Wisła, *Poland* 20 F8
Wisła →, *Poland* 20 A8
Wisłok →, *Poland* 20 E12
Wisłoka →, *Poland* 20 E11
Wismar, *Germany* 18 B7
Wismar, *Guyana* 121 B6
Wisner, *U.S.A.* 108 E6
Wissant, *France* 25 B8
Wissembourg, *France* ... 25 C14
Wissenkerke, *Neths.* 17 E3
Witbank, *S. Africa* 85 D4
Witdraai, *S. Africa* 84 D3
Witham →, *U.K.* 12 D7
Witham, *U.K.* 12 D8
Withernsea, *U.K.* 12 D8
Witmarsum, *Neths.* 16 B6
Witney, *U.K.* 13 F6
Witnossob →, *Namibia* .. 84 D3
Wittdün, *Germany* 18 A4
Witten, *Germany* 17 F10
Wittenberg, *Germany* ... 18 D8
Wittenberge, *Germany* .. 18 B7
Wittenburg, *Germany* ... 18 B7
Wittenoom, *Australia* ... 88 D2
Wittingen, *Germany* 18 C6
Wittlich, *Germany* 19 F2
Wittmund, *Germany* 18 B3
Wittow, *Germany* 18 A9
Wittstock, *Germany* 18 B8
Witzenhausen, *Germany* . 18 D5
Wlingi, *Indonesia* 57 H15
Włocławek, *Poland* 20 C9
Włodawa, *Poland* 20 D13
Włoszczowa, *Poland* 20 E9
Woburn, *U.S.A.* 107 D13
Wodian, *China* 50 H7
Wodonga, *Australia* 91 F4
Woerden, *Neths.* 16 D5
Woerth, *France* 25 D14
Woëvre, *France* 25 C12
Wognum, *Neths.* 16 C6
Wohlen, *Switz.* 23 B6
Woinbogoin, *China* 52 A2
Wokam, *Indonesia* 57 F8
Wolbrom, *Poland* 20 E9
Woldegk, *Germany* 18 B9
Wolf →, *Canada* 100 A2
Wolf Creek, *U.S.A.* 110 C7
Wolf L., *Canada* 100 A2
Wolf Point, *U.S.A.* 108 A2
Wolfe I., *Canada* 98 D4
Wolfenbüttel, *Germany* .. 18 C6
Wolfheze, *Neths.* 16 D7
Wolfsberg, *Austria* 21 J4
Wolfsburg, *Germany* 18 C6
Wolgast, *Germany* 18 A9
Wolhusen, *Switz.* 22 B6
Wolin, *Poland* 20 B4
Wollaston, Is., *Chile* 128 E3
Wollaston L., *Canada* ... 101 B8
Wollaston Pen., *Canada* . 96 B8
Wollogorang, *Australia* .. 90 B2
Wollongong, *Australia* .. 91 E5
Wolmaransstad, *S. Africa* 84 D4
Wolmirstedt, *Germany* .. 18 C7
Wolseley, *Australia* 91 F3
Wolseley, *Canada* 101 C8
Wolseley, *S. Africa* 84 E2
Wolstenholme, C., *Canada* 94 C12
Wolsztyn, *Poland* 20 C6
Wolvega, *Neths.* 16 C7
Wolverhampton, *U.K.* ... 13 E5
Wommels, *Neths.* 16 B7
Wonarah, *Australia* 90 B2
Wonck, *Belgium* 17 G7
Wondai, *Australia* 91 D5
Wondelgem, *Belgium* ... 17 F3
Wongan Hills, *Australia* . 89 F2

Wongawol, *Australia* 89 E3
Wŏnju, *S. Korea* 51 F14
Wonosari, *Indonesia* 57 G14
Wŏnsan, *N. Korea* 51 E14
Wonthaggi, *Australia* ... 91 F4
Woocalla, *Australia* 91 E2
Wood Buffalo Nat. Park,
  Canada 100 B6
Wood Is., *Australia* 88 C3
Wood L., *Canada* 101 B8
Wood Lake, *U.S.A.* 108 D4
Woodah I., *Australia* 90 A2
Woodanilling, *Australia* . 89 F2
Woodbridge, *Canada* 106 C5
Woodburn, *Australia* ... 91 D5
Woodenbong, *Australia* . 91 D5
Woodend, *Australia* 91 F3
Woodfords, *U.S.A.* 112 G7
Woodgreen, *Australia* ... 90 C1
Woodlake, *U.S.A.* 112 J7
Woodland, *U.S.A.* 112 G5
Woodlands, *Australia* ... 88 D2
Woodpecker, *Canada* 100 C4
Woodridge, *Canada* 101 D9
Woodroffe, Mt., *Australia* 89 E5
Woodruff, *Ariz., U.S.A.* .. 111 J8
Woodruff, *Utah, U.S.A.* .. 110 F8
Woods, L., *Australia* 90 B1
Woods, L., *Canada* 99 B6
Woods, L. of the, *Canada* 101 D10
Woodstock, *Queens.,
  Australia* 90 B4
Woodstock, *W. Austral.,
  Australia* 88 D2
Woodstock, *N.B., Canada* 99 C6
Woodstock, *Ont., Canada* 98 D3
Woodstock, *U.K.* 13 F6
Woodstock, *Ill., U.S.A.* .. 108 D10
Woodstock, *Vt., U.S.A.* .. 107 C12
Woodsville, *U.S.A.* 107 B13
Woodville, *N.Z.* 87 J5
Woodville, *U.S.A.* 109 K7
Woodward, *U.S.A.* 109 G5
Woody, *U.S.A.* 113 K8
Woolamai, C., *Australia* . 91 F4
Woolgoolga, *Australia* .. 91 E5
Woombye, *Australia* 91 D5
Woomera, *Australia* 91 E2
Woonsocket, *R.I., U.S.A.* 107 D13
Woonsocket, *S. Dak.,
  U.S.A.* 108 C5
Wooramel, *Australia* 89 E1
Wooramel →, *Australia* . 89 E1
Wooroloo, *Australia* 89 F2
Wooster, *U.S.A.* 106 F3
Worb, *Switz.* 22 C5
Worcester, *S. Africa* 84 E2
Worcester, *U.K.* 13 E5
Worcester, *Mass., U.S.A.* 107 D13
Worcester, *N.Y., U.S.A.* . 107 D10
Wörgl, *Austria* 19 H8
Workington, *U.K.* 12 C4
Worksop, *U.K.* 12 D6
Workum, *Neths.* 16 C6
Worland, *U.S.A.* 110 D10
Wormerveer, *Neths.* 16 D5
Wormhoudt, *France* 25 B9
Worms, *Germany* 19 F4
Wörth, *Germany* 19 F8
Wortham, *U.S.A.* 109 K6
Worthing, *U.K.* 13 G7
Worthington, *U.S.A.* 108 D7
Wosi, *Indonesia* 57 E7
Wou-han = Wuhan, *China* 53 B10
Woubrugge, *Neths.* 16 D5
Woudenberg, *Neths.* 16 D6
Woudsend, *Neths.* 16 C7
Wour, *Chad* 73 D8
Wousi = Wuxi, *China* ... 53 B13
Wouw, *Neths.* 17 E4
Wowoni, *Indonesia* 57 E6
Woy Woy, *Australia* 91 E5
Wrangel I. = Vrangelya,
  Ostrov, *Russia* 45 B19
Wrangell, *U.S.A.* 96 C6
Wrangell I., *U.S.A.* 100 B2
Wrangell Mts., *U.S.A.* .. 96 B5
Wrath, C., *U.K.* 14 C3
Wray, *U.S.A.* 108 E3
Wrekin, The, *U.K.* 12 E5
Wrens, *U.S.A.* 105 J4
Wrexham, *U.K.* 12 D4
Wriezen, *Germany* 18 C10
Wright, *Canada* 100 C4
Wright, *Phil.* 55 F6
Wrightson Mt., *U.S.A.* .. 111 L8
Wrightwood, *U.S.A.* 113 L9
Wrigley, *Canada* 96 B7
Wrocław, *Poland* 20 D7
Września, *Poland* 20 C7
Wschowa, *Poland* 20 D6
Wu Jiang →, *China* 52 C6
Wu'an, *China* 50 F8
Wubin, *Australia* 89 F2
Wubu, *China* 50 F6
Wuchang, *China* 51 B14
Wucheng, *China* 50 F9
Wuchuan, *Guangdong,
  China* 53 G8
Wuchuan, *Guizhou, China* 52 C7
Wuchuan,
  *Nei Mongol Zizhiqu,
  China* 50 D6
Wudi, *China* 51 F9
Wuding, *China* 52 E4

Wuding He →, *China* ... 50 F6
Wudu, *China* 50 H3
Wufeng, *China* 53 B8
Wugang, *China* 53 D8
Wugong Shan, *China* ... 53 D9
Wuhan, *China* 53 B10
Wuhe, *China* 51 H9
Wuhsi = Wuxi, *China* ... 53 B13
Wuhu, *China* 53 B12
Wujiang, *China* 53 B13
Wukari, *Nigeria* 79 D6
Wulajie, *China* 51 B14
Wulanbulang, *China* 50 D6
Wulehe, *Ghana* 79 D5
Wulian, *China* 51 G10
Wuliang Shan, *China* ... 52 E3
Wuliaru, *Indonesia* 57 F8
Wulumuchi = Ürümqi,
  China 44 E9
Wum, *Cameroon* 79 D7
Wuming, *China* 52 F7
Wuning, *China* 53 C10
Wunnummin L., *Canada* . 98 B2
Wunsiedel, *Germany* 19 E8
Wunstorf, *Germany* 18 C5
Wuntho, *Burma* 61 H19
Wuping, *China* 53 E11
Wuppertal, *Germany* ... 18 D3
Wuppertal, *S. Africa* 84 E2
Wuqing, *China* 51 E9
Würenlingen, *Switz.* 23 A6
Wurung, *Australia* 90 B3
Würzburg, *Germany* 19 F5
Wurzen, *Germany* 18 D8
Wushan, *Gansu, China* .. 50 G3
Wushan, *Sichuan, China* . 52 B7
Wusuli Jiang = Ussuri →,
  Asia 48 A7
Wutach →, *Germany* 19 H4
Wutai, *China* 50 E7
Wuting = Huimin, *China* . 51 F9
Wutong, *China* 53 E8
Wutonghaolai, *China* ... 51 C11
Wutongqiao, *China* 52 C4
Wuustwezel, *Belgium* ... 17 F5
Wuwei, *Anhui, China* ... 53 B11
Wuwei, *Gansu, China* ... 54 C5
Wuxi, *Jiangsu, China* ... 53 B13
Wuxi, *Sichuan, China* ... 52 B7
Wuxiang, *China* 50 F7
Wuxing, *China* 53 B13
Wuxuan, *China* 52 F7
Wuyang, *China* 50 H7
Wuyi, *Hebei, China* 50 F8
Wuyi, *Zhejiang, China* .. 53 C12
Wuyi Shan, *China* 53 D11
Wuyo, *Nigeria* 79 C7
Wuyuan, *Jiangxi, China* . 53 C11
Wuyuan,
  *Nei Mongol Zizhiqu,
  China* 50 D5
Wuzhai, *China* 50 E6
Wuzhi Shan, *China* 54 E5
Wuzhong, *China* 50 E4
Wuzhou, *China* 53 F8
Wyaaba Cr. →, *Australia* 90 B3
Wyalkatchem, *Australia* . 89 F2
Wyalusing, *U.S.A.* 107 E8
Wyandotte, *U.S.A.* 104 D4
Wyandra, *Australia* 91 D4
Wyangala Res., *Australia* 91 E4
Wyara, L., *Australia* 91 D3
Wycheproof, *Australia* .. 91 F3
Wye →, *U.K.* 13 F5
Wyemandoo, *Australia* .. 89 E2
Wyk, *Germany* 18 A4
Wymondham, *U.K.* 13 E7
Wymore, *U.S.A.* 108 E6
Wynbring, *Australia* 91 E1
Wyndham, *Australia* 88 C4
Wyndham, *N.Z.* 87 M2
Wyndmere, *U.S.A.* 108 B6
Wynne, *U.S.A.* 109 H9
Wynnum, *Australia* 91 D5
Wynyard, *Australia* 90 G4
Wynyard, *Canada* 101 C8
Wyola, L., *Australia* 89 E5
Wyoming □, *U.S.A.* 110 E10
Wyong, *Australia* 91 E5
Wyszków, *Poland* 20 C11
Wyszogród, *Poland* 20 C10
Wytheville, *U.S.A.* 104 G5

X

Xai-Xai, *Mozam.* 85 D5
Xainza, *China* 54 C3
Xambioá, *Brazil* 122 C2
Xangongo, *Angola* 84 B2
Xanten, *Germany* 18 D2
Xánthi, *Greece* 39 H7
Xanthos, *Turkey* 66 E3
Xapuri, *Brazil* 124 C4
Xar Moron He →, *China* 51 C11
Xau, L., *Botswana* 84 C3
Xavantina, *Brazil* 127 A5
Xenia, *U.S.A.* 104 F4
Xeropotamos →, *Cyprus* 37 E11
Xhora, *S. Africa* 85 E4
Xhumo, *Botswana* 84 C3
Xi Jiang →, *China* 53 F9
Xi Xian, *Henan, China* .. 53 A10
Xi Xian, *Shanxi, China* .. 50 F6

Xia Xian, *China* 50 G6
Xiachengzi, *China* 51 B16
Xiachuan Dao, *China* ... 53 G9
Xiaguan, *China* 52 E3
Xiajiang, *China* 53 D10
Xiajin, *China* 50 F8
Xiamen, *China* 53 E12
Xi'an, *China* 50 G5
Xian Xian, *China* 50 E9
Xianfeng, *China* 52 C7
Xiang Jiang →, *China* .. 53 C9
Xiangcheng, *Henan, China* 50 H8
Xiangcheng, *Henan, China* 50 H7
Xiangcheng, *Sichuan,
  China* 52 C2
Xiangdu, *China* 52 F6
Xiangfan, *China* 53 A9
Xianghuang Qi, *China* .. 50 C7
Xiangning, *China* 50 G6
Xiangquan, *China* 50 F7
Xiangshan, *China* 53 C13
Xiangshui, *China* 51 G10
Xiangtan, *China* 53 D9
Xiangxiang, *China* 53 D9
Xiangyin, *China* 53 C9
Xiangyun, *China* 52 E3
Xiangzhou, *China* 52 F7
Xianju, *China* 53 C13
Xianning, *China* 53 C10
Xianshui He →, *China* .. 52 B3
Xianyang, *China* 50 G5
Xianyou, *China* 53 E12
Xiao Hinggan Ling, *China* 54 B7
Xiao Xian, *China* 50 G9
Xiaofeng, *China* 53 B12
Xiaogan, *China* 53 B9
Xiaojin, *China* 52 B4
Xiaolan, *China* 53 F9
Xiaoshan, *China* 53 B13
Xiaoyi, *China* 50 F6
Xiapu, *China* 53 D12
Xiawa, *China* 51 C11
Xiayi, *China* 50 G9
Xichang, *China* 52 D4
Xichong, *China* 52 B5
Xichuan, *China* 50 H6
Xiemahe, *China* 53 B8
Xieng Khouang, *Laos* ... 58 C4
Xifei He →, *China* 50 H9
Xifeng, *Guizhou, China* . 52 D6
Xifeng, *Liaoning, China* . 51 C13
Xifengzhen, *China* 50 G4
Xigazê, *China* 54 D3
Xihe, *China* 50 G3
Xihua, *China* 50 H8
Xiliao He →, *China* 51 C12
Xilin, *China* 52 E5
Xilókastron, *Greece* 39 L5
Xin Jiang →, *China* 53 C11
Xin Xian, *China* 50 E7
Xinavane, *Mozam.* 85 D5
Xinbin, *China* 51 D13
Xincai, *China* 53 A10
Xinchang, *China* 53 C13
Xincheng,
  *Guangxi Zhuangzu,
  China* 52 E7
Xincheng, *Jiangxi, China* 53 D10
Xinfeng, *Guangdong,
  China* 53 E10
Xinfeng, *Jiangxi, China* . 53 D11
Xinfeng, *Jiangxi, China* . 53 E10
Xing Xian, *China* 50 E6
Xing'an,
  *Guangxi Zhuangzu,
  China* 53 E8
Xingan, *Jiangxi, China* .. 53 D10
Xingcheng, *China* 51 D11
Xingguo, *China* 53 D10
Xinghe, *China* 50 D7
Xinghua, *China* 51 H10
Xinghua Wan, *China* ... 53 E12
Xinglong, *China* 51 D9
Xingning, *China* 53 E10
Xingping, *China* 50 G5
Xingren, *China* 52 E5
Xingshan, *China* 53 B8
Xingtai, *China* 50 F8
Xingu →, *Brazil* 121 D7
Xingyang, *China* 50 G7
Xinhe, *China* 50 F8
Xinhua, *China* 53 D8
Xinhuang, *China* 52 D7
Xinhui, *China* 53 F9
Xining, *China* 54 C5
Xinjiang, *China* 50 G6
Xinjiang Uygur Zizhiqu □,
  China 54 B3
Xinjie, *China* 52 D3
Xinjin, *Liaoning, China* . 51 E11
Xinjin, *Sichuan, China* .. 52 B4
Xinkai He →, *China* 51 C12
Xinle, *China* 50 E8
Xinlitun, *China* 51 D12
Xinlong, *China* 52 B3
Xinmin, *China* 51 D12
Xinning, *China* 53 D8
Xinping, *China* 52 E3
Xinshao, *China* 53 D8
Xintai, *China* 51 G9
Xintian, *China* 53 E9
Xinxiang, *China* 50 G7
Xinxing, *China* 53 F9
Xinyang, *China* 53 A10
Xinye, *China* 53 A9
Xinyi, *China* 53 F8

Xinyu, *China* 53 D10
Xinzhan, *China* 51 C14
Xinzheng, *China* 50 G7
Xinzhou, *China* 53 B10
Xinzhu, *Taiwan* 53 E13
Xiong Xian, *China* 50 E9
Xiongyuecheng, *China* .. 51 D12
Xiping, *Henan, China* ... 50 H8
Xiping, *Henan, China* ... 50 H6
Xiping, *Zhejiang, China* . 53 C12
Xique-Xique, *Brazil* 122 D3
Xiruá →, *Brazil* 124 B4
Xisha Qundao = Hsisha
  Chuntao, *Pac. Oc.* 56 A4
Xishui, *China* 53 B10
Xituozhen, *China* 52 B7
Xiuning, *China* 53 C12
Xiuren, *China* 53 E8
Xiushan, *China* 52 C7
Xiushui, *China* 53 C10
Xiuwen, *China* 52 D6
Xiuyan, *China* 51 D12
Xixabangma Feng, *China* 61 E14
Xixia, *China* 50 H6
Xixiang, *China* 50 H4
Xiyang, *China* 50 F7
Xizang □, *China* 54 C3
Xlendi, *Malta* 37 C1
Xu Jiang →, *China* 53 D11
Xuan Loc, *Vietnam* 59 G6
Xuancheng, *China* 53 B12
Xuan'en, *China* 52 C7
Xuanhan, *China* 52 B6
Xuanhua, *China* 50 D8
Xuchang, *China* 50 G7
Xuefeng Shan, *China* ... 53 D8
Xuejiaping, *China* 53 B8
Xun Jiang →, *China* 53 F8
Xun Xian, *China* 50 G8
Xundian, *China* 52 E4
Xunwu, *China* 53 E10
Xunyang, *China* 50 H5
Xunyi, *China* 50 G5
Xupu, *China* 53 D8
Xushui, *China* 50 E8
Xuwen, *China* 53 G8
Xuyen Moc, *Vietnam* ... 59 G6
Xuyong, *China* 52 C5
Xuzhou, *China* 51 G9
Xylophagou, *Cyprus* 37 E12

Y

Ya Xian, *China* 58 C7
Yaamba, *Australia* 90 C5
Ya'an, *China* 52 C4
Yaapeet, *Australia* 91 F3
Yabassi, *Cameroon* 79 E6
Yabelo, *Ethiopia* 77 G4
Yablonovy Khrebet, *Russia* 45 D12
Yablonovy Ra. =
  Yablonovy Khrebet,
  Russia 45 D12
Yabrai Shan, *China* 50 E2
Yabrūd, *Syria* 69 B5
Yacuiba, *Bolivia* 126 A3
Yacuma →, *Bolivia* 125 C4
Yadgir, *India* 60 L10
Yadkin →, *U.S.A.* 105 H5
Yadrin, *Russia* 41 D15
Yagaba, *Ghana* 79 C4
Yagodnoye, *Russia* 45 C15
Yagoua, *Cameroon* 80 B3
Yaguas →, *Peru* 120 D3
Yaha, *Thailand* 59 J3
Yahila, *Zaïre* 82 B1
Yahk, *Canada* 100 D5
Yahuma, *Zaïre* 80 D4
Yahyalı, *Turkey* 66 D6
Yaita, *Japan* 49 F9
Yaiza, *Canary Is.* 36 F6
Yajiang, *China* 52 B3
Yajua, *Nigeria* 79 C7
Yakima, *U.S.A.* 110 C3
Yakima →, *U.S.A.* 110 C3
Yako, *Burkina Faso* 78 C4
Yakoruda, *Bulgaria* 39 G6
Yakovlevka, *Russia* 48 B6
Yaku-Shima, *Japan* 49 J5
Yakut Republic □, *Russia* 45 C13
Yakutat, *U.S.A.* 96 C6
Yakutsk, *Russia* 45 C13
Yala, *Thailand* 59 J3
Yalbalgo, *Australia* 89 E1
Yalboroo, *Australia* 90 C4
Yale, *U.S.A.* 106 C2
Yalgoo, *Australia* 89 E2
Yalinga, *C.A.R.* 73 G9
Yalkubul, Punta, *Mexico* . 115 C7
Yalleroi, *Australia* 90 C4
Yalobusha →, *U.S.A.* ... 109 J9
Yalong Jiang →, *China* . 52 D3
Yalova, *Turkey* 66 C3
Yalpukh, Oz., *Ukraine* .. 38 D11
Yalta, *Ukraine* 42 D6
Yalu Jiang →, *China* 51 E13
Yalutorovsk, *Russia* 44 D7
Yalvaç, *Turkey* 66 D4
Yam Ha Melah = Dead
  Sea, *Asia* 69 D4
Yam Kinneret, *Israel* ... 69 C4
Yamada, *Japan* 49 H5
Yamagata, *Japan* 48 E10

Yamagata □, *Japan* 48 E10
Yamaguchi, *Japan* 49 G5
Yamaguchi □, *Japan* 49 G5
Yamal, Poluostrov, *Russia* 44 B8
Yamal Pen. = Yamal,
　Poluostrov, *Russia* 44 B8
Yamanashi □, *Japan* 49 G9
Yamantau, Gora, *Russia* .. 44 D6
Yamba, *N.S.W., Australia* 91 D5
Yamba, *S. Austral.,*
　Australia 91 E3
Yambah, *Australia* 90 C1
Yambarran Ra., *Australia* 88 C5
Yâmbiô, *Sudan* 77 G2
Yambol, *Bulgaria* 38 G9
Yamdena, *Indonesia* 57 F8
Yame, *Japan* 49 H5
Yamethin, *Burma* 61 J20
Yamil, *Nigeria* 79 C6
Yamma-Yamma, L.,
　Australia 91 D3
Yamoussoukro, *Ivory C.* . 78 D3
Yampa →, *U.S.A.* 110 F9
Yampi Sd., *Australia* 88 C3
Yampol, *Ukraine* 42 B3
Yamrat, *Nigeria* 79 C6
Yamuna →, *India* 63 G9
Yamrukchal, *Bulgaria* ... 38 G7
Yamzho Yumco, *China* .. 54 D4
Yan, *Nigeria* 79 C7
Yana →, *Russia* 45 B14
Yanac, *Australia* 91 F3
Yanagawa, *Japan* 49 H5
Yanai, *Japan* 49 H6
Yan'an, *China* 50 F5
Yanbian, *China* 52 D3
Yanbu 'al Baḥr, *Si. Arabia* 64 F3
Yancannia, *Australia* 91 E3
Yanchang, *China* 50 F6
Yancheng, *Henan, China* . 50 H8
Yancheng, *Jiangsu, China* 51 H11
Yanchi, *China* 50 F4
Yanchuan, *China* 50 F6
Yanco Cr. →, *Australia* .. 91 F4
Yandal, *Australia* 89 E3
Yandanooka, *Australia* .. 89 E2
Yandaran, *Australia* 90 C5
Yandoon, *Burma* 61 L19
Yanfeng, *China* 52 E3
Yanfolila, *Mali* 78 C3
Yang Xian, *China* 50 H4
Yangambi, *Zaïre* 82 B1
Yangbi, *China* 52 E2
Yangcheng, *China* 50 G7
Yangch'ü = Taiyuan, *China* 50 F7
Yangchun, *China* 53 F8
Yanggao, *China* 50 D7
Yanggu, *China* 50 F8
Yangi-Yer, *Kazakhstan* .. 44 E7
Yangjiang, *China* 53 G8
Yangliuqing, *China* 51 E9
Yangon = Rangoon,
　Burma 61 L20
Yangping, *China* 53 B8
Yangpingguan, *China* ... 50 H4
Yangquan, *China* 50 F7
Yangshan, *China* 53 E9
Yangshuo, *China* 53 E8
Yangtze Kiang = Chang
　Jiang →, *China* 53 B13
Yangxin, *China* 53 C10
Yangyang, *S. Korea* 51 E15
Yangyuan, *China* 50 D8
Yangzhou, *China* 53 A12
Yanhe, *China* 52 C7
Yanji, *China* 51 C15
Yanjin, *China* 52 C5
Yanjing, *China* 52 C2
Yankton, *U.S.A.* 108 D6
Yanna, *Australia* 91 D4
Yanqi, *China* 54 B3
Yanqing, *China* 50 D8
Yanshan, *Hebei, China* .. 51 E9
Yanshan, *Jiangxi, China* . 53 C11
Yanshan, *Yunnan, China* . 52 F5
Yanshou, *China* 51 B15
Yantabulla, *Australia* 91 D4
Yantai, *China* 51 F11
Yanting, *China* 52 B5
Yantra →, *Bulgaria* 38 F8
Yanwa, *China* 52 D2
Yany, *China* 52 D3
Yanzhou, *China* 50 G9
Yao, *Chad* 73 F8
Yao Xian, *China* 50 G5
Yao Yai, Ko, *Thailand* .. 59 J2
Yao'an, *China* 52 E3
Yaodu, *China* 52 A5
Yaoundé, *Cameroon* 79 E7
Yaowan, *China* 51 G10
Yap I., *Pac. Oc.* 92 G5
Yapen, *Indonesia* 57 E9
Yapen, Selat, *Indonesia* .. 57 E9
Yappar →, *Australia* 90 B3
Yaqui →, *Mexico* 114 B2
Yar, *Russia* 41 B18
Yaracuy □, *Venezuela* .. 120 A4
Yaracuy, *Venezuela* 120 A4
Yaraka, *Australia* 90 C3
Yarangüme, *Turkey* 66 E3
Yaransk, *Russia* 41 C15
Yaratishky, *Belorussia* .. 40 D4
Yardea P.O., *Australia* .. 91 E2
Yare →, *U.K.* 13 E9

Yarensk, *Russia* 44 C5
Yarí →, *Colombia* 120 D3
Yaritagua, *Venezuela* 120 A4
Yarkand = Shache, *China* 54 C2
Yarker, *Canada* 107 B8
Yarkhun →, *Pakistan* 63 A5
Yarmouth, *Canada* 99 D6
Yarmūk →, *Syria* 69 C4
Yaroslavl, *Russia* 41 C11
Yarqa, W. →, *Egypt* 69 F2
Yarra Yarra Lakes,
　Australia 89 E2
Yarraden, *Australia* 90 A3
Yarraloola, *Australia* 88 D2
Yarram, *Australia* 91 F4
Yarraman, *Australia* 91 D5
Yarranvale, *Australia* 91 D4
Yarras, *Australia* 91 E5
Yarrowmere, *Australia* .. 90 C4
Yartsevo, *Russia* 40 D8
Yartsevo, *Russia* 45 C10
Yarumal, *Colombia* 120 B2
Yasawa Group, *Fiji* 87 C7
Yaselda →, *Belorussia* .. 40 E5
Yashi, *Nigeria* 79 C6
Yasin, *Pakistan* 63 A5
Yasinovataya, *Ukraine* .. 42 B7
Yasinski, L., *Canada* 98 B4
Yasothon, *Thailand* 58 E5
Yass, *Australia* 91 E4
Yata →, *Bolivia* 125 C4
Yatağan, *Turkey* 66 E3
Yates Center, *U.S.A.* 109 G7
Yathkyed L., *Canada* 101 A9
Yatsushiro, *Japan* 49 H5
Yatta Plateau, *Kenya* 82 C4
Yauca, *Peru* 124 D3
Yauya, *Peru* 124 B2
Yauyos, *Peru* 124 C2
Yavari →, *Peru* 124 A3
Yavatmal, *India* 60 J11
Yavne, *Israel* 69 D3
Yavorov, *Ukraine* 40 G3
Yavuzeli, *Turkey* 67 E7
Yawatahama, *Japan* 49 H6
Yawri B., *S. Leone* 78 D2
Yaxi, *China* 52 D6
Yayama-Rettō, *Japan* 49 M1
Yazd, *Iran* 65 D7
Yazd □, *Iran* 65 D7
Yazoo →, *U.S.A.* 109 J9
Yazoo City, *U.S.A.* 109 J9
Yding Skovhøj, *Denmark* . 9 J10
Ye Xian, *Henan, China* .. 50 H7
Ye Xian, *Shandong, China* 51 F10
Yealering, *Australia* 89 F2
Yebyu, *Burma* 61 M21
Yechŏn, *S. Korea* 51 F15
Yecla, *Spain* 29 G3
Yécora, *Mexico* 114 B3
Yedintsy, *Moldavia* 42 B2
Yeeda, *Australia* 88 C3
Yeelanna, *Australia* 91 E2
Yefremov, *Russia* 41 E11
Yegorlyk →, *Russia* 43 C9
Yegorlykskaya, *Russia* .. 43 C9
Yegoryevsk, *Russia* 41 D11
Yehuda, Midbar, *Israel* .. 69 D4
Yei, *Sudan* 77 G3
Yei, Nahr →, *Sudan* 77 F3
Yekaterinburg, *Russia* .. 44 D7
Yekaterinodar =
　Krasnodar, *Russia* 43 D8
Yelan, *Russia* 41 F13
Yelan-Kolenovskiy, *Russia* 41 F12
Yelanskoye, *Russia* 45 C13
Yelarbon, *Australia* 91 D5
Yelatma, *Russia* 41 D12
Yelcho, L., *Chile* 128 B2
Yelets, *Russia* 41 E11
Yélimané, *Mali* 78 B2
Yelizavetgrad =
　Kirovograd, *Ukraine* .. 42 B5
Yell, *U.K.* 14 A7
Yell Sd., *U.K.* 14 A7
Yellow Sea, *China* 51 G12
Yellowhead Pass, *Canada* 100 C5
Yellowknife, *Canada* 100 A6
Yellowknife →, *Canada* .. 100 A6
Yellowstone →, *U.S.A.* .. 108 B3
Yellowstone L., *U.S.A.* .. 110 D8
Yellowstone National Park,
　U.S.A. 110 D8
Yellowtail Res., *U.S.A.* .. 110 D9
Yelnya, *Russia* 40 D8
Yelsk, *Belorussia* 40 F6
Yelvertoft, *Australia* 90 C2
Yelwa, *Nigeria* 79 C5
Yemen ■, *Asia* 68 E3
Yen Bai, *Vietnam* 58 B5
Yenakiyevo, *Ukraine* 42 B8
Yenangyaung, *Burma* 61 J19
Yenbo = Yanbu 'al Baḥr,
　Si. Arabia 64 F3
Yenda, *Australia* 91 E4
Yendéré, *Ivory C.* 78 C4
Yendi, *Ghana* 79 D4
Yenice, *Turkey* 66 D2
Yenice →, *Turkey* 66 E6
Yenisaía, *Greece* 39 H7
Yenişehir, *Turkey* 66 C3
Yenisey →, *Russia* 44 B9
Yeniseysk, *Russia* 45 D10
Yeniseyskiy Zaliv, *Russia* 44 B9
Yennádhi, *Greece* 37 C9

Yenne, *France* 27 C9
Yenotayevka, *Russia* 43 C12
Yenyuka, *Russia* 45 D13
Yeo, L., *Australia* 89 E3
Yeo →, *Nigeria* 79 C7
Yeola, *India* 60 J9
Yeoryioúpolis, *Greece* .. 37 D6
Yeovil, *U.K.* 13 G5
Yepes, *Spain* 28 F1
Yeppoon, *Australia* 90 C5
Yeráki, *Greece* 39 N6
Yerbent, *Turkmenistan* .. 44 F6
Yerbogachen, *Russia* 45 C11
Yerevan, *Armenia* 43 F11
Yerilla, *Australia* 89 E3
Yerköy, *Turkey* 66 D6
Yermak, *Kazakhstan* 44 D8
Yermakovo, *Russia* 45 D13
Yermo, *U.S.A.* 113 L10
Yerofey Pavlovich, *Russia* 45 D13
Yerólakkos, *Cyprus* 37 D12
Yeropótamos →, *Greece* . 37 D6
Yeroskipos, *Cyprus* 37 E11
Yerseke, *Neths.* 17 F4
Yershov, *Russia* 41 F16
Yerushalayim = Jerusalem,
　Israel 69 D4
Yerville, *France* 24 C7
Yes Tor, *U.K.* 13 G4
Yesan, *S. Korea* 51 F14
Yeşilhisar, *Turkey* 66 D6
Yeşilırmak →, *Turkey* .. 66 C7
Yeşilkent, *Turkey* 66 E7
Yesnogorsk, *Russia* 41 D10
Yeso, *U.S.A.* 109 H2
Yessentuki, *Russia* 43 D10
Yessey, *Russia* 45 C11
Yeste, *Spain* 29 G2
Yeu, I. d', *France* 24 F4
Yevlakh, *Azerbaijan* 43 F12
Yevpatoriya, *Ukraine* .. 42 D5
Yevstratovskiy, *Russia* .. 41 F11
Yeya →, *Russia* 43 C8
Yeysk, *Russia* 42 C8
Yezd = Yazd, *Iran* 65 D7
Yhati, *Paraguay* 126 B4
Yhú, *Paraguay* 127 B4
Yhú, *Uruguay* 126 C4
Yi 'Allaq, G., *Egypt* 69 E2
Yi He →, *China* 51 G10
Yi Xian, *Anhui, China* .. 53 C11
Yi Xian, *Hebei, China* 50 E8
Yi Xian, *Liaoning, China* . 51 D11
Yialí, *Greece* 39 N10
Yialiás →, *Cyprus* 37 D12
Yi'allaq, G., *Egypt* 76 H8
Yialousa, *Cyprus* 37 D13
Yiáltra, *Greece* 39 L5
Yianisádhes, *Greece* 37 D8
Yiannitsa, *Greece* 39 J5
Yibin, *China* 52 C5
Yichang, *China* 53 B8
Yicheng, *Henan, China* .. 53 B9
Yicheng, *Shanxi, China* .. 50 G6
Yichuan, *China* 50 F6
Yichun, *Heilongjiang,*
　China 54 B7
Yichun, *Jiangxi, China* .. 53 D10
Yidu, *Hubei, China* 53 B8
Yidu, *Shandong, China* .. 51 F10
Yidun, *China* 52 B2
Yihuang, *China* 53 D11
Yijun, *China* 50 G5
Yilan, *Taiwan* 53 E13
Yıldızeli, *Turkey* 66 D7
Yiliang, *Yunnan, China* . 52 D5
Yiliang, *Yunnan, China* . 52 E4
Yilong, *China* 52 B6
Yimen, *China* 52 E4
Yimianpo, *China* 51 B15
Yinchuan, *China* 50 E4
Yindarlgooda, L., *Australia* 89 F3
Ying He →, *China* 50 H9
Ying Xian, *China* 50 E7
Yingcheng, *China* 53 B9
Yingde, *China* 53 E9
Yingjiang, *China* 52 E1
Yingjing, *China* 52 C4
Yingkou, *China* 51 D12
Yingshan, *Henan, China* . 53 B9
Yingshan, *Hubei, China* . 53 B10
Yingshan, *Sichuan, China* 52 B6
Yingshang, *China* 53 A11
Yingtan, *China* 54 D6
Yining, *China* 44 E9
Yinjiang, *China* 52 C7
Yinmabin, *Burma* 61 H19
Yinnietharra, *Australia* .. 88 D2
Yioúra, *Greece* 39 K7
Yipinglang, *China* 52 E3
Yirga Alem, *Ethiopia* 77 F4
Yishan, *China* 52 E7
Yishui, *China* 51 G10
Yíthion, *Greece* 39 N5
Yitiaoshan, *China* 50 F3
Yitong, *China* 51 C13
Yiwu, *China* 53 C13
Yixing, *China* 53 B12
Yiyang, *Henan, China* .. 50 G7
Yiyang, *Hunan, China* .. 53 C9
Yiyang, *Jiangxi, China* .. 53 C11
Yizhang, *China* 53 E9
Yizre'el, *Israel* 53 A12
Ylitornio, *Finland* 8 C17
Ylivieska, *Finland* 8 D18

Yngaren, *Sweden* 11 F10
Ynykchanskiy, *Russia* .. 45 C14
Yoakum, *U.S.A.* 109 L6
Yobe □, *Nigeria* 79 C7
Yog Pt., *Phil.* 57 B6
Yogan, *Togo* 79 D5
Yogyakarta, *Indonesia* .. 57 G14
Yoho Nat. Park, *Canada* . 100 C5
Yŏju, *S. Korea* 51 F14
Yokadouma, *Cameroon* .. 80 D2
Yokkaichi, *Japan* 49 G8
Yoko, *Cameroon* 79 D7
Yokohama, *Japan* 49 G9
Yokosuka, *Japan* 49 G9
Yokote, *Japan* 48 E10
Yola, *Nigeria* 79 D7
Yolaina, Cordillera de, *Nic.* 116 D3
Yonago, *Japan* 49 G6
Yonaguni-Jima, *Japan* .. 49 M1
Yŏnan, *N. Korea* 51 F14
Yonezawa, *Japan* 48 F10
Yong Peng, *Malaysia* 59 L4
Yong Sata, *Thailand* 59 J2
Yongampo, *N. Korea* 51 E13
Yong'an, *China* 53 E11
Yongcheng, *China* 50 H9
Yŏngchŏn, *S. Korea* 51 G15
Yongchuan, *China* 52 C5
Yongchun, *China* 53 E12
Yongdeng, *China* 50 F2
Yongding, *China* 53 E11
Yŏngdŏk, *S. Korea* 51 F15
Yŏngdŭngpo, *S. Korea* .. 51 F14
Yongfeng, *China* 53 D10
Yongfu, *China* 52 E7
Yonghe, *China* 50 F6
Yŏnghŭng, *N. Korea* 51 E14
Yongji, *China* 50 G6
Yŏngju, *S. Korea* 51 F15
Yongkang, *Yunnan, China* 52 E2
Yongkang, *Zhejiang, China* 53 C13
Yongnian, *China* 50 F8
Yongning,
　Guangxi Zhuangzu,
　China 52 F7
Yongning, *Ningxia Huizu,*
　China 50 E4
Yongping, *China* 52 E2
Yongqing, *China* 50 E9
Yongren, *China* 52 D3
Yongshan, *China* 52 C4
Yongsheng, *China* 52 D3
Yongshun, *China* 52 C7
Yongtai, *China* 53 E12
Yŏngwŏl, *S. Korea* 51 F15
Yongxin, *China* 53 D10
Yongxing, *China* 53 D9
Yongxiu, *China* 53 C10
Yonibana, *S. Leone* 78 D2
Yonkers, *U.S.A.* 107 F11
Yonne □, *France* 25 E10
Yonne →, *France* 25 D9
York, *Australia* 89 F2
York, *U.K.* 12 D6
York, *Ala., U.S.A.* 105 J1
York, *Nebr., U.S.A.* 108 E6
York, *Pa., U.S.A.* 104 F7
York, C., *Australia* 90 A3
York, Kap, *Greenland* .. 4 B4
York Sd., *Australia* 88 B4
Yorke Pen., *Australia* .. 91 E2
Yorkshire Wolds, *U.K.* .. 12 D7
Yorkton, *Canada* 101 C8
Yorktown, *U.S.A.* 109 L6
Yorkville, *U.S.A.* 112 G3
Yornup, *Australia* 89 F2
Yoro, *Honduras* 116 C2
Yoron-Jima, *Japan* 49 L4
Yos Sudarso, Pulau,
　Indonesia 57 F9
Yosemite National Park,
　U.S.A. 111 H4
Yosemite Village, *U.S.A.* 112 H7
Yoshkar Ola, *Russia* 41 C15
Yŏsu, *S. Korea* 51 G14
Yotala, *Bolivia* 125 D4
Yotvata, *Israel* 69 F4
You Xian, *China* 53 D9
Youbou, *Canada* 100 D4
Youghal, *Ireland* 15 E4
Youghal B., *Ireland* 15 E4
Youkounkoun, *Guinea* .. 78 C2
Young, *Australia* 91 E4
Young, *Canada* 101 C7
Young, *Uruguay* 126 C4
Younghusband, L.,
　Australia 91 E2
Younghusband Pen.,
　Australia 91 F2
Youngstown, *Canada* 101 C6
Youngstown, *N.Y., U.S.A.* 106 C5
Youngstown, *Ohio, U.S.A.* 106 E4
Youngsville, *U.S.A.* 106 E5
Youssoufia, *Morocco* 74 B3
Youxi, *China* 53 D12
Youyang, *China* 52 C7
Youyu, *China* 50 D7
Yoweragabbie, *Australia* 89 E2
Yozgat, *Turkey* 66 D6
Yozgat □, *Turkey* 66 D6
Ypané →, *Paraguay* 126 A4
Yport, *France* 24 C7
Ypres = Ieper, *Belgium* .. 17 G1
Ypsilanti, *U.S.A.* 104 D4

Yreka, *U.S.A.* 110 F2
Ysleta, *U.S.A.* 111 L10
Yssingeaux, *France* 27 C8
Ystad, *Sweden* 11 J7
Ysyk-Köl = Issyk-Kul,
　Ozero, *Kirghizia* 44 E8
Ythan →, *U.K.* 14 D7
Ytterhogdal, *Sweden* 10 B8
Ytyk-Kel, *Russia* 45 C14
Yu Jiang →, *China* 54 D6
Yu Shan, *Taiwan* 53 F13
Yu Xian, *Hebei, China* .. 50 E8
Yu Xian, *Henan, China* .. 50 G7
Yu Xian, *Shanxi, China* .. 50 E7
Yuan Jiang →, *Hunan,*
　China 53 C8
Yuan Jiang →, *Yunnan,*
　China 52 F4
Yuan'an, *China* 53 B8
Yuanjiang, *Hunan, China* 53 C9
Yuanjiang, *Yunnan, China* 52 F4
Yuanli, *Taiwan* 53 E13
Yuanlin, *Taiwan* 53 F13
Yuanling, *China* 53 C8
Yuanmou, *China* 52 E3
Yuanqu, *China* 50 G6
Yuanyang, *Henan, China* 50 G7
Yuanyang, *Yunnan, China* 52 F4
Yuba →, *U.S.A.* 112 F5
Yuba City, *U.S.A.* 112 F5
Yūbari, *Japan* 48 C10
Yūbetsu, *Japan* 48 B11
Yucatán □, *Mexico* 115 C7
Yucatán, Canal de,
　Caribbean 116 B2
Yucatan Str. = Yucatán,
　Canal de, *Caribbean* .. 116 B2
Yucca, *U.S.A.* 113 L12
Yucca Valley, *U.S.A.* 113 L10
Yucheng, *China* 50 F9
Yuci, *China* 50 F7
Yudino, *Russia* 41 D16
Yudino, *Russia* 44 D7
Yudu, *China* 53 E10
Yuendumu, *Australia* .. 88 D5
Yueqing, *China* 53 C13
Yueqing Wan, *China* 53 C13
Yuexi, *Anhui, China* 53 B11
Yuexi, *Sichuan, China* .. 52 C4
Yueyang, *China* 53 C9
Yugan, *China* 53 C11
Yugoslavia ■, *Europe* .. 21 M10
Yuhuan, *China* 53 C13
Yujiang, *China* 53 C11
Yukhnov, *Russia* 40 D9
Yukon →, *U.S.A.* 96 B3
Yukon Territory □, *Canada* 96 B6
Yüksekova, *Turkey* 67 E11
Yukti, *Russia* 45 C11
Yukuhashi, *Japan* 49 H5
Yule →, *Australia* 88 D2
Yuli, *Nigeria* 79 D7
Yulin, *Guangxi Zhuangzu,*
　China 53 F8
Yulin, *Shaanxi, China* .. 50 E5
Yuma, *Ariz., U.S.A.* 113 N12
Yuma, *Colo., U.S.A.* 108 E3
Yuma, B. de, *Dom. Rep.* . 117 C6
Yumbe, *Uganda* 82 B3
Yumbi, *Zaïre* 82 C2
Yumbo, *Colombia* 120 C2
Yumen, *China* 54 C4
Yumurtalık, *Turkey* 66 E6
Yun Ho →, *China* 51 E9
Yun Xian, *Hubei, China* . 53 A8
Yun Xian, *Yunnan, China* 52 E3
Yunak, *Turkey* 66 D4
Yunan, *China* 53 F8
Yuncheng, *Henan, China* 50 G8
Yuncheng, *Shanxi, China* 50 G6
Yundamindra, *Australia* . 89 E3
Yunfu, *China* 53 F9
Yungas, *Bolivia* 125 D4
Yungay, *Chile* 126 D1
Yungay, *Peru* 124 B2
Yunhe, *China* 53 C12
Yunlin, *Taiwan* 53 F13
Yunling, *China* 52 D2
Yunlong, *China* 52 E2
Yunmeng, *China* 53 B9
Yunnan □, *China* 52 E4
Yunquera de Henares,
　Spain 28 E1
Yunta, *Australia* 91 E2
Yunxi, *China* 50 H6
Yunxiao, *China* 53 F11
Yunyang, *China* 52 B7
Yuping, *China* 52 D7
Yupukarri, *Guyana* 121 C6
Yur, *Russia* 45 D14
Yurgao, *Russia* 44 D9
Yuribei, *Russia* 44 B8
Yurimaguas, *Peru* 124 B2
Yurya, *Russia* 41 B16
Yuryev-Polskiy, *Russia* .. 41 C11
Yuryevets, *Russia* 41 C13
Yuscarán, *Honduras* 116 D2
Yushanzhen, *China* 52 C7
Yushe, *China* 50 F7
Yushu, *Jilin, China* 51 B14
Yushu, *Qinghai, China* .. 54 C4
Yutai, *China* 50 G9
Yutian, *China* 51 E9

Yuxi, *China* 52 E4
Yuyao, *China* 53 B13
Yuzawa, *Japan* 48 E10
Yuzha, *Russia* 41 C13
Yuzhno-Sakhalinsk, *Russia* 45 E15
Yvelines □, *France* 25 D8
Yverdon, *Switz.* 22 C3
Yvetot, *France* 24 C7
Yvonand, *Switz.* 22 C3

Z

Zaamslag, *Neths.* 17 F3
Zaan →, *Neths.* 16 D5
Zaandam, *Neths.* 16 D5
Zab, Monts du, *Algeria* 75 B6
Žabalj, *Serbia* 21 K10
Žabari, *Serbia* 21 L11
Zabarjad, *Egypt* 76 C4
Zabaykalskiy, *Russia* 45 E12
Zabid, *Yemen* 68 E3
Ząbkowice Śląskie, *Poland* 20 E6
Zabłudów, *Poland* 20 B13
Zābol, *Iran* 65 D9
Zābolī, *Iran* 65 E9
Zabré, *Burkina Faso* 79 C4
Zabrze, *Poland* 20 E8
Zacapa, *Guatemala* 116 D2
Zacapu, *Mexico* 114 D4
Zacatecas, *Mexico* 114 C4
Zacatecas □, *Mexico* 114 C4
Zacatecoluca, *El Salv.* 116 D2
Zacoalco, *Mexico* 114 C4
Zacualtipán, *Mexico* 115 C5
Zadar, *Croatia* 33 D12
Zadawa, *Nigeria* 79 C7
Zadetkyi Kyun, *Burma* 59 H2
Zadonsk, *Russia* 41 E11
Zafarqand, *Iran* 65 C7
Zafra, *Spain* 31 G4
Żagań, *Poland* 20 D5
Zagazig, *Egypt* 76 H7
Zāgheh, *Iran* 65 C6
Zaglou, *Algeria* 75 C4
Zagnanado, *Benin* 79 D5
Zagorá, *Greece* 39 K6
Zagora, *Morocco* 74 B3
Zagorsk = Sergiyev Posad, *Russia* 41 C11
Zagreb, *Croatia* 33 C12
Zāgros, Kuhhā-ye, *Iran* 65 C6
Zagros Mts. = Zāgros, Kuhhā-ye, *Iran* 65 C6
Zaguinaso, *Ivory C.* 78 C3
Zāhedān, *Fārs, Iran* 65 D7
Zāhedān, *Sīstān va Balūchestān, Iran* 65 D9
Zahlah, *Lebanon* 69 B4
Zahna, *Germany* 18 D8
Zahrez Chergui, *Algeria* 75 A5
Zahrez Rharbi, *Algeria* 75 B5
Zaïre ■, *Africa* 80 E4
Zaïre →, *Africa* 80 F2
Zaječar, *Serbia* 21 M12
Zakamensk, *Russia* 45 D11
Zakataly, *Azerbaijan* 43 F12
Zakavkazye, *Asia* 43 F11
Zākhū, *Iraq* 64 B4
Zákinthos, *Greece* 39 M3
Zakopane, *Poland* 20 F9
Zákros, *Greece* 37 D8
Zala □, *Hungary* 21 J7
Zalaegerszeg, *Hungary* 21 J6
Zalalövö, *Hungary* 21 J6
Zalamea de la Serena, *Spain* 31 G5
Zalamea la Real, *Spain* 31 H4
Zalazna, *Russia* 41 B18
Žalec, *Slovenia* 33 B12
Zaleshchiki, *Ukraine* 42 B1
Zalingei, *Sudan* 73 F9
Zaltbommel, *Neths.* 16 E6
Zambeke, *Zaïre* 82 B2
Zambeze →, *Africa* 83 F4
Zambezi = Zambeze →, *Africa* 83 F4
Zambezi, *Zambia* 81 G4
Zambezia □, *Mozam.* 83 F4
Zambia ■, *Africa* 83 E2
Zamboanga, *Phil.* 55 H5
Zamboanguita, *Phil.* 55 G5
Zambrano, *Colombia* 120 B3
Zambrów, *Poland* 20 C12
Zamora, *Ecuador* 120 D2
Zamora, *Mexico* 114 C4
Zamora, *Spain* 30 D5
Zamora □, *Spain* 30 D5
Zamora-Chinchipe □, *Ecuador* 120 D2
Zamość, *Poland* 20 E13
Zamuro, Sierra del, *Venezuela* 121 C5
Zan, *Ghana* 79 D4
Zanaga, *Congo* 80 E2
Záncara →, *Spain* 29 F1
Zandijk, *Neths.* 16 D5
Zandvoort, *Neths.* 16 D5
Zanesville, *U.S.A.* 106 G2

Zangābād, *Iran* 64 B5
Zangue →, *Mozam.* 83 F4
Zanjan, *Iran* 65 B6
Zanjān □, *Iran* 65 B6
Zannone, *Italy* 34 B6
Zante = Zákinthos, *Greece* 39 M3
Zanthus, *Australia* 89 F3
Zanzibar, *Tanzania* 82 D4
Zanzūr, *Libya* 75 B7
Zaouiet El-Kala = Bordj Omar Driss, *Algeria* 75 C6
Zaouiet Reggane, *Algeria* 75 C5
Zaoyang, *China* 53 A9
Zaozhuang, *China* 51 G9
Zapadna Morava →, *Serbia* 21 M11
Zapadnaya Dvina, *Russia* 40 C8
Zapadnaya Dvina →, *Belorussia* 40 C4
Západné Beskydy, *Europe* 20 F9
Zapala, *Argentina* 128 A2
Zapaleri, Cerro, *Bolivia* 126 A2
Zapata, *U.S.A.* 109 M5
Zapatón →, *Spain* 31 G4
Zapiga, *Chile* 124 D4
Zaporizhzhya = Zaporozhye, *Ukraine* 42 C6
Zaporozhye, *Ukraine* 42 C6
Zapponeta, *Italy* 35 A8
Zara, *Turkey* 67 D7
Zaragoza, *Colombia* 120 B3
Zaragoza, *Coahuila, Mexico* 114 B4
Zaragoza, *Nuevo León, Mexico* 115 C5
Zaragoza, *Spain* 28 D4
Zaragoza □, *Spain* 28 D4
Zarand, *Kermān, Iran* 65 D8
Zarand, *Markazī, Iran* 65 C6
Zărandului, Munții, *Romania* 38 C5
Zaranj, *Afghan.* 60 D2
Zarasai, *Lithuania* 40 D5
Zarate, *Argentina* 126 C4
Zaraza, *Venezuela* 121 B4
Zāreh, *Iran* 65 C6
Zarembo I., *U.S.A.* 100 B2
Zaria, *Nigeria* 79 C6
Zarneh, *Iran* 64 C5
Zarós, *Greece* 37 D6
Zarqā' →, *Jordan* 69 C4
Zarrīn, *Iran* 65 C7
Zaruma, *Ecuador* 120 D2
Žary, *Poland* 20 D5
Zarza de Alange, *Spain* 31 G4
Zarza de Granadilla, *Spain* 30 E4
Zarzaítine, *Algeria* 75 C6
Zarzal, *Colombia* 120 C2
Zarzis, *Tunisia* 75 B7
Zas, *Spain* 30 B2
Zashiversk, *Russia* 45 C15
Zaskar →, *India* 63 B7
Zaskar Mts., *India* 63 C7
Zastron, *S. Africa* 84 E4
Zavārēh, *Iran* 65 C7
Zaventem, *Belgium* 17 G4
Zavetnoye, *Russia* 43 C10
Zavidovići, *Bos.-H.* 21 L8
Zavitinsk, *Russia* 45 D13
Zavodovski, I., *Antarctica* 5 B1
Zavolzhsk, *Russia* 41 C13
Zavolzhye, *Russia* 41 C13
Zawiercie, *Poland* 20 E9
Zāwiyat al Bayḍā, *Libya* 73 B9
Zawyet Shammâs, *Egypt* 76 A2
Zâwyet Um el Rakham, *Egypt* 76 A2
Zâwyet Ungeîla, *Egypt* 76 A2
Zāyā, *Iraq* 64 C5
Zayarsk, *Russia* 45 D11
Zaysan, *Kazakhstan* 44 E9
Zaysan, Oz., *Kazakhstan* 44 E9
Zayü, *China* 52 C1
Zazir, O. →, *Algeria* 75 D6
Zbarazh, *Ukraine* 40 G4
Zbąszyń, *Poland* 20 C5
Zblewo, *Poland* 20 B8
Zdolbunov, *Ukraine* 40 F5
Ždrelo, *Serbia* 21 L11
Zduńska Wola, *Poland* 20 D8
Zeballos, *Canada* 100 D3
Zebediela, *S. Africa* 85 C4
Zedelgem, *Belgium* 17 F2
Zeebrugge, *Belgium* 17 F2
Zeehan, *Australia* 90 G4
Zeeland, *Neths.* 17 E7
Zeeland □, *Neths.* 17 F3
Zeelst, *Neths.* 17 F6
Zeerust, *S. Africa* 84 D4
Zefat, *Israel* 69 C4
Zegdou, *Algeria* 74 C4
Zege, *Ethiopia* 77 E4
Zegelsem, *Belgium* 17 G3
Zégoua, *Mali* 78 C3
Zehdenick, *Germany* 18 C9
Zeil, Mt., *Australia* 88 D5
Zeila, *Somali Rep.* 68 E3
Zeist, *Neths.* 16 D6
Zeitz, *Germany* 18 D8
Zele, *Belgium* 17 F4
Zelenodolsk, *Russia* 41 D16
Zelenograd, *Russia* 41 C10
Zelenogradsk, *Russia* 40 D2
Zelenokumsk, *Russia* 43 D10

Zelënyy, *Kazakhstan* 43 B14
Zelhem, *Neths.* 16 D8
Zell, *Baden-W., Germany* 19 H3
Zell, *Rhld-Pfz., Germany* 19 E3
Zell am See, *Austria* 21 H2
Zella Mehlis, *Germany* 18 E6
Zelzate, *Belgium* 17 F3
Zembra, I., *Tunisia* 75 A7
Zémio, *C.A.R.* 82 A2
Zemmora, *Algeria* 75 A5
Zemmur, *W. Sahara* 74 C2
Zemoul, O. →, *Algeria* 74 C3
Zemst, *Belgium* 17 G4
Zemun, *Serbia* 21 L10
Zengbe, *Cameroon* 79 D7
Zengcheng, *China* 53 F9
Zenica, *Bos.-H.* 21 L7
Zenina, *Algeria* 75 B5
Žepče, *Bos.-H.* 21 L8
Zeraf, Bahr ez →, *Sudan* 77 F3
Zerbst, *Germany* 18 D8
Zermatt, *Switz.* 22 D5
Zernez, *Switz.* 23 C10
Zernograd, *Russia* 43 C9
Zerqani, *Albania* 39 H3
Zestafoni, *Georgia* 43 E10
Zetel, *Germany* 18 B3
Zetten, *Neths.* 16 E7
Zeulenroda, *Germany* 18 E7
Zeven, *Germany* 18 B5
Zevenaar, *Neths.* 16 E8
Zevenbergen, *Neths.* 17 E5
Zévio, *Italy* 32 C8
Zeya, *Russia* 45 D13
Zeya →, *Russia* 45 D13
Zêzere →, *Portugal* 31 F2
Zghartā, *Lebanon* 69 A4
Zgierz, *Poland* 20 D9
Zgorzelec, *Poland* 20 D5
Zhabinka, *Belorussia* 40 E4
Zhailma, *Kazakhstan* 44 D7
Zhambyl = Dzhambul, *Kazakhstan* 44 E8
Zhangbei, *China* 50 D8
Zhangguangcai Ling, *China* 51 B15
Zhanghua, *Taiwan* 53 E13
Zhangjiakou, *China* 50 D8
Zhangping, *China* 53 E11
Zhangpu, *China* 53 E11
Zhangwu, *China* 51 C12
Zhangye, *China* 54 C5
Zhangzhou, *China* 53 E11
Zhanhua, *China* 51 F10
Zhanjiang, *China* 53 G8
Zhanyi, *China* 52 E4
Zhanyu, *China* 51 B12
Zhao Xian, *China* 50 F8
Zhao'an, *China* 53 F11
Zhaocheng, *China* 50 F6
Zhaojue, *China* 52 C4
Zhaoping, *China* 53 E8
Zhaoqing, *China* 53 F9
Zhaotong, *China* 52 D4
Zhaoyuan, *Heilongjiang, China* 51 B13
Zhaoyuan, *Shandong, China* 51 F11
Zharkovskiy, *Russia* 40 D8
Zhashkov, *Ukraine* 42 B4
Zhashui, *China* 50 H5
Zhayyq = Ural →, *Kazakhstan* 43 C14
Zhdanov = Mariupol, *Ukraine* 42 C7
Zhecheng, *China* 50 G8
Zhegao, *China* 53 B11
Zhejiang □, *China* 53 C13
Zheleznogorsk, *Russia* 40 E9
Zheleznogorsk-Ilimskiy, *Russia* 45 D11
Zheltyye Vody, *Ukraine* 42 B5
Zhen'an, *China* 50 H5
Zhenfeng, *China* 52 E5
Zheng'an, *China* 52 C6
Zhengding, *China* 50 E8
Zhenghe, *China* 53 D12
Zhengyang, *China* 53 A10
Zhengyangguan, *China* 53 A11
Zhengzhou, *China* 50 G7
Zhenhai, *China* 53 C13
Zhenjiang, *China* 53 A12
Zhenlai, *China* 51 B12
Zhenning, *China* 52 D5
Zhenping, *Henan, China* 50 H7
Zhenping, *Shaanxi, China* 52 B7
Zhenxiong, *China* 52 D5
Zhenyuan, *Gansu, China* 50 G4
Zhenyuan, *Guizhou, China* 52 D7
Zherdevka, *Russia* 41 F12
Zherong, *China* 53 D12
Zhidan, *China* 50 F5
Zhigansk, *Russia* 45 C13
Zhigulevsk, *Russia* 41 E16
Zhijiang, *Hubei, China* 53 B8
Zhijiang, *Hunan, China* 52 D5
Zhijin, *China* 52 D5
Zhirnovsk, *Russia* 41 F14
Zhitomir, *Ukraine* 40 F6
Zhizdra, *Russia* 40 E9
Zhlobin, *Belorussia* 40 E6
Zhmerinka, *Ukraine* 42 B3
Zhodino, *Belorussia* 40 D6
Zhokhova, Ostrov, *Russia* 45 B16
Zhong Xian, *China* 52 B7
Zhongdian, *China* 52 D2

Zhongdong, *China* 52 F6
Zhongdu, *China* 52 E7
Zhongning, *China* 50 F3
Zhongshan, *Guangdong, China* 53 F9
Zhongshan, *Guangxi Zhuangzu, China* 53 E8
Zhongtiao Shan, *China* 50 G6
Zhongwei, *China* 50 F3
Zhongxiang, *China* 53 B9
Zhongyang, *China* 50 F6
Zhoucun, *China* 51 F9
Zhouning, *China* 53 D12
Zhoushan Dao, *China* 53 C14
Zhouzhi, *China* 50 G5
Zhovtnevoye, *Ukraine* 42 C5
Zhuanghe, *China* 51 E12
Zhucheng, *China* 51 G10
Zhugqu, *China* 50 H3
Zhuhai, *China* 53 F9
Zhuji, *China* 53 C13
Zhukovka, *Russia* 40 E8
Zhumadian, *China* 50 H8
Zhuo Xian, *China* 50 E8
Zhuolu, *China* 50 D8
Zhuozi, *China* 50 D7
Zhupanovo, *Russia* 45 D16
Zhushan, *China* 53 A8
Zhuxi, *China* 52 A7
Zhuzhou, *China* 53 D9
Zhytomyr = Zhitomir, *Ukraine* 40 F6
Zi Shui →, *China* 53 C9
Ziārān, *Iran* 65 B6
Ziarat, *Pakistan* 62 D2
Zibo, *China* 51 F10
Zichang, *China* 50 F5
Zichem, *Belgium* 17 F5
Zielona Góra, *Poland* 20 D5
Zierikzee, *Neths.* 17 E3
Ziesar, *Germany* 18 C8
Zifta, *Egypt* 76 H7
Zigey, *Chad* 73 F8
Zigong, *China* 52 C5
Zigui, *China* 53 B8
Ziguinchor, *Senegal* 78 C1
Zihuatanejo, *Mexico* 114 D4
Zijin, *China* 53 F10
Zile, *Turkey* 66 C6
Žilina, *Slovak Rep.* 20 F8
Zillah, *Libya* 73 C8
Zillertaler Alpen, *Austria* 19 H7
Zima, *Russia* 45 D11
Zimane, Adrar in, *Algeria* 75 D5
Zimapán, *Mexico* 115 C5
Zimba, *Zambia* 83 F2
Zimbabwe, *Zimbabwe* 83 G3
Zimbabwe ■, *Africa* 83 F2
Zimovniki, *Russia* 43 C10
Zinal, *Switz.* 22 D5
Zinder, *Niger* 79 C6
Zinga, *Tanzania* 83 D4
Zingem, *Belgium* 17 G3
Zingst, *Germany* 18 A8
Ziniaré, *Burkina Faso* 79 C4
Zinkgruvan, *Sweden* 11 F9
Zinnowitz, *Germany* 18 A9
Zion National Park, *U.S.A.* 111 H7
Zipaquirá, *Colombia* 120 C3
Zirc, *Hungary* 21 H7
Žiri, *Slovenia* 33 B11
Žirje, *Croatia* 33 E12
Zirl, *Austria* 19 H7
Ziros, *Greece* 37 D8
Zitácuaro, *Mexico* 114 D4
Zitava →, *Slovak Rep.* 21 G8
Zitundo, *Mozam.* 85 D5
Ziwa, L., *Ethiopia* 77 F4
Zixi, *China* 53 D11
Zixing, *China* 53 E9
Ziyang, *Shaanxi, China* 50 H5
Ziyang, *Sichuan, China* 52 B5
Ziyun, *China* 52 E6
Ziz, Oued →, *Morocco* 74 B4
Zizhixian, *China* 53 E8
Zizhong, *China* 52 C5
Zlarin, *Croatia* 33 E12
Zlatar, *Croatia* 33 B13
Zlataritsa, *Bulgaria* 38 F8
Zlatitsa, *Bulgaria* 38 G7
Zlatograd, *Bulgaria* 39 H8
Zlatoust, *Russia* 44 D6
Zletovo, *Macedonia* 39 H5
Zlín, *Czech.* 20 F7
Zlītan, *Libya* 73 B7
Złocieniec, *Poland* 20 B6
Złoczew, *Poland* 20 D8
Złotoryja, *Poland* 20 D5
Złotów, *Poland* 20 B7
Zmeinogorsk, *Kazakhstan* 44 D9
Żmigród, *Poland* 20 D6
Zmiyev, *Ukraine* 42 B7
Znamenka, *Ukraine* 42 B5
Znamensk, *Russia* 40 D2
Znin, *Poland* 20 C7
Znojmo, *Czech.* 20 G6
Zoar, *S. Africa* 84 E3
Zobeyrī, *Iran* 64 C5
Zobia, *Zaïre* 82 B2
Zoetermeer, *Neths.* 16 D5
Zofingen, *Switz.* 22 B5
Zogang, *China* 52 C1

Zogno, *Italy* 32 C6
Zogqên, *China* 52 A2
Zolder, *Belgium* 17 F6
Zollikofen, *Switz.* 22 C4
Zollikon, *Switz.* 23 B7
Zolochev, *Ukraine* 40 G4
Zolotonosha, *Ukraine* 42 B5
Zomba, *Malawi* 83 F4
Zomergem, *Belgium* 17 F3
Zongo, *Zaïre* 80 D3
Zonguldak, *Turkey* 42 F4
Zonguldak □, *Turkey* 66 C4
Zonhoven, *Belgium* 17 G6
Zonqor Pt., *Malta* 37 D2
Zonza, *France* 27 G13
Zorgo, *Burkina Faso* 79 C4
Zorita, *Spain* 31 F5
Zorritos, *Peru* 124 A1
Zorzor, *Liberia* 78 D3
Zossen, *Germany* 18 C9
Zottegem, *Belgium* 17 G3
Zou Xiang, *China* 50 G9
Zouar, *Chad* 73 D8
Zouérate, *Mauritania* 74 D2
Zousfana, O. →, *Algeria* 75 B4
Zoushan Dao, *China* 53 B14
Zoutkamp, *Neths.* 16 B8
Zrenjanin, *Serbia* 21 K10
Zuarungu, *Ghana* 79 C4
Zuba, *Nigeria* 79 D6
Zubayr, *Yemen* 77 D5
Zubia, *Spain* 31 H7
Zubtsov, *Russia* 40 C9
Zudáñez, *Bolivia* 125 D5
Zuénoula, *Ivory C.* 78 D3
Zuera, *Spain* 28 D4
Zuetina, *Libya* 73 B9
Zufar, *Oman* 68 D5
Zug, *Switz.* 23 B7
Zug □, *Switz.* 23 B7
Zugdidi, *Georgia* 43 E9
Zugersee, *Switz.* 23 B7
Zugspitze, *Germany* 19 H6
Zuid-Holland □, *Neths.* 16 E5
Zuidbeveland, *Neths.* 17 F3
Zuidbroek, *Neths.* 16 B9
Zuidhorn, *Neths.* 16 B8
Zuidlaarder meer, *Neths.* 16 B9
Zuidlaren, *Neths.* 16 B9
Zuidwolde, *Neths.* 16 C8
Zújar, *Spain* 29 H2
Zújar →, *Spain* 31 G5
Zújar, Pantano del, *Spain* 31 G5
Zula, *Eritrea* 77 D4
Zulia □, *Venezuela* 120 B3
Zülpich, *Germany* 18 E2
Zumaya, *Spain* 28 B2
Zumbo, *Mozam.* 83 F3
Zummo, *Nigeria* 79 D7
Zumpango, *Mexico* 115 D5
Zundert, *Neths.* 17 F5
Zungeru, *Nigeria* 79 D6
Zunhua, *China* 51 D9
Zuni, *U.S.A.* 111 J9
Zunyi, *China* 52 D6
Zuoquan, *China* 50 F7
Zuozhou, *China* 52 F6
Županja, *Croatia* 21 K8
Zurbātīyah, *Iraq* 64 C5
Zürich, *Switz.* 23 B7
Zürich □, *Switz.* 23 B7
Zürichsee, *Switz.* 23 B7
Zuromin, *Poland* 20 B9
Zuru, *Nigeria* 79 C6
Zurzach, *Switz.* 23 A7
Žut, *Croatia* 33 E12
Zutendaal, *Belgium* 17 G7
Zutphen, *Neths.* 16 D8
Zuwārah, *Libya* 75 B7
Zuyevka, *Russia* 41 B17
Zūzan, *Iran* 65 C8
Žužemberk, *Slovenia* 33 C11
Zvenigorodka, *Ukraine* 42 B4
Zverinogolovskoye, *Russia* 44 D7
Zvezdets, *Bulgaria* 38 G10
Zvishavane, *Zimbabwe* 83 G3
Zvolen, *Slovak Rep.* 20 G9
Zvonce, *Serbia* 21 N12
Zvornik, *Bos.-H.* 21 L9
Zwaag, *Neths.* 16 C6
Zwanenburg, *Neths.* 16 D5
Zwarte Meer, *Neths.* 16 C8
Zwarte Waler, *Neths.* 16 C10
Zwartsluis, *Neths.* 16 C8
Zwedru = Tchien, *Liberia* 78 D3
Zweibrücken, *Germany* 19 F2
Zwenkau, *Germany* 18 D8
Zwevegem, *Belgium* 17 G2
Zwickau, *Germany* 18 E8
Zwiesel, *Germany* 19 F9
Zwijnaarde, *Belgium* 17 F3
Zwijndrecht, *Belgium* 17 F4
Zwijndrecht, *Neths.* 16 E5
Zwischenahn, *Germany* 18 B4
Zwolle, *Neths.* 16 C8
Zwolle, *U.S.A.* 109 K8
Zymoetz →, *Canada* 100 C10
Żyrardów, *Poland* 20 C10
Zyryan, *Azerbaijan* 43 F14
Zyryanka, *Russia* 45 C16
Zyryanovsk, *Kazakhstan* 44 E9
Zyyi, *Cyprus* 37 E12

KEY TO WORLD MAP PAGES

NORTH AMERICA

ARCTIC OCEAN 4

Arctic Circle

96-97

8-9

8

14

15

12-13

16-17

24-25

30-31

26-27

32-3

36

36

28-29

100-101

98-99

104-105

106-107

112-113

74-75

36

36

ATLANTIC

OCEAN

110-111

108-109

116-117

Tropic of Cancer

114-115

PACIFIC OCEAN 92-93

102

72-73

7

120-121

Equator

SOUTH AMERICA

122-123

AFRICA

124-125

Tropic of Capricorn

PACIFIC   OCEAN

126-127

128